Real and Per-Capita Data

Less (15) Personal tax and nontax payments	Equals (16) Disposable personal income	Less personal outlays (17) Total	(18) Personal consumption expenditures	(19) Interest paid by consumers	Equals (20) Personal saving	Percentage of disposable personal income — Personal outlays (21) Total	(22) Personal consumption expenditures	(23) Personal saving	Gross national product (24) Current prices Per-capita dollars	(25) 1972 prices Billions of dollars	Disposable personal income (26) Current prices Per-capita dollars	(27) 1972 prices Billions of dollars	
Billions of dollars						Percent							
2.6	83.3	79.1	77.2	1.5	4.2	95.0	92.7	5.0	846	298	683	221	1929
2.5	74.5	71.1	69.9	0.9	3.4	95.4	93.8	4.6	734	268	605	203	1930
1.9	64.0	61.4	60.5	0.7	2.6	95.9	94.4	4.1	610	247	516	197	1931
1.5	48.7	49.3	48.6	0.5	−0.6	101.3	99.8	−1.3	464	211	390	166	1932
1.5	45.5	46.5	45.8	0.5	−0.9	102.0	100.6	−2.0	442	207	362	165	1933
1.6	52.4	52.0	51.3	0.5	0.4	99.3	98.0	0.7	514	225	414	176	1934
1.9	58.5	56.4	55.7	0.5	2.1	96.3	95.2	3.7	566	247	459	194	1935
2.3	66.3	62.7	61.9	0.6	3.6	94.6	93.3	5.4	644	283	518	218	1936
2.9	71.2	67.4	66.5	0.7	3.8	94.7	93.4	5.3	700	296	552	225	1937
2.9	65.5	64.8	63.9	0.7	0.7	98.9	97.6	1.1	652	282	504	212	1938
2.4	70.3	67.7	66.8	0.7	2.6	96.3	95.0	3.7	690	306	534	229	1939
2.6	75.3	72.0	71.0	0.8	3.4	95.5	94.2	4.5	754	344	570	244	1940
3.3	92.2	81.8	80.8	0.9	10.3	88.8	87.6	11.2	933	400	691	277	1941
5.9	116.6	89.4	88.6	0.7	27.2	76.7	76.0	23.3	1,170	461	865	317	1942
17.8	133.0	100.1	99.4	0.5	32.9	75.3	74.7	24.7	1,402	531	973	332	1943
18.9	145.6	109.0	108.2	0.5	36.6	74.8	74.3	25.2	1,518	569	1,052	343	1944
20.8	149.1	120.4	119.5	0.5	28.7	80.8	80.1	19.2	1,514	560	1,066	338	1945
18.7	158.9	145.2	143.8	0.7	13.7	91.4	90.5	8.6	1,482	478	1,124	332	1946
21.4	168.7	163.5	161.7	1.0	5.2	96.9	95.9	3.1	1,610	470	1,170	318	1947
21.0	188.0	176.9	174.7	1.4	11.1	94.1	93.0	5.9	1,767	489	1,282	335	1948
18.5	187.9	180.4	178.1	1.7	7.5	96.0	94.8	4.0	1,729	492	1,259	336	1949
20.6	206.6	194.7	192.0	2.3	11.9	94.2	92.9	5.8	1,887	534	1,362	362	1950
28.9	226.0	210.0	207.1	2.5	16.1	92.9	91.6	7.1	2,140	579	1,465	372	1951
34.0	237.7	220.4	217.1	2.9	17.4	92.7	91.3	7.3	2,211	600	1,515	383	1952
35.5	252.2	233.7	229.7	3.6	18.5	92.7	91.1	7.3	2,294	623	1,581	399	1953
32.5	257.1	240.1	235.8	3.8	17.0	93.4	91.7	6.6	2,256	616	1,583	403	1954
35.4	275.0	258.5	253.7	4.4	16.4	94.0	92.3	6.0	2,416	657	1,664	426	1955
39.7	292.9	271.6	266.0	5.1	21.3	92.7	90.8	7.3	2,501	671	1,741	446	1956
42.4	308.6	286.4	280.4	5.5	22.3	92.8	90.9	7.2	2,585	683	1,802	455	1957
42.1	319.0	295.4	289.5	5.6	23.6	92.6	90.7	7.4	2,578	680	1,832	460	1958
46.0	338.4	317.3	310.8	6.1	21.1	93.8	91.8	6.2	2,747	721	1,903	479	1959
50.4	352.0	332.3	324.9	7.0	19.7	94.4	92.3	5.6	2,800	737	1,947	489	1960
52.1	365.8	342.7	335.0	7.3	23.0	93.7	91.6	6.3	2,847	756	1,991	503	1961
56.8	386.8	363.5	355.2	7.8	23.3	94.0	91.8	6.0	3,020	800	2,073	524	1962
60.3	405.9	384.0	374.6	8.8	21.9	94.6	92.3	5.4	3,140	832	2,144	542	1963
58.6	440.6	411.0	400.5	9.9	29.6	93.3	90.9	6.7	3,309	876	2,296	580	1964
64.9	475.8	442.1	430.4	11.1	33.7	92.9	90.5	7.1	3,536	929	2,448	616	1965
74.5	513.7	477.7	465.1	12.0	36.0	93.0	90.5	7.0	3,822	984	2,613	646	1966
82.1	547.9	503.6	490.3	12.5	44.3	91.9	89.5	8.1	3,999	1,011	2,757	673	1967
97.2	593.4	551.5	536.9	13.8	41.9	92.9	90.5	7.1	4,317	1,058	2,956	701	1968
115.7	638.9	598.3	581.8	15.6	40.6	93.6	91.1	6.4	4,615	1,087	3,152	722	1969
115.8	695.3	639.5	621.7	16.7	55.8	92.0	89.4	8.0	4,795	1,085	3,390	751	1970
116.7	751.8	691.1	672.2	17.7	60.7	91.9	89.4	8.1	5,136	1,122	3,620	779	1971
141.0	810.3	757.7	737.1	19.5	52.6	93.5	91.0	6.5	5,607	1,185	3,860	810	1972
150.7	914.5	835.5	812.0	22.3	79.0	91.4	88.8	8.6	6,210	1,255	4,315	865	1973
170.2	998.3	913.2	888.1	24.1	85.1	91.5	89.0	8.5	6,666	1,248	4,667	858	1974
168.9	1,096.1	1,001.8	976.4	24.4	94.3	91.4	89.1	8.6	7,238	1,233	5,075	875	1975
196.8	1,194.4	1,111.9	1,084.3	26.7	82.5	93.1	90.8	6.9	7,991	1,300	5,477	907	1976
226.5	1,311.5	1,237.5	1,205.5	31.1	74.1	94.4	91.9	5.6	8,839	1,371	5,954	939	1977
258.8	1,462.9	1,386.6	1,348.7	37.1	76.3	94.8	92.2	5.2	9,845	1,436	6,571	981	1978
302.0	1,641.7	1,555.5	1,510.9	43.7	86.2	94.8	92.0	5.2	10,942	1,483	7,293	1,011	1979
338.5	1,821.7	1,720.4	1,672.8	46.4	101.3	94.4	91.8	5.6	11,786	1,480	8,002	1,018	1980
388.2	2,015.4	1,908.8	1,858.1	49.5	106.6	94.7	92.2	5.3	12,873	1,509	8,768	1,040	1981

Contemporary Economics

FIFTH EDITION

Contemporary Economics

Milton H. Spencer

Wayne State University

Worth Publishers, Inc.

for Cindy and Stu

Contemporary Economics, Fifth Edition

Copyright © 1971, 1974, 1977, 1980, 1983 by Milton H. Spencer

All rights reserved

Printed in the United States of America

Library of Congress Catalog Card No. 82-62690

ISBN: 0-87901-198-X

First printing, January 1983

Editor: Gunder Hefta

Production: George Touloumes

Design: Malcolm Grear Designers

Picture editor: June Lundborg

Composition: Progressive Typographers

Printing and binding: Von Hoffmann Press, Inc.

Worth Publishers, Inc.

444 Park Avenue South

New York, New York 10016

Preface

Why have enrollments in the introductory course in economics grown in the past few years? I should like to think that more and more students recognize economics as an important and exciting discipline, but there is another answer. For many students, economics is a requirement, and not merely in the sense that majors in various fields are required to take the introductory course: Many students have come to see that an understanding of economics is essential if they are to understand our complex society. Most of the great social problems that confront us are, after all, fundamentally economic—including unemployment, inflation, poverty, discrimination, urban blight, and ecological decay.

This enhanced sense of the relevance of economics has also enlarged students' expectations for the course. Students want to achieve an understanding of the economic events that affect their society and also the quality of their own lives. While they are too sophisticated to expect an introductory course to give them a set of answers and interpretations that will be valid for years to come, they want—and I want to give them—a foundation of knowledge, a systematic way of thinking about economic problems, and some useful problem-solving tools.

The Fifth Edition

With this in mind, I have attempted to provide in this edition a carefully constructed presentation of economic theory and of current economic problems and policies that I hope students will find useful now and of enduring significance. A brief summary of only the major additions and a few of the more substantial revisions will serve, I hope, to indicate how extensive are the changes in the fifth edition.

Fiscal Policy After an introduction to classical and Keynesian economics in earlier chapters, the notable successes and failures of Keynesian economics are discussed in Chapter 9. Included are modern treatments of the balanced-budget multiplier, the tax multiplier, discretionary and nondiscretionary fiscal policies, and crowding out. Students are shown how to evaluate the Keynesian model in light of today's thinking.

Foundations of Monetarism Chapter 14, a comprehensive survey of monetarism, has been written as a monetarist might have written it, not simply as an afterthought to Keynesian economics. The four pillars of monetarism—the modern quantity theory of money, the transmission mechanism and portfolio adjustments, stability in the private sector, and the focus on aggregate resource allocation—are fully explained. In addition, monetarism is compared with fiscalism, and policy implications are discussed.

Productivity and Economic Growth Chapter 15 is a comprehensive introduction to productivity and growth, with an emphasis on theories and policies. The chapter is designed to stimulate student thinking and debate. In Chapter 16, productivity trends are discussed, and the productivity of the United States is compared with that of other nations.

Supply-Side Economics Chapter 16 includes a substantial discussion of functional (as distinguished from naive) supply-side economics. It surveys our current experience with inflation and unemployment, presenting supply-side and demand-side arguments, with applications, so that students can consider alternatives as they reach their own conclusions.

The Open Economy A new chapter (Chapter 17) surveys the major economic principles underlying international trade and finance, and then it helps the student apply them to interpreting the economic problems that dominate the international news. This succinct chapter has been provided in addition to the three more detailed chapters on international economics in the last part of the book.

Public Choice Discussions of this important topic are included throughout the book (beginning in Chapter 4), and a comprehensive survey of the field has been provided in Chapter 27. Included are discussions of revealed preferences, the voting paradox, impossibility theorems, the economics of bureaucracy, and the pricing of merit goods. There is also an essay on Kenneth Arrow's work.

Antitrust and Regulatory Reform In the context of a broad discussion of government regulation of business, Chapter 28 focuses on antitrust, its achievements and shortcomings, and regulatory reform. The chapter gives up-to-date information on merger trends and the government standards that affect them. New data are given on aggregate concentration and its implications for efficiency.

Among other topics that are new or thoroughly revised are the following:

• Functional and personal income distribution and the measurement of income inequality (Chapter 3)

- Spillovers and market failures, with applications (Chapter 4 and elsewhere)

- Measuring unemployment and inflation (Chapter 6)

- Current views on public debt (Chapter 9)

- Money markets and capital markets (Chapter 10)

- Bank portfolio management, with implications for the economy (Chapters 11 and 12)

- Monetary policy, interest rates, and business investment (Chapter 12)

- Hotelling's paradox, contestable markets, and new findings on oligopoly (Chapter 23)

- Negative income tax (Chapter 30)

Special Features

Chapter Supplements Four brief supplements cover optional topics that may be appropriate to include in some courses. Each, however, is easily omitted without affecting the continuity of the text. New to this edition is the supplement to Chapter 18 on commodity-futures markets. The operations of such markets are revealed through a case study of a typical trade. This supplement will be fun for students as they learn about margin buying, speculation, and hedging—and see supply and demand in action.

Issues and Cases Many chapters contain Issues or Cases. These brief, topical essays focus on controversial questions or on real-world situations that allow the student to apply concepts learned in the chapter. Most of them end with thought-provoking questions, some intended to promote class discussion, others requiring graphing or problem solving.

Leaders in Economics As in previous editions, there are numerous brief, substantive essays on the work of many of the great economists of the past and present. These essays focus on the subject's main ideas and contributions as they relate to the topics discussed in the chapter.

Dictionary of Economic Terms and Concepts All technical terms and concepts are defined in the text where they are first discussed. In addition, all of these (and quite a few others not mentioned in the text) are included in a substantial Dictionary at the back of the book. The Dictionary has been extensively revised and expanded since the last edition, and it now contains more than 800 entries. It will serve as a convenient reference for this course and also for other courses students will take in economics and business.

Acknowledgments

It is a pleasure to acknowledge the help and cooperation I have received in the preparation of this book.

A general expression of thanks goes to Muriel Converse. She is not only the author of the accompanying *Study Guide* but also my severest critic. Her demanding standards have made the book much better than it might otherwise have been.

Mona Hersh and her students at Texas Woman's University have helped immeasurably in improving the consistency of the Dictionary.

Grace Mattheis typed a substantial portion of the manuscript and was helpful in many other ways.

Over the life of this book, I have benefited greatly from the advice and criticism of hundreds of dedicated teachers. Unfortunately, I cannot list them all. However, it is a privilege to mention the names of those who reviewed substantial portions of this edition and shared their classroom experiences with me. I thank them for their constructive suggestions and guidance. Of course, responsibility for any shortcomings in the final product is mine alone.

Dwight Blood, Brigham Young University

William W. Boorman, Palm Beach Junior College

Lilian Broner, Oakland Community College

Bruce Cofer, Louisiana College

Eugene Gendel, Lafayette College

Jack Inch, Oakland Community College

Terry Raney, U.S. Air Force Academy

David Schauer, University of Texas at El Paso

Arthur Schreiber, Georgia State University

Francis Shieh, Prince George's Community College

Milton H. Spencer
January 1983

Study Guide and Teaching Aids

The following supplements to *Contemporary Economics* are also available.

Study Guide The *Study Guide,* by Muriel G. Converse (University of Michigan), makes use of several pedagogical methods to help students learn the material covered in the text and to provide them with an opportunity to test their mastery of each topic. The *Study Guide* is written to be useful to *all* students, from those who are having difficulty (who may need to spend more time with it) to those who learn things quickly (who may be primarily concerned with self-testing to assure complete comprehension).

Instructor's Manual Each chapter of the *Instructor's Manual,* which was written by the author of the text, contains learning objectives for students (which can be reproduced and distributed, if desired). Also included are suggested answers to all of the chapter-end questions in the text and suggested answers to all of the questions in the Issues and Cases. It also contains a special supplement to Chapter 16 entitled "Explaining Stagflation: Real Aggregate Analysis Without the 'Keynesian Cross.'" This has been written for students and is ready for reproduction and distribution, if desired.

Transparency Masters All of the charts, graphs, and diagrams from the text are available in a set of masters to be used in making transparencies for overhead projectors.

Test Bank and Computerized Test-Generation System In the new edition of the *Test Bank,* which was written by the author of the text, hundreds of new questions have been added to the extensive and comprehensive assortment developed in earlier editions. Most of the questions emphasize theory and applications, while others single out important facts.

For those who adopt the fifth edition of *Contemporary Economics,* a computerized Test-Generation System is available. A magnetic tape includes all questions from the *Test Bank* and a program of access. With this tape and an on-campus computer, an instructor can obtain tailor-made exams quickly, without the need for secretarial time and without dependence on an outside source. The system, which is written in standard Fortran IV, can be used directly on nearly all computing systems and is easily adapted to others.

For those who do not use a computer, the questions in the *Test Bank* can be reproduced for use in any appropriate combination. In addition, two sets of complete model examinations have been provided for each of the book's eight parts. These examinations are ready to be reproduced and used.

Contents in Brief

Contents

Suggested Outlines for One-Semester Courses

Chapter	Macro-economic emphasis	Micro-economic emphasis	Balanced macro/micro emphasis	Problems and policy emphasis
Introduction	●	●	●	●
1. Our Mixed Economy: Resources, Goals, and Institutions	●	●	●	●
2. The Laws of Supply and Demand: The Price System in a Pure Market Economy	●	●	●	●
3. The Private Sector—Households and Businesses: Income and Industrial Structure	●	●	●	●
4. The Public Sector—Government: Public Choice and Taxation	●	●	●	●
5. National Income and Wealth: Measuring the Nation's Economic Health	●		●	●
6. Economic Instability: Business Cycles, Unemployment, and Inflation	●		●	●
7. What Causes Unemployment? Introduction to Classical and Keynesian Economics	●		●	●
8. Income and Employment Determination: The Keynesian Model	●		●	●
9. Modern Fiscal Policy: Successes and Failures of Keynesian Economics	●		●	●
10. Money, Financial Markets, and the Banking System	●		●	●
11. Commercial Banking: Money Creation and Portfolio Management	●		●	●
12. Central Banking: Monetary Policy	●		●	●
13. Macroeconomic Equilibrium in the Keynesian Model	●		●	●
14. Foundations of Monetarism: The Fiscal–Monetary Mix	●			
15. Productivity and Economic Growth	●			
16. Can We Overcome Stagflation? Supply-Side and Demand-Side Policies	●		●	●
17. The Open Economy: International Trade and Finance	●		○	
18. Working with Supply, Demand, and Elasticity: Some Interesting Applications		●	●	●
19. Looking Behind the Demand Curve: Utility and Consumer Demand		●		
20. Costs of Production		●	●	
21. Perfect Competition: Criteria for Evaluating Competitive Behavior		●	●	
22. Monopoly Behavior: The Other End of the Spectrum		●	●	
23. The Real World of Imperfect Competition		●	●	
24. Hiring Factors of Production: Marginal Productivity and Income Distribution		●		
25. Determination of Factor Prices		●		
26. Stability, General Equilibrium, and Welfare Economics		●		
27. Public Choice: Improving Public-Sector Efficiency		○	○	●
28. Business and Government: Antitrust and Regulatory Reform		●	○	●
29. Labor Economics and Labor Relations	○	●	○	●
30. Social Problems: Insecurity, Poverty, and Discrimination	○	●	○	●
31. Urban Problems: Can the Cities Be Saved?	○	○	○	●
32. Energy and Environmental Economics	○	○	○	●
33. International Economics: Foreign Trade and Protection		○		
34. International Economics: Foreign Exchange and Payments				
35. International Economics: Past and Present Policies				
36. The Less Developed Countries: Special Growth Problems of Nations in Poverty	○	○	○	○
37. Radical Viewpoints, Old and New		●	○	○
38. Economic Planning: The Visible Hand in Mixed and in Command Economies	○	○	○	○

● = Recommended chapters.   ○ = Optional chapters, time permitting.

Contemporary Economics

Overview: Our Economic System

Introduction

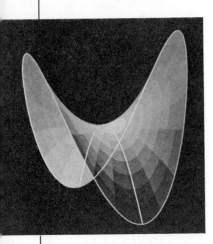

What are your greatest hopes and fears for the future?

This question is often asked in national public-opinion surveys. The answers that most people give involve economic matters. Getting or holding a good job, coping with rising prices, improving one's standard of living—these are the kinds of economic concerns that people usually express.

Most people worry about economic matters, and nearly everyone is engaged in economic activities. But economics is a subject about which relatively few people have any special knowledge. Today, such knowledge is more vitally needed than ever before. Economic issues are at the heart of most of the serious problems confronting contemporary society. These problems include inflation and unemployment; poverty, pollution, and urban decay; shortages of raw materials; and excessive corporate power.

All of us are asked to express our opinions on economic matters. Sometimes we do this by voting. More often we take part in a discussion, or we make a judgment about a current government proposal or a news item. In any case, we are continually being flooded with information and advice about economic matters, some of it right and much of it wrong.

Economics is a subject that can help us form valid opinions about many crucial problems. Although it cannot provide us with a fixed set of rules that will guarantee solutions, it does offer a systematic way of thinking and some useful tools for understanding and coping with many of society's ills.

Economic problems are all around us. We are asked frequently to make judgements about them and to express opinions.

What Is Economics About?

Anyone beginning the study of a subject likes to have a concise description of its nature and content. Here is a modern definition of economics —one you will use frequently:

> *Economics* is a social science concerned chiefly with the way society chooses to employ its limited resources, which have alternative uses, to produce goods and services for present and future consumption.

In other words, economics explains how human and material resources are used to provide people with the commodities they want. By *resources*, economists mean anything that can be used to produce goods or services. This includes human resources, such as hours of labor or a particular skill, and material resources, such as machinery, oil, or land. *Therefore, economics is concerned with the production and delivery of a standard of living.*

The definition of economics above needs some amplification.

Explaining the definition of economics.

First, why is economics a *social* science? Because it deals with the interactions of people (in particular, their interactions as they buy, sell, produce, and consume). Psychology, sociology, and the other social sciences also deal with human interactions—sometimes even economic interactions. But in economics, as you will see, the problems studied are approached from a unique standpoint and with special tools.

Second, what does it mean to say that a society's resources are limited? Simply that people everywhere want more goods and services than it is possible to produce. An economy's human and material resources are scarce when compared with society's wants. It makes no difference how affluent the society is—people will always want more goods and services than can be produced. Society must therefore decide how to use its limited resources most effectively. Economics is concerned both with these choices and with the forces that determine the choices.

Finally, what does it mean to say that resources have alternative uses? Only this: That just as you cannot use your limited time both to read at home *and* go to the movies, so society must choose between different ways of allocating its limited resources. If a society decides, for a time, to allocate more resources to the construction of highways, it will have fewer resources available for the construction of buildings.

This book will show how societies attempt to solve the three great questions of economics: What? How? and For Whom? *What* goods and services should be produced, and in what quantities? *How* should society's limited resources be used to produce the desired goods and services? And *For Whom* should the goods and services be produced? The answers to these questions affect the whole structure and nature of a society. These include its political system, the character of its institutions, the degree of choice open to its members, and the distribution of its wealth and income.

There are three great questions of economics:
What to produce?
How to produce?
For whom to produce?

Of course, every society operates according to its own rules and regulations. These determine the ways in which resources are used. Therefore, a society's laws, customs, and practices, and their relationships to its business firms, households, and government, constitute that society's *economic system*. Today, the two major types of economic systems are capitalism and socialism. The nature of these "isms," and of modern variants of them, will concern us frequently in this book.

Microeconomics and Macroeconomics

Economics is traditionally divided into two broad categories: micro-economics and macroeconomics.

Microeconomics is concerned with the specific parts or economic units that make up an economic system and with the relationships between those parts. In microeconomics, emphasis is placed on understanding the behavior of individual firms, industries, and households and the ways in which such entities interact.

Macroeconomics is concerned with the economy as a whole, or with large segments of it. Macroeconomics focuses on such problems as the rate of unemployment, the changing level of prices, the nation's total output of goods and services, and the ways in which government raises and spends money.

Stated differently:

Microeconomics looks at the trees, while macroeconomics looks at the forest. Both categories involve the construction of theories and the formulations of policies—activities that are the heart of economics.

Microeconomics studies the "trees"—the various parts of the economy and their interactions.

Macroeconomics studies the "forest"—the economy as a whole, or large segments of it.

Working with Theories and Models

Economists, like other scientists, study problems by observing the world and collecting appropriate data. The purpose of this is to discover relationships between events or between quantities called *variables*. For example, economists may study the relationship between the price of oil and the amount of oil purchased. From such a study, it may be possible to determine how changes in the price affect the quantities purchased. Ultimately, it may be possible to offer a good explanation for the relationship.

At one time, an explanation of a relationship between variables was called a *hypothesis* if there was no evidence to support it, a *theory* if there was some evidence, and a *law* or *principle* if it was certain. Scientists no longer emphasize these distinctions. They know that no hypothesis can be made about a subject of which one is completely ignorant. They know also that no scientific law is ever certain. Consequently, they tend to use the terms "theory," "law," and "principle" more or less interchangeably.

A theory may be stated in the form of a *model*. This is a representation of the essential features of a theory or of a real-world situation. A model may be expressed in the form of words, diagrams, tables of data, graphs, mathematical equations, or combinations of these. Generally, a model is easier to manipulate than the reality it represents because only the *relevant* properties of the reality are included. A road map, for example, is a model. Unlike some other maps, which are also models, a road map does not show vegetation or climatic variation because these are not relevant to its purposes. But a road map will serve better than any other type of map to guide you across the country.

A theory or model usually fits the observed facts only approximately. It might have to be revised or even discarded as time passes and the facts themselves change. In recent years, some new economic theories have revised and replaced older ones to provide better explanations of today's problems.

Scientific thinking in economics involves the use of theories, models, and principles.

Common Fallacies in Reasoning

Like physicists and chemists, economists try to use observed, verifiable facts as steppingstones to an understanding of how their portion of the world works. But physicists and chemists can usually discover rather quickly when they are in error. Typically, an experiment goes wrong; at worst, it causes an explosion. Economists, on the other hand, may labor for years under misapprehensions and may institute policies that affect thousands or even millions of people. Consequently, it is important to discern at the outset whether economic ideas are rational or misleading. One way of doing this is to examine them very carefully with the help of formal logic.

In common usage, the word *fallacy* denotes any mistaken idea or false belief. In a stricter sense, a fallacy is an error in reasoning or argument. This is what you will be looking for when you analyze economic ideas. Of course, an argument may be so incorrect that it deceives nobody. For our purposes, however, we shall reserve the word *fallacy* for certain types of reasoning that, although incorrect, are nevertheless persuasive—a dangerous combination. Here are some typical fallacies of economic thinking that will enable you to pinpoint the errors in other people's reasoning as well as in your own.

Pitfalls in economic reasoning are common. You must be careful to avoid them.

Fallacy of False Cause

Every science tries to discover cause-and-effect relationships. The fallacy of false cause, or *post hoc fallacy*, is often encountered in such efforts. (The latter name comes from the Latin expression *post hoc ergo propter hoc*, which means "after this, therefore because of this.") This fallacy is committed when a person mistakenly assumes that, because one event follows another or both events occur simultaneously, one is the cause and the other the effect.

It is common for a fallacy of false cause to be expressed in the form of an "if–then" argument:

> If A occurs, then B occurs.
> Therefore, A causes B.

Causes and effects are not always what they seem to be.

Is this sufficient reason for concluding that A causes B? Not necessarily. There are other possible explanations:

1. B may occur by chance.

2. B may be caused by factors other than A (or by a third factor, C, that is a common cause of both A and B).

3. B may cause A.

Some possibilities are illustrated in the following examples:

Example 1 Company X hired a new sales manager, and the firm's sales soared during the ensuing year.

Therefore, the growth in sales was due to the new sales manager.

This argument, consisting of both the statement and the conclusion, is obviously a false cause or *post hoc* fallacy. It fails to point out that, although some of the growth in sales may be due to the manager's efforts, much or even most of it may be the result of other factors. These may consist of lower prices for the company's products, higher incomes of buyers, or an increase in the number of buyers in the market.

Example 2 The severity of hay fever varies inversely with the price of corn. That is, the lower the price of corn, the greater the severity of hay fever, and vice versa.

Therefore, corn prices affect hay fever.

It is true that the price of corn and the severity of hay fever are inversely related. But, the fact is that ragweed is a cause of hay fever. The summer conditions that will produce an abundance of ragweed—high temperatures and adequate rainfall—will also produce an abundance of corn. This usually results in lower corn prices. Thus, it may *seem* as if corn prices affect hay fever. In reality, these factors are independent of each other, and a third factor is operating that is a common cause of both.

> Fallacious cause-and-effect relationships frequently appear in economic discussions. Because the fallacies are not often apparent, a careful study of the subject is necessary before you can learn to recognize such errors and thus avoid the fallacy of false cause.

Fallacies of Composition and Division

What is true of the parts of something is not necessarily true of the whole of it.

What is true of the whole of something is not necessarily true of the parts of it.

Two additional fallacies are often encountered in economic arguments. The *fallacy of composition* is committed when one reasons that what is true of the parts of something is also necessarily true of the whole of it. The *fallacy of division* is committed when one contends that something that is true of the whole is also necessarily true of its parts taken separately.

The following *true* statements from economics illustrate these common fallacies:

1. It may be desirable for a family to increase its savings by cutting down on its consumption expenditures. If all families do this, however, spending in the economy may decline. If this happens, firms will lay off workers, the level of total income will fall, and families will find themselves saving *less* rather than more.

2. If the prices in a specific industry were to increase tomorrow by x percent, the firms in that industry would probably experience an increase in profits. But if the prices of all goods and services throughout the economy were to increase tomorrow by x percent, no firms would experience an increase in profits.

3. Economic policies that may be wise for a *nation* are not necessarily wise for an *individual*, and vice versa.

The fallacies of composition and division are thus particularly relevant to the study of microeconomics and macroeconomics. To summarize:

> The fallacy of composition warns us that what is true of the parts is not necessarily true of the whole. Thus, generalizations of a microeconomic nature may not always be applicable to a macroeconomic problem. The fallacy of division warns us that what is true of the whole is not necessarily true of the parts. Thus, generalizations of a macroeconomic nature may not always be applicable to a microeconomic problem.

These ideas may seem obvious when they appear in a textbook. However, the fallacies can be remarkably subtle when they appear in discussions of actual economic problems.

What You Have Learned

1. Economics is a *social* science because it deals with an aspect of human behavior—how people earn a living and how society distributes the proceeds.

2. Like all sciences, social or physical, economics uses theories and models to represent reality. However, a model is a simplified version of reality. As such, it may need to be adjusted or even abandoned as facts change or as new facts come to light.

3. Many types of fallacies can be committed in economic reasoning. Perhaps the most common are the fallacy of false cause and the fallacies of composition and division.

For Discussion

1. *Terms and concepts to review:*
economics
economic system
microeconomics
macroeconomics
variables
model
fallacy of composition
fallacy of division

2. "Everyone knows that the United States is one of the richest countries in the world. Therefore, economics as it is defined may be correct for poor countries, but certainly not for America, where the problem is one of abundance, not scarcity." True or false? Explain.

3. Senator Jason is campaigning for a tax reduction. He argues that tax cuts in other major industrial nations have stimulated their rapid economic growth. Senator Blaine replies that what happens in nations thousands of miles away is no guide to what will happen here. Do you agree with Senator Blaine? Why or why not?

Identify at least one fallacy in each of the following:

4. "All rich nations have steel industries. Therefore, the surest way for a poor nation to become rich is to develop its own steel industry."

5. "The students who do best in economics have some working experience. Therefore, the surest way to receive a good grade in this course is to go out and get a job."

6. "To press forward with a properly ordered wage structure in each industry is the first condition for curbing competitive bargaining; but there is no reason why the process should stop there. What is good for each industry can hardly be bad for the economy as a whole."

Twentieth Century Socialism,
New York, Penguin Books, 1956, p. 74

7. "Each person's happiness is a good to that person, and the general happiness, therefore, a good to the aggregate of all persons."

John Stuart Mill, *Utilitarianism,* 1863

8. In a capitalist system, each manufacturing plant is free to set its own price on the product it produces. Therefore, there can't be anything wrong with all manufacturers getting together to agree on the prices of the products they produce.

9. All economics textbooks are long and dull, so we can't expect this one to be short and interesting.

10. "Roger Babson, who was best known for his predictions of the stock market, once became ill with tuberculosis. Against his doctor's advice, he chose to convalesce at his home in Massachusetts rather than remain in the West. During the freezing winter, he kept his windows open and wore a coat with an electric heating pad in the back. He had his secretary do her typing by wearing mittens and hitting the keys with rubber hammers. Babson recovered and remained a fresh-air fiend ever since. He believed that air from pine woods had chemical and/or electrical qualities of great medicinal value.

"On another occasion, Babson wrote an article in which he contended that gravity affects weather and crops, crops influence business, and business affects elections. He supported his thesis with an analysis of 27 presidential elections, [covering a period of more than 100 years]. In 75 percent of the cases, he said, the party in power remained in power when weather and business were good, and was voted out when weather and business were bad."

Martin Gardner,
Fads and Fallacies in the Name of Science,
New York, Dover Publications, 1957, p. 97

Working with Graphs

Economic ideas are often expressed with models. One of the most common ways of presenting a model is in the form of a line graph. Such a graph shows relationships between variables—that is, how one quantity varies with another. The procedure for making line graphs is illustrated in the following paragraphs and in Figures (a) through (f).

In Figure (a), a common sheet of graph paper is shown. Two intersecting straight lines at right angles to each other are drawn on the graph paper. The horizontal line is called the x *axis*, the vertical line the y *axis,* and the point of intersection the *origin.* The two lines divide the graph into four parts called *quadrants.* These quadrants are identified by starting with the upper right-hand corner and numbering them counterclockwise. Observe that positive numbers on the x axis are to the right of the origin and negative numbers are to the left. Positive numbers on the y axis are above the origin, and negative numbers are below. For brevity, we write the coordinates of a point in the form (x,y), where x is the value on the x axis and y is the value on the y axis. These procedures for labeling and numbering are used in all branches of science.

You can now locate any point on the graph with two numbers—one for x and one for y—in much the same way as you would locate a ship at sea by its latitude and longitude. The two numbers are called the *coordinates* of the point. Thus, the coordinates of point A are (3,5), those of point B are (5,2), and those of point C are (4,0). The horizontal, or x, coordinate is always stated first and the vertical, or y, coordinate second. Can you give the coordinates of the remaining points?

Graphs such as these are used to show how one quantity varies with another. In Figure (b), for example, the values of x and y are plotted from the data in the accompanying table. First, the points representing each pair of values of x and y are located and marked. The points are then connected with a smooth curve, in this case a straight line. Because the line slopes upward from left to right, the two variables are said to be *directly* related. Thus, as x increases, y increases; as x decreases, y decreases. In contrast, the line in Figure (c) slopes downward from left to right. Therefore, the two variables are said to be *inversely* related. Thus, as x increases, y decreases; as x decreases, y increases.

In economics, the lines plotted usually fall entirely in the first quadrant. This is because the data on which the lines are based are positive, although there are important exceptions. Sometimes two or more lines are plotted on the same graph in order to examine the relationships between them, as in Figure (d). Can you read the coordinates of the points determining these lines? Try filling in the table.

Different scales and labels may be used on the horizontal and vertical axes, to suit the particular purpose of the graph. This is shown in Figure (e). The vertical axis in this graph shows P, the price in dollars of a particular bond. The horizontal axis shows t, the time in number of years after the bond was purchased. The curve shows the relationship between these two variables—that is, what happened to the price, P, of a bond t years after it was purchased. For example, at $t = 0$, $P = \$1,204$; and at $t = 2$ years, $P = \$1,190$. Can you fill in the table? Where necessary, try to estimate the numbers from the graph.

Finally, Figure (f) shows the unit costs, C, that a certain firm experiences as a result of producing different quantities, Q, of a commodity. You should be able to fill in the table from the graph.

x	-3	-2	-1	0	1	2	3	4
y	-2	-1	0	1	2	3	4	5

x	-3	-2	-1	0	1	2	3	4
y	5	4	3	2	1	0	-1	-2

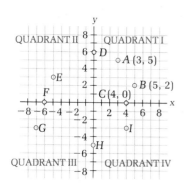

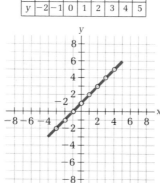

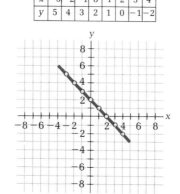

Figure (a): The two intersecting straight lines divide the graph into four quadrants, which are numbered counterclockwise. Positive values are measured to the right along the x axis and upward along the y axis. Negative values are measured to the left along the x axis and downward along the y axis. Any point on the graph can be located by its coordinates.

Figure (b): A line that slopes upward from left to right exhibits a direct relation between the two variables. As one variable increases, so does the other; as one decreases, so does the other.

Figure (c): A line that slopes downward from left to right exhibits an inverse relation between the two variables. As one variable increases, the other decreases; as one decreases, the other increases.

x	2	3		5	6
y	3			6	
y'	7	6			

t	0	4	8	12	16
P					

Q		2		4		6	
C	90		30		30		90

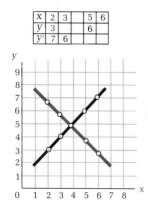

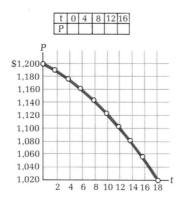

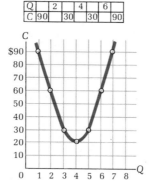

Figure (d): Two or more lines may be drawn on the same graph in order to study the relationships between them. Can you complete the table from the graph?

Figure (e): Scales should be chosen and axes labeled in the manner that best suits a particular problem. Can you use the graph to estimate the missing numbers in the table?

Figure (f): The points should be connected with care because the resulting curve may be quite pronounced. Can you fill in the table from the graph?

Exercises in Graphing

*For exercises 1–3, sketch the graphs of the
following relationships:*

1.

x	1	2	3	4	5	6	7	8
y	1	2	3	4	5	6	7	8

2.

x	1	2	3	4	5	6	7
y	7	6	5	4	3	2	1

3.

x	−2	0	2	4
y	−8	−4	0	4

4. Sketch the following data on the same
graph. Estimate the coordinates of the point
of intersection of the two lines.

x	1	2	3	4
y	2	3	4	5

x	1	2	3	4
y	5	4	3	2

5. Sketch the graph of hog prices as a function of time:

time (t)	0	1	2	3	4	5	6	7	8
hog prices (P)	8	33	40	35	24	13	8	15	40

Our Mixed Economy:
Resources, Goals, and Institutions

CHAPTER
1

Learning guide
Watch for the answers to these important questions

What are the resources of our economic system? Who owns the resources and what payments are made for their use?

What goals do we want our economy to achieve? Can we trade various goals against one another? What are the costs of doing so?

Why is our economic system called "capitalistic"? What social, political, and economic institutions constitute the basis of capitalism? How can we depict the flow of goods and resources in a capitalistic system?

This evening, it would be nice if you could (1) read this chapter, (2) do all your homework, (3) earn some money, (4) engage in some pleasant recreational activity, and (5) relax and enjoy a leisurely dinner at the best restaurant in town. But you cannot do all these things. You will have to give up one or more of them because you are faced with limitations of time and (possibly) of money.

Every economic system also faces limitations. But they are limitations of the human and nonhuman resources needed to produce the goods and services that society wants. This chapter describes the nature of those limitations and the way in which an economy adjusts to them in the light of the goals that society strives to attain.

Resources of Our Economic System: What Do We Have?

Every economic system has various resources at its disposal to produce the goods and services that society wants. These resources are of two broad types:

Resources, both material and human, are the "inputs" that every economy uses to produce "outputs."

1. Material or Property Resources These include such things as natural resources, raw materials, machinery and equipment, buildings, and transportation and communication facilities.

2. Human Resources These consist of the productive physical and mental abilities of the people who constitute the economy.

As you learn more about economics, you will find this classification of resources to be too general for some practical problems. Economists therefore divide property resources into two subcategories, "land" and "capital," and human resources into two subcategories, "labor" and "entrepreneurship." These four types of resources are known as the *factors of production.*

Factors of Production

The four factors of production—land, capital, labor, and entrepreneurship—are the basic ingredients, or "inputs," that any society must use to obtain the "outputs" it desires.

Land

Land, in economics, means all nonhuman or "natural" resources, such as land itself, mineral deposits, timber, and water. Land thus consists of all the natural physical stuff on which any civilization must be built.

You may be surprised to learn that many countries, even some of the poorest, have vast quantities of untapped natural resources. This is true because world demand for those resources is not sufficient to make their extraction profitable with existing technology. When these conditions change, as they often do, a country's natural resources may take on new economic significance.

Because of this, a nation's "stock" of natural resources should not be thought of as a fixed physical quantity. Instead, it should be viewed as a variable one whose size is determined by changing economic and technological conditions. The United States, for example, has large untapped reservoirs of oil and natural gas. However, these resources will not be extracted until higher prices resulting from increased demand, or lower costs resulting from technological advances, make their extraction profitable. Thus, the physical volume of these resources may be constant. Their economic quantity, however, may be variable, depending on prices and the costs of extraction.

Capital

Capital may be defined as a produced means of further production. By "produced" is meant that capital is made by human resources working with material resources. Thus timber is considered to be land, but lumber is capital. In this sense, capital means *capital goods* or *investment goods,* the things that are used by business. Other examples are tools, machinery and equipment, factory buildings, freight cars, and office furniture. Capital is thus an economic resource that is used to help produce consumer goods and services. Examples of consumer products include food, cars, appliances, clothing, health services, and all the other commodities typically bought by households.

It is important to note that capital, to the economist, means *physical* capital (goods used in production) and not *finance* capital (money). Business managers, *but not economists,* generally use the term "capital" to mean money—the funds owned or borrowed to purchase capital goods and to finance the operation of a business. For the economy as a whole, however, money is not a productive resource. If it were, nations could become rich simply by printing money. Instead, money's chief function is to facilitate the exchange of goods and services. Money therefore serves as a "lubricant" rather than a factor of production within the economic system.

Resources are also called "factors of production." These are land, capital, labor, and entrepreneurship.

Notice the special meaning of the term "capital."

Why isn't money a resource or a factor of production?

Labor

Land and capital are of no use unless they can be made productive. That requires *labor*, the efforts or activities of workers hired to assist in the production of goods and services. In this sense, therefore, labor refers not to the workers themselves but to the service they provide by working.

In a broader sense, however, "labor" also means the services of everyone who works for a living. We often refer to the labor force of a nation—that is, all the employable population above a certain age. The meaning of "labor force" and the notion of labor as a factor of production are different concepts in economics. Although they are sometimes related in economic discussions, you will find that the distinction between the two is clear from the context in which the terms are used.

Entrepreneurship

The three factors of production described above must be organized and combined in order to produce. In other words, labor must be given a purpose if it is to work with land and capital to turn out goods and services. This is where *entrepreneurship* enters the picture. The entrepreneur recognizes a need and the opportunities to be gained from production. Accordingly, he or she generates new ideas and puts them into effect. The entrepreneur assembles the factors of production, raises the necessary money, organizes the management, makes the basic business policy decisions, and reaps the gains of success or the losses of failure. Some entrepreneurs act as their own managers; others hire people to serve as managers. But, regardless of who acts as manager, the *entrepreneurial function* is necessary. ■

■ **Something to Think About**

Is there such a thing as "human" capital? Are scientists, engineers, teachers, doctors, lawyers, and skilled workers, for example, part of a nation's capital? What criteria would you use when deciding whether something is qualified to be called capital?

Returns to Resource Owners

In a capitalistic system, the factors of production are privately owned. In other types of economic systems, one or more of the factors of production might be owned by society. Because there is never enough land, capital, labor, or entrepreneurship to produce sufficient goods and services to satisfy everyone, the owners of these factors, in a capitalistic system, can command a price for them in the market.

For example, those who supply land receive a payment called *rent*. Those who supply finance capital, the money that business firms borrow for the purchase of physical capital, receive a return called *interest*. Workers who sell their labor receive a payment called *wages*, which includes salaries, commissions, and the like. Finally, those who perform the entrepreneurial function receive *profits* (or losses).

The yearly sum of rent, interest, wages, and profits for a country is the total annual income earned by all resource owners. This total is called *national income*.

The sum of the payments made to the owners of the factors of production is called national income.

Conclusion: Functional Classification— Economics' English Heritage

A summary of these ideas is presented in Exhibit 1. This arrangement of resources into four categories is a *functional* one. It is based on the paid-for activities or market functions that the factors of production provide in our economic system. Interestingly, the grouping rests on sociological as well as economic foundations. Thus:

Exhibit 1
Classifying the Factors of Production

Resource or factor of production	Description	Payment
Land	Natural resources (e.g., minerals, water, timber)	Rent
Capital	Produced resources (e.g., tools, factories, machines)	Interest
Labor	Physical and mental efforts (e.g., hired workers and professionals)	Wages
Entrepreneurship	Organizing and financial risk taking	Profit
Annual total		National income

The classification of factors of production and their corresponding income payments is an outgrowth of the social structure that prevailed in England during most of the nineteenth century. At that time it was customary to distinguish between landowners, capitalists, and wage earners, representing the upper, middle, and lower classes. By the turn of the century, economists recognized a fourth factor of production, enterprise. Profits then became the share of income attributed to entrepreneurship, and interest became the income received by suppliers of finance capital.

Case
Specialization: Learning More and More About Less and Less

Although the factors of production are grouped into four broad classes, you can appreciate the fact that there is generally a considerable degree of specialization within each class. Machines, for example, are designed to do specific jobs, and people are often trained to perform specific tasks. The result is a much larger volume of production, but often at the cost of substantial personal dissatisfaction.

Technically, *specialization* is the division of productive activities among people and regions so that no one person or area is self-sufficient. *Division of labor* is specialization by workers. The result of specialization is an enormous gain in productivity.

Division of Labor in a Pin Factory

The benefits of specialization and division of labor were pointed out as long ago as 1776 by Adam Smith, the founder of modern economics. Concerning the division of labor in a pin factory, Smith wrote, in what has become a classic quotation:

> A workman not educated to this business . . . could scarce, perhaps, with his utmost industry, make one pin in a day, and certainly could not make twenty. But in the way in which this business is now carried on, not only the whole work is a peculiar trade, but it is divided into a number of branches. . . . One man draws out the wire, another straights it, a third cuts it, a fourth points it, a fifth grinds it at the top for receiving the head: to make the head requires two or three distinct operations; to put it on, is a peculiar business, to whiten the pins is another; it is even a trade by itself to put them into the paper; and the important business of making a pin is, in this manner, divided into about eighteen distinct operations, which, in some manufactories, are all performed by distinct hands, though in others the same man will sometimes perform two or three of them. I have seen a small manufactory of this kind where ten men only were employed, and where some of them consequently performed two or three distinct operations. But . . . those ten persons . . . could make among them upwards of forty-eight thousand pins in a day.
>
> Adam Smith, *An Inquiry into the Nature and Causes of the Wealth of Nations* (1776)

To generalize from Smith, specialization and division of labor increase production because they:

- Allow for the development and refinement of skills.

- Eliminate the waste of time that is entailed in going from one job to another.

- Simplify human tasks, thus permitting the introduction of laborsaving machines.

Specialization has its shortcomings. It may alienate many workers because they have contributed only one small part to the completed

The assembly line was not invented by Henry Ford but by an anonymous Frenchman. This factory, observed by Adam Smith on a visit to France, increased output enormously by instituting the division of labor in the production of pins.

product. A repetitive, boring job can dull the worker's mind and can become little more than a naked means of subsistence. There is little personal satisfaction to those who must learn more and more about less and less in order to survive in an age of advancing technology.

Participatory Decision Making Today

Because of this, many companies continually seek new ways to improve workers' attitudes and to stimulate their productivity. In numerous manufacturing firms, for instance, assembly-line personnel are being given larger shares of responsibility in the management of their work. And participatory decision making between workers and managers, once considered "textbook theory," is rapidly becoming a reality.

Goals of Our Economic System: What Do We Want to Accomplish?

When we refer to the economy as a "system," we imply that it has a purpose and that there is order in its structure. What are the goals of our economic system? What do we want our economy to do?

Every economic system seeks to attain the same four goals: efficiency, equity, stability, and growth.

Every society seeks to attain certain objectives. Four goals that are fundamental to all economic systems, capitalistic as well as socialistic, are (1) efficiency, (2) equity, (3) stability, and (4) growth. The meanings of these terms are worth examining because they are universal standards used for judging the success of economic practices and policies.

Efficiency: Full Employment of Resources

Because every society possesses only limited amounts of the various factors of production, these resources must be used with maximum efficiency. What does this mean? In general, *efficiency* is the ability to make the best use of available resources to attain a desired result. This definition is adequate for most purposes. But for use in economic reasoning a clear distinction must be made between two different kinds of efficiency—technical and economic efficiency.

Technical Efficiency

Engineers measure physical efficiency by the ratio of physical output to physical input. The greater the ratio, the greater the physical efficiency. If a motor, for example, uses 100 units of energy input to produce 80 units of energy output, the motor is said to be 80 percent efficient. If the motor produces 75 units of energy output for 100 units of energy input, the motor is 75 percent efficient.

When a system has attained the greatest physical efficiency possible, it is at a point of *technical efficiency*. In economics, a firm, an industry, or an entire economy is said to be technically efficient when it is achieving maximum output by making the fullest possible utilization of available inputs. The definition works in reverse, too. That is, when a production system has attained technical efficiency, its resources are fully employed in the most effective way. Therefore, no change in the combination of inputs can be made that will increase the output of one product of the system without decreasing the output of another.

This idea can be illustrated with an example. Suppose a farmer growing as much corn as possible with the available quantities of labor, capital, and land has achieved technical efficiency. Under these circumstances, it will be impossible for the farmer to transfer some resources out of corn production and into wheat production without decreasing the farm's output of corn.

The concept of technical efficiency can be broadened from simple production systems to more complex ones, such as firms, industries, or the entire economy. An economic system, for example, is technically efficient if every firm in the system has attained technical efficiency — the greatest possible ratio of physical output to available physical input. No change in the combination of society's resources can then be made that will increase the output of one commodity without decreasing the output of another.

Economic (Allocative) Efficiency

Suppose a society has achieved technical efficiency and is making full use of its available resources. Would you give high marks to such a society if families who wanted a larger apartment had to wait ten years before one became available? Would you think the economy efficient if people who wanted to buy meat for dinner were required to spend all afternoon waiting in line outside the meat market? Most people would agree that an economic system ought to deliver the goods and services that people want and are able to pay for.

A standard that is useful in determining the success of an economy is *economic*, or *allocative*, *efficiency*. An economy is said to have achieved economic (allocative) efficiency when it is producing that combination of goods and services that people prefer, given their incomes. No change can then be made in the combination of resources or output that will make someone better off without making someone else worse off — each in his or her own estimation.

Because technical and economic efficiency are important concepts, it is useful to look at the relation between them:

1. A society that has achieved technical efficiency is making full use of its available resources. But the society is not economically efficient unless it is producing the goods that people prefer to purchase with their existing incomes.

2. A society that has achieved economic efficiency has also achieved technical efficiency. That is, the society is not only producing the largest possible output with the available resources but also satisfying consumer preferences. Economic efficiency is thus a general concept that includes technical efficiency.

These ideas suggest a useful guide for judging the success of various economic practices and policies.

One of the fundamental goals of our society is to achieve *full employment*—maximum, efficient utilization of the economy's available resources. For human resources, this means that everyone who wants to work is working, except for those who may be temporarily out of work or those who are changing jobs.

Efficiency thus means *full employment of available resources*, both human and material. You will find more complete definitions of "full employment" and "efficiency" in the Dictionary of Economic Terms and Concepts at the back of the book.

Equity: Fairness or Economic Justice

Economic efficiency refers to a society's making the best use of scarce resources to fulfill consumers' preferences. Economic efficiency does not address the question of how a society's goods are shared. This is a problem of *income distribution*—the division of a society's output (that is, the income the society earns from production) among its members. Because income distribution concerns the matter of who gets how much, it raises fundamental issues of equity or justice that every society must attempt to resolve.

Equity is justice with respect to who gets how much of the nation's goods.

Equity is both a philosophical concept and an economic goal. Unfortunately, there is no scientific way of concluding that one distribution of income is fair and therefore "good" while another is unfair and therefore "bad." For example, in the United States a neurosurgeon may earn twenty times as much as a schoolteacher; in Britain, four times as much; in Israel, twice as much; and in Cuba and China, an even smaller ratio. Which ratio is equitable depends on the rules or standards of income distribution a society establishes. You will learn about such standards in later chapters. Meanwhile, the following considerations should be kept in mind:

> Wide differences in personal income exist in our economy. Among the causes are differences between people in native ability and intelligence, in education and training, and in the extent of property ownership. In addition, the practice of racial and sexual discrimination also plays a role. One of the major goals of our society is to achieve an equitable distribution of income. Because equitable means "fair" or "just" (*not* "equal"), the attainment of equity requires that we seek reasonable methods of altering the controllable factors that cause undesirable differences in income.

Stability: Steady Average Price Level

A third economic goal of every society is to achieve stability of prices. This does not mean that *all* prices should be stable. That would be impossible in a society in which people are free to make economic decisions. However, it means that the general or *average* level of prices should be reasonably stable. This goal is important because the costs to society of a sharply rising average price level—inflation—are serious and pervasive.

Stability is the avoidance of substantial increases or decreases in the average level of prices.

Inflation hurts all of us in various ways. It impairs efficiency by lowering incentives to produce. It redistributes income arbitrarily and inequitably by reducing many people's purchasing power by disproportionate amounts. Further, it greatly weakens the nation's ability to compete in world markets when prices at home rise faster than those in other countries with which we trade. The results are losses in efficiency and greater social inequities.

Growth: Rising Output per Person

A fourth economic goal of every society is economic growth. By this is meant an increase in the quantity of goods and services produced per person—in other words, a rising standard of living.

Economic growth is tied to the goals of stability, efficiency, and equity. By maintaining stability, an economy avoids substantial price fluctuations and is better able to encourage efficiency—continuous full employment of available resources. This, in turn, leads to a robust volume of economic activity and to steady economic growth. As a result, equity is enhanced for all income groups in society because all of them can benefit even if each receives a constant proportion of an expanding economic pie.

Striving for A Proper Mix of Goals

The goals of efficiency, equity, stability, and growth seem reasonable enough. However, their realization may involve certain sacrifices—for the following two reasons.

Free Choice Versus Governmental Direction

Economic goals may conflict with one another and with our goals of political and social freedom.

In a democracy, there is a close connection between political freedom and economic freedom. Citizens vote for legislators who influence government policy, consumers choose the goods they want, workers select their occupations, and holders of wealth employ their assets as they see fit. Government, of course, may impose certain restrictions that it believes are in the public's interest. Also, social or racial discrimination may deprive some people of equal opportunities. Nevertheless, *the preservation and enhancement of freedom of choice are ideals of our democratic political and economic system.*

Unfortunately, freedom of choice does not always lead to efficiency, equity, stability, and growth. When it does not, we may be inclined to rely heavily on governmental direction and control to achieve these goals. This could cause us to sacrifice some of our political and economic freedoms. Therefore, unless we know the extent to which we are prepared to make such sacrifices, implementation of the goals outlined above will remain difficult for government policy makers.

Conflicting Goals

A second reason why sacrifices may be necessary is that certain goals tend to conflict with each other. For example, efficiency can conflict with stability if full employment, or even a high level of employment, exerts upward pressure on prices. Similarly, economic growth can conflict with equity if a rising volume of output per person benefits some groups at the expense of others.

Where such conflicts occur, government may try, through legislation or regulation, to promote the desirable goals while minimizing the undesirable consequences. However, such efforts are also likely to entail some costs. For instance, legislation that establishes a ceiling for wages and prices may very well succeed in curbing inflation, but it will also limit freedom of choice for consumers, workers, and businesspeople alike.

Conclusion: Decisions Involve Trade-Offs

It is evident from these considerations that every decision entails a choice between alternatives. If the choices are to be made rationally, we must understand the trade-offs. These consist of the alternative cost or sacrifice of choosing one objective over another, or of formulating compromises between them. Thus, an overall problem faced by society is to establish a proper mix of goals.

As a rule:

When goals conflict with one another, sacrifices or trade-offs must be made.

> The goals of nations vary according to their political as well as their economic philosophies. To achieve certain objectives, such as full employment and rapid economic growth, autocratic socialistic countries such as the Soviet Union, China, and Cuba have sacrificed much political and economic freedom. In contrast, democratic capitalistic countries, such as the United States, Canada, Japan, and many Western European nations, have tried to achieve those objectives without sacrificing political and economic freedom.

Scarcity: A Fundamental Economic Challenge

In economics, *scarcity* is the name of the game and *economizing* is the way it is played. Every society must face a fundamental economic challenge. How can limited resources best be used to satisfy unlimited wants? This is the problem of scarcity.

Scarcity of resources is what economics is all about.

For most people, scarcity is a fact of life. Most of the things they want and need are *economic goods*, in that they have a price. In this sense, they differ from *free goods*, for which the market price is zero. But even "free goods" may be scarce in some circumstances. Hawaiian sunshine and surf are free to the residents of Hawaii, but not to the tourists who must expend time, effort, and money to get there. The fish in a mountain lake may be free goods, but in a city they are scarce.

These facts suggest an important law:

> **Law of scarcity.** Economic resources are scarce. There are never enough at any given time to produce all the things that people want. Scarce resources can be increased, if at all, only through effort or sacrifice.

Scarcity of resources is what forces every economic system to make choices. A decision to produce one thing frequently implies a decision to produce less of certain other things. All societies face the basic problem of deciding what they are willing to sacrifice to get the things they want. This is the central problem of economics.

All economic systems must make decisions about the use of their scarce resources.

In general:

> Economics is fundamentally concerned with choices about the use of resources. Problems of choice arise when there are alternative ways of achieving a given objective. Economics develops specific criteria that define the conditions for making the best use of society's resources. These criteria are then used as guidelines for formulating and evaluating public policy.

The Great Questions: What? How? For Whom?

It is the task of an economic system to combine efficiently its *resources*, *wants*, and *technologies*. To do so, it must answer three fundamental and interdependent questions.

What Goods and Services Should Society Produce— and in What Quantities?

What consumer goods and what capital goods should society produce? How much should it produce of each?

How should a society's scarce resources be allocated? Should some of them be taken out of the production of consumer goods (food, clothing, automobiles, and appliances) and put into the production of capital goods (tools, machines, tractors, and factories)? Would the reverse be better? For instance, by enlarging its proportion of capital goods now, the economy will be able to produce more consumer goods in the future. It is necessary, then, to decide how much consumption should be sacrificed today to provide for increased output of consumer goods later.

A related question is: *How much* of each good should society produce? How many automobiles? How much food and clothing? How many tractors, factories, and so on? The values and priorities involved in making such decisions are extremely complex. Nevertheless, in answering this question, society is again choosing between present and future satisfactions. It is making a trade-off between the amount of consumption to be sacrificed today and the prospect of increased consumption at a later time.

How Should Resources Be Organized for Production?

How should the various consumer goods and capital goods be produced?

Most goods can be produced in more than one way by using resources in different quantities and combinations. In the early days of the United States, for example, land was in abundant supply and labor was not. Therefore, labor was the limiting factor in producing agricultural commodities. In parts of the Far East, by contrast, land is relatively more scarce than labor. Consequently, large quantities of labor are applied to limited amounts of arable land.

Similarly, it is often possible to vary the combinations of resources in manufacturing. Automobiles, for example, can be produced from different combinations of such materials as steel, aluminum, or fiber glass, as well as with different combinations of labor and capital. Any society, therefore, must decide how it will *organize* its scarce resources in order to use them efficiently.

For Whom Shall the Goods Be Produced?

How should society's output be divided?

Who is to receive what share of the economic pie? This question is of enormous significance, because an economic system is often judged by the way in which it distributes its goods and services. It is also a question of direct concern to each of us, because the answer determines our individual standards of living.

The three great questions—*what, how,* and *for whom*—are fundamental in all societies. Each society meets these challenges in different ways.

At one extreme is a *command economy*. This is one in which an authoritarian government exercises primary control over decisions concerning what and how much to produce. Government may also, but does not necessarily, decide for whom to produce. The Soviet Union, China, and Cuba are examples of countries with predominately command economies. At the other extreme is the *market economy*. In such an economy, all three questions are decided in an open market through the competitive forces of supply and demand. The market economy embodies the ideal of "pure" capitalism, also called "theoretical capitalism." It is an extremely useful model of what would happen in the absence of governmental direction. (The model's uses are examined in later chapters.) It is important to note that no countries with pure market economies exist. However:

> Between the two extremes of a command economy and a market economy is the *mixed economy*. Here the three great questions, or specific applications of them, are decided partly by the workings of a free market and partly by a central governmental authority. Most of the developed nations fall into this category. However, they vary in the degree of reliance they place on the market mechanism.

Society's Production Possibilities

For every society, the answers to the questions of *what*, *how*, and *for whom* are intimately related to the need for economizing. In reality, the problem of economizing is a complex one. Therefore, we must simplify it in order to focus on the basic concepts involved.

We may begin by constructing a model of the economizing process for a hypothetical society. The model is based on four assumptions:

A production-possibilities model rests on four assumptions.

1. Two Goods *The economy produces only two types of goods: agricultural, such as crops and livestock, and capital, such as machines and factories.* This assumption permits us to derive principles for a simple two-good economy. These principles are also applicable to a complex economy producing many goods.

2. Common Resources *The same resources can be used to produce either or both of the two classes of goods and can be shifted freely between them.* This means that labor and other factors of production can be used to produce either food or machines, or different combinations of both.

3. Fixed Conditions *The supply of resources and the state of technological knowledge are fixed.* This is an appropriate assumption for the short run. In the long run, of course, the supply of resources and the level of technological knowledge are expandable rather than fixed.

4. Full Employment *Society's resources are fully employed in the most (technically) efficient way.* This assumption emphasizes the fact that in the short run the economy may be able to increase the production of one class of goods by taking resources away from the production of another class of goods. However, the economy cannot increase the production of *both* classes of goods.

The model is depicted, both tabularly and graphically, in Exhibit 2. The table is called a *production-possibilities schedule*. Notice that, if society chooses production alternative *A*, it will be devoting all its resources to the production of agricultural goods. None of its resources will be used in the production of capital goods. Society will thus be producing 14 units of agricultural goods and zero units of capital goods.

The model can be expressed in the form of a table or in the form of a graph.

At the other extreme, if society chooses alternative *G*, it will be putting all its resources into the production of capital goods. Society will thus be producing six units of capital goods and zero units of agricultural goods.

These two alternatives are extremes. Realistically, the society must seek a balance. As society tries to increase its production of capital goods by choosing among alternatives *B*, *C*, *D*, and so on, it must *sacrifice* some agricultural goods. The amount of sacrifice for each produc-

Exhibit 2
Society's Production-Possibilities Curve: Achieving Technical Efficiency

A society that is producing a combination of goods on its production-possibilities curve has achieved technical efficiency. This means that the society has attained the largest possible output with available inputs. Therefore, no change in the combination of inputs can be made that will increase the output of one product without decreasing the output of another.

However, the society will not have achieved *economic* efficiency unless it is producing the combination of goods that people prefer to purchase with their existing incomes.

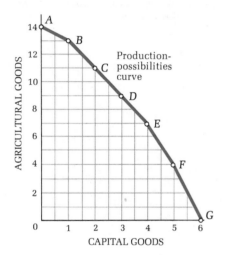

Production-Possibilities Schedule

Production alternatives	Capital goods production	Agricultural goods production	Sacrifice of agricultural goods for capital goods
A	0	14	
B	1	13	1
C	2	11	2
D	3	9	2
E	4	7	2
F	5	4	3
G	6	0	4

(**Note** When sketching a production-possibilities curve freehand, you should draw it smooth. A smooth curve is an idealization or model of a real situation and is easier to interpret than a jagged line.)

tion alternative is shown by the negative numbers in the fourth column of the table. The negative numbers therefore represent the amount of agricultural goods the economy must give up to acquire one more unit of capital goods.

All the information in the production-possibilities schedule can be transferred directly to the accompanying graph. Note that the units of capital goods are scaled on the horizontal axis and those for agricultural goods on the vertical axis. The line that connects the various production alternatives *A* through *G* is called a *production-possibilities curve* It reveals all possible combinations of maximum total output for the society it represents.

Law of Increasing Costs

The production-possibilities curve raises two challenging problems. The first concerns the attainment of an optimum combination of goods. The second concerns society's increasing sacrifice of one good for another.

Optimum Combinations

Is there a combination of agricultural and capital goods that is better than any other? The production-possibilities curve alone cannot tell us what combination of the two goods to produce. For example, some countries, such as the Soviet Union and China, have sought rapid economic growth by emphasizing the production of capital goods at the expense of consumer goods. Other nations, such as New Zealand and Uruguay, have traditionally allocated larger proportions of their resources to agricultural than to capital-goods production. Because such choices as these are based on a society's value judgments and goals, they involve questions that economics alone cannot answer.

Increasing Sacrifice

Why does an increasing amount of one good have to be sacrificed to obtain each additional unit of the other? In the model, greater and greater sacrifices of agricultural output must be made in order to get more capital goods. This is because the economy's factors of production differ and are not all equally suitable for producing the two types of goods. Fertile land, for example, is more suitable for crops than for factories, and unskilled farm workers are more adaptable to agriculture than to manufacturing. Even though an economy's resources may be substitutable within wide limits for given production purposes, the resources are relatively more efficient in some uses than in others. Thus, as society tries to increase its production of capital goods, it must take increasing amounts of resources out of agriculture. This is necessary even though, in the model, the resources are relatively more productive in agriculture.

These points suggest the operation of an important law.

Law of increasing costs. As society increases production of one good, it must sacrifice increasing amounts of an alternative good to produce each additional unit. The real cost of acquiring either good, therefore, is not the money that must be spent for it. The real cost is the amount of the *alternative* good that the society must sacrifice because it cannot have all it wants of both goods. Increasing costs are reflected in the shape of the production-possibilities curve, which is bowed outward.

Refer back to the fourth column of the table in Exhibit 2 and note again that the sacrifices are shown as negative numbers. This is because they represent the amount of agricultural goods that the society must give up in order to acquire another unit of capital goods. For example, if the society is at point D and wants to go to point E, it must give up two units of agricultural goods to gain one unit of capital goods. Similarly, if it is at point E and wants to get to point F, it must give up three units of agricultural goods to gain one unit of capital goods.

Conclusion: Opportunity Cost

The concept of a production-possibilities curve and the associated law of increasing costs point to a fundamental idea in economics:

> Because resources are scarce, the extent to which they are used for one purpose necessarily precludes their use for another. The alternative opportunity that is sacrificed is therefore the cost of their use.

Consider an example from your own experience. The more hours you devote to your schoolwork each day, the fewer hours you have available for other purposes. Therefore, the cost to you of allocating more hours to your studies is measured by the value of the time you are giving up. This value may consist of the income you could have earned from a job or even the pleasure you would have derived from additional hours of recreation.

In economics, we give a special name to this idea:

> The value of the benefit that is forgone by choosing one alternative rather than another is called *opportunity cost*. Also known as "alternative cost," it is measured by what an economic entity—such as a society, a business, a household, or a person—is not doing but could be doing. *The opportunity cost of any decision is thus the value of the sacrificed alternative.*

Some applications of production-possibilities curves are presented in Box 1.

The production-possibilities model illustrates the important concept of opportunity cost. This is the value of the alternative that is sacrificed when a decision is made to do one thing rather than another.

Capitalism and Our Mixed Economy

The economic system of our nation and of many other countries of the Western world is commonly known as "capitalism," "free enterprise," or "private enterprise." What does this mean?

> *Capitalism* is a system of economic organization characterized by private ownership of the factors of production and their operation for profit under predominantly competitive conditions.

On what theoretical foundations does capitalism rest? Is our economic system typical of theoretical (or pure) capitalism?

Capitalism means private ownership of the factors of production.

Institutions of Capitalism

If you take a course in sociology, you will learn that social systems are often characterized by their *institutions*. These may be defined as those traditions, beliefs, and practices that are well established and widely held to be fundamental parts of a culture. Because capitalism is a type of social system—or more precisely, a type of *socioeconomic* system—it has its own particular institutions. The following are the ones on which a pure capitalistic system rests.

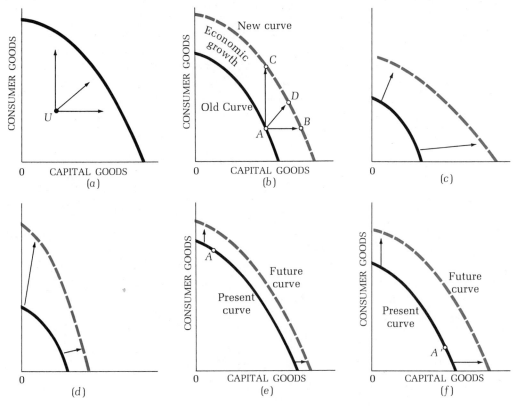

Box 1
**Applications of
Production-Possibilities
Curves**

Production-possibilities curves can be used to depict several interesting situations.

Effect of Resource Underutilization

An economy that underutilizes its resources is producing at some point, such as U, inside its production-possibilities curve. This is shown in Figure (a). Three of the moves that it can make to get back on the curve are to produce more capital goods (*horizontal arrow*), more consumer goods (*vertical arrow*), or more of both (*diagonal arrow*).

Economic Growth

Increases in resources or improvements in technology will shift an economy's pro-

duction-possibilities curve outward from the origin, as shown in Figure (b). The resulting expansion represents *economic growth*—a higher level of real output per capita. Note from Figures (c) and (d) that the new curve need not necessarily be "parallel" to the old one. Changes in resources or in technology may be such as to bring about a greater increase in one type of output than in another.

Present Goods Versus Future Goods

A society that allocates more resources in the present to the production of capital goods than to consumer goods will have more of both kinds of goods in the future.

The society will thus experience more economic growth. This is because consumer goods are used to satisfy present wants, whereas capital goods are used to satisfy future wants.

Figures (e) and (f) show how the degree of outward shift of a society's future production-possibilities curve is affected by whether it chooses to be at point A (emphasizing consumer goods) or at point A' (emphasizing capital goods) on its present curve. Note that the outward shift of the curve in Figure (f) is greater than that in Figure (e).

Private Property

The institution of *private property* is the most basic element of capitalism. It assures each person the right to acquire economic goods and resources by legitimate means, to enter into contracts concerning their use, and to dispose of them as he or she wishes.

The right to own and use property is the most fundamental institution of capitalism.

This concept of private property originated in the writings of the late-seventeenth-century English philosopher John Locke. He justified private ownership and control of property as a "natural right" independent of the power of the state. This right, he maintained, provides maximum benefits for society as a whole. (In contrast, socialist views prevailing since the nineteenth century have held that private property is a means of exploiting the working class—the so-called "proletariat.")

The granting of property rights fulfills three important economic functions:

1. It provides people with personal incentives to make the most productive use of their assets.

2. It strongly influences the distribution of wealth and income by allowing people to accumulate assets and to pass them on to others at the time of death.

3. It allows for a high degree of exchange, because people must have property rights before those rights can be transferred.

The social and economic consequences of these functions, as you will see, have been instrumental in the development of capitalism.

Self-Interest—The "Invisible Hand"

In 1776, a Scottish professor of philosophy, Adam Smith, published *The Wealth of Nations*. In this book, the first systematic study of capitalism, Smith described his principle of the *"invisible hand."* This principle states that each person, pursuing his or her self-interest without interference by government, will be led, as if by an invisible hand, to achieve the best good for society. In Smith's words:

When people are permitted to pursue their self-interest, society, as if guided by an "invisible hand," realizes its greatest good.

> An individual neither intends to promote the public interest, nor knows he is promoting it. . . . He intends only his own gain, and he is led by an invisible hand to promote an end which was no part of his intention. . . . It is not from the benevolence of the butcher, the brewer, or the baker that we expect our dinner, but from their regard to their self-interest. We address ourselves not to their humanity, but to their self-love, and never talk to them of our necessities, but of their advantages.

Self-interest drives people to action, but alone it is not enough. People must understand the effects of their decisions and their actions on their economic well-being. They must think rationally if they are to make the right decisions.

This requirement ultimately led economists to introduce the concept of *economic man*—the notion that each person in a capitalistic society is motivated by economic forces. In other words, each person will always act in such a way as to obtain the greatest amount of satisfaction for the least amount of sacrifice or cost. These satisfactions may take the form of greater profits for a businessperson, higher wages or more leisure time for a worker, and greater pleasure from goods purchased for a consumer.

Of course, these assumptions are not always realistic. People may be motivated by forces other than self-interest. Nevertheless, the idea of economic man does serve as a reasonable approximation of the way people tend to pattern their economic behavior in a capitalistic society. And in economics, as in other social sciences, reasonable approximations are often the best that can be made.

Economic Individualism—Laissez-Faire

In the late seventeenth century, Louis XIV reigned as King of France. His finance minister, Jean Baptiste Colbert, asked a manufacturer by the name of Legendre how the government might help business. Legendre's reply was "*laissez nous faire*" (leave us alone). The expression became a watchword and motto of capitalism.

"Laissez-faire" means the absence of government intervention in economic matters.

Today we interpret *laissez-faire* to mean that absence of government intervention leads to economic individualism and economic freedom. Under laissez-faire conditions, people's economic activities are their own private affairs. As consumers, they are free to spend their incomes as they choose. As producers, they are free to purchase the economic resources they desire and to use these resources as they wish.

In reality, some applications of the concept of laissez-faire are significantly limited. This is because economic freedom is almost always subject to restraints imposed by society for the protection and general welfare of its citizens. Can you give some examples indicating why such restraints are necessary?

Competition and Free Markets

Competition requires the presence of numerous buyers and sellers, each one able to exercise free choice in the marketplace.

Capitalism operates under conditions of *competition*. This means that there is rivalry among sellers of similar goods to attract customers and among buyers to secure the goods that are wanted. There is rivalry among workers to obtain jobs and among employers to obtain workers. There is also rivalry among buyers and sellers of resources to transact business on the best terms that each can get from the other.

Theoretical capitalism is often described as a free-market system. Competition and free markets are closely related. In their most complete or pure form, free markets have two characteristics:

1. There are a large number of buyers and sellers, each with a small enough share of the total business so that no individual can affect the market price of the commodity.

2. Buyers and sellers are unencumbered by economic or institutional restrictions, and they possess full knowledge of market prices and alternatives. As a result, they enter or leave markets as they see fit.

Under such circumstances, the market price of a particular commodity is established by the interacting forces of demand and supply. Each buyer and each seller, acting in his or her own best interest as an economic being, decides whether or not to transact business at the going price. No individual has control over the price because no one buyer or seller is large enough to exert any perceptible influence in the market.

In the real world, competition does not exist in this pure form. The closest we get to a pure free market is in organized exchanges such as the Chicago Board of Trade and the New York Cotton Exchange. These markets, which are open to all buyers and sellers, deal in such standardized commodities as soybeans, grains, basic metals, and cotton. Markets of this type are studied in considerable detail in microeconomics.

To summarize:

A free market performs a number of important functions. Among them:

1. It establishes competitive prices both for consumer goods and for the factors of production.

2. It encourages the efficient use of economic resources.

Free markets may fail to perform these functions if there is a growth of monopolistic or restrictive practices. When this occurs, society (through government) will frequently intervene in the market to regulate such practices.

The Price System

Who tells workers where to work or what occupations to choose? Who decides that automobiles should be made in Detroit and steel in Pittsburgh? Who declares how many cars should be produced and how many homes should be built? Who specifies the predominant style of women's dresses or men's suits?

The greater the degree of competition, the more these matters will be decided impersonally and automatically by the *price system* or the *market system*. This may be viewed as a system of rewards and penalties. Rewards consist of profits for firms and people who succeed. Penalties take the form of losses, or possibly bankruptcy, for those who fail. The price system is fundamental to the traditional concept of capitalism.

The price system basically operates on the principle that everything that is exchanged—every good, every service, and every resource—has its price. In a free market with many buyers and sellers, the prices of these things reflect the quantities that sellers make available and the quantities that buyers wish to purchase.

Thus, if buyers want to purchase more of a certain good than suppliers have available, its price will rise. This will encourage suppliers to produce and sell more of it. On the other hand, if buyers want to purchase less of a certain good, this will cause a drop in its price. Suppliers will then find it to their advantage to produce and sell less of the good.

This interaction between sellers and buyers in a competitive market, and the resulting changes in prices, are what most people refer to by the familiar phrase "supply and demand."

In a capitalistic system, the price system operates to allocate society's resources. This is what is normally meant by the familiar phrase "supply and demand."

Government: Rule-Maker, Protector, Umpire

The doctrine of laissez-faire came into prominence in the eighteenth century as a result of its popularization by Adam Smith in *The Wealth of Nations*. The concept has strong political as well as economic implications. According to this doctrine, the functions of government in a capitalistic system should be confined to certain traditional activities. These include maintaining order, defining property rights, enforcing contracts, promoting competition, and defending the realm. They also include issuing money, prescribing standards of weights and measures, raising funds to meet operating expenses, and adjudicating disputes over the interpretation of the rules.

Government is thus essential to the existence of capitalism. When society's economic, social, or political values are violated, government, usually through its system of law, takes corrective action. When personal freedoms conflict, one individual's freedom must be limited so that another's may be preserved. In theoretical capitalism, government fulfills the roles of rule-maker, protector, and umpire. Government does

Government's role in a capitalistic system is to enforce the "rules of the game."

this by imposing only those restrictions on personal freedoms that are necessary to protect the well-being of society and by reconciling conflicts of values resulting from the free exercise of property rights.

Conclusion: Our Mixed Economy

The institutions of capitalism provide a framework for the operation of our mixed but capitalistically oriented economy.

Is the doctrine of laissez-faire observed in our economy? Does the "invisible hand" perform as smoothly as Adam Smith said it would, thereby resulting in the best of all possible economic worlds?

The answers to these questions are neither completely positive nor completely negative. Over the years, our economy has become increasingly complicated and the role of government has expanded.

Through the use of legislation of various types, government has come to play a significant role as a protector and regulator of certain groups within the economy. For example: Government has promoted the interests of agriculture, labor, and the consumer. It has controlled competition among such regulated industries as domestic transportation, communication, and power. It has sought to maintain effective competition in the unregulated industries that constitute the bulk of the business sector. Government has assumed the responsibility of keeping the economy's total production and spending in balance to achieve the long-run objectives of economic growth and full employment. And government has become a major provider of many goods and services, among them education, highways, and national defense.

These historical trends suggest the following conclusion:

> The American economy is neither a pure market economy nor a pure command economy. It is a mixed but capitalistically oriented economy in which both private individuals and government exercise their economic influence in the marketplace. All countries today that call their economic systems capitalistic are actually mixed, capitalistically oriented economies.

The Circular Flow of Economic Activity

The circular-flow model depicts the movement of goods and resources between sectors of the economy.

How does a capitalistic system make products available to households and resources available to businesses? The answer is summarized in a simplified way in Exhibit 3. This model, the *circular flow of economic activity*, assumes that the total economy is divided into two sectors: households and businesses. The model shows how the two sectors meet each other in two sets of markets: the product markets and the resource markets.

In the *product markets*, households buy the goods and services that businesses sell. Payments for these goods and services are represented by consumption expenditures that become the receipts of businesses. In the *resource markets*, businesses buy the factors of production that households sell. Payments for these factors of production are costs that become the money incomes of households.

All these transactions are accomplished in free markets by a price system that registers the wishes of buyers and sellers. Through the price system, therefore, the product markets are the places where businesses decide *what* to produce, whereas the resource markets are the places where businesses decide *how* to produce.

One other feature of the diagram should be noted. The outer loop portrays the physical flow of goods and resources in one direction. The inner loop shows the corresponding flow of money in the opposite direc-

Exhibit 3
The Circular Flow of Economic Activity

Households and businesses are linked through the product markets, where goods and services are exchanged, and through the resource markets, where the factors of production are exchanged. The questions of *what* and *how* to produce are answered in these markets. Households act as buyers in the product markets and as sellers in the resource markets, whereas the reverse is true of businesses.

The outer loop shows physical flows in one direction, and the inner loop shows money flows in the opposite direction.

(**Note** The question, *For whom?* is not directly apparent in this diagram. The answer depends on factor prices, which are determined in the resource markets, and on other considerations.)

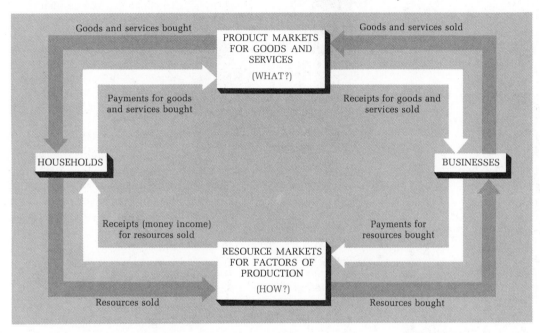

tion. If this model depicted a barter economy instead of a monetary one, only goods and resources would be exchanged and there would be no money flows.

Limitations of the Circular-Flow Model

The circular-flow model is a simplified representation of an economic system. The chief function of the model is to illustrate important aggregate economic relations. But, like any model, it is an abstraction from reality and therefore omits certain features. Among them:

1. The model says nothing about the behavior of individual buyers and sellers. Nor does it show the ways in which they react to determine prices and quantities in the product and resource markets. Hence, it is a *macroeconomic* rather than a microeconomic model.

2. The model assumes a stable, rather than a fluctuating, circular flow. It does not disclose the effects of variations in the flow on the economy's production and employment of resources. Therefore, it overlooks the problems of recession and inflation, which are among the most critical economic issues of our time.

The circular-flow model provides a broad overview of the economy's markets and sectors, not a close look at them.

Brown Brothers

Leaders in Economics

St. Thomas Aquinas
1225–1274
*The Great Scholastic
of Early Capitalism*

The period known as the Middle Ages covers approximately one thousand years—from the fall of the Roman Empire in A.D. 476 to about 1500.

Modern capitalism took root in the last three of these ten centuries. Money and credit instruments gained wider acceptance in trade among European towns and cities. The ownership of tools of production became separated from their use. And a wage system emerged with the growth of urbanization and more centralized production.

Scholasticism
The outstanding intellectual accomplishment of the late Middle Ages was the system of thought known as Scholasticism. The participants in this system are referred to as Scholastics or Schoolmen. Essentially, Scholasticism was an attempt to harmonize reason with faith. The method consisted of integrating philosophy and theology primarily on the basis of rationalism or logic rather than through science and experience.

Economic Beliefs
The greatest of the Scholastic philosophers was Thomas Aquinas, and his most famous work was the *Summa Theologica*. The English translation runs to some twenty volumes. In his writings on economic problems, Aquinas applied the principles of Aristotelian philosophy and logic to biblical teachings and canonical dogma. Thus, according to Aquinas:

• The individual's right to private property accords with natural law.

• Production under private ownership is preferred to production under communal ownership.

• Trade is to be condoned to the extent that it maintains the household and benefits the country.

• Sellers are bound to be truthful with their buyers.

• Fairness exists when goods are exchanged at equal values and at a "just" price that reflects the customary price.

• Wealth is good if it leads to a virtuous life.

• "Usury," which is defined as the charging of excess interest on loans, is among the most objectionable of trade practices.

Practical Rules
Aquinas and the Schoolmen were not in sympathy with many of the economic practices of their time. However, because they could do little to change the practices, they proceeded to make them as respectable as possible. This was done by establishing moral and ethical rules of economic behavior. Many of these rules are now an integral part of modern capitalistic philosophy.

For example, Aquinas decried usury. But he permitted the changing of *some* interest if a lender had to forgo an alternative investment that would have yielded an income. This was the principle of *lucrum cessans*—a concept similar to what is known as "opportunity cost" in modern economics. Aquinas also justified the idea that buyers on credit could pay more than the cash price and that discounts could be allowed on promissory notes. He also believed that many business transactions could entail special charges and payments.

Aquinas was canonized in 1323. For centuries his teachings have been held in high esteem by Catholic and non-Catholic educators alike.

Brown Brothers

Leaders in Economics

Adam Smith

1723–1790
*Founder of Economics
and Apostle of Economic
Liberalism*

The year 1776 was marked by two great events in the struggle for emancipation. In North America, representatives of the British colonies adopted the Declaration of Independence—an eloquent statement setting forth a doctrine of political freedom. In Europe, a former professor of philsophy at the University of Glasgow published a monumental book entitled *An Inquiry into the Nature and Causes of the Wealth of Nations.* Usually known simply as *The Wealth of Nations,* it is an eloquent statement expounding a doctrine of economic freedom. Both the Declaration of Independence and *The Wealth of Nations* stand as milestones in the Age of Enlightenment and Liberalism that blossomed during the eighteenth century.

Systematic Treatise
Born in Scotland and educated at Glasgow and Oxford, Adam Smith became a lecturer on literature and philosophy in his mid-twenties. At the age of 28, he was appointed professor of logic and moral philosophy at the University of Glasgow. His great book, *The Wealth of Nations,* took him ten years to write. It earned for him the epithet "founder of economics" because it was the first complete and systematic study of the subject.

Free Markets
The book is a masterful synthesis of centuries of accumulated but separate economic ideas. In it, Smith argues that labor, rather than land or money, is the basic source of a nation's wealth. He points out that individuals know best what is good for them. Therefore, if unrestricted by government controls or private monopolies, people will be motivated by the quest for profit to turn out the goods and services that society wants. Consequently, through free trade and free markets, self-interest will be harnessed to the common good.

Viable Topics
Smith discussed many topics in *The Wealth of Nations.* Among them: labor; value and price determination; the theory of income distribution involving wages, rent, and profit; the accumulation of capital; and the principles of government finance. These and other topics are fundamental in modern economics textbooks. However, Smith's view of "the economic problem" was somewhat narrower than the modern one.

Smith conceived the central problem of economics to be the struggle to conquer nature in the production of material wealth. Hence, Smith's concern was with increasing the productivity of labor and expanding the size of the market.

Today, on the other hand, the central problem of economics is seen to be a broader one. It is concerned with the allocation of scarce resources among different uses. The goal is to maximize consumers' satisfaction and achieve full employment of resources and steady economic growth without inflation.

Permanent Legacy
Through his approach to economic questions and his organization of the science, Smith cast a mold for the body of nineteenth-century economic thought. His substantive theory provided scores of economists with points of departure for elaboration and refinement. His views on public policy, which became the semiofficial doctrine of the British government, left their imprint on parliamentary debates and governmental reports. For these reasons, and because of his enormous influence upon succeeding generations of scholars, Smith's unique position in the history of economic thought is forever assured.

Classical Liberalism
Reading *The Wealth of Nations* today, one can see why the influence of this book reached out beyond the borders of economics. Like the Bible, Smith's treatise contains familiar concepts and well-worn truths on almost every page. As a result, "the shy and absent-minded scholar," as Smith was affectionately called, became the apostle of classical economic liberalism—meaning laissez-faire in his time. Today we refer to such ideas as "conservatism."

Despite these shortcomings, the circular-flow concept provides many useful insights. They will become increasingly apparent as we seek to amplify the underlying implications and ideas of the model in order to gain a better understanding of our modern mixed economy. (See "Leaders in Economics," pages 30 and 31.)

What You Have Learned in This Chapter

1. A society's resources are the ingredients of its production. The four classes of resources—labor, land, capital, and entrepreneurship—are commonly referred to as the factors of production. The returns received by the owners of these resources are wages, rent, interest, and profits.

2. Every economic system seeks to attain certain objectives. The chief ones are (a) *efficiency* in the use of scarce resources, (b) *equity* in the distribution of income, (c) *stability* of prices, and (d) *growth* of real output per capita. In democratic capitalistic countries, these goals are sought within a framework of political and economic freedoms. Each society, however, must decide the priorities it wishes to place on these goals and the sacrifices to be made in attaining them.

3. All societies are faced with the problem of scarcity because they have limited resources and apparently unlimited wants. Therefore, most economic problems are aspects of the three big questions that every society must answer: *What* to produce—and in what quantities? *How* to produce? *For whom* to produce? The methods by which these questions are answered differ in mixed and in command economies.

4. In an economy characterized by technical efficiency (that is, by full employment of available resources), any increase in the output of some goods and services causes a reduction in the output of others. With given resources and technology, the production choices open to an economy can be summarized by its production-possibilities curve. The shape of this curve reflects the operation of the law of increasing costs. These costs are measured by their opportunity costs, the value of the sacrificed alternatives.

5. A society's production-possibilities curve can be used to illustrate several basic economic concepts.

(a) Production at any point inside the curve indicates some underutilization of resources.
(b) An outward shift of the curve represents an increase in the supply of resources or in technological capability.
(c) At any point on the curve, a choice that alters the existing proportion of consumer goods and capital goods will affect the extent of outward shift of the economy's future curve.

6. The economic system of the United States and many other countries of the Western world is capitalistic. Capitalism is a type of economic organization in which the means of production and distribution are privately owned and used for private gain.

7. Pure capitalism rests on a foundation of certain socioeconomic institutions. These include private property, self-interest, economic individualism or laissez-faire, competition, and the price system. The economic role of government in a pure capitalistic system is relatively minor. Since the nineteenth century, however, capitalistic or market economies have become increasingly complex. As a result, the economic functions of government have gained in importance. Capitalistic economies today are mixed economies in which both private individuals and government exercise their economic influence in the marketplace.

8. The circular-flow model is a simplified representation of our economy. It focuses on aggregate relationships by depicting the streams of money, goods, and resources that link major sectors and markets.

For Discussion

1. *Terms and concepts to review:*
factors of production
land
capital
labor
entrepreneurship

division of labor
efficiency
income distribution
equity
economic goods
free goods
law of scarcity
command economy
market economy
mixed economy
production-possibilities curve
law of increasing costs
opportunity cost
capitalism
institutions
private property
"invisible hand"
economic man
laissez-faire
competition
price system
circular flow of economic activity
product markets
resource markets

2. Would entrepreneurship exist in a purely communistic society in which all citizens live and work by the motto, "From each according to his ability, to each according to his needs"?

3. "No one in a rich society has to starve or go naked. Therefore, it is incorrect to say that scarcity pervades our economy. Because enough food and clothing are available to dress and feed everyone, these goods are not scarce." True or false? Explain.

4. It is sometimes asserted that the act of exchange does not *create* wealth because it merely results in a redistribution of goods already in existence. Evaluate this argument.

5. Denmark produces some of the world's best butter. Yet most Danish butter producers use margarine in their homes instead of butter. Does this make sense? Explain.

6. "Money is a resource because a person who has it can put it to productive use. The same is true of a nation's money." Do you agree?

7. The question, *For whom shall goods be produced?* is concerned with distributing total output among the members of society. Can you suggest at least three different criteria or rules for deciding who gets how much? Which criterion is best?

8. A conventional production-possibilities curve illustrates the law of increasing costs.

Can you draw curves that illustrate (a) constant costs and (b) decreasing costs? Define the meaning of each case.

9. Suppose that an economy produces only agricultural goods and capital goods. Using production-possibilities curves, illustrate the effect of a new invention, assuming that the invention has *no direct impact* on agriculture (although it may have some indirect effects). Describe the possible adjustment paths that society may take as a result of the invention.

10. Distinguish between the concepts of *capital* and *capitalism*.

11. The "profit motive" is sometimes said to be one of the most fundamental features of capitalism. (a) What do you suppose is meant by the "profit motive"? (b) Why wasn't it explicitly listed in this chapter as one of the pillars of capitalism?

12. (a) "In a free competitive economy, the consumer is king." What does this mean? (b) "The producer, not the consumer, is king. After all, the producer is the one who advertises. Therefore, the producer is the one who creates wants and thereby influences what consumers will purchase." True or false? Explain.

13. "A shortcoming of a capitalistic society, as compared with a collectivist or socialistic one, is that people are not compensated in proportion to the usefulness and difficulty of their work." True or false? Explain.

14. If no pure market economy exists and no pure command economy exists, why does economics, which purports to be a science and to deal with reality, bother with these concepts?

Commodity market: bids and offers for meat, corn, and other commodities.

2

CHAPTER

The Laws of Supply and Demand: The Price System in a Pure Market Economy

Learning guide
Watch for the answers to these important questions

What are the "laws" of supply and demand? Do they affect the prices you pay for the things you buy?

What is a market economy? Why do we study it? How is a market economy related to a price system?

Are there advantages to a market economy? Disadvantages? How well does such an economy answer the questions, *What? How?* and *For whom?*

This chapter explains how the prices and quantities of goods are determined in a highly competitive market.

Did you know that even a parrot can answer many important economic questions with just three simple words, *supply and demand?* Here are a few examples.

Question Why are Rembrandts expensive while water is cheap—especially since everyone needs water more than Rembrandts?

Answer Supply and demand.

Question Why is the cost of medical care rising faster than prices generally?

Answer Supply and demand.

Question Why are some luxurious apartments vacant, while there is a shortage of low-cost housing?

Answer Supply and demand.

Question Why do the prices of some commodities fluctuate, while the prices of others remain stable?

Answer Supply and demand.

Such simplistic answers to complex questions are not very illuminating. Nevertheless, much of economics is concerned largely with supply and demand. In this chapter, you will discover more about this apparently simple, but actually complicated, subject.

What Do We Mean by Demand?

If pizzas were $10 each, how many would you buy per month? What if the price were $8? What if it were $6? Would you buy twice as many at $5 as you would at $10?

These are typical of the questions that arise in the study of demand. But what is demand? In economics, it has a special meaning:

Demand is a relation showing the various amounts of a commodity that buyers would be willing and able to purchase at possible alternative prices during a given period of time, all other things remaining the same.

The commodity can be anything—pizzas, shoes, television sets, haircuts, labor time, computers, or any other good or service bought by consumers, businesses, or government agencies. The definition assumes that demand means both the desire to buy and the ability to pay. Either of these taken separately is of no economic significance in the marketplace.

Thus, if you want a steak but cannot pay for it—or if you can pay for a steak but prefer to buy hamburger—you exercise no economic influence in the market for steaks. But if you have both the desire and the ability to pay, these together will affect your demand for the product.

The Demand Schedule

Suppose that you are a merchant dealing in grain—for example, wheat, corn, barley, or oats. What is your demand for a specific commodity, such as wheat?

According to the definition of demand, you must first ask, "At what prices, and for how long?" It seems likely that, within a given period, you would be inclined to buy more wheat at a lower price than you would at a higher one. Also, at a given price, you would probably be inclined to buy more in a longer period than you would in a shorter one. In view of this, you might prepare a hypothetical list of the number of bushels of wheat you would buy at different prices during a particular period of time. The period could be of any length—a day, a week, a month, or more. During this period, *your income and the prices of other commodities are assumed to remain the same.*

Exhibit 1 shows such a list, which economists call a *demand schedule.* This schedule represents your individual demand for wheat over the price range shown. The schedule tells you that, at $5 per bushel, you would buy 5 bushels per day. At a price of $4 per bushel, you would buy 10 bushels per day; and so on. The schedule can be made more detailed by extending the price scale upward and by quoting the prices in dollars and cents instead of just dollars. But such detail is not necessary. As you will see, the schedule already gives you the highlights of your demand for wheat. This is all you need in order to draw a graph.

Sketching a Demand Curve

Most people prefer to look at a graph instead of a table of figures. This preference is easily satisfied by translating numerical data (as in Exhibit 1) into graphic form (as in Exhibit 2). The graphing process is done in three steps.

Step 1 Draw the vertical and horizontal axes of the graph and put the labels on them as shown. Once you become accustomed to sketching such graphs, you may simply label the vertical axis *P* for price and the horizontal axis *Q* for quantity. The starting point or origin of the chart is always the lower left-hand corner, labeled 0 (zero).

Exhibit 1
An Individual Buyer's Demand Schedule for Wheat

A demand schedule is a list showing the number of units of a product that would be purchased at various possible prices during a given period of time.

	Price (dollars per bushel)	Quantity demanded (bushels per day)
A	$5	5
B	4	10
C	3	20
D	2	35
E	1	60

A demand curve is a graph of a demand schedule.

Exhibit 2

An Individual Buyer's Demand Curve for Wheat

A demand curve is the graph of a demand schedule. Each point along the curve represents a different price–quantity combination. A demand curve slopes downward from left to right, reflecting the fact that the quantity demanded of a product varies inversely with the price. This is called the *law of demand.*

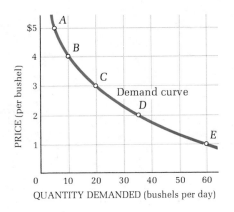

Several factors explain the reasons for the law of demand.

Step 2 Plot the corresponding prices and quantities with large dots, and label them with the appropriate letters (*A, B, C, D,* and *E*) from the demand schedule in Exhibit 1. The letters help you to identify the points. (After you gain some experience in graphing, the emphasized points and letters will no longer be necessary.)

Step 3 Connect the points with a smooth curve.

You have just drawn a *demand curve.* It is the graphic equivalent of the demand schedule in Exhibit 1. The advantage of the curve is that it enables you to "see" the relation between price and quantity demanded. Thus, you can read off the values at a glance, much as you would use a map to locate a ship at sea by its latitude and longitude.

For instance, point *C* represents 20 bushels of wheat demanded per day at a price of $3 per bushel. Would you agree that, at $1.50 per bushel, the quantity demanded is 45 bushels per day? Can you verify that, if the quantity demanded is 35 bushels per day, the *highest price* you would be willing to pay (called the *demand price*) is $2 per bushel? Can you explain why we use an agricultural product rather than a manufactured one? If you are not sure, Box 1 provides a practical answer.

The Law of Demand

A look at the demand curve in Exhibit 2 will reveal its most fundamental property. *The curve slopes downward from left to right*—from northwest to southeast. This characteristic illustrates the law of demand. The law applies to virtually all commodities: wheat, houses, cars, books, stereo records, or practically anything you care to name. Here is a definition:

> **Law of demand.** The quantity demanded of a good varies inversely with its price, assuming that other things that may affect demand remain the same. These include the buyer's income, tastes, and the prices of other commodities.
>
> (**Note** In the definition, "inversely" means that, when the price of a good decreases, the corresponding quantity demanded increases. Also, when the price of a good increases, the corresponding quantity demanded decreases.)

Why does the law of demand operate as it does? This question can be answered in several ways.

1. If the price of a good decreases, you can *afford* to buy more of it if your income, tastes, and the prices of other goods remain the same. For instance, if you like pizza but find it too expensive to buy frequently, a lower price might induce you to buy it more often.

2. When the price of a product is reduced, you may buy more of it because it becomes a better bargain than other goods are. As before, this is based on the assumption that your income, your tastes, and the prices of other goods remain constant. Thus, if the price of steak falls, you might buy more steak and fewer substitutes, such as hamburger or hot dogs. If the price of steak rises, however, you would tend to buy less steak and more substitutes.

3. Finally, the downward-sloping demand curve tells you that you would be willing to pay a relatively high price for a small amount of something. However, the more you have of it—other things remaining the same—the less you would care to pay for one more unit. Why? *Because each extra unit gives you less additional satisfaction or "util-*

ity" than the previous unit gave you. For example, however crazy you are about ice-cream sundaes, there is a limit to the number you can eat in any given period. After the first few sundaes, you would probably lose your appetite for more.

No matter how much you like a product, your demand curve will slope downward for the three sets of reasons given above. Do people in business usually act as if they believed in the existence of a law of (downward-sloping) demand? Evidently, they do. Why else would they advertise bargains that encourage people to buy more goods at lower prices?

Box 1
Why Wheat?

Why use wheat as an example? Why not use a more familiar product, such as cars or television sets?

The answer is that we want to show how the price is established for a uniform or standardized product in a highly competitive market. That is, the market should be characterized by a great many buyers and sellers, each acting independently according to his or her best interests. This type of situation will result in a *single market price* for the product at any given time. Clearly, autos and television sets do not meet these requirements, for at least three reasons.

1. Each product is produced by a relatively small number of sellers.

2. Each is nonstandardized, being differentiated by brand name, model, year, style, color, and so on.

3. Each is characterized by different prices rather than by a single price.

These conditions are true in varying degrees for nearly all the other products we buy every day.

On the other hand, such products as wheat, as well as the other commodities shown on the accompanying list, approximate the requirements of the model rather closely. Any one of them may be used to illustrate the "pure" operation of supply and demand. Prices of these commodities, which are bought and sold in national and international markets, are quoted daily in many newspapers.

Commodities: Cash Prices at National Markets (quotations as of 4 P.M. Eastern time)

	Monday	Friday	Year ago
Foods			
Flour, hard winter, per cwt.	$11.90	$12.00	$ 8.50
Coffee, Santos 4s, per lb.	.80	.76	.65
Cocoa, Accra, per lb.	.77	.79	.37
Sugar, raw, per lb.	.11	.10	.09
Butter, fresh, per lb.	.74	.75	.69
Eggs, per doz.	.64	.66	.39
Broilers, dressed "A," per lb.	.36	.39	.28
Grains and feeds			
Pepper, black, per lb.	.59	.58	.45
Wheat, No. 2, per bu.	4.50	4.92	3.40
Oats, No. 1, per bu.	1.40	1.36	.85
Rye, No. 2, per bu.	2.45	2.48	1.15
Barley, per bu.	3.80	2.90	1.65
Miscellaneous			
Cottonseed oil, per lb.	.19	.18	.10
Soybean oil, per lb.	.19	.19	.09
Peanut oil, per lb.	.24	.21	.17
Cotton, 1 in., per lb.	.72	.71	.29
Print cloth, 64 × 60, 45 in., per yd.	.50	.51	.23
Steel scrap, per ton	90.00	91.00	98.23
Lead, per lb.	.16	.16	.14
Zinc, per lb.	.20	.20	.18

Source: Adapted from *The Wall Street Journal*

Market Demand Is the Sum of Individual Demands

Adding up all of the individual demands at each price gives you the total market demand.

If you were the only buyer of wheat in the market, your demand schedule would also be the demand schedule for the entire market. In reality there are many other buyers, so the total market demand schedule is obtained simply by adding up the quantities demanded by all buyers at each possible price.

Exhibit 3 shows how this is done. This example is based on the assumption that there are only three buyers in the market—Mr. X, Ms. Y, and Mr. Z. However, the example can easily be expanded to include as many buyers as you wish. Note that the individual demand curves have all been labeled so that they can be referred to as they are needed.

What Is Supply?

You now have a basic understanding of demand and the behavior of buyers. The other half of the picture is supply and the behavior of sellers. What do we mean by supply? Is there a law of supply?

> *Supply* is a relation showing the various amounts of a commodity that sellers would be willing and able to make available for sale at possible alternative prices during a given period of time, all other things remaining the same.

Exhibit 3
Market Demand for Wheat, Assuming Three Buyers

The total market demand is obtained by summing all the individual quantities demanded at each price.

Price (dollars per bushel)	Quantity demanded (bushels per day) by Mr. X		by Ms. Y		by Mr. Z		Total market demand per day
$5	0	+	15	+	20	=	35
4	9	+	20	+	26	=	55
3	22	+	27	+	33	=	82
2	42	+	38	+	43	=	123
1	80	+	65	+	60	=	205

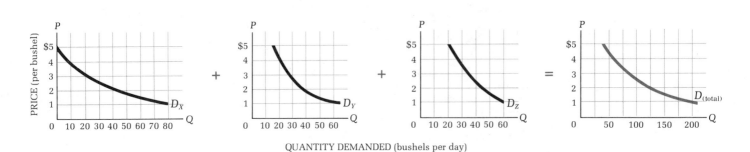

QUANTITY DEMANDED (bushels per day)

How does this definition of supply compare with the definition of demand given near the beginning of this chapter? Are there any similarities? Are there any differences?

Supply Schedules and Supply Curves

Each seller in the market has a *supply schedule* for a product, just as each buyer has a demand schedule. Thus, if you were a wheat farmer, Exhibit 4 might represent your individual supply schedule for wheat. This schedule indicates that, at a price of $1 per bushel, you would not be willing to supply any wheat at all. At a price of $2 per bushel, you would be willing to supply 21 bushels of wheat per day; and so on. Plotting these data on a chart gives the *supply curve* shown in Exhibit 5. What is your estimate of the quantity supplied at a price of $2.50 per unit? What is the *least price,* approximately, that will persuade you to supply 40 bushels per day?

Note The "least price" is more often called the *supply price.* This is the price necessary to call forth a given quantity. What do you estimate the supply price to be for 25 bushels per day?

An example of the supply schedules for three individual producers, Ms. A, Mr. B., and Ms. C, is presented in Exhibit 6. When the data are plotted, they yield the corresponding supply curves shown on the graphs. Note that the total market supply schedule is obtained by adding up the quantities supplied by all sellers at each market price. How does this compare with the way in which the total market demand schedule was derived earlier?

The Law of Supply

The supply curve as drawn has a distinguishing feature. *The curve slopes upward from left to right*—from southwest to northeast. This feature reflects the law of supply:

> **Law of supply.** The quantity of a commodity supplied usually varies *directly* with its price, assuming that all other factors that may determine supply remain the same.

> (**Note** In the definition, "directly" means that the quantity of a product produced and offered for sale will increase as the price of the product rises, and decrease as the price falls.)

Note that, according to the definition, the direct relation between quantity and price is "usually" true, but not always. This is because there can be some situations in which larger quantities are offered for sale at the *same* price as smaller quantities, or even at *lower* prices. These ideas are examined more fully in the study of microeconomics.

If you were a producer—say, a farmer cultivating both wheat and corn—the law of supply would prompt you to act in the following way. If the price of wheat were to rise relative to the price of corn, you would make greater profits by shifting your limited resources—fertilizer, land, labor, machinery, and so on—out of corn production and into wheat production. If the price of wheat were to rise high enough, you would even find it worthwhile to grow wheat on land on which you had previously grown nothing. The law of supply, therefore, does indeed affect producers' decisions concerning *what* and *how much* to produce.

Exhibit 4

An Individual Seller's Supply Schedule for Wheat

A supply schedule is a list showing the number of units of a product that sellers would be willing and able to make available for sale at various prices during a given period of time.

	Price (dollars per bushel)	Quantity supplied (bushels per day)
A'	$5	50
B'	4	42
C'	3	33
D'	2	21
E'	1	0

Exhibit 5

An Individual Seller's Supply Curve for Wheat

A supply curve is the graph of a supply schedule. Each point along the curve represents a different price–quantity combination. A supply curve slopes upward from left to right, reflecting the fact that the quantity of a product supplied varies directly with the price. This is called the *law of supply.*

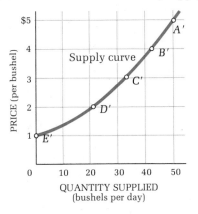

Exhibit 6

Market Supply of Wheat, Assuming Three Sellers

The total market supply of wheat is obtained by summing all the individual quantities supplied at each price.

Price (dollars per bushel)	Quantity supplied (bushels per day)							Total market supply per day
	by Ms. A		by Mr. B		by Ms. C			
$5	52	+	56	+	60	=		168
4	46	+	49	+	50	=		145
3	36	+	42	+	40	=		118
2	26	+	28	+	26	=		80
1	0	+	15	+	10	=		25

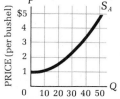
+
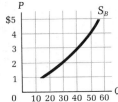
+
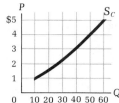
=
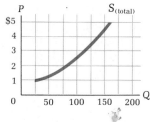

QUANTITY SUPPLIED (bushels per day)

Supply and Demand Together Make a Market

The concepts of supply and demand must be united in order to provide an explanation of how prices are determined in competitive markets.

A market exists whenever and wherever one or more buyers and sellers can negotiate for goods or services and thereby participate in determining their prices. A market, therefore, can be anywhere—on a street corner, on the other side of the world, or as close as the nearest telephone. *Competitive markets* consist of buyers and sellers so numerous that no single one can influence the market price by deciding to buy or not to buy, to sell or not to sell.

Buyers and Sellers in the Marketplace

The intersection of total market demand with total market supply determines the equilibrium market price and quantity.

By using the *total* demand and supply information derived in Exhibits 3 and 6, we can discover how the market price of a product and the quantity bought and sold are determined. The total market demand and supply schedules and their corresponding curves are reproduced in Exhibit 7. Note that the curves, abbreviated *D* and *S*, are identical with the total market curves that were graphed in Exhibits 3 and 6. The only difference is that both curves are now plotted in the same figure so that their interactions can be studied.

The most important thing to observe is that the supply and demand curves intersect at an *equilibrium* point. A dictionary will tell you that "equilibrium" is a state of balance between opposing forces. Let us see what this means in Exhibit 7.

At any price above $2.50 per bushel, the quantity supplied exceeds the quantity demanded. For example, at a price of $5 per bushel, the quantity supplied is 168 bushels per day, and the quantity demanded is 35 bushels per day. This means that, at the price of $5 per bushel, there is a *surplus* of 168 − 35 = 133 bushels per day. Because sellers have made more wheat available than buyers want, sellers will compete with one another to dispose of their product and will thereby drive the price down.

At any price below $2.50 per bushel, the quantity demanded exceeds the quantity supplied. At $1 a bushel, for example, the quantity demanded is 205 bushels per day and the quantity supplied is 25 bushels per day. At this price, there is a *shortage* of 205 − 25 = 180 bushels per day. Because buyers want more wheat than sellers will make available at this price, buyers will compete with one another to acquire the product and will thereby drive the price up.

Arriving at Market Equilibrium

At a price of $2.50 per bushel, the quantity demanded just equals the quantity supplied, 100 bushels per day. At this price there will be no surpluses or shortages. We refer to this price as the *equilibrium price* and to the corresponding quantity as the *equilibrium quantity*.

When the quantity demanded equals the quantity supplied, the market is in a state of *equilibrium*. This is because the price of the product and the corresponding quantities bought and sold are "in balance." That is, they have no tendency to change as a result of the opposing forces of demand and supply. On the other hand, when the quantities demanded and supplied at a given price are unequal or "out of balance," prices and quantities will be changing. Consequently, the market is in a state of *disequilibrium*.

Two Kinds of Changes Involving Demand

Demand and supply curves are extremely practical. You can employ them to answer many fundamental questions in economics. However, before doing so, it is important to note that there may be two kinds of changes involving demand. One is "a change in the quantity demanded," which is reflected in a movement along the demand curve. The other kind is "a change in demand," which is reflected in a movement of the demand curve itself.

Changes in the Quantity Demanded

Take another look at Exhibit 2. According to the law of demand, a downhill movement along the curve in the general direction A, B, C, . . . signifies an increase in the quantity demanded as the *price is reduced*. On the other hand, an upward movement along the curve in the general direction E, D, C, . . . signifies a decrease in the quantity demanded as the *price is raised*. Any such movement along the curve, whether downward or upward, is called a *change in the quantity demanded*. Note that this expression refers to changes in the quantities purchased by buyers due to *changes in price*.

Exhibit 7

Equilibrium Price and Equilibrium Quantity for Wheat

The intersection of the supply and demand curves determines the equilibrium price and the equilibrium quantity. At any price above the equilibrium price, the quantity supplied exceeds the quantity demanded and the price tends to fall. At any price below the equilibrium price, the quantity demanded exceeds the quantity supplied and the price tends to rise. At the equilibrium price, the quantity supplied precisely equals the quantity demanded, and hence there is no tendency for the price to change.

Price (dollars per bushel)	Total market supply (bushels per day)	Total market demand (bushels per day)
$5	168	35
4	145	55
3	118	82
2	80	123
1	25	205

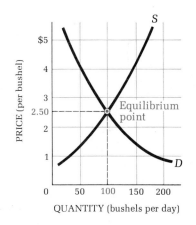

A change in the quantity demanded is a movement along the demand curve due to a change in price.

Exhibit 8
Increase in Demand

An increase in demand can be represented by a shift of the demand curve to the right. At any given price, people are now willing to buy more than they were willing to buy before.

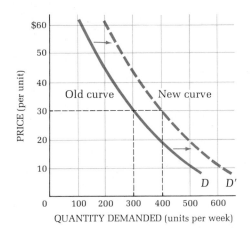

QUANTITY DEMANDED (units per week)

■ **Test Yourself 1**

An increase in demand also means that for any given quantity demanded, buyers are now willing to pay a *higher price* per unit than they were willing to pay before.

1. Can you define a decrease in demand in a parallel way?

2. Look at Exhibit 8. What is your estimate of the highest price per unit that buyers were willing to pay for 300 units per week, before and after the increase in demand?

3. Look at Exhibit 9. What is your estimate of the highest price per unit that buyers were willing to pay for 200 units per week, before and after the decrease in demand?

Changes in Demand

The law of demand says that the quantity of a good demanded varies inversely with its price, assuming that all other things remain the same. What are these "all other things"? What happens if they do not remain the same?

Among the "all other things" that will influence the demand for a good are (1) buyers' money incomes, (2) prices of related goods, and (3) nonmonetary factors. These three sets of demand determinants are not measured on the axes of the graph and hence are assumed to be constant when you draw a demand curve. Therefore, a change in any one of them will cause a shift of the demand curve to a new position. When this happens, we say that there has been a *change in demand*. The change may take either of two forms—an increase or a decrease.

1. An increase in demand can be visualized on a graph as a shift of the demand curve to the right. This is shown in Exhibit 8. The shift takes place from the old demand curve D to the new demand curve D'.
· What does this increase in demand tell you? It shows that, *at any given price, buyers are now willing to purchase more than they were willing to purchase before.* For example, the new curve indicates that, at a price of $30 per unit, buyers were previously willing to purchase 300 units per week. Now, after the increase in demand, they are willing to buy 400 units per week at the same price of $30 per unit.

2. A decrease in demand can be visualized as a shift of the demand curve to the left, as shown in Exhibit 9. This time the graph illustrates that, *at any given price, buyers are now willing to purchase less than they were willing to purchase before.* Thus, at $30 per unit, people were previously willing to buy 300 units per week. Now, after the decrease in demand, they are willing to buy only 200 units per week at the same price of $30 per unit. ■

How do changes in any of the demand determinants mentioned above (buyers' incomes, prices of related goods, and nonmonetary factors) bring about a change in demand? In other words, how do the changes cause a shift of the demand curve to the right or to the left?

Buyers' Incomes

The demand for most goods varies directly with buyers' incomes. This means the demand curves shift to the right when incomes rise and to the left when incomes fall. Goods whose demand curves behave in this way are known as *superior goods*, or more popularly as *normal goods*. They are called this because they represent the "normal" situation. Examples include most food, clothing, cars, and appliances, and other items that people typically buy.

For some goods, however, changes in consumption (prices remaining constant) vary inversely with changes in income over a certain range of income. Such goods are called *inferior goods*. Typical examples are bread, potatoes, beans, and used clothing, all of which are inexpensive and are therefore bought in quantity by poor families. As their incomes rise, these families can afford to buy goods of better quality. Thus, they spend less on bread and potatoes and more on fruits and vegetables, less on beans and more on steak, less on used clothing and more on new clothing.

Prices of Related Goods

A second factor determining the demand for any good is the price of related goods. The strength of this relation depends on the extent to which consumers regard the products as competitive with, or complementary to, each other. Thus, if buyers' incomes remain constant, the goods that consumers purchase may be placed in one of two categories.

Some products are *substitute goods*. The more that people consume of one substitute good, the less they consume of another. An increase in the price of one leads to an increase in the demand for the other. Similarly, a decrease in the price of one leads to a decrease in the demand for the other. For example, if the price of Coca-Cola increases, people will probably buy less Coca-Cola and more Pepsi-Cola. The market demand curve for Pepsi-Cola will therefore shift to the right. On the other hand, if the price of Coca-Cola decreases, people will be inclined to buy more Coca-Cola and less Pepsi-Cola. Then the market demand curve for Pepsi-Cola will shift to the left. What other substitute goods can you think of?

Some products are *complementary goods*. The more that people consume of one complementary good, the more they consume of the other. An increase in the price of one leads to a decrease in the demand for the other. Conversely, a decrease in the price of one leads to an increase in the demand for the other. For example, if the price of cameras increases, people will buy fewer cameras—and less film. The market demand curve for film will shift to the left.

Products that are neither substitutes nor complements are unrelated. The consumption of one does not affect the consumption of the other. Therefore, a change in the price of one does not cause a change in the demand for the other. Some examples are salt and pencils, chewing gum and paper clips, thumbtacks and mustard.

Keep in mind, however, that expenditures on unrelated pairs of goods must represent a relatively small percentage of the consumer's budget. Otherwise, if a buyer's expenditure on a good absorbs a relatively large proportion of his or her budget, a change in its price may affect the buyer's demand for another product. This may be true even if the latter product is neither competitive with nor complementary to the former. One example of this is housing and entertainment. Can you give some other examples?

To generalize thus far:

> Suppose that buyers' incomes remain constant. Then the market demand curve for a product will move in the same direction as a change in the price of its substitute. Conversely, the market demand curve for a product will move in the direction opposite from a change in the price of its complement. This means that, for substitute products, the relation between a change in the price of one commodity and the resulting change in demand for the other is *direct*. For complementary products, the relation is *inverse*.

Expectations Of course, buyers' *expectations* of incomes and prices can also influence their demands for goods and services. If buyers expect higher incomes or higher prices in the near future, larger quantities of goods may be bought in anticipation of the increases. This causes the demand curves for those goods to shift to the right. On the other hand, if buyers expect lower incomes or lower prices, smaller quantities of goods and services may be bought. This causes their demand curves to shift to the left. For these reasons, economists who are engaged in eco-

Exhibit 9
Decrease in Demand

A decrease in demand can be represented by a shift of the demand curve to the left. At any given price, people are now willing to buy less than they were willing to buy before.

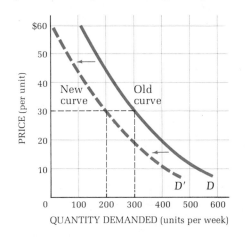

Changes in the prices of substitute and complementary goods, as well as changes in buyers expectations of incomes and prices, will cause the demand curve of a product to shift.

nomic forecasting often try to incorporate the effects of buyers' expectations in their predictive models.

Nonmonetary Factors

Many factors other than prices and incomes influence the demands for goods. These factors include all nonmonetary determinants of demand, such as the age, occupation, sex, race, religion, education, and tastes of consumers, as well as their number. Changes in these factors can affect the preferences of actual and potential consumers. However, it is customary to assume that, for large numbers of consumers, these nonmonetary factors are stable—for two reasons:

1. They vary widely among people so that their effects in the market tend to cancel out.

2. They change slowly over time because they are primarily the result of demographic characteristics and cultural traditions.

For both reasons, therefore, short-run changes in demand can be analyzed exclusively in terms of prices and incomes.

Conclusion: Important Distinctions

You have learned that demand can be represented by a schedule or curve that reflects buyers' attitudes at the time. If the demand curve does not shift, a change in price leads to a *change in the quantity demanded*, not to a change in demand. This means that there has been either an increase in the quantity demanded, as represented by a movement downward along the curve, or a decrease in the quantity demanded, as represented by a movement upward along the curve. The change is due either to a decrease or an increase in the price of the product (while all other demand determinants remain the same).

A *change in demand* means that the schedule itself has changed. Therefore, the demand curve has either shifted to the right, if there has been an increase in demand, or to the left, if there has been a decrease in demand. The shift is due to a change in any of the demand determinants that were assumed to remain constant when the curve was initially drawn.

It is easy to commit errors in economic reasoning by failing to understand the important distinctions between a change in the quantity demanded and a change in demand. ■

Two Kinds of Changes Involving Supply

As with demand, so too with supply, two types of changes may occur. One is called "a change in the quantity supplied"; the other is known as "a change in supply." On the basis of what you now know about the theory of demand, can you guess the meanings of these two concepts before they are explained?

Changes in the Quantity Supplied

Look back at Exhibit 5. According to the law of supply, an upward movement along the curve signifies an increase in the quantity supplied as the *price is raised*. On the other hand, a downward movement along

The various nonmonetary factors that can affect demand usually change slowly. Therefore, short-run changes in demand are caused by changes in prices, incomes, or both.

■ **Test Yourself 2**

Which of the following involve a change in the quantity demanded and which involve a change in demand?

1. People buy more bathing suits in the summer than in the winter.

2. Consumer incomes fall and the number of automobiles purchased declines.

3. Honda reduces the prices of its motorcycles by 10 percent and sales of Honda motorcycles increase.

4. State College raises its tuition and student enrollments fall off.

the curve signifies a decrease in the quantity supplied as the *price is reduced*. Any such movement along the curve, whether upward or downward, is called a *change in the quantity supplied*. Note that such movements are due exclusively to a *change in price*.

Changes in Supply

The law of supply says that the quantity supplied of a product usually varies directly with its price, assuming that all other things remain the same. The "other things" that may have an influence in determining supply are (1) resource prices or the costs of the factors of production, (2) prices of other goods, and (3) nonmonetary factors. If any of these factors change, a new relation is established between price and quantity offered. On a graph, this is shown by a shift of the supply curve to a new position, representing a *change in supply*.

1. An increase in supply is a shift of the supply curve to the right, as shown in Exhibit 10. *At any given price, sellers are now willing to supply more than they were willing to supply before.* For example, at a price of $30 per unit, sellers were previously willing to supply a total of 300 units per week. Now, after the increase in supply, they are willing to sell a total of 400 units per week at the same price of $30 per unit.

2. A decrease in supply is represented by a shift of the supply curve to the left, as shown in Exhibit 11. *At any given price, sellers are now willing to supply less than they were willing to supply before.* For example, they were previously willing to supply a total of 300 units per week at a price of $30 per unit. Now, after the decrease in supply, they are willing to sell a total of 200 units per week at the same price of $30 per unit.

How will a change in any of the supply determinants listed above bring about a change in supply—that is, a shift of the supply curve?

Resource Prices

Ordinarily, a decrease in resource prices (such as wages) in a particular industry will reduce production costs and thus raise the potential for profits. Firms will then be likely to increase their output at each possible price in order to capture more of these potential profits. This action will shift the total market supply curve to the right. Conversely, an increase in resource prices (such as wages) in a given industry would tend to have the opposite effect, because it raises production costs and decreases profits. This encourages businesses in that industry to reduce their output at each possible price. The market supply curve thus shifts to the left.

Prices of Related Goods

Business firms produce goods to earn profits. Changes in the relative prices of goods that a producer makes may change the relative profitabilities of those goods. This brings about changes in their respective supply curves. For instance, if the price of wheat increases relative to the price of corn, farmers may find it more profitable to transfer some land and other resources out of corn production and into wheat production. This would shift the market supply curve of corn to the left and the market supply curve of wheat to the right.

Exhibit 10
Increase in Supply

An increase in supply can be represented by a shift of the supply curve to the right. At any given price, sellers are now willing to supply more than they were willing to supply before.

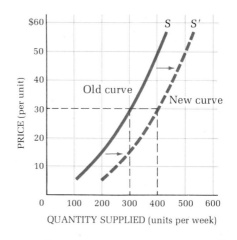

QUANTITY SUPPLIED (units per week)

Exhibit 11
Decrease in Supply

A decrease in supply can be represented by a shift of the supply curve to the left. At any given price, sellers are now willing to supply less than they were willing to supply before.

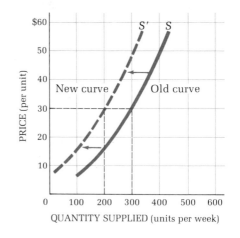

QUANTITY SUPPLIED (units per week)

Sellers' expectations of prices can affect supply curves of goods and services. So can changes in nonmonetary factors.

Expectations Of course, suppliers' *expectations* of prices will also influence their supply decisions. Some producers may decide to hold back on their current output because they expect to get higher prices for their goods in the future and, therefore, to earn higher profits. Other producers may decide to increase their current output because they expect to get lower prices for their goods in the future and, therefore, lower profits or possibly losses.

Nonmonetary Factors

Various factors other than prices can affect the supply of a commodity. The most important are the state of technology and the number of sellers in the market. For example, the adoption of a new production method, such as a new machine, can reduce the need for labor. This may improve technical efficiency and increase supply by shifting the market supply curve to the right. On the other hand, a decline in technical efficiency due to a failure to modernize can have the opposite effect. Similarly, an increase in the number of sellers in the market will result in a rightward shift of the market supply curve. A decrease in the number of sellers will cause a leftward shift of the curve.

Conclusion: Important Distinctions

You have seen that supply can be represented by a schedule or curve that reflects sellers' attitudes at the time. If the supply curve does not shift, a change in price leads to a *change in the quantity supplied*, not to a change in supply. An increase in the quantity supplied is indicated by a movement upward along the curve. Similarly, a decrease in the quantity supplied is indicated by a movement downward along the curve.

A *change in supply* means that the schedule itself has changed. That is, the curve has shifted to the right if there has been an increase in supply or to the left if there has been a decrease in supply. The shift is the result of a change in any of the supply determinants that were assumed to remain constant when the curve was initially drawn.

As with demand, so with supply, these important distinctions must be understood in order to avoid errors in economic reasoning. ∎

■ **Test Yourself 3**

An increase in supply also means that, for any given quantity supplied, sellers are now willing to accept a *lower price* per unit than before.

1. Can you define a decrease in supply in a parallel way?

2. Look back at Exhibit 10. What is your estimate of the lowest price per unit that sellers were willing to accept for a supply of 300 units per week, before the increase in supply? After the increase in supply?

3. Look at Exhibit 11. What is your estimate of the lowest price per unit that sellers were willing to accept for a supply of 200 units per week, before the decrease in supply? After the decrease in supply?

Combined Changes in Demand and Supply

Demand and supply curves rarely remain fixed for very long. This is because the factors determining them, such as buyers' incomes, resource costs, or the prices of related products, are continually changing. These changes cause the curves to shift. Because we are interested in learning about the behavior of prices and quantities in competitive markets, we must be able to analyze such shifts to evaluate their effects.

What happens when a demand or supply curve moves to a new position? The answer is that there may also be a change in the equilibrium price, the equilibrium quantity, or both. Some examples are presented in Exhibit 12, with the arrows indicating the directions of change.

Note that, in each of Figures (a) through (d) of Exhibit 12, one of the curves shifted while the other remained unchanged. The effects on the equilibrium price and quantity in each case are depicted by the arrows. In Figure (a), an increase in demand resulted in an increase in both the equilibrium price and the equilibrium quantity. The opposite occurred in Figure (b) as a result of a decrease in demand. In Figure (c), on the other hand, an increase in supply resulted in a decrease in the equilibrium price and an increase in the equilibrium quantity. The opposite occurred in Figure (d) as a result of a decrease in supply.

Can you explain, using similar terms, what happened in Figures (e) and (f)?

The Market Economy: Is It "Good" or "Bad"?

In a competitive market, prices are determined solely by the free play of supply and demand. An economy characterized entirely by such markets would be a *pure market economy* sometimes called a "competitive economy." The two expressions are often used interchangeably. They represent the "pure" model of capitalism.

What are the desirable features of such an economy? Does it have shortcomings? Is it realistic as a description of the capitalistic system?

The Principal Features of a Pure Market Economy

The answers to these questions can be expressed within the familiar framework of our society's four fundamental economic goals: efficiency, equity, stability, and growth.

Efficiency

In a competitive economy there is *consumer sovereignty*. This means that the consumer is "king"—or "queen." That is, consumers "vote" by offering more dollars for products in greater demand and fewer dollars for products in lesser demand. In this way, consumers cause shifts in demand curves. How do producers respond to these changes in demand? In general:

> In a pure market economy, resources will be used as efficiently as possible. This is true to the extent that supply and demand reflect all costs and benefits of production and consumption. The efficient use of resources occurs because firms in each industry compete for the dollar "votes" of consumers. As a result, each firm, and therefore the economy as a whole, achieves technical efficiency by making the fullest utilization of available inputs. The economy also achieves economic efficiency by fulfilling consumer preferences, producing the combination of goods that people are willing and able to purchase with their incomes.

In other words, a pure market economy achieves maximum output at the lowest prices consistent with existing costs, technology, and incomes. What is most important, perhaps, is that these results are realized without direct intervention by government. Indeed, they come about through the free interactions of market supply and demand forces. These forces, like an "invisible hand," guide the allocation of society's resources to their most efficient uses.

Equity

A second feature of a pure market economy is that it distributes society's income in proportion to each person's contribution to production. If Smith adds twice as much to the value of total output as Johnson does, then competition among employers and among suppliers of resources will see to it that Smith earns twice as much as Johnson.

Exhibit 12

Changes in Demand and Supply

Shifts in the demand or supply curves will cause changes in equilibrium price, equilibrium quantity, or both.

Increase in demand, supply remains constant

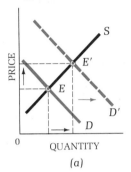

(a)

Decrease in demand, supply remains constant

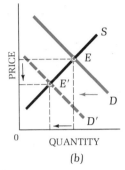

(b)

Increase in supply, demand remains constant

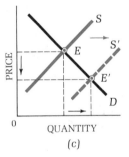

(c)

Decrease in supply, demand remains constant

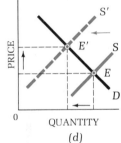

(d)

What happened here?

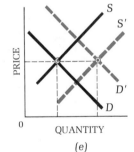

(e)

What happened here?

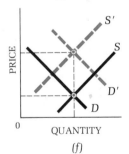

(f)

Test Yourself

In Figures (e) and (f), what would have happened to price and quantity if the change in one of the curves was not exactly "offset" by the change in the other? Try sketching a few diagrams to see for yourself. Can you suggest some general conclusions?

Note For convenience, supply and demand curves are often drawn as straight lines. Even when they are, we still refer to them as supply and demand *curves*.

The reason for this is not hard to see. No employer will pay either Smith or Johnson more than the value that each contributes. And neither Smith nor Johnson need accept less. Why? Because there is always some other employer who would find it profitable to pay them slightly more. Competition among employers would thus bid up Smith's and Johnson's earnings until each is paid precisely what he or she is worth. The result is that the "invisible hand" of competition—the forces of supply and demand—guide both Smith and Johnson into the occupations that each performs best. Stated in more general terms:

> In a pure market economy, the factors of production tend to move into their most remunerative employments. This ensures that the entire income of society is distributed to the owners of resources in proportion to their contribution to the economy's total output.

Can we conclude in any *scientific* way that this method of apportioning society's income is fair or equitable? Not really. Equity considerations are based on value judgments of what is "right" and what is "wrong," what is "good" and what is "bad." In such matters, your own opinion is not necessarily better or worse than someone else's. However, we will examine this problem in considerable detail at later points.

Stability and Growth

There are two other important features of a pure market economy. The first concerns price, output, and employment fluctuations, or the problem of economic stability. The second concerns the expansion of real output, or the problem of economic growth.

1. A pure market economy maintains a level of total spending sufficient to sustain full employment (or full utilization) of society's available resources. Of course, innovations and changes in production methods may cause lapses in full employment. However, such lapses tend to be temporary. Because of the competitive nature of both the product market and the resource market, the supplies and demands for goods and for the factors of production adjust quickly to changing economic conditions. As a result, the economy's output and employment tend to remain relatively stable while prices fluctuate around a long-run level corresponding to full employment.

2. Concerning economic growth, part of the income received by the household sector is spent for consumption. The rest is borrowed by the business sector to finance innovations. These include new production techniques, new plant and equipment, and the like. As a consequence, a society's stock of capital increases, and the economy's production-possibilities curve shifts outward to the right. This means, as you have already learned, that the society produces larger quantities of consumer goods and capital goods—that is, it experiences economic growth.

To summarize:

> With respect to stability and growth, a pure market economy has the following characteristics.
>
> **1.** Prices fluctuate relatively more than output and employment to accommodate short-run changes in the supplies of and the demands for goods and resources.
>
> **2.** Economic growth takes place in response to innovations by entrepreneurs who seek new and better ways of improving production methods.

In a pure market economy, competition assures that the owners of the factors of production will receive what their factors are worth.

In a pure market economy, prices fluctuate around a long-run level corresponding to full employment while the economy experiences economic growth.

These are among the more important features of a pure market economy. Their implications will become increasingly apparent in later chapters as you learn more about the achievements and failures of modern capitalism. Meanwhile, some further aspects of a pure market economy are pointed out in Box 2.

Some Real-World Shortcomings

A pure market economy is the prototype of theoretical capitalism. However, the ways in which modern, mixed, capitalistic economies differ from the model are many and various. Although a pure market economy may achieve a high score when judged by the standards of efficiency, equity, stability, and growth, the report card on our own capitalistic system would be far less glowing. According to the critics, defenders of real-world capitalism mislead us by attributing to it the benefits of a pure market economy. The more important criticisms may be described briefly.

Real-world capitalistic economies do not operate exactly as the model predicts they will.

Market Imperfections and Frictions

The market does not always work as neatly in the real world as the theoretical model suggests. Imperfections and frictions, such as imperfect knowledge, resource immobility, and barriers to entering markets, impede the smooth functioning of the system.

For example, buyers and sellers of goods and resources do not usually have complete information about alternative prices, working conditions, and the like. Unemployed people frequently must be retrained before they can qualify for new jobs. And even when they are retrained, they may not be willing to bear the economic or psychic costs of moving long distances to accept employment.

**Box 2
Freedom Versus Power**

A pure market economy is the prototype of capitalism. As such, it has the advantage of combining maximum economic freedom with minimum concentration of economic power—for two reasons:

1. Private Property and Economic Freedom
Freedom of enterprise is an extension of the institution of private property. Private property is the most fundamental characteristic of a capitalistic system and, hence, of a pure market economy. Freedom of enterprise means that owners of resources are free to employ them where and how they see fit. The owners are subject only to the minimal governmental restraints needed to protect the welfare of society. Unlike a command economy, therefore, a pure market economy has no central authority that decides *what, how,* and *for whom* economic resources should be used. Instead, these decisions are made individually by producers seeking to earn profits by allocating resources according to the ways in which consumers freely register their preferences through the price system.

2. Dispersion of Economic Power
Economic power exists when a single buyer or seller can exert an influence on the market price of a good or resource. The fragmentation of economic power is an integral feature of a pure market economy and is closely related to economic freedom. Theoretically, economic power does not exist in a highly competitive system. This is because the market price of a commodity is established by the bids and offers of numerous buyers and sellers. An individual buyer or seller can either accept or reject the going price but cannot influence it. Each is a passive participant whose presence or absence in the market has no influence on the economic process because each is an insignificant part of it.

Similarly, entrepreneurs and workers are often prevented from entering new industries because they lack the large amount of capital or the specialized know-how required. Or perhaps they cannot overcome monopolistic barriers, such as patent rights and apprenticeship requirements, that protect various business firms and unions from increased competition.

These and other obstacles retard the rate at which the factors of production shift out of declining industries and into expanding ones. As a result, imbalances in the form of shortages and surpluses arise in various product and resource markets. These imbalances would not ordinarily occur—or, if they did occur, they would be short-lived—if our real market-oriented economy functioned as smoothly as the theory assumes.

A number of factors help to explain why real market economies are not precisely the same as the pure market model.

Economic Inequality and Inequity

In a market economy, incomes are distributed in proportion to people's contributions to production. As we have seen, if Smith adds twice as much to the value of total output as Johnson does, then Smith's income will tend to be twice that of Johnson's.

This economic inequality can be further magnified by the right of inheritance. This fundamental institution of capitalism permits the accumulation and concentration of wealth within families. Such disparities in income and wealth can lead to economic and social inequities, differences that are not based on people's contributions. Thus, critics point out that, in a market economy, a rich person has more dollar votes than does a poor person. As a result, the former can satisfy his or her whims, whereas the latter may find it hard to satisfy even basic needs.

Technology and Large-Scale Production

The model of a pure market economy makes the assumption that each industry comprises numerous small firms, as envisioned by Adam Smith. Yet modern technology dictates that, in many industries, such as automobiles and steel, firms must be very large if they are to make use of the most efficient means of production. In such industries, a few large firms are dominant, and small firms cannot survive. In fact, the massive scale of operations imposed by modern technology helps explain why many major industries are dominated by one or a few large firms.

Social Effects and "Externalities"

"Externalities" are side effects, some favorable and some unfavorable, that arise in real market economies.

Another criticism is that the market system fails to reflect *all* the costs and benefits associated with production and consumption. As a result, there are side effects, or "externalities."

For example, production of some commodities, such as steel, rubber, and chemicals, pollutes the environment and so contributes to *social costs*. At the same time, production of other commodities, such as education, sanitation services, and park facilities, adds to community satisfactions and so contributes to *social benefits*.

These externalities may not always be fully reflected in the prices of commodities. To the extent that they are not, supply and demand curves fail to show *all* the costs and benefits of production. As a result, either too much or too little is produced, and resources are misallocated. You will learn more about this in later chapters.

Conclusion: Relevant If Not Always Realistic

For these reasons, the model of a pure market economy does not convey a true picture of the way in which the price system operates in a modern capitalistic society.

For example, in many markets we do not have large numbers of buyers and sellers in rivalry with one another, as envisioned by Adam Smith. Instead, we have big business, big unions, and big government. Consequently, concentrations of market power influence commodity and factor prices, and distort the allocation of resources. This is hardly the type of economy that Adam Smith had in mind. Nevertheless, as you will see later, the pure market model developed in this chapter provides a useful framework for evaluating the performance of a capitalistic system. Hence, the model is relevant, if not always realistic.

Despite its shortcomings, the pure market model serves as a useful guide for judging real market economies.

What You Have Learned in This Chapter

1. The purpose of studying supply and demand is to learn how a competitive or pure market economy works. This helps answer the three great questions: *What* to produce? *How* to produce? and *For whom* to produce?

2. Demand is a relation between the price of a commodity and the quantity of it that buyers are willing and able to purchase at a given time. Other things affecting demand, such as buyers' income, prices of related goods, buyers' expectations of future incomes and prices, and various nonmonetary factors, are assumed to remain the same. The law of demand states that the relation between price and quantity demanded is inverse. Therefore, demand curves slope downward from left to right.

3. Supply is a relation between the price of a commodity and the quantity of it that sellers are willing and able to sell at a given time. Other things affecting supply, such as resource costs, prices of related goods in production, suppliers' expectations of future costs and prices, and various nonmonetary factors, are assumed to remain the same. The law of supply states that the relation between price and quantity supplied is usually direct. Hence, supply curves typically slope upward from left to right.

4. The intersection of a market demand curve with a market supply curve determines the equilibrium price and the equilibrium quantity of a commodity. Demand or supply curves may shift either left or right as a result of changes in any of the determinants assumed to remain constant when the curves were drawn. When such shifts occur, we refer to them either as changes in demand or as changes in supply, depending on which curve has shifted.

5. Movements along supply and demand curves may occur. These movements result from changes in the price of the commodity while the other underlying determinants of demand and supply remain constant. Such movements are called either a change in the quantity demanded or a change in the quantity supplied, depending on the particular curve.

6. In the real world, demand and supply curves are always shifting. A change in demand or a change in supply may result in a new equilibrium price, a new equilibrium quantity, or both. The change depends on the relative shifts of the curves.

7. A market economy is highly competitive. Prices and quantities are determined by numerous buyers and sellers through the free operation of supply and demand. Organized commodity markets, such as the New York Mercantile Exchange, the London Cotton Exchange, or the Chicago Board of Trade, typify highly competitive markets. However, most of the markets in our economy differ from such competitive markets to one degree or another.

For Discussion

1. Terms and concepts to review:
demand
demand schedule
demand curve
demand price
law of demand

supply
supply schedule
supply curve
supply price
law of supply
equilibrium
surplus
shortage
equilibrium price
equilibrium quantity
disequilibrium
change in quantity demanded
change in demand
normal goods
inferior goods
substitute goods
complementary goods
change in quantity supplied
change in supply
pure market economy
consumer sovereignty
social cost
social benefit

In the following problems, use graphs whenever possible to verify your answer.

2. Do the numerical quantities of a demand schedule characterize buyers' behavior? If not, what is the fundamental property of a demand schedule?

3. Evaluate the following editorial comments on the basis of what you know about the meaning of demand and scarcity in economics.

(**Hint** How meaningful are the italicized words?)

Our community *needs* more schools and better teachers; after all, what could be more critical than the education of our children as future citizens?

Lynwood *Times*

The health of our citizens is uppermost in our minds. Ever since the rate of garbage pick-up in our northwest suburbs deteriorated to its present deplorable levels, it has been evident that our shortage of collection facilities has reached *emergency* proportions.

Lexington *Daily Explicit*

4. Some people would buy more of a good (such as jewelry or furs) at a high price than at a low price. This results in an upward-sloping "demand" curve. Would such a curve be an exception to the law of demand? Explain.

5. What would happen to the market demand curve for steak as a result of each of the following: (a) an increase in the average level of income; (b) an increase in the number of families; (c) a successful advertising campaign for veal and pork; (d) an increase in the prices of veal and pork; (e) a decrease in the prices of veal and pork?

6. What would happen to the demand for Pepsi-Cola if the price of Coca-Cola were doubled? Why would it happen?

7. Determine the effect on the supply of office buildings if each of the following things happened: (a) the price of land rose; (b) the price of steel fell; (c) the price of cement fell; (d) a new and faster method of construction were adopted; (e) the number of firms that build offices declined; (f) rents for office buildings were expected to decline.

8. Analyze the following:
(a) What would happen to the equilibrium price and quantity of butter if the price of margarine rose substantially?
(b) What would happen if there were an increase in the cost of producing butter?

9. "Wheat is wheat. Therefore, the price of wheat at any given time should be the same in Chicago as it is in Kansas City." Do you agree? Explain.

10. In organized commodity markets, buyers often become sellers and sellers often become buyers, depending on the price of the good. Examine the following schedule for five people, *A*, *B*, *C*, *D*, and *E*.

Price (dollars per unit)	Quantities that people will buy (+) or sell (−) at each market price				
	A	*B*	*C*	*D*	*E*
$1	+6	+5	+3	+8	−2
2	+3	+4	+2	+7	−5
3	0	+3	+1	+6	−8
4	−2	+2	0	+5	−10
5	−2	−3	−1	+4	−10
6	−4	−5	−2	+3	−11
7	−5	−6	−3	+2	−12

(a) Draw the market supply and demand curves, and estimate the equilibrium price and quantity.
(b) Show the effects on the supply and demand curves if *C* drops out of the market.

The Private Sector— Households and Businesses: Income and Industrial Structure

3

CHAPTER

Learning guide
Watch for the answers to these important questions

What is meant by the expression "income distribution"? Are there distinct patterns or trends that enable us to compare the shares of income that different people receive?

How is income inequality measured? What are the reasons for income inequality? Are incomes more nearly equal today than they were several decades ago?

What standards exist for judging how income should be distributed? Is it possible to judge the "fairness" of such standards? Is there a "best" distribution of income for society?

How are businesses organized in our economy? Are some businesses too big? Is big business "good" or "bad" for our society?

Our mixed economy is like a three-legged stool—one leg representing households, the second businesses, and the third government. The first two, which constitute the *private sector* of the economy, are explored in this chapter. The third is the *public sector*, which is the subject of the next and several subsequent chapters.

You and I are part of the household segment of the private sector. So too are some 80 million families. Households are the ultimate suppliers of the economy's inputs of human resources and the major purchasers of its outputs of goods and services. Businesses, of which there are more than 15 million, including farmers and professional people, are the second major group within the private sector. This group is chiefly responsible for producing the things society wants.

Households: Income, Wealth, and Equity

In the United States, concern with the distribution of income and wealth is as old as the nation itself. Alexander Hamilton believed that liberty without inequality of property ownership is impossible because the inequality "would unavoidably result from the very liberty itself." Thomas Jefferson remarked that the perpetuation of wealth through inheritance "sometimes does injury to the morals of youth by rendering them independent of, and disobedient to, their parents." And James Madison supported legislation that "would reduce extreme income and wealth toward a state of mediocrity and raise extreme indigence toward a state of comfort."

The distribution of society's income and wealth has always been a matter of great concern.

What constitutes an equitable or fair distribution of income and wealth among people? This question has been debated for centuries by economists, politicians, and social critics. Because of its fundamental importance, it is a problem that deserves our attention.

A Look at the Facts

Many people believe that income and wealth in our economy have been distributed inequitably and that this maldistribution is one of the fundamental social problems of our time. This belief is not new. It has been widely held (although its popularity has shown cyclical upswings and downswings) since the early nineteenth century. Whether it is correct is a question we shall try to answer here and in later chapters.

To begin with, we must examine the facts. This is not easy, because there are different concepts of income and wealth. To most of us, income is simply money that people receive from various sources; wealth is the value of the goods and property they own. But a significant part of many people's income consists of more than wages and salaries. Income also consists of money and nonmoney benefits that are never reported to the tax authorities or to census takers. A similar problem affects the reporting of wealth. As a result, no government or private source provides complete and accurate information about the distribution of income and wealth. With these deficiencies in mind, we can turn our attention to the available facts. First, however, we need two definitions:

> *Income* is the gain derived from the use of human or material resources; it is a flow of dollars per unit of time. *Wealth* is anything that has value because it is capable of producing income. Wealth is a "stock" of value as distinct from a "flow" of income.

Functional Income Distribution

The study of income distribution is customarily divided into two parts. One is called "functional income distribution"; the other is known as "personal income distribution."

Functional income distribution refers to the income payments made to the owners of the four factors of production. The kinds of payments made are wages, rent, interest, and profit, the sum of which is called *national income*. These payments are the compensation that resource owners receive for selling their labor, land, capital, and entrepreneurship in the marketplace.

Today it is not unusual for some individuals to receive more than one kind of income payment. For example, many people are not only workers but also landlords, creditors, and stockholders in corporations. Hence, they receive not only wages but also rent, interest, and profit. Our present concern, however, is with the percentage shares of national income going to the various owners who sell their factors of production, whatever those factors may be.

In our mixed economy, two kinds of forces determine which factor of production will receive what proportion of society's income:

1. Market Forces These are represented by demand and supply conditions. They determine the prices and quantities of human and material resources used in production.

Income is what you earn per unit of time; wealth is what you own. Be careful not to confuse the two.

The study of functional income distribution concerns the income payments made to the four factors of production.

2. Nonmarket Forces These consist of laws, customs, and contractual arrangements, such as union–management agreements. Nonmarket forces tend to modify the income shares that resource owners would have received had market forces been operating alone.

Long-Term Trends

Exhibit 1 shows the shares of national income going to each class of resource owners. These proportions change very little from one year to the next. Therefore, it is more instructive to convey the highlights of the information over intervals of several years, as has been done in the graphs.

The titles in the exhibit are those used by the U.S. Department of Commerce. This agency compiles the data shown in the graphs. It should be noted that the classification "proprietors' income" includes both the wages and the percentage return on investment earned by self-employed people. Hence, for purposes of analysis, this category may be eliminated by allocating parts of it to two of the other classes of income payments, "compensation of employees" and "net interest." This leaves the four familiar classes of income payments: wages, rent, interest, and profit.

Compensation of Employees This category of income payments, shown in Figure (*a*), represents wages. It constitutes by far the largest share of national income—more than 75 percent. The proportion has expanded steadily over the years, reflecting the growing importance of paid employment as the main source of people's income.

Proprietors' Income This class of payments, illustrated in Figure (*b*), has declined to about six percent of national income. The reason is that corporations have grown rapidly in importance during this century. As a result, they long ago replaced the proprietorship as the economically dominant form of business organization and as a significant source of people's income.

Rental Income of Persons This component, shown in Figure (*c*), has been decreasing steadily. Its share is now less than two percent of national income. One of the major reasons for the decline is that corporations, rather than individuals, have become the chief owners of property. Therefore, corporations are receiving an increasing proportion of rental income. This income becomes part of the gross income of corporations, and, after expenses have been deducted, ends up as part of corporate profits. These are shown in Figure (*e*).

Net Interest This item, illustrated in Figure (*d*), is the income that the nonbusiness sector (mostly households) receives on its loans to the business sector. For example, if you buy a Ford Motor Company bond, you are lending the company money for which it pays you interest. Net interest is thus the business sector's total interest payments to other sectors minus their total interest payments to it. The trend of net interest payments is strongly affected by monetary and credit conditions. These are matters of fundamental concern in macroeconomics.

Corporate Profits This component of national income, shown in Figure (*e*), is what is "left over." It is a residual representing a reward for entrepreneurship (that is, for organizing and risk taking) after other income

Exhibit 1

Functional Distribution of Income in the United States

(payments are shown as percentages of national income)

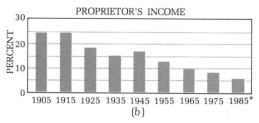

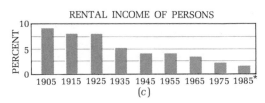

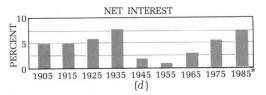

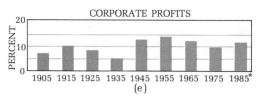

* Estimated
Source: U.S. Department of Commerce

Exhibit 2

Percentages of Aggregate Income (Total Money Income Before Taxes) Received by Each One-Fifth and the Top 5 Percent of Families*

Income rank	1950	1960	1970	1975	1980
Lowest fifth	4.5	4.8	5.4	5.4	5.1
Second fifth	11.9	12.2	12.2	11.8	11.8
Middle fifth	17.4	17.8	17.8	17.6	17.5
Fourth fifth	23.6	24.0	23.8	24.1	24.2
Highest fifth	42.7	41.3	40.9	41.0	41.5
Top 5%	17.3	15.9	15.6	15.5	15.7
Ratio of top 5% to lowest fifth	3.8	3.3	2.9	2.9	3.1

* Because figures are rounded, the sum of the five fifths in each column may not add to 100.

Source: U.S. Department of Commerce

The study of personal income distribution concerns the payments made to individual people.

Exhibit 3

Percentage of Total Wealth Held by Each One-Fifth, the Top 5 Percent, and the Top 1 Percent of Families

Wealth rank	Percent
Lowest fifth	Less than 1
Second fifth	2
Third fifth	5
Fourth fifth	18
Highest fifth	74
Top 5 percent	39
Top 1 percent	25

Source: U.S. Treasury, Internal Revenue Service.

payments, which are largely contractual, have been made. Compared with the other payments, therefore, corporate profits are the most variable. They exhibit the greatest period-to-period fluctuations when measured in terms of percentage changes.

To summarize:

> Functional income distribution refers to the allocation of national income among the classes of resource owners. The allocation is determined both by market and by nonmarket forces. Over the long run, compensation of employees averages about 75 percent of national income. Proprietors' income, rental income of persons, and net interest each average less than 10 percent. Corporate profits, which are the most variable because they are noncontractual, tend to average about 10 percent.

Personal Income Distribution

How are personal incomes distributed in the United States? Who is rich and who is poor, and what is the gap between them? This is the problem of *personal income distribution*—the allocation of income among people.

The percentage of all families in the lower-income groups has been declining in recent decades. The percentage of families in the upper-income groups has been rising. The median income has also been rising. (A *median* is a type of average that divides a distribution of numbers into two equal parts. One-half of the numbers in the distribution are equal to or less than the median and one-half are equal to or greater than the median.) However, there are still significant gaps between the median income levels of various groups—especially racial groups—within the economy. This situation causes serious equity problems for our society.

Exhibit 2 shows the relative share of total money income before taxes received by each fifth and the top 5 percent of all families in the United States. This table reveals three long-run characteristics:

> **1.** The income received by the lowest one-fifth of families has averaged slightly more than 5 percent of total *money* income. (Money income is distinguished from in-kind income, such as food stamps, subsidized housing, and subsidized medical care.) The income received by the highest one-fifth has averaged more than 40 percent of total money income. This represents a long-run ratio of approximately 8:1.
>
> **2.** The ratio of the share received by the top 5 percent to the share received by the lowest 20 percent has declined substantially. However, the former is still roughly three times as large as the latter.
>
> **3.** The entire distribution has remained remarkably stable.

Because of these long-run characteristics, many observers believe that the pattern of income distribution will continue to remain about the same as it is now. The issue of whether or not incomes should be more nearly equal involves serious ethical considerations. These will be taken up later in the chapter.

Distribution of Wealth

The distribution of income has to do with who *gets* how much. The distribution of wealth has to do with who *has* how much. The same inequality that exists in the distribution of income also exists in the distribution of wealth. However, the inequality in the distribution of wealth is more pronounced. There is a much heavier concentration of wealth at the top and a considerably thinner scattering at the bottom.

Wealth consists of both income-producing and non-income-producing assets. Stocks, bonds, savings accounts, land, houses, and automobiles are examples. Holdings of both types are important. Unfortunately, facts and figures about the distribution of wealth are limited and are not published periodically. As a result, we must rely on infrequent studies and reports.

Exhibit 3 shows that the wealthiest 1 percent of families in the United States own 25 percent of the total wealth. In fact, this small proportion of people owns about as much wealth as the lowest 80 percent of families. The wealthiest one-fifth owns somewhat less than three times as much wealth as the lowest four-fifths.

The concentration of wealth is thus considerably greater than the concentration of income. Further, the concentration of the most influential form of wealth—income-producing wealth—is even more pronounced. The top one-fifth owns the great bulk of both corporate stock and corporate and municipal bonds (not shown in the table).

This point requires some clarification. In reality, stocks and bonds are owned by millions of people. But the vast majority of these securities are owned directly by a relatively small percentage of the population. Indirectly, however, a large and growing proportion of the population owns stocks and bonds—through retirement and pension funds, which invest heavily in such securities.

Measuring Inequality and Explaining the Facts

The most commonly used device for depicting and measuring inequalities in the distribution of income and wealth is a type of graph called a *Lorenz diagram*. Such a graph depicting income inequality is shown in Exhibit 4. Both the table and the graph show what percentage of people, ranked from the poorest to the richest, received what percentage of the nation's total income in a given year.

The graph is constructed by laying off on the horizontal axis the number of income recipients—not in absolute terms but in percentages. Families, rather than individuals, are usually represented. The point marked 20 denotes the lowest 20 percent of the families; the point marked 40, the lowest 40 percent; and so on. The vertical axis measures percentages of total national income. Both axes have the same length and equal scales. Therefore, a diagonal line beginning at 0 and sloping upward from left to right at a 45° angle represents the curve of complete equality.

You can now verify certain facts from the graph. For example, along the diagonal line of equal distribution, 20 percent of the families would receive 20 percent of total income, 40 percent of the families would receive 40 percent of total income, and so on. This line is compared with the curve of actual distribution—called a *Lorenz curve*—derived from the data in the table. The area between the diagonal line of equal income distribution and the curved line of actual income distribution reflects the degree of income inequality. Thus, the more the curved line is bowed downward in a southeasterly direction, the greater is the inequality of income distribution.

How does the distribution of income compare with the distribution of wealth? The answer, given in terms of two Lorenz curves, is shown in Exhibit 5. As explained there, it is difficult to determine which curve is most responsible for the other.

Exhibit 4
Illustrating Inequality with a Lorenz Diagram

Percentage of Aggregate Income Received by Each One-Fifth of Families

Income rank	1980
Lowest fifth	5
Second fifth	12
Middle fifth	18
Fourth fifth	24
Highest fifth	42

Source: U.S. Department of Commerce.

You can use the data from the table to construct a *Lorenz curve*. This curve shows the extent of departure between an equal distribution of income and the actual distribution of income.

From the curved line showing actual distribution, can you estimate the percentage of income received by the lowest 20 percent of families? The lowest 40 percent? 60 percent? 80 percent? 100 percent? Check your estimates against the data in the table to see if you are correct.

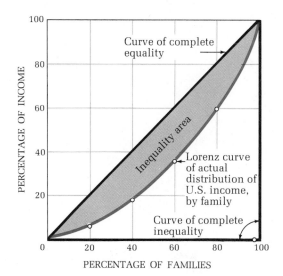

The heavy line running along the horizontal axis and up the right-hand side of the graph represents the curve of *complete inequality*. Thus, on the horizontal axis, a point near the right end of the scale is designated, showing where 99 percent of the families receive no income, and the remaining 1 percent receive it all.

Exhibit 5

Lorenz Curves of Income and Wealth Distribution

The distribution of wealth is considerably more unequal than the distribution of income. However, it is not certain which is the cause and which the effect. High income leads to higher savings, which make possible further accumulation of wealth. This in turn begets still higher income.

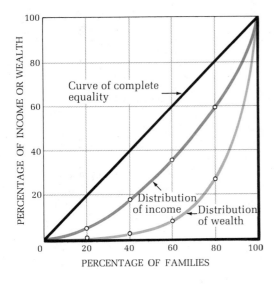

Many factors account for the differences in income among people.

Why Are Some People Rich and Others Poor?

What factors account for differences in income among households? That is, why do some people earn more money than others? There are many reasons. Among them:

1. Differences in Wealth Because wealth is a significant source of income, it appears obvious that a widely distorted distribution of wealth is perhaps the most important cause of income inequality.

2. Differences in Earning Ability and Opportunity People differ widely in education, intelligence, skill, motivation, energy, and talent. These differences translate into differences in earning ability. There are, moreover, differences in the opportunities that are available to people. Many people face job barriers because of their age, sex, race, religion, or nationality. Legislation has made some of these barriers less formidable, but they are still responsible for much of the inequality in income distribution.

3. Differences in Resource Mobility The factors responsible for differences in earning ability and opportunity also make for differences in resource mobility. Many people, for example, are prevented by a lack of information or a lack of financial means from moving into higher-paying occupations or locations. Consequently, low incomes and even poverty may persist for years in the same regions. This is true in certain parts of the United States, where sharecroppers, migratory farm workers, and some factory laborers are able at best to earn only a substandard living.

4. Differences in Luck A person born into a favorable environment and provided with opportunities to develop inherited potentials stands a greater chance of earning a higher income than one not so fortunate. This has been borne out by sociological studies of "vertical mobility"—the climb up the socioeconomic ladder. Unfortunately, what is not known is the extent to which vertical mobility may be affected by changes in income distribution.

5. Differences in Age Young people who have recently entered the job market, and old people who have left it, will have significantly lower incomes than those in midcareer.

6. Differences in Human-Capital Investment Some people make heavier investments in their future earning capacity than do others. Sales clerks, for instance, may begin earning income immediately after graduating from high school. Most professionals, on the other hand, must spend many additional years in training, often without income and living on borrowed funds, before realizing higher financial rewards for their investment of time and effort.

7. Differences in Risk, Uncertainty, and Security Some occupations are more risky, and some have more uncertain futures, than others. These differences are reflected in earnings. Many people prefer security, in return for lower incomes, in the less risky and more certain fields of employment. Witness the fact that employees in relatively stable industries, such as civil service, banking, and public utilities, generally earn less than their counterparts in more unstable industries, such as manufacturing. Admittedly, lower incomes in some stable industries may be partly offset by nonmonetary factors, such as longer vacations, shorter working hours, and better fringe benefits. But the fact remains that coal miners earn more than road-construction workers, window washers in skyscrapers command a higher wage than dish washers in restaurants, and college professors earn less (but live longer) than corporate executives. Clearly, the clash between risk, uncertainty, and security reveals itself in many ways.

These and other factors affecting people's incomes help to explain why the Lorenz curve of income distribution will always show some degree of inequality.

Measuring Inequality and Equality

Social scientists customarily express the precise degree of income inequality in terms of the *Gini coefficient of inequality* (named after an early-twentieth-century Italian statistician). Look at the Lorenz diagram in Exhibit 4. The Gini coefficient may be defined as the numerical value of the area between the Lorenz curve and the diagonal line divided by the numerical value of the entire area beneath the diagonal line. Thus, the Gini coefficient is the ratio of the inequality area to the entire triangular area under the diagonal:

$$\text{Gini coefficient of inequality} = \frac{\text{inequality area}}{\text{triangular area}}$$

The Gini coefficient of inequality is derived from a Lorenz diagram. These are the most widely used means of measuring and depicting inequality.

The value of the ratio may therefore vary from 0 to 1. For example, as incomes become more equal, the inequality area narrows relative to the triangular area under the diagonal and the Gini coefficient approaches zero. At zero there is no inequality—that is, all incomes are equal. As incomes become more unequal, however, the inequality area widens relative to the triangular area and the Gini coefficient approaches 1. At 1 there is complete inequality—that is, one family receives all the income and the rest get nothing.

The Gini coefficient thus measures the degree of inequality along a scale from 0 to 1. It follows, therefore, that a *coefficient of equality* can be derived by simply subtracting the Gini coefficient from 1:

Coefficient of equality = 1 − Gini coefficient

Long-Run Trends

Has the degree of income equality become greater or less over the years?

In 1950, the Gini coefficient of inequality for the United States was .38. Hence the coefficient of equality was .62 (=1.00 − .38). Since then, the Gini coefficient has shown a gradual downward trend, decreasing to about .35 at present. This means that, on the following scale ranging from 0 to 1, the *degree of income equality* in the United States is currently about .65.

Along a scale from 0 (no equality) to 1 (complete equality), the degree of income equality today is about .65.

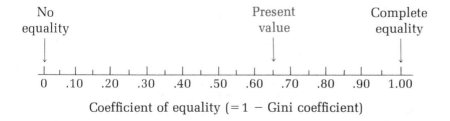

No equality   Present value   Complete equality

| 0 | .10 | .20 | .30 | .40 | .50 | .60 | .70 | .80 | .90 | 1.00 |

Coefficient of equality (=1 − Gini coefficient)

Evaluating the Data: The Trouble with Lorenz Curves

A Lorenz curve suffers from several shortcomings:

Tables of income distribution and Lorenz curves plotted from them have long been used as standard devices for measuring income inequality. Do they accomplish their objective? The answer is not a simple yes or no. This is because accurate measurements of inequality require the consideration of several factors.

Equivalent Spendable Income The data on income distribution are based on what the U.S. Census Bureau (which compiles the figures) calls "money income." This is not the same as income available for spending—for three reasons:

It is based on money income rather than spendable income.

1. Personal income taxes and social security taxes are included in money income. When these taxes are paid by families, their income available for spending is reduced.

2. Noncash income is not counted as part of money income. Noncash income consists of benefits that poor families receive in the form of government subsidies or "in-kind" transfers of goods and services. Examples are food stamps, low-income housing, rent supplements, and free medical services.

3. Money income does not reflect differences in average family size within each quintile (that is, each fifth) of the population. As a result, small families may sometimes be better off than large ones with greater income, depending on their relative *per-capita* money incomes.

In view of the difference between money income and spendable income, what happens when the money-income data are adjusted to allow for these factors? That is, how do the income-distribution figures change when (1) personal and social security taxes are subtracted from money income, (2) noncash income is added in, and (3) the data are converted to a per-capita basis to adjust for differences in average family size within each quintile? The results are startling: *The overall adjusted distribution of income shows a pronounced trend toward greater equality since 1950.* In that year, according to various studies, the lowest one-fifth of families received approximately 8 percent of total income and the highest one-fifth received about 37 percent. Since the early 1970s, the lowest fifth of families have averaged between 12 and 15 percent of total income and the highest fifth between 30 and 33 percent.

It reflects current income rather than lifetime income.

Lifetime Earnings A second difficulty concerning the measurement of income inequality with a Lorenz curve is that it reflects the distribution of income only at a given time. The curve does not reflect the incomes that people earn over their lifetimes. For example, the income of a schoolteacher and a professional athlete may be about the same over the course of their lifetimes. But the schoolteacher's income will be spread over a period of forty years, whereas most of the athlete's income will be realized in less than ten years. In any given year, therefore, the two incomes are likely to be highly unequal.

It makes no allowance for differences in the ages of income recipients.

Age Distribution of Earnings Another problem in measuring inequality is caused by the relation between age and income. To a large extent, income inequalities at any given time result from differences in the age and, therefore, in the earning power of the people in question. We do not ordinarily expect young people who have recently entered the job market, or old people who have left it, to be earning the same incomes as those in midcareer. The Lorenz curve, however, does not distinguish incomes by ages, and therefore reflects the inequalities across all ages.

The relation between age and incomes leads to an important criticism of Lorenz curves:

> The conventional Lorenz curve and the data on which the curve is based are the most common methods of measuring income inequality. These methods, however, are invalid for measuring income inequality over time. One of the main reasons for this is that the young and the old are concentrated at the low end of the income scale. To correct for this, family incomes should be calculated by age groups and comparisons should be made between members of the *same age groups at different times*. For example, the incomes of 25-year-olds several decades ago should be compared with the incomes of 25-year-olds today.

Conclusion: Substantial Gains in Equality

What happens to the data when these revisions are made? Economists who have conducted studies of income and wealth distribution in which such adjustments have been made have come up with new and interesting findings. Among them:

Unadjusted inequality data are vastly overstated. Conventional data on income and wealth inequality that have not been adjusted for age, like those in the tables and figures shown earlier, tend to overstate the degree of inequality by about 50 percent. But when the data are adjusted for age differences, there is a dramatic change. Since 1950, the overall degree of income inequality among families has actually declined by more than 25 percent, and wealth inequality has declined by more than 35 percent.

There is no "permanent state of poverty." Data on money income distribution (shown earlier in Exhibit 2) have remained stable for several decades. However, this does not prove, as some critics contend, that the lowest fifth of families is assigned to a "permanent state of poverty." On the contrary, the families on the lowest one-fifth of the income scale have raised their share of *age-adjusted* total income from 5 percent to more than 8 percent. This is an increase of more than 60 percent since 1950.

The poor receive large amounts of government assistance. The proportion of employed people among families in the upper half of the income scale has increased sharply as many more women have entered the job market. On the other hand, a strong reverse trend toward more unemployment among families in the lower end of the income scale has also occurred. Because of this, low-income families have received, during recent decades, substantial amounts of government assistance. This has taken the form of cash payments, food allotments, subsidized housing, and free health care.

These and related findings reflect the fact that, since the 1950s, our government has devoted substantial proportions of its budget to *transfer payments*. These are expenditures within and between sectors of the economy for which there are no corresponding contributions to current production. Examples include unemployment compensation, relief payments, and other "free" benefits. They are usually intended to reduce what society regards as inequities in the distribution of income and wealth.

When the shortcomings in the income-distribution data are taken into account, the degree of income equality is increased substantially.

On the basis of these findings, the "problem" of income inequality may not be as serious as some critics contend.

Note The rate of growth of transfer payments was reduced during the first two years of the Reagan administration. However, the total was held at about the same percentage of the federal budget as existed before President Reagan took office. Therefore, the preceding criticisms are still valid.

To summarize:

1. The distributions of income and wealth, adjusted for age differences, have become substantially *more equal* in recent decades.

2. The distribution of income to families as a reward for labor or paid employment has become considerably *more unequal* in recent decades. This is because there is a larger percentage of employment among families in the upper half, and a smaller percentage of employment among families in the lower half, of the income scale.

3. The conventional Lorenz standard of *age-unadjusted* inequality greatly overstates the degree of inequality. This may create the impression that the distributions of income and wealth are in more urgent need of revision than is actually the case.

Distributive Criteria and Equity— The Ethics of Distribution

The seventeenth-century English philosopher and essayist Francis Bacon remarked: "Money is like manure; not good except it be spread." But what criteria can be used for deciding how best to spread money? In other words, who should get *how much?* This is the age-old problem of economic justice. Unfortunately, the problem has no completely satisfactory solution because justice in any form is at best a tolerable accommodation of the conflicting interests of society. Nevertheless, a number of distributive standards have been proposed over the long history of discussions on the subject. Most of these standards derive from one of three criteria:

Three criteria of income distribution are (1) the contributive standard, (2) the needs standard, and (3) the equality standard.

1. Distribution based on productive contribution.

2. Distribution based on needs.

3. Distribution based on equality.

Contributive Standard

Most people would agree that a person should be paid what he or she deserves to be paid. This criterion, which fundamentally hinges on *merit*, represents one of the oldest concepts of justice.

Unfortunately, merit is a quality that is difficult to define and impossible to measure. How can we decide, in a manner acceptable to everyone, what each person merits or deserves? Surely, responsibility in a job is not the criterion, because air-traffic controllers earn far less but have much greater responsibility than heart surgeons. Nor are years of formal education a criterion, because most plumbers are more highly paid than schoolteachers. Certainly, the difficulty of a job is not the criterion, because difficulty depends on individual aptitudes and interests. More people can master advanced mathematics than can run a mile in six minutes. These, as well as almost all other standards of merit, lead to similar contradictions. However, there is one measure of merit that is unique to capitalism:

The criterion of distribution in a capitalist society can be expressed by the phrase, "To each according to what he or she produces." This may be called a *contributive standard* because it is based on the principle of payment according to contribution.

How is one's productive contribution measured? The most objective measure is the value placed upon it in a free market. Here the prices of the factors of production are established by the interactions of supply and demand. The contribution to the total product made by a particular factor of production and the payment received for the contribution can then be measured. This is done by multiplying the price per unit of the factor by the number of units supplied. Thus, under these conditions, if the market price of your labor is $6 per hour and you work 2,000 hours each year, your contribution to the total product and the payment you receive are both equal to $12,000. However, much more is involved in determining factor contributions and payments than is implied by this simple example. Nevertheless, the illustration emphasizes an important principle:

> In a capitalistic or market economy, the payment received for a factor of production is the measure of its worth. This payment, which reflects the value of the factor's contribution to the total product, is determined by the impersonal pressure of market forces—not by the judgment of a central authority.

Of course, society also recognizes obligations to its nonproducers—the aged, the disabled, the very young, the involuntarily unemployed, and so on. As a result, society employs some noncontributive criteria for apportioning income. Nevertheless, the contributive standard is the dominant one in our economy.

Contributive standard: *"To each according to the market value of what he or she produces."*

Needs Standard

The distributive principle of capitalism, as we have seen, is expressed by the phrase, "To each according to what he or she produces." In contrast, the distributive principle of pure communism may be described by the expression, "To each according to his or her needs."

It is interesting to note that the *needs standard* is not a distributive principle of communist philosophy only. This standard serves also as the criterion of distribution within most families, and, in time of war or other emergency, it is adopted by all kinds of governments as a means of rationing a severely limited supply of goods.

Distribution according to need has wide appeal. Upon close examination, however, its implementation poses two major difficulties.

1. No impersonal mechanism exists for measuring need. Thus, decisions to allocate goods according to need—whether such decisions are made within a family or on a national scale—must be based on the subjective judgment of a central authority.

2. Even if individual needs could be measured accurately, it is likely that the implementation of a needs standard would not precisely utilize the economy's entire output. There would be either shortages or surpluses, depending on whether the sum of needs was greater or less than the total product. (For example, society may "need" more cars than are produced, or society may produce more cars than are "needed.") This is less likely to occur when output is distributed according to the contributive criterion of capitalism. Under such a system, there is a tendency

Needs standard: *"To each according to his or her needs."*

for the market to equate the incomes people receive with the values of what they contribute.

To summarize:

Individual needs are impossible to measure. Therefore, if distribution of income according to needs were to be adopted, it would have to be based on some central authority's judgment of what constitutes "needs." In addition, people's different needs would somehow have to be matched up with available products if surpluses and shortages were to be avoided.

Equality Standard

Equality standard: "To each equally."

A third criterion of distribution, which was proposed as far back as biblical times, is the *equality standard*. It is expressed most simply by the phrase, "To each equally."

The equality standard is a just standard only if we assume that all individuals are alike in the *added* satisfaction or utility they receive from an extra dollar of income. In reality, an additional dollar of income may provide a greater gain in utility to some people than to others. In that case, justice is more properly served by distributing most of any increase in society's income to those who will enjoy it more.

However, there is no conclusive evidence that people are either alike or unlike in the satisfactions they derive from additional income. Therefore, the equalitarians (also called "egalitarians") argue that, because we cannot prove that people are unlike, we should assume that they are alike and distribute all incomes equally.

This conclusion, regardless of how plausible it may seem, illustrates a logical fallacy in reasoning. The fallacy is what philosophers call "argument from ignorance." It is committed whenever someone argues that a proposition is true simply because it has not been proved false, or that it is false because it has not been proved true.

In terms of the equality standard, this implies that we must go beyond the stage of theorizing about individual utilities and consider instead some of the realistic effects of an equality standard. Among the most important are the "motivational" ones:

An equal distribution of income would eliminate the incentive of rewards. There would be no economic motivation for people to develop or apply their skills, or to use economic resources efficiently, because there would be no commensurate return. The result would be declining economic progress and probable stagnation.

This argument assumes, of course, that economic progress attributable to inequality and material rewards is desirable in itself. Some critics think it is not. We shall have more to say about this issue in later chapters.

Conclusion: An "Optimal" Distribution?

The "ideal" or optimal distribution of income differs for each society, depending on its goals and institutions.

The preceding arguments suggest that there is some "ideal" degree of income inequality—a distribution that is not too extreme either way. What can be said about this hypothesis?

In a society characterized by a very unequal distribution of income, the economic surplus or savings of the rich minority can finance investment in capital. The result is material and cultural advancement. This was true of such ancient civilizations as Egypt, Greece, and Rome, whose economies were based on slavery—the most unequal distributive system of all. Because of this, they were able to produce magnificent art, architecture, and other cultural achievements.

On the other hand, in a society whose limited income is distributed equally among the masses, virtually all of its income is spent on needed consumption goods. This leaves little if any savings with which to acquire capital goods. (This is the familiar production-possibilities concept of earlier chapters. It involves the notion that every society must make choices between the proportions of consumption goods and capital goods that it wishes to have.) Such a society, although it has an equal income distribution, would tend to remain poor because of its distributive policy.

To conclude:

> Every society seeks the best compromise—the "optimum"—between two extremes of income distribution: substantial inequality and complete equality. But each society's concept of the optimum differs, depending on the society's goals and institutions. Therefore, it is impossible to state objectively whether a particular distribution of income is "good" or "bad."

Businesses—Organization and Size

The private sector includes business firms as well as households. Business is a major institution. It is powerful, and its decisions and policies influence the nature, structure, and goals of our society. This makes business highly controversial and makes its motives the subject of ceaseless debate.

Business is a major institution in our society. Therefore, it is important to understand its organizational structure.

How are business firms organized? Why are some of them large and some small? These are the questions that concern us. Before answering them, a definition of a business firm will be helpful:

> A *firm* is a business organization that brings together and coordinates the factors of production—capital, land, labor, and entrepreneurship—for the purpose of producing a good or service.

Organizational Structure

Business firms may be classified in various ways. One way is to group them according to the products they produce. Firms that turn out either similar or identical products are said to be in the same *industry*. Thus, General Motors and Ford Motor Company are in the automobile industry. But General Motors also produces trucks, buses, and diesel locomotives, among other things. Therefore, it would be correct to say that General Motors is also in the truck industry, the bus industry, and the diesel locomotive industry. Indeed, most of the largest companies make more than one product. Can you name at least five industries in which General Electric is an important producer?

Another method of classifying firms is by their legal form of organization. Three types of organizations are particularly common: the individual proprietorship, the partnership, and the corporation. More than 75 percent of all firms in the United States are proprietorships, about 10 percent are partnerships, and the remainder are corporations. Although the proportion of corporations is relatively small, this form of business organization is responsible for most of our economy's total output.

The Proprietorship

Proprietorships and partnerships are the simplest forms of business organization.

The simplest, oldest, and most common form of business is the *proprietorship*. This is a firm in which the owner (proprietor) is solely responsible for the activities and liabilities of the business. Most of the firms you see every day, such as bakeries, barber shops, beauty salons, restaurants, gas stations, and radio and TV repair shops, are examples of proprietorships. Why are proprietorships so common? Because they are relatively easy to establish. They usually do not require special business skills, experience, or large amounts of money capital (although there are some exceptions). These advantages, however, should be weighed against certain disadvantages of proprietorships. They tend to lack stability and permanence, it is difficult for them to raise funds for expansion, and their owners are personally liable for all unpaid debts of the business.

The Partnership

A partnership is simply a modified version of a proprietorship. That is, a *partnership* is an association of two or more people to carry on, as co-owners, a business for profit. A partnership has the same kinds of advantages and disadvantages as a proprietorship—but on a somewhat different scale. For example, partners can pool their funds to establish a business and they can combine their talents to manage it. However, they are jointly and personally liable for all unpaid debts of the business.

The Corporation

The corporations is the most complex form of business organization—and the most important for our purposes.

The third, and from an economic standpoint the most important form of business organization, is the corporation. Here is a definition that will be amplified in the following paragraphs:

> A *corporation* is an association of stockholders (owners) created under law but regarded by the courts as an artificial person existing only in the contemplation of law. The chief economic characteristics of a corporation are (1) the limited liability of its stockholders, (2) stability and permanence, and (3) the ability to accumulate large sums of capital for expansion through the sale of stocks and bonds.

Some of the ideas behind this definition may already be familiar to you. For example:

The owners of a corporation are its stockholders. They have limited liability—a major feature of the corporate form of organization.

The ownership of a corporation is divided into units represented by shares of *stock*. A stockholder who owns 100 shares of stock in a corporation has twice as much "ownership" as a stockholder with only 50 shares. Each stockholder participates in the profits of the corporation by receiving *dividends* in the form of a certain amount of money per share. If the corporation does not earn a profit, there may be no dividends.

One of the distinguishing features of a corporation is the *limited liability* of its stockholders. The owners of a proprietorship or partnership can be held personally liable for the debts of the business. However, stockholders in corporations cannot be held liable for any of the firm's debts. For almost all practical purposes, the most that stockholders can lose if the business goes bankrupt is the money they paid for their stock.

The corporation has durability. Stockholders may come and go, but the corporation itself lives on. Indeed, some corporations in existence today were originally chartered hundreds of years ago. This permanence makes corporations highly flexible. They can raise large amounts of capital by selling stocks and *bonds* (promises to pay money, plus interest, in future years) to the public, and they can adapt themselves to changing market needs and conditions.

Stockholders elect a board of directors, which is responsible for the management of the corporation. Each stockholder gets one vote for each share of stock owned. Some stockholders may thus elect themselves to the board if they own enough shares or if they can get the support of enough of the other stockholders. In large corporations, the board employs officers—a president and vice-presidents—to manage day-to-day operations and to report back to the board the results of these operations. In smaller corporations, it is common to find one or more members of the board also serving as officers.

Business Size: How Big Is Big?

Most corporations in the United States are "small." Their assets (cash, buildings, equipment, inventories, and so forth) total less than a few hundred thousand, or perhaps up to a few million, dollars each. At the other extreme are numerous corporations belonging to the "billion-dollar-plus club." These are companies whose total assets, annual sales, and annual net profits after taxes are far in excess of $1 billion. Each of these large corporations typically employs hundreds of thousands of workers and distributes profits to hundreds of thousands, or even millions, of stockholders. Together these companies control a large share of the nation's income-producing wealth. The names of most of the large corporations in the United States are already familiar to you. In fact, you are probably a customer for many of their products. Several of these firms are listed in Exhibit 6.

How big is big? By way of comparison, the annual sales of each of the companies shown in Exhibit 6 often ranks with the value of output produced by such countries as Argentina, Belgium, Colombia, and Denmark. And, like a number of other U.S. corporations, each of those in Exhibit 6 has annual sales exceeding, by many billions of dollars, the combined total outputs of several dozen other nations.

Is Bigness a Curse or a Blessing?

Is it "good" or "bad" to have an economy whose major industries are dominated by a few giant corporations? Are such companies as Exxon in the petroleum industry, General Motors in the automobile industry, and AT&T in the electronic communications industry beneficial or harmful? Would we be better off if we had an economy whose industries were composed of many small firms in active competition?

There are no simple answers. The best that we can do is to sketch the main aspects of the problem and leave you to think out some tentative conclusions. As you study later chapters, you may very well come to see some of these conclusions in a different light.

Stockholders Are Not Managers A striking feature of the modern large corporation is the *separation of ownership and control.* This means that the stockholders own the business and the hired managers control it. In most large corporations, stock ownership is widely dispersed among hundreds of thousands, or even millions, of people. Most of these stockholders are usually not interested in who manages the corporation. Consequently, a corporation's board of directors and officers may be able, once in power, to represent their own interests more consistently

Exhibit 6

Who's Who Among the Giants? Average Sales of America's Ten Largest Corporations, 1981

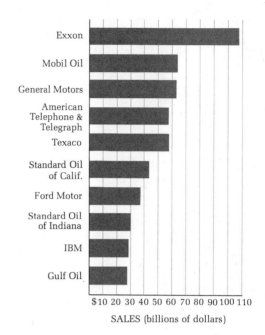

SALES (billions of dollars)

SOURCE: Forbes Directory, 1982

In most large corporations, the owners and managers are different people.

than those of the company and its stockholders. To some extent, government regulations and laws have reduced the magnitude of this problem. But the difficulty still exists in varying degrees and will probably never be eliminated completely.

Market Domination Many important industries are dominated by a few large companies. Examples include aluminum, telephone equipment, aircraft engines, and cigarettes. The giants in these industries exercise varying degrees of monopoly power over the markets in which they deal. This means, among other things, that:

- They may be able to charge prices higher than would be charged were the industries more competitive.

- They may not improve their efficiency and productivity as much as they would were they subject to greater competition.

- They may have the power to influence some of the legislators and federal agencies responsible for regulating them.

While recognizing these negative possibilities, we must also make note of some positive considerations. Many of today's corporate giants are the same companies whose productive resources and scientific know-how are vital to the country for peace as well as war. As some of the harshest critics of big business have acknowledged, these firms have been instrumental in providing us with the standard of living we now possess.

Conclusion: Free Markets for Greater Efficiency

In light of these considerations, we cannot state without qualification that big business is either "good" or "bad" for society. There are important advantages, as well as disadvantages, to large corporations, as you will see in certain of the later chapters. Meanwhile, the following conclusions should be kept in mind.

> The task of modern capitalism is not to make a choice between large firms and small ones. Both types are here to stay. The really practical problem is to find ways of making the free market work to improve the efficiency of businesses in general, both large and small. In this way, firms will utilize their resources more fully for the betterment of society.

Case
Ford Motor Company: How and Why Do Firms Become Big?

A business may expand through internal growth by plowing most of its profits back into the business. Or it can sell securities, such as stocks and bonds, to the public. In this way, it acquires the funds it needs to pay for new equipment, research, and product development.

A classic example of both types of growth is the Ford Motor Company. For several decades after its formation, it remained a privately (mostly family) held corporation. After its stock became available to the public, it often paid out as little as 33 to 40 percent of its profits as dividends to stockholders. It kept the rest of the profits for reinvestment in plant, equipment, research, and so on. At the same time, other major industrial firms were distributing between 50 and 65 percent of their profits.

The Bettmann Archive, Inc.

Henry Ford and his first car

World Headquarters of the
Ford Motor Company

Ford Motor Company.

A firm may also expand by combining or merging with others. This has been the most prevalent method of growth in American industry. Indeed, many of our largest firms achieved their present huge size through "marriages" with others.

Expansion Motives

Why do some firms become large? Their ultimate objective is usually to strengthen their financial position.

For instance, a firm may combine with other firms in the same or in related types of activity for various reasons. Among them are the desire to gain economies in production or distribution, to regularize supplies, or to round out a product line. Thus, some container manufacturers also make tin cans, glass jars, and plastic bottles. Some automobile producers also own rubber companies, iron mines, and steel mills.

Many companies have also chosen to grow by combining with firms in totally unrelated activities. This may reflect various goals on the part of the acquiring company. Among these are the desire to spread risks and to find investments for idle capital funds. Other objectives may be to add products that can be sold with the firm's merchandising knowledge and skills or simply to gain greater economic power on a broader front.

What You Have Learned in This Chapter

1. Income and wealth are among the chief measures of society's well-being. Therefore, their distribution within society and the forces determining their distribution are of central concern.

2. The Lorenz diagram and the corresponding Gini coefficient are the most commonly used devices for measuring inequality. But they are only as reliable as the data on which they are based. Therefore, the data should always be analyzed with a critical eye.

3. There are many reasons for income inequality. Among the more important are differences in such factors as wealth, earning ability and opportunity, resource mobility, luck, age, human-capital investment, and occupational risk.

4. Those who contend that the personal distribution of income has remained stable since 1950 are basing their argument on unadjusted data. When the figures are adjusted for age differences among income receivers, the results show real gains in income equality.

5. Ethical criteria exist for allocating income. Three major ones are (a) productive contribution, (b) needs, and (c) equality. The first is the primary standard of distribution in capitalistic economies. The second and third criteria are philosophical goals of pure communistic and of egalitarian societies—neither of which exist anywhere on a national scale.

6. Economic history shows that the higher a nation's real income per capita, the more that nation tends to progress toward greater income equality. This is because a high-income economy enables people to save enough to provide the capital accumulation necessary for a society's material advancement.

7. The business sector of the economy consists primarily of proprietorships, partnerships, and corporations. The number of proprietorships greatly exceeds the number of partnerships and corporations. However, corporations produce by far the largest proportion of the nation's goods and services. This is mainly because of two of their principal advantages: (a) the possibility of accumulating large sums of money to finance expansion and (b) the limited liability of their stockholders.

8. The consequences of bigness are mixed. On the one hand, it has created separation of ownership and control in the large corporation, and it has resulted in increased monopoly power for the largest firms in many industries. On the other hand, the largest firms have also been significantly responsible for some of the major advances in our standard of living and in our military preparedness.

For Discussion

1. *Terms and concepts to review:*
private sector
public sector
income
wealth
functional income distribution
national income
personal income distribution
median
Lorenz diagram
Gini coefficient of inequality
transfer payments
firm
industry
proprietorship
partnership
corporation
stock
dividend
limited liability
bond
separation of ownership and control

2. What are the chief causes of income inequality among households? Would it be better if all incomes were equal? Explain.

3. Is it a necessary condition of capitalism that some people be rich and others be poor? Is it morally right for the government to tax the incomes of the rich and redistribute them to the poor? Defend your answer.

4. We cannot distribute goods according to people's needs because we do not know how to determine those needs. Therefore, why not solve the problem by (a) distributing *incomes* according to needs, and (b) permitting goods to be allocated through the price system, thereby preserving freedom of consumer choice?

5. "The principle of payment according to one's contribution to production (that is, the contribution standard) assures that people get what they deserve. Therefore, it is more democratic than payment based on needs or on equality." Do you agree? Explain.

6. "If payments to individuals are based on needs or on equality, some people are bound to be exploited for the benefit of others." Is this statement true? What does "exploitation" mean? Explain.

7. "In a democracy, we do not allocate political votes in proportion to one's intelligence and ability to use them. Instead, everyone gets an equal vote. Therefore, the same should be true of dollar votes (income); everyone's should be equal." Do you agree?

8. "The value of a culture is measured by its peak accomplishments, not by its average level of achievement. Thus, a society of mud huts and one great cathedral is better than a society of stone huts and no cathedral. To put it differently, it is by the quality of its saints and heroes, not its common people, and by its masterpieces, not its domestic utensils, that a culture should be judged." What implications does this have for income distribution?

9. An eminent political scientist, Robert A. Dahl of Yale University, has challenged the assumption that stockholders should control the direction of a company. "I can discover absolutely no moral or political basis," he says, "for such a special right. Why investors and not consumers, workers, or, for that matter, the general public?" What implications does this statement have for the future of capitalism?

10. Can you suggest some advantages and disadvantages of "big" business?

The Public Sector—Government: Public Choice and Taxation

Internal Revenue Service archives

Learning Guide
Watch for the answers to these important questions

What is the role of government in our economy? How do we distinguish between the different types of goods that government provides?

Can goods provided by government be produced efficiently? What concepts can help us to analyze and evaluate the production of goods by the public sector?

How does the government raise money? How does it spend money? What methods can be used to achieve greater efficiency in budgeting?

What is the nature of our tax system? How might taxes be classified for purposes of analysis?

What are the fundamental principles of taxation? How are these principles used to evaluate particular taxes? How are the economic goals of efficiency, equity, stability, and growth employed in judging the consequences of particular taxes?

One of the most remarkable trends in contemporary history has been the growth in the importance of government in economic life. As measured by government purchases of goods and services, the public sector bought 10 percent of the nation's total output in 1930. By 1960, this figure had risen to 20 percent. Today it is close to 25 percent. These facts raise many problems concerning the economic functions of government in our mixed economy. This chapter examines a few of the more important ones and provides some basic concepts for understanding them.

Of course, any serious discussion of government is bound to raise questions of taxes. Taxes, if you recall from your study of history, have been the cause of wars and revolutions. Obviously, anything that can have such a powerful influence ought to be worth knowing something about.

When we speak of government, we ordinarily mean the federal government. But in this chapter we shall say some things about government at the state level and also at the local level. The local level includes counties, cities, villages, townships, school districts, and so on.

Economic Scope and Functions of Government

For centuries, political scholars have theorized about the purposes and functions of the state. In *The Wealth of Nations*, Adam Smith said that government's role should be limited to national defense, the administration of justice, the facilitation of commerce, and the provision of certain public works. Many social scientists today would agree with Smith, although some might add a few items to Smith's list. For present purposes, the economic role of government can be considered to consist of

Since the 1930s, the role of government in economic life has expanded greatly.

Adam Smith, as well as other political and economic scholars, advocated a limited role for government.

two broad functions: (1) the promotion and regulation of the private sector and (2) the provision of social goods.

Promotion and Regulation of the Private Sector

Government promotes and regulates the private sector in many ways. Sometimes it does this to the net advantage, and sometimes to the net disadvantage, of society as a whole. A complete analysis of the public sector's economic functions is impossible here. However, six major activities can be identified.

Provision of a Stable Environment

Government facilitates orderly exchanges by defining property rights, upholding contracts, adjudicating disputes, setting standards for weights and measures, enforcing law and order, and maintaining a monetary system. These conditions are so fundamental to organized society that they have existed even in the most ancient civilizations. The Code of Hammurabi (circa 2100 B.C.), and the later laws of ancient Egypt and Rome, went into considerable detail in defining property rights and related matters pertaining to commerce.

Protection of the Public Welfare

Government establishes health and safety standards in industry and regulates minimum wages for certain classes of workers. It also provides old-age, disability, sickness, and unemployment benefits for those who qualify. Of course, these social welfare measures are enacted primarily for humanitarian reasons. Nevertheless, some of the measures may be tacit admissions that the private sector has failed to fulfill society's needs in an equitable manner.

Granting of Economic Privileges

Through selective subsidies, tariffs, taxes, and other legal provisions, government favors particular consumers, industries, unions, and other segments of the economy. This elaborate network of privileges and controls results as much from political pressures as from economic logic. To a large extent, therefore, government privileges cause higher prices, reduced efficiencies, and misallocations of society's resources.

Maintenance of Competition

Specific laws forbid unregulated monopolies and unfair trade and labor practices. If government enforces these laws vigorously, it ensures the perpetuation of a strong private sector.

Encouragement of Efficiency, Equity, Stability, and Growth

Through appropriate tax, expenditure, and regulatory policies, government seeks to encourage high employment, an equitable distribution of income, stable prices, and a steady rate of economic growth. These efforts are not always successful, however, for political reasons as well as for economic ones. Much of the study of economics, as you will see, is concerned with learning to understand these reasons.

This brief sketch of the economic activities of government leads to an important observation:

The promotional and regulatory activities of government are complex and widespread. Ostensibly, some of these activities are undertaken to correct for market failures. That is, they address the inability of the private sector, if left to itself, to achieve the goals of efficiency, equity, stability, and growth to the degree that all societies seek. However, as you will see, the extent to which government activities contribute to the realization of these goals is often debatable.

Provision of Social Goods

All economic systems are concerned with the three fundamental questions: *What* will be produced? *How* will it be produced? and *Who* will receive the final output? In mixed capitalistic economies such as ours, these questions are answered primarily by the market system. But, if certain types of commodities are not adequately provided by a free market, supplying them usually becomes a function of government. We refer to such commodities as *social goods*. For present purposes, they may be classified into two groups—public goods and merit goods.

Social goods, which are provided by government, include public goods and merit goods.

Public Goods

Public goods are sometimes called "collective" goods. Examples include national defense, street lighting, disease control, the administration of justice through the courts, air-traffic control, and public safety. An essential characteristic of public goods is that you cannot be excluded from receiving their benefits, regardless of whether or not you pay for them. For instance, every person in the nation or community benefits equally from national defense, street lighting, and other public goods, even those who pay no taxes.

Public goods are those whose benefits are not subject to the exclusion principle.

Public goods can thus be distinguished from "nonpublic" goods. These consist of private goods (such as food, clothing, services, and so on) that people buy in the market and certain social goods, known as merit goods, which are described below. Someone who does not pay for nonpublic goods can conceivably be excluded from using them. Therefore, the distinction between public and nonpublic goods rests on what is called the *exclusion principle*: A good is nonpublic if anyone who does not pay can be excluded from its use. Otherwise, it is a public good.

Merit Goods

Public goods are not the only commodities supplied by government. Other social goods, called *merit goods,* are also produced. These are provided by society because it deems some minimum amount of them as meretorious, or intrinsically worthy, of production. Merit goods share, to different degrees, some of the properties of both public and private goods. Some examples of merit goods are national parks, public education, public housing, and public hospitals. Local governments may supply such merit goods as municipal libraries, tennis courts, golf courses, swimming pools, and museums.

Merit goods are those whose benefits are subject to the exclusion principle, even though the principle may not always be invoked.

In contrast to public goods, merit goods are subject to the exclusion principle, *even though the principle may not always be invoked.* Therefore, merit goods are not public goods. People could be charged for the use of merit goods instead of being given them "free" or at reduced prices. As you will see, this raises interesting questions about efficiency and equity, problems that are among the fundamental concerns of economics.

Conclusion: Achieving Efficiency Through the Market

Because social goods are not sold at market prices, methods must be found to provide them efficiently.

Throughout the nation's history, government has served as a savior, subsidizer, owner, and regulator of special interests. It has financed roads and canals, subsidized firms and industries, sheltered workers, protected consumers and businesses, stabilized credit, refereed competition, and regulated markets.

In addition, government has become the chief producer of social goods, including public and merit goods. The benefits of the former are received by everyone. The benefits of the latter are widely available and, in most cases, are provided at reduced prices. How does this affect the allocation of such goods?

> In a free market, prices perform the allocative function. A resource is always allocated to its highest-valued use, as determined by the prices that buyers offer. But the situation is different with most social goods. Because many are made available "free" or at reduced prices, it is impossible to know the value people place on the goods. Therefore, how should government decide *what* and *how much* to produce?

The answer to this question is that government should seek ways of making more effective use of market mechanisms in its pricing practices. This can be done through the use of special taxes, grants, and pricing strategies designed to test the demand for social goods. In this way, as you will see below, officials can be guided in learning how to improve efficiency in the provision of these goods. Equally important, legislators can decide whether certain social goods might better be provided through the private sector. ■

■ Something to Think About

Garbage collection is a public good in some communities, a merit good in others, and a private good in still others. Can you suggest examples of social goods that could be financed entirely by user fees and charges? Can you think of social goods that could be privatized—that is, provided by the private sector? Why might this be desirable?

Spillovers, Market Failure, and Public Choice

A characteristic of many social goods is that they create "fallout" effects, or *spillovers*. These are external benefits or costs for which no compensation is made. Spillovers, therefore, are also called *externalities*.

For example, air-traffic control at busy airports reduces noise for some nearby residents while increasing it for others. This is an unpaid-for benefit to the former and an uncompensated "cost" to the latter. In the private sector, similarly, a factory may provide income and employment to a community while polluting its environment. Thus, spillover effects exist with some private goods as well as with social goods.

It is important to separate the benefits and costs that accrue to society from those that accrue to private entities. Education, for instance, provides *social benefits*. These include not only such *private benefits* as higher incomes and other satisfactions to the recipients but also a more stable and enlightened citizenry. Likewise, the production of goods results in *social costs*. These consist not only of *private costs* to the firms that produce the goods but also of any other sacrifices that society may incur, such as environmental pollution or other dissatisfactions.

The analysis of spillover benefits and costs is part of a larger branch of economics known as *public choice*. This may be defined as the study of nonmarket collective decision making, or the application of economics to political science. As you will see in the following paragraphs, the science of public choice seeks to develop ways of improving efficiency in the public sector and, therefore, in the provision of social goods.

Resource Misallocation

How can social goods be allocated through the market system? Two primary conditions are needed.

Creation of Property Rights

Someone must be able to claim ownership of something before it can be offered for sale. Otherwise, if ownership of a good is not clearly established, it becomes a "fugitive commodity." This enables some people to benefit from using the commodity without bearing the full cost. Pollution of air and water by some business firms are obvious examples. The pollutors benefit at the expense of everyone else because air and water are free goods.

Goods must be owned before they can be sold.

Identification of Spillovers

In a competitive free market, the socially optimum price and output of a good are determined by the intersection of the supply and demand curves. This assumes that all spillover costs and benefits are reflected in the curves. What happens if this is not the case? There are two possibilities.

Supply and demand concepts can be used to analyze the effects of spillovers.

1. Suppose that the supply curve is given. Then, if you draw a demand curve that fails to include all spillover benefits to buyers, that curve will be *lower* than it would have been otherwise. Therefore, the equilibrium or market price will be "too low," and resources will thus be *underallocated* to the good. This means that society will not be getting as much of the good as it would have wanted if spillover benefits had been included in the demand curve. Can you demonstrate this proposition graphically?

2. Similarly, suppose that the demand curve is given. Then, if you draw a supply curve that fails to include all spillover costs to sellers, that curve will be *lower* than it would be otherwise. Therefore, the equilibrium or market price will also be "too low," and resources will be *overallocated* to the good. Society will thus be getting more of the good than it would have wanted if spillover costs had been included in the supply curve. Think about how you would demonstrate this proposition graphically.

These ideas lead to the following generalization (which will be illustrated shortly in a diagram):

> To the extent that spillovers exist, a competitive free market does not allocate resources efficiently. In general, it underallocates resources to the production of goods that have spillover benefits and overallocates resources to the production of goods that have spillover costs. This results in a misallocation of society's resources—a general failure of the competitive free market to provide a socially optimum level of output.

Redressing Spillovers

What can be done to correct for the effects of spillovers? Because the misallocation of resources that characterizes spillovers is a result of market failure, corrective actions to eliminate or offset them can come only from government. Three major approaches may be considered.

Promotion and Regulation

Government can promote the output of industries in which spillovers are deemed by society to be desirable. This has happened in the production of certain social goods, such as recreation, public-safety, and public-health facilities. The outputs of these goods are larger than they would be if their spillover costs were included in their supply curves. In addition, government can pass legislation—such as laws intended to discourage environmental pollution—in an effort to control undesirable spillovers.

There are several ways in which government can redress the effects of spillovers.

Mitigation

Government can seek to mitigate or reduce spillover costs that take the form of environmental damage. This can be done by undertaking clean-up campaigns, beautification programs, reclamation projects, and the like. Although such programs do not eliminate the causes of the spillovers, they do serve to decrease many of their adverse effects.

Internalization

Government can "internalize" the spillovers by imposing special charges and by granting special benefits. Exhibit 1, along with the following explanation, shows how this works.

Free-Market Model Some of the economic effects of spillovers can be analyzed in terms of a competitive free-market model, as represented by the demand and supply curves in Figure (*a*). Any point on the normal market demand curve *D* expresses the *demand price.* This is the highest price that buyers are willing to pay for a given quantity of the commodity. The curve therefore reflects only private benefits to buyers, not spillover benefits to nonbuyers or to society.

Similarly, any point on the normal supply curve *S* expresses the *supply price.* This is the least price necessary to bring forth a given output. In other words, it is the lowest price that sellers are willing to accept in order to supply a given quantity of the commodity. The supply curve thus reflects only private costs to producers of the product, not spillover costs to anyone else.

Note from the graph that the equilibrium quantity, determined by the intersection of the supply and demand curves, is at *Q*. This suggests a fundamental shortcoming of the competitive free market:

> Free-market supply and demand curves reflect only direct private costs and direct private benefits while excluding spillover costs and spillover benefits. Therefore, to the extent that the omission of these spillover costs and benefits is significant, the equilibrium quantity will not be socially ideal. That is, *if externalities exist, the competitive free market will fail to provide an optimum allocation of society's resources.*

Supply-and-demand models can show how externalities may be internalized.

Because of this, methods must be found to *internalize* the externalities. This can be done in any of three ways:

1. Internalize spillover costs by incorporating them in the market supply curve.

2. Internalize spillover benefits by incorporating them in the market demand curve.

3. Impose user fees on consumers of social goods.

Exhibit 1
Spillover Effects in a Competitive Market

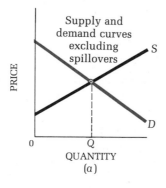

(a)

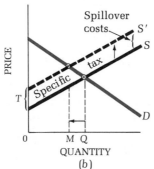

(b)

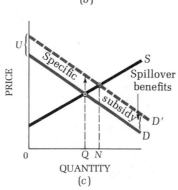

(c)

Figure (a). *No spillovers.* In a competitive free market, the demand and supply curves reflect direct private benefits and direct private costs, not spillover benefits or spillover costs. To the extent that these social consequences or spillovers exist, the equilibrium quantity at Q does not represent an optimum allocation of society's resources.

Figure (b). *Spillover costs.* A competitive free market overallocates resources to the production of goods that have spillover costs. That is, society gets more of the goods than it would want if the spillover costs were included in the supply curve.

What can society do if it wants to reduce the output at Q to the socially optimum level at M? The answer is that government can impose a specific tax on sellers equal to T per unit of output. The tax will have the same effect on sellers as an increase in the cost of production, causing the supply curve to shift from S to S'. If the tax is just high enough to equal the spillover costs, output will decrease from Q to the desired level at M.

Figure (c). *Spillover benefits.* A competitive free market underallocates resources to the production of goods that have spillover benefits. That is, society gets less of the goods than it would want if the spillover benefits were included in the demand curve.

Suppose that the socially optimum level of output is at N. In that case, government can provide buyers with a specific subsidy of U per unit of output. The subsidy will be like a cash gift to buyers, causing the demand curve to shift from D to D'. If the subsidy is just large enough to equal the spillover benefits, output will increase from Q to the desired level at N.

Internalizing Spillover Costs As shown in Figure (b), one measure that government can adopt is to require sellers to pay a *specific tax*. This is a per-unit payment on a commodity. That is, sellers would pay the tax T on each unit of the commodity produced, thereby increasing its costs of production by the amount of the tax. This would cause the supply curve to shift from S to S'. Consequently, for any given quantity, the curve would be higher by the amount of the tax. If the tax is large enough, it can compensate for any spillover costs that were not included in the supply curve. The tax will thus reduce output from the level at Q to the socially optimum level at M.

Internalizing Spillover Benefits An alternative measure that government can adopt is to give buyers a *specific subsidy*. This is a per-unit grant on a commodity. As Figure (c) indicates, buyers would receive

Exhibit 2
Growth of Government Expenditures

The size of the public sector, measured by government expenditures, has expanded rapidly—for several reasons:

1. Increased Demand for Social Goods and Services The public sector has increased its expenditures on social goods, including education, transportation, public assistance, health care, housing, and consumer protection.

2. War and National Defense A large part of the increase in federal spending can be attributed to expenditures on wars, defense-related activities, and interest on the federal debt.

3. Inflation and Lagging Productivity The costs of the social benefits provided by government have climbed with inflation. At the same time, productivity in the delivery of those services has lagged far behind rising costs. Thus, government has found that the salaries it pays out—for education, public safety, health, and so on—are growing faster than the efficiency of the services it performs.

(**Note** The vertical axis of this graph is a logarithmic scale. On this type of scale, equal distances represent equal percentage changes. Thus, because the changes from 100 to 200, 200 to 400, 300 to 600, and so on, all equal 100 percent, they are represented by equal vertical distances on the graph. This permits better comparisons to be made of both small and large—that is, *relative*—changes in the data.)

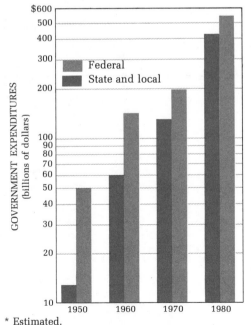

* Estimated.
Source: U.S. Department of Commerce.

the subsidy U on each unit of the commodity purchased, which would increase its consumption. This would cause the demand curve to shift from D to D'. Therefore, for any given quantity, the curve would be higher by the amount of the subsidy. If the subsidy is large enough, it can compensate for any spillover benefits that were not included in the demand curve. The subsidy will thus increase output from the level at Q to the socially optimum level at N.

Imposing User Fees Taxes and subsidies are two means by which externalities can be internalized. A third means is the imposition of user fees on consumers of social goods. This will help shift the burden of support among users. For example, those who make little use of certain social goods could pay less, and those who make the most use could pay more. To the extent that this is feasible, the prices people pay would then be more in line with the benefits they receive. This would help reduce waste and encourage efficiency by allocating goods to their highest-valued use.

Conclusion: Efficient Production and Public Choice

The public sector has limited funds available for recreational facilities, hospitals, parks, libraries, public transportation, education, and other social goods. In view of this, how much should be spent to achieve an efficient allocation of these goods? This, you will recall, is a fundamental problem of public choice.

To the extent that spillovers exist, efficient production of social goods is unlikely to occur. The reason is that the costs to society of providing social goods and the values that society places on such goods are unknown. The problem thus suggests its own solution:

> The public sector, under pressure to provide new and better social goods in the face of tight financial constraints, is looking for better management methods. Through a more sophisticated use of taxes, subsidies, and user fees, procedures can be developed for internalizing the externalities that accompany a wide variety of social goods. The greater part of the burden of paying for the goods can thus be shifted from those who make little use of them to those who receive the greatest benefits. Efficiency will thereby be improved, thus enhancing society's well-being.

Public Budgeting and Public Choice: Tools for Collective Decision Making

In the past few decades, the public sector has been characterized by a remarkable growth of expenditures at all levels of government—federal, state, and local. This means that a rising volume of the nation's output is being allocated by collective (rather than private) decision making. Several major reasons for the growth of government spending are given in Exhibit 2.

Any discussion of public-sector expenditures is bound to raise questions about public-sector revenues. The methods used by governments to manage their revenues and expenditures constitute what is known as "public budgeting." This is a branch of economics and political science concerned with governmental financial planning and control. Exhibit 3 provides some illustrations of government budgets.

Exhibit 3
Federal, State, and Local Budgets: What Happens to Your Tax Dollars?

Figure (a). The government's total revenues and expenditures for any given year are rarely equal. When they are, the budget is said to be *balanced*. When total revenues exceed total expenditures in any given year, the budget is said to have a *surplus*. When total revenues are less than total expenditures, the budget is said to have a *deficit*.

(a) FEDERAL BUDGET RECEIPTS AND OUTLAYS: 1960–1980

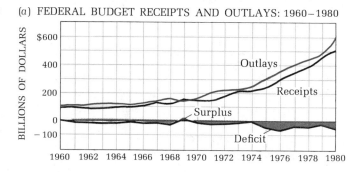

Figure (b). For the federal government, income taxes, both individual and corporate, constitute the largest source of receipts. Income security payments, including social security benefits, unemployment compensation, public assistance (welfare), and federal employment retirement and disability benefits, constitute the largest category of outlays.

(b) ANNUAL FEDERAL BUDGET: 1980 – 1981

WHERE IT COMES FROM: RECEIPTS

Excise and other taxes 12%
Individual income taxes 47%
30%
Social insurance taxes and contributions
Corporate income taxes 11%

WHERE IT GOES: OUTLAYS

Interest 12%
National defense 25%
Health and Education 15%
35%
Other 13%
Income security

Figure (c). For state and local governments combined, property taxes (on land, buildings, etc.) and sales taxes make up the chief sources of tax income. Education is the largest category of expenditure.

(c) STATE AND LOCAL GOVERNMENT BUDGETS: 1980 – 1981

WHERE IT COMES FROM: RECEIPTS

Other 28%
Individual income taxes 11%
18% Property taxes
22% 21%
Federal Government
Sales and gross receipts taxes

WHERE IT GOES: OUTLAYS

Other general expenditures 28%
Education 31%
Insurance trusts 7%
18%
Utilities and liquor stores 8%
Highways 8%
Public welfare, hospitals, and health

Figure (d). Over the long run, state and local governments have received a rising percentage share of total tax revenues, and the federal government has received a declining percentage share. These trends reflect the growing economic influence of the state and local governments relative to the federal government—and the need of the former to finance their accelerating public functions.

(d) PER CAPITA TAX REVENUE, BY LEVEL OF GOVERNMENT

Total
Federal
State and local

1950   1960   1970   1980

31 / 69   32 / 68   37 / 63   39 / 61   Percent

Source: U.S. Department of Commerce.

Exhibit 4
Application: Alternative Budget Structures for the U.S. Coast Guard

In an administrative budget, funds are allocated by administrative agencies and by activities. In a program budget, funds are allocated for the purpose of attaining certain objectives, or for undertaking specific programs. The totals in both budgets may be the same, but the ways in which the expenditures are broken down are quite different. As explained in the text, a program budget is part of a larger planning and control *system*.

Administrative budget (allocation by administrative agencies and activities)	Amount
General funds: finance division	
Operating expenses	x
Retired pay	x
Reserve training	x
Activities funds: departments	
Vessel operations	x
Aviation operations	x
Training and recruiting	x
Administration	x
Other expenses	x
Total	x

Program budget (allocation by specific objectives and programs)	Amount
Search and rescue	x
Navigational aids	x
Law enforcement	x
Military readiness	x
Merchant Marine safety	x
Oceanography projects	x
Supporting services	x
Total	x

Budgeting for a government, like budgeting for a family, is an activity dealing with hopes, daydreams, and hard facts. What is a *budget*? It is an itemized estimate of expected revenues and expenditures for a given period in the future. The federal budget covers a fiscal year. (A fiscal year is a 12-month period for which a business, government, or other organization plans the use of its revenues.) The budgets of some state and local governments cover a fiscal period that is longer than a year (typically two years).

You will often hear people complain of waste in government spending. Can financial controls be developed to reduce public-sector inefficiencies? Although improvements in budgeting have been made from time to time, two scientific techniques have gained considerable popularity at certain levels of government. The two techniques are (1) planning-program-budgeting systems and (2) benefit-cost analyses.

Planning-Program-Budgeting Systems (PPBS)

A budget is a financial road map. It tells you where revenues are expected to come from and where expenditures are expected to go. Most traditional budgets are called "administrative" budgets. They classify expected money inflows and outflows by administrative units (such as departments or agencies) or by activities (describing the work to be performed). Administrative budgets do not ordinarily explain why or how the funds are to be coordinated to fulfill objectives.

A budget that is designed to avoid this shortcoming is a "program budget." It is part of a larger complex called a *planning-program-budgeting system* (*PPBS*). This may be defined as a method of revenue and expenditure management based on:

1. Determination of goals.
2. Assessment of their relative importance to society.
3. Allocation of those resources needed to attain the goals at least cost.

Thus, PPBS is a budgetary method that relates expenditures to specific goals or programs. This is done so that the costs of achieving a particular goal can be identified, measured, planned, and controlled. You can best appreciate the difference between an administrative budget and a program budget by comparing the two tables in Exhibit 4.

In many government departments in which PPBS has been adopted, it has improved budgeting efficiency. However, it has also been found to have some important limitations. In particular:

> Outputs are usually in the form of indivisible services, which are therefore difficult to measure. For example, neither the quantity nor the quality of most governmentally provided social goods—such as education, health care, police protection, space exploration, and so on—can be broken down and measured in precise units. As a result, the establishment of budgetary goals and priorities is generally based on value judgments rather than on scientific determinations.

Despite this shortcoming, PPBS is a useful tool for facilitating overall budgetary decision making. However, when specific alternatives must be evaluated to determine whether certain large-scale projects and expenditures should be undertaken, a more scientific approach is needed.

Benefit-Cost Analysis

A scientific approach to government budgeting and financial planning is *benefit-cost analysis*. This is a method of comparing, in monetary terms, the advantages and disadvantages of alternative investment projects or spending programs to help determine which should be undertaken. Benefit-cost analysis can also be used for personal financial planning. For example, if you are thinking of buying a house, a car, or even a vacation, benefit-cost analysis can help you make the choice that best meets your needs.

Benefit-cost analysis provides a way of comparing the advantages and disadvantages of an expenditure decision.

In general terms, a typical benefit-cost study consists of three steps.

Step 1: Determine Benefits Identify the future advantages or benefits that will accrue to society as a result of the project. Then express the value of these benefits in today's dollars. For example, if the project is a government program for flood control in an agricultural area, how much will society save by reducing damage to crops, homes, and recreational facilities?

Step 2: Determine Costs Identify the sacrifices, or *opportunity costs*, that society will incur as a result of the project. In other words, what satisfactions will people have to forgo because money is being used for, say, a flood-control project rather than a job-training program?

Step 3: Determine the Benefit/Cost Ratio Divide the total dollar benefits by the total dollar costs. As an illustration, suppose the benefits equal $11 billion and the costs equal $10 billion. Then the ratio of benefits to costs is $11/$10 = 1.1. If no other project being considered by the government has a higher ratio, then this project would result in the most efficient expenditure of public funds. Why? Because it produces the largest value of benefits per dollar of costs.

Some Difficulties

This simple example conveys some of the basic ideas, but not the real difficulties, of conducting an actual benefit-cost analysis. Most of the difficulties fall into two categories—constraints and measurement.

It is difficult to measure all of the benefits and costs of an expenditure.

Constraints Government agencies are not always free to select the most socially desirable projects—the ones with the highest benefit/cost ratios. The reason is that they are subject to various administrative, financial, and legal constraints. For example, certain projects may be unable to attract enough qualified supervisors. The budgets for financing particular projects may be inadequate. And there may exist laws (such as zoning laws) that prohibit the use of particular resources for certain projects.

Measurement It is rarely possible to measure all the benefits and costs of a government spending program. This is because most projects have many secondary and intangible impacts. For example, how can we measure the value of a new educational program to a community, or the value of an antipollution program on the quality of life? Similarly, how can we measure the full opportunity costs of such programs? Because of such problems, economists conducting benefit-cost studies are often compelled either to make rough estimates of certain benefits and costs or to omit them entirely.

Conclusion: Efficiency and Public Choice

PPBS and benefit-cost analysis are two tools that are used to improve decision making in the public sector.

The growth of the public sector has fostered the development of a branch of economics called "public choice." It is concerned with methods for improving efficiency in government. Planning-program-budgeting systems (PPBS) and benefit-cost analysis are two related approaches to government budgeting that are intended to promote efficiency. Both of these techniques have been in use in certain departments and at various levels of government for several decades.

In practice, benefit-cost analysis suffers from several handicaps. Chief among them is the fact that many types of government expenditures produce benefits that are widespread, intangible, and therefore difficult to measure. As a result, the public sector's adoption of benefit-cost analysis has been limited to specific types of projects. These include flood control, electric power production, transportation systems, and certain service activities. The benefits from these kinds of projects are more clearly identifiable and measurable.

Despite limited applications, benefit-cost analysis has certain fundamental advantages:

> In a conventional budgeting system, funds tend to be allocated according to expected "needs" or "requirements." Little or no effort is made to establish, in any precise way, how those needs or requirements are determined and whether they are worth the costs. In a benefit-cost budgeting system, each expenditure is compared with the benefit it will produce. The expenditure is not undertaken unless its value is at least equaled by the value of its benefit. Scarce resources are thus allocated more efficiently—through explicit comparisons of benefits and costs rather than suppositions about "needs" or "requirements."

The American Tax System

Government budgets deal not only with expenditures but also with revenues. Governments raise revenues through taxation. In view of this, we must ask: What is the nature of our tax system?

The effects of taxes are analyzed in terms of the four goals of economics.

A *tax* is a compulsory payment to government. The purpose of a tax is to achieve one or more of four objectives:

Efficiency—full use of society's available resources to produce the goods and services that consumers want to purchase with their existing incomes.

Equity—a distribution of income and wealth that society regards as fair.

Stability—the avoidance of substantial inflations or deflations.

Growth—a rising level of output for all members of society.

Taxes can be levied and classified in many ways. In the United States and many other advanced countries, there are three principal types of taxes:

1. Taxes on income
   (a) Personal income taxes.
   (b) Corporation income taxes.
2. Taxes on wealth (including its ownership and transfer)
   (a) Property taxes.
   (b) Death (estate and inheritance) and gift taxes.

3. Taxes on activities (consumption, production, employment, and so forth)

    (a) Sales and excise taxes.

    (b) Social security taxes.

Dozens of other less important kinds of taxes exist, but nearly all can be placed in one of these three main categories.

Taxes on Income

Income taxes are based on net income—what remains after certain items are deducted from gross income. The items that can be deducted and the tax rates that are applied are specified by law, and they differ between the personal income tax and the corporation income tax.

Personal Income Tax

In poetry, spring is a time when a young man's fancy turns to thoughts of love. But in economics, spring is a much more mundane and certainly less romantic period. It is the season when millions of Americans begin to sort their previous year's income and expense records. As shown in Exhibit 5, this is the first step that must be completed in order to determine your personal income tax.

In calculating this tax, you are allowed to take specific types of deductions and exemptions. For instance, some deductions that may be made (within limits) from your income are donations to the Red Cross, to your alma mater, and to various other nonprofit organizations. You may also deduct some payments for doctor's bills, x rays, and medicine; taxes paid to state and local governments; interest paid on loans; and various other outlays. In addition, tax allowances or exemptions are permitted for support of yourself, your family, and your dependents. In this way, the government acknowledges the fact that larger families require more funds than smaller ones to meet their living costs.

The amount of income tax you must pay at a given income level depends on several things. These include whether you are single or married and what the particular tax rates happen to be at the time. The rates are usually revised by the federal government every few years. Nevertheless, certain principles underlying a tax-rate schedule never change—as explained in Exhibit 6.

Two controversial aspects of the personal income tax should be noted.

1. Incentives The steepness of the marginal tax-rate schedule (explained in the exhibit) may have serious economic consequences. It must be high enough at all income levels to yield the desired amounts of revenues. However, rates that are too high at the upper income levels may discourage investment and risk taking. Rates that are too high at the lower levels may reduce the incentive for taking on overtime work or second jobs. In view of this, is there a "best" or optimum tax-rate schedule for the economy as a whole? There probably is. But it changes with different needs and conditions, reflecting political as well as economic circumstances of the times.

2. Loopholes Through legal methods of *tax avoidance*, many taxpayers are able to reduce their average rates. This is because our tax system contains dozens of legal "loopholes" which permit relative tax advan-

Exhibit 5

Logical Structure of the Federal Personal Income Tax

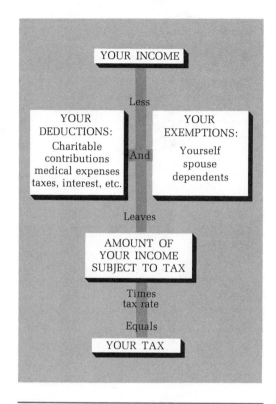

Exhibit 6

Personal Income Tax Schedule

(hypothetical data)

The income taxes people pay are determined from government tax schedules like the one shown here. Although the numbers in the table change frequently with revisions in the tax laws, certain principles on which the schedule is based remain the same. For example:

Columns (1), (2), and (3) As the level of taxable income increases, the amount paid out in income taxes also increases. The average tax rate tells you what percentage of income is paid in taxes. This percentage increases as income rises.

Columns (4) and (5) Each increase in income results in a corresponding increase in taxes. These columns enable you to compare the *amounts* of increase in both.

Column (6) This tells you the *percentage* of each increase in income that is paid out in taxes. The distinction between the *average tax rate* in column (3) and the *marginal tax rate* in column (6) is shown by the formulas beneath the table.

In comparing columns (3) and (6), note that the marginal tax rate in going from one income level to the next is always higher than the average tax rate at either income level. Observe also that, according to the marginal tax-rate schedule, you can never find yourself worse off by making an extra dollar. No matter how high your total taxable income may be, you would still be able to keep some percentage of every additional dollar you earned.

Although this is not an actual tax schedule, the basic ideas and relations conveyed are reasonably representative of one.

(1) Total taxable annual income	(2) Total personal income tax	(3) Average tax rate* (percent) (2) ÷ (1)	(4) Change in column (1)	(5) Change in column (2)	(6) Marginal tax rate† (percent) (5) ÷ (4)
$ 20,000	$ 2,600	13%			
			$ 5,000	$ 900	18%
25,000	3,500	14			
			5,000	1,300	26
30,000	4,800	16			
			5,000	1,500	30
35,000	6,300	18			
			11,000	3,500	32
46,000	9,800	21			
			14,000	5,200	37
60,000	15,000	25			
			26,000	11,000	42
86,000	26,000	30			
			30,000	14,000	47
116,000	40,000	35			
			46,000	23,000	50
162,000	63,000	39			
			54,000	27,000	50
216,000	90,000	41			

$$ \text{* Average tax rate} = \frac{\text{total personal income tax}}{\text{total taxable income}} \qquad \text{† Marginal tax rate} = \frac{\text{change in total personal income tax}}{\text{change in total taxable income}} $$

tages for people in almost every income class. For example, interest paid on debts, such as home mortgages, credit-card balances, and personal loans, is a deductible item for income-tax purposes. Although changes in the tax laws have, over the years, closed many of these loopholes, it is not likely that they will ever be entirely eliminated. (In contrast, illegal methods of escaping taxes, such as lying or cheating about income or expenses, come under the general heading of *tax evasion*.)

Nearly all taxpayers, rich and poor alike, benefit from tax loopholes of one form or another. However, the greatest share of benefits from tax loopholes goes to taxpayers with above-average incomes. This group is also the one that pays more than half the total personal income tax bill.

Case

Tax Loopholes—Something for Everyone

Our federal tax system is riddled with loopholes of various sorts. There is something for everyone—rich and poor, large taxpayers and small ones. A complete list of loopholes would consist of more than 100 items. They cost the federal government hundreds of billions of dollars in lost revenues annually.

Individuals	Corporations
Income exempt from taxes	*Exemptions, deductions, and credits*
Pension plans	Investment tax credit
Company-paid benefits	Progressive tax rate on profits
Social security benefits	Interest on municipal bonds
Interest on life insurance savings	Special employment allowances
Interest on municipal bonds	Extra depreciation deductions
Military and veterans benefits	Foreign-trade exemptions and credits
Scholarships and fellowships	Research and development expenses
Sick pay	Excess depletion allowances
Deductions and credits	Capital gains
State and local income taxes	Charitable contributions
Sales taxes	Special bad-debt reserves
Charitable contributions	Exploration and developmental costs
Mortgage interest on owner-occupied	Construction-period interest and taxes
homes	Investment credits for employee stock
State and local property taxes	plans
Medical expenses	Credit-union income exemption
Interest on debts	
Casualty losses	
Exemptions for the aged and the blind	

Source: U.S. Department of the Treasury

Corporation Income Tax

One of the federal government's important sources of revenue is the corporate income tax. (Many states also tax corporate incomes, but at lower rates.) The corporate income tax is simple to calculate because it is based on the difference between a company's total income and its total expenses—its net profit. The tax rate has varied over the years. During recent decades, it has averaged close to 50 percent.

The corporate income tax raises many important issues. Among them:

1. Some experts argue that lower rates would leave corporations with more profits to use for expanding their operations, thereby creating more jobs. Other authorities, however, contend that the rates should be higher, enabling government to reduce other taxes, especially personal income taxes.

Is the corporate income-tax rate too high?

2. There is considerable controversy over who ultimately bears the burden of the corporate income tax. Some economists believe that the tax is shifted "forward" to consumers in the form of higher prices. Other observers contend that much of the tax is shifted "backward" to resource owners in the form of lower wages, rents, and so on. Still other authorities believe that the tax is borne by the owners (stockholders) of the corporation because the tax is imposed on corporate net profit.

Who ultimately bears the burden of the corporate income tax?

Is it socially desirable to tax corporate profits "twice"?

3. The tax is actually a form of *double taxation*. This is because the corporation pays a tax on its profits, and the stockholder pays a personal income tax on the dividends received from those profits. Therefore, it is often argued not only that the tax is inequitable but that it may impede the attainment of other economic goals as well.

There are no simple resolutions for these controversial issues. Each has valid aspects that are subject to frequent debate.

The remaining two categories that make up the structure of the American tax system—taxes on wealth and taxes on activities—can be sketched briefly.

Taxes on Wealth

Taxes on wealth are imposed on what is owned (as compared to taxes on income, which are imposed on what is earned)

Property taxes are levied primarily on land and buildings to help pay for public services. The taxes vary from low rates in some rural areas where services are minor to high rates in localities with good streets, schools, and public safety facilities.

Death taxes are levied, at the time of death, on estates by the federal government and on inheritances by some state governments. An estate is the value of everything that someone owns; an inheritance is an amount that someone receives. The rates depend on values and amounts. Like income taxes, death taxes exempt small estates and inheritances but tax the unexempt portions at progressive rates. Many wealthy people would try to avoid these taxes by distributing most of their property before death. Therefore, *gift taxes* are imposed on the transfer of assets beyond certain values. However, various legal devices, such as trust funds and family foundations, have enabled many people to lighten the burden of these taxes.

Taxes on Activities

Taxes on activities are imposed on buying, selling, working, and producing.

Sales taxes are imposed by many state and local governments. These taxes are flat percentage levies on the retail prices of goods. In some states or cities, such commodities as food, medicine, and services are exempt from sales taxes. In other places, they are not. The federal government imposes no "general" sales tax on the final sale of goods. However, it does impose special sales taxes, called *excise taxes*, on the manufacture, sale, or consumption of liquor, tobacco products, gasoline, and certain other goods.

From time to time, in order to raise more money, political and economic efforts are exerted to introduce a *value-added tax (VAT)*. This is a type of national sales tax paid by manufacturers and merchants on the value contributed to a product at each stage of its production and distribution. However, this form of tax, although common in Europe, has not yet gained sufficiently wide acceptance for adoption in the United States.

Social security taxes are payroll taxes on wages and salaries levied by the federal government. The taxes finance our compulsory social insurance program covering old-age and unemployment benefits. The taxes are imposed both on employees and on employers and are based on the incomes of the former. These taxes are actually a "reverse" form of income tax. After a person has earned a certain amount each year, his or her income above that level is exempt from the tax. This assures that every income earner is taxed.

Theories of Taxation

> The power to tax is one great power upon which the whole national fabric is based. It is not only the power to destroy but also the power to keep alive.

So stated the U.S. Supreme Court in a famous case in 1899. Today hardly anyone would disagree. For this reason, economists have developed several broad standards for judging the relative merits of a tax:

1. Equity Tax burdens should be distributed justly among the people.

2. Efficiency, Stability, and Growth A tax should contribute toward improving resource allocation, economic stabilization, and the total output of goods and services.

3. Enforceability A tax should be adequate for its purpose and acceptable to the public, or else it will be impossible to enforce.

These criteria are simple and persuasive. But implementation, especially of equity, has caused much controversy. Let us see why.

Principles of Tax Equity

A good tax system should be fair. If people believe it is unfair—that too many loopholes benefit some people and not others—taxpayers' morale and the effectiveness of the tax system will deteriorate. Therefore, two standards of tax equity have evolved over the years.

The equity of a tax may be determined with respect to two standards.

Horizontal Equity "Equals should be treated equally." This means that people who are economically equal should be taxed equally. That is, if people have the same income, wealth, or other taxpaying ability, they should pay the same amount of tax.

Vertical Equity "Unequals should be treated unequally." This means that people who are economically unequal should bear equal tax burdens. To accomplish this, people with different incomes, wealth, or other taxpaying abilities should pay different amounts of tax so that everyone sacrifices equally.

Horizontal and vertical equity are standards for judging the fairness of a tax. Efforts to apply them have resulted in two fundamental principles of taxation—the benefit principle and the ability-to-pay principle.

Benefit Principle

The *benefit principle* holds that people should be taxed according to the benefits they receive. For example, the tax you pay on gasoline reflects the benefit you receive from driving on public roads. The more you drive, the more gasoline you use and the more taxes you pay. These tax revenues are typically set aside for financing highway construction and maintenance. Similarly, local governments pay for at least part of the construction of streets and sewers by taxing those residents who benefit directly from them.

The benefit principle of taxation has wide appeal, but it is often difficult to apply.

What is wrong with the benefit principle as a general guide for taxation? There are two major difficulties:

1. Relatively few publicly provided goods and services exist for which all benefits can be readily determined. For many goods and services, the benefits would be impossible to determine. The entire nation benefits from social goods, such as public education, health and sanitation facilities, police and fire protection, and national defense. How can we decide which groups should pay the taxes for these things and which should not?

2. Those who receive certain benefits may not be able to pay for them. For instance, it would be impossible to finance public welfare assistance or unemployment compensation by taxing the recipients.

Ability-to-Pay Principle

About 2,400 years ago, in his classic work *The Republic,* the philosopher Plato remarked: "When there is an income tax, the just man will be willing to pay more and the unjust less on the same amount of income."

Plato was speaking of an ideal world—a utopia in which all people strive to do what will be best for society. But with human nature being what it is, most people are not inclined to pay any more taxes than the law requires of them.

However, the *ability-to-pay principle* is actually a modern and realistic restatement of Plato's ancient dictum. It states that the fairest tax a government can impose is one that is based on the ability of the taxpayer to pay it, regardless of any benefit derived from the tax. This means that, the more wealth a person has or the higher his or her income, the greater the taxes should be. This is based on the assumption that each dollar of taxes paid by a rich person "hurts" less than each dollar paid by a poor one. The personal income tax in the United States is structured on this principle.

There are two major difficulties in the use of this principle as a general guide for taxation:

The ability-to-pay principle sounds "fair," but it may not be as fair as many people think.

1. Ability to pay is a debatable concept—difficult to determine and impossible to measure. How can we really know that an additional thousand dollars a year in income means less to a rich person than to a poor person? A rich person may not want for any material things, but he or she may derive a greater increase in satisfaction from earning an extra thousand dollars than a poor person gains from spending it. Nevertheless, we ordinarily *assume* that certain taxes should be based on ability to pay. You should keep in mind, though, that the entire concept involves psychological and philosophical issues that economics is not equipped to explore.

2. Even if we could really be clear about what we mean by ability to pay, how could we distinguish between *degrees* of ability among different individuals? You may feel that a person who earns $50,000 a year is able to pay more in taxes than someone who earns $25,000. But *how much* more? The answer is not necessarily twice as much. In fact, there is no simple answer. Indeed, as with the benefit principle, the hardest problem is to develop a way of measuring the right concepts.

Some Practical Compromises

As a result of these philosophical difficulties, it has become necessary to adopt convenient methods of implementing the benefit and ability principles. The methods may not always be ideal. Nevertheless, as explained on the next page, three major classes of tax rates—proportional, progressive, and regressive—have evolved over the years. These types of rates differ from each other according to the way in which the amount is related to the *tax base.* This is the item being taxed. Examples are the value of property (in the case of a property tax), income (in the case of an income tax), and the value of goods sold (in the case of a sales tax). When the total tax is divided by the tax base, the resulting figure, expressed as a percentage, is called the *tax rate*. Thus, a $10 tax on a tax base of $100 represents a tax rate of 10 percent. It follows that the tax base times the tax rate equals the tax yield to the government.

Proportional Tax

A *proportional tax* is one whose percentage rate *remains constant* as the tax base increases. Consequently, the amount of the tax paid is proportional to the tax base. The property tax is an example. If the tax rate is constant at 5 percent, a person who owns property valued at $10,000 pays $500 in taxes. Someone who owns property valued at $100,000 pays $5,000 in taxes.

Proportional tax: constant percentage.

Progressive Tax

A *progressive tax* is one whose percentage rate *increases* as the tax base increases. In the United States, the federal personal income tax is the best example. The tax is graduated so that, theoretically, a person with a higher income pays a greater percentage in tax than a person with a lower income. We say "theoretically" because, in reality, certain loopholes in the tax structure distort the progressive principle and sometimes even prevent it from operating over the full range of income.

Progressive tax: increasing percentage.

Regressive Tax

A *regressive tax* is one whose percentage rate *decreases* as the tax base increases. In this narrow, technical sense, there is no regressive tax in the United States. In practice, however, the term "regressive" is applied to any tax that takes a larger share of income from the low-income taxpayer than from the high-income taxpayer. Most proportional taxes, such as sales taxes, are thus seen to have regressive effects. For instance, a 6 percent sales tax is the same rate for everyone, rich and poor alike. But people with smaller incomes spend a larger percentage of their incomes. Therefore the sales taxes they pay are a greater proportion of their incomes.

Regressive tax: decreasing percentage.

To summarize:

> In the narrow, *technical* sense, definitions of proportional, progressive, and regressive taxes are expressed in terms of their actual tax bases. These are the things that are taxed, such as income, property, or value of goods sold. For *equity* purposes, however, the base chosen for reference is always income—regardless of the actual tax base.

The equity effects of a tax are always judged in relation to income.

The distinctions between the three types of tax rates are illustrated with brief explanations in Exhibit 7.

How do the foregoing principles and compromises apply to the American tax system? Generally speaking, some of our taxes tend to lean more toward the benefit principle and others more toward ability to pay. Social security, license, and gasoline taxes are some examples of the former; income and death (estate and inheritance) taxes are illustrative of the latter.

We can also find examples of progressive, regressive, and proportional taxes. Income and death taxes are progressive in both the technical sense and the equity sense because their percentage rates increase with the tax base. Property, general sales, and excise taxes are propor-

Exhibit 7

**Proportional, Progressive, and Regressive
Tax-Rate Structures in Equity Terms**
(hypothetical data)

In equity terms, the structure of a tax is *always* evaluated by comparing the tax rate to the taxpayer's income—regardless of the actual tax base to which the tax is applied.

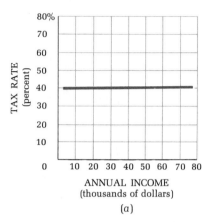

(a)

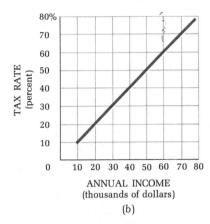

(b)

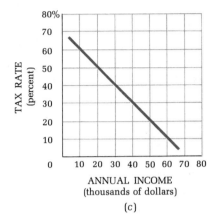

(c)

Figure (a): *Proportional tax.* The tax takes the same percentage of income from high-income taxpayers as from low-income taxpayers. In this example, the tax is 40 percent of a $10,000 income, 40 percent of a $20,000 income, and so on.

Figure (b): *Progressive tax.* The tax takes a larger percentage of income from high-income taxpayers than from low-income taxpayers. In this example, the tax is 10 percent of a $10,000 income, 20 percent of a $20,000 income, and so on.

Figure (c): *Regressive tax.* The tax takes a smaller percentage of income from high-income taxpayers than from low-income taxpayers. In this example, the tax is 60 percent of a $10,000 income, 50 percent of a $20,000 income, and so on.

tional in their technical structure, because their rates are a constant percentage of the tax base. But they tend to have regressive effects from an equity standpoint when related to the *incomes* of the taxpayers.

Tax Shifting and Incidence: Direct or Indirect Taxes?

The burdens of some taxes are not always borne by the parties upon whom they are imposed.

Surprisingly enough, the person or business firm upon whom a tax is initially imposed does not always bear its burden. For instance, a company may be able to *shift* all or part of a tax "forward" to its customers by charging them higher prices for its goods. Or it may be able to shift a tax "backward" to the owners of its factors of production by paying them less for their materials and services. When a tax has been shifted, its burden or *incidence* is on someone else. It thus proves convenient to classify taxes into two categories: direct and indirect.

A direct tax is one whose burden cannot be shifted to others.

Direct Taxes These taxes are not shifted; their burden is borne by the persons or firms originally taxed. Typical examples are personal income taxes, social security taxes paid by employees, most property taxes (excluding rental and business property), and death taxes. Certain taxes, notably those on corporate income, are probably only partially direct. Can you suggest why?

Indirect Taxes These include all taxes that can be shifted either partially or entirely to someone other than the person or firm originally taxed. The most familiar example is the sales tax. Contrary to popular belief, this tax is imposed on sellers, not buyers. Sellers, however, typically shift the tax burden to buyers. Other examples of indirect taxes are excise taxes, taxes on business and rental property, social security taxes paid by employers, and most corporate income taxes.

An indirect tax is one whose burden can be shifted to others.

In what direction will a tax be shifted, assuming that it is shifted at all? This is a thorny problem in economic theory, and the experts do not always agree. In general:

> Most taxes are like an increased cost to the taxpayer. Therefore, each taxpayer will try to pass them on to someone else. As a result, once a tax is imposed, it tends—like lightning or water—to follow the path of least resistance through the markets in which the taxpayer deals. That is, the taxpayer tries to shift the tax by altering prices, inputs, or outputs according to the least degree of opposition encountered.

Economics in the News

Higher Fees For Boat and Aircraft Users
by Darcy Lynn

WASHINGTON—Federal and local governments are under pressure to impose new user fees, and to raise existing ones, on publicly maintained and operated waterways and airports.

The increases, proponents argue, would produce the additional revenue needed to help offset the rising cost of subsidies that primarily benefit boat and aircraft operators. These subsidies, which are paid from public tax revenues, are used to maintain river harbors, channels, locks, and dams, as well as search, rescue, and navigation assistance.

Opposition to higher user fees is strong. Special-interest groups consisting of owners of recreational and commercial boats, merchant seaman, owners of private aircraft, and commercial-airline operators are lobbying hard in the federal and state capitals against most user fees. "We are already overburdened with high fuel prices," said one prominent lobbyist in Washington. "We shouldn't have to absorb further cost increases."

Some legislators disagree. According to the chairman of the Congressional committee dealing with the problem, "If the owners don't pay the costs, who should? The public?"

What You Have Learned in This Chapter

1. The economic role of government may be considered to consist of two broad functions: (a) promotion and regulation of the private sector and (b) provision of social goods.

2. Government promotes and regulates the private sector in many ways. For example, it (a) provides a stable economic environment, (b) performs social welfare activities, (c) grants economic privileges, (d) seeks to maintain competition, and (e) tries to promote high employment, and redistribute income.

3. Government provides social goods, which consist of public goods and merit goods. Public goods are those not subject to the exclusion principle. Examples are national defense, street lighting, and disease control. Merit goods are subject to the exclusion principle even though the principle may not always be invoked. Examples of merit goods are municipal libraries, national parks, and public hospitals.

4. Many social goods create "spillovers"—externalities in the form of benefits or costs. Methods for redressing spillovers consist of (a) promotion and regulation, (b) mitigation, and (c) internalization. The last can be illustrated in terms of a supply-and-demand model, which shows how efficiency can be improved by using specific taxes and subsidies to internalize spillover costs and benefits.

5. The last several decades have witnessed a remarkable growth of expenditures at all levels of government. This has been due primarily to (a) increased demand for collective goods and services, (b) increased expenditures for war and national defense, and (c) inflation and lagging productivity.

6. In the federal budget, income taxes, both individual and corporate, are the chief source of revenue. The main expenditure items are income security payments and national defense. In state and local budgets, the chief sources of revenue are property taxes and sales taxes. The main expenditure items are education (especially schools) and public welfare and health.

7. Two closely related approaches to scientific budgeting are planning-program-budgeting systems (PPBS) and benefit-cost analysis. The former method emphasizes revenue and expenditure planning based on identifiable objectives. The latter focuses on the relative worth of a program, project, or other economic activity.

8. The American tax structure consists of taxes on income, taxes on wealth, and taxes on activities. Taxes on income, both personal and corporate, are graduated or progressive.

9. A chief requirement of a good tax system is that it be fair. Accepted standards of fairness are horizontal equity and vertical equity. Two principles of taxation that seek to apply these standards are the benefit principle and the ability-to-pay principle. However, these principles are often difficult to apply. In practice, therefore, we find some taxes that are proportional, some that are progressive, and some that are regressive.

10. Those upon whom a tax is levied may sometimes be able to shift it forward or backward through changes in prices, inputs, or outputs. Thus, the burden or incidence of the tax falls on someone else. Such taxes are therefore indirect, as contrasted with direct taxes, which cannot be shifted.

For Discussion

1. *Terms and concepts to review:*
social goods
public goods
exclusion principle
merit good
social benefits
social costs
public choice
demand price
supply price
specific tax
specific subsidy
planning-program-budgeting system (PPBS)
benefit-cost analysis
double taxation
property tax
death tax
sales tax
excise tax
horizontal equity
vertical equity
benefit principle
ability-to-pay principle
proportional tax
progressive tax
regressive tax
direct tax
indirect tax

2. Public goods are not subject to the exclusion principle. How then, do you explain the fact that some public goods are, nevertheless, provided by the private sector? Give some examples.

3. Spillover benefits and costs can be redressed in different ways. One approach was illustrated in this chapter (Exhibit 1). Use the same approach to answer the following:
(a) Draw a supply-and-demand diagram that assumes no spillovers. Label the equilibrium quantity Q and write an accompanying explanation of the diagram.
(b) Draw a supply-and-demand diagram and show what happens when spillover benefits are added to the demand curve. Label the new socially optimum output M so that it can be compared with the free-market equilibrium output Q. Show how a specific subsidy U granted to *sellers* can bring about the new socially optimum output. Write an accompanying explanation of the diagram.
(c) Draw a supply-and-demand diagram. Show that, if spillover costs were known and could be added to the supply curve, a new socially optimum output could be established. Label this output N so that it can be compared with the free-market equilibrium output Q. Demonstrate that, by imposing a specific tax T on *sellers*, the socially optimum output at N can be attained. Write an accompanying explanation of the diagram.

4. What are PPBS's major problems in our system of government? How does benefit-cost analysis relate to PPBS?

5. Can you explain the formal definition of benefit-cost analysis given in the Dictionary at the back of the book? In particular, what does the word "discounted" in the definition mean?

6. How can the costs of benefits provided by the government sector be reduced?

7. Some economists and legislators contend that the present federal income tax reaches too far down into low-income brackets. Assume that you disagree with this contention, and offer arguments to defend your position.

8. If you were considering taking on an extra part-time job, would you base the decision on your average tax rate or on your marginal tax rate? Why?

9. The ability-to-pay principle of taxation may also be called the "equal-sacrifice principle." Can you explain why?

10. How can a market-oriented economy such as ours justify the large expenditures made by government on free public education?

11. Is the desire to maximize net social benefit a goal useful only to capitalistic economies, or does it apply to socialistic economies, too?

12. If you were advising a legislator on whether the government should spend an additional $2 billion on space exploration as opposed to public transportation, what approach would you use? What difficulties would you expect to encounter?

13. When the private costs of a decision are equal to its social costs, *all* the costs are borne by the decision maker. Do you agree? Explain.

14. What is wrong with using figures showing expenditures by government as a measure of the importance of government in our society?

TO APPLY FOR
BENEFITS FROM
WASHINGTON ST.
COMPLETE FORM
A & AND GO TO
WINDOW 24
These claim cards are for use when your regular cards are late. Answer all questions & include your name & SSA# on each card.
MILITARY
FEDERAL
COMPLETE
TO

National Income, Employment, and Fiscal Policy

CHAPTER 5

National Income and Wealth: Measuring the Nation's Economic Health

Learning guide
Watch for the answers to these important questions

How do we judge the nation's economic health? Are statistical measures available for evaluating the economy's overall performance?

What sort of difficulties are encountered in estimating gross national product? Does it reflect society's well-being?

What is the relation between the economy's output and its income? Is the flow of expenditures on output equal to the flow of payments for income?

How does the value of the nation's output relate to the money that households actually have available for spending? Of what practical use is this information?

In this chapter you will learn about some important measures of the economy's performance.

People are becoming increasingly concerned with their physical health. They are paying closer attention to their weight, pulse rate, blood pressure, and other measures of physical well-being. The same is true for those who are concerned with the nation's economic health. They are paying closer attention than ever before to statistical measures of the nation's output, unemployment rate, and prices. That is all to the good, for it helps make the public more aware of the nation's economic well-being.

The economy's level of activity—its state of health—is expressed in the form of data and graphs. These are published by the federal government and by various public and private organizations. Since the early 1930s, the U.S. Department of Commerce has been the nation's book-keeper. It has been responsible for developing the majority of measures used to depict the economy's overall performance. Among the chief measures are those known as "national income statistics." In this chapter, the most important types of national income statistics are described and explained.

Gross National Product—The Broadest Measure of a Nation's Output

The most comprehensive and familiar measure of a nation's economic activity, and the one referred to most frequently in newspapers and magazines, is *gross national product* (GNP). It is always stated in money terms, representing the total value of a nation's final output for the year. More precisely:

GNP is the total market value of all final goods and services produced by an economy during a year.

GNP is the most widely used measure of the economy's output.

Calculation of Gross National Product

The items that constitute GNP range from apples and automobiles to zinc and zippers. However, because you cannot add these diverse items, you must first state them in terms of their monetary values. Then, when you add x dollars' worth of automobiles to y dollars' worth of oranges to z dollars' worth of doctors' services, and so on, you arrive at a total dollar figure. If you do this for all final goods and services produced in the economy during any given year, the result is GNP. And if you repeat this process for several years, the different GNPs can be compared. In that way, you can tell whether there has been a long-run growth or decline in the economy.

However, there are several pitfalls to avoid.

Watch Out for Price Changes

If the prices of goods and services change from one year to the next, the GNP may also change—even if there has been no change in physical output. For instance, if apples cost 20 cents each this year, five apples will have a market value of $1.00. But next year, if the price rises to 30 cents each, five apples will have a market value of $1.50.

This poses a problem: How can we tell whether the variations in GNP are due to differences in prices or to differences in *real output*— that is, output unaffected by price changes? The answer is shown in Exhibit 1. Observe that GNP is expressed in two ways. One is in *current dollars*, reflecting actual prices as they existed each year. The other is in *constant dollars*, reflecting the actual prices of a previous year, or the average of actual prices in some previous period.

Price changes can affect the value of GNP in current dollars.

The use of constant dollars is thus a way of compensating for the distorting effects of inflation—the long-run upward trend of prices—by a reversing process of *deflation*. You can get an idea of how this is done by studying Exhibit 2.

Exhibit 1
Gross National Product
(current and constant dollars)

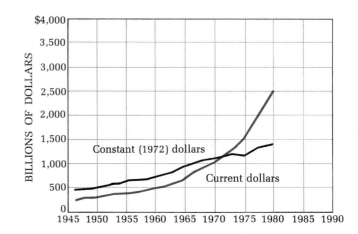

Exhibit 2
Deflating with a Price Index

How a value series in *current* dollars is converted into a value series in *constant* dollars of another year

Index numbers are percentages of some previous base period. They are widely used by government and private sources in reporting business and economic data. Column (4) expresses the prices of column (3) in the form of index numbers. Ordinarily, the base period chosen is assumed to be fairly "normal." In this illustration, because the data are hypothetical, Year 2 has been arbitrarily selected as the base.

When the value series in *current dollars* [column (5)] is divided by these index numbers, the result is a new value series in con-

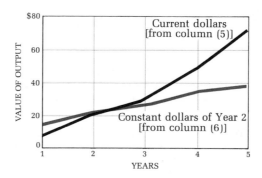

stant dollars of the base year. This is shown in column (6). The two value series are plotted for comparison in the accompanying chart.

(1) Year	(2) Units of output	(3) Price per unit of output	(4) Price index; data in column (3) as percentage of price in Year 2	(5) Value of output in *current dollars* of each year (2) × (3)	(6) Value of output in *constant dollars* of Year 2 (5) ÷ (4)
1	3	$2	2/4 = 0.50 or 50%	$ 6	6/0.50 = $12
2 = base period	5	4	4/4 = 1.00 or 100%	20	20/1.00 = 20
3	6	5	5/4 = 1.25 or 125%	30	30/1.25 = 24
4	8	6	6/4 = 1.50 or 150%	48	48/1.50 = 32
5	9	8	8/4 = 2.00 or 200%	72	72/2.00 = 36

Only final output is considered when calculating GNP, in order to avoid double counting.

Avoid Double Counting of Intermediate Goods

Note that the definition of GNP covers only *final* goods and services purchased. These are distinguished from *intermediate* goods and services, which enter into the production of final commodities. For example, if you purchase a new automobile this year, it is a final good. However, the materials of which the automobile was made, such as steel, engine, tires, and paint, are intermediate goods. Because the values of final goods include the values of all intermediate goods, only final goods are included in calculating the GNP. If you allow intermediate goods to enter the picture, you will commit the cardinal sin of *double counting*— or even triple and quadruple counting.

Exhibit 3 illustrates this with the example of the production of a loaf of bread. As you can see, the "total sales values" at the bottom of column (2) include the sales values at all the intermediate stages. This, of course, is an incorrect statement of the actual value of the product. However, the sales value of the final product, or the total *value added* for all the stages of production, given in column (3), shows the true value of the total output. It also shows the total income—the sum of wages, rent, interest, and profit—derived from the production process.

Exhibit 3
Sales Values and Value Added at Each Stage of the Production of a Loaf of Bread

(1)	(2)	(3)
		Value added (income payments: wages, rent, interest, profit)
	Sales values	
Stages of production	(dollars per loaf)	(dollars per loaf)
Stage 1: Fertilizer, seed, etc.	$ .04	$ .04
Stage 2: Wheat growing	.28	.24
Stage 3: Flour milling	.48	.20
Stage 4: Bread baking, final	.88	.40
Stage 5: Bread retailer, value	1.20	.32
Total sales values	$2.88	
Total value added (= total income)		$1.20

Stage 1 A farmer purchases 4 cents worth of seed and fertilizer, which he applies to his land.

Stage 2 The farmer grows wheat, harvests it, and sells it to a miller for 28 cents. The farmer has thereby added 24 cents worth of value. His factors of production then receive this 24 cents in the form of income: wages, rent, interest, and profit.

Stage 3 The miller, after purchasing the wheat for 28 cents, adds 20 cents worth of value by milling the wheat into flour. The miller's factors of production receive this 20 cents as income: wages, rent, interest, and profit.

Stage 4 The baking company buys the flour from the miller for 48 cents, then adds 40 cents worth of value to it by baking it into bread. This 40 cents becomes factor incomes in the form of wages, rent, interest, and profit.

Stage 5 The retailer buys the bread from the baker for 88 cents and sells it to you, the final user, for $1.20. The retailer has thus added 32 cents in value, which shows up as factor incomes in the form of wages, rent, interest, and profit.

Note that the value of the final product, $1.20, equals the sum of the values added.

We can summarize with an important principle:

GNP may be calculated by totaling either the market values of all final goods and services or the values added at all stages of production. The values added are equal to the sum of all incomes—wages, rent, interest, and profit —generated from production.

Include Productive Activities, Exclude Nonproductive Ones

The purpose of deriving GNP is to develop a measure of the economy's total output, based on the market values of final goods and services produced. However, even if all these market values are estimated, some *productive* activities still do not show up in the market. The value of these activities should, nevertheless, be included in GNP. There are also some *nonproductive* activities that do appear in the market but should be excluded from GNP.

GNP includes certain productive nonmarket activities.

Here are some examples of productive nonmarket activities:

Rent of Owner-Occupied Homes The rent that people pay to landlords enters into GNP. However, more than half the dwellings in the United States are owner-occupied. Therefore, the rental value of this housing

—the rent that people "save" by living in their own homes—may be thought of as the value of shelter produced. This value is assumed to be the same amount that individual homeowners would receive if they became landlords and rented out their homes to others. Hence, this amount is included in GNP.

Farm Consumption of Home-Grown Food The value of food that people buy is included in GNP. But the value of food that farmers grow and consume themselves is also a part of the nation's productive output and is therefore included in GNP.

Some productive nonmarket activities never enter into GNP because their values either are too difficult to estimate or involve complex definitional issues. These include such activities as the labor of a do-it-yourselfer who performs his or her own repairs and maintenance around the house. Similar activities are the productive services of homemakers in their capacities as cooks, housekeepers, tutors, dieticians, chauffeurs, and so on, for which no salaries are received. No wonder a famous British economist once remarked that, if you marry your housekeeper, you reduce the nation's output and income. Can you see why?

Here are some examples of nonproductive market activities:

Transfer Payments As you will recall, *transfer payments* are shifts in funds within or between sectors of the economy with no corresponding contribution to current production. Because these payments are not made for current output, they are excluded from GNP. Some examples of transfer payments are social security benefits, unemployment insurance, and welfare payments.

Securities Transactions When you buy or sell stocks or bonds, you exchange one form of asset for another—either money for securities or securities for money. These financial transfers add nothing to current production and therefore are excluded from GNP. (However, broker commissions on security transactions are included in GNP, because brokers perform a productive service by bringing buyers and sellers together.)

Used-Goods Sales Billions of dollars are paid each year for used automobiles, houses, machines, factory buildings, and so on. But these goods are omitted from the calculation of current GNP because each was counted as part of the GNP in the year in which it was sold new. (As with brokers, however, the value added by dealers in used-merchandise transactions is included in current GNP.)

Is GNP a Measure of Society's Well-Being?

GNP is a comprehensive indicator of the economy's output. However, it is an imperfect measure of society's well-being because it reveals nothing about three important factors:

1. The growth of leisure time—that is, the substantial reduction in the workweek that has taken place during the past several decades.

2. The quality and variety of goods and services that constitute the nation's total output.

3. The growth and distribution of total output among the members of society.

GNP excludes certain "nonproductive" market activities.

Society's "well-being" is not reflected by GNP.

On the basis of the first two factors, the long-run trend of our economy is better than the GNP figures indicate. As for the third, you will often see GNP quoted on a per-capita basis over the years. This reflects the share that each person would have in the nation's total output if it were distributed equally to every man, woman, and child. What does it mean in terms of the economy's growth if the trend of GNP per capita increases over the years? Decreases? Remains the same?

What About Gross National "Disproduct"?

The gross national product, which is our standard index of economic output, measures everything from the cost of hospital care to the wages of belly dancers. But it is an index of dollar values, not of social benefits.

In other words, GNP makes no distinction between the useful and the frivolous, regardless of the price that has been paid. For example, GNP includes cloth coats for people as well as mink coats for dogs, and life-saving antibiotics as well as useless patent medicines. Further, there is no measure of the amount of "disproduct," or *social cost*, that results from producing the GNP. Thus, to society:

GNP includes many of the "disproducts" of production—the "bads" as well as the "goods."

1. The cost of air and water pollution is the disproduct of the nation's factories.

2. The cost of treating lung-cancer victims is the disproduct of cigarette production.

3. The cost of geriatric medicine is the disproduct of good medical care in the earlier years, which results in increased longevity.

4. The cost of commuter transportation is the disproduct of living in the suburbs.

5. The cost of aspirin for headaches resulting from TV commercials is the disproduct of advertising.

Can you suggest some more examples?

If this process were carried through our whole product list, the sum would be *gross national disproduct*. And if the total were then set against the aggregate of production as measured by GNP, it would indicate our degree of progress toward (or departure from) social welfare. In fact, if we could discover a true "net" between disproduct and product, we would have our first great "social" indicator of what the country has accomplished.

The results would probably be disillusioning. We would likely find that, while satisfying human wants from today's productivity, we were simultaneously generating present and future wants to repair the damage created by current production.

Conclusion: GNP and Social Welfare

Because GNP measures the market value of final goods and services, it can only reflect the amount of money that society exchanges for commodities. As a result, many important activities that affect our standard of living are excluded from the calculation of GNP. For example, some activities that are excluded—and corresponding ones that are included—are:

GNP fails to include many important activities.

1. The nonpaid value of homemakers' services—but not the salaries paid to housekeepers.

2. The benefits received from the public sector—but not the costs of providing them.

3. The environmental pollution that results from production—but not the money spent to clean it up.

4. The social value of education—but not the expenditures incurred to acquire it.

5. The rising level of crime—but not the funds allocated to fight it.

Some economists are trying to devise a better measure of the economy's true output by incorporating the negative as well as positive contributions of production. If this can be done, GNP will come closer to measuring *social welfare* rather than just the market value of final commodities.

However, many informed observers disagree with the idea that GNP should serve as an indicator of society's well-being. They point out that "social welfare" is a multidimensional concept with too many deep economic and psychological implications to permit precise definition, let alone measurement. As a result, they conclude:

> The conversion of GNP from a measure of output to a one-dimensional summary measure of society's well-being may be dangerous. It can mislead the nation into believing that GNP is at last measuring social welfare when in fact it is not. This misunderstanding might impede progress toward urgently needed social legislation. ■

Two Ways of Looking at GNP

Because GNP is the market value of the nation's output of final goods and services, it can be expressed conceptually by the simple diagram in Exhibit 4. Equivalently, it can be expressed by the following fundamen-

■ **Something to Think About**

1. Would it be better to produce wool suits and vaccines instead of mink coats and patent medicines, so that the nation moves closer to "worthwhile" national goals?

2. Does the GNP of an advanced, interdependent economy necessarily contain a considerable amount of disproduct, in comparison to a relatively simple type of economic system?

3. Are the costs of the disproducts of our economy borne in the present or in the future?

Exhibit 4
Gross National Product = Gross National Income
(a two-sector model—without a government or foreign sector)

A simplified circular-flow model can be used to illustrate the fundamental principle that gross national product and gross national income are actually two sides of the same coin. The nation's flow of output in the upper pipeline equals the nation's flow of income in the lower pipeline. Profit is the residual or "balancing item" that brings this equality about. Can you explain why? How is the model affected if profits are positive? Zero? Negative (i.e., losses)?

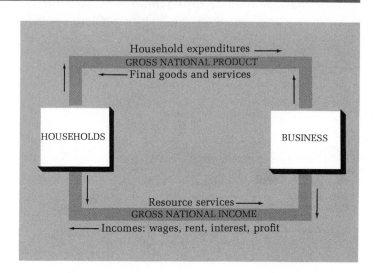

Exhibit 5
Gross National Product = Gross National Income
(a four-sector model)

The data for measuring the nation's total output can be estimated from two points of view:

• The product side—showing the value of goods and services produced and/or purchased by each sector.

• The income side—showing the costs incurred and payments received in producing those goods and services.

The product side is divided into four sectors—household, government, business, and foreign—representing the major markets for the output of the economy. The sum of their expenditures on final products constitutes GNP. The income side summarizes the payments or costs incurred by business firms to produce final products. These costs are wages, rent, interest, profit, indirect business taxes, and capital consumption allowances or depreciation. Their sum equals *GNI.*

Expenditure viewpoint: flow of product		Income viewpoint: flow of costs	
Household sector		**National income (at factor cost)**	
Personal consumption expenditures	$x	Wages	$x
+		Rent	x
Government sector		Interest	x
Government purchases of goods and services	x	Profit	x
+		+	
Business sector		**Nonincome (expense) items**	
Gross private domestic investment	x	Indirect business taxes	x
+		Capital consumption allowance (depreciation)	x
Foreign sector			
Net exports of goods and services	x		
GNP $x =			**GNI $x**

Can you explain why it must be true that, for any given period, GNP = GNI? What is the meaning of the expression "national income at factor cost"? Why is profit listed as a "cost"?

---

tal identity, which says that the *total amount spent equals the total amount received:*

$$\left.\begin{array}{c}\textit{total flow of}\\ \textit{expenditures}\\ \textit{on final output}\end{array}\right\}\text{GNP} = \text{GNI}\left\{\begin{array}{l}\textit{total flow of}\\ \textit{income from}\\ \textit{final output}\end{array}\right.$$

The left side of the identity (or the upper pipeline in Exhibit 4) shows GNP as a sum of expenditures (or a flow of product). The right side (or lower pipeline) shows *gross national income (GNI)* as a sum of incomes resulting from values added at each stage of production. GNI is the sum of wages, rent, interest, and profit earned in the production of GNP, and is always equal to GNP.

This diagram illustrates a *simple* circular-flow system consisting of only two sectors. It provides a "first look" at the relation between an economy's output and its income. A more elaborate model, consisting of four sectors, is necessary for understanding the underlying forces at work. Such a model is presented in Exhibit 5.

The total market value of final output must equal the total income earned from producing it. Thus, GNP = GNI.

GNP from the Expenditure Viewpoint: A Flow-of-Product Approach

On the left side of the table in Exhibit 5, the economy is divided into four major sectors: household, government, business, and foreign. These are the major markets for the output of the economy. In any one year, the total expenditures of these sectors constitute the nation's GNP. The historical record of these expenditures is presented in the first several columns of the front endpapers (the inside front cover) of this book. Note that the sum of the expenditure columns equals GNP. What major trends, over the past 10 years, can be discerned from the table? In particular:

1. What have been the trends of personal consumption expenditures, government purchases of goods and services, and gross private domestic investment?

2. What has been the trend of net exports?

You can answer these questions by referring directly to the front endpapers. However, you will also find it useful to prepare a chart showing the graphs of the four classes of expenditures over the past decade. Meanwhile, what can be said about the meaning of these four categories?

GNP consists of expenditures on final output by the economy's four sectors: household, government, business, and foreign.

Personal Consumption Expenditures

Frequently referred to as "consumption expenditures" or simply "consumption," this category includes household expenditures on consumer goods. Some examples are food, clothing, appliances, automobiles, services, and recreation.

Government Purchases of Goods and Services

The items in this category are purchased by all levels of government. They include guided missiles, school buildings, fire engines, pencils, and the services of clerks, administrators, and all other government employees. However, recall that a significant part of government expenditures—transfer payments—is omitted because it does not represent current output or purchases of goods and services.

Gross Private Domestic Investment

This category includes total investment spending by business firms. The term "investment" has two meanings: (1) In everyday language, a person makes an investment when buying stocks, bonds, or other properties with the intention of receiving an income or making a profit. (2) In economics, *investment* means additions to, or replacement of, real productive assets. Thus, investment represents spending by business firms on new job-creating and income-producing goods, which thereby contribute to GNP. This concept of investment is the one that concerns us in this book.

Investment goods fall into two broad classes:

Investment goods consist of new capital goods and increases in inventory.

1. New capital goods, such as machines, factories, offices, and residences, including apartment houses and owner-occupied homes. (Owner-occupied homes are included because they could just as well be rented out to yield incomes to their owners, as do apartment houses.) Recall that, when a firm buys a used machine or an existing factory, it merely exchanges money assets for physical assets. The purchase itself creates no additional GNP. But, when a firm buys *new* machines or *new* buildings, it creates jobs and incomes for steelworkers, carpenters, bricklayers, and other workers, thereby contributing to the nation's GNP.

2. Increases in *inventories* (including raw materials, supplies, and finished goods on hand). These are as much a part of a business firm's physical capital as are plant and equipment. Therefore, the market values of any additions to inventories are part of the current flow of product that makes up GNP. On the other hand, any declines in inventories are reductions from the flow of product that makes up GNP.

In the process of producing goods during any given year, some existing plant and equipment is used up, or *depreciated*. Therefore, a part of the year's gross private domestic investment goes to replace it. Any amount left over is called *net private domestic investment* because it represents a net addition to the total stock of capital. For example, if

Depreciation is the "using up" of capital goods.

$$
\begin{aligned}
\text{gross private domestic investment} &= \$400 \text{ billion} \\
\text{and replacement for depreciation} &= \underline{\$300 \text{ billion}} \\
\text{then net private domestic investment} &= \$100 \text{ billion}
\end{aligned}
$$

An economy will tend to grow, remain static, or decline according to one of three possibilities:

1. *Gross investment exceeds depreciation.* When this happens, net investment is positive. The economy is thus adding to its capital stock and expanding its productive base.

2. *Gross investment equals depreciation.* In this case, net investment is zero. The economy is merely replacing its capital stock and is neither expanding nor contracting its productive base.

3. *Gross investment is less than depreciation.* If this occurs, net investment is negative. The economy is thus diminishing, or *disinvesting*, its capital stock and is thereby contracting its productive base.

To summarize:

The term *investment* refers to spending by business firms on job-creating and income-producing goods. It consists of replacements or additions to the nation's stock of capital, including its plant, equipment, and inventories —that is, its nonhuman productive assets.

Net Exports

Some domestic expenditures are made to purchase foreign goods. These are our imports. Some foreign expenditures are made to purchase domestic goods. These are our exports. To measure GNP in terms of total expenditures, we must include the value of *exported goods and services*. This is because the value of our exports represents the amount that foreigners spent on purchasing some of our total output. Then we subtract the value of *imported goods and services* from our total expenditures, because we are interested only in measuring the value of domestic output. In performing these adjustments it is simpler to combine the separate figures for exports and imports into a single figure called *net exports,* according to the formula

Net exports equal the difference between what we sell abroad and what we purchase from abroad.

net exports = total exports − total imports

Thus, if a nation's total exports in any given year amount to $350 billion, and its total imports are $330 billion, its net exports of $20 billion are part of that year's GNP. (Look back at Exhibit 5.) Of course, the country's imports may exceed its exports in any particular year. In that case, net exports will be negative and will reduce its GNP. If you have any doubts about this, look again at Exhibit 5 and note what the effect would be on GNP if net exports were negative.

GNP from the Income Viewpoint: A Flow-of-Costs Approach

Now turn your attention to the right side of the table in Exhibit 5. This shows a second method of calculating GNP. It is expressed in terms of the flow of costs or payments that businesses incur as a result of production. The sum of these payments constitutes *gross national income* (*GNI*). However, only the first four items—wages, rent, interest, and profit—represent incomes paid to the owners of the factors of production for their contribution to the nation's output. The remaining two types of payments—indirect business taxes and capital consumption allowance (depreciation)—do not. Let us see why.

Wages

The broad category of *wages* embraces all forms of remuneration for work. Thus it includes not only wages but also executive salaries and bonuses, commissions, payments in kind, incentive payments, tips, and fringe benefits.

Rent

Income earned by persons for the use of their real property, such as a house, store, or farm, is *rent.* This category also includes the estimated rental value of owner-occupied nonfarm dwellings and royalties received by persons from patents, copyrights, and rights to natural resources.

Interest

Interest is expressed in net rather than gross terms. It represents the business sector's total interest payments to other sectors minus their total interest payment to it. All other types of interest payments are omitted from this classification. For example:

1. Interest payments within a sector, such as interest paid by one individual to another, by one business firm to another, or by one government agency to another, have no net effect on the sector. Therefore, they are excluded from this category.

2. Interest payments by government and by consumers, even when they flow between sectors (as in the case of interest paid on government debt or on consumer loans), are considered unproductive. Therefore, they are also excluded here and are counted instead as transfer payments.

Profit

Profit, in our model, combines proprietors' income and corporate profits before taxes. (These items are treated separately, however, by Commerce Department statisticians.) The former represents the earnings of unincorporated businesses—proprietorships, partnerships, and producers' cooperatives. The latter measures the profits of corporations before payments of corporate income taxes or disbursements of dividends to stockholders. To generalize:

> *National income (at factor cost)* is part of gross national income. It represents the sum of wages, rent, interest, and profit. These are the payments that business firms must make to the owners of the factors of production in return for the services provided by those factors.

The two remaining components of gross national income are indirect business taxes and capital consumption allowances (depreciation). Because these two items are not payments to the owners of productive resources, their inclusion in GNI requires some explanation.

After subtracting national income, the rest of GNI consists of certain expenses incurred from production.

Indirect Business Taxes

Indirect business taxes consist primarily of sales, excise, and real property taxes incurred by businesses. (Direct taxes on factor payments, such as employer contributions for social security or corporate income taxes, are not counted here. This is because they were already included in wages, profits, and other specific items constituting national income at factor cost.) For accounting purposes, an indirect business tax is actually "paid"—that is, turned over to the government—by a business firm. Therefore, the tax is regarded as a business expense, although the real burden of the tax may be borne by the firm's customers in the form of a higher price. Because the tax is viewed as a business expense, it is included in GNI as a cost item.

To put it somewhat differently, indirect business taxes tend to be passed on or shifted "forward" by business firms to buyers. Sales taxes are typical. If you live in a state or city that has a 5 percent general sales tax and you buy a product whose price is $1, your total *expenditure* is actually $1.05. Of this, $1 goes to pay incomes—the wages, rent, interest, and profit—earned for making the product. The remaining 5 cents goes to the local government, which has not contributed directly to production. It follows, therefore, that indirect business taxes cause the expenditure side of GNP to be greater than the income side. In view of this, indirect business taxes must be added to total incomes (or subtracted from GNP) if the two sides are to be brought closer together.

Capital Consumption Allowance (Depreciation)

In the process of producing GNP, some decline in the value of existing physical capital occurs due to wear and tear, obsolescence, and accidental loss. To reflect this decline, firms deduct as part of their costs a *capital consumption allowance*—or simply "depreciation." The allowance consists primarily of depreciation on business plant and equipment and on owner-occupied dwellings. For purposes of national-income accounting, depreciation may be thought of as the portion of the current year's GNP that goes to replace the physical capital "consumed" or used up in the process of production.

Depreciation is thus the difference between gross and net private domestic investment, as already explained. If there were no such thing as depreciation, and if the government returned all indirect business taxes to households, the nation's income from production would be identical to its output. However, because depreciation does exist, it causes the income side of GNP to be less than the expenditure side. Therefore, depreciation must be added to incomes (or subtracted from GNP) to bring the two sides closer together. To conclude:

> Business firms view indirect business taxes and depreciation as part of their costs, and hence charge higher prices for their goods in order to cover these costs. Therefore, these nonincome expense items must be added to the other income payments or expense items (wages, rent, interest, and profit) in order for the total expenditures on GNP to equal the total payments or expenses incurred in producing it.

Indirect business taxes and depreciation are reflected in higher prices charged by business firms.

Exhibit 6

**The Nation's Income Statement:
Gross National Product and Related
Accounts**
(billions of dollars)

Can you fill in the figures for the most recent
year? See the endpapers in the front of the
book.

	19__
Gross national product (GNP)	$ _____
Minus:	
Capital consumption allowance (depreciation)	_____
Equals: **Net national product (*NNP*)**	_____
Minus:	
Indirect business taxes	_____
Equals: **National income (*NI*)**	_____
Minus: Income earned but not received	
Corporate income taxes	_____
Undistributed corporate profits	_____
Social insurance contributions	_____
Plus: Income received but not earned	
Transfer payments	_____
Equals: **Personal income (*PI*)**	_____
Minus:	
Personal taxes	_____
Equals: **Disposable personal income (*DPI*)**	
Out of which come:	
Personal consumption expenditures	_____
Personal savings	_____

Four Other Concepts, All Related

What relation exists between the value of the nation's output and the
money that households actually have available for spending? We may
proceed by examining the items listed in the nation's income statement
shown in Exhibit 6.

Gross National Product to Net National Product

GNP is the total market value of the nation's annual output of final goods
and services. But, as you know, this figure does not equal the actual dollar incomes available to households. To arrive at a closer measure of the
dollars received by society, we must subtract the proportion that was
spent to replace used up capital goods. This is the *capital consumption
allowance* (or depreciation) figure. The number that results is net national product, or simply *NNP*.

Net National Product to National Income

Net national product (NNP) measures the total sales value of goods and
services available for society's consumption and for adding to its stock of
capital equipment. As such, *NNP* may be thought of as "national income at market prices."

But NNP still does not represent the dollars people actually had
available to spend. This is because NNP is overstated by the amount of
indirect business taxes—such as sales taxes. For purposes of national
income accounting, the taxes are assumed to be shifted forward by sellers to consumers in the form of higher prices. Therefore, the sum of all
indirect business taxes must be deducted from NNP in order to arrive at a
closer estimate of the dollars available to people for actual spending.
This deduction results in national income at factor cost.

National Income to Personal Income

National income (at factor cost), NI, is the total of all incomes earned by
the factors of production. Thus, NI is the sum of wages, rent, interest,
and profit earned by the suppliers of labor, land, capital, and entrepreneurship. Does NI represent the dollars that people actually had available for spending? Once again, the answer is *no*. Some people earned
income they did not receive; others received income they did not earn.

For example, the stockholders in a corporation are its owners and
hence earn the corporation's profits. However, stockholders do not receive all the profits, for two reasons. Some profits are paid to the government in the form of corporation income taxes. Some profits are also
plowed back into the business for future expansion instead of being distributed to stockholders as dividends. Likewise, social security contributions are taken out of workers' current earnings, and thus they are also
part of income earned but not received.

As for income received but not earned, the major items are transfer
payments. These are merely shifts of funds within the economy—primarily from the government sector to households—for reasons other
than current production.

To measure the dollars people actually had available for spending,
we therefore adjust the NI in two ways.

1. *Subtract* income earned but not received.

2. *Add* income received but not earned.

These two steps result in a figure called personal income.

Personal Income to Disposable Personal Income

Personal income (*PI*) is the total received by persons from all sources. It is the dollars that you and I receive for performing our jobs and thereby contributing to GNP. Does *PI* measure the dollars actually available to people for spending? The answer is still *no*, because out of personal income people must first pay their personal taxes. This amount must therefore be deducted from *PI*, leaving a figure called *disposable personal income* (*DPI*). It is this amount that people actually have available for spending. As you can see from the front endpapers of this book, the great bulk of *DPI* goes for personal consumption, while the rest is saved.

Thus, there are five measures of income and output for the economy:

1. Gross national product.

2. Net national product.

3. National income.

4. Personal income.

5. Disposable personal income—or, simply, disposable income.

All five measures are closely interrelated, can be derived from one another, and tend approximately to parallel one another over the years. In many macroeconomic discussions (except those involving specific accounting practices as described in this chapter), *economists use the term "national income" or simply "income" to represent all five terms.* A complete income-flow model is shown in Exhibit 7.

GNP is one of five measures of the economy's income. But DPI is the income you and I actually receive.

Exhibit 7
The Flow of National Income and Related Concepts

Can you fill in the data for the most recent year? See the front endpapers.

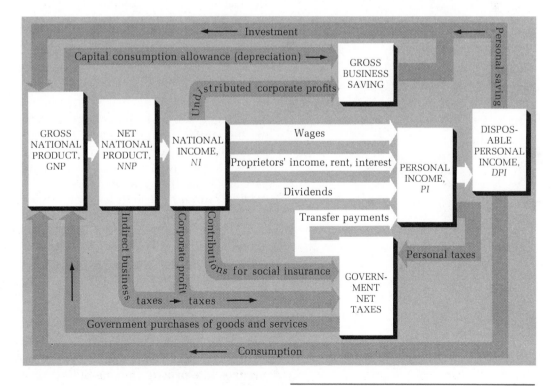

Exhibit 8
The Nation's Balance Sheet: Household, Business, Government, and Foreign Sectors
(billions of dollars)

Assets are what we own; *liabilities* are what we owe; *net worth* is the difference between the two. Can you explain why liabilities to domestic residents are the same as intangible assets?

	19__
Assets	
Tangible	
Buildings and other structures	$x
Land	x
Durable goods, equipment, and inventories	x
Intangible	
Currency and checking accounts	x
Other bank deposits and shares	x
Insurance and pension reserves	x
Credit, securities, and other claims	x
Total assets	$x
Liabilities	
To domestic residents (= intangible assets)	x
To foreigners	x
Total liabilities	$x
Net worth (or net national wealth)	
Total assets less total liabilities	$x

Wealth of a Nation: How Much Is America "Worth"?

If you wanted to buy the United States—its land, buildings, machines, people's personal belongings, government property, everything—what would you have to pay? In 1776 the answer was $3.7 billion; in 1976 it was $6 trillion. In the year 2000, according to trends in recent decades, the figure is likely to be about $13 trillion.

This sum includes only physical wealth—that is, wealth consisting of tangible assets. Such items as cash, corporate stocks and bonds, and savings and checking accounts are excluded because they represent intangible assets—claims against physical wealth.

What kinds of items enter into the calculation of a nation's wealth? You can get an idea by examining Exhibit 8. This illustrates a balance sheet for the country as a whole. When used in conjunction with the nation's income statement shown in Exhibit 6, two important types of information are revealed:

> The nation's balance sheet shows the country's financial position on a *given date*. The nation's income statement shows the country's output and income for a *given period*. Therefore, the balance sheet is like a "snapshot" of the nation's financial status, whereas the income statement is like a "motion picture."

As you may know, business firms regularly prepare balance sheets and income statements. These terms are defined *for businesses* in the Dictionary at the back of the book. How do these definitions compare with the concepts of *national* balance sheets and income statements?

In the chapters that follow, you will see how GNP, *NNP*, and related statistical measures are used for studying the economy's performance. Because of their importance, you will find it useful to learn how these measures came into existence. This is explained in "Leaders in Economics," page 112.

Case
Tax-Free GNP and the Underground Economy: Take the Money and Skip the Taxes

Fred Henderson owns his own Jeep and snowplow, earns enough during the winter months to cover an entire year's college expenses, and files no income tax return. Janet Brennan works full time as a waitress, files an annual income tax return, but generally declares only about 50 percent of her tips as income. Dr. S. J. Jackson, a physician, exchanges medical care for car maintenance services with a patient who is an automobile mechanic; as a result, no money passes between them.

Although the names in these scenarios are fictitious, the cases are not. They illustrate some of the activities that take place in the underground economy. This is a segment of the private sector in which transactions go unreported to government agencies, especially to the Internal Revenue Service.

The results are by no means trivial. Indeed, some experts estimate that the amount of unreported income each year equals as much as 30 percent of actual GNP, and that the percentage is probably growing. Further, most of this income comes from legal activities, not from illegal ones like prostitution, gambling, or drugs.

110   PART 2   NATIONAL INCOME, EMPLOYMENT, AND FISCAL POLICY

Some Implications

If the estimate is correct, or even if the true figure is only half as much, the income "lost" amounts to hundreds of billions of dollars annually. The implications for economic policy are staggering. They indicate that, if the subterranean economy is large and growing, the nation's economic health is quite different from what the official figures disclose. For example:

• Actual GNP figures are significantly higher than the official data suggest they are. Therefore, the nation's rate of economic growth—the output of its goods and services—is rising faster than is generally believed.

• The unemployment rate is much lower than is generally believed. According to some estimates, many more people, perhaps a third of those listed as unemployed, are actually working full time and earning incomes that are either unreported or understated.

• Taxes on unreported income are lost to the government. In any given year, this loss in tax revenues could be enough to erase a large portion of the deficit in the federal budget.

Because of these and other considerations, government officials are seeking ways to reduce the scope of the underground economy.

Experiences Overseas

Unfortunately, the task is not easy, as the experiences of other advanced countries bear out. Subterranean economies have thrived much longer and are considerably more extensive in western Europe and Japan than in the United States.

In Italy, where dodging the tax collector is a national sport, more than 15 percent of the labor force earns unreported income from second jobs. The Italian government, which places highest priority on full employment, prefers to ignore the matter. This is because the government prefers not to risk the loss in jobs that might occur if employers had to pay legal wages and benefits.

In France, high income and sales taxes have driven increasing numbers of workers into second jobs. Most are service occupations in which cheating on taxes is relatively easy. French officials estimate that as many as half the scientists and engineers in Paris engage in such part-time activities as television repair and automobile maintenance. "And if you go out for dinner or have your house painted," says a French tax authority, "the odds are better than even that the person who services you will be a police officer, firefighter, or schoolteacher."

Similar conditions exist in Belgium, Britain, West Germany, Denmark, Norway, Sweden, and Japan. A major reason is the steepness of tax rates in these countries. When taxes rise sharply with increases in income, the pressure on people to seek ways of escaping taxes—through illegal means, if necessary—becomes pronounced. As a result, without major tax reforms, a growing proportion of the world's economies will continue to go underground.

Questions

1. One of the chief problems of the underground economy involves the vital issue of equity. Can you explain why?

2. Can you suggest measures to eliminate the underground economy?

Businesses such as these are part of the growing underground economy.

World Wide Photos

Leaders in Economics

Simon Smith Kuznets

1901–
Father of National-Income Accounting

Few scholars in any field are capable of deciding, by their middle twenties, the precise type of work they want to do for the remainder of their professional careers. One person who made such a decision, and has earned lasting fame for his accomplishments, is Simon Kuznets.

Born in Russia, Kuznets migrated to the United States as a young man. After receiving his doctorate from Columbia University, he joined the staff of one of the nation's major research organizations, the National Bureau of Economic Research. While there, he also did occasional work for the Department of Commerce. In addition, he taught for many years at the University of Pennsylvania, Johns Hopkins, and Harvard.

Beginnings

More than anyone else, Kuznets pioneered the development of national-income data. When the nation plunged into the Great Depression of the early 1930s, the amount of factual information available was, said Kuznets, "a scandal. No one knew what was happening.

The data available then were neither fish nor flesh nor even red herring."

It remained for Kuznets to point out the kind of information that was needed. When the Senate ordered official income estimates, the Department of Commerce turned to the National Bureau of Economic Research for assistance. Kuznets went to Washington as a consultant, lecturing government economists and statisticians on his concepts. On January 4, 1934, a Senate document was published that contained the country's first national-income figures, those for the period 1929 to 1932. This was the beginning of one of the most significant advances in the history of economics. The measurement of GNP and related concepts was not fully developed by the Department of Commerce until the 1940s. Although the technical structure of GNP is quite different from that of Kuznets's original conception, he is still recognized as the person most responsible for its statistical formulation.

Shortcomings and Biases

Kuznets was well aware that national income served as an imperfect measure of society's well-being. He gave two reasons.

First, nonmarket activities, such as the services of homemakers, amateur gardeners, and others engaged in productive pursuits, do not enter the national-income accounts. As a result of these omissions, our national-income data are less than they otherwise would be.

Second, certain "occupational expenses" are included in national-income accounts, even though they may not all yield positive returns to us from the economic system. Such expenses include the

costs of commuting to work, buying banking services because we live in a money economy, and other necessary "costs" of carrying out our daily activities. Because these expenses are included, the accounts tend to be higher than they otherwise would be.

These and other shortcomings, Kuznets pointed out, introduce biases in national-income accounts. These biases make it difficult to compare one economy with another.

For example, in 1953 Kuznets wrote: "That such [errors] are hardly in the nature of minutiae may be illustrated by a tentative calculation made in attempting a comparison of per-capita income in the United States and China and purifying the former for what may be called inflated costs of urban civilization: the inflation in question amounted to from 20 to 30 percent of all consumers' outlay . . . as estimated by the Department of Commerce."

Empirical Work and Honors

Kuznets's whole career has been devoted to analyzing mountains of historical data. He has estimated the changing effects of capital, labor, income distribution, productivity, and other variables on the economic growth of this and other countries. To a degree rarely equaled by other economists, he has the ability to generate and analyze masses of data from which he draws many provocative hypotheses about long-term economic development.

Kuznets's lifework has been crowned with honors. In 1971, when he was 70, the Swedish Royal Academy of Science awarded him the Alfred Nobel Memorial Prize in Economic Science.

What You Have Learned in This Chapter

1. GNP, the basic and most comprehensive measure of a nation's output, represents the total market value of all final goods and services produced during a year.

Three pitfalls to avoid in calculating GNP are (a) failing to take the effects of price changes into account, (b) double (actually multiple) counting, and (c) the inclusion of nonproductive transactions.

2. From the expenditure standpoint, GNP is the sum of personal consumption expenditures, government purchases of goods and services, investment, and net exports. GNP can be viewed from the income standpoint as gross national income (*GNI*) or the sum of wages, rent, interest, and profit, plus two nonincome business expense items: indirect business taxes and depreciation.

3. The items that make up the nation's income accounts are GNP, *NNP*, *NI*, *PI*, and *DPI*. All five measures are closely related and can be derived from one another. They are among the most important measures of our economy's performance. In economic discussions (except those involving accounting practices) we often refer to all five measures as "national income" or simply "income."

4. The financial status of a nation is reflected by its income statement, showing gross national product and related accounts. Financial status is also reflected by a nation's balance sheet, showing assets, liabilities, and net worth. Taken together, these financial statements provide an overall picture of the economy's income and wealth.

For Discussion

1. *Terms and concepts to review:*
gross national product
real output
current dollars
constant dollars
deflation
index numbers
value added
transfer payments
gross national income
investment
inventory
depreciation
disinvestment
national income (at factor cost)
capital consumption allowance
net national product
personal income
disposable personal income

2. Suppose that a nation's GNP increased from $100 billion to $200 billion. What has happened to its *real* GNP during that period if

(a) Prices remained the same?
(b) Prices doubled?
(c) Prices tripled from their constant level in (a)?
(d) Prices fell by 50 percent of their constant level in (a)?

3. What happens when you "deflate" a *rising* current-dollar series, as in Exhibit 1? Obviously, the constant-dollar series lies below the current-dollar series for all years after the base year, and above it for all years prior to the base year. What would happen if you deflated a current-dollar series that was *declining* rather than one that was rising? Explain your answer.

4. Why is "value added" a logically correct method of measuring the nation's output?

5. The level of inventories serves as a "balancing" item between sales to final users and current production. True or false? Can sales to final users exceed current production? Can sales be less than current production? Explain your answers in terms of changes in inventories and their effects on GNP.

6. How is the growth or decline of an economy related to its net investment? Do you think an economy's percentage growth or decline is related to its percentage change in net investment? Explain.

7. What is the effect on national income if you (a) marry your housekeeper; (b) take an unpaid vacation? Is there any effect on social welfare (that is, well-being) from either act?

8. Which of the following is included, and which is not included, in calculating GNP?

(a) One hundred shares of General Motors stock purchased this week on the New York Stock Exchange.
(b) Wages paid to teachers.
(c) A student's income from a part-time job.
(d) A student's income from a full-time summer job.
(e) The value of a bookcase built by a do-it-yourselfer.
(f) The purchase of a used car.
(g) A monthly rent of $800 that a homeowner "saves" by living in his or her own home instead of renting it out to a tenant.

9. Each year the total amount of dollar payments by checks and cash far exceeds—by many billions of dollars—the GNP. If GNP is the market value of the economy's final output, how can this huge difference exist?

10. Gross business saving represents that part of business income available for various forms of investment. Examine the following hypothetical data (in billions of dollars):

Corporate profits	$90
Corporate income taxes	43
Dividends to stockholders	25
Retained profits	22
Depreciation	75

(a) How much is gross business saving? Show your method of calculation.
(b) Of what significance is depreciation in your calculation?
(c) Can gross business saving be larger than corporate profits *before* taxes and dividends? Can it be smaller? Explain.

11. Examine the following hypothetical data (all in billions of dollars) for a particular year:

(1) Gross private domestic investment	$180
(2) Contributions for social insurance	25
(3) Interest paid by consumers	9
(4) Personal consumption expenditures	600
(5) Transfer payments	60
(6) Undistributed corporate profits	45
(7) Indirect business taxes	75
(8) Net exports of goods and services	5
(9) Capital consumption allowance	60
(10) Government purchases of goods and services	175
(11) Corporate income taxes	70
(12) Personal tax and nontax payments	90

On the basis of these data, calculate (a) gross national product; (b) net national product; (c) national income; (d) personal income; (e) disposable income. (**Suggestion** You will find the front endpapers helpful.)

12. Examine the following hypothetical data (all in billions of dollars) for a particular year:

(1) Indirect business taxes	$ 90
(2) Corporate profits before taxes	150
(3) Capital consumption allowance	90
(4) Compensation of employees	675
(5) Undistributed corporate profits	60
(6) Proprietors' income	120
(7) Contributions for social insurance	40
(8) Corporate income taxes	70
(9) Net interest	15
(10) Transfer payments	80
(11) Personal tax and nontax payments	$105
(12) Rental incomes	45
(13) Personal consumption expenditures	750

On the basis of these data, calculate the five types of national income discussed in this chapter. (**Hint** Do not try to calculate GNP first.)

13. A country's gross national product rose from $285 billion in 1970 to $504 billion in 1980. During the same period, the country's Consumer Price Index (1982 = 100) rose from 72.1 to 88.7.

(a) What was the percentage increase of GNP over the decade?
(b) By how much did average prices, measured by the Consumer Price Index, rise over the decade?
(c) How would you calculate GNP for 1970 and for 1980, expressed in 1982 dollars?
(d) Is the percentage change of GNP in constant dollars greater or less than the percentage change in current dollars? Show your calculations.

14. Convert personal consumption expenditures into 1977 dollars for the years shown in the following table. What is the economic significance of your calculations? Have you "deflated" or "inflated"? Explain.

Year	Personal consumption expenditures (regional data, billions of dollars)	Consumer Price Index (1977 = 100)
1960	$191.0	72.1
1965	254.4	80.2
1970	325.2	88.7
1975	432.8	94.5

15. Which measure of national income best tells you:
(a) The amount by which the economy's production exceeds the capital equipment used up in producing it?
(b) The amount of income available to consumers for spending?
(c) The market value of commodities produced for final use?
(d) The amount of income available to people for government taxation?
(e) The incomes earned by resource owners engaged in production?
Which measure of national income is best?

Economic Instability: Business Cycles, Unemployment, and Inflation

Learning guide
Watch for the answers to these important questions

What is the nature of the fluctuations in general economic activity that are commonly referred to as "business cycles"? Why do these fluctuations occur? Can they be forecast? What methods of forecasting do economists use?

Why is unemployment a problem of continuous concern in our economy? How is unemployment measured? What are some of the causes of unemployment?

What is inflation? How does it affect each of us? Are there different causes of inflation? Why is it important for our economy to achieve greater price stability?

Fluctuations in economic activity—or "business cycles," as they are often called—have been an unending plague for mixed economies. Inflation and unemployment are the costs of that plague—costs we have paid throughout much of our history.

This chapter discusses the nature of economic fluctuations, the types of unemployment, and the consequences of rising prices.

This chapter examines the nature and interrelations of business cycles, unemployment, and inflation. Once we understand the characteristics of these problems, we can attempt to do something about the problems themselves.

Essentially, as you will learn, our government tries to keep all three problems at bay simultaneously. However, our nation's policy makers are not consistently successful, because both the problems and their solutions continue to be subjects of controversy.

Business Cycles—A Long History of Fluctuations

> Business history repeats itself, but always with a difference.
>
> Wesley C. Mitchell, *Business Cycles* (1913)

What are business cycles? You can get a preliminary idea by looking at the historical picture in Exhibit 1. You can see that, although we no longer have the frequent booms and busts that characterized the economy prior to World War II, we still have fluctuations in business activity. The following modern definition of business cycles is appropriate:

Business cycles consist of fluctuations in income, output, employment, and prices.

> *Business cycles* are fluctuations in general economic activity. The fluctuations are recurrent but nonperiodic (that is, irregular). They occur in such aggregate variables as income, employment, and prices, most of which move at about the same time in the same direction but at different rates.

**Exhibit 1
How Do Business Cycles Look?**

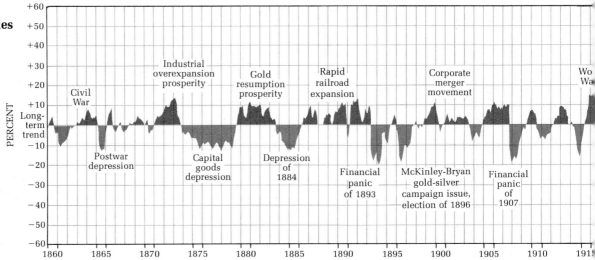

An historical picture of American business cycles. Fluctuations are recurrent but not periodic (that is, the peaks and troughs do not occur at regular intervals).

When GNP figures, sales figures, prices, employment rates, or any other figures are arranged chronologically, they are referred to as a *time series*. The measurement of "time" may be in years, months, weeks, days, or other units, and is usually scaled on the horizontal axis when depicted graphically.

According to the definition of business cycles, fluctuations may occur in production, prices, income, employment, or in any other time series of economic data. In order to measure business cycles for the economy as a whole, therefore, it is necessary to combine many different time series into a single index of business activity. Then, if the value of the index for each year is expressed as a percentage of the long-term average or trend, the resulting data when graphed might look like the fluctuations in the chart.

Note how the actual cycle differs from the idealized one. Actual business cycles are recurrent but not periodic—their scope and intensity differ. Idealized cycles are both recurrent *and* periodic—their peaks and valleys occur at regular intervals.

Can you see why the various cyclical phases are called *prosperity, recession, depression,* and *recovery*? If not, look up the meanings of these terms in the Dictionary at the back of the book.

Thus, business cycles are not simply fluctuations in the absolute level of important economic variables, but are a speeding up and a slowing down in their rates of growth. Note that the definition is important for what it excludes:

1. Business cycles are not *seasonal fluctuations,* such as the upswing in retail sales that occurs each year during the Christmas and Easter periods.

2. Business cycles are not *secular trends,* such as the long-run growth or decline that characterizes practically all economic data over a long period of years.

A more complete explanation of the nature of business cycles is given in Exhibit 1.

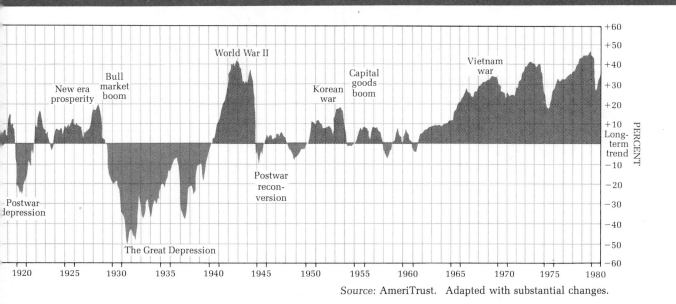

World War II

Bull
market
boom

New era
prosperity

Korean
war

Capital
goods
boom

Vietnam
war

Postwar
depression

Postwar
recon-
version

The Great Depression

+60
+50
+40
+30
+20
+10
Long-
term
trend
−10
−20
−30
−40
−50
−60

PERCENT

1920   1925   1930   1935   1940   1945   1950   1955   1960   1965   1970   1975   1980

Source: AmeriTrust. Adapted with substantial changes.

The four phases of the cycle are by no means equal in scope or intensity, and they do not always come in the order shown. For example, an economy may fluctuate between contractions and expansions for many years without experiencing either high prosperity or deep depression. Further, the transition from one phase of a cycle into the next is occasionally imperceptible; it may be almost impossible to distinguish between the end of one phase and the beginning of another. For these reasons, the names of the four phases should be viewed only as convenient descriptions and the diagram only as a highly simplified picture.

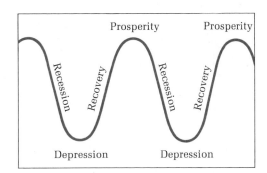

Prosperity   Prosperity

Recession
Recovery
Recession
Recovery

Depression   Depression

An Idealized Business Cycle. Fluctuations are recurrent and periodic. The peaks and troughs occur at regular intervals, like a sine or cosine curve in trigonometry, or an alternating electric current.

Some Facts About Business Cycles

Economists who have analyzed business cycles have learned a great deal about them, from studies going back to the nineteenth century. For instance:

> Over the course of a business cycle, the durable-goods (or "hard-goods") industries tend to experience relatively wide fluctuations in output and employment and relatively small fluctuations in prices. The nondurable-goods (or "soft-goods") industries tend to experience relatively wide fluctuations in prices and relatively small fluctuations in output and employment.

These observations can be attributed primarily to two factors: durability and competition.

Exhibit 2

Income and Consumer Spending During a Business Cycle

Consumer spending fluctuates with income during a typical business cycle. But expenditures for durable goods fluctuate much more widely relative to income than expenditures for nondurable goods. (**Note** A business cycle is measured from trough to trough or from peak to peak. Shaded bars denote recessions. This particular cycle covers an 11-year period.)

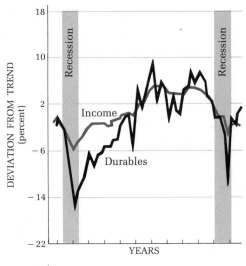

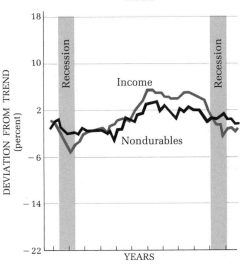

Durability

Durable goods—precisely because they are durable—do not have to be replaced at a particular time. They can be repaired and made to last longer, if necessary. What effect does this have on business executives, who buy such capital goods as iron and steel, cement, and machine tools? What effect does it have on consumers, who purchase such durable goods as automobiles, furniture, and appliances?

In a recession or depression, total demand for the economy's output is likely to be low. Business managers thus find themselves with excess production capacity. Therefore, they see little prospect of profiting from investment in capital goods. Likewise, consumers find that they can get along with their existing cars and other durable goods rather than purchasing new ones. As a result, the "hard-goods" industries experience sharp decreases in demand.

During recovery and prosperity, the opposite is true. Aggregate demand is high, and business executives and consumers are ready to replace, as well as add to, their existing stocks of capital and durable goods. The hard-goods industries, therefore, experience sharp increases in demand.

Purchase of capital goods and consumer durables can be postponed to a later date. This is less true, however, of the purchase of nondurables and semidurables—the "soft goods"—such as fresh food, some clothing, and certain services. Their purchase is not as readily postponable. Therefore, the change in demand for them over the course of a business cycle tends to be much less pronounced.

Some comparisons between income and consumer spending are shown in Exhibit 2. Note the relatively wider fluctuations for durable goods than for nondurable goods.

Competition

The degree of competition in an industry, as determined by the number of sellers, usually has a bearing on the way in which the industry adjusts its prices and outputs in response to changes in demand. In view of this, how does a fall in aggregate demand affect hard-goods producers as compared to soft-goods producers?

Many durable-goods industries tend to be characterized by relatively small numbers of dominant sellers. The aluminum, locomotive, automobile, aircraft-engine, and telephone-equipment industries, among others, are typical. The "big three" or "big four" producers in these industries control a large proportion of the total output of their commodity. Consequently, they can influence the prices they charge and can formulate relatively stable pricing policies despite fluctuations in sales. As a result, when they are confronted with a decline in aggregate demand, they try to reduce costs and maintain profit margins by cutting back production and employment. Eventually, if market sluggishness continues, some hard-pressed firms may seek to reduce their inventories by cutting prices. But even then, price decreases are likely to be small relative to the declines in output and employment.

The opposite tends to occur in industries producing nondurable and semidurable goods—such as ladies' dresses, men's suits, millinery, and toilet preparations. In these industries, unlike most durable-goods industries, a considerable number of sellers are usually competing in the same market. Each firm, therefore, is likely to have too small a share of the market to ignore the importance of price reduction as a means of countering a decrease in demand. Consequently, when aggregate demand falls, firms in such industries tend to reduce their prices while holding output and employment relatively steady. To summarize:

> Two factors—durability and competition—help account for different degrees of price and output changes when aggregate demand declines. During a recession, for example, we first hear about production cutbacks and layoffs in such industries as automobiles and steel—not in food processing or textiles. The latter industries may also reduce their output and employment, but for them the percentage decreases are usually much smaller.

Can We Forecast Business Cycles?

> If we could first know where we are and whither we are tending, we could better judge what to do and how to do it.
>
> Abraham Lincoln

These words are more than a century old, but they explain as well as any the necessity of forecasting. As long as we live in a world in which no one can predict the future with certainty, virtually all business and economic decisions rest upon forecasts.

A number of different methods exist for forecasting business cycles.

For example, if you were a business executive, would you invest without knowing something about future economic conditions in your industry or in the economy? As a consumer, would you delay buying a house or a car if you thought the price was going to drop in the near future? If you were a speculator in commodities or in common stocks, would you buy and sell if you did not expect to make a profit? If you were a member of Congress, would you vote for measures to help curb inflation if you thought that prices were going to leap upward next year?

Each of these questions involves a prediction of the future. Forecasting is a means of reducing the uncertainty that surrounds the making of business and economic decisions.

How are the forecasts made? Several methods are employed by economic forecasters working in industry, government, and universities.

Statistical Projections—Extrapolations

Suppose the GNP has increased at an average rate of 5 percent a year for a number of years. If on that basis you predict a 5 percent increase in GNP for next year, you are forecasting by statistical projection.

This simple example illustrates the idea that a statistical projection is basically an extrapolation or extension into the future of past trends, averages, or other quantitative relationships. Some statistical projection methods are quite sophisticated, employing elaborate mathematical procedures requiring computer solutions. Regardless of their sophistication, however, all extrapolation procedures are mechanical forecasting methods because they entail straightforward projections of one form or another. That is, they pay little or no attention to the underlying economic relationships that determine the data because very little is known about them.

Opinion Polling—Intentions Surveys

A second approach to forecasting is to survey a representative group of people from the business and household sectors. For example, executives and consumers might be asked: "What major economic decisions

There is no single method of forecasting that is always "right."

do you plan to make and when do you plan to make them?" The information obtained can then be blown up to a national scale in order to make predictions about the economy as a whole.

Several privately and publicly sponsored organizations conduct periodic surveys along these lines. Some of the surveys seek to determine the intentions of business managers to spend on plant, equipment, and inventories. Other surveys focus on households, their finances, and on the intentions of consumers to purchase automobiles, houses, and major appliances.

In general, surveys have frequently been successful in foretelling by a few months some of the major upward or downward turning points of business cycles. However, the surveys have not been as useful for predicting economic fluctuations over periods longer than several months. This is because people's spending decisions are affected by a wide array of economic and emotional complexities that are difficult to identify.

Forecasts based on surveys have been more successful at short-run than long-run predictions.

Econometric Models

Economics, like every science, seeks to discover relations between variables. You are already familiar with some of them. For example, the quantities demanded and supplied of a commodity are each dependent upon its price. You will learn about many other economic relationships in subsequent chapters.

Relationships may be described in terms of mathematical equations. If the equations are then verified by statistical methods, the resulting system of relationships is called an *econometric model.*

Econometric models are frequently used for forecasting. They can be constructed for firms, industries, regions, or the entire economy. In addition to being predictive devices, econometric models may also serve as guides for policy making. In order to be useful in today's complex economy, modern econometric models must contain hundreds of equations reflecting numerous relationships. Because of this, the application of such econometric models requires the use of a large computer as well as staffs of economists and statisticians to keep the models up to date. However, despite their sophistication, econometric models have not always done a better job of predicting economic fluctuations than have alternative forecasting methods.

Econometric forecasting models are gaining increasing use both in the public and private sectors.

Economic Indicators

In 1878, British economist W. S. Jevons astounded the scientific world by announcing that he had discovered a close relationship between business cycles and sunspots. These are the dark patches that appear from time to time on the surface of the sun. The explanation that Jevons gave became known as the *sunspot theory.* It held that sunspot cycles occur regularly, thereby affecting the weather. This causes cycles in agricultural production, which in turn influence total economic activity.

Jevons' theory received worldwide popularity when it was first introduced. But it soon fell into disrepute when the near-perfect 20-year correlation between sunspots and agricultural cycles that Jevons discovered did not last. The high correlation turned out to be the result of accidental rather than causal factors.

Economic science has advanced considerably since Jevons' time. Today, forecasters look at hundreds of economic time series. Among them are retail sales, new construction activity, labor productivity, and

Econometric indicators are measures of economic activity.

stock-market prices. The purpose is to judge not only what is happening but what is likely to happen. The time series that are continuously scrutinized are too numerous to list, but most of them can be classified into one of three categories:

Coincident Indicators These time series tend to move approximately in phase with the aggregate economy and therefore are measures of current economic activity. *Examples:* GNP, industrial production, retail sales.

Leading Indicators These time series tend to move ahead of aggregate economic activity, producing peaks and troughs before the economy as a whole. *Examples:* New orders for plant and equipment, new building permits, stock-market prices.

Lagging Indicators These time series tend to trail behind aggregate economic activity. *Examples:* Business loans outstanding, manufacturing and trade inventories, unit labor costs.

The trouble with all three types of indicators (especially with leading indicators) is that they often give false signals by temporarily reversing their upward or downward direction. This, of course, impairs their usefulness for interpreting and forecasting economic trends. You can appreciate this by examining the graphs in Exhibit 3 and their explanations.

Conclusion: Trade-off Between Stability and Freedom

Some people contend that the business cycle could readily be cured if only certain fundamental adjustments were made. This belief is especially popular during economic recessions. "Find a proper balance between wages and prices." "Improve labor-management relations." "Reform our tax system." If these and other measures were adopted, it is said, economic instability would be eliminated.

Exhibit 3
Forecasting with Economic Indicators: Computer, Crystal Ball, or Tea Leaves?

Ideally, the three types of indicators might look like the theoretical ones shown in Figure (*a*). They illustrate distinct leads and lags, in terms of the peaks and troughs.

In reality, the leads and lags, as shown in Figure (*b*), are not always so definite or consistent. If they were, forecasting would be a simple task.

Note that the shaded area in Figure (*a*) is a reference range. It covers a temporary downturn for the economy as a whole, represented by the coincident indicator.

The U.S. Department of Commerce publishes monthly composite indexes of leading, coincident, and lagging indicators. The leading index, for example, is an average of 12 leading indicators. Note that, for the period covered in Figure (*b*), the leading index did a better job of forecasting the peaks than the troughs.

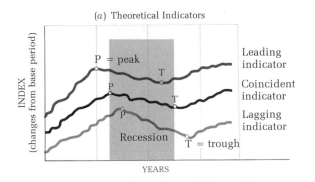

(a) Theoretical Indicators

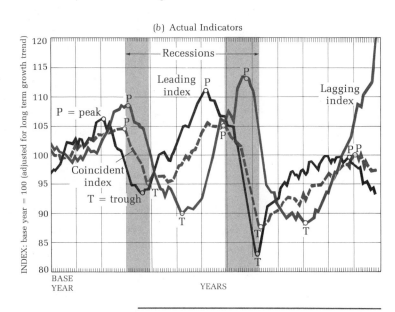

(b) Actual Indicators

Unfortunately, such beliefs are false. Even if these desirable objectives could be achieved, we would still experience economic fluctuations. The reasons are not difficult to see:

Business cycles are an inherent characteristic of mixed economies. This is because households, which express their demands for goods and services in the marketplace, are not the same as the businesses that seek to fulfill those demands. Each group is composed of different people with different motivations. Consequently, the economic actions of both groups—their decisions to spend or not to spend—generally differ. The result is that waves of economic activity are always being created.

One of the goals of macroeconomics is to improve stability by reducing the severity of business cycles.

In view of this, you will find that eliminating instability is not one of the goals of macroeconomics, because that would be impossible in our type of economy. Instead, a chief goal is to *reduce* instability without sacrificing our capitalistic institutions and freedoms. This emphasizes the fact that, at least to some extent, there is a trade-off between stability and freedom.

Unemployment

The term "unemployment" is not as simple as it may seem. There are different kinds of unemployment.

You will often hear it said that one of our primary national objectives is to maintain the economy's resources at a "full" or "high" level of employment. What do these terms mean?

Before this question can be answered, it is necessary to understand some basic terms and concepts that are part of the language of modern economics. The first is the *labor force*. It is defined as all people 16 years of age or older who are employed, plus all those unemployed who are actively seeking work. The *total* labor force includes those in the armed services as well as those in the civilian labor force. However, only the *civilian labor force* is of interest to us here, because this is the segment that experiences unemployment.

Types of Unemployment

The U.S. Department of Labor encounters certain difficulties when it tries to measure unemployment. It finds that the circumstances and conditions of unemployment vary widely among individuals. Accordingly, a distinction is made between several different kinds of unemployment.

Frictional (Transitional) Unemployment

Frictional unemployment consists of people who are "in transition" between jobs.

A certain amount of unemployment, which is of a short-run nature and is characteristic of a dynamic economy, may be called *frictional unemployment*. It exists because of "frictions" in the economic system resulting from imperfect labor mobility, imperfect knowledge of job opportunities, and the economy's inability to match people with jobs instantly and smoothly. Typically, frictional unemployment consists of people temporarily out of work because they are between jobs or in the process of changing jobs. Frictional unemployment can be reduced by improving labor mobility and knowledge, but it cannot—and in a democratic society *should* not—be completely eliminated. To do so would greatly reduce people's freedom to change jobs. In view of the nature of frictional unemployment, an equally suitable and more descriptive name for it might be *transitional unemployment*.

Cyclical Unemployment

In mixed economies such as ours, a major type of unemployment has been *cyclical unemployment*, which is a result of business recessions and depressions. Obviously, society would like to reduce cyclical unemployment as much as possible, but this can be done only by conquering the business cycle. Although substantial progress in this direction has been made in recent decades, cyclical unemployment continues to be one of our economy's most serious ills. Therefore, its treatment is a topic of major importance in subsequent chapters.

Cyclical unemployment results from slowdowns in economic activity.

Structural Unemployment

Unlike cyclical unemployment, which results from economic instability, *structural unemployment* arises from deep-rooted conditions and changes in the economy. Two major groups of people constitute the structurally unemployed.

The first group consists of the *hard-core unemployed*. These are people who lack the education and skills needed in today's complex economy and who are often the victims of discrimination. This group is composed mainly of minorities: blacks, Puerto Ricans, Mexicans, the "too young," the "too old," high-school dropouts, and the permanently displaced victims of technological change.

The second group is completely different. It consists of those skilled workers, college graduates, and professionals whose talents have been made obsolete by changes in technology, markets, or national priorities. Many mathematicians, physicists, artists, musicians, and other people whose specialized skills or training are not in strong demand are in this group.

Because the existence of both groups constitutes one of our society's major economic challenges, much of macroeconomics is concerned with efforts to solve the problems posed by structural unemployment.

Structural unemployment arises from fundamental conditions characterizing the structure of our economy.

Measuring Unemployment: Who Are the Unemployed?

The accuracy of unemployment figures is always subject to attack, especially when the figures are high. Critics point out that the overall unemployment rate may at times be either overstated or understated because of the inclusion or exclusion of three categories of workers:

Because there are different types of unemployment, the problems of measuring unemployment are considerable.

1. The Marginally Employed The jobless total is swollen by the inclusion of many people, among them some homemakers and students, who may be only marginally dependent on regular paychecks.

2. Discouraged Workers The unemployment total is understated by its failure to include "the hidden unemployed"—those discouraged people who have given up trying to find work.

3. The Partially Employed The published unemployment statistics do not reflect the fact that many jobholders are only part-time workers because they cannot find full-time jobs.

Because of these three categories of workers, unemployment data are always somewhat ambiguous. Perhaps the chief value of such data, therefore, lies not in their accuracy but in what they reveal about the direction in which unemployment is changing.

Exhibit 4
Problems of Measuring Unemployment

The length of unemployment lines is not a true indication of the extent of unemployment. The length of the lines is increased or decreased by (1) the marginally employed, (2) discouraged workers, and (3) the partially employed.

Steve Eagle/Nancy Palmer Photo Agency

Employment Ratio: A Better Measure

There are other reasons why the unemployment rate does not accurately reflect the economy's true state of health. Some of these are due to the statistical methods used by the Department of Labor to compile the data. In any case, because of the shortcomings of the unemployment rate, an alternative and considerably better measure is the *employment ratio*. This is the percentage of the working-age population that is employed.

The advantage of the employment ratio (compared to the unemployment rate) is that it focuses on the number of jobs actually held by people while ignoring those people who are entering and leaving the labor force. Thus, if businesses hire more workers, the employment ratio goes up. Meanwhile, the unemployment rate may remain constant or even rise, because it is dependent on the size of the labor force rather than on the size of the working-age population.

Of course, the employment ratio is affected by the number of part-time workers and by various other factors. These also influence the unemployment rate. But, when the proper statistical adjustments are made, economists agree that the employment ratio turns out to be a much better indicator of the economy's health.

Despite its advantages, the employment ratio cannot serve as the government's official measure unless Washington approves it. That will not happen unless Congress decides to legislate the change.

Exhibit 4 reflects some important implications of the foregoing ideas.

Full Employment and ''Normal'' Unemployment

Ideally, the economy should maintain *full employment*—maximum efficient utilization of all resources that are available for employment. In terms of society's human resources, this means that the entire civilian labor force should be working, except for the proportion that is frictionally unemployed—typically about 3 percent. This is equivalent to saying there should be no *involuntary unemployment*. This is a condition in which people who want to work are unable to find jobs at going wage rates for the skills and experiences they have to offer.

For convenience, the goal of full employment is generally expressed in terms of some percentage of the labor force. What minimum unemployment percentage is compatible with the notion of full employment? There is always some disagreement on this question, and the figure chosen by the federal government is likely to be revised upward from time to time.

For instance, it used to be widely accepted that full employment existed when the ''normal'' unemployment rate was not more than 3 percent of the labor force. Presently, we hear figures of 4, 5, or even 6 percent. This reflects the growing significance of structural unemployment and other factors discussed in the following paragraphs. You may think such relatively small differences in percentages are unimportant. However, remember that a difference of only a single percentage point can involve the employment or unemployment of more than a million people. Take a look at the recent labor-force figures that appear in the back endpapers of this book and estimate the consequences for yourself.

Causes of "Normal" Unemployment

How much higher is the "normal" unemployment level likely to go? Some experts predict that before the end of this century perhaps 15 percent unemployed will constitute "full employment." They base their beliefs on three major trends:

Several factors contribute to unemployment.

Changing Composition of the Labor Force The proportion of secondary income earners in the labor force, such as teenagers and part-time jobholders, has been increasing relative to the proportion of primary breadwinners. Because most secondary income earners are less skilled and less experienced, the percentage of unemployed within these groups is usually relatively high. In some years, the figures are as high as 20 or 30 percent. Thus the growing importance of secondary income earners within the labor force helps to boost the unemployment rate.

Rising Minimum-Wage Rate According to many studies, continued increases in the minimum-wage rate will intensify unemployment. Such increases eliminate jobs that cannot be done productively at the required wage rate. Many unskilled, low-paying occupations that could be held by teenagers will not be, simply because employers will find it unprofitable to pay the minimum wage. These jobs, therefore, will not be done unless cheaper methods can be found to do them. Various studies conducted by economists in universities and the U.S. Department of Labor support this view. The studies show that teenage unemployment rates are remarkably low or virtually nonexistent in many industrial countries that have no minimum-wage laws.

Advances in Technology Accelerations in science and technology have been occurring at particularly rapid rates in recent decades. As a result, increasing proportions of unskilled and untrained workers have been permanently displaced, thereby aggravating the problem of structural unemployment. The trend will continue unless methods are developed —through training programs, employer subsidies and tax incentives, and other devices—to absorb the displaced workers in new jobs. You will be learning more about this problem and its possible solutions in later chapters.

Conclusion: Costs of Unemployment

Several major factors are thus contributing to a rising level of "normal" unemployment. What are the costs to society of this important trend? There are two:

The costs of unemployment are borne by all of us.

> Society suffers both an economic cost and a social cost of unemployment.
>
> 1. The economic cost is what the nation forgoes and never gets back. This includes not only lost consumer goods and capital goods that society fails to produce, but deterioration of human capital resulting from loss of skills.
>
> 2. The social cost includes not only the economic cost, but also the human misery, deprivation, and social and political unrest brought on by large-scale unemployment.

Of course, social cost is usually more difficult to measure than economic cost. Nevertheless, both are important and both are matters of deep and general concern. Some interesting implications are described in Exhibit 5.

Exhibit 5
Estimating the Economic Cost of Unemployment: The GNP Gap

How much lost output does society experience from unemployment? You can obtain a rough estimate by calculating the GNP gap. This is the difference, in any given year, between potential GNP and actual GNP. Potential GNP is the output that would occur at full employment. For example, suppose that, by definition, full employment exists when 95 percent of the civilian labor force is working. Then potential GNP can be derived from the following formula:

$$\text{potential GNP} = \frac{\begin{pmatrix} \text{hours worked} \\ \text{by all persons} \\ \text{at full employment} \end{pmatrix}}{\begin{array}{c}\text{actual hours worked} \\ \text{by all persons}\end{array}} \times \begin{pmatrix}\text{actual} \\ \text{GNP}\end{pmatrix}$$

$$= \frac{\begin{pmatrix}\text{95\% of} \\ \text{civilian} \\ \text{labor force}\end{pmatrix}\begin{pmatrix}\text{average} \\ \text{weekly} \\ \text{hours} \times 52\end{pmatrix}}{\begin{pmatrix}\text{actual} \\ \text{employment}\end{pmatrix}\begin{pmatrix}\text{average} \\ \text{weekly} \\ \text{hours} \times 52\end{pmatrix}} \times \begin{pmatrix}\text{actual} \\ \text{GNP}\end{pmatrix}$$

Notice that two of the factors, *average weekly hours times 52*, will cancel out. This leaves the formula:

$$\text{potential GNP} = \frac{\begin{array}{c}\text{95\% of civilian} \\ \text{labor force}\end{array}}{(\text{actual employment})} \times \begin{pmatrix}\text{actual} \\ \text{GNP}\end{pmatrix}$$

To illustrate the calculation, suppose that, in a given year, the civilian labor force was 100 million, actual employment was 92 mil-

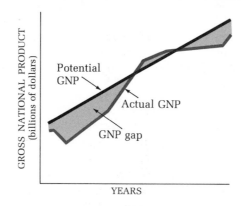

lion, and actual GNP was $2,100 billion. Applying the formula,

$$\begin{aligned}\text{potential GNP} &= \frac{(95 \text{ million})}{(92 \text{ million})} \times (\$2,100 \text{ billion}) \\ &= 1.03 \times (\$2,100 \text{ billion}) \\ &= \$2,163 \text{ billion}\end{aligned}$$

The GNP gap in any given year is then the difference between potential GNP and actual GNP:

GNP gap = (potential GNP) − (actual GNP)

Using the above example,

GNP gap = ($2,163 billion) − ($2,100 billion)
= $63 billion

The chart provides a hypothetical illustration of the GNP gap over a period of years. Can you construct a chart from actual data covering the most recent ten years? All the information you need is available in the front and back endpapers of this book.

Question How might actual GNP sometimes exceed potential GNP?

Inflation

What is it that hits the consumer's pocketbook by eroding the purchasing power of the dollar, sometimes acts as a hidden tax, reduces a nation's competitiveness in world markets, and can have a general debilitating effect on almost all types of economic activity? Answer: Inflation.

> *Inflation* is a rise in the general price level (or the average level of prices) of all goods and services. The general price level thus varies inversely with the purchasing power of a unit of money (such as the dollar). For example, if prices double, purchasing power decreases by one-half; if prices halve, purchasing power doubles. Therefore, inflation is also a reduction in the purchasing power of a unit of money.

The opposite of inflation is *deflation*. Can you formulate your own definition?

Does inflation mean that all prices rise? Clearly not. In almost any period of inflation, some prices rise, some are fairly constant, and some even fall. However, the "average" level of prices—the *general price level*—rises.

Types of Inflation: Is the United States Inflation-Prone?

Different explanations for inflation have been given from time to time. Here are the more common types you are likely to encounter in the news media and should know something about. Note that some of them may be overlapping in their causes and effects.

Demand-Pull Inflation

The traditional type of inflation, known as *demand-pull inflation*, takes place when aggregate demand is rising while the available supply of goods is becoming increasingly limited. Goods may be in short supply because resources are already fully utilized or because production cannot be increased rapidly enough to meet the growing demand. As a result, the general level of prices begins to rise in response to a situation sometimes described as "too much money chasing too few goods."

This is the meaning behind the conventional "demand-pull" model in Exhibit 6. It assumes a time period in which the stock of resources and their productivity are constant. The model can be analyzed in terms of its three stages.

No-Inflation Phase In this stage the economy has excess resources. Therefore, as total demand rises from a depressed level, producers can increase the output of goods while competitive pressures remain strong enough to keep prices from rising.

Inflation Phase In this stage the economy comes closer to utilizing all its available labor and other productive factors. Less efficient resources are brought into use, and some inputs become substantially scarcer than others. Consequently, businesses find it easier to raise prices and also to pass on cost increases to buyers. Output and employment thus reach a point where further increases in aggregate demand cause more than proportional increases in the general price level.

Hyperinflation Phase Once the full-employment level of labor and other resources is attained, additional increases in output are no longer possible during the given period of time. Any further rise in aggregate demand, therefore, drives the economy into a hyperinflationary phase. This is characterized by spiraling prices as producers bid against each other for the same fixed supply of resources.

Cost-Push (Market-Power) Inflation

A second type of inflation is *cost-push inflation*. It occurs when prices increase because factor payments to one or more groups of resource owners rise faster than productivity or technical efficiency. Typical forms of cost-push inflation are "wage-push," "profit-push," and "commodity inflation."

Exhibit 6
Relation Between Inflation and Employment: Conventional Demand-Pull Model

Increases in aggregate demand or total spending may result in moderate increases in the general price level as full employment is approached. Thereafter, further increases in total spending result in pure inflation (or hyperinflation) as the general price level rises without any increases in output.

(**Note** This does not mean that hyperinflation is synonymous with full employment. As suggested in the text, the underlying conditions of each are vastly different.)

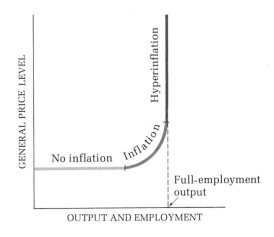

Wage-push inflation occurs when strong labor unions manage to force wage increases in excess of productivity gains. This raises unit costs of production and exerts pressure on sellers to increase prices to maintain profit margins.

Profit-push inflation occurs when sellers try to increase their profit margins by raising prices rather than by reducing costs through improved efficiency. This effort may not always be successful. Nevertheless, rising prices prompt workers and other factor owners to "catch up" by seeking higher resource payments. That increases unit costs of production and stimulates inflation.

Commodity inflation occurs when prices of material inputs rise sufficiently to cause significant increases in costs of production. This prompts firms to respond by raising the prices of finished goods. Worldwide commodity inflations that have resulted from rising costs of energy and other raw materials provide common examples.

These facts suggest the following conclusion:

> Cost-push inflation is usually attributable to monopolistic "market power." This is the degree of discretion that those who control resources, such as unions or firms, have in setting wages and prices. Market power is generally stronger in prosperity periods because labor is in relatively short supply and consumers are less sensitive to price increases. Conversely, market power tends to be weaker in recession periods, and for the opposite reasons. Because of the existence of market power, it is likely that our society will have to tolerate some degree of cost-push inflation while seeking to attain high levels of income and employment.

Structural Inflation, Creeping Inflation, and Hyperinflation

All the types of inflation arise either from demand-pull or from cost-push factors.

Demand-pull and cost-push inflation are the fundamental types of inflation. Any other kinds of inflation that you may read or hear about in the news media are simply different variations on these basic themes. The ones that are most often mentioned are structural inflation, creeping inflation, and hyperinflation. On the basis of what you have already learned, can you formulate definitions of these terms? Explanations are given in the Dictionary at the back of the book.

Inflations in our economy have resulted at various times from demand-pull as well as from cost-push factors. These forces have been at work in different degrees, suggesting that our nation is inflation-prone or that it has a built-in inflationary bias. Some of the implications of this will be examined shortly.

Who Suffers from Inflation? Who Benefits?

Inflation affects people differently. Most people suffer from it, but sometimes certain people benefit.

Everyone is aware that many things cost more today than they did a few years ago. This fact suggests that the long-run trend of prices has been upward. By how much? You can gain some idea from the graphs in Exhibit 7 showing important price indexes.

The *Consumer Price Index* (CPI) is an average of the prices of various goods and services commonly purchased by families in urban areas. Generally referred to as a "cost-of-living index," the CPI is published monthly by the Bureau of Labor Statistics of the U.S. Department of Labor.

The *Producer Price Index* (PPI) is an average of selected items priced in wholesale markets. The items whose prices are averaged include raw materials, semifinished products, and finished goods. The PPI, like the CPI, is also published monthly by the Department of Labor.

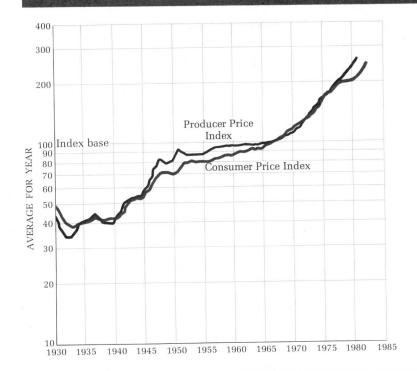

Exhibit 7
Price Indexes (1967 = 100)

The Consumer Price Index and the Producer Price Index are prepared by the U.S. Department of Labor. They are the most widely used measures of inflationary price trends in our economy. Can you project the indexes to the year 2000? What are you assuming when you make such projections?

[**Technical Note** The vertical axis of this figure is scaled logarithmically. This facilitates comparison of relative (percentage) changes in the graphs. To understand why, look up the meaning of *logarithmic scale* in the Dictionary at the back of the book.]

Source: U.S. Department of Labor.

Should we conclude from the graphs that the rising trend of the price indexes imposes an inflationary burden on all of us? Not necessarily. The effects of inflation are not distributed equally. Most people suffer from it, but others sometimes benefit.

To see why this is so, we must understand the difference between two kinds of income:

1. *Money income.* This is the amount of money received for work done.

2. *Real income.* This is the purchasing power of money income as measured by the quantity of goods and services that it can buy.

Clearly, your money income may be quite different from your real income. This is because the latter is determined not only by your money income but also by the prices of the commodities you buy.

Expected Versus Unexpected Inflation

If the rate of inflation were fairly steady, it would be easier for people to plan for it. They could do this by *anticipating* future increases in the average prices of goods and services. Then they could adjust their *present* earning, buying, borrowing, and lending activities in such ways as to overcome the expected depreciation of the dollar. However, if they failed to forecast the rate of inflation correctly, they might inadvertently transfer some of their wealth to other groups in society.

As an illustration, suppose that you lend a friend $100 for one year. If you expect the general price level to remain stable, and if you want to earn a real return (in terms of constant purchasing power) of 5 percent, you will charge 5 percent interest on the loan. Assume, however, that you expect the average level of prices to rise by 10 percent. In that case, you should charge your friend about 15 percent interest on the loan. Of this, 5 percent represents a real return and 10 percent represents compensation for your loss in purchasing power.

Failure to forecast inflation correctly can lead to a redistribution of wealth between borrowers and lenders.

In practice, redistributions of wealth between debtors and creditors are always occurring during inflationary periods.

Suppose that a year elapses and your friend pays you what is owed, but the rise in prices has been greater than you anticipated. Are you better or worse off? Obviously, the repaid loan plus interest has not provided full compensation for your decreased purchasing power. Hence, your change in real wealth is less than you anticipated. You have suffered a loss from inflation. Your friend, on the other hand, has repaid the loan in terms of less purchasing power than was originally borrowed. Your friend has thus experienced an increase in wealth—a gain from inflation. On the whole, therefore, there has been a redistribution of wealth—in this case from you to your friend—because of your failure to make a full adjustment to inflation.

Conversely, if the rise in prices has been less than you anticipated, you are better off. You will experience an increase in wealth—a redistribution from your friend to you. Can you explain why?

To generalize:

> People who do not predict inflation correctly are unable to adjust their economic behavior to compensate for it. As a result, some people experience gains while others experience losses. The net outcome is a redistribution of wealth between debtors and creditors.

Redistributive Effects: Problems of Equity

What, then, is wrong with unanticipated inflation? One of the chief criticisms is that it redistributes wealth arbitrarily—that is, in a manner that may not always accord with society's goals. As shown below, this can be explained in terms of the net monetary financial position of the economy's sectors. The explanation rests on the following distinction.

1. A sector is a *net monetary debtor* if it owes more than it is owed.

2. A sector is a *net monetary creditor* if it is owed more than it owes.

The public sector and the nonfinancial business sector are net monetary debtors. Therefore, these sectors benefit from unanticipated inflation.

Public Sector This sector—particularly because of the federal government—has long had a rising national debt. (The national debt, which is the debt owed by the federal government, is also called the public debt. It is incurred by selling U.S. Treasury securities, such as bonds, to the public. The size of the debt is listed in the back endpapers of this book.) Government is by far the largest net monetary debtor in our economy and it therefore benefits from unanticipated inflation. Because government belongs to all of us, the gains that accrue to it are passed along to everyone. *But the distributions are not equal.* Your income, wealth, age, occupation, or certain other factors can affect the various forms and amounts of benefits you receive from government. These benefits include subsidies, financial aids, and even the benefit of reducing your taxes through legal loopholes.

Nonfinancial Business Sector This sector (that is, the business sector, excluding banks, insurance companies, and other financial businesses) is also a net monetary debtor, but on a much smaller scale than the public sector. Therefore, the owners (stockholders) of those firms that are net monetary debtors are the ultimate beneficiaries of unanticipated inflation. (Keep in mind, however, that even though the nonfinancial business sector as a whole is a net monetary debtor, many business firms within the sector are net monetary creditors.)

Household Sector This sector is the economy's largest net monetary creditor. This is because it is the ultimate source of most of the funds borrowed by the public and private sectors. Consequently, those households that are net monetary creditors suffer from unanticipated inflation. (Keep in mind, of course, that many individual households are net monetary debtors, even though the sector as a whole is a net monetary creditor.)

To summarize:

The business and household sectors consist of units that may be net monetary creditors or net monetary debtors. As a result, unexpected price-level changes cause a redistribution of wealth among these units by taking from some and giving to others. The redistribution is not on the basis of income levels, number of dependents, or other socially acceptable economic criteria. Instead, the redistribution is haphazard and inequitable in a manner unrelated to society's objectives.

International Impacts: Efficiency and Growth

In today's interdependent world, inflation may also have adverse international consequences. If prices and costs rise faster in this country than abroad, our ability to compete in world markets is impaired. This may cause a decrease in exports, an increase in imports, and therefore a general decline in efficiency and growth. As you will learn in later chapters, situations of this type occur frequently and create international economic problems of major significance.

Measuring Inflation: The Declining Value of Money

You have probably heard it said that the dollar today is worth only 60 cents, or 50 cents, or perhaps even less. Such statements try to convey the idea that today's dollar buys only a fraction of what a dollar bought during some period in the past. What fraction? It depends on which past period you choose as a reference point. The decline in the purchasing power of the dollar is much greater during high inflationary years than during low ones.

For example, the most widely used measure of the general price level is the Consumer Price Index (CPI). It tells you the average level of prices in a given year as a percentage of the average level of prices in some other year, called the "base year." In the base year, of course, the average is 100 percent of itself. In any given year, therefore, the average may be greater than, equal to, or less than 100 percent, depending on whether prices have risen, remained constant, or fallen in relation to the base year.

To illustrate, look at the hypothetical data shown in the first two columns of Exhibit 8. Suppose we arbitrarily select Year 1 as the base year. This means that the CPI for that year equals 100.

Note that the CPI in Year 2 was 125 percent of its value in Year 1. This tells you that the average level of prices was 25 percent higher in Year 2 than in the base year. In Year 3, the CPI was 87 percent of its value in Year 1. That is, the average level of prices was 13 percent lower in Year 3 than in the base year.

Using this information, the value or purchasing power of the dollar is calculated in the third column. This is done by expressing the CPI in decimal form and taking its reciprocal. (The reciprocal of a number is 1 divided by that number.) The answer is given for each year in the fourth column.

The household sector is a net monetary creditor. Therefore, it suffers from unanticipated inflation.

The declining value of the dollar due to inflation is measured by the reciprocal of the CPI.

Exhibit 8
Measuring the Value of the Dollar

Year	CPI	Reciprocal		Value of $1
1 (base)	100	$1 \div 1.00$	=	1.00
2	125	$1 \div 1.25$	=	0.80
3	87	$1 \div 0.87$	=	1.15

Exhibit 9
**Tracking Inflation: The Value of
Money and Consumer Prices**

The Consumer Price Index (CPI) is an
average of the prices of various goods and
services commonly purchased by families
in urban areas. The reciprocal of the CPI
thus provides a measure of the "value,"
or purchasing power, of the dollar.

HOW MUCH IS A DOLLAR WORTH?

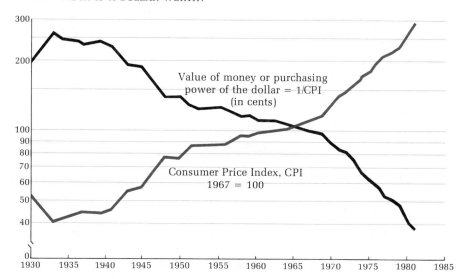

Value of money or purchasing
power of the dollar = 1/CPI
(in cents)

Consumer Price Index, CPI
1967 = 100

The actual CPI is shown in the back endpapers of this book. From
these data, long-run comparisons of the CPI and the value of money are
graphed in Exhibit 9.

To summarize:

The value of a unit of money, such as the dollar, is defined in terms of its
purchasing power. This is measured as the reciprocal, or inverse, of the
general price level. Thus, the higher the level of prices, the lower the value
or purchasing power of a unit of money, and vice versa.

Conclusion: The Need for Price Stability

*Stable prices are one of the major goals of
our economy because price stability encourages greater efficiency and growth.*

The term "inflation" means rising prices. However, it is important to
distinguish between anticipated and unanticipated inflation.

If *all* prices rose at a fairly steady rate, people would learn to anticipate inflation and to adjust their asset and liability holdings accordingly. The impact of inflation on unsuspecting individuals and groups
would thus be greatly reduced.

In reality, *all* prices do not rise at the same rate, nor does the average
price level expand at a steady pace. As a result, inflation tends to be
erratic and unanticipated, leaving far more losers than winners within
the household sector. In fact, even if households could anticipate inflation perfectly, they would still lose wealth to the extent that they held
money during periods of rising prices.

This leads to the following conclusion:

Unanticipated inflation has three major adverse consequences:

1. It creates general economic instability.

2. It results in individual inequities and costs. (The inequities are the result
of haphazard redistributions of wealth. The costs are the efforts that people
must put forth to forecast and adjust their asset and liability holdings to
unanticipated increases in prices.)

3. It retards efficiency and growth by impairing productive capacity and the
ability to compete in world markets.

For these reasons, a major goal of society is to achieve sufficient price stability in order to encourage a steady high level of economic activity. A number of subsequent chapters are devoted to understanding the difficulties of achieving this goal.

Case
Inflation: The 6% Solution

When can you take a friend to dinner at a modest restaurant, hand the waiter a $50 bill, and not get back enough change to leave an appropriate tip? Answer: Pretty soon, if inflationary trends of 6 to 12 percent—or even more—are as common in the future as they have been in the past.

Table 1 shows average prices of some familiar commodities in 1980. If inflation proceeded at an annual rate of "only" 6 percent—the rate often heralded as reasonable—prices by 1990 will have nearly doubled. By the year 2000 they will have more than tripled.

6% Is No Solution

How does inflation affect you personally? You can get an idea from Table 2. At a 6 percent rate of inflation, for example, your dollar today will lose half of its value in only 12 years. At higher inflationary rates, the loss will occur much faster. Unfortunately, your income is not likely to keep up with inflation. The conclusion, therefore, is that inflation hurts all of us to the extent that we are unable to anticipate it and adjust accordingly. Unfortunately, hardly anyone can.

This raises two questions for those who want to "beat" inflation:

1. What can you do in order to avoid inflation's adverse effects?

2. What are *real assets* as distinguished from *monetary assets*? Is this distinction important in light of your answer to the first question? (*Suggestion* Look up the meanings of these terms in the Dictionary at the back of the book.)

Table 1. What Things Will Cost (rounded to the nearest dollar)

Goods and services	1980	Future cost, assuming 6% inflation	
		1990	2000
House	$60,000	$107,460	$192,420
Boat	10,000	17,910	32,070
Automobile	6,000	10,746	19,242
Tuition cost—state college	1,300	2,328	4,002
Two-week vacation	1,000	1,791	3,207
Steak dinner	15	26	56
Haircut	10	18	32
Pizza	4	7	13
Paperback novel	3	5	10
Hamburger, french fries	2	4	6

Table 2. Purchasing Power of the Dollar at Various Rates of Inflation

Years hence	Inflationary rate at:					
	2%	4%	6%	8%	10%	12%
0	$1.00	$1.00	$1.00	$1.00	$1.00	$1.00
2	.96	.92	.89	.86	.83	.80
4	.92	.85	.79	.74	.68	.64
6	.89	.79	.70	.63	.56	.51
8	.85	.73	.63	.54	.47	.40
10	.82	.68	.56	.46	.39	.32
12	.79	.62	.50	.40	.32	.26
14	.76	.58	.44	.34	.26	.20
16	.73	.53	.39	.29	.22	.16

What You Have Learned in This Chapter

1. Mixed economies suffer from recurrent but nonperiodic fluctuations in economic activity known as business cycles. The four phases of such cycles are prosperity, recession, depression, and recovery.

2. Industries in the economy react to business cycles in different ways. Most durable-goods industries tend to be less competitive than nondurable-goods industries. Therefore, they experience relatively wide fluctuations in output. The opposite tends to occur in many nondurable-goods industries. In these, prices fluctuate relatively more than output and employment.

3. If economists can learn how to forecast business cycles, they will be in a better position to recommend government policies for avoiding downturns in economic activity. Today the most scientific methods of business-cycle forecasting involve the use of surveys and opinion polling, econometric models, and economic indicators.

4. The rate of unemployment is expressed as a percentage of the labor force. A jobless rate of 4 to 5 percent is generally regarded as constituting "full" to "high" employment. Unemployment rates may continue to rise in future years because of (a) the changing composition of the labor force, (b) a rising level

of minimum-wage rates, and (c) advances in technology.

5. Inflation is a rise in the general price level or a reduction in the purchasing power of a unit of money. Inflations are commonly attributed to demand-pull or cost-push forces. Although there is widespread agreement on the former as a cause of inflation, there is much disagreement over the latter. In general, inflation tends to redistribute wealth haphazardly without regard to social goals. It may also impair a nation's efficiency, growth, and competitiveness in world markets.

6. There is considerable evidence that virtually all mixed economies, including our own, have an "inflationary bias." This means they are inflation-prone. Therefore, a desirable social objective is not only to reduce inflation, but to make it less erratic. People would then be better able to adjust to inflation by altering their asset and liability holdings, thereby minimizing adverse redistributive effects.

For Discussion

1. *Terms and concepts to review:*
business cycles
seasonal fluctuations
trend
labor force
frictional unemployment
cyclical unemployment
structural unemployment
employment ratio
involuntary unemployment
inflation
time series
econometrics
economic indicators
general price level
demand-pull inflation
cost-push inflation
Consumer Price Index
Producer Price Index
money income
real income

2. If business cycles were recurrent and periodic, would they be easily predictable? Why? What, precisely, would you be able to predict about them?

3. If you were to compare two industries, automobiles and agricultural products, over the course of a business cycle, which would be more stable with respect to (a) output and employment and (b) prices? Explain why.

4. It is customary to remove both the seasonal and long-term trend influences from time-series data before undertaking an analysis of cyclical forces. Although there are no unusual controversies concerning removal of the seasonal factor, there is considerable disagreement among economists over removal of the trend. Can you suggest why?

5. Can you suggest how the interaction of changes in consumption and investment may cause business cycles?

6. What do you suppose are some of the chief difficulties in using leading indicators for forecasting purposes?

7. Is an increasing level of aggregate demand likely to cure the problems of cyclical unemployment and structural unemployment—without encouraging inflation? Explain.

8. Is it better to have full employment with mild inflation or moderate unemployment with no inflation? Explain.

9. "Because of the changing composition of the labor force, a single measure of full employment proves to be an inadequate goal." In view of this statement, what alternatives can you suggest? Discuss.

10. It is often said that our economy has a built-in inflationary bias and is inflation-prone. Can you give reasons to account for this statement?

11. Minimum-wage legislation, despite its good intention, has been called "the most racially discriminating law on the books." Can you explain why? Can you show, with supply and demand curves, how minimum-wage legislation results in unemployment? What market solution can you suggest to increase employment among low-skilled members of the labor force?

12. "Reduce working hours. Spread the work. That's the way to solve the unemployment problem." So say many critics, union leaders, and social reformers. They argue for a reduction in working time—with no loss of pay—as a cure for unemployment. Do you agree with them?

What Causes Unemployment? Introduction to Classical and Keynesian Economics

Learning guide
Watch for the answers to these important questions

Can our mixed economy achieve and maintain economic efficiency, or *full employment* of resources? How did the so-called "classical economists" of the nineteenth and early twentieth centuries answer this question? Are their ideas useful today?

What happened during the 1930s to change the thinking of most economists? How did developments since then contribute to the formulation of new ideas for studying today's economic problems?

In modern macroeconomics, what basic variables are used for analyzing the central problems of efficiency, stability, and growth? What are the relationships between these variables? How do the relationships together provide the basis for a model of the macroeconomy?

In our mixed economy, we face an awesome task. We must find ways to put millions of unemployed people to work. At the same time, we must learn how to reduce upward pressures on prices. These are the problems of unemployment and inflation. In a broader sense, as you already know, they are the fundamental problems of efficiency and stability. Both are at the heart of most macroeconomic problems.

To solve these problems, we first need a logical explanation of why they occur. Such an explanation is provided by a body of macroeconomic principles known as the theory of income and employment. The theory is built on three types of economic activity: consumption, saving, and investment. Each plays a distinctive role in the economy. Acting in combination, they help to determine our society's material well-being. Therefore, they are the foundations upon which much of modern macroeconomic policy is built.

The twin problems of modern macroeconomics are unemployment and inflation.

The Classical Explanation of Income and Employment

As you have already learned, the modern discipline of economics began with Adam Smith in the late eighteenth century. It developed until, by the 1930s, it was the predominant body of economic theory in the non-Communist world. The ideas that Smith formulated, and that were refined and extended by Smith's followers, constitute what is known as "classical economics."

In the late 1930s, a British scholar, John Maynard Keynes (pronounced "canes"), introduced certain macroeconomic ideas that came to be known as "Keynesian economics." The theories formulated by

Classical economics began with Adam Smith.

Keynes, like those of Smith, have undergone substantial refinement and revision. Today, many of the analytical tools and ideas provided both by classical and by Keynesian economics are widely used by practically all economists.

But in the social sciences, great theories, like the phenomena they try to describe, rarely remain constant. Much of today's economic thinking represents a modern synthesis and extension of the best ideas from classical and Keynesian economics, as the following pages and chapters point out.

Say's Law: "Supply Creates Its Own Demand"

In the early nineteenth century, a French economist, Jean Baptiste Say, wrote:

> . . . a product is no sooner created than it, from that instant, offers a market for other products to the full extent of its own value. . . . Thus, the mere circumstance of the creation of one product immediately opens a market for other products.

This conclusion has come to be known as *Say's Law*. But the idea has been expressed more pointedly by David Ricardo, a British contemporary of Say and a great pioneer in economic thought:

> No man produces but with a view to consume or sell, and he never sells but with an intention to purchase some other commodity which may be immediately useful to him or which may contribute to future production. By producing, then, he necessarily becomes either the consumer of his own goods, or the purchaser and consumer of the goods of some other person.

Say's Law—whether as originally expressed by Say or as restated by Ricardo—amounts to saying that *supply creates its own demand*. This occurs because in a specialized, or exchange, economy, as distinct from a self-sufficient "Robinson Crusoe" economy, people are interdependent. That is, people work at the occupations in which they are relatively most efficient. They then exchange the surplus of what they produce above their own needs for the products of other people's efforts. Thus, as Ricardo put it, the shoemaker, the butcher, and the baker acquire one another's wares by exchanging the portions of their outputs that they do not consume themselves.

These ideas can be expressed in monetary rather than in barter terms. Thus, the income a person receives from production is spent to purchase goods produced by others. For the economy as a whole, therefore, total income equals total production and aggregate demand equals aggregate supply. Consequently, any addition to output generates an equal addition to income, which in turn is spent on the added output. Hence:

> It follows from Say's Law that firms will always find it profitable to hire unemployed resources up to the point of full employment. This is true provided that the owners of unemployed resources are willing to be paid no more than their physical productivities justify. If this condition is granted, there can be no prolonged period of unemployment—for two reasons:
>
> **1.** Workers and other resource suppliers will be receiving what they are worth, as measured by the value of their contribution to production.
>
> **2.** The additional income earned from increased production will be spent on purchasing the additional output.

This belief was central to classical economic thought of the nineteenth and early twentieth centuries. It is a belief that is widely held with varying degrees of conviction today. In view of this, what does the classical model really tell us? What are its implications for our economic system? The answers to these questions are fundamental to modern economics.

Essentials of the Classical Theory: An Overview

The classical model assumes the operation of a free-enterprise, highly competitive economic system. This is a system in which there are many buyers and sellers, both in product markets and in resource markets. It is also a system in which all prices are flexible so that they can quickly adjust upward or downward to changing supplies and demands in the marketplace. In this type of economic system, the product and resource markets will automatically adjust to full-employment levels as if guided by an "invisible hand." This is because *aggregate demand equals aggregate income or output*. Let us examine this idea more closely.

Classical economics rests on certain assumptions and can be expressed as a set of propositions.

Aggregate Demand = Aggregate Income or Output

You have learned that an economy's aggregate output (GNP) equals its aggregate income (GNI). But the classicists argued that the purpose of earning income is to spend it on output. Hence, the level of *aggregate demand*—the total value of output that all sectors of the economy are willing to purchase—always equals the level of aggregate income or output.

Society's income is the measure of total demand for society's output.

This does not mean that oversupply of some particular items cannot occur. Overproduction of specific commodities can and does occur when business managers misjudge the markets for their goods. But these errors are temporary and are corrected as entrepreneurs shift resources out of production of less profitable commodities into production of more profitable ones. According to the classical view, only *general* overproduction, or a deficiency in aggregate demand, is impossible.

But what if households choose to *save*—that is, not to spend a certain proportion of their income on goods and services? Will these savings represent a withdrawal or "leakage" of funds from the income stream? Will aggregate demand then fall below aggregate output or supply, resulting in excess production, increasing unemployment, and decreasing incomes? The classical economists' answer is no, because *all savings are invested*. Let us see why.

All Savings Are Invested

Say's Law tells us that total spending will always be high enough to maintain full employment. Thus, if some people save part of their income, there will always be businesspeople who will borrow those savings and pay a price for them called *interest*. This borrowed money will be invested in capital goods in order to carry on profitable production. In classical theory, therefore, saving by households leads directly to spending by businesses on capital or investment goods. Because aggregate income is always spent, part of it is spent for consumption and part for investment.

Exhibit 1
Markets in the Classical Theory of Income and Employment

In the classical model, all markets are assumed to be competitive and all resources mobile. Therefore, prices and quantities are flexible and adjust *automatically* to their full-employment equilibrium levels through the free play of market forces.

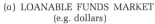

(a) LOANABLE FUNDS MARKET
(e.g. dollars)

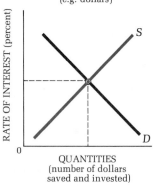

QUANTITIES
(number of dollars
saved and invested)

(b) PRODUCT MARKETS
(e.g., wheat)

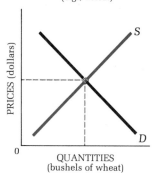

QUANTITIES
(bushels of wheat)

(c) RESOURCE MARKETS
(e.g., labor)

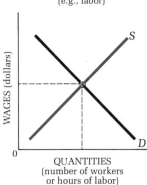

QUANTITIES
(number of workers
or hours of labor)

What mechanism ensures that all money saved is invested at full employment? The classicists' answer is *interest,* which they view as a reward for saving. That is, interest is a price that businesses pay households to persuade them to consume less in the present so that they can consume more at a later date. Current interest rates are determined in the economy's financial markets, collectively called the "loanable funds" market. In this market, households' supply of savings interacts with businesses' demand for them.

This is illustrated in Figure (a) of Exhibit 1. The model is based on the classical assumption that no household will save (and thereby forgo the pleasure of spending) unless it is offered interest in return. Also, no businessperson will borrow (and thereby pay interest) unless he or she plans to invest. Therefore, a flexible interest rate assures that every dollar saved by households will be borrowed and invested by businesses, thus *automatically* maintaining a full-employment level of aggregate spending.

Prices and Wages Are Flexible

But suppose some unemployment *did* develop, causing a decline in aggregate income or purchasing power. Would such a situation be more than temporary? The classicists answered no, because *prices and wages are flexible.* In classical theory, prices in *all* markets—the loanable funds market, the product markets, and the resource markets—are assumed to move freely. Therefore, they *automatically* adjust to their individual full-employment equilibrium levels.

These ideas are shown in Exhibit 1. As you can see, if the price in any market is below its particular equilibrium level, the quantity demanded will exceed the quantity supplied. Competition among buyers (demanders) in that market will therefore drive the price up. If the price in any market is above its equilibrium level, the quantity supplied will exceed the quantity demanded. Competition between sellers (suppliers) in that market will therefore drive the price down. At the equilibrium price in each market, the quantity that sellers want to sell is equal to the quantity that buyers want to buy. At these prices, *there are no shortages and no surpluses* in any of the product, resource, or loanable funds markets. Therefore, there must be full employment and full production throughout the economy.

Classical Conclusion: Capitalism Is a Self-Regulating Economic System

In the classical economists' view it follows that a capitalistic economic system will tend *automatically* toward full employment through the free operation of the price system. Therefore, the functions of government, as Adam Smith emphasized, should be limited to national defense, the administration of justice, the facilitation of commerce, and the provision of certain public works. Adherence to such a policy would establish *laissez-faire* (freedom from government intervention) as the watchword of capitalism. It would place government in an economically neutral position, leaving the economy to allocate its resources optimally as if guided by an "invisible hand."

To summarize:

Classical economics dominated the Western world from the late eighteenth century until the late 1930s. Among its chief early proponents were Adam Smith (1723–1790), Jean Baptiste Say (1767–1832), and David Ricardo (1772–1823). It emphasized people's self-interest and the operation of universal economic laws. These would tend automatically to guide the economy toward full-employment equilibrium if the government adheres to a policy of laissez-faire or noninterventionism.

It would be a mistake to infer from the foregoing discussion that, prior to the 1930s, all economists presented a united classical front. In fact, many economists differed substantially in their beliefs. For example, some adhered to the classical tradition but advocated government spending programs as short-term measures to stimulate production and employment. Others departed from the classical tradition by adopting socialistic ideologies (that is, government ownership of the means of production). Still others turned to descriptive studies of the economy based on sociological and legal institutions. However, despite these dissentions from orthodox theory, the basic ideas of classicism represented the mainstream of economic thinking prior to the birth of Keynesian economics in the 1930s.

The Keynesian Response to Classical Theory

The Great Depression of the 1930s was long and painful. At the bottom of the business cycle in 1933, unemployment in the United States reached almost 13 million, approximately 25 percent of the labor force. For the remainder of the decade, it never dropped lower than 8 million, or 14 percent of the labor force. Comparable rates of unemployment existed in the United Kingdom during this period.

Keynesian economics, which was born in the 1930s, was a reaction to classical beliefs.

The occurrence of such a prolonged and deep depression was contrary to classical thinking. As a result, many economists were inclined to explain the situation away by saying it was the "world" and not the theory that was at fault. For example, one of the most distinguished classicists of that era, Professor Arthur C. Pigou of England's Cambridge University, in a famous book entitled *The Theory of Unemployment* (1933), wrote:

> With perfectly free competition . . . there will always be a strong tendency toward full employment. The implication is that such unemployment as exists at any time is due wholly to the fact that frictional resistances [caused by monopolistic unions and firms maintaining rigid wages and prices] prevent the appropriate wage and price adjustments from being made instantaneously.

A flexible wage and price policy, Pigou and other classical economists contended, would "abolish fluctuations of employment" entirely. In America, many orthodox economists added the proviso that the government under President Franklin Delano Roosevelt's administration should also stop interfering with the free operation of the markets through its extensive regulatory legislation and activities. Thus:

During the depression of the 1930s, most classicists argued that high unemployment was due mainly to monopolistically rigid wages and prices.

> The classicists strongly believed that the economic system *automatically* tends toward full-employment equilibrium. They contended that frictional maladjustments alone are responsible for temporary short-run fluctuations.

In response to this general view—and to Pigou's book in particular —an eminent British scholar named John Maynard Keynes published in 1936 a monumental treatise, *The General Theory of Employment, Interest and Money*. In this book, Keynes strongly criticized the classical theory and formulated a theory of his own. This new theory soon revolutionized economic thinking.

From Keynes to Modern Macroeconomics

Keynesian ideas have been greatly refined and extended over the years.

Much of modern macroeconomic theory is rooted in the work done by Keynes. However, the theory has been greatly refined and extended since then—in many instances by some of Keynes's strongest critics. In addition, a good deal of non-Keynesian thinking has been integrated in modern macroeconomics. Today, most of the major controversial economic issues you read and hear about—such issues as taxes, inflation, national debt, unemployment, balance of payments, interest rates, and so forth—are analyzed within the framework of modern macroeconomic theory.

The remainder of this chapter deals with the basic macroeconomic relationships that Keynes and his followers developed. Subsequent chapters will then bring the relationships together and build upon them. The result will be a comprehensive view of macroeconomics as it exists today.

Before beginning, a brief sketch of Keynes's background and ideas will prove helpful. See "Leaders in Economics," p. 144.

Essentials of the Keynesian Theory: An Overview

Keynesian economics rests on certain assumptions and can be expressed as a set of propositions.

How does modern macroeconomic theory—the theory of income and employment determination—contrast with the classical theory? We may answer by formulating several propositions showing how Keynes responded to the classicists' arguments.

Aggregate Demand May Not Equal Full-Employment Aggregate Income

Keynesian theory rejects the classical notion that aggregate demand always equals full-employment aggregate income and that the economic system automatically tends towards its full-employment equilibrium level. Keynesian theory demonstrates that the economic system may be in equilibrium at less than full employment and may remain so indefinitely.

Changes in aggregate demand play a critical role in the Keynesian theory. An economy may be operating at a level equal to or below full employment. If the economy then experiences a drop in aggregate demand, there will be a consequent decline in real output and resource use. On the other hand, an economy may be operating at a level below full employment. If the economy then experiences an increase in aggregate demand, there will be a consequent rise in real output and resource use. Further, if aggregate demand continues to increase above full-employment levels, the result will be rising prices and demand-pull inflation. As you will see in later chapters, this is a situation sometimes described as "too much money chasing too few goods."

Savers and Investors Are Different People with Different Motivations

An important feature of the Keynesian theory concerns the roles of saving and investment.

Keynes pointed out that, in a primitive economy, saving and investing are undertaken largely by the same groups for the same reasons. But in an advanced economy, saving and investing are undertaken by different groups for different reasons.

In our own economy, for example, households such as yours and mine may save for several reasons—among them, to purchase a new car, to finance an education, to make a down payment on a house, or to pay for a vacation. Households may also save to provide for future security, to amass an estate that can be passed on to future generations, or to buy stocks and bonds for income or future profit. And, of course, many households may save simply to accumulate funds without a specific purpose in mind.

Business firms save when they retain some of their profits instead of distributing them to stockholders. Their reasons for saving, however, are different from those of households. Businesses usually save in order to invest in plant, equipment, and inventories; they may also borrow for the same purposes. In any case, they invest primarily on the basis of the rate of profit they anticipate. Thus:

> Savers and investors are different people with different motivations. Most of the economy's saving is done by households, whereas its investment is done primarily by businesses on the basis of profit expectations. The amount businesses want to invest fluctuates widely from year to year and is not likely to equal the amount households want to save. The interest rate, therefore, is *not* a mechanism that brings about the equality of saving and investment at full employment, as the classicists assumed.

The household sector does most of the saving. The business sector does most of the investing in plant, equipment, and inventories.

Prices and Wages Are Not Flexible

Do prices and wages exhibit the flexibility the classicists assumed? The answer is no. Our economy is characterized by big unions and big businesses, and there is great resistance to reductions in prices and wages. We almost always hear of prices and wages going up, but we rarely hear of them going down.

Nevertheless, let us assume for the moment that wages and prices are flexible and that the fall in wages during a period of employment is greater than the fall in prices. This is what the classical economists postulated. If wage decreases are experienced by one firm only, its profits will increase and it will be encouraged to expand its production and employment. But if wage decreases are experienced by all firms in the economy, *real wages* (that is, money wages relative to the general price level) or general purchasing power will decline. The result is likely to be a further reduction in output and employment instead of the reverse. And if the interest rate happens to be "sticky" rather than flexible, as is often the case, its failure to adjust downward helps to perpetuate or worsen an already depressed situation. To summarize:

> A reduction in real wages within a single firm is not likely to affect the overall demand for that firm's product. However, it cannot be assumed that a general reduction in real wages of *all* workers throughout the economy will have no effect on aggregate demand.

Inflexible prices and wages prevent rapid market adjustments.

The classical economists failed to recognize this distinction between the "particular" and the "general." They thereby committed a logical fallacy in their thinking. Can you name the fallacy?

Keynesian Conclusion: Laissez-Faire Capitalism Cannot Ensure Full Employment

Keynesian ecomonics concludes that the economy does not tend automatically toward full employment.

In contrast to the classicists, Keynes concluded with these ideas:

A capitalistic economy provides *no automatic tendency* toward full employment. The levels of aggregate output and employment are determined by the level of aggregate demand, and there is no assurance that aggregate demand will always equal full-employment aggregate income. As aggregate demand increases, so do aggregate output and employment—up to the level of full employment.

Many economists since Keynes have subscribed to these beliefs. In view of this, let us now see what the Keynesian theory says about the concept of *aggregate demand.* This, you recall from the study of national-income accounting, is the sum of expenditures by all sectors of the economy.

Consumption Demand

Consumption demand is by far the largest component of aggregate demand. What factors determine *consumption* demand, that is, personal consumption expenditures on goods and services in our economy?

Exhibit 2
A Family's Consumption and Saving Schedule
(annual data)

How Do Consumption and Saving Relate to Income?

(1) Disposable income (after taxes), *DI*	(2) Consumption, *C*	(3) Saving, *S* (1) − (2)	(4) Average propensity to consume, *APC* (2) ÷ (1)	(5) Average propensity to save, *APS* (3) ÷ (1)	(6) Marginal propensity to consume, *MPC* **Change in (2) Change in (1)**	(7) Marginal propensity to save, *MPS* **Change in (3) Change in (1)**
$ 8,000	$ 9,200	− $1,200	1.15	−0.15		
					0.70	0.30
10,000	10,600	− 600	1.06	−0.06		
					0.70	0.30
12,000	12,000	0	1.00	0.00		
					0.70	0.30
14,000	13,400	600	0.96	0.04		
					0.70	0.30
16,000	14,800	1,200	0.93	0.07		
					0.70	0.30
18,000	16,200	1,800	0.90	0.10		
					0.70	0.30
20,000	17,600	2,400	0.88	0.12		
					0.70	0.30
22,000	19,000	3,000	0.86	0.14		
					0.70	0.30
24,000	20,400	3,600	0.85	0.15		

These hypothetical figures show that, as a family's disposable income increases, the amount it spends on consumption and the amount it saves also increase. The meanings of the various columns are explained in the text.

Take your own case. What determines the amount spent by your family on goods and services? You can probably think of several factors, but first and foremost is your family's disposable income—the amount it has left after paying personal taxes.

The situation is much the same with other families. *Disposable income is usually the single most important factor affecting a family's consumption expenditures.* Other conditions, such as the size of the family, the ages of its members, its past income, and its expectations of future income, will also have some influence.

The Propensity to Consume

No two families spend their incomes in exactly the same way. However, the relation between a hypothetical family's disposable income and its consumption expenditures is illustrated by the schedule in the first two columns of Exhibit 2. The difference between disposable income and consumption is saving, which is shown in column (3). The first thing to notice is that as disposable income increases, consumption increases and so does saving.

The consumption and saving data are graphed in Exhibit 3. Let us consider the upper figure first. Note that consumption expenditures are measured on the vertical axis and disposable income on the horizontal. Observe also that both axes are drawn to the same scale. Therefore, the 45-degree diagonal is a line along which consumption C is 100 percent of disposable income DI. That is, the ratio $C/DI = 1$.

The consumption curve C is the graph of the data in columns (1) and (2) of the table. The intersection of this curve with the diagonal line is the family's "break-even point." This is the point at which consumption is exactly equal to disposable income. At this level the family is just getting by, neither borrowing nor saving.

To the right of the break-even point the vertical distance representing consumption is less than the horizontal distance denoting disposable income. The difference, saving, is represented by the vertical distance between the consumption line and the diagonal.

To the left of the break-even point the family is consuming more than its disposable income. The difference is called *dissaving*. How does a family dissave or live beyond its means? Either by spending its previous savings, by borrowing, or by receiving gifts from others (that is, by being subsidized).

Here are some important ideas to remember:

> The level of consumption depends on the level of income (that is, disposable income). The dependency is such that, as income increases, consumption increases, but not as fast as income. This relation between consumption and income is called the *propensity to consume,* or the *consumption function.* The word "function" is thus used here in its mathematical sense. It means a quantity whose value depends on the value of another quantity. (For example, we say that the amount of consumption *depends* on, or is a function of, the level of income.)

Note that the consumption curve C is the family's propensity-to-consume curve. It assumes that, apart from income, *all other factors that may affect consumption remain constant.* Do you recall these factors? If not, refresh your memory by referring back to the top of this page.

Exhibit 3

A Family's Consumption and Saving in Relation to Its Income
(annual data)

The vertical distances show how much will be consumed and saved at each income level. For example, at an income of $22,000, the amount spent on consumption is $19,000 and the amount saved is $3,000.

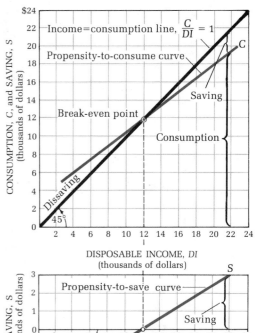

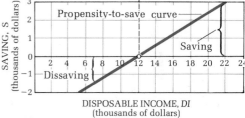

United Press International

Leaders in Economics

John Maynard Keynes
1883–1946
Founder of a "Revolution"

"You have to know that I believe myself to be writing a book on economic theory which will largely revolutionize . . . the way the world thinks about economic problems." So wrote John Maynard Keynes to the Irish wit and author George Bernard Shaw in 1935.

Keynes was right. He did indeed write a book that revolutionized economic thinking. As a result, he became recognized as one of the most brilliant and influential economists of all time. In fact, as one who helped shape the thinking of future generations of scholars, Keynes ranks with Adam Smith and Karl Marx.

Keynes was born in Cambridge, England, the son of a noted economist, John Neville Keynes. The younger Keynes was educated at Eton and Cambridge, where he first majored in mathematics but later turned his attention to philosophy and economics. After college, he took a civil service post in the India Office. (In those years, India was subject to British rule.) Later, he returned to England

and served as a teaching fellow at Cambridge, where his talents were quickly recognized. He became editor of the *Economic Journal,* Britain's most distinguished economic publication—a position that he held for 33 years.

Many-Sided Genius
To say that Keynes was brilliant is an understatement. He was a genius with diverse talents who combined teaching at Cambridge with an active and highly successful business life in the fields of insurance, investments, and publishing. In addition to his many publications in economics, he wrote a remarkable book on the philosophical foundations of probability that has long been required reading by graduate students in mathematical logic and philosophy. And he amassed a fortune of more than $2 million by speculating in the international currency and commodities markets. Perhaps most impressive, however, is the fact that he accomplished these feats in his "spare time." He wrote his mathematics book while employed in government service, and he accumulated his fortune by analyzing financial reports and phoning orders to his broker for a half-hour each morning before breakfast.

Unconventional Ideas
Keynes's most celebrated work, *The General Theory of Employment, Interest and Money* (1936), is one of the most influential books ever written in economics. Here Keynes made it clear that he was departing significantly from traditional economic theory. This theory held that there is a natural tendency for the economy to reach equilibrium at full employment. In-

deed, Keynes showed that equilibrium can be reached and maintained at a level of output less than full employment.

Because of this, Keynes advocated reduction in the bank interest rate to stimulate investment. He also believed in progressive income taxation to make incomes more equal and thereby increase the percentage of aggregate income that people spend on consumption. And he argued for government investment through public works as a "pump-priming" process when private investment expenditures fall off. Today, these and several related ideas are part of a larger family of concepts that make up modern macroeconomic theory and policy.

Depression vs. Inflation Theory
Nowadays, practically all economists use many of the fundamental theoretical tools and concepts that Keynes developed. However, economists may not always agree on the ways in which those ideas should be implemented in matters of public policy.

For example, many informed observers agree that Keynesian economics works well when applied to deflation and depression. In these situations, expenditures (and, therefore, purchasing power) can be increased to stimulate demand and to promote higher employment and production. But the Keynesian model seems less than adequate for coping with inflation. This is especially true if a high level of employment is to be maintained. Consequently, much effort continues to be devoted to developing tools for dealing with these and related problems of today's economy.

The Propensity to Save

You know that saving is the difference between income and consumption. You also know that consumption depends on income. Therefore, you may correctly conclude that saving depends on income. (Keep in mind that the term "income" as used here means disposable income.)

The data on saving in column (3) of Exhibit 2, taken together with the data in column (1), are shown in the graph in the lower panel of Exhibit 3. Here, disposable income is again measured on the horizontal axis, but saving is now scaled vertically. The saving curve S depicts the vertical differences between the diagonal line and the consumption curve in the upper chart.

> The level of saving depends on the level of income. This relation between saving and income is called the *propensity to save,* or the *saving function.*

Thus, the saving curve S is the family's propensity-to-save curve.

Average Propensities to Consume and to Save

What will the family's *average* consumption be in relation to its income? What will be its *average* amount of saving? The answers are given in columns (4) and (5) of Exhibit 2.

The *average propensity to consume* (APC) is simply the ratio of consumption to income:

$$APC = \frac{\text{consumption}}{\text{income}}$$

The APC tells you the proportion of each income level that the family will spend on consumption. Similarly, the *average propensity to save* (APS) is the ratio of saving to income. The APS tells you the proportion of each income level that the family will save—that is, will not spend on consumption:

$$APS = \frac{\text{saving}}{\text{income}}$$

For example, at an income level of $20,000, the family will spend 88 cents of each dollar, or a total of $17,600. It will save 12 cents of each dollar, or a total of $2,400. In other words, the family will spend 88 percent of its income and save 12 percent.

Note that as income increases, APC decreases. Therefore, APS increases because both must total 1 (or 100 percent) at each income level. What can you learn from the fact that APC declines with rising incomes? Basically, this tendency confirms the everyday observation that the rich save a larger proportion of their incomes than the poor. You probably would have guessed this without looking at the figures in the table. Nevertheless, they help to fix this important idea more firmly in your mind.

Marginal Propensities to Consume and to Save

You will see later that it is important to know both the amount of each *extra* dollar of income that the family will spend on consumption and the amount it will save. These amounts are shown in columns (6) and (7) of Exhibit 2.

Your APC is the percentage of your income that you spend. Your APS is the percentage that you save.

The *marginal propensity to consume* (MPC) is the change in consumption resulting from a unit change in income. As you can see from the table, the formula for calculating MPC is

$$MPC = \frac{\text{change in consumption}}{\text{change in income}}$$

The MPC tells you the *fraction of each extra dollar of income that goes into consumption.* An MPC of 0.70, for instance, means that 70 percent of any increase in income will be spent on consumption.

The *marginal propensity to save* (MPS) is the change in saving resulting from a unit change in income:

$$MPS = \frac{\text{change in saving}}{\text{change in income}}$$

The MPS tells you the *fraction of each extra dollar of income that goes into saving.* An MPS of 0.30, for example, means that 30 percent of any increase in income will be saved.

What is the difference between APC and MPC? What is the difference between APS and MPS? At any given level of income, the APC relates total consumption to total income. On the other hand, the MPC relates a *change* in the amount of consumption to a *change* in the amount of income. The "average" may thus be quite different from the "marginal," as you can see from the table in Exhibit 2. The same kind of reasoning applies to the difference between APS and MPS. The "average" and the "marginal" tell you two distinctly different things. Note from the table, however, that, just as APC and APS must always total 1 (or 100 percent) at any income *level,* MPC and MPS must always total 1 (or 100 percent) for each *change* in income.

The MPC and MPS are of great practical value. For example, suppose that the nation is in recession and the MPC for the economy as a whole is 0.70. This means that, to increase the volume of consumption by $700 million in order to move the economy closer to full employment, the level of aggregate disposable income must be raised by $1 billion. As shown in later chapters, government can adopt various economic measures to achieve such a goal.

"Marginals" Are Slopes

By now you have probably recognized an important feature of MPC. Because it is the change in total consumption resulting from a unit change in income, it measures the *slope* (steepness) of the consumption function or line. The slope of any straight line is defined as the number of units it changes vertically for each unit of change horizontally. Thus, in Exhibit 4, the line rises 4 units on the vertical axis for a run of 6 units on the horizontal. Therefore, the slope, which is measured by the rise over the run, is ²/₃.

Similarly, the MPS measures the slope of the saving line. You should be able to verify that the slope of a straight line is the same at every point. This is why the table shows all values of MPC as equal and all values of MPS as equal. That is, the consumption and saving functions in this example are each straight lines.

Exhibit 4
Slope of a Line

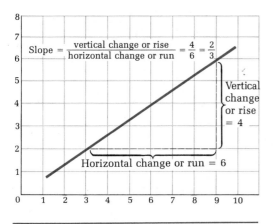

Two Kinds of Changes Involving Consumption

The consumption function (propensity-to-consume curve) expresses a relation between consumption expenditures and income. Your understanding of this concept can serve as a basis for distinguishing between two kinds of variations in consumption. One is called a change in the amount consumed. The other is a change in consumption.

Change in the Amount Consumed

Examine the figures in Exhibit 5. In the upper figure, any movement along the consumption curve represents a *change in the amount consumed*. The change will consist of an increase in the amount consumed if income rises and a decrease in the amount consumed if income falls. This is indicated by the vertical dashed lines. Thus:

1. A movement to the right always signifies an increase in income and hence a movement upward along the existing C curve.

2. A movement to the left indicates a decrease in income and therefore a movement downward along the existing C curve.

Note also in the lower figure that saving, like consumption, varies directly with income. Therefore, a change in the amount saved—either an increase or a decrease—occurs for the same reason as a change in the amount consumed: namely, because of a change in income.

Change in Consumption

A second type of movement, shown in Exhibit 6, is a *change in consumption*. This may take the form of an increase in consumption, whereby the curve shifts to a higher level. Or it may take the form of a decrease in consumption, shown by a shift of the curve to a lower level. An increase in consumption from curve C to curve C' means that, at any given level of income, people are now willing to consume more and save less than before. What does a decrease from curve C to curve C'' mean?

As with supply and demand curves, the consumption curve may shift as a result of a change in any one of the "all other" things that were assumed to remain constant when the curve was initially drawn. What are these factors? Some of the more important ones are:

1. The volume of liquid assets (for example, currency, stocks, or bonds) owned by a household.

2. Expectations of future prices and incomes.

3. Anticipation of product shortages (resulting, for example, from a war or a strike).

4. Credit conditions.

An increase in any one of these factors (and several others that you may be able to think of) can cause an increase in consumption and shift the curve upward. Likewise, a decrease in any one can cause a decrease in consumption and shift the curve downward. Because these factors do not remain constant over the long run, the *true* consumption function for the economy is likely to vary. Some further implications are pointed out in Box 1.

Exhibit 5

Changes in the Amounts Consumed and Saved

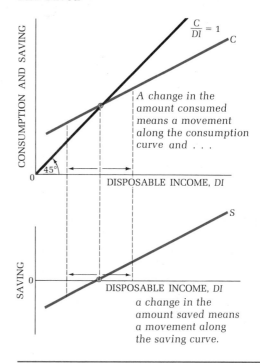

A change in the amount consumed means a movement along the consumption curve and . . .

a change in the amount saved means a movement along the saving curve.

Exhibit 6

Changes in Consumption and Saving

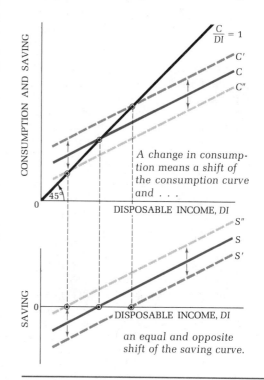

A change in consumption means a shift of the consumption curve and . . .

an equal and opposite shift of the saving curve.

Private Investment Demand

Investment spending on plant, equipment, and inventories is done by the business sector.

"The economy turns on capital investment, and capital investment turns on confidence, and confidence turns on certainty, and certainty turns on predictability." These words, spoken by a major corporation president, suggest that investment is of critical importance to our economy.

Investment, of course, means spending by business firms on physical capital, such as additions to plant, equipment, and inventories. As you know, the private sector's consumption demand and investment demand are the two major components of aggregate demand. Therefore, having studied consumption demand, we must now turn our attention to investment demand.

Investment and Rate of Return

Investment spending depends on expected profitability.

If you were a business executive, what would determine your decision to invest? The fundamental answer, of course, is your profit expectation. If you think a new machine would add to your profit, you will try to purchase it. If you believe that an additional wing on your factory would yield greater profits, you will try to build it.

In the business world, the money you get back each year from an investment, in relation to the investment, is called the *rate of return*. It is always expressed as a percentage. Thus, if you buy land for $1,000 and rent it out for $100 a year, the annual rate of return on your investment is 10 percent:

$$\text{rate of return} = \frac{\text{annual receipts}}{\text{investment}} = \frac{\$100}{\$1,000} = 0.10, \text{ or } 10\%$$

Box 1
The Consumption Function: Three Ideas in One Principle

There is general agreement that consumption depends on income. But the nature of the dependency has long intrigued economists. Over the years, three proposed explanations—called "hypotheses" —have been explored.

Absolute-Income Hypothesis
A family's consumption depends on its *level* of income —the absolute amount available for spending. This concept of the propensity to consume was the one used by Keynes.

Relative-Income Hypothesis
A family's consumption depends on its previous peak level of income and/or the relative position that the family occupies along the income scale. In other words, spending behavior is influenced by the highest past income levels to which people have become accustomed, and by the spending behavior of other individuals in the same socioeconomic environment.

Permanent-Income Hypothesis A family's consumption depends on its anticipated long-run or permanent income. This is the average income expected to be received over a number of years. In

addition, a family's consumption expenditures are approximately proportional to its permanent income.

All three theories fit the definition of the *propensity to consume*—the law stating that consumption increases with income, but not as fast. However, the two latter explanations have been found, for certain purposes, to be significant improvements over the first.

For example, the relative-income hypothesis recognizes that people try to maintain their previous higher standard of living when their incomes decline. The theory also acknowledges that a fam-

ily's consumption patterns are influenced by social pressures as well as by income.

The permanent-income hypothesis helps explain why people's expectations of their long-run income determine their purchases of large-expenditure items, such as houses, expensive jewelry, and furs.

As you can see from these theories, *consumer behavior is strongly affected by psychological as well as economic factors.*

Instead of using the expression "rate of return," economists employ the phrase "marginal efficiency of investment." Although it involves the same idea, it is a more precise and more meaningful term—as you will come to appreciate.

These concepts are worth repeating for emphasis.

> The profit from an investment, in relation to the investment, is expressed as a percentage. It measures the rate of return on the investment. Economists call the expected rate of return on an addition to capital investment the *marginal efficiency of investment* (MEI). More precisely, it is the expected rate of return over cost of an additional unit of a capital good. Thus, you might have an *MEI* or expected rate of return of 25 percent for one type of investment, 15 percent for another, and so on.

Understanding the MEI

You can gain a better understanding of the *MEI* by studying its graph in Figure (*a*) of Exhibit 7. The figure shows that, at any given time, a business firm is faced with a number of investment opportunities. These may include renovating its existing plant, purchasing new machines, acquiring additional power facilities, or installing a computer system. Each project competes for a firm's limited funds. However, some projects are expected to be more profitable—that is, to have a higher rate of return (or *MEI*)—than others. In view of this, which projects should management select? Or, to put it differently, how much investment expenditure should management undertake?

The first step in answering this question is to imagine that the managers of a firm *rank* alternative investment projects in decreasing order of their *MEI*s. In Figure (*a*), each project's cost and corresponding *MEI* are shown. The most attractive investment open to the firm is the renovation of its plant at a cost of $2 million. For this, the firm anticipates a rate of return, or *MEI*, of 27 percent, which is read from the vertical axis. The next most profitable investment is the addition of a new wing to its factory at a cost of $1 million, for which the *MEI* is 20 percent. Each remaining investment project is interpreted similarly. If we assume that the risks of loss associated with these investments are the same, the descending order of *MEI*s suggests two things:

1. Fewer investment opportunities are available to a firm at higher rates of return than at lower ones. For example, it is harder to find investments yielding 25 percent than to find investments yielding 10 percent.

2. A firm will tend to choose those investment projects that have the highest *MEI*s. Therefore, a project with a higher anticipated rate of return over cost is likely to be selected over a project with a lower one.

Cost of Funds: The Rate of Interest

Once the *MEI* (or rate of return) on an investment is estimated, the next step is to establish the cost of funds needed to finance the investment. Only then can you decide if the investment is worth undertaking.

The cost of funds needed to finance an investment is expressed as a *percentage*. Thus, if a business firm borrows money for investment and agrees to pay an annual interest charge of, say, 10 percent, then that is the firm's cost of funds. Alternatively, if the firm uses its own money instead of borrowing, the interest return sacrificed by not lending the

Exhibit 7
Investment Demand in the Private Sector

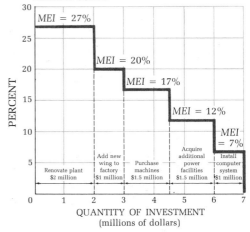

(*a*) MARGINAL EFFICIENCY OF INVESTMENT FOR AN INDIVIDUAL FIRM: A FIRM'S INVESTMENT DEMAND CURVE

Figure (*a*). The solid stepped line is an individual firm's *MEI* (or rate-of-return) curve. It shows the amount of investment the firm will make at various interest rates or cost of funds at any given time. The *MEI* curve is thus the firm's demand curve for investment.
There are many such stepped curves at any given time, one for each firm in the economy.

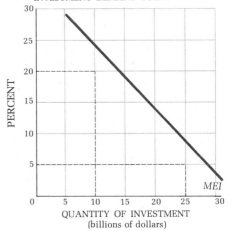

(*b*) MARGINAL EFFICIENCY OF INVESTMENT FOR ALL FIRMS: THE PRIVATE SECTOR'S INVESTMENT DEMAND CURVE

Figure (*b*). The *MEI* curve for all firms is a smooth line obtained by summing individual *MEI* curves. It shows the total amount of private-sector investment that will be made at various interest rates or costs. The *MEI* curve in this chart is the economy's aggregate demand curve for private-sector investment.

money in the financial markets (through the purchase of bonds or other securities) may be thought of as the company's cost of funds. This cost, of course, is the *opportunity cost* of the funds. In any case:

> The *MEI* and the cost of funds are each quoted as percentages. Therefore, they can be easily compared. This makes it possible to determine the amount of investment that will take place.

The *MEI* and the Interest Rate

The amount of investment spending that is undertaken is determined by the expected rate of return relative to the cost.

How much investment will the firm undertake? To answer this, we must understand that at any given time there is an interest rate in the market that represents the current cost of funds to the firm. We will assume that this interest rate or cost of funds is the same whether the firm borrows the money or uses its own. It follows that a higher interest cost will mean a lower expected return and therefore a smaller volume of investment. Conversely, a lower interest cost will mean a higher expected return and hence a larger volume of investment. In general terms, we may conclude:

> Investment by a firm occurs when the *MEI* (expected rate of return) on an addition to investment exceeds the rate of interest or cost of funds that is incurred in making the investment.

For example, look again at Figure (a) of Exhibit 7. The graph tells you that, at an interest cost (shown on the vertical axis) of, say, 13 percent, this particular firm would demand $4.5 million for investment. Of this amount, $2 million would be spent on renovating its plant in anticipation of a return or *MEI* of 27 percent. In addition, $1 million would be allocated to a new wing for its factory for an expected *MEI* of 20 percent. Finally, $1.5 million would be used to buy new machines in anticipation of an *MEI* of 17 percent. If the interest cost should fall to 6 percent, the firm will demand an *additional* $2.5 million, or a *total* of $7 million. The extra amount would be invested in the next two projects—power facilities and a computer system. In general, therefore, the firm's total amount demanded for investment funds depends on its *MEI* relative to the interest rate or cost of funds.

This analysis leads to two important principles. *At any given time:*

The investment demand curve, whether for a firm or for the entire business sector, relates the amount of investment to the interest rate (cost of funds).

1. A demand curve relates the quantities of a commodity that buyers would be willing and able to purchase at various prices. For business investments, the prices are interest rates (costs of funds) to business firms. Hence, the *MEI* curve shows the amounts of investment that a firm would be willing and able to undertake at various interest rates. This is illustrated by the solid irregular line in Figure (a) of Exhibit 7. It follows that *a firm's MEI curve is its demand curve for investment.*

2. Each firm's own *MEI* curve is based on its particular investment needs and expectations. If the individual *MEI* curves are summed horizontally, we get the *MEI* curve for all firms in the economy. As a result, the irregularities disappear, giving a smooth continuous line like the one in Figure (b) of Exhibit 7. *The aggregate MEI curve depicts total private investment demand at different rates of interest.* For example, at an interest rate of 20 percent, the amount of private-sector investment would be $10 billion. If the interest rate fell to 5 percent, the amount of private-sector investment would increase to $25 billion.

Determinants of the *MEI*: Shifts of the Curve

The *MEI* curve is an investment demand curve. Therefore, like any demand curve, it may shift to the right or left as the result of a change in one or more of the factors that determine it. At least four factors are particularly important:

1. Expected Product Demand To businesses, the *expected* net return on an investment will depend largely on the demand that is anticipated for the product produced by the investment. For example, if you are a shoe manufacturer, your expected *MEI* for shoe machinery will be influenced by your anticipated demand for shoes. Similarly, for the economy as a whole, the expected return on new investment will be influenced by business executives' anticipations of total consumer spending on the products of businesses.

2. Technology and Innovation Advances in technology and the introduction of new products generally require the construction of new plants or the installation of new equipment. This stimulates the demand for additional capital.

3. Cost of New Capital Goods Changes in the cost of new plant or equipment affect business firms' demand for them. Thus, a rise in the cost of new capital goods shifts the *MEI* curve to the left; a fall in cost shifts the curve to the right.

4. Corporate Income Tax Rates Businesses are interested in expected rates of return on investment expenditures *after* allowances for corporation income taxes. Hence, an increase in the tax rates, other things being equal, shifts the *MEI* curve to the left; a decrease in the tax rates shifts the curve to the right.

These, as well as other economic and psychological conditions, affect businesses' expected rates of return on investment. Because one or more of these factors is always changing, the *MEI* curve is continually shifting either to the right or to the left. As a result, the level of private investment in the economy fluctuates widely over the years, as shown in Exhibit 8.

Indeed:

> In Keynesian theory, fluctuation in private investment is the single most important cause of fluctuations in income and employment. This, in turn, is the major reason for periods of prosperity and recession.

Government Demand and Net Foreign Demand

The remaining components of aggregate demand stem from government and from international sources. Government demand, which consists of public investment expenditures, depends to a large extent on public needs. These include such things as highways, schools, welfare benefits, and defense requirements. The volume of government demand is independent of profit expectations and, beyond the minimum levels required by society, is determined at will by government. No scientific law or guiding set of principles exists to predict changes in the level of public investment.

Net foreign demand, which is the difference between our exports and our imports, is another factor affecting aggregate demand. In the

Exhibit 8
The Instability of Private Investment

The *MEI* curve is continually shifting, owing to changes in the factors that determine it. As a result, private investment spending fluctuates widely over the years.

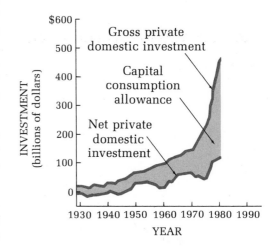

next several chapters, attention will be focused entirely on domestic factors affecting the economy. Therefore, the influence of net foreign demand on the nation's income and employment will be neglected for the time being.

Conclusion: Reviewing the Basic Relationships

You now have the basic building blocks necessary for understanding the Keynesian theory of income and employment. This theory will be developed further in the following chapters. In the meantime, you can test your knowledge of the basic relationships explained thus far by making sure you understand the equations presented in Exhibit 9.

Exhibit 9

Some Key Relations in the Keynesian Theory of Income and Employment

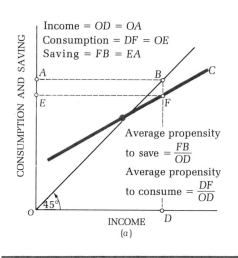

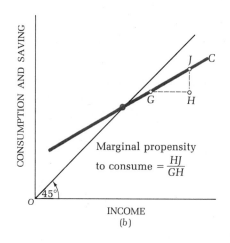

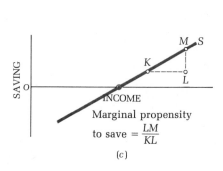

What You Have Learned in This Chapter

1. The classical theory of income and employment holds that, in a competitive capitalistic system, supply creates its own demand. That is, aggregate demand equals aggregate income or output. Therefore, the economy automatically tends toward full employment through the free operation of the market system. In this system, prices, wages, and interest rates are free to adjust to their full-employment levels.

2. The Keynesian theory of income and employment is rooted in several fundamental ideas. Among them:

• Aggregate demand may be greater than, equal to, or less than full-employment aggregate income.

• The interest rate need not equate intended saving and intended investment, because these are done by different people for different purposes.

• Prices and wages are not flexible—especially on the down side—because of resistance by business monopolies and unions and also because of minimum-wage legislation and other institutional forces.

For these reasons, the economy may not necessarily adjust itself to full-employment equilibrium.

3. The propensity to consume, or the consumption function, expresses a relationship between consumption and income. The relationship, based on observation and experience, is such that, as income increases, consumption increases, but not as fast as income.

4. At any given level of income, the average propensity to consume (APC) is the proportion of income spent on consumption. Similarly, the average propensity to save is the proportion of income saved. Therefore, APC + APS = 1 (or 100 percent). Out of any given increase in income, the marginal propensity to consume (MPC) is the proportion of the increase spent on consumption. Similarly, the marginal propensity to save is the proportion of the increase saved. Hence, $MPC + MPS = 1$ (or 100 percent).

5. A *change in the amount consumed* means a movement along the consumption curve due to a change in income. A *change in consumption* means a shift of the entire consumption curve to a new level. This occurs because of a change in one or more of the "all other" things that are assumed to be constant when the curve is initially drawn. These factors include the volume of liquid assets owned by households, expectations of future prices and income, anticipation of product shortages, and credit conditions.

6. Investment demand, like consumption and saving, is a major variable in income and employment theory. The expected rate of return on an investment is called the marginal efficiency of investment (MEI). Investment occurs when the MEI exceeds the rate of interest or the cost of funds that is incurred in making the investment. In general, private investment spending depends on the profit expectations of businesses. These expectations are determined by such factors as expected product demand, the rate of technology and innovation, cost of new capital goods, and corporate income-tax rates. For these reasons, private investment tends to be highly volatile over the years and is the major cause of fluctuations in economic activity.

For Discussion

1. *Terms and concepts to review:*
classical economics
Keynesian economics
Say's Law
aggregate demand
aggregate supply
saving
interest
consumption
dissaving
propensity to consume
propensity to save
average propensity to consume
average propensity to save
marginal propensity to consume
marginal propensity to save
slope
change in amount consumed
change in consumption
absolute-income hypothesis

relative-income hypothesis
permanent-income hypothesis
investment
marginal efficiency of investment

2. Of what significance are interest rates and prices in the classical model?

3. Does Say's Law apply to *individual* goods? Explain.

4. Why do people save? Why do businesses invest?

5. "During a recession, a firm will probably increase its sales if it cuts its prices, and it will reduce its costs if it cuts its wages. It follows that the whole economy will be better off if all firms do this." True or false? Comment.

6. Look up the meaning of *Engel's Laws* in the Dictionary at the back of the book. Then express Engel's Laws in terms of the average propensity to consume (APC).

7. Why does the APC differ from the MPC? Why does the APS differ from the MPS?

8. What factors other than income are likely to be most important in determining consumption?

9. Complete the following table on the assumption that 50 percent of any increase in income is spent on consumption. Sketch the graphs of consumption and saving. Label all curves.

DI	C	S	APC	APS	MPC	MPS
$100	$150					
200						
300						
400						
500						
600						

10. Would you expect expenditures on consumer durable goods to fluctuate more widely than expenditures on consumer nondurable goods? Explain your answer.

11. What would be the effect on aggregate consumption if social welfare expenditures on public hospitals, parks, medical care, and so on were financed entirely by our progressive income tax system? Does it make any difference if there are tax loopholes?

12. How would you distinguish between a "change in the amount invested" and a "change in investment"? Explain.

Portfolio

The Classical Economists: Adam Smith's "Sons" and "Daughters"

Dictionaire de l'Economie Politique, Paris: Librarie de Guillaumin, 1864

Adam Smith

"I am a beau only to my books," remarked Adam Smith. Little did the shy, absent-minded scholar suspect that, though he would never marry and probably never have any love affairs, his offspring would include numerous "children" and "grandchildren."

Smith was a professor of philosophy at the University of Glasglow. His masterpiece, *The Wealth of Nations* (1776), marked the beginning of *classical economics*. This body of thought dominated the Western world during the nineteenth and early twentieth centuries. Classical economists typically emphasized people's self-interest and the operation of universal economic laws. These laws tend automatically to guide the economy toward full-employment equilibrium if the government adheres to a policy of laissez-faire or noninterventionism.

During the nineteenth century these ideas, initiated by Adam Smith, were refined and expanded by more than a dozen of his "sons" and "daughters." Among them were seven who, for different reasons, are especially worthy of mention.

Jean Baptiste Say (1767–1832)

"Supply creates its own demand." This was the famous Law of Markets expounded by the French economist Jean Baptiste Say in his *Treatise on Political Economy* (1803). This work presented the first popular and systematic presentation of Adam Smith's ideas. As a result, it established Say as one of the leading economists of the early nineteenth century.

Say's Law became central to classical economic thinking. In modern terminology the Law meant simply that

Dictionaire de l'Economie Politique, Paris: Librarie de Guillaumin, 1864

Jean Baptiste Say

the level of aggregate output (GNP) always equaled the level of aggregate income (*GNI*). This income enabled society to buy (that is, to demand) the output produced. Therefore, general overproduction of goods (due to a deficiency in aggregate demand) was impossible.

But what if businesses misjudged the markets for their goods? In that case, the classicists contended, overproduction of specific commodities could and would occur. But such errors would only be temporary and would be corrected as entrepreneurs strove to fulfill consumers' preferences by shifting resources out of the production of unprofitable goods and into the production of profitable ones.

Say's Law was occasionally challenged by some nineteenth-century dissenters. However, it took almost a century and a half for the Law of Markets to be put to rest. This was done by John Maynard Keynes in *The General Theory of Employment, Interest and Money* (1936).

Thomas Robert Malthus (1766–1834)

As the eighteenth century drew to a close, England found itself facing mounting

Brown Brothers

Thomas Malthus

social problems. Among them were widespread poverty, the growth of urban slums, and massive unemployment. These social problems resulted from economic dislocations caused by years of war with France. In addition, the factory system of production had begun and was displacing numerous workers.

It befell a hitherto unknown English clergyman, Thomas Robert Malthus, to explain these problems. In his famous *Essay on Population* (1798, revised 1803), he expounded the belief that population would tend to outrun the food supply. The result would be bare subsistence for the laboring class. This prophecy, of course, has become a stark reality in many of the overcrowded, poor countries of the world.

Malthus also contributed significantly to economic thought. In his *Principles of Political Economy* (1820), he developed the concept of "effective demand," which he defined as the level of aggregate demand necessary to maintain full production. If effective demand declined, he said, overproduction would result. Malthus thus not only disagreed with Say on the Law of Markets but anticipated the Keynesian concept of full-employment aggregate demand by more than a century.

David Ricardo (1772–1823)

Generally considered to be the greatest of the classical economists, David Ricardo was the first to view the economy as an analytical model. That is, he saw the economic system as an elaborate mechanism with interrelated parts. His task was to study the system and to discover the laws that determine its behavior. In so doing, Ricardo formu-

David Ricardo

lated theories of value, wages, rent, and profit. These theories, although not entirely original, were for the first time stated completely, authoritatively, and systematically. Portions of them became the basis of many subsequent writings by later scholars, including Marx and Keynes.

Ricardo, an English businessman rather than an academician, wrote a number of brilliant papers. His ideas were largely incorporated in his work, *Principles of Political Economy and Taxation* (1817). The book was an immediate success, and it attracted many disciples. As a result, Ricardo's influence became pervasive and lasting. Indeed, Ricardian economics became a synonym for classical political economy (or "classical economics," as we call it today). Fifty years were to pass before that influence waned.

Like his predecessors, Ricardo was mainly concerned with the forces that determine the production of an economy's wealth and its distribution among the various classes of society. But he was not only a "pure" theorist, as were some of the other classical economists. He also made major policy recommendations to Parliament concerning the dominant social and economic problems of his day. As a result, many of Ricardo's ideas have become pillars of economics and are as relevant today as when he first expressed them.

John Stuart Mill (1806–1873)

Known equally well as a political philosopher and as an economist, the Englishman John Stuart Mill was the last of the major classical economists. His great two-volume treatise, *Principles of Political Economy* (1848), was a masterful synthesis of classical ideas. As a consequence, the book became a standard text in economics for several decades. Numerous students in Europe and America obtained their knowledge of economics from this basic work. So, too, did a number of American presidents—including Abraham Lincoln—although they did not always correctly apply the principles they learned.

Mill's major objective was economic reform. Although he believed in laissez-faire, he went beyond the "natural law of political economy." He did so by advocating worker education, democratic producer cooperatives, taxation of unearned gains from land, redistribution of wealth, shorter working days, improvements in working conditions, and social control of monopoly. These measures, Mill felt, would assure to the individual worker the benefits of his or her contribution to production without violating the "immortal principles" of economics laid down by Ricardo.

It is easy to see why contemporaries of Mill often labeled him a socialist. In reality, however, he believed too strongly in individual freedom to advocate major government involvement in the economy. By today's standards, Mill probably would be classified as a moderate conservative.

Jane Haldimand Marcet (1769–1858)

In addition to his four famous "sons" (and to many others who were not so famous), Adam Smith had three "daughters" who, in the nineteenth century, distinguished themselves in the classical tradition. Their fame, however, rests on their achieve-

ments in economic education —the teaching of economics —rather than on the formulation of economic principles. As Dorothy Thomson of City University of New York has remarked, "At a time when it was considered unfeminine for women to show that they have brains, it required courage for anyone to attempt to break the mold."

The first woman to break the mold in economics was an English writer, Jane Haldimand Marcet. In 1816, she published one of several economics books, *Conversations on Political Economy*. In this and subsequent works she conveyed in dialogue form the teachings of her predecessors and contemporaries—Smith, Say, Malthus, and Ricardo. Marcet thus became one of the first popular synthesizers of economic ideas. In doing so, she established an original approach to economic education and to the writing of elementary-school textbooks. Many teachers and writers subsequently adopted her style of presentation.

Harriet Martineau (1802–1876)

Among the many people influenced by Jane Marcet's *Conversations*, there was one who saw in it the possibility

John Stuart Mill

Harriet Martineau

of conveying the basic principles of economics in yet another lively dimension. That person was Harriet Martineau. To this popular English author, economics was more than a collection of principles. It was a living experience conveyed through the "natural workings of social life."

This belief led to the publication of her pioneering *Illustrations of Political Economy* (in 9 volumes, 1832–1834). Unlike any prior work in economics, this one was written in narrative form, almost like a collection of short stories, and it was illustrated throughout with applications. The basic principles of economics were thus integrated with real-life experiences instead of being taught separately. Today the teaching of many business and some economics courses by the "case method" owes much of its success to the path-breaking approach initially established by Harriet Martineau.

Millicent Garrett Fawcett (1847–1929)

The last great synthesis of classical economics was written by John Stuart Mill in 1848. This huge, two-volume work, however, was not the kind of book to be read and absorbed easily. What was needed was a more concise and simplified version— one that would present the most important principles of economics in a brief and readily understandable way.

It fell to Millicent Garrett Fawcett to write that book. A well-known English author and strong supporter of women's rights, she and her husband (a professor of political economy at Cambridge University) were close friends and admirers of Mill. Her

Political Economy for Beginners (1870), based on Mill's treatise, was an enormous success. It went through 10 editions—an average of one every four years—thus ranking as one of the most enduring textbooks in publishing history.

In subsequent years, Fawcett published a number of other books—two of them dealing with economic principles and issues. In these, as in the successive editions of her *Political Economy for Beginners*, she analyzed and interpreted important economic issues of her time. Her viewpoints, however, were always "classical," with an emphasis on the desirability of social reform in the spirit that John Stuart Mill would have advocated. As stated in her text, "The present system does not work so well as to be absolutely incapable of improvement. We ought to be ready to admit that some improvement is necessary in a community in which a considerable proportion of the population are either paupers or on the brink of pauperism."

Neoclassical "Grandchildren"

In today's terminology, it would be correct to say that the classical economists tended to be mostly concerned with macroeconomic problems. But in the 1870s, approximately 100 years after the appearance of *The Wealth of Nations*, economic thinking began undergoing a revolutionary change. A new point of view and a powerful new tool called "marginal" analysis came into existence. You have already learned about the marginal propensity to consume and the marginal propensity to save. These are only two of many marginal

concepts that abound in economics.

The new view that was born in the 1870s is known as "neoclassical economics." It became the foundation of today's microeconomics. In general, neoclassical economists revised, refined, and extended many classical concepts and developed numerous new ones as well. The founders of, and contributors to, neoclassical economics, many of whose ideas are studied in modern microeconomics, may therefore be thought of as Adam Smith's "grandchildren."

Conclusion: Continuing Problems

Neoclassical economics dominated Western thought for seven decades—from the 1870s to the 1930s. In 1936, Keynes's great treatise, *The General Theory of Employment, Interest and Money*, gave birth to modern macroeconomics. Since then, enormous advances have been made both in macroeconomics and in microeconomics, providing much deeper insights into how our economic system operates. However, many of the same problems that have always concerned economists are still with us. This suggests that, in economics as in other social sciences, it is not usually the problems themselves that change; rather, it is our understanding of them that changes.

Millicent Garrett Fawcett

Income and Employment Determination: The Keynesian Model

Learning guide
Watch for the answers to these important questions

What is the nature of the Keynesian model? How are consumption, saving, and investment brought together to determine the economy's equilibrium levels of output and employment?

Are there alternative ways of explaining the concept of equilibrium? If so, what are they? How are they depicted graphically?

How do changes in investment relate to the level of income? What is this relationship called? What, essentially, does the relationship show?

Why might an increase in saving be undesirable for the economy? What must happen to assure that it will *not* be undesirable?

What is meant by inflationary and recessionary gaps? How are they defined? How are they illustrated graphically?

You have already learned that the crucial factor in determining whether we live in a state of full employment or a state of unemployment is the level of investment. The reasons for this will become increasingly evident in the following pages. There the level of investment is discussed in conjunction with the levels of consumption and saving. This will enable you to see how the three variables interact to bring about equilibrium in the economy as a whole.

After completing this chapter you will have a better understanding of the way in which economic fluctuations arise and of government policies designed to minimize them. Those policies are of great importance. They can help determine whether our economy will achieve the goals of full employment, price stability, and economic growth.

The Basic Keynesian Model of Income and Employment

The time has come to examine a model that relates the concepts of consumption, saving, and investment. The model shows how these variables interact to determine the overall level of income and employment. This is the model that Keynes and his followers formulated in an effort to explain the workings of the modern macroeconomy.

The model is "basic" in that it focuses on the barest essentials. That is, it covers only the household and business sectors while neglecting, for the time being, the public and foreign sectors. With this model, you can learn how the simplest system works before you are introduced to additional factors that make the model more representative of the real world.

The Keynesian model describes a set of relationships between consumption, saving, and investment.

Exhibit 1

Determination of Income and Employment Equilibrium

(hypothetical economy, billions of dollars)

Explanation of the Table:

Columns (1) and (2) It is *assumed* that, for every level of aggregate supply or output, there is a corresponding level of employment. Further, these variables are directly related: As aggregate supply increases, employment increases; as aggregate supply decreases, employment decreases.

(**Note** The assumption of a close relationship between output and employment is both plausible and useful for our present model. However, some exceptions will be noted in later chapters.)

Columns (3) and (4) Consumption and saving vary directly with income [column (1)]. It is useful to think of consumption and saving as the amounts that households *plan* or *intend* to consume and save at each income level.

Column (5) Net investment is used rather than gross investment because we are dealing with NNP in column (1) rather than GNP as a measure of the economy's output. (You should recall that net investment equals gross private domestic investment minus the capital consumption allowance; actual figures are found in the front endpapers of this book.) As explained in the text, the level of net investment is assumed to be independent of NNP or DI [column (1)] and therefore constant *in relation to them*.

Column (6) Aggregate demand is simply the sum of intended consumption and investment at each level of income in column (1). Aggregate demand thus denotes total desired spending on output or, in other words, the total amount of consumption and investment that all sectors of the economy *plan* to undertake at each income level.

Columns (7) and (8) The change in inventory is the difference between aggregate supply and aggregate demand, or between saving and investment. As explained in the text, the change in inventory level tends toward equilibrium—that is, zero *unplanned* or undesired accumulation or depletion. When this inventory level is reached, income and employment are also in equilibrium, with no tendency to change.

You will find that, despite its simplicity, the model is by no means an oversimplification of reality. Indeed, it sheds considerable light on some fundamental and rather complex economic problems.

Structure of the Model

We begin by examining the structure of the model shown in Exhibit 1. The explanation accompanying the table should be read carefully because it describes the meanings of the columns and their relationships. Once these are understood, you can turn your attention to Exhibit 2, which shows the graphs of the data from the table in Exhibit 1.

Factors in Determination of Equilibrium (dollar amounts in billions)

(1) Aggregate supply (output = income),* NNP = DI	(2) Level of employ-ment (millions)	(3) Consump-tion, C	(4) Saving, S (1) − (3)	(5) Net invest-ment, I	(6) Aggregate demand, AD (3) + (5)	(7) Inventory accumu-lation (+) or deple-tion (−) (1) − (6) or (4) − (5)	(8) Direction of income and employment
$100	30	$140	− $ 40	$40	$180	− $80	increase
200	35	220	− 20	40	260	− 60	increase
300	40	300	0	40	340	− 40	increase
400	45	380	20	40	420	− 20	increase
500	50	460	40	40	500	0	equilibrium
600	55	540	60	40	580	+ 20	decrease
700	60	620	80	40	660	+ 40	decrease
800	65	700	100	40	740	+ 60	decrease
900	70	780	120	40	820	+ 80	decrease

* Includes only the private sector (households and firms), not the public sector (government) or the foreign sector. Also, households are assumed to be the sole source of saving. Therefore, NNP as a measure of aggregate supply equals NI, PI, and DI because there are no taxes, transfer payments, and so on (that is, there is no government sector). Thus, the total income received by households (DI) equals the net value of the economy's output (NNP).

Some important features of the graphs in Exhibit 2 should be noted:

Figure (a) This depicts both aggregate supply and aggregate demand. The graph of aggregate supply is the 45° line. It shows the amount of total output (consisting of consumption and investment goods), measured on the vertical axis, that will be made available for sale at each level of income or net national product (NNP), shown on the horizontal axis. The graph of aggregate demand shows the amount that will be spent for consumption and investment (measured on the vertical axis) at each level of income (measured on the horizontal axis).

Figures (a) and (b) These show that the graphs of consumption and saving vary directly with income. This is what you would expect from your knowledge of the propensities to consume and save.

Figure (b) This also depicts the graph of net investment—a horizontal line. Why is net investment the same at all levels of aggregate supply?

As emphasized in the previous chapter:

> The investment plans of businesses depend on the marginal efficiency of investment (*MEI*) relative to the interest rate. The *MEI* is determined by such factors as expected product demand, the rate of technology and innovation, the cost of new capital goods, and corporate income tax rates. Therefore, the level of investment that businesses *plan* or *intend* to undertake is assumed to remain constant in relation to output. This level, however, varies widely over time, as you have already seen.

The assumption of a constant level of investment with respect to output plays a fundamental role in the present "basic" Keynesian model. Later, the assumption will be modified to permit the introduction of more complex considerations.

The amount of investment undertaken by the business sector will be assumed to remain constant with respect to the economy's income.

The Equilibrium Level of Income and Employment

You now have the information needed to interpret the model. The question to be answered is: *What will be the equilibrium levels of income and employment—and why?* In other words, where will the level of output and the corresponding level of employment finally settle? As you can see, there are two parts to the question.

1. Columns (7) and (8) of the table in Exhibit 1 show that, at the *equilibrium level of output*, business firms are holding the precise level of inventory they desire. That is, at the equilibrium level, businesses are neither accumulating nor depleting their stock. This is because the factor determining the change in inventory—namely, the difference between aggregate supply and aggregate demand or between planned saving and investment—is zero.

The equilibrium point *E* in the figures in Exhibit 2 depicts these notions graphically. The vertical line shows that, in this hypothetical economy, equilibrium occurs at an output level of $500 billion and an employment level of 50 million persons. The *what* part of the question above has thus been answered. The next part concerns the *why*.

2. The best way to understand why income and employment tend toward equilibrium is to ask yourself what happens when they are not in equilibrium. For example, suppose that *NNP* or *DI* is greater than $500 billion—say, $600 billion. This means that businesses are paying $600 billion in the form of wages, rent, interest, and profit. At the same time, the corresponding level of total spending or aggregate demand, *C* + *I*, which is the amount that business firms are taking in, is $580 billion. As you can see from the table and the figures, aggregate supply exceeds aggregate demand, and the amount that households intend to save exceeds the amount that businesses intend to invest. Therefore, businesses find their sales to be less than anticipated. This imbalance causes firms to accumulate inventories beyond desired levels, so managers cut back on production and lay off workers. As a result, output, income, and employment decrease toward their equilibrium levels, as shown by the arrows in the figures.

Conversely, at any output less than the equilibrium level—say, $400 billion—the reverse occurs. In Figure (*a*), aggregate demand exceeds aggregate supply, and in Figure (*b*), businesses' intended investment exceeds households' intended saving. Households are consuming

In disequilibrium, aggregate supply is not equal to aggregate demand and intended saving is not equal to intended investment.

Exhibit 2

Determination of Income and Employment Equilibrium

(based on data in Exhibit 1)

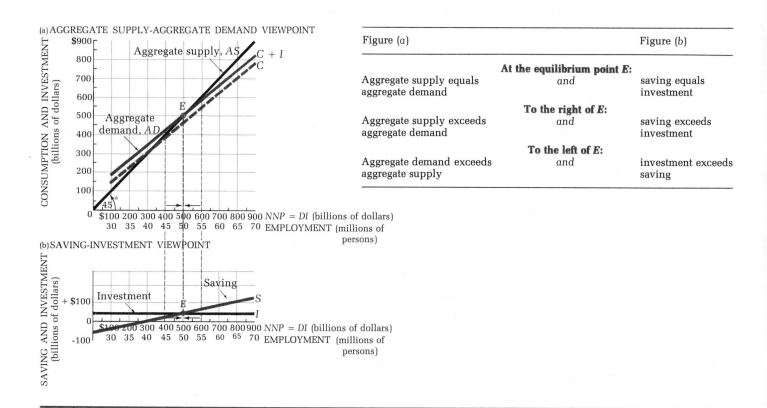

(a) AGGREGATE SUPPLY-AGGREGATE DEMAND VIEWPOINT

CONSUMPTION AND INVESTMENT (billions of dollars)

Aggregate supply, AS
C + I
C
Aggregate demand, AD
E
45°

$100 200 300 400 500 600 700 800 900 NNP = DI (billions of dollars)
30 35 40 45 50 55 60 65 70 EMPLOYMENT (millions of persons)

(b) SAVING-INVESTMENT VIEWPOINT

SAVING AND INVESTMENT (billions of dollars)

+$100
Investment
Saving
E
S
I
0
-100

$100 200 300 400 500 600 700 800 900 NNP = DI (billions of dollars)
30 35 40 45 50 55 60 65 70 EMPLOYMENT (millions of persons)

Figure (a)		Figure (b)
At the equilibrium point E:		
Aggregate supply equals aggregate demand	*and*	saving equals investment
To the right of E:		
Aggregate supply exceeds aggregate demand	*and*	saving exceeds investment
To the left of E:		
Aggregate demand exceeds aggregate supply	*and*	investment exceeds saving

goods at a faster rate than firms are producing them. As a result, business inventories are being depleted—they are falling below desired levels. Managers then seek to expand production and to hire more workers. This causes output, income, and employment to increase toward their equilibrium levels, as indicated by the arrows in the charts.

Thus, three fundamental conclusions may be drawn from this model:

1. Income and employment tend toward an equilibrium level at which aggregate supply equals aggregate demand and intended saving equals intended investment.

2. The movement toward equilibrium takes place as businesses seek to eliminate unplanned inventory changes.

3. Equilibrium can occur at *any* level of employment, not necessarily at full employment. This is because equilibrium is determined by the intersection of aggregate demand with aggregate supply (or saving with investment), as shown in the figures.

Injections and Withdrawals: The "Bathtub Theorem"

A further understanding of these ideas can be gained by expressing them in terms of a physical analogy.

For example, suppose that we use the notions of "injections" and "withdrawals" to account for expansions and contractions in the economy's circular flow of income. These terms can be defined in the following way:

1. Injections These are expenditures that are not dependent on income. Examples are investment, government spending, and exports. The effects of these expenditures are to increase aggregate demand and thus to raise the economy's level of income and employment.

2. Withdrawals These are "leakages" from total income. Examples are household saving, business saving, taxes, and imports. The effects of such leakages are to decrease aggregate demand and thus to reduce the economy's level of income and employment.

The significance of these terms can be visualized by referring back to the figures in Exhibit 2. Injections may be represented by investment (I), and withdrawals or leakages may be represented by saving (S). As you have already learned, equilibrium will occur where $I = S$, the level of income and employment at which injections and withdrawals are equal.

We can now illustrate these ideas by means of the "bathtub theorem"; see Exhibit 3.

Planned and Realized Saving and Investment: Another View of Equilibrium *

The concept of equilibrium may be approached from yet another point of view. For example, it has been emphasized above that, in equilibrium, *intended* saving equals *intended* investment. What does this mean? How do adjustments in inventory levels bring about stability of income and employment?

When you studied the operation of supply and demand in an earlier chapter, you saw that buyers and sellers are each influenced by different factors. Consequently, their plans or intentions as reflected by market schedules or curves do not coincide. That is, the number of units of a commodity actually purchased is always equal to the number actually sold. However, the quantities that buyers *plan* to buy and that sellers *plan* to offer will always differ over the full range of their curves—except in equilibrium, where the scheduled amounts intersect.

A similar idea exists with respect to saving and investment. As you have seen, *savers and investors are different people with different motivations.* Therefore, their plans to save and invest are not identical at all levels of output. Although saving always equals actual or realized investment, saving seldom equals *planned* investment—except at the equilibrium level of output.

You can get a better understanding of these ideas by recalling the meaning of investment. As you have already learned in the study of national-income accounting, *investment consists of replacements or additions to the nation's stock of capital, including its plant, equipment, and inventories.* Against this background, investment expenditures may be divided into two parts:

1. Planned Investment Expenditures on plant, equipment, and inventories undertaken *intentionally* by businesses.

2. Unplanned Investment Changes in inventory that occur unexpectedly because businesses experience unplanned differences between the

* **Note to Instructor** This section is optional. It may be omitted without affecting continuity.

Exhibit 3
Injections and Withdrawals:
The "Bathtub Theorem"

Investment may be thought of as an injection into the income stream; saving may be thought of as a withdrawal. Hence, the water in the bathtub can be in equilibrium at any level as long as the inflow equals the outflow. If the inflow exceeds the outflow, the level in the tub will rise. If the outflow exceeds the inflow, the level in the tub will fall.

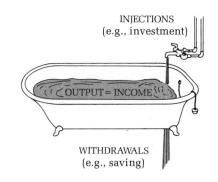

INJECTIONS
(e.g., investment)

OUTPUT = INCOME

WITHDRAWALS
(e.g., saving)

Exhibit 4
Planned and Realized Saving and Investment

Figure (a): Unplanned investment (and disinvestment), reflected by changes in inventory, occurs at output levels at which aggregate demand differs from aggregate supply.

Figure (b): Saving and investment, as shown by the S and I curves, are planned by different people with different motivations. Hence, saving and investment are not equal —except in equilibrium, where the curves intersect. But for any realized level of income, saving always equals realized investment.

aggregate demand for goods and the aggregate supply to them. [**Note** Refer back to Exhibit 1, column (7), of this chapter to see how unexpected inventory changes arise.]

These concepts are summarized by the following equation:

Actual or realized investment

= planned investment + unplanned investment

intentional expenditures on plant, equipment, and inventories — unexpected inventory changes

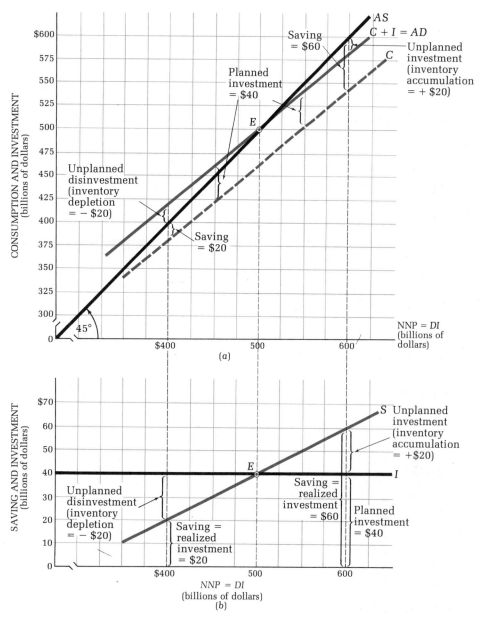

(a)

(b)

Three Possible Cases

It has been emphasized that buyers and sellers, as well as savers and investors, are each influenced by different factors. For this reason, their plans to buy and sell, or to save and invest, are rarely identical.

These concepts are illustrated graphically in Exhibit 4. The model is the same as the one in Exhibit 2, but the scales have been magnified so that you can see the important details more readily. Three possible cases are considered—those in which aggregate supply (AS) is either equal to, greater than, or less than aggregate demand (AD).

Three examples illustrate why the economy's saving is always the same as its realized investment.

Case 1: $AS = AD$ It is clear from Figure (a) that, if businesses plan to sell an output of $500 billion, this is also the amount of $C + I$ that the household and business sectors plan to purchase at that output. Therefore, aggregate supply equals aggregate demand, and there is no inventory accumulation or depletion. Likewise, in Figure (b), the amount that households plan to save at that output equals the amount that businesses plan to invest. There are thus no unplanned or unexpected changes in inventory.

Case 2: $AS > AD$ Figure (a) shows that, if businesses plan to sell $600 billion of NNP, households and businesses combined plan to purchase $580 billion of $C + I$ at that output. The business sector will therefore experience unplanned investment or inventory accumulation of +$20 billion. In Figure (b), household saving exceeds planned investment of businesses by this $20 billion, which is the amount of this unplanned investment. But saving equals actual or *realized* investment because the latter always includes both planned and unplanned (inventory) investment.

Case 3: $AS < AD$ Figure (a) shows that, if businesses plan to produce $400 billion of NNP, households and businesses combined plan to purchase $420 billion of $C + I$ at that output. Aggregate demand thus exceeds aggregate supply, and the difference represents unplanned *disinvestment,* or negative investment. This is because the stock of inventory is being used up faster than it is being replaced. In this case it amounts to an inventory depletion of $20 billion (that is, a change of −$20 billion). In Figure (b), saving falls short of planned investment by that amount. But saving still equals actual or *realized* investment because the latter includes both the planned amount of $40 billion and the negative unplanned (inventory) disinvestment of −$20 billion.

Note that planned investment is reduced by the amount of negative investment or inventory depletion.

Conclusion: Fundamental Identities

These ideas can now be summarized briefly:

• Saving and investment are planned by different people with different motivations. Hence, their schedules or curves are not likely to be equal —except in equilibrium.

• Saving (like consumption) depends on the level of aggregate income or output. Saving is simply that part of society's income not consumed. Therefore, no distinction is made between planned saving and realized saving because both concepts are the same.

• Investment is independent of aggregate income. Some investment consists of *planned* or intentional expenditures on plant, equipment, and inventories. Some investment may also consist of *unplanned* or unexpected inventory changes. Once society incurs a given level of aggregate income, the amount of realized investment from that income includes both planned and unplanned (inventory) investment.

As a result of these conditions, the following simple equations express the key concepts that you have learned thus far. Out of any *realized* level of income, it is always true that

income = consumption + saving

It is also true that

income = consumption + realized investment

Therefore,

saving = realized investment

These are actually fundamental identities of national-income accounting. You can verify them for any given year from the front endpapers of this book. However, you must first make the proper calculations to reflect the fact that government and the foreign sector are excluded from this basic model.

The Multiplier Principle

The multiplier principle tells you that a change in investment spending can produce a multiplied change in aggregate income.

One of the most critical problems of macroeconomics concerns the question of how changes in net investment affect the level of income. You already know that an increase in net investment can cause an increase in income. Likewise, a decrease in net investment can cause a decrease in income. But what you may not know is that *investment spending may have an amplifying effect on economic activity:*

> An increase in net investment may cause a magnified increase in income and output. Similarly, a decrease in net investment may cause a magnified decrease in income and output. The amount by which a change in investment is multiplied to produce an ultimate change in income and output is called the *multiplier*

For instance, if a permanent increase in investment of $5 billion per year causes an increase in income and output of $10 billion, the multiplier is 2. If, instead, the increase in income and output is $15 billion, the multiplier is 3. How does the multiplier work? It can be illustrated in three ways: numerically, in the form of a table; graphically, in the form of a diagram or figure; and algebraically, in the form of an equation.

Before looking at the ways in which the multiplier can be illustrated, it is necessary to recall two important concepts that you learned in the previous chapter.

1. The *marginal propensity to consume (MPC)* is the fraction of each additional dollar of income that is spent on consumption.

2. The *marginal propensity to save (MPS)* is the fraction of each additional dollar of income that is saved.

You will now see how these two fundamental ideas can be put to use.

Numerical Illustration

Suppose that businesses decide to spend $5 billion more per year on construction of new plants and equipment. This means that unemployed workers, materials suppliers, and so on, will be hired to perform the construction. If we assume that they have an MPC of 4/5 and hence an MPS of 1/5, they will tend to spend four-fifths and save one-fifth of any additional income they receive.

The ultimate effect on income is illustrated in Exhibit 5. In the first round of expenditures, the increase in investment of $5 billion becomes increased income to the owners of the newly hired resources. Because their MPC is 4/5 and their MPS is 1/5, they utilize 80 percent, or $4 billion, for increased consumption and 20 percent, or $1 billion, for increased saving.

In round 2, when the four-fifths is spent on consumption, firms find their sales increasing and their inventories decreasing. Therefore, firms hire more resources in order to increase their production, thereby creating $4 billion of income for the owners of the resources. These income recipients then utilize four-fifths, or $3.2 billion, for increased consumption and one-fifth, or $0.8 billion, for increased saving.

In round 3 and in each subsequent round, the process is repeated. Four-fifths of each increase in income is spent in the following round and is thereby added to the income stream.

Thus, a permanent increase in investment of $5 billion in round 1 has brought about an ultimate increase in income of $25 billion. The multiplier is therefore 5. This overall increase in income consists of a $20 billion increase in consumption plus a $5 billion increase in saving. The total saving increase is always the amount of the original investment, as you can verify from the table.

Note from the table that the greatest increases in income occur during the first few rounds. After that, however, the income effects tend to fade away gradually—like the ripples produced by a stone dropped into a pond.

Graphic Illustration

Exhibit 6 represents the same multiplier concept graphically. It shows how an increase in investment, represented by an upward shift of the C + I curve in Figure (a), or by an upward shift of the I curve in Figure (b), causes a magnified increase in output. As before, the model is based on the assumption that the MPC is 4/5 and the MPS is 1/5. That is, the aggregate demand curve has a slope of 4/5 and the saving curve has a slope of 1/5.

Point E in both charts represents the initial equilibrium level at which aggregate demand equals aggregate supply and saving equals investment. Point E' defines a new equilibrium resulting from an increase in investment. Note from the description accompanying the charts that the increase in income is a *multiple* of the increase in investment. The multiplier, as you can see, is 5.

Can you also see that the multiplier works in reverse? What happens to income if investment falls back to its initial level? What happens if investment falls below its initial level?

Exhibit 5
The Multiplier Illustrated Numerically
(all data in billions)

$$MPC = 4/5$$
$$MPS = 1/5$$
$$\text{multiplier} = 5$$

Expenditure rounds	Increase in income	Increase in consumption, MPC = 4/5	Increase in saving, MPS = 1/5
1 increase in investment = $5 billion	$ 5.00	$ 4.00	$1.00
2	4.00	3.20	0.80
3	3.20	2.56	0.64
4	2.56	2.05	0.51
5	2.05	1.64	0.41
6	1.64	1.31	0.33
All other rounds	6.55	5.24	1.31
Total	$25.00	$20.00	$5.00

Exhibit 6
The Multiplier Illustrated Graphically

$MPC = \frac{4}{5}$
$MPS = \frac{1}{5}$
multiplier = 5

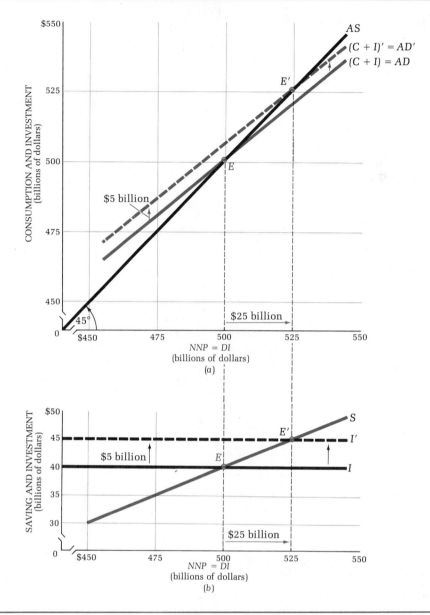

Figure (*a*): An increase in the level of investment by $5 billion causes an increase in the level of income, or *NNP*, by $25 billion. Hence, the multiplier is 5.

Figure (*b*): What happens to income, or *NNP*, if investment falls back to $40 billion? To $35 billion?

Algebraic Illustration

The tabular and graphic illustrations of the multiplier demonstrate that the increase in income is related to the marginal propensities to consume and to save. For example, you have already learned from the study of the consumption function that

$$MPC + MPS = 1$$

Therefore,

$$MPS = 1 - MPC$$

From the previous illustrations, you know that *MPC* is $\frac{4}{5}$ and *MPS* is $\frac{1}{5}$.

Therefore, you can easily verify that

$$\text{multiplier} = \frac{1}{^1/_5} = \frac{1}{1 - ^4/_5} = 5$$

This is the same value of the multiplier obtained previously in the numerical and graphic illustrations.

These ideas have been stated in the form of a specific example. To be useful, they can now be expressed in terms of a general formula. Thus:

$$\text{multiplier} = \frac{1}{MPS} = \frac{1}{1 - MPC}$$

This means that, if you know either the *MPC* or the *MPS*, you can determine the multiplier immediately. (This is what was done above to determine a multiplier of 5.) Then, once you know the value of the multiplier, you can predict the ultimate change in income that may result from a change in investment by the formula

The size of the multiplier is the reciprocal of the MPS.

multiplier × change in investment = change in income

The same formula applies to a decrease as well as an increase in investment. Go back and check it out in the illustrations above, just to make sure that you see how it works.

Notice that *the multiplier is the reciprocal of the MPS.* (The reciprocal of a number is 1 divided by that number.) Thus, the lower the *MPS*, the less withdrawal or "leakage" into extra saving that occurs at each round of income and the greater the *MPC*. Therefore, the greater the value of the multiplier. Conversely, the greater the *MPS*, the lower the *MPC*. Therefore, the lower the value of the multiplier.

To summarize:

The *multiplier* principle states that changes in investment can bring about magnified changes in income. This idea is expressed by the equation: multiplier × change in investment = change in income. The formula for the multiplier coefficient is thus

The essential idea of the multiplier is that the change in aggregate income is a function of (or is dependent upon) the change in investment spending.

$$\text{multiplier} = \frac{\text{change in income}}{\text{change in investment}} = \frac{1}{MPS} = \frac{1}{1 - MPC}$$

where *MPS* stands for the marginal propensity to save and *MPC* for the marginal propensity to consume. (**Note** This multiplier is also sometimes called the *simple multiplier,* the *expenditure multiplier,* or the *investment multiplier.* These names are used to distinguish it from other types of multipliers in economics.)

The Paradox of Thrift

The multiplier principle is one of the pillars of the Keynesian model. The principle tells you that any increase (or decrease) in investment can set in motion a multiple expansion (or contraction) of income. But can changes in saving or consumption also bring about a multiplier effect on income? The answer is yes—as your intuition would probably lead you to believe. But you can sharpen that intuition with some illustrations.

Take a look at Figure (*a*) in Exhibit 7. It illustrates the effect of an increase in saving (or equivalently, the effect of a decrease in consump-

Exhibit 7
Effect of an Increase in Saving:
The Paradox of Thrift

Figure (a): An increase in saving causes a multiplied decrease in output or income. Note that, at the new equilibrium point E', saving is the same as it was previously at E.

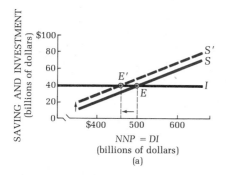

(a)

Figure (b): Suppose that investment depends on income so that the I curve slopes upward. Then the shift from S to S' reduces income and therefore causes investment to fall. Note that saving is less at E' than it was at E. People have tried to save more, and society has ended up saving less!

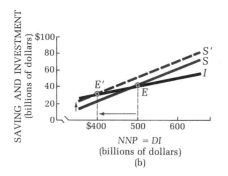

(b)

tion) on the nation's income or output. An increase in saving, such as from S to S', means that, at any given level of income, households now plan to save more than before. This might occur if they expect a recession and want to be better prepared for future contingencies.

Figure (b) in Exhibit 7 reflects the same idea as Figure (a), but now the investment curve is drawn with a moderate upward tilt. This shows more realistically that investment is not completely *autonomous*. That is, until now it was assumed for simplicity that investment is independent of income, output, and general economic activity. However, with expanding income and output, investment will probably grow because businesspeople become more optimistic and are willing to spend more on investment goods. The rigorous assumption of a horizontal investment curve is thus being relaxed, as was promised earlier.

This tendency of rising economic activity to stimulate higher levels of investment is called *induced investment*. Note in Figure (b) that, because of a rising I curve, the multiplier effect on output resulting from an increase in saving is even greater than in Figure (a).

Looking at both figures, you can see that the new equilibrium at E' reveals a curious phenomenon. *A small upward shift of the saving curve (or downward shift of the consumption curve), when not offset by an upward shift of the investment curve, causes a multiplied decrease in income or output.* This results in an interesting paradox.

> An increase in thrift may be desirable for an individual family because it can lead to greater saving and wealth. However, it may be undesirable for all of society because it leads to reductions in income, output, and employment if it is not offset by an increase (upward shift) in investment. Also, where the investment curve is upward-sloping, an increase in thrift, unless offset by an increase in investment, will actually lead to a *reduction in society's rate of saving*. This is the *paradox of thrift*. Thus, what is good for an individual is not necessarily good for everyone. (What logical fallacy is demonstrated by this paradox?)

The paradox of thrift leads to a remarkable economic implication. If the saving curve rises because households decide to save more (consume less), they should be doing exactly the opposite to improve their own and society's economic well-being. This is true unless the increase in saving can be offset by an upward shift in the investment curve. You will learn more about this implication shortly.

Inflationary and Recessionary Gaps

The Keynesian theory of income and employment demonstrates that the level of aggregate demand may be greater than, equal to, or less than the level of aggregate supply. These three possibilities, shown in Exhibit 8, are always defined with reference to full employment. Thus:

1. The amount by which aggregate demand *AD* (equal to *C* + *I*) exceeds aggregate supply *AS* at full employment is called the *inflationary gap*. This is shown in Figure (a). The excess volume of total spending when resources are already fully employed creates inflationary pressures. Their effect is to pull up prices and hence the *money* value (rather than the *real* value) of NNP.

2. When aggregate demand equals aggregate supply at full employment, there is no gap. This is shown in Figure (b).

Exhibit 8
Inflationary and Recessionary Gaps

Inflationary and recessionary gaps are always measured at the full-employment level and are shown by the vertical distances. This model assumes, for simplicity, that prices are constant up to the level of full employment and turn up sharply thereafter. In reality, they would tend to turn up before the economy reached full employment and continue to rise at steeper and steeper rates.

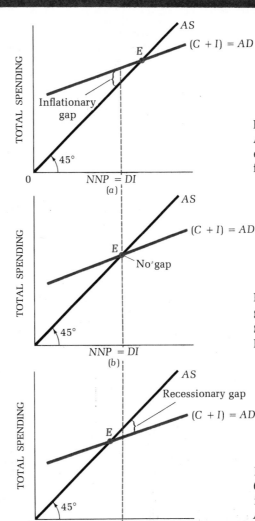

Figure (a): *Inflationary Gap.* Aggregate demand AD exceeds aggregate supply AS at full employment.

Figure (b): *No Gap.* Aggregate demand AD equals aggregate supply AS at full employment.

Figure (c): *Recessionary Gap.* Aggregate demand AD is less than aggregate supply AS at full employment.

---

3. The amount by which aggregate demand falls short of aggregate supply at full employment is called the *recessionary gap.* This is shown in Figure (c). The gap occurs because the deficiency of total spending pulls down the *real* value of NNP.

Conclusion: Closing the Gaps

The Keynesian model thus leads to the conclusion that the economy does not move automatically toward full-employment equilibrium, where AS = AD. Therefore, if the economy is not at full-employment equilibrium, either of two undesirable conditions is possible:

1. AS < AD This creates an inflationary gap, which may trigger further price increases. Such increases could occur if people learn to expect inflation and then include that expectation in their economic decisions.

2. *AS* > *AD* This results in a recessionary gap accompanied by serious unemployment. The problem may last indefinitely, leaving the economy in a prolonged state of stagnation.

To avoid these possibilities, and to correct them if they occur, what does the Keynesian model suggest?

> To close an inflationary gap, measures are needed to *decrease* aggregate demand. To close a recessionary gap, measures are needed to *increase* aggregate demand.

As you will see in the next chapter, Keynesian thinking contends that *government* is the logical source of measures aimed at closing inflationary and deflationary gaps. Thus, in Keynesian economics, government has an important role to play in formulating policies for achieving efficiency, stability, and growth.

What You Have Learned in This Chapter

1. The equilibrium level of NNP occurs where aggregate supply is equal to aggregate demand. This is also the output at which saving equals investment. At this output, businesses are holding the level of inventories desired.

2. If aggregate supply exceeds aggregate demand, or if planned saving exceeds planned investment, unwanted inventories accumulate. Businesses seek to reduce these surpluses by cutting back production. As a result, output, income, and employment fall.

Conversely, if aggregate supply is less than aggregate demand, or if planned saving is less than planned investment, inventories are depleted. Businesses try to replenish these shortages by expanding production. The result is an increase in employment as output and income rise.

3. Because saving and investment are planned by different people with different motivations, they are not likely to be equal—except in equilibrium, where the amounts intersect. By definition, saving is that part of income not spent on consumption. Therefore, out of any realized level of income, saving always equals the amount of realized investment because the latter consists of both planned and unplanned investment.

4. Any increase (or decrease) in investment can cause a multiple expansion (or contraction) of income. Any changes in consumption (or saving) can similarly produce multiple effects on income. All such effects are called multiplier effects. The simple multiplier is also called the investment multiplier. It shows how changes in investment may cause magnified changes in income. The multiplier is equal to the reciprocal of the marginal propensity to save.

5. The paradox of thrift tells us that an increase in saving may be desirable for an individual. However, it also tells us that a general increase in saving by society, unless it is offset by an increase in investment, can actually reduce the economy's income and employment. Therefore, what is good for an individual is not necessarily good for society.

6. The amount by which aggregate demand exceeds the full-employment aggregate supply is called the *inflationary gap*. The amount by which aggregate demand falls short of the full-employment aggregate supply is called the *recessionary gap*. There is no automatic tendency for aggregate demand to equal the full-employment aggregate supply. Hence, methods must be found to close inflationary and recessionary gaps if our mixed economy is to maintain full employment.

For Discussion

1. *Terms and concepts to review:*
realized investment
multiplier
autonomous investment
induced investment
paradox of thrift
inflationary gap
recessionary gap

2. Complete the following table for a hypothetical economy. (All figures are in billions of dollars.) Assume that the propensity to consume is linear and that investment is constant at all levels of income.

NNP = DI	C	S	I	APC	APS	MPC	MPS
$100	$125		$25				
$200	200						
300							
400							
500							

(a) From the data in the table, draw a graph of the consumption function and of the consumption-plus-investment function. Underneath this graph, draw a graph of the saving and investment curves. Then connect the two sets of break-even points with vertical dashed lines.

(b) Has there been a multiplier effect as a result of the inclusion of investment? If yes, by how much? What is the numerical value of the multiplier?

(c) What is the equilibrium level of income and output before and after the inclusion of investment?

(d) What will income be if investment increases by $10 billion?

3. How does the size of the multiplier vary with MPC? How does it vary with MPS? Explain why, without using any equations.

4. Distinguish between the individual and community viewpoints concerning the desirability of thrift.

5. Can you suggest at least one method of closing inflationary or recessionary gaps?

6. A student remarked to his instructor: "First you say that saving and investment are never really equal. Then you say they are always really equal. Why don't you economists make up your minds?" Can you help the student out of his muddle?

7. Suppose that a consumption function is given by the equation

$C = 120 + 0.60\, DI$

(a) What will be the amount of consumption at an income level of 100?

(b) How much income is required to support a consumption level of 420?

(c) What will be the amount of consumption if income is taxed 100 percent? How can consumption be financed under such circumstances?

(d) What is the value of the MPC? What is the value of the MPS?

(e) Prepare a consumption and saving schedule, and graph the consumption and saving functions for income levels from $DI = 100$ to $DI = 500$. What is the equilibrium level of income?

8. If planned investment in Problem 7 were 50, what would be the equation for aggregate demand? Draw the aggregate demand curve and investment curve on your graphs. Can you estimate the equilibrium level of income from your graphs?

9. Refer to your graphs from Problem 8.

(a) At a realized income of 500, how much is unplanned investment? How much is realized investment? Is this an equilibrium situation? Explain.

(b) At a realized income of 400, how much is unplanned investment? How much is realized investment? Is this an equilibrium situation? Explain.

(c) At the realized-income levels in (a) and (b), does saving equal investment? Explain.

10. How does the size of the MPC and the size of the MPS, or the steepness of the consumption curve and that of the saving curve, affect the size of the multiplier? Explain.

11. Adam Smith wrote that a spendthrift is an enemy of society, but a frugal person is its benefactor. Benjamin Franklin advised that "a penny saved is a penny earned." Evaluate these statements in light of the paradox of thrift.

Modern Fiscal Policy: Successes and Failures of Keynesian Economics

U.S. Treasury, Washington, D.C.

Learning guide
Watch for the answers to these important questions

How is the Keynesian model applied to the problem of reducing unemployment? In what ways do government spending and taxing policies affect the levels of output and employment?

What is the balanced-budget multiplier? What lesson does it teach us? Does it always work as expected?

How does fiscal policy operate? What is the full-employment budget, and of what significance is it?

Has discretionary fiscal policy been successful in achieving its economic goals? Why or why not?

How do budget policies relate to Keynesian economics? What are the burdens and benefits of a national debt? Are there some practical guidelines for managing it?

This chapter shows you how Keynesian economics, through the use of what is called fiscal policy, seeks to close recessionary and inflationary gaps.

How does Keynesian economics explain the occurrence of recessionary and inflationary gaps? The answer, you will recall from Chapter 8, is that gaps between aggregate demand and aggregate supply occur when the two are not equal at full employment.

How does Keynesian economics seek to remedy these conditions? The answer is largely the concern of this chapter. Through the use of what is known as "fiscal policy," government measures are considered whose aim is to achieve both full employment and price stability. Once these measures are understood, it becomes possible to evaluate various aspects of Keynesian economics. This will be done in the present chapter and in several later ones, based on our own experiences as well as those of other nations.

The English noun *fisc* (from the Latin *fiscus*, translated as basket, money basket, treasury) means a state or royal treasury. The adjective *fiscal* refers to all matters pertaining to the public treasury, particularly its revenues and expenditures. In broad terms, therefore, *fiscal policy deals with the deliberate exercise of the government's power to tax and spend for the purpose of closing recessionary and inflationary gaps.*

Introducing Government: Enlarging the Model

The proper economic role of government is always controversial. Should taxes be raised or lowered? Should government spending be increased or reduced? These are among the fundamental issues of fiscal policy. They are also typical of the questions you read and hear about almost every day in the news media. In this chapter, therefore, the Keynesian model is enlarged to include the role of government.

Increased Government Spending Raises Aggregate Demand; Decreased Spending Lowers It

Government fiscal policy affects the basic Keynesian model through two major variables—taxes and spending. Let us assume for the moment that *taxes are held constant.* Then government spending (G) on goods and services becomes a net addition to total spending or aggregate demand. That is, government spending supplements household consumption expenditures (C) and business investment expenditures (I).

Exhibit 1
Effect of Increased Government Spending on Net National Product

Assumptions: $MPC = 4/5$ and $MPS = 1/5$; therefore,

$$\frac{\text{expenditure}}{\text{multiplier}} = \frac{1}{1 - 4/5} = \frac{1}{1/5} = 5$$

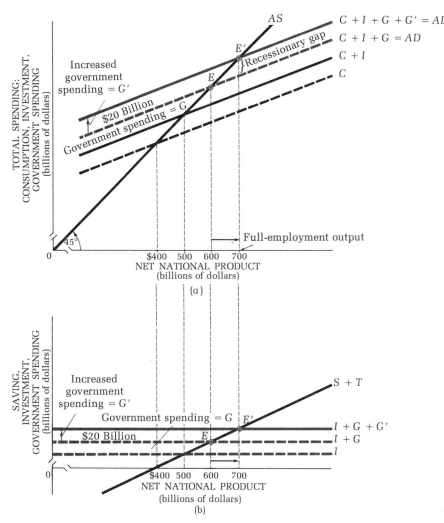

Figure (a): Increased government spending by the amount G' raises aggregate demand from AD to AD' and produces a multiplier effect on net national product. Because the multiplier is 5, increased government spending of $20 billion increases NNP by $5 \times 20 billion = $100 billion: from $600 billion to $700 billion. This closes the recessionary gap.

Figure (b): The multiplier effect of increased government spending G' can also be seen in terms of a saving–investment diagram. A $20 billion increase in government spending raises the equilibrium NNP by 5 times the increase in spending: from $600 billion to $700 billion.

This is illustrated in the hypothetical case of Exhibit 1, Figure (a).

The $C + I + G$ curve shows total spending at each level of national product. The new equilibrium point at which aggregate demand AD equals aggregate supply AS occurs at E. The corresponding information in terms of saving and investment is given in Figure (b). Observe that the upward-sloping line now represents saving plus taxes $(S + T)$. This is because taxes, like saving, denote a portion of income not spent on consumption.

Note Because the basic model is now enlarged to include the public sector instead of just the household and business sectors, the existence of taxes must be recognized. Therefore, NNP in the enlarged model does not equal DI as in the basic model of the previous chapter. (Do you remember why—in terms of national-income accounting?)

Notice in Figure (*a*) that the *AD* curve includes a certain amount of government spending. However, the equilibrium *NNP* of $600 billion is still short of the $700 billion needed to reach the full-employment level of output. This means that, in order to achieve full employment, the aggregate demand curve must be raised high enough to close the recessionary gap. This can be done by increasing any of the components of *AD*— namely, *C*, *I*, or *G*. If we assume that the *C* and *I* curves remain constant, an increase in *G* by the amount *G'* will close the recessionary gap by raising the aggregate demand curve from *AD* to *AD'*.

Multiplier Effect

The multiplier principle, which you learned in the previous chapter, shows how changes in government spending can have a multiplier effect on NNP.

Note that an increase in government expenditure, with taxes held constant, has a multiplier effect on *NNP* just as does an increase in private investment expenditure. In the diagram, an increase in aggregate demand of $20 billion, from *C + I + G* to *C + I + G + G'*, increases *NNP* by $100 billion. We can infer from this that a rise in government demand has the same multiplier effect on *NNP* as a rise in consumer demand or a rise in investment demand. This is because a rise in government demand enhances the sales and profits of firms that sell to the government. This, in turn, causes further increases in output throughout the economy. Because of this, the multiplier in Exhibit 1 may be called an "expenditure multiplier." Thus:

> Increased government spending may be used to raise the level of aggregate demand from an unemployment to a full-employment level. However, any additional spending that raises aggregate demand above full-employment levels will be inflationary.

Observe how the multiplier principle actually comes into play. In Exhibit 1, we know from the constant slope of the consumption curve that *MPC* is ⁴/₅ at every point. Therefore, the multiplier is 5. Given this information, and knowing that the increase in *NNP* must be $100 billion to reach full employment, the increase in government spending must be $20 billion in order to achieve the desired goal. This is because 5 × $20 billion = $100 billion. Summarizing:

> A rise in government expenditures has the same multiplier effect on *NNP* as a rise either in consumption expenditures or in investment expenditures. Therefore, the multiplier in Exhibit 1 may be thought of as an *expenditure multiplier*. Its influence on *NNP* is affected by the amount of change in *AD*, whose components are *C*, *I*, and *G*.

Increased Taxes Reduce Aggregate Demand; Decreased Taxes Raise It

Changes in taxes can also have a multiplier effect on NNP, but the effect is inverse.

What happens to the equilibrium level of *NNP* when government spending is constant and taxes vary? Your intuition tells you that an increase in taxes will reduce disposable income and, hence, consumption expenditures. This, in turn, will decrease output and employment.

Of course, the many different kinds of taxes—direct or indirect, proportional or progressive, personal or business—may all have different effects on income and employment. For simplicity's sake, however, let us assume that a net increase in personal income taxes of $20 billion is imposed on consumers in our hypothetical economy. We may represent this net amount of the tax increase by the letter *T*.

In Exhibit 2, the consumption curve C, whose MPC is ⁴/₅, is shifted downward and parallel until it becomes C′ as a result of the tax T. But has the consumption curve shifted downward by the exact amount of the tax? The answer is no:

> The first effect of the $20 billion increase in taxes is to reduce people's disposable income by $20 billion. However, because *consumption depends on income* and the MPC is ⁴/₅, consumption expenditures decrease by ⁴/₅ of $20 billion = $16 billion. It follows, therefore, that saving decreases by ¹/₅ of $20 billion = $4 billion.

The tax thus causes a downward shift of the C curve according to the value of the MPC. *The amount of the downward shift equals MPC × T.* What will be the effect of T on NNP? Because the expenditure multiplier is 5, it follows that a decrease in consumption expenditures of $16 billion will reduce NNP by 5 × $16 billion = $80 billion. This is shown in Exhibit 2, where the equilibrium NNP changes from E at $400 billion to E′ at $320 billion, a decrease of $80 billion.

As you might expect, a decrease in taxes of $20 billion would have had the opposite effect. Such a decrease would have stimulated consumer spending, raised aggregate demand, and thereby increased NNP by $80 billion.

Varying G and T Together

Suppose that we now allow government spending, G, and taxes, T, to vary simultaneously. For instance, what will be the effect if G and T are both increased simultaneously by the same amount—in our example, by $20 billion?

• The increase in G will raise NNP by 5 × $20 billion = $100 billion. The magnified effect of the expenditure change, called the *expenditure multiplier*, has a numerical value of 5.

• The increase in T will lower NNP by 4 × $20 billion = $80 billion. The magnified effect of the tax change, which may be called the *tax multiplier*, has a numerical value of 4.

• Therefore, the *net* effect of equal increases in G and T together will be to increase NNP by 1 × $20 billion = $20 billion, which is the amount of the initial increment.

The reason for this result is that the $20 billion increases in G and T are precisely equal, but their effects are opposite. The two multiplier processes thus cancel each other out—except on the first round, when the full amount of G ($20 billion) is added to NNP. This is why the *net* multiplier effect of equal increases in G and T is 5 − 4 = 1.

Summarizing:

> Changes in taxes cause changes in disposable income. These, in turn, can cause magnified changes in the nation's output, depending on the MPC. In general, the larger the MPC, the larger the proportion of any decrease in income that is withdrawn from consumption. Therefore, the larger the decrease in NNP.

To verify this, look again at Exhibit 2 and ask yourself what would have happened if the MPC had been larger than ⁴/₅. Would NNP have decreased by more than $80 billion or by less?

Exhibit 2
Effect of Increased Taxes on Consumption and on Net National Product

Assumption: MPC = ⁴/₅ and MPS = ¹/₅; therefore, expenditure multiplier = 5. T = tax increase of $20 billion.

As a result of the tax increase, the consumption curve shifts downward from C to C′, and hence the equilibrium point changes from E to E′. The amount of change equals MPC × T. Thus, because MPC = ⁴/₅ and the tax increase is $20 billion, the C curve shifts downward by ⁴/₅ × $20 billion = $16 billion.

However, because the expenditure multiplier is 5, NNP on the horizontal axis decreases by a multiple of the decrease in spending—by 5 × $16 billion = $80 billion. Note too that, although the decrease in NNP is equal to 5 times the $16 billion decrease in spending, it is equal to 4 times the $20 billion increase in taxes. The number 4 may therefore be called the *tax multiplier.*

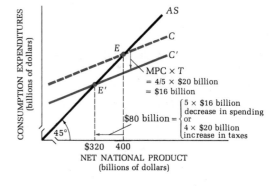

The Balanced-Budget Multiplier

When the expenditure multiplier is combined with the tax multiplier, the result is called the balanced-budget multiplier.

The multiplier effects of government spending and taxes thus interact with each other in affecting NNP. In fact, as you have seen, there are actually *two* multipliers operating simultaneously—an expenditure multiplier and a tax multiplier.

1. Expenditure Multiplier (M_E) This tells you the multiple by which an increase in total spending, by raising aggregate demand, may be expected to expand NNP.

2. Tax Multiplier (M_T) This tells you the multiple by which an increase in personal income taxes, by lowering total consumption (and hence aggregate demand), may be expected to contract NNP.

We can now summarize all of the foregoing ideas in this way:

If G and T are increased (or decreased) simultaneously by equal amounts, NNP will be increased (or decreased) by the same amount. For example, a simultaneous increase in G and T by \$20 billion will raise NNP by $1 \times \$20$ billion = \$20 billion. Similarly, a simultaneous decrease by \$20 billion will lower NNP by $1 \times \$20$ billion = \$20 billion. Thus, the numerical value of the expenditure multiplier, M_E, minus the numerical value of the tax multiplier, M_T, may be called the *balanced-budget multiplier*, M_B. In general, it is always true that

$$M_B = M_E - M_T = 1$$

Fiscal-Policy Formulas: Three Simple Multipliers

It is easy to see why the balanced-budget multiplier equals 1.

Economic ideas can often be expressed concisely in terms of equations. The following simple equations will help provide a more precise understanding of the balanced-budget multiplier concept.

The Expenditure Multiplier The first multiplier you learned about was the expenditure multiplier. As you recall, it is the reciprocal of the MPS. Thus:

$$M_E = \frac{1}{MPS}$$

The Tax Multiplier You also learned that increased taxes on consumers reduce their incomes. This in turn reduces their consumption expenditures because consumption depends on income. The decrease in consumption is determined by the MPC. Therefore, the tax multiplier, M_T, is simply a fraction (equal to MPC) of the expenditure multiplier:

$$M_T = MPC \times \frac{1}{MPS} \quad \text{or simply} \quad \frac{MPC}{MPS}$$

The Balanced-Budget Multiplier You can now show that $M_B = 1$ by substituting in the equation for the balanced-budget multiplier. Thus:

$$M_B = M_E - M_T$$
$$= \frac{1}{MPS} - \frac{MPC}{MPS}$$
$$= \frac{1 - MPC}{MPS}$$

But you already know that MPS is the same as $1 - MPC$. Therefore, substituting in the last equation,

$$M_B = \frac{1 - MPC}{1 - MPC} = \frac{MPS}{MPS} = 1$$

Conclusion: Does the Balanced-Budget Multiplier Work?

If the government would raise taxes and use the additional revenues to pay for additional expenditures, it would balance the budget while still adhering to an expansionary policy. Therefore, the effect on the economy would be stimulative—not neutral as is often believed.

Is this quotation from a newspaper editorial correct? The answer is *yes*—according to the balanced-budget multiplier theory. As you have learned, this theory concludes that equal increases in G and T are expansionary, not neutral.

But does the theory always work as expected? In other words, is the balanced-budget multiplier always equal to 1, or can it be larger or smaller? The answer depends on the theory's underlying assumptions. Among them:

Because of the dubious assumptions on which the balanced-budget multiplier rests, it may not always work as expected.

1. Government Spending Must Be Noncompetitive The increase in government spending should not compete with private spending. But in reality, it often does. Consequently, if government, for example, spends more on education, transportation, health, and so on, the private sector may spend less on these. In that case, private-sector consumption expenditures will decrease, saving will increase, and hence the expansionary effect will be reduced.

2. Taxes Must Not Create Disincentives The increased taxes needed to pay for enlarged government spending should not be counterproductive. In reality, however, they may be. For example, if people feel that taxes are already high, further increases may reduce the incentives of households to work and save and of businesses to invest. Some critics believe that this has happened at various times. If so, it has reduced the expansionary effect of the balanced-budget multiplier.

3. *MPCs* Must Be the Same The group that receives the benefits of increased government spending must have the same *MPC* as the group that pays the increased taxes. In reality, however, this is not likely. Therefore, the tax multiplier may actually be greater than, equal to, or less than the expenditure multiplier. This alters the expansionary effect.

Dubious Assumptions

The balanced-budget multiplier theory is an integral part of fiscal policy. However, because of some questionable premises on which the theory is based, it has not gone without criticism. In general:

The balanced-budget multiplier theory rests on some dubious assumptions. Therefore, although it is logically correct *within the Keynesian model,* it may not always work as expected. For example, increased government spending and taxes may at times impede rather than stimulate the private sector's growth. The effect of this will be to increase rather than to decrease unemployment and inflation. This helps to explain why it is not always possible to predict accurately what the consequences of economic policies will be.

Overview of Fiscal Policy

Discretionary fiscal policy uses expansionary measures to combat recession and contractionary measures to combat inflation.

The foregoing analyses suggest some guides for discretionary *fiscal policy*. This may be defined as deliberate actions by the government in its spending and taxing activities to achieve price stability, to help dampen the swings of business cycles, and to bring the nation's output and employment to desired levels.

Fiscal policy, as we know it today, is largely a direct result of Keynesian beliefs. These ideas hold that fiscal policies should differ over the course of a business cycle. Government spending and taxing policies designed to cure recession should not be the same as those aimed at curbing inflation. That is, two distinct classes of policies are necessary.

Antirecessionary Measures: Expansionary Policy

During recession, the goal is to raise aggregate demand to a full-employment noninflationary level. Therefore, an *expansionary* fiscal policy is needed to close the gap. This may involve either an increase in G, a decrease in T, or some combination of both. If the federal budget is balanced to begin with, an expansionary fiscal policy will require a budget *deficit*, because the government's expenditures will exceed its revenues.

Anti-inflationary Measures: Contractionary Policy

During inflation, the goal is to lower aggregate demand to the full-employment noninflationary level. Therefore, a *contractionary* fiscal policy is needed to close the inflationary gap. This may entail either a decrease in G, an increase in T, or some combination of both. If the federal budget is already in balance, a contractionary fiscal policy would require a budget *surplus*, because the government's revenues will exceed its expenditures. Of course, a relatively small surplus may not be sufficient to do the job. The budget surplus must be large enough to induce deflationary effects if a contractionary fiscal policy is to operate effectively.

Nondiscretionary Controls: Automatic Fiscal Stabilizers

Nondiscretionary fiscal policy relies on automatic fiscal stabilizers to keep the economy on a desired course.

Not all fiscal activity is discretionary. Much is *nondiscretionary*, meaning that it is neither deliberate nor planned. Significant changes in government spending and taxes occur automatically over the business cycle without any explicit decisions by the President or Congress.

In fact, the U.S. economy has certain "built-in" stabilizers. These *automatic fiscal stabilizers* help to cushion the economy against a recession by retarding a decline in disposable income, and they help to curb an inflation by retarding an increase in disposable income. They thereby contribute to keeping the economic system in balance without human intervention or control, much as a thermostat helps to maintain an even temperature in a house.

Three of these stabilizers are particularly important:

Tax Receipts

The federal government's chief sources of revenue are personal and corporation income taxes. The rates on these taxes—especially those on personal income taxes—are progressive. Thus, when national income rises, there is a more than proportional increase in government tax receipts. This will tend to dampen an economic boom. On the other hand, a declining national income results in more than proportional decreases in government tax receipts. This will tend to soften an economic recession.

Unemployment Taxes and Benefits

During times of prosperity and high employment, total tax receipts to finance the unemployment-insurance program exceed total benefits paid out. This creates a surplus. During recession and unemployment, the reverse occurs. This creates a deficit.

Corporate Dividend Policy

Corporations generally maintain fairly stable dividends in the short run. That is, their dividend payouts to stockholders do not fluctuate with each reported increase or decrease in profits. As a result, retained corporate earnings or undistributed profits, to the extent that they are saved and not invested, tend to have a stabilizing influence in expansionary and contractionary periods alike.

> On the whole, the automatic stabilizers tend to reduce the severity of business cycles. Some studies suggest that all the automatic stabilizers acting together may reduce the amplitudes of cyclical swings by about one-third. But automatic stabilizers merely curb the highs and lows of business cycles. To limit their spread, Keynesian economics concludes that certain discretionary methods of fiscal policy (to be described shortly) are needed.

Exhibit 3 explains how automatic stabilizers tend to limit the peaks and troughs of business cycles. As you can see, because of our progressive tax structure, an increase or decrease in NNP can *automatically* push the budget toward a surplus or deficit.

The Full-Employment Budget

What fiscal implications do automatic surpluses and deficits entail? They assume that, under certain circumstances, the actual budget surplus or deficit in any particular year is not necessarily the same as the one that would occur in a year of full employment. The reason can be shown by an example.

For instance, suppose that tax rates and the amount of government spending are held constant. Then, in a specific year in which the economy is operating at less than full employment, the government may incur a budgetary deficit. But, with the same tax rates and the same amount of federal spending, there might have been a budgetary surplus if the economy had operated at full (or nearly full) employment. Why? Because the greater level of national income during a period of high employment would have produced a larger volume of tax revenues for the government.

Thus we can introduce a new concept called the *full-employment budget*. It may be defined as an estimate of what annual government expenditures and revenues would be if the economy were operating at full employment. Any resulting surplus (or deficit) in this budget is called a *full-employment surplus* (or *deficit*).

Exhibit 3
Automatic Stabilizers

Suppose that government expenditures remain constant at all levels of the nation's output. Then, as NNP rises or falls, the government's tax receipts increase or decrease correspondingly.

Thus, starting with a balanced budget at an output of NNP_0:

1. An increase in output from NNP_0 to NNP_1 causes tax receipts to rise. This *automatically* creates a budget surplus, which tends to dampen an economic expansion.

2. A decrease in output from NNP_0 to NNP_2 causes tax receipts to decline. This *automatically* creates a budget deficit, which tends to soften an economic contraction.

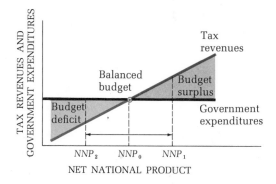

Like the effect of any other surplus, the effect of a full- or even high-employment surplus is contractionary. This is because the government has taken more purchasing power out of the income stream through taxes than it has put back through spending. Under inflationary conditions, this serves to dampen price increases. And, if GNP is rising, its rate of growth will tend to be slowed. Therefore, policy measures are needed to assure proper utilization of any full- or high-employment surpluses.

Fiscal Drag and Fiscal Dividends

Fiscal drag occurs when tax revenues exceed government expenditures. To offset this, government can seek ways to spend more money or to reduce taxes.

What policy measures are appropriate? The answer is best understood by expressing the problem and its solution in the form of two propositions:

1. The automatic and more rapid increases in tax revenues relative to expenditures that an expanding economy experiences will tend to impede the economy's growth. This phenomenon is called *fiscal drag*.

2. The federal government can offset the effect of fiscal drag by declaring a "fiscal dividend." This can be done in several ways:
    (a) Increased federal spending on various social goods, such as education, regional development, and health.
    (b) Reduced taxes on the private sector in order to increase consumption and investment.
    (c) Larger unrestricted revenue grants to the state and local governments, which can be used by those governments to meet their expenditure needs.

All of these methods of reducing fiscal drag have been employed by Washington at various times. As you will see, there is some disagreement among critics as to how well the methods have succeeded in achieving their goal.

Conclusion: Which Budget?

The actual budget is not the same as the full-employment budget.

You can now see that, within the framework of Keynesian economics, the actual budget and the full-employment budget involve two distinctly different concepts. Which one should be used for judging the effectiveness of fiscal policy? Finding the answer involves three considerations:

1. The actual budget tells you the government's revenues and expenditures for a particular year. If the amount of government spending is constant, deficits and surpluses are affected mainly by changes in NNP, not by discretionary fiscal policy. Therefore, there is no way of knowing from actual deficits or surpluses whether the government is following either an expansionary or a contractionary policy.

2. The full-employment budget tells you what the government's revenues and expenditures would be in a particular year if the economy operated at full employment. If the amount of government spending is constant, deficits and surpluses in the full-employment budget are determined by the structure of tax rates. Therefore, at full employment, one type of tax-rate structure may create a budget surplus, which is contractionary. Another type may create a budget deficit, which is expansionary.

3. Deficits and surpluses in the actual budget are independent of those in the full-employment budget. For example, during recession the government's tax revenues may be reduced, causing the actual budget to have a deficit. This might suggest that the government's fiscal policy is expansionary. However, the full-employment budget may have a surplus. In that case, the government's fiscal policy is actually contractionary.

The implications for judging the effectiveness of discretionary fiscal policy are therefore clear:

> Keynesian economics concludes that surpluses or deficits in the full-employment budget provide a more accurate reflection of the government's fiscal-policy thrust than do surpluses or deficits in the actual budget.

Keynesian economics argues that the full-employment budget is the only appropriate one for judging the effectiveness of fiscal policy.

Discretionary Fiscal Policy in Action: Managing Budget Deficits and Surpluses

The two basic prescriptions of discretionary fiscal policy seem to be simple and straightforward:

1. To expand the economy, cut taxes and raise government expenditures. This creates a budget deficit.

2. To contract the economy, raise taxes and cut government expenditures. This creates a budget surplus.

Thus, the principal concerns of discretionary fiscal policy are the ways in which the federal government, *represented by the Treasury,* manages its budget. But these depend on the manner in which the government raises and spends money and on the economic consequences of such activities. Therefore, let us examine these activities.

How the Government Raises Money

Basically, the government has three sources of revenue: taxation, borrowing, and printing new money.

The ways in which the government raises money play a critical role in discretionary fiscal policy.

Taxation

Taxes are the most familiar source of government revenue, because practically everyone pays them in one form or another. When taxes are to be changed, it is necessary to consider simultaneously both the type of tax and the tax rate.

Type of Tax There are many different kinds of taxes—sales taxes, property taxes, income taxes, and so forth. However, for purposes of fiscal policy, income taxes, both personal and corporate, are the most important by far. This is because changes in income taxes, as you have seen, directly affect consumption and investment expenditures. Therefore, income-tax changes also affect the overall level of economic activity.

Tax Rate Changes in the rate structure of income taxes can affect both government revenues and the level of economic activity. The effect of a change in the rate structure depends on the *MPCs of the income groups affected by the change.*

For instance, suppose tax rates are reduced for lower-income groups and raised for higher-income groups. There may be two possible consequences:

1. To the extent that lower-income groups have a higher *MPC*, the net effect will stimulate total consumer spending. (Can you explain why?)

2. The increased tax rates on higher-income groups may reduce their saving and, hence, the funds they make available for investment.

For these reasons, a change in income-tax rates of the type assumed would probably reduce government tax revenues as well as the levels of output and employment. On the other hand, a tax-rate change that puts a heavier burden on lower-income groups and a lighter burden on higher-income groups could have other kinds of consequences. Can you suggest some?

Borrowing

Heavy borrowing by the Treasury can cause interest rates to rise. This may force many potential borrowers out of the market.

A second method by which the government can raise money, and thereby finance a deficit, is borrowing. This consists of selling Treasury securities, such as bonds, to the public. When the Treasury engages in this activity, two consequences are likely to occur:

1. Higher Interest Rates Treasury bonds compete with corporation bonds for investors' dollars. As a result, if all other things remain the same, heavy sales of bonds drive up interest rates. Both the Treasury and business borrowers find that they must offer increasingly higher interest rates to lenders in order to persuade them to purchase additional bonds.

2. Crowding Out Because deficit spending, which is an expansionary fiscal policy, creates upward pressure on interest rates, it raises borrowing costs. Many businesses, of course, are not able to pay the higher costs. Consequently some private investment is reduced because numerous business firms are "crowded out" of the financial markets by government deficit spending.

Heavy government borrowing can therefore be a significant cause of inflation. Crowding out reduces the growth of the private relative to the public sector as scarce resources are transferred from the former to the latter. Inflationary pressures are thus likely to be created over the long run unless the private sector can offset its relative decline by increasing its productive efficiency. This may require government "incentive" legislation designed to spur more private-sector investment and production. Tax reduction is one example of such legislation. This and other examples will be discussed in later chapters.

Printing

A third way in which the government can raise money is simply to print it. This is actually a monetary action rather than a fiscal one, as you will learn subsequently in the study of banking. However, it is appropriate to say a few words about it here.

By printing money, a government can engage in deficit spending—that is, spend more than it collects in taxes. It can thereby pay for the resources it wants without depressing private consumption and investment spending. This may seem like a delightful and painless way to finance public expenditures. In fact, *the great majority of countries* (the United States is one of relatively few exceptions) *turn frequently to the printing presses to pay for armies, highways, schools, and so on.* These countries usually lack the other two means of obtaining funds—an adequate tax system for raising revenues and an organized system of financial markets in which to sell securities.

But the results of printing additional money are not likely to be painless—for two reasons:

1. Inflationary Pressures Inflation arises from a condition described as "too much money chasing too few goods." Therefore, printing money to finance deficit spending can cause prices to rise during cyclical downturns as well as at cyclical peaks. Here is why:

Printing money to finance government deficits can be inflationary because there will be "too much money chasing too few goods."

• During times of recession, most firms have excess capacity. Nevertheless, it generally takes many months for management to plan future increases in output and to organize the resources needed to achieve new production goals. Consequently, output cannot expand rapidly enough to fulfill the higher aggregate demand created by the enlargement of government spending made possible by printing new money.

• During periods of high employment, the effects of printing new money will be inflationary unless private spending can be reduced. This can be accomplished by raising taxes enough to offset the increase in government spending.

2. Hidden Tax What happens if taxes are not raised sufficiently to offset the increased spending? In that case the resulting inflation will act as a disguised "tax." Prices will rise throughout the economy, thereby causing real incomes to shrink.

How the Government Spends Money

The second important aspect of discretionary fiscal policy has to do with the ways in which the government spends money. There are two forms that government spending may take: transfer payments and social-goods expenditures.

The ways in which government spends money play a critical role in discretionary fiscal policy.

Transfer Payments

Transfer payments, you will recall, are expenditures within or between sectors of the economy for which there are no corresponding contributions to current production.

Certain types of transfer payments act as automatic stabilizers. For example, unemployment compensation and old-age retirement benefits rise and fall more or less inversely with the nation's income. Other transfer expenditures, such as veterans' benefits and interest payments on the national debt, are independent of the nation's income and do not have this automatic stabilizing characteristic.

What is the net effect of transfer payments? Evidence suggests that, over the long run, they have been inflationary. On the one hand, they are spent for goods and services, thereby raising aggregate demand. On the other hand, a large portion of transfer payments has been financed by income taxes and by government borrowing. The first, some critics contend, has left a smaller amount of savings available for investment. The second, as already explained, may create inflationary pressures.

Social-Goods Expenditures

A second outlet for government spending is *social goods*. These are products provided by the public sector because society believes that such goods are not provided in sufficient quantity by the private sector. Examples of social goods are highways, parks, public buildings, slum-clearance projects, and regional development. In addition, social-goods expenditures include money used to create public-service employment in government agencies. The jobs may range from lawn mowing to social work, but the purpose is to provide temporary employment for people until they can find jobs in the private sector.

What are the economic effects of social-goods expenditures? Two major ones are these:

1. If properly planned, spending on social goods can stimulate the capital-goods and construction industries, in which unemployment rates are among the highest. In addition, these expenditures can provide society with some socially useful goods like those mentioned above.

2. Depending on how the spending is financed—by taxation, borrowing, or printing money—and on the stage of the business cycle in which they are undertaken, social-goods expenditures may turn out to be inflationary. In that case, society will be trading reductions in unemployment for higher prices.

Conclusion: Need for Budget Policies

A budget surplus is anti-inflationary. However, a budget deficit is not necessarily inflationary. It may or may not be, depending on how it is financed.

The ways in which the federal government raises and spends money thus determine whether the federal budget will have a surplus or a deficit. How should these be managed?

> A budget surplus means that the government has taken more money out of the economy in taxes than it has put back via spending. A surplus is therefore anti-inflationary. A budget deficit means that the government has put more money into the economy via spending than it has taken out in taxes. A deficit *may* therefore be inflationary. Whether it is or not depends on how the deficit is financed, the use to which it is put, and the stage of the business cycle in which it is incurred.

How can government reverse the contractionary effect of a budget surplus? One way is to use it to retire some of the national debt. This means that, if you and other government creditors have Treasury bonds that are due to mature, the government can pay them off without borrowing additional funds to do so. To the extent that you and the other recipients of the money then spend it on goods and services, the results are likely to be expansionary.

How can government reverse the possible inflationary effect of a budget deficit? This question is extremely practical, because deficits are far more common than surpluses. One answer is that the private sector's *productivity* may have to be stimulated with appropriate policies. These are explored in considerable detail in later chapters. Meanwhile, can you suggest some government policies that would encourage businesses and workers to increase their production?

Does Discretionary Fiscal Policy Really Work? Some Difficulties of Implementation

The Keynesian model, as you have seen, provides two simple fiscal-policy prescriptions:

Certain obstacles arise in putting discretionary fiscal policy to use.

1. To expand the economy, raise aggregate demand by decreasing taxes and increasing government expenditures.

2. To contract the economy, lower aggregate demand by increasing taxes and decreasing government expenditures.

In both cases, the expenditure and tax multipliers tell you how large the changes in spending must be to achieve full employment at stable prices.

How well do these principles of discretionary fiscal policy actually work? Because they require implementation by Washington, many complicated economic and political issues arise. Several classes of difficulties may be identified.

Cyclical Forecasting and Policy Timing

The most practical problems facing legislators concern (1) the forecasting of cyclical turning points and (2) the timing of countercyclical fiscal policies.

The difficulties of forecasting business cycles and therefore the timing of appropriate policies are some of the major obstacles to employing effective discretionary fiscal policies.

Forecasting Cyclical Turning Points

Substantial advances have taken place in economic model building over the years. Nevertheless, business-cycle forecasting remains an inexact science. Economists can usually explain reasonably well why past recessionary or inflationary trends have occurred and why present trends seem to be what they are. However, even economists working with elaborate computer models cannot predict with much accuracy or consistency the future turning points of business cycles. Yet these turning points—the peaks and troughs—must be forecast before attempts can be made to moderate their impact with appropriate fiscal policies.

Timing Countercyclical Policies

Because of the difficulty of forecasting cyclical swings, appropriate timing of countercyclical fiscal policies is complicated by a variety of delays. Three types of delays are especially important.

1. Identification Lag It generally takes many months before a cyclical turning point can be identified. By that time a recession or inflation, or perhaps both, may be well underway.

2. Action Lag Even after a cyclical turning point has been identified, it takes many more months before Washington decides on what action is to be taken. The President, the President's advisers, and Congress are all involved in the seemingly interminable debates and compromises that major fiscal-policy decisions entail.

3. Multiplier Lag By the time government expenditure and tax policies are eventually implemented, additional months must pass for their effects to be realized. In fact, it may be necessary for a year or more to elapse before the successive multiplier rounds are completed and their full economic impact is felt.

Because of these factors, the sum of all three lags usually amounts to a total delay of 2 to 3 years.

Unknown Multiplier Effects

A lack of knowledge about the sizes of tax and expenditure multipliers impedes the employment of effective discretionary fiscal policies.

A second source of difficulties with fiscal policy arises from the uncertain consequences of government spending and taxation. In reality, no one really knows the sizes, and therefore the effects, of the expenditure and tax multipliers. Among the main reasons for this are a lack of knowledge about (1) household *MPCs* and (2) the impact of business taxes on investment.

Household *MPCs*

The expenditure and tax multipliers are usually calculated on the assumption that there is an "average" *MPC* for the entire household sector. This may be a vast oversimplification. In reality, the *MPCs* of households can differ widely according to their income levels, their tax brackets, and various other factors. This makes any estimates of the two multipliers very uncertain. As a result, any predictions based on them are open to considerable question.

Taxes and Investment

How do changes in corporate income-tax rates affect business investment? Does an additional dollar of corporate income tax reduce the amount of business investment by some fraction of a dollar? If so, by what fraction? The answer is unknown. However, it is known that at least three factors—taxes, investment, and corporate liquidity—are relevant to the question. In general, when corporations have abundant liquid assets (such as cash and marketable securities), they have more investable funds available relative to their investment opportunities. In such a case, an increase in corporate tax rates will have a smaller impact on investment spending than it will when corporations are relatively illiquid.

Restrictive Effects: Crowding Out

Crowding out can cause a serious decline in private-sector investment expenditures.

One of the most serious consequences of discretionary fiscal policy concerns the problem of "crowding out." As you learned earlier, this can occur when the federal government pursues an expansionary policy by cutting taxes and raising expenditures.

For example, in order to finance its budget deficits, the Treasury borrows in the financial markets by selling debt securities, such as bonds. The Treasury thus competes with private borrowers in bidding for available funds. This causes interest rates—the prices of the funds—to rise. Private borrowers who are unable to pay the higher interest rates find themselves crowded out of the market. Therefore, to the extent that private investment is decreased, the resulting negative multipliers will reduce the positive multipliers arising from the government's spending and tax policies.

Public-Choice Problems: Political Business Cycles

In addition to the economic difficulties of implementing discretionary fiscal policies, there are political problems to overcome. These arise mainly from the nature of our democratic system. Because they deal with the interface between economics and political science, they come under the heading of what is known in both fields as "public choice."

One of the most significant problems concerns the way in which elected officials respond to their constituents. Political leaders know that voters are concerned with the *personal short-term effects* of economic policies. Therefore, in order to seek re-election, legislators will often adopt policies designed to achieve favorable short-term results, regardless of what the unfavorable long-term consequences may be.

For example, it is not unusual for the government to follow conservative spending policies (aimed at curbing inflation) during the early years of an administration and liberal spending policies (intended to stimulate employment) in the later years, as election time draws closer. This has resulted in what economists and political scientists call a "political business cycle"—a type of instability *caused* by discretionary fiscal policies.

Our type of political system tends to encourage inappropriate fiscal policies.

Conclusion: Some Successes and Failures

For these and other reasons, discretionary fiscal policy, which is a logical consequence of Keynesian economics, has been the subject of many critical evaluations. Their main conclusions, based on studies of recessions and inflations since the 1950s, may be summarized briefly.

The evidence shows that Keynesian policies have helped to reduce the depths of recessions, but they have also produced serious inflationary consequences.

Antirecessionary Policies

Attempts to curb recessions have had only limited success. Government taxation and spending programs were generally adopted too late— usually after the worst of a recession was over—to be very effective. Nor have government spending programs succeeded in achieving sustained full employment. However, over the long run, the growing importance of transfer payments (particularly unemployment insurance, welfare assistance, and social-security benefits) has contributed to reducing the severity of business recessions. This is because transfer payments enable recipients to maintain higher levels of consumption expenditures than would be possible otherwise.

Anti-inflationary Policies

Attempts to achieve price stability have been less successful than measures aimed at curbing recession. This is because budget deficits have usually been financed simultaneously by borrowing and by creating money through the banking system. As you have already learned, government borrowing is sufficient to bring about rising prices. And, as you have learned (and will read more about in the next several chapters), creating money is very likely to cause prices to rise. As a result, the economy has experienced prolonged periods of inflation.

To conclude:

On the whole, discretionary fiscal policy has produced some benefits to society as well as some costs:

1. On the benefit side, evidence suggests that, with the help of transfer payments, the severity of recessions has been moderated and their frequency has been reduced.

2. On the cost side, the methods used to finance deficit spending appear to have usually produced serious inflationary consequences without achieving full employment.

On balance, because subjective judgments are involved, there is no scientific way of concluding that the benefits of discretionary fiscal policy have, or have not, been worth the costs.

Some trends in total federal welfare spending—that is, transfer payments—are shown in Box 1.

Case
Reagan's Tax Policies

When Ronald Reagan assumed the presidency in 1981, one of the primary economic goals of his administration was to increase savings. This, it was argued, would make more funds available for business investment, thereby stimulating total production and, hence, employment. To help meet these objectives, Congress passed what has popularly been called "the Reagan Tax Cut of 1981."

Critical Views

Many Keynesians argued that the tax cut would not achieve its stated goal. They contended that tax cuts stimulate consumption, not saving. At best, they argued, there may be a temporary increase in the saving rate—until people adjust their spending to their higher levels of income. Then they splurge on goods and services.

Reagan's advisers disagreed. Referring to "the Kennedy Tax Cut of 1964," the only other major tax reduction in recent history, they supported their arguments with the accompanying graphs.

The Kennedy Tax Cut of 1964

Figure (*a*): This figure shows the difference between actual and predicted consumer expenditures (both in constant dollars) after the tax cut. The predicted line is based on a model developed by the Federal Reserve Bank of San Francisco. Note that, by 1967, actual consumption was almost $18 billion less than predicted—an amount larger than the tax cut. This means that the average propensity to consume declined after the tax cut.

Figures (*b*) and (*c*): It follows, therefore, that the amount of saving, as well as the saving rate, should have increased sharply. The fact that this indeed occurred is verified by Figures (*b*) and (*c*).

What happened to capital investment after the tax cut? It leaped from an average annual rate of 4.2 percent before the cut to 12.9 percent afterward. It then declined as tax rates rose in the late 1960s.

Promote Incentives to Produce

Where did the Keynesian critics of Reagan's policies go wrong? Their thinking, according to Reagan's supporters, neglected the important distinction between average tax rates and marginal tax rates.

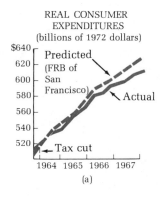

REAL CONSUMER
EXPENDITURES
(billions of 1972 dollars)

(a)

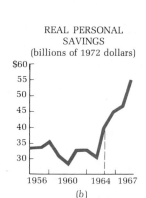

REAL PERSONAL
SAVINGS
(billions of 1972 dollars)

(b)

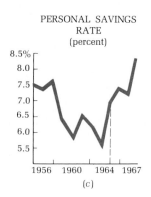

PERSONAL SAVINGS
RATE
(percent)

(c)

Thus, Keynesians advocated lower *average* tax rates in order to encourage more spending, thereby offsetting some "fiscal drag." They should also have stressed reductions in *marginal* tax rates—the taxes paid on the last few dollars of wages, interest, and dividends in each tax bracket. This would promote incentives to produce *additional* income, thereby overcoming the "tax break" of rising marginal tax rates on saving, investing, and working.

Tax Increase of 1982

The Reagan tax cut was coupled with a huge increase in government spending, especially on national defense. This would have led to a massive expansion of the federal deficit. To prevent this, Washington passed the "Reagan Tax Increase of 1982." This law was designed to recapture nearly one-fourth of the taxes lost by the Treasury because of the previous cut. However, most of the new revenues were to have come from the closing of tax loopholes and from stricter measures to ensure compliance with the tax laws. Therefore, according to supporters of the tax increase, the overall objective of Reagan's tax policies remains the same—to increase savings, production, and employment.

Box 1
Total Federal Welfare Spending
(billions of dollars)

Total spending in the form of transfer payments has continued to increase, but the rate of growth has slowed down during the early 1980s. (**Note** Data from 1982 to 1984 are based on forecasts made in 1982.)

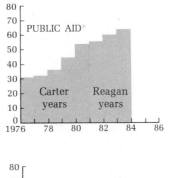

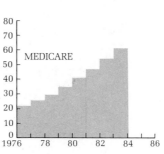

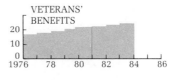

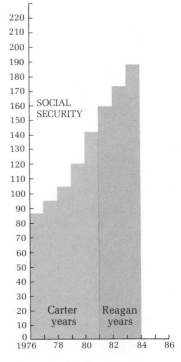

* Includes spending on Medicaid, food stamps and other nutritional programs, housing subsidies, supplemental security income, and aid to families with dependent children.

Alternative Budget Policies

Different types of budget policies are possible. Each has its own economic consequences.

Keynesian fiscal theory calls for budget deficits to ward off recessions and budget surpluses to combat inflations. This is the essence of countercyclical fiscal policy. What does it mean as far as balancing the budget is concerned? Should the federal budget be balanced frequently, occasionally, or not at all?

In attempting to answer this question, four distinctly different policies may be considered:

1. An annually balanced budget.

2. A cyclically balanced budget.

3. "Functional finance."

4. A full-employment balanced budget.

Let us see what each of these policies involves.

Annually Balanced Budget

An annually balanced budget would be procyclical.

Some people argue that the budget should be balanced every 12 months. That is, annual revenues and expenditures should be equal. This policy, its advocates claim, would place the government in an economically "neutral" position by providing a constraint on runaway spending and fiscal disorder.

Is this argument correct? Obviously not. If the federal government balanced the budget each year without regard to fluctuations in the private sector, its actions would not be neutral. Such actions would, in fact, accentuate cyclical swings for two reasons:

1. In recessionary periods, when tax revenues are falling, tax rates would need to be increased and spending would need to be reduced in order to balance the budget.

2. Conversely, during inflationary periods, when tax revenues are rising, tax rates would need to be reduced and spending would need to be increased in order to achieve budgetary balance.

Obviously, therefore, if the budget is to be used as a tool for countercyclical fiscal policy, adherence to annually balanced budgets is impossible.

Cyclically Balanced Budget

Most Keynesians would prefer a cyclically balanced budget, but that is impossible to attain.

Another philosophy holds that the budget should be balanced over the course of the business cycle. This belief, which most Keynesians have always supported, requires the government to incur budget deficits during depression in order to stimulate the economy. Those deficits would need to be offset with budget surpluses during prosperity in order to curb inflationary pressures and help pay off the public debt.

Would such a policy turn the budget into a countercyclical fiscal tool, while preserving the long-term objective of budgetary balance? In theory, the answer is *yes*.

In practice, unfortunately, business cycles are recurrent but not periodic, and their peaks and troughs are not ordinarily equal. Hence, it would be virtually impossible for the government to forecast its revenues and expenditures over the length of a business cycle. Further, it would be very unlikely for the surplus in any given period of prosperity to equal or even approximate the deficit of a previous recession.

Functional Finance

Proponents of the *functional-finance* philosophy contend that the government should pursue whatever fiscal measures are needed to achieve noninflationary full employment and economic growth—without regard to budget balancing per se. The federal budget is thus viewed in a functional sense. That is, it is seen as a flexible fiscal device to be manipulated for achieving economic objectives, not merely as an accounting statement to be balanced periodically.

In reality, functional finance has been the policy usually followed.

Functional finance is a belief that has been most strongly supported by "liberal" Keynesians. However, functional finance has not been without its critics. In their opinion, a balanced budget serves as a rough fiscal guide that should be applied with discretion. By accepting functional finance as a budget policy, the long-run goal of a balanced budget is consigned to oblivion. When this happens, both the means and criteria for preventing runaway spending and inflation are lost.

Full-Employment Balanced Budget

Can a budget policy incorporate the best features of the foregoing proposals? Many experts think so. Their plan is simple. First, determine a level of expenditures based on long-term merits without regard to stabilization considerations. Second, set tax rates to cover those expenditures at full or high employment and, perhaps, to yield a moderate surplus besides.

The full-employment balanced budget does not rely on discretionary fiscal policies.

This plan has two major advantages:

1. It produces an approximately balanced budget over the full course of a business cycle.

2. It rejects the use of discretionary fiscal policy, which is often difficult to apply for both political and economic reasons. Instead, it relies on the use of automatic stabilizers to keep the economy at a high level of employment.

According to critics, however, a full-employment balanced budget has two major disadvantages. First, reliance on automatic stabilizers may not be enough to keep small swings from developing into big ones. Second, there are times when the private sector is either too weak or too strong, so that stabilization may require more substantial and intentional federal deficits or surpluses than the plan would permit.

Conclusion: A Practical Compromise

Which of these alternative budget policies should the federal government follow? Which policy has Washington tended to follow? Which policy would be most practical?

In general, most informed observers agree on these points:

• Ideally, the government should adhere to a policy of cyclically balanced budgets. Realistically, this has proven to be impossible, for reasons explained above.

Exhibit 4
The Public Debt and Interest Payments

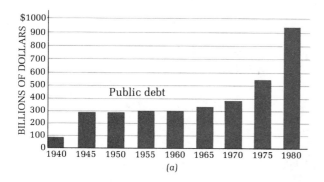

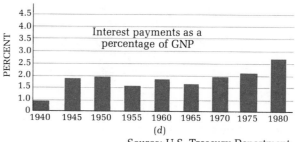

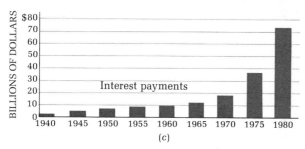

Source: U.S. Treasury Department.

Figure (a): Sharp increases in the national debt have occurred at different times and for different reasons. The main causes of the increases have been the need to pay for wars, national defense, other social goods, and income security benefits to the poor and the disabled. General inflation combined with lagging productivity in the public sector have also been major factors contributing to the increasing costs of government.

Figure (b): The trend of a nation's debt relative to its income or GNP is the best indicator of its ability to carry that debt. Note that the long-run trend has been downward.

Figure (c): The chief burdens of a public debt are the annual interest payments. The long-run trend of these payments has been upward in recent decades.

Figure (d): The long-run trend of interest payments as a percentage of GNP has been fairly stable. Note that the percentage is still relatively low.

• Historically, the government has usually adhered to the practice of functional finance. This has proven to be the most expedient policy in a society whose political leaders, in order to be elected (and re-elected), must satisfy the voters in the short run.

Therefore:

As a practical measure, the most suitable policy is one that strives for a full-employment balanced budget. This would not necessarily assure full or even high employment. Nevertheless, most experts agree that, if consistent efforts were made to adhere to a full-employment budget policy, the results would be more favorable over the long run than those attained from the policies that have actually been followed.

The Public Debt: Myths and Realities

For more than half a century, the number of budget deficits has far exceeded the number of surpluses. As a result, the government has accumulated a substantial national debt. The size of this debt—also called the public debt—has been the subject of a good deal of controversy and criticism. Before exploring the issues that are involved, you should examine the facts by studying the figures and the accompanying comments in Exhibit 4.

Is our present public debt too large? What are its economic consequences? These are the kinds of questions that thoughtful people ask. Some of the answers, as you will see, are contrary to what is widely believed.

The Bankruptcy Myth

One of the most popular misconceptions about a large national debt is that it endangers the nation's credit and may lead to bankruptcy. This belief is a myth. It is rooted in people's emotions rather than in their ability to reason and to interpret facts.

The credit standing of the government of the United States is determined, as it is for any borrower, by those who lend it money. These are the banks, insurance companies, corporations, and households that buy the bonds and other securities sold by the Treasury. Despite its large debt, the government is able to borrow (that is, to sell securities) in competitive markets at the lowest interest rates.

Bankruptcy is a term applied to a borrower who is unable to repay debts. But the federal government need never go bankrupt. Even if it is unable to borrow new funds to pay off old debts, it can always raise taxes or even print money. Therefore:

> The economic consequences of government debt policies will depend on the nation's productive output, such as its real GNP, and not on the size of the debt per se. Hence, objections that a large public debt may endanger the nation's credit rating, or lead to bankruptcy, are based on psychological fears, not economic facts.

A nation's productive output, rather than the size of its debt per se, determines the economic consequences of a large public debt.

It Burdens Future Generations: Myth and Reality

Many people argue that, when the government incurs long-term debt, it burdens future generations with the cost of today's policies. There is some merit to this argument, but several aspects of it need to be examined.

To begin with, keep in mind that the basic idea of cost involves the idea of sacrifice. The real cost of something is not the dollars you spend for it but the value of the alternative that you give up. In view of this, what are the real costs of public debt? The answer depends on whether the debt was incurred to cushion a recession or to help pay for war.

The burden of the national debt depends on the reasons for which the debt was incurred.

Case 1: Antirecession Policy

Suppose the debt is increased by deficit spending during a period of unemployment. To the extent that resources that would otherwise have remained idle are thereby put to work, the increase in debt levies no real cost. That is, there is no added burden, either on the generation that incurs the debt or on future generations. Society has benefited from the greater output, and some of the output has even added to that portion of the nation's capital stock that will be inherited by later generations.

Case 2: Paying for War

The situation is somewhat different if debt is increased to help finance war. In that case, those people living during the war bear the heaviest sacrifice because they must go without civilian goods in order to buy military ones. (Think in terms of the production-possibilities curve.) In addition, spending on war usually starves the nation of capital goods, which are not replaced as fast as they are used up. That burden, more than the burden of increased debt, may be the significant one borne by later generations.

What Are the Real Burdens?

Once we are aware of these myths and realities, attention can be focused on the main burdens of a public debt.

External-Debt Burden: Do We "Owe It to Ourselves"?

A significant proportion of the national debt is owed to foreigners.

In 1960, only about 5 percent of the national debt was owed to foreign creditors. In 1970, the figure was still less than 10 percent. In those days, therefore, it was generally accepted that the debt posed no particular burden because we "owed it to ourselves." That is, the debt was largely owed *by* the people of the United States *to* the people of the United States.

In 1980, approximately 15 percent of the national debt was owed to foreign creditors. Because of this trend, the assertion that we "owe it to ourselves" has become much less meaningful than it once was.

Does a debt owed to foreigners impose a burden on future generations? The answer is that it can. This is because future generations must pay interest and principal without necessarily receiving corresponding benefits in return. The foreign bondholders may well spend their incomes in their own country rather than here. However, an exception can occur if the sums originally borrowed were spent here to buy capital goods and to create jobs. In that case, the resulting current output may be large enough to cover most if not all of the interest and principal payments on the debt.

Income-Redistribution Burden: Do the Rich Get Richer?

The effect of the national debt on income distribution is not a particularly relevant issue.

Of course, the greater part of the nation's debt is owed to domestic bondholders. To the extent that this is so, the payment of interest and repayment of principal are transfer payments. They are financed by tax revenues drawn from all income groups and paid to bondholders who are predominantly in the higher-income groups.

Does this mean that the rich get richer at the expense of everyone else? Many critics answer *yes*. However, the question is largely irrelevant—for three reasons:

1. People in the higher-income groups bought the bonds in the first place, and they are therefore entitled to the principal and interest payments initially agreed upon. (Remember that a bond is a contract between the lender and the borrower and that both parties entering into a contract agree to the stipulated conditions.)

2. A large portion of the national debt is incurred to provide social goods. The benefits of these accrue primarily to people in the lower- and middle-income groups, who pay most of the taxes, rather than to those in the higher-income groups, who hold most of the bonds.

3. If enough people believe that the interest and principal repayments on government bonds tend to favor the rich, society can alter the results through taxation and income-redistribution policies. Indeed, this often happens when the tax laws are changed every few years.

For these reasons, the argument that a growing national debt leads to an inequitable distribution of income is much less significant than is widely believed.

Inflationary Burden: Do Deficits Cause Rising Prices?

A rising public debt results from deficit financing. Critics contend that this can contribute to inflation in three ways.

1. Creating Money If spending is financed by creating money to meet deficits, the inflationary impact is direct. The situation becomes one of "too much money chasing too few goods." You have already encountered this phenomenon, and you will learn much more about it in later chapters.

2. Crowding Out If spending is financed by borrowing from the public and by taxes, the inflationary impact is indirect and takes longer to occur, but it is nevertheless real. Both public borrowing and taxes crowd out private spending, transferring resources from the private sector to the public sector. This creates upward pressure on interest rates while reducing incentives to work, save, and invest. The nation's productivity and economic growth are thereby inhibited.

3. Irresponsible Spending A number of studies covering several decades of history have concluded that deficits foster inefficient and wasteful government spending. (Some of the most critical of these studies have been done by the General Accounting Office, a government agency.) One does not have to be an economist to know that wasteful government spending can be a significant cause of inflation.

A rising debt thus tends to contribute to inflationary pressures. However, *there is no concrete evidence that an increasing debt by itself always causes inflation.* It depends on how the deficits are financed and how they are used. Many countries, including our own, have sometimes experienced relatively stable prices during periods of rising national debt.

The inflationary effect of the national debt depends on how the debt is financed.

Benefits of a Public Debt

In addition to the burdens, there are some benefits of a national debt.

The national debt also has certain benefits.

Financial Investment Advantages

Negotiable Treasury bonds and other securities provide assured safety of principal, interest payments, and frequently a high degree of liquidity. Because of this, these securities are a desirable financial investment for many families and large institutions.

Fiscal-Policy Tool

Within the Keynesian model, changes in the public debt can have desirable effects when used as a tool for discretionary fiscal policy. Indeed, modern countercyclical fiscal theory relies heavily on debt manipulation to achieve and maintain economic efficiency and stability.

However, it should be emphasized that this is a Keynesian argument. As you have learned, *the way in which the debt is financed and used, not the size of the debt itself,* affects economic efficiency and stability. The reasons for this involve issues pertaining to money creation, productivity, and related matters that are taken up in later chapters.

Conclusion: Practical Debt-Management Guidelines

Three practical rules of debt management should be followed.

On the basis of these arguments, should the public debt be allowed to grow without limit? There is no simple answer. However, certain principles of debt management may be formulated. They suggest that the government's ability to meet its payments of interest and principal is determined by the taxable capacity of the nation. This, in turn, depends on the growth of GNP. Therefore:

> There need be no adverse consequences of an indefinitely large public debt, provided that:
>
> **1.** The public debt does not, over the long run, grow faster than GNP. That is, the public debt as a percentage of GNP should not rise for a prolonged period.
>
> **2.** Interest payments on the debt are a relatively small percentage of GNP.
>
> **3.** The debt is incurred for constructive purposes and is financed by noninflationary means.

Looking back at Exhibit 4, can you judge the extent to which some of these guidelines have been followed?

What You Have Learned in This Chapter

1. Fiscal policy is a logical outgrowth of Keynesian economics. The goal of modern fiscal policy is to achieve economic efficiency and stability—that is, full employment without inflation.

2. According to fiscal-policy theory, government spending and tax policies can be used to alter aggregate demand in order to close inflationary or recessionary gaps. For example, an increase in government spending, with taxes held constant, will raise aggregate demand. An increase in taxes, with government spending held constant, will reduce aggregate demand. And a simultaneous and equal change in government spending and taxes will alter national income by the amount of the change. This is because of the operation of the balanced-budget multiplier principle.

3. The balanced-budget multiplier theory rests on some questionable assumptions. Among them are the ideas that (a) government spending does not compete with private spending, (b) increased taxes to finance government spending do not create disincentives, and (c) the *MPCs* of tax-paying and benefit-receiving groups are the same. Because these assumptions are not always realized, increased government spending and taxes may at times impede the private sec-

tor's growth. This would cause unemployment and inflation to worsen rather than improve.

4. Fiscal policy may be discretionary or nondiscretionary. Discretionary fiscal policy is "active," in that it involves conscious changes in government spending and taxation to create expansionary or contractionary effects. Nondiscretionary fiscal policy is "passive," because it relies on automatic or built-in stabilizers to keep the economy on course. Modern fiscal policy embraces some degree of both kinds of policies. However, there are differences of opinion as to the proper combination. The controversy hinges on the extent to which government should be involved in economic activity.

5. There is a difference between the actual budget and the full-employment budget. The latter is an estimate of annual government revenues and expenditures at full employment. It may therefore reveal budgetary surpluses when the actual budget is experiencing deficits, or vice versa. Because of this, Keynesian economics concludes that the full-employment budget provides a more meaningful and reliable guide for judging the thrust of government fiscal policies.

6. In carrying out discretionary fiscal activities, the government's sources of funds may include taxation, borrowing, or printing money. Its spending may include transfer payments and financing of social goods. In brief and general terms, a budget surplus is anti-inflationary, whereas a budget deficit *may* be inflationary. Whether a deficit will actually turn out to be inflationary depends on how it is financed, the use to which it is put, and the stage of the business cycle in which it is incurred.

7. The implementation of discretionary fiscal policies poses several difficulties. They include: (a) business-cycle forecasting and policy timing; (b) the lack of knowledge of multiplier effects; (c) such adverse fiscal-policy consequences as "crowding out"; and (d) such public-choice problems as the creation of "political business cycles." Because of these difficulties, fiscal policy has experienced limited successes as well as serious failures.

8. There is an erroneous tendency to associate some of the dangers of private debt with those of public debt. Thus, it is often argued that a large public debt can endanger the nation's credit standing, lead to bankruptcy, and inevitably shift a burden of principal and interest payments to future generations. In fact, the real burdens of a debt depend on several factors. Among them: whether it (a) is externally held, (b) results in using up capital that is unreplaced, and (c) causes inflation.

9. A large public debt may have adverse psychological consequences. However, its principal and interest must be assessed in relation to GNP and to the growth of the economy as a whole before a meaningful evaluation can be made.

For Discussion

1. *Terms and concepts to review:*
expenditure multiplier
tax multiplier
balanced-budget multiplier
fiscal policy
automatic fiscal stabilizers
full-employment budget
full-employment surplus
full-employment deficit
fiscal drag
crowding out
social goods
annually balanced budget
cyclically balanced budget
functional finance
full-employment balanced budget

2. Assume that the economy is in recession, the MPC is $1/2$, and an increase of $100 billion in output is needed to achieve full employment. Then, using diagrams if necessary, and assuming that private investment is constant, answer the following questions:
(a) How much should government spending be increased to achieve full employment?
(b) What would happen if taxes were reduced by $10 billion? Is this enough to restore full employment? If not, how much of a tax reduction is needed?
(c) What would be the effect of a simultaneous increase in government spending and taxes of $50 billion? Of a simultaneous decrease of $50 billion? Explain why. Would the situation be different in the case of a simultaneous increase in G and T under full employment? Explain.

3. What are our chief automatic stabilizers, and how do they operate?

4. What are the government's sources of revenue and its outlets for expenditures? Which are expansionary? Which are contractionary?

5. In view of the difficulties of applying fiscal policies, it has been suggested that a law involving an automatic tax-rate formula be enacted. In this way, tax rates could be tied to GNP and perhaps to other measures, and they would vary automatically when these measures changed by given percentages. What are some of the chief advantages of such a proposal?

6. What fiscal-policy advantages do you see in the concept of a full-employment budget?

7. "Some increases in government expenditures, such as those for health, education, and welfare, are inflationary, whereas other government expenditures, such as those incurred for national defense and public works, are not." Do you agree? What central questions must be considered to determine whether some government expenditures are more inflationary than others?

8. Evaluate the following argument about the public debt: "No individual or family would be wise to continue accumulating indebtedness indefinitely, for eventually all debts must either be paid or repudiated. It follows that this fundamental principle applies equally well to nations, for, as Adam Smith himself said, 'What is prudence in the conduct of every private family can scarce be folly in that of a great kingdom.'"

Monetary Economics and Macroeconomic Equilibrium

Money, Financial Markets, and the Banking System

Learning guide

Watch for the answers to these important questions

What is money? What forms does it take? How is it defined and measured?

Are credit and debt related to money? What types of credit (or debt) instruments are used as money? In what markets are these instruments exchanged? What economic functions do these markets perform?

Why do financial intermediaries exist? What are they? Why are there different types of financial intermediaries? What economic functions do they perform?

Why was the Federal Reserve System created? What is it? What are its objectives? In general, what minimum functions does a central bank perform that a commercial bank does not?

This chapter explains the meaning of money and its use in our economy.

What is *money*? Most people want it, but few can define it. The average person will probably say: "It's cash, and whatever you've got in the bank." An economist may describe money in terms of its four basic functions—the needs it fulfills in every society:

1. A medium of exchange—money used as a means of payment for things.

2. A measure of value—money used to express the prices of things.

3. A standard of deferred payment—money borrowed or loaned, until it is repaid in the future with interest.

4. A store of value—money saved so that it can be spent in the future.

But money and credit—which is an "extension" of money—are even more important than these functions indicate. For money and credit have a direct influence on the level of economic activity, and some economists argue that the supply of money is the chief determinant of the economy's health.

The reason for this is not hard to see. A monetary system's primary task is to provide society with money that is widely acceptable. This money should also be flexible enough in supply to meet the needs of economic activity. The long history of money shows that this is no easy task. As a result, there has been a continuous evolution of monetary systems designed to achieve these two objectives.

What does it mean to say that the supply of money must be flexible? Interestingly enough, this question can only be answered in terms of the demand for money. Indeed, the demand for money, as this and the following chapters show, poses the most fundamental problem faced by our monetary and banking sytem.

Defining and Measuring Money

If you think you know exactly what money is, you are way ahead of most economists. For economists are always in the midst of a painstaking search for "M"—an ideal measure of the quantity of money available in the United States.

Currently there are several basic measures of the quantity of money. Each of these basic measures seeks to identify a particular component of the money supply. This is illustrated by the following classifications.

Money can be classified into narrow, medium, and broad categories.

M1: Narrow-Transactions Money, the Basic Money Supply

The most familiar form of money is that used by people for routine spending. This classification of money is symbolized $M1$. It is called "narrow-transactions money," which means simply that it is readily spendable. Its components are the currency (and coins) in circulation plus checkable deposits. Narrow-transactions money is also commonly referred to as the "basic money supply."

Currency and checkable deposits are the types of money with which we are most familiar.

Currency

Paper money or *currency*—$1 bills, $5 bills, and so on—makes up roughly 30 percent of the money supply. Any paper money you have will almost certainly say "Federal Reserve Note" across the top. This signifies that it is issued by one of the Federal Reserve Banks. You will read more about them later. Federal Reserve Notes represent more than 99 percent of the total value of paper money in circulation. The rest consists of other types of paper money—some dating far back in history—which are collectors' items.

Note Coins, which are not part of currency, constitute less than 1 percent of the total money supply. Because coins are interchangeable with currency, they are part of $M1$. However, they are a very trivial component, and hence are neglected in discussions of the money supply.

Checkable Deposits

The remaining component of $M1$ is checkable deposits. If you write checks to pay for some of the things you buy, you may have one of several kinds of checkable deposits. It is helpful to distinguish between them.

Demand Deposits If you have a *demand deposit* with a bank, it means that the bank promises to pay immediately an amount of money specified by you, the owner of the deposit. A demand deposit is thus a type of "checkbook money," because it permits transactions to be paid for by check rather than with currency. However, unlike other checkable deposits discussed below, a demand deposit does not pay interest to its owner.

Demand deposits constitute about two-thirds of the basic money supply. Hence they are a major medium of exchange. However, because they are used primarily for business transactions, demand deposits are relatively more important to the financial operations of large banks than to small, consumer-oriented ones.

Demand deposits are the main component of the money supply.

Demand deposits are only one form of checkable deposits.

NOW, Share-Draft, and ATS Deposits In addition to demand deposits, other types of checkable deposits exist. Their most distinguishing feature is that they are actually savings-type checking accounts. These are of three types.

1. Negotiable-Order-of-Withdrawal (NOW) Accounts These are essentially interest-bearing checking accounts. They are offered by most banks, savings and loan associations, and other depository institutions.

2. Share-Draft Accounts These are basically the same as NOW accounts, but they are provided by credit unions.

3. Automatic-Transfer-Services (ATS) Accounts These are a combination of interest-bearing savings and zero-balance checking accounts. They are offered by many commercial banks. If you have an ATS account, your bank will simply switch funds from your savings account to your checking account when the checks you write are presented to the bank for payment. Therefore, a more apt description would be "automatic-transfer-of-savings" accounts.

> The largest component of checkable deposits, as well as of the basic money supply, is demand deposits. Because they are immediately convertible into cash, the *narrowest* measure of money within the $M1$ category is currency and demand deposits.

M2: Medium-Range Money

Savings deposits and certain short-term credit instruments are also money.

You can think of $M1$ as the narrowest class of monetary assets that people own. Therefore, a broader class would consist of $M1$ plus certain other assets. This enlarged category, symbolized $M2$, may be regarded as medium-range money. Among the components of $M2$ are savings deposits and certain short-term credit instruments.

Savings Deposits

Savings deposits may take different forms, such as passbook accounts, savings certificates, and certificates of deposit. All, however, are simply different kinds of time deposits.

A *time deposit* is money held in a depository-institution account of an individual or firm. Several types of time deposits have specified maturity dates, at which times the principal with accumulated interest becomes payable to the owner. For other kinds of time deposits, the depository institution may require advance notice of withdrawal. Small-denomination time deposits—the types that are counted in $M2$— are those under $100,000.

Repurchase Agreements (RPs)

Certain borrowers and lenders often make contracts involving the sale and buyback of short-term credit instruments. Such contracts are called *repurchase agreements* (RPs). The borrower sells the securities to the lender and agrees to repurchase them on a later date at the same price plus interest.

RPs are used extensively by commercial banks.

RPs frequently arise when a bank is temporarily in need of funds and a corporation has idle cash balances to lend. The bank borrows by contracting to sell and repurchase some of its short-term government securities, such as U.S. Treasury bills. All banks hold government securities, including Treasury bills and bonds, in their portfolios as part of their income-earning assets. By selling some of these assets to the lending corporation, the bank acquires the temporary funds it needs and the corporation earns a return on what amounts to a secured loan to the bank. The terms of RPs may range from one day to several months. Those included in M2 are overnight RPs held by commercial banks.

Money-Market Mutual-Fund Shares

The *money market* is a center where short-term credit instruments, such as U.S. Treasury bills, corporations' commercial paper or promissory notes, and other types of financial claims described later, are bought and sold. A mutual fund is an organization that pools people's money and uses it to buy securities, such as stocks and bonds. Putting the two terms together, a money-market mutual fund is one that buys money-market securities.

Money-market mutual-fund shares have become an important type of money.

If you own shares (that is, a deposit account) in a money-market mutual fund, as do millions of individuals and corporations, you can write checks against your account. The minimum amount of the check must usually be $500. Therefore, an account of this type is like a checkable deposit included in M1, but it is somewhat more restrictive. Because of this, it is counted as part of M2.

Eurodollars

Many dollar deposits are held in banks outside the United States, mostly in Europe. These deposits are called *Eurodollars*. They are owned by American and foreign banks, corporations, and individuals. Eurodollars represent dollar obligations that are constantly being shifted from one country to another in search of the highest return. Because of their growing importance in our financial system, overnight Eurodollars held by U.S. residents are included in the measure of M2.

M3: Wide-Range Money

A still broader classification of money is obtained by extending the conditions of certain items in the previous category. This classification, symbolized M3, may be thought of as wide-range money. It includes these two additional components:

Large deposits and paper claims that are easily convertible to cash constitute still another form of money.

1. Large-denomination time deposits at all depository institutions. A large-denomination time deposit is one of $100,000 or more.

2. Term repurchase agreements. These are RPs arranged for at least two days and as long as three months, and sometimes even longer.

L: Liquid and Near-Liquid Assets

The broadest classification of money is symbolized L. It consists of the most liquid asset, cash, plus near-liquid assets—paper claims that are easily convertible to cash. The L classification thus includes M1, M2, and M3, as well as three additional types of assets:

1. U.S. savings bonds and other government obligations, such as Treasury bills and Treasury bonds.

2. Term Eurodollar deposits (that is, those with terms longer than one day) held by U.S. residents other than banks.

3. Certain business obligations, such as commercial paper issued by major corporations and banker's acceptances (explained later in the chapter) issued by banks.

Conclusion: Money Is a Spectrum of Assets

Just as there is no single color that characterizes a rainbow, so too there is no adequate single measure of money. A rainbow is a spectrum of colors; money is a spectrum of assets.

Against this background, what does it mean to ask such questions as "What is money?" and "How is it measured?"

> Currency and checkable deposits are readily convertible one into another. Therefore, they constitute money in the *narrow* sense.

In a broader sense, some other assets are also "money." But they are often called *near-monies*. Their values are known in terms of money, and they can easily be converted into money, if this is desired. Some important examples are time deposits, such as savings certificates, and U.S. government short-term securities held by individuals and businesses. Other examples include the cash value of insurance policies, high-grade commercial paper, and similar near-liquid assets.

The concept of near-monies is important, because people who possess near-monies may feel wealthier and hence have higher propensity-to-consume curves. This, as you already know, will affect the levels of income and employment for the economy as a whole.

Thus, the answers to the questions "What is money?" and "How is it measured?" are by no means simple. Because there are different concepts of money, its definition and measurement are subject to controversy. The issues are examined in later chapters. Meanwhile, you will find it helpful to think about money in the following way:

> Money is more than just paper currency and coins. *Money is a spectrum of assets ranging from currency and checkable deposits through various types of time deposits to financial claims against businesses and the U.S. Treasury.* Because of this, many economists are seeking to develop an ideal measure of money—one that best explains its influence on the levels of income, employment, and prices.

The foregoing ideas are summarized in the description and illustrations of Exhibit 1.

Financial Markets

> Who goeth a borrowing goeth a sorrowing.
>
> Benjamin Franklin

> Let us all be happy and live within our means, even if we have to borrow the money to do it.
>
> Anonymous

One of the reasons why money is a complex concept is that it is closely related to debt and credit. This is what you would expect, because credit replaces money, supplements money, and, in the final analysis, provides the base of the nation's money supply.

Most people do not realize that debt and credit are the same thing looked at from two different sides. If a friend lends you money, his credit to you is the same as your debt to him. In general, the term *credit* implies a promise by one party to pay another for money borrowed or for goods or services received. Credit may therefore be regarded as an extension of money.

A significant part of credit is that part represented by *credit instruments*. These are written or printed financial documents that serve either as promises to pay or as orders to pay. They provide the means by which funds are transferred from one party to another.

The most familiar example of a credit instrument is an ordinary *promissory note,* or simply a *note.* It is an "I.O.U."—a promise made by one party to pay another a specified sum of money by a given date, usually within a year. Such notes are issued by individuals, corporations, and government agencies. Firms make heavy use of notes in order to borrow working capital from banks at certain busy times of the year. The interest on such loans is a chief source of income for many financial institutions, such as banks.

Various other types of credit instruments exist. The most important ones are traded in the nation's financial markets, whose components are the money market and the capital market. As you will see, both of these markets perform the important economic function of exchanging claims for liquidity. That is, in the financial markets, organizations that have surplus funds can purchase claims against organizations that are in need of funds.

The Money Market

Markets exist for many types of credit instruments, just as for commodities. As you have learned, a *money market* is a center where short-term credit instruments issued by banks, corporations, and governmental entities are bought and sold. A variety of credit instruments are traded in the money market. Among the most important are the following.

L = LIQUID AND NEAR-LIQUID ASSETS
  Treasury obligations,
    including bills and bonds.
  Term Eurodollars, high-grade
    commercial paper, and
    banker's acceptances.

M3 = WIDE-RANGE MONEY
  Large-denomination time deposits.
  Term repurchase agreements.

M2 = MEDIUM-RANGE MONEY
  Savings (time) deposits.
  Repurchase agreements (overnight).
  Money market mutual-fund shares.
  Eurodollars (overnight).

M1 = NARROW-TRANSACTIONS MONEY:
  BASIC MONEY SUPPLY
  Checkable deposits:
    Demand, NOW, share-draft, and
    ATS accounts.

  Currency

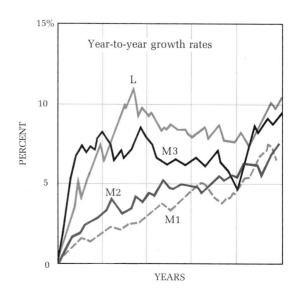

Treasury Bills

U.S. Treasury bills are the major instruments sold in the money market.

Each week, in order to help finance its operations, the U.S. Treasury issues marketable obligations known as *Treasury bills.* They have minimum denominations of $10,000, and they usually mature in 3 months, 6 months, or 1 year. The Treasury sells the bills in weekly auctions at a discount from face value. This means that, if you buy a 1-year Treasury bill today for $9,000, you will receive $10,000 at maturity—a rate of return of about 11%.

The money that the Treasury raises from the sale of its bills helps the federal government to meet its operating expenses. These include the salaries of civil-service employees and armed-forces personnel, the costs of supplies for government offices, and numerous other things for which the government disburses money. In terms of dollar volume, Treasury bills are by far the dominant money-market instrument.

Other Instruments

Various other instruments of the money market are becoming increasingly important.

Government agencies, banks, and corporations sell a variety of other interest-earning money-market securities. The more important ones may be identified briefly.

Federal Agency Discount Notes These are sold by certain government agencies. Among them are the Federal Home Loan Bank, the Federal National Mortgage Association, and the Federal Farm Credit Bank System. The money raised by these agencies is used to provide mortgages and other types of loans.

Negotiable Certificates of Deposit (CDs) These are large-denomination notes ($100,000 or more) issued by major banks. The banks sell these securities to corporations and large individual investors, who buy them for their interest payments. (As you may know, most banks also sell deposit or savings certificates for smaller investors. However, these are merely special types of time deposits. They are smaller in size and are not resalable, unlike negotiable CDs.)

Commercial Paper This consists of promissory notes, in minimum denominations of $10,000, sold by several hundred major corporations. The most familiar example is GMAC paper, issued by General Motors Acceptance Corporation, to finance the purchase of General Motors cars.

Banker's Acceptances These instruments arise both in domestic trade and in international trade. In effect, a *banker's acceptance* (BA) is a bank-guaranteed "postdated check" written by one of its customers. If the bank stamps the check "accepted," it becomes a BA. This means that the bank assumes the customer's debt and guarantees payment on the postdated day. (The customer, of course, must eventually repay the bank the full amount plus interest.) In the interim, if the bank should need short-term funds, it can sell the check at a discount from face value in the money market.

Repurchase Agreements Popularly known as RPs or "repos," these constitute a kind of collateralized loan. As mentioned earlier, in a *repurchase agreement* the borrower sells the lender a credit instrument, usually a government security. In addition, the borrower simultaneously agrees to buy the instrument back on a later date at the same price plus interest at a specified rate. The lender (investor) thus holds a security as collateral for a loan with a fixed maturity and a fixed interest rate. Banks, often in need of short-term funds, are major users of RPs. The RPs are sold to corporations and large individual customers who have surplus cash balances to lend.

Tax-Exempt Instruments These are short-term obligations sold by some state and local governments and by local housing and urban-renewal agencies. They are issued in anticipation of future tax revenues. Banks are among the major purchasers of these instruments. One reason is that they are considered safer from default than some other money-market instruments. Another is that their interest payments are exempt from federal income taxation.

Federal Funds Unlike the credit instruments described so far, *federal funds* are not represented by paper claims that change hands in the money market. Instead, they are unsecured loans that banks and certain other depository institutions make to one another, usually overnight, out of their excess reserves. Although federal funds are an integral part of the money market, the purchase and sale of such funds is limited to banks, savings institutions, and certain government agencies.

The Capital Market

Besides the money market, the other important type of financial market is the *capital market*. This is where long-term financial instruments that mature in more than 1 year are bought and sold.

Many borrowers turn to the capital market for long-term loans that mature in more than a year.

For example, bonds of various types are among the major credit instruments traded in the capital market. A *bond* is an agreement to pay a specified sum of money (called the principal) either at a future date or periodically over the course of a loan. During this time, a fixed rate of interest may be paid on certain dates. Bonds are issued by corporations (corporate bonds), state and local governments (municipal bonds), and the federal government (government bonds). Bonds are used for long-term financing.

Five major types of instruments are bought and sold in the capital market:

1. U.S. government bonds—issued by the Treasury and by certain government agencies, such as the Federal National Mortgage Association, and the Federal Home Loan Bank.

2. Municipal bonds—issued by state and local governments.

3. Corporate bonds.

4. Mortgages.

5. Corporate stock.

The yields on these securities differ from one another at any given time. The differences reflect maturity dates, coupon rates, risk of default, tax treatment, and other factors.

In general, municipal bonds tend to have the lowest yields. This is because the interest received by purchasers of such bonds is exempt from federal income taxes. Therefore, these bonds can be sold at lower yields than comparable Treasury and corporate taxable bonds.

The yields on capital-market securities depend on a number of factors. Therefore, there is no single yield (or interest rate) in the capital market.

Exhibit 2
Capital-Market Yields

Yields on securities tend to differ from one another at any given time, depending on risk of default, maturity dates, tax advantages, and many other factors. Note that the various yields tend to rise and fall at about the same time.

Long-term Treasury bonds generally have a lower yield than comparable corporate bonds. The reason is that Treasury bonds carry no risk of default. Yields on high-quality corporate bonds are, in turn, lower than those on mortgages, which cost more to administer and are not so easily marketed.

A comparison of interest yields for these different types of securities is shown in Exhibit 2.

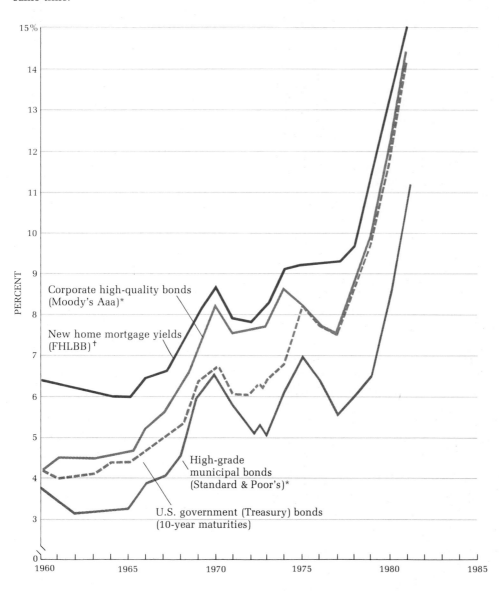

* Moody's and Standard & Poor's are private companies that rate the quality of bonds issued by corporations and government agencies. A rating of Aaa represents the highest quality—that is, the lowest risk of default.

† FHLBB stands for the Federal Home Loan Bank Board, a governmental agency.

Conclusion: Important Economic Functions

The business and government sectors are continually seeking funds to finance production of goods and services. The acquisition of these funds is made possible through financial markets, namely the money market and the capital market. Taken together, these markets perform the task of transferring funds from lenders to borrowers. More specifically:

The *financial markets* provide important economic functions:

1. The money market primarily enables firms and government entities (federal, state, and local) to obtain liquidity. This happens when these organizations acquire funds by selling short-term claims against themselves.

2. The capital market primarily facilitates the transfer of funds from savers to borrowers. This occurs when borrowing institutions acquire funds by selling long-term claims against themselves.

To some extent, these functions overlap. In general, however, *the money and capital markets allocate financial resources between borrowers and lenders and between short-term and long-term uses.*

The money and capital markets allocate financial resources.

The world's largest financial markets are in New York City. Other major markets exist in London, Paris, Hong Kong, Tokyo, and certain other cities. These markets attract funds from numerous countries and perform a vital function in financing the needs of businesses and governments.

Financial Intermediaries

The institutions that serve the money and capital markets are known as *financial intermediaries.* These organizations constitute a connecting link between lenders and borrowers. How? By creating and issuing financial obligations or claims against themselves in order to acquire profitable financial claims against others.

Financial intermediaries "connect" borrowers and lenders, thereby serving as wholesalers and retailers of funds.

A chief function of financial intermediaries, therefore, is to provide *liquidity.* This refers to the ease with which an asset can be converted into cash quickly without loss of value in terms of money. In this and the next few chapters, you will learn how financial intermediaries fulfill this function.

For our purposes, financial intermediaries may be divided into two broad classes: (1) commercial banks and (2) all other financial institutions. These include mutual savings banks, savings and loan associations, credit unions, insurance companies, private pension funds, finance companies, mortgage companies, and so on. As indicated above, all financial intermediaries serve as wholesalers or retailers of funds.

Commercial Banks

All banks deal in money and credit instruments. However, a *commercial bank* is the only type of bank engaged in making short-term loans by creating demand deposits. (Remember that a demand deposit is the technical term for a checkable deposit that does not pay interest to its owner.) In addition, a commercial bank may engage in many of the same activities carried on by other financial institutions. These activities include taking savings accounts or time deposits and providing life insurance. However, a commercial bank's fundamental business is handling demand deposits.

A major purpose of commercial banks is to lend money by creating demand deposits.

When you establish a demand-deposit account with a commercial bank, the bank creates and issues a financial obligation or claim against itself. It does this by agreeing to honor your checks on demand up to the amount of the deposit.

When a bank accepts your savings or time deposit, it creates a claim against itself that is legally payable after a specified time. For example, although a bank rarely does so, it can, if it wishes, require notice of intended withdrawal from a passbook savings deposit—usually 30 days or more. Hence, any time deposit, of which a passbook savings deposit is perhaps the most familiar type, may be thought of as a claim that possesses a stipulated maturity date.

Other instruments representing time-deposit claims are savings bonds and savings certificates. However, none of these are as liquid as demand deposits. In fact:

Demand deposits are the single most important component of the money supply.

> Demand deposits are among the most liquid of all claims created and issued by financial intermediaries. Because checks written against them are instantly acceptable in exchange, demand deposits are included with currency as the *narrowest* measure of the money supply. As you have learned, currency and checkable deposits, of which demand deposits are by far the largest component, constitute what has been called "narrow-transactions money," or the *basic money supply*.

The role played by commercial banks in expanding and contracting demand deposits is of enormous importance in understanding how the economy works. Therefore, commercial banking will occupy a considerable part of our attention in this and in subsequent chapters.

Other Financial Intermediaries

Like commercial banks, other kinds of financial intermediaries seek to accommodate the particular needs and preferences of borrowers by creating and issuing claims against themselves.

For example, mutual savings banks and savings and loan associations issue time-deposit claims. These are very much like those provided by commercial banks—except, in some cases, for differences in maturities and yields. The assets or claims against others that the issuing institutions acquire with the funds consist primarily of real-estate mortgages, corporate bonds, and government securities.

Likewise, credit unions issue savings-deposit claims to their members and acquire claims against others primarily in the form of consumer loans. Insurance companies issue claims in the form of policies against themselves and use most of the funds collected in premiums to purchase real-estate mortgages, corporate securities, and government bonds. In like manner, other financial intermediaries generate obligations against themselves in order to acquire funds with which to purchase profitable, but often less liquid, obligations against others.

Some Economic Implications

One of the most important economic functions of financial intermediaries is to provide the economy with liquidity.

In view of the activities of financial intermediaries, a few facts about their role in our economy should be mentioned.

> Financial intermediaries perform important economic functions. They provide the economy with the money supply and with near-liquid assets. Financial intermediaries thus facilitate investment in plant, equipment, and inventories.

As issuers of claims against themselves and as suppliers of funds to other sectors, financial intermediaries, especially banks, must strive to maintain their liquidity. They can do this by observing certain practical rules for survival. Two are especially important:

Rule 1: Lend Short and Borrow Long

Banks should make short-term loans, usually for less than a year, and finance them by issuing claims against themselves for longer periods. This would give banks greater control over their short-term interest income while "locking in" their long-term interest expenses. In reality, banks sometimes do the opposite—they "borrow short and lend long." During certain periods, for instance, some banks may have 10- to 20-year loans outstanding, often to small African and Asian countries. However, the banks will be financing the loans with 90-day certificates of deposit, or with other short-term funds.

Rule 2: Spread Loans Widely

A second rule is to diversify loans among different types of borrowers. In this way, by not "placing all of their eggs in one basket," banks can reduce the risks of borrowers defaulting on their loans. In practice, banks sometimes bend this rule in order to expand their loans. As a result, when an industry that has experienced much growth suddenly takes a turn for the worse, those banks that engaged too heavily in financing the industry's expansion are likely to participate in its decline.

Some banks do not always adhere to the rules of good banking practice. The result can be bank failure—that is, bankruptcy.

Conclusion: Maintaining Liquidity

Because the claims acquired by financial intermediaries are frequently less liquid than the claims they issue, it seems plausible that these intermediaries may sometimes find themselves temporarily illiquid. This means that they are unable to meet unexpected demands for payment out of their own assets. Situations of this type occurred frequently in American history and were especially serious during the depression of the 1930s. Sometimes they gave rise to financial crises or panics.

Legislation has been passed to minimize the chances of financial intermediaries becoming even temporarily illiquid.

To help remedy this problem, legislation designed to protect the public has been passed. It has provided insurance for bank deposits and set minimum financial requirements for banks, insurance companies, and certain other financial intermediaries. In addition, federally sponsored institutions have been created to provide liquidity to some financial intermediaries by lending to them or by purchasing assets from them. Notable among these have been special federal banks that supply funds to savings and loan associations and make intermediate-term loans to farmers. Most important for our purposes, however, have been the Federal Reserve Banks. They supply funds to depository institutions as one of the functions of the Federal Reserve System.

The Federal Reserve System

On December 23, 1913, President Woodrow Wilson signed the Federal Reserve Act. It was, according to its preamble, "An Act to provide for the establishment of Federal Reserve Banks, to furnish an elastic currency, to afford means of rediscounting commercial paper, to establish a more effective supervision of banking in the United States, and for other purposes." Section 4 of the new statute charged the Federal Reserve Banks with making ". . . such discounts, advancements, and accommodations as may be safely and reasonably made with due regard for . . . the maintenance of sound credit conditions, and the accommodations of commerce, industry, and agriculture."

The act marked the beginning of a new era in American banking. Periodic money panics—"runs" on banks by depositors fearing that the banks were failing—had plagued the country for many years. Based on what was learned from the great panic of 1907, one of the worst in American history, the act was designed to end extreme variations in the money supply and thus avoid panics. It did succeed in contributing to economic stability.

Case
Money Panics and the Banking System: How the Federal Reserve System Came About

American banking history records a series of attempts to provide a currency that could expand or contract according to the demands of business. Theoretically, the ability of commercial banks, through the lending process, to expand or contract the amount of money available should have provided for the demands occasioned by changes in business activity.

Commercial banks, however, while they could expand credit, could not add to the amount of available currency. Inasmuch as bank depositors had a legal right to withdraw their money in the form of currency and coin, banks provided for ordinary withdrawals by retaining a part of their total deposits in the form of reserves. These reserves usually consisted of currency, coin, and deposits in other banks.

Money Panics

Occasionally there would be a general increase in demand by depositors for their money at a time when demand deposits created by loans were already high. This would create a situation in which the available amount of currency and coin might not cover the percentage of reserves that the banks had set up. An unusual demand by depositors forced banks to exchange their assets, such as securities and deposits

Brown Brothers

The money crisis of October 1907 brought thousands of nervous investors to New York City's Wall Street, the financial center of the world.

On October 29, 1907, in the midst of the crisis, business buccaneer and financial tycoon John Pierpont Morgan wrote a personal guarantee on his library stationery to support the credit of New York City.

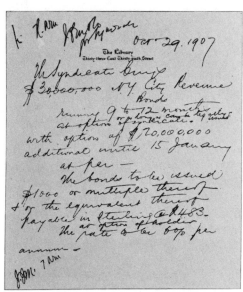

Brown Brothers

Photoworld/F.P.G.

with other banks, for currency. An attempt by one bank to supply itself with currency by withdrawing its reserve balance from another all too frequently set up a "chain reaction," which resulted in a widespread shortage of currency among many banks.

Some banks were forced to close, although their assets could have been converted into currency if sufficient time had been allowed. A widespread closing of banks resulting from unusual demands by depositors invariably brought on a period of economic depression. These unusual demands were called "money panics," and one that occurred in 1907 set into motion a thorough study of our nation's money system.

Congressional Commission

The congressional commission charged with this study found that almost all countries with a money supply that could be expanded or contracted to meet the needs of the depositors also had some form of central bank. This bank had the power to issue a currency that depositors would accept. As a result of this and other studies, Congress in 1913 passed the law that created the Federal Reserve System.

Objectives, Organization, and Functions of the Federal Reserve System

The *Federal Reserve System* is the nation's central bank. This means that, like other central banks throughout the world, the Federal Reserve's chief responsibility is to regulate the flow of money and credit in order to promote economic stability and growth. It also performs many service functions for commercial banks and other depository institutions, the Treasury, and the public. In specific terms, the Federal Reserve System seeks to provide monetary conditions favorable to the realization of four national objectives: high employment, stable prices, economic growth, and a sound international financial position.

The Federal Reserve System is organized essentially like a pyramid, as illustrated in Exhibit 3. It consists of (1) member banks, (2) Federal Reserve Banks, (3) a Board of Governors, (4) a Federal Open Market Committee, and (5) other committees.

Member Banks

At the base of the Federal Reserve pyramid are the System's *member banks*. All national banks (chartered by the federal government) must be members, and state banks (chartered by their respective states) may join if they meet certain requirements. Of some 14,000 commercial banks, less than 6,000 are members. However, these member banks are for the most part the larger banks in the country, holding the great bulk of all demand deposits.

Today the number of member banks relative to nonmember banks is not particularly significant. This is because legislation enacted in 1980 requires *all* depository institutions, members as well as nonmembers, to meet the same standards with respect to reserve requirements. In addition, all institutions can purchase, on equal terms, any of the System's services, such as check clearing and wire transfer of funds. Therefore, although more than half the banks in the nation do not belong to the Federal Reserve System, this does not affect the System's ability to influence the economy by controlling the money supply.

Nearly 70 years later, in the mid-1970s, New York City once again teetered on the brink of bankruptcy. Unable to redeem its bonds, owing to years of financial mismanagement, the city had to be rescued by the State of New York and forced to put its financial house in order.

The major function of the Federal Reserve System is to regulate the nation's money supply.

Exhibit 3
Organization and Map of the Federal Reserve System

Note Alaska is in the Seattle Branch territory and Hawaii is in the territory served by the Head Office of the Federal Reserve Bank of San Francisco. Both are in the Twelfth District.

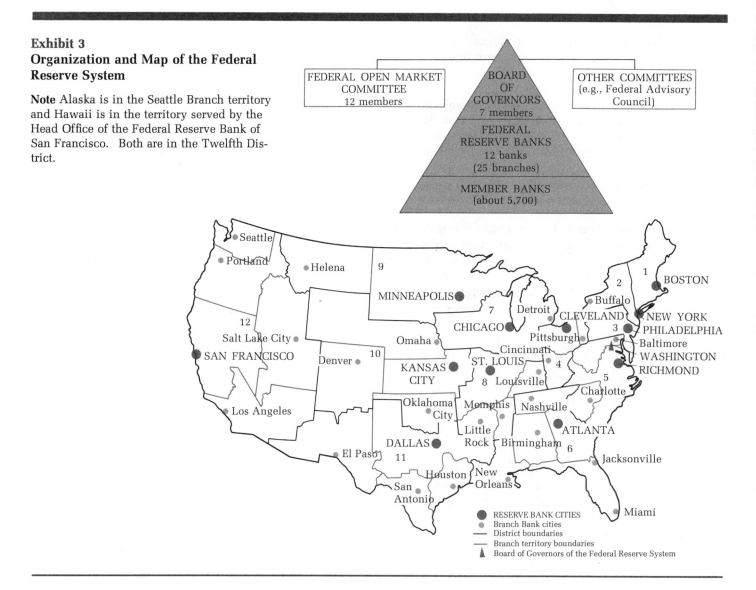

Federal Reserve Banks

The country is divided into twelve Federal Reserve districts, each with a *Federal Reserve Bank.* There are also twenty-five Federal Reserve Bank branches serving areas within the districts. (See the map in Exhibit 3.)

Technically, each Federal Reserve Bank is owned by its member banks, which are the stockholders. But, unlike most private institutions, the Reserve Banks are operated in the public interest rather than for profit. However, they are, in fact, highly profitable because of the interest income they earn on the government securities that they own. Thus, after meeting their expenses, they pay a relatively small part of their earnings to the member banks as dividends, and the major portion is returned to the U.S. Treasury. Note that the district Federal Reserve Banks (and branches) constitute the second level of the pyramid.

Board of Governors

At the peak of the pyramid is the *Board of Governors* in Washington. It consists of seven members appointed by the President and confirmed by the Senate. Members are appointed for fourteen years, one term expiring every two years. Because members do not come and go with every election, political influences on the Board are thus reduced. The chairperson of the Board, who is also a member of the Board, is appointed by the President for a four-year term.

The Board supervises the Federal Reserve System and sees that it performs effectively. But its prime function is to influence the amount of money and credit within the economy. The Board does this by engaging in certain special activities that are explained and evaluated in subsequent chapters.

Federal Open Market Committee

The most important policy-making body within the System is the *Federal Open Market Committee*. It consists of twelve members—the seven Governors plus five Presidents of the major Federal Reserve Banks. Its chief function is to make policy for the System's purchase and sale of government and other securities in the open market in New York. Actual transactions are carried on by the "Trading Desk" of the Federal Reserve Bank of New York. Government securities bought outright are then allocated among the twelve Reserve Banks according to a formula based upon the reserve ratios of the various Reserve Banks.

Several committees assist the Fed in its regulatory and policy-making activities.

Other Committees and Functions

Several other committees play a significant role in the System's operations. One of these is the *Federal Advisory Council*, which advises the Board on important current developments.

To conclude:

The Federal Reserve System is the central banking system of the United States. *The primary purpose of the "Fed" is to regulate the flow of money and credit in order to promote economic stability and growth.* In addition, it provides a number of important services to the Treasury, the public, and depository institutions. These services include:

1. Performing the function of fiscal agent for the Treasury,

2. Operating a nationwide "clearing-house" for checks.

3. Providing for the wire transfer of funds from one depository institution to another anywhere in the country.

4. Supplying coin and currency for circulation.

Organization of the Banking System

How is the nation's banking system structured and supervised? This question is important because the banking industry is the largest and most important financial institution in our economy.

Banking Structure: Our Dual Banking System

The United States has long had what is known as a *dual banking system*. This unusual structure, not found in any other country, grew out of legislation passed during the 1860s, whose purpose was the creation of federally chartered banks. As a result, our dual banking system consists of two classes of commercial banks—national banks and state banks.

You can always tell a national bank from a state bank. A national bank is required to have either the word "national" in its title or the letters "N.A." (for *national association*) after its name. If it has neither, it is a state bank.

Our banking system is regulated by several government agencies, resulting in waste of resources and duplication of effort.

National Banks These are commercial banks chartered by the federal government. Such banks are required to belong to the Federal Reserve System. About one-third of all commercial banks today are national banks; the rest are state banks. Although fewer in number, national banks hold considerably more than half the deposits of the banking system and are larger than most state banks.

State Banks These are commercial banks chartered by state governments. State banks may or may not be members of the Federal Reserve System. Today, only a relatively small minority of state banks (about 10 percent) are member banks. ■

Banking Supervision: A Regulatory Thicket

Our dual banking system, which is rooted in America's political history, has led to the nation's banks being regulated by several government agencies.

Comptroller of the Currency This federal agency charters all national banks. It also oversees the operations both of national banks and of those state banks that are members of the Federal Reserve System.

Federal Reserve System The "Fed," as it is popularly known, exercises some degree of regulation over all banks, national as well as state. In addition, the Fed exerts some control over thrift institutions, such as savings banks and savings and loan associations.

Federal Deposit Insurance Corporation (FDIC) This agency (described below) supervises the operations of all insured banks. These include national banks, state banks that belong to the Fed, and insured banks that do not. Relatively few banks, however, are uninsured. The FDIC, therefore, has regulatory authority over almost all banks.

State Banking Commissions All fifty states exercise varying degrees of control over their state-chartered banks. The only banks not subject to state regulations are national banks. This is because they are federally chartered and hence subject to federal regulations.

Thus:

> All banks in the United States are regulated by at least two government agencies, most are regulated by three, and many are regulated by four. As a result, there is considerable overlapping and conflicting supervisory responsibility among the regulatory agencies. This leads to much waste of resources and duplication of effort.

The complex network of regulation is illustrated in Exhibit 4.

Deposit Insurance: Protecting Your Money

The FDIC is a government agency that insures bank deposits.

What happens to your money if a bank in which you have a deposit fails? Chances are you will be protected by insurance, because of the existence of the *Federal Deposit Insurance Corporation* (FDIC). This government agency came into existence in 1934 when the country was in the throes of a major depression. More than 9,000 banks had failed during the years 1930–1933, leaving depositors unprotected. The FDIC was created to correct this problem and thereby help improve bank stability.

The primary function of the FDIC is to insure deposits (demand and time) at commercial and savings banks. Each insured bank pays an annual premium equal to a fraction of 1 percent of its total deposits. In return, the FDIC insures each account up to $100,000 against loss due to bank failure. In addition to its insurance function, the FDIC supervises insured banks and presides over the liquidation of banks that do fail. Two parallel agencies that perform similar functions are the Federal Savings and Loan Insurance Corporation (FSLIC), which insures deposits in savings and loan associations, and the National Credit Union Administration, which provides deposit insurance for federally chartered credit unions.

All national banks must be insured by the FDIC, and state banks may apply for coverage if they wish. Since the late 1930s, practically all banks (more than 98 percent) have been covered by this insurance. Banks have thus become much more stable than they were before the creation of government insurance. As a result, widespread runs on banks by panicky depositors seeking to withdraw their funds have ceased to occur.

Exhibit 4
The Bank-Regulation Thicket

Bank regulatory agencies exchange some of their information and accept one another's audits for certain purposes. Nevertheless, duplication of efforts in the regulation of banking leads to much inefficiency and waste of resources.

Note that this diagram provides a partial illustration of the regulatory maze. It includes only commercial banks and no other types of depository institutions, such as credit unions and savings and loan associations. These are regulated by the Fed as well as by other agencies not shown.

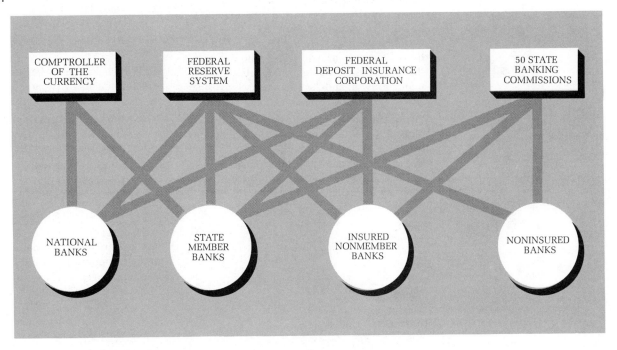

What You Have Learned in This Chapter

1. Money is a medium of exchange, a measure of value, a standard of deferred payments, and a store of value. The demand for money is the most fundamental problem of our monetary and banking system.

2. Money should be thought of as a spectrum of assets. "Narrow-transactions money," M1, is readily spendable money. It constitutes the basic money supply and consists of currency and checkable deposits. The largest component of checkable deposits is demand deposits. Because these are immediately convertible into cash, the *narrowest* measure of money is currency and demand deposits.

3. Broader measures than M1 also exist. They include savings deposits, money-market mutual-fund shares, and various kinds of near-monies that consist of highly liquid assets.

4. The two major financial markets are the money market and the capital market. Short-term credit instruments are bought and sold in the former, long-term instruments in the latter. These markets thus perform the economic function of allocating financial resources between borrowers and lenders and between short-term and long-term uses.

5. Financial intermediaries, such as banks, insurance companies, credit unions, and other financial institutions, are connecting links between lenders and borrowers. They create and issue financial claims against themselves in order to acquire proceeds with which to purchase profitable financial claims against others. In general, they serve as wholesalers or retailers of funds.

6. The Federal Reserve System is the central bank of the United States. It consists essentially of about 5,700 member (commercial) banks scattered throughout the nation, 12 Federal Reserve Banks (plus 25 branches) located in various cities, and a seven-member Board of Governors appointed by the President and confirmed by the Senate. The function of the System is to foster a flow of credit that provides for stable prices, orderly economic growth, and strong international financial relationships.

7. The United States has a dual banking system consisting of national banks and state banks. Practically all banks are supervised by several government agencies, and almost all bank deposits (demand and time) are insured by the FDIC.

For Discussion

1. *Terms and concepts to review:*
money
currency
demand deposit
time deposit
repurchase agreement
money market
Eurodollars
near-monies
credit
credit instrument
promissory note
Treasury bill
negotiable certificate of deposit
commercial paper
banker's acceptance
federal funds
capital market
bond
financial markets
financial intermediaries
commercial bank
Federal Reserve System
member bank
Federal Reserve Bank
Board of Governors
Federal Open Market Committee
Federal Advisory Council
dual banking system
national bank
state bank
Federal Deposit Insurance Corporation

2. Which function of money is most important in today's society? Explain.

3. Which function does money perform least efficiently?

4. How would the functions of money be affected if the value of the dollar increased from year to year?

5. The more money you have, the richer you are. Similarly, the more money a nation has, the richer it is. Therefore, nations can become rich simply by printing more money. Do you agree?

6. What economic reasons can you give for the existence of money markets?

7. Money-market instruments must possess certain characteristics in order to function *efficiently*. Can you think of three? What does "efficiently" mean in this case?

8. What economic reasons can you give for the existence of capital markets?

9. Capital markets have played an important role in our nation's growth. Can you explain why?

10. Financial intermediaries play a much more important role in today's economy than they did several decades ago. They are also more significant in the United States than in, say, African, Asian, or Latin American countries. Why?

11. Every nation has its own central bank. Why? What minimum functions does a central bank perform that a commercial bank does not?

Commercial Banking: Money Creation and Portfolio Management

Learning guide
Watch for the answers to these important questions

How do we define money for the purpose of studying deposit expansion and contraction? What is the goldsmiths' principle and how does it relate to fractional-reserve banking?

Why is an individual bank in a banking system unable to lend more than its excess reserves? What would happen if it tried to do so?

Can the banking system as a whole lend more than its excess reserves? What is the deposit-expansion multiplier, and what does it tell you? What factors tend to reduce the potential expansion of bank deposits?

What goals do banks seek in the management of their portfolios? How do these goals impinge on one another? What is the nature of the conflict between liquidity, profitability, and safety?

How do banks allocate their funds among different classes of reserves? Which particular types of securities are likely to be found in a typical bank's portfolio?

The average person probably thinks of a bank as a place in which to deposit and from which to withdraw money. But banks are much more than mere depositories for people's funds. They play a fundamental role in the financial and monetary structure of our economy.

In a more specific sense, banks deal in money and credit instruments. A commercial bank, as we learned earlier, is a financial institution chartered by the federal government or a state government. It is primarily engaged in making short-term commercial and industrial loans by creating demand or checking deposits, and retiring loans when demand deposits are repaid. In addition, a commercial bank may or may not carry on functions performed by other financial institutions. Examples include providing life insurance, holding time (that is, savings) deposits, making long-term mortgage loans, renting safe-deposit boxes, operating a trust department, and so on.

The present chapter is concerned with surveying the basic economic functions of commercial banking.

This chapter surveys the functions and operations of commercial banks.

The Fundamental Principle of Deposit Banking

You have already learned that there are different measures of money, depending on what is included in its definition. For example, you will remember from the previous chapter that $M1$ is called "narrow-transactions money." This means that it is readily spendable money because it consists of currency (and coin) and checkable deposits. Thus, according to the definition of $M1$,

money = currency + checkable deposits

Checkable deposits, you will recall, consist of demand deposits and savings-type checking deposits. The latter category includes NOW accounts, ATS accounts, and credit-union share-draft accounts.

In this chapter, we are interested in learning how banks expand and contract the money supply. But, because demand deposits constitute the largest component of checkable deposits, it will be easier to focus on what was defined in the previous chapter as the *narrowest* measure of money. Thus we will assume that

money = currency + demand deposits

As you will see, the principles associated with this simpler measure of money can be easily extended to include the broader definition represented by M1.

Proportions of Currency and Demand Deposits

Of course, most of us are more familiar with currency than with demand deposits. So it is appropriate to ask: Who determines the amount of currency in circulation?

The answer is "the public"—you and I and everyone else. This is because currency and demand deposits are interchangeable. Therefore, you will generally cash a check when you need currency and deposit currency in your checking account when you have more cash than you need.

Everyone behaves in much the same way. As a result, the public always holds the exact amount of cash that it wants, shifting its holdings back and forth between currency and demand deposits. As you might expect, over the course of a year the economy holds a smaller proportion of M1 in currency than in demand deposits. But at certain times of the year, such as Christmas and Easter, the proportion of currency in circulation increases significantly because people desire more cash for spending. After the holidays, the proportion of currency in circulation decreases significantly as businesses deposit their cash receipts in checking accounts.

The Goldsmiths' Principle

Because demand deposits are by far the largest part of our money supply, it is important for us to know how they come into existence and what role they play.

The credit-creation process of deposit banking is based on the following fundamental principle:

> Not all of the customers of a bank will withdraw their funds at the same time. On any given day, some customers will decrease their deposits by withdrawing funds in the form of cash and checks drawn on the bank while others will increase their deposits by depositing funds in the form of cash and checks drawn on other banks. Under normal conditions, the volume of deposits and withdrawals will tend to be equal over a period of time.

This is a modernized version of what may be called the *goldsmiths' principle*—because it was discovered centuries ago by the English goldsmiths. They found that, when people deposited gold for safekeeping, it was not usually necessary to store all the gold away. Instead, only a portion of it needed to be kept in reserve for those individuals who might want to withdraw their gold. The rest of it could be "put to work" earning interest by being loaned to others with the promise of repayment.

In a bank, of course, there is always the possibility that, during some periods, withdrawals will exceed deposits. To meet such contingencies, reserves equal to less than 5 percent of deposits are usually more than adequate. However, for reasons of monetary control that will be explained later, the percentage of reserves that banks actually keep on hand is considerably higher than 5 percent.

The Goldsmiths' Principle and Fractional Bank Reserves

The ways in which demand deposits are expanded and contracted can best be illustrated in terms of changes in a bank's assets, liabilities, and net worth. These terms have special meanings.

The goldsmiths' principle is the basis of modern fractional-reserve banking.

For any economic entity such as an individual, household, or firm:

Assets are things of value that are owned—cash, property, and the rights to property.

Liabilities are monetary debts or things of value that are owed to creditors.

Net worth, or owners' equity, is the difference between assets and liabilities.

Thus, for any individual, household, or firm,

assets − liabilities = net worth

Therefore, it is also true that

assets = liabilities + net worth

As you will see shortly, the second equation is the form in which these concepts will be presented.

When these three classes of data are grouped together for analysis and interpretation, the financial statement on which they appear is called a *balance sheet*. For example, on a bank's balance sheet, the principal assets are government securities and loans; the principal liabilities are demand deposits.

As stated above, the English goldsmiths discovered by experience that they could run a banking business by maintaining a fractional—rather than a 100 percent—reserve in gold against their deposits. Although U.S. banks today do not hold their reserves in gold, the law requires them to maintain fractional reserves of liquid assets against their deposit liabilities. There are three types of reserves: legal, required, and excess. The first type includes the other two.

Legal Reserves

Legal reserves are assets that a bank or other depository institution (such as a savings and loan association or a credit union) may lawfully use as reserves against its deposit liabilities. For a member bank of the Federal Reserve System, legal reserves consist of currency held in the vaults of the bank—called *vault cash*—plus deposits held with the district Federal Reserve Bank. Any other highly liquid financial claims, such as government securities, are classified as *nonlegal reserves*. For a nonmember bank or other depository institution, legal reserves consist of vault cash plus deposits with the district Federal Reserve Bank or with an approved institution. The latter is any depository institution (such as a member bank) that holds a reserve balance with the Federal Reserve.

Required Reserves These are the minimum amount of legal reserves that a bank is required by law to keep behind its deposit liabilities. For example, if the required reserve ratio is 1:5, or 20 percent, a bank with demand deposits of $1 million must hold at least $200,000 of required legal reserves.

Excess Reserves These are the quantity of a bank's legal reserves over and above its required reserves.

As you can see from these definitions,

legal reserves = required reserves + excess reserves

and therefore

excess reserves = legal reserves − required reserves

It follows that anything that changes either a bank's legal reserves or its required reserves will change its excess reserves. But excess reserves, as you will see, are the determinants of a bank's lending power. Therefore, as you study the processes by which banks expand and contract demand deposits, you should keep in mind the simple equations above.

Note The preceding definition of legal reserves is a result of the *Monetary Control Act of 1980*—a major piece of bank legislation. It makes *all* depository institutions subject to uniform reserve requirements on similar classes of deposits. Prior to 1980, only member banks had to meet legal reserve requirements as defined above. Nonmember institutions were subject to less stringent and more heterogeneous requirements that varied by state.

Deposit Expansion by a Single Bank

The easiest way to understand the deposit-banking process is to examine the transactions of a single bank over successive stages. To keep the arithmetic simple, a reserve requirement of 20 percent will be assumed. In reality, the average requirement for depository institutions as a whole is closer to 10 percent. However, rather than employing this figure in the following examples, it will be used instead for some of the problems at the end of the chapter.

Stage 1 Let us begin by assuming that Bank A has the following simplified balance sheet:

Bank A: Balance Sheet
Stage 1: Initial Position

Assets			Liabilities and Net Worth	
Legal reserves		$ 5,000	Demand deposits	$20,000
Required	$4,000		Net worth	1,000
Excess	1,000			
Loans (Claims)		16,000		
		$21,000		$21,000

The first thing to notice is that the balance sheet "balances." That is, the totals always conform to the equation: assets = liabilities + net worth.

On the right side of the balance sheet, observe that demand deposits are a liability. This is because the bank is obligated to honor checks drawn by its depositors up to the amount shown.

On the left side, legal reserves (which consist of vault cash plus demand deposits with the district Federal Reserve Bank) are assets. Loans are also classified as assets because they represent financial claims held by the bank against borrowers. These claims are "IOUs," usually in the form of promissory notes.

Return to the right side of the balance sheet. Note that net worth is the difference between total assets and total liabilities. It is thus a "balancing item" representing stockholders' ownership in the bank.

Note also that, with $20,000 of demand deposits and a reserve requirement of 20 percent, required reserves (on the left side) are $4,000. Because legal reserves are $5,000, excess reserves are equal to $1,000.

Stage 2 Because the bank has $1,000 in excess reserves, it can make loans equal to this amount. Suppose you, a businessperson, borrow the funds and give the bank your promissory note in exchange. The bank then credits your account for $1,000. *Before* you write any checks, how does the bank's balance sheet look?

A bank can lend up to the amount of its excess reserves.

Bank A: Balance Sheet
*Stage 2: After the bank grants a loan of $1,000
but before checks are written against it*

Assets		Liabilities and Net Worth	
Legal reserves	$ 5,000	Demand deposits	$21,000
Loans (Claims)	17,000	Net worth	1,000
	$22,000		$22,000

As shown above, demand deposits have risen to $21,000. This reflects the bank's commitment (liability) to honor your checks up to $1,000. In addition, loans have increased to $17,000, reflecting the promissory note (asset) you gave the bank for $1,000. As a result of this transaction, *the bank has created $1,000 of new money.*

Stage 3 Of course, you can take your $1,000 out in currency if you wish. However, because you are in business, you will probably find it more convenient to write checks in order to pay your bills.

Suppose that you write a check for the full $1,000 and give it to a supplier from whom you purchased materials. The supplier then deposits the check in its own bank, Bank B, which in turn presents it to Bank A for payment. The effect on Bank A, as shown in the following balance sheet, is to reduce its demand deposits to $20,000 and its legal reserves to $4,000. Note that required reserves are 20 percent of demand deposits, or $4,000—which equals the bank's legal reserves. The bank, in other words, no longer has excess reserves.

A bank is in equilibrium, or fully loaned up, when its excess reserves are zero.

Bank A: Balance Sheet
Stage 3: Final Position

Assets			Liabilities and Net Worth	
Legal reserves		$ 4,000	Demand deposits	$20,000
Required	$4,000		Net worth	1,000
Excess	0			
Loans (Claims)		17,000		
		$21,000		$21,000

The foregoing analysis leads to an important conclusion:

> No individual bank in a banking system can lend more than its excess reserves. In other words, when a bank's excess reserves are zero, it has no unused lending power. The bank, therefore, is "in equilibrium" or *fully loaned up.*

Of course, the supplier to whom you gave your $1,000 check might have had an account in Bank A instead of in Bank B. In that case, the *total* demand deposits of Bank A would have been unaffected. The bank, when processing the check, would simply have reduced your account by $1,000 and increased the supplier's account by the same amount. In the great majority of cases, however, this situation does not exist. Instead:

> As a borrower writes checks against a deposit, his or her bank is likely to lose reserves and deposits to other banks within the banking system. Hence, a bank cannot afford to make loans in an amount greater than its excess reserves.

Deposit Expansion by the Banking System

Although a single bank cannot make loans totaling more than its excess reserves, the banking system can lend several times the amount. This provides another interesting example of the familiar fallacy of composition. That is, *what is true of the individual is not necessarily true of the whole.* Let us examine the reasons for this by continuing with the foregoing illustration. In order to keep matters simple, we will focus our attention on the relevant balance-sheet *changes* while disregarding all other items. As before, the reserve requirement is assumed to be 20 percent.

Stage 4 The $1,000 check you paid your supplier is deposited in the supplier's account in Bank B. Bank B's demand deposits increase by $1,000 and its legal reserves increase by $1,000 (after the check clears). Assuming that Bank B was fully loaned up prior to this transaction, it sets aside 20 percent or $200 in required reserves, and hence has 80 percent or $800 in excess reserves.

Bank B
Stage 4: Bank B receives $1,000 deposit lost by Bank A

Assets			Liabilities	
Legal reserves		+ $1,000	Demand deposits	+ $1,000
Required	+ $200			
Excess	+ 800			
		+ $1,000		+ $1,000

Stage 5 Bank B, of course, will try to lend $800—an amount equal to its excess reserves. Assuming it grants such a loan, its balance sheet *before* any checks are written will show demand deposits have risen from $1,000 to $1,800 and, therefore, loans have increased by a corresponding amount. Thus:

Bank B

Stage 5: After Bank B grants a loan for $800 but before checks are written against it

Assets		Liabilities	
Legal reserves	+$1,000	Demand deposits	+$1,800
Loans (Claims)	+ 800		
	+$1,800		+$1,800

The credit expansion process continues as each bank receives deposits and lends up to the amount of its excess reserves.

Stage 6 If we assume that the borrower writes a check for the entire amount of the loan, the check will be deposited by its recipient in Bank C. This will cause Bank B to lose $800 in deposits and (after the check clears) $800 of legal reserves to Bank C. This leaves Bank B with the following net changes:

Bank B

Stage 6: After checks for $800 are written against Bank B

Assets		Liabilities	
Legal reserves (net change = +$1,000 − $800)	+$ 200	Demand deposits (net change = +$1,800 − $800)	+$1,000
Loans (Claims)	+ 800		
	+$1,000		+$1,000

Notice that the change in Bank B's legal reserves is equal to 20 percent of the change in its demand deposits. Therefore, its excess reserves are zero. Hence, Bank B is "in equilibrium," or fully loaned up.

Stage 7 Bank C receives the $800 deposit that was lost by Bank B in Stage 6, thus gaining (after the check clears) $800 in legal reserves. Assuming Bank C had been fully loaned up, it sets aside 20 percent, or $160, as required reserves and therefore has 80 percent, or $640, in excess reserves.

Bank C

Stage 7: Bank C receives $800 deposit lost by Bank B

Assets			Liabilities	
Legal reserves		+$800	Demand deposits	+$800
Required	+$160			
Excess	+ 640			
		+$800		+$800

Stage 8 Suppose that Bank C now grants a loan equal to the amount of its excess reserves. *Before* any checks are written, both its demand deposits and loans will have risen by $640.

Bank C

Stage 8: After Bank C grants a loan for $640 but before checks are written against it

Assets		Liabilities	
Legal reserves	+$ 800	Demand deposits	+$1,440
Loans (Claims)	+ 640		
	+$1,440		+$1,440

Stage 9 After the borrower writes a check against the loan and deposits the check in Bank D, demand deposits and legal reserves in Bank C go down by $640 (once the check clears). This leaves Bank C with the following net changes:

Bank C
Stage 9: After checks for $640 are written against Bank C

Assets		Liabilities	
Legal reserves (net change = +$800 − $640)	+$160	Demand deposits (net change = +$1,440 − $640)	+$800
Loans (Claims)	+ 640		
	+$800		+$800

Because the increase in Bank C's legal reserves is equal to 20 percent of the increase in its demand deposits, its excess reserves are zero. The bank, therefore, is in equilibrium, or fully loaned up.

Through lending, the banking system's excess reserves are eventually "used up."

Stage 10 and Beyond You can see by now that a logical expansionary process is taking place. It is sufficient, therefore, to illustrate a few further steps in the sequence by noting the changes experienced by each bank on its partial balance sheet, assuming that each bank is initially fully loaned up. (All data are rounded to the nearest dollar.)

Bank D

Assets		Liabilities	
Legal reserves	+$128	Demand deposits	+$640
Loans (Claims)	+ 512		
	+$640		+$640

Bank E

Assets		Liabilities	
Legal reserves	+$102	Demand deposits	+$512
Loans (Claims)	+ 410		
	+$512		+$512

Bank F

Assets		Liabilities	
Legal reserves	+$ 82	Demand deposits	+$410
Loans (Claims)	+ 328		
	+$410		+$410

And so on.

The deposit-creation process thus continues until all excess reserves in the system are "used up." That is, until no bank in the system has legal reserves greater than its required reserves.

The entire process of deposit expansion is illustrated in Exhibit 1. Note that the *total* expansion of deposits created by the banking system as a whole is a multiple of the initial deposit or increase in excess reserves—in this case, $5,000 for $1,000, or a ratio of 5:1.

This is the same process that was illustrated above in terms of changes in the bank's balance sheets. Either approach can be used to illustrate what may be called the principle of *multiple expansion of bank deposits*. Can you express this principle in your own words? (You may want to check your definition against the one given in the Dictionary at the back of the book.)

The Deposit-Expansion Multiplier

You may have noticed that the expansion in demand deposits by the banking system as a whole is determined by two factors: (1) the required reserve ratio and (2) the initial amount of excess reserves. You can verify this from Exhibit 1 by demonstrating that the reciprocal of the required reserve ratio—that is, the number 1 divided by the required reserve ratio—gives what may be called the "deposit-expansion multiplier." Thus, letting R represent the required reserve ratio,

$$\text{deposit-expansion multiplier} = \frac{1}{\text{required reserve ratio}} = \frac{1}{R}$$

Hence, if you know the required reserve ratio, you can determine the deposit-expansion multiplier immediately. For instance, in our example, the required reserve ratio was 20 percent, or $1/5$. Therefore,

$$\text{deposit-expansion multiplier} = \frac{1}{1/5} = 5$$

Exhibit 1
Multiple Expansion of Bank Deposits Through the Banking System
(rounded to the nearest dollar)

The table shows the cumulative expansion of deposits in the banking system as a whole, assuming an initial deposit or increase in legal reserves of $1,000 and a required reserve of 20 percent.

If all banks in the system are aligned in decreasing order of new deposits created, the multiple-expansion process can be expressed clearly in the form of a bar graph.

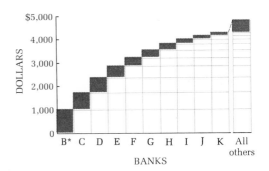

Banks	New deposits	Required reserves at 20%	New loans (= excess reserves)	Cumulative deposits
B	$1,000*	$ 200	$ 800	$1,000
C	800	160	640	1,800
D	640	128	512	2,440
E	512	102	410	2,952
F	410	82	328	3,362
G	328	66	262	3,690
H	262	52	210	3,952
I	210	42	168	4,162
J	168	34	134	4,330
K	134	27	107	4,464
All other banks	536	107	429	5,000
Totals	$5,000	$1,000	$4,000	

* This deposit came from Bank A in Stage 4.

This means that an increase of $1,000 in the banking system's *excess* reserves may result in a total expansion of new deposits for the banking system as a whole of as much as $1,000 × 5 = $5,000. The same formula also applies in a downward direction. That is, a $1,000 contraction in the banking system's *legal* reserves can cause as much as a $5,000 reduction in deposits for the entire system.

These ideas can be generalized and incorporated in a simple formula. Let D represent the change in demand deposits for the banking system as a whole, E the amount of excess reserves, and R the required reserve ratio. Then,

$$D = E \times \text{deposit-expansion multiplier}$$

or

$$D = E \times \frac{1}{R}$$

To illustrate, if $R = 10$ percent, or $1/10$, the deposit-expansion multiplier is 10. Therefore, excess reserves E of $1,000 can result in an increase in the banking system's demand deposits D of as much as $1,000 \times 10 = $10,000.

You can use the preceding formula to answer practical questions involving deposit expansion and contraction. For the latter, E would represent deficient reserves and have a negative sign.

The following definition helps summarize the basic ideas:

Deposit-expansion multiplier. An increase in *excess* reserves of the banking system may cause a larger or magnified increase in total deposits. Similarly, a decrease in the banking system's *legal* reserves may cause a larger or magnified decrease in total deposits. However, the total cumulative expansion (or contraction) will at most be equal to the reciprocal of the required reserve ratio.

The deposit-expansion multiplier enables you to calculate the amount by which an increase in the banking system's excess reserves can result in a much larger increase in total bank deposits.

How does this multiplier principle compare with the simple multiplier pertaining to investment and income that you studied in an earlier chapter? Do you see any analogy between the required reserve ratio and the marginal propensity to save? Now is a good time to turn back and refresh your knowledge of the simple multiplier. However, be careful not to confuse the two multiplier concepts. They involve different assumptions and applications.

A "Monopoly Bank" and the Banking System

It is interesting to observe how the principle of multiple expansion of bank deposits would operate if there were just one bank—a monopoly bank—instead of many independently owned banks.

A monopoly bank would behave exactly as the banking system as a whole behaves. It would receive all deposits and grant all loans. However, since it would be the only bank in the system, there would be no other banks to which it could lose reserves when checks that were drawn upon it were presented for payment. Thus, assuming a reserve requirement of 20 percent, the monopoly bank would simply continue to lend on the basis of its excess reserves until it produced a 5:1 expansion of bank deposits. It would therefore be able to do what each individual bank in a system of many banks could not do.

Three Qualifications

The principle of multiple expansion of bank deposits assumes that the banking system will produce a magnified expansion in deposits. The expansion may be 5:1 or some other ratio, depending on the reserve requirement and the assumption that banks always make loans equal to the full amount of their new excess reserves. Actually, this principle is modified in practice by at least three factors.

Leakage of Cash into Circulation A business borrowing money from a bank may take part of it in cash. Or, someone who is paid a debt by check may "cash" some or all of it rather than deposit the entire amount. For these reasons, some money that would otherwise serve as excess reserves will tend to leak out of the banking system, thereby leaving less new reserves available for banks to lend.

Idle Excess Reserves Banks do not always make loans equal to the full amount of their excess reserves. They may sometimes maintain idle excess reserves because they desire a "safety margin" or because they are unable to find good investments. Thus, if the reserve requirement were 20 percent, banks might have available an average reserve of 25 percent. This, of course, would reduce the deposit-creating ability of the banking system from 5:1 to 4:1.

Willingness to Borrow and to Lend The principle of multiple expansion of bank deposits assumes, of course, that businesses are willing to borrow and that banks are willing to lend. This may not always be so. During a recession, for example, when business executives are gloomy about the future, they may not borrow all that banks have available for lending. Further, banks may prefer the safety of liquidity and hence decide to maintain a higher level of excess reserves rather than risk being unprepared for heavy withdrawals by the public or an unusual amount of defaulting on loans by borrowers.

As a result of these three factors:

The multiple expansion of deposits actually created by the banking system is always somewhat less than the theoretical amount determined from the formula. The formula establishes the upper limit of deposit expansion, not the amount actually realized in all cases.

Deposit Contraction

Does the multiple expansion of bank deposits work in a downward direction? If a bank loses a deposit when all banks are fully loaned up, would this cause a cumulative contraction of demand deposits throughout the system? The answer is *yes*—for reasons that are essentially the reverse of those given for deposit expansion.

For example, the most obvious way for a bank to lose a deposit is for a depositor to withdraw his or her money in currency instead of by check. (A less obvious but more significant way, which will be examined subsequently, is for the Federal Reserve System to sell government securities.) Suppose, for instance, that you withdraw $1,000 in currency from Bank A. The bank's balance sheet will show a reduction in demand deposits and in legal reserves (vault cash) by that amount. Thus:

The actual size of the deposit-expansion multiplier is reduced by these three factors.

The deposit-contraction process works in the same way as the deposit-expansion process, but in reverse.

Bank A
After depositor's withdrawal of $1,000 in currency

Assets		Liabilities	
Legal reserves (vault cash)	− $1,000	Demand deposits	− $1,000

If the reserve requirement is 20 percent, the decrease in demand deposits of $1,000 reduces Bank A's required reserves by $200. But

Exhibit 2
Multiple Contraction of Bank Deposits Through the Banking System

(rounded to nearest dollar)

Banks	Demand deposits	Required reserves at 20%	Earning assets (e.g., government securities)
A	−$1,000	−$ 200	−$ 800
B	− 800	− 160	− 640
C	− 640	− 128	− 512
D	− 512	− 102	− 410
E	− 410	− 82	− 328
All other banks	− 1,638	− 328	− 1,310
Totals	−$5,000	−$1,000	−$4,000

The ways in which banks manage their portfolios affect the economy as a whole.

Bank A still has a reserve deficiency of $800 against its remaining deposits. Therefore, one way for it to correct this deficiency is to sell some of its earning assets—primarily government securities. If the buyer of the securities pays for them with a check written against his or her deposit in Bank B, the latter institution experiences a deposit decrease of $800. Of this, 20 percent, or $160, represents a decrease in required reserves, and 80 percent, or $640, is a reserve deficiency against the bank's remaining deposits.

Bank B, like Bank A, may make up this deficiency by selling some of its earning assets. Assuming that all banks remedy their reserve deficiencies by selling their earning assets, the deposit-contraction process continues, as indicated by the table in Exhibit 2.

Note that the same end result—a reduction in deposits by $5,000 for the banking system as a whole—could have been reached by using the deposit-expansion multiplier. To illustrate, because the reserve requirement is assumed to be 20 percent, the multiplier is 5. Therefore, an initial change (decrease) in demand deposits, and hence in legal reserves, of −$1,000 results in a change in demand deposits for the entire banking system of −$1,000 × 5 = −$5,000.

To conclude:

> The multiple contraction of bank deposits works in essentially the same way as a multiple expansion, but in reverse. However, the contraction process is based on two assumptions:
>
> **1.** *All banks are fully loaned up.* In reality, to the extent that they are not, reductions in deposits can be met out of excess reserves.
>
> **2.** *Banks always sell their earning assets in order to raise short-term money.* In reality, banks in need of temporary funds can often borrow either from the Fed or from other banks.
>
> For both reasons, therefore, the deposit-contraction multiplier is almost always significantly lower than the deposit-expansion multiplier.

An interesting implication of our fractional-reserve system is explained in Box 1.

Managing a Bank's Portfolio

As a bank expands and contracts its demand deposits, it also acquires and disposes of income-earning assets. These assets, plus the bank's cash, make up what is known as its "portfolio." Income-earning assets—or simply earning assets—are of two types:

1. Securities issued by the federal government, municipal governments, and governmental institutions (such as the Federal National Mortgage Association and the Farm Credit Bureau, among others).

2. Financial obligations, such as promissory notes, issued by firms.

Taken together, earning assets typically constitute between one-fourth and one-third of a commercial bank's total assets. The remaining portion of its total assets consists primarily of other loans and, to a lesser extent, of demand deposits with other banks (including Federal Reserve Banks) and vault cash.

A bank's earning assets are thus an important source of its income. The manner in which banks as a whole manage their portfolios, acquiring and disposing of earning assets as the need arises, can have important impacts throughout the financial markets and on the borrowing and expenditure practices of households and businesses. It is desirable, therefore, that we look into some features of bank portfolio management before we go on to examine its economic effects in later chapters.

Objectives: Liquidity, Profitability, and Safety

Imagine yourself responsible for managing a bank's portfolio. Because one of your major tasks is to acquire earning assets, the problem you continually face is to achieve a proper balance between liquidity, profitability, and safety. What do these terms mean?

Liquidity

Liquidity is a complex concept, the precise meaning of which sometimes differs among economists and financial managers. For our purposes, however, *liquidity* may be defined as the ease with which an asset can be converted into cash quickly without loss of value in terms of money. Liquidity is thus a matter of degree. Money (that is, cash) is an asset that is perfectly liquid. It can be used as a medium of exchange, and it always retains the same value in terms of itself. A short-term government obligation is an asset that is almost as liquid as money, because it can be readily sold for cash with little or no loss of value. On the other hand, a bank building is a relatively illiquid asset. It cannot easily be sold, and it may yield a loss when it is. In general, the relative liquidity of an asset is associated with three interrelated factors:

**Box 1
Why Not 100 Percent Reserves?**

What would happen if banks were required to maintain 100 percent reserves against demand deposits? Improvements in banking efficiency would be dramatic, because practically all other government regulations could be dropped. Among them: a tangled web of rules and laws governing such factors as reserve levels, capital requirements, permissible types of asset holdings, and deposit insurance.

Would the elimination of such regulations usher in an era of financial panics similar to those that occurred before the 1930s? Clearly not. Panics occur when the public fears the inability of banks to honor their commitments. This has not happened since the creation of federal deposit insurance in 1934. Prior to that time, in the opinion of

many experts, the panics that occurred were caused mainly by a government policy that promised but failed to protect bank liabilities. Under a 100 percent reserve plan, depositors would always be protected because their deposits would be fully backed. Therefore, neither deposit insurance nor many other complicated banking regulations designed to protect the public would be needed.

Despite the apparent advantages, most bankers oppose a 100 percent reserve system. One main reason is that demand-deposit inflows would no longer yield excess reserves, because demand deposits and required reserves would be the same. Demand deposits, and the interest return that banks earn, would thus be reduced. So too would the profitability of

banks, because they would no longer be able to create money through new deposits. Instead, banks' incomes would have to depend more heavily on fees charged for services performed (such as providing checking accounts) and on interest earned from loans made out of depositors' savings accounts.

In fact, only the Federal Reserve System would be able to expand or contract the money supply, by buying or selling government securities in the market. You will learn how this is done in the next chapter. Meanwhile, opposition to a 100 percent reserve system remains strong. Therefore, despite its benefits, the system is never likely to be adopted, even though many economists have long advocated it.

---

1. **Marketability** An asset that is bought and sold in an organized market —such as a security traded on the New York Stock Exchange—is highly salable and hence more liquid than one that is not.

2. **Collateral Value** An asset is likely to be more liquid if it is readily acceptable to lenders as security for a loan.

3. **Contractual Terms** An asset's liquidity is affected by the contractual conditions under which it is issued. The liquidity of a bond, for example, is greater if it has an earlier maturity date than a later one, or if it is paid off in installments over its life (amortized) instead of in a lump sum at maturity.

Profitability

Earning profits is a second goal of a bank's portfolio. Profitability is measured by the difference between what you pay for an asset and what you realize when you redeem or sell it, plus any returns you receive in the interim. In the case of government (including federal and municipal) bonds, which are a major form of earning assets for banks, these variables are reflected by a single percentage figure called *yield to maturity*. A bond's yield to maturity may be 10 percent, 15 percent, or some other amount—and it will fluctuate according to market conditions. Portfolio managers, therefore, are continually changing the compositions of their earning assets, selling bonds and other securities that have lower yields in order to purchase those that have higher ones.

Safety

In managing their portfolios, banks seek to obtain the best combination of liquidity and profitability at a prescribed level of safety.

Maintaining safety is a third goal in bank portfolio management. Safety refers to the probability that the contractual terms of an investment— such as the interest and principal payments on a bond—will be fulfilled by the borrower. Safety is thus a matter of degree. The safest of all financial obligations are Treasury bills, Treasury notes, and Treasury bonds. This is because these securities are backed by the good faith and taxing power of the federal government. Bonds issued by many municipal governments also rank very high on the safety scale. Interestingly enough, however, safety and liquidity do not always go together. Market prices of U.S. Treasury bonds, for example, may fluctuate substantially, thereby impairing their liquidity. However, the safety of Treasury securities—that is, payment of interest and principal—is never in doubt.

The Conflict Between Liquidity and Profitability

The ideal commercial-bank portfolio is liquid, profitable, and safe. But it is impossible to maximize all three objectives—for two reasons.

First, a bank's most immediate obligation is to pay cash upon demand. The moment it is unable to convert demand deposits into cash, it must close its doors. Consequently, the holding of a certain portion of its assets in the form of vault cash helps a bank to meet its liquidity needs.

Second, a bank is in business to make a profit for its owners (stockholders). The holding of earning assets is an important means of attaining this goal.

Therefore:

Because a bank's vault cash yields no return, a conflict exists between liquidity and profitability. Thus:

• Too large a proportion of a bank's assets in the form of cash provides greater liquidity but an unnecessary loss of income.

• Too small a proportion of a bank's assets in cash permits higher income from investment in earning assets, but at the risk of illiquidity and failure.

Evidently, a compromise between these two extremes is needed. Moreover, the compromise must be achieved with a relatively high degree of safety. This is because banks are subject to a variety of legal and conventional constraints that limit the types of earning assets they can acquire.

The nature of the conflict between liquidity and profitability is illustrated in Exhibit 3. The axes of the figure denote the two alternatives available to a bank at any given time. For example, if you are a portfolio manager, you can keep all the bank's funds in cash, in which case the amount is represented by the vertical distance 0M. Alternatively, you can invest all the bank's funds in earning assets, in which case the amount is shown by the horizontal distance 0N. However, neither one of these extreme choices is acceptable. Why? Because the former would leave the bank in too liquid a position to earn income, whereas the latter would leave it completely illiquid and hence unable to pay cash on demand.

If we connect the two points, the resulting line MN shows all the combinations of cash and earning assets in which it is possible to invest the bank's funds. Therefore, it may be called an "investment-possibilities line." Of course, there is some point along the line—some combination of cash and earning assets—that is the optimum for a particular bank. The challenge faced by every bank's portfolio manager, therefore, is to find that point—thereby achieving the highest possible level of earnings consistent with liquidity and safety.

Priorities for Allocating Bank Funds

The fundamental goals of a bank portfolio are liquidity, profitability, and safety. However, these goals are in conflict. Therefore, priorities for allocating a bank's funds must be established. That is, criteria are needed for deciding how banks are to utilize their limited funds. Four classes of uses may be distinguished:

Primary Reserves

This category of assets receives the highest priority. It consists of a bank's legal reserves and the demand deposits it may have with other banks. In other words, a bank's primary reserves consist of liquid assets. They are instantly available to meet depositors' needs.

Secondary Reserves

This category of assets, which receives the second highest priority, provides "protective investment." It is made up of earning assets that are *readily convertible into cash on short notice without substantial loss.* Secondary reserves are thus slightly less liquid than primary reserves.

Exhibit 3
Investment-Possibilities Line

Each point along the line MN denotes a different combination of cash and earning assets. Thus, point A denotes G dollars of cash and H dollars of earning assets; point B denotes J dollars of cash and K dollars of earning assets. The portfolio manager of a bank seeks to obtain an optimum combination of cash and earning assets, subject to various legal constraints designed to assure a high degree of safety.

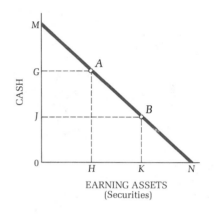

To help achieve the best combination of liquidity, profitability, and safety, banks allocate their funds in decreasing order of priorities.

Secondary reserves consist of such short-term financial obligations as U.S. Treasury bills, high-grade commercial paper (such as promissory notes issued by large corporations), banker's acceptances, and call loans to brokers on stock-market purchases. The main purpose of this application of a bank's funds is to meet expected and more or less regular seasonal demands for liquidity, such as occur during the peak business periods of Christmas and Easter.

Customer Loan Demands

The third priority in allocating a bank's funds is meeting customer credit needs. This is the fundamental purpose for which a bank is created. By fulfilling this objective, a bank enhances its profits because interest rates on loans are usually higher than on securities.

Investments for Income

After banks take care of their liquidity and lending needs, any remaining reserves are invested in securities that yield steady income.

The fourth priority concerns the use of a bank's funds after the three previous priorities have been satisfied. Thus, any funds that a bank has available after fulfilling the foregoing requirements are invested in long-term securities aimed at providing additional income. These investments, of course, are also subject to constraints of safety. Therefore, they consist primarily of government securities—namely, notes and bonds issued by the federal government and by state and local governments.

This order of priorities applies to all commercial banks. However, the relative distribution of funds for these four purposes differs somewhat among individual banks. In general:

> The proportions of its funds that a bank allocates to cash and earning assets, and the proportions that it allocates among different types of earning assets, depend on three major factors. These are (1) legal requirements, (2) local business needs, and (3) the bank's ability to find a compromise between the conflicting goals of liquidity and profitability at the required level of safety.

Types of Bank Investments

The types of securities in which banks invest are usually called "governments" and "municipals".

The types of investment a commercial bank can make are regulated by law. Consequently, three classes of securities are likely to be found in a typical bank's portfolio:

1. U.S. Government Securities These consist of *Treasury bills*, *Treasury notes*, and *Treasury bonds*. All are readily marketable if the bank should wish to sell them, and they differ from each other in their periods of maturity. They thus contribute greatly to satisfying the liquidity requirements of commercial banks.

2. Municipal Securities These are marketable financial obligations issued by state and local governments. Called simply *municipals*, these securities provide holders with interest income that is exempt from all federal income taxes. This is a major reason banks purchase them.

3. "Quasi-governmental" Securities These consist of notes and bonds issued by various agencies of the federal government, such as the Federal Home Loan Bank and the Federal National Mortgage Association.

For the past several decades, the holdings of municipals in commercial-bank portfolios have increased substantially relative to U.S. government and quasi-governmental securities. This is largely because of the tax-exempt features of municipals.

As you will learn in the following chapters, the way in which banks manage their portfolios, buying and selling earning assets as the need arises, has profound effects on the financial system and the economy.

What You Have Learned in This Chapter

1. Commercial banking rests on the goldsmiths' principle. This enables banks to maintain a fractional—rather than a 100 percent—reserve against deposits, because not all customers will withdraw their funds at the same time. Hence, the banks can earn interest by making loans equal to their unused or excess reserves.

2. A single bank in a banking system cannot lend more than its excess reserves. When a bank's excess reserves are zero, it is in equilibrium, or fully loaned up.

3. The banking system as a whole can expand deposits by a multiple of its excess reserves. This process is known as the principle of multiple expansion of bank deposits. It is of fundamental importance in banking.

4. The amount by which the banking system as a whole can expand or contract demand deposits depends on the required reserve ratio and the initial amount of excess reserves. The required reserve ratio determines the deposit-expansion multiplier, which, when multiplied by initial excess reserves, tells the maximum amount of expansion that can take place.

5. The objectives of a commercial-bank portfolio are liquidity, profitability, and safety. The portfolio manager seeks an optimum combination of cash and earning assets consistent with a high level of safety. Hence, he or she is largely limited to three major classes of investments: U.S. government securities, municipal government securities, and quasi-governmental securities.

For Discussion

1. *Terms and concepts to review:*
goldsmiths' principle
assets
liabilities
net worth
balance sheet
legal reserves
required reserves
excess reserves
multiple expansion of bank deposits
deposit-expansion multiplier
liquidity
yield to maturity
primary reserves
secondary reserves
Treasury bills
Treasury notes
Treasury bonds
municipals

2. What is meant by "fractional-reserve banking"? How did it come into existence? Is it relevant today?

3. An individual bank cannot lend more than its excess reserves. Let us see why—by observing what would happen if it tried to do so.

Suppose that the reserve requirement is 20 percent, and Bank Z is holding:

Assets		Liabilities	
Vault cash	$ 50,000	Demand deposits	$200,000
Loans and other assets	160,000	Net worth	10,000
	$210,000		$210,000

(a) How much are Bank Z's excess reserves?

(b) Since the reserve requirement is 20 percent, or $1/5$, show the effect on Bank Z's balance sheet after it expands its loans in a 5:1 ratio—that is, by five times its excess reserves—but before borrowers spend their new deposits. What is the percentage of reserves to demand deposits?

(c) Suppose that borrowers write checks against their new deposits and the checks are deposited in other banks. Show the effect on Bank Z's balance sheet after all the checks are presented to it for payment. What has happened to the bank's reserves against deposits?

(d) What can Bank Z do to correct the situation? If it succeeds, how would its balance sheet look?

(e) What do you conclude from this exercise?

4. Suppose that you borrow $1,000 in currency from Midwest Bank and give the bank your promissory note in return.

(a) Show the effects on the following balance sheets:

Your Balance Sheet

Change in Assets	Change in Liabilities and Net Worth

Midwest Bank's Balance Sheet

Change in Assets	Change in Liabilities and Net Worth

(b) Complete Balance Sheet 2 below.

Balance Sheet 1—Midwest Bank
Before making $1,000 loan

Assets		Liabilities and Net Worth	
Cash	$ 3,000	Demand deposits	$20,000
Reserves	4,000	Other liabilities	25,000
Loans	15,000	Net worth	27,000
Other assets	50,000		
	$72,000		$72,000

Balance Sheet 2—Midwest Bank
After $1,000 in cash is withdrawn by borrower

Assets		Liabilities and Net worth	
Cash	_____	Demand deposits	_____
Reserves	_____	Other liabilities	_____
Loans	_____	Net worth	_____
Other assets	_____		
	_____		_____

(c) How would Balance Sheet 2 be affected if you had written $1,000 in checks against your deposit instead of withdrawing the money in cash?

5. Some people argue that "loans create deposits," while others contend that "deposits permit loans." Which statement is correct? Which is likely to be defended by economists? By bankers? Explain.

6. Assume that the reserve requirement is 10 percent. There are no currency withdrawals. Bank A's partial balance sheet is as follows:

Bank A

Assets		Liabilities	
Legal reserves	$ 16	Demand deposits	$100
Loans	84		
	$100		$100

(a) How much can Bank A expand demand deposits? Explain.

(b) If all other banks are in equilibrium, how much can Bank B lend? How much can Bank C lend? What is the maximum for the whole banking system? Explain.

7. What is the deposit-expansion multiplier when (a) required reserves are 1 percent; (b) required reserves are 10 percent; (c) required reserves are 100 percent?

8. For Bank A, legal reserves are $1,000, required reserves are $800, and demand deposits are $8,000. All other banks are in equilibrium. By how much can the banking system expand its demand deposits?

9. Will the *actual* amount of deposit expansion by the banking system equal the *predicted* amount? Why or why not? Explain.

10. Fill in the gaps for the omitted banks in the following table, assuming a 15 percent reserve requirement against demand deposits. What fundamental principle does the table illustrate?

	Amount added to checking accounts	Amount lent	Amount set aside as reserves
Bank 1	—	$10,000	—
Bank 2	$10,000	8,500	$_____
. . .	. . .	. . .	. . .
Bank 11	2,315	1,968	347
. . .	. . .	. . .	. . .
. . .	. . .	. . .	. . .
. . .	. . .	. . .	. . .
. . .	. . .	. . .	. . .
Bank 20	537	457	80
All other banks	_____	_____	_____
Totals—all banks	$_____	$_____	$_____

Case
Northfield Bank and Trust Co.: Portfolio Management by Linear Programming

One of the most challenging tasks faced by banks is the management of their portfolios. These consist of cash and earning assets. The latter include various types of financial claims—such as government securities, promissory notes issued by businesses, and other obligations. Banks continually change the composition of their portfolios, striving to achieve the best balance between three conflicting objectives: liquidity, profitability, and safety.

The method that many banks use to attain an optimally balanced portfolio involves a scientific technique known as linear programming. The theory underlying linear programming is mathematical, and its effective application usually requires the use of a computer. Nevertheless, you can gain some appreciation of the nature of linear programming from the following simplified example of an actual bank portfolio problem.

Investment-Possibilities Line

Northfield Bank and Trust Company has $100 million to allocate between two classes of assets—loans and securities. This task is represented in Figure (*a*) by the line *AB*, called an "investment-possibilities line." Each point along this line denotes a different possible combination of loans and securities totaling $100 million.

For example, at point *A*, the bank allocates $100 million to securities and nothing to loans. At point *B*, the bank allocates $100 million to loans and nothing to securities. At any point between *A* and *B*, the bank allocates some money to loans and some money to securities, the sum allocated to both equaling $100 million.

Of course, line *AB* represents the maximum attainable combinations of loans and securities totaling $100 million. If the bank decides to spend less than that amount, the combination chosen will be represented by a point to the left, or "inside," line *AB*.

Security/Loan Line

The bank seeks to obtain the most profitable combination of loans and securities. At the same time, it does not want to incur the risk of investing too much in one of these alternatives relative to the other. From experience the bank has concluded that a minimum ratio of $30 in negotiable securities to $100 in loans provides a satisfactory balance. Therefore, line 0*E* represents what may be called a "security/loan line." Each point along this line denotes a different combination of loans and securities such that the volume of securities is always 30 percent of the volume of loans. For example, point *H* represents $20 million in loans and $6 million in securities. Point *E* represents $100 million in loans and $30 million in securities.

Minimum-Loan Line

Banks are in business to lend money. Although they also earn income from other sources, lending is their most important activity. Every bank, therefore, seeks to accommodate its principal customers by fulfilling their requests for loans. In the case of Northfield Bank and Trust, it has been found that customers' aggregate demand for

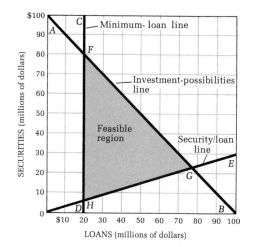

Figure (*a*): *Constraints and Feasibility*. Three intersecting straight lines establish the conditions of the bank's portfolio. The problem is to select the most profitable portfolio consisting of a combination of loans and securities. This combination is represented by a point somewhere on the feasible region.

loans totals at least $20 million for the period under consideration. This is shown by line *CD*, called a "minimum-loan line." The fact that this line is vertical, intersecting the horizontal axis of the chart at $20 million, means that the bank's portfolio cannot contain less than that amount in loans, irrespective of the amount allocated to securities.

The Feasible Region

You probably realize by now that the three lines defined above represent constraints. That is, the lines impose limiting conditions on the problem. For example, the investment-possibilities line tells you that the size of the portfolio is limited to a maximum of $100 million. The security/loan line tells you that the amount of money allocated to securities is limited to a minimum of 30 percent of the amount allocated to loans. And the minimum-loan line tells you that the amount allocated to loans must be at least $20 million.

When these ideas are put together on the chart, we obtain the shaded area *FGH*. This area may be called the "feasible region" because it designates the field within which portfolio decisions can be made. Thus, any portfolio represented by a point outside the feasible region violates one or more of the constraints. Conversely, any portfolio represented by a point within the feasible region or on any of its boundaries satisfies all the constraints. Therefore, the bank's portfolio will consist of some combination of loans and securities that can be represented by a point on the feasible region.

Income Line

In order for the bank to select the most profitable portfolio, the rate of return on loans and securities must be known. These returns will vary according to market conditions. However, suppose that, for the present period, the bank is earning a 10 percent return on its loans and a 5 percent return on its securities. Then, the level of income that can be earned from the portfolio depends on the amounts allocated to loans and securities.

These ideas are depicted in Figure (*b*). Each line, called an "income line," shows the amount of funds that must be allocated to loans and securities to earn a given income based on the above rates of return. At point *J*, for example, the bank allocates $20 million to securities. Assuming a 5 percent rate of return, this produces an income of $1 million. At point *K*, the bank allocates $10 million to loans. Assuming a 10 percent rate of return, this also yields an income of $1 million. Therefore, if we connect the two points, we get the income line *JK*. Each point along this line denotes a different allocation of funds to securities and to loans, the combined income from which totals $1 million.

In a similar manner, line *LM* is an income line representing $2 million. As you can see, therefore, the bank's income increases as the income line shifts outward from the origin of the chart.

The Optimum Portfolio

We now have the information needed to determine the bank's optimum portfolio. This is done by combining the essential ideas from the two previous charts, as shown in Figure (*c*).

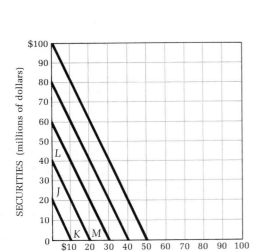

Figure (*b*): *Income Lines.*
The downward-sloping lines are called "income lines." Each line shows the amount of funds that must be allocated to loans and securities to earn a given income, based on a 10 percent return on loans and a 5 percent return on securities.

The bank's goal is to select an optimum portfolio—a combination of loans and securities that yields the highest income obtainable. As you have already learned, there are two considerations to keep in mind:

1. The optimum portfolio will be represented by a point located somewhere on the feasible region.

2. The highest income obtainable will be represented by an income line that lies as far as possible to the right while still touching the feasible region.

Does the income line *RS* determine the optimum portfolio? Evidently not. Although the line contains points that are on the feasible region, none of these points represents the most profitable portfolio.

The income line *TU*, however, does determine the optimum portfolio. This line just touches the feasible region at point *G*. Therefore, the most profitable portfolio is the one indicated by this point. It represents a portfolio consisting of $77 million in loans and $23 million in securities.

What will be the bank's income from this portfolio? As stated earlier, the bank earns 10 percent on loans and 5 percent on securities. Therefore, earnings will be $7.7 million on loans and $1.15 million on securities, or a total of $8.85 million on the entire portfolio.

Conclusion: A Practical Tool

Northfield Bank and Trust Co. is one of many banks that utilize linear programming as a management tool. In practice, banks' assets are broken down into detailed categories and grouped in various ways to achieve a balance between three conflicting objectives: liquidity, profitability, and safety. Numerous constraints are then introduced which set limits on the ways in which the variables in a problem may be combined to attain the optimum result. By the use of a computer, answers are thus obtained to complex problems that would otherwise be impossible to solve.

Questions

1. On the basis of what you have read, formulate a general definition of linear programming. In the light of your definition, can you suggest how a business firm might use linear programming to improve efficiency in production?

2. (a) What constraints does Northfield Bank and Trust Co. face in its efforts to attain an optimum portfolio? (b) Is the portfolio affected by a change in any of the constraints? Explain.

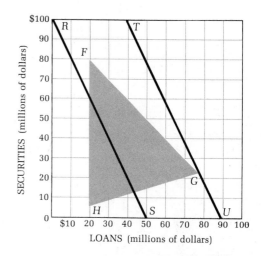

Figure (*c*): *The Optimum Portfolio.* The optimum portfolio is determined by an income line *TU* that lies as far as possible to the right while still touching the feasible region. This occurs at point *G*. The optimum portfolio thus consists of $77 million in loans and $23 million in securities.

Central Banking: Monetary Policy

Learning guide
Watch for the answers to these important questions

What is the meaning of monetary policy? What institution is responsible for conducting monetary policy?

How does the Federal Reserve influence economic activity? What *general* tools are available to the Fed for controlling the money supply?

What *selective* tools are available to the Fed for supplementing its general tools? Can all of the tools be coordinated so as to maximize their overall effectiveness?

Which monetary policies are likely to result in higher and in lower interest rates? How do changes in interest rates affect business investment?

Do Treasury actions have an impact on monetary policy? What would happen to the banking system if the Treasury disbursed funds without concern for monetary influences?

How useful is monetary policy? What are its advantages and limitations?

This chapter explains the means available to the Fed for performing its most important economic function—controlling the money supply.

FED RAISES RESERVE REQUIREMENTS

DISCOUNT RATE INCREASED BY FED

FED TO SELL U.S. SECURITIES

The financial press often contains headlines like these. They emphasize that the *Federal Reserve System* plays not one role but two. It is a "banker's bank," performing for depository institutions much the same services that these institutions perform for the public. But the Fed is also an important influence on the nation's economic and monetary policy. In a previous chapter, we examined the Fed's banking role. In this chapter, we shall look at the part it plays in making and implementing economic decisions.

Essentially, the Fed can utilize five instruments to modify or even reverse the direction of the economy. They are (1) reserve ratios, (2) the discount rate, (3) open-market operations, (4) margin regulations, and (5) moral suasion. The first three are broad controls because they influence the nation's money supply and the overall availability of credit. The fourth is a device used specifically to try to regulate the purchase of stock. The fifth is a psychological technique that relies on personal talk and public opinion. It is convenient, therefore, to classify the first three as "general" controls and the remaining two as "selective" controls.

Before beginning, it helps to understand what is meant by monetary policy. The following definition indicates the central concern of this chapter:

> *Monetary policy* is the deliberate exercise of the monetary authority's (that is, the Federal Reserve's) power to induce expansions or contractions in the money supply. The purpose of monetary policy is to achieve price stability, to help dampen the swings of business cycles, and to bring the nation's output and employment to desired levels.

General Controls

Three types of general controls are available to the Federal Reserve for influencing the level of economic activity. These controls consist of (1) changes in bank reserve ratios, (2) changes in the discount rate, and (3) open-market operations. Let us see how each helps to shape the nation's monetary policy.

Changing Reserve Ratios

You already know that banks are required to maintain legal reserves against demand-deposit liabilities. Why? Primarily to provide the monetary authorities—those who manage the central banking system—with one of several mechanisms for controlling the money supply.

As you have seen, commercial banks must maintain reserves equal to a minimum percentage of their deposits. Member banks of the Federal Reserve System may hold this minimum reserve as a deposit in a Reserve Bank and as cash in their own vaults. Nonmember banks may hold the minimum reserve as deposits in approved institutions (such as member banks) and as vault cash. In any case, the percentages of reserve requirements are graduated according to the size of banks' deposits. For the banking system as a whole, the average reserve requirement is approximately 10 percent.

You can readily see the implications of this from the following partial balance sheets. If the average required reserve ratio for all banks were 15 percent, $15 million of reserves would be needed to support $100 million of demand deposits:

By altering the reserve ratio, the Fed can exercise a powerful influence over the money supply. But the reserve ratio is a blunt tool, and it is therefore seldom changed.

All Banks			
Assets		Liabilities	
Required reserves	$15	Demand deposits	$100
Excess reserves	0		
Legal reserves	$15		

But if the average required reserve ratio for all banks were reduced to 10 percent, the amount of required reserves would decline from $15 million to $10 million. This would make $5 million of excess reserves available for lending.

All Banks			
Assets		Liabilities	
Required reserves	$10	Demand deposits	$100
Excess reserves	5		
Legal reserves	$15		

The existence of excess reserves, as you already know, can lead to a multiple expansion of demand deposits for the banking system as a whole.

The reverse of this process is also true. For example, an increase in the average required reserve ratio from 10 percent to 15 percent would absorb the $5 million of excess reserves. If banks were fully loaned up and had no excess reserves, an increase in the average required reserve ratio would force them to sell some of their earning assets, such as Treasury bills and commercial paper, in order to raise the necessary funds to cover their reserve deficiency. This, as you have seen, causes a multiple contraction of demand deposits for the banking system as a whole.

Thus, changes in the required reserve ratio affect the economy as a whole in the following way:

> A *decrease* in the required reserve ratio tends to be expansionary because it permits banks to enlarge the money supply. An *increase* is contractionary because it requires banks to reduce the money supply—depending on the degree to which they have excess reserves. The Federal Reserve System can thus affect the supply of money and the availability of bank credit through its control over reserve ratios and the volume of bank reserves.

The ability to alter the required reserve ratio is the Federal Reserve System's most powerful monetary tool. But it is a fairly blunt tool, and it is employed relatively seldom. The reason is that other instruments of control can be applied with greater flexibility and more refinement.

Changing the Discount Rate

Federal Reserve Banks can lend money at interest to banks and other depository institutions just as these depository institutions can lend money at interest to the public. Thus, it may be said that the Federal Reserve Banks are wholesalers of credit, while banks and other depository institutions are retailers.

No Federal Reserve policy tool is as well known or as poorly understood as the *discount rate*. In reality, it is simply the interest rate charged depository institutions on their loans from the Reserve Banks. However, it is called a "discount rate" because the interest on the loans is discounted or deducted from the loan when it is made, rather than added on when the loan is repaid.

When a bank borrows, it gives its own secured promissory note to the Federal Reserve Bank. The Reserve Bank then increases the borrowing bank's reserves by the appropriate number. Why would a bank want to borrow from the Fed? Usually, the bank wants to replenish its reserves, which may have "run down" for one or more reasons. Some examples:

Seasonal, or Short-Term, Changes in Business Conditions These may cause some banks to gain reserves during certain busy periods of the year and lose reserves when conditions slacken.

Trend, or Long-Term, Forces Over a period of years, a bank that grows less rapidly than its nearby competitors will often find itself with too large a pool of reserves. Conversely, a bank that grows faster than its competitors will frequently experience a diminishing pool of reserves.

Irregular, or Random, Forces Unexpected short-term occurrences sometimes cause sharp changes in a bank's reserves. For example, natural disasters, such as floods or storms, or large-scale transfers of funds by corporate depositors may subject some banks' reserves to severe pressures.

You can see, therefore, that the Federal Reserve's policy at the "discount window" (an expression widely used in banking circles) can be quite significant. It can affect not only banks' reserves but also credit conditions in the economy as a whole.

The direct effect of changes in the discount rate is to raise or lower the price of admission to the discount window. An increase in the discount rate makes it more expensive for banks to borrow; a reduction has the opposite effect. Indirectly, increases in the discount rate are usually associated with a rise in market interest rates and a general tightening of credit. Decreases in the discount rate tend to be associated with a reduction in market interest rates and an overall easing of credit.

The discount rate was the preeminent tool of monetary policy in the early years of the Federal Reserve System. This is no longer the case. One reason is that the Federal Reserve is very selective—its loans are deemed a privilege and not a right. As a result, banks often find it easier to replenish their reserves by selling earning assets (for example, government securities) or by borrowing from other banks rather than by seeking loans from the Federal Reserve.

Open-Market Operations: "The Fed Is in the Market"

"The Fed is in." This expression is heard frequently on Wall Street when the Federal Reserve Bank of New York buys or sells securities. Examples of such securities are Treasury bills, Treasury bonds, banker's acceptances, repurchase agreements, and so on.

Buying and selling Treasury bills and bonds and certain other securities in the open market is the Fed's most important monetary tool.

The Fed deals in these securities, sometimes as agent for the Federal Open Market Committee, or for the U.S. Treasury, or for other banks (as part of the services rendered by the Federal Reserve System). Such transactions are commonly referred to as *open-market operations*. They directly affect the volume of bank reserves and hence the overall cost and availability of credit. *These transactions are the Fed's most important monetary tool for day-to-day operations and for economic stabilization.*

Here, essentially, is the way in which open-market operations work.

Buying Securities

When the Fed *buys* securities in the open market, banks' reserves are increased in the following ways.

1. If the Fed buys securities directly from banks, it pays by increasing the banks' reserves with the Federal Reserve Banks by the amount of the purchase.

2. If the Fed buys securities from nonbanks (such as individuals or corporations), it pays with checks drawn on itself. The sellers then deposit these checks in their own banks, which, in turn, send the checks to the Federal Reserve Banks for collection. The Reserve Banks pay by increasing the reserves of the banks.

Selling Securities

When the Fed *sells* securities in the open market, banks' reserves are thereby decreased:

1. If the Fed sells securities directly to banks, the banks pay by reducing their reserves with the Federal Reserve Banks by the amount of the purchase.

2. If the Fed sells securities to nonbanks, they pay with checks drawn mainly on commercial banks. The Federal Reserve Banks collect on these checks by reducing the reserves of the commercial banks. The commercial banks, in turn, return the canceled checks to their depositors and reduce their deposit accounts accordingly.

Illustrations with Balance Sheets

You can gain a firmer grasp of these ideas by seeing them conveyed in terms of partial balance sheets. Here are some examples. (All data are in millions of dollars.)

When the Fed buys securities in the open market, the effect is to increase banks' reserves.

Case 1 Suppose that the Federal Reserve Bank purchases $1 million worth of government securities in the open market. If the seller of the securities is a commercial bank, the Reserve Bank pays the commercial bank by increasing its reserve deposit:

Reserve Bank

Assets		Liabilities	
Government securities	+ $1	Commercial bank reserve deposits	+ $1

Commercial Bank

Assets		Liabilities
Government securities	− $1	
Reserves with Federal Reserve Bank	+ $1	

Case 2 If the seller of the securities is a nonbank—such as an individual or corporation—the check received in payment from the Federal Reserve Bank will most likely be deposited at the seller's commercial bank. That bank, in turn, sends the check to the Reserve Bank for credit to its reserve account:

Reserve Bank

Assets		Liabilities	
Government securities	+ $1	Commercial bank reserve deposits	+ $1

Commercial Bank

Assets		Liabilities	
Reserves with Federal Reserve Bank	+ $1	Demand deposits	+ $1

Note that the effect on reserves is the same in both cases. That is:

Whether the seller of securities is a bank or a nonbank, the legal reserves of the bank are increased. The amount of the increase will be the value of the securities purchased by the Federal Reserve authorities.

Case 3 The opposite situation occurs when the Federal Reserve Bank sells $1 million of government securities in the open market. If the buyer is a commercial bank, it acquires $1 million in government securities and loses $1 million of reserves:

Reserve Bank

Assets		Liabilities	
Government securities	−$1	Commercial bank reserve deposits	−$1

Commercial Bank

Assets		Liabilities
Government securities	+$1	
Reserves with Federal Reserve Bank	−$1	

Case 4 If the buyer of the security is a nonbank, the Federal Reserve Bank receives payment with a check drawn on the buyer's bank. After the check "clears," that bank's deposit at the Reserve Bank and the buyer's deposit at his or her bank are both reduced by the value of the securities transacted:

Reserve Bank

Assets		Liabilities	
Government securities	−$1	Commercial bank reserve deposits	−$1

Commercial Bank

Assets		Liabilities	
Reserves with Federal Reserve Bank	−$1	Demand deposits	−$1

Note that the ultimate effect is the same in cases 3 and 4.

The legal reserves of the commercial bank have been reduced by the value of the securities sold by the Federal Reserve Bank.

Although these open-market operations have been illustrated for only one commercial bank, the same ideas apply to all banks within the banking system. The overall economic effects of such transactions can be summarized briefly:

Open-market purchases of government securities are expansionary. They increase bank reserves and therefore permit a multiple growth of deposits. Conversely, open-market sales of government securities are contractionary. They reduce bank reserves and hence force a multiple decline of deposits.

Selective Controls

In addition to its general controls, the Federal Reserve can make use of certain selective tools. These, like the others, are designed to influence the supply of money and the overall level of economic activity. The principal selective controls available to the Fed involve margin regulations and moral suasion.

When the Fed sells securities in the open market, the effect is to decrease banks' reserves.

The various selective controls available to the Fed are not as effective as the general ones.

Margin Regulations

The Federal Reserve Board is empowered to set the so-called *margin requirement*. This is the percentage down payment that must be made when borrowing to finance purchases of stock. This power was granted by Congress during the early 1930s because the excessive use of credit to purchase stocks was a significant factor in the great stock-market crash of 1929. The higher the margin requirement, the larger the proportion of a stock purchase that must be paid for in cash. Therefore:

> An increase in margin requirements discourages speculation on borrowed credit; a decrease may encourage security purchases.

The margin requirement is altered infrequently because it is not as important as it once was. Nevertheless, it is a device for dampening or stimulating activity in the stock market. This, in turn, can affect the ability of firms to sell stocks in order to finance new investment.

Moral Suasion

Of course, the Federal Reserve's Board of Governors can always exert pressure on bankers by using oral and written appeals to expand or restrict credit. This process, called *moral suasion*, does not compel compliance. Nevertheless, it has been successful on a number of occasions. During recessions, it has sometimes stimulated the expansion of credit by encouraging banks to lend more. During inflations, it has sometimes discouraged lending and restricted the expansion of credit. In a more general sense, the Federal Reserve exercises moral suasion every day when it advises individual member banks on ordinary loan policy.

Summarizing:

> To be effective, all the foregoing methods of general and selective monetary control are coordinated by the Federal Reserve. Its goal is to promote economic growth and stability through the money supply. You can gain some appreciation of the Fed's task of coordination by examining Exhibit 1.

How Monetary Policy Affects Interest Rates and Business Investment

The Fed's monetary policy, particularly with respect to its open-market operations, affects interest rates in the economy.

The tools of monetary policy are important. Through the proper use of general and selective controls, the Fed can strongly influence the nation's level of economic activity.

Two of the Fed's tools—the discount rate and open-market operations—are especially significant because they are actively used and are closely connected with interest rates. This connection can best be seen by examining the relationship between the prices of bonds and their yields. Keep in mind that a bond, like any other credit instrument, is also a debt instrument. It is an asset to the party who owns it and a liability to the party who issues it.

If you buy a credit instrument, such as a bond, the effective rate of interest on the security is called the *yield*. Exhibit 2 shows the relationship between the market price and effective yield of a $100 bond maturing one year hence with a nominal interest rate of 8 percent (paying its holder an interest of $8 per annum). The chart shows that, if you could buy the bond in the market today for around $99, you would receive $100 upon maturity plus $8 in interest. This is an effective yield of

Exhibit 1
Flow of Federal Reserve Influence

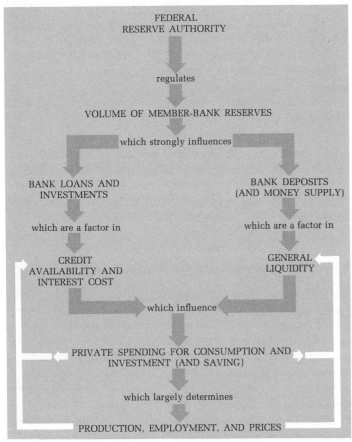

Source: Board of Governors of the Federal Reserve System. Adapted.

Exhibit 2
Bond Prices and Bond Yields Vary Inversely

A bond pays its owner a fixed amount of dollars annually. Therefore, the lower the price at which you can buy a bond, the higher the percentage return or *yield* you will receive, and vice versa.

This figure shows the price–yield relationship for a $100 bond paying 8 percent (that is, $8) annually to its owner. As explained in the text, if you can buy the bond for $99, the yield to you will be approximately 9 percent. At $101, the yield will be approximately 7 percent.

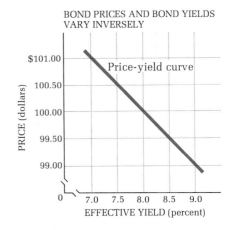

about 9 percent. On the other hand, if you bought the bond today at a market price of $101, you would still get $100 back at maturity (thereby losing $1 from your purchase price) plus $8 in interest. This makes an effective yield of about 7 percent. Thus:

> *The price of a bond varies inversely with its yield.* This is because the annual dollar payments received on a bond are a fixed amount. Therefore, the higher the market price of a bond, the lower its yield, and vice versa. This principle applies to all credit (or debt) instruments, not just to bonds.

Bank Portfolio Effects and Business Investment

What bearing does this inverse relationship have on longer-term interest rates? The answer can be understood in terms of the impacts of securities on banks' portfolios:

1. When the discount rate is increased, banks find it more costly to borrow. Therefore, they usually replenish their reserves by selling some of their short-term securities instead. The increased sale of securities tends to lower security prices and raise their yields. These higher market yields (that is, effective rates of interest on existing short-term securi-

Banks respond to changing interest rates by altering their portfolios of cash and securities.

ties) tend to push up longer-term market interest rates on new securities. Why? Because *all* securities compete for investors' dollars. The result of higher short-term and long-term interest rates is to discourage business investment.

2. Similar effects occur when the Fed, in order to dampen economic activity, sells securities in the open market. When short-term credit instruments, such as Treasury bills and repurchase agreements, are sold by the Fed, the prices of these securities decline. Therefore, their yields increase, raising short-term interest rates and putting upward pressure on long-term interest rates.

3. On the other hand, when the discount rate is lowered, banks are likely to maintain their borrowings at a higher level because of cheaper rates. Further, when the Fed tries to stimulate the economy by purchasing short-term securities in the open market, their prices are bid up. This reduces short-term interest rates, which, in turn, puts downward pressure on longer-term rates. The result is to encourage business investment by making it less costly.

Conclusion: Money and Interest Rates

The Fed controls the money supply, but not interest rates. Interest rates are determined in the financial markets.

A number of monetary-management tools are available to the Federal Reserve. Nevertheless, the ones you read and hear about most often in the news media are the discount rate and open-market operations.

The discount rate is an important monetary tool. However, as stated earlier, it is not as important as it was in the early days of the Federal Reserve System. With the development of open-market operations in the 1920s, the Fed came to depend increasingly on this latter device as the best short-term means of controlling the money supply.

Through its week-to-week open-market operations, the Fed exercises strong control over the money supply. This control is reinforced, from time to time, with changes in the discount rate and, on rare occasions, with changes in reserve requirements. In this way, by controlling the money supply, the Fed plays a powerful role in influencing interest rates. But note this important point:

> Contrary to widespread popular opinion, *the Fed does not directly determine interest rates.* The Fed only determines the money supply. Interest rates are determined directly in the financial markets through the interactions of lenders (such as banks) and borrowers (such as businesses) as they respond to changes in the money supply.

Impact of the Treasury on Monetary Management

Interestingly enough, the Federal Reserve is not the only organization that can influence monetary management. The U.S. Treasury can, too. You can appreciate this when you consider that the Treasury raises and spends hundreds of billions of dollars annually, conducting its activities through commercial and Federal Reserve Banks. Ordinarily, such huge financial operations would wreak havoc with the banking system. To avoid this possibility, the Treasury plans its decisions very carefully so as to minimize the impact of its actions on Federal Reserve monetary management. Occasionally, however, the Treasury deliberately synchronizes its activities with the Federal Reserve's in order to supplement the latter's monetary policies.

To understand the Treasury's influence in monetary matters, we will examine its practices with respect to deposit banking. The ways in which its actions can be used for contractionary or expansionary purposes will then become clear.

Treasury Deposits in the Banking System

The Treasury maintains demand deposits with almost every commercial bank in the country as well as with the Federal Reserve Banks. If you send a check to the Treasury in payment of your income tax, the Treasury deposits the check in one of its approximately 14,000 commercial-bank accounts. On the other hand, if the Treasury sends you an income-tax refund, its check will usually be drawn on one of its deposits at a Federal Reserve Bank. This practice is adhered to by the Treasury for virtually all its receipts and expenditures.

For example, if you have a checking account at your local bank, chances are that the Treasury does too. Therefore, when you send a check to the Internal Revenue Service (a division of the Treasury) to pay your income tax and the check is presented to your bank for payment, the bank simply transfers the funds from your account to the Treasury's. Because no money leaves the bank, the bank experiences no loss of reserves.

The Treasury, however, is constantly disbursing funds—for government payrolls, national defense, and many other purposes. In order to manage its expenditures efficiently, it periodically makes what are technically known as "calls on the banks." These are communications to banks informing them that, on a certain date, the Treasury intends to transfer a specified amount of funds from its commercial accounts to its Federal Reserve accounts. The banks know they must have the money available on that date. Then, when the transfers are made, the reserves of commercial banks are reduced. However, when the Treasury disburses the funds with checks written against its Federal Reserve Bank accounts, the recipients deposit the checks in commercial banks, thereby increasing their reserves. On the whole, the Treasury is able to maintain fairly constant balances with the Reserve Banks because it can plan with reasonable accuracy the amount and timing of its disbursements.

To summarize:

> The great bulk of the Treasury's deposits are with the nation's commercial banks. On the other hand, almost all of the Treasury's checks are drawn against the Federal Reserve Banks. This is because the money that the Treasury receives—say, from tax collections or from the sale of bonds—is deposited to its accounts in commercial banks. However, the money that the Treasury disburses—say, for tax refunds, welfare, or defense—is first transferred to its accounts at the Federal Reserve Banks, and then checks are issued against those Federal Reserve deposits.

This may seem to be a strange way for the Treasury to conduct its transactions. However, the Treasury adheres to this policy in order to minimize the possible disruptive effects that its large-scale transactions would have on the banks and the money market. In general, the reductions in reserves created by the Treasury's transfers are approximately offset by the increases in reserves that result from its outlays. In this way, a reasonable degree of stability among the banks and financial markets is maintained.

The ways in which the Treasury manages its bank balances can also affect monetary policy. These balances fluctuate according to Treasury collections and disbursements of funds.

Contractionary and Expansionary Actions

In general, the Treasury tries to stabilize its fiscal operations in order not to disrupt Federal Reserve monetary policy.

You can see that the ways in which the Treasury manages its cash balances can exercise important influences on monetary policy. For example:

1. Suppose that the Treasury wishes to *contract* the availability of commercial-bank credit. In that case, the Treasury can increase its average balance at the Federal Reserve Banks by transferring from its commercial accounts to its Federal Reserve accounts more funds than it intends to disburse. The effect is to reduce the volume of commercial-bank reserves and hence create a multiple contraction of demand deposits.

2. If the Treasury wishes to *expand* the availability of commercial-bank credit, it can follow the reverse procedure. That is, it can decrease its average balance at the Federal Reserve by transferring deposits from these banks to the commercial banks. This action is not quite as flexible as the contractionary process, because the Treasury must always maintain a minimum level of Federal Reserve balances sufficient to carry on its day-to-day operations. Nevertheless, the shifting of funds into commercial accounts provides the banking system with increased reserves. This procedure may, of course, produce a multiple expansion of bank deposits.

To summarize:

There are various ways in which the Treasury can manage its cash balances with the intention of influencing monetary policy. In practice, however, the Treasury rarely uses any of the techniques for that purpose. Instead, it tries to perform its fiscal operations without disrupting the banks and the money market, and leaves matters of monetary management to the Federal Reserve authorities.

Is Monetary Policy Really Useful?

How effective is monetary policy in influencing economic activity? As with all policy areas of economics, this question is the subject of continuous debate. The principal arguments for and against the usefulness of monetary policy can be outlined briefly.

Advantages of Monetary Policy

The advantages of monetary policy outweigh those of fiscal policy.

In evaluating the usefulness of monetary policy, it is often instructive to make comparisons with fiscal policy. This is an alternative and sometimes complementary method of fighting inflation and unemployment.

Monetary Policy Is Nondiscriminatory (in Principle)

Monetary controls are ordinarily employed in a general way to influence the total volume of credit. The Fed is nondiscriminatory *in principle* with respect to the borrowers or activities that are to be encouraged or discouraged, and it leaves it to the market to be "discriminatory." The home-construction, automobile, and major appliance industries, for example, feel the effects of tight credit more quickly than most other industries because of their dependence on the ability of buyers to borrow. Fiscal policy, on the other hand, involves changes in taxation and government spending. These changes can directly alter the composition of total production as well as its overall level.

Monetary Policy Is Flexible in Application

Because the Board of Governors controls monetary policy, changes can be made quickly and smoothly without getting snarled in administrative red tape. In contrast, fiscal policy involves budgetary considerations of taxation and spending. On such matters, Congress usually deliberates for many months before arriving at a decision.

Monetary Policy Is Nonpolitical (in Principle)

Congress gave the Federal Reserve System political independence to assure its effective performance. It provided fourteen-year terms of office for appointed Board members, made them ineligible for reappointment, staggered their terms of office, and provided for the election of Reserve Bank presidents by their own boards of directors, subject to the approval of the Federal Reserve Board. As a result, although the institution is sometimes pressured by the White House, the Fed *can* nevertheless base its day-to-day decisions on economic rather than on political grounds. In contrast, fiscal policy is *always* strongly influenced by politics.

Limitations of Monetary Policy

Whereas the advantages of monetary policy are fairly general, most of its limitations arise out of specific situations and circumstances.

The limitations of monetary policy are not entirely comparable with those of fiscal policy.

Monetary Policy Has Incomplete Countercyclical Effectiveness

During an inflation, the Federal Reserve can use its instruments of control to choke off borrowing and to establish an effective tight-money (high-interest-rate) policy. But during a recession, even an easy-money (low-interest-rate) policy cannot ensure that businesspeople will want to borrow. If they regard the business outlook as poor, the desired increase in loans and spending will not be realized. Further, there is the possibility that commercial bankers may be unwilling to lend when they have excess reserves. For these reasons, monetary policy is far more effective and more predictable as an anti-inflationary device than as an antirecessionary one.

Monetary Policy Cannot Correct Cost-Push or Profit-Push Inflation

Some observers contend that inflation often results from upward pressure on wages and prices. This pressure arises because of the monopolistic power that large unions and business firms are able to exert in the market. If this argument is true, monetary policy can do little to correct the situation. At most, actions taken by the Federal Reserve may help dampen either a cost-push or profit-push inflation, but they will not eliminate either.

Monetary Policy May Conflict with Treasury Objectives

Every debtor likes low interest rates. This is especially true of the U.S. Treasury, which is the biggest debtor of all. Because the Treasury is continually "refunding" maturing securities by selling new ones, it wants to keep the interest cost as low as possible. Indeed, a difference of one percentage point in the interest rate on government securities can cost the Treasury many billions of dollars annually.

Reserve officials, on the other hand, regard high interest rates as an important anti-inflationary weapon. In the past, these two distinctly different goals have at times resulted in a policy conflict between the Treasury and the Federal Reserve. Although compromises or "accords" were eventually worked out, they tended to reduce somewhat the full effectiveness of anti-inflationary monetary policies.

Monetary Policy May Be Offset by Changes in the Velocity of Money

Discretionary monetary policy, as you have seen, requires that the Federal Reserve authorities follow a two-pronged approach:

1. In prosperity, decrease the money supply to curb inflation.

2. In recession, increase the money supply to stimulate recovery.

The Fed's control over monetary policy is weakened by such factors as changes in the velocity of money, the growth of financial intermediaries, and the difficulty of forecasting economic changes.

Unfortunately, the effectiveness of these actions may sometimes be at least partially reduced by opposite changes in the velocity, or turnover, of money. This is simply the average number of times per year that a dollar is spent. As you might expect, the velocity of money is affected by the public's confidence in the future course of the economy. For example, in prosperity, when people are optimistic, they often tend to spend more freely. Hence, velocity may increase at a time when the money supply should be reduced. In recession, when people are pessimistic, they often tend to curb their spending. Hence, velocity may decrease at a time when the money supply should be increased.

Significant changes in the velocity of money can therefore exert a direct influence on the price level. How? By causing prices to rise when velocity increases and to decline when velocity decreases. As a result, changes in velocity may offset, to some extent, the monetary authorities' efforts to stabilize the economy by contracting or expanding the money supply. You will be learning much more about these concepts in subsequent chapters.

The Fed Lacks Complete Control Over Lending

During the past several decades, two types of situations have made it more difficult for the Reserve authorities to exercise as much control over the total volume of lending as they would like.

1. There has been a substantial growth of *financial intermediaries*. Some examples are such nonbank lenders as insurance companies, personal finance companies, and credit unions. These institutions hold large volumes of savings, which they are continually trying to "put to work" by investing or lending to the public. This helps to offset restrictive monetary policies of the Reserve officials.

2. Large holdings of money-market securities are in the hands of commercial banks and business corporations. These organizations can sell off the securities as needed to obtain additional cash.

Because both of these situations are largely outside the Fed's control, they tend to increase the velocity of money. This, in turn, can weaken the effectiveness of monetary policies.

Forecasting and Timing Are Difficult

Although monetary policies may be implemented more quickly than fiscal policies, monetary policies nevertheless suffer from similar kinds of forecasting and timing problems. As a result, the Federal Reserve has often managed the money supply too erratically, thereby causing further instability. Thus:

> Monetary policy has shortcomings as well as benefits. The fact that there are more limitations than advantages should not lead you to believe that monetary policy is useless. It is a powerful force for stabilization and will continue to play an important role in the economy.

Case
Problems of the Fed: Money + Power ≠ Happiness

Most people, if asked to name Washington's most influential agency, would probably say the FBI or the CIA. In reality, the Federal Reserve Board has more influence because it is both rich and powerful.

The Fed's income is derived primarily from the interest it receives on the billions of dollars' worth of securities that it holds. (Most of this interest is returned to the Treasury after the Fed deducts dividend payments to member banks plus any operating expenses deemed necessary.)

The Fed's actions directly determine or influence such things as the interest rate charged on a bank loan, the minimum "down payment" needed to purchase a stock, the ability of a potential home buyer to obtain a mortgage, and many other conditions affecting people's lives.

However, despite its money and power, the Fed is almost always beset with problems. One of the most enduring of these is the question of "independence versus regulation."

Independence: Is More Regulation Needed?

When the Federal Reserve Board was created in 1913, no one perceived that it would some day exercise a powerful influence on government economic policy. In that pre-Keynesian era, the economic system was thought to be basically stable. Therefore, the Fed's primary purpose was to provide business with a proper supply of money. If that were done, it was believed, lapses from prosperity would then be temporary, and the economy would automatically restore itself to full employment.

The Great Depression of the 1930s changed these beliefs. Legislation was passed that strengthened substantially the Fed's economic powers. The Reserve Board, for example, was given complete control over open-market operations and was granted greater authority in setting reserve requirements.

This new independence has since been resented by many political leaders. One group argues that fiscal policy—government tax and expenditure actions—should take precedence over, and be accommodated by, the Fed's monetary policies. Another group believes that monetary policy should have priority over fiscal policy because the Fed's instruments of control are more powerful and faster acting. And some critics who subscribe to neither of these points of view contend that the Reserve Board's term of office should be changed to coincide with the President's. This would enable each President to choose a Board whose policies are consistent with national purpose.

These and related issues of Federal Reserve independence have been debated among political leaders for years.

Whatever the outcome, it is likely to have profound economic effects on everyone's life.

What You Have Learned in This Chapter

1. The chief responsibility of the central banking system—the Federal Reserve System—is to regulate the supply of money and credit so as to promote economic stability and growth. The ways in which this responsibility is fulfilled determine our monetary policy.

2. The chief instruments of monetary policy available to the Federal Reserve System are reserve requirements, the discount rate, open-market operations, margin regulations, and moral suasion. These tools are usually coordinated by the Reserve officials to achieve the System's overall objectives of promoting stable economic growth through the money supply.

3. Monetary policy has important effects on interest rates and business investment. Through open-market operations and the discount rate, the Fed affects prices of credit instruments, which, in turn, affect interest rates. This, of course, influences business investment decisions.

4. The U.S. Treasury, like the Federal Reserve, can also influence monetary management. However, it usually carries on its operations in a manner that creates minimum disruption within the banking system and the money market.

5. Monetary policy has advantages and limitations as a method of economic stabilization. Its chief advantages are that it is (a) nondiscriminatory, (b) flexible, and (c) nonpolitical. Its main limitations are that it (a) may serve as an incomplete countercyclical weapon, (b) is relatively ineffective in combating inflationary forces caused by cost-push pressures, and (c) sometimes conflicts with Treasury goals. Also, it (d) may be offset by changes in the velocity of circulation of money, (e) lacks control of nonbank lending and credit operations, and (f) suffers somewhat from a lack of precision. Despite these shortcomings, monetary control will continue to play an integral role in our general stabilization policy.

For Discussion

1. *Terms and concepts to review:*
monetary policy
discount rate
open-market operations
margin requirement
moral suasion
yield

2. How do changes in reserve requirements, the discount rate, and margin requirements affect economic activity? Explain.

3. How do open-market operations work? When might they tend to be expansionary? Contractionary?

4. Suppose that the reserve requirement is 15 percent. If the Federal Reserve Bank purchases $1 million of government securities in the open market, a bank increases both its legal reserves and demand deposits by that amount. (Do you remember why?) Using the axes below, construct a bar graph showing the initial net new deposit and the *potential* cumulative expansion of bank deposits that may take place at each "round" of deposit creation. (**Suggestion** You may find it helpful to construct a table showing the multiple expansion of bank deposits. The table can then be used to sketch the graph.)

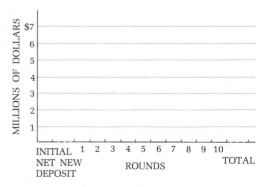

5. Suppose that the Treasury issues more paper currency than people want. (a) What will happen to bank reserves? (b) What can the Federal Reserve authorities do to offset the consequences?

6. Using two long "T-accounts" arranged side by side as shown, depict the positive (+) or negative (−) changes represented by each of the following transactions.

Federal Reserve Banks		Commercial Banks	
Assets	Liabilities	Assets	Liabilities

(a) The Federal Reserve buys $100 of government securities from a dealer. The Fed pays the dealer with a check drawn on itself, which the dealer deposits in the bank.
(b) The bank sends the $100 check to the Federal Reserve, which credits the bank's reserve deposit.
(c) The Federal Reserve buys $100 of government securities from a bank and pays with a check on itself.
(d) The bank sends the $100 check to the Federal Reserve for credit to its account.
(e) The Federal Reserve lends $100 to a bank by discounting the latter's note.
(f) A depositor writes a check for $100 against a demand deposit and cashes it at his or her bank.

(g) A depositor adds $100 in currency to a demand deposit.
(h) The Treasury sells $100 of securities to the nonbanking public and deposits the checks it receives in commercial banks.
(i) The Treasury transfers $100 of deposits from commercial banks to Federal Reserve Banks.
(j) The Treasury pays $100 for services by writing a check against its deposit at the Federal Reserve.
(k) The party to whom the check was paid deposits it. The bank sends the $100 check to the Federal Reserve for collection.

13
CHAPTER

This chapter shows the interrelationships among the key variables in the Keynesian model.

Macroeconomic Equilibrium in the Keynesian Model

Learning guide
Watch for the answers to these important questions

How does money affect output and prices? Is there a relationship between the quantity of money in circulation, its velocity or rate of turnover, and GNP?

What factors affect interest rates? What are the differences between the classical and liquidity-preference theories of interest?

According to the liquidity-preference theory, how do changes in the interest rate come about? How do these changes affect the volume of investment spending by businesses?

What basic relationships exist among the variables constituting the Keynesian model? How does a change in the money supply affect interest rates, investment expenditures, and hence aggregate demand?

> The importance of money essentially flows from its being a link between the present and the future.

So wrote J. M. Keynes in *The General Theory of Employment, Interest and Money* in 1936. The following year he went on to say: "The possession of actual money lulls our disquietude; and the premium which we require to make us part with money is the measure of the degree of our disquietude."

The "link between the present and the future"—the "premium" to which Lord Keynes referred—is the rate of interest. This variable plays a strategic role in the explanation of income and employment determination. This fact was pointed out in an earlier chapter but it must now be examined in closer detail.

It is important to understand the relationship between money and interest. In this chapter, you will learn how the rate of interest may be directly influenced by changes in the money supply. Once the relationship between money and interest is established, the Keynesian macroeconomic model of income determination will be complete. You will then see how the strategic variables in the model interrelate within the system as a whole.

Money Affects Output and Prices

You have already learned how the Federal Reserve can influence the level of economic activity by its discretionary actions. For example, to encourage economic expansion, the Fed can increase the supply of money by engaging in open-market purchases of government securities. To initiate economic contraction, the Fed can decrease the supply of money by undertaking open-market sales of government securities. Thus, there is a *direct* relationship between the money supply and the level of economic activity: Changes in the former can produce similar changes in the latter.

The idea that changes in the money supply lead to changes in the price level was fundamental to classical economic thinking. But it was not stated with precision until the early 1900s. At that time, a distinguished American economist at Yale University, Irving Fisher (1867–1947), expressed the link between money and prices by means of an equation that soon became famous. A modernized version of that equation can be developed in the following way.

Equation of Exchange

You may not be able to see how fast individual dollars are spent. However, you can measure the average speed of money movements as a whole rather easily.

The equation of exchange relates the quantity of money and the velocity of money to total spending.

Let V stand for the *income velocity of money*. This is the average number of times per year each dollar is spent on purchasing the economy's annual flow of final goods and services—its GNP. Further, let M denote the nation's money supply as measured by the amount of money, including currency and checkable deposits, in the hands of the public. Then, the income velocity of money is measured by the formula

$$V = \frac{GNP}{M}$$

For example, if in a certain year the GNP was $800 billion and the stock of money was $200 billion, V = $800/$200 = 4 per year for that year. In other words, each dollar must have been used an average of four times to purchase the economy's GNP.

The letter M in the equation above can, of course, be "transposed" to the left side. Then the equation becomes

$$MV = GNP$$

As you will recall, it is also true that gross national income (*GNI*) is equal to GNP. Therefore, *MV* is obviously the same as *GNI*.

Suppose, however, that we make the equation more refined by expressing GNP in terms of its component prices and quantities. Let P stand for the average price of final goods and services produced during the year and let Q represent the physical quantity of those goods and services. The *value* of final output is then price times quantity. That is, GNP = $P \times Q$, because, for example, GNP = price of apples times number of apples, plus price of haircuts times number of haircuts, plus . . . and so on for all final goods and services produced. The equation can therefore be written

The equation of exchange tells you that the nation's income is equal to the market value of final output.

$$MV = PQ$$

This is known as the "equation of exchange." For example, imagine a highly simplified case in which the students in your class constitute an economy whose total supply of money, M, is $80. Further, assume that the class produces a quantity of output, Q, equal to 60 units of a good and that the average price, P, of this output is \$4 per unit. Then the equation of exchange tells you that V must equal 3, because

$$MV = PQ$$

or,

$$(\$80)(3) = (\$4)(60)$$

Each dollar is thus spent an average of three times per year on the class's output.

The equation of exchange is actually an identity. It states that the total amount of society's income *spent* on final goods and services, MV, is equal to the total amount of money *received* for society's final goods and services, PQ.

To summarize:

> **Equation of exchange.** The quantity of money (M) multiplied by the average number of times (V) each unit of money is spent on purchasing the economy's output of final goods and services is MV. The average price (P) of final goods and services multiplied by their quantity (Q) is PQ. During a given period, society's income and expenditure are equal. Therefore, $MV = PQ$.

The equation tells us that the given flow of money can be looked at from either the buyers' or the sellers' point of view. The aggregate flow is the same in either case. As in demand-and-supply analysis, the quantity of a commodity purchased is equal to the quantity sold.

The Quantity Theory of Money

What does the equation of exchange tell us about the role of money in influencing national income and expenditure? To answer this, we have to examine some of the components of the equation.

1. Suppose we assume that V *remains constant.* This means that by controlling M we could control GNP. For instance, if M is increased, either P or Q or both will have to increase in order to maintain equality between the right and left sides of the equation. The changes in P or Q will depend on the state of the economy. In a period of recession, Q will tend to rise relatively more than P as unemployed resources are re-employed. In a period of high employment, P will tend to rise more than Q as full utilization of resources is approached. What do you suppose would happen in a period of full employment?

2. Suppose we assume that *both V and Q remain constant.* This, in fact, is what the classical economists believed. They assumed that V was constant because it was determined by the long-run money-holding habits of households and business firms. These habits, the classicists argued, were fairly stable. Further, they assumed that Q was constant because the economy always tended toward full employment. The classical economists thus concluded that P depends directly on M. As a result, their theory has come to be known as the "quantity theory of money."

> **Quantity theory of money.** The level of prices in the economy is directly proportional to the quantity of money in circulation. That is, a given percentage change in the stock of money will cause an equal percentage change in the price level in the same direction.

The statement that $MV = PQ$ *is the same as saying that GNI = GNP.*

In the classical theory, V and Q were assumed to be constant. Therefore, changes in P were directly proportional to changes in M.

The quantity theory states, for example, that a 10 percent increase in M will cause a 10 percent increase in P. Likewise, a 5 percent decrease in M will cause a 5 percent decrease in P. In general, according to the quantity theory of money, *changes in the price level are directly proportional to changes in the money supply.*

What Does the Evidence Show?

How well does the quantity theory of money correspond with the facts? Can changes in M be used to predict changes in P?

In evaluating the theory, it is necessary to distinguish between long-term and short-term changes. The evidence falls into two major classes of findings.

1. During a number of long-run periods, changes in P have appeared to be closely tied to changes in M. For example, in the late sixteenth century, the Spanish importation of gold and silver from the New World caused major price increases in Europe. Likewise, the discovery of gold in the United States, Canada, and South Africa during the latter half of the nineteenth century brought sudden expansions in the money supply and rapidly rising prices in these countries. During more recent history, the excessive borrowing and printing of money by most countries has resulted in periods of upward-spiraling prices. In these and various other cases, prices rose directly with increases in the quantity of money, without any corresponding increases in output.

2. In the short run, V varies a good deal, even though its long-run trend has been steadily rising. This is shown in Exhibit 1. And output, of course, may also vary substantially from year to year. In addition, even if P increases as a result of an increase in M, the rise in prices might encourage an increase in V as people spend money more quickly for fear of future price increases. If this happens, P is no longer merely a passive variable dependent on M, but a *causal* variable contributing to changes in other factors.

Because of such complexities, the quantity theory of money has not yet proved suitable for predicting short-run changes in P from changes in M. However, as pointed out above, the theory provides a useful guide for judging the influence of monetary forces on changes in the general price level.

Modernizing the Quantity Theory: The Importance of Velocity

The quantity theory of money played a critical role in classical economic thinking. Since the 1950s, it has undergone substantial revision by various economists. Notable among them has been Nobel laureate Milton Friedman, Professor Emeritus of the University of Chicago.

The revised, or "modern," quantity theory retains much of the traditional doctrine but reorients it toward the importance of V. For example, V is not assumed to remain constant as in the old theory but is believed instead to be influenced by certain specific factors. One of these (which, for the time being, may be expressed in general terms) is *public confidence in the economy.*

Exhibit 1
Income Velocity of Money:
$$V = \frac{GNP}{M1}$$

The income velocity of money (V) usually fluctuates considerably within any given year. Its long-run trend, however, has been steadily upward. This graph shows the velocity of $M1$, which is the most widely used measure of the money supply.

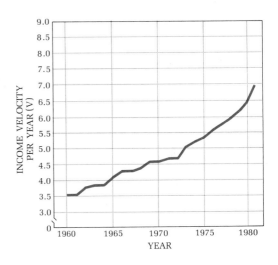

In the modern quantity theory, much interest focuses on the predictability of V.

Thus, if people fear unemployment or are pessimistic about the future, they will tend to refrain from spending. Therefore, they will increase their percentage of income saved. The larger the proportion of saving that occurs without a corresponding increase in investment, the more slowly money turns over. Hence, the lower its velocity.

Conversely, if people are optimistic about the future, they will increase their spending and thus reduce their percentage of income saved. Money thus turns over faster and its velocity is higher.

Predictability of Velocity

Modern quantity theorists argue that the Fed should increase the money supply at a steady rate sufficient to stabilize the economy at full employment.

Modern quantity theorists believe that, although V fluctuates over time, its range of short-run variation is limited and, given sufficient knowledge, *predictable*. Therefore, the underlying determinant of GNP (or *PQ* in the equation of exchange) is still the quantity of money. This conclusion has important policy implications. It suggests the following "rule":

> The central bank (that is, the Federal Reserve) should use its monetary policies—such as open-market operations and control over the discount rate and reserve requirements—in a consistent manner. That is, *it should provide a continuous expansion in the money supply at a rate sufficient to assure steady economic growth and full employment.* Failure to follow this "rule," say the modern quantity theorists, leads inevitably to economic instability.

Does this mean that diverse fiscal and monetary measures should be discarded in favor of a uniform, consistent policy that provides for steady growth in the money supply at an established rate? Many informed observers would answer *yes*. But many others believe that an optimum fiscal–monetary mix must be found that will assure economic stability at a high level of income and employment. However, the difficulties of attaining such a mix are considerable—for reasons that will be pointed out subsequently. (See "Leaders in Economics," page 261.)

Determination of the Interest Rate

Interest rates and the factors determining them are fundamental to understanding the role of money in the economy.

Any study of money must inevitably lead to a discussion of the rate of interest and to an analysis of the forces determining it. This is a matter of great importance. As you will recall from the study of investment in the Keynesian model, businesses invest because they expect to earn profits. That is, they acquire capital goods only as long as the anticipated rate of return on an additional unit of investment—called the *marginal efficiency of investment*—exceeds the cost of money, or the rate of interest. In view of this, what determines the rate of interest? The answer, as you will see, provides the final link in the Keynesian model of the macroeconomy.

What Is Meant by "the" Interest Rate?

As you have already learned from the previous chapters, there is no such thing as "the" interest rate. That is, there is no single rate on all financial instruments traded in the money and capital markets. Instead, there are many different rates on specific types of notes, bonds, and so on.

Leaders in Economics

Irving Fisher
1867–1947

Wide World Photos

Fisher demonstrates one of his many inventions: a two-way map that could be folded into a globe or spread flat.

Irving Fisher, a professor of economics at Yale University, was one of America's foremost economists prior to World War II. A mathematician as well as an economist, he was a profound scholar and a prolific writer. In addition to twenty-eight published books, he wrote dozens of articles in professional journals. Of his books, eighteen covered diverse areas of economics and statistics. The remainder consisted of some well-known mathematics textbooks, plus several popular volumes on diet and on health—subjects that interested him because he suffered from tuberculosis as a young man.

Fisher also invented many mechanical devices. The only one to achieve commercial success was a card index system mounted on a rotary stand. Fisher received about $1 million for this, which he subsequently parlayed into $9 million in the stock market. He lost it all in the crash of 1929.

Equation of Exchange
Among Fisher's major interests was the study of money and prices. In a book entitled *The Purchasing Power of Money* (1911), he stated the *equation of exchange*—which also subsequently became known as the *Fisher equation:*

$$MV + M'V' = PT$$

Here M is the quantity of currency, V its velocity of circulation, M' the quantity of demand deposits, V' their velocity of circulation, P the average price level of all goods sold, and T the volume of transactions or total quantity of all goods sold. Economists often shortened the equation to $MV = PT$ by redefining M to include "money"—currency plus demand deposits.

Modern Version: $MV = PQ$
The equation of exchange, formulated long before national-income data were available, is theoretically interesting but of little practical use because it encompasses *all* transactions involving payment in money. It covers not only the sale of final goods but also the sale of raw materials, partly finished goods, securities, real estate, and used goods. Hence, it may be called the "transactions-velocity" formulation, to distinguish it from the modern and much more practical "income-velocity" formulation,

$$MV = PQ$$

This equation encompasses only transactions for *final* goods and uses readily available GNP data. Both this equation and the original one, however, have similar structural properties and permit similar interpretations.

Application
Fisher employed his equation to explain a cause-and-effect relationship between the quantity of money and the price level. He assumed that the velocity of circulation (V) and the volume of transactions (T) were constant—or at least that they always tended toward equilibrium. Therefore, he concluded, if there is "a doubling in the quantity of money . . . it follows necessarily and mathematically that the level of prices must double." Or, in general, *"one of the normal effects of an increase in the quantity of money is an exactly proportional increase in the general level of prices."* From this it is evident, according to Fisher, that business cycles are not inherent in the economy but are due almost entirely to excessive expansions and contractions in the money supply—"especially in the form of bank loans." This conclusion, we shall see, is now widely accepted among many informed observers.

Many Achievements
Fisher made important contributions to the study of business cycles, capital, and interest. He also did pioneering work in the fields of mathematical economics and statistics, the integration of which is known as *econometrics.* He was honored for his many achievements by being elected president of each of the three major professional organizations concerned with the advancement of economic science—the American Economic Association, the American Statistical Association, and the Econometric Society.

The interest rates for financial instruments depend on numerous factors, including risks of default, maturity dates, and tax advantages. Despite such differences, however, interest rates are interrelated in that they tend to increase or decrease together, although differentials between them often vary. Therefore, it proves convenient to talk about "the" interest rate, thinking in terms of the *whole structure of rates* as rising or declining.

Classical Explanation: Fisher's Theory

In the classical (Fisherian) theory, interest is the price that businesses pay in order to attract savings from households. An important distinction exists between the real rate of interest and the market rate.

People usually think of interest as a payment for the use of money. This interpretation is adequate for most purposes. To the classical economists, however, interest had a special and quite different meaning.

You will recall that, in the simplified circular-flow model, the total economy is divided into two parts—a household sector and a business sector. The household sector supplies the saving that the business sector borrows. The business sector uses the borrowed funds to invest in capital goods for the purpose of carrying on profitable production. Interest, therefore, is a price that businesses pay households to persuade the latter to consume less in the present so that they can consume more at a later date.

Thus:

> Interest is a payment for "saving," for "abstinence" from consumption, or for overcoming people's preference for present as opposed to future consumption.

Why is interest necessary? The classicists believed that no household will save, and thereby forgo the pleasure of spending, unless it is offered interest in return. Likewise, no business will borrow, and thereby pay interest, without investing in profitable production. Saving, in classical theory, therefore leads automatically to spending on capital or investment goods. A flexible interest rate in the competitive financial markets (the money and capital markets) assures this. That is, the interest rate, determined by the free play of supply and demand, adjusts to the level where every dollar saved by households is borrowed and invested by businesses.

The Real Rate and the Market Rate

These ideas of classical economics were further developed in the early part of this century by Irving Fisher. The classical explanation of interest is also sometimes called the Fisher theory of interest. It rests fundamentally on a distinction between two interest rates: the real rate and the market rate.

The real rate of interest is the rate that would prevail in the market if prices remained stable.

Real Rate The *real rate of interest* is the interest rate measured in terms of goods. That is, it is the rate that would prevail in the market if the general price level remained stable. Under such circumstances, if you lend a friend $100 today with the understanding that he will repay you $105 one year from today, you give up $100 worth of goods now for what you expect will be $105 worth of goods a year from now. The *real* rate of interest is therefore 5 percent.

According to the classicists, this rate is established by real economic forces of demand and supply. The "real demand" for funds by businesses is determined by the productivity (and therefore the profitability) of borrowed capital. The greater its productivity, the larger the amount of funds that businesses will want to borrow. The "real supply" of funds by households is determined by the willingness of consumers to abstain from present consumption. The greater their willingness, the larger the amount of funds that households will want to lend.

Market Rate The *market rate of interest* is the actual or money rate that prevails in the market at any given time. Unlike the real rate, which is not directly observable, the market rate is the one we actually see in the markets. This is because the market rate reflects the quantity of loans measured in units of money, not goods. Hence, it is the rate people ordinarily have in mind when they talk about "the" interest rate.

A crucial point in classical theory is that the real rate and the market rate usually are not equal. Only if borrowers and lenders expect the general price level (that is, the value of a unit of money) to remain constant will both rates be the same. This does not ordinarily happen. People are always expecting prices either to rise or to fall. Therefore, the market rate of interest will depart from the real rate, depending on either of two conditions.

1. Anticipated Inflation If people believe that prices will rise—and hence that the purchasing power of a unit of money will decline—the market rate of interest will be higher than the real rate. For example, if lenders and borrowers expect the price level to rise 5 percent per year, the market rate of interest will be the real rate plus 5 percent. This "inflation premium" is necessary to compensate lenders for their loss in purchasing power. At the same time, borrowers will be willing to pay the premium because they will be repaying their loans with money worth 5 percent less per year than the money they borrowed.

2. Anticipated Deflation If people believe that prices will fall—and therefore that the purchasing power of a unit of money will rise—the market rate of interest will be below the real rate. The difference is a "deflation discount" (or negative inflation premium). This is necessary to compensate borrowers for their loss in purchasing power. At the same time, lenders will be willing to grant the discount because they will be repaid with money worth 5 percent more per year than the money they initially lent.

These ideas can be summarized briefly:

In classical theory, the market rate of interest may be greater than, equal to, or less than the real rate. The difference depends on whether households and businesses expect the general price level to rise, remain constant, or decline. Any differential between the market rate and the real rate represents the amount necessary to compensate lenders or borrowers for adverse changes in purchasing power resulting from anticipated inflation or deflation.

The determination of the market rate of interest is illustrated in Exhibit 2. The upward-sloping saving-supply curve S of households intersects the downward-sloping investment-demand curve D of businesses. This determines the equilibrium interest rate r on the vertical axis. Of course, if the demand curve shifts to a new position, such as D', a new equilibrium rate of interest occurs at r'.

Exhibit 2
The Market Rate of Interest in Classical Theory

In the classical theory, the interest rate is the price paid for the use of loanable funds. Like any other price, the interest rate rations the supply of a commodity—in this case, loanable funds—among those who want to use it. Only those borrowers who are willing and able to pay the market interest rate can acquire the funds that are wanted. This rate is at r.

The classicists theorized that, if there were a change in the investment-demand curve—say, from D to D'—then the intersection with the existing saving-supply curve would determine the new rate of interest, r'.

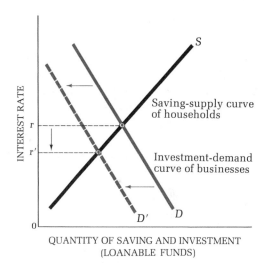

QUANTITY OF SAVING AND INVESTMENT
(LOANABLE FUNDS)

The market interest rate is the sum of the real interest rate and the inflation premium.

This classical view of interest is held today by many informed observers. They believe that the interest rates you see quoted in the market contain an inflation premium. This premium reflects the public's beliefs about future prices. As a result, market interest rates and prices tend to move together, just as the classicists theorized.

On the basis of this idea, you can use classical theory to estimate the real interest rate from the following equation:

$$\text{market interest rate} = \text{real interest rate} + \text{inflation premium}$$

Therefore, the real interest rate is equal to the market interest rate minus the inflation premium:

$$\text{real interest rate} = \text{market interest rate} - \text{inflation premium}$$

To illustrate, here is how the real interest rate might be estimated.

First, in order to obtain a measure of the market interest rate, you should use the yield on 3-month Treasury bills. This is because 3-month Treasury bills, unlike other securities, provide the best combination of high marketability, short maturities, and zero default risk. For this reason, their yield represents a "pure" rate of interest. The average annual yield on 3-month Treasury bills is shown in the back endpapers of this book.

Second, in order to obtain a measure of the inflation premium, you should estimate borrowers' and lenders' *expectations* of future prices. But expectations are subjective and changeable, so any estimate will be at best a reasonable "guess" based on recent trends. A rather simple approach that illustrates the basic idea can be accomplished in two steps.

The inflation premium is difficult to calculate because it depends on expected as well as recent price trends.

Step 1 Choose a measure of the overall level of prices. One such measure, as you know, is the Consumer Price Index (CPI). However, there is an even broader indicator called the *Implicit Price Index* (IPI). Popularly known as "the GNP deflator," the IPI is the most comprehensive measure of the general price level available. Constructed by the U.S. Department of Commerce, the IPI consists of an average of the various price indexes used to deflate the components of GNP. The IPI is shown in the endpapers at the back of the book.

Step 2 Calculate the latest percentage change in the IPI to obtain the inflation premium in the current period. For example, suppose the IPI increased from 120 in Year 1 to 126 in Year 2, the current year. Then, as shown in the table, the percentage change or inflation premium for the current year is $(126 - 120)/120 = 0.05$, or 5%. This procedure thus *assumes* that the inflation premium in the current year is best estimated by the percentage change in the general price level from the previous year. Of course, other assumptions could also be made. In fact, the inflation premium may depend on a number of factors, not just on the most recent rate of change in the general price level.

Year	IPI	Inflation premium (percentage change in IPI)	Market interest rate	Real interest rate
1	120	5%		
2 (current)	126		9%	4%

Once you have the necessary information, the formula is easily applied. For instance, if in the current year the market interest rate is, say, 9 percent and the inflation premium for the year (calculated as in step 2) is 5 percent, the real interest rate in the current year is 4 percent.

Conclusion: Prices and Interest Rates Move Together

Is the connection between prices and interest rates valid? Today's classical economists believe that it is. They point out that, historically, interest rates in the United States have risen when prices increased over a period and have declined when they decreased for some time. This indicates that high market interest rates reflect actual as well as expected inflation. Evidence of this can be seen in many nations. Countries that traditionally experience steep inflations generally have much higher interest rates than countries whose price levels are relatively more stable.

Classicists conclude that a correct monetary policy will reduce inflation and, therefore, interest rates.

To conclude:

> According to the classicists, increases in the quantity of money result in "too much money chasing too few goods." Consequently, prices and interest rates rise. By reducing the rate of growth in the money supply, the monetary authority (the central banking system) can retard inflation and bring about reductions in the market rate of interest.

Liquidity-Preference Explanation: Keynes's Theory

As you learned earlier, much of traditional economic thinking underwent major changes in the Great Depression of the 1930s. The person initially responsible for this restructuring of ideas was the British economist John Maynard Keynes. The revised theory, which Keynes called a "general theory," resulted in the birth of *Keynesian economics*. You will find it helpful to refresh your understanding of this term by looking it up in the Dictionary at the back of this book.

The liquidity-preference (Keynesian) theory of interest is a distinct departure from the classical theory. The latter, Keynes argued, provided a "special" explanation of business cycles and of interest-rate determination rather than a general explanation.

What did Keynes have to say about the role of the interest rate and the factors determining it? We already know part of the answer:

> Capital spending or investment by businesses is the strategic determinant of the level of income and employment. Such spending is undertaken as long as the marginal efficiency of investment exceeds the rate of interest. Therefore, the rate of interest is crucial in relation to investment.

As for the factors determining the rate of interest, Keynes argued that the classical theory is correct for an economy that tends automatically toward full employment. His own theory, on the other hand, is more general because it applies to an economic system that may be in equilibrium at *any* level of employment.

Keynes and the Classicists

These ideas can best be understood by comparing some of Keynes's views with those of the classicists. For example, in the classical theory, the investment-demand curve illustrated earlier in Exhibit 2 shows the amount of capital spending that businesses are willing to undertake at each rate of interest. This demand curve is the same as the marginal-efficiency-of-investment (*MEI*) curve that you studied in earlier chapters as part of the Keynesian model. You should recall, however, that in the Keynesian model *investment expenditures by the business sector are part of the economy's aggregate demand*. Therefore, Keynes argued, the classicists erred by assuming that the investment-demand curve could

Exhibit 3
Keynesian Model:
Changes in Investment Affect
Aggregate Demand and Income

In the Keynesian model, the equilibrium level of NNP (or aggregate income) is determined by the intersection of aggregate demand, AD, with aggregate supply, AS. But aggregate demand includes the business sector's investment demand. Therefore, *a decline in investment demand will result in a decrease in aggregate demand*, say, from AD to AD', and *a simultaneous drop in NNP from N to N'*. Keynes thus concluded that the classicists were wrong in believing that a change in investment demand would affect only the interest rate (as shown in Exhibit 2), not the level of aggregate income.

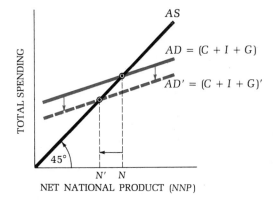

NET NATIONAL PRODUCT (NNP)

shift *without causing simultaneous changes in the aggregate demand curve*. Such changes would, in turn, affect the level of income and hence the saving-supply curve. These ideas are illustrated in Exhibit 3. Note that, because AD includes I, a decrease in I will reduce AD to, say, AD'. This causes a decrease in NNP (or aggregate income) from N to N'.

Thus, the classical economists simply viewed interest as a "price" that equates the demand for investment with the supply of saving at the full-employment level of income. Keynes argued that, because *the saving-supply curve will shift if the investment-demand curve shifts*, the rate of interest and the equilibrium quantity of saving and investment cannot be determined from the classical scheme. The information provided in the classical model is insufficient to allow for a complete solution. In view of this, let us see how Keynes restructured the theory of interest.

Statement of the Theory

In classical theory, interest is a reward for "waiting"—for "abstinence" from consumption. *In Keynes's theory, interest is a reward for "parting" with liquidity. Because of this the rate of interest is determined entirely by the demand for and supply of money.* But two factors underlying demand and supply must be understood: liquidity preference and the quantity of money.

On the demand side, in Keynes's view, money is wanted because it is the only perfectly liquid asset. People would rather hold some of their assets in money than in any other form. Therefore, if you are to be persuaded to give up some of your perfectly liquid assets, you must be paid a reward. *Interest is the price that must be paid to overcome liquidity preference.* To put it slightly differently, *interest is the reward for not hoarding money.*

On the supply side, according to Keynes, the quantity of money is the important factor. As you already know, the quantity of money is determined by the monetary authority (central bank) through its control over open-market operations, reserve requirements, and other factors. The monetary authority can use these mechanisms to increase the money supply if the public wants to hold a larger proportion of its assets in the form of money. If the public desires to hold a smaller proportion, the monetary authority can decrease the money supply. *In Keynes's view, therefore, expansions and contractions in the money supply play a strategic role in the determination of the interest rate.*

Determinants of Demand and Supply

The demand for money is a demand for liquidity. Why should you and I and everyone else prefer to hold assets in liquid form? Keynes provided three reasons, which he called the transactions, precautionary, and speculative motives.

Transactions Motive Households and businesses must hold some of their assets in the form of money (currency and checkable deposits). This is because they purchase goods and services more or less continuously from day to day, whereas they receive income only at intervals, such as weekly or monthly. Therefore, a certain amount of money must be held to bridge the gap. The amount required—the transactions demand for money—does not depend on the interest rate. Instead, it is directly related to the level of economic activity. Thus, as aggregate income rises, so does the need for money for transactions purposes.

Precautionary Motive A second reason why households and businesses want to hold part of their assets in liquid form is to meet unforeseen developments. Examples are illnesses, accidents, losses of employment, strikes, or market fluctuations. Although individuals and firms may be able to convert other assets into money at such times, the possibility of loss due to forced liquidation under unfavorable market conditions prompts them to prefer money for reserve contingencies. The precautionary demand for money is influenced primarily by aggregate-income levels rather than by changes in the interest rate. Hence, most precautionary demand may be combined with the transactions demand for money, because both depend mainly on income. This is shown in Exhibit 4.

Speculative Motive Finally, households and businesses may prefer to hold part of their assets in the form of money to enable them to take advantage of changes in interest rates. Individuals and firms tend to hold more securities—especially long-term bonds—and less money when the interest rate is high, to take advantage of higher returns. Conversely, individuals and firms tend to hold more money and fewer securities when the interest rate is low, because the risk of holding bonds—the possible fall in their prices—more than offsets the interest returns. As Exhibit 5 demonstrates, the interest rate is inversely related to the quantity of money wanted for speculative purposes.

The transactions, precautionary, and speculative motives determine the total demand for money. What factors determine supply? As you know, the supply of money is simply the stock of money available to satisfy the demand. The supply of money is determined by the monetary authority through its control over open-market operations, reserve requirements, and discount-rate policy. Hence, at any given time the supply or stock of money is fixed. This means that it can be represented by a vertical—or, in the language of economics, a "perfectly inelastic"—supply curve, as explained in Exhibit 6.

The reason for this terminology is not hard to see. Unlike most supply curves, which are upward-sloping, this one is vertical. This means that increases or decreases in the interest rate (the "price" of money) do not cause changes in the stock of money. Therefore, we may say that the quantity of money supplied is unresponsive to changes in the interest rate.

Exhibit 4
Transactions and Precautionary Demands for Money

Households and businesses want to hold some of their assets in the form of money in order to carry on day-to-day transactions and to meet unforeseen contingencies. These reasons for holding money are called the *transactions motive* and the *precautionary motive*, respectively. Both demands for money depend primarily on the total level of money payments or aggregate income. The straight line in this chart means that money demanded for transactions and precautionary purposes rises by some constant proportion of NNP (or aggregate income).

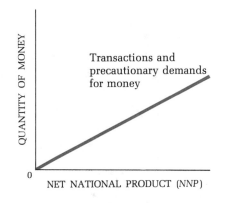

Exhibit 5
Speculative Demand for Money

Households and businesses (which constitute the private sector) desire to hold some of their assets in the form of money to take advantage of changes in interest rates. The private sector's speculative demand for money varies inversely with the interest rate. At a high interest rate, households and businesses will hold less money and more securities. At a low interest rate, more money and fewer securities will be held. Note that the line is curved rather than straight and that it tends to flatten out at its lower right end. The reasons for this are explained later.

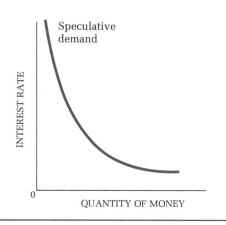

Exhibit 6
Supply of Money

At any given time, there is a quantity or stock of money available to satisfy the public's demand. This quantity, M, is determined by the monetary authority through its open-market operations, discount-rate policy, and reserve requirements. Hence, the supply curve is a vertical line, indicating that the quantity of money supplied is unresponsive to changes in the interest rate. That is, the quantity supplied is the same at higher interest rates as it is at lower ones.

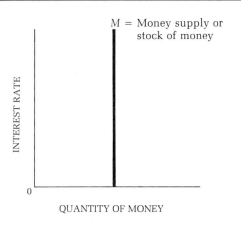

Exhibit 7
Determination of the Interest Rate by Total Demand for Money (*L*) and Supply of Money (*M*)

At a given level of aggregate income, the equilibrium rate of interest r is determined by the intersection of the L curve, representing the total demand for money, with the M curve, representing total supply. Note that the L curve consists of two components. One is the transactions and precautionary demands, which depend mainly on the level of aggregate income (but not on the interest rate). The other is the speculative demand, which depends on the interest rate and hence causes the L curve to be downward-sloping. The entire L curve is the sum of both components.

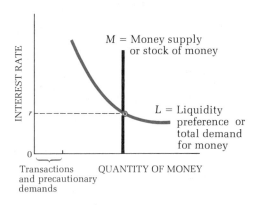

Determining the Interest Rate

Of course, as in any supply-and-demand problem, either variable by itself cannot determine the price. The two must be combined in order for a price to be established. This is shown in Exhibit 7. As you can see, the equilibrium rate of interest r is determined by the intersection of the liquidity-preference curve L, representing the total demand for money, with the money supply curve M, representing the stock of money. If the interest rate is higher than the equilibrium level, the quantity supplied exceeds the quantity demanded. This drives the rate down. If the interest rate is below the equilibrium level, the quantity demanded exceeds the quantity supplied. This drives the rate up. Note that the demand curve for money includes all three components of demand, as explained in the exhibit.

Like all demand and supply curves, those in Exhibit 7 are drawn on the assumption that all other things (besides the interest rate) that may affect demand and supply remain constant. If one of the factors changes, the relevant demand or supply curve will shift. This will bring about a new equilibrium rate of interest. For example:

1. If aggregate income rises, the quantity of money demanded for transactions and precautionary purposes also rises. This causes an increase in liquidity preference, or the demand for money, at all interest rates. The money-demand curve, in other words, shifts to the right from L to L ', as in Exhibit 8. Therefore, the interest rate rises from r to r '. The same result might be obtained if there were a decline in business expectations. In that case, households and businesses might attempt to increase their holdings of money for precautionary purposes.

2. If the monetary authority increases the supply of money, the money-supply curve in Exhibit 8 will shift to the right from M to M '. The interest rate, therefore, will decline from r to r".

To summarize:

The *liquidity-preference theory of interest* was formulated by J. M. Keynes. The theory contends that households and businesses want to hold some of their assets in the most liquid form, namely cash or checking accounts. The reason is to satisfy three motives: (1) the transactions motive, (2) the precautionary motive, and (3) the speculative motive. These motives determine the demand for money, whereas the monetary authority determines its supply. The demand for and supply of money together determine the equilibrium rate of interest.

Practical Implications of the Liquidity-Preference Theory

The liquidity-preference theory of interest is the final link in the entire Keynesian system. Without it there would be no determinate solution to our general economic model. You will gain a better appreciation of this fact as we proceed to point out the practical implications of the theory of interest within the framework of what we have already learned.

Marginal Efficiency of Investment and the Interest Rate

You will recall from the study of the Keynesian model that the *marginal efficiency of investment (MEI)* is the expected rate of return on an investment. More precisely, it is the *expected rate of return over the cost of an additional unit of a capital good.*

Each business firm has its own *MEI* curve. The curve shows the amount of investment a firm will undertake at various costs of money capital, expressed as interest rates. Hence, *a firm's MEI curve is its demand curve for investment.*

It follows that at any given time the sum of all firms' *MEI* curves will yield an aggregate *MEI* curve. This shows the total amount of private investment that will be undertaken at various rates of interest. Therefore, *the aggregate MEI curve is the business sector's demand curve for investment.*

This idea is illustrated in Exhibit 9. In Figure (a), the equilibrium rate of interest r is determined by the intersection of the demand and supply curves of money—the L and M curves—as you have already learned. This rate is the cost of money capital to firms. Hence, in Figure (b), the amount of investment undertaken by the business sector at this rate of interest, shown by the aggregate *MEI* curve, is I.

What happens if this volume of investment is insufficient to achieve full employment? In that case the monetary authorities can lower the rate of interest by increasing the money supply—say, from Q to Q'. As-

Exhibit 8

Changes in the Interest Rate Resulting from Shifts in the Money-Demand and Money-Supply, or L and M, Curves

If the money-supply or M curve remains fixed, an increase in aggregate income will shift the liquidity-preference or demand-for-money curve rightward from L to L'. This causes the equilibrium rate of interest to rise from r to r'. If the money-demand or L curve remains fixed, an increase in the stock of money will shift the money-supply curve rightward from M to M'. This causes the equilibrium rate of interest to decline from r to r''.

Of course, a decrease in aggregate income or a decrease in the money supply will correspondingly shift the L and M curves leftward. Can you show what happens to the equilibrium rate of interest under such circumstances? What may happen if the L and M curves shift simultaneously in the same direction? In opposite directions?

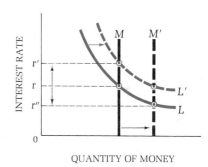

QUANTITY OF MONEY

(a) DEMAND FOR, AND SUPPLY OF, MONEY   (b) BUSINESS-SECTOR INVESTMENT

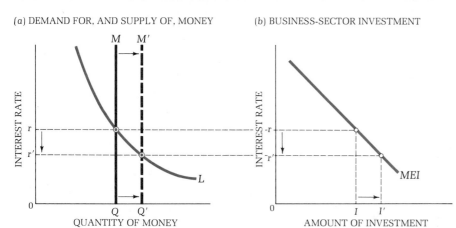

Exhibit 9

The Interest Rate and Investment

In Figure (a), an increase in the money-supply curve from M to M' increases the quantity of money from Q to Q'. Therefore, the rate of interest decreases from r to r'. This increases the amount of investment from I to I' in Figure (b), because businesses invest to the point where the *MEI* equals the interest rate (or cost of money capital).

Exhibit 10
The Liquidity Trap

Because the L curve "flattens out" at its right end, there is some low rate of interest (say, 2 percent) beyond which an increase in the supply of money cannot reduce the rate further. Hence, the total demand for money at this low interest rate is infinite. That is, everyone would prefer to hold money in idle balances rather than risk the loss of holding long-term securities offering such poor yields.

In geometric terms, the *liquidity trap* exists at the rate of interest at which the liquidity-preference curve becomes perfectly horizontal.

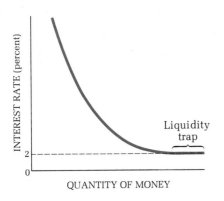

suming that the L curve remains fixed, the equilibrium rate of interest will decline from r to r', causing the amount of investment to increase from I to I'. This increase in investment, as you know, will have a magnified effect on income, owing to the operation of the investment multiplier. Further, since the liquidity-preference (L) curve depends on income, it will shift to the right when income rises—as you have already learned.

You can see, therefore, that the effectiveness of monetary policy for stimulating economic activity poses some challenging questions. For example:

1. To what extent will the interest rate fall as a result of an increase in the money supply?

2. To what extent will the amount of investment increase as a result of a decline in the interest rate?

3. To what extent will income rise as a result of an increase in investment?

The answer to the first question depends on the relative steepness of the L curve. The answer to the second question depends on the relative steepness of the MEI curve. And the answer to the third question depends on the size of the investment multiplier.

For instance, referring back to Exhibit 9, what would be the effect on the change in the interest rate and on the change in the amount of investment if both the L curve and the MEI curve were flatter? Steeper? You can answer these questions by sketching some curves yourself and comparing the differences. As for the size of the investment multiplier, you will recall that it depends on the marginal propensity to consume or to save. This is because the investment multiplier, as you have learned, equals $1/(1 - MPC)$, or $1/MPS$.

The Liquidity Trap

Should we infer from Exhibit 9 that increases in the quantity of money will always lower the rate of interest and, therefore, increase the amount of investment? The answer is not a simple *yes* or *no*. As pointed out above, other factors must be considered. One of them is the shape of the L curve, which, as you saw in previous diagrams, is assumed to flatten out at its right end. As a result, the lower the rate of interest, the more resistant it becomes to further reductions, until a point is reached at which the L curve becomes perfectly horizontal. From then on, it is impossible to reduce the interest rate further merely by increasing the supply of money.

This concept is illustrated in Exhibit 10. The flat portion of the curve signifies that, at a low rate of interest (say, 2 percent), everyone prefers to hold money rather than risk any loss from holding long-term securities yielding poor returns. Therefore, this horizontal segment of the curve is called the *liquidity trap*. It has been used by some economists to explain why monetary policy may not be effective in inducing recovery from a deep recession if the rate of interest, although low absolutely, is still too high relative to the marginal efficiency of investment. Under such circumstances, these economists contend, there is no stimulus for business executives to increase the amount of their investment, despite low interest rates. It should be emphasized, however, that this is a hypothesis; there is no concrete evidence to support it.

Conclusion: Importance of the Interest Rate

The preceding analysis is based on a *given level of aggregate income*. If aggregate income is allowed to change, the problem becomes more complicated. This is because a change in aggregate income will affect the rate of interest as well as the volume of saving and investment. To the extent that the amount of investment is responsive to a change in the interest rate, aggregate demand and, therefore, the overall level of employment will also be affected. Further, a change in aggregate income will influence the transactions and precautionary demands for money—which, in turn, influence the total demand for money for liquidity purposes.

This suggests an important conclusion:

In the Keynesian model, the interest rate is influenced directly by monetary policy and plays a specific role in affecting economic activity.

> The rate of interest is of strategic importance in the Keynesian model. It is the mechanism that establishes equilibrium between the supply of money in the economy and the amounts that people wish to hold as cash balances. Because the rate of interest is affected by the money supply, which, in turn, is controlled by the monetary authority, expansionary or contractionary monetary policies can influence the level of economic activity.

How does the rate of interest fit into the overall picture of income determination? As you will now see, the rate of interest is one of several variables that are instrumental in establishing macroeconomic equilibrium.

Macroeconomic Equilibrium: Putting the Pieces Together

The macroeconomic theory of income determination which we set out to study at the beginning of Part 2 is now completed. (You will find it helpful to refer to the table of contents at the front of the book to get an overview of the ground covered thus far.) We will now review the major components of the theory. This will permit us to integrate certain fundamental relationships between key variables into a meaningful whole.

Outline of the Keynesian Theory

A summary of the Keynesian theory of income determination is outlined in Exhibit 11. The relationships may be stated briefly in the form of several propositions:

Several propositions express most of the main ideas of the Keynesian model. These can also be diagrammed.

1. The level of income depends on consumption expenditure and investment expenditure.

2. Consumption expenditure depends on the propensity to consume in relation to income. Investment expenditure depends on the marginal efficiency of investment relative to the rate of interest.

3. The propensity to consume (or consumption function) expresses a relationship between consumption and income. The relationship is such that, as income increases, consumption increases, but not as fast as income. Two related concepts are (a) the average propensity to consume, or ratio of consumption to income, and (b) the marginal propensity to consume, or change in consumption relative to the change in income.

4. The marginal efficiency of investment depends on expected rates of return on capital investment. The rate of interest depends on liquidity preference and the quantity of money.

Exhibit 11
Outline of the Keynesian Theory of Income Determination

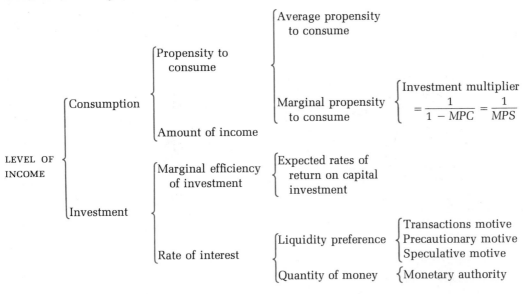

5. The marginal propensity to consume affects the size of the investment multiplier. This, in turn, affects the amount by which an increase in investment causes a multiplied increase in income.

6. Liquidity preference—the demand for money—is determined by the transactions, precautionary, and speculative motives. In contrast, the quantity of money is controlled by the monetary authority.

These propositions contain only the main features of the theory. They do not express all the interrelations between the variables, many of which were discussed in this and earlier chapters.

Some Basic Relationships

Many of the key relationships in the Keynesian model can be expressed in the form of three interrelated graphs.

Exhibit 12 shows an integration of important relationships. This highly simplified model conveys many of the essential ideas of Keynesian macroeconomic equilibrium. In Figure (a), the equilibrium rate of interest is determined by the intersection of the demand or liquidity-preference curve for money L with the supply curve of money M. In Figure (b), this interest rate is brought together with the marginal efficiency of investment MEI to determine the amount of investment I. In Figure (c), this volume of investment is superimposed on the consumption function C. Hence, the intersection of the C + I or aggregate-demand (AD) curve with the 45° aggregate-supply (AS) curve determines the equilibrium level of income.

If this level of income is either too low or too high to correspond to full employment, the result, as you learned in the study of income and employment determination, is either a recessionary or an inflationary gap. To close the gap, some combination of fiscal and monetary policy is needed. But government faces problems of considerable difficulty when it tries to choose a proper blend of policies, as you shall soon see.

Exhibit 12

Simplified Keynesian Model of Income Determination

This model emphasizes the interrelations among key variables by showing the four basic determinants of income or *NNP*. These are (1) liquidity preference, *L*; (2) money supply, *M*; (3) marginal efficiency of investment, *MEI*; (4) consumption function, *C*.

In Figure (*a*), the equilibrium rate of interest is determined by the intersection of the liquidity-preference (*L*) and quantity of money (*M*) curves. In Figure (*b*), the amount of investment (*I*) is determined by the interest rate and the marginal efficiency of investment (*MEI*) curve. In Figure (*c*), the volume of in-

vestment is superimposed on the consumption function to give the *C + I* or aggregate-demand (*AD*) curve. (Government spending, *G*, has been omitted in order to keep the diagram simple.) The intersection of this curve with the 45° line or aggregate-supply (*AS*) curve determines the equilibrium level of income.

As you can see from these figures, there can be no change in income, or *NNP*, without a shift of one or more of the four basic curves, *L*, *M*, *MEI*, and *C*.

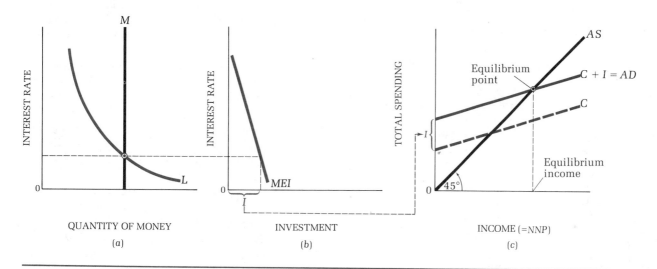

(a)   (b)   (c)

What You Have Learned in This Chapter

1. The equation of exchange is $MV = PQ$. It states, in effect, that the economy's gross income ($=MV$) is spent on purchasing the economy's final output of goods and services ($=PQ$). The equation is thus a truism or identity because it tells us that the same flow of money can be looked at either from the buyers' or the sellers' point of view.

2. The quantity theory of money, as originally formulated by Irving Fisher, assumes that the velocity of money and the volume of output are constant. Therefore, in terms of the equation of exchange, changes in the general price level are directly proportional to changes in the quantity of money. Modern quantity theorists have extended Fisher's ideas. They believe that the income velocity of money fluctuates over time, but its range of short-run variation is limited and, given

sufficient knowledge, *predictable*. Therefore, their attention is focused on the factors influencing velocity and on the role of the money supply as a determinant of GNP.

3. In classical theory, the market rate of interest will depart from the real rate if households and businesses expect the general price level to rise or decline. Any differential between the market rate and the real rate represents the amount necessary to compensate lenders or borrowers for adverse changes in purchasing power resulting from anticipated inflation or deflation.

4. In the classical view, interest is the reward that businesses pay households for abstaining from consumption. The equilibrium rate of interest is determined in a competitive money market where the supply of funds saved by households equals the demand for funds invested by businesses.

5. In the Keynesian view, interest is the payment made to households and businesses to overcome liquidity preference. The equilibrium rate of interest is determined by the intersection of the liquidity-preference (or demand) curve for money with the money-stock (or supply) curve of money.

6. Among the basic factors determining income or *NNP* are the state of liquidity preference, the money supply, the marginal efficiency of investment, and the consumption function. No change in *NNP* can occur without a change in one or more of these factors. In macroeconomic equilibrium, all four variables are synchronized. Hence, a change in one of them, such as the money supply (because it is controlled by the monetary authority), creates economic instability until a new equilibrium is reached.

For Discussion

1. *Terms and concepts to review:*
income velocity of money
equation of exchange
quantity theory of money
interest
marginal efficiency of investment
real rate of interest
market rate of interest
Implicit Price Index
transactions motive
precautionary motive
speculative motive
liquidity-preference theory of interest
liquidity trap

2. What basic differences are there between the equation of exchange as Fisher formulated it and the modern equation as it is used today? Is there any advantage to the modern equation as compared to Fisher's equation?

3. What has been the long-run trend of the income velocity of money (that is, *V* in the equation of exchange) since the 1950s? Can you give the reasons for this trend?

4. Suppose that the Federal Reserve buys securities in the open market and that the securities are sold by a nonbank, such as an individual or corporation. As a result of this transaction alone, what will be the directions of change, if any, of *M, P, Q, V* (in that order), and *MV* in the equation $MV = PQ$? Explain.

5. In terms of the equation $MV = PQ$, what are likely to be the effects on *P, Q,* and *PQ* if there is a large increase in the money supply under conditions of (a) substantial unemploy-

ment, or (b) high or full employment? Explain your answer.

6. If the interest rate on short-term loans is the same as that on long-term loans, what are the advantages and disadvantages to lenders of being in short-term as opposed to long-term investments? Discuss.

7. If the yield on long-term securities is greater than on short-term securities, why would anyone want to invest in the latter?

8. "The classical theory holds that the equilibrium rate of interest equates the supply of, and demand for, savings in a competitive financial market. The Keynesian theory holds that the equilibrium rate of interest equates the demand for money with its supply. Therefore, there is no essential difference between the two theories." Do you agree? Explain.

9. Do the transactions and precautionary demands for holding money depend entirely on income? If not, on what else do they depend? Explain.

10. If a reduction in the interest rate does not result in an expansion of investment, what might this suggest in terms of the Keynesian theory of interest?

11. If the economy is in a liquidity trap, would an increase in the quantity of money stimulate investment? Explain.

12. Assume that the economy is in macroeconomic equilibrium. What effect would each of the following changes, considered separately and without regard to secondary results, have on income? Explain why.
  (a) Increase in the money supply.
  (b) Increase in liquidity preference.
  (c) Increase in the marginal efficiency of investment.
  (d) Decrease in consumption.
  In general terms, how would secondary effects have influenced your answers?

Issue
Should Interest Rates Be Controlled?

Until near the end of the 1960s, the United States was traditionally regarded as a low-interest economy. Credit was cheap and plentiful, and three decades of a rising trend of interest rates had been tolerated because the level never got too high. But in recent history the level during some periods was well over 15 percent, causing considerable distress for consumers, home buyers, farmers, and some businesspeople.

According to traditional doctrine, interest rates are the price of funds. Therefore, like any price, interest rates perform an allocative function: They ration the supply of scarce funds—the flow of savings—to the ultimate users. Those borrowers with the most promising investment opportunities, who are willing to pay a high interest rate, bid funds away from their competitors. In this way, the interest-rate structure allocates funds among households, businesses, and government, and between private and public uses.

Reasons for Controls

Of course, when interest rates rise too high, the painful effects are felt by a widening circle of individuals, industries, states and localities, and the federal government itself. Pressures are then placed on political leaders to control lending charges by legislating interest ceilings. Two major reasons for imposing controls are usually advanced:

1. Interest payments are a significant cost to business firms. Like other costs, an increase in interest rates is passed along to consumers in the form of higher prices, thereby furthering cost-push inflation.

2. Interest payments are incomes to those who grant loans. Therefore, increases in interest rates unjustly benefit lenders—especially banks—at the expense of borrowers.

Some "Cons"

Most economists do not find these arguments convincing. They believe that interest rates are a reflection of inflation rather than a cause. As a result, they oppose interest ceilings, for several reasons.

First, despite the trend of rising rates, interest charges play only a minor role in cost-push inflation. Net interest charges average less than 3 percent of total production costs of nonfinancial corporations. In contrast, labor costs average between 60 and 70 percent.

Second, an increase in interest rates may be necessary to help choke off inflation. Although a rise in borrowing costs need not immediately deter spending, it sooner or later deters some consumers from buying houses, automobiles, and major appliances, and some businesspeople from buying new plant and equipment.

But regardless of the pros and cons, the really fundamental issue is the question of free versus controlled markets. What the United States must decide is whether it prefers a government-controlled economy or an economy in which supply and demand forces are dominant in every field—including money.

Macroeconomic Problems and Policies

4
PART

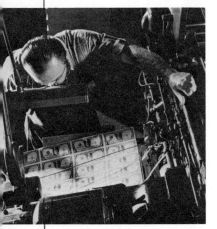

14
CHAPTER

Foundations of Monetarism: The Fiscal–Monetary Mix

Learning guide
Watch for the answers to these important questions

What are the distinctions between the two points of view known as "fiscalism" and "monetarism"? Are there fundamental features that characterize each?

Of what significance is the modernized quantity theory of money? How is the public's demand for money related to its income?

What is meant by the "transmission mechanism"? Why is the transmission mechanism in the monetarist model described as a portfolio-adjustment process?

In the opinion of monetarists, how do erratic monetary growth rates affect the private sector's stability? Can the effects of monetary policy be forecast for specific sectors of the economy?

How do the fiscalist and monetarist models differ? What are the effects of these differences on the goal of achieving an optimum fiscal–monetary mix?

This chapter focuses on the importance of money and monetary policy in affecting economic activity. The monetary concepts form a body of ideas known as "monetarism."

On New York City's Wall Street, the nation's financial center, the news that is usually awaited most eagerly concerns the money-supply figures released each Friday by the Federal Reserve. These data can affect not only the money and capital markets but Washington's economic policies as well.

The reasons are not hard to see. You have learned that changes in the quantity of currency and credit play a decisive role in influencing price levels and economic activity. Therefore, many economists believe that the money supply should be expanded at a steady rate in order to accommodate the needs of business. Monetary expansions that occur at too fast or too slow a rate will be destabilizing. They will cause inflation when there is too much money chasing too few goods, or recession when there is not enough money relative to the stock of goods available.

This suggests that there must be some optimum rate of monetary expansion—one that is sufficient to assure continuous high employment at stable prices. If this is true, the task of monetary policy is to identify that rate and adhere to it. But this poses difficulties, both economic and political, that must be understood before it is possible to evaluate the role played by the nation's monetary authority.

Of course, any practical discussion of monetary policy requires some understanding of the role played by fiscal policy. As you will see, the task confronting Washington's policy makers is to arrive at what is believed to be the "best" fiscal–monetary mix.

The Fiscal–Monetary Mix: Overview of the Issues

Two broad policy approaches have guided the implementation of government measures aimed at achieving full employment and price stability. The relative importance of the two policies in attaining the desired goals has been the subject of much controversy. At the heart of the debate are three basic questions:

How important are fiscal policy and monetary policy as means of achieving economic stability? Which type of policy is of greater importance?

• Is it mainly *fiscal policy*—the design of the federal budget—that determines the economy's levels of output, employment, and prices?

• Or is it mainly *monetary policy*—the rate at which the Federal Reserve adds to the nation's money supply—that makes the major difference?

• Or, as a third possibility, does the answer lie somewhere in between?

The central issue, therefore, can best be understood by reducing it to a fundamental problem:

What is the optimum fiscal–monetary mix—the best combination of fiscal and monetary policy?

The most convenient way of dealing with the problem is to distinguish between two points of view called "fiscalism" and "monetarism."

Fiscalism

Do you read the business and editorial sections of *Time, Newsweek, The Wall Street Journal,* or other major news publications? If so, you may wonder why certain political leaders, economists, and social critics are often referred to as "fiscalists" or "Keynesians."

Fiscalists are people whose ideas follow in the Keynesian tradition. They think in terms of aggregate demand (AD) as the sum of consumption demand (C), investment demand (I), and government demand (G). Their beliefs are thus rooted in the fundamental equation

$AD = C + I + G$

Fiscalists contend that a capitalistic economy is *inherently unstable* and does not tend automatically toward full employment. This is because the level of aggregate demand does not always remain high enough to absorb the nation's full-capacity output. Therefore, the fiscalists believe, government should take up the slack by stimulating enough spending to raise aggregate demand to the full-employment level.

How can government accomplish this task? There are several ways:

1. Reduce Taxes This leaves the private sector with more income to spend.

Fiscalists believe that government should play an active role in stimulating the economy.

2. Increase Public Spending This adds directly to the total demand for goods and services.

3. Utilize Monetary Policies These should supplement and complement the major shifts in economic activity brought about by changes in fiscal policy.

By thus adhering to an appropriate blend of fiscal and monetary policies, it is possible, in the opinion of the fiscalists, to stabilize the economy and perhaps even to "fine-tune" it.

Exhibit 1
Aggregate Demand and Economic Policy in the Keynesian Model

As you will recall, aggregate demand (AD) is the sum of consumption demand (C), investment demand (I), and government demand (G). The intersection of aggregate demand with aggregate supply (AS) determines the prevailing level of output and employment.

The line (C + I + G) represents the objective of a well-coordinated fiscal and monetary policy. It expresses the full-employment level of *total* spending by households, businesses, and government. A lower level of total spending such as (C + I + G)' will produce a recessionary gap; a higher level will produce an inflationary gap.

What kinds of fiscal and monetary policies should be employed to close these gaps?

If a recessionary gap exists, as represented by the aggregate demand curve AD', then:

1. An appropriate fiscal policy would increase government expenditures and reduce taxes. This would increase G, and probably C and I as well. (Why do we say "probably" C and I? Why not "surely"?)

2. An appropriate monetary policy would increase the money supply by easing credit, thereby further encouraging business firms to increase I.

The result of these combined policies would be to shift the aggregate demand curve back up toward the full-employment level represented by the AD curve.

On the other hand, an inflationary gap as represented by the aggregate demand curve AD" requires a different approach to fiscal and monetary policy. Can you suggest the proper guidelines?

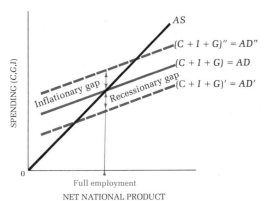

SPENDING (C,G,I)

Inflationary gap

Recessionary gap

AS

(C + I + G)" = AD"

(C + I + G) = AD

(C + I + G)' = AD'

0

Full employment

NET NATIONAL PRODUCT

These are only a few of the fundamental notions underlying fiscalist or Keynesian thinking. Other fiscalist ideas will be developed later in the chapter. Meanwhile, the following summary provides a review of some familiar concepts.

> *Fiscalism* or *Keynesian economics* is an outgrowth of ideas that emerged in the 1930s from the work of John Maynard Keynes. In contrast with classical economics, the Keynesian model argued that a capitalistic economy does not tend automatically toward full employment. Therefore, the government should pursue active fiscal policies, supported by appropriate monetary policies, to achieve and maintain full employment, stable prices, and steady economic growth.

You can gain a fuller appreciation of these conclusions by reviewing the explanation and diagram in Exhibit 1.

Monetarism

In contrast to fiscalists, there is a *monetarist* group, which marches to a distinctly different tune. The beliefs of the monetarists stem from the ideas expressed by Irving Fisher. These include the familiar quantity theory of money and the equation of exchange:

$$MV = PQ$$

In this equation, you will recall, M represents the quantity of money, V its velocity of circulation, P the average price of final goods and services, and Q the quantity of those goods and services. Therefore, PQ represents the market value of all final goods and services produced, and is the same as GNP.

Monetarists believe that V is relatively stable. Therefore, they say, changes in the economy's output or income (PQ) are due to changes in the quantity of money, M.

Note To refresh your understanding of these concepts, look up the meanings of *quantity theory of money* and *equation of exchange* in the Dictionary at the back of the book.

The monetarists contend that a capitalistic economy is *inherently stable*. Therefore, the system is not necessarily subject to business-cycle fluctuations. Major inflations and recessions, it is argued, are due primarily to one factor: *large swings in the rate of growth of the money supply*. Consequently, the monetarists conclude, fiscal policy cannot be used as a stabilizing device. Only monetary policy, in the form of consistent rather than erratic changes in the supply of money, can enable the economy to stabilize itself.

Like fiscalists, monetarists do not always agree on every point. However, monetarists are unanimous in their belief that money exercises a major influence on the economy. You can see why by examining the main features of their argument:

1. According to monetarist theory, the amount of money people wish to hold is closely related to their level of income. Hence, if the supply of money (that is, currency and demand deposits) increases faster than income, people will spend away the excess. This will cause inflation. On the other hand, if the supply of money increases more slowly than income, the opposite effect will occur. People will try to build up their money balances by cutting back on their expenditures, thereby causing unemployment. Therefore, monetarists conclude:

> Changes in the money supply cause people to alter their spending in relation to their income, thereby generating business cycles.

2. Monetarists do not claim that business cycles result exclusively from changes in the money supply. Like the fiscalists, monetarists recognize that the economy is always in the process of adjusting to changes in such things as population, consumer habits, and competition within industries. But monetarists nevertheless believe:

> Erratic changes in the supply of money are the dominant cause of business cycles.

3. In view of the fundamental role of money in the economy, monetarists believe that government fiscal actions by themselves exert little, if any, influence on total spending. It is when these actions are accommodated by the Fed through monetary expansions or contractions that changes in the money supply exert a strong independent influence on total spending. Therefore, because business cycles are primarily the result of erratic fluctuations in the money supply, monetarists contend:

> Control of the rate of monetary expansion or contraction is the appropriate means of stabilizing the economy.

4. In line with the rest of their theory, monetarists believe that the market interest rate rises and falls with the general price level. The reason, they say, is that borrowers and lenders add an "inflation premium" to the real interest rate—the rate that would prevail if prices remained stable. Monetarists therefore argue:

> An increase in the money supply raises prices and therefore the market interest rate; a decrease in the money supply does the opposite.

In contrast, as you will recall, the Keynesian model supports the idea that an increase in the money supply *decreases* the rate of interest. This encourages business investment and economic expansion. Conversely, a decrease in the money supply has the opposite effect.

The Money-Supply Rule

The monetarists' views are strong and persuasive. To support their beliefs, monetarists cite detailed studies, some going as far back as the nineteenth century, analyzing the behavior of money and prices. Monetarists contend these studies show that changes in the money supply have larger, more predictable, and quicker effects on GNP than do fiscal-policy changes in tax rates, government expenditures, and the federal deficit.

In the monetarists' opinion, therefore, the government should help the economy achieve its full-employment potential by adhering to a simple and well-defined guide:

> The Federal Reserve should expand the nation's money supply at the economy's desirable long-run growth rate or capacity to produce. This is about 3 to 4 percent per year. A faster rate of increase in the money supply would lead to strong inflationary pressures. Conversely, a slower rate would tend to be stagnating. This guide for economic expansion advanced by monetarists is called the *money-supply rule*.

Monetarists believe that monetary policy is of far greater importance than fiscal policy in affecting economic stability.

Monetarists believe that there is an optimum rate of monetary expansion and that the Fed should adhere to it.

Conclusion: The Monetarist Revolution

Monetarists have modernized the classical quantity theory of money. In the modern theory, M represents the public's demand for money in the form of real purchasing power.

Monetarists thus believe that the Federal Reserve has the power to stabilize the economy—or at least to permit the economy to stabilize itself. How? By controlling bank reserves and therefore the rate of growth of the money supply. Monetarists also believe that most of the fluctuations in economic activity that have occurred since the establishment of the Federal Reserve System in 1913 can be attributed to well-meant but inappropriate monetary policies. As a result, these policies have magnified rather than mitigated business cycles. Some examples will be shown later in this chapter.

Modernizing the Theory

Monetarists have undertaken a revision of the classical quantity theory, and have made it an integral part of monetarist beliefs. Two fundamental ideas on which the modern theory rests may be presented briefly.

1. The chief function of money is to serve as a medium of exchange. This means that money is wanted because it fulfills the *transactions motive*. This is the desire of the public to hold some of its assets in liquid form—that is, as cash balances—in order to carry on day-to-day spending. However, the public's purchasing power depends on the amount of its *real*, rather than nominal, cash balances. Therefore, monetarists contend:

> The demand for money is a demand for real cash balances.

2. Discrepancies quite commonly arise between the actual and desired real cash balances held by the public. For example, when there is an excess supply of money, people have greater cash balances than they desire. Hence they spend the excess cash for assets. These include consumption goods, investment goods, and securities (such as stocks and bonds). The increased spending leads to higher prices, thereby reducing people's actual real cash balances. This brings those balances back to their desired level, thereby eliminating the initial excess supply of money. Thus:

> The public must frequently adjust its actual real cash balances to desired levels. These adjustments cause economic instability.

Monetarist ideas have been adopted by a large proportion of business people, economists, and legislators. Consequently, much more attention is devoted to monetary policy today than was the case in previous decades. The result has been a monetarist revolution in economic thinking. Although fiscal policy and fiscalist beliefs are still important, they no longer overshadow Federal Reserve actions. Indeed, as you will see, such actions are among the topics most frequently discussed by business and political leaders.

Pillars of Monetarism: A Closer Look

The essential feature of monetarism is the dominant role it assigns to changes in the money supply as the chief factor affecting economic activity. To understand the implications of this, it is necessary to analyze the structure of monetarist thinking. This can best be done by examining the main propositions of monetarism—the pillars on which the system rests.

The Quantity Theory of Money

The most fundamental tenet of monetarism is the *quantity theory of money*. As you will recall, this proposition states that a given percentage change in the stock of money (*M*) will cause an equal percentage change in the average level of prices (*P*) in the same direction. It follows that changes in the stock of money will also cause changes in society's nominal income (*PQ*). Because money thus affects income, the role of money in monetarist thinking must be examined more closely.

To begin with, monetarists redefine *M* to represent the amount of money people want to hold in the form of real cash balances. The question they then ask is: *What determines the public's demand for real cash balances?* The answer, monetarists say, depends in a predictable fashion on a few key variables. Among them:

Nominal Income The amount of money people want to hold rises and falls with the economy's nominal income—its GNP. In terms of the equation of exchange, this means that the public's demand for money varies *directly* with *PQ*.

Monetarists contend that the amount of money (real cash balances) people want to hold depends mainly on three factors: nominal income, inflationary expectations, and real interest rates.

Inflationary Expectations If people expect prices to rise, they will spend away their cash balances now in order to avoid losing the purchasing power of that cash in the future. Conversely, if people expect prices to decline, they will hold onto their cash balances in order to have more purchasing power later. Therefore, the public's demand for real cash balances varies *inversely* with inflationary expectations.

Real Interest Rates Cash balances are assets. The public's decision to hold them depends in part on how profitable they are in comparison with other assets, such as securities, property, and so on. Thus, if the returns on other assets, measured by real interest rates, rise relative to the returns on real cash balances, people will reduce their holdings of real cash balances in order to take advantage of the higher returns elsewhere. The reverse, of course, occurs when the returns on other assets decline. In general, therefore, the public's demand for real cash balances varies *inversely* with real interest rates.

These factors, according to monetarists, determine the public's demand for money—that is, real cash balances. What about the supply? This, as you know, is determined by the monetary authority. Monetarists thus contend:

> The public's demand for real cash balances varies *directly* with nominal income and *inversely* with inflationary expectations and real interest rates. Under normal conditions, the public's demand for real cash balances tends to be stable in relation to those variables. The supply of money, however, has historically been unstable. Therefore, *discrepancies between the public's actual and desired holdings of real cash balances arise from changes in the supply of, not the demand for, money.*

Velocity and the Frequency of Payments

According to the equation of exchange,

$$MV = PQ \qquad \text{and therefore} \qquad V = \frac{PQ}{M}$$

When the equation is expressed in the latter form, it focuses attention on *V*. What is the connection between this variable and the public's demand for money—that is, cash balances? One of the key factors is the *frequency with which people are paid.*

Exhibit 2
The Public's Demand for Money Depends on Nominal Income (GNP)

At any given time, the public's demand for money is equal to some fraction (k) of nominal income (GNP). Therefore, an increase in the money-supply curve from M_S to M_S' provides people with excess cash balances. These balances are then spent, causing the equilibrium level of nominal income to rise from GNP_1 to GNP_2.

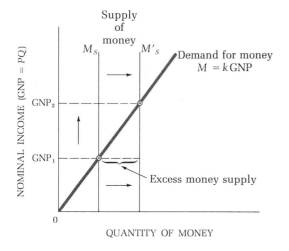

Take your own case as an example. Your income velocity of money is the ratio of your annual income to your average cash balance:

$$\text{Velocity} = \frac{\text{annual income}}{\text{average cash balance}}$$

If you were paid once each month, you would need to hold a considerable average cash balance in order to tide you over from one paycheck to the next. On the other hand, if you were paid every two weeks, your average cash balance would be much smaller. Your velocity, therefore, would increase. And if you were paid weekly, your average cash balance would be still smaller, thereby further increasing your velocity. Of course, the same is true for everyone else. Therefore:

> The income velocity of money varies directly with the frequency of payments. The more frequently people are paid, the smaller the average cash balances that must be held. Hence, the greater the velocity of money.

Demand for Money and the Nation's Income

How does society's demand for money relate to income? To find out, we can take the equation of exchange

$$MV = PQ$$

and rewrite it in terms of M. Thus:

$$M = \frac{PQ}{V} \qquad \text{or equivalently} \qquad M = \frac{1}{V} PQ$$

Expressed in this form, the equation on the right emphasizes the relation between the demand for money and the nation's income. To see why, suppose we let k stand for the ratio $1/V$. Then the right-hand equation becomes

$$M = kPQ$$

Of course, because PQ is the same as GNP, this equation can also be written

$$M = k\text{GNP}$$

What does this equation tell us? The answer can be expressed in words:

> People want to hold an amount of money (M) equal to a fraction (k) of their nominal income (PQ, or GNP). This is simply another way of saying that *the public's demand for real cash balances varies directly with nominal income.*

This proposition, as you have already learned, is one of the fundamental tenets of monetarism. The same idea is developed graphically in Exhibit 2. Society's nominal income, GNP, is measured on the vertical axis, and the quantity of money is measured on the horizontal axis. The figure conveys the following points:

1. The money-demand curve is an upward-sloping straight line. This indicates that the public wants to hold an amount of money equal to a specified fraction (k) of the nation's nominal income.

2. The money-supply curve, M_S, is a vertical line. This indicates that, at any given time, the quantity of money (determined by the Fed) is a fixed amount and is unresponsive to changes in income.

3. The equilibrium income at GNP$_1$ is determined by the intersection of the demand curve and the supply curve. If the Federal Reserve now decides to increase the money supply from M_S to M_S', it will create an excess supply of money relative to what people want. They will therefore spend the excess, causing nominal income to rise to the new equilibrium at GNP$_2$.

The Stability of Velocity

Another important feature of monetarist thinking is revealed in Exhibit 2.

The fact that the money-demand curve is a straight line (that is, its slope is constant) means that the amount of money people want to hold is equal to a constant fraction (k) of GNP. But, as you have already learned, k represents the ratio $1/V$. That is, $k = 1/V$. Therefore, because k is constant, V must also be constant in order for the equation to hold true. Further, if $k = 1/V$, then $V = 1/k$.

To illustrate these ideas, suppose that people want to hold 25 percent of their income in the form of cash balances. Then, $k = ¼$. And, since $V = 1/k$, $V = 4$. This means that each dollar is spent an average of four times during the year to purchase the economy's GNP.

Similarly, if people want to hold 20 percent of their income as cash, then $k = 1/5$. Hence, $V = 5$. Each dollar is thus spent an average of five times per year.

In general, k is the reciprocal of V, V is the reciprocal of k, and both are constants. In view of this, what determines V?

In general:

> Monetarists believe that the income velocity of money is stable. That is, although velocity can and does fluctuate over the years, it nevertheless bears a stable relationship to the variables that determine it. The main ones are: (a) the frequency of payments; (b) people's expectations about inflation; and (c) real interest rates. The last two factors, which, as you saw earlier, help to determine the public's demand for M, also contribute to determining V. On the other hand, the frequency with which people are paid, such as weekly or biweekly, remains fairly constant over long periods of time. Therefore, *the major causes of changes in V are inflationary expectations and real interest rates.*

Monetarists believe that, although velocity fluctuates over time, it is a stable function of the variables determining it. The major ones that change frequently are inflationary expectations and real interest rates.

Conclusion: Three Modern Monetarist Propositions

Monetarists have modernized the neoclassical quantity theory of money. This theory held that, in the equation of exchange, both V and Q were constant. V was constant because it depended on gradual, evolutionary changes. These included the frequency with which people are paid and the long-run money-holding habits of the public. Q was constant because the economy always tended toward full employment of its resources. Therefore, the theory concluded, government policies that increase the money supply will cause proportional increases in the general price level.

Monetarists have revised these ideas in several ways:

> The modern monetarist version of the quantity theory of money rests on three propositions:
>
> **1.** The public's demand for money is a demand for real (as distinguished from nominal) cash balances.

2. Changes in people's spending behavior result from discrepancies between actual and desired real cash balances. These discrepancies are brought about by changes in the supply of money, which affect nominal income.

3. The income velocity of money depends on: (a) frequency of payments; (b) inflationary expectations; and (c) real interest rates.

You may conclude from this that the modern quantity theory of money is not radically different in its basic tenets from the neoclassical one. To a large extent this is true. However, the chief function of the revised quantity theory is to place certain crucial variables in a different light. This, as you will see, permits them to be analyzed and interpreted in newer and more meaningful ways.

The Transmission Mechanism: Portfolio Adjustments

The second major pillar of monetarism is the *transmission mechanism.* This is the process by which changes in the money supply bring about changes in people's spending behavior, thereby affecting prices, interest rates, and other economic variables.

The transmission process, as the monetarists see it, can be summarized in three steps.

First, our economy is composed of decision-making units—individuals, households, and firms. These economic entities hold their wealth (that is, things of value) in the form of portfolios of assets. Examples are cash, property, and the rights to property. Thus, some of the things you might own, including both financial and nonfinancial assets, are money, a car, a stereo system, some securities, a house, furniture, and perhaps even a business. Because all of these items constitute wealth, each is a part of your portfolio.

Second, erratic changes in the supply of money cause discrepancies between people's actual and desired real cash balances. To restore equilibrium, individuals adjust the composition of assets in their portfolios. For example, if a disequilibrium is caused by an unexpected increase in the money supply, people will reduce their excess cash balances by purchasing any of a wide range of other assets.

Third, individuals are always shifting their holdings of wealth between different assets in an effort to obtain satisfactory relative rates of return on their entire combination of assets. For example, if returns in the securities market are relatively higher than returns in the real-estate market, people will shift some of their funds out of buildings and land and into stocks and bonds. These reallocations of wealth are reflected by changes in the relative prices of assets as spending patterns shift over a wide range of goods and services.

Thus:

> Monetarists believe that the transmission mechanism by which changes in the money supply cause changes in total spending is essentially a *portfolio-adjustment process.* Individuals are seen as disposing of their excess money balances over a broad spectrum of existing assets. These include stocks, bonds, consumer goods, and producer (capital) goods. As a result, the relative prices of these goods are always changing in response to shifts in people's spending patterns caused by changes in the money supply.

When people's real cash balances become too large because of erratic increases in the money supply, they spend the excess away on a wide range of goods and services. This is why monetarists describe inflation as "too much money chasing too few goods."

Stability of the Private Sector

A third pillar of monetarism is the belief that the private sector is inherently stable. That is, if left to its own devices, the economy will adjust to high levels of employment unless it is disturbed by erratic monetary growth.

In other words, monetarists see the private sector as basically resilient. It is thus capable of absorbing random shocks, such as strikes, boycotts, natural disasters, even limited wars, and adjusting to them over a period of time. However, the economy's ability to transform such random shocks into steady economic expansion is greatly influenced by the rate of growth of the money supply.

These ideas may be stated briefly:

> Monetarists believe that the private sector is capable by itself of attaining high levels of employment, provided that the Federal Reserve avoids erratic monetary policies.

Monetarists believe that the private sector will automatically adjust to full employment if the Fed avoids erratic monetary expansion.

Focus on Aggregate Resource Allocation

A fourth pillar of monetarism is its emphasis on the overall allocation of resources. That is, monetarists are not usually concerned with what is happening in particular sectors of the economy. This is because monetarist theory focuses on changes in the money supply and its impact on people's overall spending behavior, their real cash balances, and the general price level.

In fact, monetarists make a sharp distinction between movements in the general price level, which is affected by the quantity of money, and the behavior of relative prices, which are influenced by particular market conditions within the various sectors. According to monetarist belief, and contrary to fiscalist or Keynesian contentions, the channels through which monetary factors operate cannot be specified. Consequently, there is no way of predicting, as some Keynesian models try to do, the impact of monetary policy on different sectors and industries, such as the housing and automobile industries.

This philosophy largely explains why monetarists generally prefer to work with small-scale computer models for analyzing and predicting GNP, employment, prices, and other measures of aggregate economic activity. Such models utilize fewer variables—those that are believed to play key roles in influencing overall market forces. Fiscalists, on the other hand, typically focus on what is happening in specific sectors and segments of the economy. Hence they have tended to construct large-scale models, most of them containing hundreds of equations. These models provide detailed information on the way various sectors and industries influence overall economic behavior. However, there is no evidence that the large-scale models do a better job of predicting aggregate economic variables than the small-scale ones.

To summarize:

> Monetarists believe that erratic shifts in the money supply lead to price changes in all sectors of the economy, but in some more quickly than in others. However, the effects on specific sectors are unknown. Therefore, monetarists contend, only the overall impact of monetary policy on resource allocation can be judged.

Monetarists are concerned mainly with resource allocation in the economy as a whole, rather than in its various sectors, because monetary policy affects people's total spending behavior.

Conclusion: Major Propositions of Monetarism

The main ideas of monetarism can be summarized in terms of six propositions.

Monetarist ideas play an important part in today's economic policies. It is useful, therefore, to review some of the major propositions of monetarism.

1. The roots of monetarist belief go back to the quantity theory of money and to the equation of exchange. Both were formally expressed in the early part of this century by the distinguished American classical economist Irving Fisher (1867–1947).

2. Both the classical quantity theory of money and the equation of exchange have been reinterpreted by modern monetarists. They contend that M, the public's demand for money, is a demand for real cash balances. M is not, as in the classical view, merely an explanation of how changes in the money supply affect the price level and, therefore, nominal income (PQ or GNP). In addition, the modern theory, unlike the older one, does not assume full employment.

3. The public's demand for M is stable with respect to a few key variables. These are (a) nominal income, (b) inflationary expectations, and (c) real interest rates. The income velocity of money V is also stable with respect to a few key variables. These are (a) the frequency of payments, (b) inflationary expectations, and (c) real interest rates. The last two factors are thus common determinants of M and V. They are also the major short-run factors affecting V, because the frequency with which people are paid remains relatively constant for long periods of time.

4. The transmission mechanism—the effect of an increase in the money supply on the public's spending behavior—is viewed by monetarists as a *portfolio-adjustment process*. This means that the public spends its excess money balances on consumer goods as well as on investment goods, and not just on the latter because of lower interest rates or borrowing costs.

5. The private sector is inherently stable if left to its own devices. Therefore, the Fed should not subject the private sector to erratic monetary growth rates.

6. Erratic changes in the money supply cause complex spending fluctuations throughout the economy. Therefore, the effects of monetary policy can be estimated and predicted only for the economy as a whole, and not for specific sectors.

Today's monetarist views are a reaction to fiscalist-Keynesian ideas. In many ways, monetarism is a direct attack on the Keynesian model, and therefore on its conclusions pertaining to public policy. Consequently, the logic underlying the following conclusion is apparent.

Monetarists contend that "inflation is always and everywhere a monetary phenomenon"—caused by erratic increases in the money supply. Therefore, to achieve stability, the monetary authority should adhere to a policy of steady monetary expansion at a rate consistent with the economy's desirable long-run growth of GNP—about 3 to 4 percent annually. This fundamental idea has been called the *money-supply rule*. It serves as a practical guide for Federal Reserve monetary policy and as a basis for judging the Fed's overall performance.

Fiscal–Monetary Issues: Some Unresolved Questions

Many of the ideas advanced by the monetarists have become an integral part of modern economic thinking. Nevertheless, certain fundamental difficulties remain. The major ones can be expressed in terms of three questions:

1. Which transmission mechanism is correct?

2. Is velocity stable?

3. Is the private sector stable?

The answers to the foregoing questions determine many of the federal government's most important economic policies. Therefore, it is instructive to compare the fiscalists' and monetarists' viewpoints on the underlying issues.

Which Transmission Mechanism Is Correct?

As you will recall, the transmission mechanism is the process by which a change in the money supply causes changes in total spending.

The fiscalist or Keynesian model utilizes the liquidity-preference theory of interest, which you have already studied. (You can refresh your understanding of it by looking it up in the Dictionary at the back of the book.) In this theory, the interest rate is determined by the supply of, and demand for, money. Therefore, an increase in the money supply will lower the interest rate relative to the marginal efficiency of investment. This will stimulate business investment spending and cause a rise in aggregate demand. The result will be an increase in output, and subsequently in prices, as the economy approaches full employment. Thus, the chain of causation is:

The fiscalist (Keynesian) view holds that the transmission mechanism runs from money to interest rates to prices.

Fiscalist View

> **Money → Interest Rates → Prices**

Monetarists, on the other hand, see the transmission mechanism as one in which monetary influences affect spending decisions through a *portfolio-adjustment process.* An erratic increase in the money supply causes the public's actual money balances to be out of line with its desired money balances. People react by spending away the excess portion on a wide range of financial and nonfinancial assets—stocks, bonds, goods, and services. This causes prices to increase. As a result, the market rate of interest rises relative to the real rate—the rate that would prevail if prices were stable. This is because lenders charge an "inflation premium" on loans in order to compensate for their expected loss of purchasing power. And borrowers, you will recall, are willing to pay the premium because they expect to repay the loans in the future with dollars that are worth less. Therefore, the chain of causation is:

The monetarist view holds that the transmission mechanism runs from money to prices to interest rates.

Monetarist View

> **Money → Prices → Interest Rates**

The two theories thus lead to dramatically different conclusions.

For instance:

> The fiscalist and monetarist theories agree that changes in the money supply will initiate a series of effects. The two theories differ, however, about what the transmission mechanism or chain of causation is.

> • The fiscalist theory says that an increase in the money supply will reduce interest rates. This will encourage investment, thereby raising output and employment.

> • The monetarist theory says that an expansion of the money supply will increase prices and inflationary expectations. This will cause interest rates to rise, thereby discouraging investment, and hence reducing output and employment.

Is Velocity Stable?

A second source of controversy between fiscalist and monetarist views concerns the stability of velocity.

Fiscalists contend that V is unstable and that the effects of its fluctuations are unpredictable.

You learned that, in the Keynesian model, a decrease in the money supply causes the interest rate to rise. This prompts people to spend some of their cash holdings in order to acquire more interest-earning securities, such as bonds. Consequently, velocity increases.

Conversely, an increase in the money supply causes the interest rate to decline. Therefore, people sell some of their securities in order to hold more cash. Hence, velocity decreases.

But by how much does velocity increase or decrease with changes in the interest rate? How is the level of prices affected by changes in the money supply? The fiscalists' answers to these questions can be summarized in terms of three propositions:

1. Velocity is an unstable quantity that fluctuates with the interest rate, but the amount of fluctuation is unknown.

2. Because of the instability of velocity, the effect of any change in the money supply may be more than offset by a change in velocity.

3. Therefore, it is impossible to predict the extent to which any change in the money supply will affect the price level.

Monetarists contend that V is a stable function of the factors determining it. Therefore, the effects on the price level of changes in the money supply are measurable.

How do monetarists respond to these arguments? As you will recall, they contend that, although velocity fluctuates over time, it is stable with respect to its determining variables. Therefore, changes in the money supply are not offset by changes in velocity. Indeed, changes in the money supply exert direct influences on future price levels.

Summarizing:

> In the fiscalist view, velocity is unstable. Therefore, it is impossible to know the extent to which changes in the money supply will produce changes in the price level.

> In the monetarist view, velocity is stable with respect to its causal variables. Therefore, changes in the money supply will produce definite and measurable effects on the price level.

Is the Private Sector Stable?

A third fundamental difference between fiscalism and monetarism concerns the stability of the private sector.

As you recall, Keynesian economics was born in the depression of the 1930s. In response to the classical beliefs of his time, Keynes advanced several ideas:

• Aggregate demand may not necessarily equal full-employment aggregate income. Consequently, the economic system may be in equilibrium at less than full employment and may remain so indefinitely.

• Economic fluctuations result from wide swings in the business sector's demand curve for investment—the marginal-efficiency-of-investment or *MEI* curve. Shifts of the curve occur frequently because of changes in expected product demand, technology, corporate income-tax rates, and other factors.

• The inherent instability of the economy makes it necessary for the government to play an active role. Thus, through appropriate fiscal and monetary policies, stable levels of prices and full employment can be achieved.

Fiscalists conclude that government should pursue active stabilization policies.

These ideas, of course, are at odds with monetarist belief. This viewpoint holds that the economy is inherently stable at a high level of employment unless disturbed by erratic monetary growth. Therefore, the central bank should adhere to a consistent monetary policy. The dynamic structure of the private sector would then enable the system to absorb shocks and transform them into stabilizing motion.

Monetarists conclude that government efforts to stabilize the economy turn out to be destabilizing.

Summarizing these beliefs:

There are two distinct differences of opinion on the question of stability:

1. Modern Keynesians contend that the economy is not particularly resilient. Hence, it does not readily revert back to its normal growth path when subjected to disturbances. Therefore, stabilization actions, consisting of fiscal policies accompanied by appropriate monetary policies, are needed to achieve and maintain full employment.

2. Monetarists believe that, if the money supply is expanded at a steady rate, the economy will rapidly absorb the adverse effects of disturbances. This will enable output to resume its long-run growth path. Therefore, no active stabilization policies should be undertaken. Indeed, such policies actually turn out to be *destabilizing*.

Some important relationships involving money, velocity, and other variables are discussed in Exhibit 3.

Recapitulation: The Critical Role of Money

You can now appreciate that certain differences between fiscalism and monetarism have far-reaching implications. For practical policy-making purposes, the fundamental difference concerns the effects of changes in the money supply on interest rates and prices. Two classes of effects may be distinguished.

Fiscalism in Brief

In the fiscalist model, a change in the money supply has a direct effect on the interest rate, but not on the price level. Further, no distinction is made between market and real rates of interest. Following in the tradition of Keynes, fiscalists contend that an increase in the money supply

Fiscalism can be characterized by three important features.

Exhibit 3

Tracking Economic Trends: The Fed and Inflation

Monetarists contend that the Fed has too often focused attention not on controlling the money supply but on controlling interest rates. This, however, is something it has been unable to accomplish.

Figure (*a*): This figure, say the monetarists, demonstrates the instability of the money supply, M1, and the Consumer Price Index, CPI, both measured in percentage changes. The relationship shows that increases in the monetary growth rate cause increases in the inflation rate about two years later.

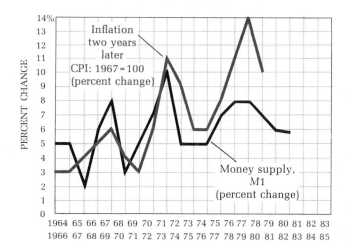

Figure (*b*): Monetarists agree that, over a period of a few months, increases in the money supply may reduce interest rates and decreases in the money supply may raise them. But over a period of years, as this figure shows, the relation is different. In accordance with monetarist belief, rapid monetary growth rates result in higher inflation, which in turn produces higher interest rates. Slow monetary growth rates result in lower inflation and, therefore, in lower interest rates.

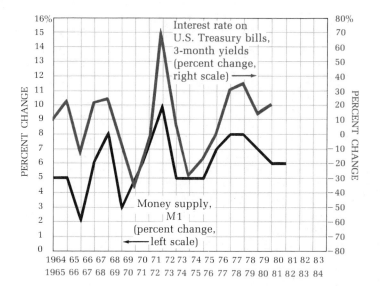

Figure (*c*): Monetarists contend that interest rates respond to inflation. Higher prices lead to higher interest rates because lenders want to be compensated for the purchasing power they expect to lose due to inflation. And borrowers are willing to pay higher interest rates because they expect to be repaying their loans with cheaper dollars. (**Note:** The recent *inverse* relation may be only temporary. It reflects the Reagan administration's tight money and easy fiscal policies, which resulted in higher interest rates and a reduced rate of inflation.)

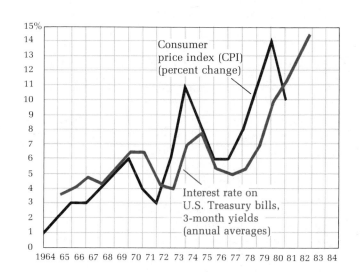

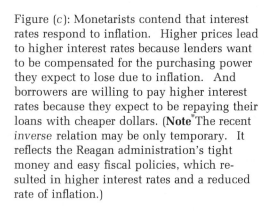

leads to a reduction in the interest rate. This causes an increase in the amount of business investment and therefore in aggregate demand. Unemployed resources are drawn into production, and the economy moves toward full employment while prices adjust accordingly.

Thus:

Fiscalism is characterized by (1) a predominantly monetary explanation of the interest rate, (2) a predominantly nonmonetary explanation of the price level, and (3) no distinction between market rates and real rates of interest.

Monetarism in Brief

In the monetarist model, a change in the money supply has a direct effect on the price level but not on the interest rate. Further, a distinction is made between market rates and real rates of interest. Following in the tradition of Fisher, monetarists believe that an increase in the money supply leads to an increase in prices. This causes the actual or market rate of interest to rise relative to the "real" rate—the rate that would exist if prices were stable. The difference between the market rate and the real rate represents an "inflation premium." This is an amount that lenders charge and borrowers are willing to pay because both expect prices to continue rising. Thus:

Monetarism is characterized by (1) a predominantly monetary explanation of the price level, (2) a predominantly nonmonetary explanation of the interest rate, and (3) a distinction between market rates and real rates of interest.

Monetarism can be characterized by three important features.

Which Model? Some Agreement and Some Disagreement

The way in which Washington manages the money supply is thus critical for public policy. Which of the two models, fiscalist or monetarist, is correct? As with all complex questions, there is no simple answer. However, monetarists believe that the Fed should adhere to at least three basic rules:

Provide an Optimum Monetary Growth Rate

The Fed should stabilize the expansion of the money supply at about 3 to 4 percent a year. This would "feed" money to the business sector at a rate consistent with the economy's long-run growth of GNP. When the monetary growth rate increases much faster than this, as it often has, the result is inflationary.

In addition, a rate of monetary expansion that is substantially greater than 3 to 4 percent annually should be reduced slowly. The reason is that a gradual reduction rather than a rapid one is more likely to permit a slower rate of business contraction. Therefore, it will be less destabilizing and will create less unemployment.

Monetarists argue that, if the Fed adheres to three basic rules, it will achieve both efficiency and stability.

Do Not "Monetize" the Debt

As you know, bond prices and interest rates are inversely related. Consequently, when the Treasury borrows from the public by selling securities, their prices decline and interest rates rise.

High interest rates, as you will recall, may lead to *crowding out* of business investment and thereby bring on a recession. The Fed, therefore, will often buy securities in the open market in order to maintain their prices and stabilize interest rates. But this action is inflationary—the same as printing money. Why? Because open-market purchases of government securities increase banks' reserves. This enables banks to expand demand deposits and hence the money supply.

When the Fed buys securities in the open market, it thus "monetizes" some of the national debt by converting it into money. This policy, monetarists emphasize, should be avoided in order to reduce inflationary pressures. *The Fed should concentrate instead on stabilizing the monetary growth rate and leave interest rates to be determined in the market.*

Watch the Monetary Base, Not the Federal Funds Rate

Monetarists believe that the Fed should focus on stabilizing the monetary base.

It is interesting to note that an increasing number of economists, including many diehard fiscalists, have come to agree with these prescriptions. Unfortunately, however, a chief difficulty in implementing them arises from the ambiguity of the notion of "money."

As you know, there are several different measures of money, including M1, M2, and M3. Which of these should the Fed try to stabilize? There is growing recognition that some sort of representative or "compromise" measure is needed. One that is often recommended is called the "monetary base."

> The sum of legal reserves and currency in circulation constitutes the *monetary base*. It may be called "high-powered" money because it supports the money supply (currency + checkable deposits), which, because of our fractional-reserve banking system, is a multiple of the monetary base. Thus, by controlling the monetary base, the Fed could exercise a stronger influence over the total monetary assets of the public.

According to critics, the Fed has often devoted too little effort to stabilizing the monetary base and too much to influencing the *federal funds rate*. This is the interest rate at which banks borrow excess reserves from other banks' accounts at the Fed, usually overnight, to keep required reserves from falling below the legal level. The Fed pays close attention to this rate. It is an indicator of what is happening to other short-term interest rates, because they all tend to move with the federal funds rate.

Conclusion: The Optimum Fiscal–Monetary Mix

The optimum fiscal–monetary mix is one that reduces budgetary deficits while stabilizing monetary expansion.

The Fed, of course, cannot control interest rates. It can only control the supply of money, which, when combined with the public's demand for money, determines the level of interest rates in the market. Critics thus conclude that frequent efforts by the Fed to influence interest rates by manipulating the money supply have been destabilizing and inflationary. As a result:

> All informed observers agree that, to achieve economic stability, an optimum fiscal–monetary mix is needed. The optimum mix aims at reducing budgetary deficits while providing a reasonably steady expansion of the money supply—that is, the monetary base. To do so requires two things:

Leaders in Economics

Milton Friedman
1912–
America's Best-Known Monetarist

United Press International

Nowadays, relatively few economists advocate the abolition of welfare, social security, graduated income taxes, and professional licensure—including the licensing of medical doctors. Milton Friedman is one who does. A Nobel laureate (1976) and professor emeritus at the University of Chicago, he is not only one of America's leading economists but also the foremost exponent of what is known as the "Chicago School" of economic thought. Like his distinguished predecessors at that renowned institution, he has an abiding faith in free enterprise and an unshakable conviction that the free market is the best device ever conceived for allocating society's resources and for ordering human affairs.

Friedman is more than a maverick economist. He has been called the most original economic thinker since John Maynard Keynes. This reputation has been earned largely because of Friedman's exhaustive criticisms of Keynesian ideas. As a result, Friedman is believed by many to equal, if not to outrank, Keynes as the most influential economist of the twentieth century.

Money-Supply Rule
This belief is based primarily on Friedman's approach to money and his unique position as America's best-known monetarist. Using carefully documented research going back to the late nineteenth century, he argues that the crucial factor affecting economic trends has been the quantity of money, not government fiscal policy. Accordingly, he opposes the use of discretionary monetary policy by the Federal Reserve to achieve economic stability. Friedman advocates instead a *money-supply rule*—an expansion of the nation's money supply at a steady rate in accordance with the economy's growth and capacity to produce. Friedman gives four major reasons for this view.

1. Past Performance of the Fed
Throughout its history, the Fed has proclaimed that it was using its monetary powers to promote economic stability. But the record often shows the opposite. Despite the Fed's well-intentioned efforts, it has been a major cause of instability by permitting the quantity of money to expand and contract erratically. Therefore, the urgent need is to prevent the Fed from being a source of economic disturbance.

2. Limitation of Our Knowledge
Economic research has established two propositions:

(a) There are close, regular, and predictable relations among the quantity of money, national income, and prices over a number of years. Therefore, a stable price level over the long run requires that the quantity of money grow at a fairly steady rate roughly equal to the average rate of growth of the nation's output—its real GNP.

(b) The relation between the quantity of money and economic activity is much looser in the short run (from month to month or from quarter to quarter) than it is over a number of years. Therefore, any attempt to use monetary policy for fine-tuning the economy is bound to create economic instability because not enough is known about short-run relationships between money and prices.

3. Promotion of Confidence
An announced, and adhered to, policy of steady monetary growth would provide the business sector with a firm basis for confidence in monetary stability. This is more than any discretionary policy could provide even if it happened to produce roughly steady monetary growth.

4. Neutralization of the Fed
An independent Fed is at times too removed from political pressures and at other times unduly affected by them. Hence, a money-supply rule would insulate monetary policy both from the arbitrary power of a small group of people not subject to control by the electorate and from the short-run pressures of partisan politics.

Conclusion: Feasible Policy
Is the adoption of a money-supply rule technically feasible? Friedman claims that it is. Although he admits that the Fed could not achieve a precise rate of growth in the money supply from day to day or from week to week, it could come very close from month to month and quarter to quarter. If and when it does, he says, it will provide a monetary climate favorable to economic stability and orderly growth. And that, Friedman concludes, is the most we can ask from monetary policy at our present state of knowledge.

1. The government should strive to narrow the gap between spending and taxes.

2. The Fed should keep a close watch on the monetary base, rather than the federal-funds rate, as a guide for short-term policy.

Although there is now considerable uniformity of opinion on these beliefs, much less agreement exists concerning the short-run and long-run effects of changes in the fiscal–monetary mix on interest rates and prices. Because of these differences in views, fiscal and monetary policy can often be influenced by political pressures—both Republican and Democratic. Consequently, you will find many controversial discussions of these issues in the news media. (See "Leaders in Economics," p. 295.)

What You Have Learned in This Chapter

1. Which combination of fiscal and monetary policy is best? This question has concerned economists and political leaders since the birth of Keynesian economics in the 1930s. Two distinct viewpoints or schools of thought—called "fiscalist" and "monetarist"—have evolved.

2. Fiscalists are neo-Keynesians. They follow the Keynesian tradition. This means that their beliefs are rooted in the fundamental equation

$$AD = C + I + G$$

and in the equation's implications. Among them:

(a) A capitalistic economy is inherently unstable and does not tend automatically toward full employment. Therefore:

(b) An active fiscal policy involving taxation and budgetary changes is needed to bring aggregate demand to full-employment levels. In addition:

(c) An appropriate monetary policy should supplement and complement the major shifts in economic activity brought about by changes in fiscal policy.

3. Monetarists are neo-Fisherians. They build upon the writings of Irving Fisher, one of the great American neoclassical economists of the early 1900s. Monetarist beliefs are rooted in the basic equation of exchange

$$MV = PQ$$

and in the quantity theory of money. These concepts have undergone substantial revision by monetarists, who emphasize the following ideas:

(a) A capitalistic economy is inherently stable and not necessarily subject to substantial business-cycle fluctuations. Major inflations and recessions are due primarily to one factor: *erratic changes in monetary growth.* This causes people to alter their spending in relation to income, thereby generating wide swings in business activity.

(b) In the equation of exchange given above, the velocity (V) of money is relatively stable with respect to the variables determining it. Therefore, the quantity of money (M) is of critical importance in affecting the economy's prices and output (PQ), or GNP. (In contrast, fiscalists contend that, because of the speculative demand for money, V is relatively unstable and, therefore, unpredictable.)

(c) Because of the importance of monetary growth, the Federal Reserve should adhere to a "money-supply rule." That is, the money supply should be increased at the same rate as the economy's capacity to produce—about 3 or 4 percent a year. More than this would be inflationary; less would cause stagnation.

4. Looking more closely at monetarism, its essential features can be summarized in terms of several related propositions. Among them:

(a) The classical quantity theory of money is reinterpreted as a theory of the demand for real cash balances rather than as an explanation of the level of nominal income.

(b) The public's demand for money (M) depends on a few key variables. These include nominal income, inflationary expectations, and real interest rates. The velocity of money (V) depends on frequency of payments, inflationary expectations, and real interest rates. M and V are thus influenced largely, but not entirely, by the same factors.

(c) The transmission mechanism is viewed as a portfolio-adjustment process. That is, people spend their excess money balances on a wide range of both consumer and investment goods.

(d) Because the economic system is inherently stable, the Fed should avoid erratic monetary growth rates. These can only lead to spending fluctuations, and therefore to inflation and unemployment, throughout the economy.

5. The fiscalist and monetarist models leave some unresolved questions. For example:

(a) *Which transmission mechanism is correct?* The fiscalist model depicts the chain of causation as money → interest rates → prices. The monetarist model contends that the causal chain is money → prices → interest rates. In reality, there is some evidence to suggest that both possibilities often occur, but with varying time lags. For example, an erratic increase in the money supply may sometimes reduce interest rates for a month or two, or perhaps even for several months. However, the rates then begin to rise as lenders and borrowers see prices increasing and expect them to continue.

(b) *Is velocity stable?* The fiscalist model concludes that V is relatively unstable and can be more than offset by changes in M. The monetarist model concludes that V is relatively stable and, therefore, that only changes in M can affect PQ. In reality, the evidence indicates that V exhibits some degree of stability. But there is disagreement between some fiscalists and monetarists over just how stable is stable.

(c) *Is the private sector stable?* The fiscalist model contends that the economy is inherently unstable in that it does not necessarily tend toward full employment. Therefore, active stabilization policies are needed to achieve and maintain full employment. The monetarist model argues that the economy is inherently stable and that it tends toward full employment if the money supply is expanded at a slow steady rate. Therefore, no active stabilization policies should be undertaken.

6. There is substantial agreement among most experts that reductions in budgetary deficits and a reasonably steady expansion of the money supply are necessary to achieve stability. There is much less agreement, however, concerning the influence of money growth on other economic variables. Nevertheless, there is considerable uniformity of opinion that the monetary base is more important than the federal-funds rate as a guide for short-term Federal Reserve policy.

For Discussion

1. *Terms and concepts to review:*
fiscal policy
monetary policy
money-supply rule
transactions motive
quantity theory of money
equation of exchange
transmission mechanism
fiscalism
monetarism
crowding out
monetary base
federal-funds rate

2. Monetarists are more critical of erratic changes in the money supply than of its rapid growth. The former, they contend, is a far more serious problem. Can you explain why?

3. "If the money supply increased at a steady rate of about 4 percent a year, would business cycles still occur?" How would a monetarist answer this question?

4. There is a close relationship between GNP and the money supply. Can you offer an explanation as to why either one may be the cause of the other?

5. "The equation $AD = C + I + G$ says fundamentally the same thing as the equation $MV = PQ$." Do you agree? Explain.

6. Which is more important, the size of the nation's budgetary deficit or its rate of growth? Assume that the deficits are monetized by the Fed.

7. Is it possible for the fiscalists and monetarists to agree on public policy even though they disagree on certain fundamental matters of theory?

8. "Government budgetary deficits are not necessarily a cause of inflation. It depends on how they are financed." Explain.

9. "The Fed cannot simultaneously control both the money supply and interest rates." Is this statement true? Explain.

10. The Fed gains greatest control over the money supply by focusing attention on the monetary base. Why?

15
CHAPTER

Productivity and Economic Growth

Learning guide
Watch for the answers to these important questions

What is productivity? How is it measured? What sorts of difficulties arise in estimating productivity? Why and how do changes in productivity affect economic growth?

How is economic growth defined? How is it measured? How may it be depicted in terms of a production-possibilities curve?

What factors determine economic growth? What difficulties are encountered in trying to measure it?

Can economic growth be depicted with a model? What is the significance of the capital-output ratio? Can the full-employment growth rate be measured? If so, how?

This chapter is concerned with ways of improving efficiency in the use of resources, especially labor and capital.

The greater thing in this world is not so much where we stand as in what direction we are going.

Oliver Wendell Holmes

After years of steep inflation, high taxes, sluggish economic growth, and weak international competitiveness, many informed observers have concluded that the nation must somehow achieve a massive gain in efficiency. It must seek to increase its output from existing labor and capital, and it must look for ways to offset rising wage and materials costs with new and better production methods.

Many things can be done to help the country realize these goals. Revising the tax system to instill more production incentives is one approach. Increasing the quantity of physical capital with which labor can work is another. And improving the quality of labor as well as the efficiency with which labor and capital are combined is still another. These and related measures enhance the nation's *productivity* and, therefore, its *economic growth*. Hence it is important to understand the meanings and implications of these concepts.

What Is Productivity?

How many miles does your car get to a gallon of gasoline? What is the average amount of wheat produced per acre of land? Does the Japanese steel industry produce more tons of steel per dollar of investment than the American steel industry does? Which brand of typewriter enables a typist to produce the largest number of letters per hour?

These and similar questions concern problems of productivity. What is *productivity*? It is the relationship between output of goods or services and one or more of the inputs used to produce the output. Productivity is thus measured by a ratio of output to input:

$$\text{productivity} = \frac{\text{output}}{\text{input}}$$

Productivity, simply stated, is "what you get out for what you put in."

In order to understand productivity (and to avoid common misconceptions about it), it is important to note what is not included in the concept.

First, productivity is not a measure of the total volume of output. Neither does it disclose how hard anyone works. Therefore, measures of actual productivity neither imply nor support judgments about what is "good" or "bad" (unless they are judgments of performance relative to established productivity goals).

Second, a measure of productivity is not necessarily a measure of efficiency. For example, a lawyer may be able to type more letters per day than his or her typist. But is typing letters the most efficient use of the lawyer's time? Probably not. Therefore, the lawyer hires a typist to do the typing. The lawyer is then able to be more efficient by devoting full time to the practice of law. Of course, it might be possible to increase the typist's productivity by providing better equipment, such as a larger desk or a faster typewriter. But it might be more *efficient* (that is, more profitable) for the lawyer to send fewer letters per day, which would require less of the typist's time.

Thus:

Measures of productivity are measures of the use of resources or of the degree of their use. Consequently, measures of productivity may or may not serve as indicators of the volume of output or of efficiency. Whether or not they do depends on how the measures are constructed and employed.

Two Measures of Productivity

As used in economics, productivity is simply a ratio of output to input. Higher productivity can thus be attained either by (a) getting more output with the same amount of input or (b) getting the same output with less input.

Although many different measures of productivity can be formulated, the two that have gained the widest use are partial productivity and total-factor productivity.

Partial Productivity

The concept of *partial productivity* uses only one input in its denominator. Although labor is the input most commonly employed, land and capital are also frequently utilized. Thus, such ratios as output per worker, yield per acre, and production per machine are examples of partial-productivity measures.

Partial productivity is a measure of output based on a single measurable input.

The most familiar measure of labor productivity in the United States is the index of output per hour of all persons employed in the private business sector. This is shown in the back endpapers of the book. The index, published by the U.S. Department of Labor, is calculated by dividing real GNP (that is, GNP in constant dollars) originating in the private business sector by labor-hours employed in that sector.

Why are the contributions of government to GNP excluded from the measure? Because, unlike the private sector, which sells readily identifiable products to individuals at market prices, most of the products of the public sector consist of hard-to-measure services. These goods are given away "free" or at below-market prices. Some examples include national defense, police and fire protection, and subsidized health care. These, unlike the products produced by the private sector, are provided in order to fulfill collective rather than individual wants.

Total-Factor Productivity

Total-factor productivity is a measure of output based on the sum of all measurable inputs.

A second measure of productivity is called *total-factor productivity*. The denominator of this index is the sum of all the measurable inputs (labor, land, capital) used in production. However, because some inputs may be more important than others in a particular production process, it is necessary to "weight" the inputs according to their relative significance.

For example, certain heavy industries, such as the automobile and steel industries, have become increasingly capital-intensive, using more machines and fewer workers. Consequently, greater numerical weight must be given to the importance of capital relative to labor when measuring such industries' total-factor productivity. On the other hand, in such high-technology industries as the biomedical and microelectronics industries, improvements in productivity depend heavily on research and development. Hence, the time and money spent on these activities must be given relatively greater weight than other inputs when estimating the gains in total-factor productivity of these industries.

Searching for the Right Measure

Attempts to measure productivity are complicated by problems pertaining to the measurement of output, input, and level of coverage.

It is usually easier to define a concept than to measure it. Productivity is no exception. Efforts to quantify it have been the subject of much controversy, leading to the conclusion that any measure is at best a tolerable compromise between conflicting objectives.

For instance, if your car gets 25 miles to a gallon of gasoline and your friend's car gets 20, then your car is more productive than your friend's with respect to gasoline consumption. On the other hand, if your friend's car uses a quart of oil per thousand miles while yours uses the same amount in 500 miles, then your friend's car is more productive than yours with respect to oil consumption.

But which car is more productive overall? There is no simple answer. To understand why, it is necessary to clarify certain practical problems associated with the measurement of three components of productivity—output, input, and level of coverage.

Output Measurement and Its Problems

Of the two figures from which a productivity ratio is derived, output is usually the more difficult one to determine. There are three major reasons for this:

1. Dissimilar Products Some products are sufficiently uniform that their outputs can be measured in physical units, such as tons of steel or bushels of wheat. But most products are dissimilar. Therefore, to derive a measure of total output, the outputs of these goods must be combined into a composite number. The most common procedure is to use the money value of products as the measure of output. But then the figures must be deflated by an appropriate price index in order to eliminate the effects of inflation. The results obtained are a measure of *real* output—that is, output expressed in constant dollars of a past period. An illustration is presented in Exhibit 1.

2. Changes in Quality The quality of most goods does not remain constant. Because of advances in technology, the durability, design and appearance of many products tend to improve over time. These improvements are not always reflected in the price indexes used as deflators of value figures. As a result, measures of productivity often understate such actual gains in productivity.

3. Nonquantifiable Services The provision of many types of services cannot be divided into well-defined units. Consequently, their production is often extremely difficult, if not impossible, to measure. How, for example, can the outputs of teachers, musicians, scientists, and numerous other producers of services be quantified in order to provide a basis for estimating their productivities? The answer is that usually they cannot. Because of this, useful productivity measures have been developed for only a few industries in the service sector.

Input Measurement and Its Problems

"Input" constitutes the denominator of the productivity equation. Although a variety of specific inputs may be used, they generally fall into one of three categories—labor, capital, and land.

1. Labor Productivity The improvement of human resources has always been a fundamental concern of economics. Consequently, the most common types of productivity ratios are those that measure labor productivity. This may be expressed alternatively as (a) output per hour of employed persons and (b) output per worker-hour. Both measures are widely used, mainly because they utilize data that are relatively easy to obtain when compared to other types of inputs.

2. Capital Productivity Another measure of productivity is output per unit of capital. In terms of tangible capital, some common formulations of productivity include output per plant, output per machine, and output per square foot of factory space. In terms of intangible capital, expressions such as output per dollar of current assets (that is, cash and near-liquid assets) or output per dollar of inventory serve as measures of capital productivity. As you can see, the concept of capital is complex. Consequently, there is no single measure that serves all purposes.

3. Land Productivity A third measure of productivity is output per unit of land. Agriculture provides the most common examples. Data expressing yields per acre for wheat, corn, oats, and other grains are published regularly by the U.S. Department of Agriculture. So too are figures reporting the value per acre of land and the value of buildings per acre of land. These and similar measures provide indicators of the intensity of land use. That is, they reveal the extent to which a unit of land is fulfilling the purposes to which it is being put.

Level of Coverage

In addition to the problems of measuring output and intput, the scope or comprehensiveness of any measure of productivity must also be consid-

Exhibit 1
Deflating Output with a Price Index
(hypothetical data)

When the outputs of dissimilar products are combined to form a composite number, that measure is commonly expressed in terms of money value. Gross national product (GNP) provides a typical example. However, the results may have to be "deflated" to remove the influence of price increases. This is done by dividing the value series in current dollars [column (1)] by an appropriate price index [column (2)], thereby obtaining a "real" series expressed in constant dollars of a base period [column (3)].

Note that the price index expresses each year's average price level as a percentage of the average in the base period. For example, in Year 2, which is the base period, the average price level was 100 percent of itself. In Year 1, the average was 91.4 percent of what it was in Year 2. In Year 3, the average was 116 percent of what it was in Year 2. And so on.

	(1)	(2)	(3)
	GNP (billions of current dollars)	General price index	Real GNP (billions of constant dollars of Year 2)
Years			(1) ÷ (2)†
1	$ 982.4	91.4	$1,075
2*	1,171.1	100.0	1,171
3	1,412.9	116.0	1,218
4	1,702.2	133.7	1,273
5	2,127.6	152.1	1,399

* Base period. The general price index [column (2)] equals 100 for this period.
† Before dividing, move decimal place in column (2) two places to the left.

ered. This is because measures of productivity can be prepared for almost any level of activity.

For example, at the lowest (that is, the simplest) level, many firms prepare productivity measures for their own operations. These are compared with industry averages and trends to reveal how well the company is performing relative to the industry. Among the more familiar measures of productivity at this level are output per worker, output per worker-hour, and output per department or division of the firm.

At the next higher level, trade associations consisting of groups of firms in the same industry often publish productivity data for their entire industry. The measures are typically expressed in the form of *index numbers*. As you have already learned, these are figures that disclose the relative changes in a series of numbers, such as prices or production, from a base-period value usually designated as 100. All other numbers in the series, both before and after the base period, are expressed as percentages of that value. Industry productivity data thus reflect the productivity gains of individual firms within the industry. These gains can occur when firms improve their efficiency or when they increase their utilization rates of specific inputs.

Productivity is most difficult to measure at the national level. Therefore, there are only a few measures of the economy's overall productivity.

Finally, the highest or most general measures of productivity are those made at the national level. No perfect indicator of national productivity exists—for at least three reasons:

1. The most comprehensive measure of the economy's output, namely GNP, excludes certain productive activities. (Can you recall some examples?)

2. Government productivity cannot be measured completely. This is because many of the services government provides, such as national defense, public safety, education, and cultural opportunities, are given away "free" rather than sold.

3. Some of the factors used in production cannot be classified and combined with other quantifiable resources to produce a comprehensive, unambiguous measure of input. Capital, as you have seen, provides an example. Can you think of others?

Because of these and other difficulties, there exist relatively few measures of productivity at the national level. The most widely quoted are (a) output per hour of all persons in the private business sector and (b) output per worker-hour. Both sets of data are published regularly by the U.S. Department of Labor. The figures, along with other statistics, are widely used as guidelines for wage and salary negotiations by unions and management.

Changes in Productivity

If we all produce more, the economy's productivity increases and the nation as a whole grows richer. Yet our economy has gone through long periods when it has experienced declines in productivity relative to some advanced countries. What are the reasons for this? There are many, but among the more important are these:

Growth of Service Industries The banking, entertainment, retailing, health-care, insurance, and other service industries have expanded rapidly. Productivity in the service sector is difficult to measure because outputs and inputs are not usually as easy to identify as they are in manufacturing.

Inefficient Labor and Management Practices Over the long run, many unions have been able to negotiate shorter workweeks, longer vacations, and more paid holidays, thus reducing production without corresponding reductions in wages. In addition, the managements of many firms have been remiss in eliminating outmoded business practices and procedures, thereby failing to fulfill their functions as efficient coordinators of their firms' resources. These factors have been important contributors to declines in productivity.

Restrictive Government Policies Through such selective measures as tariffs, subsidies, regulations, and controls, government has promoted certain industries while hampering others. Through tax legislation favoring consumption over capital formation, government at times has reduced incentives to work, save, and invest. Taken together, these policies have often had dampening effects on the economy, reducing productivity and causing resources to be misallocated.

Conclusion: Stimulating Productivity

It is easy to understand why today's most thoughtful business, labor, and political leaders are seeking ways to increase the economy's productivity. They realize that rising levels of output relative to input is a key to improving living standards. Therefore, if productivity does not increase, workers will have to put in more hours, or else a larger number of workers will be needed, to provide a rising volume of output per person.

Growth in productivity is thus the key source of living standards. An increase in productivity means that the economy is producing more goods and services with its existing factors of production. The nation's real income therefore rises. A decrease in productivity means the opposite—and, consequently, leads to a decline in the nation's real income.

The most common measures of productivity are partial measures based usually on one factor of production, labor. For example, labor productivity is measured by output per employed person or output per worker-hour. However, a more comprehensive view of how well the economy is utilizing its productive resources is provided by a different index, total-factor productivity. This is a measure of output relative to nonhuman resources as well as human ones.

Unfortunately, total-factor productivity is a more difficult concept to quantify because it combines in its denominator a weighted sum of *all* inputs used in production. Thus, partial-productivity measures, based mainly on labor inputs because they are typically the largest and easiest to quantify, remain the most widely used indexes of productivity.

> What can be done to step up gains in productivity? The greatest single need is for more investment in new plant and equipment. Over the long run, the largest increases in productivity come from the adoption of improved technology. This requires that economic policies be formulated to encourage more rapid advances in technology, thereby stimulating productivity, which in turn leads to faster economic growth.

Productivity is thus the key to economic growth. This fact will become increasingly evident throughout the remainder of this chapter.

To encourage increases in productivity, economic policies are needed that will stimulate business investment in new plant and equipment.

Exhibit 2

Economic Growth Can Be Seen As an Outward Shift of an Economy's Production-Possibilities Curve

Economic growth is not a movement along a given curve, such as from S to T, because this is merely a change in the composition of total output. Nor is economic growth a movement from a point of unemployment, such as U, to the production-possibilities curve. Economic growth is an *outward shift* of the curve.

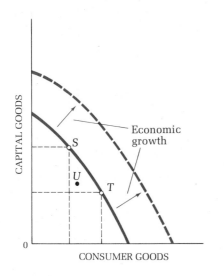

What Is Economic Growth?

Productivity and economic growth go hand in hand. However, there is often confusion about the meaning of economic growth. This is because politicians and economists are fond of hurling statistics at each other showing growth rates of various countries or regions over different periods. Hence, an accurate definition is needed.

> *Economic growth* is the rate of increase in an economy's full-employment real output or income over time. That is, economic growth is the rise in an economy's full-employment output in constant prices. Economic growth may be expressed in either of two ways:
>
> **1.** As the increase in total full-employment real GNP or *NNP* over time.
>
> **2.** As the increase in per-capita full-employment real GNP or *NNP* over time.

The first of these measures is usually employed to describe the expansion of a nation's economic output. The second is used to express the development of its material standard of living and to compare it with that of other nations.

In the most fundamental sense, the study of economic growth is concerned with policy measures aimed at expanding a nation's *capacity* to produce. It thus contrasts with monetary and fiscal policies, which seek to make full and efficient use of a nation's existing capacity.

The concept of economic growth can be illustrated in terms of the familiar production-possibilities curves in Exhibit 2. Since each curve represents an economy's capacity to produce, an outward shift of the curve is a measure of a nation's economic growth.

Measuring Economic Growth

Is the economy of the United States growing, declining, or stagnating? How does its growth compare with that of the economy of the USSR? With that of the economy of Japan? The answers are determined by the way in which we measure growth. Although the definition seems clear-cut, experts do not always agree on the results, because the methods of calculation can involve some slippery procedures. Economists, therefore, simply use past measures of output or income, as suggested by the definition of economic growth, and derive long-term growth trends from these historical records. Frequently, the trends are projected into the future at various assumed compound rates of growth—like money growing at compound interest in a savings account.

What Factors Determine Economic Growth?

Suppose we assume that aggregate demand is sufficient to maintain full employment and that government will take the necessary monetary and fiscal measures to assure this. The growth of real GNP will then be determined by improvements in the nation's resources and the "environment" in which they are used. These major growth-determining factors include:

1. Quantity and quality of human resources.

2. Quantity and quality of "natural" resources.

3. Accumulation of capital.

4. Specialization and scale of production.

5. Rate of technological progress.

6. Environmental factors.

These are also the kinds of factors that influence an economy's production-possibilities curve. Over the next several pages, we shall examine each of them in turn.

Quantity and Quality of Human Resources

On the basis of our earlier definition of economic growth, the following simple formula is a convenient guide for discussion:

$$\text{real GNP per capita} = \frac{\text{total real GNP}}{\text{population}}$$

The rate of economic growth is measured by the rate at which the left side of this equation, at full employment, increases over time. This in turn will depend on the rate at which the numerator of the right side of the equation, at full employment, increases relative to the denominator.

> The faster the rate of increase in total real GNP at full employment as compared to the rate of increase in population, the greater the rise in real GNP per capita. Hence, the rate of economic growth will be faster also.

The formula above uses population only in quantitative terms. But there are quantitative and qualitative considerations alike that should be taken into account. For instance, increases in population will bring about increases in the size of the labor force—that is, in the number of people working or looking for work. The productivity of the labor force will influence the rate of economic growth. The chief factors determining labor productivity include:

The quality of human and natural resources, like their quantity, is an important factor in a nation's economic growth.

• Time spent at work, such as the average length of the workweek.

• Education, health, and skills of workers.

• Quantity and quality of the tools and capital equipment used by workers.

Over the past several decades, modern industrial nations have experienced a steady decline in the first of these factors along with a continuous increase in the last two.

Thus, the *quality* of a country's human resources (as well as their quantity) influences the country's economic growth.

Quantity and Quality of "Natural" Resources (Land)

An economy's output and economic growth also depend on the quantity and quality of its soil, minerals, water, timber, and so on. These are commonly referred to as natural resources. In economics, however, they are classified under the general heading of "land" as a factor of production.

Some economists contend that there is no such thing as a "natural" resource. They argue that resources provided by nature are of no value to society unless people are able to put them to use. When that happens, the resources are no longer natural. A nation may be rich in resources, but its material well-being or rate of economic growth will not be influenced in the slightest if these resources remain "natural," or untapped. Consequently, demand and cost conditions must be favorable if a resource is to be converted from a natural (or "neutral") to a positive state. This means that there must be a high enough level of demand for the products that the resource will help to produce. There must also be an adequate supply of capital, labor, and technical skills to transform the resource by putting it to a profitable use.

Of course, the quantity and quality of a nation's natural resources are not necessarily fixed. By diverting some of its *existing* labor and capital into research, a society may be able to discover or develop *new* natural resources within its own borders that will enhance its future rate of economic growth. In terms of the production-possibilities curve, this means that some consumer goods must be sacrificed in the present to enable the economy to reach a higher curve in the future.

Accumulation of Capital

By saving a larger proportion of its income (or by consuming a smaller proportion of it), a society acquires the funds it needs to finance capital accumulation.

A society must also forgo some current consumption in order to build capital goods such as factories, machines, transportation facilities, dams, and educational institutions. The rate at which a nation can add to its stock of capital will influence its economic growth.

Why is the rate of capital accumulation greater in some countries than in others? You have already learned in the study of macroeconomic theory that many considerations may influence investment. Two, however, are fundamental: (1) profit expectations of business executives and (2) government policies toward investment. Although the influence of these conditions differs among nations, one aspect of the process of capital accumulation is relevant to all—the necessity for sacrifice.

Thus, capital accumulation is closely related to the volume of savings. This is the portion of a society's income that is not spent for consumption. In order to add to their long-run stock of capital goods, the people of a country must refrain from consuming a portion of their current output (or income) so that a larger proportion of it can be devoted to new investment. This principle helps to explain why poor countries, like poor families, are ordinarily unable to save as much as rich ones and, hence, experience little or no economic growth. In general:

> The *cost* of economic growth to a society is the consumption that it must sacrifice in order to save for the purpose of accumulating capital.

Specialization and Scale of Production

> The greatest improvement in the productive powers of labor and the greater part of the skill, dexterity, and judgment with which it is anywhere directed, or applied, seem to have been the effects of the division of labour.

So said Adam Smith in *The Wealth of Nations*. Smith then gave the celebrated example of a pin factory: "One man draws out the wire, another straights it, a third cuts it, a fourth points it, a fifth grinds it . . ." and, as a result, there is a far greater output than if each man were to make the entire pin himself.

Smith also made the interesting point that the division of labor is limited by the "extent of the market." He observed that, in a small isolated economy, there will be less division of labor and a smaller scale of operations to satisfy local needs than in a large exchange economy, such as Glasgow's, or a still larger one, such as London's.

These comments on specialization and scale of production provide significant insights into the process of economic growth. In the early stages of a nation's economic development, production is relatively non-specialized and the scale of operations is small. In such circumstances, businesses often produce only to supply the needs of the surrounding community, without advancing to the factory stage of production.

Gains in technology permit advances in the scale of production, resulting in larger volumes of output at lower unit costs and prices.

This situation prevailed in the United States until the end of the eighteenth century. But, with the expansion of the market and advances in the technology of production, more specialization and a greater scale of operations became possible. Larger volumes of output and lower unit costs were thus realized. This has become a continuing process in the economic growth of nations and regions.

> Economic growth is not just an increase in the quantity of the factors of production. Economic growth involves fundamental changes in the organization and techniques of production. These include changes in the *structure* of production as represented by the input–output relationships that characterize an economy's firms and industries.

A nation's economic growth, therefore, will be determined in part by the potential it has for increasing the specialization of its resources and the scale of its production. Thus, there are qualitative as well as quantitative considerations that determine economic growth.

Rate of Technological Progress

One of the most important qualitative factors influencing economic growth is the rate of technological progress. This is the speed at which new knowledge is both developed and applied to raising the standard of living.

Technological progress must be accompanied by appropriate institutional and economic innovations in order to stimulate high rates of growth.

If you remember your study of American history, you will recall that the early nineteenth century was a period of rapid technological advancement. The invention of the cotton gin, the steamboat, the milling machine, the locomotive, and numerous other devices contributed enormously to the young nation's economic progress.

It must be kept in mind, however, that these technological advances were accompanied by legal and economic innovations that also had important consequences for the nation's development. Two particularly spectacular advances that occurred during the early 1800s were critical:

1. *The rapid growth of banking, including the creation of a government bank as well as several dozen state-chartered banks.* These provided new and important sources of credit for business transactions.

2. *The rapid adoption of the corporate form of business organization.* This provided opportunities for accumulating large amounts of finance capital (money) with limited liability on the part of owners.

In an expanding economy in which risk taking was a vital element of growth, these features made possible the financing and adoption of the technical innovations mentioned above. Clearly, therefore:

Technological progress involves more than just invention. Technological progress embraces an effort on the part of society as a whole to get the most out of existing resources and to discover new and better resources through continuous improvements in education, engineering, management, and marketing.

Environmental Factors

Many environmental factors, such as the banking, legal, and tax systems, play essential roles in encouraging economic growth.

All of the points considered thus far lead to an important conclusion: *The political, social, cultural, and economic environment must be favorable if significant growth is to occur.* This means, among other things, that there must be a *banking and credit system* capable of financing growth. There must be a *legal system* that establishes the ground rules of business behavior. There must be a *tax system* that does not discourage new investment and risk taking. And there must be a *stable government* that is sympathetic to economic expansion.

It is no accident that such countries as the United States, Canada, the United Kingdom, Japan, and the USSR have experienced periods of rapid economic growth despite their different political systems. Some Latin American and Asian countries, on the other hand, have had little or no significant economic growth for many years—and in some cases even for many decades.

Conclusion: The Problem of Measurement

Of the six factors discussed here, how important is each in determining a country's economic growth? Can we measure their separate influences? These questions are extremely difficult to answer, because some causes of growth are qualitative rather than quantitative. Consequently, there is a tendency among economists to reduce the determinants of growth to three sets of "measurable" factors:

Since the early 1900s, "technical progress," defined as all factors other than labor and capital, has been responsible for most of the increase in the nation's output per person.

1. Growth of the labor force.

2. Growth of capital.

3. Technical progress (that is, "all other things").

The first two factors can be measured quite precisely, whereas the third cannot. Therefore, in measuring the causes of an economy's growth, the contributions of the first two factors to total economic growth are estimated quantitatively. Then the contribution of the third factor is viewed as a "residual" or catchall for all determinants other than labor and capital.

As a simple example, if an economy grows at the rate of 6 percent annually over a given period and 4 percent of that growth is estimated to have been due to the growth of labor and capital combined, the remaining 2 percent might be attributed to technical progress. For purposes of measurement, therefore, "technical progress" includes such things as better machinery and technology, better management, and greater labor skills.

How important is technical progress?

It has been estimated that, in the United States, more than 80 percent of the increase in output per capita since the early part of the century has been due to technical progress. This leaves less than 20 percent to be explained by the other two factors. In terms of *total* output (as distinct from output per capita), technical progress has accounted for approximately 50 percent of the growth of production in the United States and various other industrial nations.

This suggests that economic growth is best envisioned as a continuous development and discovery of new and better ways of doing things. Economic growth is *more* than just a quantitative expansion of existing inputs or outputs.

Case
Technological Progress: Classic Examples in America's Early Development

A remarkable series of events took place in the United States within the short space of thirteen years, between 1790 and 1803. It demonstrates how the rate of technological progress can influence the evolution of a national economy.

In 1790, a brilliant young Englishman, Samuel Slater, employed by a merchant firm in Rhode Island, began spinning cotton thread by machine, thus marking the first effective introduction of the factory system in this country. In the same year, John Fitch constructed and operated successfully the world's first regularly scheduled steamboat. When this was later employed on Western waters, it cut the costs of transportation remarkably and enabled the West to become part of the national economy.

In 1793, Eli Whitney invented the cotton gin, which made possible the extensive cultivation of cotton and subsequently transformed the economy of the South. In 1800, this same young graduate of Yale College contracted to manufacture 10,000 rifles for the government. He succeeded in producing them with precisely made interchangeable parts—the first step toward assembly-line production.

In 1803, a Philadelphia inventor named Oliver Evans achieved almost complete automation in the milling of wheat into flour by an ingenious system of machines that weighed, cleaned, ground, and packed the flour with virtually no human assistance.

These and other inventions of the era played a key role in the nation's economic growth during the nineteenth century.

The Bettmann Archive

Carding, drawing, roving, and spinning in Slater's Mill, 1790.

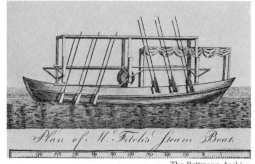
The Bettmann Archive

John Fitch's first steamboat, Philadelphia, 1790.

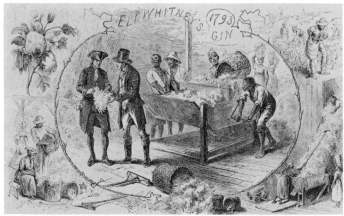
The Bettmann Archive

Eli Whitney's first cotton gin, 1793.

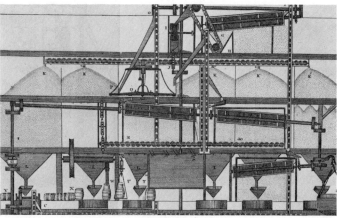
The Historical Society of Pennsylvania

Oliver Evans's automated mill, Philadelphia, 1803.

Exhibit 3

Investment and the Growth of Capacity at Full Employment

In the upper figure, let the output at N_1 be the full-employment NNP in Year 1. Then saving in that year will be C_1S_1. This amount, when invested in plant and equipment, will increase productive capacity in Year 2 by N_1N_2. Saving and investment must then rise to C_2S_2. This in turn will increase productive capacity in Year 3 by N_2N_3. Investment must thus rise by *increasing amounts,* as emphasized in the lower figure, in order to sustain full employment of a *growing productive capacity.*

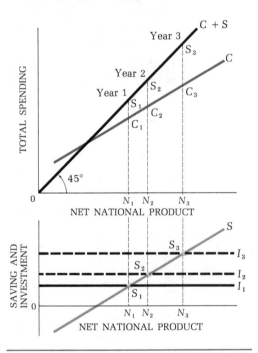

A Simple Growth Model

Modern approaches to the theory of economic growth are closely tied to analysis of business cycles. The reasons are obvious. When we studied business cycles, we learned that an economy's rate of growth will vary in different stages of the cycle. We also learned that, if the consumption function is assumed to be stable, the level of income and employment is determined by net investment.

But in the study of economic growth, net investment has yet another function: *It adds to the economy's capacity.* Therefore, the more the net investment undertaken in any one period, the greater will be the productive capacity of the economy in the next period. Consequently, as you will see, the level of investment will have to be raised again to sustain aggregate demand and full employment at the new capacity output.

The Capital–Output Ratio

This point is illustrated by the familiar consumption-function diagram in the upper figure in Exhibit 3. For simplicity, only the private sector is represented; the influence of the public sector (government) is excluded. Let us suppose that the output at N_1 represents the economy's full-employment NNP in Year 1. Hence, the corresponding level of consumption is, N_1C_1 and the corresponding level of saving is C_1S_1. We assume that this volume of saving flows into new investment—that is, that planned saving equals planned investment—so that the output at N_1 is maintained.

As a result of this new investment, the economy's capacity to produce is enlarged in Year 2 to the output at N_2. In order to produce this output, the volume of planned saving C_2S_2 must flow into new investment. If it does, the capacity of the economy will be further enlarged in Year 3 to the output at N_3.

If this process continues, the economy's ability to produce will expand by increasing amounts. Therefore, *increasing levels of investment* will be needed to sustain full employment of a *growing productive capacity.* This is further emphasized by the lower figure in Exhibit 3. Here the level of investment each year shifts upward by larger and larger amounts.

How much will the economy's productive capacity rise each year? The answer depends on the *capital–output ratio.* This is the relationship between the economy's stock of real capital and the resulting output or productive capacity. A ratio of 3:1, for instance, which has been the approximate long-run trend in the United States, means that 3 units of capital produce 1 unit of output per period.

Full-Employment Growth Rate

We can extend the foregoing ideas to develop an important formula that is widely used as an expression of economic growth at full employment. In addition to assuming full employment, let us also assume that *saving equals investment* and that all investment results in an increase in *capital.*

On this basis, if we know the *average propensity to save*—that is, the proportion of the economy's income or output that is not spent on consumption—we can tell how much savings will flow into investment and hence into the creation of additional capital. Then, if we also know the capital–output ratio, we can calculate the expected full-employment growth of NNP.

The procedure is illustrated in Exhibit 4. Columns (1) and (2) show the full-employment output for each year represented by NNP. For convenience, we begin with an arbitrary NNP of $100 in Year 1. In column (3) of the table, saving equals investment or the increase in capital, and the average propensity to save, APS, is assumed to be 10 percent. This is equivalent, of course, to saying that the average propensity to consume is 90 percent. If we assume that the capital–output ratio is also 3:1, the resulting increase in output will be one-third of the increase in capital, as shown in column (4). This increase in output then becomes the next year's addition to NNP in column (2), as emphasized by the arrows. The table can thus be extended very easily by simply continuing the pattern. That is, take 10 percent of NNP, calculate one-third of that, and add the result to the current year's NNP to get next year's NNP.

You may be able to estimate from the table that the full-employment output of NNP is growing at a rate of something more than 3 percent per year. However, a closer estimate can be made in terms of the variables in the model by applying a simple formula. Thus:

$$\text{full-employment growth rate} = \frac{\text{average propensity to save}}{\text{capital–output ratio}}$$

This basic formula is widely used in modern theories of economic growth. It can be applied for any average propensity to consume and for any capital–output ratio. In the model above, for example, we assumed a long-run APS of 0.10 and a capital–output ratio of 3. Hence, the full-employment growth rate is 0.10/3 = 0.033, or 3.3 percent per year. Of course, a larger or smaller growth rate can be obtained, depending on the values of the APS and the capital–output ratio used in the formula.

The growth-rate formula and the simple model on which it is based are useful primarily because they illustrate important relationships. But it should be kept in mind that they assume a number of simplifying conditions. Among them:

1. A fixed capital–output ratio.

2. A fixed average propensity to save.

3. A neglect of such real-world factors as business taxes, government monetary and fiscal policies, and changes in technology.

These assumptions are the subject of much debate among economists.

International Comparisons and the Sources of Growth

How does America's growth rate compare with that of other relatively advanced nations? Some information for selected countries covering different periods of time is presented in Exhibit 5, Figures (a) and (b).

As the facts indicate, nations may differ widely in their rates of growth. This is because growth is determined by various interacting factors, as explained earlier. For convenience, they may be summarized broadly in terms of the classification given in the table in Exhibit 5, which shows sources of U.S. economic growth. This table provides

Exhibit 4
The Full-Employment Rate of Economic Growth

What will be the full-employment NNP for Year 5? To find out, take 10 percent of Year 4's NNP, then calculate one-third of that, and add the result to the NNP for Year 4. The arrows illustrate the pattern to be followed.

(1) Year	(2) Full-employment output, NNP	(3) Saving = investment = increase in capital (APS = 0.10) [10% of column (2)]	(4) Resulting increase in output (capital/output = 3/1) [⅓ of column (3)]
1	$100.00	$10.00	
			$3.33
2	103.33	10.33	
			3.44
3	106.77	10.68	
			3.56
4	110.33		

Exhibit 5
Comparative Growth Rates and Sources

The growth rates of advanced countries can vary considerably over the years. This is because the various sources of growth, both quantitative and qualitative, differ markedly from one nation to another.

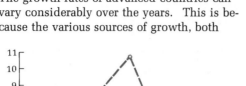

Figure (a): Growth rates of real GNP. Figure (b): Growth rates of real GNP per capita.

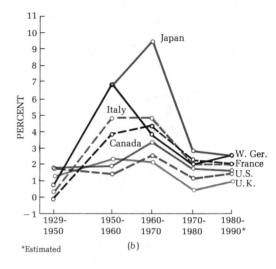

*Estimated   (a)

*Estimated   (b)

Figures (c) and (d): *Educational attainment and expenditures on public elementary and secondary education in the U.S. A rising level of educational attainment is the same as an increase in human-capital investment. The productive potential of workers is enhanced, thereby benefiting employers, employees, and society as a whole.*

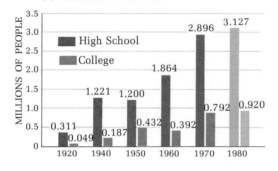

(c) NUMBER OF GRADUATES

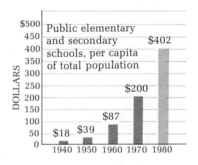

(d) EXPENDITURES

Sources of U.S. economic growth. The factor that has been contributing most significantly to economic growth since 1929 has been a "qualitative" one: improved education and training of human resources.

Contributions to real national income	1909–1929	1930–1949	1950–1979	1980–2000*
Quantitative factors				
Increase in quantity of labor†	39%	30%	26%	22%
Increase in quantity of capital	26	21	15	12
Qualitative factors‡				
Improved education and training	13	25	30	36
Improved technology	12	18	22	25
All other things§	10	6	7	5
Total growth in real national income	100%	100%	100%	100%

* United Nations estimates.
† Adjusted for decreases in the workweek.
‡ Some qualitative factors are at least partially quantitative. Improvements in education, for example, depend on the number of years of schooling as well as on the quality of schooling.
§ Consists primarily of increased economies of large-scale production resulting from the expanding size of the market.

Source: Adapted with changes from Edward Denison, *The Sources of Economic Growth in the United States* (New York: Committee for Economic Development, 1962); Joint Economic Committee of the Congress, 1972; United Nations periodic reports.

rough estimates of the contribution that each factor makes to the nation's total economic growth.

Note that before 1929, increases in the *quantitative* factors—the supplies of labor and capital—accounted for about two-thirds of the economy's expansion. The remaining one-third resulted from increases in such qualitative factors as improvements in education and training, technology, and "all other things." Since 1929, the situation has been almost reversed. The *qualitative* factors have played a more important role in economic growth while the quantitative factors have been less important.

Conclusion: Investment in Human Capital

The information suggests that improvements in education and training have become the single most important factor contributing to economic growth. In other words, the scarcest resource for our society is not land or muscle power, but brain power. The advances of modern science and technology are making this increasingly evident. Hence:

> Our investment in human capital reflects rising long-run trends in the number of high-school and college graduates and in expenditures on public elementary and secondary education. These trends will continue to rise in the years to come. The reason is that society's returns from investment in human capital are higher than its returns from investment in capital goods.

Economics in the News

WHY GAINS IN PRODUCTIVITY DECLINE

Choose One or More Reasons, or All of the Above

by Craig Pernick

Washington—When there is a slowing of the rate of increase in the nation's productivity (the gain in its output per worker), everybody suffers. Society gets less production from employed resources.

Why might the growth of productivity become sluggish? The answer can depend on many factors. Here are the ones that are most often cited.

Rapidly Expanding Labor Force
The United States experienced an unprecedented increase in the number of job seekers since the 1960s as many more women and young people entered the labor market. The relatively large proportion of these less skilled workers reduced overall productivity. This trend, however, should reverse itself in the coming years as the average age of the work force increases and the number of job applicants declines.

Insufficient Capital Investment
Business expenditures on new plant and equipment are the lifeblood of the economy. When these shrink, as sometimes happens, the results can show up in lower productivity. This is why business executives emphasize the importance of maintaining a rising level of investment per worker. By providing workers with more and better equipment, labor productivity increases.

Government policies designed to encourage investment are therefore important. Favorable tax and depreciation policies are the first things that come to mind. But policies that encourage savings are also needed in order to provide the funds for new investment.

Research and Development
Advances in technology are the result of scientific efforts. These require growing expenditures on research and development. If spending slows, the rate of technological advance is retarded, dragging productivity with it. Therefore, government tax policies should treat expenditures on research and development as capital investments, permitting accelerated write-offs in order to encourage new technology.

Employee Motivation
Capital investment alone cannot generate productivity gains. Workers must want to make use of the capital support that management provides. Otherwise, gains in productivity will be small (if not negative). This is why many companies are experimenting with new approaches to labor relations and new forms of job organization. Workers are being given greater opportunities than ever before to express their views about how job assignments should be allocated and how work programs should be organized. Progressive managers want workers to see themselves not as cogs in a wheel but as members of a team striving for achievement and recognition.

What You Have Learned in This Chapter

1. Productivity is the ratio of output to input. Although there are different indexes of productivity, all seek to measure the ways in which resources are used and the extent of their use.

2. Economists are interested in measuring partial-factor productivity as well as total-factor productivity. The former is usually based on one input, whereas the latter is based on all inputs. Because of the difficulty of measuring *all* inputs used in production, partial-factor productivity indexes are much more widely employed than total-factor productivity indexes.

3. Productivity is the key to economic growth —a rising level of real income per person. A major step toward improving productivity is the promotion of new investment in plant and equipment. This requires the adoption of economic policies aimed at encouraging rapid advances in technology.

4. Many factors determine a nation's economic growth. Among them are the quantity and quality of human and natural resources, the rate of capital accumulation, the degree of specialization and scale of production, the rate of technological progress, and the nature of the socioeconomic and political environment. For measurement purposes, however, these are usually reduced to three sets of factors: (a) growth of the labor force, (b) growth of capital, and (c) technical progress (or "all other things" not represented by the previous two measurable factors).

5. The full-employment growth of an economy's productive capacity depends on its capital–output ratio. For the United States, the ratio has had a long-run trend of about 3:1. A basic approach for measuring the full-employment growth rate is to divide the average propensity to save by the capital–output ratio. This formula is based, however, on a number of simplifying conditions, thus making it useful only for illustrating some important relationships.

For Discussion

1. *Terms and concepts to review:*
productivity
partial productivity
total-factor productivity
index numbers
economic growth
capital–output ratio

2. It is often contended that increased government spending, as a percent of GNP, slows down productivity and, therefore, the rate of growth of real output. Can you suggest at least three reasons why?

3. It is often said that pollution controls hurt productivity. Can you explain why this may be true?

4. Is our economic definition of growth "better" than the biological definition, which expresses growth as an *organic process*—a transference of material from one part of an organism (such as the human body) to another? Explain.

5. What are the shortcomings of the economic definition of growth? That is, what sort of "amenities" does the definition omit as far as the growth of a society is concerned?

6. The factors that determine an economy's growth are both quantitative and qualitative. The quantitative factors are susceptible to measurement and can be incorporated in a growth model. Does this mean that such models are incomplete to the extent that qualitative factors are omitted? What can be done about correcting the situation? Explain your answer.

7. How is the full-employment growth rate of an economy influenced by the size of its *APS* relative to its capital–output ratio? Can you suggest some general policies that the government can adopt through the tax system to reduce the capital–output ratio and thus stimulate economic growth?

8. (a) It has been suggested that the income tax system, which provides equal deductions for each dependent, might be revised with the objective of regulating family size by taxation. How might this be done? Develop a specific example.
(b) What do you think of a population-control plan that parallels several decades of American agricultural policy, giving subsidies for "fallow acres" and penalties for "overcropping"?

The Classical Explanation of Growth: How Economics Became the "Dismal Science"

In the late eighteenth and early nineteenth centuries, certain classical British economists formulated theories that dealt in large part with economic development. These economists included Adam Smith, David Ricardo, and Thomas Malthus. The conclusions of Ricardo and Malthus were basically pessimistic. They argued that a country's economic growth must end in decline and stagnation. The ideas of these men compose what may appropriately be called the "classical" theory of economic growth. Their views are interesting and can help us to understand modern economic problems of growth.

The classical explanation of growth provides some interesting insights into today's overpopulation problem in many parts of the world.

The Subsistence Theory and Diminishing Returns

The classical model of economic growth is based on a *subsistence theory*. In its simplest form the classical model can be expressed in terms of two basic propositions:

1. The population of a country tends to adjust to a subsistence level of living.

2. Increases in population, with technology and natural resources (land) held constant, result *eventually* in decreasing incomes per capita as a result of the operation of the "law of diminishing returns."

These concepts are illustrated in Exhibit 1. The population of a country is scaled on the horizontal axis, and its material standard of living (as measured by real income per capita) is scaled on the vertical. The curve labeled *L* shows the actual level of living that the society can maintain for various levels of population applied to the fixed quantity of

Exhibit 1
The Subsistence Theory and Diminishing Returns

In the classical model of Ricardo and Malthus, the actual level-of-living curve L depends on the size of the population (or number of workers) applied to a fixed amount of land. The population tends toward an equilibrium level at M. This corresponds to the subsistence level represented by the distance MR. Even an upward shift of the actual level-of-living curve from L to L', due to the development of new resources or new production techniques, is of short-run duration. The population simply expands to the new size at K, leaving the average output per person, KT, at the same subsistence level as before.

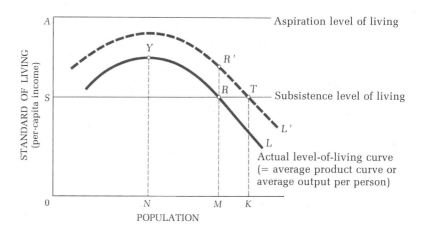

other resources. The L curve may therefore be thought of as an *average product curve* representing the average output per person (or per worker). It results from adding more and more people to a given amount of land while production techniques are held constant.

The average product or actual level-of-living curve (L) rises to a maximum and then declines. This represents the eventual tendency for "diminishing returns" to set in as a growing population is applied to a fixed amount of resources. The ideal or *optimum population* is therefore at N, because this yields a level of living equal to the distance NY. This is the highest level attainable on the curve. Any other combination of population and fixed resources is not optimal because it yields a lower output per person.

The classical economists contended that there was some standard of living at which the population—especially the working population—would just maintain itself, with no tendency to increase or decrease. They called this the "subsistence level." Although determined primarily by physical or biological requirements, this level is also determined by social and customary needs, which in turn influence the rearing of children.

Thus, the classicists argued that, if wages per worker fell below the subsistence level, people would tend to stop having children and the population would decline, thereby increasing real income per capita. Conversely, if wages per worker rose above the subsistence level, people would tend to start having more children and the population would increase, thereby lowering real income per capita. This early-nineteenth-century classical theory is known as the *subsistence theory of wages* (also called the *iron*, or *brazen, law of wages*).

Although the early classical economists did not use graphs, these ideas can be expressed as shown in Exhibit 1. Thus, suppose the standard of living at S represents the subsistence level of living. Then the equilibrium size of the population, according to the classicists, is $0M$ ($=SR$). The reason is that if the population is larger than $0M$, the actual level of living will be below the subsistence level. Hence, the population will decline and real income per capita will therefore increase. On the other hand, if the population is less than 0M, the actual level of living will be above the subsistence level. Consequently, the population will increase and real income per capita will therefore decrease. Thus, it is apparent that the "subsistence level" in the classical model is a long-run equilibrium level of living for the population as a whole.

Economics—The "Dismal Science"

Because of this pessimistic theory, economics (or political economy, as it used to be called) came to be known as the "dismal science." Clearly, if the subsistence level of living is a long-run equilibrium toward which society is always tending, there is no hope of ever improving the future of humankind. Even the discovery of new natural resources or the implementation of new production techniques would at best provide only temporary benefits until the population had time to adjust to these new developments. Then, a larger number of people would be left living in the same minimal circumstances as before.

The gloomy conclusions of the classical theory led to economics being called "the dismal science."

For example, suppose that new natural resources are discovered, or more land becomes available, or new production techniques are developed. The effect, as shown in Exhibit 1, is to raise the average product curve from L to L', for now the same population has more or better fixed resources with which to work. However, this increase in benefits per person from MR to MR' will be of limited duration. Because average product is now above the subsistence level, the population will increase until it reaches a new equilibrium at K. At this point, more people will be living at the same subsistence level $0S$ (=KT) than before.

The Malthusian Specter

Among the early English classical economists, there was one whose theory of population (illustrated by the above model) is especially well known. His name was Thomas R. Malthus, and his famous theory is often encountered in various social-science courses.

Malthus theorized that, unless preventive measures are taken, population growth will outrun the food supply, thereby leading to misery and poverty.

> *The Malthusian theory of population* (first published by Malthus in 1798 and revised in 1803) stated that population increases faster than the means of subsistence. That is, population tends to increase as a geometric progression (1, 2, 4, 8, 16, 32, and so on) while the means of subsistence increase at most only as an arithmetic progression (1, 2, 3, 4, 5, 6, and so on). This is because a growing population applied to a fixed amount of land results in eventually diminishing returns to workers. Human beings are therefore destined to misery and poverty unless the rate of population growth is retarded. This may be accomplished either by preventive checks, such as moral restraint, late marriages, and celibacy; or, if these fail, by positive checks, such as wars, famines, and disease.

Has the prediction of Malthus been realized? There is no doubt that it has in certain crowded, underdeveloped areas of Asia, Africa, and South America. In these regions, the Malthusian specter hangs like a dark cloud. Here, industrialization and economic growth are impeded because agriculture is inefficient and unable to feed both the people on farms and those who live and work in the cities. In many of these areas, wars, famines, and disease are the main curbs on population, although major efforts are being made to encourage use of contraception.

Some Proposed Solutions

Can the underdeveloped, overpopulated countries escape from the "Malthusian trap"? Three ways out may be suggested.

One solution would be to shift millions of people from overpopulated to underpopulated regions—from the small farms in Southeast Asia, for example, to the vast jungles of South America that await development. But the many obvious political and social obstacles make this policy unrealistic.

A second possibility would be to develop new resources and production techniques. This would need to be done at a sufficiently rapid rate so that the upward shifts of the average product curve would more than offset the growth in population. In this way, the population would never catch up with the rising level of output per person, and the level of living would continually increase.

A third approach would be to seek ways of raising the "subsistence level" to the point at which it becomes an *aspiration level,* a target or a goal for which to strive. In Exhibit 1, for example, the standard of living (which is measured along the vertical axis of the graph) might be raised from the level at S to the level at A. Note that this new level is above the maximum possible level of living that is attainable with any present combination of population and resources. Therefore, there might be continual pressure on people to reduce the existing population in order to rise higher on the average product curve. Alternatively, there might be sufficient pressure on people to discover and develop new resources and production techniques that the entire average product curve is shifted upward. It is more likely, however, that some combination of both possibilities would probably occur.

The "Hot-Baths" Hypothesis

There may be a relationship between population and living standards that automatically causes a nation's population to stabilize at its economically optimum size.

The second and third solutions, in varying degrees, have occurred and are continuing to occur in the economic development of some of today's advanced nations. The third approach, that of raising the subsistence level to an aspiration level, is based on a fascinating assumption. It suggests that a relationship may exist between population growth and living standards in many overpopulated, underdeveloped countries. This "connection," so to speak, can be called—facetiously—the *hot-baths hypothesis:*

> There may be a significant relationship between human fertility rates and "hot baths." That is, once a society reaches a certain minimum level of living at which it has a reasonable abundance of the creature comforts of life—adequate food, clothing, housing, sanitation, and so on—its desire for more and better material things, as measured by its aspiration level, continually rises. If this is true, then the society's population will tend automatically to seek its economically optimum size through the practice of birth control. But this assumes that the society's living conditions can first be brought (probably with outside help from other nations) to the minimum threshold level.

To repeat, this is only an hypothesis—a tentative proposition that has yet to be explored and tested in different nations under varying cultural and social conditions. Nevertheless, it is an interesting and important concept. Indeed, foreign aid to poor, overpopulated nations has sought, in large part, to raise living conditions in those countries to some

minimum level at which their economies can break out of their stationary states and enter a new phase of more self-sustaining and self-propel-
ling economic growth.

Capital Deepening and Diminishing Returns

The subsistence theory of wages in the classical model implies the existence of a *subsistence theory of profits* as well.

For example, the model of population growth that was developed in
Exhibit 1 may be adapted to serve as a model of the growth of nonhuman
capital. This includes buildings, machines, inventories, and so on.
This can be done by measuring the rate of return along the vertical axis
and the total stock of capital along the horizontal axis. The curve L is
then the "profitability" curve of capital, which results from applying different amounts of capital to a fixed quantity of other resources.

When looked at in this way, the model indicates that capital is accumulated in anticipation of future interest returns or profits. Thus, when
the stock of capital in the economy is relatively low, the anticipated return on capital is high, thereby encouraging further accumulation. As
capital is accumulated, however, the law of diminishing returns eventually sets in. If we suppose that $0S$ represents the "subsistence rate" of
profits, capital accumulation will proceed to the level at M. Improvements in any of the fixed resources or in production techniques will, of
course, shift the profit curve upward from L to L', thereby bringing about
a further accumulation of capital to the amount at K.

> An increase in the stock of capital relative to other resources, especially
> labor, is called *capital deepening*. What are the effects of such a deepening,
> assuming that there are no changes in technology? Clearly, with the opera-
> tion of the inexorable law of diminishing returns, the interest or profit rate
> on capital must *decline*. Simultaneously, the real wages of labor must *rise*
> as this resource becomes more and more scarce relative to the growing stock
> of capital.

The Wages-Fund Theory

These ideas gradually led to a reformulation of the subsistence theory of
wages in the classical model. The reformulation, known as the "wages-
fund" theory, existed or was implied in the writings of Smith (1776) and
Ricardo (1817). However, it was best articulated several decades later,
in 1848, by John Stuart Mill—not only the greatest economist of his time
but also one of history's most distinguished intellectuals.

The *wages-fund theory* was a mid-nineteenth-century classical theory of wages. The theory held that the producer sets aside, from his capital, funds with which to hire the workers needed for production. The
producer does this because of the indirect or "roundabout" nature of the
production process: It takes time for goods to be produced, sold, and
paid for. Therefore, workers must be given advance payments—out of
the producer's "wages fund"—to meet their basic needs. The amount of
the wages fund, and hence the real wage of labor, depends directly on
the size of the capital stock relative to the number of workers. But in the
long run, as we have seen in the classical model, the accumulation of
capital tends to be determined by the minimum subsistence rate of profits. Hence, the only effective way to raise real wages is to reduce the
number of workers or the size of the population.

*The classical model concluded that profits
will decline to a minimum "subsistence"
level as the stock of capital grows relative to
other resources, especially labor.*

Leaders in Economics

Thomas Robert Malthus
1766–1834

Brown Brothers

In the last third of the eighteenth century, two great problems occupied the attention of most thinking people in England. One was widespread poverty; the other was how many British subjects there were. Socialists called attention to the poverty problem with a promise of a Utopian world—a paradise—in which all would be well. The population problem had prompted Adam Smith to remark in *The Wealth of Nations* (1776) that "No society can surely be flourishing and happy, of which the far greater part of the members are poor and miserable."

Famous Theory
Were England's resources adequate to bring about a fulfillment of the socialists' dreams? A theretofore unknown English clergyman, Thomas Robert Malthus, thought not. In 1798, he published a treatise of fifty thousand words entitled *An Essay on the Principle of Population, As It Affects the Future Improvement of Society*. The essay was based on his observations and travels in various countries. From these he expounded his

famous rule that "population, when unchecked, goes on doubling every twenty-five years or increases in a geometric ratio," but the means of subsistence can only increase in an arithmetic ratio.

Malthus became a professor of history and published a revision of his essay in 1803. In this he moderated his rigid "formula" and spoke more of a *tendency* of population to outrun the supply of food. Human beings, he concluded, were destined to misery and poverty unless the rate of population growth is retarded either by preventive checks (such as moral restraint, late marriages, and celibacy) or, if these fail, by positive checks (such as wars, famine, and disease).

Grim Consequences
Malthus and his population theory were severely criticized by people in nearly every walk of life—politicians, clergymen, philosophers, and journalists. All of them raised cries of heresy. Some, like an editor of the *Quarterly Review* (July 1817), admitted that it was easier simply "to disbelieve Mr. Malthus than to refute him." But some, notably Ricardo and other classical economists, made Malthus's theory the basis of their own theories of wages and rent.

The generalizations expressed by Malthus have been recognized by governments throughout the world and by the United Nations in its efforts to assist the overpopulated, underdeveloped countries. Although there may be a tendency to dismiss the gloomy forebodings of the Malthusian theory, its warnings cannot be pushed aside. They are a stark reality for millions of people in many nations today.

Other Achievements: Anticipating Keynes
In addition to his population theory, Malthus made outstanding contributions to economics, notably in his *Principles of Political Economy* (1820). He was an intimate friend of David Ricardo, and it is impossible to disassociate their economic views, even though the two men were often in substantial disagreement. For one thing, Ricardo was as incapable of grasping the pragmatic and empirical approach of Malthus as Malthus was incapable of appreciating the rigor and subtle deductive reasoning of Ricardo.

Among the notable contributions that Malthus made to economic thought was the concept of "effective demand." He defined this as the level of aggregate demand necessary to maintain continuous production. More than a century was to pass before the problem of effective demand would rise again to public notice. In his *General Theory*, John Maynard Keynes paid tribute to the pioneering work of Malthus on this subject.

Conclusion: The Classical View of Growth

These ideas led the English classical economists—especially Ricardo—to the conclusion that the development of an economy depends on the relative growth of two critical variables: *population* and *capital*. If population grows faster than capital, wages fall and profits rise. Conversely, if capital grows faster than population, profits fall and wages rise. From time to time, one of these variables may grow faster than the other, thereby causing an upward shift in the level-of-living curve of population or in the profit curve of capital. Eventually, however, both wages per worker and profits per unit of capital must tend toward a long-run level of subsistence. Land, on the other hand, remains fixed in supply, according to the classical theory. Therefore, landlords stand to benefit over the long run as rents continue to rise with increases in population and in output per worker.

Two critical variables in the classical model of growth are population and capital. When they are in equilibrium in relation to one another, the returns to both, consisting of wages and profits, are at the subsistence level.

What Are the Long-Run Trends?

Have the foregoing predictions been vindicated by history? For most of the advanced or developed economies of the Western world, the answer is *no*. Since the nineteenth century in the United States, for example, three very long-run patterns have been evident:

1. The trends of real wages and of output per worker have been sharply upward, not downward. These trends result mainly from rapid expansion in technology and growth of the capital stock at a rate faster than the growth of population, thus resulting in a deepening of capital.

2. Interest rates or profit have fluctuated in the business cycle, with no particular upward or downward trend.

3. Land rents have moved upward relatively slowly, while actually declining in relation to other factor prices.

In general terms, the average product curve of the economy has shifted upward over time at a pace rapid enough to more than offset tendencies toward diminishing returns and Malthusian subsistence equilibrium. This upward shift can be attributed to changes in the conditions that are assumed to remain "fixed" when the curve is drawn. In broad terms, these include improvements in the quality of labor, discoveries of new and better natural resources, and technological advances in production. These are actually the kinds of factors that determine a nation's economic growth. As a result, the classical, or "Ricardian," model is useful not only for what it includes but also for what it excludes in explaining many of the dynamic processes of economic history. (See "Leaders in Economics," pages 320 and 322.)

In the advanced nations, the long-run trends of real wages, output per worker, interest rates, profit, and land rents have not borne out the classical model's predictions. Nevertheless, the model provides an instructive exercise in the interpretation of economic history.

What You Have Learned in This Perspective

1. The classical explanation of economic growth rests on a subsistence theory of wages and on the law of diminishing returns. As a result of these two principles, classical economics concluded that society is destined to remain at a minimum level of existence.

2. In the classical theory, the development of an economy depended on the relative growth rates of population and capital. However, the returns to both in the form of wages and profit tended toward subsistence levels over the long run.

Leaders in Economics

John Stuart Mill
1806–1873

The Bettmann Archive

John Stuart Mill was an eminent philosopher and social scientist and the leading economist of the mid-nineteenth century. In many ways, he was one of the most unusual men who ever lived.

Any discussion of Mill must make mention of his remarkable education, based on the experiences reported in his famous *Autobiography*. He was the son of James Mill, a noted philosopher, historian, and economist. James Mill was also an intimate friend of David Ricardo and of the great utilitarian philosopher Jeremy Bentham. This intellectual background exercised a profound influence on the younger Mill, who was educated at home by his father.

Extraordinary Education
At the age of three, before most children can even recite the alphabet, John Stuart was reading English fluently and beginning the study of Greek. By the time he was seven, he had read the dialogues of Plato; the great books of the ancient Greek historians Herodotus and Xenophon; the philosophical writings of Diogenes; and most of the nearly eighty works of Lucian, a Greek satirist of the second century.

At the age of eight, Mill took up the study of Latin. Before he was twelve years old, he had already digested, among other things, the major writings of Aristotle, Aristophanes, Horace, Lucretius, Sallust, and Socrates. He then made a comprehensive survey of algebra, calculus, and geometry and embarked on a serious study of logic through the writings of Thomas Hobbes, a British philosopher of the early seventeenth century. In the meantime Mill wrote, in addition to some verses, a "History of Rome," a "History of Holland," and the "Abridged Ancient Universal History."

Economic Education
At the age of thirteen, John Stuart was introduced by his father to the writings of Smith, Ricardo, and Malthus. Thus began his education in political economy—an education that eventually established him as one of the abler critics of classical economic liberalism. For although Mill is considered a member of the classical school, he actually repudiated some of its most basic premises.

In contrast to Smith, for example, Mill did not believe that laissez-faire led to the best of all possible worlds. Instead, he advocated social reforms. These included the taxation and redistribution of wealth, a shorter working day, abolition of the wage system, and the establishment of democratic producers' cooperatives in which the workers would own the factories and elect the managers to run them. It should be emphasized, however, that Mill believed too strongly in individual freedom ever to go far as a socialist. He distrusted the power of the state, and his reason for favoring producers' cooperatives was not to exalt the laboring class but to assure workers the fruits of their labor.

Classical Synthesis
Mill's chief contribution to economics was his collection and systemization of its literature. His major two-volume work, *Principles of Political Economy*, published in 1848, was considered to be a masterful synthesis of post-Ricardian economic writings. The book offered a calm prescription for peaceful progress and served as a standard text in economics for several decades. A noteworthy coincidence is that, in the same year, an incendiary pamphlet entitled *Communist Manifesto* was published by a then relatively unknown prophet of socialism, Karl Marx, whose ideas ultimately shook the world.

As for Mill himself, few individuals were ever held in higher esteem. Like the great and beloved Greek philosopher Plato of some 2,200 years earlier, Mill was a selfless man with a gentle, kind, and reasonable manner that endeared him to everyone. He was regarded with the deepest affection and respect —indeed, he was almost worshiped—by his contemporaries throughout the world. And, like Plato, when he died, an entire nation mourned his passing.

---

3. For advanced nations, empirical evidence has not borne out the classical explanation of growth. The theory, nevertheless, is extremely useful for understanding many of the dynamic processes of economic history.

For Discussion

1. *Terms and concepts to review:*
subsistence theory of wages
Malthusian theory of population
wages-fund theory

2. If Ricardo and Malthus had been living in the United States rather than England during the early nineteenth century, do you think they would have developed the same theory of economic growth? Explain your answer. (**Hint** Think in terms of the subsistence theory and the supply of relatively scarce resources as compared to fairly plentiful ones.)

3. What is meant by an "optimum population"? Do you believe there really is such a thing? Is it as applicable to the United States as it is to India? Why or why not?

Can We Overcome Stagflation? Supply-Side and Demand-Side Policies

Learning guide
Watch for the answers to these important questions

Unemployment and inflation are the chief economic problems of our time. Is there a relationship between these two phenomena? If there is, how useful is it as a guide for public policy?

What is the rational-expectations theory? According to this theory, which kinds of fiscal–monetary policies are effective?

What is supply-side economics? What is demand-side economics? How do they differ? What are the implications of these differences for policy purposes?

What is stagflation? What major proposals and policies have economists and political leaders advanced for overcoming it? What are the difficulties in implementing the various proposals?

It is a gloomy moment in the history of our country. Not in the lifetime of most men has there been so much grave and deep apprehension; never has the future seemed so incalculable as at this time. The domestic economic situation is in chaos. Our dollar is weak throughout the world. Prices are so high as to be utterly impossible.

The political cauldron seethes and bubbles with uncertainty. Russia hangs as usual, like a cloud, dark and silent, upon the horizon. It is a solemn moment. Of our troubles no men can see the end.

Harper's Weekly (October 1857)

Everyone agrees that times change. Yet people often see uncanny parallels between adverse economic conditions today and those of some period in the distant past. Perhaps this is because many social problems do not really change with time; rather, it is our understanding of them that changes.

This is especially true of macroeconomics. Problems of unemployment and inflation have been with us for decades. Only the scope and the intensity of the problems, and our understanding of them, have changed.

Because of this, new policies for coping with unemployment and inflation are continually being proposed by economists and political leaders. What sorts of policies are these? Can they accomplish what they are designed to do? These are the fundamental questions that this chapter seeks to answer.

This chapter explains alternative policies for coping with stagflation—that is, unemployment and inflation.

Understanding Stagflation: Recession and Inflation

We must understand the interactions of recession and inflation before we can devise policies to cope with them.

For many years, the chief macroeconomic problem facing our own and most other mixed economies has been *stagflation*. As the name suggests, it is a combination of two words—"stagnation" and "inflation." Stagnation is a condition resulting from slow economic growth and high unemployment. Inflation, of course, means rising prices. Other names for stagflation, therefore, are "recessionary inflation" or "inflationary recession." All of these expressions are used frequently in the news media.

Phillips Curves: Short-Run Trade-Offs

Many economists believe that, because inflation and unemployment can exist at the same time, there may be a relationship between them. If this is true, the relationship can be expressed by a *Phillips curve*. This idea is named after A. W. Phillips, a British economist who proposed the concept several decades ago.

The relationship is illustrated in Exhibit 1. It emphasizes the notion that, if a Phillips curve actually represents reality, there can be only one such curve for the economy at any given time. Let us see why.

Conventional Curve: The "Old" Type

The conventional Phillips curve depicts a clear trade-off between unemployment and inflation.

Figure (a) of Exhibit 1 shows a "conventional" Phillips curve, a type that was widely believed, a few decades ago, to represent reality. Each point on a particular curve, such as curve 1, designates a specific *combination* of unemployment and inflation. The point labeled *A*, for instance, represents an unemployment rate of 4 percent and an inflation rate of 5 percent.

What would happen if there were a shift—for reasons to be explained shortly—from curve 1 to curve 2? In that case, a given point on the higher curve denotes at least as much of one variable plus more of the other, when compared to a point directly below or to the left of it on the lower curve. Thus, point *B* represents the same unemployment rate as point *A* (4 percent), but it denotes the higher inflation rate of 9 percent. Point *C*, on the other hand, denotes the same inflation rate as point *A* (5 percent) but an unemployment rate of 7 percent. The same notion applies to any other point you may choose. Any point on curve 2 between *B* and *C*, however, represents a higher rate of both unemployment and inflation as compared with point *A* on curve 1. These ideas suggest that lower curves are "better" and higher curves are "poorer" for the economy as a whole.

You can now see why a Phillips curve can be defined in the following way:

> A *Phillips curve* represents a trade-off between unemployment and inflation. Every point along the curve denotes a different combination of unemployment and inflation. A movement along the curve measures the reduction in one of these at the expense of a gain in the other.

The conventional Phillips curve—*if it actually represented reality* —would thus provide government policy makers with a menu of choices between inflation and unemployment. As one goes up, the other goes down, and vice versa. The trick, therefore, would be to choose the fiscal and monetary policies needed to achieve the desired balance.

Modified L Curve and the Natural Unemployment Rate: A Newer View

Many observers believe that the situation described by the conventional Phillips curve was real but that it was only a temporary phenomenon. It may have existed, for example, during the 1960s. Since then, there have been periods in which inflation and unemployment have shot up simultaneously. This indicates two possibilities: Either the conventional curve has shifted so far outward as to be meaningless, or a new type of curve with a distinctly different shape has emerged. There is evidence to support both these beliefs. One possibility, as shown in Figure (b) of Exhibit 1, is that the new curve may be approximately L-shaped. Thus:

> The modified L-shaped Phillips curve depicts a limited trade-off between unemployment and inflation. Along the lower-right segment of the curve, increased government spending through fiscal–monetary policies will raise aggregate demand and hence the inflation rate. At the same time, the increased spending will also create more jobs and thereby reduce the unemployment rate. But at some critical level of unemployment, the curve becomes vertical. Thereafter, further government spending is purely inflationary and does not reduce unemployment.

Exhibit 1
A Curve Named Phillips— Then and Now
(hypothetical data)

Figure (a): *Conventional Curve.* Along any given curve, a reduction in the unemployment rate can be achieved through expansionary fiscal–monetary policies. These increase aggregate demand and create more jobs, but they also raise the inflation rate. This "traditional" type of Phillips curve which at one time may have seemed plausible, has been generally discredited because unemployment and inflation rates have frequently risen simultaneously.

Figure (b): *Modified L Curve.* Along the lower-right end of the curve (that is, the trade-off segment), a reduction in the unemployment rate may be achieved at the expense of an increase

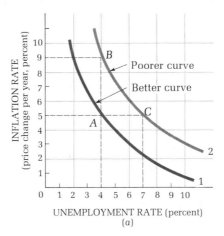

(a)

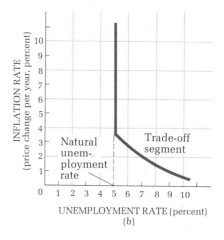

(b)

In Figure (b) of Exhibit 1, the critical level occurs at a 5 percent *natural unemployment rate.* This is the employment level at which only frictional and structural unemployment exist, not cyclical unemployment arising from a deficiency in aggregate demand. The natural unemployment rate, therefore, is not some irreducible minimum. It can be lowered by improving labor markets—through job training, combatting discrimination in hiring, and so on—but not by overexpansionary fiscal and monetary policies.

Acceleration Curves: Short-Run "Paths"

Does a modified L-shaped Phillips curve really represent reality? Many economists think so. However, they agree that the reality it represents is at best only a short-run phenomenon.

Another possibility is that the Phillips curve that truly represents reality is a vertical line at the natural unemployment rate. If that is the case, continued attempts to reduce unemployment through fiscal–monetary measures are not only futile but lead to accelerating inflation.

in the inflation rate. However, at some critical level of unemployment—called the *natural unemployment rate*—the Phillips curve becomes vertical. Thereafter, further fiscal–monetary expansion merely increases the inflation rate without reducing the unemployment rate. (**Note** The critical level in the figure—the natural unemployment rate—is 5 percent. In reality, this level cannot usually be determined so precisely. More likely, the natural unemployment rate today is somewhere between 5 and 6 percent.)

Conclusion. There is empirical evidence to suggest that the unemployment–inflation relationship for our economy can perhaps be represented by a modified L curve. Of course, the entire curve may shift outward, thereby reflecting a higher natural unemployment rate, for reasons that are explained in the text.

Exhibit 2

Acceleration Curves: Up and Down the Phillips Curve—Another View

Many economists believe that the Phillips curve that best describes reality is a vertical line at the natural unemployment rate. The line *ACE* in the figures is an example of a vertical Phillips curve. The dashed lines, such as *ABC*, are *acceleration curves*. They show the temporary unemployment–inflation "path" (indicated by arrows) that the economy might follow in response to fiscal–monetary stimulation.

This is the meaning of the "acceleration curves" shown in Exhibit 2. In Figure (*a*), the economy is assumed to be at point *A*, representing a natural unemployment rate *N* and a zero inflation rate. What happens if government undertakes expansionary fiscal and monetary policies to reduce the unemployment rate? The answer can be obtained by following the short-run dashed curve, representing the temporary "path" of unemployment and inflation as it passes through several stages.

Stage 1 Along the path from *A* to *B*, the increase in aggregate demand, which was unanticipated by the public, pulls up prices relative to wages. Business profits thus rise, prompting firms to increase production and hire more workers. At point *B*, the unemployment rate reaches its lowest level.

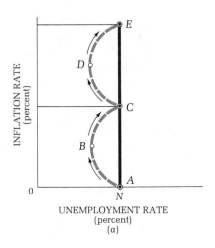

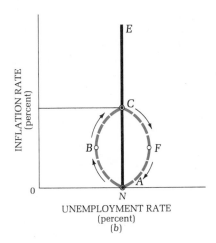

Figure (*a*): Increases in government spending might temporarily reduce unemployment as the economy moves from its assumed initial equilibrium position at point *A* along the path to point *B*. However, as inflation accelerates, uncertainty mounts. Consequently, business investment declines, the unemployment rate increases, and the economy moves to a new equilibrium at *C*. Renewed fiscal–monetary stimulation might then push the economy into a new cycle along the path *CDE*. Notice that each new equilibrium position, such as *C* or *E*, represents the same natural unemployment rate accompanied by a higher inflation rate.

Figure (*b*): If the economy is at *C*, it can return to *A* along the path *CFA*. This would happen if government ended its fiscal–monetary stimulation, thereby causing aggregate demand to decline relative to aggregate supply. The unemployment rate would increase until the point *F* was reached and then decrease as the inflation rate continued declining.

Stage 2 Workers now begin to realize that prices have been increasing faster than money wages, causing *real* wages to decline. Although unions manage to negotiate higher money wages, real wages continue to suffer. As unanticipated inflation continues, production costs rise, uncertainty mounts, and business profitability and investment incentives decline. Unemployment thus starts to increase while prices continue rising. The economy moves from point *B* to point *C*. At this point, unemployment is back to its natural rate, and inflation, now fully anticipated by the public, is at a higher level. With respect to workers, money wages have "caught up" with prices so that real wages are constant. In general, the equilibrium at *C* is *stable* (that is, it has no tendency to change).

Stage 3 Of course, the equilibrium *can* change if government again employs stimulative fiscal–monetary measures. The economy would then follow the inflation–unemployment path shown by the dashed line *CDE*.

How does the economy get back to point *A*? The answer is shown in Figure (*b*). Let us assume that the economy is at *C*, which corresponds to *C* in Figure (*a*). If government ends fiscal–monetary stimulation, aggregate demand declines relative to aggregate supply. As a result, the inflation rate declines and the unemployment rate increases following the path *CFA*. At point *A*, the economy is again in stable equilibrium, this time at the same natural unemployment rate but at a zero inflation rate.

Against this background, we can identify some important ideas in terms of the charts.

1. The dashed lines are *acceleration curves.* These are short-run unemployment–inflation relationships showing the rapid rise in inflation that may result from attempts to increase employment through fiscal–monetary stimulation.

2. The vertical line is a Phillips curve. It connects the points *A*, *C*, and *F* as the economy moves from one of these stable equilibrium positions to another.

Conclusion: Today's Phillips Curve

The conventional Phillips curve was conceived on the assumption that a permanent trade-off existed between unemployment and inflation. This meant that fiscal and monetary policies could be used to bring about reductions in unemployment, but only at the expense of higher rates of inflation. Conversely, reductions in inflation could be achieved only at the cost of increases in unemployment.

The modified L curve depicts a limited trade-off between unemployment and inflation.

Subsequent experiences have shown these beliefs to be incorrect. There is substantial evidence to indicate that, if a trade-off exists between unemployment and inflation, it is a short-term one at best. Therefore:

> Today's Phillips curve, assuming that it represents present realities, is likely to be either a modified L curve or a vertical line. With either curve, the vertical portions correspond to the natural rate of unemployment. This means that the trade-off opportunities between unemployment and inflation are extremely limited. Consequently, expansionary fiscal–monetary policies aimed at reducing unemployment are virtually certain to create strong inflationary pressures without achieving durable gains in employment.

Rational Expectations: What You Foresee Is What You Get

> Inflation does give a stimulus . . . when it starts from a condition that is noninflationary. But if the inflation continues, people get adjusted to it. Then, when they *expect* rising prices, the mere occurrence of what has been expected is no longer stimulating.
>
> Sir John R. Hicks (1967)

Hicks, a distinguished British economist and Nobel laureate, knows that much of economics is concerned with predicting human behavior. Therefore, when government policy makers try to stabilize the economy, they must predict how people will respond.

But this appears to be impossible—according to a controversial theory called "rational expectations." The theory holds that people form expectations about government fiscal–monetary policies on the basis of past experiences, and then include these expectations in their economic decisions. Consequently, by the time the government's policies are initiated, the public has already acted on them, thereby offsetting the effects. As the quotation from Hicks implies, the only

The rational-expectations theory says that widely expected policy moves are ineffective because they have already been incorporated in peoples' decisions. Therefore, only surprise moves are effective.

policy changes that can work are those that come as surprises, because they force people to revise their expectations.

Two examples will illustrate how the theory of rational expectations works.

1. If the economy is in recession, businesspeople will expect the Fed to take steps toward reducing interest rates. They will therefore tend to defer investment expenditures on new plant and equipment until interest rates decline. This deferral worsens the recession. When the rates finally do come down they will stimulate a greater volume of investment than policy makers intended. The result will be more rather than less cyclical instability, caused by too much rather than too little government intervention.

2. From time to time, Washington proposes a reduction in corporate income taxes in order to spur business investment. According to the rational-expectations theory, such talks prompt executives to postpone many planned projects, waiting for the tax change to occur. When the change finally comes, capital spending may pick up—if a recession has not intervened.

The correct policy, according to rational-expectations theory, combines balanced budgets with steady monetary expansion. Such a policy would assure stability.

Do these and similar examples mean that, according to rational-expectations theory, the only correct public policy should be no public policy? Not quite. Proponents contend that only *systematic* economic policy is impotent. Therefore, the only effective policy is balanced budgets and steady money growth, because this, proponents argue, will keep the economy on its stable long-run growth path.

The essential ideas of *rational-expectations theory* can be summarized in terms of three propositions.

> **1.** Widely expected or *systematic* policy moves have no impact when made because they have already been incorporated into people's decisions.
>
> **2.** The only policy moves that cause changes in people's behavior are the ones that are not expected—the *surprise* moves.
>
> **3.** To assure economic stability, government should choose the right policy and stick to it. This means that government should adhere to a policy of balanced budgets and steady growth of the money supply. Failure to do so will lead to public policies that are self-defeating and inflationary.

As stated above, rational-expectations theory is controversial. Nevertheless, it is attracting a growing number of scholars who believe there is considerable merit in what the theory says.

Conclusion: Searching for Stability

In certain respects, rational-expectations theory out-monetarizes monetarism.

You have probably noticed that Phillips curves, acceleration curves, and rational-expectations theory have much in common. They try to explain, although in somewhat different ways, how inflation may result from fiscal–monetary stimulation designed to reduce unemployment.

These ideas are also related to *monetarism*. As you have learned, this doctrine holds that monetary policy is much more important than fiscal policy in affecting the economy's levels of income, employment, and prices. Because of this, sudden increases in the money supply aimed at lowering interest rates or financing government deficits may help reduce unemployment. But such measures, as acceleration curves show, are likely to work only in the short run.

In the long run, the similarity between monetarist and rational-expectation views is worth noting:

> Both the monetarist and rational-expectations theories end up with basically the same conclusion—the rejection of neo-Keynesian interventionism. But the reasons differ. Monetarist theory contends that we do not know enough about the workings of the economy to fine-tune it. Rational-expectations theory holds that the public rejects fine-tuning because everyone expects it and therefore undertakes actions that thwart its effectiveness.

Supply-Side Economics

> The encouragement of mere consumption is no benefit to commerce, for production alone furnishes the means for consumption. Thus, it is the aim of good government to stimulate production, of bad government to encourage consumption.
>
> Jean Baptiste Say (1803)

What drives the economy? The answer can depend on whether the economy is viewed from the demand side or from the supply side.

Demand-side economics consists of measures aimed at devising policies to regulate purchasing power. Keynesian economics, because it focuses on fiscal and monetary policies to control aggregate demand, may be characterized as demand-side economics.

Supply-side economics consists of measures aimed at devising policies to stimulate production. Although there are many policies that may encourage increased production, some of the most fundamental supply-side policies are those that make direct use of *incentives*. For example, reductions in marginal tax rates—the taxes paid on the last few dollars of wages, interest, and dividends—provide direct incentives to work, save, and invest.

Supply-side economics makes heavy use of incentives to stimulate investment, production, and employment.

Whereas demand-side economics is an outgrowth of Keynesian theory and policy, supply-side economics harks back to classical thinking. In fact, to a large extent, supply-side economics is a reconsideration of the ramifications of *Say's Law*—the proposition that "supply creates its own demand." You can appreciate the significance of this by examining the major pillars on which supply-side economics rests. These include:

1. Rejection of Keynesian demand-management policies.
2. Tax reduction to stimulate production.
3. Nonmonetization of government deficits.
4. Deregulation of industries and markets.

Rejection of Keynesian Demand-Management Policies

Supply-side economists point out that the Keynesian model provides an *underconsumption* explanation of recessions. That is, Keynesian theory attributes the cause of unemployment to insufficient aggregate demand, resulting in a recessionary gap. Therefore, to restore full employment, government policy should stimulate aggregate demand through budget deficits and easy money (low interest rates).

Supply-side economists object to government policies aimed at manipulating purchasing power.

Government policies designed to stimulate demand have, in the opinion of critics, led to inflation.

Keynesian ideas attained a firm foothold in the United States in the late 1940s. Since then, except for some brief periods, Washington has made extensive use of fiscal and monetary policies to stimulate demand. But these policies have led to mounting inflationary pressures. As a result, after years of soaring prices, many economists have come to feel that Keynesianism might be a "one-way street." In theory, government deficits are supposed to expand in recessions and decline during prosperities. However, attempts to reverse years of extravagant spending have often proved to be difficult politically.

When President Reagan took office in 1981, he appointed supply-siders to important government positions. Their views on monetary and tax policies contrast in important ways with the policies that have been studied thus far.

Supply-Side Monetary and Tax Policies

As you know, Keynesian demand-management policies are implemented through changes in the money supply and in taxes. Supply-siders reject such policies—for several reasons.

1. Experience shows that the Fed is unable to control the money supply. Therefore, it should give up trying to do so. Instead the country should return to a genuine *gold standard*. Under such a standard, the dollar would be defined by law in terms of a fixed weight of gold. This would stabilize the dollar, both domestically and internationally, because the nation's currency would be tied directly to gold, whose quantity is relatively fixed. Under these circumstances, Washington's ability to inflate the money supply in order to finance huge budget deficits would be severely limited. (A more complete explanation of the idea of

2. Whenever people's incentives to produce are stifled, any form of demand stimulation will lead to inflation. Therefore, policies should be a gold standard is given in the Dictionary at the back of the book.) formulated to increase the supply of goods by encouraging increases in *productivity*.

3. Contrary to Keynesian belief, not all income tax cuts are the same. Only those that emphasize reductions in *marginal* (rather than average or total) tax rates provide maximum incentives to work, save, and invest. This is because marginal tax rates—the taxes paid on the last few dollars of income—determine people's willingness to undertake *additional* work, saving, and investment.

Supply-siders advocate tight monetary policy accompanied by selective tax cuts.

4. Contrary to Keynesian belief, a reduction in taxes is not likely to have the same effect as an increase in government spending. A reduction in taxes, if properly designed, can exert a substantial impact on incentives to produce. An increase in government spending, on the other hand, absorbs resources from the private sector and thus expands the size of government relative to business.

Summarizing these ideas:

In contrast with Keynesian demand-side economics, the basis of supply-side economics is (a) tight monetary control (preferably through a return to the gold standard) to curb inflation and (b) tax cuts to encourage greater output. The taxes that are most important to reduce are marginal tax rates on personal and business income. This is because the goal is to stimulate supply rather than demand.

Tax Reduction to Stimulate Production

Exorbitant taxes destroy industry by producing despair. An attentive legislature will observe the point when the revenue decreases and the prejudice begins.

David Hume (1756)

High taxes, sometimes by diminishing the consumption of the taxed commodities and sometimes by encouraging smuggling, afford a smaller revenue to government than what might be drawn from more moderate taxes.

Adam Smith (1776)

I can make a profit if I sell a car for $500 and I can make a profit if I sell a car for $1,500. But I can make the most profit when I sell a car for some price in between.

Henry Ford (1930)

Hume was an eighteenth-century philosopher. Smith was the founder of modern economics. And Ford was a twentieth-century industrialist. Yet all three had something in common: They understood human nature as it relates to taxation and spending.

For instance, all three would have agreed with the idea underlying Figure (a) of Exhibit 3. The diagram, called a *Laffer curve*, expresses a relationship between tax revenues and the marginal tax rate—the rate on the last few dollars of income. The relationship shows that, as the tax rate increases from zero to 100 percent, government revenues from taxation correspondingly rise from zero to some maximum level and then decline to zero. Thus, the optimum tax rate—the one that produces the largest revenue—is somewhere between the two extremes.

An important feature of the curve is that it covers both a "normal" range and a "prohibitive" range. In the normal range, a higher tax rate brings higher revenues. In the prohibitive range, the tax rate is so high that it impairs incentives. Therefore, a tax cut would actually increase revenues by spurring the incentive to work and invest.

Exhibit 3
Professor Laffer's Famous Curve

"Except for the optimum rate, there are always two tax rates that yield the same revenues." So says the University of Southern California's Arthur Laffer, whose controversial curve has received a great deal of attention from legislators and economists.

Figure (a): The "Laffer curve" is one of the pillars of supply-side economics. Although the concept is neither new nor complicated, it may have powerful implications. Basically, it says that, if marginal tax rates are in the "normal" range, increases in the rates will yield more tax revenues. But if marginal tax rates are in the "prohibitive" range, *decreases* in the rates will actually produce more revenues by stimulating the incentive to work, save, and invest.

Figure (b): In reality, neither the optimum tax rate nor the true shape of the Laffer curve is known. For instance, curve A and curve B are two of many possible shapes. Consequently, in order to maximize revenues, the present tax rate, r, must be either decreased

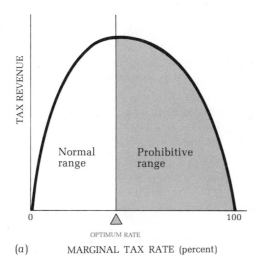

(a)   MARGINAL TAX RATE (percent)

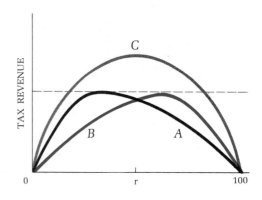

(b)   MARGINAL TAX RATE (percent)

"The Wedge" and Marginal Tax Rates

Supply-siders contend that an economy's stagflation can be due to various causes. One of them is that personal and corporate income tax rates may be so high as to be in the prohibitive range. If that is the case, a cut in taxes may be warranted—for two reasons:

or increased, depending on whether curve A or curve B is correct. On the other hand, by reducing tax deductions and exemptions, the curve can be shifted upward to C. This curve yields higher revenues at *all* tax rates.

1. The difference between before-tax and after-tax incomes of resource owners may be too wide. If so, this difference, called "the wedge," reduces incentives to work and invest.

2. The decision whether or not to work, save, or invest depends on *after-tax marginal incomes*. These are the last few dollars of wages, interest, and dividends available for spending in each tax bracket. The more that is available, the greater people's incentive to work, save, and invest.

These beliefs lead to the following conclusion:

Supply-siders contend that, if *marginal* tax rates are in the prohibitive range, they should be cut. This action would make working, saving, and investing more rewarding, thereby stimulating economic activity. The result would be greater economic growth and employment, leading to higher, not lower, tax revenues.

Difficulties for Public Policy

Different kinds of Laffer curves are possible. Each kind might suggest a different policy.

The Laffer curve is an interesting idea. Unfortunately, no one knows where the optimum point is located or even what the true shape of the curve is. This can pose difficulties for public policy.

For example, in Figure (*b*) of Exhibit 3, the actual Laffer curve might be either curve *A* or curve *B*. If the present tax rate is *r* and the goal is to maximize revenues, tax rates should be *decreased* if *A* is the correct curve and *increased* if *B* is correct. Alternatively, by revising the tax laws and closing tax loopholes (by reducing exemptions and deductions), the entire curve can be shifted to a higher level—say, *C*. Along curve *C*, revenues would be greater at *all* tax rates.

Because of these possibilities, it is easy to understand why the Laffer curve, which is a fundamental part of supply-side economics, is also highly controversial.

Nonmonetization of Government Deficits

Supply-siders contend that rising deficits per se *are not inflationary: Deficits become inflationary when the Fed monetizes them.*

Supply-siders recognize that, in the short run, a reduction in marginal tax rates may result in increased budget deficits until the positive effects of the tax cuts take hold. Are the rising budget deficits likely to be inflationary? The answer, say the supply-siders, depends on how the Federal Reserve reacts to the Treasury's fiscal policy.

As you will recall, the Treasury incurs a budget deficit by spending more than it collects in taxes. Its excess spending is financed (that is, paid for) by selling debt instruments (such as bills and bonds) to the public. The increased supply of debt instruments on the market causes their prices to decline and, therefore, interest rates to rise. (Remember that prices of debt instruments and interest rates are inversely related.) As a result, many firms that cannot afford to borrow at higher interest rates may be forced out of the financial markets—a process known as *crowding out.*

The Fed, seeing interest rates rising and fearing the possibility of recession, may engage in open-market purchases of Treasury securities in an effort to bring interest rates down. This action, of course, enlarges banks' reserves. As a result, banks seek to expand their lending, thereby increasing demand deposits and hence the money supply. Thus, through its purchase of Treasury securities in the open market, the Fed *monetizes* the Treasury's deficits by making them part of the money supply. (The term monetize means to convert into money.)

Supply-siders thus conclude that rising deficits are not by themselves inflationary. This is because they represent transfers of purchasing power from the public to the Treasury with no net increases in total spending. However, if the Fed monetizes the Treasury's deficits, the results will be inflationary because *monetization transforms the deficits into money.*

Policy Implications

Supply-side ideas provide an interesting contrast to Keynesian beliefs:

> According to Keynesian policy, a tax cut without a spending cut creates a budget deficit. This results in a fiscal stimulus that becomes even more pronounced when the Fed monetizes the deficit.

> According to supply-side policy, a tax cut without a spending cut may create a short-term deficit. However, it does not become inflationary unless monetized by the Fed. *The purpose of the tax cut is to improve production incentives, not to provide a fiscal stimulus. Therefore, the deficit should not be monetized.*

Does this mean that mounting deficits are harmless as long as they are not monetized? Supply-siders answer *no*. They emphasize two points.

1. Reduced government spending should accompany tax reduction Cutbacks in government spending are desirable because they encourage the increase in private savings resulting from tax reduction to flow into private investment. Otherwise, the increased savings may be used to purchase Treasury securities, thereby financing the growth of government spending.

Tax reduction will be ineffective, and may even be counterproductive, if not accompanied by reduced government spending.

2. If government spending is not reduced, increased budget deficits may crowd out private investment This could happen if the additional savings from tax reduction are less than the increased deficits, forcing the government to borrow in order to make up for lost tax revenues. But, if the extra savings either equal or exceed the enlarged deficits, the gain in savings would be used to finance additional capital investment. This will stimulate the economy and boost the government's tax revenues within a short time.

Supply-siders contend that fiscal—monetary policies should encourage more savings so as to finance increased business investment.

To summarize:

> Supply-siders emphasize that in order to encourage increased production and employment without inflation, two fiscal—monetary policies are necessary:

> **1.** Government deficits should not be monetized.

> **2.** Reductions in government spending should equal or exceed reductions in taxes, thereby providing more savings to finance business investment.

Depreciation Reform

Policies concerning tax reduction are closely related to those concerning depreciation. What is *depreciation?* It is the decline in the value of a fixed asset, such as plant or equipment, due to wear and tear, destruction, or obsolescence resulting from the development of new and better techniques.

Companies treat depreciation as a cost. That is, the tax laws allow firms to deduct from their income each year a certain amount of depreciation on buildings, machines, vehicles, and other capital goods as a cost of doing business.

For example, suppose that a firm owns a building that cost $1 million. If the tax laws require the firm to "write off" the building over 20 years, the firm could deduct from its income $50,000 a year as a depreciation expense. If the tax laws allow the firm to accelerate depreciation over 10 years, however, it could deduct $100,000 a year.

Obviously, the more a firm can deduct each year for depreciation, the smaller will be its profit and, therefore, the less it will pay in income taxes. The same is true for other firms. Therefore:

> Laws permitting accelerated depreciation—that is, faster write-offs of plant and equipment—can be an important part of a tax-reduction policy. Accelerated depreciation gives firms a greater incentive to undertake new investment in order to replace existing capital equipment. However, accelerated depreciation also (1) reduces tax revenues to the Treasury and (2) benefits capital-intensive firms while neglecting labor-intensive ones. (Examples of the latter are firms that specialize in high technology, research, and development.) Because of this, there is always controversy over any proposal that involves changes in depreciation rates.

Deregulation of Industries and Markets

One of the most remarkable developments of recent decades has been the enormous growth of government regulations. These have imposed heavy burdens on large and small businesses, discouraged productivity, and contributed to inefficiency. It is easy to see, therefore, why the desire for deregulation is strong among a wide spectrum of economists and political leaders, not just supply-siders.

The maze of regulations is staggering. There are literally millions of federal and state laws, rules, and specifications that must be met in order to produce the nation's GNP. These laws pertain, among many other things, to occupational safety and health, consumer products, food, drugs, cosmetics, transportation, energy production, finance, and marketing.

As an example, the production and sale of an ordinary cheeseburger entails more than 40,000 regulations. These range from numerous laws controlling the feeding and slaughtering of cattle and the processing of the meat to detailed specifications of the fat content of the meat and cheese, the chemical composition of the bun, the texture and freshness of the lettuce, tomatoes, and pickles, and the color and density of the ketchup and mayonnaise. It has been estimated that all of the rules and regulations together may add as much as 20 percent to the price you pay for a cheeseburger.

Steps Toward Regulatory Reform

Of course, regulations usually provide benefits as well as costs. The problem, therefore, is to compare the two as part of an overall scheme designed to improve the regulatory process. There are a number of measures that could go a long way toward achieving regulatory reform. Among the most promising are:

1. Impose regulations only when a careful analysis reveals that the benefits exceed the costs.

2. Identify the specific goals of regulation; then choose the least costly method of achieving the goals.

3. Make greater use of economic incentives and penalties, and less use of rigid rules, to encourage compliance by firms.

4. Broaden the use of "sunset" legislation, which requires Congress to evaluate periodically, and then either renew or terminate, existing regulatory laws and agencies.

5. Shift a greater proportion of regulatory responsibilities from the federal government to the states, especially when the problems in question are more local than national.

These and other steps toward regulatory reform have been adopted gradually in varying degrees. However, progress probably will continue to be slow—for the most basic of reasons:

> Bureaucrats (that is, government officials and administrators) tend to resist major regulatory reforms. This is because reforms (1) threaten jobs, power, or status and (2) are sometimes difficult to implement. For example, if most government regulations could be subjected to careful analyses of benefits and costs, the efficiency of regulation would be greatly improved. This would reduce the need for, and size of, many government agencies.

> However, there are numerous benefits and costs of regulations, such as health and safety rules, that are often impossible to measure. Consequently, detailed analyses of benefits and costs are employed in government on a relatively limited basis.

Conclusion: From Limited Keynesianism to Reaganomics

It is interesting to note that these and other supply-side beliefs are not new. Many of them were expressed by Keynes and others as long ago as the 1930s. Further, they have been adopted and implemented in varying degrees since President Reagan took office in 1981. Thus:

> It would be a mistake to conclude that supply-side and demand-side views are the result of opposing theories. Indeed, policies aimed at improving incentives to invest and produce are measures that demand-siders as well as supply-siders have always supported. In a larger sense, therefore, supply-side economics is not so much a rejection of Keynesian economics as a necessary reminder of its limitations and a different emphasis on some of its ideas.

Some interesting views on supply-side economics are expressed in Box 1.

Curing Stagflation Through the Market

Faint hearts, it is often said, do not win elections. Political leaders are acutely aware of this. In recent history, some American presidents, responding to the mounting pressures of inflation and unemployment, have resorted to desperate proposals and measures. These have included diverse policies aimed at limiting price increases, adjusting to them, and promoting more jobs.

In general, all antistagflation policies can be classified in either of two categories—market and nonmarket. Market policies, which will be considered first, seek to minimize if not avoid the bureaucracy of complex regulations that arises when nonmarket measures are employed.

Box 1
Naive and Functional Supply-Side Economics (continued)

Monetary and supply-side economics are based on the proposition that private initiative is the source of wealth and the source of higher standards of living.

What has been characterized as the supply side of our economic policy deals with the effect government spending and financing has on the willingness and ability of individuals to take a chance on productive ventures.

Beryl Sprinkel
Under Secretary of the Treasury
for Monetary Affairs

Supply-side economics has grown out of the frustration that U.S. policy makers and business leaders have felt about the inability of demand-drive economic policies to produce non-inflationary economic growth in our country.

William F. Ford
President, Federal Reserve
Bank of Atlanta

The fundamental effort to shift resources and decision-making from the government to the private sector is as needed and meritorious as ever.

Reducing the burden of taxation and regulation and slowing the growth of government spending and credit are essential steps to achieving a stronger economic performance.

Murray Weidenbaum
Professor of Economics
Washington University
(Formerly Chairman, President's
Council of Economic Advisers)

Fiscal and Monetary Guidelines

Several practical guidelines have been proposed for fiscal and monetary policy.

Most authorities agree that both fiscal and monetary actions determine the level of economic activity. Although there are differences of opinion about their relative importance, neither policy can be pursued effectively to the exclusion of the other.

The reason is not hard to see. When unemployment rises to undesirable levels, government spending is increased in order to stimulate the economy. Gradually, prices start to rise as the economy approaches high employment. To keep a lid on interest rates, the monetary authority expands the money supply. This may succeed in reducing interest rates for a while. But it also promotes further inflation, causing subsequent upward pressure on interest rates. The process thus continues until government budgetary and monetary policies are revised in an effort to check inflation. Then the economy enters a recession and the cycle starts over again.

This scenario, more or less, has been the typical pattern for several decades. If it is to be avoided in the future, measures are needed to assure greater control over government revenues and expenditures. This is part of a larger goal of limiting the size of government. An expanding federal deficit may be an indication that government is growing. If it grows faster than the national economy, command over resources is shifted from the private sector to the public sector.

What can be done to avoid this possibility? Four major monetary and fiscal guidelines aimed at curing stagflation have been proposed.

Stabilize Monetary Growth

Practically all experts agree that steady, as opposed to erratic, monetary expansion is a first step toward achieving stability. Therefore, if the monetary growth rate is excessive, it should be reduced gradually until it equals the long-run desired growth rate of the economy—approximately 3 to 4 percent annually. As you will recall, this prescription is the familiar *money-supply rule*. By adhering to a policy of gradual rather than sudden monetary reduction, the possibility of causing economic disturbances is minimized.

Balance the Federal Budget Annually

This frequently heard proposal is often advocated as a constitutional amendment. Its intention is to eliminate budget deficits, but not necessarily budget surpluses. If the proposal were adopted, it would prevent the use of government deficit spending, unless constitutionally approved by a specified majority of Congress. Consequently, monetary policy would become the key means of achieving economic stability.

Limit Federal Spending

A constitutional amendment that would place an upper limit on federal spending has often been proposed. This measure would limit federal spending to a certain percentage of GNP. Figures ranging from 18 to 21 percent, which are somewhat less than historical trends, are typically suggested. Of course, a spending limit is concerned only with the level of spending, not with budget balance or with the relationship between spending and revenues. Therefore, passage of the measure would not necessarily eliminate deficits or surpluses. On the other hand, it would restrict the activities of government and weaken its ability to utilize antirecessionary fiscal policy. Thus it might lead government to adopt undesirable alternatives, such as increased regulations and controls.

Limit Federal Revenues

Another measure sometimes advocated as a constitutional amendment is to restrict federal tax revenues to some percentage of GNP. This form of revenue limit would not eliminate deficits or surpluses because it would deal with the level of revenues, not with spending or the budget balance. Further, it would restrict somewhat the activities of government and reduce its ability to use antirecessionary fiscal policy. However, it would not encourage increased regulations and controls because tax incentives and additional spending to increase GNP could be employed when deemed necessary.

You can see from this analysis that guidelines of any type have certain advantages and disadvantages. Nevertheless:

> The purpose of any set of guidelines is to provide a stable framework for making decisions. This is especially important in a democratic, free-enterprise system. Without appropriate guidelines for fiscal and monetary policies, political control can flounder indefinitely. The costs of this to society are the prolonged losses that result from the failure to attain higher levels of efficiency, stability, and growth.

Reward and Punishment: TIP

Do conventional fiscal and monetary measures work well enough to control today's endemic problem, stagflation? Many critics think not. A strong dose of government spending, prescribed by the Keynesian doctors to cure recession, is likely to bring the patient to an inflation high. A slow but steady increase in the money supply, the treatment ordered by the monetarist physicians, may induce a case of excessive sluggishness. And resorting to radical surgery, in the form of rigid government controls over wages and prices, is regarded by many as alien to our democratic system.

It therefore comes as no surprise that economists continue to search for stagflation remedies. One of the more imaginative proposals is known as a *tax-based incomes policy* (TIP). Its novelty is that it uses a carrot and stick—reward and punishment—to cope with the stubborn problem of stagflation.

TIP uses a system of reward and punishment —through taxes—as a way of curing stagflation.

How TIP Works

TIP is based on the assumption that price increases are influenced strongly by wage increases. Therefore, by limiting gains in wages, upward pressure on prices will be reduced.

To implement the idea, TIP would set an annual guideline for wage increases. Through tax rewards and penalties, firms and employees would be encouraged to adhere to the guideline.

For example, each year the government would announce what it considers to be a noninflationary standard or guideline for wage increases. The figure would be somewhere between the gain in the economy's productivity and the current rate of inflation—perhaps an average of both. A figure of about 5 percent might be typical.

Firms and employees approving average wage increases in excess of the guideline would be penalized by paying additional corporate and personal income taxes on the difference. Firms and employees approving average wage increases below the guideline would be rewarded with corporate and personal tax cuts. Because the penalty or reward in each firm depends only on the *average* wage increase, individual promotions and raises are not discouraged.

Some Pros and Cons

TIP is by no means a simple solution to the problem of stagflation.

Would the adoption of TIP help solve the economy's stagflation problem? Those who believe it would offer three basic arguments.

1. It Reduces Wage Inflation TIP would make larger wage increases more expensive to employers and employees. Therefore, both groups would be more inclined to resist such increases.

2. It Reduces Price Inflation TIP is based on the observation that, for the economy as a whole, the margin between prices and unit labor costs has long remained virtually constant. Consequently, because wage increases tend to be associated with price increases, reduction of wage inflation will also reduce price inflation.

3. It Permits Free-Market Decisions TIP allows business and labor to negotiate wage increases. Therefore, the market mechanism is not restricted, and hence output and employment are not adversely affected.

In contrast, critics of TIP disagree with the entire concept. Among their many reasons, three are sufficient to indicate why.

1. It Assumes "Cost-Push" Inflation TIP is based on the premise that inflation is caused by labor and business, particularly by wages pushing up prices. This assumption contradicts the monetarist view. This view holds that excessive monetary growth is responsible for inflation, which, in turn, causes workers to press for wage increases in order to maintain real incomes.

2. It Causes Inefficiencies TIP would require all industries, some of which are expanding and some declining, to adhere to a single guideline. This would cause resource misallocation because the hiring decisions of the firms would be influenced strongly by the guideline rather than by market forces alone.

3. It Causes Inequities TIP requires for its administration a method of measuring the equivalent *average* wage-rate increase resulting from improved fringe benefits. Examples of these are pension rights, medical plans, executive stock options, and numerous other nonwage enrichments that companies provide for their employees. Any method devised to measure the monetary values of these benefits would obviously be enormously complex and would create inequities that would lead to untold numbers of court tests.

Conclusion: TIP Is a Short-Term Solution at Best

TIP would not provide a permanent solution to stagflation.

TIP is a form of wage–price policy designed to reduce inflation without interfering with the market system. In essence, TIP provides tax benefits for those workers and firms that curb wage increases, and tax penalties for those that do not.

Would the adoption of TIP lead to a permanent cure for inflation? Probably not:

> TIP is at best a short-term anti-inflationary measure. This is because it deals with the symptoms of inflation, not its cause. Among the fundamental causes of inflation are government deficit spending financed by excessive monetary growth. Therefore, these are the activities that must ultimately be curbed if inflation is to be controlled.

Employment Programs: Putting People to Work

Our economy faces an awesome challenge. Each year it must generate many millions of new jobs. That is what is needed to lift the country out of the quagmire of unemployment.

How can the task be accomplished? Many specific proposals have been offered. They range from the conservative position advocating a hands-off government policy to the liberal view that government should become more deeply involved. Most of the proposed measures can be grouped into one of three approaches: (1) public employment, (2) employment-training policies, and (3) employment subsidies (vouchers).

Several methods have been proposed for putting people to work. But difficulties may arise from the ways in which these methods are administered and financed.

Public Employment

There is a need for people to clean up parks, assist in hospitals, and fill other types of public-service jobs. Therefore, a direct way to reduce unemployment is for Washington to appropriate in advance the necessary funds for public employment. Then, when unemployment reaches a certain critical level—say, 6 percent—the money could be used to put unemployed people to work.

This statement is correct as far as it goes. However, it considers only the direct effects of a public-employment program. The indirect ones, which can be considerable, arise from the ways in which the program may be financed. These are discussed below.

Employment-Training Policies

A second approach to dealing with unemployment is through *employment-training policies*. These are deliberate efforts undertaken in the private and public sectors to develop and use the capacities of human beings as actual or potential members of the labor force. Employment-training policies have been financed largely by government. Such policies aim at improving job skills, thereby enhancing worker motivation and mobility.

Employment Subsidies (Vouchers)

Somewhat related to employment-training policies as a means of reducing unemployment are employment subsidies. These are grants given to employers who hire and train unemployed people. One way of implementing subsidies would be for government to issue vouchers to the unemployed and unskilled. Those who find jobs at the minimum wage would give the voucher to their employer, who would present it to the government for redemption. The redemption value might be, say, 40 percent of the minimum wage. The employer would then be required to spend the payment on training the new workers.

A voucher system could be an effective means of implementing employment subsidies.

Rifle or Shotgun Approach?

Critics contend that most such employment programs are simply disguised "make-work" schemes. To some extent this may be true. However, well-designed employment programs can greatly reduce, if not eliminate, inefficiency and waste.

For example, by focusing on unemployment problems among particular age groups and industries, selective rather than general programs can be formulated. Several European countries, among them Sweden and the Netherlands, have followed this course, making effective use of selective labor-market techniques. These include free training programs, progressive incentive payments, and relocation grants for people willing to work in certain occupations and regions. These countries have also made some use of public-employment programs for people unable to find work in the open market. For the most part, however, a rifle approach that targets on specific problems, rather than an indiscriminate shotgun approach, has proved to be the most effective way of attacking the unemployment problem.

Conclusion: We Need Better Employment-Training Programs

Despite the high cost of effective employment-training policies, the alternative cost of poor ones, or none at all, may be greater.

What are the economic consequences of employment programs? Historically, they have tended to be inflationary because they have been financed by creating money—that is, by borrowing through the banking system. Oftentimes, they have also been poorly administered. Nevertheless, well-designed programs, especially employment-training programs, yield two major benefits.

1. They lower the cost to employers of hiring workers who might otherwise remain unemployed because of their low productivity.

2. They enable young people to be employed and trained for higher-paying jobs.

In view of this, what can we conclude about the desirability of employment-training policies? The following practical answer is based on realistic considerations.

> A comprehensive employment-training strategy would be difficult and expensive to establish. But the alternative should be recognized. Government now spends many billions of dollars annually on unemployment insurance and welfare benefits. Most of the funds produce neither new jobs nor additional output. The money could be used instead to put people to work.

Productivity: Steps Toward Improving Efficiency

Finding ways to improve productivity is fundamental to curing stagflation.

Almost everyone agrees that if the nation is to make substantial progress toward reducing inflation, greater efforts will be needed to cut the costs of producing things. This means increasing the productivity of the factors of production.

Productivity is the output of goods and services obtained from a given amount of the factors of production. A rise in productivity means that the economy is getting more output, and therefore more real income, from its productive resources. A decline in productivity means the opposite. Productivity is thus a measure of an economy's technical efficiency. It follows that widespread increases in productivity make it possible for everyone to enjoy better living standards. Without such increases, efforts to provide more goods and services for the growing population must inevitably produce mounting inflationary pressures.

Comparisons and Trends

Although every nation recognizes the importance of achieving high rates of productivity, not all are able to do so. There are numerous reasons for this, and the reasons differ from country to country. In the United States, for example, management blames unions for establishing make-work rules and wasteful labor practices. Unions, on the other hand, blame management for its indifference toward, and callous disregard of, labor's needs. And both blame government for failing to pass legislation that would be conducive to stimulating greater production.

Regardless of who is at fault, there is widespread agreement that unemployment and inflation result, to a large extent, from a drag on output. This helps to explain why America's stagflation has, for many years, been accompanied by productivity growth rates that are among the lowest of the major industrial nations. Some interesting comparisons and trends are shown in Exhibit 4.

Causes of Decline

What are the reasons for America's relatively low productivity? Experts offer a number of explanations, but four are especially important:

Inadequate Investment Private-sector expenditures on new plant and equipment have not increased rapidly enough to sustain a high rate of growth of real output. Business executives attribute the main causes of sluggish investment to lack of confidence engendered by excessive government regulations, high business taxes, and erratic inflation.

Excessive Regulations Government rules have required firms to spend large amounts of money on expensive health, safety, and environmental-protection equipment. Regardless of their worthiness, these expenditures have left firms with less to spend on modernizing and expanding their plant and equipment.

Increased Services The economy's service sector has grown so much that it now accounts for approximately 50 percent of GNP. Because it is harder to increase the productivity of a service worker (such as a barber, a police officer, a teacher, or a lawyer) than it is to increase that of an assembly-line worker, significant gains in productivity have become more difficult to attain.

Protected Inefficiencies Import quotas, tariffs, subsidies, and occasional loan guarantees to failing firms are measures that have been used by government to support and protect weak firms. Many have thus been preserved, or allowed to die slowly, thus retarding the flow of their resources into high-productivity occupations.

Work Incentives: What Can We Learn from Japan?

What can be done to improve the nation's productive efficiency and thereby achieve fuller utilization of resources and lower prices? Many of the answers have already been given. They include revision of the fiscal–monetary mix, broad-scale tax reductions, effective employment-

Exhibit 4
U.S. Productivity

America's gains in productivity have lagged far behind those of most industrial nations. Until the right steps are taken to improve the situation, a permanent solution to the stagflation problem is unlikely.

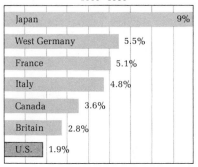

INCREASE IN OUTPUT PER WORKER-HOUR, 1965–1980

Japan 9%
West Germany 5.5%
France 5.1%
Italy 4.8%
Canada 3.6%
Britain 2.8%
U.S. 1.9%

Source: U.S. Department of Labor.

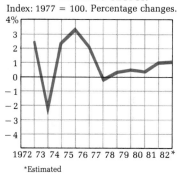

OUTPUT PER HOUR OF ALL PERSONS, BUSINESS SECTOR
Index: 1977 = 100. Percentage changes.

1972 73 74 75 76 77 78 79 80 81 82*
*Estimated

training policies, and special tax incentives. Adoption of these measures on a systematic basis would go a long way toward achieving efficiency and stability.

But there is more that can be done. Most experts agree that one of the surest ways of improving productivity is through the use of *incentives*. Without them, workers will not be motivated to fulfill more than their minimum job requirements.

No country has had more success with incentive systems than Japan. There are several reasons for this. Among them:

Japan has made use of several policies to stimulate incentives.

1. Lifetime Employment The Japanese worker is guaranteed a job for life. The introduction of new labor-saving machinery, therefore, is not a threat. The worker will simply be assigned to a different job within the company if his or her job is eliminated for any reason.

2. People-Related Wage Rates Wage rates are assigned to the individual rather than to the job. Bonuses consist of money, prizes (such as gifts or extra vacation days), and praise. They are based on increases both in productivity and in corporate profitability.

3. Labor-Saving Initiatives Workers are encouraged to seek ways of reducing the amount of labor used in production. Teams of workers meet periodically to discuss methods of increasing efficiency and improving their company's products.

In contrast, most American workers view labor-saving machinery as a potential threat to employment. They may be aware that gains in productivity can lead to higher wages, but they perceive the connection between the two as loose and remote. Consequently, American workers often have little incentive to increase productivity. Indeed, they have frequently looked for ways to curb productivity by resisting technical change, imposing restrictive work rules, and limiting the introduction of innovations. Because of this:

> Investment in new plant and equipment is a necessary but not a sufficient condition for achieving substantial gains in technical efficiency. If America is to close the productivity gap between itself and leading industrial nations, it will have to devise new incentive systems for labor and management. *Only when workers expect to benefit from change, not to be penalized by it, will they be eager to support it.*

There is growing evidence that this principle is gaining increasing acceptance in modern labor—management relations.

Curing Stagflation: Can Nonmarket Measures Work?

Various nonmarket measures for coping with stagflation have been proposed from time to time.

> The inflation came in various forms—sometimes led by wages, sometimes by prices. Sometimes it was domestic and sometimes imported. Many programs have been launched to stop it—without durable success. Inflation seemed a hydra-headed monster, growing two new heads each time one was cut off.
>
> President's Council of Economic Advisers

The various policies described thus far work directly through the market to overcome stagflation. As a result, these measures do not tend to limit our economic freedoms. Certain other policies, however, replace the operation of the market with extensive laws and regulations. These not only limit personal choices but often reduce them. The chief examples of such nonmarket measures are (1) wage–price controls and (2) economic planning.

Wage–Price Controls: Incomes Policies

One way in which government can try to cure stagflation is to impose wage and price controls. Measures of this type provide examples of what is known as *incomes policies*. These are laws aimed at curbing inflation by establishing conditions under which businesses' production costs (especially wages), prices, and profits may be allowed to increase. As you might expect, incomes policies in general, and wage–price controls in particular, are the subject of frequent debate.

Incomes policies do not provide a permanent cure for stagflation. At best, they act as a temporary palliative, and they lead to gross inefficiencies and inequities in the long run.

Arguments Against Wage–Price Controls

Those who oppose government wage and price controls believe they have a number of undesirable effects:

Misallocation of Resources Under a system of controls, resource and product prices are determined by specific governmental rules or orders. Buyers' and sellers' responses to the free-market forces of supply and demand are thus replaced by government edicts. The wage–price structure becomes frozen. This prevents producers from responding to changes in tastes and technology, as would happen if markets were unregulated. As a result, resources are misallocated and economic efficiency is impaired.

Reduction of Productivity Controls put a lid on wages and prices, keeping them from rising to their free-market levels. This diminishes productivity in three ways:

1. Millions of working hours in government and industry are wasted on administering controls.

2. To the extent that wage increases are restrained, workers' incentives are reduced and employers are prevented from paying more for the high-quality workers that are wanted.

3. If ceilings are imposed on profit margins, as they were during some previous periods of control, businesses lose much of their incentive to improve efficiency. The reason is that profits above the ceiling are taxed at prohibitive rates. As a consequence, firms look for frivolous ways to increase costs. This can be done by spending lavishly on advertising and promotion, buying corporate jets, providing generous expense accounts for executives, and so on—all for the purpose of cutting down profits.

Institutionalization of Inflation Wage and price controls provide at best only a temporary palliative rather than a permanent cure for inflation. They lull society into accepting inflation as a way of life instead of encouraging the public to press for eradication of the root causes. Those causes are found, as you have already learned, in fiscal and monetary policies. But they are also found in the monopoly power wielded by

With wage and price controls, an acceptable level of inflation could be "built into" the economy.

large firms and trade unions and in government legislation that establishes minimum wages, subsidies, tariffs, and import quotas. These restrictive elements interfere with the effective functioning of a free market. Therefore, public policy should be directed toward eliminating them in order to achieve price stability.

The Case for Controls

Arguments in favor of wage-and-price controls are not based on strong evidence.

On the other side of the fence, most advocates of wage and price controls are generally sympathetic with the competitive market philosophy. However, they believe that the inflationary bias has become entrenched by our failure to eliminate monopolistic elements, represented by large corporations and unions, within the economy. As a result, they believe, it is unrealistic to assume that these elements, which are now deeply embedded, will ever be significantly reduced. Therefore, the choice is not between free markets or public controls; it is between free markets and *some degree* of public controls. As many advocates of controls contend:

> Less than half the economy's private sector is responsive to reasonably competitive market forces. Within the remainder of the private sector, prices are essentially set by the great corporations in conjunction with the unions. It follows that public controls can be confined to the less competitive segment, where market power is greatest. They are not needed in the more competitive segment, where the market still functions.

As it happens, there is no strong evidence to support this point of view. As a result, critics have proposed other approaches—among them economic planning—as a way of reducing unemployment and inflation.

Economic Planning

Economic planning replaces private decision making with government decision making. There is no evidence that government can plan better than businesses can, and there is much evidence that government may plan more poorly.

Another method of coping with unemployment and inflation is economic planning. It may be—and often is—employed in conjunction with wage–price controls. Hence, the two approaches should not necessarily be thought of as mutually exclusive.

> An *economic plan* is a detailed method, formulated beforehand, for achieving specific economic objectives. The plan governs the activities and interrelations of those economic institutions—firms, households, and governments—that have an influence on the desired outcome.

To repeat, the purpose of economic planning is to achieve certain objectives. Those who advocate national economic planning believe that a federal agency should be established to perform the task—both for government activities and for the private sector's actions. The government planning board would thus be directly involved in dealing with the three fundamental problems of every economic system. These problems, you recall, are *what* to produce, *how* to produce, and *for whom*.

As you would expect, there is much controversy over the desirability of planning. Proponents contend that the government's central planning board would act purely in an *advisory* capacity to major industries and government agencies. The board would merely point out long-run goals or targets and suggest how they might be realized. Opponents of planning disagree strongly. They offer such arguments as the following:

1. Planning would create a new federal bureaucracy to administer economic activity. The free market—and with it consumer sovereignty—would be replaced by governmental authority and coercion.

2. The government's planning office would probably come to be dominated by the major corporations whose activities are planned. This is evidenced by the fact that many government regulatory agencies have long been influenced by the industries that are regulated. Collaboration and collusion between big business and government would thus be promoted rather than discouraged.

3. There is no evidence that government is more adept at planning than private industry is. On the other hand, there is considerable evidence, based on experiences in some mixed economies, that government involvement in economic planning may at best result in improvements in equity. However, this may be achieved at the cost of seriously impairing economic efficiency, price stability, and perhaps growth.

For these and other reasons, the controversy over national economic planning is likely to continue. As a result, you will often read and hear a great deal about it in the news media.

Conclusion: Economics, Politics, and Rationality

Stagflation is today's most serious economic problem. To help overcome it, numerous policy proposals have been made. Those explained in this chapter are among the most important.

Stagflation is likely to persist until Washington develops some basic rules for budget deficits and monetary expansion.

Practically all of these proposals have been adopted, in varying degrees, during recent history. For example, since the early 1970s the nation has experimented with wage–price controls, wage-and-price guidelines, tax reduction, public-employment schemes, employment-training policies, and economic planning. Without evaluating specific measures, it can be said that these programs usually attack the symptoms of stagflation rather than the cause.

> Stagflation is caused mainly by improper fiscal and monetary policies and by insufficient incentives to produce. These conditions lead to greater economic uncertainty, reduced private investment, and slower economic growth. Therefore, policies that fail to recognize the real causes of stagflation will not be successful in curing it.

Today these beliefs are held by practically all informed observers. But, unfortunately, there is no consistent agreement on what constitutes the "right" fiscal–monetary mix or the "right" combination of incentives. However, there is widespread agreement that, at the very least, a reasonably steady expansion of the money supply and a continuous reduction in budget deficits are necessary to promote greater long-run stability.

Despite this understanding, it is characteristic of our type of democracy that political considerations often outweigh economic logic. Few political leaders are willing to risk their careers on policies designed to curb inflation at the cost of increased joblessness. Consequently, legislators usually find that budget deficits accompanied by rapid monetary expansion is the easiest way of combatting unemployment. Therefore:

Some practical guidelines are needed for relating government spending to revenues.

> Until Congress develops some rational rules for relating government spending to revenues, stagflation resulting from large deficits and erratic fluctuations in the money supply will continue to plague the economy.

What You Have Learned in This Chapter

1. For many years, the chief macroeconomic problem facing our own and some other mixed economies has been stagflation. Another name for stagflation is "recessionary inflation."

2. Economists have long debated the possibility of a trade-off between unemployment and inflation. This concept is represented by a Phillips curve. A widely held view today is that the most realistic Phillips curve has a modified L shape. The vertical portion coincides with the natural unemployment rate, while the lower-right segment—the "stem"—is downward-sloping. The curve thus depicts a limited trade-off along the stem.

3. Another view—one held by many monetarists—is that the most realistic Phillips curve is a vertical line at the natural unemployment rate. Along this line, therefore, fiscal–monetary stimulation to reduce unemployment leads to accelerating inflation as represented by acceleration curves.

4. The search for stability has led to some new ideas concerning public policy. One theory, the rational-expectations theory, holds that people form expectations about government fiscal–monetary policies and then include these expectations in their economic decisions. As a result, systematic (or widely expected) policies become ineffective. Therefore, the best policy, according to the theory, is for government to achieve stability and then maintain it by adhering to balanced budgets and steady growth of the money supply. Failure to do so will lead to public policies that are self-defeating and inflationary.

5. In matters of macroeconomic policy, traditional Keynesian economics focuses on measures designed to control aggregate demand. An alternative approach, known as "supply-side" economics, emphasizes policies aimed at influencing aggregate supply. The major pillars of supply-side economics are: (a) rejection of Keynesian demand-management policies; (b) tax reductions to stimulate production; (c) nonmonetization of government deficits; and (d) deregulation of industries and markets. Nowadays practically all economists concur with these ideas to varying degrees. However, there are differences of opinion on the relative importance of each and the extent to which they should be implemented at any given time.

6. A number of market measures for curing stagflation have been proposed. The chief ones are:

(a) *Fiscal and monetary policies.* These should seek to stabilize the growth of the money supply. They should also help establish closer ties among government tax revenues, government spending, and the nation's income. Four guidelines for achieving these goals have been proposed by various groups: (1) stabilize monetary growth; (2) balance the federal budget annually; (3) limit federal spending; and (4) limit federal revenues.

(b) *Tax-based incomes policy (TIP).* Government should provide tax benefits for those workers and firms that keep wage increases within a certain guideline, and tax penalties for those that do not. The guideline, announced annually by the government, would be somewhere between the economy's productivity rate and the current rate of inflation—perhaps an average of both.

(c) *Employment programs.* A comprehensive employment-training policy designed to promote the employment and training of people for higher-paying jobs should be adopted. Although such a program would be expensive, the alternative is for government to continue spending many billions of dollars annually on unemployment insurance and welfare. Most of these expenditures produce neither new jobs nor additional output.

(d) *Productivity improvement.* Measures designed to stimulate investment in physical and human capital should be undertaken. In addition, new incentive systems for labor and management must be devised. Such measures would improve productive efficiency and boost the economy's long-run growth rates, thereby helping to absorb unemployed resources and to curb inflation.

7. In addition to the market measures for curing stagflation, some observers have proposed two major nonmarket policies:

(a) *Wage–price controls: incomes policies.* These are laws aimed at curbing inflation by establishing limits within which businesses' production costs, prices, and profits may be allowed to increase.

(b) *Economic planning.* This is a program for achieving specific economic goals. A comprehensive plan would embrace the activities of households, firms, and government in a unified effort to attain desired objectives.

8. Nearly all of the foregoing proposals have been adopted in varying degrees since the early 1970s. However, because stagflation is fundamentally caused by an improper mix of government fiscal and monetary policies, these are the activities that must ultimately be modified. Otherwise, any other measures can yield only temporary benefits at best and may even be harmful in the long run.

For Discussion

1. *Terms and concepts to review:*
stagflation
Phillips curve
natural unemployment rate
acceleration curves
rational-expectations theory
demand-side economics
supply-side economics
gold standard
Laffer curve
depreciation
money-supply rule
tax-based incomes policy (TIP)
employment-training policies
incomes policies
economic plan

2. Explain carefully the difference between an acceleration curve and a vertical Phillips curve.

3. What legislative and fiscal actions can you recommend to *improve* the economy's Phillips curve? Before answering, explain precisely what is meant by "improve."

4. If you take a course in finance or in investments, you will learn how a modified version of the rational-expectations theory, called the "efficient-market theory," applies to the stock market. From your understanding of rational expectations, what do you suppose the efficient-market theory says about the prediction of stock-market prices?

5. Many economists want to limit government spending by tying it to some percentage of tax revenues. For example, spending might be limited to, say, 103 percent of tax revenues. (a) What is the reason for allowing spending to exceed revenues? (b) Why not set the figure at 100 percent or even less? (c) Can we limit government spending by putting a ceiling on taxes?

6. Tax reduction is often seen as a device to stimulate demand. But it can also stimulate supply. Can you explain how?

7. "Indexation of the income tax and of government bonds would lower the Treasury's tax revenues. This reduction in the benefits government receives from inflation would stimulate incentives to curb inflation." Explain this statement. How does government benefit from inflation? (**Note** Look up the meaning of *indexation* in the Dictionary at the back of the book.)

8. Can you give at least two arguments against indexation and two rebuttals in favor? What are your conclusions?

9. How would the position or location of our economy's Phillips curve be affected by each of the following? Explain your answers.
    (a) A reduction in tariffs.
    (b) A decrease in import quotas.
    (c) A new law making labor unions illegal.
    (d) A merger of the largest firm in each major industry (for example, automobiles, steel, and so on) with the second largest firm in its industry.
    (e) A new law prohibiting any firm's sales from exceeding 50 percent of its industry's.
    (f) Significant advances made in automation throughout most of industry.

10. Some economists and political leaders contend: "Inflation promotes growth and diminishes unemployment. We must recognize that the costs of inflation are much less than the costs of avoiding it. Therefore, we should accept inflation and learn to live with it. This can be done by recognizing that it is easier to compensate the victims of inflation than the casualties of recession." What specific compensatory measures can you propose to make inflation less painful and inequitable? Discuss.

17
CHAPTER

The Open Economy: International Trade and Finance

Learning guide
Watch for the answers to these important questions

Why do nations trade? How important is international trade in today's economy?

What is meant by "comparative advantage"? How do a country's terms of trade differ from its gains from trade? Is there a connection between specialization, comparative advantage, and gains from trade?

What is the foreign-trade multiplier? How is it affected by the marginal propensity to save? The marginal propensity to import?

What is the balance of payments? Why do nations prepare balance-of-payments statements?

Where is foreign exchange bought and sold? What determines the price of foreign exchange?

In what ways do imports create jobs? In what ways does import protection eliminate jobs?

Why must fixed exchange rates result either in overvalued or undervalued currencies, and therefore balance-of-payments deficits or surpluses? Why do nations today engage in managed floating?

This chapter focuses on international aspects of macroeconomics, including both commercial and financial problems and policies.

We work in order to earn income with which to buy the goods we want. Nations export in order to earn income with which to buy the imports they want. Thus, just as we work in order to buy, nations export in order to import—*not the other way around.*

The study of macroeconomics would be incomplete without an understanding of our nation's role in the world economy. Until now we have neglected this consideration by assuming that ours is a "closed" economy, insulated from the economies of other nations. It is time to broaden this outlook by recognizing that we live in an "open" economy. This means that many of our nation's economic actions affect other countries and are affected by them.

The study of the world economy is known as "international economics." It embraces three broad areas of interest:

1. International trade—the commerce of nations.

2. International finance—the payments of nations.

3. International commercial and financial problems.

This chapter surveys the major economic principles and ideas underlying international trade and finance. It then applies these concepts in a macroeconomic setting, thereby enabling you to analyze and interpret many practical international economic problems. These problems, you will find, are the kinds you read and hear about almost every day in the news media.

International Trade: The Commerce of Nations

World trade is gaining increasing significance among nations. You can see the growing importance of trade for the United States by noting the trend shown in Exhibit 1.

The graph shows that, until the 1960s, the dollar sum of U.S. imports and exports was less than 10 percent of GNP. By 1970 the proportion had climbed to more than 12 percent. Within a decade the figure approximately doubled, reaching 25 percent in 1980. During the 1990s, according to some experts, the proportion will range between 30 and 40 percent. These sharp increases reflect the growing trend of economic interdependence between the United States and other countries.

Why Trade?

Why do nations trade? Why, for example, does not the United States produce all of the cars, motorcycles, electronic goods, and cameras that it wants so that Americans would not have to buy these products from Japan? In return, why does not Japan produce all of the food, machinery, transportation equipment, and chemicals that it wants so that the Japanese would not have to buy these goods from the United States?

The answer is that nations have different quantities and qualities of economic resources and different techniques of combining them. As a result, each country can produce certain goods more efficiently, or at relatively lower costs, than others.

This idea can be stated somewhat differently. Imagine a world consisting of only two countries, each producing the same two commodities. Under such circumstances, the alternative or *opportunity cost* to each country of producing more of one commodity is the amount of the second commodity that must be sacrificed. In view of this, which of the two commodities should the countries produce?

The answer is that each should *specialize*. How? By producing the commodity with the lower opportunity cost and trading with the other country for the commodity with the higher opportunity cost. In that way, the combined output of both commodities will actually be larger, and each country will get more of them than it would if it tried to be self-sufficient by producing both.

Comparative Advantage

These concepts can be illustrated by an example. Exhibit 2 shows hypothetical production-possibilities curves (the solid lines) for meat (*M*) and wine (*W*) for the United States and France. To simplify the analysis, the production-possibilities curves are drawn as straight lines instead of being bowed outward. This means that *constant* rather than increasing opportunity costs of production are assumed. Note that opportunity cost is measured by the *slope* of the line—the change in the vertical distance per unit of change in the horizontal.

Domestic-Exchange Equations

What does the assumption of constant opportunity costs imply?

In Figure (*a*), any point along the United States' production-possibilities curve reveals a different output combination of meat and wine.

Exhibit 1
Share of U.S. Economy Involved in Foreign Trade

International trade has assumed an increasingly important role in the economy of the United States since 1970. The sum of imports and exports as a percentage of GNP will continue to grow in future years.

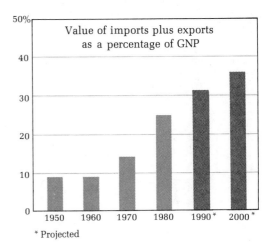

Value of imports plus exports as a percentage of GNP

* Projected

Source: U.S. Department of Commerce.

Exhibit 2
Production and Trading Possibilities: Terms of Trade and Gains from Trade

For each country, the opportunity cost (or domestic-exchange equation) for meat and wine is represented by the slope of the production-possibilities curve. The *terms of trade*, on the other hand, are represented by the slope of the trade-possibilities curve. Each country, by specializing in production of the good with the lowest opportunity cost and then trading, can end up with more of both goods than it would if it produced them both itself.

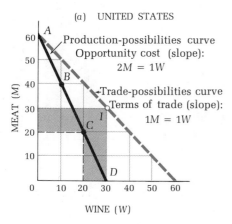

(a) UNITED STATES

Production-possibilities curve
Opportunity cost (slope):
$2M = 1W$

Trade-possibilities curve
Terms of trade (slope):
$1M = 1W$

For example, suppose that each country tried to be self-sufficient. In Figure (a), the United States might produce a combination of meat and wine represented by point C. In Figure (b), France might produce a combination shown by point F. By specializing and trading, however, the United States could end up with the products at point I, and France with those at point J. The net benefit or increase in consumption for each country thus represents its *gains from trade*. These are shown by the shaded areas. Thus, for the United States, the gains are 10 units of meat and 10 units of wine. For France, the gains are 10 units of meat and 30 units of wine.

For instance, point A denotes an output of 60M and 0W; point B, an output of 40M and 10W; point C, an output of 20M and 20W; and point D, an output of 0M and 30W. In general, at any point along its production-possibilities curve, the United States must sacrifice meat for wine at the rate of 20M to 10W. This is equivalent, of course, to a rate of 2M to 1W. The opportunity cost of the two products is therefore $2M = 1W$.

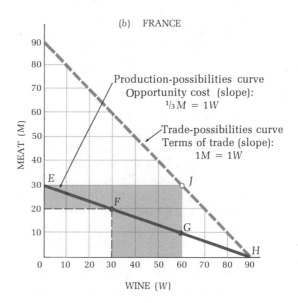

(b) FRANCE

Production-possibilities curve
Opportunity cost (slope):
$\frac{1}{3}M = 1W$

Trade-possibilities curve
Terms of trade (slope):
$1M = 1W$

In Figure (b), on the other hand, France's production-possibilities curve reveals a different opportunity cost for the two products. For example, in order to go from point E to point F, France must sacrifice 10 units of meat to gain 30 units of wine. Similarly, a movement from F to G entails sacrificing another 10M for an additional 30W. In order to go from G to H, the sacrifice is again the same. Therefore, the rate of sacrifice in France is 10M to 30W. This is the same, of course, as a rate of 1M to 3W, or $\frac{1}{3}M$ to 1W. The opportunity cost of the two products is therefore $\frac{1}{3}M = 1W$.

Opportunity costs in the United States and France thus determine each country's domestic-exchange equation. The equation expresses each country's opportunity costs—the rate at which either commodity can be "exchanged" for the other. The two equations are therefore:

United States:	$2M = 1W$	or equivalently	$1M = \frac{1}{2}W$
France:	$\frac{1}{3}M = 1W$	or equivalently	$1M = 3W$

You can now see two facts that are evident from these equations:

1. Wine is more expensive in the United States than in France. In the United States, it costs 2M to acquire 1W whereas in France it costs only $\frac{1}{3}M$ to acquire 1W.

2. Meat is less expensive in the United States than in France. In the United States, 1M can be acquired for only $\frac{1}{2}W$, whereas in France 1M can be acquired only at the higher cost of 3W.

Because of these cost relationships, it can be said that France has a comparative advantage in wine production and that the United States has a comparative advantage in meat production. That is:

> Given any two products, a country has a *comparative advantage* in the product that has the lower opportunity cost.

Specialization and the Gains from Trade

If the two countries were self-sufficient, each would produce its own meat and wine. The amounts produced in each country would depend on consumer preferences as reflected through the price system. For example, the United States might produce at point C, representing 20 units of meat and 20 units of wine. France, on the other hand, might produce at point F, representing 20 units of meat and 30 units of wine.

Suppose, however, that each country were to specialize by producing the product in which it has a comparative advantage and then were to trade with the other. In that case, the United States would allocate all of its resources to meat and none to wine, producing at point A ($60M$ and $0W$). Likewise, France would allocate all of its resources to wine and none to meat, producing at point H ($90W$ and $0M$). By trading, each country would then end up with more meat and more wine, as represented perhaps by points I and J.

Thus:

- At point I, the United States consumes 30 units of meat and 30 units of wine. This is greater than the consumption level at point C (20 units of meat and 20 units of wine), which existed before trade was undertaken. For the United States, therefore, the *gains from trade* are 10 units of meat and 10 units of wine.

- At point J, France consumes 30 units of meat and 60 units of wine. This is greater than the consumption level at point F (20 units of meat and 30 units of wine), which existed before trading began. For France, therefore, the *gains from trade* amount to 10 units of meat and 30 units of wine.

In other words, through specialization and trade, the United States produces 60 units of meat and France produces 90 units of wine. The United States then exports 30 units of meat to France, and France exports 30 units of wine to the United States. As a result, both countries end up with more meat and more wine than they would if each tried to be self-sufficient in both products.

Summarizing:

> By specializing in the good in which it has a comparative advantage, each nation is able to produce enough of the good so that it can exchange some of it for the other. Both nations can thereby incur *gains from trade*. These are the net benefits or increases in goods that a country receives as a result of trading with others.

Law of Comparative Advantage

You can now appreciate the meaning of *comparative advantage*. It refers to the *relative* benefit of producing one good instead of another. The idea can be expressed as a law—one of the oldest in economics.

By specializing in the production of those products they can produce most efficiently and then trading, nations can reap greater benefits than if they try to be more self-sufficient.

To achieve efficiency, nations should pro-duce those goods for which they have the lowest opportunity costs and then trade with other nations.

Law of comparative advantage. A basis for trade exists when each of two nations, both capable of producing the same two goods, specializes in producing the one good that is *relatively* cheaper for it to produce. This is the good in which the country has a lower opportunity cost—a comparative advantage. The two countries can then have more of both goods by engaging in trade. This is a general principle applicable not only to nations but also to regions and even to individuals.

The law of comparative advantage accounts for the benefits that nations receive from engaging in trade. Therefore, as you will see shortly, the law also accounts for the costs that nations incur when they erect barriers to trade.

Terms of Trade

When two parties engage in a transaction, the sacrifice that each makes to obtain something from the other is called the "terms of trade." For example, in order to buy this textbook, you might have had to give up five visits to the movies. Your terms of trade, therefore, are 5 movies = 1 book. On the other hand, if you bought four fewer pizzas in order to accumulate enough money to purchase this book, your terms of trade are 4 pizzas = 1 book. The *terms of trade* for a given transaction equal the number of units of goods that must be given up for one unit of goods received by each party to the transaction.

Using these ideas, what are the terms of trade for meat and wine between the United States and France? To begin with, you have already learned that the domestic exchange equations are:

The terms of trade are measured by what each party to a transaction must sacrifice in order to acquire what it wants.

$$\text{United States:} \quad 2M = 1W$$
$$\text{France:} \quad \tfrac{1}{3}M = 1W$$

In Exhibit 2, of course, these equations simply represent the *slopes* of the production-possibilities curves (solid lines). They express the sacrifice of one good for the other that each country incurs if it chooses to produce both commodities.

On the other hand, the terms of trade (dashed lines) express the actual exchange rate between the two countries' goods. The *slopes* of the lines for both countries, as you can see from the figures, are given by $1M = 1W$. These lines may therefore be called *trade-possibilities curves*.

Limits of the Terms of Trade

Keeping these facts in mind, you can now see the importance of the following proposition and the examples illustrating it:

> The terms of trade must fall somewhere between the two domestic-exchange equations, or slopes, in order for both countries to experience gains from trade. Otherwise, one of the countries will not find it advantageous to trade.

Two examples illustrate why this is true.

Example 1 Suppose the terms of trade are $3M = 1W$. Trade would then be advantageous to France but not to the United States. Why? Because, by specializing and trading, France could import 3 units of meat in return for exporting 1 unit of wine. This is a better value than obtaining only $\tfrac{1}{3}$ unit of meat for 1 unit of wine by producing both commodities domestically.

The United States, on the other hand, would have to export 3 units of meat in order to import 1 unit of wine. This is more expensive than producing both commodities domestically at a cost of only 2 units of meat for 1 unit of wine.

Example 2 Suppose the terms of trade are $\frac{1}{5}M = 1W$. In that case, trade would be advantageous to the United States but not to France. The United States, by specializing and trading, could export $\frac{1}{5}$ unit of meat in order to import 1 unit of wine. This is cheaper than producing both products domestically at a cost of 2 units of meat for 1 unit of wine.

France, however, would have to export 1 unit of wine in order to import $\frac{1}{5}$ unit of meat. This is not as good a value as producing both commodities domestically at a cost of 1 unit of wine for $\frac{1}{3}$ unit of meat.

Thus, international trade will not occur in either of these examples because only one country would experience gains from trade. However, if the terms of trade fall *between* the two domestic-exchange equations, as does $1M = 1W$, trade will occur because both countries will be able to realize gains.

What determines the terms of trade? In general:

A nation's terms of trade are determined in world markets by the supply of, and the demand for, its goods.

> The terms of trade for nations' goods are determined in world markets by international forces of supply and demand. The larger the overall global demand for a product relative to its supply, the higher its price—or terms of trade—in relation to other goods. Conversely, the smaller the overall global demand for a good, the lower its price—or terms of trade—relative to other goods. However, *the terms of trade must lie within the range of the nations' domestic-exchange equations in order for trade to occur.*

Increasing Costs and Incomplete Specialization

You can see from the foregoing analysis why nations find it profitable to trade. *A basis for trade exists when there are differences in opportunity costs between countries.* Thus, with respect to the United States and France, the difference in the opportunity costs of producing meat and wine reflects the different slopes of their production-possibilities curves.

In reality, increasing (rather than constant) costs prevail. This is likely to lead to incomplete international specialization and reduced world trade.

In view of this, what would happen if the curves bowed outward? This, as you will recall from your study of production-possibilities curves near the beginning of the book, is the typical situation. It means that costs are *increasing* rather than constant because resources are not perfectly substitutable between alternative uses.

In other words, as each country expands production of its specialty, its opportunity cost (sacrifice) in terms of the alternative good rises. A point can eventually be reached at which the two opportunity costs are equal. When that happens, the basis for trade, and hence the need for further specialization, is eliminated. Thus:

> When increasing costs result in equal opportunity costs between countries, there are two effects:
>
> **1.** *Incomplete specialization.* Both countries stop short of complete specialization because further increases in specialization cease to be economic.
>
> **2.** *Reduced trade.* Each country continues to produce both products—its specialty as well as some of its nonspecialty. Although trade is still carried on, its total volume is less than it would be if costs were constant.

The Foreign-Trade Multiplier

International trade can thus affect the level of a nation's income and employment. Indeed, international trade can have a *multiplier* effect on these variables. To see why, it helps to refresh your understanding of some basic concepts.

Exhibit 3
Injections and Withdrawals: The "Bathtub Theorem" in an Open Economy

Exports may be thought of as an injection into the income stream; imports may be thought of as a withdrawal. Hence, the water in the bathtub can be in equilibrium at any level as long as the inflow equals the outflow. If the inflow exceeds the outflow, the level in the tub will rise. If the outflow exceeds the inflow, the level in the tub will fall.

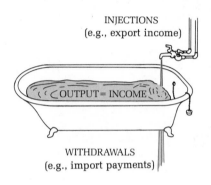

INJECTIONS
(e.g., export income)

OUTPUT = INCOME

WITHDRAWALS
(e.g., import payments)

We must examine the changes in a country's net exports to determine their effects on output.

First, recall (from the study of macroeconomic equilibrium) the meanings of the terms "injections" and "withdrawals." These ideas, you will remember, were illustrated with a physical analogy or model called the *"bathtub theorem."* The model is reproduced in Exhibit 3, but the inflows and outflows are now represented by export income and import payments. Summarizing the concepts briefly:

• *Injections* are expenditures that expand the nation's circular flow of income, thus raising the level of water in the tub. Examples are investment spending, government spending, and exports (that is, foreign spending for domestic goods).

• *Withdrawals* are "leakages" that contract the nation's circular flow of income, thus lowering the level of water in the tub. Examples are saving, taxes, and imports (that is, domestic spending for foreign goods).

Second, a distinction must be made between "closed" and "open" economies. A closed economy is one that is not engaged in international trade. This is the type of economy that occupied our attention in *all* of the previous chapters. In contrast, an open economy is one that is engaged in international trade. This is the type of economy that concerns us in this chapter.

Open-Economy Model

Against this background, how does international trade affect the level of a nation's income and employment? In order to answer this question, it helps to simplify the problem. This can be done by making two assumptions about the determinants of a nation's imports (M) and exports (X).

1. *Imports* (like saving) depend on the level of income. As the nation's income increases, so do domestic expenditures on imports of foreign cars, electronics products, steel, and other goods. We can thus define the *marginal propensity to import, MPM,* as the change in imports resulting from a unit change in income:

$$MPM = \frac{\text{change in imports}}{\text{change in income}}$$

The MPM is thus the fraction of each additional dollar of income that is spent on imports.

2. *Exports* are independent of the domestic level of income. That is, the dollar volume of exports is assumed to depend on the level of income in the importing country, not the exporting one.

It follows that the difference between a country's total exports and its total imports is its *net exports* (X_N). Thus:

$$X_N = X - M$$

Obviously, X_N may be positive, zero, or negative, according to whether the country's total exports are greater than, equal to, or less than its total imports.

Three Possibilities for Net Exports

With these ideas in mind, take a look at Exhibit 4. The AD_0 curve represents aggregate demand in a closed economy. Note that the intersection of AD_0 with aggregate supply, AS, determines an equilibrium level of NNP at $600 billion.

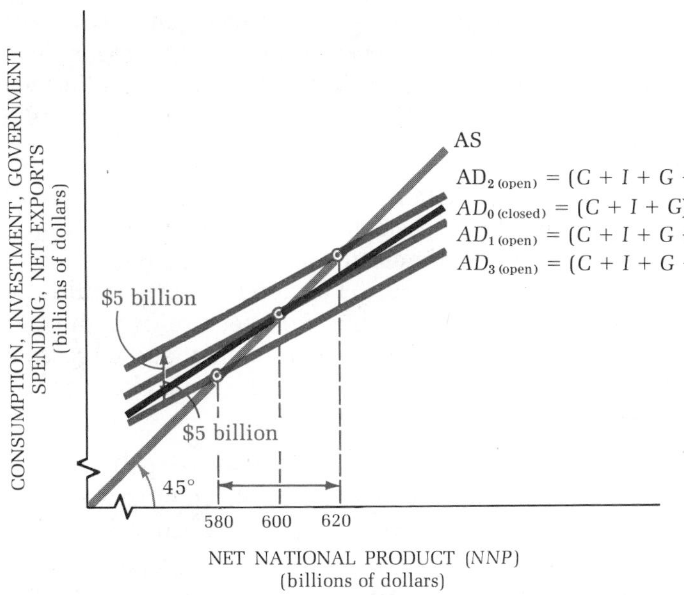

Exhibit 4

Aggregate Demand and the Foreign-Trade Multiplier

An open economy engages in international trade. Therefore, its AD curves are not as steep as the AD_0 curve for a closed economy. The reason is that, in an open economy, a part of each increase in income is spent on imports instead of on domestic goods. Therefore, the MPC is lower.

The lower MPC (and, therefore, the higher MPS) reduces the size of the multiplier, as explained in the text.

Labels on graph:

CONSUMPTION, INVESTMENT, GOVERNMENT SPENDING, NET EXPORTS (billions of dollars)

AS

$AD_{2 \text{ (open)}} = (C + I + G + X_N)_2$
$AD_{0 \text{ (closed)}} = (C + I + G)_0$
$AD_{1 \text{ (open)}} = (C + I + G + X_N)_1$
$AD_{3 \text{ (open)}} = (C + I + G + X_N)_3$

\$5 billion

\$5 billion

45°

580 600 620

NET NATIONAL PRODUCT (NNP)
(billions of dollars)

If the economy is now opened to trade, one of three possibilities may occur:

1. Neutral Effect: Net exports equal zero ($X_N = 0$) and *NNP* does not change. If exports equal imports, net exports are zero. This signifies that the export "injection" into the economy's circular flow of income has been exactly offset by the import "withdrawal" or "leakage." In terms of the bathtub theorem, therefore, the level of water in the tub, representing NNP, remains the same.

The aggregate demand curve, AD_0, may shift to AD_1. This new curve is less steep than the previous one because the AD_1 curve reflects the fact that some goods are now being purchased from abroad. Therefore, the slope or MPC of AD_1—the demand for *domestically* produced goods—is smaller because *part of each increase in income is spent on imports rather than on domestic goods*. Thus, spending on imports or foreign NNP is assumed to be a substitute for spending on domestic NNP.

2. Expansionary Effect: Net exports are positive ($X_N > 0$) and *NNP* rises. If exports are larger than imports, net exports are positive. This causes the AD curve to rise, say, to AD_2, signifying an "injection" into the nation's circular flow of income. In terms of the bathtub theorem, the water (NNP) in the tub rises to a new and higher level.

3. Contractionary Effect: Net exports are negative ($X_N < 0$) and *NNP* falls. If exports are less than imports, net exports are negative. This causes the AD curve to decline, perhaps to AD_3, signifying a "withdrawal" or "leakage" from the nation's circular flow of income. Therefore, the level of water (NNP) in the tub declines.

The effects of a change in net exports on NNP may be neutral, positive, or negative.

Summarizing:

International trade may have a neutral, expansionary, or contractionary effect on an economy's output and income. The effect of international trade on a country's NNP is neutral if net exports are zero, expansionary if net exports are positive, and contractionary if net exports are negative.

Multiplier Effect

In an open economy, the multiplier is the reciprocal of the MPS and the MPM—the total leakage.

If you look again at Exhibit 4, you can see how a change in net exports can have a multiplier effect on NNP. Before examining the reason, however, it will help you to review certain fundamental concepts that you learned a number of chapters back when you first studied the notion of macroeconomic equilibrium.

1. Closed Economy Assuming there are no taxes, how is an increase in society's income allocated? In a closed economy, you will recall, part of the increased income is spent on domestic goods and the rest of the increase is saved. Thus, $MPC + MPS = 1$. Further, the simple multiplier (also called the investment multiplier) equals the reciprocal of the MPS —that is, $1/MPS$. The MPS, of course, is the fraction of any increase in income that "leaks" into saving. Therefore, the multiplier may be thought of as the *reciprocal of the leakage*.

2. Open Economy In contrast to a closed economy, an open economy (assuming again that there are no taxes) may allocate any increase in income to a third spending alternative—imports. Therefore, $MPC + MPS + MPM = 1$. The MPM is the fraction of any increase in income that "leaks" into imports. This suggests the existence of a foreign-trade multiplier, which, like the simple multiplier for a closed economy, is the *reciprocal of the leakage*. But the leakage now includes imports as well as saving. Thus:

$$\text{foreign-trade multiplier} = \frac{1}{MPS + MPM} = \frac{1}{\text{leakage}}$$

This means, for example, that, if the MPS is 0.20 and the MPM is 0.05, the total leakage is 0.25. Therefore, the foreign-trade multiplier is $1/0.25 = 4$. In contrast, the simple multiplier (for a closed economy) is $1/0.20 = 5$.

Because of the existence of imports, the size of the multiplier in an open economy is smaller than in a closed one.

What do these numbers imply? In terms of Exhibit 4, a change in the open economy's aggregate demand curve of $5 billion, *whether due to a change in investment or to a change in net exports,* changes NNP by 4 times that amount, or by $20 billion. In a closed economy, on the other hand, the same change in aggregate demand (due, of course, to a change in investment) would have resulted in a change in NNP of $25 billion. The difference, as you have already learned, is due to a lower MPC in the open economy. This is because part of any increase in income is spent on imports, leaving a smaller portion to be spent on domestic goods.

To summarize:

The *foreign-trade multiplier* is a principle that states that fluctuations in net exports (= exports − imports) can generate magnified variations in national income. In general, an increase in net exports tends to raise domestic income—the same as an increase in net investment expenditures would. But the increased income also induces some imports, or "leakages." These tend to reduce the full multiplier effect on income that would exist if imports remained constant.

Conclusion: The Case for Free Trade

The study of international trade is among the oldest branches of economics. Adam Smith, in *The Wealth of Nations,* devoted considerable attention to the subject.

Among the concepts that Smith emphasized was that each country has different quantities and qualities of resources. These differences enable each country to produce at least one low-cost product it can sell to others. Therefore, it behooves nations to specialize in what they can produce most efficiently, and to engage in free (that is, unrestricted) trade. In that way, all countries can share in the gains from trade.

Absolute Advantage

This principle subsequently became known as the *law of absolute advantage*. It states that a basis for trade exists when one nation is more efficient than another in producing a good that the other wants. Each country can then specialize in producing the good it can produce most efficiently. By trading, nations can acquire one another's goods more cheaply than they can if they produce the same goods at home.

Absolute advantage exists when a nation can produce a good more efficiently than another.

This law accounts for much of the world's trade. For example, Brazil has an absolute advantage over the United States in the production of coffee. However, the United States has an absolute advantage over Brazil in the production of computers. Therefore, Brazil finds it advantageous to specialize in coffee and the United States finds it advantageous to specialize in computers. By trading, Brazil gets computers more cheaply and the United States gets coffee more cheaply than if each produced both products itself.

Similar illustrations can be given with many other goods. For instance: French perfume and Arabian oil; Bolivian tin and Peruvian cotton; Florida oranges and Nebraska wheat. Can you think of other examples?

Comparative Advantage

But what if a country can produce *two* goods, such as meat and wine, more cheaply than another country? Is there still a basis for trade in those goods between the two countries? This question was asked by the English economist David Ricardo in *The Principles of Political Economy and Taxation* (1817). Ricardo's answer was *yes*, and his brilliant reasoning helped to establish him as the greatest of the classical economists.

Comparative advantage exists when a nation can produce two goods more efficiently than another and it is more efficient in the production of one of these than it is in the production of the other.

Ricardo showed that, even if one country has an absolute advantage in the production of two products, it is the *relative* advantage—the *comparative* rather than absolute advantage—that counts. Ricardo proved this by demonstrating that it pays for each country to specialize in producing the good in which it has the greatest "degree" of advantage. The two countries can then trade for the alternative good.

The law of comparative advantage accounts for the logic of international trade, and it underlies the meat-and-wine example used earlier. Thus, because the United States had a comparative advantage in meat and France had one in wine, it paid for them to specialize and trade. More meat and wine were thereby consumed by the two countries than if each tried to produce both goods.

Can you think of similar illustrations for individuals? For example, if you were a doctor as well as an expert gardener, you might nevertheless employ a gardener who is less competent than yourself. Why? Because you could be more productive as a doctor than as a gardener. Similarly, if you were a lawyer as well as a good typist, you would probably find it more profitable to hire a typist—even one who is less proficient than you.

The Argument for Free Trade

But suppose a law prohibited you from hiring a gardener (or a typist), so that you were compelled to do the gardening (or typing) yourself. In that case, you would be less efficient as a doctor (or as a lawyer).

The same principle applies to countries. Through specialization and free (unrestricted) trade, nations achieve a more efficient allocation of world resources. As a result, all nations end up with more goods, and hence with a higher standard of living, than if they imposed legislation restricting free trade.

> The effect of free trade on nations is the same as the effect of increases in resources or improvements in technology. That is, the effect on nations is the same as if they experienced outward shifts of their production-possibilities curves. Therefore, legislation that restricts free trade also reduces nations' standards of living.

International Finance: The Payments of Nations

The study of international economics deals not only with the flow of goods between nations but with the flow of money. This involves the area of international finance, a vast and complex subject. You can gain some appreciation of its nature by learning about two of its main components—the balance of payments and the foreign-exchange market.

The Balance of Payments

Most countries publish a periodic financial report called the *balance of payments*. This is a statement of the money value of all transactions between a nation and the rest of the world during a given period, such as a year. These transactions may consist of imports and exports of goods and services and movements of short-term and long-term investments, gifts, currency, and gold. The transactions can be classified into several categories, of which the two broadest are the current account and the capital account.

The balance of payments for the United States is shown in Exhibit 5. Note that the monetary results of transactions are recorded either as debits (−) or as credits (+). A *debit* is any transaction that results in a flow of money out of the country. A *credit* is any transaction that results in a flow of money into the country. Thus, an import is a debit and an export is a credit.

The balance-of-payments statement is easy to comprehend. By reading each line and the accompanying explanations, you will understand how the various items are obtained. If you do that now, the following additional comments will prove helpful.

Line (4) This discloses what is popularly known as the *balance of trade*. It is that part of a nation's balance of payments dealing with merchandise imports and exports. You will sometimes hear it said that a nation has either a "favorable" or an "unfavorable" balance of trade, depending on whether the value of its merchandise exports is greater or less than the value of its merchandise imports. In reality, however, as you will discover shortly, this statement is meaningless. It neglects the fact that other items in a nation's balance of payments will necessarily offset either a surplus or a deficit in the balance of trade, because the *balance of payments always balances*.

Exhibit 5

United States Balance of Payments, 1980—Summary of International Transactions
(billions of dollars)*

	Debits (−), money outflows. Credits (+), money inflows.
(1) CURRENT-ACCOUNT TRANSACTIONS	
(2) Merchandise exported	$ 224.0
(3) Merchandise imported	−249.3
(4) Balance on merchandise trade: (2) + (3)	**−25.3**
(5) Services exported	120.7
(6) Services imported	−84.6
(7) Balance on services: (5) + (6)	**36.1**

Services exported (+) include: travel expenditures by foreigners here (which is the same as "scenery exported by the U.S."), interest and dividends received from abroad, banking and insurance services rendered to foreigners by domestic institutions, and expenditures by foreign governments here.

Services imported (−) include the opposite, such as travel expenditures by Americans abroad (i.e., "scenery imported by the U.S."), interest and dividends paid to foreigners, and so on.

(8) Balance on goods and services: (4) + (7)	**10.8**
(9) Unilateral transfers, net	**−7.7**

These are "one-way" gifts and grants involving no return commitments or claims. Money outflows (−) consist of U.S. private remittances sent abroad plus U.S. governmental military and nonmilitary grants to other countries. Money inflows (+) are the opposite. The net result (i.e., balance) has generally been negative.

(10) Balance on current accounts: (8) + (9)	**3.1**
(11) CAPITAL-ACCOUNT TRANSACTIONS	
(12) U.S. official reserve assets abroad, net	−8.2

Includes major currencies, gold, and other internationally accepted reserve assets. They are held at the International Monetary Fund, an arm of the United Nations. The assets are owned by the central bank of the United States, the Federal Reserve System. They are used for settling accounts with the central banks of other countries, such as the Bank of England, the Bank of Japan, etc.

(13) U.S. government assets abroad, other than (12), net	−5.2

Includes U.S. government loans and other long-term claims, less repayments.

(14) U.S. private assets abroad, net	−71.5

Includes direct investment by U.S. individuals and companies in foreign property and securities, plus other financial claims.

(15) U.S. assets abroad, net: (12) + (13) + (14)	**−84.8**

Note: Net increases in U.S. assets abroad are money outflows (−). Net decreases are money inflows (+).

(16) Foreign official assets in the U.S., net	15.5

Includes U.S. Treasury securities and other official claims against the U.S. government held by foreigners.

(17) Other foreign assets in the U.S., net	34.8

Includes direct investment by foreigners in U.S. property and securities, plus other financial claims.

(18) Foreign assets in the U.S., net: (16) + (17)	**50.3**

Note: Net increases in foreign assets in the U.S. represent money inflows (+). Net decreases represent money outflows (−).

(19) Balance on capital accounts: (15) + (18)	**−34.5**
(20) Balance on current and capital accounts: (10) + (19)	**−31.4**

This line would equal zero if there were no errors or omissions in the data, as explained below for line (21).

(21) Statistical discrepancy	31.4

Includes errors and omissions that arise because the balance of payments summarizes millions of individual international transactions. Hence, accuracy down to the last dollar is impossible. Note that the statistical discrepancy, which is simply the number on line (20) with the sign reversed, serves as a balancing factor. It assures that the balance shown on line (22) below is zero—i.e., that the balance of payments balances.

(22) Overall balance (20) + (21)	**$ 0.0**

* Data may not always add exactly to the balances shown because of rounding and omissions of some minor items.
Source: U.S. Department of Commerce.

Line (10) This reflects the net effect of all short-term transactions. The number may be either positive or negative, disclosing how much money the United States received from, or paid to, the rest of the world.

Line (19) This reflects the net effect of all long-term transactions. Here, too, the number can be either positive or negative.

Line (20) This is where the current and capital accounts are combined into a single number. If the number is positive, it means that the value of what the nation sold to the rest of the world, such as goods, services, securities, or other assets, exceeded the value of what it purchased. If the number is negative, the value of what the nation bought from abroad exceeded the value of what it sold.

Lines (21) and (22) Finally, these entries show you why the balance of payments always balances *in an accounting sense.* As you can see from the explanation accompanying line (21), the statistical discrepancy assures that the overall balance on line (22) is zero.

The Foreign-Exchange Market

The foreign-exchange market is a world market in which nations' currencies, as well as certain other financial instruments, are bought and sold.

It is impossible to use the information provided in the balance of payments without an understanding of *foreign exchange.* This consists of instruments used for making international payments. Such instruments include currency, checks, drafts, and bills of exchange (which are orders to pay currency). Foreign exchange is bought and sold in a world market called the "foreign-exchange market."

Thus, if you take a trip to France, you will have to sell some dollars to buy French francs. The francs are needed in order to pay for lodging, food, and anything else you purchase while you are in France. If you travel from France to Italy, you can buy Italian lire with any francs or dollars you may have. And if you go from Italy to Britain, you can purchase British pounds with francs, lire, or dollars.

The same principle applies to any country you visit. You can always buy one currency with another.

Graphic Illustration

The market for a currency, like the market for wheat, copper, and other raw-material commodities, can be represented by an ordinary supply-and-demand model. The reason is easy to see.

1. There are numerous participants in the market for each currency. Most of the participants are banks and other dealers who buy and sell currencies on their own behalf as well as for their customers. These include importers, exporters, multinational corporations, tourists, and so forth.

2. The product, whether it be dollars, francs, lire, or pounds, is standardized. Therefore, like raw-material commodities, buyers and sellers of currencies are concerned only with their prices.

3. The market participants' knowledge of currency prices is "perfect." This means that buyers and sellers are completely informed about bids and offers throughout the world, because information is transmitted immediately by telex and telephone.

Because of these conditions, the determination of a currency's price, such as the U.S. dollar price of Japanese yen, can be illustrated as in Ex-

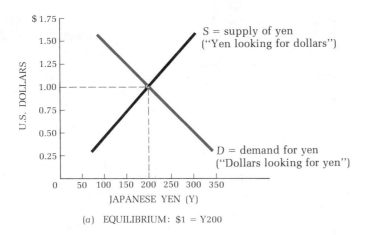

(a) EQUILIBRIUM: $1 = Y200

Exhibit 6
The Foreign-Exchange Market: Dollar Prices of Japanese Yen

Equilibrium prices and quantities are determined by the interactions of supply and demand.

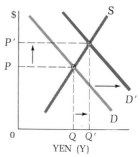

(b) INCREASE IN DEMAND

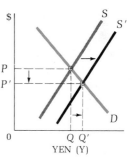

(c) INCREASE IN SUPPLY

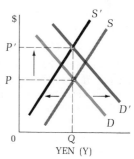

(d) INCREASE IN DEMAND
     DECREASE IN SUPPLY

hibit 6. Thus, in Figure (a), the demand curve for yen is downward-sloping, indicating that buyers will purchase more yen at lower prices than at higher ones. The supply curve is upward-sloping, signifying that sellers will offer more yen at higher prices than at lower ones.

> At any given time, the demand curve for yen represents *"dollars looking for yen"* and the supply curve of yen represents *"yen looking for dollars."* The equilibrium price of yen is determined by the intersection of the two curves. In the figure, this price is $1 = Y200.

Shifts of the Curves: Causes and Effects

As with all supply-and-demand models, certain factors are assumed to be constant when the curves are drawn. A change in one or more of these factors may cause a change in demand or in supply—*a shift of the curves*. The result, of course, is a new equilibrium price, a new equilibrium quantity, or both, as you learned when you first studied supply and demand.

Which factors are assumed to be constant? There are many, but three are especially important. They are: (1) relative real income levels, (2) relative price levels, and (3) relative interest rates.

1. Relative Real Income Levels Suppose that the level of real income in the United States rises in relation to that of the "rest of the world"—specifically, Japan. This enables Americans to purchase more Japanese-made products: Hondas, Sonys, steel, "scenery" (that is, trips to Japan), and so on. The result will be an increase in "dollars looking for yen," causing the demand for yen to increase. In Figure (b), the curve shifts from D to D', leading to a higher equilibrium price and a larger equilibrium quantity of yen. The yen thus *appreciates*, or increases in value, relative to the dollar. This, of course, is equivalent to saying that the dollar *depreciates* relative to the yen.

Conversely, if Japan's real income rises in relation to that of the United States, the supply curve of yen will shift to the right. There will be an increase in "yen looking for dollars" as Japanese seek to buy more American goods. In Figure (c), the supply curve shifts from S to S', causing the equilibrium price of yen to decline and the equilibrium quantity to increase. The yen thus *depreciates* relative to the dollar, which means that the dollar *appreciates* relative to the yen.

2. **Relative Price Levels** How do changes in each country's general price level affect foreign-exchange rates? Because the effects are somewhat more complicated, it helps to analyze them in two steps.

Step 1 If inflation in the United States is higher than it is in Japan, many Japanese products (such as cars and televisions) will be cheaper than similar American products. In Figure (*d*), therefore, the demand for yen increases from *D* to *D'* as Americans substitute more of these Japanese goods for American goods.

Step 2 Because these Japanese goods are cheaper than their American substitutes, some Japanese buyers will switch from American goods to their own domestic goods. In Figure (*d*), the supply curve shifts from *S* to *S'* because there are fewer "yen looking for dollars." The result is a higher equilibrium price of the yen—an *appreciation* of the yen—and hence a *depreciation* of the dollar. What about the equilibrium quantity? This may remain the same or it may change, depending on the relative shifts of the curves.

3. **Relative Interest Rates** Government economic (fiscal and monetary) policies may cause interest rates to be higher in the United States than in Japan. The Japanese, therefore, may decide to increase their supply of "yen looking for dollars" in order to purchase American interest-earning securities. In Figure (*c*), the price of the yen will fall in terms of the dollar. That is, the yen will *depreciate* and the dollar will *appreciate*.

Various other conditions can affect foreign-exchange rates. Economic and political policies in each country and expectations about future developments are some of the factors that may play a role. However, relative income-level, price-level, and interest-rate changes are of major importance, as you will see shortly.

Conclusion: Important Ideas and Potential Problems

In the world of international finance, two concepts are of fundamental importance. One of these is the balance of payments; the other is the foreign-exchange market.

The balance of payments discloses the inflows and outflows of money that a nation experiences during a given period. These flows result from the purchase and sale of goods, services, securities, and other assets, and from gifts and grants. In general, a nation's balance of payments is affected by the price of its currency relative to others in the foreign-exchange market.

The foreign-exchange market is a world market in which various nations' currencies (and certain other financial claims) are bought and sold. In an unregulated foreign-exchange market—one in which governments do not interfere—equilibrium prices and quantities are determined by the forces of supply and demand. When the price of one currency rises relative to the price of another, the more valuable currency is said to *appreciate* and the less valuable one is said to *depreciate*. It follows that changes in exchange rates affect the prices that domestic buyers pay for foreign goods as well as the prices that foreign buyers pay for domestic goods.

In general:

An *appreciation* of a nation's currency makes its exports dearer and its imports cheaper. A *depreciation* does the opposite: It makes a country's exports cheaper and its imports dearer. Therefore, changes in exchange rates may influence substantially a country's balance of payments. This can create fundamental policy problems of deep concern to the community of nations.

International Commercial and Financial Problems

No modern economy is self-sufficient. All are engaged in international trade and in making international payments. Consequently, external conditions affecting a nation's efficiency, stability, and growth are always occurring.

In view of this, what international policies should countries pursue in order to achieve their desired economic goals? This is a question of fundamental importance and a problem of enormous practical significance. Indeed, it occupies the attention of political leaders everywhere. The question, as you will see, involves two broad but related issues:

1. Free trade versus import protection.
2. Flexible versus fixed exchange rates.

Free Trade Versus Import Protection

The law of comparative advantage demonstrates a fundamental principle. *By engaging in free trade, nations make efficient use of the world's scarce resources, thereby raising standards of living.*

This principle is universally acknowledged. Despite this fact, all nations impose trade restrictions of one form or another, especially on imports, to protect some of their domestic industries. The restrictions may be of several types:

Despite the universally acknowledged benefits of free trade, all nations engage, to varying degrees, in import protection.

Tariffs These are customs duties or taxes imposed by a government on the importation (or exportation) of a good. Tariffs may be (1) specific, in the form of a tax per unit of the commodity, or (2) ad valorem, based on the value of the commodity.

Import Quotas These are laws that limit the number of units of a commodity that may be imported during a specified period. An import quota (sometimes simply referred to as a "quota") is thus an example of a nontariff barrier to free trade.

Nontariff Barriers These are any laws or regulations, other than tariffs, that nations impose in order to restrict imports. For instance, to "protect the health and safety" of their citizens, many countries establish much higher standards of quality for various kinds of imported goods than for similar goods produced domestically. Food products and automobiles provide typical examples. Actually, nontariff barriers (other than import quotas) are direct but subtle protective devices that are never publicly stated as such. Hence they have become a major form of trade protection and are used to different degrees by nearly all countries.

Visible and Invisible Effects

If the world's political leaders know that free trade leads to greater efficiency, why do they impose protective trade restrictions? The most common reason among the advanced countries is obvious: *In the industries affected, imports cause unemployment.* For example, the American automobile and steel industries, as well as their suppliers, have suffered substantial increases in unemployment due to the importation of foreign cars and steel.

But these are the visible effects. There are also invisible ones that must be taken into account.

The visible effect of imports may be to cause unemployment in the industries directly affected. But there are invisible effects of imports and of protection that must be considered.

1. Imports Create Jobs It is not usually obvious that imports provide a significant source of new jobs. These occur in those industries producing the exports that foreigners buy with the money earned from our imports. Some major American exporting industries include those producing various kinds of agricultural, mineral, fuel, chemical, and manufactured goods.

2. Protection Reduces Exports It follows that the volume of our exports suffers from import restrictions. By making it harder for foreigners to sell to us, we reduce their income and therefore their ability to buy our goods. As a result, although we may be reducing unemployment in our protected industries, we may also be increasing it in our exporting industries.

3. Protection Reduces Consumer Choice Import restrictions narrow the range of choices available to consumers. They are denied the privilege of purchasing what they believe is the best product for their money. Instead, they are required to pay higher prices either for similar products or for what they regard as less desirable products.

4. Protection Reduces Competition Import restrictions limit competition from foreign producers. This permits protected domestic industries to become more inefficient and perhaps to gain more monopolistic control over their markets. It is interesting to note that, in the opinion of many experts, unrestricted trade is a far more effective means of promoting competition and efficiency than the federal antitrust (antimonopoly) laws designed for those purposes.

Unemployment and Trade-Adjustment Assistance

It is logical to conclude, therefore, that nations will always experience the greatest gains from trade by engaging in free trade. In that way, countries will produce and exchange those goods in which there are the greatest comparative advantages.

Trade-adjustment assistance to affected workers has often been poorly administered.

But what happens to workers who become unemployed due to increased foreign competition? In most cases they become eligible for governmentally financed trade-adjustment assistance. This consists of extended unemployment compensation, job retraining programs, and moving allowances to help cover the costs of re-employment in distant locations.

In theory, trade-adjustment assistance is based on the assumption that the benefits or gains from trade more than offset the costs of the assistance provided. In practice, however, this is often not true. The various assistance programs have frequently been poorly managed and inadequately funded. But this is a criticism of governmental administrative failures, not of free trade.

Flexible Versus Fixed Exchange Rates

Another of the fundamental financial problems facing an open economy concerns its balance-of-payments adjustments to surpluses and deficits. How do adjustments in the balance of payments take place? The answer depends on whether foreign-exchange rates are flexible or fixed.

Flexible (Floating) Exchange Rates

Flexible exchange rates are also called floating exchange rates. They are simply exchange rates that are free to fluctuate in response to market forces of supply and demand.

Exhibit 7 provides an illustration in terms of U.S. dollars and British pounds (£). Suppose that the equilibrium exchange rate is $2 = £1 and the equilibrium quantity is £300 million. If U.S. imports from Britain now increase, the demand curve for pounds will shift to the right from D to D'. The pound will thus *appreciate* to $3 = £1, and the dollar will therefore *depreciate*.

What will be the economic effects? Because the pound is now more expensive, American imports of British goods will decline. Also, because the dollar is now cheaper, British imports of American goods will rise. Therefore, at the new equilibrium price of $3 per pound, any disequilibrium (either a deficit or a surplus) in either country's balance of payments will be *automatically* corrected, as shown in the figure.

In reality, under a system of flexible exchange rates, a nation's balance of payments at any moment may be temporarily in disequilibrium. But the balance will always be *tending* toward equilibrium. This idea is thus analogous to the market price of a commodity (such as wheat) traded in competitive markets. The market or actual price of the commodity at any given instant is always tending toward its equilibrium or "normal" price.

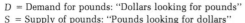

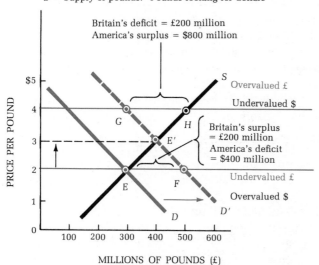

MILLIONS OF POUNDS (£)

D = Demand for pounds: "Dollars looking for pounds"
S = Supply of pounds: "Pounds looking for dollars"

Britain's deficit = £200 million
America's surplus = $800 million

Britain's surplus = £200 million
America's deficit = $400 million

Exhibit 7

The Foreign-Exchange Market and the Balance of Payments: American Dollars and British Pounds

An increase in the demand for pounds from D to D' raises their free-market equilibrium price from $2 = £1 to $3 = £1.

In order to hold down (undervalue) the price of a pound to $2, the Bank of England can increase the supply of pounds. This is done by printing and selling the amount EF (= £200 million) in the foreign-exchange market. Britain will thereby receive $400 million.

In order to raise (overvalue) the price of a pound to $4, the Bank of England can increase the demand for pounds. This is done by buying up the amount GH (= £200 million) in the foreign-exchange market. Britain will thereby spend $800 million.

Fixed Exchange Rates

Despite the advantage of automatic balance-of-payments adjustment under a system of flexible exchange rates, many countries have often maintained fixed exchange rates. Under a system of fixed exchange rates, a country's currency may be either undervalued or overvalued in relation to its free-market price.

Undervaluation An undervalued currency is one whose price is held *below* the price that would exist in a free market. This makes the currency cheaper, thereby encouraging exports. It also makes other currencies dearer, thereby discouraging imports.

For example, look again at Exhibit 7. Suppose Britain wants to offset the increase in demand by keeping the price of the pound at $2. This is easily done. Britain's central bank, the Bank of England, can increase the supply of pounds in the foreign-exchange market simply by printing and selling an amount equal to the excess demand EF (= £200 million). This action will have several effects.

1. Exports and Imports Because the pound is now undervalued in terms of the dollar, British goods will be cheaper for Americans to buy. However, the dollar is now overvalued in terms of the pound. Therefore, American goods will be more costly for Britons to buy. Thus, undervaluation of the pound relative to the dollar encourages British exports and discourages British imports.

2. Terms of Trade Britain's terms of trade with the United States will worsen. That is, Britain will have to export more units of goods (such as textiles) for each unit of goods imported (such as food). On the other hand, the United States' terms of trade with Britain will improve. This is because the United States will have to export fewer units of goods for each unit of goods imported.

3. Balance of Payments Because of the undervalued pound, Britain will experience a surplus in its balance of payments with the United States. And in turn, due to the overvalued dollar, the United States will experience a deficit in its balance of payments with Britain. As you can see from Exhibit 7, the amount of the surplus or deficit is EF = £200 = $400 million.

Overvaluation An overvalued currency is one whose price is held *above* the price that would exist in a free market. This makes the currency dearer, thereby discouraging exports. It also makes other currencies cheaper, thereby encouraging imports.

Intentional overvaluation may be as common as intentional undervaluation. For example, some major oil-exporting nations, in order to hasten industrialization, have at various times overvalued their currencies. The purpose was to use the money (such as dollars, yen, and marks) earned from oil exports to pay for imports of technology, capital, and other goods from more developed countries.

How does overvaluation work? For illustrative purposes, look at what would happen in Exhibit 7 if Britain were to fix the exchange rate at $4 = £1. The Bank of England would then have to buy up the excess supply of pounds—equal to the amount GH = £200 = $800 million. The Bank could do this only as long as it had enough dollars, gold, or other internationally acceptable reserve assets with which to purchase the pounds. Once the assets were spent, the price of pounds would fall to the free-market level unless other countries were willing to lend additional reserves to the Bank.

What would be the results of an overvalued pound? The effects would be the opposite of those listed above for an undervalued one. Try working your way through the various effects to make sure you understand them.

Managed or "Dirty" Floating

It is obviously easier for a country to maintain an undervalued currency than an overvalued one. Undervaluation requires the nation's central bank simply to continue printing and selling its own currency. Overvaluation, on the other hand, requires the central bank to continue receiving an inflow of internationally acceptable reserve assets sufficient to buy its own excess currency in the foreign-exchange market.

Most countries today "manage" their currencies, preventing prices from fluctuating too widely in the foreign-exchange market.

Are today's foreign-exchange rates flexible or are they fixed? The answer is that they are some of both. Many nations' central banks intervene in the foreign-exchange market to prevent unwanted fluctuations beyond a few percentage points. This is called "managed" or "dirty" floating. Both terms are commonly used.

Countries engaged in managed floating thus incur, at least partially, a major benefit of flexible rates—namely, automatic balance-of-payments adjustments. At the same time, by keeping foreign-exchange-rate fluctuations within a relatively narrow range, these countries also realize, at least partially, two of the chief advantages of fixed exchange rates: reduced uncertainty and stable terms of trade.

1. Reduced Uncertainty Fixed exchange rates can encourage international trade and investment. If you are an importer or an exporter, for example, you like to know that the prices at which you do business today will yield an anticipated rate of profit in the coming months. If exchange rates fluctuate, you may realize unexpected losses (as well as gains) when merchandise is paid for upon delivery—say, 30 or 60 days later. The same principle applies if you are a long-term foreign investor. Your objective is to earn future profits on your investment abroad. You do not want to incur the *additional* risk of fluctuations in the foreign-exchange rate when you eventually convert your foreign profits into dollars in order to "bring them home."

Managed exchange rates enable countries to maintain greater stability in their international economic dealings.

2. Stable Terms of Trade A nation's terms of trade tend to vary directly with the international value of its currency. For example, a decrease in the value of the pound will encourage British exports while discouraging imports. Britain will thus give up more units of goods to other countries for each unit of goods imported from them. Of course, an increase in the value of the pound will have the opposite effect. Managed floating, therefore, helps countries to stabilize their terms of trade rather than allowing them to vary substantially.

Thus:

In the opinion of many experts, a system of managed exchange rates combines the advantages of flexible and fixed rates. However, the validity of this conclusion depends on (1) the range of exchange-rate fluctuations that countries permit and (2) the frequency of their intervention.

Conclusion: Today's Problems and Policies

Today's international economic system is characterized by managed or *relatively* fixed exchange rates. However, like all supply and demand curves, those in the foreign-exchange market frequently shift. As a result, the currencies of some countries become overvalued, causing balance-of-payments deficits. The currencies of other countries become undervalued, causing balance-of-payments surpluses. Sooner or later, realignments of exchange rates take place. These occur in either of two ways:

Managed exchange rates may, from time to time, be readjusted in order to cure balance-of-payments deficits or surpluses.

1. Devaluation This is an official act that makes the price of a country's currency cheaper in terms of other currencies. History shows that a country whose currency is significantly overvalued will eventually be forced to devalue it in order to reduce a balance-of-payments deficit.

2. Revaluation This, the opposite of devaluation, serves to appreciate (rather than depreciate) a country's currency in the foreign-exchange market. History shows that a country whose currency is undervalued is not particularly prone to revalue it in order to reduce a balance-of-payments surplus.

Devaluation and revaluation are relatively temporary corrective measures.

Evidently, devaluation and revaluation are not *lasting* corrective measures. To achieve such corrections, nations must adopt appropriate long-term policies. Three that can be employed are (1) fiscal and monetary policies, (2) trade controls, and (3) exchange controls.

Fiscal and Monetary Policies

As you learned in previous chapters, government actions pertaining to taxing, spending, and growth of the money supply are known as fiscal and monetary policies. Depending on the ways in which they are used, they can have either contractionary or expansionary effects. How might a nation employ fiscal and monetary policies to correct either a deficit or a surplus in its balance of payments?

Fiscal—monetary policies and trade controls are long-run corrective measures. But the former involve sacrifices that nations are not usually inclined to take. Therefore, trade controls are often utilized.

1. Deficit Nation: Contractionary Policies A *deficit* nation can lower the price of its overvalued currency by pursuing contractionary fiscal and monetary policies. By reducing its prices at home relative to those in surplus nations, the deficit nation will discourage imports and encourage exports. However, contractionary fiscal and monetary policies will also cause increased unemployment at home. The deficit nation will thus be sacrificing domestic employment stability for balance-of-payments equilibrium.

2. Surplus Nation: Expansionary Policies A *surplus* nation can raise the price of its undervalued currency by pursuing expansionary fiscal and monetary policies. If prices in the surplus nation rise faster than those in deficit nations, imports will be encouraged and exports will be discouraged. However, the surplus nation will then be sacrificing domestic price stability in order to reduce other countries' deficits. This, of course, is not something that the surplus nation is likely to do.

Thus:

A nation's balance of payments is affected by its fiscal and monetary policies. The use of these policies to achieve balance-of-payments equilibrium entails a sacrifice of some domestic stability. This is a trade-off that countries are usually reluctant to make.

Trade Controls

A second approach to reducing payments imbalances is through trade controls. A deficit nation, for example, can contract imports by imposing tariffs, quotas, and other trade barriers. A surplus nation, on the other hand, can expand exports by subsidizing the industries it wants to encourage and by providing them with special tax benefits.

All countries, to varying degrees, engage in such policies. Their effects, of course, are obvious. Because they impede the operation of the law of comparative advantage, they misallocate resources. As a result, inefficiency is enhanced and the volume of world trade is reduced.

Exchange Controls

Finally, nations can reduce imbalances, or at least manage them more effectively, through exchange controls. These are commonly utilized by command economies. They require exporters to sell their foreign exchange to the government, which then uses the scarce funds to purchase needed imports. These may include such staple goods as foods, raw materials, and capital goods deemed necessary for economic growth, rather than such "luxury" goods as foreign sports cars, stereos, and liquors.

Exchange controls are usually employed in command economies as a way of managing their balances of payments.

As with trade controls, exchange controls misallocate resources and therefore contract the volume of world trade. In addition, they reduce consumer choice and are likely to encourage the growth of black (illegal) markets. Hence, exchange controls are not commonly employed by market-oriented economies, except perhaps in wartime emergencies.

In conclusion:

International economic policies are strongly influenced by economic and noneconomic (including political and military) considerations. Because of this, all nations, in varying degrees, impose trade restrictions and engage in managed floating. As a result, most political leaders are continually seeking to establish a set of workable rules for improving the efficiency of the international economic system.

What You Have Learned in This Chapter

1. The study of international trade is concerned with the commerce of nations. In today's interdependent world, international trade is becoming increasingly important.

2. By engaging in free or unrestricted trade, nations receive the greatest gains from trade. These gains are measured by the increases in goods that a country receives as a result of trading with others.

3. Trade involves sacrifice. A nation must give up some goods in order to receive others. These sacrifices are the terms of trade, and they are measured by the slope of a trade-possibilities curve.

4. A basis for trade exists when there are differences in opportunity costs between countries. Therefore, when no differences exist, there will be incomplete international specialization and hence a reduced volume of world trade.

5. Fluctuations in net exports—the difference between exports and imports—can generate magnified variations in national income. This proposition is demonstrated by the foreign-trade multiplier.

6. The law of comparative advantage is among the oldest principles of economics. The law shows why it pays for each nation to specialize in producing the goods in which it has the greatest *relative* advantage. Then, by trading with others, nations can have more goods than if each nation tried to be self-sufficient. The law thus leads to the conclusion that the effect on nations of international specialization and free trade is the same as if those nations experienced outward shifts of their production-possibilities curves.

7. The study of international finance is concerned with the payments of nations. Such payments are reported in a country's balance of payments, a periodic financial report.

8. The balance of payments summarizes all of a country's money inflows and outflows resulting from international transactions, public and private. A disequilibrium in a nation's balance of payments means that the outflows exceed the inflows. Disequilibrium can occur only when exchange rates are not free to fluctuate.

9. Adjustments in the balance of payments take place through the foreign-exchange market, where currencies are bought and sold. The prices of currencies are determined by international forces of supply and demand. Consequently, the currencies of nations may appreciate or depreciate relative to one another in the foreign-exchange market.

10. Two problems are fundamental in international economics:

(a) *Free trade vs. import protection.* Imports can be a visible cause of unemployment in the industries directly affected. However, imports can also be an invisible cause of increased employment in other industries. These industries are the ones that produce the exports that foreigners buy with the money earned from our imports.

(b) *Flexible vs. fixed exchange rates.* Flexible exchange rates permit automatic adjustments to balance-of-payments equilibrium. Nevertheless, most countries today adhere to managed exchange rates in order to maintain their overvalued or undervalued currencies. Under such circumstances, balance-of-payments adjustments to equilibrium may not occur automatically.

11. Because of trade restrictions and managed exchange rates, resources are misallocated and world trade is reduced. Consequently, most political leaders are continually seeking workable rules for improving the efficiency of the international economic system.

For Discussion

1. *Terms and concepts to review:*
opportunity cost
specialization
terms of trade
gains from trade
trade-possibilities curve
"bathtub theorem"
marginal propensity to import
foreign-trade multiplier
law of absolute advantage
law of comparative advantage
balance of payments
balance of trade
foreign exchange
import quota
nontariff barrier
devaluation
revaluation

2. Suppose that, with the same resources, the United States can produce either 40 cars or 40 tons of food per unit of time. With the same resources, Japan can produce either 60 cars or 20 tons of food in the same time. Assume that both countries have constant costs of production (their production-possibilities curves are straight lines).

(a) Plot the production-possibilities curves on separate graphs. To facilitate uniformity for classroom discussion, use the vertical axes for cars and the horizontal axes for food. Label the axes and curves.

(b) What is each country's domestic-exchange ratio? Are there any comparative advantages? Explain.

(c) Suppose that each country is self-sufficient. Then the United States might produce, say, 30 cars and 10 tons of food. Japan, on the other hand, might produce, say, 15 cars and 15 tons of food. On your respective graphs, label these points A and A'.

(d) If the United States and Japan each specialize and trade, what combinations of goods will each produce? Label the points B and B', respectively.

(e) Suppose the United States and Japan trade 20 tons of food for 40 cars. What combinations of goods will each country consume? Label these points E and E' on the countries' trade-possibilities curves. What are the gains from trade for each country and for the "world"?

(f) Explain the gains from trade in terms of the *slopes* of the production-possibilities curves and the trade-possibilities curves. Label these curves along with their slopes.

3. Assume the following conditions:

• National income (NI) is below its full-employment level.

• Exports (X) equal imports (M).

• $MPS = 0$ and $MPM = 0.1$.

Suppose that X, which is independent of NI, rises by \$100 and remains at its new higher level.

   (a) What is the size of the foreign-trade multiplier (K)?
   (b) Will the increase in X affect NI? If so, by how much?
   (c) What will happen to M?
   (d) Describe in *words*, rather than equations, the nature of the income-adjustment process.
   (e) What would have been the effect if NI had initially been at its full-employment level?

4. Referring to problem 3, suppose that $MPS = 0.15$.

   (a) Calculate the size of K.
   (b) Calculate the increase in NI.
   (c) Calculate the increase in M.
   (d) Is the income adjustment complete? Explain.

5. What are the sources of demand for foreign exchange? What are the sources of supply?

6. State whether each of the following transactions is a debit or a credit on the U.S. balance of payments.

   (a) An American firm imports \$100,000 worth of French perfume.
   (b) An American tourist flies via British Airways from New York to London.
   (c) A British tourist flies via Pan American Airlines from London to New York.
   (d) A British tourist flies via Pan American Airlines from New York to London.
   (e) An American buys stock in a Swiss corporation.
   (f) An American sells stock in a German corporation.
   (g) The Federal Reserve Bank of New York reduces its debt to the Bank of Japan.

7. Evaluate the following arguments commonly heard in defense of protection (for example, tariffs and quotas).

   (a) "We must protect domestic labor from cheap foreign labor."
   (b) "Protection is needed to reduce domestic unemployment."
   (c) "Protection is necessary for young industries until they mature sufficiently to meet foreign competition."
   (d) "We must protect steel and other vital industries necessary for national defense."

8. Why do nations engage in managed floating?

ECONOMICS IN THE NEWS

PESO PANIC
Why Mexico Devalued

by Mike Rouff

Mexico City—Why might a country devalue its currency? What happens when devaluation occurs? Mexico's recent experience provides some interesting answers.

Huge oil reserves, second only to those in Saudi Arabia, were discovered in Mexico during the late 1970s. This prompted the government to launch a bold program of economic expansion.

To pay for needed imports of industrial goods, Mexican private and governmentally owned corporations borrowed heavily from abroad. By mid-1982, however, Mexico found itself caught in a financial squeeze. A worldwide recession and an oil glut cut sharply into Mexico's export revenues. At the same time, high interest rates in the United States and Europe increased the carrying cost of Mexico's debt.

The result of the squeeze was a dollar hemorrhage—a flight of U.S. currency out of Mexico to safer havens. When its dollar reserves were finally exhausted, the Bank of Mexico, which had been maintaining an overvalued price for the peso in order to finance essential imports, was forced to let it "float." The effect was an immediate fall in its price—a *devaluation* of the peso in terms of the dollar.

Rescue Operation

Mexico is one of America's major trading partners, and it is considered a bulwark against communism in the Western Hemisphere. Therefore, neither Washington nor U.S. banks (which held some \$22 billion of Mexican debt), were willing to accept default. To prevent it, new loans from the central banks of various Western nations and from the International Monetary Fund were arranged. However, Mexico had to agree to some belt-tightening measures aimed at curbing inflation. These include wage freezes, import restrictions, and reduced government subsidies.

Si, Aceptamos Pesos

Meanwhile, at the U.S.– Mexican border, business boomed on the southern side and languished on the northern side. With the price of the peso down by more than 50 percent, Americans streamed into Mexico from Texas, Arizona, and southern California. After picking stores clean, they returned home with carloads of bargains.

For American shopkeepers, the reverse was true. When the peso was stronger, they had depended on Mexican consumers for much of their livelihood. After devaluation, however, streets in many downtown shopping areas were deserted, despite signs in the shop windows that read, "Si, aceptamos pesos."

Using Supply and Demand:
The Laws of Production
and Cost

18
CHAPTER

Working with Supply, Demand, and Elasticity: Some Interesting Applications

Learning guide
Watch for the answers to these important questions

What is elasticity? How is it measured? Of what practical value is it? What factors determine elasticity?

How can basic supply-and-demand models be used to explain such concepts as shortages and surpluses? What are the effects of taxes and subsidies on the prices and quantities of goods? Can supply-and-demand models be used to illustrate these effects?

What is the income elasticity of demand? What is the cross elasticity of demand? How are they interpreted? Can they be applied to practical problems? Are all measures of elasticity basically similar?

What assumptions underlie the use of supply-and-demand models? How does the market price of a good differ from its normal price? In what way does the price system serve as a rationing or allocative mechanism?

The purpose of this chapter is to explain how changes in quantities supplied and demanded, and how changes in supply and demand, respond to changes in prices and incomes.

Is there a distinction between pure and applied science? In answer to this question, the nineteenth-century French scientist Louis Pasteur replied:

> No, a thousand times no. There does not exist a category of science to which one can give the name applied science. There are only science and the applications of science, bound together as the fruit to the tree which bears it.

Supply and demand can be viewed in much the same way. You are already familiar with the "pure" side of the subject from your study of it early in this book. Now you can take a few moments to brush up on the basic concepts by reviewing the brief presentation in Exhibit 1.

In this chapter, we explore the "applied" aspects of supply and demand by solving some interesting problems. When you complete this chapter, you will probably agree with Pasteur that the principles and applications of supply and demand, like those of any science, are indeed "bound together as the fruit to the tree."

The Concept of Elasticity: A Measure of Responsiveness to Changes in Price

You already know from Exhibit 1 that the relationship between the price and quantity of a good is *causal*. For instance, a rise in price will cause a decrease in the quantity demanded and an increase in the quantity supplied. A fall in price will produce the opposite effects—an increase in the quantity demanded and a decrease in the quantity supplied.

Exhibit 1
Brief Review of Supply and Demand

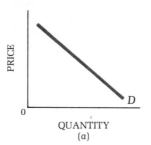

(a)

(b)

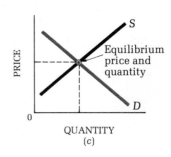

Equilibrium price and quantity

(c)

Figure (a): The *law of demand* states that the quantity demanded of a good varies inversely with its price. This means that people will buy more of a good at a lower price than at a higher price.

Figure (b): The *law of supply* states that the quantity supplied of a good usually varies directly with its price. Thus, sellers are willing to supply larger quantities at higher prices than at lower prices.

Figure (c): When demand and supply curves are graphed, their intersection determines the equilibrium market price and quantity. Any price above this equilibrium level results in the quantity supplied exceeding the quantity demanded, thereby driving the price down. Any price below the equilibrium level results in the quantity demanded exceeding the quantity supplied, thereby driving the price up. At the equilibrium level there are no product surpluses or shortages. Thus, the market is precisely cleared.

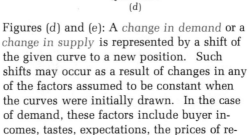

(d)

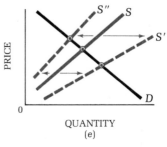

(e)

Figures (d) and (e): A *change in demand* or a *change in supply* is represented by a shift of the given curve to a new position. Such shifts may occur as a result of changes in any of the factors assumed to be constant when the curves were initially drawn. In the case of demand, these factors include buyer incomes, tastes, expectations, the prices of related goods, and the number of buyers in the market. In the case of supply, they are resource costs, technology, sellers' expectations, the prices of other goods, and the number of sellers in the market. Changes or shifts in demand or supply may bring about new equilibrium prices and quantities.

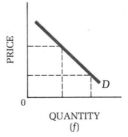

(f)

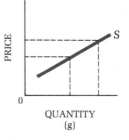

(g)

Figures (f) and (g): If the demand curve remains fixed, a movement along the curve from one point to another denotes a *change in the quantity demanded*. Likewise, if the supply curve remains fixed, a movement along the curve denotes a *change in the quantity supplied*. Such changes are always associated with changes in price.

But by *how much* will a change in price affect the quantities supplied or demanded? The answer depends on the particular good. There is a big difference, for example, between a commodity such as salt and a commodity such as vacation trips. In the case of salt, the quantity demanded varies relatively little with changes in price. In the case of vacation trips, however, changes in price may cause relatively large changes in the quantity demanded.

How can we measure these changes? One way is to use a concept called "elasticity." This reflects the responsiveness of a change in one variable to a change in another.

The following interpretive definition of *elasticity* can be used to understand and explain its meaning:

> *Elasticity* is the percentage change in quantity (demanded or supplied) resulting from a 1 percent change in price.

The following mathematical definition of elasticity can be used to calculate elasticities of supply or demand, as illustrated later:

> *Elasticity* is the ratio of the percentage change in quantity (demanded or supplied) to the percentage change in price:

$$\text{elasticity} = \frac{\text{percentage change in quantity}}{\text{percentage change in price}}$$

You already know that the law of supply expresses a *direct* relation between price and quantity supplied. Therefore, the coefficient you get when you calculate supply elasticity will be positive. On the other hand, the law of demand expresses an *inverse* relation between price and quantity demanded. Therefore, the coefficient of demand elasticity will be negative. In practice, however, it is customary to disregard the negative sign and express all elasticities as if they were either positive or zero.

Visualizing Elasticities from Graphs

Because elasticity measures the responsiveness of changes in quantity to changes in price, it is helpful to distinguish among the different degrees of responsiveness. This is done in Exhibit 2, where five types of elasticity are illustrated. Study these diagrams and the following definitions carefully.

Figure (a): *Perfectly Elastic* An infinitesimally small percentage change in price results in an infinitely large percentage change in the quantity demanded or supplied. The numerical elasticity is infinite. Thus, a change in price from P_1 to P_2 produces a change in quantity demanded or supplied from zero to a positive amount. In terms of percentages, this is an "infinite" change.

Figure (b): *Relatively Elastic* A given percentage change in price results in a larger percentage change in quantity. The numerical elasticity is greater than 1. Thus, a change in price from P_1 to P_2 causes a more than proportionate change in quantity from Q_1 to Q_2.

Figure (c): *Unit Elastic* A given percentage change in price results in an equal percentage change in quantity. The numerical elasticity is 1. Thus, a change in price from P_1 to P_2 causes an equal proportionate change in quantity from Q_1 to Q_2.

Exhibit 2
Five Different Kinds of Elasticity

Elasticity is a measure of the *responsiveness* of a change in quantity to a change in price. The changes can be visualized from the graphs.

Note that E = numerical elasticity (that is,

negative signs are disregarded). Therefore, an elasticity coefficient will always be either a positive number or zero, but never a negative number. (The symbol $<$ means "less than"; the symbol $>$ means "greater than.")

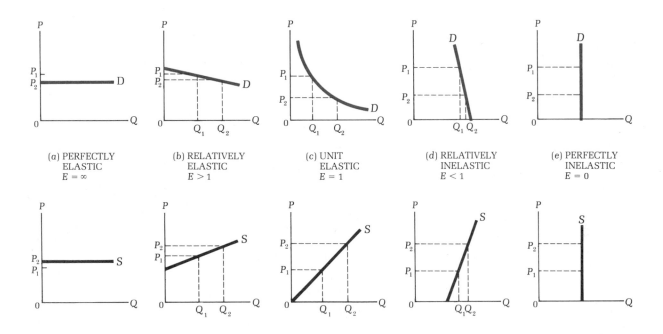

(a) PERFECTLY ELASTIC
$E = \infty$

(b) RELATIVELY ELASTIC
$E > 1$

(c) UNIT ELASTIC
$E = 1$

(d) RELATIVELY INELASTIC
$E < 1$

(e) PERFECTLY INELASTIC
$E = 0$

Technical note (optional) If you are mathematically inclined, you may be able to see that the slope and elasticity of a curve would be the same if the *logarithms* of price and quantity were plotted in the figures. Or, equivalently, the slope and elasticity of a curve would be the same if the curve were plotted on a special type of graph paper whose vertical and horizontal axes were both scaled in *logarithms*. The reason for this is that, on a logarithmic scale, equal distances represent equal proportional (or *relative*) changes. Because elasticity is nothing more than a measure of relative change, the slope of a straight line on logarithmic scales is the same as its elasticity. It is an interesting exercise to prove these ideas algebraically.

Figure (d): *Relatively Inelastic* A given percentage change in price results in a smaller percentage change in quantity. The numerical elasticity is less than 1 (but greater than zero). For example, a change in price from P_1 to P_2 causes a less than proportionate change in quantity from Q_1 to Q_2.

Figure (e): *Perfectly Inelastic* A given percentage change in price results in no change in quantity. The numerical elasticity is zero. Thus, a change in price from P_1 to P_2 causes no change in quantity.

There is an easy way to remember the charts in Exhibit 2. Think of them as the frames of a motion picture. In the first "frames," both curves are in a horizontal position. In successive frames, the demand curve gradually tilts downward while the supply curve tilts upward until both curves end up in a vertical position.

Exhibit 3
Calculating the Elasticity of Demand

The following procedures illustrate the calculation of elasticity for the segment AB in the accompanying figure.

Change from A to B:

At A: $Q_1 = 20$, $P_1 = 52$
At B: $Q_2 = 80$, $P_2 = 17$

$$E_D = \frac{\dfrac{Q_2 - Q_1}{Q_2 + Q_1}}{\dfrac{P_2 - P_1}{P_2 + P_1}} = \frac{\dfrac{80 - 20}{80 + 20}}{\dfrac{17 - 52}{17 + 52}}$$

$$= \frac{0.60}{-0.51} = -1.2, \text{ or } 1.2 \text{ numerically}$$

Change from B to A:

At B: $Q_1 = 80$, $P_1 = 17$
At A: $Q_2 = 20$, $P_2 = 52$

$$E_D = \frac{\dfrac{Q_2 - Q_1}{Q_2 + Q_1}}{\dfrac{P_2 - P_1}{P_2 + P_1}} = \frac{\dfrac{20 - 80}{20 + 80}}{\dfrac{52 - 17}{52 + 17}}$$

$$= \frac{-0.60}{0.51} = -1.2, \text{ or } 1.2 \text{ numerically}$$

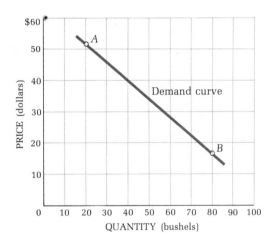

Interpretation A 1 percent change in price results in a 1.2 percent change in quantity demanded. (Similarly, a 10 percent change in price results in a 12 percent change in quantity demanded.) Because the change in quantity demanded is more than proportional to the change in price, demand is said to be relatively elastic.

Do the five different definitions of elasticity in Exhibit 2 sound intuitively reasonable? They should. After all, elasticity is nothing more than the "stretch" in quantity compared with the "stretch" in price, with both stretches being measured in percentages.

Caution Do not confuse elasticity with slope. They are not the same. The slope of a curve at any point is its steepness (or flatness) at that point. A straight line has the same slope at every point, but not necessarily the same elasticity. Therefore, *you cannot always infer the elasticity of a curve from its slope alone.* The figures in Exhibit 2 are merely intended to help you visualize the five different kinds of elasticity. (See, however, the technical note beneath the graphs if you are interested in the mathematical relationship between elasticity and slope.)

Measuring Elasticity

A hypothetical demand curve is shown in Exhibit 3. Our objective is to estimate the elasticity of demand for this curve. We may choose two points near the ends of the line, such as points A and B, because they are conveniently located on at least one of the grid lines, and calculate the elasticity for the segment AB.

How does the change in quantity demanded compare with the change in price over this segment? In answering this question, you can disregard for the time being the calculations accompanying the figure. Observe from the figure alone that a movement along the curve from A to B is measured by two changes: an increase in quantity from 20 bushels to 80 bushels and a corresponding decrease in price from about $52 to about $17. An increase in quantity of 60 bushels is thus associated with a decrease in price of $35. The change in quantity per unit change in price, therefore, is $60/(-35) = -1.72$, or 1.72 if the sign is disregarded.

Is this the elasticity of demand? The answer is *no*, because the result is obviously affected by the units in which the quantities and prices are measured. The solution would have been different, for example, if quantities had been expressed in millions of bushels or if prices had been expressed in British pounds or in French francs. Because a chief purpose of calculating elasticity is to permit comparisons to be made between products, a measure of elasticity is needed that is unaffected by the units in which the data are quoted. That is, what is needed is a *coefficient of elasticity.*

The Coefficient of Elasticity

You will recall from the definition of elasticity that its measurement is simply the percentage change in quantity divided by the percentage change in price. The most common method of measuring these percentage changes is to divide the observed change in quantity by the average of the two quantities, and the observed change in price by the average of the two prices. This enables us to express the definition by the formula

$$\text{elasticity} = \frac{\text{percentage change in quantity}}{\text{percentage change in price}} = \frac{\dfrac{\text{change in quantity}}{\text{average quantity}}}{\dfrac{\text{change in price}}{\text{average price}}}$$

You can use this formula in calculating the elasticity of demand in Exhibit 3. In doing so, however, substitute the letters P for price and Q

for quantity in the formula and attach subscripts to the letters so that you do not mix up your Ps and Qs. Thus, let

Q_1 = old quantity, or quantity before change
Q_2 = new quantity, or quantity after change
P_1 = old price, or price before change
P_2 = new price, or price after change

The formula for elasticity of demand E_D is then

$$E_D = \frac{\frac{Q_2 - Q_1}{(Q_2 + Q_1)/2}}{\frac{P_2 - P_1}{(P_2 + P_1)/2}} = \frac{\frac{Q_2 - Q_1}{Q_2 + Q_1}}{\frac{P_2 - P_1}{P_2 + P_1}}$$

Notice, from the middle part of the equation, that the average quantity is the sum of the two quantities divided by 2 and the average price is the sum of the two prices divided by 2. These 2s then cancel out, leaving the complex fraction at the end.

An application of this formula is illustrated by the equations in Exhibit 3. Observe that the same result is obtained whether the change is from A to B or from B to A. This is an important advantage, because many practical situations arise in which we know only two prices and two quantities without knowing which price and quantity came first.

Example The Savemore Paint Company sold an average of 300 gallons of paint per week at $10 per gallon and 500 gallons of paint per week at $8 per gallon. What is the elasticity of demand for their paint?

The answer is −2.25, or 2.25 numerically, regardless of the values you choose for your initial price and quantity. Work it out both ways and see for yourself. How do you interpret this answer? What would you expect the percentage change in quantity to be if the price were to change by 10 percent? (**Hint** Refer back to Exhibit 3.)

What about elasticity of supply E_S? Do we measure it in the same way? The answer is *yes*. We also use the same formula. However, we let Q_1 and Q_2 stand for the quantities supplied before and after the change and P_1 and P_2 represent the corresponding prices. ∎

Elasticity of Demand and Total Revenue

In many practical situations involving the study of demand, economists find it convenient to have a simple guide for judging whether demand is elastic or inelastic. An easy method that can be used for this purpose is to compare the change in the price of the commodity with the corresponding change in the seller's gross receipts. These receipts are customarily called "total revenue." It is important to keep in mind that a seller's total revenue (abbreviated TR) is equal to price (P) per unit times the quantity (Q) of units sold. That is, $TR = P \times Q$. Thus, if a necktie manufacturer charges $10 per tie and sells 100 ties, the total revenue is $1,000.

Exhibit 4 provides useful visual illustrations of the relation between demand elasticity and total revenue. These charts are similar to three of the five types of demand elasticities described in Exhibit 2.

Demand elasticity and inelasticity can often be judged from changes in total revenue.

Exhibit 4
Demand Elasticity and Total Revenue

A seller's total revenue is equal to the price per unit multiplied by the number of units sold. Therefore, total revenue in all three figures can be measured by the rectangular area under the demand curve. Thus, at a price equal to the distance 0P, quantity de-manded is represented by the distance 0M. Therefore, total revenue is the area of the rectangle 0PSM. At a price of 0T, quantity demanded is 0N. Therefore, total revenue is the area of the rectangle 0TVN.

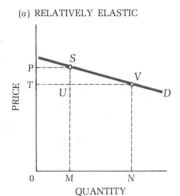

(a) RELATIVELY ELASTIC

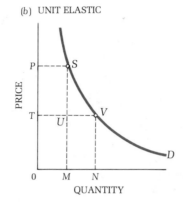

(b) UNIT ELASTIC

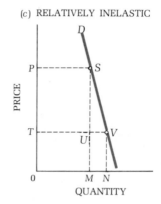

(c) RELATIVELY INELASTIC

Figure (a): *Relatively Elastic.* When demand is relatively elastic, a decrease in price results in an increase in total revenue, and an increase in price results in a decrease in total revenue.

Figure (b): *Unit Elastic.* When demand is unit elastic, a decrease or increase in price results in the same total revenue.

Figure (c): *Relatively Inelastic.* When demand is relatively inelastic, a decrease in price results in a decrease in total revenue, and an increase in price results in an increase in total revenue.

When demand is relatively elastic, changes in price cause opposite changes in total revenue.

Relatively Elastic Demand

Exhibit 4, Figure (a), illustrates a relatively elastic demand curve. Suppose that the price is at P, which is represented by the distance 0P. Then the corresponding quantity demanded is at M, measured by the distance 0M. The seller's total revenue is therefore price times quantity, or $0P \times 0M$. This is also the area of the rectangle 0PSM, because the area of *any* rectangle is the product of its base and height.

Suppose that the selling firm lowers its price to 0T. The quantity demanded then increases to 0N. Hence, the seller's new total revenue is again equal to price times quantity, or the area of the rectangle 0TVN. This new rectangle is larger in area than the old one. That is, as a result of a price reduction, the seller has lost a relatively small amount of total revenue represented by the rectangle TPSU. However, the seller has also gained a larger amount of total revenue represented by the rectangle MUVN. Because the gain more than offsets the loss, the seller's final total revenue is larger after the price reduction than before.

What happens if price increases, say from 0T to 0P? The result is exactly the opposite. Total revenue declines from 0TVN to 0PSM. In other words, the large loss more than offsets the small gain.

The relationship between changes in price and changes in total revenue can be readily explained in terms of elasticity. When demand is relatively elastic:

1. A given percentage decrease in price is more than offset by a corresponding percentage increase in quantity demanded. Therefore, total revenue rises.

2. A given percentage increase in price is more than offset by a corresponding percentage decrease in quantity demanded. Therefore, total revenue falls.

Unit-Elastic Demand

A second type of situation is illustrated in Exhibit 4, Figure (b). Here demand is unit elastic. At a price of 0P, the quantity demanded is 0M. Hence, the seller's total revenue is the area of the rectangle 0PSM. On the other hand, at a price of 0T, the quantity demanded is 0N. Therefore, the seller's total revenue is the area of the rectangle 0TVN.

It is interesting to note that the rectangles are equal in area. That is, 0PSM = 0TVN. This suggests an important principle:

When demand is unit-elastic, revenue remains constant with changes in price.

> In any situation involving a unit-elastic demand curve, the rectangular areas associated with each corresponding price and quantity are always equal. This means that a given percentage decrease (or increase) in price is exactly offset by an equal percentage increase (or decrease) in quantity demanded. Consequently, the total revenues remain the same.

This principle helps to explain why a unit-elastic demand curve has such a special shape. It is the only type of mathematical curve (called a "rectangular hyperbola") that permits percentage changes in price to be exactly offset by equal percentage changes in quantity demanded. As a result, the elasticity remains equal to 1 and hence the total revenue stays constant.

Relatively Inelastic Demand

What happens in the case of a relatively inelastic demand, as in Exhibit 4, Figure (c)? The relationships are obvious. When price is reduced from 0P to 0T, total revenue decreases from 0PSM to 0TVN. Clearly, the percentage decrease in price more than offsets the percentage increase in quantity demanded. This causes total revenue to fall. The opposite occurs in the case of a price increase, say from 0T to 0P. Total revenue rises because the percentage increase in price more than offsets the percentage decrease in quantity demanded.

The foregoing ideas are helpful for analyzing and predicting the effects of price changes on sellers' total revenues. You will encounter many practical situations in later chapters in which such predictions are a useful guide to policy formulation. A brief summary of these basic concepts is appropriate.

> The relationship between price and total revenue depends on whether the elasticity of demand is greater than, equal to, or less than 1. Thus:
>
> • If demand is relatively elastic, a change in price causes a change in total revenue in the *opposite* direction.
>
> • If demand is unit elastic, a change in price causes *no* change in total revenue.

■ Some Practical Applications

1. Public transit systems often raise their rates to offset increased costs. Some of these systems find that their gross incomes decline in the first few weeks after the rate increase, and then rise. What does this suggest about the elasticity of demand for these services?

2. A country's currency may decline in value and therefore become cheaper for foreigners to buy. When this happens, the country may experience both (a) an increase in exports and (b) an influx of tourists. How would you interpret these occurrences?

3. If your college football stadium is drawing less-than-capacity crowds, under what conditions might a price increase be desirable? A price decrease? No change in price?

The number and closeness of available substitutes is the chief determinant of elasticity.

• If demand is relatively inelastic, a change in price causes a change in total revenue in the *same* direction.

How well do you understand these basic ideas? You can judge for yourself by answering several relevant questions. ■

What Determines Elasticity?

Once you have learned how to calculate elasticity, you have mastered only half the job. The other half is to understand the factors that determine elasticity so that you can put this important concept to use.

For example, what makes some demand or supply curves elastic and others inelastic? The answers involve three key words—*substitutes, inexpensiveness,* and *time.*

Substitutes

The most important determinant of demand elasticity and supply elasticity is the number and closeness of available *substitutes.* That is, the elasticity of demand for a product depends on the ease of substitution in consumption.

For example, if a product has good substitutes, and if the prices of these substitutes remain the same, a rise in the price of the product will divert consumer expenditures away from the product and over to the substitutes. A fall in the product's price will swing consumer expenditures away from the substitutes and back to the product. Thus, the demand for the product tends to be elastic.

On the other hand, if a product has poor substitutes, consumers will not respond significantly to changes in its price. Thus, the demand for the product tends to be inelastic.

The foregoing principle can be applied to the elasticity of supply, which depends on the ease of substitution of *resources* used in production.

For example, suppose that the resources (such as labor and capital) that are used in the production of a certain product can easily be increased by hiring similar resources away from other occupations. Then, if the price of the product rises relative to its costs of production while the prices of other products remain the same, producers of the higher-priced product will find it profitable to produce more of it. By hiring *substitutable* resources away from other occupations, the producers will increase the output of the more profitable product significantly.

Conversely, a fall in the price of the product relative to its costs will cause many resources engaged in its production to shift into other occupations. This will decrease output significantly.

In both instances, supply tends to be elastic because of the *ease of substitution* of the resources—that is, the ease with which they can be transferred from one occupation to another. On the other hand, if it is difficult for resources to enter or leave a particular occupation, the supply curve will tend to be inelastic.

Inexpensiveness

The more *inexpensive* a product—that is, the smaller the fraction of their total expenditures that consumers allocate for it—the more inelastic the demand for it is likely to be. For example, the demand for such things as salt, matches, and toothpicks tends to be relatively inelastic. This is because each of these products accounts for such a relatively small part of consumers' total expenditures that changes in prices result in less-than-proportional changes in the quantities demanded.

Time

Elasticities of demand and supply for a given product tend to increase over time. That is, elasticities tend to be greater in the long run than in the short run, because buyers and sellers have more time to adjust to changes in price.

Elasticities usually tend to be greater over longer periods of time, because buyers and sellers can adjust more easily to price changes.

This principle is based on the observation that, the longer the time that elapses after a change in price, the easier it may become for buyers and sellers to use substitutes. Demands for specific products may therefore tend to become more elastic as buyers develop new tastes and habits of consumption. Supplies of specific products may tend to become more elastic as sellers find alternative resources for production of their outputs.

Of course, you may think of exceptions to some of these principles. This is true of almost any principle in the social sciences. However, there is ample evidence to indicate that the principles work in most cases.

Models of Supply and Demand

Most people find it more enjoyable to learn about a subject when they can see how it works in the world around them. After studying supply and demand, we can apply its principles to the solution of many practical problems. Some are illustrated here in the form of real-world models involving government price fixing, taxes, and subsidies.

Price Fixing by Law

Government may interfere with the normal operation of supply and demand. The reason may be to establish a price that is either lower or higher than the price that would be established normally in an unregulated market. For example, price ceilings have been placed on many consumer goods during war or other critical inflationary periods to keep prices from going "too" high. Likewise, price floors have been used to keep the hourly wages (labor prices) of many workers from going "too" low. What are some of the economic effects of these legally established prices?

Price Ceilings Cause Shortages

An example of a price ceiling is provided by rent control on apartments, which has been instituted in some parts of the country. The nature of such a price ceiling is illustrated by the normal supply and demand curves in Exhibit 5. The equilibrium price that would be established in the market if there were no outside interference would be at P, represented by the distance $0P (= NP')$. The equilibrium quantity would be at N, represented by the distance $0N$.

What happens if the government regards the equilibrium price as too high? In that case, the government might establish a ceiling price,

Exhibit 5
Price Ceilings Result in Product Shortages

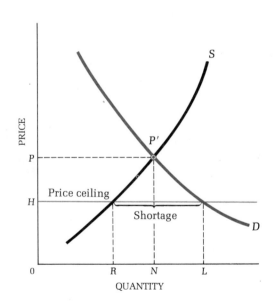

Exhibit 6
Price Floors Result in Product Surpluses

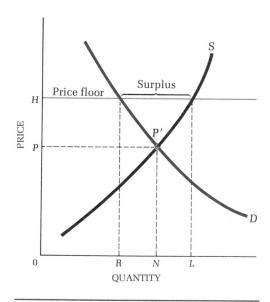

Minimum-wage legislation provides an example of how a price floor can cause a surplus (which, in this case, takes the form of unemployment).

making it illegal to sell the product at any price higher than the price at H. The result will be a *shortage* equal to the amount RL, because this represents the excess of quantity demanded over quantity supplied at the ceiling price.

When this situation occurs, the limited amount of the product, equal to the distance 0R, will be snatched up by the early buyers. This will leave nothing for later customers who want to buy a quantity of the product equal to the amount RL at the ceiling price. The government, therefore, may find it necessary to introduce some form of *rationing* as an equitable method of allocating the limited good among all the buyers who want it.

Price Floors Cause Surpluses

Price floors, which are the opposite of price ceilings, are designed to prevent a price from falling below a specified level. Although price ceilings have typically (but not exclusively) been a wartime phenomenon in the United States (but not in some other countries), price floors have played a continuing role in our daily lives. Two types have been particularly common: agricultural price supports and minimum-wage legislation.

In the general model of Exhibit 6, the equilibrium price and quantity that would emerge from an unregulated market are at P and N, represented by the distances 0P and 0N, respectively. But now the price at H represents a government-imposed price floor. At this price the quantity supplied will exceed the quantity demanded, resulting in a *surplus* of the amount RL.

What can be done about this surplus? In agriculture, where price floors for certain commodities have been employed during some periods, surpluses have been a recurrent phenomenon. As a result, government at various times has sought to cope with the situation in three major ways:

1. Restrict Supply Acreage allotments have been imposed on farmers, thereby limiting the amount of land they can use to grow certain agricultural commodities.

2. Stimulate Demand Research into new uses for agricultural products has been encouraged.

3. Buy up Surpluses Certain agricultural commodities have been bought and stored by the government for future sale or disposal.

Of course, the government could have eliminated the surpluses by removing the price floor, thus allowing the price to settle at P. But that would have nullified the government's objective of raising farm prices in order to help farmers.

With respect to minimum wages, Exhibit 6 may be thought of as a model of the supply and demand for labor. For example, let the horizontal axis measure the quantity of labor in terms of hours of labor time, and let the vertical axis measure the price of labor in terms of dollars per hour. The surplus is then the volume of unemployment RL occurring at the minimum-wage level at H. Therefore, one way to reduce this labor surplus is to *lower* the hourly wage rate. What would this do to total payrolls if the demand for labor were relatively elastic? What would it do to them if the demand were relatively inelastic? Can you suggest other possible methods of reducing the unemployment surplus?

Effects of Specific Taxes and Subsidies

Supply and demand analysis can be helpful in solving problems involving certain kinds of commodity taxes and subsidies. As the following examples demonstrate, different degrees of elasticities affect in surprising ways the prices and quantities of some of the things we buy every day.

Specific Taxes

Suppose a *specific tax* is imposed on the sale of a commodity. That is, for each unit of a commodity sold a fixed amount of money must be paid to the government. A specific tax is thus a *per-unit tax* that is independent of the price of the product. Some of the taxes on cigarettes and gasoline are of this kind.

The effect of a specific tax on a commodity may be to increase its equilibrium price and to decrease its equilibrium quantity.

How does a specific tax on a product affect its market prices and quantities? Is the *incidence*, or burden, of such a tax borne by those upon whom it is initially imposed, or is it *shifted* to others? These are the practical questions that the analysis will answer.

You can proceed by first examining the model in Exhibit 7, Figure (a). The curves D and S are the market demand and supply curves before the tax is imposed. The equilibrium quantity is therefore at N; the equilibrium price is the distance NP.

Suppose that sellers are required to pay a tax of T per unit. The results of such a tax can be analyzed in two steps:

1. The supply curve shifts upward to the parallel position S', showing that less will be supplied at any given price. This is because the tax is an added cost to the producer at all levels of output. Hence, the *supply price*—the price necessary to call forth a given output—will be higher by the amount of the tax. For example, before the tax, consumers paid a price equal to NP to obtain the quantity at N. After the tax they must pay a price of NR to call forth the same quantity at N. When the selling firm receives NR, it will pay a tax of PR (=T) to the government, leaving itself with NP, the old price.

2. The tax will therefore cause the equilibrium point to shift from P to H. This movement will be associated with a decrease in quantity from ON to OL and an increase in price from NP to LH, where GH is the amount of the tax.

Importance of Elasticities

Are there any general principles that can tell us the extent to which prices and quantities will be altered as a result of the tax? Figures (b), (c), and (d) in Exhibit 7 will help answer this question.

You can use the concept of elasticity to interpret the effects on quantities that result from changes in price.

In Figure (b), demand is perfectly elastic. That is, any increase in price will cause sales to drop to zero. Therefore, the same price is maintained after the tax as before, but sellers compensate for the added cost of the tax by reducing their quantity. Consumers, therefore, will get fewer units of the good, even though they will continue to pay the same price per unit.

In Figure (c), the demand curve is perfectly inelastic. That is, no one will stop buying the product (nor will anyone buy less of it) if the price is raised. Therefore, the entire burden of the tax is shifted forward from sellers to buyers in the form of a higher price, with no reduction in the equilibrium quantity.

Exhibit 7
Effects of Specific Taxes and Subsidies

Taxes will affect the equilibrium prices and quantities of commodities, depending on the relative elasticities of demand and supply. Subsidies have effects that are opposite to the effects of taxes, but their influence is also determined by the relative elasticities of demand and supply.

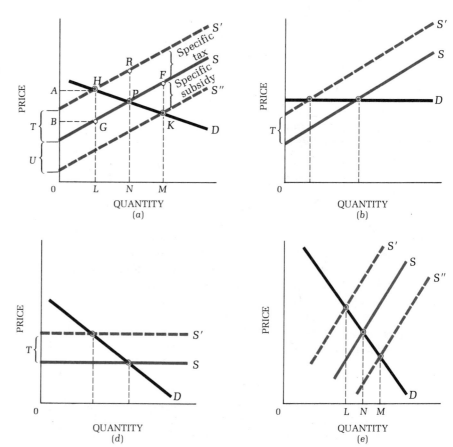

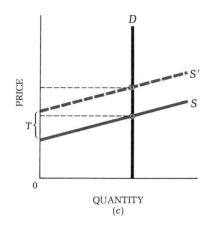

In Figure (d), supply is perfectly elastic, and both price and quantity are affected as a result. The burden of the tax is shifted entirely to buyers, *and* the equilibrium quantity is reduced. Note how this compares with the case in Figure (c), in which only price is affected, not quantity. What would have happened in Figure (d) if the demand curve had been perfectly inelastic?

We can now establish two important principles:

1. The more *inelastic* the demand and the supply of a commodity, the smaller will be the decline in output resulting from a given tax. [This is illustrated in Figure (e), where the letters have the same meaning as before.]

2. The relative burden of a tax among buyers and sellers tends to follow the path of least resistance. That is, the tax is shifted in proportion to where the *inelasticity* is greatest.

The first principle leads to the following practical conclusion:

If government wants to minimize disruptions in production, industries whose commodities are inelastic in demand and supply are better suited to commodity taxation. This is because they suffer smaller contractions in output and hence in employment.

From what you have learned, you should be able to illustrate this proposition with supply and demand curves. The second principle results in another useful conclusion:

> In most supply-and-demand situations (except the extreme ones involving perfect elasticity or inelasticity), the tax will be shared by consumers and producers. The proportions will vary according to the relative elasticities of demand and supply.

As with the previous proposition, you should be able to illustrate this one with supply and demand curves. Thus, as a result of the tax, the consumer's price will rise, but by less than the amount of the tax. Similarly, the producer's net price will fall, but by less than the amount of the tax. However, the *relative* changes in prices and quantities will depend on the *relative* elasticities of demand and supply.

Note Exhibit 7 does not demonstrate the effect of a tax in the case of a perfectly inelastic supply curve. Can you illustrate such a case and explain it? Be careful; this is a tricky question. (**Hint** If the supply curve is perfectly inelastic, can it shift as a result of the tax?) You will learn more about this problem in a subsequent chapter when you encounter a concept known as the "single tax." This idea once played an interesting role in American politics. In the meantime, see if you can deduce the answer yourself.

Subsidies

A *subsidy* is a payment a government makes to businesses or households to achieve a particular purpose. The subsidy enables them to produce or consume a product in larger quantities or at lower prices than they would be able to otherwise. Government subsidies have been granted, and in some cases continue to be granted, to farmers, airlines, railroads, shipping companies, shipbuilding firms, low-income households, and certain other groups in the economy.

A *specific subsidy* is a per-unit subsidy on a commodity. It is thus the opposite of a specific tax. In fact, a specific subsidy can be thought of as a "negative" specific tax because the government is giving money to the seller or to the consumer rather than taking it away.

The effects of a specific subsidy on sellers are illustrated in Exhibit 7, Figure (a). As a result of a subsidy equal to the amount U, the supply curve shifts downward from its normal position S to the new position S″. This is because the subsidy is like a reduction in cost to the producer at all levels of output. Therefore, the supply price will be lower by the amount of the subsidy.

For instance, the subsidy causes the equilibrium point to shift from P to K. Hence, the equilibrium price decreases from NP to MK and the equilibrium output increases from 0N to 0M. At this new and larger output, buyers will pay the price MK but sellers will receive the additional amount KF (=U). This, of course, is the amount of the subsidy per unit of output.

Our analysis leads us to an important principle:

> The more elastic the supply and demand curves, the greater will be the expansion in output and the less will be the reduction in price resulting from a subsidy.

This can be verified by comparing Figures (a) and (e) in Exhibit 7.

The economic purposes of a subsidy are to reduce prices or to increase output. The latter objective is usually the primary one when the

The effect of a specific subsidy for a commodity may be to decrease its equilibrium price and to increase its equilibrium quantity.

product is to be used wholly for domestic consumption. These ideas suggest a practical conclusion:

> If government wants to increase production through the use of a subsidy, industries whose commodities are relatively elastic in demand and supply are better suited to subsidies. This is because such industries experience larger expansions in output and therefore in employment.

Subsidies are also quite common in international trade. They occur when a government subsidizes a firm or even an entire industry in order to help it penetrate foreign markets at lower prices. For example, at various times Japan has been accused by its trading partners of subsidizing the production of automobiles, steel, electronic products, and cameras in order to encourage their export to the United States and other countries.

Other Types of Elasticities: Similar Ideas and Measures

The income elasticity of demand measures the responsiveness of a change in the quantity purchased of a good to a change in income.

Early in this chapter you learned that elasticity is a measure of the responsiveness of changes in quantity to changes in price. Actually, this type of elasticity, called "price elasticity," is one of many used in economics. However, it is the most common of all elasticity measures. Therefore, in any economic or business discussion, the term "elasticity" always means price elasticity unless otherwise indicated.

What are some other types of elasticity? Two that are especially useful are (1) the income elasticity of demand and (2) the cross elasticity of demand.

Income Elasticity of Demand

When you draw a demand curve that shows a relationship between price and quantity demanded, one of the things you assume to be constant is buyers' incomes. But if incomes change, the demand curve shifts—that is, there is a change in demand. How much of a change? The answer depends on the income elasticity of demand.

> The *income elasticity of demand* is the percentage change in the quantity purchased of a good resulting from a 1 percent change in income. This type of elasticity thus measures the responsiveness of changes in demand to changes in income.

Note that the formula for income elasticity is analogous to the formula for price elasticity.

The method of measuring income elasticity is the same as that for measuring price elasticity. As you will recall, price elasticity is simply the ratio of the percentage change in quantity (demanded or supplied) to the percentage change in price. Similarly, the income elasticity of demand is the ratio of the percentage change in quantity purchased to the percentage change in income. Thus,

$$\text{income elasticity of demand} = \frac{\text{percentage change in quantity purchased}}{\text{percentage change in income}}$$

It follows that the formula used for measuring income elasticity is the same as that for price elasticity—except for some differences in symbols. Thus, let

Q_1 = old quantity, or quantity purchased before the change in income

Q_2 = new quantity, or quantity purchased after the change in income

Y_1 = old income, or income before the change

Y_2 = new income, or income after the change

The formula for the income elasticity of demand is then

$$_yE_D = \frac{\dfrac{Q_2 - Q_1}{Q_2 + Q_1}}{\dfrac{Y_2 - Y_1}{Y_2 + Y_1}}$$

Note Economists usually employ the letter Y to represent income because I is customarily used to represent investment.

Measurement and Interpretation

How is the income elasticity of demand interpreted? What are its uses?

Before you can answer these questions, you need to understand how the income elasticity of demand is measured in a real-life situation. Exhibit 8 provides an example.

The data suggest that goods can be classified according to their income elasticity of demand. One such classification distinguishes between "superior" and "inferior" goods.

Superior Goods: $_yE_D > 0$ The income elasticity of demand for some goods may be greater than zero. That is, the coefficient may be positive. Such products are called *superior goods*. They are commodities whose consumption varies directly with money income, prices remaining constant. In the hypothetical illustration of Exhibit 8, record albums, hamburgers, and magazines are examples of superior goods. Each has an income elasticity of demand greater than zero. As you might expect, most goods are superior goods. That is, their consumption increases with income. Therefore, such goods are also called *normal goods*, because they represent the "normal" situation.

Superior goods can be subclassified in terms of income elasticity. If the value of the income elasticity coefficient is greater than 1, the demand for the commodity is said to be income elastic. If the coefficient is less than 1 but greater than 0, the demand is said to be income inelastic. In Exhibit 8, record albums are income elastic while magazines are income inelastic. Hamburgers, being a borderline case, may be classified as income unit-elastic.

Inferior Goods: $_yE_D < 0$ The income elasticity of demand for some goods may be less than zero. That is, the coefficient may be negative. Such products are called *inferior goods*. Their consumption varies inversely with money income (prices remaining constant) over a certain range of income. Potatoes, used clothing, and other "cheap" commodities bought in relatively larger quantities by poorer families are examples. The consumption of these commodities declines in favor of fancier foods, new clothing, and the like as the incomes of low-income families rise. In the hypothetical example of Exhibit 8, pizza is an illustration of an inferior good.

Exhibit 8
Measuring the Income Elasticity of Demand

Suppose that your monthly income, and some of the things you spend it on, are shown in the table. You can calculate your income elasticity of demand for each item quite easily. The following calculation, involving record albums, provides an example.

$$_yE_D = \frac{\dfrac{Q_2 - Q_1}{Q_2 + Q_1}}{\dfrac{Y_2 - Y_1}{Y_2 + Y_1}} = \frac{\dfrac{2 - 1}{2 + 1}}{\dfrac{\$1,500 - \$1,000}{\$1,500 + \$1,000}}$$

$$= \frac{\dfrac{1}{3}}{\dfrac{1}{5}} = 1.67$$

You should verify the remaining elasticities shown in the table in the same way. For each good, however, be careful to pair Q_1 with Y_1 and Q_2 with Y_2, to avoid errors.

Item	Quantity purchased per month at $1,000 income per month	Quantity purchased per month at $1,500 income per month	$_yE_D$
Albums	1	2	1.67
Hamburgers	10	15	1.00
Magazines	4	5	0.56
Movies	3	3	0
Pizzas	4	3	−0.71

In general, income elasticities of demand vary widely from commodity to commodity and from person to person. Indeed, a good that is superior for one individual may be inferior for another, and vice versa. Nevertheless, a few overall tendencies may be mentioned.

Usually, commodities that consumers regard as "necessities" tend to be income inelastic. Examples are food, fuel, utilities, and medical services. Commodities that consumers regard as "luxuries" tend to be income elastic. Examples are sports cars, furs, costly vacation trips, and expensive foods. Therefore, the income elasticity of demand provides an approximate guide for judging the importance of commodities to consumers.

Cross Elasticity of Demand

The cross elasticity of demand measures the responsiveness of a change in the quantity purchased of a good to a change in the price of another good.

When you draw a demand curve, you assume that buyers' incomes and the prices of other goods remain constant.

Of course, buyers' incomes may vary. If they do, the resulting change in demand is measured by the income elasticity of demand, as you have just seen. But what if prices of other goods vary? In that case, the resulting change in demand is measured by a new relationship—the cross elasticity of demand.

The *cross elasticity of demand* is the percentage change in the quantity purchased of a good resulting from a 1 percent change in the price of another good. This type of elasticity thus measures the responsiveness of changes in the demand for a good to changes in the price of a different good.

Note that the formula for cross elasticity is analogous to the formulas for price and income elasticity.

Like every other type of elasticity, the cross elasticity of demand is simply a ratio of two percentage changes. Therefore, its formula is the same as all other elasticity formulas, except for the choice of symbols. Thus, let

Q_{X1} = quantity purchased of product X before a change in the price of product Y

Q_{X2} = quantity purchased of product X after a change in the price of product Y

P_{Y1} = price of product Y before the change

P_{Y2} = price of product Y after the change

The cross elasticity of demand, $_+E_D$, is thus measured by the formula

$$_+E_D = \frac{\dfrac{Q_{X2} - Q_{X1}}{Q_{X2} + Q_{X1}}}{\dfrac{P_{Y2} - P_{Y1}}{P_{Y2} + P_{Y1}}}$$

Measurement and Interpretation

How is the formula used? Three practical applications are shown in Exhibit 9. The diagrams are derived from several business studies. As they show, the cross elasticities of demand for products will differ according to whether the products are substitutes, complements, or independent.

Substitutes: $_+E_D > 0$ Substitute goods are goods that compete with one another. The more you consume of one, the less you consume of the other. Examples are butter and margarine, coffee and tea, automobile and bus transportation.

The cross elasticity of demand for substitute goods is significantly greater than zero. The coefficient is thus positive. The reason is that a price increase for one of the goods causes people to buy less of that good and more of the substitute. Hence, the quantity purchased of the substitute increases.

This idea is illustrated in Figures (a), (b), and (c) of Exhibit 9. Figure (a) shows a hypothetical demand curve for Coca-Cola. Similarly, Figure (b) shows a hypothetical demand curve for Pepsi-Cola.

What happens if there is an increase in the price of Coca-Cola? Obviously, less of it will be bought. In other words, there will be a *decrease in quantity demanded*, a movement "up" the curve. However, many people who previously bought Coca-Cola will now switch to Pepsi-Cola. As a result, there will be an *increase in demand* for Pepsi-Cola, shown as a shift of the demand curve to the right. Thus, the overall effect of an increase in the price of Coca-Cola is to reduce its sales while increasing the sales of Pepsi-Cola.

The opposite effects occur, of course, if there is a decrease in the price of Coca-Cola: The demand curve for Pepsi-Cola shifts to the left.

Figure (c) shows the actual consequences of changes in the price of Coca-Cola. These results are derived from a set of demand studies conducted for a chain of supermarkets. Note that higher prices of Coke result in increased purchases of Pepsi. Therefore, the cross elasticity of demand is positive. You should verify this result by applying the cross-elasticity formula to the data in the chart.

Complements: $_+E_D < 0$ Complementary goods are goods that "go together." The more you consume of one, the more you consume of the other. Examples are cameras and film, gasoline and tires, textbooks and notebooks.

The cross elasticity of demand for complementary goods is significantly less than zero. The coefficient is therefore negative. The reason is that, as the price of a good increases, people buy less of it. Therefore, they also buy less of the complementary goods. The opposite effects occur, of course, if the price of a good decreases.

These ideas can be seen in Figures (d), (e), and (f) of Exhibit 9. Figures (d) and (e) show hypothetical demand curves for shirts and ties. In Figure (d), an increase in the price of shirts causes a *decrease in quantity demanded*. In Figure (e), therefore, there is a *decrease in demand* for ties, as shown by a leftward shift of the curve.

Some actual relationships, based on demand studies conducted for a department store, are shown in Figure (f). The downward-sloping curve tells you that the cross elasticity of demand must be negative. You should verify the estimate by applying the cross-elasticity formula to the data in the figure.

Independent: $_+E_D = 0$ Independent goods, as the name implies, are unrelated. The consumption of one is not directly influenced by the consumption of the other. Consequently, changes in the price of one have no significant effect on quantities purchased of the other. The cross elasticity of demand is therefore zero.

For substitute goods, the cross elasticity is significantly positive.

For complementary goods, the cross elasticity is significantly negative.

For independent goods, the cross elasticity is not significantly different from zero.

Exhibit 9
Measuring the Cross Elasticity of Demand

(a) COCA-COLA

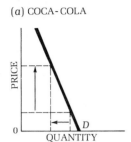

(b) PEPSI-COLA

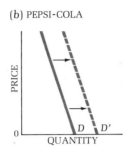

(c) SUBSTITUTES
(Coke and Pepsi)

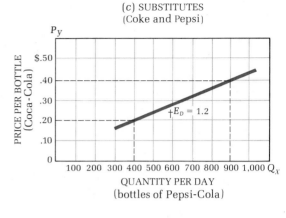

QUANTITY PER DAY
(bottles of Pepsi-Cola)

Substitute Goods: In Figure (a), an increase in the price of Coca-Cola causes a *decrease in quantity demanded.* This, in turn, leads to an *increase in demand* for Pepsi-Cola, shown

in Figure (b). Figure (c) estimates the cross elasticity of demand for Pepsi-Cola relative to the price of Coca-Cola.

(d) SHIRTS

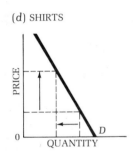

(e) TIES

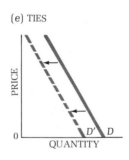

(f) COMPLEMENTS
(shirts and ties)

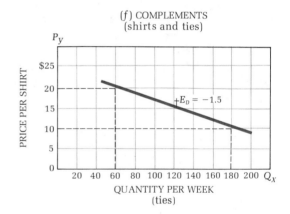

QUANTITY PER WEEK
(ties)

Complementary Goods: In Figure (d), an increase in the price of shirts causes a *decrease in quantity demanded.* In Figure (e), therefore, there is a *decrease in demand* for ties as

the curve shifts to the left. Figure (f) estimates the cross elasticity of demand for ties relative to the price of shirts.

(g) INDEPENDENT

Independent Goods: In Figure (g), changes in the price of lettuce have no effect on the demand for catsup, beer, or milk. Therefore, as shown in the graph, cross elasticities of demand for these products relative to the price of lettuce are zero.

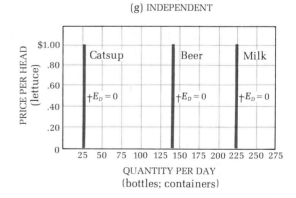

QUANTITY PER DAY
(bottles; containers)

An illustration of the cross elasticity of demand for independent goods is provided in Exhibit 9, Figure (g). Some examples of other pairs of independent or unrelated goods are pizza and jewelry, books and dishes, egg rolls and wristwatches.

Simple Rules to Remember

The following rules will help you remember these ideas:

The cross elasticity of demand provides a measure of *substitutability* between products. In general:

1. Goods whose cross elasticities of demand are significantly greater than zero may be thought of as "positive substitutes." (Examples are competing brands of goods in the same industry, such as soaps, toothpastes, and television sets.)

2. Goods whose cross elasticities of demand are approximately zero may be thought of as "weak substitutes" or "nonsubstitutes."

3. Goods whose cross elasticities of demand are significantly less than zero are complements. Such goods, therefore, may be thought of as "negative substitutes."

Here are some practical rules for remembering the different types of cross elasticity.

Some Assumptions and Conclusions

Before concluding this study of supply and demand, it is important that you recognize certain assumptions that underlie the previous models. In addition, it is useful for you to understand some implications about the overall role of supply and demand in a market economy.

Two Underlying Assumptions

Two special assumptions are relevant to the kinds of models developed in this chapter. These serve as warnings about the limitations of the analysis.

Simple Versus Complex Considerations

Theoretical models of supply and demand assume that a particular economic action—such as the imposition of price ceilings, price floors, taxes, or subsidies—can be analyzed in terms of economic considerations alone. These models thus neglect multiple considerations involving both economic and noneconomic factors. In reality, of course, both types of conditions are usually at work.

Basic supply-and-demand models focus on quantities and prices while assuming that all other things remain the same.

For example, a tax on cigarettes may prompt some people to give up smoking for psychological reasons because they associate the unpleasant task of paying taxes with the act of smoking. This will cause the demand curve to shift to the left, resulting in a different equilibrium from the one in our model.

Likewise, in analyzing the effects of taxes, subsidies, and so on, it must be remembered that conditions vary in the real world. Supply and demand curves are always changing over time due to changes in technology, tastes, and other factors ordinarily assumed constant.

Hence, although our models have purposely been kept simple, it should be apparent that complexities such as these must be introduced if the models are to be made more realistic.

Static Versus Dynamic Models

Another important limitation of supply and demand models is that they are *static* rather than *dynamic*. Stated in simple terms, a static model examines the effects of a change *after* it occurs. A dynamic model, however, examines the effects of a change *while* it is occurring. Thus, in a dynamic model, the influence of expectations by buyers or sellers would be recognized. This is because the process of moving toward an equilibrium might itself cause changes in the supply and demand curves.

As an example, a fall in price might prompt consumers to postpone their purchases in anticipation of further price decreases. This would cause a shift to the left of the demand curve. On the other hand, the supply curve might shift to the right as suppliers sought to offset the future effects of the expected price drop by producing and selling more now at the higher price. Situations such as these continually occur in the stock and commodities markets, making it extremely difficult to predict future prices.

Fortunately, these limitations do not make static models too simple to be useful. They merely remind you that any model is a simplification of reality, and that care should be taken not to claim that a model is more than it really is.

Market Price and Normal Price

You have learned how prices and quantities are determined under competitive market circumstances. It will be useful at this point to summarize what you know.

1. Central to supply and demand is the idea that competition among many buyers and sellers will cause market prices and quantities to move toward equilibrium.

2. Prices in a market reflect the *eagerness* of people to buy or sell. In competitive markets there will be a tendency for equilibrium prices to establish themselves automatically through the free operation of supply and demand.

3. Once equilibrium prices are established, they will have no tendency to change unless there are changes in the factors that determine supply and demand.

The third point requires some amplification. In reality, the equilibrium price is rarely, if ever, the actual price that exists at any given instant. The forces that are at work to determine an equilibrium price are always changing, thus causing the equilibrium price to change. In view of this, it helps to distinguish between two kinds of price:

> The *market price* is the actual price that prevails in a market at any particular moment. The *normal price* is the equilibrium price toward which the market price is always tending but may never reach. (Normal price may thus be viewed as a dynamic equilibrium price.)

You can think of the market price as pursuing the normal price in much the same way as a guided missile pursues a moving target. The missile may never reach the target, just as the market price may never reach the dynamic equilibrium price. Yet the target is necessary to explain where the missile is heading, just as the concept of a normal price is necessary to explain where the market price is heading.

Exhibit 10

How a Market Economy Rations (Allocates) Goods or Resources Among Buyers and Sellers

The equilibrium price serves as a highly selective filter. It admits to the market only those buyers whose demand price is greater than, or equal to, the equilibrium price and those sellers whose supply price is less than, or equal to, the equilibrium price. All buyers and sellers who are not able and willing to deal at the going price are excluded.

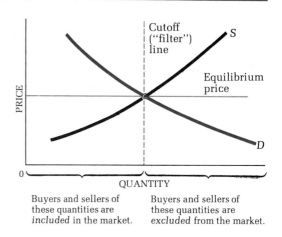

Buyers and sellers of these quantities are *included* in the market.

Buyers and sellers of these quantities are *excluded* from the market.

Conclusion: The Price System As a Rationing (Allocative) Mechanism

We now come to one of the most significant conclusions in the study of economics. It consists of an explanation of how the market system allocates scarce goods among competing buyers.

You already know that scarcity—the inability of limited resources to produce all the goods and services that people want—is an economic fact of life. In a command economy some central authority—perhaps a king, a commissar, or a committee—decides the alternative uses to which these limited resources will be put. To a large extent the central authority may also ration the fruits among the members of society. In that way, a command economy answers the three big questions: *what* to produce, *how* to produce, and *for whom* to produce.

In a pure market economy, on the other hand, these questions are answered by a competitive price system through the free operation of supply and demand. The concept, described in Exhibit 10, shows that the equilibrium price automatically admits certain buyers and sellers to the marketplace while simultaneously excluding others. The cost of admission to the market is the *demand price* for buyers and the *supply price* for sellers—two terms that are already familiar to you. The diagram and its accompanying description thus lead to the following conclusion:

> A *price system* is a mechanism that allocates scarce goods and resources among competing uses. The price system accomplishes this by rationing goods among those buyers and sellers in the marketplace who are willing and able to deal at the market price.

A price system in a competitive market thus allocates goods and resources through the free play of supply-and-demand forces. These, in turn, result from the interaction of many sellers and buyers. But what about "noncompetitive" price systems, in which buyers or sellers are relatively few? As will be shown in later chapters, such systems result in pricing situations quite different from those that occur in the familiar supply-and-demand models studied so far.

Through the price system, scarce goods and resources are allocated to their highest-valued uses.

Case
The DuPont Cellophane Case: Using Cross Elasticity in the Courtroom

What is the meaning of *monopoly?* It is a term that many people have heard but that few understand.

Monopoly is the absence of competition. Every business firm would like to be a monopoly in order to have greater control over its prices and profits. But monopolies, if unregulated by government, could exploit their market power at the expense of the public. For this reason, government has passed laws, called antitrust laws, that prohibit firms from obtaining or seeking a monopoly.

Defining the Relevant Market

In order to enforce the laws, the government sometimes must specify the market for a particular product. This can be difficult. If substitution were not possible, every brand of every product would have a monopoly. If substitution were extremely easy, monopoly would be virtually nonexistent. The problem is to draw the proper boundaries— that is, to *define the relevant market.*

For example, are rugs, carpets, and linoleum sold in separate markets? Or are they all sold in the floor-covering market? Should toasters and blenders be classified in separate industries? Or are they part of the electrical appliance industry?

The task of defining the relevant market has been undertaken by the courts in numerous cases. One of the most famous, which occurred in 1956, involved the use of cellophane. The E. I. DuPont Corporation, producer of cellophane, was charged by the U.S. Department of Justice with monopolizing the market.

Was the company guilty or innocent? The answer depended on the definition of the market.

1. The government (that is, the Justice Department) argued that the relevant market was that for cellophane. Therefore, DuPont clearly had a monopoly because it controlled the entire output of the product.

2. DuPont countered with the argument that the relevant market was that for flexible packaging materials. These included cellophane, waxed papers, parchment papers, aluminum foil, pliofilm, and glassine. In that market, cellophane accounted for only 18 percent of the total, a figure hardly large enough to constitute a monopoly.

Conclusion: Substitutability Is Relevant

A Federal District court found in favor of DuPont. The case was appealed to the Supreme Court, and that body upheld the lower court's verdict. In both trials, the courts concurred that "a relevant market exists when commodities are reasonably interchangeable by consumers for the same purposes."

Both courts also agreed that the relevant market determined the boundaries of the industry. According to the Supreme Court's majority opinion, "The cross elasticity of demand for cellophane was high and competition intense. . . . The relevant market, therefore, was not that for cellophane produced by the defendant . . . but for flexible packaging materials produced by various firms."

Flexible packaging materials:
substitutes for cellophane.

Robert Rattner

Questions

1. For several decades prior to the case, the price of cellophane was often substantially higher than the prices of other flexible packaging materials. In view of this, why would business firms, which were the main purchasers of cellophane, buy this product instead of the cheaper substitutes?

2. In the Supreme Court's minority opinion, the statement was made that "cross elasticities are not engraved in stone." Was this intended as a criticism of the majority opinion? What did it mean?

What You Have Learned in This Chapter

1. Elasticity is a basic concept in supply-and-demand analysis. It may be defined interpretively as the percentage change in quantity (demanded or supplied) resulting from a 1 percent change in price. Elasticity may also be defined mathematically as a ratio: elasticity = (percentage change in quantity)/(percentage change in price).

2. The coefficient of elasticity is commonly expressed in its absolute-value or numerical form. This means that any minus signs are disregarded. There are five types of elasticity, ranging from zero to infinity:

perfect elasticity	$(E = \infty)$
relative elasticity	$(E > 1)$
unit elasticity	$(E = 1)$
relative inelasticity	$(E < 1)$
perfect inelasticity	$(E = 0)$

These five types apply both to supply and to demand.

3. Because elasticity is a measure of relative changes, it may vary for each segment along a curve. The formula used for elasticity gives a type of "average" elasticity over an entire segment.

4. Elasticity is *not* the same as slope. Therefore, the elasticity of a curve cannot always be judged from its slope alone. An exception occurs in the case of vertical and horizontal curves. In most other cases, the exact elasticity must be calculated.

5. You can tell whether demand elasticity is greater or less than 1 by observing the effect of a price change on total revenue. If price and total revenue change in opposite directions, demand elasticity is greater than 1. If price and total revenue change in the same direction, demand elasticity is less than 1.

6. The availability of good commodity substitutes tends to make demand more elastic. Similarly, the availability of good resource substitutes tends to make supply more elastic. Goods that are relatively inexpensive tend to be more inelastic in demand. This is because they account for only a small part of the consumer's total expenditures.

7. Elasticities of demand and supply tend to be greater over longer periods of time. The reason is that buyers and sellers can eventually adjust to the use of substitutes or to changes in price.

8. Price ceilings are imposed to keep the market price of a commodity below its normal (free-market) equilibrium price. Price floors, on the other hand, are imposed to keep the market price of a commodity above its normal (free-market) equilibrium price. Price ceilings cause product shortages and the need for rationing. Price floors cause product surpluses, which may require government action to absorb them.

9. Specific taxes tend to be shifted between buyers and sellers according to where the inelasticity is greatest. Industries whose commodities are inelastic in demand are better suited to commodity taxation because they suffer smaller contractions in output and hence in employment. On the other hand, industries whose commodities are elastic in demand are better suited to subsidies because they experience larger expansions in output and hence in employment.

10. The term "elasticity" always means price elasticity, unless otherwise indicated. In addition to price elasticity, two important kinds of elasticity are (a) the income elasticity of demand and (b) the cross elasticity of demand. The first measures the responsiveness of quantity purchased of a good to changes in income. The second measures the responsiveness of quantity purchased of a good to changes in the price of another good.

11. Some important lessons are to be learned from supply-and-demand concepts:
(a) Simple supply-and-demand models do not take into account complex economic and noneconomic considerations, and they are static rather than dynamic.
(b) The competitive market is always tending toward the equilibrium price, but it may never reach that price because the underlying forces are always changing.
(c) In a market economy, the price system allocates goods and resources by rationing

them among those buyers and sellers whose demand and supply prices are sufficient to admit them to the market.

For Discussion

1. *Terms and concepts to review:*
elasticity
shortage
rationing
surplus
specific tax
incidence
supply price
subsidy
specific subsidy
income elasticity of demand
superior good
inferior good
cross elasticity of demand
market price
normal price
price system

2. Several studies have found that the overall demand for automobiles has an elasticity of about 1.3. (a) How do you interpret this coefficient? (b) After hearing about these studies, a Ford dealer in Chicago cut prices by 10 percent and sold 22 percent more cars. What is the elasticity of demand in this case? Does it mean that the estimate of 1.3 is incorrect? Explain.

3. Suppose that we are given the following demand schedule for a commodity:

	Price (cents)	Quantity demanded
A	20	50
B	15	100
C	10	200
D	5	400

(a) Calculate the elasticity between points A and B, B and C, C and D. (**Suggestion** Sketch the demand curve and label it with the points A, B, C, D in order to help you "see" what you are doing.)
(b) How will your results compare if you calculate the elasticity in reverse directions (that is, from B to A, C to B, and D to C)? Explain.

4. Fill in the blank cell in each of the following rows:

Price	Total revenue	Elasticity
increases		>1
decreases	decreases	
decreases	no change	
	increases	<1
	decreases	>1
increases		1

5. "At a given price ceiling or price floor, the size of a shortage or surplus varies directly with the elasticity of the demand and supply curves." Demonstrate this proposition graphically.

6. Many people criticize public transit systems (subways, buses, and so on) for being too crowded during rush hours. From what you know about the price system as a rationing mechanism, how would you correct the situation?

7. The R. H. Lacy Co., a department store, conducted a study of the demand for men's ties made from low-cost synthetic fibers. The store found that the average daily demand D in terms of price P is given by the equation $D = 60 - 5P$.
   (a) How many ties per day can the store expect to sell at a price of $3 per tie?
   (b) If the store wants to sell 20 ties per day, what price should it charge?
   (c) What would be the demand if the store offered to give the ties away free?
   (d) What is the highest price that anyone would be willing to pay for these ties?
   (e) Plot the demand curve.

8. The demand D for sugar in the United States in terms of its price P was once estimated to be $D = 135 - 8P$. If this equation were valid today:
   (a) How much would be demanded at a price of 10?
   (b) What price would correspond to a demand of 95?
   (c) How much would be demanded if sugar were free?
   (d) What is the highest price anyone would pay?

9. The demand D for a certain product in terms of its price P is given by the equation $D = 3a - 3bP$, in which a and b are positive constants.

(a) Find the price if the quantity demanded is $a/2$.
(b) Find the quantity demanded at a price of $a/3b$.
(c) How much will be demanded if the product is free?
(d) What is the highest price anyone will pay for the good?

10. Principles or Proverbs? Many statements of an economic nature are accepted as principles when, in reality, they are hardly more than proverbs. The differences between the two are by no means trivial. For one thing, principles are never contradictory, whereas proverbs often are. (**Example** *"Look before you leap"*; however, *"He who hesitates is lost."*) Statements such as the following are often heard. Are they principles or proverbs? Explain. Rephrase if necessary to improve the statement. Use examples.
   (a) "Inexpensive products tend to have inelastic demands."
   (b) "The demands of rich consumers are less elastic than the demands of poor consumers."
   (c) "Products whose purchases are closely correlated with income are elastic in demand."

11. "Demand elasticity measures percentage changes in quantity demanded relative to percentage changes in price. It follows that, with 10 equal demanders for a product, the elasticity will be 10 times as great as it is for one." True or false? Explain.

12. "The elasticity of demand for a product usually increases with the length of time over which a price change persists. Thus, a 1 percent decrease in price may result at first in an increase in quantity demanded of less than 1 percent, but eventually the quantity may increase by 2 percent, 5 percent, or even more." True or false? Explain why.

13. Are the following statements true or false? Explain.
   (a) "For most consumers, the income elasticity of demand for restaurant meals is probably lower than the income elasticity of demand for ball-point pens."
   (b) "For some commodities, the price elasticity of demand may be greater than 1 (that is, relatively elastic) while the income elasticity of demand is negative."
   (c) "The cross elasticity of demand for commodity A relative to the price of commodity B may be quite different from the cross elasticity of demand for commodity B relative to the price of commodity A."

Commodity Futures Markets: Supply and Demand in Action

This supplement describes the operations of supply and demand in an important market of the economy.

Buy low and sell high. And if it don't go up, don't buy it.

Will Rogers

Will Rogers, a famous comedian and "cowboy philosopher" of the early 1900s, offered this foolproof advice for people who wanted to invest in the stock market.

However, Rogers's advice does not necessarily apply to commodity-futures markets. The reason is that, "if it don't go up," you may still be able to make a huge profit—even if it goes down.

Thus, if you have a few thousand dollars to spare, there are not many places where you can find faster action than in the commodity-futures markets. Profits are big if you guess right, and losses are fast if you do not. To see why, it helps to understand some basic facts about this remarkable institution.

What Are Commodity-Futures Markets?

Organized trading in commodity futures dates back to antiquity. Active markets in the sale of grain and certain other agricultural products existed in Arabia, China, and Egypt as long ago as 1000 B.C. The operations of today's commodity-futures markets resemble in many ways the procedures for trading in rice developed by the shoguns of Japan in the late seventeenth century.

What are commodity-futures markets—or simply "commodities markets" or "futures markets," as they are often called? They are places where contracts to deliver certain standardized products are bought and sold. Among the contracts traded are those for foreign currencies, gold, copper, silver coins, and U.S. Treasury bills (short-term debt instruments issued by the Treasury). In addition, contracts are also traded for many agricultural products. The more popular ones include grains, coffee, sugar, eggs, butter, live cattle, live hogs, frozen turkeys, and frozen pork bellies (uncured, unsliced slabs of bacon).

Auction Markets

The scene in a commodity-futures market resembles a huge public auction in which market prices are determined by the forces of supply and demand. Transactions are conducted by public outcry. Brokers, representing buyers and sellers, shout their bid and ask prices in the trading pits on the floor of the exchange. These prices, like those in all competitive markets, rarely remain constant for very long. They fluctuate almost continuously in response to buyers' and sellers' expectations of future market conditions. You can see the day-to-day changes in commodity-futures prices by looking them up in many of the major daily newspapers, such as *The Wall Street Journal*.

Prices are the result of "bids" by buyers and "asks" by sellers.

Trading Example

The best way to gain an understanding of the commodity-futures markets is to examine a typical trade. Such a trade consists of three parts: transaction, delivery, and settlement. Let us begin by assuming that, because you are interested in being a market participant, you have already opened an account with a broker. The broker is likely to be a member of one or more of the several dozen commodity exchanges that operate throughout the world. One of these is shown in Box 1 on page 410.

1. Transaction

On April 5, you look in the morning paper and note that the previous day's closing price of corn for delivery in December (that is, the December futures contract) is $2 per bushel. Feeling that corn production in the coming months will decrease and that the price will rise, you instruct your broker to *buy* a contract of December corn. By purchasing the contract, you are agreeing to accept delivery and pay $2 per bushel for corn in December. The trader who sells the contract agrees to deliver corn in December for $2 per bushel.

2. Delivery

What is the nature of the contract? It is an agreement that specifies several conditions. The main ones are: (1) the commodity, (2) the price per unit, (3) the number of units, (4) the quality or grade, and (5) the delivery date, place, and terms of payment. In the case of corn and other grains, the standard contract is for 5,000 bushels and the place of delivery is a public warehouse designated by the commodity exchange.

Thus, unlike stocks or bonds, you cannot buy a commodity-futures contract and hold it indefinitely. Nor are you likely to will it to your heirs. Every futures contract has a relatively short life span, usually less than a year. When the contract period is over, you must accept delivery if you are a buyer or make delivery if you are a seller.

Delivery months differ for each commodity. Generally, they are tailored to seasonal production times and to the needs of the buyers and sellers of the particular commodity. For example, delivery months for corn and other grains are March, May, July, September, and December.

For live cattle, the delivery months are January, February, and alternate months thereafter. Delivery contracts for eggs can be written for any month.

3. Settlement

A couple of months pass, and it is now June. You look in the paper and see that contracts for December corn are trading for $2.10 per bushel. (Remember that you paid $2 per bushel for a 5,000-bushel contract on April 5.) Because you believe that the price will not go any higher, you phone your broker to sell your 5,000-bushel contract "at the market"— which means the highest price obtainable. Your gross profit on the purchase and sale is thus 10¢ per bushel, or $500. After subtracting the broker's commission for buying *and* selling—about $21 (which is a fraction of 1 percent on the total value of the transaction)—you are left with a net of $479. But what if the price of December contracts had fallen, say, to $1.90? In that case, if you had sold, your loss would have been $500 plus the commission—a total of $521.

What will happen if, instead of selling the contract, you hold it until the December delivery month? Contrary to popular myth, a huge trailer truck will not arrive at your house in December and dump 5,000 bushels of corn on your front lawn. You will simply receive notice from a public warehouse that you hold title to the corn. Therefore, it must be paid for in full (you made only a down payment when you purchased the contract), and you must begin paying a storage charge to the warehouse. If, at a later date, you default on the payment, the warehouse can sell the corn, deduct all handling and unpaid storage expenses, and return any remaining balance to you.

Two-Way Transaction

The futures market thus differs from the everyday cash market:

> In the cash market, transactions between buyers and sellers entail actual delivery of the goods. The nation's farmers, for example, sell their grain in the cash market to thousands of country storage facilities known as granaries or grain elevators. These firms, in turn, resell the wheat in a cash market to major terminal markets in Chicago and Kansas City and to food-processing companies, such as Kellogg's, General Mills, and Pillsbury.

The object of most futures trading is *not* to deliver actual commodities. In fact, less than 3 percent of the contracts are ever settled by delivery of goods. Many transactions in the futures market are undertaken for speculation, as you have seen. However, as you will see shortly, much trading is also done on behalf of producers and middlemen who want to protect themselves against price fluctuations. Transactions made for protection are settled by an offsetting contract.

For example, you could have settled your purchase of a corn contract by selling an offsetting contract for the same quantity of corn in the same delivery month. On the other hand, if you had initially sold a futures contract for corn, you could have offset it by buying another one for the same quantity of corn in the same delivery month. In either case, your purpose, as you will learn later, would have been to avoid the profit or loss you might have realized as a result of changes in prices.

In the cash market, physical commodities are bought and sold. In the futures market, contracts for later delivery of physical commodities are bought and sold.

Margin Buying

Trading in futures involves large amounts of commodities. To illustrate, the contract size for corn, oats, wheat and soybeans is 5,000 bushels. For live cattle, it is 40,000 pounds. For cocoa, it is 30,000 pounds; for cotton, 50,000 pounds; for eggs, 18,000 dozen; and for lumber, 40,000 board feet. Other commodities are traded in similarly sizable units, usually based on freight-carload quantities.

Because of the considerable expense that would be involved if contracts were acquired for cash, futures contracts are bought on *margin*. The *margin requirement* is the percentage down payment you have to make in order to purchase a contract. This requirement, which is set by the board of the commodities exchange, normally averages between 10 percent and 20 percent of the initial value of the contract. The balance is due only if delivery is actually taken. If the price declines before delivery, then so does the market value of your contract. Therefore, the broker will require you to make additional payments in order to maintain your margin balance.

"Margin" is the percentage down payment that a buyer must make in order to purchase a futures contract.

Speculation and Protection

Trading in futures contracts may be conducted for two purposes—speculation and protection.

If you are a speculator, you will buy futures when you think their prices are going up, hoping to sell later at a profit. However, you also take the risk of a loss if prices go down.

If you are a protective trader—a farmer, for instance—you will want to shield yourself against changes in the price of the physical commodity that you produce. Therefore, as you will see shortly, you will protect your future financial position by being both a buyer and a seller of the physical commodity, entering into opposite sales and purchases of futures. You hope that, in this way, a possible loss in one will be offset by a gain in the other, so that you will neither lose nor profit from changes in prices.

Basis = Futures Price − Cash Price

Before considering an illustration of how this is done, it will help you to keep certain facts in mind.

First, the cash market and the futures market are separate markets. Although they deal in the same commodities, a purchase or a sale in either market does not necessarily entail a transaction in the other.

Second, under normal circumstances, when there are abundant supplies of a commodity available, the futures price will exceed the cash price. This difference is called the *basis*. It is an amount approximately equal to the carrying costs (including freight, insurance, storage, and so on) of moving the product from local rural markets to major terminal markets, such as Chicago, Omaha, and Kansas City.

These facts give rise to two important propositions:

1. Cash and futures prices of a commodity tend to move in the same direction. When the cash price changes, the futures price usually changes by about the same amount, reflecting the carrying costs of the commodity up to the delivery date.

The "basis," or the difference between the futures price and the cash price, is approximately equal to the carrying costs of the commodity up to the delivery date.

2. Cash and futures prices of a commodity tend to converge as the delivery date approaches. That is, the basis typically narrows as the delivery time nears, reflecting the declining carrying costs of the good.

Cash prices reflect only current market conditions, whereas futures prices reflect both current and expected market conditions.

It should be remembered that these are tendencies, not certainties. In reality, exceptions often occur because commodity cash prices and futures prices alike are affected by worldwide influences.

The implications of this are not hard to see. For instance, futures prices reflect both current and *expected* supply-and-demand conditions. Cash prices, on the other hand, reflect only *current* supply-and-demand conditions. Therefore, expectations of supply disruptions caused by wars, strikes, droughts, or political turmoil, whether at home or abroad, can influence futures prices. These expectations can cause futures prices to deviate from cash prices by more or less than the amount of the carrying charges. Indeed, the futures price of a contract may sometimes be even less than the commodity's cash price, resulting in a negative basis. This could happen, for example, if an unusually large increase in supply of the commodity is expected to occur in the coming months.

Hedging

Hedging is a widely used method for minimizing the risks associated with unforeseen price changes in the cash market.

Despite the real possibility that the basis may not always remain constant over a period of months, it is useful, for the time being, to assume that it does. This helps to explain the concept of hedging, one of the most interesting aspects of commodity-futures trading.

Two types of hedging transactions may be distinguished—the selling hedge and the buying hedge.

The Selling Hedge

Suppose that you own a grain elevator—a storage facility—in a rural area whose closest terminal market is Chicago. One of your trading experiences might proceed as follows.

Step 1 On October 15, a farmer brings you 5,000 bushels of soybeans. In order to determine the price you should pay, you start with the Chicago terminal price on that day—say, $3.18 per bushel. From this you subtract the sum of the freight expense to Chicago, the terminal commission fee, and your handling charges, which include your profit margin. Assuming these costs amount to 18 cents per bushel, you pay the farmer $3 per bushel.

Because you want to protect yourself against the possibility of a price decline during the next few months, after which you expect to sell the soybeans, you *sell* a May futures contract for soybeans at $3.10 per bushel. These transactions are illustrated in Exhibit 1, Table (a).

Step 2 Several months pass, and it is now January 10. You decide to *sell* your soybeans at the current market price. Suppose it has declined 10 cents to $2.90 per bushel. This means that the price of soybean futures has also declined 10 cents to $3.00 per bushel, because it is assumed that cash and futures prices exactly parallel one another. Therefore, to offset your loss in the cash market, you *buy* a May futures contract for soybeans at $3 per bushel.

Result What is the net outcome of these transactions? As Table (*a*) in Exhibit 1 shows:

1. In the cash market, you incurred a loss of 10 cents per bushel on your buying and selling transactions for the physical commodity—soybeans.

2. In the futures market, you incurred a gain of 10 cents per bushel on your selling and buying transactions for futures contracts—paper claims against soybeans.

Because the same quantity is involved in both futures contracts, they cancel each other out. Thus, your 10 cent loss in the cash market was offset by your 10 cent gain in the futures market, enabling you to break even.

Note The actual cancellation of your two futures contracts is nothing more than a bookkeeping procedure. It is done in the accounting office of the commodity exchange where the contracts were traded.

What would have happened if the price in the cash market had gone up to, say, $3.10 per bushel instead of down to $2.90? In that case you would have made a gain instead of a loss in the cash market, and an offsetting loss instead of a gain in the futures market. The numbers illustrating this are shown in Table (*b*).

By conducting a selling hedge in the futures market, you try to avoid incurring an overall *net* loss or gain resulting from unforeseen price changes in the cash market. However, you still earn a profit from your grain-elevator operations, which is why you are in business. (Remember that you included the profit margin in your handling charges when you bought the soybeans from the farmer.)

The Buying Hedge

Suppose that you continue to engage in successful transactions such as these and that your business prospers. Consequently, you decide to expand operations by becoming an exporter of soybean oil. Here is a typical set of transactions you are likely to conduct.

On June 20, you agree to export 300,000 pounds of soybean oil, at a price of 10 cents per pound, to a foreign buyer. This price consists of the cash market price on June 20 plus your handling charge (including a profit margin) of 2 cents per pound. (To avoid confusion, the handling charge will be disregarded for the time being and will be recognized at the end.)

The oil is to be shipped nearly four months later, on October 5. Because you cannot be sure what the market price of soybean oil will be at that time, you consider the following alternatives:

1. Buy the oil now and store it until the shipping date. But this will require you to pay almost four months' inventory carrying costs, including storage, insurance, and interest charges. These costs can reduce your profits substantially.

2. Take a chance that the price of soybean oil will drop by early October, so you can buy it more cheaply when it is time to ship. But, if you guess wrong, you may lose money. If the price goes up by only 1 cent per pound, you will lose $3,000. To avoid this risk, you can utilize a buying hedge in futures. This action will establish your cost of soybean oil without requiring you to incur the cost of carrying physical inventory.

Exhibit 1

Hedging in the Futures Market: The Selling Hedge

Table (*a*)

Cash Market Soybeans	Futures Market Soybeans Contracts
October 15 Buy 5,000 bu. @ $3.00	October 15 Sell 5,000 bu. May futures @ $3.10
January 10 Sell 5,000 bu. @ $2.90	January 10 Buy 5,000 bu. May futures @ $3.00
Loss 10¢	Gain 10¢

Table (*b*)

Cash Market Soybeans	Futures Market Soybeans Contracts
October 15 Buy 5,000 bu. @ $3.00	October 15 Sell 5,000 bu. May futures @ $3.10
January 10 Sell 5,000 bu. @ $3.10	January Buy 5,000 bu. May futures @ $3.20
Gain 10¢	Loss 10¢

Exhibit 2
Hedging in the Futures Market: The Buying Hedge

Table (a)

Cash Market Soybean oil		Futures Market Soybean oil contracts	

June 20
  Sell
  300,000 lbs. to be shipped Oct. 5
	8¢	June 20
		  Buy
		  300,000 lbs. (five contracts) Oct. futures @
			12¢

Oct. 5
  Buy
  300,000 lbs. and ship as per agreement
	11¢	Oct. 5
		  Sell
		  300,000 lbs. (five contracts) Oct. futures @
			15¢

Loss	3¢	Gain	3¢

Table (b)

Cash Market Soybean oil		Futures Market Soybean oil contracts	

June 20
  Sell
  300,000 lbs. to be shipped Oct. 5
	8¢	June 20
		  Buy
		  300,000 lbs. (five contracts) Oct. futures @
			12¢

Oct. 5
  Buy
  300,000 lbs. and ship as per agreement
	5¢	Oct. 5
		  Sell
		  300,000 lbs. (five contracts) Oct. futures @
			9¢

Gain	3¢	Loss	3¢

Step 1 Because you want to make a handling profit on your export business without risking unforeseen changes in market prices, you choose the second alternative. You will hedge your forward sales by buying the equivalent amount in futures contracts at the time of the export agreement. Therefore, on June 20, you *sell* in the cash market for October shipment 300,000 pounds of soybean oil at 8 cents per pound. At the same time, you *buy* for October delivery five futures contracts for soybean oil at 12 cents per pound. (The size of a futures contract in soybean oil is 60,000 pounds.) These transactions are shown in Exhibit 2, Table (a).

Step 2 When October 5 arrives, it is time to export the soybean oil. You therefore *buy* the required 300,000 pounds in the cash market at the prevailing price, which is now 11 cents per pound, and ship it to the importer. This fulfills your export agreement. At the same time, you *sell* five contracts in the futures market at 15 cents per pound. Note that the price in the futures market has gone up by the same amount as in the cash market—namely, by 3 cents per pound.

Result The net outcome of these transactions is shown in Table (a):

1. In the cash market, you have incurred a loss of 3 cents per pound on your selling and buying transactions for the physical commodity—soybean oil.

2. In the futures market, you have incurred a gain of 3 cents per pound on your buying and selling transactions for futures contracts—paper claims against soybean oil.

The *net* result of the combined transactions in both the cash and futures markets is that you have broken even. The loss in one market was precisely offset by the gain in the other. What if the price in the cash market had gone down, say, to 5 cents per pound instead of up to 11 cents? In that case, you would have made a gain instead of a loss in the cash market and an offsetting loss instead of a gain in the futures market. This is shown in Table (*b*).

> Your purpose in undertaking a buying hedge is the same as your purpose in undertaking a selling hedge. You want to avoid incurring an overall *net* loss or gain resulting from unforeseen price changes in the cash market. However, you may still earn a profit on your export operations, which is why you decided to go into that business. (Remember that you allowed for a profit margin in your handling charges when you agreed to export the soybean oil.)

Economics of Futures Markets

You have probably guessed from these explanations of hedging that the futures market has many interesting economic implications. A few of the more important ones are worth noting.

Who Benefits?

Is the futures market simply a huge gambling casino? Many people who do not understand it think it is. In reality, as you saw from the illustrations of hedging, there are distinct advantages to futures markets. For example:

Society benefits from futures markets because they reduce costs to firms that conduct futures transactions.

1. They enable firms to reduce their inventory costs and to operate on narrower margins of profit.

2. They provide the flexibility that firms need to liquidate their positions in the face of changing market conditions.

3. They help to assure firms of future supplies of physical commodities (such as raw materials) needed for production.

These benefits, of course, accrue directly to those firms whose businesses are such that they can participate in futures trading. Not all firms can do so, because the products with which they deal are not traded in futures markets. Ultimately, however, the advantages of such markets are reflected throughout the economy in the form of lower prices.

Against this background, the following definition of hedging helps to reinforce basic ideas.

> *Hedging* consists of a purchase and a sale of a commodity in two different markets at the same time and a corresponding offsetting sale and purchase of the same commodity in those two markets at a later time. The markets in question are the cash or spot market, in which a physical commodity is bought and sold, and the futures or forward market, in which contracts for subsequent delivery of the physical commodity are bought and sold. Hedging helps firms to reduce inventory costs, to adjust to changing market conditions, and to plan for the acquisition of future supplies of goods needed for production. Hence, it also leads to lower prices.

Who Hedges?

What types of businesses hedge in the futures market? Why do they hedge? The answers may be given by classifying firms and their motives in terms of the two types of hedges—selling and buying.

Many people and businesses engage in hedging operations.

The Selling or "Short" Hedge

A selling hedge is commonly referred to as a "short" hedge. It is a transaction conducted by businesses when they want protection against a possible price decline. Some firms that use short hedges are:

• Farmers, who sell futures contracts against their crops.

• Grain-elevator operators and other merchants, who buy the outputs of farmers and other producers and simultaneously sell futures contracts against these purchases while holding them for later sale to industrial buyers.

• Processors and manufacturers, who sell futures contracts against purchases of physical commodities intended for conversion into manufactured products.

The Buying or "Long" Hedge

A buying hedge is commonly known as a "long" hedge. It is undertaken when a firm wants to protect itself against a possible price increase. Two types of businesses make the widest use of long hedges:

• Exporters and other merchants, who purchase futures contracts against fixed-price sales of commodities that are to be bought and shipped by the seller at a later date.

• Manufacturers, who buy futures contracts against sales of manufactured goods for which, at time of sale, the raw materials have not yet been purchased.

Limits of Protection: Varying Basis

Although hedging reduces risks, it cannot offer complete price protection.

Can we conclude that hedgers are always completely protected from possible adverse price changes? The answer is *no*. Hedging does not always work as neatly as in the numerical examples presented earlier. These examples demonstrated what may be called a *perfect hedge*—one in which the hedger breaks even. In reality, the hedger occasionally experiences an *imperfect hedge*—one in which there is a net gain or loss due to fluctuations in the spread between cash and futures prices.

This spread, you will recall, is known as the basis. Although it is usually constant, it can sometimes vary for a particular commodity from time to time. This may be due to actual and expected changes in supply-and-demand conditions affecting the commodity, unstable political conditions in countries that are major producers of the commodity, and so on. Because of these factors, hedging offers substantial, but not always complete, price insurance. See Exhibit 3.

Who Speculates?

There are two types of participants in futures markets—hedgers and speculators. As you have seen, hedgers buy and sell futures contracts in an effort to avoid the risks of possible price changes. But what about speculators?

As it is commonly understood, speculation means any business transaction involving considerable risk for the chance of receiving large gains. In the futures market, however, speculation is a more complex concept.

Exhibit 3
Basis = Futures Price − Cash Price

In a normal market with adequate supplies, the basis will tend to reflect the carrying cost of the commodity to the delivery month. But markets are not always "normal." When they are not, the basis can vary considerably, or even become negative.

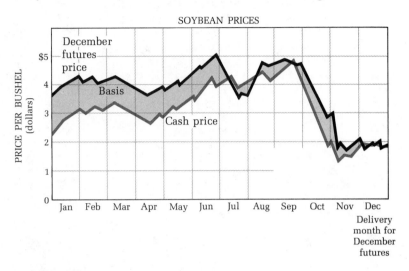

SOYBEAN PRICES

In the futures market, *speculation* is the act of buying or selling a futures contract without having an offsetting interest in the actual commodity. An increase in the price of the futures contract creates a profit for buyers of the contract (who are called "longs") and a corresponding loss for sellers of the contract (who are called "shorts").

A large proportion of total futures trading is done by speculators. They perform an important economic function because their continuous trading interest and activity contribute to the maintenance of broad and smoothly operating markets. This, in turn, permits effective hedging, because *speculators are risk bearers who assume the risks that hedgers seek to avoid.*

Conclusion: Economic Efficiency

When you purchase a magazine subscription or make payments on a car, you are buying the future benefits of a product. When a firm purchases or sells a futures contract, it is also buying future benefits. However, the benefits are derived from a claim involving subsequent delivery of a product. The opportunity to acquire these benefits exists because of the presence of many hedgers and speculators, whose combined actions make possible the operation of organized futures markets.

Hedging is an important aspect of such markets. The hedger exchanges a major risk—the entire cost or price of a commodity—for a much smaller one—the difference between the cash and futures price of the commodity. The *total* risk in the market for all participants is still the same. However, the proportions have been shifted between the hedger and the speculator.

Hedging shifts the proportions of risk among the hedger and the speculator. However, the total risk remains the same.

Box 1
Trading Floor of the Chicago Mercantile Exchange

A huge public auction in commodities and currencies

Source: Chicago Mercantile Exchange.

1. Cash and statistical boards indicate the latest cash prices and production and storage figures for commodities traded at major markets. They keep floor brokers informed of the latest trends in the cash market.

2. Transjet tickers carry the latest information from the major stock and commodity exchanges.

3. Board markers record transactions in board-traded commodities on sales panels.

4. Brokers in trading pits openly cry out bids and offers. Here, the forces of supply and demand meet and the market level is established.

5. Electronic price-quotation boards at both ends of the trading floor and on the face of the vistors' gallery instantly report prices of the latest trades, as well as the day's and the season's highs and lows.

6. Teletype machines (at both ends, behind the member stations) receive sales orders and send trade confirmations. Printers of major commodity and financial news services provide steady streams of worldwide data.

7. The spacious vistors' gallery accommodates dozens of people in seats, plus many more who are standing.

8. Pit clerks write trade data on cards, time-stamp them, and hand them to a computer input operator for permanent recording and worldwide transmission.

9. Runners relay orders from desk clerks and brokers to traders in the pits and return confirmations of completed trades to desks for forwarding to customers.

10. Personnel at member stations receive orders from all over the country, confirm sales, and advise clients on the latest futures prices and trends.

Thus:

A hedger who is *certain* that a commodity's price will go up and stay up has no need for a selling hedge. Likewise, a hedger who is *certain* that a commodity's price will go down and stay down has no need for a buying hedge. In reality, hedgers can rarely be certain, or even confident, that a commodity's price will go either up or down. Therefore, they and speculators enable futures markets to perform the economic function of allocating goods between present and future uses. This, of course, is a necessary condition for achieving economic efficiency.

What You Have Learned in This Supplement

1. Commodity-futures markets are places where contracts to deliver certain standardized products are bought and sold. Among the contracts traded are those for U.S. Treasury bills, foreign currencies, and gold. Other contracts traded are for grains, butter, coffee, sugar, cotton, soybeans, and various other agricultural products.

2. Trading in futures contracts is conducted for two purposes—speculation and protection. The speculative purpose is to earn a profit. The protective purpose is to minimize the risks of future price changes in the physical commodity.

3. Commodity-futures markets provide opportunities for hedging. Hedging consists of making simultaneous transactions in a physical commodity and in futures contracts. Firms that engage in hedging do so in order to minimize the risks of unforeseen price changes. The existence of speculators makes it possible for hedging to occur, because speculators assume the risks that hedgers seek to avoid. Hedging and speculation, therefore, improve the efficiency of futures markets.

For Discussion

1. *Terms and concepts to review:*
margin requirement
basis
hedging
speculation

2. If you were a farmer, a grain-elevator operator, a processor, or an exporter, you would often have to borrow money to help finance your operations. You would find that banks are much more willing to lend you money if you hedge your inventory (using the warehouse receipts as collateral) than if you do not. Why?

3. A "premium market" is one in which the futures price of a commodity exceeds its cash price. A "discount market" is the opposite. Why do such market conditions occur? When is the premium or discount equal to zero?

4. Is speculation essentially the same as gambling? Explain.

19
CHAPTER

Looking Behind the Demand Curve: Utility and Consumer Demand*

Learning guide
Watch for the answers to these important questions

Why do demand curves slope downward? Does "common sense" provide an adequate answer? Do such concepts as income effects and substitution effects provide an answer?

What is the meaning of utility? How does it enter into the determination of consumer equilibrium?

What is meant by consumer surplus? How is it measured on a demand graph? How is it measured on a marginal-utility graph?

How do the shortcomings of utility theory affect the law of demand? Is the law useless because of these shortcomings?

This chapter explains the meaning of demand in terms of the consumer's utility for goods.

In economics, the term *demand*, with reference to market demand, has a specific meaning. Demand is a dependent relationship revealing the quantity of a particular commodity that will be purchased at various prices—other things remaining the same. This relationship, as you have seen, can be portrayed numerically in the form of a demand schedule or graphically in the form of a demand curve. (It can also be represented algebraically in the form of an equation, but this is not usually necessary for understanding the basic ideas.)

What are the underlying factors that account for the law of (downward-sloping) demand? This is a question we have not yet considered. To answer it, we must turn our attention to the study of consumer behavior. This topic, which draws partially on psychology, has played an interesting and important role in the development of economic ideas.

Explaining Utility and Consumer Demand

Economists have long been interested in the factors that account for the shape of demand curves. Until now it has been taken pretty much for granted that such curves typically slope downward from left to right. Upon closer examination, we find several reasons for their negative inclination.

One explanation is based on "common sense," by which we mean observation and intuition. On the basis of our experiences, it seems reasonable to expect that a reduction in the price of a product will enable a buyer to purchase more of it. Conversely, an increase in the product's price will reduce that ability.

---

* **Note to Instructor** This chapter is optional. It may be omitted without affecting continuity.

Income and Substitution Effects

A second explanation can be given in terms of what economists call "income effects" and "substitution effects."

The *income effect* tells us that a decrease in the price of a given product, while the prices of other goods and services and the consumer's money income and tastes remain the same, will enable the consumer to buy more of the product and perhaps more of other products as well. Therefore, such a decrease in price results in an increase in the consumer's real income.

The *substitution effect* says that a reduction in the price of a product, with the consumer's income, tastes, and other prices remaining constant, makes the product whose price has been reduced seem relatively more attractive. This enables the consumer to substitute more of that product for other products.

These concepts can be summarized in more formal terms:

The total effect of a price change may be divided into two parts.

1. Income effect. This is a change in quantity demanded by a buyer due to the change in his or her real income resulting from a change in the price of a good. The income effect assumes that the buyer's money income, the buyer's tastes, and the prices of all other goods remain the same.

2. Substitution effect. This is the change in quantity demanded by a buyer resulting from a change in the price of a good while the buyer's real income, the buyer's tastes, and the prices of other goods remain the same.

The concepts of income and substitution effects thus provide further insights into the shape of a consumer's demand curve. They tell us that the demand curve slopes downward because of the substitution effect. This means that the consumer is willing to purchase more of a product when its price declines relative to other prices. The consumer's willingness is reinforced by the income effect. This is the ability of a consumer to buy more of a product due to the gain in his or her real income resulting from the price decline. Taken together, therefore, both effects explain how a price change influences a consumer's *willingness* and *ability* to buy. These two terms, you will recall, were emphasized when we first studied the nature of demand.

The income and substitution effects account for the existence of downward-sloping demand curves.

The Meaning of Utility

A third (and in many ways much more fundamental) explanation of the downward-sloping demand curve can be given in terms of utility. *Utility* refers to the ability or power of a good or service to satisfy a want. That is, the utility of a good or service is the satisfaction one receives from consuming it—whether it be a pizza, a pair of jeans, a vacation trip, or a stack of textbooks.

The concept of utility was employed by the classical economists of the eighteenth and early nineteenth centuries. But the theory of utility as such did not come into full flower until the late nineteenth century, when it was formulated by certain neoclassical economists. As you study the theory in the following paragraphs, be careful not to confuse "utility" with "usefulness." At any given time, water may be much more useful than diamonds. However, the utility of either one may be quite different for various individuals.

The concept of utility provides an alternative explanation for downward-sloping demand curves.

Exhibit 1
Total and Marginal Utility

The table and charts convey the same fundamental relations. That is, as consumption of the product is increased, both total utility and marginal utility rise to a maximum and then decline. The marginal-utility curve is more important, for it reveals the operation of *the law of diminishing marginal ability.* The vertical dashed line emphasizes the fact that marginal utility equals zero when total utility is at a maximum.

Note The marginal-utility curve is plotted to the *midpoints* of the integers on the horizontal axis. This is because marginal utility reflects the *change* in utils from one unit of product to the next.

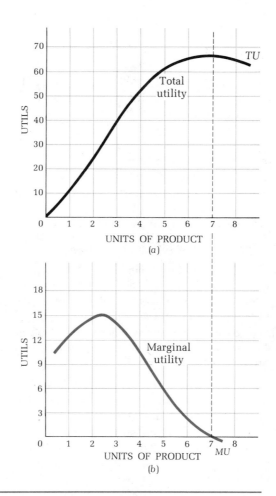

(1)	(2)	(3) Marginal utility, MU Change in (2) / Change in (1)
Units of product consumed	Total utility, TU	
0	0	
1	10	10
2	24	14
3	39	15
4	52	13
5	61	9
6	64	3
7	65	1
8	64	−1

Total Utility and Marginal Utility

Although no one knows how to measure utility, it is interesting to *assume* that it can be measured. Suppose, for example, that a "utility meter" could be strapped to your arm to measure the units of satisfaction, called *utils,* that you get from consuming a product. This is the same idea as a doctor strapping a meter to your arm to measure your blood pressure. What would such a utility meter reveal?

The answer is suggested by the data and curves in Exhibit 1. The table and figures show the utils, or units of satisfaction, that you might experience from consuming a hypothetical product. This model assumes that your consumption is taking place at a *given period of time during which your tastes are constant.* Otherwise, as you will soon see, it would make no sense to talk about the utility of different quantities of a product.

The exhibit illustrates that 1 unit of the commodity (for example, ice-cream cones) yields a certain amount of total utility, 2 units yield a larger amount, 3 units still more, and so on. Eventually, a level of intake is reached at which total utility is at a maximum. The consumption of any additional units then results in a decline in total utility. This is clearly seen from the graph of total utility in the exhibit. (The fact that the curve turns downward after the consumption of 7 ice-cream cones means that any more of them will make you sick.)

Much more important than total utility is *marginal utility*. This is defined as the change in total utility resulting from a unit change in the quantity of the product consumed. As you can see from column (3) of the table, marginal utility may be measured by the equation

Marginal utility is analogous to other marginality concepts, and it is measured in a similar way.

$$\text{marginal utility} = \frac{\text{change in total utility}}{\text{change in quantity consumed}}$$

Marginal utility is thus measured by the *ratio of change* in the two variables. This is emphasized by the way its values are recorded in column (3) of the table—a half-space between those shown for columns (1) and (2). Note that its graph is plotted in the same way—to the *midpoints* of the integers on the horizontal axis—as explained in the exhibit.

Observe from the figures in Exhibit 1 that the marginal-utility curve reaches a maximum and then turns downward while the total-utility curve is still rising. When the total-utility curve reaches its maximum height, the marginal-utility curve is at zero height. That is, the marginal-utility curve intersects the horizontal axis, as emphasized by the vertical dashed line. The reason for this relationship is a technical one that will be explained in a later chapter—after you have learned some more about "marginal" and "total" curves.

Law of (Eventually) Diminishing Marginal Utility

It is important to emphasize that, although marginal utility may at first increase, it must *eventually* decrease as more units of the product are consumed. What this means, for example, is that you might very well gain more satisfaction from the second unit of a commodity (for example, a slice of pizza) than you gained from the first. And you might even gain more from the third than from the second. However, you must eventually reach a point at which each successive unit gives you less gain in satisfaction than the previous one. This idea can be expressed more formally by an important law:

The law of (eventually) diminishing marginal utility is fundamental both to utility theory and to demand theory.

> **Law of diminishing marginal utility.** In a given period of time (during which tastes are assumed to remain constant), the consumption of a product may at first result in increasing marginal utilities per unit of the product consumed. However, a point will be reached beyond which the consumption of additional units of the product will result in decreasing marginal utilities per unit of the product consumed. This is the point of diminishing marginal utility.

As suggested by the word "diminishing" in this law, it is the *decreasing* part of the marginal-utility curve that is relevant. In effect, the law means that, on the downward side of the curve, the more you have of something, the less you care about *one* unit of it.

Consumer Equilibrium

How can the concepts of total and marginal utility be used to describe the economic theory of consumer behavior and the existence of downward-sloping demand curves? This is the question we set out to answer at the beginning of this chapter.

Imagine that you are a consumer with a given amount of money to spend on two commodities, A and B. Let us designate your marginal utility for product A as MU_A and the price of product A as P_A. Similarly, let your marginal utility for product B be represented by MU_B and the price of product B by P_B.

Now, keep in mind that it is the *downward* side of a product's marginal-utility curve that is relevant. In view of this, how should you distribute your expenditures on these two products so as to maximize your total satisfaction or utility? The answer is that you must allocate your expenditures so that the marginal utility *per dollar* spent on the two commodities is equal. That is,

$$\frac{MU_A}{P_A} = \frac{MU_B}{P_B}$$

In other words, to achieve this result you will adjust the quantities you buy. For example, suppose that you have a combination of A and B such that the left-hand ratio is greater than the right-hand ratio. Then you can increase your total utility by giving up some of product B (thereby moving up on your MU curve of B) and buying more of product A (thereby moving down on your MU curve of A). It can be demonstrated that the gain will more than offset the loss.

To illustrate, suppose that you have a combination of products A and B such that

$$\frac{MU_A}{P_A} = 30 \text{ utils per dollar}$$

$$\frac{MU_B}{P_B} = 10 \text{ utils per dollar}$$

If you spend a dollar less on B, you will lose 10 utils. If you spend a dollar more on A, you will gain 30 utils. The transfer of a dollar from B to A will therefore result in a net gain of 20 utils. Hence, you will make the transfer. As the transfer proceeds, the marginal utility per dollar of B rises as the amount purchased decreases. At the same time, the marginal utility per dollar of A falls as the amount purchased increases. When the two ratios are equal—say, at 20 utils per dollar—there is no further gain by transferring expenditures from B to A. At this point your total utility is at a maximum.

But what about your *money*, which is being exchanged for these products? You can think of money (symbolized m) like any other commodity. That is, the marginal utility of money to you, the consumer, is represented by MU_m and its price by P_m. The foregoing marginal-utility equation, to be complete, should now be extended to read

$$\frac{MU_A}{P_A} = \frac{MU_B}{P_B} = \frac{MU_m}{P_m}$$

Because the price of a dollar is $1, the denominator in the last ratio may be omitted so that the equation becomes

$$\frac{MU_A}{P_A} = \frac{MU_B}{P_B} = MU_m$$

This equation expresses your market equilibrium as a consumer. That is, the equation defines the conditions that exist when you have allocated your money and commodities, in the face of market prices, in such a way as to maximize your total utility. This equation is also equivalent to the following statement:

> For the consumer to be in equilibrium with respect to utilities and market prices, the last dollar spent on A must yield the same marginal utility per dollar's worth of A as the last dollar spent on B. This, in turn, must equal the marginal utility of money (per dollar of expenditure).

This principle can be extended to any number of commodities. The point is that, in order for you to be in equilibrium, your marginal utility per dollar of expenditure must be equal for all commodities, which, in turn, must equal your marginal utility for money. Otherwise, you will be able to increase your total utility by reshuffling your expenditures.

Marginal Utility and Demand Curves

We now wish to derive your consumer's demand curve for a specific commodity based on your utility data. The preceding equation says that, for any particular commodity, say commodity A,

$$\frac{MU_A}{P_A} = MU_m$$

If we "transpose" and solve for P_A, we get

$$P_A = \frac{MU_A}{MU_m}$$

Suppose that we now simplify by assuming that in the short run your marginal utility for money is a constant positive amount. For example, let us assume that MU_m is any positive number—say, 3. (The number itself makes no difference for our present purposes; any positive number can be chosen, as will be seen momentarily.) Your individual demand curve for commodity A can then be derived if your marginal-utility schedule is known.

This is illustrated in Exhibit 2, in which the price data in column (4) are obtained from the given information in the other columns. As you can see from the explanation in the exhibit, the demand curve represents the demand schedule from columns (1) and (4) of the table. This curve is downward or negatively sloped, a fact that is not influenced by the constant positive value chosen for MU_m.

Some Applications of Utility Theory

The development of utility theory in general, and the concept of marginal utility in particular, permit us to interpret more precisely problems that would otherwise be handled in relatively crude ways.

For example, a question suggested earlier was, "Why is the price of water low and the price of diamonds high, especially since everyone needs water but no one really needs diamonds?" If we knew nothing about utility theory, the answer would be given simply in terms of "sup-

Exhibit 2

Deriving a Consumer's Demand Curve for a Commodity, Based on Utility Data

The demand curve is graphed from columns (1) and (4) of the table. The curve will be negatively inclined regardless of the constant positive value chosen for MU_m.

(1) Units of product, A (given)	(2) Marginal utility of money, MU_m (given)	(3) Marginal utility of product, MU_A (given)	(4) Price of product, P_A (3) ÷ (2)
1	3	15	5
2	3	12	4
3	3	9	3
4	3	6	2
5	3	3	1

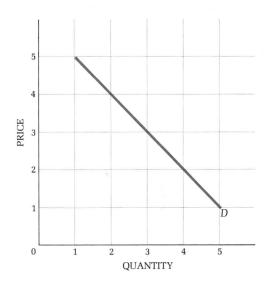

Exhibit 3
Measuring Consumer's Surplus from a Demand Curve and from a Marginal-Utility Curve

The rectangular and triangular areas, respectively, measure total expenditure and consumer's surplus. This is true whether they are measured in dollars, as in Figure (a), or in utils, as in Figure (b).

(a) DEMAND CURVE

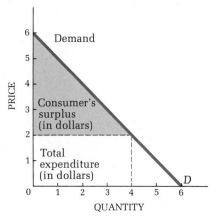

(b) MARGINAL UTILITY CURVE

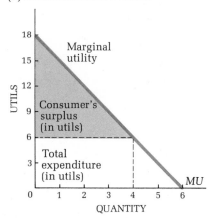

ply and demand." But we can go a step further. We can say that the marginal utility of water is ordinarily low because it is usually available in ample quantities. That is, the more we have of something, the less we care about *one* unit of it. Hence, we do not usually hesitate to use the extra water we need to sprinkle our lawns and wash our cars. The marginal utility of diamonds, on the other hand, is relatively high and their supply is scarce. Therefore, a single unit has considerable value. In a desert or on a battlefield, however, the circumstances might be exactly reversed. In those situations, we might be quite willing to trade a diamond for a pint of water, or perhaps a kingdom for a horse.

This suggests an interesting point:

> For some products, total utility may be high while marginal utility is low or even zero. Examples include an urban freeway during off-peak hours, a fire department when there is no fire, and a doctor's service when there is no need for it.

Can you think of other illustrations?

Consumer's Surplus

A concept directly related to utility theory is *consumer's surplus*. In everyday language, a consumer's surplus is simply a bargain. In more formal terms, it may be defined as any payment made by a buyer that is less than the maximum he or she would have been willing to pay for the quantity of the commodity purchased. Consumer's surplus thus represents the difference between the buyer's *demand price* and the price actually paid.

The concept of consumer's surplus is illustrated in Exhibit 3. There the surplus is measured from a buyer's demand curve and marginal-utility curve, both based on the data given previously in Exhibit 2. In both cases, however, the curves have been extended to touch the axes. Notice that, although the curves seem to look alike, the scales on the vertical axes of the two figures are in different units.

In Figure (a), the demand curve tells us that, as a consumer, you would be willing to pay $2 for the fourth unit of the commodity. However, you would have been willing to pay more, if necessary, for the first, second, and third units. You therefore get a consumer's surplus—a net amount of "pure" satisfaction—by paying only $2 for each of the four units. Your total expenditure is therefore $8. This is the rectangular area (equal to base × height) shown in the diagram. Your consumer's surplus, which is the right-triangular area (equal to ½ base × height), also happens to be $8 in this case. These two amounts, of course, need not always be the same, depending on the slope of the demand curve.

In Figure (b), we can calculate the same information in utils. Thus, your total expenditure *in utils* equals 4 × 6 = 24 utils. Likewise, your consumer's surplus *in utils* equals (4 × 12)/2 = 24 utils. Suppose that we now invoke our earlier assumption that the marginal utility of money is equal to 3 utils per dollar. Then your total expenditure in dollars comes to $8, and your consumer's surplus in dollars also comes to $8. These amounts, of course, are the same as those calculated previously from the demand curve in Figure (a).

The concept of consumer's surplus has a long and interesting history. For our present purposes, it poses two important questions.

1. Because consumer's surplus represents the "extra" value of satisfaction to a buyer, could the government tax it away without affecting either the quantity purchased or its price?

2. Suppose that a seller could measure a buyer's demand curve. Would the seller then be able to capture the consumer's surplus? For instance, could the seller charge the highest possible price for the first unit, the next highest price for the second unit, and so on—instead of charging the *same* price per unit for *all* units?

The answer to these questions is *yes*. However, there are limitations and conditions. Some of these are spelled out in the next section. The rest must wait until we have covered more ground in a later chapter.

Conclusion: Two Major Shortcomings of Utility Theory

As mentioned earlier, the theory of utility provides one of the more fundamental explanations of why a demand curve is downward-sloping. However, the theory suffers from serious shortcomings, at least two of which are especially important.

1. Indivisibility of Products The theory assumes that commodities are sufficiently divisible to be consumed in small units—such as ice-cream cones, candy bars, or cups of coffee. To the ordinary consumer who may buy one house or one piano in a lifetime or a new and different type of car every several years, the idea of marginal utility has little or no application. This is because it is a concept that, by definition, refers to the consumption of increasing units of the *same commodity within a given period of time while tastes remain constant*. The theory of utility is thus weakened by the fact that many products bought by consumers are large and indivisible and cannot be consumed in small, successive doses.

2. Immeasurability of Utility A more fundamental difficulty, as mentioned at the beginning of the chapter, is that no method has yet been devised for measuring a consumer's intensity of satisfaction. That is, utility cannot be measured in the same way we might measure the weight of an object in pounds or kilograms, or the distance between two points in miles or meters. In other words, we cannot measure utility in terms of *cardinal* numbers like 10, 23, 32.7, and so on, as the theory of utility assumes.

In view of the theory's rather tenuous assumptions, must we conclude that one of its most fundamental features—the law of diminishing marginal utility—is invalid? Most economists think not. They contend that the law of diminishing marginal utility is valid for the following reason.

> Were it not for the law of diminishing marginal utility, we would spend all of our money on the one commodity that gave us the greatest gain in satisfaction (or marginal utility) relative to its price. We know, of course, that this does not actually happen. Therefore, even though there is no absolute measure of utility, the theory nevertheless permits the development of meaningful principles pertaining to consumer demand and equilibrium.

Two interesting and, in some respects, opposing viewpoints on this matter are described in "Leaders in Economics," pages 420 and 421).

The trouble with utility theory is that its conclusions cannot be proven. This is because most products are not divisible into small units and because consumers' satisfactions are not measurable.

Despite its shortcomings, utility is a useful concept for economics.

Leaders in Economics

William Stanley Jevons
1835–1882
*Marginal-Utility Theorist
and Mathematical
Economist*

BBC Hulton Picture Library

"Repeated reflections and inquiry have led me to the somewhat novel opinion that *value depends entirely upon utility.* Prevailing opinions make labor rather than utility the origin of value; and there are even those who distinctly assert that labor is the *cause* of value. I show, on the contrary, that we have only to trace out carefully the natural laws of the variation of utility, as depending on the quantity of commodity in our possession, in order to arrive at a satisfactory theory of exchange, of which the ordinary laws of supply and demand are a necessary consequence."

These were the words with which the great English economist William Stanley Jevons introduced his major work in economics, *Theory of Political Economy.* First published in 1871, it was followed by three other editions.

Major Contributions

Jevons is one of the towering figures in the development of economic thought. He made many significant contributions to value and distribution theory, capital theory, and to statistical research in economics. But he is perhaps best known as a leading contributor to marginal-utility analysis. In one of the key passages of his book, he points out that exchange between two individuals will cease when "the ratio of exchange of any two commodities is . . . the reciprocal of the ratio of the final degrees of utility of the quantities of commodity available for consumption." This is just a complicated, technical way of saying that, *in equilibrium, marginal utilities will be proportional to prices.*

Economics: A Mathematical Science

Jevons was educated in England. He majored in chemistry and the natural sciences but maintained a strong interest in philosophy, science, logic, mathematics, and political economy (that is, economics). He served as Professor of Political Economy at Owens College, Manchester, and at University College, London. In addition to a famous study called *The Coal Question* (1865), which gained him recognition as an economist, Jevons wrote a distinguished text entitled *Elementary Lessons in Logic and Principles of Science* (1870). His main work, however, was *Theory of Political Economy,* in which he made clear his desire to develop economics as a mathematical science. In his own words:

"It is clear that Economics, if it is to be a science at all, must be a mathematical science. There exists much prejudice against attempts to introduce the methods and language of mathematics into any branch of the moral sciences. Many persons seem to think that the physical sciences form the proper sphere of mathematical method, and that the moral sciences demand some other method—I know not what.

"My theory of Economics, however, is purely mathematical in character. Nay, believing that the quantities with which we deal must be subject to continuous variation, I do not hesitate to use the appropriate branch of mathematical science, involving though it does the fearless consideration of infinitely small quantities. The theory consists in applying the differential calculus to the familiar notions of wealth, utility, value, demand, supply, capital, interest, labour, and all the other quantitative notions belonging to the daily operations of industry. As the complete theory of almost every other science involves the use of that calculus, so we cannot have a true theory of Economics without its aid."

Economic Forecasting

Jevons also did pioneering work in statistics and business forecasting. He formulated statistical correlations and forecasts of economic data that he sold to businesses—an idea that was at least 50 years ahead of its time.

Jevons's productive efforts were brought to an untimely end. In his late thirties, he began to suffer ill health, and, at the age of forty-seven, he drowned while visiting a health resort.

Leaders in Economics

Thorstein Bunde Veblen
1857–1929
Great Iconoclast —
Institutionalist —
"Antimarginalist"

Brown Brothers

Theories in economics are not always accepted without reservation. Throughout their development, economic doctrines have been challenged and criticized. But few people have ever been more challenging and more critical than Thorstein Veblen—philosopher, anthropologist, sociologist, economist, "compleat" social scientist, and prophet extraordinary. Indeed, Veblen ranks as one of the most creative and original thinkers in the history of economics. He also influenced an entire generation of brilliant economic scholars who succeeded him.

Veblen was eccentric, found it difficult to get along with people, and earned a reputation for being an extremely dull and uninteresting teacher. As a result, he stumbled from one precarious teaching position to another, never reaching a rank higher than associate professor, which he held at Stanford University from 1906 to 1909. In later years, he taught at the University of Missouri and at the New School for Social Research in New York City.

Institutionalist Views

Veblen was part of what is known as the "institutionalist" school of economic thought. He believed that human behavior could best be understood in terms of the practices and customs of society, its methods of doing things, and its ways of thinking about things, all of which compose "settled habits of thought common to the generality of men." These habits become institutions—deeply ingrained patterns of thought and action on which all material civilization is built.

Institutions, however, are not permanent. They unfold and grow into new patterns of change. In this sense, socioeconomic behavior is more evolutionary and dynamic than it is mechanistic—more like biology than physics—because it is devoid of the "natural," "normal," "controlling principles" that are found in the writings of marginal-utility theorists and other neoclassical economists.

"Antimarginalist"

This is the type of argument that Veblen used in hammering away at accepted economic doctrines. Thus, parodying the pseudoscientific style of some of the marginal-utility theorists of his time, Veblen wrote:

"What does all this signify? If we are getting restless under the taxonomy of a monocotyledonous wage doctrine and a cryptogamic theory of interest, with involute, loculicidal, tomentous and moniliform variants, what is the cytoplasm, centrosome, or karyokinetic process to which we may turn, and in which we may find surcease from the metaphysics of normality and controlling principles?"

No wonder Veblen was once referred to as "the archdisturber of the economist's academic peace of mind."

Conspicuous Consumption

Veblen wrote more than a dozen books, all of them interesting and controversial. His first and best-known work, *The Theory of the Leisure Class* (1899, rev. 1918), is often required reading even today for students taking courses in sociology. In this book he coined a famous phrase, *conspicuous consumption*. This meant the tendency of those above the subsistence level (that is, the "leisure class") to be mainly concerned with impressing others through standards of living, taste, and dress—that is, through what Veblen called "pecuniary emulation" —which is the hallmark of society. This, Veblen argued, is a "commonly observed pattern of behavior" that is contrary to marginal-utility theory. Stated differently, conspicuous consumption clearly implies that people may sometimes buy more of a good at higher prices than at lower prices in order to impress others.

Critic and Prophet

Thorstein Veblen, more perhaps than any other social scientist, criticized practically every aspect of social life. Throughout his writings there are prophecies about the changing structure of society, many of which have materialized with astounding accuracy. History may someday record that Veblen was one of the greatest prophets of social and economic change who ever lived.

What You Have Learned in This Chapter

1. An explanation of the law of (downward-sloping) demand can be given on the bases of observation and experience, substitution and income effects, or the theory of utility. The last assumes that utility can be measured in cardinal numbers, thus giving rise to the law of diminishing marginal utility—one of the most famous laws in economics.

2. The theory of utility shows how consumer equilibrium is obtained when the marginal utility per dollar of expenditure is equal for all commodities, including money. On the basis of this principle, a consumer's demand curve for a commodity can be derived and the concept of consumer's surplus can be demonstrated.

For Discussion

1. *Terms and concepts to review:*
income effect
substitution effect
utility
marginal utility
law of diminishing marginal utility
consumer's surplus
demand price
conspicuous consumption

2. Assume that Mr. R is rich, that Ms. P is poor, and that both have the same marginal-utility-of-money curve (MU_m), as shown in the figure. Let Mr. R's income be equal to the distance 0R and Ms. P's income be equal to the distance 0P.

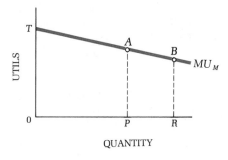

QUANTITY

(a) What is Mr. R's marginal utility for money? What is Ms. P's?
(b) What is Mr. R's total utility for money? What is Ms. P's?
(c) If you could reallocate the total incomes of these two people, how would you do it so as to maximize their *combined* total utility for money? Illustrate on the figure.
(d) Which person would experience a loss in total utility for money as a result of this income reallocation? Which person would experience a gain?
(e) Is the *net* effect of income reallocation a gain or a loss in the total utility for money?
(f) Does this problem suggest any implications for society as a whole? Discuss.

3. "A proportional income tax is a fair tax because, other things being the same, people with equal incomes pay equal taxes and therefore make equal sacrifices." On the basis of this chapter, do you agree? Discuss. (**Note** Look up the meaning of *proportional tax* in the Dictionary at the back of the book.)

4. Suppose that, after some minimum level of income is attained, each person's marginal utility of income changes in one of the following ways.
(a) It decreases at a rate *equal to* the percentage increase in income.
(b) It decreases at a rate *faster than* the percentage increase in income.
(c) It decreases at a rate *slower than* the percentage increase in income.
In a single figure, sketch the three curves depicting the conditions outlined above. Which type of taxation—progressive, proportional, or regressive—would you suggest in order to assure equal subjective sacrifice by taxpayers? Explain your answer. (**Note** Look up the meanings of *progressive tax*, *proportional tax*, and *regressive tax* in the Dictionary at the back of the book.)

5. Fill in the empty cells in the following table:

Total utility	Marginal utility
increasing at a constant rate	
	increasing
increasing at a decreasing rate	
	zero
decreasing	

Indifference Curves

The law of diminishing marginal utility has long been used to explain the existence of downward-sloping demand curves. The chief difficulty with this explanation, as noted earlier, lies in our *inability to measure utility*. Unlike the weight of an object or the distance between two points, utility cannot be measured in terms of cardinal numbers. It was largely because of this shortcoming that economists devised an alternative approach for explaining demand phenomena. This approach makes use of a concept known as *indifference curves*.

This supplement provides a new and different way of thinking about demand.

The Price Line or Budget Line

Imagine that you are a consumer with $2 and that you are entering the market to spend your money on goods. You are confronted with two commodities, X and Y. The price of X is $2 per unit; the price of Y is $1 per unit. Thus, the price of X is twice the price of Y. Algebraically, if P denotes price, then $P_X = 2P_Y$.

Now you could spend your entire $2 on X, in which case you could buy only 1 unit and have nothing left to spend on Y. Or, you could spend your whole $2 on Y, in which case you could buy 2 units and have nothing left to spend on X. The table in Exhibit 1 shows a few of the combinations of X and Y that you could purchase with your $2. Of course, you could also purchase any other combinations that will total $2.

The diagram in Exhibit 1 illustrates the same situation graphically. In this chart, the vertical axis represents the different quantities of commodity Y that you can purchase, and the horizontal axis shows the amounts of X that can be had.

Exhibit 1
A Consumer's Alternative Purchase Combinations

Assumptions: consumption budget = $2; price of X = $2; price of Y = $1.

The price line represents all the possible combinations of commodities X and Y that you the consumer can purchase at a particular time, given the market prices of the commodities and your money budget.

Purchase combinations	Units of X	Units of Y	Total amount spent
N	1	0	$2 + $0 = $2
Q	½	1	$1 + $1 = $2
M	0	2	$0 + $2 = $2

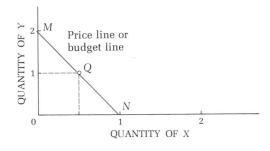

Exhibit 2
An Increase in the Price Line

An increase in your income results in the price line being shifted outward, thus enabling you to buy more of X and Y at the given market prices.

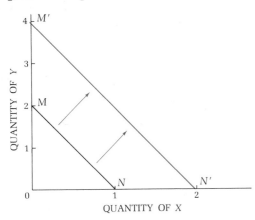

The diagram shows that, if you spend your entire $2 on Y, you can purchase 2 units or an amount equal to the distance $0M$. If you spend your $2 on X, you can purchase 1 unit or an amount equal to the distance $0N$. If we connect these two points, the resulting line MN is called a "price line," or "budget line."

Just what does this price line tell us? It indicates all the possible combinations of X and Y that could be purchased for a total of $2, assuming that P_X = $2 and P_Y = $1. Thus, point Q shows that you could purchase 1 unit of Y and ½ unit of X for a total of $2. The same is true of any other point on the line MN. Notice, however, that, as we move along the line from M to N, more of X can be purchased and less of Y. This is just as we should expect. Out of any given money income, the more we spend on one commodity, the less we have to spend on other things. Thus:

> A *price line* (or budget line) represents all the possible combinations of two commodities that a consumer can purchase at a particular time, given the market prices of the commodities and the consumer's money budget or income.

Many Possible Price Lines

Suppose now that you have $4 instead of only $2. Because you have twice as much money, you can buy twice as much of each commodity, provided that their prices do not change. Thus, for $2, you were able to buy as much as $2Y$ or $1X$, or any combination in between. Now you can buy as much as $4Y$ or $2X$, or any combination in between. This fact is shown in Exhibit 2, in which the line $M'N'$ represents the new price line at a higher income or budget of $4 and MN represents the old price line at a lower income or budget of $2. Obviously, for every level of income there will be a different price line corresponding to that income level. If income rises, so does the price line; if income falls, the price line falls too. Thus, because an infinite number of budgets or income levels are possible, an infinite number of price lines are possible.

The Nature of Indifference Curves

Next, even though you are a consumer confronted with two commodities, X and Y, you will probably not spend your entire income on only one of these items. Instead, you will probably purchase some combination of the two. Because there are many possible combinations of X and Y that can be bought, the question is: Just which of the many possible combinations will you purchase?

Let us disregard the price relationships that were described earlier and pay attention solely to the satisfaction you would derive from possessing commodities X and Y. That is, let us forget for the moment that P_X = $2 and P_Y = $1 and that you have a given income.

We start by constructing what is called an *indifference schedule*. This is a list showing the various combinations of two commodities that would be equally satisfactory to you at a given time. Column (1) of the table in Exhibit 3 is an example of a possible indifference schedule for two commodities X and Y.

In this column, each combination of X and Y is equally satisfactory to you. Thus, you would just as soon have combination 1, consisting of 60Y and 1X, as you would combination 2, consisting of 50Y and 2X, or combination 3, 41Y and 3X, and so on. This is true because each combination yields the same total satisfaction or utility. Hence, you are completely *indifferent* about which combination to choose because you prefer no one combination. All combinations are equally desirable because they *all yield the same total utility.*

Now there is an important thing to notice about an indifference schedule. Because each combination yields the same total utility, it follows that, if you were to increase your X intake by one unit at a time, you would have to decrease your Y holdings by some amount in order that each successive combination would continue to yield the same total utility. For example, when you possess combination 1, 60Y and 1X, you derive a certain amount of total utility. If you were to have 60Y and 2X, your total utility would be greater than the total utility of 60Y and 1X, because you would have the same amount of Y plus more of X. Therefore, in order to keep your total utility the same, you must give up a certain amount of Y for each unit increase in X. Column (1) in Exhibit 3 shows this relationship.

Marginal Rate of Substitution

Next, notice that, as you increase your X intake, the amount of Y that you are willing to give up *decreases*. Thus, when you possess combination 1, 60Y and 1X, you are willing to give up 10 units of Y for 1 unit of X. This leaves you with 50Y and 2X, or combination 2. At this point, you are willing to give up only 9 units of Y for 1 more unit of X, which would leave you at combination 3. Column (2) indicates this relationship. It shows us the amount of Y you are willing to surrender for every unit increase in your X holdings so that the new combination yields you the same satisfaction as the previous one—that is, the same total utility.

> The rate at which the consumer is willing to substitute commodity X for commodity Y is called the *marginal rate of substitution* (MRS). It may be defined as the change in the amount of one commodity that will just offset a unit change in the holdings of another commodity, so that the consumer's total utility remains the same. Since the ratio of the change in Y to the change in X is negative (because the amount of one commodity decreases when the other increases), the marginal rate of substitution may be expressed by the formula

$$MRS = -\frac{\text{change in } Y}{\text{change in } X}$$

As a general rule, the minus sign is understood and may be omitted in written and oral discussions.

Why does the MRS, as shown in column (2) of the table, decrease? You will remember that a demand curve slopes downward from left to right because the marginal utility of the commodity decreases as more of the commodity is consumed. (The more you have of something, the less you care about having an additional unit of it.)

The concept of a decreasing MRS is similar to that of decreasing marginal utility. As X *increases* (one unit at a time), the marginal utility of X *decreases*. As Y *decreases*, the marginal utility of Y *increases*.

Exhibit 3

A Consumer's Indifference Schedule, Indifference Curve, and Marginal Rate of Substitution

Each combination in column (1) yields the same total utility to you, the consumer. Hence, you are indifferent as to which combination you prefer.

In column (2), the marginal rate of substitution measures the amount of commodity Y you must give up in order to get 1 unit of commodity X, while maintaining the same total utility. The numerical value of this ratio decreases as additional units of X are acquired.

An *indifference curve* is a graph of an indifference schedule. Any point on the curve denotes a particular combination of commodities X and Y that yields the same total utility.

Note that, as X increases 1 unit at a time, the amount of Y that you are willing to give up decreases. This reflects a decreasing marginal rate of substitution of X for Y.

Combina-tions	(1) Indifference schedule	(2) Marginal rate of substitution of X for Y
1	60Y and 1X	10/1
2	50Y and 2X	9/1
3	41Y and 3X	8/1
4	33Y and 4X	7/1
5	26Y and 5X	6/1
6	20Y and 6X	5/1
7	15Y and 7X	4/1
8	11Y and 8X	3/1
9	8Y and 9X	2/1
10	6Y and 10X	1/1
11	5Y and 11X	

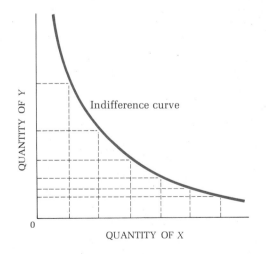

QUANTITY OF Y

Indifference curve

0

QUANTITY OF X

Exhibit 4
Two Indifference Curves

The higher a consumer's indifference curve, the greater the total utility. The points S and R, in comparison with the point Q, each represent as much of one commodity plus more of the other. Any point between S and R, such as T, represents more of *both* commodities. Although this figure depicts only two indifference curves, an infinite number of such curves exist for every consumer.

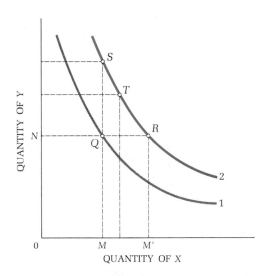

Thus, the more you have of X, the less you want one more unit of it, and the less you have of Y, the less you are willing to give up one more unit of it. That is, as you give up Y for X, the less of Y you are willing to give up for additional units of X.

For example, when you had 60Y and 1X, you were willing to give up a relatively large amount of Y, namely 10Y, for another unit of X. After that, you were willing to give up only 9Y, then 8Y, and so forth, for additional units of X. This is because you care less and less for additional units of X, and hence you are willing to give up less and less of Y. (Or, conversely, you care more and more for your smaller holdings of Y and you are willing to give up fewer units of it to acquire one more unit of X.)

Many Possible Indifference Curves

Suppose now that we were to plot the various combinations in the indifference schedule on a chart. The result would be a curve similar to the one in Exhibit 3. This curve is called an *indifference curve* because every point on it represents a particular combination of the two commodities X and Y that is equally satisfactory to you. That is, each point on the curve yields you the same total utility.

Just as it is possible to have an infinite number of price lines, so is it possible to have an infinite number of indifference curves. This is suggested in Exhibit 4, in which point Q represents a combination of 0M of X and 0N of Y. This combination yields the same total utility as any other combination on the same curve. On the higher curve at point R, however, the consumer possesses the same amount of Y, namely 0N, plus more of X, namely 0M'. Therefore, this combination must yield a higher total utility than any of the previous combinations to be found on curve 1.

If you now compare point S on the higher curve with point Q on the lower one, you will see that point S represents the same amount of X plus more of Y. Finally, if you pick any point between S and R on the higher curve, say point T, you will note that there is more of *both* X and Y than there is in *the combination denoted by point Q* on the lower curve.

These ideas suggest three important conclusions about indifference curves:

1. The higher an indifference curve—that is, the farther it lies to the right—the greater the consumer's total utility. This is because any point on a higher curve will always denote *at least* the same amount of one commodity plus more of the other.

2. A consumer will always try to be on the highest possible indifference curve. This is because it is assumed that the consumer will always try to maximize total utility.

3. Each indifference curve represents a *different* level of total utility. Therefore, indifference curves can never intersect at any point.

The Equilibrium Combination

Now let us combine the concepts of price lines and indifference curves. Superimposing one upon the other, we get a result such as the one depicted in Exhibit 5.

The price line *MN* shows the possible combinations of *X* and *Y* that could be purchased with given prices of *X* and *Y* at a given income. Each indifference curve, 1, 2, and 3, shows various combinations of *X* and *Y* that yield the same total utility along a given curve. The higher the indifference curve, the greater the total utility. Therefore, you, the consumer, will always try to be on the highest possible indifference curve.

Given these price lines and indifference curves, precisely what combination of *X* and *Y* will be purchased? The answer is based on the following fundamental notions:

1. The indifference curves represent the consumer's *subjective* valuations of *X* and *Y*. These valuations have no relationship to the *objective* facts that *X* and *Y* have certain prices and that the consumer has a certain money income to spend. These objective facts are shown by the price line.

2. Subjectively, the consumer will try to be on the highest possible indifference curve. Objectively, this goal is limited by the price line. The problem, therefore, is to reconcile this difference.

Because the price line shows all the possible combinations of quantities of *X* and *Y* that can be purchased for a given money income, it follows that there will be only one point on the price line that will also be on the highest possible indifference curve. This is point *Q*, at which the price line is tangent to curve 2. Point *Q*, therefore, shows the particular quantities of *X* and *Y* that will be purchased, namely 0*L* units of *Y* and 0*P* units of *X*.

Thus, as a consumer, you would not want to be on curve 1, where you would purchase a combination determined by *D* or *E*, because your purchasing power (as determined by the price line) permits you to be on a higher indifference curve. The highest curve that you can be on and yet remain within your income is curve 2. And the only point at which the price line touches the highest indifference curve within your means is point *Q*. This point, therefore, indicates the combination of *X* and *Y* that you will purchase at the prevailing prices, given your income.

Along an indifference curve, therefore, you are in a position not unlike that of Buridan's ass. The ass (according to a legend attributed to the fourteenth-century French philosopher Jean Buridan) stood equidistant between two equal bundles of hay and starved to death because it could not choose between them.

Similarly:

All combinations on any one indifference curve are equally desirable. It is the point of tangency of an indifference curve with a price line that determines the equilibrium–purchase combination.

What Happens When Income Changes?

Suppose now that your income increases while the prices of *X* and *Y* remain the same. You would now purchase more of both *X* and *Y*. This condition is shown in Exhibit 6, in which the price line shifts to the right from *MN* to *M'N'* to *M"N"*, indicating that a greater combination of both commodities can be purchased. At each new level of income, there is a tangency with a new and higher indifference curve. Connecting these points of tangency, we get the line *QRS*. Then, extending vertical

Exhibit 5
The Equilibrium–Purchase Combination

The tangency of the price line with an indifference curve determines the consumer's equilibrium–purchase combination. Thus, because the tangency is at point *Q*, you will buy 0*P* units of *X* and 0*L* units of *Y*.

A given price line may intersect any number of indifference curves, but it can be tangent to only one indifference curve.

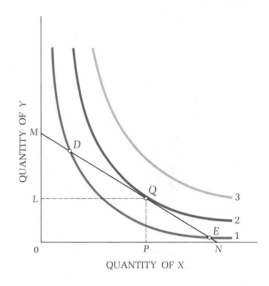

Exhibit 6
Income–Consumption Curve

An increase in income may increase your purchases of both X and Y. The line QRS connects the tangency points of price lines and indifference curves as your income increases. It is called an income-consumption curve (ICC).

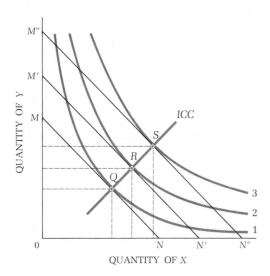

and horizontal lines from each of these points to the *X* and *Y* axes shows us by how much you increase your purchases of both *X* and *Y* as your income rises.

The line *QRS* may be called an *income-consumption curve* (*ICC*). It connects the tangency points of price lines and indifference curves by showing the amounts of two commodities that you will purchase if your income changes while their prices remain constant.

It is possible, however, that, as your income increases, your consumption of one commodity may increase while your consumption of the other commodity decreases. This is shown in Exhibit 7. In Figure (*a*), as your income rises, your consumption of *Y* also rises, and, although your consumption of *X* at first increases, it gradually falls off. The opposite is seen in Figure (*b*). As your income rises, your consumption of both *X* and *Y* at first increases, but your consumption of *Y* soon decreases.

A good whose consumption varies inversely with money income (prices remaining constant) over a certain range of income is called an *inferior good*. Some classic examples are potatoes, used clothing, and other "cheap" commodities bought by low-income families. The consumption of these commodities by low-income families declines in favor of fancier foods, new clothing, and so on, as their incomes rise. It should be noted, however, that almost any good may become, in a larger sense, "inferior" at some income level. Thus, when a family "steps up" from a lower-priced to a higher-priced car because of an increase in income, the lower-priced car becomes an inferior good.

On the other hand, a good whose consumption varies directly with money income (prices remaining constant) is called a *superior good*. Most consumer goods are of this type. Superior goods are also sometimes called *normal goods* because they represent the "normal" situation. Examples include most foods, clothing, appliances, and other nondurable and durable items that people typically buy.

Exhibit 7
Superior and Inferior Goods

As your income increases, you may buy more of one commodity (a superior good) and less of another commodity (an inferior good). [**Note** The inferior good in each graph is inferior only over the range in which the income-consumption curve (*ICC*) has a negative slope. This occurs where the curve bends "backward" in Figure (*a*) and "downward" in Figure (*b*).]

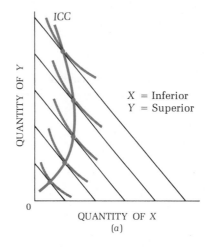

(a)

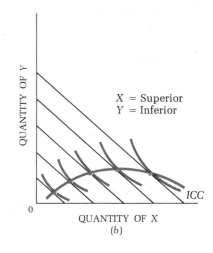

(b)

Exhibit 8

Price–Consumption Curve

With your income and the price of Y constant, decreases in the price of X result in
your buying more of it. The line QRS connects the tangency points of price lines and
indifference curves under these circumstances. It is called a *price–consumption
curve* (PCC).

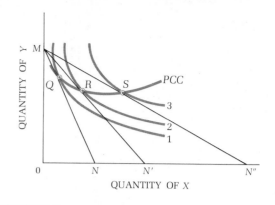

What Happens When Price Changes?

The previous case assumed that you, the consumer, had an increase in
income while the prices of X and Y remained constant. Let us now assume that both your income and the price of Y remain constant while the
price of X decreases. What happens?

The result is seen in Exhibit 8. The lower end of the price line shifts
to the right from MN to MN' to MN". This indicates that, as P_X falls,
more of X can be purchased. The price line thus fans outward as a result
of decreases in P_X.

We can work the same idea in the other direction by permitting the
lower end of the price line to shift left. For instance, let us assume that
the price line to begin with is MN". Then suppose that the price of X
gradually rises while the price of Y and your income remain the same.
As P_X rises, less of X can be bought, until finally the price of X is so high
that it is not purchased at all. The price line then becomes the vertical
line 0M, indicating that you spend your entire income on Y.

The line QRS in the diagram is thus a *price–consumption curve*
(PCC). It connects the tangency points of price lines and indifference
curves. The PCC curve thus shows the amounts of two commodities
that you will purchase when your income and the price of one commodity remain constant while the price of the other commodity varies.

Deriving a Demand Curve

How do the principles of indifference curves and price lines relate to the
law of demand? As you will recall, this is the question we started out to
answer.

The answer is that these two principles are together used to derive a
demand curve. This is illustrated in Exhibit 9, where numbers are used
with letters so that the computations can be followed easily.

In Figure (a), the price line MN signifies an income of $10, with
$P_Y = \$1$ and $P_X = \$2$. As a consumer, you can thus purchase either 10
units of Y, or 5 units of X, or various combinations in between. The
tangency of the price line with your indifference curve, however, shows
that you will maximize your total utility by purchasing 4 units of Y and
3 units of X.

Exhibit 9

Derivation of a Demand Curve from Indifference Curves

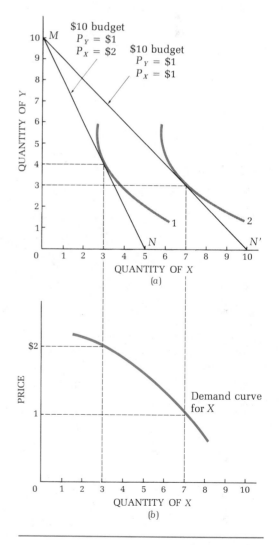

Suppose now that the price of X falls to $1 while your income and the price of Y remain constant. The tangency of the new price line MN' with the higher indifference curve indicates that you will be in equilibrium by purchasing 3 units of Y and 7 units of X.

This kind of information is needed to derive a demand curve. For example, in Figure (b), you see the relationship between the price of X and the quantity demanded of X while all other things—namely, your income and the price of Y—remain the same. Thus, the dashed lines emphasize the fact that you will purchase 3 units of X at a price of $2 per unit and 7 units of X at a price of $1 per unit. Connecting these two points (as well as all the in-between points that may be similarly derived), gives us the demand curve for X. Clearly, then, this curve obeys the law of demand. That is, the curve is downward-sloping, indicating that the lower the price, the greater the quantity demanded.

Conclusion: Only Consumers' Preferences Are Needed

The properties of a demand curve can be derived from indifference−curve analysis.

The theory of indifference curves had its origins in the late nineteenth century and reached maturity in the 1930s. It marked a major advance in the history of economics, because it freed the concept of demand from a reliance on the older and controversial concept of utility.

You can easily see the reason for this. In the indifference-curve approach, it need only be assumed that, as a consumer, you know your own preferences. That is, you must know whether you prefer one combination of goods to another or whether you regard them as equivalent. You do not have to know by *how much* you prefer one good to another. Hence, the older approach to demand theory, which rested on the less realistic assumption of a cardinal utility relationship (1, 2, 3, and so on), is replaced by the more realistic assumption of an ordinal preference relationship (first, second, third, and so forth).

The significance is clear:

> From the standpoint of indifference-curve analysis, the inability to measure utility is no longer a problem because such a measure is no longer needed. *A downward-sloping demand curve can be derived directly from a consumer's indifference curves and price lines without using or even assuming a "law" of utility.*

What You Have Learned in This Supplement

1. The theory of indifference curves relates *objective* facts determined by market prices and the consumer's income to the consumer's *subjective* valuations of commodities. The key mechanisms employed in the theory are price lines and indifference curves.

2. Through indifference-curve analysis, we can show how the consumption of goods changes when a buyer's income increases while prices are held constant. We can also illustrate how a buyer's consumption of a good changes when its price varies, while income and all other prices remain the same.

3. A consumer's demand curve can be derived directly from the tangency points of indifference curves and price lines. The law of demand can thus be established without relying on the controversial theory of utility.

For Discussion

1. *Terms and concepts to review:*
price line (budget line)
indifference schedule

marginal rate of substitution
indifference curve
income–consumption curve
inferior good
superior good
price–consumption curve

2. We have drawn indifference curves so that they are *convex* to the origin. What would it mean to draw an indifference curve that is *concave* to the origin? Would it make sense? Explain. (**Hint** Think in terms of the *MRS.*)

3. Draw a consumer's indifference curve that represents the situation that exists with each of the following combinations of commodities:

(a) Two commodities that are perfect complements (that is, commodities that are used in 1:1 proportions, such as left shoes and right shoes).

(b) Two commodities that are perfect substitutes, such as nickels and dimes in the ratio 2:1.

4. Such commodities as diamonds and furs are sometimes cited as exceptions to the law of demand because some people will buy more of these at a higher price than at a lower price. Does this mean that the "demand" curve for these products is upward-sloping? Explain. (**Warning** Be careful in your thinking. This is a much deeper question than is immediately apparent.)

5. In terms of indifference-curve analysis, what might be the effects of each of the following: (a) an increase in taxes; (b) an increase in the cost of living; (c) the expectation of inflation.

20
CHAPTER

Costs of Production

Learning guide
Watch for the answers to these important questions

What does the word "cost" mean? Is the term employed in different senses? What specific meanings of cost are necessary for understanding production problems?

How are costs related to production? What relationships exist between the inputs and outputs of production?

How do we distinguish between short-run and long-run costs? What are the relationships between costs and production in the short run? What are they in the long run? How does this information help us understand the economic behavior of business firms?

This chapter explains the relation between inputs and the outputs of production, and between outputs and the costs of production.

According to a familiar saying, you have to spend money in order to make money. In the business world, this can be translated to mean that a company must be willing to incur costs if it is to receive revenues.

What do we mean by *costs?* The term is by no means as simple as most people think. Engineers, accountants, and economists are all concerned with the nature and behavior of costs, but they all deal with different cost concepts in solving different problems.

For example, suppose that you were the president of a corporation and were interested in constructing a new manufacturing plant. You might employ an industrial engineer to study the cost of designing the plant, and you might hire a cost accountant to classify and analyze production costs after the plant was in operation. You might also hire an economist to advise you on the ways in which the plant's costs of production would be affected by changes in its volume of output. The economist could also provide advice about how these costs could be used as a guide in helping you to achieve the volume of production that would bring maximum profits.

Thus, analyses of costs by engineers, accountants, and economists may be done for very different purposes. This chapter explains the basic cost concepts and relationships that are of interest to economists.

What Do We Mean by "Cost"?

There are many different concepts of costs, but sacrifice is common to all of them.

As long ago as 1923, a famous economist, J. M. Clark, wrote, "A class in economics would be a success if the students gained from it an understanding of the meaning of cost in all its many aspects." Clark was prompted to make this statement because the general concept of cost embraces a wide variety of specific concepts. However, one general meaning is common to all specific concepts of cost:

> Cost is a sacrifice that must be made in order to do or to acquire something. The nature of the sacrifice may be tangible or intangible, objective or subjective. Also, it may take one or more of many forms, such as money, goods, leisure time, income, security, prestige, power, or pleasure.

Let us amplify this definition by describing and illustrating the notion of cost.

Outlay Costs Versus Opportunity (Alternative) Costs

To most of us, the concept of cost that readily comes to mind is what we may call *outlay costs*. These are the moneys expended in order to carry on a particular activity. Some examples of outlay costs to a business are wages and salaries of its employees and expenditures on plant and equipment. Other examples are payments for raw materials, power, light, and transportation; disbursements for rents, advertising, and insurance; and taxes paid to the government. Outlay costs are also frequently called *explicit costs, historical costs,* or *accounting costs*. This is because they are the objective and tangible expenses that an accountant records in the company's books.

The real cost of anything is measured by the value of the sacrificed alternative.

Economists use a more basic concept of cost: *opportunity cost*. It is defined as the value of the benefit that is forgone by choosing one alternative rather than another. This is an extremely important concept because the "real" cost of any activity is measured by its opportunity cost, not by its outlay cost. How do you identify opportunity costs? By making a comparison between the alternative that was chosen and the one that was rejected. Here are some examples:

1. To a student, the cost of attending college full time includes more than the outlay costs for tuition and books. It also includes the opportunity cost of income forgone by not working full time.

2. To a business firm, the cost of advertising includes more than its outlay costs for magazine space or television time. It also includes the opportunity cost of earnings sacrificed by not putting these funds to some other use. This might consist of the purchase of new equipment or the training of more salespeople.

3. To a city, the cost of a public park includes more than the outlay costs for construction and maintenance. It also includes the opportunity cost of the tax revenues forgone by not zoning the land for residential, commercial, or industrial use.

You can probably think of other examples. It should be evident, however, why opportunity costs are often called "alternative costs."

Sacrificed alternatives are opportunity costs.

The concept of opportunity cost arises whenever the inputs of any activity are scarce and have alternative uses. The real cost or sacrifice is then measured by the value of the forgone alternative. This principle applies at all levels of economic activity—macroeconomic as well as microeconomic. Thus:

> For any economic entity—a society, a business, a household, or an individual—it is incorrect to confine the cost of an activity or a decision to what the entity is doing. *What the entitiy is not doing but could be doing is the correct cost consideration.*

Nonmonetary alternatives also involve cost considerations.

The principle of opportunity cost raises some important questions. For example, is it not true that the alternative cost of a given action may often involve nonmonetary considerations, such as riskiness, working conditions, prestige, and similar factors? The answer is *yes*. This explains, to some extent, why window washers in skyscrapers earn more than dishwashers in restaurants. It explains why college professors, on the average, earn less—but probably have fewer headaches—than corporation executives. It explains why the prices of "glamour" securities in the stock market fluctuate much more widely than the prices of public utility shares. It also explains why some people may be willing to work for smaller returns in their own businesses, where they can be their own bosses, rather than for higher returns in other people's businesses.

Of course, the nonmonetary elements that help make the differences in resource allocation are often difficult to measure. But, *in principle*, the monetary returns plus or minus the various nonmonetary advantages and disadvantages determine the ways in which the owners of the factors of production put their human and material resources to use.

Economic Cost Includes Normal Profit

Economic costs consist of explicit and implicit costs. The latter constitute normal profit.

Once we recognize the existence of opportunity costs, it becomes apparent that there is a sharp distinction between costs in accounting and costs in economics. *Economic costs* are payments that must be made to persuade the owners of the factors of production to supply the factors for a particular activity. This definition emphasizes the fact that economic costs are supply prices or "bids" that buyers of resources must offer to attract the desired factor inputs.

Thus, a firm buys its resouces, such as capital, land, and labor, in the open market. Expenditures for these resources are part of the firm's economic costs. These money outlays are the *explicit costs* that an accountant records in the company's books.

But there are other types of economic costs, called *implicit costs* because they are the costs of self-owned or self-employed resources that are not entered in a company's books of account. For example, if you own a business, including the building and its real estate, and if you manage the business yourself, part of your cost includes the following implicit items.

1. The *interest* return on your investment that you are forgoing by not putting your money into an alternative investment of equal risk.

2. The *rental* receipts that you are passing up by not renting the land and building to another firm.

3. The *wages* (including the return for entrepreneurship) that you would earn if you could be hired to manage the same kind of business for someone else.

The sum of implicit costs equals normal profit.

These implicit costs of ownership constitute what may be called *normal profit*. This is the least payment the owner of an enterprise would be willing to accept for performing the entrepreneurial function, including risk taking, management, and the like. Normal profit is thus part of a firm's total economic costs, because it is a payment that will keep the owner from withdrawing capital and managerial effort and putting them into some other alternative. Further, economic costs include

Exhibit 1
Economic Costs and Economic Profit

Suppose that you own your own business, including the building and its land. If you sell an item for $1, your economic costs and economic profit might look like this:

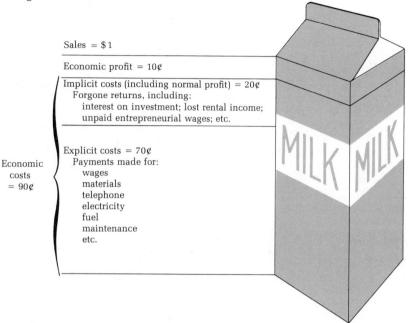

Sales = $1

Economic profit = 10¢

Implicit costs (including normal profit) = 20¢
 Forgone returns, including:
  interest on investment; lost rental income;
  unpaid entrepreneurial wages; etc.

Economic costs = 90¢

Explicit costs = 70¢
 Payments made for:
  wages
  materials
  telephone
  electricity
  fuel
  maintenance
  etc.

both explicit costs and implicit costs, and implicit costs include normal profit. Therefore, any receipts that a firm may get over and above its economic costs represent *economic* or *pure profit*. These ideas are illustrated in Exhibit 1.

Short Run and Long Run

Of course, the costs of resources are strongly influenced by the ways in which they are used. Because of this, any discussion of costs must include an explanation of two useful concepts—the short run and the long run. These refer not to clock or calendar time but to the time necessary for resources to adjust fully to new conditions. This is true regardless of how many weeks, months, or even years the adjustment may take.

At any given time, a firm has available a certain *capacity* to produce. This is determined by the quantity of the firm's equipment or the scale of its plant. If the firm experiences unexpected increases or decreases in the demand for its products, it can change its level of output by using existing plant and equipment either more or less intensively. But it cannot alter plant scale or production capacity with equal speed. Business firms do not put up new factories or discard old ones with every increase or decrease in demand, any more than colleges and universities erect new classroom buildings or abandon old ones with every rise or fall in enrollment.

The short run and the long run are defined in operational terms, not in terms of time.

The distinction between the short run and the long run is based on operational considerations, not on "time."

This leads to an important distinction between the short run and the long run. The *short run* is a period in which a firm can vary its output through a more or less intensive use of its resources. However, it cannot vary its capacity because it has a fixed plant scale. The *long run* is a period long enough for a firm to enter or leave an industry or to vary its output by varying *all* its factors of production, including plant scale.

These concepts of the short run and the long run suggest an appropriate passage from Henry Wadsworth Longfellow's famous poem "The Day Is Done":

> And the night shall be filled with music,
>   And the cares that infest the day,
> Shall fold their tents, like the Arabs,
>   And as silently steal away.

In economics, business firms can come and go like the Arabs to whom Longfellow referred. By our definition, however, businesses can do this *only* in the long run, not in the short run.

The Production Function

The production function expresses a relation between inputs and outputs.

Every businessperson is well aware that costs of production depend on two things: the quantity of resources purchased and the prices paid for them. At this point, our concern is with the quantity purchased. Therefore, it will be useful to analyze a concept known as the *production function*. This is a relationship between the number of units of inputs that a firm employs and the corresponding units of output that result.

The Law of (Eventually) Diminishing Returns

You have probably heard of the *law of diminishing returns*. This law is as famous in economics as the law of universal gravitation is in physics. But you are not likely to have a precise understanding of the law of diminishing returns without a prior course in elementary economics, any more than you would have a clear understanding of the law of universal gravitation without a basic course in physics.

Exhibit 2 displays a production function based on only one variable input. The table and chart enable you to "see" the operation of the law of diminishing returns as well as to understand it in terms of the following definition.

> **Law of (eventually) diminishing returns.** Assume that the state of technology is constant. Then, the addition of a variable factor of production, keeping the other factors of production fixed, will yield increasing marginal returns per unit of the variable factor added. This will continue until an input point is reached beyond which further additions of the variable factor yield diminishing marginal returns per unit of the variable factor added. (**Note** This law is also known by the more general name of the *law of variable proportions*.)

The law of diminishing returns was first discovered (by the great English classical economist David Ricardo) in agriculture in 1815. Considered a heroic advance in the history of economics, the law is one of the most widely held and best-developed principles in all of economics. This is because it encompasses many kinds of production functions. These range from agriculture and automobiles through retailing and textiles to zinc and zippers. The law thus has enormous significance as well as generality.

Two sets of features should be observed:

1. Note that columns (1) and (2) of Exhibit 2 are in general terms. In order to put them into specific terms, the variable input in column (1) of the table might represent pounds of fertilizer applied to an acre of land. Then the corresponding output in column (2) could be bushels of wheat. Or the variable input might be the number of workers on an assembly line in a factory and the output could be the number of units of the finished good produced. Practically any simple type of "input–output" relationship or production process could be used to illustrate the basic concepts.

2. The curves in the figure are actually "idealized" or smoothed-out versions of the data given in the table. This enables us to focus most of our attention on the graphs rather than on the numbers. Thus, the horizontal axis shows the variable factor from column (1) of the table, and the vertical axis represents the corresponding output from the remaining columns.

How Is the Law Interpreted?

The first thing you probably noticed in the figure in Exhibit 2 was the shape of the total product, or *TP*, curve. As the variable input increases from zero, the *TP* curve goes through three phases. At first it rises rapidly, then it tapers off until it reaches a maximum, and finally it declines.

These three phases are reflected by the *marginal product*, *MP*. This is defined as the change in total product resulting from a unit change in a variable input. Hence, marginal product can be calculated by the formula

$$MP = \frac{\text{change in total product}}{\text{change in variable input}}$$

You can verify these changes in *MP* from the table. *Average product*, *AP*, on the other hand, is simply the ratio of total product to the amount of variable input needed to produce that product:

$$AP = \frac{\text{total product}}{\text{variable input}}$$

For example, if Exhibit 2 is taken to represent the number of people working a given parcel of land in order to produce tomatoes, the results could be interpreted in the following way.

The efforts of the first person (whom we will call *A*), applied to the fixed amount of land, must be spread too thinly in covering all the land. Consequently, the total output is only 6 boxes of tomatoes. If a second person, *B*, is added who is *equally as efficient* as *A*, both persons can work the same amount of land and thereby increase total output to 14 boxes of tomatoes. The average output is then 7 boxes of tomatoes per person. However, the marginal product or gain in output is 8 boxes of

Exhibit 2
Production Function

(1) Units of variable factor, F	(2) Total product, TP	(3) Average product, AP (2) ÷ (1)	(4) Marginal product, MP Change in (2) / Change in (1)
A 1	6	6	
B 2	14	7	8
C 3	26	8.7	12
D 4	37	9.3	11
E 5	46	9.2	9
F 6	52	8.7	6
G 7	57	8.1	5
H 8	60	7.5	3
I 9	61	6.8	1
J 10	58	5.8	−3

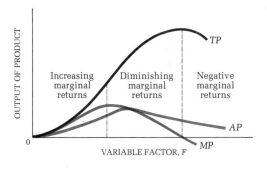

tomatoes. Adding workers increases the total output. But, as you can see in Exhibit 2, a point is eventually reached at which there are so many workers that they get in each other's way and even trample the tomatoes. When this happens, the *TP* curve passes its maximum point and turns downward. The gain in output or marginal product then becomes negative.

Marginal Returns Are the Most Important

Note, therefore, that the *MP* curve at first rises and eventually begins to fall, even though *all the workers are equally efficient*. This is an extremely important idea. The reason the *MP* curve declines is not that the last person hired is less efficient than the previous one. It declines solely for quantitative reasons. That is, the *MP* curve declines because of the changing proportions of variable factors to fixed factors, while all qualitative considerations are assumed to remain equal. This is why the term "law of variable proportions" is more often employed than "law of diminishing returns."

Mathematically, of course, the *MP* curve is derived from changes in the *TP* curve. Indeed, the *MP* curve represents the *slope* of the *TP* curve. This is because the slope of any curve is the change in its vertical distance per unit of change in its horizontal distance. Thus, the fact that the *TP* curve first increases at an increasing rate and then at a decreasing rate is what causes the *MP* curve to rise to a maximum point and then fall. The resulting three phases—*increasing marginal returns, diminishing marginal returns,* and *negative marginal returns*—are labeled in the figure. It is to these phases—especially the first two—that the definition of the law of diminishing returns refers.

> Because all three curves rise to a maximum and then decline, it can be said that *a law of diminishing returns applies to the total product, the average product, and the marginal product curves.* Indeed, from the time the law was initially formulated in 1815 until about the end of the nineteenth century, it was often stated in general terms without distinguishing between total, average, and marginal returns. But it then came to be realized that *marginal* returns are of key importance for decisions involving changes in the quantities of input or output. This idea will become increasingly apparent in subsequent chapters.

It is clear from Exhibit 2 that the point of diminishing marginal returns occurs at the input level where the *MP* curve is at its maximum. Where is the point of diminishing average returns? Where is the point of diminishing total returns?

Short-Run Costs

You have seen that in the short run some resource inputs for a firm are variable while others are fixed. This is because it may be possible in a given production process, for example, to vary the number of unskilled workers or to draw down large or smaller quantities of raw materials available in inventory. However, it may take considerable time to add a new wing to a plant or to have machines built to specification.

In view of this, what are the nature and behavior of a firm's costs in the short run? We shall answer this question by analyzing three families of cost concepts: *total cost, average cost,* and *marginal cost.*

Diminishing returns occur for the total, average, and marginal curves. But the marginal curve is the most important one for decisions involving changes in inputs and outputs.

Short-run costs are those that vary with output.

Cost Schedules and Curves

The table in Exhibit 3 presents a company's cost schedule. It illustrates the relationship between quantities of output produced per day, as shown in column (1), and the various costs per day of producing these outputs, as shown in the remaining columns. The accompanying figures are graphs of the cost data presented in the table. Note that, as usual, output is measured on the horizontal axes and costs are measured on the vertical axes. Also, the graphs are idealized to show their interrelations more clearly.

Costs are related to output in different ways.

Our objective is to see how the different costs in Exhibit 3 are related to output. That is, we want to know how they do or do not vary with changes in output. Because the cost curves have a number of important properties, it is important to examine them closely. Remember that we are assuming that *a firm's total costs are its economic costs and hence include normal profit.*

The Family of Total Costs

The first class of costs to be considered is the "total" group shown in columns (2), (3), and (4) of the table.

Total Fixed Cost *TFC* in column (2) represents those costs that do not vary with output. Examples include rental payments, interest payments on debt, property taxes, and depreciation of plant and equipment. Also included are the wages and salaries of a skeleton staff that the firm would employ as long as it stayed in business—even if it produced nothing. The *TFC* figure is $25 at all levels of output in the table and hence appears as a horizontal line in Figure (*a*).

Total Variable Cost *TVC* in column (3) consists of those costs that vary directly with output. These costs rise as output increases over the full range of production. Examples are payments for materials, labor, fuel, and power. Note from Figure (*a*) that, as output increases, *TVC* increases first at a decreasing rate and then at an increasing rate. This reflects the operation of the law of diminishing (total) returns, as explained earlier.

Total Cost *TC* in column (4) represents the sum of total fixed cost and total variable cost. Thus, we have the basic equation

Total cost is simply the sum of total fixed costs and total variable costs.

$$TC = TFC + TVC$$

This means that

$$TFC = TC - TVC$$

and

$$TVC = TC - TFC$$

You should also note from the table and Figure (*a*) that *TC* equals *TFC* at zero output. This is because there are no variable costs when there is no production. Observe too that the shape of the *TC* curve is the same as—or "parallel" to—the shape of the *TVC* curve. The only difference between them is the constant vertical distance represented by

Exhibit 3
Short-Run Cost Schedules and Curves for a Firm

(1) Quantity of output per day, Q	(2) Total fixed cost, TFC	(3) Total variable cost, TVC	(4) Total cost, TC (2) + (3)	(5) Average fixed cost, AFC (2) ÷ (1)	(6) Average variable cost, AVC (3) ÷ (1)	(7) Average total cost, ATC (4) ÷ (1) or (5) + (6)	(8) Marginal cost, MC Change in (4) / Change in (1)
0	$25	$ 0	$ 25	$ —	$ —	$ —	
1	25	10	35	25.00	10.00	35.00	$10
2	25	16	41	12.50	8.00	20.50	6
3	25	20	45	8.33	6.67	15.00	4
4	25	22	47	6.25	5.50	11.75	2
5	25	24	49	5.00	4.80	9.80	2
6	25	27	52	4.17	4.50	8.67	3
7	25	32	57	3.57	4.57	8.14	5
8	25	40	65	3.13	5.00	8.13	8
9	25	54	79	2.78	6.00	8.78	14
10	25	75	100	2.50	7.50	10.00	21

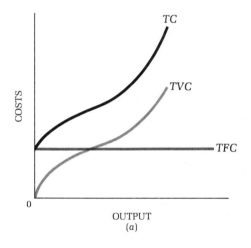

(a)

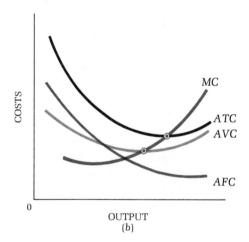

(b)

TFC. In other words, because total fixed cost is constant, changes in total cost are due entirely to changes in total variable cost.

The Family of Average Costs

Columns (5), (6), and (7) give us three different types of average costs. These are represented by Figure (b), which accompanies the table.

Average Fixed Cost AFC is the ratio of total fixed cost to quantity produced:

$$AFC = \frac{TFC}{Q}$$

Note from Figure (b) that AFC continually decreases as output increases. This is because TFC in the foregoing equation is constant. Hence, increases in output will always reduce the value of the ratio.

Average Variable Cost AVC is the ratio of total variable cost to quantity produced:

$$AVC = \frac{TVC}{Q}$$

Notice that, as output increases, the AVC curve falls to a minimum point and then rises. The AVC curve thus reflects the operation of the law of diminishing (average) returns described earlier.

Average Total Cost ATC is the ratio of total cost to quantity:

$$ATC = \frac{TC}{Q}$$

Hence, it is also equal to the sum of AFC and AVC:

$$ATC = AFC + AVC$$

Of course, you can transpose the equation to express either AFC or AVC in terms of the other variables.

Note Businesspeople often use the terms "unit cost" or "cost per unit" when they mean average *variable* cost. If you were a shirt manufacturer, for example, you might figure your cost per shirt to be $6 based on the cost of labor, materials, and other variable resources used. You would then set a "markup" price of perhaps an additional $6 per shirt to cover "overhead" or fixed costs. Economists, on the other hand, include fixed costs with total costs right from the outset. Hence, they use unit cost, or cost per unit, to mean average *total* cost.

Notice that the vertical distance between ATC and AVC diminishes as output increases. That is, ATC and AVC come progressively closer together. This is because the difference between them, AFC, continually decreases as output expands.

Marginal Cost

There is an important lesson to be learned from the table and charts of Exhibit 3. The lesson is that *total cost always increases as output increases.* That is, the more a firm produces, the greater its total costs of production. This is because increased production always requires the use of more materials, labor, power, and other variable resources. Only average costs—in particular ATC and AVC—decrease as output increases until some "optimum" or best level of production is reached. Thus, when you hear a businessperson say that production needs to be increased in order to lower costs, he or she is talking about unit costs—either ATC or AVC—not TC or TVC.

The fact that total cost changes with variations in production gives rise to an important cost concept called *marginal cost*, MC. It is defined as the change in total cost resulting from a unit change in output. The formula for determining marginal cost is thus similar to that for determining marginal product, except that "change in TP" becomes "change in TC;" and "change in variable input" becomes "change in output." Thus, marginal cost may be measured by the formula

$$MC = \frac{\text{change in } TC}{\text{change in } Q}$$

Marginal cost is especially important. It measures the change in total cost due to a change in output.

Exhibit 4
The Average–Marginal Relationship and the Total–Marginal Relationship

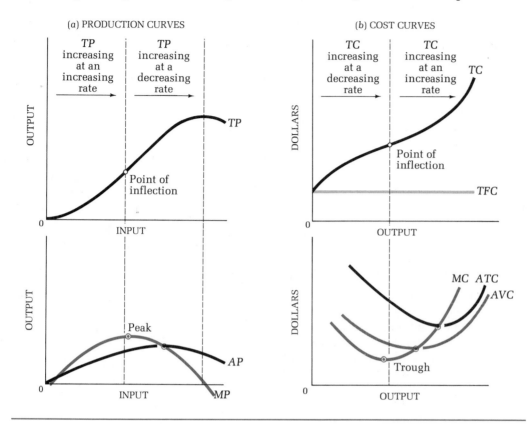

(a) PRODUCTION CURVES

TP increasing at an increasing rate

TP increasing at a decreasing rate

OUTPUT

Point of inflection

TP

0   INPUT

OUTPUT

Peak

AP

0   INPUT   MP

(b) COST CURVES

TC increasing at a decreasing rate

TC increasing at an increasing rate

TC

DOLLARS

Point of inflection

TFC

0   OUTPUT

DOLLARS

MC ATC

AVC

Trough

0   OUTPUT

Of course, changes in *TC* are due to changes in *TVC*, because *TFC* remains constant as production varies. Hence, marginal cost can also be measured by dividing the change in *TVC* by the change in *Q*.

What does marginal cost really mean?

Mathematically, marginal cost represents the *slope* of the total cost curve (just as you saw earlier that marginal product represents the slope of the total product curve). Economically, it tells you, for any given output, the *additional* amount of cost a business firm would incur by increasing its output by one unit.

You will see later that, *for economic decisions involving changes in output, marginal cost is the single most important cost concept.*

The Average–Marginal Relationship

By this time you may have noticed an interesting geometric principle that characterizes all average and marginal curves. For convenience, Exhibit 4 groups the foregoing production curves and cost curves together, so that they may be examined simultaneously. However, we are interested for the moment only in the average and marginal curves, so these curves are shown separately below their corresponding total curves.

If you refer to these lower curves, you will note an important set of relationships.

1. When an average curve is rising, its corresponding marginal curve is above it.

2. When an average curve is falling, its corresponding marginal curve is below it.

3. When an average curve is neither rising nor falling, that is, is either at a maximum or at a minimum, its corresponding marginal curve intersects (is equal to) it.

This set of relationships constitutes what may be called the *average–marginal relationship*.

The sense behind the average–marginal relationship can be appreciated by a simple example. If to a class of students we add an extra, or "marginal," student whose age is above the average age of the class, the average will increase. If we add a student whose age is below the average, the average will decrease. And if we add a student whose age is equal to the average, the average will remain the same.

Does the average–marginal relationship hold true for both the production-function and cost curves? The figures in Exhibit 4 indicate that it does. But in the production figure the marginal curve intersects the average curve at its maximum point, whereas in the cost figure the marginal curve intersects the two average curves at their minimum points.

In later chapters you will encounter other types of average and marginal curves, but the underlying principle stated here characterizes them all.

The Total–Marginal Relationship

A geometric principle is also common to all total and marginal curves. It is based on the fact that every marginal curve is a graph of the *slope* of its corresponding total curve, as you have already seen.

If you refer again to Exhibit 4, this time to both the upper and lower figures, you will see an interesting relationship. This is emphasized by the vertical dashed lines. Thus:

The short-run cost curves obey certain laws of behavior with respect to changes in output.

1. When a total curve is increasing at an increasing rate, its corresponding marginal curve is rising.

2. When a total curve is increasing at a decreasing rate, its corresponding marginal curve is falling.

3. When a total curve is increasing at a zero rate, as occurs when it is at its maximum, its corresponding marginal curve is zero.

This set of relationships is called the *total–marginal relationship*

Observe from the diagrams that the point at which the rate of change of the total curve changes direction is called the *point of inflection*. This point corresponds to either a peak or a trough in the marginal curve, as shown by the vertical dashed lines.

To avoid confusion, you might make note of an important aspect of the total–marginal relationship. It is not necessary to include the fact that when the total curve is falling—as in the case of the *TP* curve at its right end—the corresponding *MP* curve is negative. Although negative marginal curves may exist from a theoretical standpoint, they do not ordinarily have any economic significance. A rational employer, for example, will not knowingly hire so many units of an input as to yield the firm a negative marginal product.

As with the average–marginal relationship, there are several kinds of total–marginal relationships that you will encounter in later chapters. However, the underlying principle presented here characterizes them all.

Long-Run Costs

It was emphasized earlier that an important difference exists between the short run and the long run. In the *short run* a firm can vary its output but not its plant capacity. Therefore, the firm will have some variable costs and some fixed costs. In the *long run* a firm can vary not only its output but also its plant capacity. Therefore, the firm has no fixed costs. That is, *in the long run all costs are variable.*

Of what practical value is this in the study of costs? The previous analysis of short-run costs reveals how a firm's costs will vary in response to output changes within a period short enough that the size of the plant remains fixed. If we now extend the logic one step further, we can develop a firm's *long-run cost curve.* This shows how costs vary with output in a period long enough for all resource inputs, including plant and equipment, to be freely variable in amount. Once the long-run cost curve is derived, the knowledge gained from it can be of use to businesspeople in determining the most economical size of a plant and its general operational standards.

Alternative Plant Sizes

Look at the problem in this way. Suppose that you were a manufacturer whose plant had gone through a series of additions and expansions over a period of years. For each plant size with its associated complement of equipment there would be a different production function and hence a different cost structure. Each of these cost structures would be represented by a different set of short-run cost curves of the type we have already studied. To illustrate, Exhibit 5, Figure (a), presents five short-run average total cost curves. Each curve, labeled ATC_1, ATC_2, and so on, represents one of five different plant sizes. Theoretically, there could be infinitely many such curves, one for each possible plant size.

These short-run curves can be looked at from still another point of view. Suppose that you were a businessperson planning to construct and equip a plant for the production of a good. In that case, all your factors of production—and therefore all your costs—would be variable. Each possible plant size or "layout" would then be represented by a different cost structure, as illustrated by these short-run average total cost curves. As before, it should be borne in mind that from a theoretical standpoint there can be infinitely many such curves, one for each possible layout.

Plant Utilization

Some important lessons may be learned from Figure (a). On the basis of the information presented, it seems intuitively clear that the "optimum" output level is at N. Also, the lowest-cost or optimum-size plant for pro-

---

Long-run costs exhibit a pattern of behavior that is different from that of short-run costs.

Exhibit 5

Short-Run Average Total Cost Curves and the Long-Run Average Cost (or Planning) Curve

Figure (a): Each short-run plant size or "layout" represents a different plant-cost structure. The optimum level of output is at N. Theoretically, there may be infinitely many such curves, one for each possible plant size.

Figure (b): The planning curve, or long-run average cost curve, is tangent to all the short-run curves. But it can only be tangent to the minimum point of the *lowest* short-run curve. For every other short-run curve, the tangency occurs on either the declining or the rising side.

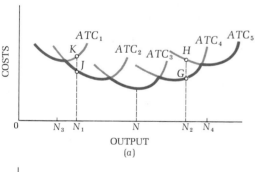

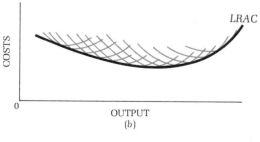

ducing this output is represented by ATC_3. However, for all other levels of output two interesting principles exist—based on the assumption of infinitely many ATC curves:

1. *At any output less than the optimum output at N, it pays better to "underuse" a larger plant than to "overuse" a smaller one.* For example, suppose that you want to produce the output at N_1. Obviously, it is cheaper to use the larger-scale plant ATC_2 at an average production cost of N_1J per unit than to use the smaller-scale plant ATC_1 at an average cost of N_1K per unit.

2. *At any output greater than the optimum output at N, it pays better to "overuse" a smaller plant than to "underuse" a larger one.* For instance, suppose that you wish to produce the output at N_2. Clearly, it is cheaper to use the smaller-scale plant ATC_4 at an average cost of N_2G per unit than to use the larger-scale plant ATC_5 at an average cost of N_2H per unit.

The choice of the "right" size for a plant depends on the level of output.

It should be noted that these principles are true for *all* outputs—even for outputs like those at N_3 and N_4. Why? Because of the assumption that infinitely many ATC curves may be drawn. Therefore, you can sketch in the possible ATC curves for the outputs at N_3 and N_4 to demonstrate the validity of these concepts.

The Planning Curve

These principles suggest that the lower portions of the short-run average total cost curves are the only ones economically relevant to the selection of a particular plant. What would happen to these lower portions if, instead of having just five short-run curves, there were an infinitely large number of them, as was theoretically assumed? To find out, look at Figure (b) along with the following explanation.

The heavy line, called a *planning curve,* is a *long-run average cost curve* (*LRAC*) that is tangent to each of the short-run average total cost curves from which it is derived. The reason for calling the *LRAC* curve a "planning curve" has already been indicated. When the plant is still in the blueprint stage and all costs are variable, the *LRAC* curve tells you the average total cost of producing a given level of output. Thus, it can be thought of as a curve that shows what costs would be like at the present time for alternative outputs if different-sized plants were built.

You can think of the LRAC curve as the "envelope" of infinitely many ATC curves.

The Behavior of Long-Run Average Cost: Economies and Diseconomies of Scale

These ideas give rise to an important question: What causes the *LRAC* curve (or the successive ATC curves of which it is composed) to decrease to a minimum and then rise? Or, to put the question in terms of real-world examples: Why are steel mills larger than machine shops? Why do some firms remain small while others become large?

A firm's long-run average cost curve reflects economies and diseconomies of scale.

The answers are based on what may be called *economies and diseconomies of scale* These are simply decreases and increases in a firm's long-run average costs as the size of its plant is increased. Let us see why these decreases or increases occur.

Economies of Scale

Economies of scale arise from the advantages of being "big."

Several factors may give rise to economies of scale—that is, to decreasing long-run average costs of production.

1. Greater Specialization of Resources As a firm's scale of operation increases, its opportunities for specialization are greatly enhanced. This is because a large-scale firm can often divide the tasks and work to be done more easily than can a small-scale firm.

2. More Efficient Utilization of Equipment In many industries, the technology of production is such that large units of expensive equipment must be used. The production of automobiles, steel, and refined petroleum are notable examples. In such industries, companies must be able to afford whatever equipment is necessary and must be able to use it efficiently by spreading the cost per unit over a sufficiently large volume of output. A small-scale firm cannot ordinarily do these things.

3. Reduced Unit Costs of Inputs A large-scale firm can often buy its inputs—such as its raw materials—at a cheaper price per unit. This is because large firms buy in large quantities and can obtain discounts from their suppliers. And for certain types of equipment, the price per unit of capacity is often much less when larger sizes are purchased. Thus, the construction cost per square foot for a large factory is usually less than for a small one. The price per horsepower of electric induction motors varies inversely with the amount of horsepower.

4. Utilization of By-products In certain industries, large-scale firms can make effective use of many by-products that would be wasted by a small firm. A typical example is the meat-packing industry. Here, major firms make glue from cattle hoofs, as well as pharmaceuticals, fertilizer, and other products from the remains of livestock.

5. Growth of Auxiliary Facilities An expanding firm may benefit from, or encourage other firms to develop, ancillary facilities, such as warehousing, marketing, and transportation systems. These facilities save the growing firm considerable costs. For example, urban colleges and universities benefit from nearby public libraries and restaurants. Individual farms benefit from common irrigation and drainage ditches. Similarly, growing businesses often encourage the development of, and receive the benefit from, improved transportation facilities.

Diseconomies of Scale

Diseconomies of scale arise from the disadvantages of being "too big."

At the same time that economies of scale are being realized, a point may be reached at which diseconomies of scale begin to exert a more-than-offsetting effect. As a result, the long-run average cost curve starts to rise, primarily for two reasons.

1. Limitation on Decision-Making Capacity of Management As a firm becomes larger, heavier burdens are placed on management. Eventually, this resource input is overworked relative to the others, and "diminishing returns" to management set in. Of course, management may be able to delegate authority to others, but ultimately decisions must emanate from a final center if there is to be uniformity in performance and policy. Even the modern principles of scientific management do not eliminate these diseconomies. At most, they may be postponed, or perhaps their seriousness may be lessened.

2. Competition for Resources Long-run average costs can rise as a growing firm increasingly bids labor or other resources away from other industries. This may raise the prices the firm pays for its inputs and cause increases in unit production costs.

Summary: Classifying Economies and Diseconomies as Internal or External

These causes of increasing and decreasing returns to scale may be classified according to whether they are internal or external to the firm. The distinction is important, because the internal factors may be subject to a certain amount of managerial control, whereas the external factors are not. The following classification illustrates these ideas while summarizing important concepts.

Internal economies and diseconomies are those conditions that bring about decreases or increases in a firm's long-run average costs or scale of operations as a result of size adjustments *within* the firm as a producing unit. They occur regardless of adjustments within the industry and are due mainly to physical economies or diseconomies. Thus, reductions in long-run average costs occur largely because the indivisibility of productive factors is overcome when size and output are increased. On the other hand, increases in long-run average costs occur because of adverse or conflicting factor interaction between management and other resources.

External economies and diseconomies are those conditions that bring about decreases or increases in a firm's long-run average costs or scale of operations as a result of causes that are entirely *outside* the firm as a producing unit. The causes depend on adjustments of the industry and are related to the firm only to the extent that it is part of the industry.

On the basis of this distinction, you should be able to classify each of the various economies and diseconomies of scale listed in the two previous sections as either internal or external.

Conclusion: What Does the Evidence Show?

How have business firms adjusted to the existence of economies of scale? Do the long-run average cost curves of firms actually look like the ones shown earlier? Or do their shapes vary according to the economics of the industry in which they operate? The answer to both questions is *yes*.

In all industries, the long-run average cost curves of firms decline, reach a minimum, and eventually rise. However, some curves do so more quickly than others, depending on the particular industry and the types of economies and diseconomies that characterize it. Three basic variations of such curves are shown in Exhibit 6.

Case
Sunshine Dairy Products Corporation: Constructing New Plants

Sunshine Dairy Products Corporation is a leading producer of milk, ice cream, cheese, and various other dairy products. After many years of research, the company succeeded in developing a very low calorie, low-

Exhibit 6
Three Typical Long-Run Average Cost Curves

The shapes of different firms' long-run average costs vary in different industries.

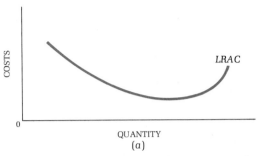

Figure (a): A situation in which economies of scale outweigh the diseconomies over a wide range of output. Examples are the aluminum, automobile, cement, and steel industries.

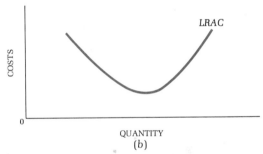

Figure (b): A situation in which diseconomies of scale set in quickly and many small firms exist side by side. Examples are the retailing, metal-fabrication, and publishing industries.

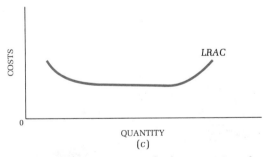

Figure (c): A situation in which economies of scale are either quickly exhausted and diseconomies take a long time coming, or else the economies and diseconomies tend to cancel each other out. Examples are the chemical, food-processing, furniture, and appliance industries.

cost, synthetic "ice cream." Extensive taste tests have indicated that this new ice cream is every bit as delicious as any of the leading regular brands. Accordingly, the management of the company has decided to produce and market the new ice cream on a test basis within one region of the country and to construct the necessary production facilities for that purpose.

The Sunshine Corporation conducted a market survey of the three largest population areas of the region. The results indicated that the company should package the product in liter-size containers, and that sales would average about 10,000, 5,000, and 2,500 liters per week in the three areas. An economic consultant for the company has suggested either of two alternatives with respect to the construction of ice-cream plants:

1. Construct a single plant equidistant between the three population areas, with a production capacity of 20,000 liters per week at a fixed cost of $5,000 per week and a variable cost of 70 cents per liter.

2. Construct three plants (one in each market area) with weekly capacities of 12,000, 6,000, and 3,000 liters, weekly fixed costs of $4,000, $3,000, and $2,000, and a variable cost of only 60 cents per liter (due to the reduction of shipping costs).

Questions

1. Assuming that the market survey is correct, which alternative should management select? At a price of $1.99 per liter, what would be the profit (or loss) per liter and in total?

2. If demand were to increase to production capacity, which alternative would be better?

3. Suppose that management selects the second alternative rather than the first and that demand is at the level of production capacity in all three markets. If the company wanted to make a profit of $1 per liter in each of the three markets, what price per liter would it have to charge in each of these markets? Can management be sure of realizing its expected profit? Explain why.

4. Instead of constructing a new plant, the management of Sunshine is contemplating the purchase of an existing plant. An economic consultant has provided the following cost estimates for the plant under consideration:

   (a) ATC of 5,000 liters is $12,600.
   (b) AVC of 4,000 liters is $10,000.
   (c) TC rises by $13,000 when production rises from 5,000 to 6,000 liters.
   (d) AFC of 5,000 liters is $2,000.
   (e) The increase in TC from producing nothing to producing 1,000 liters is $15,000.
   (f) TC of 8,000 liters is $170,000.
   (g) TVC increases by $25,000 when production rises from 6,000 to 7,000 liters.
   (h) AFC plus AVC for 3,000 liters is $16,000.
   (i) ATC falls by $6,000 when production increases from 1,000 to 2,000 liters.

On the basis of this information, complete the following cost schedule. [*Hint* First fill in all the data given in items (a) through (i).]

Ted Feder/Editorial Photocolor Archives

Cost Schedule of an Ice-Cream Plant

Output (thousands of liters per week)	Cost (thousands of dollars per week)						
	TFC	TVC	TC	AFC	AVC	ATC	MC
0	$ ___	$ ___	$ ___	$ ___	$ ___	$ ___	
1	___	___	___	___	___	___	$ ___
2	___	___	___	___	___	___	___
3	___	___	___	___	___	___	___
4	___	___	___	___	___	___	___
5	___	___	___	___	___	___	___
6	___	___	___	___	___	___	___
7	___	___	___	___	___	___	___
8	___	___	___	___	___	___	___

What You Have Learned in This Chapter

1. Cost is a sacrifice that must be made in order to acquire something. The sacrifice may include monetary and nonmonetary elements.

2. Opportunity costs are critical in economics because they measure the value of a forgone alternative. Opportunity costs arise because resources are limited and have alternative uses.

3. Economic costs are payments that must be made to attract resources. Such costs include not only explicit costs or money expenditures for resources but also the implicit costs of self-owned or self-employed resources.

4. The law of diminishing returns—more accurately called the law of variable proportions—states what happens to output when a variable input is combined with fixed inputs. Although the law covers total, average, and marginal returns, the last is most important where output changes are involved. Graphically, marginal product always intersects average product at its maximum point.

5. There are three families of costs: total, average, and marginal. The family of total costs consists of total fixed cost, which does not vary with output, and total variable cost, which increases as output increases. The family of average costs consists of average fixed cost, which is the ratio of total fixed cost to quantity, and average variable cost, which is the ratio of total variable cost to quantity. Marginal cost is a one-member family consisting of marginal cost alone. It is the change in total cost resulting from a unit change in output. Graphically, marginal cost always intersects average variable cost and average total cost at their minimum points.

6. The short run is a period long enough to vary output but not plant capacity. The long run is a period long enough to vary plant capacity. Therefore, in the short run some of a firm's costs are fixed and some are variable. But in the long run all of a firm's costs are variable because all its factors of production are variable.

7. The long-run average cost curve, or planning curve, tends to be U-shaped, reflecting first economies and then diseconomies of scale. Economies of scale result from greater specialization of resources, more efficient utilization of equipment, reduced unit costs of inputs, and fuller utilization of by-products. Diseconomies of scale arise mainly from the increasing complexities of management as a firm grows larger. Each of these economies and diseconomies can be classified as either internal or external to a firm.

8. The actual shape of a planning curve tends to vary within different industries. For example, in heavy industries, such as autos and steel, internal economies extend over a wide range of output. Hence, such industries tend to have small numbers of large firms. In light industries, such as textiles and retailing, internal economies are exhausted rather quickly over a narrow range of output. Consequently, such industries tend to have large numbers of small firms.

For Discussion

1. *Terms and concepts to review:*

cost
outlay costs
opportunity cost
economic costs
explicit costs
implicit costs
normal profit
economic (pure) profit
short run
long run
production function
law of diminishing returns (law of variable
   proportions)
marginal product
average product
total fixed cost
total variable cost
total cost
average fixed cost
average variable cost
average total cost
marginal cost
average–marginal relationship
total–marginal relationship
long-run average cost curve (planning curve)
economies and diseconomies of scale
internal economies and diseconomies of scale
external economies and diseconomies of scale

2. Complete the accompanying table, showing the cost schedule of a firm. Graph the family of total costs in one figure and all the remaining costs in another. (**Note** When you graph the marginal cost curve, plot each *MC* value to the midpoint between successive outputs. Thus, the first *MC* value in your figure corresponds to an output of 0.5, the second to 1.5, the third to 2.5, and so on.) Discuss the various curves in terms of their shape as influenced by the law of diminish-

ing returns. (**Hint** Sketch the family of total costs on one figure and the family of average and marginal costs on a figure directly beneath it. Then see if you can draw a vertical dashed line through both figures such that the stage of increasing marginal returns is on the left side of the vertical line and the stage of decreasing marginal returns is on the right.) In your answer, account for the relative distances between *ATC* and *AVC* at different levels of output, and explain the reason for the intersection of *MC* with *ATC* and *AVC* at their minimum points.

3. Are opportunity costs entered in the accounting records of a firm? If so, what are the cost figures used for? If not, what good are they?

4. In estimating the annual cost of owning a fully paid-up $9,000 automobile, you might show the following cost entry on your books: "Interest on investment at 6 percent: $540." What would this mean? Explain.

5. Why do you suppose that some professors, who could earn considerably more by working in industry, continue to accept a lower salary by remaining in education?

6. "As a firm becomes larger and decision making becomes more complex, the long-run average cost curve turns upward because the burden of administration becomes disproportionately greater and 'diminishing returns' to management set in." Would this statement be true of firms that are very well managed? Of what significance are technology, organizational structure, managerial ability, and similar factors?

7. The law of diminishing returns was originally intended to serve as an explanation of a historical process. In England, for example, as the population grew during the eighteenth

Cost Schedule of a Firm

(1) Quantity of output	(2) Total fixed cost	(3) Total variable cost	(4) Total cost	(5) Average fixed cost	(6) Average variable cost	(7) Average total cost	(8) Marginal cost
0	$100	$ 0	$_____	$_____	$_____	$_____	$_____
1	____	40	_____	_____	_____	_____	_____
2	____	64	_____	_____	_____	_____	_____
3	____	80	_____	_____	_____	_____	_____
4	____	88	_____	_____	_____	_____	_____
5	____	96	_____	_____	_____	_____	_____
6	____	108	_____	_____	_____	_____	_____
7	____	128	_____	_____	_____	_____	_____
8	____	160	_____	_____	_____	_____	_____
9	____	216	_____	_____	_____	_____	_____
10	____	300	_____	_____	_____	_____	_____

and nineteenth centuries, it was predicted (by the early classical economist David Ricardo in 1817) that the marginal productivity of labor on land would decline. If this were true:

(a) What would happen to aggregate values of agricultural land?

(b) What would happen to total land rent as a percentage share of the nation's total income?

(c) What would happen to the price of food relative to nonfood goods?

(d) How would you answer these questions with respect to the United States during most of the nineteenth century?

8. What is the effect of a technological improvement on a company's production function?

9. "If it were not for the law of diminishing returns, it would be possible to grow all the world's food in a flowerpot." Do you agree? Explain.

10. The most common type of production function is one characterized by "constant returns to scale." This means that, if *all* inputs to a production process are increased in the same proportion, output is increased in that proportion. For example, if *all* inputs are expanded by 10 percent, output is expanded by 10 percent; if *all* inputs are doubled, output is doubled; and so on. In view of this, how do you account for the following situation?

(a) A suit-manufacturing firm doubled the size of its factory, the number of machines in it, the number of workers, and the quantity of materials employed. As a result, output increased from 200 to 420 suits per day. Is this an example of *increasing returns to scale,* that is, economies of large-scale production?

(b) The company then doubled the quantity of managers and found that output fell to 370 suits per day. What do you suppose might have happened?

11. Physical-Growth Analogies of Returns to Scale

(a) There is a relationship between the volume V and the surface area A of regular physical bodies. This relationship may be approximated by the "square-cube" law:

$$V = A^{3/2} = \sqrt{A^3}$$

For example, if the surface area of an object increases 4 times, its volume should increase about $\sqrt{4^3} = 8$ times. Can you use this notion to explain why there are no small warm-blooded animals in the Antarctic or in the ocean? Can you use it to explain why the largest insect is about as large as the smallest warm-blooded animal?

(b) There is often a tendency to think that constant returns of scale should be common in economic life, yet variable returns (both increasing and decreasing) are frequently encountered. For example, we should expect that, by doubling *all* inputs to a production process, we will double the output. Yet there are examples from nature to illustrate why this is not so. Thus, if a house were scaled down so that it stood in the same proportion to a flea as it now stands to a person, the flea would be able to jump over the house. However, if a flea were scaled up to the size of a person, the flea would not be able to jump over the house. In fact, it could not jump at all because its legs would break. Can you explain why?

(c) What conclusions relevant to the size and growth of organizations can you draw from these notions? (**Hint** It has been said that some prehistoric monsters became extinct because they could not adjust to their changing environment. Why not?)

(d) Do you see any connection between questions (a) through (c) and the following quotation?

> There is a story of a man who thought of getting the economy of large-scale production in plowing, and built a plow three times as long, three times as wide, and three times as deep as the ordinary plow and harnessed six horses to pull it, instead of two. To his surprise, the plow refused to budge, and to his greater surprise it finally took fifty horses to move the refractory machine. In this case, the resistance, which is the thing he did not want, increased faster than the surface area of the earth plowed, which was the thing he did want. Furthermore, when he increased his power to overcome this resistance, he multiplied the number of his power units instead of their size, which eliminated all chance of saving there, and since his units were horses, the fifty could not pull together as well as two.
>
> J.M. Clark, *Studies in the Economics of Overhead Costs*, Chicago, University of Chicago Press, 1923, p. 116

The Economics of the Firm:
How Are Prices and Outputs
Determined?

21
CHAPTER

Perfect Competition: Criteria for Evaluating Competitive Behavior

Learning guide
Watch for the answers to these important questions

What is perfect competition? Why do we study it? Is it a fantasy or is it real?

How do a firm's costs and revenues affect its production decisions? What is the fundamental principle of profit maximization? Why does this principle "work"? Can it be explained in practical terms? How are supply curves derived from marginal cost curves?

What are the long-run equilibrium conditions of a firm in perfect competition? How does the adjustment to equilibrium come about? How are constant-, increasing-, and decreasing-cost industries distinguished? Why is $MC = P$ the condition of economic (or allocative) efficiency?

What are the favorable consequences of perfect competition? The unfavorable consequences? How are the consequences evaluated in terms of the economy's goals?

This chapter develops a theoretical model of pure capitalism.

You know that economics is concerned with how society allocates its limited resources, which have alternative uses, to the production of goods and services. Economists have always wanted to see this task accomplished with maximum efficiency—that is, with the least amount of waste. Hence, they have developed a theory that explains how this can be done.

This is the theory of "perfect competition," also called "pure competition." The two terms may be regarded as synonymous. (However, a technical distinction that is sometimes made between them is explained in the Dictionary at the back of the book.) The theory underlies the operation of supply and demand that we studied in previous chapters. It attempts to explain how a *"perfect"* market economy or *"pure"* free-enterprise system tends to operate.

What Is Perfect Competition?

Perfect competition is a type of market structure.

When a scientist tries to describe a complicated problem, he or she starts by constructing a simplified picture of the situation—a *model.* In this chapter we shall develop a model or theory of perfect competition.

Let us begin with a definition.

> *Perfect* (or *pure*) *competition* is the name given to an industry or market structure characterized by a large number of buyers and sellers all engaged in the purchase and sale of a homogeneous commodity. Each buyer or seller has perfect knowledge of market prices and quantities; there is no discrimination; and there is perfect mobility of resources.

The expression "perfect competition" can be used in discussing either an industry or a market. The distinction is always clear from the context in which the term is used. Now let us analyze the definition.

Explaining the Definition

The definition of perfect competition contains five essential conditions. Each of them requires separate examination.

Large Numbers of Buyers and Sellers

What do we mean by a "large" number of buyers and sellers? Is 1,000 large and 999 small? To answer *yes* would be silly; the words "large" and "small" are relative rather than absolute. Hence, the definition does not establish the size of a perfectly competitive market in terms of numbers. Instead, it uses the word "large," as we have discussed in earlier chapters, to mean *large enough that no one buyer or seller can affect the market price by offering to buy or not to buy, to sell or not to sell.* Therefore, whether it takes 1,000 or 1 million buyers or sellers is of no relevance. The only requirement is that the market price for any buyer or seller is *given.* The individual can accept the market price or reject it, but cannot alter it by going into or out of the market.

No one buyer or seller can affect the market price.

Homogeneous Commodity

This means that all units of the commodity that sellers make available must be identical in the minds of buyers. The reason for this requirement, as will be shown later, is that buyers must be indifferent about which seller they deal with. They must be willing to purchase from the seller who offers the good at the lowest price.

The product being bought and sold is standardized.

Notice, therefore, that we are referring to *economic homogeneity,* not physical homogeneity. Two sellers may be selling the same physical product, but buyers may be willing to pay more to seller A than to seller B. This may be true because seller A provides service with a smile, or offers the commodity in a more attractive package, or perhaps uses a brand name. In such cases, the two products are *not* economically homogeneous.

This point can be illustrated with a concrete example. Beet sugar and cane sugar are virtually identical for all practical purposes. That is, they look and taste the same. Yet, in some regions of the country, beet sugar sells for less than cane. Why? Because buyers do not think of them as the same. Instead, they believe that beet is somehow inferior to cane. And, because the law requires that a package of sugar must be labeled either "beet" or "cane," there sometimes is a price difference between them. In this case, the two products are physically homogeneous but *economically heterogeneous.* That is, they are similar but not identical. How about butter and margarine? Two nickels and a dime? Are they homogeneous? Heterogeneous?

Perfect Knowledge of Market Prices and Quantities

The third condition—"perfect knowledge"—means that all buyers and sellers are completely aware of the prices and quantities at which transactions are taking place in the market and that all have the opportunity to participate in those transactions. For example, perfect knowledge

Buyers and sellers know the market prices of goods.

does not exist if buyers do not know that sellers across the street are charging a lower price for a certain commodity. Likewise, perfect knowledge does not exist if sellers do not know that buyers across the street are offering a higher price for a certain product. In both instances, the buyers and sellers on one side of the street are not competing with the buyers and sellers on the other side. Hence, they are not even in the same market.

No Discrimination

Buyers and sellers deal solely on the basis of price.

This condition of no discrimination requires that buyers and sellers be willing to deal openly with one another. This means that they must be willing to buy and sell at the market price with any and all that may wish to do so. It also means that buyers and sellers must not offer or accept any special deals, discounts, or favors that are not available to everyone on equal terms. Discrimination thus has an economic meaning, not just a social one.

Perfect Mobility of Resources

Resources and goods can be moved quickly and easily into their most remunerative uses.

The condition of perfect resource mobility requires that there be no obstacles—economic, legal, technological, or others—to prevent firms or resources from entering or leaving the particular market or industry. Further, there must be no impediments to the purchase or sale of commodities. This means that firms, resources, and commodities can be shifted about swiftly and smoothly without friction. For example, the land, labor, capital, and entrepreneurship used in wheat production can be moved quickly and easily into corn production if it is more profitable. Similarly, potatoes stored in Idaho can be sold instantly in New York or in San Francisco if the price is right. In general, owners of resources and commodities are free and able to take advantage of the best market opportunities as they arise.

Is Perfect Competition Realistic?

The model serves as a guide for judging real-world market structures.

Is the concept of perfect competition realistic or a fantasy? After all, no market or industry anywhere in the world exactly meets the five requirements just described. Should you infer, therefore, that the notion of perfect competition is "theoretical and impractical"?

The answer is *no*. As you shall see shortly, the concept of perfect competition is a *theoretical extreme*—like the concept of a perfect vacuum or the assumption of a frictionless state in physics. For example, in elementary physics it is expressly assumed, in many problems of motion, that there is *no friction*. This assumption is made even though everyone knows that friction always exists in the real world. The assumption creates an idealized situation that permits simplification of a problem in order that it may be analyzed. Similarly, the theory of perfect competition assumes a "frictionless" economic system in which the movement of goods and resources is unobstructed. Thus, like physics, economics uses idealized models in order to simplify and analyze specific problems.

But the model developed in this chapter, although it represents a theoretical extreme, is not completely unreal. Some markets do approach the conditions of perfect competition at least roughly, although none meets all the conditions precisely. The examples that come closest to the ideal are the organized commodity and stock exchanges in New York, Chicago, and many other cities, and, to a lesser extent, some industries producing standard raw materials. The approximation to perfect competition varies in these markets, but it is close enough to make the theory and conclusions of this chapter both meaningful and useful.

Costs, Revenues, and Profit Maximization in the Short Run

It follows from the explanation of perfect competition that the market price of a commodity under such circumstances would be established independently through the free operation of total supply and total demand. You have already seen how this happens. No individual buyer or seller can influence the price, yet the price emerges automatically as a reflection of the interaction of numerous buyers and sellers.

Prices and quantities respond to supply-and-demand forces.

This leads to a vital question. How does a seller in perfect competition, faced with a market price over which he or she has no influence, decide how much of a commodity to produce? The answer to this question is one of the most fundamental principles of economics.

Total Cost and Total Revenue

To begin with, turn your attention to the table in Exhibit 1. This table gives the costs and revenues of a firm in perfect competition. The only costs shown are those needed for the present analysis.

Columns (1) and (2) represent familiar concepts, because they contain quantities produced and their corresponding levels of total cost. As always, total cost increases as the quantity increases.

Column (3) denotes *average revenue* (AR). This is the price per unit of output or, as you will see momentarily, the ratio of total revenue to quantity. In this case, the average revenue is $10 per unit. Thus, it is

Exhibit 1
Cost and Revenue Schedules of a Firm Under Perfect Competition

(1) Quantity per day, Q (given)	(2) Total cost, TC (given)	(3) Price per unit, or average revenue, P = AR (given)	(4) Total revenue, TR (3) × (1)	(5) Average total cost, ATC (2) ÷ (1)	(6) Marginal cost, MC Change in (2) / Change in (1)	(7) Marginal revenue, MR Change in (4) / Change in (1)	(8) Net revenue, NR (4) − (2)
0	$ 25	$10	$ 0	$ —			−$25
1	35	10	10	35.00	$10	$10	− 25
2	41	10	20	20.50	6	10	− 21
3	45	10	30	15.00	4	10	− 15
4	47	10	40	11.75	2	10	− 7
5	49	10	50	9.80	2	10	1
6	52	10	60	8.67	3	10	8
7	57	10	70	8.14	5	10	13
8	65	10	80	8.13	8 ← $10 → 10		15
9	79	10	90	8.78	14	10	11
10	100	10	100	10.00	21	10	0

assumed that the price established in the market through the free interaction of supply and demand is $10. Hence, this is the price with which the firm is faced and over which it has no control. Or, to put it somewhat differently, the firm finds that it can sell all the units it wants to at the market price P of $10.

Column (4), called *total revenue* (*TR*), is simply the price per unit times the number of units sold. Looking at the headings of columns (3) and (4) together, you will see that only the simplest arithmetic is needed to describe the connection between average revenue, total revenue, and price:

$$AR = \frac{TR}{Q} = \frac{P \times Q}{Q} = P$$

Finally, you can skip temporarily to column (8) of the table and examine *net revenue* or net profit—the difference between total revenue and total cost. Note that it is at first negative, but that it then rises to a peak of $15 at 8 units of output and falls thereafter.

Graphic Illustration of Total Cost and Total Revenue

The graphs provide a complete view of price and output determination.

The *TC* and *TR* values are graphed in Figure (*a*) of Exhibit 2. The *TC* curve has a familiar shape, but note that the *TR* curve is a straight line. This reflects the fact, as stated earlier, that the firm receives the same price per unit for all the units it sells.

The points labeled B_1 and B_2 are called *break-even points*. They designate levels of output at which a firm's revenue equals its cost. Thus, the firm is incurring neither an economic profit nor an economic loss. At any output between these two points, the firm's profit or net revenue is positive. At any output beyond the break-even points, it has a net loss (or negative net revenue) because its costs exceed its revenues.

Finally, it should be pointed out that net revenue, as represented by the vertical distance *GH*, is a maximum at 8 units of output. At this output, the *slope* of the total cost curve, as measured by the slope of the tangent at *H*, is equal to the *slope* of the total revenue curve. This suggests an important fundamental concept:

The *slope* (steepness) of a line is the change in its vertical distance per unit of change in its horizontal distance. The slope of a straight line (such as the *TR* curve) is the same at every point, but the slope of a curved line (like the *TC* curve) differs at every point. Geometrically, you can find the slope of a curve at a point by drawing a straight line tangent to the curve at that point. The slope of the tangent will then be the slope of the curve at the point of tangency. As you will recall from elementary mathematics, parallel lines have equal slopes. Thus, the tangent at *H* is parallel to the *TR* curve.

This important concept is amplified further in the next section and in the descriptions in Exhibit 2.

Marginal Cost and Marginal Revenue

Total revenue and total cost are not suitable for evaluating changes in output.

The use of total revenue and total cost is a valid and practical way in which to determine the most profitable level of output for a firm. However, it is not the method that economists usually employ. They prefer to use an approach that may seem a bit strange at first but that is actually much more useful for understanding and interpreting *changes* in production and costs.

458

PART 6   THE ECONOMICS OF THE FIRM: HOW ARE PRICES AND OUTPUTS DETERMINED?

Exhibit 2

Cost and Revenue Curves of a Firm Under Perfect Competition*

Profit Maximization: Three Viewpoints

Figure (a). Total Curves The most profitable level of output is determined where the difference between curves TR and TC, as represented by the distance GH, is greatest. This occurs at an output of 8 units. At this output, a tangent to the TC curve, such as the tangent at H, is parallel to the straight-line TR curve. At smaller or larger outputs, such as 7 or 9 units, a tangent to the TC curve would not be parallel to the TR curve.

The break-even points are at B_1 and B_2, at which $TC = TR$. The break-even outputs are thus 5 units and 10 units.

Figure (b). Marginal Curves The most profitable level of output is the point at which $MC = MR$, as explained in the text. This can also be seen by following the vertical dashed line downward at 8 units of output.

The break-even points are at B_1 and B_2, at which $ATC = AR$.

Figure (c). Net Revenue Curve The most profitable level of output is the point at which the net revenue curve NR ($= TR - TC$) is at a maximum. The vertical dashed line at 8 units of output emphasizes these profit-maximizing principles in all three figures.

Technical Note (Optional) You should recall from high-school mathematics that parallel lines have equal slopes. Therefore, the most profitable output in the top figure is the one at which the *slope* (steepness) of the TC curve, measured by the slope of the straight-line tangent at H, equals the *slope* (steepness) of the TR curve. In the middle figure, marginal cost is the graph of the *slope* of total cost and marginal revenue is the graph of the *slope* of total revenue. Hence, at the level of maximum profit,

$$MC = MR$$

which is the same as saying that

slope of TC = slope of TR

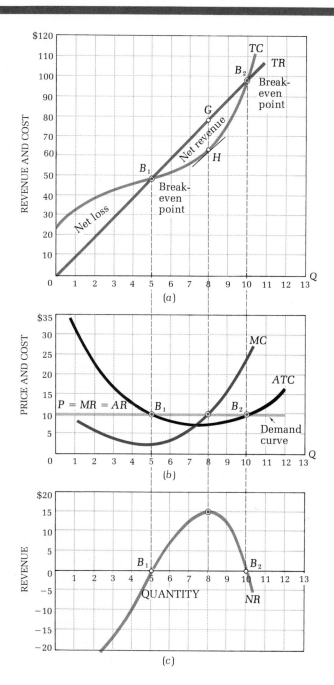

(a)

(b)

(c)

* The curves have been smoothed to enhance readability, so at some points they may not correspond precisely to the data in the table.

Referring back to the table in Exhibit 1, observe that column (5) gives average total cost and column (6) presents marginal cost. Column (7), however, has a new term, *marginal revenue* (*MR*). This is defined as the change in total revenue resulting from a unit change in output. Therefore, the formula for measuring marginal revenue is

$$MR = \frac{\text{change in } TR}{\text{change in } Q}$$

Marginal revenue is thus a concept exactly analogous to marginal cost.

What is the connection between slopes and "marginals"? As you know, the slope of a curve is the change in its vertical distance resulting from a unit change in its horizontal distance. Therefore, it should now be clear that *marginal cost measures the slope of a total cost curve, and marginal revenue measures the slope of a total revenue curve.*

Observe that the marginal revenue figures in column (7), namely $10, are precisely the same as the average revenue or price figures in column (3). Thus, $MR = AR = P$. This is no accident. If price remains constant while quantity increases, total revenue (which equals $P \times Q$) will have to increase by the amount of the price, and this amount of change will also be the same as marginal revenue. You can verify this relationship by experimenting with a few different numbers yourself.

Finally, note that columns (1) and (3) taken together constitute a *demand schedule*. This is because the two columns disclose the price per unit that buyers will pay (and the seller will receive) for various quantities of the commodity.

Now let us see how these data look in graphic form.

"Marginals" are simply slopes. They measure rates of change.

The demand curve facing a perfectly competitive firm is a perfectly elastic line at the market prices.

Graphic Illustration of Marginal Cost and Marginal Revenue

When the ATC, MC, and the $MR = AR$ data are graphed, the results are as shown in Figure (b) of Exhibit 2. The first thing to notice is that the horizontal revenue line at the price of $10 is a demand curve based on columns (1) and (3) of the table in Exhibit 1. Indeed, it is a *perfectly elastic demand curve*. Therefore, the curve is labeled $P = MR = AR$, to emphasize the fact that it represents price, marginal revenue, and average revenue—all at the same time. However, this is a special property that exists only under perfect competition. As you will see in subsequent chapters dealing with other types of competition, a different situation arises when the demand curve slopes downward instead of being horizontal.

Note For graphing purposes, you should recall from previous chapters that marginal values, in this case MC and MR, are plotted to the *midpoints* of the integers on the horizontal axis. This is because MC and MR reflect, respectively, the *change* in total cost and the *change* in total revenue resulting from a unit *change* in quantity. Notice also from the footnote in the exhibit that the curves have been smoothed. Therefore, some parts of the curves may differ slightly from the data in the table.

What is the firm's most profitable level of output? You already know that the answer is 8. But you can verify it further by extending the vertical dashed line at 8 units of output from Figure (a) in Exhibit 2 down to Figure (b) and then to Figure (c). This last figure shows the graph of net revenue NR from column (8) of the table. Figure (b), along with the other two supporting figures, reveals the operation of one of the most important principles in all of economics:

The most profitable level of output for a firm occurs where its $MC = MR$. This is a *general* principle that applies under all types of competition. Under the special case of perfect competition, however, it is also true that the most profitable level of output is the one at which $MC = MR = P = AR$, because the last three terms are one and the same. It is only at the output at which $MC = MR$ that a firm's net revenue, as measured by the difference between its total revenue and total cost, is greatest.

This $MC = MR$ rule is of such great importance that it may appropriately be called the *fundamental principle of profit maximization*. You may also verify the principle from the table in Exhibit 1. The demarcated section at 8 units of output shows that, when NR reaches a maximum of $15, MC rises from $8 to $14 while MR remains constant at $10. Thus, at 8 units of output, $MC = MR = \$10$. The figures in Exhibit 2, of course, reveal the relationships more clearly. You should study them and their accompanying explanations carefully.

Interpreting the $MC = MR$ Rule

The $MC = MR$ rule must be elaborated more fully. Why does the rule "work" as a guide for profit maximization? How does a firm react to the rule within the setting of a competitive market?

Part of the answer is given in Exhibit 3. In Figure (*a*), the market price at P and market output at N are determined by the intersection of the *total*-demand and *total*-supply curves, representing the interactions of many buyers and many sellers. In Figure (*b*), any individual seller finds that, by producing to the point at which $MC = MR$, the net revenue or profit is maximized. Also, the output measured by the distance 0J is an infinitesimal proportion of the industry's output measured in Figure (*a*) by the distance 0N. We may note this important principle:

Under perfect competition, each seller faces a perfectly elastic demand curve at the market price—for two reasons:

1. Because the product is homogeneous, buyers will purchase the commodity from the seller who offers it at the lowest price.

2. Because only an infinitesimal part of the total market is supplied by each seller, *all* of that seller's output can be sold at the going market price. The seller cannot sell any output for more than that price and has no reason to sell any of it for less.

Exhibit 3

An Industry and a Firm in a Perfectly Competitive Market

Figure (*a*): *A Perfectly Competitive Market with Many Buyers and Sellers.* The market price at P and market output at N are determined by the intersection of the *total* market demand and supply curves. The total market demand curve is downward-sloping, because the quantity demanded will be greater at lower prices.

Figure (*b*): *A Typical Firm in a Perfectly Competitive Market.* Each firm is confronted with a perfectly elastic demand curve at the market price. By producing at the point at which its $MC = MR$, this firm's most profitable output at J is an *infinitesimal fraction* of the industry's total output at N in Figure (*a*).

(**Note** The horizontal scales differ for the two figures.)

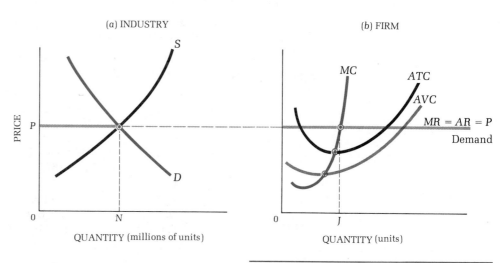

(a) INDUSTRY   (b) FIRM

A firm maximizes its profit at the output at which MC = MR.

Thus, at any output less than the output at J, each 1-unit increase in output adds more to total revenue than it adds to total cost. That is, MR exceeds MC, so it pays to expand production. Conversely, at any output greater than the output at J, each 1-unit decrease in output reduces total cost more than it reduces total revenue. That is, MC is greater than MR, so it pays to cut back production. Only at the point at which MC = MR do you find the most profitable output equal to the distance 0J. Hence, this MC = MR point may be called the seller's *equilibrium* position. It determines the profit-maximizing output that the firm will seek to achieve and maintain under the given market conditions and the company's existing cost curves.

This concept can be illustrated with a simple example. Suppose that you were a manufacturer of bicycles. You knew that by increasing your production by a specific amount you would raise your total revenue by $10 and your total cost by $8. In that case you would try to expand output and thereby increase net profit by $2. On the other hand, if you knew that by decreasing production by a given amount you would cut total cost by $15 and total revenue by $10, you would try to reduce output in order to increase net profit by $5. As a general rule, the only time you would not want to alter the production rate is when profits were already at a maximum. In that case the *changes* in TC and TR would be the same—which is the same as saying that MC would equal MR.

Analyzing Short-Run Equilibrium

What is the nature of the profit-maximizing or equilibrium position that the firm is trying to attain? Some of its important properties are illustrated by the figure in Exhibit 4.

First, note that the figure depicts the firm in short-run equilibrium. This means that, under the existing market conditions for the inputs the firm buys and the output it sells, and the given set of cost curves with which it operates, the most profitable output is at J. Why? Because at this output MC = MR for this particular firm. You will see later that in the long run certain market conditions, as well as the seller's cost curves, are likely to change. This will result in a different equilibrium position for the firm.

Next, you should verify that, at the most profitable level of output 0J, the following geometric cost and revenue conditions exist.

1. The average total cost of producing output 0J is represented by the vertical distance JK (= 0T).

2. The average revenue received from the sale of this output is the vertical distance JL (= 0U).

3. The difference between these two amounts, of course, is the net revenue per unit—that is, average net revenue—as represented by the vertical distance KL (= TU).

Therefore, the total net revenue, which can be found by multiplying the net revenue per unit by the number of units, is the area of the rectangle TULK.

The same result can also be arrived at in a different way. The average revenue per unit (JL) times the number of units (0J) equals total revenue, which is the area of the large rectangle 0ULJ. Similarly, average total cost (JK) times the number of units (0J) equals total cost or the area

Exhibit 4
Profit Maximization in the Short Run for a Perfectly Competitive Firm

At the output at which a firm's MC = MR, the area of its net-revenue rectangle TULK is greatest. This is the largest net-profit rectangle that can be drawn.

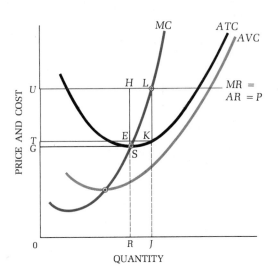

of the rectangle 0TKJ. Therefore, when you subtract the total-cost rectangle from the total-revenue rectangle, the difference is the net-revenue rectangle TULK.

Finally, it is important to observe that profits are maximized at the output at which $MC = MR$, even though this output may be beyond the point of minimum average total cost. Profit, in other words, is *not* maximized at output 0R, despite the lower average total cost of that output, namely RS. For by increasing output from 0R to 0J, the seller increases the net-revenue rectangle from GUHS to TULK. The rectangle thus gains the larger area EHLK while losing the smaller area GTES. In general, the output at which the largest net-profit rectangle can be drawn is determined by the point L, at which $MC = MR$, and by the corresponding point K on the ATC curve. Or, to put it differently, it can be proved mathematically that any other net-profit rectangle must of necessity be smaller than the one determined by points K and L. But this is equivalent to saying that the net-revenue curve reaches a maximum at the output at which $MC = MR$, which is a fact that you already know.

Deriving Supply Curves from Marginal-Cost Curves

When you first studied the operation of supply and demand, you learned that a supply curve expresses a relation between the price of a product and the amount that sellers would be willing and able to produce at each price. You are now in a position to see how a perfectly competitive firm's supply curve is actually derived, based on what you know about the $MC = MR$ rule.

Suppose that a firm in perfect competition is represented by the cost curves shown in Exhibit 5. If the market price of the product is at P_1, the firm will produce an output at N_1, because this is determined by the point at which MC is equal to MR_1. If the price falls to P_2, the firm will reduce its output to N_2, following its marginal-cost curve. At a price of P_3 it will produce the amount N_3. However, because this price is tangent to the firm's average total-cost curve at its minimum, the firm will not be earning a positive net revenue. Rather, its net revenue will be zero. This means that the firm is only normally profitable, because *average total cost includes normal profit.* Thus:

A perfectly competitive firm maximizes its profit by always adjusting its output so that it follows the marginal-cost curve.

Minimizing Short-Run Losses

What will the firm do if the price falls below P_3, say, to P_4? The answer is the same as before. The firm will decrease its output following its marginal cost curve, thus producing the amount at N_4. At this output the firm's net revenue will be negative; but the firm will be *minimizing its losses,* for the following reason.

In the short run, the firm has certain fixed costs, such as rent, property taxes, and utilities. It must continue to pay these expenses as long as it remains in business, regardless of how much it produces. Therefore, as long as the firm can get a price that is at least high enough to cover its average variable (or "out-of-pocket") costs, anything that it earns over and above this amount will go toward paying its fixed costs, which it is "stuck" with in any case.

![Exhibit 5 graph]

Exhibit 5

In Perfect Competition, a Firm's Supply Curve Is Its *MC* Curve Above Its *AVC*

The firm will always produce the quantity determined by the point at which $MC = MR$. Therefore, as the market price falls from P_1 to P_4, the firm reduces its output from N_1 to N_4, following its marginal cost curve. At P_4, the firm is just covering its average variable (out-of-pocket) costs and hence will remain in business in the short run. At a price below P_4, the firm will go out of business—as shown by the shutdown point.

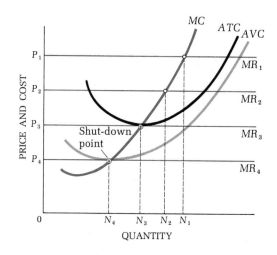

The MC = P (= MR) rule determines the
firm's supply curve. From this, the industry's supply curve can be easily derived.

As you can see, therefore, at any price above P_4, the firm will lose
less in the short run by operating and producing N_4 than by shutting
down—as would happen if the market price were to fall to, or below, the
shut-down point shown in the figure. In the long run, on the other
hand, the firm must receive a price at least high enough to cover all its
costs, including a normal profit, if it is to stay in business. The firm
must, in other words, cover its ATC in the long run.

We can now summarize these ideas in an important principle:

A perfectly competitive firm will produce the output determined by the
point at which $MC = P (= MR)$. The firm will thus increase or decrease its
output by following its marginal-cost curve. In this way the firm will maximize its profit (or minimize its loss).

This principle enables us to formulate two important propositions.

1. A perfectly competitive firm's supply curve is the same as its marginal-
cost curve above the level of average variable cost.

The reason is that the MC curve tells you how many units of the
good the firm will make available at various possible prices. This, however, is the meaning of a supply curve, as you will recall from your initial study of supply and demand. (You should refresh your understanding by looking up the definition of supply curve in the Dictionary at the
back of the book.)

2. The industry's supply curve is the horizontal sum of the firms' marginal-
cost curves above their levels of average variable cost.

In other words, you can derive a perfectly competitive industry's
supply curve by summing the quantities that firms will make available at
each price. This method, you should recall, was used to derive a total
market supply curve when you first studied supply and demand earlier
in this book.

Long-Run Equilibrium of a Firm and an Industry

You have seen that, in the short run, a firm in a perfectly competitive
industry may earn profits in excess of normal profits. Can this also happen in the long run? The answer is no, because the conditions that are
assumed in the definition of perfect competition prevent it from occurring. Let us see why.

The Adjustment Process

All firms in the industry adjust to long-run
equilibrium.

An industry is said to be in equilibrium—that is, in a state of "balance"
—when there is no tendency for it to expand or to contract. This means
that the least profitable firm in the industry, usually called the "marginal" (or borderline) firm, is only normally profitable.

For instance, if any firms in the industry are earning less than their
normal profit in the long run, then by definition of normal profit their
owners are receiving less than the least return they are willing to accept
on the basis of their opportunity costs. The owners will therefore leave
the industry, causing the industry supply curve to shift to the left and
the market price to rise. The firms suffering the greatest losses will shut
down first. The remaining firms will then become more profitable.
This exodus of firms will continue until the least profitable firm is just

normally profitable. When that happens, the industry will have no further tendency to contract.

The opposite situation occurs when the least profitable firm is earning more than normal profits. New firms will then be tempted to enter the industry to get a share of those profits. The industry will thus expand. That is, its total output will increase as the industry supply curve shifts to the right. At the same time, the market price will fall, thereby making existing firms less profitable. This entry of new firms will continue until the least profitable firm is just normally profitable, at which point the industry will have no further tendency to expand.

Graphic Illustration of Long-Run Equilibrium

The final adjustment to long-run equilibrium for every firm in perfect competition is illustrated in Exhibit 6. Each firm will have an average total cost curve and a corresponding marginal cost curve for each possible scale of plant. It follows that if some firms in the industry operate with optimum-size plants when the price is higher than the long-run equilibrium level, they will earn above-normal profits. This in turn will attract new firms into the industry. Market supply will increase, market price will fall, and supernormal profits will disappear. Firms with plants that are larger or smaller than the optimum size will thus suffer losses, whereas those with optimum-size plants will earn normal profits. Therefore:

> In perfectly competitive industries, firms have no choice of whether to build large-scale or small-scale plants. Firms in these industries must eventually build optimum-size plants if they are to survive in the long run.

The firm's optimum-size plant is thus ATC_3. Its long-run equilibrium price is at P, and the firm's rate of output is at N. These conditions are also true for every other firm in the industry. Thus, although Exhibit 6 represents a model of a single firm, a diagram similar to this could be made for each firm in the industry.

The Long-Run Industry Supply Curve

We now know enough about the operation of supply and demand in competitive markets to introduce a new concept pertaining to the long-run supply price of an industry.

Each of the diagrams in Exhibit 7 represents the supply and demand situation for a different industry. We assume, in each case, that the industry is in equilibrium at point E. This represents the intersection of the industry's supply and demand curves, thus defining the industry's equilibrium price and output. Remember that the long-run supply curve of an industry is made up of the individual supply curves of all its sellers. The problem now is to examine the nature of each industry's long-run supply curve or supply price.

Referring to the three diagrams, suppose that there is an increase (shift) in demand from D to D'. If the costs of the firms in the industry remain the same, the equilibrium point shifts from E to E'. This represents a higher market price and a larger market output than before. This expanded output occurs because firms that are already in the industry find it profitable to increase their production in response to the higher market price.

Exhibit 6

Long-Run Equilibrium for a Firm in Perfect Competition

At any given time, a firm may be represented by an ATC curve and a corresponding MC curve.

In the long run, competition will force each firm in the industry to end up with an optimum-size plant, such as ATC_3. At the optimum level of output for each firm, such as the output at N for this particular firm,

$$MC = P = MR = AR = ATC = LRAC$$

This equation defines the long-run conditions of equilibrium for every firm in a perfectly competitive market or industry.

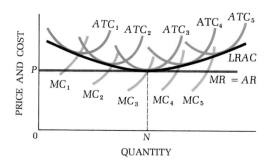

An industry's long-run supply curve may be constant, increasing, or decreasing.

Exhibit 7
Long-Run Supply Curves for Constant-, Increasing-, and Decreasing-Cost Industries

The immediate effect of an increase in demand from D to D' is to change the industry's equilibrium from the long-run point E to the short-run point E'. At this higher price, new firms will find it profitable to enter the industry and the supply curve will shift to the right until it reaches S'. The industry's final equilibrium will thus settle at the long-run point E''. *The long-run industry supply curve S_L is therefore defined as the locus or "path" of the industry's long-run equilibrium points.*

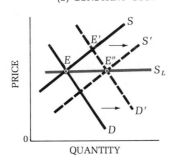

(a) CONSTANT COST

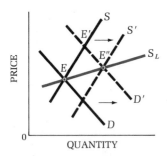

(b) INCREASING COST

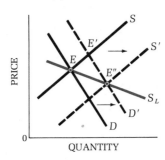

(c) DECREASING COST

The equilibrium at E', however, is likely to be of relatively short duration. This is because the higher and more profitable price will soon attract new firms into the industry. As this happens, the supply curve of the industry will shift to the right and the market price will be driven down along the D' curve until it is no longer profitable for new firms to enter the industry. The supply curve will ultimately settle at S', and the final equilibrium will be at E'', where the new supply and demand curves intersect. The point E'' represents the *long-run equilibrium* position of the industry.

This analysis suggests an important principle.

> If we connect each industry's initial and final long-run equilibrium points E and E'', we get the *long-run industry supply curve*, labeled S_L. This curve may be either horizontal, rising, or falling, depending on whether the industry is one of constant, increasing, or decreasing costs.

This principle requires an explanation of constant-cost, increasing-cost, and decreasing-cost industries.

Constant-Cost Industries

A *constant-cost industry* experiences no increases in resource prices or costs of production as new firms enter the industry. This tends to happen when an industry's demand for the resources it employs is an insignificant proportion of the total demand for those resources. In that case, new firms will be able to enter the industry and buy the labor, capital, and other inputs they need without bidding up the prices of these factors of production. The long-run industry supply curve will thus be perfectly elastic. Unspecialized resources (such as unskilled workers) that are in wide use by many industries are examples of such inputs. Janitors, retail-sales clerks, and office receptionists provide a few familiar illustrations.

Increasing-Cost Industries

An *increasing-cost industry* experiences rising resource prices and therefore increasing costs of production as new firms enter the industry. This happens because the industry's demand for resources is a significant proportion of the total demand. Therefore, any new firms must bid up the prices of the factors of production in order to acquire them from other firms. Specialized resources (such as skilled workers) provide examples of such inputs; their supplies are not readily expanded as the demand for them increases.

In general, increasing-cost industries are more common than constant-cost industries. This is especially true in our expanding scientific and technological age, in which firms must make growing use of highly specialized resources. The computer, electronic, and aircraft industries are a few prominent examples of increasing-cost industries.

Decreasing-Cost Industries

A *decreasing-cost industry* experiences declining resource prices and therefore falling costs of production as new firms enter the industry and the industry expands. This, of course, is not as common as the two previous cases. However, it could exist for a while as a result of substantial external economies of scale, as you have already learned. Can you think of some examples?

Understanding Equilibrium

The concept of equilibrium is as fundamental in economics as it is in other sciences. It is important, therefore, to understand the meaning of equilibrium in the context in which it has been used here. Once you have achieved this understanding, you will be able to evaluate the social consequences of perfect competition—its effects on society as a whole.

The Equilibrium Conditions

Look back at Exhibit 6 and note carefully the properties that characterize a perfectly competitive firm in long-run equilibrium. As you can see, these properties may be described succinctly by the equations

$$MC = P = MR = AR = ATC = LRAC$$

These equations are called *equilibrium conditions*. They constitute a set of relationships that define the equilibrium position of an economic entity—in this case, a firm in perfect competition. In certain advanced courses in economic theory, other sets of equilibrium conditions are studied—not only for firms, but also for households, and even for entire economies.

Our purpose is to analyze and interpret the meaning of the foregoing equations. In so doing, we will see some important results of perfect competition. You may find it helpful to refer back to Exhibit 6 while reading the following explanation. Keep in mind that these characteristics apply to *every* firm in the industry.

The equilibrium of an industry can be expressed succintly in terms of equations.

1. $MC = P$ This is an indicator of *economic efficiency*. It tells you that the additional cost of the resources used by the firm to produce the last unit of the product is just covered by the price that the firm receives. In other words, the value of the last unit of the good to the consumer (measured by the price he or she pays for the last unit, which is equal to the price paid for any other unit) is equal to the value of the resources used to produce that unit. Consequently:

The meaning of economic efficiency can be seen clearly in the equation MC = P.

> At a level of output at which $MC = P$, the firm's resources are being allocated to the product in precise accordance with consumer preferences. At any smaller output, MC is less than P. Therefore, resources are being underallocated relative to consumer preferences. At any larger output, MC is greater than P. Therefore, resources are being overallocated relative to consumer preferences. The $MC = P$ condition is thus a *standard of economic (allocative) efficiency*. It measures the extent to which the firm is making full utilization of its resources to fulfill the preferences of consumers, given their incomes.

2. $MC = MR$ This means that the firm is maximizing its profits and there is no incentive for it to alter its output. The firm is thus in short-run (as well as long-run) equilibrium.

The remaining equations disclose other characteristics of equilibrium.

3. $MR = AR (= P)$ This tells you that the firm is selling in a perfectly competitive market. As we shall see in the following chapters, any other type of market situation results in a firm's marginal revenue always being less than its average revenue or demand price.

4. $ATC = AR$ This says that the firm is earning only normal profits. Therefore, there is no incentive for other firms to enter or leave the industry.

5. MC = ATC This means that the firm is operating at the minimum point on its average total cost curve. Hence, the firm is combining the variable resources available to it with its given plant so as to produce at the least cost per unit.

6. MC = ATC = LRAC This tells you that the firm is producing the optimum output with the optimum-size plant. Therefore, the firm is allocating *all* its resources in a *technically efficient* manner.

These equilibrium conditions are at the heart of microeconomics. Their implications and importance will become increasingly evident in the following pages and chapters.

Economic Goals: Efficiency, Equity, Stability, Growth

What are the economic consequences of perfect competition? That is, to what extent does perfect competition fulfill society's four economic goals—efficiency, equity, stability, and growth? The question can be answered by distinguishing between the various favorable and unfavorable features of a perfectly competitive system.

Favorable Features of a Perfectly Competitive Price System

Perfect competition tends to lead to economic efficiency, depending on whether certain conditions are met.

The equilibrium conditions listed above serve as a basis for describing the favorable features of an economic system composed entirely of perfectly competitive markets. Such a system would yield certain beneficial consequences in long-run equilibrium:

1. Consumer preferences, as reflected in the marketplace, would be fulfilled with the largest amount of goods consistent with the minimum (average cost) prices and known production techniques of business firms.

2. Society's resources would be allocated in the most efficient way, both within and between industries.

3. Flexible factor and product prices would assure full employment of all resources.

4. Competition among employers for inputs and among factors for jobs would cause factor owners to be paid their opportunity costs. These would be determined by the market value of the respective contributions to total output of each factor.

5. With consumer incomes and tastes assumed to be constant, aggregate consumer satisfaction would be maximized because goods would be distributed among consumers according to their demands.

These desirable features of a perfectly competitive price system in long-run equilibrium, and other characteristics that we have not mentioned, can be formulated as theorems that are actually proved in more advanced theoretical discussions. For our purposes, however, it is sufficient that the favorable consequences be described as they are above so that they can be compared with the shortcomings discussed in the next section.

Unfavorable Features of Perfect Competition

Several undesirable consequences of a perfectly competitive price system were pointed out when we first studied the laws of supply and demand early in the book. At that time, you did not have a formal knowledge of the theory of perfect competition, nor did you know that it is the basis for supply-and-demand analysis. Now, however, you are in a better position to understand the shortcomings of perfect competition.

Perfect competition may fall short of achieving the goals of efficiency, equity, stability, and growth, depending on how the means of achieving them are implemented.

Incomplete Reflection of Consumer Desires

In a perfectly competitive system, sellers react only to those preferences that consumers register through their "dollar votes" in the marketplace. Consequently, this type of system does not measure the desire of consumers for "collective" or public goods, such as national defense, highways, parks, and unpolluted air and water.

Further, to the extent that incomes are unequally distributed, the competitive price system will reflect the dollar votes of the rich more than those of the poor. Charles Dickens portrayed this situation in *A Christmas Carol* (1843). As you may recall, Ebenezer Scrooge could buy milk for his cat that poor Bob Cratchit could not afford to buy for his frail, crippled son, Tiny Tim.

Inadequate Reflection of Social Welfare

A chemical company disposes of its waste products in a nearby lake. A steel mill's smoke permeates the air of a neighboring city. A drive-in theater discharges its patrons onto a highway at the end of a movie. In each of these and many other situations, two types of costs, called "private costs" and "social costs," are involved.

Private costs are the economic costs to a firm of performing a particular act. *Social costs* are the reductions in incomes or benefits that accrue to society as a result of a particular act. In the examples above, the social costs would include the suffering of the community due to water pollution, air pollution, and congested highways.

A similar distinction can be made in terms of benefits. If you get a good education, this act will lead to *private benefits* for you in the form of higher income. However, society will also incur *social benefits* because you will (ideally) become a more enlightened and informed citizen. Likewise, if you maintain an attractive lawn, your neighbors will be pleased. And if you bathe regularly, you are less likely to become a social outcast.

Of what significance are these distinctions between private and social benefits and costs? Because economics is a social science, a perfectly competitive price system must be evaluated in terms of its effects on society. As you know, competitive prices tend to reflect private costs and private benefits and may exclude some social costs and social benefits. Therefore, the equilibrium condition $MC = MR$ only guarantees maximum profit for a firm; it does not guarantee maximum welfare for society. To achieve the latter, the costs and benefits of production *to society* must be incorporated in firms' activities. To the extent that they are not, the $MC = MR$ condition fails to reflect the full effect of production on social welfare.

The $MC = MR$ condition may not reflect all of the effects of production on society.

This distinction between the private and social consequences of economic activities is important. It is discussed more fully in a number of other places in this book.

Insufficient Incentives for Progress

A third major criticism frequently leveled against a perfectly competitive system is that it dampens incentives to innovate and therefore retards economic progress. This happens because the typical firm in perfect competition is relatively small. Therefore, it is not likely to have access to the considerable financial resources needed to support the substantial research and development projects that often lead to major innovations. Further, even if a firm had the money to finance large-scale research, it would probably refrain from undertaking the needed capital investment because the innovation, if successful, would be adopted quickly by competing firms.

Life Under Perfect Competition—Dismal and Dull?

Deciding whether perfect competition is "good" or "bad" requires a value judgement.

What would it be like to live in a perfectly competitive world? Most of us might find it monotonous. For example:

Goods would be standardized in each industry and the range of consumer choices would be severely limited.

At the grocery store, bread would be just plain bread, and ketchup would likewise be just ketchup. The modern supermarket with its endless and colorful varieties of goods would cease to exist.

The choice of an automobile, like eggs in the dairy case, might be confined to "small," "medium," and "large." In all other respects, cars would be alike.

Because products in each industry would be homogeneous, there would clearly be no need for advertising (except perhaps for industry-wide or institutional advertising, such as "Eat more bread" or "Drink more milk"). Nor would there be any trademarks or brand names; and imaginative promotional campaigns, for good or evil, would be lost.

There would be no commercial television as we now know it, and newspapers and magazines would cost more.

In general:

In a world of perfect competition, consumers would know their alternatives. Therefore, the only type of advertising needed would be the kind that informs rather than persuades. There would be no need for anything other than, perhaps, classified advertising and the Sears, Roebuck catalog.

Conclusion—And a Look Forward

Is this the kind of world you want? You must answer for yourself. In economics, the most that can be done is to identify the alternatives and their probable consequences. As you have already seen, although a perfectly competitive economy would have various beneficial consequences, it would also have what many people would undoubtedly regard as undesirable features.

If the imaginary world of perfect competition is so unreal, why do we study it? Does it have any practical value? The answer is simple:

We do not learn about perfect competition in the vain hope of making it a reality. Instead, we study perfect competition because it provides us with a guide for evaluating and improving the real world of imperfect competition, which we shall analyze later.

Some further implications of the significance of perfect competition are pointed out in "Leaders in Economics," p. 471.

Leaders in Economics

Alfred Marshall
1842–1924
Synthesizer and Pioneer in Microeconomics

Historical Pictures Service

In the last quarter of the nineteenth century, there arose in Europe and America a system of economic thought known as the *neoclassical* school. One of the leaders of this school was Alfred Marshall, a British scholar whose landmark treatise, *Principles of Economics* (1890), will forever be regarded as a masterwork.

Marshall was born in London and educated at Cambridge University, where he majored in the classics and mathematics. "My acquaintance with economics," he once wrote, "started in 1867–1868. It commenced with reading John Stuart Mill and David Ricardo while I was still earning my living by teaching mathematics at Cambridge; and translating the doctrines into differential equations as far as they would go; and, as a rule, re-

jecting those which would not go."

Several decades later, John Maynard Keynes, himself a leading scholar and at one time a student of Marshall's at Cambridge, referred to his former teacher "as a scientist . . . who, within his own field, was the greatest in the world in a hundred years."

Major Contributions
Marshall's *Principles*, which went through eight editions, was a leading text in economics for several decades. Among the major contributions of this and other works by Marshall were the distinction between the short run and the long run, the extensive use of diagrams and models to describe economic behavior, and the equilibrium of price and output resulting from the interaction of supply and demand. Marshall also systematized the use of elasticity, the distinction between money cost and real cost, and many other ideas. In short, almost everything we read today pertaining to supply and demand analysis, equilibrium, and related notions was originally formulated precisely and definitively by Marshall. Few students today realize or appreciate the significant role that Marshall's ideas play in their economics education.

Although he was an adept mathematician, Marshall chose the less rigorous method of elementary geometric analysis because it served to make economic science a better "engine for discovery" in the investigation of specific problems. His approach to his predecessors was unusually conciliatory, and throughout his career he tended to phrase his own doctrines so as to minimize the change from the classical tradition. In contrast to the

earlier utility theorists, he did not take supply for granted but considered it as "the other blade of a pair of scissors." Underlying demand was marginal utility as reflected in the price offers of buyers. Underlying supply was marginal cost, reflected in the supply prices of sellers in the marketplace.

Ceteris Paribus
Marshall's preference for dealing with "one market at a time" rather than with "all markets simultaneously" is illustrated in typical fashion by his discussion of demand. Because the demand schedule related solely to the relationship between price and quantity demanded, other things must be held constant, or, as Marshall has it, "impounded in *ceteris paribus*" (Latin for "other things being equal"). Thus, the taste of consumers, their money incomes, the number of buyers, and the prices of other commodities are held constant in the discussion of the equilibrium determination of supply and demand. This procedure is still the accepted method of analyzing changes in demand.

Enduring Structure
By the time he retired from his professorship at Cambridge, Marshall had trained several generations of England's greatest economists. These disciples went on to assume major positions in universities and government service. Much has changed in economics since the eighth edition of *Principles of Economics* was published in 1920. However, these changes have for the most part been gradual. As a result, Marshall's neoclassical structure is still clearly identifiable today throughout the whole body of economic literature.

What You Have Learned in This Chapter

1. A perfectly competitive industry or market is characterized by many buyers and sellers engaged in the purchase and sale of a homogeneous commodity. Each buyer and seller has perfect knowledge of market prices and quantities, there is no discrimination, and there is perfect mobility of resources. Perfect competition is thus a theoretical extreme rather than a real-world phenomenon, although some of its features are roughly approximated in the organized commodity and stock markets.

2. In perfect competition, prices are established in the market through the interaction of many buyers and sellers. Each firm thus finds itself faced with a market price over which it has no influence. It cannot sell any of its output at a price that is the slightest bit above the market price. Because it can sell its entire output at the market price, there is no inducement for it to sell at any lower price.

3. In terms of costs and revenues, each firm's most profitable level of output is the level at which its marginal cost equals its marginal revenue. This is the output at which its total revenue minus its total cost is greatest.

4. In perfect competition, a firm's supply curve is its marginal cost curve above its average variable cost. The industry's short-run supply curve is thus derived by summing all the firm's marginal cost curves at each price above average variable cost. In the short run, a firm will operate as long as the market price is at least equal to its average variable (out-of-pocket) costs, since any price it gets over and above that will go to pay at least part of its fixed costs. In the long run, the firm will have to receive a price high enough to cover all costs, including a normal profit, if it is to remain in business.

5. In the long run, competition will force all firms to earn only normal profits and to operate with optimum-size plants. When this occurs, the industry as well as all firms in it will be in long-run equilibrium, with no tendency to expand or contract.

6. The industry's long-run supply curve connects all of its long-run supply-and-demand equilibrium points. The long-run supply curve may be constant (that is, perfectly elastic), increasing, or decreasing.

7. In long-run equilibrium, a perfectly competitive economy will have allocated its resources in the most efficient way so as to maximize consumer satisfactions. This is assured by the equations

$$MC = P = MR = AR = ATC = LRAC$$

If these equations are analyzed separately, they tell us that firms are maximizing their profits and making the most efficient use of their resources, given the distribution of consumers' incomes and tastes.

8. Among the favorable features of a perfectly competitive price system are the following:

(a) It fulfills consumer preferences with the largest amount of goods in the most efficient way.

(b) It allocates resources optimally and, as a result of flexible product and factor prices, tends to encourage full employment of all resources.

(c) It provides for factor payments at their opportunity costs as determined by their respective marginal productivities.

Among the unfavorable features are the following:

(a) It reflects consumer desires incompletely.

(b) It does not always measure social costs and social benefits.

(c) It provides insufficient incentives for economic progress.

For Discussion

1. *Terms and concepts to review:*
perfect competition
average revenue
total revenue
net revenue
break-even points
marginal revenue
long-run industry supply curve
constant-cost industry
increasing-cost industry
decreasing-cost industry
equilibrium conditions
private costs
social costs
private benefits
social benefits

2. What is the "fundamental principle of profit maximization"? Explain. What special application of this rule applies to perfect competition? Why?

3. Is the price of a product determined by its cost of production, or is the cost of production determined by the price?

4. If new firms enter an industry, they will compete for factors of production and thereby raise the prices of those factors. How will this affect the cost curves of firms in the industry? Discuss.

5. "The farmer must receive a living price for milk." Discuss this statement in terms of what you have learned in this chapter.

6. If you owned a shoestore and the shoes you carried cost you $40 per pair, would you stay in business if the highest price you could get for them were $40 per pair? Explain your answer in terms of this chapter.

7. The long-run history of the automobile industry reveals an enormous growth of output and a substantial reduction in real (inflation-adjusted) prices. How do you account for this, since we have usually assumed that larger outputs come only from higher prices?

8. Insert words in the following sentences to make them *true*. Do not delete any words. Underline your inserted words.
(a) A firm is in equilibrium when its costs and revenues are equal.
(b) A perfectly competitive firm is in equilibrium when it is producing at its minimum average cost.
(c) A perfectly competitive firm cannot earn supernormal profits.
(d) A perfectly competitive firm's supply curve is its marginal curve.

9. What are the "equilibrium conditions" for a perfectly competitive industry in long-run equilibrium? Explain their meaning.

10. "It is an indictment of our economic system that our country can spend more on such unimportant things as cosmetics or liquor than it spends on education." Evaluate this statement.

Our Farm Problem: A Case Study

This supplement surveys the economic problems of American agriculture—an industry that has certain features characteristic of perfect competition.

American society has staggered from crisis to crisis for more than a century. Although government has spent billions of dollars to alleviate farm problems, there have been few satisfactory solutions. Instead, politics has become intertwined with economics, resulting in public policies toward agriculture that have often impaired—rather than improved—the quest for efficiency, equity, stability, and growth.

The nature of the so-called "farm problem" is best understood by examining the underlying economics of agriculture as a whole.

Economics of Agriculture

The problems that farmers have traditionally faced stem largely from four conditions that characterize the agriculture sector: (1) price and income inelasticities, (2) highly competitive structure, (3) rapid technological change, and (4) resource immobility.

These conditions are not unique to American agriculture. They are prevalent in the industry in other advanced mixed economies, where they cause problems similar to those in the United States.

Price and Income Inelasticities

The demands for most farm products tend to be both price inelastic and income inelastic.

The demand for most farm products, including foods and fibers, is largely unresponsive to changes in price. As a result, people usually do not buy much larger quantities of farm commodities when their prices fall or much smaller quantities when their prices rise. In more technical terms, this means that *the demand for most agricultural goods is relatively inelastic (unresponsive) with respect to changes in price.*

The supply of most agricultural goods, especially within a given year, *is also relatively inelastic.* This is because production cannot be increased greatly in a single season. If prices are high, additional feed and fertilizer can be applied and land can be farmed more intensively. But the industry's "plant"—the land itself—cannot be expanded very much.

Agricultural products tend also to be income-inelastic in demand. The *income elasticity of demand* is the percentage change in the quantity of a good purchased resulting from a 1 percent change in income. For practically all farm food products, this elasticity is less than 1.0 —somewhere between 0.1 and 0.2. We may, therefore, expect a 10 percent rise in real disposable income per capita to cause only a 1 to 2 percent rise in the purchase of most agricultural food commodities.

Some Implications of Price and Income Inelasticities

Three important implications of these inelasticities should be noted.

1. Price inelasticities of demand and supply mean that small fluctuations in the output of farm products lead to large fluctuations in their prices.

2. Income inelasticity of demand means that total consumption of basic farm food products is limited largely by the rate of growth of total population. This characteristic holds in all wealthy nations. The proportion of any increase in income spent for food is always smaller in well-fed countries than in poorly fed ones.

3. As a result of both price and income inelasticities, increases in the rate of growth of farm production that exceed increases in the rate of growth of consumption will cause a downward trend in farm prices and in farmers' incomes. This has been the long-run trend in the United States. The effects are illustrated in Exhibit 1, which shows three variables:
   (a) An index of prices received by farmers for products sold.
   (b) An index of prices paid by farmers for products bought.
   (c) A parity ratio. This is simply an index of prices farmers receive divided by an index of prices paid. The parity ratio thus provides a measure of agriculture's economic well-being, as you will see shortly.

Exhibit 1
How Well-off Are Farmers?

The long-run trend of the parity ratio, expressed in decade averages, reached a peak in the 1940s (during World War II). This was because American farmers had to supply domestic agricultural needs as well as those of war-torn countries. Since the 1940s, the long-run trend of the parity ratio has been downward.

Note from Exhibit 1 that, since the 1940s, the long-run trend of the parity ratio has been downward. Despite this, however, farmers *as a group* are not as poor as the figures show—for three reasons:

Unreported Income A huge proportion of farmers' incomes—as much as 30 percent, according to some government estimates—comes from cash sales that are never reported for income tax purposes. More conservative estimates place the figure as low as 15 percent.

Future Capital Gains Farm property values have soared in recent decades. This increases farm owners' net worth—and eventually increases their income when capital gains (profits) are realized from sale of the property.

Tax Benefits Farm firms receive special privileges under our tax laws that are not granted to other businesses.

> For these reasons, *reported* farm income is not a true measure of farmers' economic well-being.

Highly Competitive Structure

Agriculture is characterized by numerous sellers (and buyers), homogeneous products, and relative ease of entry.

In addition to price and income inelasticities, a second major characteristic of American agriculture is competition. Here, competition means three things:

1. There are many farms in the United States—more than 2 million. As a result, virtually no single farm can influence the market price by deciding to sell or not to sell. (**Note** We say "virtually" because today there are some large farms that can exert an influence on the market price of certain commodities. This has been true only since the 1960s.)

2. Agricultural products are homogeneous—at least within broad categories. Grains, for example, are not branded products, and hence cannot be identified with the farm from which they came. Milk, meat, and produce may carry the name of a store or processor, but not usually the name of the producer. Agricultural products within each class are therefore highly substitutable, and each farmer is faced with a perfectly elastic demand curve at the market price for the goods sold.

3. As with many areas of retailing, there are few barriers to entering the agricultural industry. No licenses, union membership, or formal education are required. Anyone who wants to farm, and has a modest amount of capital, can get into the business—at least on a relatively small scale. (Large-scale farming, on the other hand, requires a considerable amount of capital.)

Rapid Technological Change

Our agricultural industry has experienced enormous technological changes in the past several decades.

American agriculture has made striking gains in productivity since 1930 —greater gains, indeed, than were made in the previous two centuries.

What has been the nature of these advances? They have consisted of the introduction of new seeds, fertilizers, and pesticides; of improved breeds of livestock and poultry; of improved feeds for farm animals; and of the mechanization and electrification of farming. These advances have gone hand-in-hand with the development of improved capital and

Exhibit 2
Farms and Farm Output

In the United States, over the long run, the farm population, the number of farms, and the labor input on farms have been decreasing, while the average size of farms, their total output, and their output per worker-hour have been increasing.

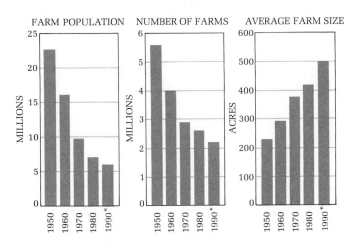

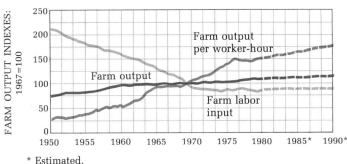

* Estimated.

Source: U.S. Departments of Agriculture and Commerce.

credit facilities and with the emergence of more technically trained and educated farmers—most of them graduates of land-grant colleges. Many of these gains have been fostered by government through special taxation and subsidization programs favorable to agriculture.

These changes have wrought profound social and economic effects, as illustrated in Exhibit 2. The farm population and the number of farms have dropped over the long run, while the average size of farms, their total output, and their output per worker-hour have steadily risen. However, improvements in agriculture have not been uniform. Many farmers are still poor because they lack the capital and knowledge to become efficient producers. This, as you will see, has been the traditional crux of the farm problem.

Resource Immobility

Although the number of farms and the number of farmworkers have been declining, there are still too many farmers on too many farms. Why should this be? Why has agriculture, which has experienced a long-run trend of declining prices and incomes relative to the rest of the economy, failed to reduce sufficiently its stock of human and nonhuman resources? Is not this failure contrary to what the laws of supply and demand would lead us to expect?

The fundamental difficulty is that agricultural resources are relatively immobile. Farmers and farmworkers, for example, cannot use many of their skills in other activities. Hence, they tend to remain in farming because it is the only type of work they know. Further, many of them prefer to make a modest living in rural areas rather than to seek better-paying work in the cities.

Box 1
Agriculture: A Declining Industry Responds to Adversity

The late nineteenth century saw the growth of big business and monopoly, the exaltation of commerce and the machine, and the first phase of a long-run decline of agriculture.

In the industrial sector, labor responded to its grievous loss of status by forming unions. The best known ones were the Knights of Labor and the American Federation of Labor. In the agricultural sector, farmers responded through the formation of the National Grange and the Farmers' Alliance. Both organizations worked to improve the economic position of farmers.

In several western states, the Grangers were successful in getting laws passed that set upper limits on railroad and warehouse charges and in persuading Congress and state legislatures to create regulatory commissions. Our federal Interstate Commerce Commission (established in 1887), charged with regulating railroads and subsequently trucks and other surface transportation, was initially the result of the Granger movement.

"Gift for the Grangers" was published in Cincinnati in 1873. It exalts the virtues of farmers and emphasizes their role as the "source" of society's wealth.

The Granger Collection

Newspaper cartoon (1873) of a farmer trying to rouse the public to the railroad menace. Railroads often engaged in economic discrimination against farmers, charging them as much as the traffic would bear instead of setting uniform rates based on distance.

The Granger Collection

Granger meeting in Illinois in 1873. The purpose of the meeting was to protest monopolies, tariffs on imports of manufactured goods, and low farm prices.

Recently, farmers expressed their economic dissatisfactions and demanded more government support by organizing tractor cavalcades to Washington.

Conclusion: Agriculture—A Declining Industry

In an advancing economy, the agricultural sector declines relative to the industrial sector.

The four major economic characteristics of agriculture—price and income inelasticities, a highly competitive structure, rapid technological change, and resource immobility—are universal in all developed countries. Such countries experience a special problem:

> As an economy grows in wealth, it devotes less of its total resources to agriculture, and more to manufacturing and services.

The reason is simple. In technologically advanced societies, farmers can produce enough not only for themselves and their families but also for many other people. In less developed countries, on the other hand, nearly everyone is forced to farm. Productivity is so low that farmers have little left to sell after growing food and fibers to feed and clothe themselves and their families. The *relative* magnitude of the agriculture resource base is thus smaller in rich societies than in poor ones, and this base is being constantly "squeezed" as the society grows. Agriculture then becomes a declining industry in a growing economy, with the *proportion* of total resources employed in agriculture continually contracting.

A brief pictorial history of American agriculture's response to such adversity is shown in Box 1.

Our Farm Policies

Several types of government policies designed to assist farmers have been in use for decades.

You can see from the information presented earlier in Exhibit 1 that prices paid by farmers have usually exceeded prices received. As a result, since the late 1920s, government has employed policies designed to improve farmers' real incomes and to stabilize prices. Three alternative approaches that have constituted the core of our farm policy have been price supports, crop restrictions, and direct payments. All of these have long been used, either separately or in combination, to reduce the effects of market adversities on farmers.

Price Supports

One way in which farmers can receive higher real incomes is for the government to maintain price supports for agricultural commodities. Such price supports are, in reality, price "floors," established at levels above those that would prevail in free markets.

The basic idea is illustrated in Exhibit 3. The diagram shows a situation at harvest time. Therefore, the demand curve *D* has a customary downward slope, whereas the supply curve *S* is vertical—*perfectly inelastic*. This indicates that the quantity supplied is fixed or unresponsive to changes in prices. The diagram demonstrates an important conclusion:

> Under a price-support program, consumers do not pay, nor do producers receive, the lower free-market equilibrium price at which there are no surpluses or shortages. Instead, consumers pay and producers receive the higher "parity-support price." This results in a surplus of the commodity that government must purchase, store, and administer.

A price-support policy of this type has existed for a variety of farm products since the 1930s. The program has at times been terminated for certain products and then reinstated because of political pressures from farm groups. In general, price supports have involved two major problems—selecting parity prices and disposing of continually mounting commodity surpluses.

Selecting Parity Prices

There is a story of a farmer who, during a television interview, was asked the meaning of parity. He replied: "If you could take a bushel of wheat to the market in 1912, sell it, and use the money to buy a shirt, then you ought to be able to do the same today. That's parity."

A dictionary will tell you that parity means the same thing as "equivalence." When applied to agriculture, therefore, a *parity price* is one that gives a commodity the same purchasing power, in terms of the goods that farmers buy, that it had in a previous base period. The period traditionally used has been 1910–1914 because it represents the "golden age of agriculture"—an era in which farmers prospered.

Over the years, the term "parity" also came to be used in a different sense to mean *parity ratio*. This, as you saw earlier in Exhibit 1, is the ratio of prices received to prices paid by farmers. It serves as an economic indicator of agricultural well-being. The parity ratio, whose components are updated from time to time, is calculated by the Department of Agriculture and is often quoted in the news media. A parity ratio of 80, for example, might be interpreted by some people to mean that the prices of farm products are 20 percent "too low." As a result, various farm programs are often proposed with the objective of raising farm commodity prices to 100 percent of parity, on the grounds that this would restore the fair economic status of agriculture.

Surplus Disposal

A price-support policy has, at various times, resulted in the accumulation by the government of huge surpluses—billions of bushels of wheat, millions of tons of feed grain, and so on. The costs to taxpayers, including the costs of acquisition, transportation, storage, losses on sales, and interest on investment, have amounted to many billions of dollars. To alleviate the pressure, government has sought ways to reduce accumulated surpluses. The most common methods have been:

1. Foreign dumping—the sale of foods and fibers abroad at much lower prices than at home.

2. Domestic dumping—the free distribution of foods to poor families and to charitable institutions.

3. Foreign aid—the donation of foods and fibers to countries in need.

4. Waste and spoilage—the willful destruction, or neglect and consequent deterioration, of large quantities of agricultural commodities in order to keep them out of commercial markets.

5. Industrial uses—the expenditure of much time and effort by government and businesses to find new industrial uses for food and fibers.

Have these methods of disposing of excess farm products been socially desirable? For the most part, they have not.

Exhibit 3
Price-Support Policy

At harvest time, the quantity supplied is already determined. Therefore, the supply curve S is "fixed" or perfectly inelastic—unresponsive to changes in price—while the demand curve D is downward-sloping.

The diagram shows how a price-support plan establishes a price floor at some level above the free-market equilibrium price. Consumers pay and producers receive the higher parity-support price, and the resulting surplus is purchased and stored by the government.

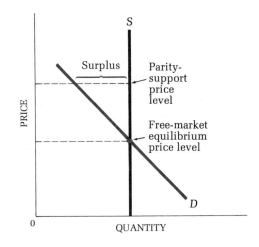

Exhibit 4
Crop-Restriction Policy

If government requires farmers to curb output, the supply curve at harvest time is not the free-market curve S but the restricted curve S'. As a result:

Total output is at M rather than N.

Price is at J rather than H.

Farmers' total revenue (equal to price times quantity) is the area of the larger rectangle 0JKM rather than the small one 0HLN.

(**Note** Remember that the demand curve for most farm products is relatively inelastic. Therefore, higher prices result in larger total revenues. You can see that, by raising the price from H to J, the gain in total revenue, HJKR, more than offsets the loss, MRLN.)

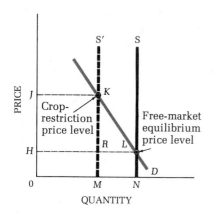

Informed observers generally agree that government has been inefficient in managing farm surpluses. Even foreign aid and domestic dumping, which may be desirable on humanistic grounds, frequently have been poorly administered. These practices, it is contended, should be adopted on their own merits instead of being made incidental to the disposal of surpluses resulting from inappropriate farm policies.

Crop Restriction

A second way in which agricultural prices might be raised above free-market levels—and agricultural incomes thereby improved—is for government to legislate restrictions on farm production. In that way, society gets less output and consumers pay higher prices. However, farmers receive larger total revenues because the demand for most agricultural goods is relatively inelastic. The basic idea is explained and illustrated in Exhibit 4.

At various times since the depression of the 1930s, government has attempted several methods of output restriction. The most important have been acreage curtailment, marketing quotas, and land retirement.

Acreage Curtailment

When farm surpluses accumulated in the past, government frequently sought to limit production by curtailing the amount of acreage that could be planted in particular crops. Surprisingly, however, such policies generally failed to reduce output significantly and often even increased it. The reasons are not hard to find. When farmers are required to reduce their volume of acreage, they retire their poorest land and retain their best. They then cultivate the land more intensively by utilizing additional labor and capital. In this way, they increase their yields per acre and often maintain, if not expand, their total output.

Marketing Quotas

Because acreage curtailment generally has not reduced output, it has been suggested that marketing quotas based on physical units would be a better method of control. Each farmer would be given certificates permitting the sale of a certain number of units of a commodity at the support price. Any production in excess of these legal quotas would be subject to high taxes.

Such marketing quotas existed for tobacco, cotton, and potatoes during the early 1930s. Similar plans have subsequently been proposed for other commodities. Congress, however, has rejected the idea under the pressure of middle- and upper-income farm groups who would be made worse off under such a scheme.

Land Retirement

Government has repeatedly tried, with little success, to reduce output by removing land from agricultural use. Unlike acreage curtailment, which may vary over the years, land retirement is usually fairly permanent. Many millions of acres of farm land have been retired as a result of the government purchasing and renting not only portions of farms but also entire farms.

Land retirement is convenient, it is cheaper than price supports, and it is easier to administer than production controls. However, it has had limited, and sometimes inverse, effects on output. This is because farmers usually sell or rent their poorest lands and increase their production on the superior land they retain. When the government retires land, therefore, it must do so on a scale large enough to avoid engaging in what would otherwise be a costly and largely self-defeating activity. Failure to do so will result in the government offering higher and higher purchase prices or rental fees in order to acquire the more productive land. The people who benefit from this government action are landowners, who are not usually farmers.

Direct Payments

A third way of protecting farmers from price declines while improving farm incomes is to adopt a system of *direct payments*. This plan would eliminate parity payments to farmers and allow the prices of agricultural products to be determined in a free market by supply and demand. Government would compensate farmers for the difference between the market price they receive and some higher target price established according to a selected base period in the past. The fundamental idea is illustrated and further explained in Exhibit 5.

Direct payments are not a new idea. They were introduced on a significant scale in the 1950s and have been expanded and contracted since then for a variety of basic farm products.

Are Direct Payments Good or Bad?

Under a direct-payments plan, market prices adjust freely to whatever levels are necessary to move the entire supply into consumption. As a result, the plan has the following favorable and unfavorable features.

On the positive side, the principal advantages are these:

1. It does away with the cost of storage as well as the wastes of destruction and spoilage.

2. It brings lower prices to consumers on the domestic market.

3. It eliminates the pressure for export dumping at low prices and the resulting resentment of foreign governments, who want to protect their own farmer's incomes.

4. It makes the farm subsidy visible, requiring it to be debated and voted upon periodically by Congress.

The principal disadvantages, on the other hand, are largely matters of costs. Direct payments are more costly to the government (and hence to the taxpayer) than price supports, because direct payments cover more commodities. These costs grow as production increases. Therefore, direct payments tend to lead to stricter production controls. Land, for example, can still be taken out of crop production if the Secretary of Agriculture determines that farm output is likely to be excessive.

In general, therefore:

> Under a system of direct payments, government subsidies to farmers are costly to taxpayers as long as free-market prices of farm commodities are below target prices. But if total (world) demand for farm goods increases to the point at which free-market prices are equal to or greater than target prices, no subsidies or direct payments are required. In that case, little land (if any) will be diverted from production, and the farm economy will be essentially a free-market economy.

Exhibit 5
Direct-Payments Policy

This plan permits consumers to pay the lower free-market equilibrium price and producers to receive the higher support or target price set by the government. The difference between the two prices is the distance *RT*. This distance times the number of units *RV* equals the area of rectangle *RTUV*. This area represents the total subsidy or direct government payments to farmers.

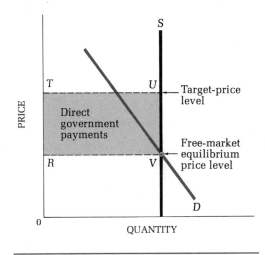

In reality, total world demand for farm crops is rarely high enough for sufficiently long periods to eliminate *all* direct payments. As a result, subsidies to farmers, some of whom are quite rich, continue to be considerable.

Conclusion: Efficiency and Equity

Our agricultural-assistance policies have contributed to resource misallocation and inequities.

The economics of agriculture is such that, in an advancing economy, the proportion of resources devoted to farming tends to decline. Although this has been the long-run trend, it has been retarded by our agricultural policies. These have inhibited rather than encouraged the orderly exodus of resources from the farm sector, thus impeding agriculture's adjustment to changing supply-and-demand conditions. The results have been distortions in the utilization of farm inputs and misallocations of productive resources—at considerable costs to society.

Our agricultural policies have also created inequities among farmers by doing relatively little to correct the fundamental problem of agricultural *poverty*. Thus, despite the long-run decline in the farm population, a substantial proportion of the people living on farms may be classified as "poor." They are concentrated mostly in the South—particularly in the Appalachians and in the Mississippi Valley. For these families, who consume most or all of what they produce rather than selling it, our farm policies have had relatively little effect. Instead, it is largely middle- and upper-income farmers—the ones who sell most of what they produce—who have benefited from government price- and income-support programs.

Box 2
Farm Policy: Political Economy or Economic Analysis?

Many people in Congress who participate in formulating agricultural policy have personal interests in the legislation that is drafted. For example:

• The family farm of former Senator James O. Eastland, a Mississippi Democrat who served on the Senate Agriculture Committee, at times received cotton-support payments averaging about $180,000 annually.

• Former Texas Representative W. R. Poage, who headed the House Agriculture Committee and was himself a farmer, benefited financially

James O. Eastland   World Wide Photos

W. R. Poage   World Wide Photos

from farm legislation. He once remarked: "It may be only a rationalization, but if you have—and I think you should have—people with the greatest familiarity with the situation, you get the benefit of the most knowledge. I also think that people [in Congress] who are directly involved in the truck business, the railroad business, and so forth ought to be on the committees writing transportation legislation."

For these reasons, it is easy to see that the task of formulating a sound agricultural policy may be more a problem of *political economy* than of economic analysis.

Despite these facts, our agricultural policies have been promoted as measures aimed at helping *all* farmers on the grounds that they are all poor. In reality, only *some* farmers are poor; others are actually quite well off. The latter, however, are the ones who dominate agricultural organizations and political-pressure groups. This explains why Congress has done little to correct the inequities that our farm policies have created. (See Box 2.)

Solution: Subsidize Exodus

It is clear, therefore, that new policies are needed to correct imbalances existing in the agricultural sector. The long-run trend of American farm exports is increasing as the world demand for food continues to rise. Nevertheless, there is no reason to believe that the growing volume of exports will be sufficient to solve our *long-run* agricultural problem— that of *reducing the proportion of resources on farms*. To do this we need a different strategy, as the following conclusion suggests:

> The solution to our farm problem is not to provide price supports or income-maintenance programs that keep agricultural resource owners where they are. The solution is to *subsidize them to get out and relocate*. It would be cheaper and healthier for agriculture, and for the economy as a whole, if the government would spend money this way instead of continuing costly programs that serve to protect an artificially large agricultural sector.

What You Have Learned in This Supplement

1. Agriculture in the United States is characterized by (a) products that are price-inelastic and income-inelastic in demand, (b) a highly competitive structure, (c) rapid technological change, and (d) resource immobility. These characteristics mean that small fluctuations in output lead to large fluctuations in prices. Further, as the economy grows, the proportion of its total resources that it devotes to agriculture declines and the proportion that it devotes to manufacturing and services increases.

2. For many decades, prices paid by farmers have usually exceeded prices received. As a result, since the late 1920s, government has employed various policies designed to improve farmers' real incomes and to stabilize prices. Three major policies that have long been in use, separately or in combination, are price supports, crop restrictions, and direct payments.

3. Our agricultural policies have had several adverse effects. Among them:
(a) The orderly exodus of resources out of agriculture has been inhibited rather than enhanced, thereby impeding the farm sector's adjustment to changing supply and demand conditions;

(b) The policies have created inequities that have largely benefited middle- and upper-income farmers while doing relatively little or even nothing for poor ones. Society has thus borne the costs of policies that have proved to be inefficient and inequitable for agriculture as a whole.

4. Despite the world food shortages that occur from time to time, America's *long-run* agricultural problem is to reduce the proportion of resources on farms. This can best be done by subsidizing farmers to leave agriculture rather than "paying" them (through price supports or income-maintenance programs) to remain in it.

For Discussion

1. *Terms and concepts to review:*
income elasticity of demand
parity price
parity ratio
direct payments

2. "The aggregate demand for agricultural products is relatively inelastic. Over the long run, aggregate demand has not increased as fast as aggregate supply. Hence, the pressure on prices has generally been downward." Illustrate this proposition graphically.

3. "Agricultural products are relatively inelastic in demand, whereas many manufactured goods are relatively elastic in demand. Therefore, a technological improvement in agriculture that results in a price reduction will bring about a decrease in the total revenue received by farmers. On the other hand, a technological improvement in manufacturing that results in a price reduction will often bring about an increase in the total revenue received by producers. This helps to explain why agriculture must decline in a technologically advancing society." Illustrate this proposition with the use of demand curves.

4. "The demand for agricultural products is such that small increases in output resulting from improved technology result in relatively large decreases in price and income (that is, total revenue)." What type of elasticity is indicated in this statement? Illustrate your answer with a demand curve.

5. Which is likely to have the most favorable effect on agriculture as a whole: a 10 percent decrease in farm prices, a 10 percent increase in real disposable personal income, or a 10 percent increase in population? Explain.

6. "It is only humanitarian to help the poor. Therefore, we should help farmers because they are poor." Do you agree? Explain.

7. "The government should accumulate stockpiles of agricultural goods when crops are plentiful and sell the goods when crops are scarce. This would help stabilize farm prices and incomes without discouraging production." Discuss.

Monopoly Behavior: The Other End of the Spectrum

Learning guide

Watch for the answers to these important questions

What is the meaning of monopoly? How does monopoly come about? Are there different types of monopolies?

How does a monopoly, seeking to maximize profit, determine its price and output? What fundamental rule of profit maximization does the monopoly follow? Why is a monopoly's marginal revenue not the same as its price? Why is its marginal cost not the same as its supply?

What criticisms may be leveled against monopoly? How does monopoly behavior affect society's economic goals?

How is price discrimination defined? Are there different types of price discrimination? What conditions are necessary for effective price discrimination? Is price discrimination legal?

Market structures are usually classified into several categories. Each of these categories may be regarded as occupying a position along a spectrum. Up to now we have studied only the market structure called perfect competition, which may be visualized at the left end of the competitive spectrum:

This chapter explains the economics of monopoly—a type of market structure characterized by the absence of competition.

Perfect competition	Pure monopoly

In this chapter you will turn your attention to the extreme opposite of perfect competition—pure monopoly. You will find that this type of market structure is, like perfect competition, a theoretical extreme and that it is virtually nonexistent in its pure (unregulated) form.

Does this mean that the study of monopoly is impractical, or even useless? The answer is *no*. The theory of monopoly provides many useful tools and concepts for understanding the behavior of actual business firms. Against this background, the next chapter will show how the features of perfect competition and monopoly can be combined. This will help to explain the competitive behavior of firms in the real world. For the time being, this "real" world is represented by the blank space in the spectrum above.

The Meaning and Types of Monopoly

What is meant by the term *monopoly*? How do monopolies come into existence? What conditions must prevail in order for monopolies to survive? How does a monopolist determine price and output? What is wrong with monopoly, and what can be done about it?

The answers to these questions constitute the basic aspects of the study of monopoly.

What Is Monopoly?

A monopoly's product is unique because it has no close substitutes.

A *monopoly* is defined as a single firm producing a product for which there are no close substitutes. This means that no other firms produce a similar product. Hence, the monopoly firm constitutes the entire industry and is thus a "pure" monopoly. A buyer who wants this particular product must either buy it from the monopolist or do without it.

Pure monopolies are relatively rare, but they do exist. The electric, gas, and water companies in your locality are good examples, since each produces a product for which there are no close substitutes.

Can a firm's degree of monopoly vary from one market to another? The answer is *yes*. For instance, the electric company has a monopoly in the production of electricity for lighting purposes, but for heating purposes its electricity may compete with gas, coal, and fuel oil sold by other producers. An electric company may thus be a pure monopoly in the lighting market but a "partial" monopoly in the heating market, in the sense that it faces some degree of competition from sellers of reasonably adequate substitute goods. Similarly, railroads, bus companies, taxi companies, and airlines are not pure monopolies, but they are certainly partial monopolies, depending on the extent to which buyers can substitute the products of these industries in meeting their transportation needs.

In view of this, most firms in our economy, as we shall see, may be characterized as "partial monopolies." In this chapter we shall develop a theory of pure monopoly. Many of its principles and conclusions, however, are applicable to partial monopolies as well.

Sources and Types of Monopoly

Monopolies may arise in different ways.

What are the origins of monopoly, and why do monopolies continue to exist? There are several possible explanations, all of which amount, in one form or another, to "obstacles to entry." These are economic, legal, or technical barriers that permit a firm to monopolize an industry and prevent new firms from entering. These obstacles give rise to the following common types of monopolies, which are not mutually exclusive. That is, a monopoly firm may fall into more than one category.

Natural Monopoly

A *natural monopoly* is a firm that experiences increasing economies of scale—long-run decreasing average costs of production—over a wide range of output. This enables the firm to supply the entire market at a lower unit cost than two or more firms could do. Electric companies, gas companies, and railroads are classic examples of natural monopolies. The technology of these public utilities is such that, once the heavy fixed-cost facilities are established (such as power generators, gas transmission lines, or railroad tracks and terminals), additional customer service reduces average total costs over a wide range of output. This permits the construction of more optimum-size plants, which lowers long-run average costs.

Legal and Government Monopolies

In some industries, unrestricted competition among firms may be deemed undesirable by society. In such cases, government grants one firm in an industry an exclusive right to operate—a status of *legal monopoly*. In return for this, government may also impose standards and requirements pertaining to the quantity and quality of output, geographic areas of operation, and the prices or rates that are charged. Investor-owned or privately held (as distinguished from governmentally owned) public utilities are typical examples of legal monopolies.

Some monopolies are privately owned and governmentally regulated. Some are both governmentally owned and governmentally regulated.

The justification of legal monopoly is based on judicial opinions handed down over many decades by the courts. These opinions have held that a "business affected with a public interest" may qualify as a public utility (and therefore a legal monopoly) because the welfare of the entire community is directly dependent on the manner in which the business is operated.

In some states the result of this vague definition has been the establishment of numerous types of businesses as public utilities. Some familiar examples are water, gas, electricity, telephone, and telegraph companies, as well as common carriers of all kinds. Other, less familiar examples are bridges, warehouses, cemeteries, gristmills, sawmills, grain elevators, stockyards, hotels, docks, cotton gins, refrigeration plants, markets, and news services.

Whereas legal monopolies are privately owned but governmentally regulated, there are other monopolies that are both owned and regulated by the federal or local government. These are called *government monopolies*. Examples are the U.S. Postal Service, the water and sewer systems of almost all local municipalities, the electric power plants of many cities, and the central banks of most countries.

Strategic-Resource Monopoly

A firm that has gained control of an essential input to an important production process is said to have a *strategic-resource monopoly*. The possibility of this happening, however, is extremely remote. One of the very few examples is the International Nickel Company of Canada, which at one time owned almost the entire known world supply of nickel. Another illustration is the De Beers Company of South Africa, which once owned almost all of the world's diamond mines but today owns a substantially smaller share.

Patent Monopoly

A *patent monopoly* is a firm upon which government has conferred the exclusive right—through issuance of a patent—to make, use, or vend its own invention or discovery. A patent therefore enables a firm to profit from its invention while preventing its adoption by competitors. Several decades ago, the National Cash Register Company and the United Shoe Machinery Company each held a series of patents on their line of products. These patents enabled them to monopolize their respective industries for many years. Today, IBM, Xerox, Polaroid, and others have varying degrees of monopoly power through patent protection.

Over the years, these companies have lost a good deal of their monopoly power, owing to product innovations by competitors.

As these examples suggest, a patent gives one an exclusive right to produce a specifically defined product, but it does not preclude others from producing a closely related substitute good. For example, Xerox Corporation has the exclusive right to produce copiers that function in a particular way, as described in the patents they hold. However, a number of other firms produce competing copying machines. Thus, though patents sometimes enable firms to establish pure monopolies, more often they only provide partial monopolies.

Price and Output Determination

You learned in the study of perfect competition that sellers in a perfectly competitive industry have no influence over the price at which they can sell their output. Each is faced with a perfectly elastic demand curve at the market price, and each maximizes profit by producing the output at which $MC = MR (= P)$.

A pure monopolist is in a different situation. Because the monopoly constitutes the *entire* industry rather than just a small part of it, the monopolist can exercise complete control over the price at which output is sold. The monopolist will thus find that more of the product can be sold at a lower price than at a higher one. This means that the market demand curve for the product will be less than perfectly elastic. *The market demand curve will slope downward instead of being horizontal.* On the other hand, we may assume that the *shapes* (curvatures) of the monopoly's production function and cost curves are similar to those studied in previous chapters. This is because both the variable and fixed factors must be purchased in the input markets and then combined in order to produce a product. These activities are subject to the same laws of production and cost as those of any other seller.

Cost and Revenue Schedules

The cost and revenue data of a monopoly, illustrating the ideas discussed above, are shown in Exhibit 1. It should be apparent from this table that columns (1) and (2) actually compose the demand schedule facing the monopolist. Note that average revenue (= price) is inversely related to quantity. This means that, *in order to sell more units of a product, the monopolist must charge a lower price per unit for all units sold.*

Because the average revenue or price varies inversely with quantity, total revenue rises to a maximum and then begins to fall. The changes in total revenue, as always, are reflected by marginal revenue [column (7)]. These figures turn out to be different from average revenue because of the changes in price.

The cost schedules in the table are those used in the previous chapter for a perfectly competitive firm. This is because, as already noted, we are assuming that the *shapes* or curvatures of the monopolist's cost curves are similar to those of any other seller. Besides, by using the same cost data, we shall be able to see more clearly that the chief differences between the two firms originate in the output market where goods are sold, rather than in the input market where factors are bought.

Exhibit 1
Cost and Revenue Schedules of a Monopoly

(1) Quantity per day, Q (given)	(2) Average revenue or price, AR = P (given)	(3) Total revenue, TR (1) × (2)	(4) Total cost, TC	(5) Average total cost, ATC (4) ÷ (1)	(6) Marginal cost, MC Change in (4)/Change in (1)	(7) Marginal revenue, MR Change in (3)/Change in (1)	(8) Net revenue, NR (3) − (4)
0	$16	$ 0	$ 25	$ —			−$25
					$10	$15	
1	15	15	35	35.00			− 20
					6	13	
2	14	28	41	20.50			− 13
					4	11	
3	13	39	45	15.00			− 6
					2	9	
4	12	48	47	11.75			1
					2	7	
5	11	55	49	9.80			6
					3 ←— $4 —→	5	
6	10	60	52	8.67			8
					5	3	
7	9	63	57	8.14			6
					8	1	
8	8	64	65	8.13			− 1
					14	−1	
9	7	63	79	8.78			− 16
					21	−3	
10	6	60	100	10.00			− 40

A look at the table shows that the fundamental principle of profit maximization still holds. The monopolist's most profitable level of output—the output at which net revenue [column (8)] is a maximum—is at 6 units, which is also where $MC = MR = \$4$. Why is this so? Because as you learned in the previous chapter, at any output less than this, the added cost of an additional unit is less than the added revenue. Therefore, it pays to increase production. At any output greater than this, the opposite is true. Only where $MC = MR$ is the firm's output at its most profitable level.

A monopoly's profits are maximized at the price and output at which MC = MR.

Looking at the Graphs

You can visualize these ideas more easily by examining the graphs of the cost and revenue schedules rather than the data. In Exhibit 2, the monopolist's total-revenue and total-cost curves are shown in Figure (a), the appropriate average and marginal curves in Figure (b), and the net-revenue curve in Figure (c). The vertical dashed line that passes through all three figures emphasizes the fact that, at the most profitable level of output:

1. $TR - TC$ is greatest.
2. $MC = MR$, since the tangents to TC and TR are parallel.
3. NR is greatest.

Note also in the middle figure that the average-revenue or demand curve facing the monopolist slopes downward, which was not the case for a perfectly competitive seller. As explained earlier, this means that, in order to sell more units of a product, the monopolist must charge a lower price per unit for *all* units sold. Since the AR curve is downward-sloping, the MR curve lies below the AR curve because of the *average–marginal relationship,* as you learned in a previous chapter. You can verify this for yourself by experimenting with a few prices and quantities on your own and then sketching their graphs.

Exhibit 2
Cost and Revenue Curves
of a Monopoly*

Profit Maximization: Three Viewpoints

Figure (a): Total Curves The most profitable level of output is determined where the difference between the curves TR and TC, as represented by the distance GH, is greatest. This occurs at an output of 6 units. At this output, a tangent to the TR curve is parallel to a tangent to the TC curve, as at G and H. At smaller or larger outputs, such as 5 or 7 units, the tangents would not be parallel.

Figure (b): Marginal Curves The most profitable level of output is determined where $MC = MR$, as explained in the text. You can verify this by simply following the vertical dashed line downward at 6 units of output.

Figure (c): Net-Revenue Curve The most profitable level of output is determined where the net-revenue curve NR ($= TR - TC$) is at its highest point. The vertical dashed line emphasizes these profit-maximizing principles in all three figures.

Technical Note (Optional) If you like to think in geometric terms, remember that parallel lines have equal slopes or steepness. Hence, the most profitable output in the top chart is determined where the *slopes* of the TC and TR curves are equal, which is where the tangents are parallel. In the middle figure, marginal cost is the graph of the *slope* of total cost, and marginal revenue is the graph of the *slope* of total revenue. Therefore, it is true that, at the level of maximum profit,

$$MC = MR$$

or, equivalently,

$$\text{slope of } TC = \text{slope of } TR$$

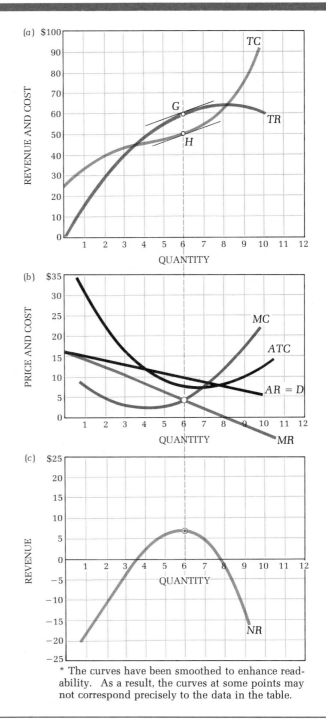

* The curves have been smoothed to enhance readability. As a result, the curves at some points may not correspond precisely to the data in the table.

Note For graphing purposes, you should recall from previous chapters that the MC and MR curves are plotted to the *midpoints* between the integers on the horizontal axis. This is because they reflect, respectively, the *change* in total cost and in total revenue resulting from a unit *change* in output. Notice also, from the footnote to the exhibit, that the curves have been smoothed. Therefore, some parts of the curves may differ slightly from the data in the table.

Using the MC = MR Principle

We must examine the profit-maximizing behavior of a monopoly more closely so that we are in a better position to evaluate the consequences of its actions. Let us therefore analyze its performance in terms of the fundamental $MC = MR$ principle, which is illustrated by the figures in Exhibit 3.

In Figure (a), the monopoly finds that the $MC = MR$ rule leads it to produce the output at N. At this output, the demand curve indicates that the highest price that can be charged is NG (= 0P). Total profit, or net revenue, is thus the area of the shaded rectangle in the figure.

In Figure (b), the monopoly's costs are relatively high compared to its revenues. This may be due to an increase in the prices of the monopoly's factors of production (which causes its cost curves to shift upward), or to a decrease in demand for its output (which causes its revenue curves to shift downward), or to both. Thus, at the $MC = MR$ output, namely N, the corresponding price P is just high enough to yield a normal profit. Because the ATC curve is tangent to the AR curve at this output, the monopolist knows that any other level of production would yield losses because ATC would be greater than AR.

In Figure (c), the monopoly's ATC curve is everywhere higher than its AR curve. As before, this can be the result of an increase in costs, a decrease in demand, or both. Thus, at least for the short run, the $MC = MR$ rule still prevails because the output N and the corresponding price P *will minimize losses*. That is, any other price and output will yield a larger loss area than the shaded rectangle in the figure.

You can see from these types of problems that it is essential to sketch correctly both average-revenue and marginal-revenue curves. Therefore, here is a convenient geometric rule to remember when the curves are straight lines (as they usually are):

> *An MR curve always bisects any horizontal line drawn from the vertical axis to the AR curve. Thus, in Figure (a), the distance PW = WG, and similarly for any other horizontal line that may be drawn.*

This rule is based on a theorem that we shall not prove here. However, you can easily verify it for yourself by constructing your own tables and plotting the graphs. Actually, all that this rule means is that, *at any given price, an MR curve is twice as steep as (or has twice the slope of) its corresponding AR curve.*

Marginal Revenue Is Not Price; Marginal Cost Is Not Supply

You are now in a position to discover an important distinction between a monopoly firm and a perfectly competitive firm. When you studied the theory of perfect competition, you learned that the seller's marginal-revenue curve and average-revenue (= price) or demand curve were the same. You also learned that the marginal-cost curve was the supply curve above the level of minimum average variable cost. Do these conditions also apply to a monopolist? The answer is *no*. You can verify this from the cost and revenue schedules shown earlier in Exhibit 1 and the figures in Exhibit 3.

Exhibit 3
Three Possible Profit Positions for a Monopolist

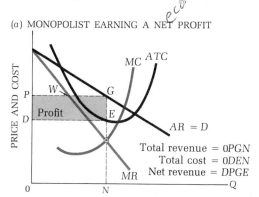

(a) MONOPOLIST EARNING A NET PROFIT

Total revenue = 0PGN
Total cost = 0DEN
Net revenue = DPGE

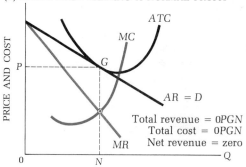

(b) MONOPOLIST EARNING A NORMAL PROFIT

Total revenue = 0PGN
Total cost = 0PGN
Net revenue = zero

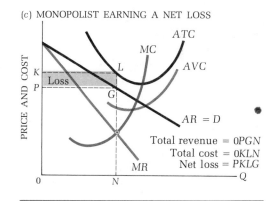

(c) MONOPOLIST EARNING A NET LOSS

Total revenue = 0PGN
Total cost = 0KLN
Net loss = PKLG

Exhibit 4
No Supply Curve for a Firm with a Downward-Sloping Demand Curve

For any given marginal-cost curve, the most profitable price and output depend on the firm's particular average-revenue curve and its corresponding marginal-revenue curve. Thus, in Figure (a), the single output at N corresponds to the two prices at P and at S. In Figure (b), the two outputs at N and at L correspond to the single price at K. This suggests the following principle:

A firm faced with a downward-sloping (or less than perfectly elastic) demand curve has no supply curve. This is because there is no single quantity that the firm will necessarily supply at a given price and no single price at which the firm will necessarily supply a given quantity.

(a) SINGLE OUTPUT AT MULTIPLE PRICES

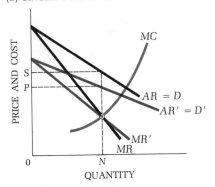

(b) MULTIPLE OUTPUTS AT A SINGLE PRICE

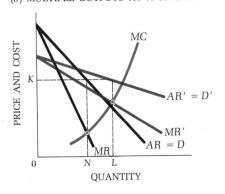

When a seller's demand (AR) curve is downward-sloping:

1. Marginal revenue falls faster than average revenue (= price) or demand. Thus, *marginal revenue is not price.*

2. The most profitable level of output for the seller and the most profitable price that can be charged for that output are determined by $MC = MR$, not by $MC = AR (= P)$. Thus, *marginal cost is not supply.*

The reasons for these differences between price and output determination by a monopolist as compared to a perfectly competitive seller are explained further in Exhibit 4. Each diagram compares a given MC curve of a monopolist with two arbitrarily different demand or AR curves and their corresponding MR curves. A study of these diagrams and the accompanying analysis leads to the conclusion that *a less than perfectly competitive firm has no supply curve.*

In view of this, is it possible to conclude that, strictly speaking, prices are determined by supply and demand *only* under perfect competition? You will have an opportunity to discuss this important question in a problem at the end of this chapter.

Do Monopolies Earn "Large" Profits?

You now know enough about the behavior of a monopoly to draw three important conclusions about monopoly pricing:

1. The price charged by an unregulated monopoly is not, as Adam Smith once remarked, "the highest which can be got." This fact may surprise many people. Instead, the monopoly's price is the highest that is consistent with maximizing profits. For instance, the monopoly of Exhibit 3, Figure (a), could produce somewhat less than N and charge a price higher than P. Then, as long as its ATC did not exceed its AR, the firm would still make a profit, but it obviously would not make the maximum profit possible.

2. A pure monopoly does not necessarily receive "high" profits just because it is a monopoly. In fact, if its profits are relatively high, the monopoly may find that the owners of some of its factors of production, for example workers or landlords, will absorb part of the surplus by demanding larger payments. This will cause the monopoly's ATC curve to rise, possibly to the point at which the firm is earning a "small" profit or perhaps only a normal profit. This is shown in Exhibit 3, Figure (b).

3. In the short run, a monopoly may earn less than a normal profit and still remain in business. This is the situation depicted in Exhibit 3, Figure (c). In the long run, however, the monopoly would have to earn at least a normal profit to continue in operation.

Thus, having a pure monopoly does not in itself assure extraordinary profit, although a monopoly is likely to be more profitable than a perfectly competitive firm. A monopolist is faced with certain market restraints that affect decisions about price and output. The ability of the monopolist to cope with these restraints will affect the profitability of the firm. By adhering to the $MC = MR$ principle, the monopolist will always maximize profits (or minimize losses). However, the $MC = MR$ principle in itself does not guarantee that those profits will be large (or that losses will be small).

Evaluating Monopoly: What's Wrong with It?

You have probably heard that monopoly is "bad," but may not know exactly why. Now, however, on the basis of what you have learned from economic analysis, you can give some significant reasons.

Efficiency: It Misallocates Resources

The basic economic criticism of pure monopoly is this:

> A monopoly adheres to the $MC = MR$ principle of profit maximization. Therefore, a monopoly misallocates society's resources by restricting output and charging a higher price than it would if it followed the $MC = P$ standard of perfect competition.

This basic criticism embodies the following fundamental ideas, all of which are best understood in terms of Exhibit 5.

Monopoly Price: $MC = MR$

In seeking to maximize profit, the monopoly produces the equilibrium output at Q and charges the equilibrium price QJ. The latter is called the *monopoly price* because it is determined by the intersection of the MC and MR curves. Note that this price is greater than the monopoly's marginal cost at that output. Therefore: *The value of the last unit to the marginal user (measured by the price he or she pays for the last unit, which is equal to the price paid for any other unit) is greater than the value of the resources used to produce that unit.* In other words, because $MC < P$, society is not getting as much of the good as it wants in relation to the resources sacrificed to produce the good.

Marginal-Cost Price: $MC = AR\ (=P)$

If the monopoly followed the $MC = AR\ (= P)$ rule of perfect competition, it would produce the larger output at N and charge the lower price NK. The latter is called the *marginal-cost price*. It is the optimum price for society because at this price, the value of the last unit to the marginal user is equivalent to the value of the resources used to produce that unit. Therefore, society is getting as much of the good as it wants in relation to the resources sacrificed to produce it.

Technical Inefficiency

By adhering to the $MC = MR$ principle of profit maximization, the monopoly is technically inefficient. This is because it typically "underuses" the plant by producing on the declining side of the ATC curve. Because the entry of other firms into the industry is blocked, the monopoly can remain in this equilibrium position indefinitely. In contrast, you will recall that firms in perfect competition are technically efficient because they operate in the long run at the minimum point of their ATC curves. Thus, society's resources are ordinarily used relatively less efficiently in monopoly markets than they are in perfectly competitive markets.

The Natural-Monopoly Case

Does this criticism mean that a monopoly produces less, and charges more, than a perfectly competitive industry with the same total demand curve? Not necessarily. In fact, the opposite may often be true.

Exhibit 5
Price and Output Effects of Monopoly Behavior

The *monopoly price* at J maximizes the firm's profit, but it results in resource misallocation.

The *marginal-cost price* at K is the optimum price for society, but it is usually impossible to determine because marginal costs cannot ordinarily be estimated from a firm's accounting records.

The *full-cost* (or *average-cost*) *price* at L results in the largest output and lowest price consistent with earning a normal profit. Because average costs can be roughly estimated from a company's accounting records, the full-cost price is the one that government usually tries to impose on regulated monopolies.

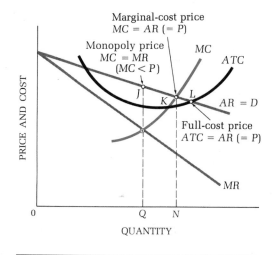

In some industries, technology may widen the "spread" of the cost curves by bringing about increasing economies of scale over a broad range of output. If that happens, one firm may be able to supply the entire market at a lower unit cost (and perhaps at a lower price) than several. This, you will recall, is the basis of most natural monopolies, especially public utilities such as electric companies, gas companies, and railroads.

Full-Cost (Average-Cost) Price: $ATC = AR (= P)$

You can see from the foregoing analyses that an unregulated monopoly will seek to maximize its profits. This means that it will charge the so-called monopoly price determined by $MC = MR$. As a result, output will be smaller, and the price higher, than it would be if other pricing policies were followed.

Which policies? In most cases government agencies that regulate monopolies would like to require them to charge the marginal-cost price. In practice, however, marginal costs are ordinarily impossible to estimate from a firm's accounting records. Therefore, the price that regulatory agencies usually strive to impose is the *full-cost* (or *average-cost*) price, which is shown in Exhibit 5. This price has two important characteristics:

1. It enables the firm to cover all its costs, both fixed and variable, and thus to earn a normal profit while producing the largest output consistent with that profit.

2. It is easier to determine than the marginal-cost price because average costs of production can be roughly estimated from a company's accounting records.

Equity: It Contributes to Income Inequality

A second criticism of monopoly is that it tends to create greater income inequality than would exist in a perfectly competitive economy. By restricting output and charging a higher price, the monopoly may make supernormal profits. These go to its owners or stockholders. These people thus benefit at the expense of the many consumers and resource owners who make up the rest of society.

Growth: It Lacks Incentives for Innovation and Progress

A third major criticism is that a monopoly, unlike a perfectly competitive firm, is not under constant pressure to develop better methods of production. Therefore, it may retard economic progress. This is because the obstacles to entry make the monopoly relatively secure in its position. Competitive pressures that would otherwise stimulate innovation are absent for monopolies.

Public utilities—especially the railroads and telephone companies—are often cited as illustrations. These monopolies, critics contend, have intentionally retarded the development of new and improved products to avoid increasing the rate of obsolescence of their existing equipment. Further, they have been able to do this because of their protected status as legal monopolies.

Conclusion: What Can Be Done About Monopoly?

The general criticisms of monopoly are rooted in the fundamental notion of resource misallocation resulting from the restriction of output and higher prices. In view of this, what do you think can be done about monopolies in our society? The four major possibilities are discussed below.

Various measures may be proposed for correcting the deficiencies of monopolies.

1. Do Nothing Sooner or later a monopoly that is not insulated by patents or other protective legislation is likely to see its position weakened. This will happen as new firms enter the industry in order to capture a share of the monopoly's market. The history of American business is replete with examples of companies that lost their dominant position as a result of competition from other firms, both domestic and foreign.

2. Break Monopolies Up into Competing Firms In the United States and some other developed countries, *antitrust* legislation exists for dealing with monopolies by breaking them up into smaller firms. But the problems of implementing the laws are many and complex.

3. Tax Away All the Profits of Monopolies Above Their Normal Profits If all of the excess profits of monopolies were taxed, their revenues could be distributed to the public through increased or improved government services. This would not drive monopolies out of business, because they would still be normally profitable. However, it would effectively reduce the tendency for monopolies to contribute to income inequality.

4. Treat All Monopolies as Public Utilities The outputs and prices of monopolies can be regulated by government agencies. The agencies could require monopolies to produce more and charge less than they would if they were completely free and unregulated. This, you have already learned, is the way in which legal monopolies are administered, as illustrated earlier in terms of the discussion of full-cost pricing.

Would the adoption of these policies "solve" the so-called monopoly problem? The answer is *no*. In fact:

> No one of these approaches, nor any combination of them, would overcome completely the fundamental problem of resource misallocation. However, each would tend to reduce somewhat the adverse effects of misallocation.

Price Discrimination

Until now we have assumed that a monopoly sells its entire output at the *same* price per unit. However, a monopoly may sometimes find it more profitable to charge different prices instead of a single price for the units it sells. It is then engaging in what is known as price discrimination— one of the most interesting problems in the theory of monopoly.

Price discrimination is one way in which a monopoly may be able to increase its revenues.

> *Price discrimination* may be defined as the practice of charging different prices to buyers for the same good. Hence, it is also sometimes called *differential pricing*. In general terms, price discrimination or differential pricing is a method that some sellers use to maximize profits by tailoring their prices to the specific purchasing situations of the buyers. The price may vary according to the amount purchased or according to the market in which the good is purchased.

Exhibit 6
Price Discrimination Based on Quantity

A monopoly can charge a different price to the same buyer (or to the same homogeneous class of buyers) according to the quantity purchased. In that case, the total revenue will be larger (shown by the shaded areas) than it would be if the monopoly charged the same price per unit for all units purchased.

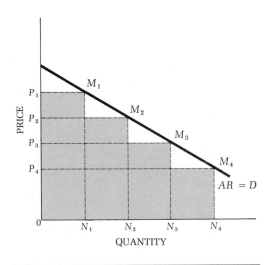

Dumping is a form of price discrimination that occurs both in domestic and in international trade.

"Tapping" the Demand Curve

An example of price discrimination occurs when a monopolist "taps" the demand curve of the buyer by charging lower prices for larger quantities instead of a single price per unit for all units purchased. The monopolist may also charge different prices to different classes or groups of buyers.

For example, an electric company does not usually charge all buyers the same price per unit for electricity. Instead, it *segments* the total market—that is, divides it into homogeneous submarkets consisting, say, of residential users, commercial users, and industrial users—and charges a different price to each class of user. In this way it earns more money than it would if all users paid the same price. This concept is illustrated in Exhibit 6.

Assuming that the AR curve is the demand curve of a single buyer or of a single homogeneous class of buyers, the monopoly may simply charge a price of P_4 per unit and sell N_4 units. In this case there is no discrimination, and the firm's total revenue is price times quantity, or the area of the rectangle $0P_4M_4N_4$.

However, the monopoly can enlarge total receipts considerably if it discriminates in price. Thus, it may charge a price of P_1 for the first N_1 units, giving it a total revenue of $0P_1M_1N_1$. Then it may lower the price to P_2 per unit and sell additional units equal to the distance N_1N_2. After that, it can lower the price to P_3 and sell additional units equal to the distance N_2N_3. Finally, it can lower the price to P_4, at which it sells further units equal to the distance N_3N_4. Although the monopoly still ends up selling the same total number of units, namely N_4, its total revenue is now the entire shaded area instead of the area $0P_4M_4N_4$, its revenue was when it charged a price of P_4 per unit without discrimination.

Evidently:

> The smaller the reductions in price, the narrower the steps under the demand curve become and hence the larger the total revenue. Theoretically, the limit would be a total revenue equal to the entire area under the curve. But this would require an infinite number of price reductions of infinitesimal amounts. In practice, the reductions are in finite amounts for blocks of units, and the sales are made simultaneously to different classes of buyers at different price scales.

Dumping

Another form of price discrimination occurs when a monopolist sells the same product in different markets at different prices. This practice is known in international trade as *dumping*, but its underlying principles are equally applicable to domestic trade.

The basic concept is illustrated by the diagrams in Exhibit 7. A firm that has a monopoly in the domestic market, for example, will probably find that the demand for its product at home is more inelastic than the demand abroad. This is because foreign buyers have a greater number of alternative sources from which to purchase the product. Consequently, their demand for the monopolist's product is more elastic.

Exhibit 7 shows the demand curve in the domestic market to be more inelastic than that in the foreign market. The curve for the total marginal revenue of both markets, namely $MR_1 + MR_2$, may be obtained by summing the horizontal ordinates to the MR_1 and MR_2 curves, or, in other words, by adding together the quantities in the two markets at each marginal revenue.

The most profitable level of *total* output must be determined first. This is done in Figure (*c*), in which the *MC* curve in the total market is the monopoly's marginal-cost curve. The firm's most profitable total output is at N_3 because this is where the marginal cost of the output equals the total marginal revenue.

It should be emphasized that only one marginal-cost curve is assumed to exist in this case, because it makes no difference to costs whether the product is sold at home or abroad. That is, the product is still the same, and the marginal cost is determined by the total output. Hence, for the output at N_3, the monopolist's marginal cost is equal to the distance N_3L_3, and this is equal to the distance N_1L_1 in the domestic market and to the distance N_2L_2 in the foreign market.

Equilibrium in the Submarkets

How will the monopolist divide total output among the two submarkets? What price will be charged in each market? The answers to these questions follow from the $MC = MR$ principle you have already learned. In order to maximize profit, the monopolist will sell N_1 units in the domestic market at the price N_1P_1 because this is where the marginal revenue in that market is equal to the marginal cost N_1L_1. Likewise, the monopolist will sell the remaining N_2 units in the foreign market at the price N_2P_2 because this is where the marginal revenue in that market equals the marginal cost N_2L_2.

Applications

There are many illustrations of dumping at both the domestic and international level. For example, some manufacturers of appliances and various other products sell part of their output to mail-order firms and department stores (such as Sears and Montgomery Ward) at lower prices under different brand names. Milk cooperatives frequently sell milk at a higher price to consumers and at a lower price to butter and cheese manufacturers. Tire manufacturers often sell identical tires under their own brand names in the domestic market and under different brand names through other marketing channels in both domestic and foreign markets. In each case, the seller earns a higher profit by making fuller utilization of excess plant capacity. However, this assumes that the extra or marginal cost of the additional output does not exceed the extra or marginal revenue.

The Conditions for Price Discrimination

Price discrimination is thus a practice of charging different prices to different *segments* of a market for the same good, where each segment represents a distinct market or submarket for the product. If you were a seller, what practical conditions would have to exist to enable you to practice price discrimination effectively? There are three: (1) multiple demand elasticities, (2) market segmentation, and (3) market sealing.

Multiple Demand Elasticities

There must be differences in demand elasticity among buyers due to differences in income, location, available alternatives, tastes, or other fac-

Exhibit 7
Illustration of Dumping

To allocate the product between the domestic and foreign markets, the most profitable level of *total* output must be determined first. This is done in Figure (*c*). By adhering to the $MC = MR$ principle, the monopolist maximizes profit by allocating the total equilibrium output at N_3 among the two submarkets in Figures (*a*) and (*b*). The monopolist then charges a higher price in the submarket where the demand elasticity is smaller (or the inelasticity is larger).

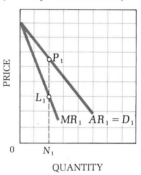

(*a*) DOMESTIC MARKET (relatively inelastic demand)

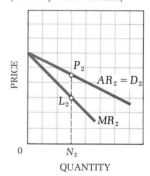

(*b*) FOREIGN MARKET (relatively elastic demand)

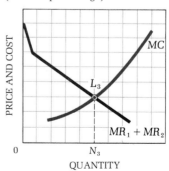

(*c*) TOTAL MARKET (domestic plus foreign)

tors. Otherwise, if the underlying conditions that normally determine demand elasticity are the same for all purchasers, the separate demand elasticities for each buyer or group of buyers will be approximately equal, and a single rather than multiple price structure may be warranted.

Market Segmentation

The key to price discrimination is to partition the total market into homogeneous submarkets according to demand elasticity.

A second condition for price discrimination is that the seller must be able to partition (segment) the total market. How? By segregating buyers into groups or submarkets according to elasticity. Profits can then be enhanced by charging a different price in each submarket. There are many ways in which a total market can be effectively segmented into submarkets. For example:

1. Segmentation by Income A doctor may charge a rich patient more than a poor patient for the same operation.

2. Segmentation by Quantity of Purchase A manufacturer may offer quantity discounts to large buyers.

3. Segmentation by Geographic Location A state university may charge out-of-state students a higher tuition than in-state residents.

4. Segmentation by Time A theater, tennis club, or telephone company may charge more at certain hours than at others. Similarly, a resort hotel, restaurant, or clothing store may charge higher prices during certain seasons of the year.

5. Segmentation by Brand Name The same product may be sold under different brand names at different prices.

6. Segmentation by Age An airline may charge less for children than for adults, despite equal costs of serving them.

Segmentation by race, religion, sex, and education provide still further opportunities for partitioning a market into relatively homogeneous subgroups. Can you suggest some examples?

Market Sealing

After partitioning a total market, methods must be found to seal each submarket so as to prevent "leakage."

A third condition for price discrimination is that the seller must be able to seal the market. That is, the seller must be able to prevent—or natural circumstances must exist that will prevent—any significant resale of goods from the lower- to the higher-priced submarket. Any leakage in the form of resale by buyers between submarkets will, beyond minimum critical levels, tend to neutralize the effect of differential prices. The result will be to narrow the effective price structure so much that it approaches that of a single price to all buyers.

For example, a movie theater may use tickets of different color for matinees and for evenings, or for children and for adults. In this way, it seals the segmented markets and prevents buyers from purchasing at the lower price and selling or using the product at the higher price. Similarly, some publishers of magazines, newspapers, and professional journals sell subscriptions to students at special rates. Of course, market sealing cannot always be accomplished with 100 percent perfection. When it is not, a certain amount of leakage will occur between submarkets, thereby reducing the effectiveness of price discrimination.

Conclusion: Is Price Discrimination Legal?

Price discrimination is a practical way for sellers to increase their profits. By identifying relevant demand elasticities and by effectively segmenting and sealing markets, firms can discover new and larger sources of profit. However:

Some forms of price discrimination are expressly illegal; some are not.

> Certain types of price discrimination are expressly illegal under our antitrust laws. The legality of some other forms is not clearly defined, and those who practice these other forms of price discrimination may therefore be open to legal action by the government. As a consequence, sellers must be cautious about employing certain discriminatory practices in their pricing policies.

Case
Cartels: "International Monopolies" and Commodity Power

In the early 1970s, the Organization of Petroleum Exporting Countries (OPEC)—a twelve-member group dominated by Arab oil nations—succeeded in escalating the world price of oil. Since then the attention of economists and political leaders has focused frequently on cartels and on the role these organizations can play in affecting global-resource allocation.

What Is a Cartel?

A cartel is often popularly referred to as an "international monopoly." More precisely, a *cartel* is an association of producers in the same industry that has been established to increase the profits of its members by adopting common policies affecting production, market allocation, or price. A cartel may thus be either domestic or global in scope. However, in the United States (but not elsewhere) the term "cartel" generally applies only to producer associations operating across national boundaries.

Cartels have had a long and interesting history. The evidence indicates that cartels are generally difficult to form and even more difficult to sustain. In the past, concerted efforts by major producers to raise commodity prices substantially above free-market levels have rarely been successful for any extended period. Nevertheless, efforts at cartelization continue to be made from time to time, often for political as well as economic reasons.

How to Succeed

When a cartel is established, the goal is to raise each member's long-run profits to higher levels than would prevail under competitive conditions. To be successful, therefore, a cartel must have certain characteristics:

1. *Dominant Market Share* A cartel must control the bulk of an industry's total output. Otherwise, the members will not have sufficient power to influence market prices.

2. *Cohesiveness* If the number of cartel members is relatively small, it is more likely that the group will be cohesive and that the members will cooperate with one another for the good of the group. A member nation will be less likely to cut its price in order to boost sales and profits at other members' expense.

Saudi Arabia's oil minister and delegates at the 59th OPEC Conference, Hong Kong, 1980.

United Press International

3. *Income-Inelastic Demand* The demand for the cartel's product must remain fairly stable over the long run—during recessions as well as prosperities. This is necessary in order to discourage members from violating the agreement when general economic circumstances change. More precisely, this means that the demand for the cartel's product must be largely unresponsive or relatively inelastic with respect to changes in buyers' income.

4. *Price-Inelastic Demand* The quantity demanded of the cartel's product must also be fairly unresponsive or relatively inelastic with respect to changes in price. This means that, if the price of the product is increased by some given percentage, quantity sold declines by a smaller percentage so that total revenue (price times quantity) rises.

OPEC and Other Cartels?

It is easy to see why a cartel must possess *all* of these characteristics in order to succeed. The OPEC cartel, for example, was founded in 1960, but it was not especially effective because it lacked cohesiveness—a spirit of cooperation among members. Not until the early 1970s was the needed cohesion achieved—owing partly to the Middle East war and partly to the feeling among oil-exporting countries that they had too long been exploited by the developed nations. Whether or not OPEC continues to be effective depends on its ability to retain the necessary characteristics of a cartel.

The success achieved by OPEC has encouraged many other mineral-producing nations to consider making cartelization agreements. Several cartels—not necessarily successful—involving some of the commodities shown in the accompanying table have existed for years.

Ultimately, the true measure of any cartel rests on its ability to restrict output in order to sustain prices during periods of low demand. Since cartel policy is usually based on detailed negotiation and cooperation among sovereign states with widely divergent economic and political interests, successful cartels have been relatively rare. Most, in fact, have ended up being not much more than information clearinghouses for their members.

Beating the System: Sealed Bids

But what if a cartel does succeed? Can anything be done to weaken its position and thereby bring about a reduction in prices?

One idea that merits serious consideration is the use of sealed competitive bids. A major buying nation, for example, could auction off transferable quota tickets to governments (or cartel members) that want to bid for the right to export their commodity to the importing country. The cartel members would then have to compete in mutual ignorance, each unable to know who may be betraying the rest. At the very least, even if the cartelists agree to boycott the importing nation, a secret auction system would upset customary international market shares and exert pressure on exporters to reduce their prices. This, it seems, would be preferable to doing nothing at all.

Questions

1. Suppose a cartel maintains high prices over a long period of time. Then the demand for the cartelized product is likely to become more elastic—and the cartel thereby weakened. Can you explain why?

2. What do you see as the single biggest economic factor capable of making or breaking a cartel?

Producers of Selected Minerals

Commodity	Major producing countries
Bauxite-alumina	Jamaica, Surinam, Canada, Australia
Chromium	South Africa, USSR, Turkey
Cobalt	Zaïre, Zambia, Norway, Finland
Copper	Canada, Peru, Chile
Iron ore	Canada, Venezuela
Lead	Canada, Australia, Peru, Mexico
Manganese	Brazil, Gabon, South Africa, Zaïre
Nickel	Canada, Norway
Oil	Saudi Arabia, Iran, Venezuela, Kuwait
Potash	Canada
Sulfur	Canada, Mexico
Tin	Malaysia, Thailand, Bolivia
Tungsten	Canada, Bolivia, Peru, Australia, Thailand
Zinc	Canada, Mexico, Peru

Source: U.S. Bureau of Mines.

What You Have Learned in This Chapter

1. A monopoly is a single firm producing a product for which there are no close substitutes. Major types are natural monopolies, legal monopolies, government monopolies, strategic-resource monopolies, and patent monopolies.

2. The most profitable output of a monopoly is determined where its $MC = MR$. Unlike a firm in perfect competition, any firm faced with a downward-sloping demand curve is a partial monopoly. Such a firm finds that its marginal-revenue curve is not a demand curve and that its marginal-cost curve is not a supply curve.

3. The basic economic criticism of monopoly is that it misallocates resources. By adhering to the $MC = MR$ principle of profit maximization, a monopoly restricts output and charges a correspondingly higher price than it would if the $MC = P$ standard of perfect competition were followed. In addition, monopolies contribute to income inequality and they may lack incentives to be innovative and progressive. Four possible "solutions" are to do nothing, to tax away their supernormal profits, to break them up into competing firms, and to regulate them as public utilities. If monopolies were regulated as public utilities, their rates would tend to accord with principles of full-cost pricing rather than monopoly pricing or marginal-cost pricing.

4. Price discrimination enlarges revenues by segmenting the market into submarkets and allowing sellers to charge different prices in each according to relative demand elasticities. Markets may be segmented by income, brand names of products, locations of buyers, and various other criteria. Dumping is a typical form of price discrimination.

For Discussion

1. *Terms and concepts to review:*
monopoly
natural monopoly
legal monopoly
government monopoly

strategic-resource monopoly
patent monopoly
average–marginal relationship
monopoly price
marginal-cost price
full-cost (average-cost) price
dumping

2. Evaluate the judicial definition that a monopoly is "a business affected with a public interest."

3. Answer *true* or *false,* and explain why:
(a) A monopoly is secure because, by controlling its price and output, it can guarantee a profit.
(b) A perfect monopoly is almost as unlikely as perfect competition.
(c) A monopoly's price is higher than a perfect competitor's price in the long run.
(d) A monopoly maximizes its profit by charging the highest price it can get.

4. "A monopoly is most likely to be successful when the demand for its product is relatively inelastic." True or false? (**Hint** Prove that a monopoly will never produce at an output at which the elasticity of demand is numerically less than 1. You can do this by first proving that, when marginal revenue is positive, the elasticity of demand is numerically greater than 1.)

5. What is the most profitable output for a monopolist faced with a unit-elastic demand curve throughout the entire length of the curve? (**Hint** What is marginal revenue when demand is unit elastic?) Explain.

6. If the government wanted to extract the maximum revenue from a monopoly without driving it out of business, should the government tax profits or should it tax each unit of output? Explain.

7. "The prices of automobiles, TV sets, and corn flakes are each determined by supply and demand." Evaluate this statement in light of the fact that a less than perfectly competitive firm has no supply curve. What do "supply" and "demand" actually mean in this case?

8. Complete the table below, which shows cost and revenue data of a monopolist. Sketch the following curves on three separate figures, one beneath the other, as was done in this chapter:
(a) Total revenue and total cost.
(b) Marginal cost, average total cost, average revenue, and marginal revenue.
(c) Net revenue.
In the figures, draw vertical dashed lines showing the most profitable level of output and the two break-even points. (**Note** You will have to "project" the curves to obtain the second break-even point.) Label all the curves and explain their significance. Remember that marginal curves are plotted to the midpoints between the integers on the horizontal axis.

9. Suppose that you were an economic advisor to a monopoly. Can you suggest ways in which the firm could engage in price discrimination by segmenting the market on the basis of (a) quantity, (b) geographic location, and (c) "time"?

10. Some critics have suggested that firms with strong monopoly power should be subsidized, or even governmentally owned, in order to have them adhere to a socially desirable pricing policy. What do you think of this argument? Be specific.

Problem 8
Cost and Revenue Schedules of a Monopolist

Quantity per day, Q	Average revenue or price, AR = P	Total revenue, TR	Marginal revenue, MR	Total cost, TC	Average total cost, ATC	Marginal cost, MC	Net revenue, NR
0	$21	$ 0	$_____	$22	$_____	$_____	$_____
1	20	20		37			
2	19	38	_____	42	_____	_____	_____
3	18	54	_____	45	_____	_____	_____
4	17	68	_____	47	_____	_____	_____
5	16	80	_____	50	_____	_____	_____
6	15	90	_____	54	_____	_____	_____
7	14	98	_____	59	_____	_____	_____
8	13	104	_____	65	_____	_____	_____
9	12	108	_____	72	_____	_____	_____
10	11	110	_____	80	_____	_____	_____
11	10	110	_____	89	_____	_____	_____
12	9	108	_____	99	_____	_____	_____

The Real World of Imperfect Competition

Learning guide

Watch for the answers to these important questions

What types of market structures constitute imperfect competition?

What is monopolistic competition? Why is advertising a particularly important activity in monopolistic competition? Is advertising good? Is it bad? What are the economic consequences of monopolistic competition?

What is oligopoly? How does oligopoly differ from monopolistic competition? Why may oligopoly lead to collusive behavior? Why may it lead to price leadership? What are the economic consequences of oligopoly?

Is it reasonable to assume that firms seek to maximize profit? What other assumptions are reasonable? Why does economic theory assume profit-maximizing behavior?

If the world of perfect competition is largely imaginary and the world of monopoly is relatively limited and regulated, what does the *real* world look like? This question can be answered by constructing models that come closer to approximating the kinds of markets in which most firms and industries in the economy operate. You will find that your knowledge of perfect competition and monopoly provides a basis for comparing and evaluating the consequences of these more realistic situations.

To give yourself a bird's-eye view of where you are and where you will be heading in this chapter, simply examine the following spectrum of market structures:

This chapter explains the economics of market structures that fall "between" perfect competition and pure monopoly.

Perfect competition	Varying degrees of imperfect competition: monopolistic competition and oligopoly	Pure monopoly

You have already analyzed the cases of perfect competition and monopoly at the extreme ends of the spectrum. Now you will be turning your attention to the broad middle range in order to examine what is known as "imperfect competition." This includes market structures that are classified as "monopolistic competition" and "oligopoly." These names arise from the fact that *imperfect competition* consists of various "mixtures" of perfect competition and pure monopoly. You will find that these mixed structures characterize most of the markets in our economy.

Monopolistic Competition: Many Sellers, Similar Products

Monopolistic competition takes place all around us. Retailing is a typical example.

You know that perfect competition consists of many firms producing a homogeneous product and that monopoly consists of one firm producing a unique product for which there are no close substitutes. Both are important for economic analysis. Some industries, such as agriculture, standardized raw materials, and the organized commodity and stock exchanges, operate under conditions that exhibit many characteristics of perfect competition. Other industries, such as electric and gas utilities, have certain features similar to those of a pure monopoly.

In reality, most of the nation's economic activity occurs under conditions of imperfect competition. This market structure consists of industries and markets that fall between the two extremes of perfect competition and pure monopoly. One such intermediate type that exists throughout the economy is called *monopolistic competition*. It may be defined as an industry or market characterized by (1) a large number of firms of different sizes producing heterogeneous (similar but not identical) products and (2) relatively easy entry for firms. This type of competition will be studied first. The other subcategory of imperfect competition, known as "oligopoly," is examined later in the chapter.

Product Differentiation Is a Key Factor

Very often, only slight differences in a product or in its "packaging" distinguish it from another.

Does the term "monopolistic competition" contradict itself? How can a market be both monopolistic and competitive at the same time?

The answer is based on the fact that, in an industry characterized by monopolistic competition, the products of the firms in the industry are *differentiated*. But product differentiation, like beauty, is in the eye of the beholder. And, in economics, the beholder is always the buyer. Consequently, products may be differentiated by brand name, color of package, location of the seller, customer service, credit conditions, or the smile of the salesperson—even if the products themselves are physically the same. As a result, each firm has a partial monopoly of its own differentiated product.

Monopolistic competition is found in many industries. Retailing provides a good general illustration. Some more specific examples include the manufacture of clothing, household goods, shoes, and furniture. In some areas, the services provided by most barbers, doctors, and dentists are also good examples. In each of these industries the products sold are usually only moderately differentiated. This helps to explain why similar kinds of goods in monopolistic competition tend to have similar prices. In most markets, for example, the prices of haircuts are similar, as are the prices of appendectomies and the prices of dental fillings. In general, the less the degree of product differentiation in the minds of buyers, the less the disparity in prices.

Price and Output Determination

When we apply these ideas to the construction of a model, we find that the theory of monopolistic competition is as much a *theory of the firm* as it is a theory of market or industry behavior. Thus:

1. Because each seller has a partial monopoly due to product differentiation, there will be a separate *AR* or demand curve for each firm. These curves will be downward-sloping, indicating that a firm can raise prices to some degree without losing all of its sales.

2. You learned in the study of monopoly that a firm with a negatively inclined demand curve has no supply curve. This is because a given price may be associated with multiple outputs and a given output may be associated with multiple prices, depending on the position of the *AR* curve. Hence, there can be no industry supply curve. In fact, the whole concept of an industry becomes somewhat cloudy and vague in monopolistic competition because of the existence of product differentiation.

3. Because the products of competitors are close but not perfect substitutes, it can be assumed that their elasticities of demand are relatively high. (Examples include competing brands of soap, toothpaste, and soft drinks.) Indeed, the elasticity will vary inversely with the extent of product differentiation. And, of course, the less the degree of product differentiation and the greater the number of sellers, the closer the model will be to pure competition.

The *MC* = *MR* Principle Again

As always, to maximize profit, firms will seek to produce the quantity at which *MC* = *MR*. But this does not necessarily mean that they will be highly profitable. Because there are many firms in the industry and entry is relatively easy, some firms will, in the short run, earn only modest supernormal profits.

In the long run, however, there will be a *tendency* for most surviving firms to be approximately normally profitable. Again, this is only a general tendency. Profitability will depend on the degree of product differentiation and the number of firms. For example, a small retail store might continue to be considerably more than normally profitable because it happens to be in a particularly good location. On the other hand, a similar kind of store in a different location may continue to be considerably less than normally profitable. Why? Because the seller would prefer to be his or her "own boss"—despite the economic loss that may result—rather than hire out to do the same job at a higher salary for someone else. Therefore, although most firms in a monopolistically competitive industry *tend* to earn approximately normal profits in the long run, some firms do not. These possibilities are illustrated and explained for the firms in Exhibit 1.

The Importance of Selling Costs

Because product differentiation plays a key role in monopolistic competition, many firms spend money on advertising, merchandising, sales promotion, public relations, and the like in order to increase their profits. Marketing expenditures of this type, which are aimed at adapting the buyer to the product, are termed *selling costs*. This distinguishes them from production costs, which are designed to adapt the product to the buyer. For purposes of analysis, economists generally view all sales outlays or selling costs as synonymous with advertising.

The seller in monopolistic competition who engages in advertising seeks to attain a delicate balance between commodity homogeneity and heterogeneity. To attract customers away from competitors, the seller must convey two ideas:

Exhibit 1

Firms in Monopolistic Competition

Firm *A* is earning above-normal profits, firm *B* is receiving only normal profits, and firm *C* is earning below-normal profits. In the long run most firms in monopolistic competition will *tend* to be approximately normally profitable. However, there may be some exceptions due to locational factors or other special circumstances.

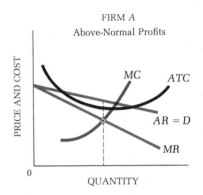

FIRM *A*
Above-Normal Profits

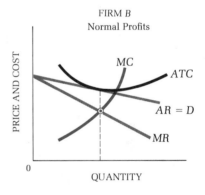

FIRM *B*
Normal Profits

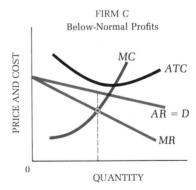

FIRM *C*
Below-Normal Profits

Exhibit 2
Advertising and Demand

The purpose of advertising is *not* to make the demand curve more inelastic so that a higher price can be charged. If that were the case, D_1 would be preferable to D_2. However, if N_2 is the most profitable volume of output, D_2 permits a higher price to be charged than D_1 does. The opposite is true if N_3 is the most profitable output.

Thus:

The purpose of advertising is to shift the demand curve to a higher *level*, such as D_3. This permits a higher price to be charged for *any* volume of output.

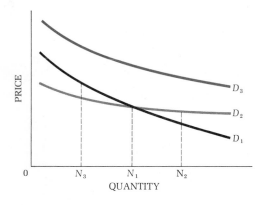

Advertising is a common phenomenon in monopolistic competition as each firm tries to distinguish its product from the products of its competitors.

1. The firm's product is not sharply differentiated from competing products, so that buyers will find it feasible to purchase the product instead of those of competitors.

2. The product is somehow superior to those of competitors, so that buyers believe there is greater heterogeneity than exists in fact.

Clearing Up a Misconception

These objectives of advertising account for an erroneous statement that is sometimes made about it. Marketing experts, for example, often contend that the seller's purpose in advertising is to make the demand curve more inelastic. This would allow a higher price to be charged for each unit sold.

If this statement were true, it would mean that the seller would prefer to be confronted with the demand curve D_1 in Exhibit 2 rather than D_2. Yet if output is most profitable beyond the level at N_1, say at N_2, then D_2 is clearly preferable to D_1. Why? Because it allows for sales at a higher price, even though D_2 is more elastic than D_1. On the other hand, if output is most profitable at N_3, then D_1 would be preferred to D_2. Therefore, the argument that advertising is desirable for the seller because it results in a more inelastic demand curve may be only partially true, and in many instances may be completely false.

The statement can be correctly reformulated by noting that what the seller really wants is not necessarily a more inelastic demand curve but rather a new and higher curve *level*. This is illustrated by D_3. With this demand curve, the seller can charge a higher price per unit relative to either D_1 or D_2, regardless of the most profitable output volume indicated in the figure.

Is Advertising "Good" or "Bad"?

Advertising has been a subject of much debate among economists. The arguments have revolved around three major issues:

1. Information Versus Persuasion Those in favor of advertising argue that it educates and informs buyers about firms, products, and prices. Therefore, advertising tends to make markets more perfect than they otherwise would be. Those who oppose advertising reply that it seeks to persuade buyers rather than to inform them, thereby creating wants that result in a distortion of "natural" preference patterns.

2. Competition Versus Concentration Defenders of advertising argue that it encourages competition. It does this by exposing consumers to competing products and enabling firms to gain market acceptance for new products more rapidly than they could without advertising. Critics of advertising contend that the opposite is true. Advertising, they say, facilitates the concentration of monopoly power because large firms can usually afford continuous heavy advertising, whereas new and small firms cannot.

3. Efficiency Versus Waste Proponents of advertising contend that it familiarizes consumers with products and thereby broadens the market for goods. This encourages not only further capital investment and employment but also large-scale operations that result in low-cost mass production. Critics of advertising reply that it encourages artificial product differentiation among goods that are physically similar and that advertising among competing firms tends to have a canceling effect. This duplication of effort results in a waste of resources, higher product costs, and higher prices. Consequently, any real economies of scale—if they exist—are lost through inefficiencies. This argument of efficiency versus waste is explained further in Exhibit 3.

These arguments indicate the fundamental nature of the controversy. Because both points of view are persuasive, the issues will probably never be resolved.

Conclusion: Monopolistic Competition and Efficiency

From what we already know about the results of perfect competition and monopoly, the more relevant social effects of monopolistic competition may be stated briefly. Note that these effects pertain mainly to efficiency.

Resource Misallocation

Monopolistically competitive firms determine their production volumes and prices by the $MC = MR$ rule of profit maximization. They therefore *misallocate resources* by restricting outputs and charging higher prices than they would if they adhered to the economically efficient $MC = P$ standard of perfect competition. Note that *this is the same basic criticism that was given for monopoly.* However, in the case of monopolistic competition, the extent of resource misallocation with its associated output restriction and higher prices will depend, in each industry, on the degree of product differentiation and the number of sellers.

Nonprice Competition

A second consequence of monopolistic competition is that it encourages *nonprice competition.* This consists of methods of competition that do not involve changes in selling price. Examples include advertising, sales promotion, customer services, and product differentiation. Nonprice activities that result in greater innovation and product improvement may be desirable. However, to the extent that they result in higher production costs due to the duplication of resources, excessive style changes, and so on, they tend to cause technical inefficiencies and are therefore undesirable.

Wasteful Excesses

A third adverse consequence is that monopolistically competitive firms create what economists have called the *"wastes" of monopolistic competition.* This refers to the existence of "sick" or inefficient industries. They are characterized by chronic excess capacity resulting from too many sellers of differentiated products dividing up markets, operating inefficiently at outputs less than their minimum average costs, and charging higher prices. Examples abound in the retail trades, such as grocery stores, clothing shops, and restaurants. Other examples are found in the light manufacturing industries, such as textiles, shoes, and plastics.

Why do chronically sick industries of monopolistic competition continue to exist? There are several reasons. They include relatively

Exhibit 3
Advertising and Economies of Scale

Figure (a): In the short run, advertising raises a firm's average total cost curve by the advertising cost per unit. Thus, for the output at M, if the advertising cost per unit is DC, total advertising expenditures are equal to the area of the rectangle $ABCD$.

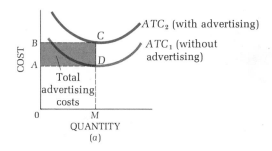

Figure (b): Advertising may also shift a firm's demand curve to the right and raise its long-run average costs. This, in turn, affects the firm's economies of scale. For example, suppose that without advertising the firm would have produced the output at J for a unit cost of JE. Then, as a result of advertising, there may be several possible effects:

1. Advertising may give the firm economies of scale, enabling it to produce the larger ouput at K for the lower unit cost KG, even though point G is on a higher $LRAC$ curve than point E.

2. Advertising may have a canceling effect, leaving output unchanged at J and simply increasing unit costs from JE to JF.

3. Advertising may cause diseconomies of scale, causing the firm to produce the output at L for unit costs of LH. This case is not very likely, however, since monopolistic competition results in firms of less than optimum size, as pointed out in the text.

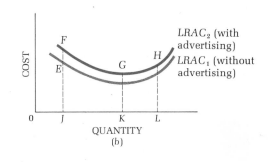

low initial capital requirements, little need for financial or marketing knowledge, and the desire to own a business and "be your own boss." As a result, new firms enter the industry as fast or even faster than the unprofitable ones leave it.

Conclusion: Hotelling's Paradox—More Is Less

The struggle for product differentiation leads to more products with fewer differences.

Product differentiation is a fundamental characteristic of monopolistic competition. But the nature of the market is such that, in order for products to survive, they can be only minimally different.

For example, why do department stores in the same city usually tend to locate near each other? Why are banks, brokerage firms, and other financial institutions in New York City concentrated in the Wall Street area of lower Manhattan? Why do hotels and restaurants in the same market tend to offer, within the same price range, similar services and products? And why are there many similar kinds of breakfast cereals, frozen foods, canned goods, cosmetics, and liquor?

The answer to all of these questions is the same. It was demonstrated analytically as long ago as 1929 by a prominent American economist and statistician, Harold Hotelling.

> **Hotelling's paradox: principle of minimum differences.** Monopolistically competitive firms must, in order to attract each other's customers, make their products as similar to existing products as possible without destroying the differences. Therefore, as a type of market structure, monopolistic competition leads to maximum differentiation of products with minimum differences between them. (**Note** Because the theory of monopolistic competition had not yet been formulated in 1929, Hotelling's model was based on what he called "industries composed of many firms and similar goods.")

Oligopoly: Competition Among the Few

Oligopoly, like monopolistic competition, is also a common type of market structure. Many of the products we use every day are made by oligopolies.

When you drive a car, open a can of tuna fish, replace a light bulb, buy cigarettes, wash your hands with soap, purchase gasoline, type a term paper, or talk on a telephone, you are using products manufactured by oligopolistic industries. An *oligopoly* is an industry composed of a few firms. The industry produces either (1) a homogeneous product, in which case it is called *perfect oligopoly*, or (2) heterogeneous products, in which case it is called *imperfect oligopoly*. Oligopolistic industries are typically characterized by high obstacles to entry. These are usually in the form of substantial capital requirements, the need for technical know-how, patent rights, and the like.

Examples of perfect oligopoly are found primarily among producers of such industrial goods as aluminum, cement, copper, steel, and zinc. These goods are bought by other manufacturers who usually order them by specification. That is, the goods are ordered in a particular form, such as sheet steel, structural steel, or cold-rolled steel of a specific temper (i.e., hardness and plasticity). A specified type of steel is the same whether it is made by U.S. Steel, Bethlehem Steel, Republic Steel, or any other steel company.

Examples of imperfect oligopoly are found among producers of consumer goods. These include automobiles, cigarettes, gasoline, major appliances, soaps and detergents, television tubes, rubber tires, and typewriters.

In both perfect and imperfect oligopolies, the majority of sales go to the "big three" or the "big four" companies in each industry. Can you name the three or four leading firms in some of the oligopolistic industries mentioned above?

Some Characteristics of Oligopolies

In addition to fewness of sellers, high obstacles to entry, and similar if not identical products, most oligopolistic industries tend to have several other characteristics in common.

Oligopolies have certain common economic characteristics.

1. Substantial Economies of Scale Firms in oligopolies typically require large-scale production to obtain low unit costs. If total market demand is sufficient only to support a few large firms of optimum size, competition will ensure that only a few such firms survive.

2. Growth Through Merger Many of the oligopolies that exist today have resulted from mergers of competing firms. In some cases, the mergers occurred as long ago as the late nineteenth or early twentieth centuries. In 1901, for example, the U.S. Steel Corporation was formed from a merger of eleven independent steel producers. The purpose, as in most mergers, was to gain a substantial increase in market share, greater economies of scale, larger buying power in the purchase of inputs, and various other advantages that smaller firms did not possess to the same extent.

3. Mutual Dependence The fewness of sellers in an oligopolistic industry makes it necessary for each seller to consider the reactions of competitors when setting a price. In this sense, the behavior of oligopolists in the marketplace may be somewhat similar to the behavior of players in such games of skill as chess, checkers, and bridge. In these games, the participants try to win by formulating strategies that recognize the possible responses of their opponents.

4. Price Rigidity and Nonprice Competition Oligopolistic firms usually find it more comfortable to avoid price competition by maintaining constant prices. These firms may prefer instead to engage in various forms of nonprice competition, such as advertising and customer service, in order to hold, if not increase, their market shares. Price reductions, when they occur, are sporadic. They usually come about only under severe pressures resulting from lessened demands or excessive inventories. These features give rise to a "live and let live" policy in many oligopolistic industries.

Price and Output Determination

With these characteristics as a background, how do oligopolistic firms determine their prices and outputs?

Many oligopolies are faced with kinked demand curves.

A number of different models may be used to portray various types of oligopolistic situations. One of the most interesting possibilities is demonstrated by the model in Exhibit 4. It illustrates what is commonly known as the *kinked demand curve*. This is a "bent" demand curve, accompanied by a corresponding discontinuous marginal-revenue curve, facing an oligopolistic seller.

Thus, suppose that an oligopoly's current price is at P and its output

Exhibit 4

A Kinked Demand Curve Facing an Oligopolist

Given the kink at *K*, any price reduction below the level at *P* will increase sales slowly along *KD*. This is because other firms will probably match any price cuts.

A price increase above the level at *P* will reduce sales rapidly along *LK* because other firms will probably not match the price rise.

Because marginal cost can fluctuate widely between the points *G* and *H*, the equilibrium price at *P* and output at *N* tend to be stable. However, this model leaves some price uncertainty because it does not explain why the kink happens to occur at the point *K* rather than at some other point.

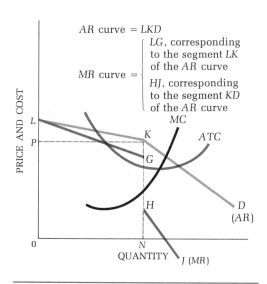

A duopoly is a type of oligopoly that consists of two firms. Their cost curves may be either identical or different.

is at *N*. When contemplating a change in price, either up or down, the firm must consider how its rivals will react. Hence, management might visualize the firm's demand curve by reasoning in the following way:

> If we reduce our price below the level at *P*, our competition will lose some of their customers to us and this will probably prompt them to match our price cut. Therefore, our sales will increase relatively little following the curve *KD*. On the other hand, if we increase our price above the level at *P*, our competitors probably won't match the increase and we'll lose some of our customers to them. Therefore, our sales will fall off rapidly along the curve *KL*.

In other words, *the kinked demand curve reflects the greater tendency of competitors to follow price reductions than price increases.* Price reductions take sales away from other firms and prompt them to cut prices in retaliation. Price increases do not usually invite such responses, because other firms will take sales from the firm that raises its price. It follows that the more homogeneous or standardized the product, the sharper the kink. This is because customers will shift more readily and sellers will therefore react more quickly to changes in prices.

As you can see, the large discontinuity in the *MR* curve between the points *G* and *H* permits the *MC* curve to fluctuate widely within this range. This helps explain why oligopolies exhibit a high degree of price stability. But there is also this seeming paradox:

> The kinked-demand-curve model leaves oligopolists with a considerable degree of price uncertainty. The model demonstrates that once the kink is given, the price at that point will tend to be stable. However, it does not say anything about *why* the kink happens to occur where it does instead of at some other point.

Some oligopolies have tried in various ways to reduce the state of uncertainty in which they operate. Two such methods have been collusion and price leadership.

Oligopolies in Collusion

Oligopolists in some industries have occasionally colluded. That is, they have "gotten together" and agreed on a single industry-wide price that they would all charge. This situation is most probable when the firms in the industry are faced with similar demands, as might occur in a case of perfect oligopoly. The result may then be much the same as in monopoly, except that there is more than one firm. Two interesting models, both illustrated in Exhibit 5, can be employed to demonstrate these possibilities.

Duopoly with Identical Costs

For simplicity, we will assume a case of perfect oligopoly, in which the industry consists of only two firms producing a standardized product. An industry composed of two sellers is also called a *duopoly*. It may be either a perfect or an imperfect duopoly, depending on whether the product is standardized or differentiated.

In Figure (*a*), we will further suppose that the products and the prices of the two firms are identical. Therefore, each firm will have a 50 percent chance of selling to any buyer. Hence *the market will be divided equally between the two companies.*

Of course, as is typically the case, the *AR* curve of the industry will be downward-sloping. At any given price such as the price at P, the quantity sold by each firm will be one-half the industry's total (because each firm is assumed to have 50 percent of the market). Also, you should recall a mathematical rule learned in the study of monopoly. *For all straight-line MR and AR curves, the marginal-revenue curve must bisect any horizontal line drawn from the vertical axis to the average-revenue curve.* Hence the AR curve of each firm corresponds to the MR curve of the industry, and so the distance PW is equal to the distance WK. Similarly, the MR curve of each firm is such that PL = LW.

If we assume that the two firms have identical marginal-cost curves, it follows that each firm will maximize its profits by following the MC = MR rule. This means that each firm will produce N units of output and charge a price of P per unit. The two firms might also collude by agreeing not to deviate from the MC = MR rule and to maintain a single-price policy even in the face of changing business conditions.

Duopoly with Different Costs

The identical demand conditions are also illustrated in Figure (b). Now, however, it is assumed that the two duopolists X and Y have different costs. Thus, duopolist X is a larger-capacity producer than duopolist Y because the marginal-cost curve of firm X, as represented by MC_X, is farther to the right than the marginal-cost curve of firm Y, as represented by MC_Y. This means that, for any given marginal cost, firm X can produce more than firm Y.

In this case, by following the MC = MR rule, firm X will maximize its profit by producing N units and charging a price of P per unit. Firm Y will maximize its profit by producing N' units and charging a price of P' per unit.

The two firms are thus in conflict. If firm X charges its preferred lower price, firm Y *must* charge the same price or else lose sales. If firm Y charges its preferred higher price, firm X need not do the same, in which case firm Y will again suffer the consequences.

What will the two firms do? They might collude by agreeing on a single price for both, thereby avoiding an uncomfortable price war. The agreed-upon price may be at P, or at P', or at some price in between. And it may be a price that is profitable for both firms as long as each is earning at least normal profits.

In practice, a number of real-world factors can reduce the tendency toward collusion. They include:

1. The antitrust laws (to be studied in a later chapter), which make such behavior illegal.

2. A large number of firms in an industry—because the larger the number, the harder it may be for sellers to "get together."

3. A wide range of product differentiation—because greater differentiation makes collusion more difficult.

Despite these obstacles to collusion, cases of it are often uncovered by the government. (See Box 1.)

Price Leadership

Oligopolistic firms need not formally agree on a mutually satisfactory price, as concluded above with respect to Exhibit 5, Figure (b). It is pos-

In Figure (a), each firm maximizes its profits by adhering to the MC = MR rule. Each firm thus produces an amount equal to N units and charges a price of P per unit. Both firms may also agree to stick to this rule at all times, thereby always charging a single, industry-wide price. This policy would assure price stability and leave the firms free to engage in nonprice competition.

(a) IDENTICAL DEMANDS AND COSTS

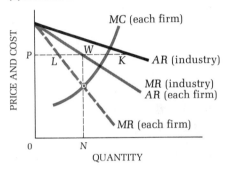

In Figure (b), if each firm followed the MC = MR rule, firm X, represented by MC_X, would prefer a price of P. Firm Y, represented by MC_Y, would prefer a price of P'. By colluding, both firms might agree on a price within this range. But through price leadership by firm X, which is the larger firm, firm Y may be willing to adopt firm X's price of P. This policy, like the previous one, would also assure price stability while permitting nonprice competition.

(b) IDENTICAL DEMANDS AND DIFFERENT COSTS

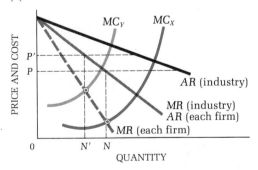

sible instead that firm Y might accept a policy of *price leadership*. This is a situation in which all firms in an oligopolistic industry adhere, often tacitly and without formal agreement, to the pricing policies of one of its members. Usually, but not always, the price leader will be the largest firm in the industry, and other firms in the industry will simply go along with the leader.

Thus, in Figure (b) firm X, which is the largest of the two, would probably be the price leader. It could therefore set a price at P to maximize its own profit, and firm Y would follow the leader by charging the same price. This policy avoids unprofitable price wars, and it is not regarded as illegal by the courts unless it is proved to be the result of collusion or other monopolistic practices. It also leaves the price followers earning at least normal, although not maximum, profits. This explains why price leadership has at one time or another been a widespread practice in most oligopolistic industries. Examples include cigarettes, steel, anthracite coal, farm equipment, newsprint, tin cans, lead, sulfur, and sugar.

Oligopoly and Efficiency

Oligopoly is a major form of market structure in our economy. What can be said about its social consequences? Unfortunately, the issues are extremely complex and the conclusions are by no means clear-cut. Nevertheless, several aspects of oligopoly are worth noting.

Box 1
Oligopolies in Collusion

FTC NEWS RELEASE
Federal Trade Commission
Washington, D.C. 20580

FTC CHARGES FOUR MAKERS OF "ANTIKNOCK"
COMPOUNDS WITH UNFAIR COMPETITION

The FTC announced a complaint charging that the nation's four producers of lead-based "antiknock" additives for gasoline have engaged in practices that unlawfully reduced or eliminated competition.

The complaint alleges that the companies—Ethyl Corp., E. I. du Pont de Nemours & Co., PPG Industries, Inc., and Nalco Chemical Co.—facilitated maintenance of uniform prices by, among other things, "signaling" future price changes to competitors.

In addition to "signaling," the Commission complaint alleges that each company lessened uncertainty about price movements and facilitated maintenance of substantially uniform prices by selling only on a uniform delivered price basis. With the exception of PPG Industries, the companies are also alleged to have used "most favored" customer agreements, promising a buyer the lowest price the seller charges other buyers.

The Commission released a proposed order which, among other things, prohibits:

• The present delivered price system and systematic freight equalization.

• The public announcement of antiknock compound prices as well as any advance notice of price changes.

• "Most favored" customer clauses.

The basic criticism of oligopoly, as a type of market structure, is the same as that of monopoly and monopolistic competition. Oligopoly misallocates resources by restricting output short of the point corresponding to $MC = P$.

With this fundamental criticism in mind, what are the consequences of oligopoly? A number of studies have come up with the following conclusions.

Various studies of oligopolies have arrived at a number of important findings.

Concentration and Competition

Oligopolistic industries vary widely in the extent of their market dominance. The degree of market dominance is commonly measured by the *concentration ratio*. This is the percentage of an industry's output (such as sales or value of shipments) accounted for by its four largest firms. (More or fewer firms may be used to calculate a concentration ratio, but the four-firm ratio is the one most commonly employed.)

In some relatively concentrated oligopolistic industries, the "big four" firms are responsible for more than 80 percent of the industry's sales. Examples are the aluminum, flat glass, and cereal breakfast-foods industries. In a number of less concentrated oligopolistic industries, such as the computer, television picture tube, and tire industries, the concentration ratios are considerably below 80 percent.

Are industries with high concentration ratios less competitive than industries with low ones? Not necessarily. A concentration ratio only provides an indication of market dominance by an industry's four largest firms. It says nothing about the *intensity* of competition between firms or about the fact that a high ratio may result from product innovation and low prices.

Economies of Scale and Lower Costs

As stated above, the basic criticism of oligopoly is output restriction and higher prices. Does this mean that a particular oligopoly produces less, or has higher unit costs and prices, than a perfectly competitive industry would have if it produced the same product?

Economies of scale permit larger outputs, lower costs, and lower prices.

Once again the answer is *not necessarily*. In some oligopolistic industries, technology may be such that economies of scale are very important, as they are in automobile and steel production. The firms in such industries achieve larger outputs and lower long-run unit costs than they would if their industries were perfectly competitive. An automobile manufacturer, for example, could not gain significant reductions in unit costs without the technology and economies of assembly-line mass production. These, in turn, would not be possible if the manufacturer were required to share the market with numerous competitors.

High Concentration and Lower, More Stable Prices

It has been traditionally assumed that large oligopolies are a chief cause of higher prices in high-concentration industries. It has also long been assumed that the largest firms in such industries are prone to increase their prices when economic conditions permit. Are these assumptions borne out by the facts? Several studies done by leading scholars have come up with two surprising sets of findings.

First, high concentration ratios may be a result of lower prices, not a cause of higher ones as has usually been believed. The reason is that, in many oligopolistic industries, the largest firms are often the ones that gained their position by maintaining the lowest prices. In such industries, therefore, lower prices have actually been a *cause* of high concentration.

Second, the overall level of prices tends to be more stable in high-concentration industries than it does in low-concentration industries. Moreover, there is no evidence that the largest firms in high-concentration industries increase their prices more frequently than the largest firms in low-concentration industries.

Profitability and Economies of Scale

Profits are often the result of economies of scale rather than the result of price-raising ability.

The relation between profitability and economies of scale has also been the subject of some investigations. The evidence indicates that, among large oligopolies, profitability is influenced more by economies of scale than by market power (that is, price-raising ability). Firms with substantial economies of scale and limited market power tend to be more profitable than firms with limited economies of scale and substantial market power.

Contestable Markets and Ease of Exit

An implicit requirement of perfect competition is ease of entry. This condition opens the market to competition, helping to assure efficiency. Does this mean that high-concentration industries with steep entry barriers cannot operate efficiently? The answer depends on the "contestability" of their markets.

There are other competitive factors that help to reduce the market power of many oligopolies.

A *contestable market* is one that is characterized by ease of exit—the ability to leave the market with little cost. Under such circumstances, companies already in the market are under pressure to maintain a low-price policy. This discourages outsiders from swooping in, capturing some of the industry's profits, and getting out quickly. Trucking and airlines provide good examples of contestable markets. Although the required investment in trucks and planes is high, these assets are both mobile and readily resalable.

Countervailing Power and Offsetting Influences

The economic influence of oligopoly may be somewhat offset by the growth of *countervailing power*. This term means that the growth of market power by one group may stimulate a reaction by another group on the other side of the market that offsets the influence of the first group. For instance, powerful labor unions have grown up to face oligopolistic industries across the bargaining table. Chain stores have emerged to deal with large processing and manufacturing firms. And even the government has grown larger, partly in response to the growth of big business and big labor. Countervailing power therefore has some favorable competitive effects within the economy. However, it does not exist with equal effectiveness in all oligopolistic industries.

Research and Development

Oligopolistic industries are more progressive in research and development (R&D) than perfectly competitive industries. The evidence shows, however, that oligopolistic industries tend to be considerably more progressive in development than in research. This is because it is usually more profitable to leave the job of product creation to independent inventors, research firms, and universities, so that limited funds can be used to finance product improvement and marketing.

In contrast to industrial oligopolies, research and development is also extensive in agriculture—an industry illustrative of perfect competition. But agricultural R&D is financed largely by government and conducted mainly by agricultural experiment stations and land-grant colleges rather than by privately owned farms.

Conclusion: Learning to Love Oligopolies

Oligopoly is subject to the same basic criticism as monopoly and monopolistic competition. The criticism is that it results in *resource misallocation* caused by output restriction and higher prices. However:

> There is growing recognition that oligopolies are much more efficient than has been traditionally believed. Summarizing the major evidence:
>
> **1.** High concentration ratios can result from innovation and low prices, and are not necessarily indicative of market power.
>
> **2.** Economies of scale play a more important role than market power in bringing about higher profitability, lower prices, and price stability.
>
> **3.** Contestable markets and countervailing power reduce the market independence of large oligopolies, while their R&D expenditures contribute significantly to our standard of living.

On the basis of these findings, there is considerable agreement that the offsetting benefits of oligopolies are much greater than has customarily been assumed.

There is growing evidence that oligopolies are much more efficient than has been customarily assumed.

Do Firms Really Maximize Profits?

The study of business behavior under imperfect competition is now completed. It is thus appropriate to ask: Do firms really strive to maximize profits as economic theory assumes? In other words, do businesspeople actually behave the way the theory says they do, equating their *MC*s and *MR*s?

This question often comes up in discussions of politics, labor—management relations, and other areas of current social and economic interest. Therefore, it is necessary to look closely at three classes of problems involving profit maximization. These are (1) definitional problems, (2) measurement problems, and (3) environmental problems.

Definitional Problems: Which Concept of Profit?

It is easy to define profit as total revenue minus total cost. But is this all there is to the concept of profit? The answer is not as simple as it may seem, because business executives do not always know whether they are seeking to maximize short-run profit or long-run profit. Nor do executives always view the approach to profit management in the same way. As a result of these *definitional* problems, it becomes difficult to state unequivocally that firms in the real world either do or do not strive to maximize their profits.

For example, firms often adopt policies that may reduce short-run profits but that are designed to establish a better long-run situation. Illustrations of such policies include (1) costly research and development programs for creating new products and new markets, and (2) fringe benefits to employees aimed at developing long-run loyalties. At the same

Which definition of profit, short-run or long-run, is appropriate?

time, these firms may exploit short-run market situations to the fullest advantage at the risk of adversely affecting their corporate image in the long run.

Likewise, any two firms may very well view the profit problem in discordant ways. Many studies conducted by business economists and management researchers have found that corporations tend to approach the formulation of profit policies differently. A policy that may seem wise to one firm may seem foolish to another. A typical illustration of this is found in the field of employee relations. One firm may regard pension programs, health and accident plans, and even coffee breaks as important means of raising labor morale and productivity. Another firm may consider them at best a necessary evil.

Measurement Problems: Which Indicator of Profit?

Which measure of profit is correct?

The problems of defining the concept of profit are closely tied to the problems of measuring it. Economic theory assumes that businesses know their marginal costs and marginal revenues and can adjust their outputs to the most profitable levels—the levels at which $MC = MR$.

But in a dynamic economic environment, where changes in technology, tastes, and other underlying forces constantly influence costs and demands, a firm's executives cannot possibly have a precise understanding of how changes in output will affect costs and revenues. At best, executives may be able to gain a rough idea of costs at a few "typical" or standard volumes of output. But even this would be of relatively limited value as a guide to profit maximization in the manner described by economic theory.

As a result of these and other difficulties, business firms in imperfect competition do not, as economic theory assumes, set prices with full knowledge of their marginal costs and marginal revenues. Instead, managers establish prices on the basis of experience, trial and error, and the customs and practices of the industry of which they are a part. And prices are not usually set with the direct objective of maximizing profits. Rather, pricing strategies often aim at attaining other objectives, including the following ones, which may (or may not) indirectly maximize profits:

1. To achieve a certain target or percentage return on investment.

2. To stabilize a firm's prices and outputs over a period of time long enough to permit effective planning of production and resource utilization.

3. To achieve a certain target or percentage share of the market.

4. To meet or match the prices of competitors.

None of these objectives is a substitute for profit maximization. All, however, influence a firm's net revenue, and all are usually easier for executives to use as "tools" for profit management and control. Hence, these goals serve as *practical guides* for profit rather than measures of profit. In studies of pricing practices of large corporations, it has been found that the first of the goals listed above is dominant, but that the others also play important roles.

Environmental Conditions: Reasons for Limiting Profits

A firm may actively avoid maximizing its short-run profits for long-run reasons. Four such practical long-run considerations may be noted as follows.

1. To Discourage Competitive Entry If a company has a moderately strong market position, management may prefer lower profits in order to discourage potential competitors from entering the industry. In this case a long-run price policy that is in line with the rest of the industry will be more advantageous to the firm than one that exploits current market conditions for immediate profit.

2. To Discourage Antitrust Investigation Profits are one of a number of criteria used by the government as evidence of firms' illegal monopolistic market control. This can seem somewhat paradoxical when contrasted with the previous consideration. On the one hand, management may maintain lower profits in order to exclude competitors and thereby strengthen its monopoly control. Yet the federal government's prosecutors may consider high profits, not low profits, as one of several indexes of monopoly power.

3. To Restrain Union Demands Reducing the possibility of having to pay higher wages is another factor prompting management to restrain profits. This is particularly applicable in industries with strong labor unions. As long as the economy is prosperous and profits are rising, unions can more easily demand higher wages without inflicting damage on the firm. But if, in a recession, prices are falling faster than wages, the profit margin is squeezed at both ends. Those companies that curbed wage increases in the beginning would then have a better opportunity to cope with changing market conditions.

4. To Maintain Consumer Goodwill Management may choose to limit profits in order to preserve good customer relations. Consumers frequently have their own ideas of "fair" prices, and some firms make conscious efforts to identify and adhere to those prices.

Evidence shows that some firms may actually seek to limit their profits.

Conclusion: Maximize or "Satisfice"?

The profit problem is complex. This makes it extremely difficult to state unequivocally that firms in imperfect competition do or do not seek to maximize profits. Perhaps in reality they do not seek to maximize but to "*satisfice.*" What this means is that firms may often try to attain targets of satisfactory performance. These may include a specific rate of return on investment, a particular share of the market, or a defined average annual growth of sales. However:

> In economic theory, it is always *assumed* that the firm's underlying objective is to maximize profit. The reason is that this assumption, as already shown, enables us to evaluate the social performance of the firm as a resource allocator.

The theories underlying many of the foregoing ideas are still relatively young. To understand why, see "Leaders in Economics," pages 520 and 521.

The assumption of profit maximization is used in economic theory in order to evaluate the firm's market performance.

Leaders in Economics

Edward Hastings
Chamberlin
1899–1967

Joan Robinson
1903–

Harvard University News Office

"It is this latter problem which is of especial interest and importance. In all of the fields where individual products have even the slightest element of uniqueness, competition bears but faint resemblance to the pure competition of a highly organized market for a homogeneous product."

In the same year, quite independently (the two were unknown to each other), an eminent economist at Cambridge University in England, Joan Robinson, published a volume entitled *The Economics of Imperfect Competition.* This book and Chamberlin's formed the basis of what we know today about economic behavior in monopolistically competitive markets.

Ramsey & Muspratt

The theory of monopolistic competition had its origin in the early 1930s. Prior to that time there was only a theory of perfect competition and a theory of monopoly.

In the United States, the person responsible for the development of the theory was a professor at Harvard University, Edward Chamberlin. His distinguished treatise, *The Theory of Monopolistic Competition,* was published in 1933. As Chamberlin put it, the theory was needed because:

"With differentiation appears monopoly, and as it proceeds further the element of monopoly becomes greater. Where there is any degree of differentiation whatever, each seller has an absolute monopoly of his own product, but is subject to the competition of more or less imperfect substitutes. Since each is a monopolist and yet has competitors, we may speak of them as 'competing monopolists,' and of the forces at work as those of 'monopolistic competition.'

Many Similar Ideas

Both authors stressed the joint influence of competitive and monopolistic elements in the determination of equilibrium. They pointed out that the distinguishing characteristics of imperfect markets are product differentiation and consumer preferences rather than the absence of a large number of sellers. This makes each firm a "partial" monopoly, regardless of the number of competitors in its industry.

Although there were some differences in their views, both used the critical concepts of marginal cost and marginal revenue, and both showed how the firm maximizes profits by equating these two variables. They also discussed short-run and long-run equilibrium, barriers to entry into an industry, and the role of normal profits. Chamberlin, in addition, provided a substantial analysis of the role of advertising.

Stackelberg Model

One year later, in 1934, a German economist named Heinrich Von Stackelberg published a book entitled *Marktform und Gleichgewicht* (*Market Structure and Equilibrium*), which emphasized the interdependence of firms and the problems of oligopoly. One of Stackelberg's chief conclusions was that a democratic state cannot eliminate market structures that fail to achieve a socially desirable equilibrium, whereas authoritarian states can. He thus developed a defense of government intervention in the economy in order to bring about the results deemed best by society. Some of these ideas played a role in the economic policies of Nazi Germany during the late 1930s.

Leaders in Economics

Herbert Alexander Simon
1916–
*Decision Doctor's R$_X$:
"Satisfice," Not Maximize*

Wide World Photos

The Nobel Prize is not awarded in the fields of psychology, sociology, public administration, computer science, or applied mathematics. If the award were granted in any of these disciplines, Herbert Simon would already have received it. Instead, he is a recipient of the 1978 Nobel Prize in Economic Science.

A professor of psychology and computer science at Pittsburgh's Carnegie-Mellon University, Simon has been called by other leading scholars a "renaissance man" and "one of the few geniuses in the social sciences."

Decision Theorist
Simon is best described as a behavioral scientist. His chief interest (and the field

that most of his pioneering research has dealt with) is the mental operations of decision making. This has led him to the study of rational behavior, human thinking processes, the creation of artificial intelligence through computer technology, and related activities.

Simon carried some of his research into economics. He challenged one of its most basic assumptions—that economic man must maximize for satisfaction. "That," according to Simon, "is an extravagant definition of rationality." According to the conventional view of economics, he wrote in his widely read book, *Administrative Behavior*:

"Economic man has a complete and consistent system of preferences that allows him to choose among the alternatives open to him; he is always completely aware of what these alternatives are; there are no limits on the complexity of computations he can perform in order to determine which alternatives are best; probability calculations are neither frightening nor mysterious to him."

This assumption, according to Simon, "bears little discernible relationship to the actual or possible behavior of flesh-and-blood humans."

Conflict Versus Harmony
Simon thus criticizes the traditional microeconomic belief that firms seek to obtain maximum profits. In the modern corporation, he concludes, decision making is diffused among many departments and individuals. This often leads to conflict and dissension, not harmony. Therefore, corporate policy makers are forced to make de-

cisions without enough accurate information to maximize profits. As a result, they aim for "satisfactory" profits rather than maximum profits. They seek to *satisfice* rather than maximize.

Most economists, however, find it difficult to accept this view. That is, they prefer to adhere to the traditional notion that firms seek to maximize profits. Otherwise, many of the conclusions and policy decisions that emerge from economists' models, both in industry and government, would be difficult to justify.

Issue
Advertising: Which Half Is Wasted?

Dozens of advertising slogans have become part of American folklore, the subject of countless jokes and of almost as many solemn academic investigations, theories, and theses. In all capitalistic industrial nations, advertising is pervasive, and it often accounts for a surprisingly high proportion of a firm's costs.

Advertising provokes passionate polemics from proponents and opponents. Is it a vital source of information about available products, processes, and services? Or is it a dishonest form of promotion that either misinforms or creates a legend about a company's offerings without saying much about the reality? Those are the main lines of the debate.

Some Important Issues

Social critics generally view advertising as wasteful. They argue that it does not increase aggregate demand but is primarily a means of one company's holding or gaining a certain share of the market. In this view, advertising of, say, freezers is a cost passed on to consumers, who are unwittingly paying for the battle for market shares waged by General Electric, Westinghouse, Frigidaire, and so on.

But is that view really correct? Certainly, each of those companies wants to increase its market share. But an important reason for advertising a *class* of product is to increase total sales. Ideally, in the minds of the industry's management, promoting the *idea* of a freezer will make many consumers regard it as a virtual "necessity."

But what happens when almost every household has a freezer? At that point, aggregate freezer sales are determined chiefly by population growth, by family incomes, and by the frequency with which households replace freezers. At that stage, it is probably true to say that advertising has only a small effect on aggregate sales.

Unfortunately, nobody knows what proportion of advertising expenditures goes to increasing aggregate sales and what proportion goes to maintaining or increasing individual firms' market shares. As an eminent English businessman once said: "I know that half my advertising expenditures are wasted, but I don't know which half."

For most products, advertising helps to reduce distribution costs as well as production costs, because products that have rapid turnover produce more revenue per unit of storage space.

Advertising, Competition, and Truth

The need to advertise greatly increases the "cost of entry" for small firms seeking to break into markets dominated by large firms. In some industries, notably the cosmetics and the non-prescription pharmaceuticals industries, advertising and packaging costs are a high proportion of total costs. In those industries, only large firms can afford the heavy cost of advertising, and small firms are barred, whatever the virtues of their products. However, advertising expenditures are only *one* cost of entry. The costs of entry are also high in certain industries that advertise rather little, notably steel, aluminum, and other industries that require heavy capital investment and large-scale production.

A further charge against advertising is more ethical than economic in nature. Much advertising, it is contended, is untruthful in the sense

Joel Gordon/DPI

that it tells us nothing about the product but a great deal about the people at whom the advertising is directed. Some critics of advertising charge that such practices are even more dishonest than the old hard sell, because there is nothing to prove or disprove.

Although the trend is disturbing, there are those who maintain that advertising can only persuade a consumer to make the first purchase. No amount of advertising, it is argued, can sell a product a second time if the product is unsatisfactory to consumers.

Questions

1. "Advertising serves to protect existing products. It is therefore a barrier to competition and a means of monopolizing markets." Evaluate.

2. The Federal Trade Commission has charged some oligopolistic firms with (a) conspiring to share markets and (b) maintaining market shares through advertising. Are these charges logically consistent?

3. Do you agree with those critics who contend that advertising should inform rather than persuade? Do you believe that advertising bamboozles consumers into buying unwanted things? Discuss.

What You Have Learned in This Chapter

1. Monopolistic competition exists in industries characterized by many firms producing heterogeneous products. Product differentiation, which is largely a matter of buyers' perceptions, is thus a key factor among firms in such industries. Monopolistically competitive industries are a major segment of our economy.

2. The $MC = MR$ principle serves as a guide for profit maximization in monopolistic competition. Because there is reasonable freedom of entry, firms will *tend* to earn approximately normal profits in the long run, but there may be exceptions.

3. Advertising plays a major role in monopolistic competition because of the importance of product differentiation. The pros and cons of advertising have centered around three major issues: information versus persuasion; competition versus concentration; efficiency versus waste.

4. Monopolistic competition is subject to the same basic criticism as monopoly: Resource misallocation resulting from output restriction and higher prices. This is due to adherence to the $MC = MR$ standard rather than the $MC = P$ standard of production and pricing. In addition, monopolistic competition encourages nonprice competition, which may or may not be undesirable, and it results in

"wastes" as well as the perpetuation of "sick" industries that are overcrowded and inefficient.

5. Oligopolistic industries consist of several firms producing either homogeneous products (perfect oligopoly) or heterogeneous products (imperfect oligopoly). These industries play a major role in our economy. Oligopolistic firms usually tend to be characterized by substantial economies of scale, a history of growth through merger, mutual dependence, price rigidity, and nonprice competition.

6. The $MC = MR$ principle applies to oligopolistic firms that seek to maximize profit. In addition, each firm may see itself as being faced with a kinked demand curve, indicating that competitors will follow a price decrease by any one seller, but not a price increase.

7. The kinked demand curve results in a stable price, but it leaves the seller uncertain about the determination of the price itself. This has prompted oligopolists to reduce price uncertainty either by colluding with competitors or by accepting one of the competitors as a price leader and matching that firm's price.

8. Oligopolies are subject to the same basic criticism as monopolies: they result in resource misallocation caused by output restric-

tion and higher prices. This is due to their adherence to the $MC = MR$ standard rather than the $MC = P$ standard of production and pricing. However, there is growing evidence that oligopolies are more efficient, and that their social costs are therefore less significant, than has been traditionally assumed.

9. It is difficult to state unequivocally that firms in imperfect competition either do or do not seek to maximize profits. In reality, it is quite likely that they strive to "satisfice" rather than to maximize. Nevertheless, the assumption of profit maximization is fundamental in microeconomic theory because it permits an evaluation of the social function of the firm as a resource allocator.

For Discussion

1. *Terms and concepts to review:*
imperfect competition
monopolistic competition
selling costs
nonprice competition
"wastes" of monopolistic competition
Hotelling's paradox
oligopoly
kinked demand curve
duopoly
price leadership
concentration ratio
contestable market
countervailing power
"satisfice"

2. Firms in monopolistic competition tend to be only normally profitable in the long run. The same is true of firms in perfect competition. Therefore, why criticize monopolistic competition?

3. Why should firms in monopolistic competition spend so much money on advertising if much of it has canceling effects?

4. Is the kinked demand curve an objective fact of the marketplace, or is it a subjective phenomenon in the mind of each oligopolist? Explain.

5. Why is there a tendency toward some type of externally imposed price decision in oligopoly? What are some examples?

6. The need for self-protection is one reason often given for the rise of labor unions, consumer cooperatives, and agricultural cooperatives. Can you explain why in the light of this chapter?

7. One could easily argue that, because it is more *ethical* for people to cooperate than to compete, the same standard should apply to business firms. Do you agree?

8. "Economic theory is unrealistic because it assumes that firms seek to maximize profits. Yet we know that in reality this assumption is not a valid one." Evaluate this statement.

9. Are prices determined by costs of production or are costs of production determined by prices? Discuss. (**Suggestion** Think in terms of both perfect and imperfect competition.)

10. Case Problem: Saturn Publishing Co.
Saturn Publishing Co. publishes two monthly magazines, called *Action* and *Brisk*. The company charges the same price for both magazines, but the sales of *Brisk* are about twice those of *Action*. Both magazines are among the leaders in their field, with combined sales of 5 to 6 million copies per month. In this sales range, therefore, the marginal cost of producing the two magazines is practically constant. Further, it has been established, on the basis of previous pricing experiments in various markets, that the elasticity of demand is equal for the two magazines at the present price.

Recently, the president of the company posed the question of whether it is consistent with profit maximization for the two magazines to carry the same price. The sales manager replied that, in order for Saturn to maximize its profits, it ought to charge a higher price for *Brisk* than for *Action*, since demand is greater for the former.

The president has called you in as a consulting economist to settle the question. Both the president and the sales manager studied a considerable amount of economics while in college and both are fairly familiar with such concepts as average revenue, marginal revenue, and marginal cost. Can you provide them with an analytical (graphic) solution to the problem?

11. In the book publishing business, it is inherent in the royalty arrangement that the publisher's pricing policy results in an economic conflict between the author and the publisher. Thus, in the great majority of cases, the author's royalty is a percentage of the total revenue that the publisher receives on the sale of the book. The publisher, however, determines the price of the book (and also incurs all costs of manufacturing, promotion, and distribution). It follows that *the price that maximizes profit for the publisher is higher, and the output lower, than the price and output that maximize royalty payments for the author.* Why? Demonstrate this proposition graphically, using marginal analysis.

12. Case Problem: Scrumptious Pizza Co.

Scrumptious Pizza Co. operates a national chain of pizza parlors on a franchise basis. The company maintains a closely controlled, uniform set of production standards and selling prices as a condition for granting franchises. One of the unique features of Scrumptious pizzas is that they are made with a special blend of fine imported cheeses.

Recent cost increases of cheeses, dough, and other ingredients have made it necessary for the company to consider a revision of its pricing and product policies for all its franchises. Three alternatives have been proposed:

(a) Increase price by some specified percentage, but maintain quantity and quality.

(b) Reduce quantity by some specified percentage, but maintain price and quality.

(c) Reduce quality, but maintain price and quantity.

The company hired an economic consulting firm to estimate the effects on profits of each of these choices. In its report, the consulting firm submitted the following *payoff matrix.* This is a table showing the probable level of profit that will result from each alternative and its associated sales level.

For example, suppose that the company chooses alternative A and that its average daily national sales are 6,000 pizzas. Then its *expected profit* on those sales will be 15 percent of $2,000, or $300. On the other hand, if its sales are 7,000, its expected profit will be 25 percent of $2,800, or $700. By extending this idea, you can see that the total expected profit of any alternative is simply the *sum* of the separate expected profits that comprise it. (Notice that for each alternative, the probabilities must add to 1.0, or 100 percent.)

(a) Which alternative should the company choose, assuming that it wants to maximize its profit?

(b) Which alternative should the company choose in order to maximize its sales?

(c) Is it possible to have a situation in which one alternative would maximize profit and another would maximize sales, or must the same alternative do both? Explain.

Alternatives, profits, and probabilities	Average daily national pizza sales			
	6,000	7,000	8,000	9,000
Alternative A				
Profit	$2,000	$2,800	$4,000	$4,200
Probability*	0.15	0.25	0.30	0.30
Alternative B				
Profit	$1,500	$3,000	$5,000	$5,100
Probability*	0.25	0.25	0.40	0.10
Alternative C				
Profit	$1,200	$2,500	$4,500	$4,800
Probability*	0.05	0.05	0.40	0.50

* The probability of an outcome is the likelihood of its occurrence. It can be expressed as a percentage by multiplying by 100.

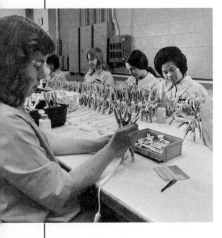

24
CHAPTER

Hiring the Factors of Production: Marginal Productivity and Income Distribution

Learning guide
Watch for answers to these important questions

What considerations determine a firm's decision to hire factors of production? How do a firm's inputs, outputs, and revenues relate to one another? What fundamental principle determines the price paid for a factor of production?

How do you distinguish between a change in demand for a factor of production and a change in the quantity demanded? What determines the former? What determines the latter? How do these affect the elasticity of demand?

What is the equilibrium condition, or equation, that expresses a firm's minimum cost in the input market? What is the equilibrium condition, or equation, for maximum profit?

How does the marginal-productivity theory serve as a guide for equitable income distribution in a pure capitalistic system? What are the difficulties of employing the theory for this purpose?

This chapter explains a basic principle that determines the hiring of productive resources.

Until now we have focused on the behavior of firms in the *output* markets. This has been done by examining the principles of product pricing and production under the three main types of market conditions—perfect competition, monopoly, and imperfect competition.

But to produce their products, firms must buy factors of production. Therefore, the behavior of firms in the *input* markets must be examined in order to see how principles of resource employment can be developed. That is the purpose of this chapter. It establishes microeconomic principles pertaining to the input side of the market rather than the output side. As you will soon see, the most interesting aspect of input principles is the way in which they parallel the ones that you learned about earlier. As a result, the various pieces will fit together like those of a large jigsaw puzzle.

The Marginal-Productivity Theory: How the Firm Buys Factors of Production

If you were a business executive, what principles would guide you in deciding how much of a resource you should purchase? After all, buying too little can be just as unprofitable as buying too much. A major problem facing a firm that wishes to maximize its profits is to utilize precisely the right combination of inputs. In order to do this, management must understand the nature of its demand for resources.

The demand for any resource is a *derived demand*. That is, the demand for a resource is based on what a particular factor of production contributes to the product for which it is used. For example, the demand for steel is derived in part from the demand for automobiles. The demand for land in the heart of a city is derived from the demand for the office buildings and stores that will be built upon it. The demand for college professors is derived mostly from the demand for education as measured by college enrollments. As a general rule, and as you will see shortly, the concept of derived demand embraces the following principles:

The number of units of a factor of production that a firm employs depends on the profitability of that factor relative to other factors of production.

> Other things being equal, the quantity of a factor of production that a firm demands will depend on three things:
>
> **1.** The productivity of the factor.
>
> **2.** The value or price of the product that the factor is used to make.
>
> **3.** The price of the factor relative to the prices of other factors.

These principles make a good deal of practical sense. For instance, they tell you the following (all other things remaining constant):

1. An increase in the output of a factor of production relative to its input will result in an increase in the demand for that factor by the firms that use it.

2. If improvements in a product or reductions in its price create a greater demand for it, the need for the factors that produce or use that commodity will also increase. *Example:* electronic computers and computer programmers.

3. If the price of a factor of production becomes cheaper relative to other factors, the quantity demanded of the lower-priced factor will increase if producers begin to substitute it for the more expensive inputs. *Example:* labor-saving machinery relative to high-cost labor.

Physical Inputs, Outputs, and Revenues

Exhibit 1 provides a more precise understanding of a firm's demand for an input. The first three columns illustrate the familiar law of variable proportions, which you learned in the study of production. They show how the total and marginal physical products change when a variable input such as labor is applied to fixed inputs such as land and capital.

The remaining columns of the table convert these physical data into revenues. In these columns, the assumption has been made that the firm is perfectly competitive in the sale of the product to which the variable factor is contributing. This is why the price of the product [column (4)] is assumed to be constant at $10 per unit.

The last two columns of the table are based upon the total revenue figures [column (5)]. They introduce two new terms. The first is *marginal revenue product* (MRP), defined as the change in total revenue resulting from a unit change in input. The second is *average revenue product* (ARP), which is the ratio of total revenue to the quantity of the variable input employed.

The marginal revenue product of a factor of production tells you the value of that factor's contribution to production.

Because the firm is operating under perfect competition in the input market, the supply of labor resources is so large that the firm cannot influence the price by buying or not buying. The firm can purchase as many units as it wants at the given price. Hence, *the marginal cost of the resource will be the same as its price.*

The Most Profitable Level of Input

A firm will hire a factor of production up to the point at which the marginal cost of the factor equals its price (or marginal revenue product).

When the revenue data from the table in Exhibit 1 are graphed, they yield the curves shown in the figures. In this case, since we want to relate the firm's revenues to the labor that it hires, it is easier to plot the revenue curves against input rather than output on the horizontal axis. It also helps simplify matters a bit to assume, as stated in the footnote to column (1) of the table, that there are no fixed costs. That is, the firm's fixed factors of production are available free. This means that the firm's total variable costs are the same as its total costs. Therefore, the TC curve emanates from the origin of the figure rather than from a point higher up on the vertical axis.

What is the most profitable level of input for the firm? The answer depends on the *marginal cost of the input as compared with its marginal revenue product.* In other words, the answer depends on the amount each additional unit of the input adds to the firm's total cost as compared to the amount it adds to the firm's total revenue.

For example, Figure (*a*) shows that, when the marginal cost or price of labor is $20 per person, the most profitable input level is 4 persons. At this input the TC_1 curve in the figure is parallel to a tangent drawn to the TR curve at D. At the same time, Figure (*b*) shows that at this level of input the marginal cost of the factor (MCF), which is the same as the price of the factor (P_F), is equal to its marginal revenue product MRP.

Similarly, at $39 per person, the firm's most profitable input is 3 persons. This is again determined in Figure (*b*), where $MCF = P_F = MRP$. On the other hand, if the factor were available free, the most profitable input level would be 5 persons, because the TC curve in Figure (*a*) would lie along the horizontal axis and would be parallel to a horizontal tangent drawn at the peak of the TR curve at E.

Finally, at $61 per person, the firm would just be covering its variable costs, because TC_3 is tangent to TR. Hence, the most profitable input would, theoretically, be 2.2 persons. This is again determined in Figure (*b*), where $MCF = P_F = MRP$. (**Note** If you dislike the idea of measuring "fractions of persons," you can think of the horizontal axis as being scaled in terms of hours of labor time instead of numbers of persons.)

> Because the MCF or P_F line tells you the number of workers available to the firm at the particular wage, it is a *supply curve* of labor. The firm is thus faced with a horizontal supply curve of the factor in the input market just as it is faced with a horizontal demand curve for its product in the output market.

Two Important Principles

The fundamental input principle of profit maximization is: MCF = P_F = MRP.

Two important principles follow directly from these marginal concepts. As you will see in the following paragraphs:

> When there is perfect competition in the input market, the marginal cost of an input will be the same as its price. Therefore:
>
> **1.** The firm's demand curve for an input will be its *MRP* curve below the maximum point of its *ARP*.
>
> **2.** The firm will maximize its profits by purchasing factors of production up to the point at which $MCF = P_F = MRP$.

Exhibit 1

Demand for a Resource by a Firm

(assuming perfect competition in the output market and perfect competition in the input market)

(1) Units of variable factor, F (labor)*	(2) Total physical product, TPP	(3) Marginal physical product, MPP **Change in (2)** / **Change in (1)**	(4) Product price, P	(5) Total revenue, TR (2) × (4)	(6) Marginal-revenue product, MRP **Change in (5)** / **Change in (1)**	(7) Average-revenue product, ARP (5) ÷ (1)
0	0		$10	$ 0		$?
		4			$40	
1	4		10	40		40.0
		8			80	
2	12		10	120		60.0
		5			50	
3	17		10	170		56.7
		3			30	
4	20		10	200		50.0
		1			10	
5	21		10	210		42.0
		−1			−10	
6	20		10	200		33.3

* Labor is assumed to be the only variable input. All other inputs are fixed and are available free. Therefore, total (labor) cost equals total variable cost.

Figure (a): The most profitable input level occurs where the distance between the TR and TC curves is a maximum. This is where a tangent to the TR curve is parallel to the TC curve. (For example, at $20 per person, the most profitable input is 4 persons, because this is the input at which the tangent at D is parallel to the straight-line TC_1 curve.)

Figure (b): By following the vertical dashed lines downward, it can be seen that the most profitable input also occurs where the marginal cost of the factor (MCF) or its price (P_F) equals its marginal-revenue product (MRP). Therefore, given the marginal costs or prices of the factors of production, the firm will maximize its profits by hiring each factor of production up to the point where its $MCF = P_F = MRP$. The firm's demand curve for an input is thus the MRP curve up to the maximum point on the ARP curve. As the price of the input falls, the firm hires more of it by following its MRP curve. (**Note** The MRP curve, like the marginal curves in previous chapters, is plotted to the *midpoints* between the integers on the horizontal axis. This is because the curve reflects the *change* in total revenue from one unit of input to the next.)

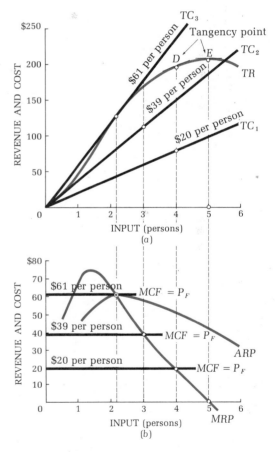

Technical Note (Optional) Here is a simple explanation in geometric terms. Each MCF curve in the lower figure is a graph of the *slope* of its corresponding TC curve in the upper figure. Likewise, the MRP curve in the lower figure is a graph of the *slope* of the TR curve in the upper figure. The input at which the slopes are equal (or at which a tangent in the upper figure is parallel to a TC curve) is the one at which net profit is maximized. You can verify these profit-maximizing principles by following the vertical dashed lines downward at each level of input.

By this time you may have noticed a certain symmetry between the input and output markets. For example, the two input propositions above are analogous to two output propositions that you learned a few chapters earlier in the study of perfect competition. As you will recall:

1. A perfectly competitive firm's MC curve is its supply curve above the minimum point on its AVC curve.

2. A perfectly competitive firm maximizes its profit by producing to the level at which its $MC = P = MR$.

Therefore, in order to visualize the symmetry between the input market and the output market, try to imagine what the curves in Figure (*b*) of Exhibit 1 would look like if the diagram were flipped upside down on its horizontal axis. Or, if you have trouble visualizing this, try turning the book upside down and looking through the back of the page while holding it up to the light. You will see that the ARP and MRP curves resemble the AVC and MC curves of a firm in perfect competition. This suggests that there is a symmetry, in the theory of perfect competition, between the input market and the output market. *Indeed, the curves in one market are the reciprocals of the corresponding curves in the other market.*

In economic terms, why does the firm maximize its profit at the input level at which $MCF = P_F = MRP$? Because at any input less than this the added cost of an additional unit is less than the added revenue, so it pays to hire another unit. At any input greater than this, the opposite is true. Therefore, the fundamental principle of profit maximization—the $MC = MR$ rule, which you learned in previous chapters—applies here as well. In addition, a principle of fundamental importance can now be stated:

> In competitive input markets, the price paid to hire a factor of production will equal its marginal productivity. Therefore, the owners of each factor will be paid the value of what their factor contributes. This is called the *marginal-productivity theory of income distribution*

Demand for Inputs

You learned in the study of supply and demand that the market demand curve for a product is derived by summing the individual demand curves of all buyers in the market. A parallel situation exists in the market for inputs. Other things remaining the same, the market demand curve for a factor is derived by summing the individual demands or MRP curves of all firms in the market. Like any other demand curve, this aggregate MRP curve for a factor of production will be subject to two kinds of changes. One kind consists of changes in demand. The other type consists of changes in the quantity demanded.

Changes in Demand

The market MRP curve for a given factor may shift from one position to another for several reasons:

1. A Change in Demand for the Final Product For example, a change in demand for houses will affect the price of houses and may also change the demand for lumber, bricks, carpenters, and other resources.

2. A Change in Productivity Improvements in the quantity and quality of the fixed factors of production will increase the productivity of the variable factor. Thus, workers who have more and better machines and land are more productive than those who do not.

3. A Change in the Prices of Substitute or Complementary Factors Some resources may be substitutable, some may be complementary, and some may be neither. Labor and machines provide typical examples of all three possibilities. Changes in the price of one relative to the other may encourage firms to use more or less of either or both. The choice depends on the proportions in which they must be used—such as the number of workers needed to operate a machine.

Changes in the Quantity Demanded: Elasticity of Demand for Factor Services

There are also conditions that will determine changes in the quantity demanded of a given factor. As you will recall, these changes represent movements along the curve due to a change in price. Hence, these movements reflect the sensitivity or elasticity of demand for the resource. What determines this elasticity?

Several conditions determine the elasticity of the MPP curve.

1. The Rate of Decline of Marginal Physical Product The rate at which the *MPP* curve declines as the variable factor is added to the fixed factors depends on the technological nature of the production process. The faster it declines, the more inelastic the resulting *MRP* curve will be and hence the less will be the change in the quantity of input demanded relative to a change in its price.

2. The Elasticity of Demand for the Final Product The greater the elasticity of demand for the final product, the more elastic the demand for the factors used in making it. For instance, if the demand for a final product is relatively elastic, a small increase in its price will result in a more-than-proportional decrease in the purchase of it. This will cause a relatively large drop in the quantity demanded of the resources that are used to produce it.

3. The Proportion of the Factor's Cost Relative to Total Production Cost The larger the cost of a factor of production relative to the total cost of the product, the more elastic the demand for the factor. For example, if labor costs are only 10 percent of the cost of a product, a 10 percent wage increase will raise production costs by 1 percent. Hence, the effect on the final price of the product should be small, and the quantity demanded of the factor should be relatively little affected. On the other hand, if labor costs are 90 percent of production costs, a 10 percent wage increase will have a more substantial impact on production costs as well as on final prices and sales. Therefore, the decrease in the quantity demanded of the factor is likely to be relatively large.

4. The Ease of Factor Substitutability The greater the number of different factors that can be substituted for one another in a given production process, the larger will be the elasticity of demand for any one of these factors. Thus, if copper, aluminum, and other light metals had equal conductive properties, the demand for each of them by the electrical industry would be highly elastic. But the fact is that copper is a superior conductor and hence the demand for it is relatively inelastic within its typical price ranges.

The Optimum Allocation of Inputs

The foregoing principles apply to all factors of production that the firm may purchase. Let us assume, therefore, that the firm is buying two factors of production, labor and capital, and that these factors are substitutable for one another. There are two questions to be answered:

1. What is the least-cost combination of factors needed to produce a given output?

2. Which combination of factors yields the largest profits to the firm?

The first question is concerned with cost minimization; the second is concerned with profit maximization.

Cost Minimization

A firm minimizes the costs of its inputs by equating the ratios of marginal physical product to price for all of the factors that it hires.

If you were a manufacturer interested in producing a certain volume of output, in what proportion would you use the various inputs? The question is important because, although many different combinations will produce a given level of output, only one combination is cheapest. Clearly, the cheapest combination depends on the relative prices of the inputs. As a manager, therefore, you would adhere to the following fundamental principle:

> **Least-cost principle.** The least-cost combination of inputs is achieved when a dollar's worth of any input adds as much to total physical output as a dollar's worth of any other input.

To illustrate, suppose that you are buying only two factors of production, A and B, in a perfectly competitive market. Letting MPP_A represent the marginal physical product of A, and P_A the price of A, and similarly for factor B, the equation of minimum cost is

$$\frac{MPP_A}{P_A} = \frac{MPP_B}{P_B} \tag{1}$$

This indicates that, if the price of an input rises, less of it should be used, thereby increasing its marginal product. Simultaneously, more of the other input should be used, thereby decreasing its marginal product. As an example, suppose that P_A and P_B are each $1, and at some given volume of output,

MPP_A = 10 units
MPP_B = 8 units

Assuming that you want to minimize costs at the prescribed output level, you should proceed as follows:

1. Buy $1.00 less of B, thereby reducing production by 8 units.

2. Buy $0.80 more of A, thereby increasing production by 8 units (= 4/5 of the marginal product of a dollar's worth of A).

3. Save $0.20.

This example shows how you would go about minimizing total costs for a given volume of output. Equation (1), of course, can be extended to include any number of inputs and corresponding prices. When all the ratios are equal, total costs are minimized at the established output volume. If a change should then occur in the price of one of the factors, the equality will no longer hold. This means that the cheaper factor will have to be substituted for more expensive ones until equality is restored. These ideas help explain why business firms are always seeking to change the composition of their inputs, replacing more costly ones (such as labor) with less costly ones (such as machines).

Profit Maximization

The second problem concerns the following question: Of all possible factor combinations, which one yields the largest profits for the firm? The answer has already been indicated, and it may now be expressed as a general principle:

A firm maximizes profits on its inputs by equating the ratios of marginal revenue product to price for all of the factors that it hires.

> **Maximum-profit principle.** The most profitable combination of inputs is achieved by employing each factor of production up to the point at which the marginal cost of the factor is equal to its marginal revenue product.

This principle was demonstrated in Exhibit 1. When the firm is hiring a resource in a perfectly competitive market, it will employ further units of the resource as long as the *MRP* of the factor is greater than its price (or marginal cost). Why? Because each additional unit adds more to the firm's total revenue than to its total cost. Conversely, the firm will release some units of the resource if the *MRP* of the factor is less than its price. This is because each reduction of one unit of the input lowers the firm's total cost by more than it lowers total revenue.

These ideas can be summarized with a formula. You know that the firm will maximize profits by hiring units of factor A up to the point at which the marginal revenue product of that factor, MRP_A, is equal to its price, P_A:

$$MRP_A = P_A$$

If both sides of this equation are divided by P_A (or in other words, if P_A is "transposed" to the left side), then

$$\frac{MRP_A}{P_A} = 1 \tag{2}$$

Similarly, the firm will buy units of factor B up to the point at which the marginal-revenue product of that factor, MRP_B, is equal to its price P_B:

$$MRP_B = P_B$$

If you divide both sides by P_B (or transpose P_B to the left side),

$$\frac{MRP_B}{P_B} = 1 \tag{3}$$

Because each of their ratios is each equal to 1, equations (2) and (3) can be expressed as a single equation for maximum-profit equilibrium:

$$\frac{MRP_A}{P_A} = \frac{MRP_B}{P_B} = 1 \tag{4}$$

Equation (4), like equation (1) for least cost, can be extended to include any number of inputs and their corresponding prices. In general, equation (4) defines the profit-maximizing or equilibrium conditions of a firm in a perfectly competitive input market. It shows that:

> The most profitable level of input for a firm in a perfectly competitive input market is attained when the firm earns the same increment in revenue *per dollar of outlay* from each of the factors that it hires, with each ratio equal to 1. That is, the firm hires each factor up to the point at which the marginal revenue product of the factor equals its price.

It helps to translate these ideas into concrete terms. For example, suppose a firm is hiring two factors of production, labor L and capital C. If these factors are substitutable for one another, equation (4) says that the company will maximize profits in a perfectly competitive input market by hiring to the point at which

$$\frac{MRP_L}{P_L} = \frac{MRP_C}{P_C} = 1$$

In general, the firm can be thought of as juggling all of its factors of production simultaneously.

What would happen if this equality did not occur? In other words, suppose the first ratio in this equation were greater than the second and the employment of capital were already in equilibrium at the point at which $MRP_C/P_C = 1$. Then the firm would be earning more of an increment in revenue on its labor relative to the price of labor than it would be earning on its capital relative to the price of capital. Graphically, this means that the firm would be to the *left* of its optimum input point for labor. Hence, it would pay for the company to hire more workers, thereby reducing MRP_L until the ratios were equal.

Conversely, what would happen if the first ratio were less than the second? Graphically, this means that the firm would be to the *right* of its optimum input point for labor. Therefore, it would pay for the company to reduce its number of workers, thereby raising MRP_L until the ratios were again equal.

In a more general sense, neither factor need be in equilibrium to start. You can think of the firm as juggling all its factors of production simultaneously until it achieves the desired equilibrium ratio, which is noted above.

Marginal Productivity, Income Distribution, and Equity

You have seen that, when there is perfect competition in the input market, each firm will purchase factors of production up to the point at which the price or marginal cost of the factor is equal to its marginal-revenue productivity. Expressed in real terms, this means that the owners of each factor will be paid a value equal to what their factor contributes to the national output. Stated differently, the owners of the factor will be paid what their factor is "worth." This concept, as you have learned, is known as the *marginal-productivity theory of income distribution*.

The theory itself was first introduced near the turn of the present century by a distinguished American economist, John Bates Clark. It was widely supported because it showed that a competitive (capitalistic) system distributed the national output in a socially "just" and "equitable" manner. However, economists and social critics have pointed out, over the years, three fundamental criticisms of this interpretation.

Imperfect Markets A large part of the market for inputs is imperfect rather than perfect. Thus, certain factors of production tend to be relatively immobile, and in some markets there may be only one or a few firms buying inputs instead of a large number of firms. In addition, union restrictions, patent controls, tariff barriers, and other limitations also create obstacles to a smoothly functioning market for inputs as envisioned in the competitive model.

Complex Production Processes Most production processes involve complex interrelations among inputs. Consequently, when a variety of factors are employed, it is usually impossible to divide the total output into the amounts contributed by each class of factors, such as labor and capital.

Normative Versus Positive Standards Such terms as "just" and "equitable" involve normative rather than positive concepts—what *ought* to be rather than what *is*. Their meanings may also vary from time to time and from place to place according to the customs and beliefs of society. Thus, in a philosophical sense, it is not necessarily "just" that a person who is twice as productive as another should be paid twice as much. It might equally well be argued, for example, that it is "just" for a family of six to receive twice as much as a family of three—regardless of their relative productivities. In other words, the *normative* question of what constitutes a just distribution of income is quite different from the *positive* question of what specific steps can be taken to alter the distribution of income. The former is a philosophical question; the latter is an economic one.

It is appropriate to conclude, therefore, with an important generalization:

> The central idea of the marginal-productivity principle is that an employer will not pay more for a unit of input—whether it be a person, or an acre of land, or a dollar's worth of borrowed capital—than it is worth to the firm. The employer will continue to acquire an input as long as each unit purchased adds more to the firm's total revenue than it adds to its total cost. Because it is assumed that the units can be infinitesimally small, the net result is that the employer's profit is maximized at the point at which the added (or marginal) cost of the input equals its added (or marginal) revenue product.

In short, the marginal-productivity principle is correct in the sense that it can be deduced logically from given assumptions. However, it should be understood for what it is: *a guide for maximizing a firm's profits in the input market under prescribed market conditions.* (See "Leaders in Economics," page 536.)

The marginal-productivity theory provides an explanation of income distribution under pure capitalism.

What You Have Learned in This Chapter

1. The marginal-productivity theory explains how a firm purchases its inputs in the factor market. In general, a firm's demand for any factor of production is a derived demand based on the productivity of the factor, the price of the final product, and the price of the factor relative to the prices of other factors.

2. The aggregate MRP curve for a factor of production is determined by summing the individual MRP curves. Like any demand curve, the MRP curve is subject to changes in demand for a factor and to changes in the quantity demanded. The latter is based on a change in price and reflects the elasticity of demand for a factor.

Leaders in Economics

John Bates Clark
1847–1938
Marginal-Productivity Theory

Brown Brothers

"It is the purpose of this work to show that the distribution of the income of society is controlled by a natural law, and that this law, if it worked without friction, would give to every agent of production the amount of wealth which that agent creates."

In these words, J. B. Clark outlined the general plan for his book, *The Distribution of Wealth,* which was published in 1899. This was the first American work in pure economic theory. Prior to that time, American economists were generally interested in the socioeconomic problems of their period and in the achievement of social reforms. Clark's book still stands as one of the great landmarks in economic theory.

Natural Law
Clark began by asking: "Is there a natural law according to which the income of society is divided . . . ? If so, what is that law? This is the problem which demands solution."

As he proceeded to answer this question, he developed a distinction between static and dynamic forces in the economy. The static forces, he said, are the result of "universal economic laws" which are always applicable to the economy, such as the law of diminishing returns, the law of diminishing utility, and so on. But the dynamic forces that exist in society—changes in population, capital, production techniques, and forms of industrial organization—are constantly causing fluctuations in production, prices, and the like. In Clark's words, "Static forces set the standards, dynamic forces produce the variations."

Marginal Analysis
Clark went on to say: "Each unit of labor . . . is worth to its employer what the last unit produces. When the force is complete, no one body of a thousand men can withdraw without lessening the product of the whole society by the same amount that we have attributed to the one that we last set working. The effective value of any unit of labor is always what the whole society with all its capital produces, minus what it would produce if that unit were to be taken away. This sets the universal standard of pay. A unit of labor consists, in the supposed case, of a thousand men, and the product of it is the natural pay of a thousand men. If the men are equal, a thousandth part of this amount is the natural pay of any one of them." This "one", Clark pointed out, is the *marginal* worker.

"Marginalist School"
Actually, Clark had much in common with his great British contemporary, Alfred Marshall. Each used the static analysis, but Marshall was more realistic and analyzed many problems of dynamics and change. Clark, however, raised marginal-productivity analysis to its highest standard of perfection. In so doing, he founded a "marginalist school" of thought, which established a pattern for teaching and research in economics that is at the heart of microeconomics.

The modern version of the marginal-productivity theory is essentially due to Clark's treatment. His theory of wages is a demand theory that assumes a given quantity of labor in its analysis of the marginal product of labor. It was this theory, with its impeccable logic, that was widely employed by others to support the contention that a (perfectly competitive) capitalistic system distributes incomes in a "just" manner according to what each of the factors contributes.

In later decades, the development of the theory of imperfect competition and the growing power of labor unions made some of the unrealistic assumptions of Clark's theory more apparent.

3. If a firm's production function and the market prices of the resources it purchases are given (that is, if it is hiring factors in a perfectly competitive market for inputs), it can seek the factor combination that assures (a) least cost and (b) maximum profit. The least-cost combination requires that the marginal physical product per dollar spent on every factor be equal. The maximum-profit combination requires that the marginal-revenue product per dollar spent on all factors be equal to 1. Both equilibrium conditions can be achieved simultaneously.

4. The marginal-productivity theory of income distribution is a guide for profit maximization in the input market. It does not purport to say what pattern of income distribution is "just" or "equitable." That is a normative question based on philosophical rather than economic considerations.

For Discussion

1. *Terms and concepts to review:*
derived demand
marginal-revenue product
average-revenue product
marginal-productivity theory of income
 distribution
least-cost principle
maximum-profit principle

2. What analogies do you see between a firm in the output market and a firm in the input market with respect to each of the following: (a) the profit-maximizing rule; (b) marginal cost and average variable cost, and marginal-revenue product and average-revenue product.

3. Distinguish between a change in demand for an input and a change in the quantity demanded. What are the causes of each?

4. "The way to eliminate poverty and unemployment is through minimum-wage legislation. By raising the minimum wage, workers are given more purchasing power. This creates a greater demand for goods and services, thereby putting unemployed people to work." Evaluate this argument using the graphic tools employed in this chapter. (**Hint** There are *two* issues involved here. Can you identify them?)

5. "The marginal-productivity theory of income distribution is a *fair* theory because it demonstrates that each worker gets what he or she deserves." Evaluate.

6. "It is meaningless to say that the equilibrium factor price will equal the marginal-revenue product, since the latter varies with the number of factor units employed." Comment. Rephrase if necessary.

25
CHAPTER

Determination of Factor Prices

Learning guide

Watch for the answers to these important questions

Have wages and productivity increased at about the same rate over the long run? Why are there different wage-determination models? Is any one of these models the appropriate one for today?

Is rent a price-determined or price-determining payment? Is rent a cost or a surplus? How does rent arise?

How does the loanable-funds theory of interest differ from the liquidity-preference theory? Are the two theories mutually exclusive? What economic function does the interest rate perform?

What are the three major theories of profit? What economic function does profit perform?

This chapter explains how wages, rent, interest, and profit are determined in a capitalistic economy.

Most of our nation's income consists of wages and salaries paid to workers. The rest of the economic pie is sliced into rent, interest, and profit. These incomes are the payments made to resource owners who sell their factors of production—labor, land, capital, and entrepreneurship—in the economy's markets.

What determines the levels of wages, rent, interest, and profit? In this chapter we seek answers to these questions by deriving basic principles. You will find that many of the ideas from previous chapters dealing with supply and demand, competition, market structures, cost and demand curves, and the like play an integral role in determining factor prices.

What will not be so apparent, however, is that, although the theory of wages and (to a somewhat lesser extent) the theory of rent are fairly well established in modern economics, the theories of interest and profit involve various unsettled questions. These questions are the subject of more advanced discussions. We shall not delve into them in much detail, because our purpose at this time is to concentrate on the main features of the various theories rather than on the controversies that surround them.

Theory of Wages

Wages constitute about three-fourths of the national income. But what determines their level? Let us begin with some definitions.

Wages are the price paid for the use of labor. They are usually expressed as time rates, such as a certain amount per hour, day, or week, or, less frequently, as piece rates, such as a certain amount per unit of work performed or product produced.

Labor, as defined in economics, means all personal services, including the activities of wage-workers, professional people, and independent businesspeople. Thus, "laborers" are workers of any sort, whether they receive compensation in the form of hourly wages or in the form of annual salaries, bonuses, or commissions. Our interest in this chapter is in wages as defined above, especially in wages expressed as time rates.

Money wages are the amount of money received per unit of time, such as cash wages received on an hourly, weekly, or monthly basis. In contrast, *real wages* are the quantity of goods that can be bought with money wages. Real wages thus depend on money wages and on the prices of the goods that are purchased with money wages. For instance, it is quite possible for your money wages to increase while your real wages either rise, remain the same, or fall, depending on what happens to prices.

The Trends of Wages and Productivity

Most of us know that wages differ between occupations and individuals. Nevertheless, it is reasonable to expect a long-run relationship between the wages of workers and their productivity. Over the years both should increase at roughly the same rate. In reality, wage gains have often outstripped increases in productivity, as shown in Exhibit 1.

The gains in productivity are due partly to improvements in the quality of labor, which result from better education, training, and health. The gains are also due partly to the remarkable growth in the quantity and quality of the other factors of production with which labor works. Because an economy's real income is the same as its real output, its income per worker is likely to keep pace with its output per worker over the long run if its markets are reasonably free and competitive. Therefore, it follows that, if income and output per worker do not keep pace, we should look for reasons why.

Wages have increased much faster than productivity over the long run.

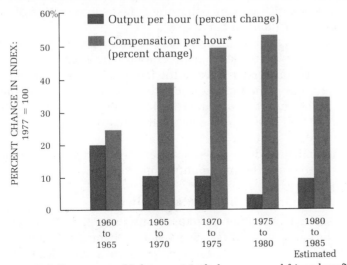

Source: U.S. Department of Labor   * Includes wages and fringe benefits.

Exhibit 1
Output and Earnings in the Private Business Sector

Wages and productivity used to increase at about the same rate. But the gap between them has widened over the years.

Exhibit 2
A Competitive Model of Wage Determination

In the competitive model, the wage at W and the corresponding quantity at M for a particular type of labor are determined in the market through the free interaction of supply and demand. Each firm can buy all the labor it wants at the market wage. Therefore, the supply curve of this factor to any individual firm is perfectly elastic and is the same as the marginal cost of the factor. The firm's most profitable input at N and the corresponding wage at W are determined where the company's $MCF = MRP$.

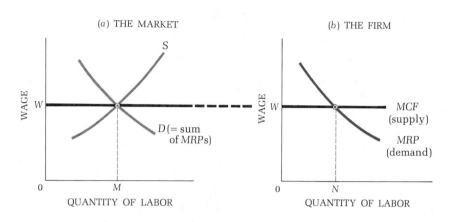

(a) THE MARKET

(b) THE FIRM

Some Wage-Determination Models

How are wages determined in the market at any given time? The answer depends on the type of market model that is assumed to exist in a particular situation. There are several interesting possibilities.

Competitive Model: Many Buyers, Many Sellers

Suppose that there is such a large number of employers hiring a certain type of labor and such a large number of employees selling it that no single employer or employee can influence the wage rate. We would then have a competitive model of wages, as illustrated in Exhibit 2.

In Figure (a) the downward-sloping market demand curve for this type of labor represents the sum of the individual MRPs (marginal revenue products) of the buyers. The upward-sloping market supply curve reflects the fact that, if these workers are already employed, the firms buying labor will have to offer higher wages to attract workers from other occupations and localities. The equilibrium wage at W and the equilibrium quantity at M are determined by the intersection of the labor supply and labor demand curves.

In Figure (b) the buying firm is faced with a perfectly elastic supply curve of labor at the market wage. The horizontal supply curve represents the marginal cost or price of the factor (MCF), as you learned earlier in the study of marginal-productivity analysis. Since the firm's most profitable input is obtained by following the $MCF = MRP$ rule, management will hire N units of labor at the corresponding market wage of W per unit.

What analogies do you see between this model and that of a perfectly competitive seller in the output market?

Monopsony Model: One Buyer, Many Sellers

A *monopsony* is a market structure consisting of a single buyer and many sellers of a good or service. Hence, it may be thought of as a "buyer's monopoly." (The term *monopsony* comes from the Greek *mono-*, "one," and *opsōnia*, "a buying.") An example would be a firm

In a competitive model, wages are determined by the supply of, and the demand for, labor.

Exhibit 3
A Monopsony Model of Wage Determination

In order to acquire more labor, the monopsonist must offer a higher price per unit for all units hired. The average cost of labor will thus rise, and the marginal cost of labor will be different from the average cost.

Cost Schedule of Labor Factor

Units of labor factor, F	Average cost of labor factor (= wage rate or supply price of labor), ACF or S	Total cost of labor factor, TCF	Marginal cost of labor factor, MCF
1	$5	$ 5	
			$ 7
2	6	12	
			9
3	7	21	
			11
4	8	32	
			13
5	9	45	

The MCF curve lies above the average-cost curve ACF, which is also the labor-supply curve S. By hiring to the point at which MCF = MRP, the monopsony firm employs L units and pays the lowest price per unit consistent with that volume of input, namely LT.

The monopsony firm thus restricts its employment of resources and pays a lower price per unit of input *than it would if it were a perfectly competitive buyer in the factor market.*

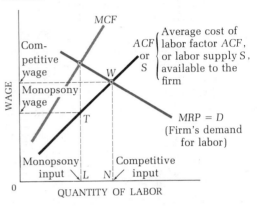

that is the sole employer in a company town, as has been the case in many mining towns. Similarly, in some farm areas a single food-processing plant dominates employment for many miles around.

A monopsony wage model is shown in Exhibit 3. Note from the second column of the table that the monopsonist must offer a higher wage rate or price per unit for *all* units in order to acquire more labor. (This is thus the "reverse" of the monopolist in the output market, who must charge a lower price per unit for *all* units in order to sell more products.) The result is that the marginal cost of labor will be greater than the average cost at each input, as shown in the figure.

The most profitable input level is determined, as always, by the location of the point at which MCF = MRP. Thus, the monopsonist will employ L units of labor and pay the lowest possible price for that quantity of labor, namely LT per unit. As a result, input, as compared to the amount at N, will be restricted. Further, the price per unit, as compared to the wage NW, will be lower than it would have been if the monopsonist were a perfectly competitive buyer in the input market.

What analogies do you see between this model and that of a pure monopolist in the output market?

In a monopsony model, both the wage paid and number of workers hired are less than they would be under perfect competition.

Monopoly Model: One Seller, Many Buyers

Suppose that a labor monopoly, such as a craft union whose members include all skilled workers in a particular trade (such as printing or plumbing), faces a market consisting of many buyers of that particular skill. What level of wages and what corresponding volume of labor output will result?

Exhibit 4

A Monopoly Model of Wage Determination

A monopoly union, such as a craft union composed of skilled workers like plumbers or electricians, will behave like any monopolist. It will restrict the supply of labor in order to command a higher price or wage rate than could be commanded in a perfectly competitive market.

The curves S and D represent the free-market or unrestricted supply and demand curves. By restricting the supply of labor from S to S', the monopoly union reduces the equilibrium output from N to N' and raises the equilibrium wage from W to W'.

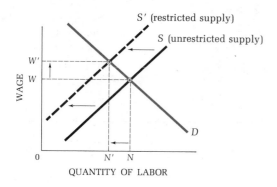

Exhibit 5

A Bilateral Monopoly Model of Wage Determination

In a bilateral monopoly, both parties may agree on some quantity, such as the amount at M. However, the theory does not predict the exact price. At best, we can say that the price of labor will be somewhere between the monopsony's preferred wage at U and the monopoly's preferred wage at V.

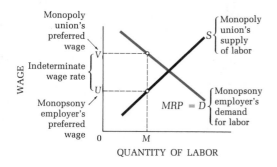

The model is illustrated in Exhibit 4. The curves S and D represent the normal supply and demand curves for labor in a free market. The equilibrium quantity of labor will be at N and the equilibrium wage will be at W. A monopoly union, however, will seek to restrict the supply of its labor in order to attain a higher wage for its members. The union will thus shift the supply curve to the left from S to S'. This will reduce the equilibrium quantity of labor to the level at N' and raise the equilibrium wage to the level at W'.

This analysis helps explain why some labor unions, especially certain craft unions, have established long apprenticeship requirements, high initiation fees, and similar obstacles to entry. The same is true of certain professional associations in such fields as medicine, law, and engineering. Their motives, at least partly, have been to curb the supply of labor in the market and thus to boost wage rates. Of course, there are also unions that do not seek to maximize wages. They may try to maximize membership instead so that they can wield more market power. In order to portray such cases, the model in Exhibit 4 would have to be modified to reflect these objectives.

Bilateral Monopoly Model: One Buyer, One Seller

A *bilateral monopoly* is a market structure in which a monopsonist buys from a monopolist. The simplest version, which *combines the main features of the previous monopsony and monopoly models*, is shown in Exhibit 5. Both the buyer and the seller are seeking to maximize their net benefits from the transaction. Therefore, let us assume that the two parties can agree on a given quantity to be exchanged, say the amount at M. It follows that the monopsonist will wish to purchase that quantity for the lower price at U, while the monopolist will want to sell that quantity for the higher price at V. What will be the transaction price?

Economists have been trying to solve this problem for decades. Many years ago a fascinating series of controlled experiments was conducted by an economist and a psychologist at Pennsylvania State University. In the experiments, numerous pairs of students participated in bargaining for real money. Out of these and other studies, there has emerged a fair amount of agreement that, although the quantity figure may be determinate in a bilateral monopoly model, the price level is not. The reason is that, even if the two traders agree on a quantity that maximizes their *joint* net benefits, the highest price acceptable to the buyer will give the whole net benefit to the seller, and vice versa.

The solution, therefore, is logically indeterminate. That is, the price will end up somewhere between the monopsony wage rate at U and the monopoly wage rate at V. However, the theory does not predict the precise level within this range. That may depend on psychological or other noneconomic considerations not represented by the model.

Conclusion: Which Wage Model Exists Today?

All these models are applicable to the modern economy. In the input markets, just as in the output markets, there are *degrees* of competition and monopoly. Hence, these models, or mixtures and modifications of them, can be useful in describing fundamental patterns of wage determination.

The majority of the American labor force is not organized in any labor union. Among agricultural and white-collar workers, for example, union membership is relatively slight and the situation conforms roughly to the competitive model. On the other hand, in some of the service industries, significant segments of the labor force are unorganized and relatively immobile for long periods. Here, the monopsony model provides a good approximation—with an allowance for the legal minimum wage (which does not apply to many farmworkers).

What about the minority of the labor force that is organized into unions? Here there are some industries, such as the garment and building trades, coal mining, and stevedoring, in which the balance of power is with the unions rather than with the employers. The situation in those industries approximates that of monopoly. In most of manufacturing, transportation, and related sectors, strong unions face strong employers or employers' associations, and the bilateral monopoly model applies. In these cases, collective bargaining (negotiations between unions and management) is the chief means of settling issues. Thus:

> A wide variety of situations exist in American labor markets. No single model can be used to depict all types of conditions and circumstances. Nevertheless, each model can go a long way toward explaining and predicting the consequences of various outcomes.

America's labor markets provide examples of several different wage-determination models.

Theory of Rent

In the early nineteenth century, a political controversy arose that was responsible for producing one of the great theoretical advances in the history of economics. The place was England. The period was 1814–1816.

For most of the previous century, from 1711 to 1794, the price of "corn" (the generic term in England for all grains) had been extremely stable. But between 1795 and 1800 the price tripled, and it continued to rise over most of the following two decades. Because grain was a primary source of food, the rise in price created great hardship and considerable political unrest. Many people starved, and employers reluctantly raised wages because of soaring food prices.

"Rent is price determined, not price determining," said David Ricardo in 1815. This view is still held today.

One group argued that the landlords were in a "conspiracy" to keep up corn prices by charging high rents to farmers. (Most of the corn was grown on rented land.) Another group, represented by the great English classical economist David Ricardo, argued exactly the opposite: Corn prices are high, said the "Ricardians," because of shortages resulting from the Napoleonic Wars. The high price of corn makes corn cultivation more profitable. This increases the demand for land and hence the price paid for the use of the land—namely, rent. If the price of corn fell, corn cultivation would become less profitable, and this would bring decreased rents. In Ricardo's own words:

> "Corn is not high because a rent is paid, but a rent is paid because corn is high." Ricardo meant that the price of land is determined by demand and supply, and that rent is *price-determined, not price-determining.*

Ricardo and his followers carried on a vigorous battle for the repeal of the English Corn Laws (tariffs) of 1815. Their goal was to bring more corn into the country, thereby increasing the supply and lowering the price.

Exhibit 6
The Determination of Rent

Figure (*a*): The landlord's opportunity cost is zero. Hence, the total amount received, the area 0PRN, represents economic rent, since the landlord would be willing to supply the same amount of land for any price greater than zero.

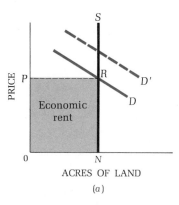

(*a*)

Figure (*b*): The total amount received by the bus drivers is the area 0PRN. However, only the "Nth" driver is getting his or her exact opportunity cost. Those "to the left" are getting more than their opportunity costs, as represented by their total economic rent, the triangular area *KPR*.

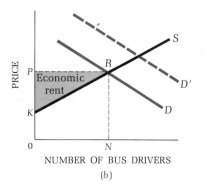

(*b*)

Economic Rent Is a Surplus

Ricardo's argument was based on three assumptions:

1. The amount of land available is fixed.

2. Land used for growing corn has no alternative uses.

3. A landlord would prefer to receive *any* payment for the use of land rather than to leave it idle and receive nothing.

In the language of modern economics, these statements amount to saying that the *supply of land is perfectly inelastic,* as illustrated in Exhibit 6, Figure (*a*).

The intersection of the supply curve *S* with the demand curve *D* establishes the equilibrium quantity at *N* and the corresponding equilibrium price at *P*. It follows that this price (or rent) per unit of land must be a *surplus* to the landlord. This is because the landlord would be willing to supply the same amount of land at a lower price, down to any price greater than zero, depending on where the demand curve intersects the supply curve. We call this surplus "economic rent" and define it as follows:

> Economic rent is any payment made to the owner of a factor of production, in an industry in equilibrium, in excess of the factor's supply price or opportunity cost. That is, economic rent is a payment above the minimum amount necessary to keep that factor in its present occupation.

Note that this definition restricts the concept of economic rent to an *equilibrium* surplus. This is because the owners of some factors may receive surpluses while those factors are in a transitory stage from one equilibrium position to another and because such surpluses may exist even in long-run equilibrium. It follows that the entire rectangular area in Figure (*a*), 0PRN, represents the total economic rent received by the landlord.

Originally, "rent" meant the payment made for the use of land. But economists eventually realized that the owners of any factor of production, not just the owners of land, may receive a surplus above the opportunity cost of that factor. Hence, they coined the expression "economic rent" to represent all such differentials. (Sometimes the term "producer's surplus" is also used.)

Exhibit 6, Figure (*b*), is a hypothetical model of the supply and demand for bus drivers under perfect competition. According to the figure, a quantity of bus drivers equal to 0N would each receive a wage equal to 0P. But only for the Nth bus driver is this wage the supply price or opportunity cost. Each of the others that make up the amount equal to 0N would have been willing to work for less, as determined by the height of the segment *KR* of the supply curve. Therefore, all the other drivers are receiving a total economic rent equal to the triangle *KPR*. You should be able to see from the demand curves in both diagrams in Exhibit 6 that, if the supply curves remain the same, an increase in demand from *D* to *D'* will enlarge the amount of economic rent. On the other hand, a decrease in demand will reduce it.

This leads to an important conclusion:

> Economic rent arises because the owners of the various units of a particular factor of production differ in the eagerness with which they are willing to supply those units. That is, the owners differ in their supply price. If all owners had equal supply prices, the supply curve would be perfectly elastic and there would be no economic rent.

Thus, in Exhibit 6, Figure (b), the area of economic rent would diminish to zero if the supply curve were to pivot on point R so as to approach the horizontal.

Economic rent is a concept similar to that of net revenue, inasmuch as both represent surpluses. The difference between them is merely a matter of reference. When the surplus is received by the owner of a factor of production, it is called economic rent. When the surplus is received by a firm, it is referred to as net revenue.

Is Rent a Cost or a Surplus?

Contrary to Ricardo's assumptions, units of land often have alternative uses and are of different quality. This explains why the demand for an acre of real estate in the heart of a city's business district may be quite different from the demand for an acre of farm land or an acre of desert land elsewhere in the country. These differences in demand also account for the differences in rent that are paid by the users of the land.

Are these rents a cost or a surplus? The answer depends on the point of view you take.

> From the firm's viewpoint, rent is the price that must be paid to attract land from its alternative uses. Hence, rent is a *cost*. From the economy's viewpoint, rent is the value that society receives for making available the land provided free by nature, regardless of the alternative uses to which the land is put and the rents that are paid. Hence, rent is a *surplus*.

Rent is a cost to those who pay it, but it is a surplus to society.

The fallacy of composition thus plays a role in the interpretation of rent from the individual versus social viewpoint. Some interesting implications of this are pointed out in "Leaders in Economics," page 546.

Theory of Interest

If you incur a debt in order to buy a car or to pay your tuition, you must pay interest to the lender for the credit given you. Therefore, *interest* is defined as the price paid for the use of credit or loanable funds over a period of time.

Interest is always expressed as a percentage of the amount of the loan. Thus, an interest rate of 10 percent means that the borrower pays 10 cents interest per $1 borrowed per year, or $10 per $100 borrowed per year, and so on.

Interest is paid for the use of credit, which in turn is used to buy productive resources or capital goods. Therefore, you will often hear reference made to the interest on capital. What this really means, of course, is the interest on the value of the capital in which the investment was made.

Interest rates, which are the prices paid for the use of credit or loanable funds, are based on several factors. Therefore, it proves convenient to talk of "the" interest rate—that is, the pure interest rate—on a riskless loan.

In our economy there are many different interest rates on debt instruments of all types—notes, bonds, mortgages, and so on. The rates vary according to several factors:

1. Risk—the chance of the borrower's defaulting on the loan.

2. Maturity—the length of time over which the money is borrowed.

3. Liquidity—the ease with which the creditor can convert the debt instrument into cash quickly without loss of value in terms of money.

4. Competition—the extent to which lenders compete for borrowers in particular money markets.

Leaders in Economics

Henry George
1839–1897
The Single Tax

Culver Pictures, Inc.

Henry George was born in Philadelphia and raised there by middle-class, strongly devout parents. His religious background was to be reflected in a certain missionary tendency in all his writings. After quitting school at thirteen he worked as an errand boy and clerk, went to sea while in his teens, and then lived in stark poverty in San Francisco for a number of years.

He became interested in politics and ran for the state legislature, but he was defeated through the opposition of the Central Pacific Railroad. George vehemently opposed the land subsidy the company was receiving from the state and the speculation occasioned by the completion of the railroad between Sacramento and Oakland.

At this time the seeds of George's opposition to land monopoly and exploitation were sown. In 1871 he sketched the bare outlines of his later theory in a pamphlet entitled *Our Land and Land Policy*. However, he did not elaborate the theme until 1879, when his famous book *Progress and Poverty* was published.

Successful Book
Ironically, George had had difficulty in finding a publisher. But the book turned out to be a work that brought him great fame, for it was an immediate success both at home and abroad. Many millions of copies have been sold throughout the world, and it is undoubtedly the most successful popular economics book ever published.

The central concept in George's writing is that poverty is caused by the monopolization of land by the few, who deprive the rest of the people of their birthright. Since land is endowed by nature, all rent on land is unearned surplus. The injustice to the landless grows when, as a result of natural progress, the value of land is augmented and rent increases correspondingly. The solution, therefore, is the confiscation of rent by the government through a *single tax* on land. No other taxes would be necessary, according to George.

Great Debates
Famous economists, including Alfred Marshall and J. B. Clark, debated with Henry George over the single-tax issue. Their conclusions, and those of later economists, suggested that a land tax would probably have fewer adverse effects on the allocation of society's resources than other taxes. However, a single tax on land alone would have three major shortcomings:

1. It would not produce enough revenue to meet governments' needs.
2. It would be unjust, because surpluses or economic rent may accrue to other resource owners besides landlords if the owners can gain monopolistic control over the sale of their resources in the marketplace.
3. It might be impossible to administer, because it does not distinguish between land and capital—that is, between the proportion of rent that represents a surplus and the proportion that results from improvements made on the land.

George entered politics again in 1886 as a candidate of the Labor and Socialist parties for mayor of New York City. By this time he was enormously popular, and it took the maximum efforts of a coalition of parties to defeat him at the polls. He became a candidate again in 1897, but the strain of campaigning was too much for him. He died before the election at the age of 58.

Other things being equal, interest rates will tend to vary directly with the first two factors and inversely with the second two. If you are not sure of the reasons for this, ask yourself how these factors would affect the interest rate that you would charge if you were a banker making loans.

> As a result of the wide structure of interest rates, economists find it convenient to talk about "the" rate of interest. By this they mean the theoretical *pure interest rate* on a riskless loan. This rate is best approximated by the interest on negotiable government securities.

Because the interest rate is the price of credit or loanable funds, we shall see shortly that it is determined by the interaction of demand and supply forces. But first, what are the sources of demand and supply?

Demand for Loanable Funds

You and I and people everywhere want credit. But from the economy's viewpoint we fall into three major groups: businesses, households, and government.

Businesses

Businesses are the largest source of demand for loanable funds. Corporations borrow because they want to purchase new capital goods, some of which are used to build up inventories. A firm undertakes such purchases as long as it expects to receive a yield that exceeds the cost of its funds. The expected yield or rate of return on investment projects can be depicted by the marginal revenue product (*MRP*) curve of capital expressed in terms of percentages.

This is illustrated in Exhibit 7. You can see from the diagram that the *MRP* curve should be viewed as a cumulative investment-demand curve. It tells you, for example, that the firm can earn 18 percent on the first $200,000 of investment and 16 percent on the next $100,000. Therefore, it can earn *at least* 16 percent on the first $300,000. Similarly, it can earn *at least* 14 percent on the first $400,000 invested.

When the *MRP* curve is interpreted in this way, you can see that, because the rate of interest on borrowed funds is also expressed as a percentage, *the points on the curve show the amount of investment the firm will undertake at various interest rates.* For example, at an interest rate on borrowed funds of 10 percent, the firm will demand $600,000 for investment. If the rate is lowered to 8 percent, the firm will increase the amount of funds demanded for investment to $700,000.

The diagram thus suggests a familiar marginal principle:

> Under competitive conditions, a firm will demand loanable funds up to the point at which the marginal-revenue productivity of the capital purchased with those funds is equal to the interest rate (or price) that must be paid for the loan. *The MRP curve of capital is therefore the firm's demand curve for capital* (that is, loanable funds used to purchase capital).

Households

Households are the second major source of demand for loanable funds. Households borrow such funds to buy automobiles, washing machines and other appliances, vacation trips, homes, and so forth. There is some limited evidence to suggest that the household demand curve for loan-

Exhibit 7
A Firm's Demand Curve for Loanable Funds

In a competitive market, the firm will demand loanable funds with which to purchase capital up to the point at which the *MRP* of capital equals the interest rate (or price). Thus, a decrease in the interest rate from 10 percent to 8 percent will increase the quantity of capital (or the amount of loanable funds) demanded from $600,000 to $700,000. (**Note** In macroeconomics, a firm's *MRP* curve of capital is called its marginal efficiency of investment, *MEI.*)

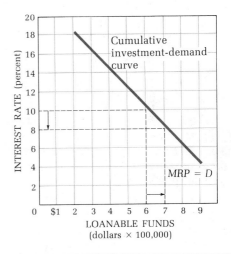

The business, household, and government sectors are the main sources of demand for loanable funds.

able funds is downward-sloping. This indicates that households will tend to borrow larger amounts of money at lower interest rates.

Government

The public sector is the third major source of demand for loanable funds. Governments at all levels—national, state, and local—borrow in order to finance national defense, highways, schools, welfare benefits, and so forth. The federal government borrows in order to finance a budget deficit. Therefore, we cannot assume that the federal government's demand for loanable funds depends on the interest rate. However, there is ample evidence to support such an assumption about state and local governments. They tend to borrow more when interest rates are low than when they are high.

In general, many studies point to the following conclusion:

> For all three sources—businesses, households, and government—taken together, the total market demand curve for loanable funds is downward-sloping. In addition, various studies have concluded that the demand curve is probably relatively inelastic. Therefore, changes in the interest rate are likely to result in less-than-proportional changes in the quantity demanded of loanable funds.

Supply of Loanable Funds

The central banking system, households, and business are the main sources of the supply of loanable funds.

We must now turn our attention to the supply side of the picture and ask: What are the sources of loanable funds? There are two.

The Central Banking System

A country's central bank (the Federal Reserve System in the United States) exercises a great deal of influence over the supply of money and hence the supply of loanable funds. This influence is intertwined with government economic measures, including taxation and spending policies, for combating recessions and inflations.

Households and Businesses

These sectors of the economy supply some loanable funds to the money market out of their past or present savings. Household savings are that part of household income not spent on consumption. Business savings are mainly undistributed (plowed-back) profits and depreciation reserves. Most businesses reinvest their savings in new plant and equipment, but some savings find their way into the money market. In general, very little is known about the effects of interest rates on household and business saving, but the influences are believed to be relatively slight.

Determination of the Interest Rate

The interest rate is determined by the supply of, and the demand for, loanable funds.

The demand and supply forces generated by government, businesses, and households combine to determine the equilibrium interest rate in the market. This is shown by the familiar supply-and-demand diagram in Exhibit 8.

As mentioned above, the downward-sloping demand curve *at any given level of national income* reflects the willingness on the part of businesses to demand more funds for investment at a low interest rate than at a high interest rate. The upward-sloping supply curve, although it is based on much more complex and uncertain factors, *assumes* that household and business savers will make available somewhat larger quantities of loanable funds at a high interest rate than at a low one.

Actually, the determination of the interest rate has much deeper implications than is apparent from this simple supply-and-demand diagram. Further, government monetary, taxation, and spending policies, as explained in macroeconomics, exercise a powerful influence on the forces that help to determine the interest rate. As a result, the interest rate tends to be more stable and does not fluctuate as freely as do the prices of commodities that are determined by supply and demand in perfectly competitive markets.

The Rationing or Allocating Function of Interest

Because the interest rate is a price, it performs the same rationing function as any other price. *The interest rate allocates the economy's scarce supply of funds among those who are willing to pay for them.*

Thus, in a free market, only the most profitable investment projects —those projects whose expected return or productivity is equal to or greater than the rate of interest—are undertaken. Any project whose prospective yield is below the interest rate is dropped from consideration. In this way the interest rate decides the critical question of *who* shall provide the economy with its limited supply of capital. In so doing, the interest rate directs the growth of productive capacity in a capital-using economy.

Does the interest rate actually perform this function in our economic system? For the most part the answer is *yes*, but there are some qualifications:

> The interest rate in our economy is not the sole mechanism for allocating scarce funds—for two reasons:
>
> **1.** The government allocates some of the available capital to projects that it believes to be in the public interest, regardless of their financial profitability.
>
> **2.** The unequal distribution of bargaining power among borrowers may enable many large firms to borrow on more favorable terms (at lower interest rates) than most small firms. This is true even when the latter have relatively greater prospects for growth.

Conclusion: Two Major Theories of Interest

Two main theories of interest have been an integral part of economics since the 1930s. One is the loanable-funds theory; the other is the liquidity-preference theory.

Loanable-Funds Theory

The *loanable-funds theory of interest* holds that the interest rate is determined by the demand for, and the supply of, loanable funds only, as distinguished from *all* money. The sources of demand for loanable funds are businesses that want to invest (that is, purchase capital), households that want to pay for consumer purchases, and government agencies that want to finance deficits. The sources of supply of loanable funds are the central banking system, which influences the supply of money (and

Exhibit 8
Determination of the Interest Rate

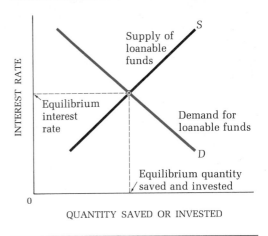

The interest rate is the price that allocates scarce funds among alternative uses.

Both the loanable-funds theory and the liquidity-preference theory are fundamental to modern economics.

hence the supply of loanable funds) in the economy; and households and businesses, which make loanable funds available out of their past or present savings.

Liquidity-Preference Theory

The *liquidity-preference theory of interest* contends that people would rather hold their assets or wealth in the most liquid form, namely cash. This is necessary to satisfy three motives: the "transactions motive" to carry out everyday purchasing needs, the "precautionary motive" to meet possible unforeseen conditions, and the "speculative motive" to take advantage of a rise in interest rates. Accordingly, interest is the price or reward that must be paid to overcome liquidity preference. The equilibrium rate of interest is determined by the demand for, and the supply of, money.

> The loanable-funds and liquidity-preference theories should not be regarded as mutually exclusive explanations of interest. The two theories involve many complexities that are treated in greater detail in macroeconomic theory. However, they tend to supplement and complement each other rather than to compete.

Theory of Profit

Three major explanations of profit have existed for many decades.

You have learned that *profit* or net revenue represents the difference between total revenue and total cost. Profit is thus a *residual* or *surplus* over and above normal profit, and it accrues to the entrepreneur after all costs, including explicit costs and implicit costs, have been deducted from total revenue. What does economic theory tell us about the determinants of profit? What functions does profit perform?

The history of economics reveals a number of theories of how profits are derived. Today, three are generally recognized as being particularly relevant:

1. Friction and monopoly theory.

2. Uncertainty theory.

3. Innovation theory.

This system of classification is not all-inclusive and any one of the theories may contain elements of the others. The system merely emphasizes the main lines that have been followed in the course of thinking on the subject.

Friction and Monopoly Theory

The friction and monopoly theory attributes profits to institutional rigidities and market failure.

By the end of the nineteenth century, the theory of a perfectly competitive economy was well on its way toward becoming a unified body of thought. Against this setting the noted American economist J. B. Clark (1847–1938) constructed a model of the economy that was intended to reconcile the static laws of theory with the dynamic world of fact.

According to Clark's "stationary" model (or the theory of perfect competition, as it is called today), the economy is characterized by a smooth and frictionless flow of resources. Theoretically, the system automatically clicks into equilibrium through the free play of market forces. Of course, changes may occur that cause a departure from equilibrium. But as long as resources are mobile and opportunities are equally accessible to all economic entities, the adjustment to change and a new equilibrium will be accomplished quickly and smoothly. In this type of economic equilibrium all of the owners of the factors of production would receive their opportunity costs. The revenues of each enterprise would exactly equal its costs (including the implicit wages and interest of the owner), and no economic surplus or profit residual could result.

In the real world, however, surpluses do occur. According to the theory, they can be attributed only to the frictions (or obstacles to resource mobility) and monopoly elements that actually characterize a dynamic economy. In the long run, according to the theory, the forces of competition would eliminate any surpluses. But in reality, however, the surpluses recur because new frictions and new monopoly elements continually arise. Therefore:

> Profits are the result of institutional rigidities in the social and economic system that prevent the working out of competitive forces. To the extent that these rigidities cause profits or surpluses, therefore, they are to the temporary advantage of the surplus recipient.

Many illustrations from real life substantiate the existence of friction and monopoly as a cause of economic surplus. The construction of military posts brings profit bonanzas to neighboring cities. Foreign crises often rescue domestic industries from threatening oversupplies of their products. The existence of patents and franchises enables many firms to reap profits by legally excluding competitors from the field. A favorable location for a business often results in the value of the site exceeding the rental payment for it. In general, the control of any resource whose supply is scarce relative to the demand for it provides a basis for pure or windfall profits.

Of course, a surplus would not arise if resources were sufficiently mobile to enter the market or if the economy were frictionless (perfect) in its competitive structure. At best, any surpluses that did arise would be short-lived and would vanish entirely when the adjustments had time to exert their full effect in the market. But social processes—customs, laws, and traditions—make such rapid adjustments impossible.

Uncertainty Theory

The uncertainty theory of profit was introduced by Professor Frank Knight (1885–1972) of the University of Chicago. The theory, formulated in a remarkable doctoral thesis entitled *Risk, Uncertainty, and Profit* (1921), is rooted in a distinction between "risk" and "uncertainty."

The uncertainty theory of profit is based on a distinction between risk and uncertainty.

The Meaning of Risk

Risk is defined as the quantitative measurement of the probability that a particular outcome, such as a gain or a loss, will occur. Because the distinguishing feature of risk is predictability, the firm can "insure" itself against expected losses by incorporating them in advance into its cost structure. This is true whether the risk is of an *intrafirm* or an *interfirm* nature.

Intrafirm Risk Such risk occurs when management can establish the probability of loss because the number of occurrences within the firm is large enough to be predicted with known error. For example, a factory may experience a loss of about 2 machine-hours out of every 100 machine-hours due to equipment breakdown. In this case, the cost of the production lost can be added to the cost of the production resulting from the remaining 98 machine-hours, and the profit rate can be altered by the revision in the cost structure. In other words, where the average expected loss for the company can be predicted for the coming period, the loss can be "self-insured" by treating it as a cost of doing business. Therefore, no insurance from outside sources is necessary.

Thus, small-loan companies expect a certain percentage of defaults. Banks regularly charge off as bad debts a portion of their loans. And many companies institute self-insurance programs against risks for which they can prepare themselves through proper reserve accounting.

Interfirm Risk For some risks the number of observations or experiences is not large enough within any one firm for management to feel that it can predict the loss with reasonable confidence. However, when many firms are considered, the observations become numerous enough to exhibit the necessary stability for prediction.

Examples of such risks are losses caused by floods, storms, fires, or deaths. Because managers are unable to predict such losses for themselves, they are able to shift the burden of the risk to insurance companies whose function is to establish the probability of such losses based on a large number of cases. Although insurance companies cannot establish that a particular individual will die or that a particular building will burn, they can predict with small error what fraction of the population will die next year or how many buildings out of a given number will burn. It follows that, because a firm pays a risk premium for insurance, it can and does treat this risk premium as a cost of doing business.

The Meaning of Uncertainty

Profits are the rewards, and losses are the penalties, for bearing uncertainty.

Uncertainty is defined as a state of knowledge in which the probabilities of outcomes resulting from specific actions are not known and cannot be predicted. Unlike risk, therefore, uncertainty is a subjective phenomenon rather than an objective one. No two individuals who forecast a particular outcome based on given facts will necessarily arrive at the same result. This is because there is not enough information on which to base a strong probability estimate.

Under conditions characterized by uncertainty, decision makers must make choices based on incomplete knowledge. They may do this by forming mental images of future outcomes that cannot be verified quantitatively. It follows from this that uncertainty is not insurable and cannot be integrated within the firm's cost structure, as can risk. At best, each manager may harbor his or her own subjective probability about a future outcome, but it is nothing more than a strong hunch. According to this theory:

> The great majority of events in our society are unpredictable—they are uncertainties. Therefore, *profits are the rewards, and losses are the penalties, of bearing uncertainty.*

The uncertainty theory concludes that, in a market economy, entrepreneurs undertake an activity because they *expect*, but do not necessarily *receive*, profits. Like a dog chasing a rabbit, the expectation of gains is the incentive that keeps entrepreneurs running.

Leaders in Economics

Joseph Alois Schumpeter
1883–1950

The "Crumbling Walls" of Capitalism

Bettmann Archive

One of the most famous economists of the twentieth century was Joseph Schumpeter. His reputation rests as much on his total achievements as a social scientist as on his contributions to the advancement of economics. Although many scholars have excelled in special fields, Schumpeter was one of the few who was extraordinarily well versed in many, including economics, mathematics, philosophy, sociology, and history. In addition to a varied and successful career as a professor, cabinet minister, banker, and jurist, he was a professor of economics at Harvard University from the early 1930s until his death in 1950.

Schumpeter's output of books, essays, articles, and monographs was enormous, but his most important works fell broadly in the field of business-cycle theory. Perhaps his greatest theoretical contribution was the model he developed to describe how business cycles result from *innovations* by a business system under capitalism. This innovation theory was subsequently adopted by many economists as a partial explanation of how profits (surpluses) arise in a capitalistic system.

Capitalism's Decay
In one of his classic works Schumpeter discussed the "crumbling walls" of capitalism. By this he meant the eventual decay of the system due to the obsolescence of the entrepreneurial function. In his own words:

"The economic wants of humanity might some day be so completely satisfied that little motive would be left to push productive effort still further ahead. Such a state of satiety is no doubt very far off even if we keep within the present scheme of wants; and if we take account of the fact that, as higher standards of life are attained, these wants automatically expand and new wants emerge or are created, satiety becomes a flying goal, particularly if we include leisure among consumers' goods. However, let us glance at that possibility, assuming, still more unrealistically, that methods of production have reached a state of perfection which does not admit of further improvement.

"A more or less stationary state would ensue. Capitalism, being essentially an evolutionary process, would become atrophic. There would be nothing left for entrepreneurs to do. They would find themselves in much the same situation as generals would in a society perfectly sure of permanent peace. Profits and along with profits the rate of interest would converge toward zero. The bourgeois strata that live on profits and interest would tend to disappear. The management of industry and trade would become a matter of current administration, and the personnel would unavoidably acquire the characteristics of a bureaucracy. Socialism of a very sober type would almost automatically come into being. Human energy would turn away from business. Other than economic pursuits would attract the brains and provide the adventure."

No "School"
Schumpeter was widely respected, and his many pioneering works were studied by scholars throughout the world. However, he never founded a "school" of economic thought or gathered a following that could eventually assume the status of a school. In other words, no "Schumpeterians" ever emerged to carry on and elaborate his ideas, although many other leading scholars inspired disciples to follow them. Various reasons may be advanced for this. Perhaps the most significant is that his theory contained no *cause célèbre*—no fundamental challenge that could offer a rallying point. Although his innovation theory of business cycles was developed on a high theoretical plane, it offered no concrete solutions to the world's economic problems.

Innovation Theory

The innovation theory attributes profits to the application of new ideas or techniques.

In the 1930s, one of the most distinguished economists of this century, Joseph Schumpeter, introduced a theory of business cycles based on innovations. This theory has often been extended to include the notion of innovation as a cause of profits.

An *innovation*, as economists define it, is "the setting up of a new production function." That is, an innovation is a new relation between the output and the various inputs (capital, land, labor, and entrepreneurship) in a production process. Innovations may thus embrace such wide varieties of activities as the discovery of new markets, differentiation of products, or, in short, new ways of doing old things or different combinations of existing methods to accomplish new things. There is an important distinction between invention and innovation. Invention is the creation of something new; innovation is the adaptation of an existing thing, such as an invention, to a new use. Many inventions never give rise to innovations.

Schumpeter's original purpose in propounding the innovation theory was to show how business cycles result from these disturbances and from successive adaptations to them by the business system. He began by assuming a stationary (perfectly competitive) system in equilibrium—in which all economic life is repetitive and goes on smoothly, without disturbance.

Into this system a shock—an innovation—is introduced by an entrepreneur who foresees the possibility of extra profit. The quietude and intricate balance of the system is then shattered as if the system had been invaded by a Hollywood-staged cattle stampede. The successful innovation causes herds of businesspeople (followers rather than leaders) to plunge into the new field by adopting the innovation, and these mass rushes create and stir up secondary waves of business activity.

When the disturbance has finally run its course, the system settles into equilibrium once again, only to be disturbed later by another innovation. Profit making and economic activity are thus experienced as series of fits and starts (cycles) rather than as smooth and continuous progressions.

The innovation theory was only one of Schumpeter's many ideas. He also had much to say about other aspects of economics, including the future of capitalism. (See "Leaders in Economics," page 553.)

Functions of Profits

As mentioned earlier, there is no single "correct" theory of profit. All three theories contribute to explaining the cause of profit. They also help us understand the two major functions of profits in our economy:

> **1.** Profits stimulate innovation by inducing business managers to undertake new ventures and to improve production methods.
>
> **2.** To the extent that markets are free and competitive, the desire for profits induces business executives to allocate their resources efficiently in accordance with consumer preferences.

As a result of these functions, you can see that profits and the profit system account for a fundamental distinction between capitalistic and socialistic systems. Indeed, as you will learn in a later chapter, attitudes toward profit are crucial in determining the economic success of any economic system.

What You Have Learned in This Chapter

1. The long-run trend of real wages in our economy has been upward, based mainly on the increased productivity of labor resulting from improvements in the quality and quantity of the factors of production.

2. Wages are determined in the market under different competitive conditions. Four models that explain most of the wage arrangements that exist in our economy are the competitive model, the monopsony model, the monopoly model, and the bilateral monopoly model. The bilateral monopoly model may yield a determinate solution on quantity, but it yields an indeterminate solution on price.

3. Economic rent is a surplus that is price-determined, not price-determining. To an individual firm, rent is a cost of production just like any other cost; but to society rent is a surplus that is received for making available nature's free land.

4. Interest is the price paid for the use of credit or loanable funds over a period of time. Although the interest rate is determined by the supply of, and the demand for, loanable funds, it can be influenced by government borrowing and by central-bank credit-creation policies. The chief function of the interest rate is to allocate scarce funds for alternative uses, thus directing the flow of capital.

5. Profit is a residual or surplus over and above all costs, including normal profit. It may result from frictions and monopoly elements in our economy, from uncertainty, and from innovations. The chief functions of profit are (a) to stimulate economic progress by inducing business managers to invest in plant and equipment; and (b) to the extent that markets are competitive, to allocate resources in accordance with consumer preferences.

For Discussion

1. *Terms and concepts to review:*
wages
labor
money wages
real wages
monopsony
bilateral monopoly
economic rent
interest
single tax
pure interest rate
loanable-funds theory of interest
liquidity-preference theory of interest
profit
risk
uncertainty
innovation

2. Why has the long-run trend of real wages been upward, especially since the supply of labor today is so much larger than it was years ago?

3. Which wage-determination model best explains each of the following? Illustrate and explain each with an actual model. (a) The wages of file clerks and secretaries; (b) the wages of unskilled farmworkers; (c) the wages of typographers and stevedores.

4. A union official once advised the members of his union to ask for a 10 percent wage cut. Was he crazy? What economic factors might have prompted him to offer such advice?

5. "Wages are determined by the marginal productivity of labor, just as prices are determined by costs of production." True or false? Explain.

6. Do you see any similarity between the concept of economic rent received by the owners of a factor of production and net revenue received by a firm? Explain.

7. Henry George ran for mayor of New York in 1886. If you had been a voter at that time, how would you have reacted to his single-tax idea?

8. Money itself is not a resource, and it is unproductive. Why, then, should people be willing to pay a price in the form of interest in order to acquire it? What determines the interest rate that is paid? What functions does interest perform?

9. Classify each of the following as an inter-firm or intrafirm risk: (a) glassware and china breakage in a restaurant; (b) egg breakage on a chicken farm; (c) absenteeism in a factory; (d) "acts of God" (cite examples).

10. (a) From a chicken farmer's standpoint, is the price of eggs (which is determined in competitive markets) a risk or an uncertainty? (b) Is the sale of next year's Chevrolets by General Motors a risk or an uncertainty? Why?

11. "Economic profits should be taxed away because they result from frictions and monopolistic influences." Evaluate.

Reading

Ricardo on Rent

[In 1817, the greatest of the English classical economists, David Ricardo, published his *Principles of Political Economy and Taxation.* In this treatise he developed the theory of economic rent. This theory has remained essentially the same since that time. The following brief selection has been adapted, with minor changes, from Ricardo's monumental book.]

Rent is that portion of the produce of the earth which is paid to the landlord for the use of the original and indestructible powers of the soil.

It is often, however, confounded with the interest and profit of capital, and, in popular language, the term is applied to whatever is annually paid by a farmer to his landlord.

If, of two adjoining farms of the same extent, and of the same natural fertility, one had all the conveniences of farming buildings, and besides, were properly drained and manured, and advantageously divided into hedges, fences, and walls, while the other had none of these advantages, more remuneration would naturally be paid for the use of one, than for the use of the other. Yet in both cases the remuneration would be called rent. But it is evident that a portion only of the money annually to be paid for the improved farm would be given for the original and indestructible powers of the soil. The other portion would be paid for the use of the capital which had been employed in ameliorating the quality of the land, and in erecting such buildings as were necessary to secure and preserve the produce.

On the first settling of a country, in which there is an abundance of fertile land, a very small proportion of which is required to be cultivated for the support of the actual population, or indeed can be cultivated with the capital which the population can command, there will be no rent. For no one would pay for the use of land, when there was an abundant quantity not yet appropriated, and, therefore, at the disposal of whosoever might choose to cultivate it.

If all land had the same properties, if it were unlimited in quantity, and uniform in quality, no charge could be made for its use, unless where it possessed peculiar advantages of situation. It is only, then, because land is not unlimited in quantity and uniform in quality, and because in the progress of population, land of an inferior quality, or less advantageously situated, is called into cultivation, that rent is ever paid for the use of it. When in the progress of society, land of the second degree of fertility is taken into cultivation, rent immediately commences on that of the first quality, and the amount of that rent will depend on the difference in the quality of those two portions of land.

When land of the third quality is taken into cultivation, rent immediately commences on the second, and it is regulated as before, by the difference in their productive powers. At the same time, the rent of the first quality will rise, for that must always be above the rent of the second, by the difference between the produce which they yield with a given quantity of capital and labor.

With every step in the progress of population, which shall oblige a country to have recourse to land of a worse quality, to enable it to raise its supply of food, rent on all the more fertile land will rise.

The reason, then, why raw produce rises in comparative value, is because more labor is employed in the production of the last portion obtained, and not because a rent is paid to the landlord. The value of corn is regulated by the quantity of labor bestowed on its production on that quality of land, or with that portion of capital, which pays no rent. Corn is not high because a rent is paid, but a rent is paid because corn is high; and it has been justly observed, that no reduction would take place in the price of corn, although landlords should forgo the whole of their rent. Such a measure would only enable some farmers to live like gentlemen, but would not diminish the quantity of labor necessary to raise raw produce on the least productive land in cultivation.

Stability, General Equilibrium, and Welfare Economics

Learning guide

Watch for the answers to these important questions

How do we distinguish between stable, unstable, and neutral equilibria? How do we distinguish between statics and dynamics? Why are such distinctions important?

What is the difference between partial equilibrium and general equilibrium? In what way is a general-equilibrium model a "system"?

What is welfare economics? How does it relate to the idea of Pareto optimality? What implications do these concepts have for efficiency and equity in a capitalistic system?

Equilibrium is a concept of fundamental importance, and we have already made considerable use of it. But what does "equilibrium" really mean? How significant is it in economic analysis?

Equilibrium was defined in earlier chapters as a state of balance between opposing forces. An object is in equilibrium when it is at rest; it has no tendency to change its position because the forces acting upon it are canceling each other. In economics, as we have seen, the "objects" may be prices, quantities, incomes, or other variables. You cannot consider a problem solved if, at the point you terminate your analysis, the variables that are germane to the particular problem are still changing. Only when the variables settle down to steady levels, or only when their future equilibrium positions can be predicted, can you consider the solution complete.

However, the study of equilibrium is not an end in itself. We must also understand the forces that can disturb an equilibrium and the measures that may have to be undertaken to restore it. These ideas will become more meaningful as we explore the ramifications of equilibrium in this chapter.

This chapter explains the meanings of stability, the characteristics of a microeconomy in equilibrium, and some applications of these ideas to maximizing society's satisfactions.

Stability of Equilibria

If the forces acting upon an object at rest suddenly change, the object may or may not have the ability to reestablish its position. If it does, the equilibrium is stable; if it does not, the equilibrium may be either unstable or neutral. Let us examine these ideas in both a physical and an economic context.

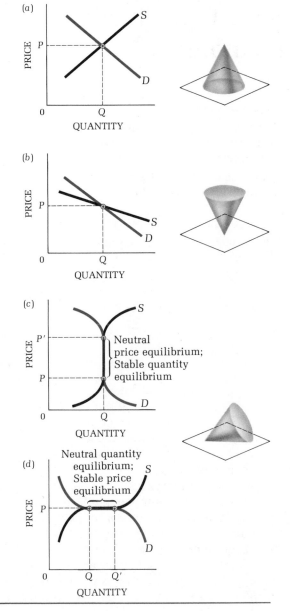

(a)

(b)

(c)

(d)

Exhibit 1

Stable, Unstable, and Neutral Equilibria: Static Models

Figure (a): *Stable Equilibrium.* The equilibrium at P is stable—like a cone resting on its base. A "shock" sufficient to disturb the equilibrium brings into play self-corrective forces that automatically restore the initial position.

Figure (b): *Unstable Equilibrium.* The equilibrium at P is unstable—like a cone balanced on its vertex. If the equilibrium is disturbed, the system is forced away from its initial state. Thus, at any price higher than the level at P, the quantity demanded exceeds the quantity supplied, so the price continues to rise. At any price below the level at P, the reverse is true. Note, however, that the equilibrium at P would be stable if the downward-sloping supply curve cut the demand curve from above instead of from below. Can you illustrate and explain this?

Figures (c) and (d): *Neutral Equilibrium.* In Figure (c), any price equilibrium between P and P′ is neutral. In Figure (d), any quantity equilibrium between Q and Q′ is neutral. Within their neutral ranges, price and quantity are indeterminate; they may take on any values. Hence, the situation is analogous to a cone rolling on its side.

Stable, Unstable, and Neutral Equilibria

An equilibrium may be stable, unstable, or neutral.

Exhibit 1 provides some interesting examples of the stability of equilibria in terms of supply and demand curves.

Figure (a) illustrates a case of stable equilibrium. This represents the normal situation. In physical terms, it may be depicted by a cone resting on its base. In economic terms, it can be represented by the interaction of ordinary supply and demand curves. If the system is subjected to an external "shock" or disturbance sufficient to dislodge it from equilibrium, self-corrective forces will cause it to return to its initial position. If the price, for example, should for some reason rise above its equilibrium level at P, the quantity supplied of the product will exceed the quantity demanded, thereby driving the price down. If the price should fall below P, the quantity demanded will exceed the quantity supplied, thereby driving the price up.

Although Figures (b) through (d) do not depict typical situations, they are useful for providing deeper insights into the concept of equilibrium.

Figure (b) presents a case of unstable equilibrium. A physical example is a cone balanced on its vertex. An economic example is one in which price is determined by the intersection of supply and demand but the supply curve is downward-sloping *and* cuts the demand curve from below. As you can see from the diagram, the system is in a delicate state of balance. If the equilibrium is disturbed, the object will be forced away from its initial state. As an example, suppose that for some reason the price rises above its equilibrium level. Then the quantity demanded will exceed the quantity supplied and the price will continue to rise. Conversely, if the price falls below its equilibrium level, the quantity supplied will exceed the quantity demanded and the price will continue to fall.

It is interesting to note that these conclusions would not hold if the downward-sloping curve cut the demand curve from *above* instead of from below. In that case the equilibrium would be stable. You should be able to demonstrate this by sketching the curves.

Figures (c) and (d) provide illustrations of neutral equilibrium. The physical situation can be depicted by a cone lying on its side. If the cone's equilibrium is disturbed, it simply "rolls" to some other neutral position. The analogous economic situation occurs in those ranges of price and quantity in which the supply and demand curves happen to coincide. Thus, in Figure (c), any price between P and P' is in neutral equilibrium—the price is "rolling" or indeterminate within this range. Similarly, in Figure (d), any quantity between Q and Q' is in neutral equilibrium—and therefore the precise quantity is indeterminate within this range.

The different types of equilibrium may be understood in terms of supply-and-demand models.

Statics and Dynamics

The concepts of stable, unstable, and neutral equilibrium can also be depicted by the charts in Exhibit 2. Note from the titles of Exhibits 1 and 2 that Exhibit 1 consists of static models, whereas Exhibit 2 consists of dynamic ones. Let us examine these concepts more closely.

A *static model* is one in which economic phenomena are studied without reference to time—without reference to preceding or succeeding events. In a static model, time is not permitted to enter into the analysis in any manner that will affect the results. When we construct a static model, therefore, we are taking a "snapshot" and analyzing its essential features. Each of the diagrams in Exhibit 1, and most of the other theoretical situations and figures you have studied in this book, are static models.

Of course, in many practical situations, you want to analyze the effects of a change in one or more of the determining conditions in a static model. This method is known as *comparative statics*. It consists of comparing two "snapshots"—one taken before the change and one taken after. For example, when you analyzed supply and demand situations in previous chapters by comparing equilibrium prices and quantities before and after a shift in one or both of the curves, you were using comparative statics. Statics and comparative statics encompass most of the theory in this book—and by far the larger part of economic theory in general.

Static models are analogous to "snapshots," dynamic models to "motion pictures."

Exhibit 2
Stable, Unstable, and Neutral Equilibria: Dynamic Models

Stable Equilibrium. Price converges toward the equilibrium level at P. Price may oscillate, or it may approach equilibrium from above or below.

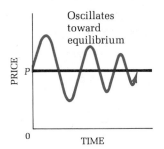

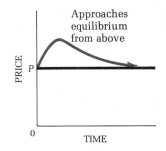

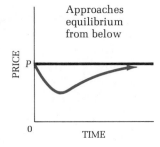

Unstable Equilibrium. Price diverges from the equilibrium at P. Price may oscillate, or it may "explode" upward or downward from the equilibrium level.

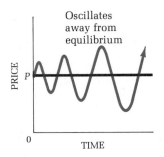

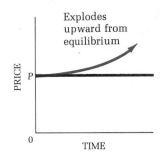

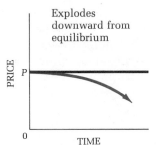

Neutral Equilibrium. Price fluctuates around the equilibrium level at P. Price has no permanent tendency to converge toward equilibrium or to diverge from it.

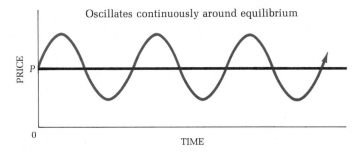

A *dynamic model* is one in which economic phenomena are studied by relating them to preceding or succeeding events. The influence of time is taken explicitly into account. Illustrations of the results of dynamic models are shown in Exhibit 2. Each figure depicts a possible way in which price may behave in relation to its equilibrium level over a period of time. Each of these dynamic models, therefore, is like a "motion picture," as distinguished from the "snapshot" of Exhibit 1.

Fluctuations in prices like those shown in Exhibit 2 do not continue in the same pattern indefinitely. Why? Because the underlying supply and demand curves that determine prices tend to change fairly frequently, so that different patterns are generated. At any given moment the pattern may be tending toward stable, unstable, or neutral equilibrium. However, over a period of time, prices in most markets tend toward some stable equilibrium level.

This suggests the following definition:

Stable equilibrium is a condition in which an object or system (such as a price, firm, industry, or market) in equilibrium, when subjected to a shock sufficient to disturb its position, returns toward its initial equilibrium as a result of self-restoring forces. (In contrast, an equilibrium that is not stable may be either unstable or neutral.)

As you can see from this explanation, the concept of stable equilibrium is of fundamental importance. Indeed, it has occupied the interest of a number of scholars. Among them has been Paul Samuelson, whose pioneering work on stability analysis contributed significantly to his being the first American to receive the Nobel Prize in Economic Science. (See "Leaders in Economics," page 562.)

General Equilibrium: "Everything Depends on Everything Else"

Although *equilibrium* means a state of balance, there are different and interesting ways of thinking about it. For example, in the early part of this century, a famous American economist, Henry J. Davenport, investigated relationships between the prices of corn, pork, and land. He noted part of his conclusions in a verse:

The concept of general equilibrium is that of a system of interdependent markets.

> The price of pig
> Is something big;
> Because its corn, you'll understand
> Is high-priced, too;
> Because it grew
> Upon the high-priced farming land.
> If you'd know why
> That land is high
> Consider this: its price is big
> Because it pays
> Thereon to raise
> The costly corn, the high-priced pig.

Long before Davenport observed connections between these three variables, a prominent mid-nineteenth-century French economist Frederic Bastiat expressed amazement about the Paris of his day. Hundreds of thousands of people, he remarked, live in the city, yet each day a wide variety of goods and services are provided in approximately correct quantities without coordination or planning by any single agency. "Imagination," Bastiat wrote,

> is baffled when it tries to appreciate the vast multiplicity of commodities which must enter tomorrow to preserve the inhabitants from famine. Yet all sleep and their slumbers are not disturbed for a single minute by the prospects of such a frightful catastrophe.

What Davenport and Bastiat (and many other observers as well) were commenting upon is the notion that a complex economy is a vast system of interrelated components—a system in which "everything de-

Leaders in Economics

Paul Anthony Samuelson
1915—
America's First Nobel Laureate in Economic Science

Wide World Photos

In 1935, an extraordinary young man, born in Gary, Indiana, received his B.A. degree from the University of Chicago. He went on to pursue graduate work at Harvard University, from which he received a Ph.D. in economics in 1941. During that six-year period he published eleven major professional journal articles, most of which became classics in their own time. In addition, he produced a pathbreaking doctoral dissertation that later appeared as a book, *Foundations of Economic Analysis* (Harvard University Press, 1947). The impact of this treatise, which was largely conceived and written in 1937 by the then-23-year-old author, was noted in 1970 by the Swedish Royal Academy of Science when it bestowed upon Samuelson the Alfred Nobel Memorial Prize in Economic Science.

Renowned Scholar
Paul Samuelson is probably the world's most widely known economist. Several generations of college students in the United States and abroad took their first course in economics using his introductory textbook. Millions of readers of American and foreign newspapers and magazines have been exposed to his articles on current economic policies. Professional economists throughout the world have studied, and have been stimulated toward further research by, the extraordinary range of his scientific work. This includes hundreds of profound papers and several books dealing with theoretical topics in consumer behavior, business cycles, public finance, international trade, linear programming, and other technical subjects. In all these fields, Samuelson's originality has been evidenced by his ability to develop sophisticated formulations of economic concepts through the use of advanced mathematics.

Accelerator–Multiplier Interactions
For example, among his many classic publications is a mathematical essay on the interaction of the multiplier and the accelerator—an important topic of macroeconomic theory. Samuelson wrote this celebrated article when he was a graduate student. It was initially prepared as a term paper for a seminar course in business cycles. The article reflected Samuelson's early interest in the important concept of stability.

Correspondence Principle
In the *Foundations,* which immediately established Samuelson's reputation as a highly creative mathematical economist, he presented a systematic analysis of static and dynamic economic theory. His approach was to describe, in mathematical form, the "state" of an economic system in equilibrium and the process or path of adjustment from one state to another. He then linked statics and dynamics by what he called the *correspondence principle*. This is a proposition that demonstrates that, in order for comparative statics (the comparison of equilibrium positions in static states) to be meaningful, it is first necessary to develop a dynamic analysis of stability.

Storehouse of Insights
In general, Paul Samuelson's scientific contributions—developed in precise mathematical rather than literary form—have greatly deepened our understanding of how the economic system works. He has shown the general applicability of the concept of maximization, subject to constraints, to many branches of economics.

For example, the consumer tries to maximize satisfactions, subject to such constraints as income and the prices of the goods purchased. The business firm tries to maximize profit, subject to the constraints of technology, resource limitations, and costs. Similarly, government tries to maximize net social benefits, subject to various economic (not to mention political) constraints. These and many other ideas had long been part of economics, but Samuelson revealed them in new and provocative ways. As a result, he has provided a storehouse of theoretical insights that have both stimulated and facilitated important research by others.

Now an Institute Professor at the Massachusetts Institute of Technology, Paul Samuelson has been on the faculty of that renowned institution since 1941. He has also been active as a government consultant and as an invited speaker on many public platforms.

pends on everything else." You can gain a better appreciation of this idea by examining some of the features of what is known as general-equilibrium theory.

Partial- and General-Equilibrium Theory

Until now, almost all of our attention in microeconomics has been focused on "partial-equilibrium" theory, as distinguished from "general-equilibrium" theory. What do these terms mean?

> *Partial-equilibrium theory* analyzes and develops models of a particular market on the assumption that other markets are in balance. It thus ignores the interrelations of prices and quantities that may exist between markets.

For example, ordinary supply-and-demand analysis is normally of a partial-equilibrium nature. The reason is that it focuses on a single market while neglecting others. This method of investigation can be extremely useful for gaining a better understanding of how a market works. In particular, it is invaluable for analyzing the effects of such things as price control, rationing, minimum wages, and commodity taxes, as was done in earlier chapters. However, by ignoring the ramifications and repercussions of price and quantity changes that may occur in other markets, we are overlooking the fact that such changes could have a significant influence on the market we are studying.

In view of this, it is necessary to think of the price system as an interrelated whole and to recognize that partial analyses can provide only approximations of a full explanation. This being the case, a "general" approach, which simultaneously takes into account all product and resource markets in the economy, is needed.

> *General-equilibrium theory* analyzes the interrelations between prices and quantities of goods and resources in different markets. It demonstrates the possibility of simultaneous equilibrium between all markets. Thus it views the economy as a system composed of interdependent parts.

In general-equilibrium theory, the structure of the economy is analyzed as a *system* of interrelated markets. The theory assumes that, if all participants are given such information as consumer demand schedules, resource supply schedules, production functions, and the demand for money for each particular market, equilibrium forces will cause commodity and resource prices to adjust themselves in a mutually consistent manner. The entire system can then settle down in a stable equilibrium of supply and demand.

However, any change in the determinants affecting the price and quantity of a good or resource can upset the entire system. This will have widespread repercussions on the equilibrium prices and quantities of all other goods and resources. Thus, these ideas emphasize the fact that in the real world there is often a significant degree of interdependence among various markets.

Most economic concepts relate to partial equilibrium rather than to general equilibrium. The same idea is true in all other sciences.

A General-Equilibrium Model: Two Commodities

A full explanation of general equilibrium requires the use of mathematics. However, many of the basic notions can be conveyed without mathematics by a simple supply-and-demand analysis involving only two commodities—say, meat and fish.

Exhibit 3
General Equilibrium—A Two-Commodity Model: Demand and Supply Curves for Meat and Fish

In Figure (a) the demand curve for meat (D_M) is drawn on the assumption that the equilibrium price of fish (P_F) in Figure (b) is given. Similarly, in Figure (b) the demand curve for fish (D_F) is drawn on the assumption that the equilibrium price of meat (P_M) in Figure (a) is given. The supply curves of meat S_M and of fish S_F are drawn under the same assumptions.

In Figure (a), if a specific tax of T per unit is imposed on meat sellers, the supply curve shifts from S_M to S'_M to reflect the cost increase. The equilibrium price of meat rises to P'_M and the equilibrium quantity falls to Q'_M. Consumers, therefore, substitute fish for meat, causing the demand curve for fish in Figure (b) to shift to the right from D_F to D'_F. As a result, the equilibrium price of fish increases to P'_F and the equilibrium quantity to Q'_F.

In addition to these changes, some resources (not shown in the diagrams) are likely to move out of meat production and into fish production. This will cause the supply curves in both industries to shift. This process will continue until a new state of general equilibrium is reached.

In Exhibit 3, Figure (a), there is a market demand curve for meat, D_M, and a market supply curve for meat, S_M. Their intersection determines the equilibrium price of meat, P_M, and the equilibrium quantity of meat, Q_M. Similarly, in Figure (b), the intersection of the market demand and supply curves of fish, D_F and S_F, determines the equilibrium price of fish, P_F, and the equilibrium quantity of fish, Q_F.

Before considering any changes in the curves, it is important to note some of the assumptions on which they rest. Basically, each curve in any one market is drawn on the assumption that the equilibrium price of the commodity in the other market remains constant. For example, in Figure (a) the demand curve for meat assumes that the price of fish in Figure (b) is at its equilibrium level P_F. Similarly, in Figure (b) the demand curve for fish assumes that the equilibrium price of meat in Figure (a) is at its equilibrium level P_M.

Other assumptions not evident from the diagrams are also made. In particular, it is assumed that (1) consumer preferences for commodities are given, (2) the stock of resources available for production is fixed, and (3) the techniques of production (the production functions for commodities) are given. These conditions are among the basic determinants of the system being described. Therefore, a change in any one of them will disturb the existing equilibrium pattern.

Effect of a Specific Tax

Now suppose that a *specific tax*—a tax per unit of commodity—is imposed by government on sellers of meat. In Figure (a), if the tax is equal to T per unit, it will increase the cost to suppliers by shifting the supply curve from S_M to S'_M. This will cause the equilibrium price of meat to rise to P'_M and the equilibrium quantity to fall to Q'_M.

(a) MEAT

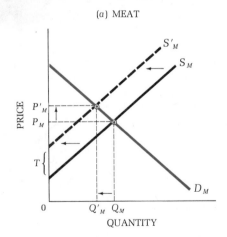

(b) FISH

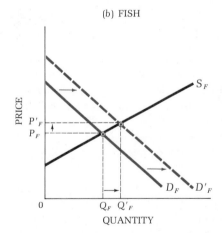

Because the price of meat compared to fish is now *relatively* higher than before the tax, consumers will substitute some fish for meat in their consumption patterns. This will cause an increase in the demand for fish—a shift of the demand curve in Figure (b) to the right from D_F to D'_F. Therefore the equilibrium price of fish will rise from P_F to P'_F and the equilibrium quantity will increase from Q_F to Q'_F. As a result of the tax, therefore, both the price of meat and the price of fish have risen. But the quantity of meat produced and consumed has decreased while the quantity of fish produced and consumed has increased.

Other Changes

Under normal circumstances, various other repercussions, not shown in the diagrams, will occur. For example, after the tax, fewer resources are needed to produce the smaller quantity of meat, while more resources are needed to produce the larger quantity of fish. Therefore, the price and employment of resources in meat production will decline. At the same time, the price and employment of resources in fish production will rise. As a result, some resources will move out of meat production and into fish production.

As these movements occur, the supply curves in the two industries will shift. This will cause market prices and quantities to change. In addition, the change in relative resource prices will cause shifts in the pattern of income distribution, and this will have further repercussions on the demand for the two commodities. This adjustment process will continue until the system is once again in general equilibrium.

Interdependence and the Circular Flow

The interdependence that exists between markets in the economy can be extended beyond what is shown in the model in Exhibit 3. However, the model would then be considerably more complicated. It is sufficient, therefore, to convey the overall nature of the interrelations by means of a familiar circular-flow diagram. This is done in Exhibit 4.

The model is self-explanatory. Note that it lists the conditions that are assumed to be given or fixed in the household sector and in the business sector. The important thing to observe is that it emphasizes the interdependence between households, businesses, product markets, and factor markets.

In general:

> The overall concept conveyed by the circular-flow model is that the quantities supplied and demanded for each product and for each factor of production must be equal. When this occurs, the economy is in a state of general equilibrium.

The circular-flow model depicts, in a simplified way, the idea of market interdependence. This is at the heart of general-equilibrium theory.

The earliest notion of general equilibrium was developed in the eighteenth century by a group of French economists called the physiocrats. Foremost among them was an economist named François Quesnay. In 1758, he presented a circular-flow model to depict what he called the "natural order" of an economic system. These ideas were subsequently developed in much greater depth and with mathematical precision in the late nineteenth century by a Swiss-French economist, Leon Walras (1834–1910). Although he was a college dropout, he nevertheless ranks as one of the greatest economists of all time.

Welfare Economics

The concept of general equilibrium provides us with an overview of a perfectly competitive economy. But what are the main characteristics of such an economy? Is perfect competition "good" or "bad"? In answering these questions, you will gain some insights into what is known as *welfare economics*. This is a branch of economic theory concerned with the development of principles for maximizing society's satisfactions (that is, its social welfare).

Welfare economics is concerned with the development of principles for maximizing society's satisfactions.

Exhibit 4
Economic Interdependence– General Equilibrium and the Circular Flow

Households and businesses are linked through the product markets, where goods and services are exchanged, and through the resource markets, where the factors of production are exchanged. The economy is in a state of general equilibrium when the quantities supplied and demanded of goods and services and of factors of production are equal.

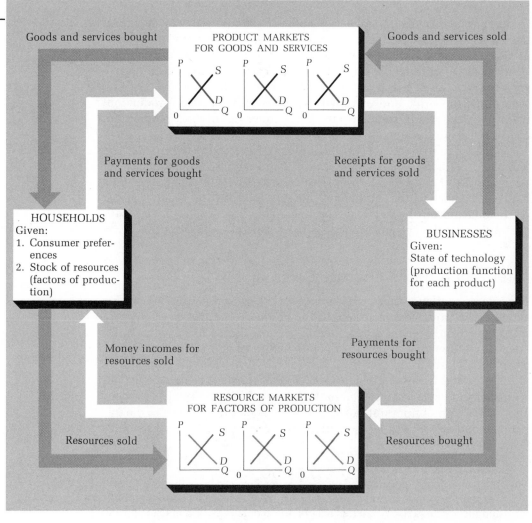

Goods and services bought

PRODUCT MARKETS
FOR GOODS AND SERVICES

Goods and services sold

Payments for goods and services bought

Receipts for goods and services sold

HOUSEHOLDS
Given:
1. Consumer preferences
2. Stock of resources (factors of production)

BUSINESSES
Given:
State of technology (production function for each product)

Money incomes for resources sold

Payments for resources bought

RESOURCE MARKETS
FOR FACTORS OF PRODUCTION

Resources sold

Resources bought

Pareto Optimality

The criterion of social-welfare maximization is known as Pareto optimality.

To begin with, what do we mean by social welfare? The concept cannot be precisely defined, and therefore it is impossible to measure. As a result, we cannot assert objectively that any particular economic situation represents greater or lesser welfare for society than another. One of the main reasons for this difficulty is that *we cannot make interpersonal comparisons of utility* or satisfactions. That is, the welfare of one person cannot be compared with that of another.

For example, as a rational consumer, I would feel better off if I could keep all my income so that I could spend more for consumption. But, as a good citizen, I might feel better off if I gave up part of my income (through taxes and charitable contributions) and thereby consumed less so that others who were not as fortunate as I could consume more. Similarly, some people argue that as a nation of consumers we are better off keeping all our income for ourselves. Others contend, however, that we should contribute part of our national income as foreign aid to less developed countries.

Therefore, even though we cannot make interpersonal comparisons of utility, such comparisons are made all the time. Indeed, it would be virtually impossible to have any social policy without them. Why? Because almost any social policy makes some people better off while making others worse off. Ideally, what we usually want are social policies that make some people better off *without making others worse off*. This involves what economists and other social scientists call "Pareto optimality."

> *Pareto optimality* is a condition that exists in a social organization when no change can be implemented that will make someone better off without making someone else worse off—each in his or her own estimation.

This concept, named after a famous Italian-Swiss sociologist and economist, Vilfredo Pareto (1848–1923), leads to two important principles:

1. Any social action that benefits at least one person without harming someone else will clearly increase social welfare. Therefore, any such action should be undertaken.

Pareto optimality is an intriguing concept but a difficult one to implement.

2. The effect on social welfare of any action that benefits some while harming others—the *numbers* of people are immaterial—cannot be determined. The reason is that we cannot compare satisfactions and dissatisfactions among people. That is, *we cannot make interpersonal comparisons of utility.*

The first principle provides a useful guide for formulating public policies, while the second contains some interesting implications. The second principle tells us, for example, that, even though a particular policy (such as the imprisonment of criminals) benefits a large majority of the people while harming a small minority, we cannot be sure that adherence to it results in an increase in social welfare. At best we can only *assume* that it does, but we cannot prove it in any objective, scientific way.

General Equilibrium and Pareto Optimality— Economic Efficiency and Equity

What are the implications of Pareto optimality for an economic system? The answer can be stated in the form of a proposition:

Pareto optimality and economic efficiency go hand in hand.

> When a perfectly competitive economy achieves a general equilibrium of prices and quantities, no economic entity (individual, household, or firm) can be made better off without some other entity being made worse off. The system has therefore attained a Pareto optimum—it has achieved an *economically efficient* allocation of resources. (**Note** Certain qualifications to this statement are pointed out in the following sections.)

The proof of this proposition requires considerably more advanced economic theory than is covered in this book. However, you can appreciate the sense of it on the basis of what was learned in previous chapters. For example, suppose that a perfectly competitive economy has settled down in general equilibrium. Keeping in mind the conditions that are "given"—namely, the pattern of consumer preferences, the stock of productive factors, and the state of technology—what are the main characteristics of the resulting state of balance?

Efficiency of Consumption in the Household Sector

In the household sector, each consuming unit spends its income on the goods and services it wants most, given the prices it must pay. Each consuming unit therefore allocates its income in such a way that it maximizes total utility or satisfactions. In terms of Pareto optimality, this means that society has achieved efficiency in consumption. This is because *no transfer of commodities can be made between any two consuming units that will make one consuming unit better off without making the other worse off.*

Efficiency of Production in the Business Sector

In the business sector, as you learned in the study of perfect competition, each firm in the long run ends up producing in the output market at the level of production at which certain efficiency conditions apply. Among them:

1. $MC = P$ This means that the value of the last unit of the good to the consumer (measured by the price the consumer pays for the last unit, which is equal to the price paid for any other unit) is equal to the value of society's resources used to produce that unit.

2. $MC = ATC = LRAC$ This means that the firm is producing the optimum output with the optimum-size plant. Therefore, it is allocating all its resources in a technically efficient manner.

Equity and Efficiency in the Economy

In the input markets, firms also achieve equilibrium by adhering to marginal principles. Thus, every firm hires each factor of production up to the point at which the marginal cost or price of the factor is equal to the value of what it contributes (its marginal revenue product). Each factor thus receives what it is "worth"—the value of what it contributes to total output—as determined in free markets by supply and demand. According to the *contributive standard*, therefore, society has achieved equity (economic justice) in the distribution of income. (**Note** To refresh your understanding, look up the meaning of *contributive standard* in the Dictionary at the back of the book.)

What else do the above equilibrium conditions (equations) mean? Fundamentally, they tell us that society has achieved *technical efficiency* in production by producing the largest possible volume of output with available resources. Therefore, *no transfer of resources can be made between the production of any two commodities that will increase the output of one commodity without decreasing the output of the other.* In other words, the economy is producing on its production-possibilities curve instead of at some point inside it. Therefore, there is full employment of all resources. Moreover, society has also achieved *economic efficiency* because the goods that are being produced are those that people want to buy with their available incomes.

General equilibrium and economic efficiency thus go hand in hand. It is particularly interesting, however, to realize the remarkable way in which these end results come about:

> All participants in the economy—consumers, businesspeople, resource owners—acting *independently* in their own self-interest and without direction from government, make millions of market decisions daily. These determine *what, how,* and *for whom* goods shall be produced. Yet the economic system, because it is perfectly competitive, is guided by Adam Smith's "invisible hand" toward general equilibrium and economic efficiency. This is an end result that, as Smith pointed out, is "no part of anyone's intention."

Efficiency conditions can be expressed by some familiar equations.

General equilibrium and economic efficiency go hand in hand. They occur through the free play of market forces under perfect competition.

Implications for Social Welfare

Should we conclude from this that perfect competition leads to the best of all possible worlds? As pointed out earlier, when a perfectly competitive economy is in general equilibrium, it has attained a Pareto optimum. This is a situation in which no person can be made better off without someone else being made worse off, each in his or her own estimation. However, there are some qualifications. The more important ones have already been discussed in several earlier chapters. Therefore, it is sufficient to summarize them briefly at this time.

General equilibrium may be "good" or "bad," depending on society's values.

Social Costs and Social Benefits

Competitive prices tend to reflect private costs and private benefits, but they may exclude some social costs and social benefits. Environmental pollution arising from production is a typical example of a cost to society that may not be included in a manufacturer's private costs. Likewise, flood control and conservation practices undertaken by a seller provide illustrations of benefits that accrue to many people other than those who buy the producer's product.
   Therefore:

Market failures may give rise to externalities —social costs and social benefits that are not reflected in market supply and demand curves.

> To the extent that *all* social costs and benefits are not incorporated in firms' activities, general equilibrium will not provide an optimum allocation of society's resources.

Income Distribution and Equity

In a system of perfect competition, the owners of each factor of production are paid according to the "contributive standard." That is, the owners of each factor are paid what their factor is "worth," as measured by what it contributes to total output. This is known as the *marginal-productivity theory of income distribution.*
   According to this principle, a person who is twice as productive as another is paid twice as much. Whether or not this is a just or equitable standard of income distribution is a normative question rather than a positive one. Therefore, each society must answer the question for itself. Some might argue, for example, that it is "just" for a family of six to be paid twice as much as a family of three—regardless of their productivities. Therefore:

The distribution of income in accordance with marginal productivities may or may not be considered "fair."

> To the extent that society regards the contributive standard as *unjust*, general equilibrium will *not* provide an equitable distribution of the economy's income.

Conclusion: Norms of Efficiency for Welfare Economics

You can now appreciate more fully the role played by modern welfare economics. In broad terms, welfare economics deals with the normative aspects of microeconomics. Welfare economics is concerned not with what the perfect world would look like but with the changes that may be undertaken to improve the well-being of consumers and producers in *today's* world. Welfare economics does this by providing us with a norm or standard expressed in terms of economic efficiency. This enables us to state unambiguously whether one equilibrium position is better or worse than another.

From what we now know about microeconomics, it is clear that perfect competition leads (with some qualifications) to an optimum allocation of society's resources. This is assured by Smith's "invisible hand." Other types of market structures—such as unregulated monopoly, monopolistic competition, and oligopoly—do not achieve an optimum allocation. This suggests that the norm provided by welfare economics can serve as a guide for government intervention in markets. Intervention can occur through taxes, subsidies, direct regulation, or other means. The purpose of government intervention is to correct for costs and gains that result when the norm is violated. In other words:

> In markets in which supply and demand forces serve efficiently as mechanisms for allocating society's resources, no intervention by government is needed. But when markets fail to perform efficiently, certain types of intervention may be called for.

The nature and effects of various kinds of intervention pose many interesting problems that will occupy our attention in the following chapters. Meanwhile, see "Leaders in Economics," page 572.

Case
Rat Economics

What motivates people? This is a question that psychologists often ask. In recent years, economists have also become concerned with the question. And, like psychologists, some economists are conducting experiments in the hope of finding answers. In doing so, they are discovering results that lend support to conclusions derived from many diverse areas of economic theory.

Income Distribution

Two economists who have done pioneering work along such experimental lines are Ray Battalio and John Kagel, both of Texas A&M University. In one of their investigations, they constructed a token economy in a women's ward of a New York state psychiatric hospital. There, patients were paid tokens for performing various jobs, such as sweeping the floor, making the beds, working in the laundry, and so on.

One of the remarkable results of the study was that the *pattern of earnings among the patients closely resembled the distribution of income in the United States as a whole.* For example, the highest fifth of the income earners at the hospital got 41 percent of all the earnings, compared with 42 percent for the highest fifth in the nation. The lowest fifth at the institution got 7 percent, compared with a little more than 5 percent for the country as a whole.

Kagel and Battalio also came up with some fascinating findings in studies of mixed (male–female) token economies. In one of their studies they found that the median token income of women was 69 percent that of men. This compares with about 60 percent for the economy as a whole. The results led them to conclude that, among the participants in their experiment, most of the income difference between the sexes could not be explained by sex discrimination. Other factors, such as physical stamina or desire for leisure, might have accounted for most of the difference, but not discrimination. Kagel and Battalio, however, do not draw any inferences from this for the economy as a whole.

Income–Leisure Tradeoff

Do rising wages encourage workers to work harder, or do workers reduce their efforts as wages increase? Economic theory has sometimes assumed the latter. This is because it has been found that, as wages rise, the amount of time or effort put forth by workers increases—but only up to a point. Thereafter, further increases in wages result in a reduction in work because workers are "satisfied" with the incomes they are already earning. This relationship gives rise to what is known as a "backward-bending labor supply curve," illustrating a tradeoff between income and leisure.

Kagel and Battalio, along with several psychologists, decided to test the income–leisure tradeoff under controlled laboratory conditions. Using pigeons and rats in Skinner boxes (devised by Harvard psychologist B. F. Skinner), the experimenters taught the animals to peck at buttons and to push levers in order to earn rewards of food.

As a result of this approach, the research team confirmed the existence of a backward-bending labor supply curve for the animals. As their wage rate (measured in terms of servings of food) went up, hungry pigeons and rats pecked and pushed harder and faster—but only up to a point. The point differed with each animal. But beyond their respective points, even though the animals were not satiated, their efforts slowed down as they traded off some work for more leisure.

Negative Income Tax

The research team also used Skinner boxes to investigate the effects of a negative income tax. This is a type of reverse income tax that some economists and legislators have proposed. It would provide government payments to poor people whose incomes are below a certain minimum level. As the recipients' income from work rises towards the minimum, the government's payments decline to zero.

By programming the boxes to provide varying amounts of "free" food intermittently while the animals were working, the team observed several interesting results:

1. The animals reduced their work effort approximately in proportion to the quantity of free food they received.

2. Work reduction was relatively greater among the low-wage rats. These were rats that had to work longer for less food. High-wage rats, on the other hand, seemed to enjoy working and reduced their efforts relatively less.

3. Total income, consisting of both earned and free food, was less when free food was provided than when it was not.

Conclusion: Food for Thought

As with all creative research, these and similar studies have been viewed skeptically by some. The critics contend that the experiments are too simple and unrealistic to permit generalizations about human behavior.

The experimenters, of course, disagree. They reply that economic theory often fails to predict the outcome of real-world policies, which can be viewed as complex experiments conducted on a large scale. Therefore, theories should first be able to predict simple laboratory behavior before they are used as a basis for policy prescriptions.

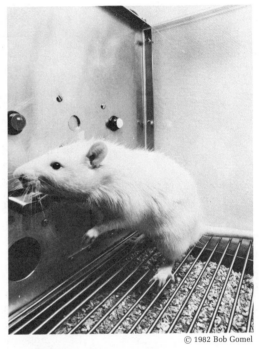

© 1982 Bob Gomel

In a Skinner box, the animals learned to "buy" food in exchange for work and to trade off food for leisure.

Leaders in Economics

Marie Esprit Leon Walras
1834–1910

Vilfredo Pareto
1848–1923
*The "Lausanne School":
General Equilibrium and
Welfare Economics*

Charles Phelps Cushing

Marie Esprit Leon Walras

Historical Pictures Service

Vilfredo Pareto

Leon Walras, as he is commonly known, ranks as one of the most significant figures in the history of economic thought. His fame rests on his formulation of the theory of general equilibrium, which he developed rigorously through the use of mathematics. He thus became one of the founders of an approach to economics known as mathematical economics, which has flourished to this day.

Born and educated in France, Walras studied to be a mining engineer but left engineering school before his training was completed in order to become a free-lance journalist. In this capacity he wrote many articles advocating economic, and especially agrarian, reform. In 1870, he was appointed to the chair of political economy at the University of Lausanne, Switzerland, where he remained until 1892.

General Equilibrium
A few years after his arrival at Lausanne, Walras published his great work, *Elements of Pure Economics*. In this book he showed how, given the mathematical equations of demand and supply at equilibrium and the *numéraire* (the unit of accounting), the solution of the problem of general equilibrium is determinate. That is, there is a set of simultaneous equations whose number equals the number of unknowns, with the number of prices to be ascertained. The problem, however, is determinate in a formal sense only. The necessary data cannot be obtained, and the number of simultaneous equations that would have to be solved is virtually infinite. Nevertheless, this does not destroy the value of general-equilibrium theory, for the virtue of the concept lies in the precise way in which it demonstrates the mutual interdependence of economic phenomena.

Welfare Economics
Walras was succeeded at Lausanne by Vilfredo Pareto, an Italian scholar who abandoned a career as an engineer to devote time to scholarly pursuits. Heavily influenced by Walras, Pareto contributed significantly to the literature of pure economics. His expositions in mathematical economics are even today considered extremely elegant and erudite.

In his major work, *Manual of Political Economy*, Pareto presented economic theory in an aridly pure, static, and general way, in the sense that it can be applied to any economic system. Pareto's formulation of theory, like Walras's, is one of general equilibrium under static conditions. However, Pareto was also concerned with the problem of how to maximize total satisfactions in an economy. He developed the concept now commonly referred to as Pareto optimality—a notion that is fundamental to modern welfare economics. In passing, it should be noted that Pareto also made notable contributions to sociology. In fact, his reputation in that field is as strong as his reputation in economics.

Important Influence
Together, Walras and Pareto constitute what is known as the "Lausanne School" of economic thought. The influence of this school on subsequent writers—especially in mathematical economics, general-equilibrium theory, and welfare economics—has been enormous. Indeed, modern microeconomic theory owes much of its present content to the pioneering scientific work first done at Lausanne.

What You Have Learned in This Chapter

1. The concept of equilibrium is of fundamental importance in economics. An equilibrium position may be stable, unstable, or neutral—in a static or in a dynamic sense.

2. A static model provides a "snapshot" of the essential features of an economic phenomenon at an instant in time, whereas a dynamic model provides a "motion picture" over a period of time. Although static analysis encompasses most of economic theory, many important problems cannot be analyzed without the use of dynamics.

3. General equilibrium, as distinguished from partial equilibrium, emphasizes the interdependence that exists between markets and sectors of the economy. The notion of general equilibrium can be depicted by a circular-flow diagram.

4. The concept of general equilibrium goes hand in hand with the science of welfare economics. The latter is concerned with the development of principles for maximizing social welfare. Thus, when a perfectly competitive economy achieves a general equilibrium of prices and quantities, it has attained a Pareto optimum—an efficient allocation of resources—and therefore has maximized social welfare. Some qualifications to this conclusion may be needed, however, depending on such factors as the inclusion of social costs and social benefits in firms' activities and the extent to which society regards the contributive standard of income distribution as inequitable.

For Discussion

1. *Terms and concepts to review:*
equilibrium
static model
comparative statics
dynamic model
stable equilibrium
partial-equilibrium theory
general-equilibrium theory
correspondence principle
specific tax
welfare economics
Pareto optimality
contributive standard
economic efficiency
marginal-productivity theory of income distribution

2. Which is more important—the stability of an equilibrium position or its "location"? Explain.

3. You have already learned the concepts of *demand price* and *supply price* in previous chapters. (To refresh your memory, look up their meanings in the Dictionary at the back of the book.) Using these notions, and thinking in terms of supply and demand curves, formulate definitions of stable and unstable *quantity* equilibrium. (**Hint** You may find it helpful first to formulate definitions of stable and unstable *price* equilibrium in terms of quantity supplied and quantity demanded. Then use a parallel procedure to define stable and unstable quantity equilibrium in terms of demand price and supply price.)

4. In terms of supply and demand curves, can a price equilibrium be stable for an upward movement and unstable or neutral for a downward movement, and vice versa? Is the same true for a quantity equilibrium in terms of a leftward or rightward movement? Explain.

5. "If the world economy were perfectly competitive, a tariff (tax on imports) would result in a misallocation of resources and a reduction in net social welfare for the world community." Do you agree? Why?

6. Nations sometimes employ rationing as a means of distributing scarce goods. Usually, consumers are given ration coupons entitling them to purchase, say, 1 pound of meat and 1 pound of fish per week. In this way, an equal amount of each good is assigned to each consumer. Is this "fair"? Can you propose an alternative method of rationing that is more equitable?

7. It is contended by some social critics that, because we do not know the actual distribution of income that will maximize satisfaction, it must be assumed that an equal distribution of income out of any given level of national income would most likely maximize satisfaction. Evaluate this argument.

Microeconomic Problems
and Policies

27
CHAPTER

Public Choice: Improving Public-Sector Efficiency

Learning guide
Watch for the answers to these important questions

What are social goods? Can measures be taken to improve efficiency in the provision of social goods?

How are public goods allocated? What practical difficulties arise in the allocation process? How are these difficulties overcome?

What voting rules does our society employ to reveal consumers' preferences for public goods? How is the size of government affected by our voting rules? Is it possible to devise a voting system that is always fair and rational?

What is the nature of government bureaucracy? Why does it exist? How does it function? What can be done to improve the effectiveness of government bureaucracies?

Should people pay for the use of merit goods? Can pricing strategies be developed for merit goods? What are the advantages and difficulties of such strategies?

This chapter surveys major principles and issues concerning the economics of the public sector.

Since its beginnings in the eighteenth century, economics has often been called "political economy." The latter term is more descriptive. It affirms that economic decisions are often rooted in politics and that political processes are at the heart of most economic policies.

Economics and politics, therefore, share some common ground. The piece of common ground that concerns us at this point is called *public choice*. This may be defined as the branch of economics that deals with nonmarket collective decision making, or the application of economics to political science. The goal of public choice is to develop means of improving efficiency in the public sector and in the provision of social goods.

Public Choice and Social Goods

In our mixed economy, society's resources are allocated to the production of private goods in accordance with market forces. But what about *social goods*? As you have already learned, these may be defined as products provided by government, usually because society believes that such goods are not adequately provided by the free market. The nature and economic implications of social goods are best understood by dividing them into two classes—public goods and merit goods.

Public Goods

Certain goods provided by government are *public* (or *collective*) *goods*. Examples include national defense, public safety, disease control, and the administration of justice through the court system. Public goods have three important characteristics: (1) their benefits are indivisible, (2) their benefits are provided at zero marginal cost, and (3) they create spillover effects.

Indivisible Benefits

Unlike "private goods," which are sold in the marketplace only to those who buy them, public goods are available to all. Consequently, you cannot be excluded from using a public good, regardless of whether or not you pay for it. For example, the benefits of national defense are available equally to everyone in the nation, just as are the benefits of public health.

The benefits of public goods are available to everyone, regardless of payment.

This differentiation of goods rests on what may be called the *exclusion principle*. It provides a basis for distinguishing between nonpublic and public goods. Thus, a good is nonpublic if anyone who does not pay for it can be excluded from its use. Otherwise, it is a public good.

Benefits Provided at Zero Marginal Cost

A second characteristic of public goods is that their benefits can be provided to an additional user without additional costs. Thus we say that the marginal cost of a public good's benefits is zero.

For example, the cost of providing electric power to a community does not increase because of the addition of one more person. Nor does the cost of maintaining an army and navy rise when the population increases by one. This characteristic, however, is also shared by certain private goods. For instance, within wide limits, up to the point of overcrowding, the marginal cost to the owners of a football stadium or a movie theater does not increase with the admittance of one more patron. The same is usually true of buses, concert halls, museums, marinas, and the like.

Two further (but not unique) characteristics of public goods are (1) that benefits provided at zero marginal cost and (2) that they create spillover effects or externalities.

Spillover Effects

A third characteristic of public goods is that they create *spillovers*. These are external benefits or costs for which no compensation is made. Spillovers are also referred to as *externalities*. For example, air-traffic control at busy airports reduces noise for some nearby residents while increasing it for others. This is an unpaid-for benefit to the former and an uncompensated "cost" to the latter. Similarly, in the private sector, a factory may provide income and employment benefits to a community while polluting its environment. Thus, spillover effects, like zero marginal costs of benefits, are not unique to public goods.

These characteristics provide the basis for a definition:

> *Public goods* are those not subject to the exclusion principle. This is because the benefits of public goods are indivisible. No one can be excluded from receiving them, whether he or she pays for them or not. For this reason, public goods are commodities that the private sector is usually unable or unwilling to produce. Two additional (but not unique) characteristics of public goods are (1) zero marginal costs of benefits and (2) spillover effects.

Note Virtually all radio transmissions and most television transmissions are public goods because they are not subject to the exclusion principle. Yet they are provided (in the United States and in some other countries) by the private sector. Can you suggest why? Can you think of some other exceptions?

Merit Goods

Merit goods have some of the characteristics both of public goods and of private goods.

In addition to public goods, government produces what may be called *merit goods.* These are goods provided by society because it deems some minimum amount of them intrinsically worthy (or meritorious) of production. Examples of merit goods are public education, highways, museums, hospitals, recreation facilities, libraries, low-cost housing, and public transportation.

Merit goods share, to different degrees, some of the properties of public goods and private goods. For instance:

1. Like public goods, merit goods are characterized either by benefits whose marginal costs are zero, or by spillover effects, or by both. Can you give some examples?

2. Like private goods, merit goods are subject to the exclusion principle. This is true *even though the principle may not always be invoked.* In other words, people could conceivably be charged for the use of merit goods instead of being given them "free" or at reduced prices.

You can see from the preceding examples of merit goods that they are provided in varying degrees by federal, state, and local governments. This raises some interesting questions about the financing and administration of such goods. For instance, even though the public sector now pays all or most of the cost of merit goods, could greater efficiency be achieved if these goods were produced and distributed by the private sector? If so, how might such "privitization" policies be implemented? The solutions to these and related problems affect all of us. Hence they are among the most fundamental concerns of informed citizens.

Conclusion: Revealed Preferences Needed

The study of public choice is concerned with improving efficiency in the provision of social goods.

In a competitive market, the forces of supply and demand operate to allocate the factors of production efficiently. This means that society attains full utilization of its available resources and that firms produce the goods that consumers want to purchase with their given incomes. Under these conditions, it follows that no change in the allocation of resources can be implemented that will make someone better off without making someone else worse off.

Is this happy state of affairs actually experienced in the real world? The answer, of course, is *no.* Efficiency is one of the goals of our economic system. Like the other goals—equity, stability, and growth—efficiency is a "moving target" that we would like the economy to reach but that we know is unattainable. Therefore, much of our concern in economics must focus on the development of legislation and government policies aimed at reducing waste and promoting the *tendency* toward greater efficiency. With respect to social goods, this has the following implications.

> A distinguishing feature of social goods is that they are provided either "free" or at reduced prices. Consequently, consumers' preferences for these goods (in contrast with private goods provided in the marketplace) are usually unknown. For this reason, many social goods tend to be produced inefficiently. *Therefore, a necessary step toward achieving efficiency is to develop some means of revealing people's preferences for social goods.*

Allocating Public Goods

> The less government we have, the better: the fewer laws, and the less confided power.
>
> Ralph Waldo Emerson (1833)

> As new conditions and problems arise beyond the power of men and women to meet as individuals, it becomes the duty of government itself to find new remedies.
>
> Franklin Delano Roosevelt (1933)

Emerson, a nineteenth-century essayist, did not see the role of government in the same way as did Roosevelt, a twentieth-century president. Roosevelt's view, of course, is the one that society has adopted. Consequently, government's place in the economy has expanded enormously since the 1930s.

Public goods (not to mention merit goods) have played an important role in this expansion. Because they are not subject to the exclusion principle, the production of public goods raises special problems concerning the allocation of society's resources. We can learn a great deal about the nature of these problems by examining them in terms of a few simple supply-and-demand models.

Deriving Demand Curves ✗

When you studied demand and supply curves, you saw how the total market demand curve for a commodity is derived by summing horizontally the individual demand curves. A similar procedure is used to derive the total market supply curve. To refresh your memory, the idea is illustrated in Exhibit 1 for a demand curve. For simplicity, this model assumes there are only three people in the market—*A*, *B*, and *C*. The conclusions can then be extended to include a market consisting of any number of people.

In Figure (*a*), the total demand for a private good is simply the *horizontal sum* of the individual demand curves, D_A, D_B, and D_C. For example, at a price of $2 per unit, *A* will demand 4 units, *B* will demand 8 units, and *C* will demand 10 units. Therefore, the total market demand at a price of $2 will be $4 + 8 + 10 = 22$ units. Similarly, at a price of $6 per unit, the specific quantities demanded will be $2 + 4 + 8 = 14$ units. If you connect each pair of points for each person with a straight line, you will get the three individual demand curves. The total market demand curve is then seen to be the horizontal sum of the individual curves at each price.

In contrast, Figure (*b*) shows the individual demand curves for a public good. Unlike a private good, whose benefits must be purchased by those who want them, the benefits of a public good—such as guided missiles, street lighting, and disease control—are shared by everyone. As a result, the total demand curve for a public good must be derived in a different way.

Thus, in Figure (*b*), the total demand for the good is the *vertical sum* of the individual demand curves D_A, D_B, and D_C. For example, to share in the benefits of 1 unit of the good, such as 1 missile, person *A* would be willing to pay (in the form of increased taxes) $2. Similarly, *B* would be willing to pay $4, and *C* would be willing to pay $5. Therefore, the total *demand price*—the highest price per unit that buyers are willing to pay

The demand curve for a public good is derived by obtaining the vertical sum of individual demand curves at each quantity.

Exhibit 1

Deriving Demand Curves and Allocating a Public Good

Figure (a): For a private good, each point on the total demand curve is obtained by starting with a given price and finding the horizontal sum—the total quantity that individual buyers are willing to purchase.

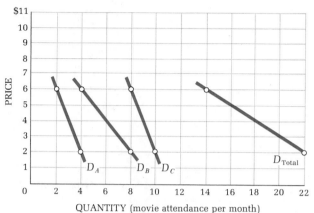

(a) DERIVING A DEMAND CURVE FOR A PRIVATE GOOD
(example: movie attendance)

Figure (b): For a public good, each point on the total demand curve is obtained by starting with a given quantity and finding the vertical sum—the total price (in the form of taxes) that individuals are willing to pay.

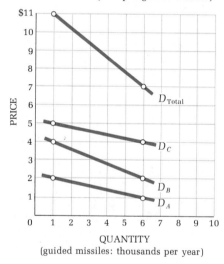

(b) DERIVING A DEMAND CURVE FOR A PUBLIC GOOD (example: guided missiles)

Figure (c): For many public goods, the supply curve is horizontal—that is, perfectly elastic. This indicates that the additional or marginal cost to the government of providing one more unit of the good remains constant. (*Example:* guided missiles.) Given the supply curve, the actual amount provided and the price are determined by the intersection of the supply curve with the total demand curve [derived in Figure (b)]. Thus, the equilibrium quantity is at M, and the equilibrium price is at P.

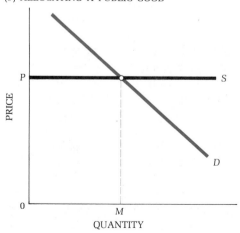

(c) ALLOCATING A PUBLIC GOOD

for a given quantity of the commodity—is $2 + $4 + $5 = $11 for 1 unit. For a quantity of 6 units, the total demand price is $1 + $2 + $4 = $7. As before, if you connect each pair of points for each person with straight lines, you will get three individual demand curves. The total curve, of course, is simply the vertical sum of the individual curves at each quantity.

You can now use supply and demand curves to determine the equilibrium quantity of a public good. The equilibrium quantity is the amount that society will produce with its limited resources. This is shown in Figure (c). Note that the supply curve in this case is horizontal. This is true of many public goods. *The horizontal supply curve tells you that the additional or marginal cost of supplying one more unit of the good remains the same.* Therefore, government is willing to supply additional units at a constant price per unit.

How much will actually be supplied, and at what price? The answer is determined by the intersection of the demand and supply curves. Thus, the equilibrium quantity of the good will be at M units and the equilibrium price at P dollars per unit.

These ideas can be summarized briefly:

> For a *private good*, each point on the total demand curve is obtained by starting with a given price and finding the *horizontal sum*—the total quantity that people are willing to purchase. For a *public good*, each point on the total demand curve is obtained by starting with a given quantity and finding the *vertical sum*—the total price that people are willing to pay. If the public's supply and demand curves are known, the equilibrium price and quantity are determined in the same way as for a private good—by the intersection of the two curves. ∎

Practical Difficulties: False Demand Curves and the Free-Rider Problem ✓

The preceding analysis of how a public good is allocated may seem strange if not confusing. The reason is that it involves at least two practical problems.

1. The demand curves shown in Figure (b) are actually "false" or "counterfeit" demand curves. This is because they are based on the unrealistic assumption that consumers voluntarily state their demand prices for public goods. If this were in fact the case, government could achieve greater efficiency and equity in the financing of public goods by charging consumers the amounts they were willing to pay. Instead, public goods are usually financed through taxes and subsidies. For reasons shown later in the chapter, these methods of financing may often fall far short of achieving maximum efficiency and equity.

2. A second problem arises from the fact that a public good is one that is not subject to the exclusion principle. Therefore, no individual can be prevented from receiving the benefits of a public good, whether he or she pays or not. In view of this, why would anyone be willing to state a demand price for a public good, as was assumed in Figure (b)?

This second difficulty results in what is known as the *free-rider problem*. It may be defined as the tendency of people to avoid paying for a good's benefits when the benefits can be obtained free. The free-rider problem exists because public goods, more than any others, create extensive spillover benefits. Those who receive the benefits without

Although the supply curves of most public goods are horizontal, those of some public goods are vertical.

■ **Test Yourself**

1. For a private good, the supply curve is likely to be upward-sloping. What does such a curve tell you? (Think in terms of the law of supply.)

2. For some public goods, the supply curve is horizontal. For other public goods, the supply curve may be upward-sloping or even vertical. What would a vertical curve tell you? Does it conform to the law of supply? What types of supply curves characterize such public goods as fighter planes, free parks, and free polio vaccinations?

paying are thus "free riders." It follows that, if many people become free riders, the demand curves shown in Figure (b) become ineffective. That is, they serve as a useful guide for thinking about the problem of allocating a public good, but they do not provide a practical means for doing so. Thus, an alternative approach is needed.

Conclusion: Allocation by Collective Action

In democratic societies, public goods are allocated by voting—that is, by collective action.

The inability of the market system to allocate resources for the production of public goods is an example of *market failure*. When markets fail, democratic societies resort to various nonmarket methods to provide the desired goods. Because voters as well as their elected representatives have different attitudes about what constitutes the optimal amount of public goods, differences of opinion must be reconciled through the political process. How is this accomplished? In general:

> The nonmarket method used by democratic societies to allocate resources for the production of public goods is *collective action*—the rule of majority vote. This method does not always lead to equitable results because it may not be capable of reconciling conflicting preferences of voters. However, through vote trading and compromise by legislators, collective action has proven to be a workable and relatively "fair" system—as evidenced by its long history of acceptability.

Voting Rules and Revealed Preferences

There are various voting rules and practices whose purpose is to reflect the public's preferences.

In our economy's private sector, people express their preferences in the marketplace by casting dollar "votes" for the goods they want. In the public sector, people express their preferences at the polls by casting political votes for the candidates and issues they support. Public choice deals with the study of decision making in the public sector. It is appropriate, therefore, to examine some alternative voting systems. This helps to explain how people's preferences for social goods are revealed in a democratic society.

Unanimity Rule

What is the "best" way of deciding whether a proposed law or other measure should be enacted? One possibility is to require unanimous approval by the voters. This would assure that every person is satisfied —that no person's welfare is reduced by the proposed action. In other words, it would guarantee that the proposal is Pareto optimal.

Note You should recall the meaning and implication of *Pareto optimality.* It is a condition that exists in a social organization when no change can be implemented that will make someone better off without making someone else worse off—each in his or her own estimation. Therefore, when society has achieved Pareto optimality, its level of well-being, or welfare, is at a maximum.

A voting system that adhered to a unanimity rule would achieve welfare outcomes corresponding to those of perfect competition. If a proposed measure failed to obtain unanimous agreement, the drafters of the legislation would have to continue modifying the proposal until it met the approval of all voters. Thus, when the measure finally passed, no person would be worse off as a result of its passage. Society, therefore, would not suffer a net loss of welfare.

Despite this benefit, the unanimity rule of voting has two major shortcomings:

1. Costliness The legislative body would have to spend much time and effort modifying a proposal and resubmitting it until it met everyone's approval. Under such circumstances, government would rarely get any bills passed, and society would bear the high costs of inaction and delay.

2. "Blackmail" Any person or group could effectively extract concessions from the other voters by threatening to vote against a proposal that the other voters support. The final outcome will thus depend on the relative bargaining strength of the two negotiating parties—the "blackmailer" and the other voters.

These shortcomings of the unanimity rule have often been sufficient to outweigh its advantages. Although the unanimity rule is employed in certain circumstances, democratic societies have found it necessary to develop other kinds of voting rules.

Majority Rule

Most voting systems stipulate that a majority of voters must approve a proposal in order for it to be enacted. But what constitutes a majority? Two types, called "simple" and "qualified," may be distinguished.

Under a *simple majority* rule, each person gets one vote. A proposal is passed if the number of "yes" votes exceeds the number of "no" votes. The U.S. Congress and the state and local legislatures usually adhere to this form of majority rule. It is employed for making most types of routine decisions.

Of course, certain decisions are not routine. They require special consideration because of their exceptional nature. Examples include the impeachment of an elected official, the overriding of a presidential veto, and the passage of a constitutional amendment. For such purposes, legislatures and other voting groups require the approval of a "substantial" or *qualified majority* —such as two-thirds or three-fourths of the qualified voters.

Logrolling: Vote Trading

Voting provides people with a means of expressing their preferences. But the *intensities* of voter preferences on specific issues are not the same. As a result, the benefits received by a winning majority may sometimes be less than the minority's losses. To reduce the chances of this happening, legislators frequently engage in vote trading, or logrolling. It may be either explicit or implicit. Senator A may make similar agreements with Senators C, D, and E, as long as those Senators' proposals do not conflict with the desires of A's constituents. The less conflict there is, the more likely A is to trade votes. However, if Senator F's proposal is repugnant to A's constituents, A will not want to trade votes with F. Thus may the intensity of voter preferences be registered in the legislative process.

Explicit logrolling is usually obvious and straightforward. It consists of a well-defined exchange of votes between politicians. In the simplest case, Senator A agrees to vote for Senator B's proposal if Senator B will vote for Senator A's proposal.

Logrolling provides a way of reflecting the intensities of voter preferences on specific issues.

Implicit logrolling, by contrast, is often subtle and indirect. Its occurrence depends on the way in which the proposed legislation is structured. For instance, a bill that contains various separate measures, each of which is favored by a large number of legislators, may have a better chance of approval than one that does not. By voting for the entire bill, legislators in effect "exchange" votes with one another in order to obtain the specific measures they want.

Logrolling is a common practice in all democratic societies. It evidences the existence of unequal intensities of feeling among voters. Without logrolling, the majority would always win over the minority on each issue, even when the minority's preferences were more intense. Through logrolling, however, minorities are able to express the intensity of their preferences in much the same way as people express their preferences in trading private goods.

> By combining vote trading and majority rule, a democratic society tends to produce legislation that reflects the preferences of the people. Therefore, contrary to much popular opinion, logrolling is not a disreputable practice. It is a constructive factor in political decision making because it usually results in a more efficient choice, and hence in an improvement in society's net welfare.

Some Implications

Various other types of voting systems and practices exist. However, those based on the unanimity rule and on majority rule are the most familiar because they are the most common. What are some of the important implications of these rules?

The purpose of voting is to enable people to express their preferences. It follows that the type of voting rule adopted can have important implications. Two of them, stated as propositions, are particularly interesting.

> **1.** The size and scope of government tends to vary inversely with the extent of agreement required for the passage of legislation.

The fewer the number of voting approvals required, the greater will be the tendency toward big government.

This means that those who desire an expanded role for government should be in favor of reducing the proportion of approvals required for the passage of legislation. The reason is that the fewer the number of people who must agree on a proposal, the more likely it is to pass. Consequently, many more proposals could be voted upon and approved, thereby creating a growing need for government to administer the new laws.

Conversely, those who want to restrict the size of government should be in favor of increasing the number of approvals required for the passage of legislation. This would cut down on the number of proposals that could be approved, thereby reducing the need for government.

> **2.** Even if each voter has rational and consistent voting preferences, a group of voters using a simple majority rule may produce a collective result that is irrational and inconsistent.

The preferences of a group may not always be consistent with the preferences of its members.

This proposition may be called the "voting paradox." It suggests the interesting conclusion that, under a voting system of majority rule, the preferences of a group may turn out to be inconsistent with those of its members. Let us see why.

Voting Paradox

The dictionary tells you that a paradox is a seeming contradiction. To understand how this can occur in voting, imagine a committee of three legislators deciding how their city should finance improvements for a public recreation area. They must vote on whether the city should acquire the needed funds by charging admission fees, by borrowing, or by raising taxes.

Suppose that one of the legislators prefers fees to borrowing and borrowing to taxes. The second prefers borrowing to taxes and taxes to fees. The third prefers taxes to fees and fees to borrowing. Each of the legislators thus has a different order of preferences:

Legislator 1: fees, borrowing, taxes
Legislator 2: borrowing, taxes, fees
Legislator 3: taxes, fees, borrowing

If the legislators' preferences are viewed in pairs in order to determine the majority choice, a contradictory result occurs. For example:

• A majority of the committee, namely legislators 1 and 3, prefers fees to borrowing.

• A majority of the committee, namely legislators 1 and 2, prefers borrowing to taxes.

• Thus, a majority prefers fees to borrowing and a majority prefers borrowing to taxes. Therefore, it is logical to *deduce* from these preferences that the committee prefers fees to taxes.

However, if the legislators now exercise their individual preferences, the opposite result occurs. Despite the seemingly logical conclusion that the committee prefers fees to taxes, a majority consisting of legislators 2 and 3 prefers taxes to fees.

Inconsistencies can arise between individual and group preferences.

The voting paradox thus leads to an interesting conclusion:

> In voting, each voter may be logically consistent in his or her preferences. Nevertheless, the group may produce a collective result that seems illogical and inconsistent.

Conclusion: Impossibility Theorem— No System Is Perfect

These and related ideas have been expressed by Nobel laureate Kenneth Arrow in much more sophisticated form. Using advanced mathematics and symbolic logic, he developed what has come to be called *Arrow's impossibility theorem*. The proposition proves that no voting system is perfect because group decisions cannot be both rational and fair. The reason is that five conditions are needed in order to meet all requirements of rationality and fairness:

It is impossible to construct a voting system that is completely fair and rational.

1. The voter must be able to rank alternatives in a consistent order of preferences. (For example, if a voter prefers candidate A to candidate B and candidate B to candidate C, then the voter must prefer candidate A to candidate C.)

2. The voter must be free to choose any possible ranking of alternatives.

Collective decisions can result in inefficient and inequitable taxes and policies and thus impose high costs on people. Society's net welfare may thereby be seriously reduced. Therefore, careful selection of voting rules is needed to arrive at efficient collective decisions.

This is one of many propositions demonstrated by Kenneth Arrow in his monumental treatise, *Social Choice and Individual Values* (2nd ed., 1970). In this extraordinarily sophisticated book, as well as in many of his writings, Arrow has displayed exceptional creative ability. He has formulated, with mathematical elegance and rigor, deep theoretical concepts integrating economics and related social sciences. In recognition of his accomplishments, he was awarded a Nobel Prize in 1972, and he has frequently been called an "economist's economist."

One of Arrow's many contributions is an analysis of the way in which individual preferences may affect outcomes in collective decision making. The so-called "voting paradox" provides an interesting example. Although Arrow did not originate the concept, he was the first to demonstrate how it relates to economic efficiency. He did this by showing that, in the marketplace as well as in the voting booth, similarity of preferences (both consumers' and voters') affects the efficiency of results. In general, the more similar the preferences, the greater the net gains in benefits that society experiences from collective action.

Arrow's research and writings have been wide-ranging. In addition to his many contributions to economics, his work on voting behavior has been a foundation for further investigations in political science, psychology, and sociology. As a result, Arrow's ideas are as well known in these fields as in economics.

3. The voting outcome must please as many people as possible while displeasing as few as possible.

4. No person may dictate a decision to the voting group.

5. The addition of a new set of alternatives must broaden the voter's choice without altering the consistency or the order of previously ranked alternatives.

Arrow's theorem demonstrates that, because of logical inconsistencies, these conditions cannot be applied simultaneously. Consequently:

> It is impossible to construct a "perfect" voting system—one that is completely rational and fair. Nevertheless, public-choice scholars have shown that some types of voting systems are better than others. Because voter preferences affect the efficiency of outcomes and hence society's well-being, research efforts are continually under way to develop better voting systems.

On the basis of this, you can see why people's voting behavior is of interest where problems of collective decision making are involved. The reasons are discussed further in "Leaders in Economics," above.

The Economics of Bureaucracy

In our democracy, the people vote for their political leaders. But these elected officials constitute a relatively small part of the total government work force. The work of government is accomplished chiefly through bureaus or agencies staffed by nonelected civil servants. Some of these people are appointed by elected officials, but most are selected on the basis of impersonal examinations. As a general rule, the bureaus are characterized by diffusion of authority among numerous officials, inflexible rules of operation, and complex procedures that impede effective action.

This generalization points to some interesting problems of efficiency in government, problems that become increasingly complex as the size of government expands. The difficulties are best understood within a framework provided by the answers to certain basic questions:

1. What is the nature of government bureaucracy? Why does it exist? How does it function?

2. Can the effectiveness of government bureaus be enhanced? How can they be made more responsive to the public's preferences? In general, what can be done to improve their efficiency?

Distinguishing Features of Government Bureaucracy

Bureaucracies are not confined entirely to the public sector. There are bureaucracies in corporations also. But our interest, in the study of public choice, is in the bureaucracies in government. Three major distinguishing features of such organizations may be identified. (1) They are monopoly suppliers of their services. (2) They are not motivated by profits. (3) They tend to produce an excessive supply of their services.

Monopoly Supplier

A government bureau is usually given the exclusive responsibility of providing a particular service. Therefore, it is a monopoly supplier of the service. Like any monopoly, it may operate relatively inefficiently compared with the way it would perform if it had to compete in the marketplace with other firms.

For example, the U.S. government has a Department of Energy whose function is to "administer, in the public interest, resources and policies pertaining to the production and distribution of energy." However, because there are no other government bureaus that are charged with this task, it is extremely difficult to determine the department's efficiency. Therefore, Congress can never really know whether its annual appropriation to the Department of Energy is too large—that is, whether the same services could be provided on a substantially smaller budget.

Government bureaucracies tend to be the sole suppliers of their services.

No Profit Motive

A second distinguishing feature of government bureaus is that they are nonprofit organizations. Consequently, they do not have the incentive to reduce costs that the profit motive would provide. In fact, if a bureau is able to provide its services for less than its appropriation, it will usually be "penalized" by having the following year's budget reduced by the amount of the cost saving. That is why, in practically all federal, state, and local government agencies, there is a rush, near the end of each fiscal year, to spend whatever funds are left over. Failure to do so is likely to result in a reduction in the next year's budget.

Unlike managers in the private sector, those in government do not maximize profits. What, then, do they maximize? In other words, what do they seek to attain?

Managers in both the private sector and the public sector have many objectives. Among them are higher salaries, better working conditions, and improvements in prestige, power, and service. In the private sector, executives have the best chance of attaining these goals by maximizing profits. But in the public sector, where the profit motive is absent, the

Government bureaucracies are not motivated by profit.

most likely means of achieving those objectives is to maximize *size*. Therefore, public-choice experts generally conclude that *the goal of government bureaucrats is to obtain the largest possible budget for their bureaus.*

Excessive Supply

A third distinguishing feature of government bureaus is that they are inclined to produce an excessive supply of public services. There are several reasons:

Bargaining Strength Most bureaus combine monopoly power with the goal of budget maximization. These characteristics strengthen the bargaining position of bureaus before legislative appropriations committees.

Visible Benefits, Invisible Costs Practically all voters know that they benefit, at least in a general way, from such public services as police and fire protection, education, and national defense. But few if any voters are aware of how much additional tax they pay for an additional fire truck, school building, or nuclear submarine.

Concentrated Benefits, Dispersed Costs Many types of public services and subsidies are designed to benefit only particular groups, while the costs are dispersed among all taxpayers. Farmers, welfare recipients, and some industries provide examples of groups that benefit from public assistance. It is often easier for beneficiaries to organize and vote for legislators who support particular bureaus and policies than it is for taxpayers as a whole to resist such support. This is an important characteristic of, and often a serious flaw in, our democratic political process.

Conclusion: Improving Efficiency

The term "bureaucracy" refers mainly to the administration of government through bureaus or agencies staffed with nonelected officials. As bureaucracies grow, they become increasingly characterized by a diffusion of authority among numerous officials, inflexible operating rules, and complex procedures that impede effective action. This accounts for the public's considerable dissatisfaction with the performance of most bureaus.

What can be done to enhance the effectiveness of government bureaus? As a general rule, bureaucratic efficiency can be improved by promoting competition within the public sector and between the public and private sectors. Three measures may be recommended.

Private Contracting of Public Services

Public provision of a service should not be equated with public production. Government can provide a service without necessarily producing it. That task can be left to the private sector, where competition among producers is likely to provide goods at lower costs than if government produced them. In fact, most of today's government services were at one time or another produced and provided by private sources. In more recent times, many communities have found it far less costly to contract with private firms for the production of certain public services than to produce those services themselves. Garbage collecting, street cleaning, health care, and fire protection provide some examples.

Competition with Private Firms

In those fields in which government chooses actually to produce the public services it provides, competition with private producers could be encouraged. Public education, provided by state and local governments, is an example. To promote efficiency in public education, from the elementary school through the university level, the state could give money, in the form of "vouchers," to students (or to their parents, if the students are minors). Recipients would be free to present their vouchers for tuition payment at any accredited school—public, parochial, or private. The vouchers would be equivalent in value to the community's expenditures per public-school student, and the state could reimburse the school by the amount of the voucher. This plan would give people a wider choice of schools, thereby pressuring the institutions either to state their objectives and live up to them or to risk being forced out of the market.

Competition within the public sector and between the public and private sectors can be enhanced in various ways.

Decentralization of Bureaus

A third method of improving efficiency within government would be to decentralize certain bureaus. This would reduce their monopoly power, make them more responsive to the needs of the groups they serve, and provide improved information about the cost-effectiveness of bureau operations. Of course, decentralization may not be warranted where distinct benefits are derived from pronounced economies of scale. But the reverse condition is frequently the case. That is, there is evidence that, because of their cumbersome size, many large bureaus actually suffer from *diseconomies* of scale. Therefore, more often than not, the advantages of decentralization are likely to outweigh the disadvantages.

To summarize:

Most public services are supplied by government bureaus at the federal, state, and local levels. These agencies tend to be characterized by diffusion of authority among numerous officials, rigid rules of operation, and complex administrative procedures. To improve their efficiency, three steps can be taken to introduce competition into government bureaucracy. These include: (1) private contracting of public services, (2) promotion of competition with private firms, and (3) decentralization of large bureaus.

These measures, of course, are not mutually exclusive. They can be adopted in various combinations to achieve greater efficiency in the public sector. ■

Allocating Merit Goods √

You will recall that, in addition to public goods, government provides merit goods. Some examples of merit goods are waterways, highways, public transportation, public education, and municipally owned libraries, museums, and recreation facilities.

Merit goods, unlike public goods, are subject to the exclusion principle. This means that people could be charged for the use of merit goods instead of receiving them "free" or at reduced prices. Would the imposition of appropriate prices be a step toward improving efficiency and equity in the provision of merit goods? Before exploring the answer to this question, it helps to examine briefly the different kinds of prices that can be imposed.

■ **Some Interesting Questions**

1. Why do teachers' unions usually favor general income taxation rather than local property taxation as a source of educational financing?
2. Why do most government bureaucracies tend to grow rather than to decline?

Types of User Charges ✓

The basic issue in pricing merit goods is whether users should be required to pay the fees necessary to cover the costs of maintaining and operating the facilities. The fees that users would be required to pay are called "user charges." Although there are many specialized types of user charges, most tend to fall into one of several general categories.

License Fees

A license fee is a one-time payment that permits the licensee to use a facility for a specified period of time. License fees paid for the use of waterways and highways are good examples. Such licenses can be uniform or they can vary with the weights and capacities of vessels and vehicles. For example, license fees for automobiles are considerably lower than those for trucks.

Congestion Charges

Whenever the quantity demanded of a product exceeds the quantity supplied, it is an indication that the price at that moment is too low. This is a common occurrence with public transit facilities, such as buses and trains, during rush-hour periods. To the extent that congestion charges could be imposed, they would alleviate the problem. As explained later, congestion charges are an example of what is called "peak-load pricing." It provides a way of distributing the use of facilities more evenly over a 24-hour period.

Weight-Distance Taxes

A tax based on weight and distance, such as ton-miles, could be imposed on barges and trucks for the use of waterways and highways. A tax of this sort would have some effects that are similar to those of license fees. Unlike license fees, however, a weight-distance tax could be designed to reflect the quantity of waterway or highway actually used. As a result, users who transport heavier loads, or those who transport goods over greater distances, would receive greater benefits from the use of a given right-of-way. They would, therefore, pay a higher tax than those who receive lesser benefits.

Entrance Fees

The most familiar user charges are entrance fees. The beneficiary pays an admission charge in order to gain access to a facility. Toll highways are an obvious example. However, many national parks, municipal golf courses, and municipal swimming pools, among other merit goods, also levy entrance fees. In general, like some other user charges, an entrance fee requires users to help pay the costs of a facility from which benefits are derived. Under such circumstances, the following alternative approach can often turn out to be much more suitable.

"Two-Part" Tariffs

When the consumption of a product can be separated into complementary components, the charging of two prices may be the most efficient way of allocating the good. An illustration is provided by the *two-part tariff.* This pricing technique requires the consumer to pay two different sums: a fixed charge representing an access fee and another charge that varies with use.

For example, public utilities charge a minimum fee and then levy an additional charge based on services rendered. An amusement park may charge an entrance fee and then impose separate charges for individual attractions. Can you think of other examples?

Such a pricing method could be employed successfully with many merit goods. Municipal libraries and museums, for instance, could levy general admission fees supplemented by extra charges for the use of special collections and exhibits. Similarly, many waterways, highways, public recreation areas, and public transportation systems, among other types of merit goods, could make rational use of two-part tariffs. In each case, the fixed fee could be used to cover installation and maintenance costs of buildings and equipment, while the variable charges could be imposed to pay the operating costs of the specific services actually consumed.

Review of Pricing Principles

Before an attempt is made to allocate merit goods by the implementation of user charges, the effects on resource allocation of specific pricing policies should be known. This requires an understanding of certain pricing principles that are already familiar to you from the study of monopoly. They are summarized in Exhibit 2.

There are various pricing principles that can be used in allocating merit goods.

It is obvious from the explanation in Exhibit 2 that the marginal-cost price, which is the socially optimum price for society, would leave the firm suffering a loss of KW per unit. This is because the marginal-cost price is below the average total cost.

In view of this, what can be done to cover the difference between MC and ATC? The most feasible alternative is to finance the deficit ($= KW$ per unit) out of tax revenues. As a practical matter, however, any increase in taxes to finance the deficit might interfere with efficient resource allocation elsewhere in the economy, thus imposing losses on society. Because of this, and even more because of the difficulties of measuring marginal cost, the full-cost price is the one that government regulatory commissions typically impose on natural monopolies.

Pricing Strategies and Policies

Which types of pricing practices are most appropriate for merit goods? There is no general answer. Different pricing strategies are needed for different purposes. Because of this, the most feasible approach is to develop some overall guidelines that can be adapted to the pricing of specific types of merit goods. In each case, the strategy followed and the actual policy adopted depend on the objectives pursued.

No single pricing method is applicable to all merit goods.

Full-Cost Pricing

If the goal is to recover all costs of operation, then a full-cost ($ATC = P$) pricing policy should be adopted. There are three reasons:

1. **Ease of Application** Full-cost prices are based on a company's average total costs of production. These figures can be roughly estimated from the firm's accounting records.

Exhibit 2
Merit Goods: Determining Prices and Outputs

Three types of pricing policies can be employed for allocating merit goods. These are illustrated in Figure (a):

1. Monopoly Price: $MC = MR$. This price maximizes the firm's profit. The intersection of MC and MR determines the output at Q and the price at J that yield the largest net revenue to the seller.

2. Marginal-Cost Price: $MC = AR$ ($= P$). This price (at K), which is the standard of perfect competition, maximizes society's welfare. It is the only price at which the added resource cost (MC) to society of producing an additional unit equals the added value ($AR = P$) of that unit to the consumer.

3. Full-Cost Price: $ATC = AR$ ($= P$). This price enables the firm to "break even" by covering its average total cost, both fixed and variable. The intersection of the ATC and AR curves thus determines the output at S and the corresponding price at L that yield a normal profit to the seller.

Decreasing-Cost Industry: Natural Monopoly

Some merit goods, such as certain public utility services, are provided by natural monopolies. As shown in Figure (b), the producer's ATC curve may thus exhibit increasing economies of scale over a wide range of output, enabling the firm to supply the entire market. Under such circumstances, the marginal-cost price, which is the optimum one for society's welfare, will result in a net loss of KW per unit to the firm. Can you see why?

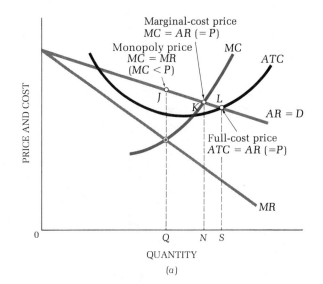

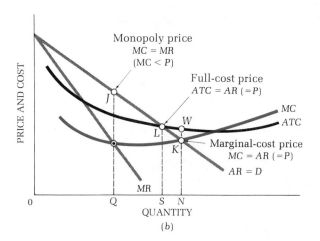

Conclusion: Full-Cost Price Is Most Likely

In practice, the full-cost price is likely to be the one adopted for most merit goods—for two chief reasons:

1. Average total cost is easier to estimate than marginal cost. The former can be roughly approximated from the company's accounting records, whereas the latter requires technical information that is not generally available or even known.

2. Prices based on average total cost (which includes normal profit) permit replacement of plant and equipment at desired rates. Because merit goods are provided for the benefit of society, the usual goal is to earn at most a normal profit so that there will be enough to replace fixed assets as needed.

2. Subsidization of Losses Full-cost prices can be set so that profits on some operations subsidize losses on others. For example, the prices of hospital services can be set so that they cover the full costs of those services while providing a sufficient margin to offset losses on emergency and clinical care for indigents.

3. Replacement of Capital Full-cost prices can be set so that they cover average total costs of production and yield a "fair" rate of return on the company's capital investment (that is, its plant and equipment). For example, public utilities make extensive use of full-cost pricing. Government regulatory commissions usually allow utilities to set rates high enough to generate the funds that are needed to replace buildings and machines as they wear out. Because of this, utilities' profits are strongly influenced by the amount of their capital investment. They are therefore motivated to misallocate resources by expanding their acquisitions of plant and equipment relative to other inputs in order to enhance their profitability. The same tends to be true of other facilities providing merit goods at full-cost prices.

Marginal-Cost Pricing

If the goal is to achieve efficiency in resource use, then a marginal-cost pricing policy ($MC = P$) is the appropriate one to employ. As you will recall, the *marginal-cost price* is the one at which the value of the last unit sold to the marginal user (measured by the price he or she pays for the last unit, which equals the price paid for any other unit) is equivalent to the value of the resources used to produce that unit. Therefore, *the marginal-cost price requires the user to pay for the additional resources needed to provide the product.*

The marginal-cost price will achieve efficient resource use; but it may be difficult to implement and (under some circumstances) socially undesirable for equity reasons.

In reality, marginal-cost pricing may be difficult to implement for some types of merit goods. There are three reasons:

1. Low Marginal Costs of Services For certain merit goods, such as national parks, public zoos, museums, buses, and trains, the total fixed costs of operation are high. However, within wide limits, up to the point of congestion, the marginal cost of servicing additional users is relatively low or even zero. For such goods, therefore, a policy of marginal-cost pricing may cause the facility to suffer an economic loss. This is because revenues may not be high enough to recover the investment in buildings, machinery, and certain other fixed assets. In that case, the method of measuring marginal cost would have to be revised. The new measure would have to include not only operating and maintenance costs but depreciation and depletion costs based on economic (including opportunity-cost) considerations.

2. Congestion Costs The consumption of certain merit goods sometimes results in their "overuse." This creates congestion costs—reductions, due to overcrowding, in the satisfaction that people experience from a merit good (such as a park, museum, or library). Because of congestion, the notion of marginal cost requires further revision. The concept must be restructured to include not only economic depreciation and depletion costs, which were mentioned in the previous paragraph, but congestion costs as well. These costs, however, may be especially difficult to estimate.

3. Income-Redistribution Goals Even if the necessary cost data can be estimated, strict adherence to marginal-cost pricing may not always be socially desirable. Should national parks and public zoos charge the same prices for children as for adults? Should senior citizens living on social security, and poor people living on welfare, pay the same prices as everyone else for hospital services and health care?

If efficiency is to be achieved, the answer to all of these questions is *yes*. This is because the marginal cost to each user is about the same. However, if society chooses, in such cases, to rank equity above efficiency, it may seek to redistribute income by offering preferential prices to children, the aged, the infirm, and to other special groups. The prices of certain merit goods are, in fact, often set with these goals in mind.

Peak-Load Pricing

It is possible to overcome some of the difficulties of marginal-cost pricing. For example, one of the most practical ways of reducing congestion costs is to adjust the prices of a product over time according to the product's intensity of use. This type of variable pricing is known as *peak-load pricing*. It makes use of the fact that consumers' demand for a good may be more inelastic at certain times than at others. Therefore, by charging higher prices when demand is relatively inelastic and lower prices when demand is relatively elastic, a more even use of the facility can be obtained.

Telephone companies and some other utilities have long employed variable pricing systems in order to ration their limited services during peak periods. Similarly, many municipal governments that provide merit goods, such as golf courses, swimming pools, recreation areas, and zoos, often impose higher fees on weekends and holidays in order to achieve a more balanced use of facilities.

Conclusion: A Practical Solution

The two-part tariff, because of its adaptability to different circumstances, offers the best compromise pricing strategy for most merit goods.

There is no single pricing strategy that is appropriate for all merit goods. Each strategy must be judged in terms of the objectives that are sought. In general, however:

> The best *practical* solution to the pricing of most merit goods is the two-part tariff. It requires the user to pay two types of charges:
>
> **1.** A fixed "entrance" fee to help cover installation and maintenance costs of buildings and equipment.
>
> **2.** Separate or variable fees to pay the operating costs of specific services actually consumed.
>
> If properly devised, the two-part tariff can largely avoid the disadvantages of other pricing strategies while approximating the advantages of marginal-cost and peak-load pricing. On the whole, the two-part tariff is best suited for facilities characterized by high fixed cost, large capacity, and low marginal costs. Most merit goods are provided by facilities with these characteristics.

MAJORITY VOTING NOT ALWAYS DEMOCRATIC
But Who Wants Vegetarians?

By Bernard Feigen

New York—Marjority rule is democratic because victory for a political candidate depends on voters' preferences. Right?

Wrong. It can depend as much on the type of voting system used. So says Dr. Kenneth Arrow, a Nobel prizewinner in economics.

Professor Arrow, a renowned expert on voting systems, thinks we should look for ways to make the electoral process more equitable. Many political scientists agree. They point out that, when political candidates are up for election, voters will often behave inconsistently. For example, the same voters, faced with the need to choose one of three candidates for office, may:

1. Select one candidate after ranking all the candidates.
2. Choose a different candidate when voting favorites.
3. Select a third candidate when using another electoral process.

Proportional Balloting
To minimize such inconsistencies, Dr. Arrow and certain political scientists advocate a type of voting system called "proportional balloting." It allows voters to rank the candidates and then cast ballots reflecting this ranking. The ballots may then be redistributed among candidates according to a predetermined dates representing a wider formula. As a result, candispectrum of viewpoints can be elected to fill vacant positions.

In contrast, the present voting system tends to be more limiting. Voters' choices are narrowed to electing either Democrats or Republicans.

Bruce Roberts/Rapho/Photo Researchers, Inc.

Limited Use
A few cities, among them Cambridge, Massachusetts, and Ann Arbor, Michigan, have used proportional balloting. Australia is perhaps the only democracy that employs it in national elections.

Those who favor the system say that it is fairer because it allows all constituencies, including third-party candidates and even lesser ones, full representation in government. But this is precisely why major political parties oppose it. "After all," says one Republican state chairman, "who wants to see the Vegetarian Party's candidate elected to an important office? Under proportional balloting, this could happen." Neither Democrats nor Republicans are likely to advocate replacement of the present voting system. Any step taken toward the adoption of proportional balloting would simply dilute the relative influence of the two dominant parties in government.

Questions
1. What is the main idea of this article?
2. Would it be possible to devise an equitable voting system if voters were always consistent in their preferences?
3. Do the three choices listed in the third paragraph of the article relate to the "voting paradox" explained in the chapter?

What You Have Learned in This Chapter

1. Public choice is a branch of economics dealing with nonmarket collective decision making. The study of public choice involves the application of economics to political science. That is, public choice seeks to develop means of improving efficiency in the production and distribution of goods and services provided by government.

2. Governmentally provided goods and services are known as social goods. They include public goods and merit goods. A unique feature of public goods is that they are not subject to the exclusion principle. Two additional (but not unique) characteristics of public goods are (a) zero marginal costs of benefits provided and (b) spillover effects.

3. Merit goods share, to different degrees, some of the properties of public goods and private goods. Thus, merit goods may be characterized by relatively low, or sometimes zero, marginal costs of benefits provided and by spillover effects. Merit goods are, however, subject to the exclusion principle, even though it may not always be invoked. That is, people could conceivably be charged for the use of merit goods instead of receiving them free or at reduced prices.

4. Unlike private goods, public goods and many merit goods are not "sold" in the market. Consumers' preferences for most social goods are therefore not known. Many social goods thus tend to be produced inefficiently —either in "too large" or in "too small" a quantity in relation to society's preferences. Consequently, to improve efficiency, methods are needed for revealing people's preferences for social goods.

5. The allocation of a public good can be thought of in terms of a demand-and-supply model. Each point on the total demand curve is obtained by starting with a given quantity and finding the *vertical* sum—the total price that people are willing to pay. If the supply curve is known (that is, given), the equilibrium price and quantity are determined in the same way as for a private good —by finding the intersection of the two curves.

6. The demand-and-supply approach to allocating a public good does not lend itself to practical application. One reason is that consumers do not state their demand prices. Another is that no individual can be excluded from receiving the benefits of a public good. Therefore, such nonmarket methods as collective action in the form of voting must be used to decide *what* public good to produce, and *how much*.

7. There are a number of possible voting systems. The most common are based either on unanimity rule or on majority rule. In systems based on majority rule, the *intensities* of voters' preferences are not measured—only the numbers of voters are counted. Therefore, logrolling or vote trading occurs, which helps to produce more efficient choices. Two propositions concerning voters' preferences are instructive:

(a) The size and scope of government tends to vary inversely with the extent of agreement required for passage of legislation.

(b) Even if each voter has logical and consistent voting preferences, a group of voters using a simple majority rule may produce a collective result that seems illogical and inconsistent.

These and related ideas have given rise to what is known as Arrow's impossibility theorem. This proposition demonstrates that no voting system is perfect because group decisions cannot be both rational and fair.

8. Through the voting process, we elect our political leaders. They, in turn, delegate most of the work of government to bureaus or agencies. These bureaus are generally monopoly suppliers of their services. They are not motivated by profit, and they are typically oversized. Therefore, steps should be taken to improve the efficiency of bureaucracies. Three practical measures are: (a) private contracting of public services, (b) promotion of competition with private firms, and (c) decentralization of large bureaus.

9. The allocation of merit goods raises problems that are different from those associated with the allocation of public goods. Merit goods are subject to the exclusion principle. Therefore, proper pricing techniques are needed to allocate merit goods efficiently. Appropriate pricing strategies usually include full-cost pricing, marginal-cost pricing, and peak-load pricing. (Monopoly pricing is not typically employed for merit goods because they are provided by government on either a "nonprofit" basis or a limited-profit basis.) Each has certain advantages and disadvantages, and each may be designed to achieve specific objectives. There is no single pricing method that is suitable in all cases. However, a practical compromise for pricing most merit goods is the two-part tariff.

For Discussion

1. *Terms and concepts to review:*
public choice
social goods
exclusion principle
spillovers (or externalities)
public goods
merit goods
free-rider problem
Pareto optimality
Arrow's impossibility theorem
two-part tariff
full-cost price
marginal-cost price
peak-load pricing

2. The following article has been adapted from a newspaper editorial.

NO ZONING IN HOUSTON
Result: Better Land Use

By Robin Carol

Houston—Practically every city in the nation has zoning laws. One of their major purposes is to protect land values by classifying neighborhoods for residential, commercial, and industrial construction. In that way, property owners are assured that undesirable construction—such as a rubber factory or a sewage plant—will not be built in a residential area.

Houston is the only major city in the country without zoning laws. Instead, land buyers and developers sign contracts agreeing to maintain the land parcels in their current use. These agreements can be changed only if 51 percent of the landowners in a development agree to it.

Is this a better system than zoning? Several studies conclude that it is. Land in Houston is allocated more efficiently for residential, commercial, and industrial uses than in other large cities that have zoning. And land prices are not artificially high in some areas and low in others, as occurs with zoning.

Look up the *Coase theorem* in the Dictionary at the back of the book.
(a) Does Houston's experience conform to what the Coase theorem predicts?
(b) Would you say that land-use agreements in Houston result in an economically efficient allocation of land?
(c) Do the forces of supply and demand determine land use in Houston? What effect would zoning laws have?

(d) In light of the Coase theorem, how does zoning legislation affect landowners?

3. "The existence of government is a response to the free-rider problem." Do you agree?

4. What sort of practical difficulties tend to limit the widespread applicability of the *Coase theorem*? (Look up this concept in the Dictionary at the back of the book.) Give examples. In terms of supply and demand curves, how might government, through legislation, require producers to "pay" for their adverse externalities? What would be the effects on equilibrium price and output?

5. A committee of three people, Candy, Randy, and Sandy, wishes to select by majority rule one of three alternatives, x, y, or z. The committee decides to do it by voting in turn on pairs of these alternatives, the losing alternative being eliminated. Suppose the individuals rank the alternatives in the following orders of preference:

Candy: x, y, z
Randy: y, x, z
Sandy: z, y, x

(a) Assume that the committee agrees to vote first on the pair of alternatives y and z and that the winner is then to be matched against x. What will be the final outcome?
(b) Note that Candy prefers y to z. Nevertheless, she would be wiser to vote for z instead of y. Can you explain why?

6. In court cases, a unanimity rule of voting is often required of juries. Can you explain why?

7. Government programs are often adopted even though their marginal costs exceed their marginal benefits. Why does this happen?

8. National parks in the Rocky Mountain region have found that (a) usage is influenced more by general conditions in the economy as a whole than by the entrance fees charged and (b) within wide limits, the entrance fees have little effect on public use. On the other hand, the managers of municipal recreation facilities (such as swimming pools, golf courses, and tennis courts) in less affluent areas have found that even small changes in entrance fees can have substantial influences on usage. What do these findings suggest with respect to the price and income elasticities of demand for these recreation facilities? Try to formulate your answer in terms of a few general propositions.

28
CHAPTER

U.S. Department of Justice, Washington, D.C.

This chapter focuses on government regulation of business and the effects of regulation on business efficiency.

Business and Government: Antitrust and Regulatory Reform

Learning guide
Watch for the answers to these important questions

Are big business and monopoly the same thing? What is the nature of the "monopoly problem"?

What are the nation's main antitrust laws? How are they enforced?

What has been the attitude of the courts toward restrictive agreements? Toward "good" monopolies and "bad" ones? Toward mergers, both large and small?

How have patents and trademarks been used by some companies to inhibit competition? What has been the trend of court decisions in such matters?

What measures are customarily used to determine the extent of competition in an industry? In the economy? What is wrong with these measures? What have been the overall trends of concentration in recent decades?

Have the antitrust laws succeeded in attaining their objective? What criticisms have been leveled against them?

How does economic regulation differ from social regulation? What steps can be taken to reform both types?

More than two hundred years ago, Adam Smith remarked in a famous passage in *The Wealth of Nations*:

> People of the same trade seldom meet together, even for merriment and diversion, but the conversation ends in a conspiracy against the public, or in some contrivance to raise prices. It is impossible indeed to prevent such meetings, by any law which either could be executed, or would be consistent with liberty and justice. But though the law cannot hinder people of the same trade from sometimes assembling together, it ought to do nothing to facilitate such assemblies; much less to render them necessary.

According to Smith, competition in business is not a "natural" practice. Given the opportunity, business executives would prefer to seek ways of avoiding competition if they could strengthen their market positions by doing so.

The history of American business suggests that this is indeed the case. As a result, the American government has, since the late nineteenth century, been engaged in constructing a body of laws and policies to assure that competition in our economy is at least maintained if not enhanced. This chapter sketches the main features of these laws, notes the interesting ways in which they have been applied in some exciting court cases, and evaluates the chief economic issues pertaining to problems of competition and monopoly in our society.

Big Business and the Monopoly Problem

In economic theory, a market is said to be monopolized when it consists of a single firm producing a product for which there are no close substitutes. This narrow definition is usually adequate for analyzing market structures. But when it comes to matters of public policy, economists, government officials, and judges in courts of law take a much broader view. They regard a market as being monopolized if it is dominated by one or a few firms—that is, if it is "oligopolized."

For regulatory purposes, a market may be viewed as monopolized when it is actually "oligopolized."

In the American economy, the automobile, aluminum, chemical, and steel industries, as well as many others, provide notable examples of oligopoly. In each of these industries the sales of two, three, or four large firms account for a major share of the total market. This leaves a relatively minor share for smaller competitors to divide among themselves. According to this interpretation, therefore, such big businesses as General Motors, Aluminum Company of America (Alcoa), DuPont, U.S. Steel, and their chief competitors qualify as "monopolies."

Big Businesses as "Monopolies": Some Pros and Cons

The arguments for and against big-business monopolies have been debated for decades. Among the chief objections to monopolies are these:

The arguments for and against monopoly are often applied to big businesses in general.

1. They maximize profit by restricting output and charging higher prices than they would if they were more competitive. Monopolies thereby misallocate resources and contribute to income inequality.

2. They retard economic progress and technological advance because they are protected from the pressures of competition.

3. They exert disproportionate influences at all levels of government, giving rise to an "industrial-political complex" that favors big business at the expense of the rest of society.

Arguments in defense of big-business monopolies are these:

1. Monopolies are effectively more competitive than the numbers of firms alone indicate. This is because there is rivalry among particular products in specific markets (for example, aluminum versus copper, steel, and plastics), as well as countervailing power on the opposite side of the market exerted by labor unions and other monopolistic sellers of resources.

2. Monopolies permit mass-production economies at lower unit costs and prices than would be possible with large numbers of small firms.

3. Monopolies have the financial ability to support extensive research and development.

4. Monopolies have the ethical and moral sense not to exploit their monopoly power.

To repeat:

The foregoing arguments are often applied to today's big businesses, which the public usually equates with "monopoly." Therefore, this consideration should be kept in mind as you analyze the facts in each case before judging the relative merits of the arguments.

Reactions to Monopoly: The Antitrust Laws

Society has reacted to the growth of big businesses, and in some cases to monopolies, by passing legislation designed to maintain competition.

During the last two decades of the nineteenth century, the American economy underwent an extraordinary transformation. The period 1879–1904 saw the first great merger movement in American history. During these years, an unprecedented number of firms expanded by combining or merging with others, thereby forming new single-business units with huge investments, capacities, and outputs. These new business organizations were called monopolies or "trusts." In reaction to them and to subsequent economic developments, Congress has passed a body of legislation known as the "antitrust laws."

The *antitrust laws* passed since 1890 commit the government to preventing monopoly and maintaining competition. There are also antitrust laws in almost every state in the country. But these are frequently ineffectual and erratically enforced. This is because states are powerless to control agreements or combinations in major industries whose activities extend into interstate commerce. Coupled with the states' lack of funds, this weakness has left the task of maintaining competition almost entirely to the federal government. Thus, it is the federal antitrust laws that will be of concern to us here. These laws consist mainly of the Sherman Antitrust Act, the Clayton Antitrust Act, the Federal Trade Commission Act, the Robinson–Patman Act, the Wheeler–Lea Act, and the Celler Antimerger Act.

The Sherman Antitrust Act (1890)

The Sherman Antitrust Act prohibited monopolization, but it was not specific enough in its wording.

The *Sherman Antitrust Act* was the first attempt by the federal government to regulate the growth of monopoly. The provisions of the law were concise (probably too concise) and to the point. The act declared the following things to be illegal:

1. Every contract, combination, or conspiracy in restraint of trade that occurs in interstate or foreign commerce.
2. Any monopolization or attempts to monopolize, or conspiracy with others in an attempt to monopolize, any portion of trade in interstate or foreign commerce.

Violations of the act were made punishable by fines, imprisonment, or both, and persons injured by violations could sue for triple damages.

The act was surrounded by a cloud of uncertainty because it failed to state precisely which kinds of actions were prohibited. Also, no special agency existed to enforce the law until 1903, when the Antitrust Division of the U.S. Department of Justice was established under an Assistant Attorney General. (See Box 1.)

The Clayton Antitrust Act and the Federal Trade Commission Act (1914)

The Clayton Antitrust Act and the Federal Trade Commission Act were passed in order to correct the deficiencies in the Sherman Antitrust Act.

In 1914, in order to put some teeth into the Sherman Antitrust Act, Congress passed both the Clayton Antitrust Act and the Federal Trade Commission Act. These were aimed at practices of *unfair competition*, defined as deceptive, dishonest, and injurious methods of competition. The *Clayton Antitrust Act* was concerned with four specific areas: price discrimination, exclusive and tying contracts, intercorporate stockholdings, and interlocking directorates.

Box 1
Alphabet of Joyous Trusts

Although the Sherman Antitrust Act was passed in 1890, some big businesses continued to monopolize certain industries. Consequently, popular resentment toward trusts became increasingly pronounced over the next several decades. The plethora of trusts that existed around the turn of the century prompted cartoonists to depict the more objectionable monopolies in sardonic ways.

R is the Railroad Trust, always on time To Run over the People, and get their last dime.

O is the Oil Trust, a modern Bill Sikes; He defies the police, and does just as he likes.

B is the Beef Trust. This heartless old sinner Makes the People pay double or go without dinner.

U 's the United States Rubber Trust. He Twists himself into knots, while he sobs the C. P.

S is the Shipping Trust; when he's afloat There's a mighty poor show for the poor People's boat.

A is the Asphalt Trust. This is the way He shakes down the People and makes the thing pay.

The Granger Collection

Price Discrimination

For sellers to discriminate in pricing by charging different prices to different buyers for the same good is *illegal*. However, such discrimination is permissible under certain circumstances:

1. If there are differences in the grade, quality, or quantity of the commodity sold.

2. If the lower prices make due allowances for cost differences in selling or transportation.

3. If the lower prices are offered in good faith to meet competition.

According to the law, illegality exists whenever instances of such discrimination "substantially lessen competition or tend to create a monopoly."

Exclusive and Tying Contracts

For sellers to lease, sell, or contract for the sale of commodities on condition that the lessee or purchaser not use or deal in the commodity of a competitor is *illegal* if such exclusive or tying contracts "substantially lessen competition or tend to create a monopoly."

Intercorporate Stockholdings

For corporations engaged in commerce to acquire the shares of a competing corporation, or the stocks of two or more corporations competing with each other, is *illegal* if such intercorporate stockholdings "substantially lessen competition or tend to create a monopoly."

Interlocking Directorates

For corporations engaged in commerce to have the same individual on two or more boards of directors is an interlocking directorate. Such directorships are *illegal* if the corporations are competitive and if any one has capital, surplus, and undivided profits in excess of $1 million.

> Thus:

> Price discrimination, exclusive and tying contracts, and intercorporate stockholdings were not declared by the Clayton Antitrust Act to be absolutely illegal. Rather, in the words of the law, they were unlawful only when their effects "may be to substantially lessen competition or tend to create a monopoly." On interlocking directorates, however, the law made no such qualification. The fact of the interlock itself is illegal, and the government need not find that the arrangement results in a reduction in competition.

The *Federal Trade Commission Act* served primarily as a general supplement to the Clayton Antitrust Act by stating broadly and simply that "unfair methods of competition in commerce are hereby declared unlawful." In addition, it provided for the establishment of the *Federal Trade Commission* (FTC), a government antitrust agency with federal funds appropriated to it for the purpose of attacking unfair competitive practices in commerce.

The FTC is also authorized under the act to safeguard the public by preventing the dissemination of false and misleading advertising of foods, drugs, cosmetics, and therapeutic devices used in the diagnosis, prevention, or treatment of disease. It thus supplements in many ways

The Clayton Antitrust Act made certain specific trade practices illegal.

The Federal Trade Commission Act declared all forms of unfair competition illegal, and it established a commission to regulate the market practices of businesses.

the activities of the Food and Drug Administration, which, under the Food, Drug, and Cosmetic Act (1938), outlaws adulteration and misbranding of foods, drugs, medical devices, and cosmetics moving in interstate commerce.

The Robinson–Patman Act (1936)

Frequently referred to as the "Chain Store Act," the *Robinson–Patman Act* deals with trade practices. It was passed for the purpose of providing economic protection to independent retailers and wholesalers, such as grocers and druggists, from "unfair discriminations" by manufacturers, who might otherwise charge chain stores lower prices "because of their tremendous purchasing power." The law was an outgrowth of the increasing competition faced by independents when chain stores and mass distributors developed during the 1920s.

The Robinson–Patman Act made illegal certain market practices that injure independent retailers and wholesalers.

Supporters of the bill contended that the lower prices charged by large organizations were attributable less to lower costs than to sheer weight of bargaining power. This enabled the large organizations to obtain unfair and unjustified concessions from their suppliers. The act was thus a response to the cries of independents who demanded that the freedom of suppliers to discriminate be more strictly limited.

The act, which amended the Clayton Antitrust Act, Section 2, relating to price discrimination, contained the following provisions:

Brokerage Fees

The payment of brokerage fees where no independent broker is employed is *illegal*. This was intended to eliminate the practice of some chains of demanding the regular brokerage fee as a discount when they purchased directly from manufacturers. The argument posed was that such chains obtained the discount by their sheer bargaining power and thereby gained an unfair advantage over smaller independents that had to use and pay for brokerage services.

Concessions

The making of concessions by sellers, such as manufacturers, to buyers, such as wholesalers and retailers, is *illegal* unless such concessions are made to all buyers on proportionally equal terms. This provision was aimed at preventing advertising and promotional allowances from being granted to large-scale buyers without similar allowances being made to small competing buyers.

Discounts

Other forms of discrimination, such as quantity discounts, are *illegal* where they substantially lessen competition or tend to create a monopoly, either among sellers or among buyers. However, price discrimination is not illegal if the differences in prices make "due allowances" for differences in cost or if lower prices are offered "in good faith to meet an equally low price of a competitor." But even where discounts can be justified by lower costs, the FTC is empowered to fix quantity limits beyond which discounts may not be granted, if it believes that such discounts would be "unjustly discriminatory or promotive of monopoly in any line of commerce."

Predatory Behavior

Sellers are prohibited from preying upon one another. Thus it is *illegal* to charge lower prices in one locality than in another for the same goods or to sell at "unreasonably low prices" where either of these practices is aimed at "destroying competition or eliminating a competitor."

The Wheeler–Lea Act (1938)

The Wheeler–Lea Act aimed at protecting consumers from unfair business practices.

An amendment to part of the Federal Trade Commission Act, the *Wheeler–Lea Act* was passed for the purpose of providing consumers, rather than just business competitors, with protection against unfair practices. The act makes "unfair or deceptive acts or practices" *illegal* in interstate commerce. Thus, a consumer who may be injured by an unfair trade practice is, before the law, of equal concern with the merchant who may be injured by an unfair competitive practice. The act also defines "false advertising" as "an advertisement other than labeling which is misleading in a material respect." This definition applies to advertisements of foods, drugs, curative devices, and cosmetics.

The Celler Antimerger Act (1950)

The Celler Antimerger Act limited the ability of firms to merge with others through acquisition of their assets.

The *Celler Antimerger Act* is an extension of Section 7 of the Clayton Antitrust Act relating to intercorporate stockholdings. The Clayton Act, as stated earlier, made it illegal for corporations to acquire substantial amounts of the stock of competing corporations. But that law, the FTC argued, left a loophole through which monopolistic mergers could still be effected. A corporation could acquire the *assets* of a competing corporation, or it could first acquire *some* of the stock and, by voting or granting of proxies, acquire the assets.

The Celler Antimerger Act plugged the loophole in the Clayton Antitrust Act by making it illegal for a corporation to acquire the stock *or assets* of a competing corporation if such acquisitions "substantially lessen competition or tend to create a monopoly." Thus the Celler Antimerger Act could, depending on the circumstances, ban all types of mergers. These include:

1. Horizontal Mergers Plants producing similar products are brought together under one ownership. *Example:* the merging of two or more steel mills.

2. Vertical Mergers Plants in different stages of production are integrated under one ownership. *Example:* the acquisition of a steel mill by an automobile company.

3. Conglomerate or Circular Mergers Dissimilar plants and unrelated product lines are placed under one ownership. *Example:* the purchase of a food-processing firm by a transportation company.

These three types of mergers can be banned, provided the Commission can show that the effects may substantially lessen competition or tend to create a monopoly.

It should be noted, however, that the intent of Congress in passing the Celler Antimerger Act was that there be a *maintenance of competition*. Accordingly, the act was intended to apply to mergers between large firms or between large and small firms. The Act was not designed to apply to mergers of small firms, which may be undertaken by such firms to strengthen their market position.

Enforcement of the Antitrust Laws

In general, the antitrust laws are applied on a *case-by-case* basis. That is, an order or decision resulting from an action is not applicable to all of industry, only to the defendants in the particular case. Cases may originate in the complaints of injured parties, in suggestions made by other government agencies, or in the research of the Antitrust Division of the Department of Justice and of the Federal Trade Commission. Both of these agencies are responsible for enforcing the antitrust laws. However, most of the cases arise from complaints issued by injured parties.

The antitrust laws fix the responsibility for the behavior of a corporation on its officers and directors and make them subject to the penalties of heavy fine or imprisonment for violating the laws. Business executives who do not want to risk violation of the law may present their proposed plans for mergers or other such practices to the Justice Department. If the plans appear to be legal, the Department may commit itself not to institute future criminal proceedings, but it will reserve the right to institute civil action if competition is later restrained. The purpose of a civil suit is not to punish but to restore competition by providing remedies. Typically, three classes of remedies are employed:

1. Dissolution, Divestiture, or Divorcement Examples of these provisions include an order to dissolve a trade association or combination, to sell intercorporate stockholdings, or to dispose of ownership in other assets. The purpose of these actions is to break up a monopolistic organization into smaller and more competitive units.

2. Injunction This is a court order requiring that the defendant either refrain from certain business practices or perhaps take a particular action that will increase rather than reduce competition.

3. Consent Decree This is an agreement usually worked out between the defendant and the Justice Department without a court trial. The defendant in this instance does not admit guilt, but agrees nevertheless to abide by the rules of business behavior set down in the decree. This device is the chief instrument employed in the enforcement of the Sherman and Clayton Antitrust Acts.

Finally, the laws are also enforced through private suits by injured parties (individuals, corporations, or states), who may sue for treble damages including court costs. This approach to enforcement has become quite common in recent years.

Exemptions and Interpretations

A compact summary of the antitrust laws is presented in Exhibit 1. A few industries and economic groups are exempt from antitrust laws. The most important of these are the transport industries and the labor unions. Transporters—including companies operating railroads, trucks, ships, and barges—are excluded because they are largely subject to the control of other regulatory agencies, such as the Interstate Commerce Commission. The exemption of labor unions was originally justified on the ground that they do not normally seek to monopolize markets or to engage in methods of unfair competition. They seek instead to protect and enhance the position of labor. However, labor unions may be subjected to antitrust prosecution if they combine with management to violate the antitrust laws.

Exhibit 1
The Antitrust Laws in a Nutshell

1. It is flatly *illegal*, without any qualification, to:

(a) Enter a contract, combination, or conspiracy in restraint of trade (Sherman Antitrust Act, Sec. 1).

(b) Monopolize, attempt to monopolize, or combine or conspire to monopolize trade (Sherman Antitrust Act, Sec. 2).

2. When and if the effect may be substantially to lessen competition or to tend to create a monopoly, it is *illegal* to:

(a) Acquire the stock of competing corporations (Clayton Antitrust Act, Sec. 7).

(b) Acquire the assets of competing corporations (Clayton Antitrust Act, Sec. 7, as amended by the Celler Antimerger Act in 1950).

(c) Enter exclusive and tying contracts (Clayton Antitrust Act, Sec. 3).

(d) Discriminate unjustifiably among purchasers (Clayton Antitrust Act, Sec. 2, as amended by the Robinson–Patman Act, Sec. 1).

3. In general, it is also *illegal* to:

(a) Engage in particular forms of price discrimination (Robinson–Patman Act, Sec. 1 and 3).

(b) Serve as a director of competing corporations of a certain minimum size (Clayton Antitrust Act, Sec. 8).

(c) Use unfair methods of competition (Federal Trade Commission Act, Sec. 5).

(d) Use unfair or deceptive acts or practices (Federal Trade Commission Act, Sec. 5, as amended by the Wheeler–Lea Act, Sec. 3).

Thus, the laws taken as a whole are designed not only to prevent the growth of monopoly but to maintain competition as well.

To summarize:

1. The Sherman Antitrust Act (1890) forbids restraints of trade, monopoly, and attempts to monopolize.

2. The Clayton Antitrust Act (1914) forbids practices whose effects may be to lessen substantially the degree of competition or to tend to create a monopoly.

3. The Federal Trade Commission Act (1914) forbids unfair methods of competition.

Although Congress succeeded in passing these laws, it failed to define many of the essential terms. Instead, it left it to the courts to interpret in their own way the meaning of such terms as "monopoly," "restraint of trade," "substantial lessening of competition," and "unfair competition." As a result, judicial interpretations have been crucial in determining the economic applications and effects of the antitrust laws. In view of this, we shall attempt to sketch briefly some major issues, court decisions, and trends that have emerged in the past few decades.

Restrictive Agreements—Conspiracies

Restrictive agreements, or conspiracies, have always been struck down by the courts.

The state of the law regarding restrictive agreements or conspiracies of virtually any type among competitors is reasonably clear, and the courts have almost always upheld the government in such cases.

In general, a *restrictive agreement* is defined by the government as a conspiracy of firms that results in a restraint of trade among separate companies. It is usually understood to involve a direct or indirect, explicit or implicit form of price fixing, output control, market sharing, or exclusion of competitors by boycotts or other coercive practices. It makes no difference whether the agreement was accomplished through a formal organization such as a trade association, whether it was arrived at informally, or whether it was simply the result of "similar patterns of behavior." This expression, or the one used by the courts, *conscious parallel action*, means identical price behavior among competitors. Thus, the effects of market actions, more than the ways of conducting them, are judged.

For instance, in a major case against the American Tobacco Company in 1946, the government charged that the "big three" cigarette producers exhibited striking uniformity in the prices they paid for tobacco and in the prices they charged for cigarettes. Despite the fact that not a shred of evidence was produced to indicate that a common plan had even so much as been proposed, the Supreme Court declared that conspiracy "may be found in a course of dealings or other circumstances as well as in an exchange of words." Hence, the companies were held in violation of the law.

Thus:

> No secret meetings in a smoke-filled room and no signatures in blood are needed to prove the conspiracy provisions of the Sherman Antitrust Act. Any type of agreement, explicit or implicit, any practice, direct or indirect, or even any action with the knowledge that others will act likewise to their mutual self-interest, can be interpreted as illegal. This is especially true if the act results in exclusion of competitors from the market, restriction of output or of purchases, division of markets, price fixing, elimination of the opportunity or incentive to compete, or coercion.

The doctrine of conscious parallel action was partially repudiated by judges in some subsequent cases. However, although it has been used infrequently in recent decades, it is still invoked from time to time in some antitrust cases. (See Box 2.)

Combination and Monopoly

Concerning monopoly, the state of the law is less certain and the position of the courts less consistent than in cases involving restrictive agreements. There are three aspects of monopoly to be considered: monopoly per se, vertical and horizontal mergers, and conglomerate mergers.

Monopoly Per Se

With respect to monopoly per se, the attitude of the courts has changed fundamentally since 1945. Before then the courts held that the mere size of a corporation, no matter how impressive, was no offense. For a firm to be in violation of the law, "unreasonable" behavior in the form of actual exertion of monopoly power, as shown by unfair practices, was required. Since the Standard Oil case in 1911, this had been called the *rule of reason* or, what is roughly equivalent, the "good trust versus bad trust" criterion.

The courts today still make some use of the "rule of reason" in deciding the fate of monopolies.

Box 2

Department of Justice

News Release

TUESDAY, MARCH 6, 1979

The Department of Justice has terminated a civil antitrust case against Brink's Incorporated and Wells Fargo Armored Service Corporation.

Both companies provide armored car services. The firms had been charged with conspiring among themselves and co-conspirators to allocate customers and rig bids and price quotations for armored car services in the United States.

Both Brink's and Wells Fargo pleaded no contest to the criminal charges and were sentenced to pay fines of $625,000 and $375,000, respectively.

But a major decision handed down near the end of World War II reversed this outlook almost completely. In a 1945 case against the Aluminum Company of America (Alcoa), Judge Learned Hand turned the trend in judicial thinking on monopoly. It was his opinion that:

1. To gain monopolistic power even by growing with the market (that is, by reinvesting earnings rather than by combining with other companies) is nevertheless illegal.

2. The mere size of a firm is indeed an offense, for the power to abuse and the abuse of power cannot be separated.

3. Alcoa's market share was 90 percent and that "is enough to constitute a monopoly; it is doubtful whether 60 or 64 percent would be enough; and certainly 33 percent is not."

4. Prior to 1945, the good behavior of the company would have been an acceptable defense to the court. However, this is no longer valid, for *"Congress did not condone 'good' trusts and condemn 'bad' ones; it forbade all."*

With this decision, Judge Hand greatly tempered the rule-of-reason criterion. Subsequent court decisions have not repudiated his doctrines, although the decisions have softened his conclusions somewhat. At the present time, the judgment of monopoly is based on many factors. They include the number and the strength of the firms in the market, their size from the standpoint of economies of scale, and the extent of competition with substitutes and with foreign trade. They also include the need to maintain strong productive facilities and vigorous scientific-research efforts in the interest of national security and the public's interest in lower costs and uninterrupted production.

> The case against the Aluminum Company of America (1945) was a major milestone in the history of antitrust. It suggests that a monopoly firm *may* be held to be in violation of the law even if there is no proof that the firm intended to monopolize the market and even if the power to do so were lawfully acquired. It further implies that power may be condemned even if never abused, especially if it tends to limit or prevent access to the market by other firms. Although the rule of reason is still an important criterion employed by the courts, it has been used with greater discretion since 1945 than it was before that time. (See Box 3.)

Mergers

A merger is an amalgamation of two or more firms under one ownership. It may result from one of three types of integration:

1. Vertical Mergers These unite firms engaged in different stages of production of the same or similar goods from raw materials to finished products. Such mergers may take the form of forward integration into buyer markets or backward integration into supplier markets. They may result in greater economies by combining different production stages and regularizing supplies, thereby increasing profit margins. *Example:* A clothing manufacturer merges with a chain of retail clothing stores and a textile plant.

2. Horizontal Mergers These unite firms producing similar products. The products may be close substitutes, like cement from different plants, or moderate substitutes, like tin cans and glass jars. The objective of such a merger is to round out a product line that is sold through the same distribution channels, thereby offering joint economies in sales and distribution efforts.

3. Conglomerate Mergers These unite dissimilar firms producing unrelated products. Such mergers may reflect a desire by the acquiring company to spread risks, to find outlets for idle capital funds, or to add products that can be sold with the firm's merchandising knowledge and

---

Box 3
The Rule of Reason

The Sherman Antitrust Act outlawed every contract, combination, and conspiracy in restraint of trade. In both the Standard Oil and the American Tobacco cases of 1911—which were among the most famous in the history of antitrust—the Supreme Court upheld the government. But the Court went on to write the "rule of reason" into law, contending that a distinction should be made between "good" trusts and "bad" trusts.

skills. Alternatively, they may simply reflect a desire to gain greater economic power on a broader front.

The courts have often upheld the government by disapproving of mergers that resulted in a substantial lessening of competition or a tendency toward monopoly. This has been true regardless of the type of merger involved. However, the changes in the law on corporate acquisition made in the Celler Antimerger Act of 1950 were given specific meaning in a landmark 1962 decision by the Supreme Court known as the Brown Shoe case.

The Brown Shoe Case

The courts are inclined to allow mergers as long as they do not impair competition significantly. But the Brown Shoe case was an exception.

In the Brown Shoe case, which involved both a horizontal and a vertical merger, the Supreme Court ruled against the defendant. The Brown Shoe Company was the nation's fourth-largest shoe manufacturer, with 4 percent of the industry's total, and it also controlled a number of retail outlets. Seven years earlier, in 1955, it had merged with the G. R. Kinney Corporation. This company operated the nation's largest retail shoe chain, accounting for 1.2 percent of national shoe sales, and also served as the nation's twelfth-largest shoe manufacturer.

Chief Justice Earl Warren spoke for the Court in upholding a federal district court's decision ordering Brown to divest itself of Kinney. He pointed out that, despite the relatively small market shares of the companies, the merger was significant. Thus:

1. The vertical aspect of the merger of Brown's manufacturing facilities with Kinney's retail outlets would probably "foreclose competition from a substantial share of the markets for men's, women's, and children's shoes, without producing any countervailing competitive, economic, or social advantages."

2. The horizontal aspect of the merger—the marriage of Brown's retailing outlets with Kinney's outlets—involved a retail market that could be the entire nation or a single metropolitan area. "The fact that two merging firms have competed directly on the horizontal level in but a fraction of the geographic markets in which either has operated does not, in itself, place their merger outside the scope of Section 7" of the Clayton Antitrust Act. The Court must recognize "Congress' desire to promote competition through the protection of viable, small, locally owned businesses."

Recent Trends

This point of view, as you will see shortly, has changed considerably since the Brown Shoe case in 1962. In general:

> The government's policy today is not to wage an all-out war on mergers. Instead, it applies its own judgment to the merits of each situation. However, both vertical and horizontal mergers are likely to be declared illegal if it can be proven that the mergers will tend to decrease competition.

Conglomerate or "circular" mergers, where the merging firms are neither competitors nor have a supplier–customer relationship, have proved to be the most popular form of combination. This is shown in Exhibit 2. Some of today's well-known conglomerates are International Telephone and Telegraph, Gulf and Western, Litton Industries, and Radio Corporation of America. These and many other firms own numerous companies engaged in different types of businesses.

Exhibit 2
The Merger Movement—Recent Trends

Conglomerate mergers outweigh both vertical and horizontal mergers—in number as well as in value of assets. The most recent tidal wave of mergers occurred during the late 1960s. In that period many of today's well-known, diversified corporate giants were born.

ACQUISITIONS OF MANUFACTURING AND MINING FIRMS WITH ASSETS OF $10 MILLION OR MORE

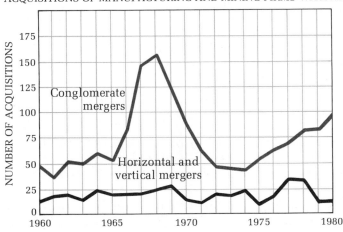

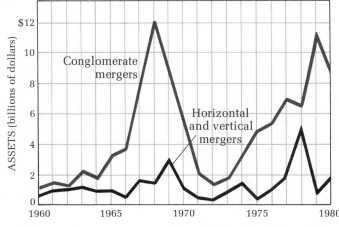

Source: Federal Trade Commission.

Conclusion: Today's Merger Guidelines

Mergers of all types, vertical, horizontal, or conglomerate, raise many difficult antitrust issues. This is because mergers can have adverse effects on competition in various ways. For example, mergers may:

Some mergers can have seriously adverse effects on competition.

• Reduce the number of firms capable of entering a particular market.

• Decrease the number of firms with the capability and incentive for competitive innovation.

• Increase the barriers to the entry of new firms in a particular market.

• Diminish the vigor of competition by increasing actual and potential customer–supplier relationships among leading firms in a particular market.

Because of this, the Department of Justice watches mergers closely. In general, the legality of any merger is judged primarily by its effect on *efficiency.* Therefore:

1. *Vertical mergers,* in which one company buys another in the same production or marketing chain, are likely to be approved—especially if they permit greater economies of scale.

2. *Conglomerate mergers,* in which one company buys another in an entirely different line of business, are likely to be approved if the markets for the products those companies produce remain reasonably competitive and there are many potential entrants.

3. *Horizontal mergers,* in which one company acquires a direct competitor, will be scrutinized and probably contested if there is a likelihood of a significant decrease in competition.

In summary:

Barring any unusual effects that are likely to lead to future monopoly, any type of merger that is not anticompetitive is acceptable. In most cases, vertical and conglomerate mergers are not anticompetitive, but horizontal mergers are. As a rule, the Justice Department's evaluation of a merger is based on many factors. They include: (1) the rate of technological change in the industry; (2) the size of the industry and the market share held by the major firms, domestic and foreign; (3) the existence of barriers to entry by potential competitors; and (4) contestability or ease of exit by existing competitors.

Patents

The Constitution of the United States (Art. 1, Sec. 8, Par. 8) empowers Congress "To promote the progress of Science and useful Arts, by securing for limited Times to Authors and Inventors the exclusive Right to their respective Writings and Discoveries. . . ." Although this power was not denied to the states, it came in time to be exercised solely by the federal government. Upon this authority the American patent and copyright system is based.

What are the economic implications of patents?

A *patent* is an exclusive right conferred on an inventor by government, for a limited time. It authorizes the inventor to make, use, transfer, or withhold an invention, which can be done even without a patent. But it also gives the inventor the right to exclude others or to admit them on specific terms, which can be done only with a patent.

Patents thus promote invention by granting temporary monopolies to inventors. But the patent system has also been employed as a means of controlling output, dividing markets, and fixing prices of entire industries. Because these perversions of the patent law have a direct effect on competition, they have been criticized by the antitrusters, and the courts have increasingly limited the scope and abuses of patent monopoly. The trends based on court decisions in each of the following areas may be sketched briefly.

Right of Nonuse

The right of a patentee to withhold an invention from use has been upheld by the courts. In numerous cases tried since the turn of the century, the courts have viewed a patent as a form of private property and hence have upheld the patentee's right to refuse to put it to use. In response, it has been argued by some that a patent is a privilege and not a right, that nonuse may retard technological progress and economic development, and hence that the courts should exercise more judgment and discretion in such cases. And even the courts in recent decades have spoken of patents as privileges contingent upon the enhancement of public welfare. But the right of nonuse appears nevertheless to be supported by the law. As stated by the Supreme Court in the Hartford Empire case several decades ago: "A patent owner is not . . . under any obligation to see that the public acquires the free right to use the invention. He has no obligation either to use it or to grant its use to others."

What do you think? Is a patent a privilege or a right? Would society be better off if the law were changed so as to eliminate the right of nonuse? How would such a measure affect inventors' incentives and technological progress?

Tying Contracts

A seller uses a *tying contract* (or tie-in sale) to require the buyer to purchase one or more additional or "tied" products as a condition for purchasing the desired or "tying" product. For the tie-in sale to be effective, the major or tying product must be difficult to substitute, not easily dispensed with, and relatively more inelastic in demand than the subsidiary or tied item. A good example occurred in block-bookings of motion pictures. Movie theaters were once required to take a certain number of "B" films as a condition for obtaining "A" films. Many other examples can be cited.

A patent makes it possible for a seller to "tie" the sale of the patented product to other products.

An ideal opportunity for tie-in sales exists when the seller possesses an exclusive and essential patent. A classic example is the United Shoe Machinery Company, which once compelled shoemakers to purchase other materials and intermediate products as a condition for purchasing shoe machinery. In the United Shoe case, as well as in a number of subsequent cases involving such firms as Radio Corporation of America, International Business Machines, and International Harvester, the courts have struck down tying contracts that were found substantially to lessen competition within the meaning of the Clayton Antitrust Act. On the whole:

> The trend of the courts is to disallow a tying contract if it is anticompetitive. This occurs if the effect of the contract is to extend the scope of a patent monopoly or cause substantial injury—or even the probability of such injury—to competition.

Restrictive Licensing

Under a *restrictive license*, a patentee sells a patented product to a licensee with certain restrictions. Typically, the restrictions include the patentee's fixing the geographic area of the licensee, the level of output, or the price at which the patented good may be sold. Usually, such licensing is motivated by considerations of reciprocal favor (for example, the exchange of patents among competitors). It may also be undertaken for the purpose of minimizing the incentive of the licensee to develop an alternative process. In any case, three major trends based on various court cases may be noted:

A patent enables a seller to license the sale of the patented product under restrictive conditions.

1. The right of a patentee to fix the licensee's prices on patented products has been, and still is, upheld by the courts.

2. The right of the patentee to fix the prices charged for unpatented products made by patented processes (for example, a patented machine) is generally doubtful.

3. The use of restrictive licensing is illegal when employed for the purpose of eliminating competition among many licensees.

In general, the extent to which patent owners may license their patents is quite strictly limited. When each of several licensees accepts restrictive terms on condition or with the knowledge that others will do likewise, they are committing a conspiracy in restraint of trade in the opinion of the Court and hence are guilty of violating the law.

Cross-Licensing and Patent Pooling

The existence of patents can make it desirable for sellers to share their patented products. But this practice can also be anticompetitive.

Such "sharing" devices as the cross-licensing of patents or the pooling of patents for mutual benefit are not held to be illegal as such. However, they are generally declared illegal when, in the eyes of the courts, they are used as a means of eliminating competition among patent owners and licensees.

But what constitutes elimination of competition? Three landmark cases provide an answer.

1. In the Hartford Empire case (1945), it was held that Hartford Empire employed the patents in its pool to dominate completely the glass-container industry, to curtail output, to divide markets, and to fix prices through restrictive licenses. The company's use of patent pooling was therefore declared an unlawful conspiracy.

2. In the National Lead case (1947), a cross-licensing agreement that divided markets and fixed the prices of titanium pigment was also declared illegal.

3. In the Line Material case (1948), the Court was most emphatic in its denunciation of a cross-licensing arrangement that fixed the price of fuse cutouts used in electric circuits.

> On the whole, it appears that patent pooling per se is not illegal. (The automobile industry is frequently cited as an outstanding example of successful and desirable patent pooling.) However, the courts will declare that abuse exists under certain circumstances:
>
> **1.** When the pool is restricted to certain competitors or available only at excessive royalty payments.
>
> **2.** When the pool is used as a device to cross-license competitors for the purpose of fixing prices and allocating markets.

Concentration of Patent Ownership

Firms may illegally monopolize a market by concentrating the ownership of patents.

Patent concentration within a single firm has been frowned on increasingly since the late 1940s. Prior to that time, the ownership of many patents by a single firm was held to be legal. Since then, the courts have held that the concentration of patents by a dominant firm in an industry —regardless of whether the firm's patents were achieved by research, assignment, or purchase—may constitute monopolization and hence may violate the antitrust laws. This is true *even if the firm did nothing illegal and did not use the patents to hinder or suppress competition.*

The courts have provided strong remedies in such cases. These include compulsory licensing, sometimes on a royalty-free basis for a company's existing patents and on a reasonable-royalty basis for future patents. They also include the provision of necessary know-how, in the form of detailed written manuals and even technical consultants, at nominal charges to licensees and competitors. Thus, in a number of cases involving Eastman Kodak, Standard Oil of New Jersey, the Aluminum Company of America, Merck & Co., A. B. Dick, Libbey-Owens-Ford,

Owens-Corning Fiberglas, American Can, General Electric, and many other firms, measures of these types have been adopted.

In conclusion, therefore:

> Through compulsory licensing and the provision of technical knowledge, hundreds of patents for inventions in a wide variety of manufacturing industries have been freed. Because competition has thereby been significantly enhanced, it is likely that the courts will continue this policy in the future.

Trademarks

The purpose of a trademark, as originally conceived, was to identify the origin or ownership of a product. In an economic sense, however, managements have come to look upon trademarks as a strategic device for establishing product differentiation, and, through advertising, consumer preference. In this way some firms have been able to establish a degree of market entrenchment that has remained substantially unrivaled for as long as several decades. Moreover, by establishing product differentiation through trademarks, firms have exploited this advantage in various ways with the aim of enhancing long-run profits. Five classic examples may be noted in view of their antitrust significance.

Trademarks are a means of differentiating products. Some firms have used this fact to gain illegal market control at the expense of competitors and consumers.

1. Price Discrimination This has been implemented through the use of trademarks. Until the court decided against it, Rohm & Haas sold methyl methacrylate as Lucite and Crystalite to manufacturers at 85 cents per pound, and as Veronite and Crystalex to dentists at $45 per pound. Many firms today sell branded products in one market at higher prices than they sell the same product—unbranded—in other markets.

2. Output Control Output control can be accomplished through the use of trademarks. United States Pipe and Foundry once licensed companies to produce pipe under its patents at graduated royalty rates on the condition that they stamp their products with the trade name "de Lavaud." Because of the restrictive nature of this agreement, the courts ruled against the company for using a trademark to control output.

3. Exclusive Markets These can be attained through the use of trademarks. General Electric was able to persuade industrial and government buyers to establish specifications requiring the use of Mazda bulbs. It licensed Westinghouse to use the name but denied its other licensees the same right. A court subsequently ruled that General Electric had used the trademark as a device for excluding competitors from markets.

4. Market Sharing Market-sharing cartels have been accomplished through the use of trademarks. A *cartel* is an association of firms in the same industry, established to increase the profits of its members by adopting common policies affecting production, market allocation, or price. A cartel may be domestic or international in scope. Thus, a cartel member may be granted the exclusive right to use a trademark in its own territory. If it oversteps its market boundary, it is driven back by an infringement suit. Many familiar trade names have identified such regional monopolies at various times. Examples are Mazda, Mimeograph, Merck, and Timken, and the trademarks of General Storage Battery, New Jersey Zinc, American Bosch, and S. K. F. Industries.

For many years, the courts have found such arrangements to be in violation of the Sherman Antitrust Act. As a result, the courts have sometimes forbidden cartel members to grant their foreign partners exclusive trademark rights abroad, to sell in American markets, and to interfere with American imports.

5. Resale-Price Maintenance This practice, popularly referred to as "fair trade," permits the manufacturer or distributor of a branded product to set the minimum retail price at which that product can be sold. It thereby eliminates price competition for the good at the retail level. Although no longer as significant as it was several decades ago, this practice still exists in some industries or lines of commerce. Fair trade has been implemented by the use of trademarks even where patents and copyrights have failed.

Concentration of Economic Power

You have now examined the main antitrust laws and their applications. However, some basic questions remain to be answered:

1. To what extent does monopoly power exist in the United States?

2. What should public policy be with respect to competition and monopoly?

How Much Market Concentration Is There?

As a measure of market dominance, concentration ratios are subject to important criticisms.

The growth and importance of big business in the United States have resulted in three charges, frequently made and widely believed:

1. Economic or market power is concentrated in the hands of a few corporate giants.

2. Market concentration has grown over the years.

3. Therefore, there has been a general "decline of competition."

Upon close examination the evidence shows the first of these charges to be at best only partially true and the second and third to be highly debatable if not unfounded. Let us see why.

A measure that is extensively used by economists and government antitrust agencies to evaluate the monopoly power of a firm is *market share*. This is the percentage of an industry's output accounted for by an individual firm. For example, if 1,000 units of a commodity were sold in a particular year, and one firm in the industry sold 500 of those units, the firm's market share for that year would be 50 percent. In practice, a company's market share is usually measured on the basis of sales. But other measures, such as value added at each stage of production or value of shipments, are also sometimes used.

In developed industrial societies such as ours, where many industries tend to be dominated by a few large firms, economists and antitrust agencies have found it useful to expand the concept of market share to a measure called the *concentration ratio*. This is simply the percentage of an industry's output accounted for by its four largest firms. As in the measurement of market share, a concentration ratio is usually based on sales, value added, or value of shipments. Other measures of size, however, such as assets or employment, are also sometimes used. An illustration of concentration ratios is presented in Exhibit 3.

Note Unless otherwise stated, the term *concentration ratio* always refers to the four largest firms in an industry. When concentration ratios are employed for smaller or larger numbers of firms, the numbers are always given. Thus, 2-firm, 8-firm, and even 200-firm concentration ratios are sometimes used.

Do concentration ratios measure "monopoly power"? In most cases they do not, because the results can differ according to the way in which the calculations are made. Three fundamental considerations are involved: (1) the choice of an industry base, (2) the choice of a producing unit, and (3) the choice of a measure of output.

Choice of Industry Base

The degree of concentration will vary depending on the industry base chosen. Concentration ratios are tabulated by the Census Bureau, which classifies industries on the basis of physical similarities of goods produced rather than on the basis of their substitutability in the marketplace. For example, metal cans and glass jars are identified as being in two different industries, even though the products are effective substitutes and usually fall within the same market. As a result, if a concentration ratio were calculated for the food-container industry, the figure would be quite different from those for either the metal-can or the glass-jar industry. The same idea applies to many other industries. Thus:

Concentration ratios often fail to indicate the true degree of market influence and monopoly power.

Choice of Producing Unit

The degree of concentration will vary depending on the producing unit chosen (for example, whether it is a single plant or a whole firm comprising several plants). Similarly, the concentration will vary from a single-product firm to a multiple-product firm. Concentration ratios apply to a heterogeneous conglomeration of industries, some of which are highly competitive, some moderately so, and some virtually monopolized. Further, the ratios are obscured because they pertain to a group consisting of the four largest firms in an industry, without revealing the degree of domination by any single firm. Thus:

Concentration ratios disclose little about the extent of competition or monopoly.

Choice of Measure of Output

The degree of concentration will vary depending on the measure of output chosen. In some cases, the concentration ratio will be seriously understated if the output figures are national and the markets are regional, or if heterogeneous goods are lumped together into a single category. In other cases the ratios will be greatly overstated if the figures are limited to domestic production, with competition from imports ignored. Thus:

Concentration ratios may reveal little about either the structure of the markets for particular goods or about the index of concentrated power.

It is apparent, therefore, that measures of economic concentration are not measures of "monopoly power," as is often contended. At best, concentration ratios may reveal the results of innovation, market development, and lower costs and prices. But these ratios may also conceal the influence of potential competition, and the existence—on the other side of the market—of countervailing power. Nevertheless:

Exhibit 3

Concentration Ratios: Percentage of Industry Output Produced by the Four Largest Firms in Each of Several Selected Industries

Industry	Value of shipments (percent of industry output)
High-Concentration Industries	80–100
Primary aluminum	
Cigarettes	
Aircraft engines and parts	
Metal containers	
Television broadcasting	
Medium-Concentration Industries	60–79
Photographic equipment	
Tires and inner tubes	
Aircraft	
Motor vehicles	
Industrial chemicals	
Low-Concentration Industries	Less than 60
Soap and detergents	
Electronic computing equipment	
Radio and television sets	
Construction machinery	
Toilet preparations	
Petroleum refining	
Pharmaceutical preparations	
Fluid milk	
Bottled and canned soft drinks	
Women's and misses' dresses	

Source: U.S. Bureau of the Census.

Exhibit 4
Aggregate Concentration: Market Domination Across Sectors and Subsectors of the Economy
(latest data)

	1955	1965	1975
Manufacturing Sector			
Largest 50 firms			
Percent of value added	23	25	24
Percent share of assets	—	—	—
Largest 100 firms			
Percent of value added	30	33	34
Percent share of assets	44	47	45
Largest 200 firms			
Percent of value added	38	42	44
Percent share of assets	53	57	58
Nonmanufacturing Sector			
Electric & Gas Utilities: Largest 40 firms			
Percent share of assets	56	60	
Percent share of net income after taxes	52	53	
Transportation: Largest 50 firms			
Percent share of sales revenues	56	66	
Percent share of employment	35	37	
Banking: Largest 50 firms			
Percent share of assets	39	36	
Percent share of deposits	38	34	
Life Insurance: Largest 50 firms			
Percent share of assets	86	80	
Percent share of insurance in force	77	71	
Retail Trade: Largest 50 firms			
Percent share of sales revenues	17	21	
Percent share of employment	17	21	

Source: U.S. Bureau of the Census; U.S. Department of Commerce; Federal Deposit Insurance Corporation; American Council of Life Insurance; *Fortune*; American Gas Association; Lawrence White. "Aggregation Concentration in the United States," *Journal of Industrial Economics*, vol. 29, March 1981; *Forbes* directory.

Despite the shortcomings of concentration ratios, they are the most commonly available measures of market power. As a result, government agencies charged with enforcing the antitrust laws continue to rely on these indicators as the major single source of information on monopolization of markets.

What About Aggregate Concentration?

A concept different from market concentration is aggregate concentration. This is the share of sales, assets, value added, profits, employment (or any other indicator of size) accounted for by the largest firms across entire sectors or subsectors of the economy. The number of "largest firms" may range from 40 or 50 to 200, depending on the size of the sector being measured. An *aggregate-concentration ratio* thus provides an indication of the relative size of firms within a large segment of the economy.

Various studies of aggregate concentration have been made from time to time. Exhibit 4 provides an example of the data from the most recent such study. Has the long-run trend of concentration been increasing, stable, or decreasing? A synthesis of this and other studies reveals the following:

1. In the manufacturing sector, the overall pattern of aggregate concentration has exhibited two long-run trends:
  (a) A slight decrease for the period 1900 to 1950.
  (b) Stability or possibly a slight increase since 1950.

2. In the nonmanufacturing sector, regulated industries, including utilities and transportation, have experienced a modest increase in aggregate concentration since 1950. In contrast, the finance industry has undergone a significant decrease in aggregate concentration since 1950, while retail trade has undergone a substantial increase since then. Overall, however, both the finance and the trade subsectors of the economy are characterized by relatively low degrees of aggregate concentration.

Conclusion: Stable Trends

These trends are consistent with those derived from other studies of monopoly and competition in the American economy. The trends indicate that the overall degree of concentration has remained approximately stable for a very long period. Thus:

> Aggregate-concentration ratios for the largest companies across the entire economy have shown no strong tendency to rise or decline during the present half-century. Thus, the frequently heard contention that the economy as a whole has become more monopolized in recent decades is not supported by the facts.

Dump Antitrust?

If the antitrust laws have not succeeded in enhancing competition, have they been a failure? If not, are they at least an idea whose time has gone?

Many economists and political leaders, liberals as well as conservatives, would answer *yes* to the first question. Considerably more would answer *yes* to the second. They would contend that the fear of market concentration has been oversold. They would also argue that the benchmark or reference point of perfect competition is too removed from the real world of monopolistic competition and oligopoly.

Critics of the antitrust laws base their position on several arguments:

1. International Competition Our modern economy is not as isolated from foreign competitors as it used to be. The automobile industry, the banking industry, the steel industry, and numerous others now face much more competition from abroad than they have faced in the past.

2. Irrelevant "Relevant Markets" Antitrusters have always been concerned with defining the relevant market for a monopolized product. For example, is cellophane a unique product, or is it competitive with other flexible wrapping materials, such as glassine, waxed paper, aluminum foil, and so forth? In today's economy, in which there are numerous substitutes for most products, monopolization of a "relevant market" is usually a meaningless concept.

3. Potential Competition and Contestable Markets Most markets today are vulnerable to potential competitors. Many domestic and foreign firms are waiting in the wings with sufficient resources to take on a firm that is earning monopoly profits. In addition, contestable markets— those characterized by ease of exit—create further pressure on existing firms to keep prices down.

4. Questionable Benefits of "Deconcentration" When government succeeds in breaking up a large firm, the result may be more harmful than beneficial. One large IBM may be much better than four or five small ones, especially if the breakup sacrifices economies of scale. In such a case, foreign computer manufacturers would be the major beneficiaries.

5. Nonprice Competition Antitrusters have traditionally looked more favorably on price competition than on nonprice competition. The latter consists of advertising, product differentiation, customer service, and other forms of competition that do not involve differences in selling price. However, there is no strong evidence that, when given the choice, the general public prefers price competition to nonprice competition. Therefore, both types of competition should be accepted as valid.

Some critics contend that the antitrust laws are largely out of date and, with some exceptions, should be abolished.

Conclusion: More Antitrust or Less?

On the basis of such arguments as these, attitudes toward our antitrust laws are undergoing extensive reconsideration. In general:

> The antitrust laws have had one major purpose—*to improve efficiency.* There is no strong evidence that most of them have done this. Therefore, many critics contend that, except for the purpose of combating restrictive agreements (which are conspiracies against the public), horizontal mergers that reduce competition significantly, and various anticompetitive market practices, the enforcement of existing antitrust laws should be minimized. Instead, *the federal government should seek to promote competition by putting greater reliance on the marketplace and less on the courts.*

It should be noted that this is only one of several points of view on this topic. Another, equally contemptuous of the antitrust laws, favors a completely different solution. See "Leaders in Economics," page 620.

The antitrust laws should be judged by whether they have enhanced efficiency.

Leaders in Economics

John Kenneth Galbraith
1908–
Painless Socialism

United Press International

"Economics, as it is conventionally taught, is in part a system of belief designed less to reveal truth than to reassure its communicants about established social arrangements."

"Scientific truth in economics is not always what exists; often it is what can be handled by seemingly scientific methods."

These are typical of the criticisms John Kenneth Galbraith has leveled against traditional economic thinking. A retired Harvard professor, former ambassador to India (1961–1963), and a stimulating teacher as well as scholar, the towering 6-foot 8-inch iconoclast has devoted most of his professional career to assailing the conventional wisdom of economic theories and policies. As a result, he has become a leading social critic, fulfilling in the late twentieth century a position occupied by economist-sociologist Thorstein Veblen in the early 1900s.

Capitalism's Failures
Galbraith has set forth his ideas in various books and articles. His arguments, concerning not only the failure of the American economic system but the failures of economics as well, can be summarized with disturbing simplicity:

The modern industrial state is not an economy of free enterprise or of consumer sovereignty. It is an economy dominated by a relatively small number of large corporations—in the United States, about 500—most if not all of them directly or indirectly dependent on government contracts. These corporations have long since experienced a separation of ownership and control so that they are governed today not by capitalists or stockholders but by a highly bureaucratic "technostructure" composed of the managerial and technological elite. This elite constitutes the corporate sector's "organized intelligence."

The goal of the technostructure is not to maximize profits, since these would not accrue to it anyway, but to seek its own security and to produce the "minimum levels of earnings" necessary to assure corporate growth. In its quest for these goals, the technostructure *plans* the organization's future in two ways:

1. It finances corporate growth with retained earnings rather than with new security issues, thereby freeing the firm from reliance on the capital market.

2. It engages in the "management of demand" through advertising, thereby insulating the firm from the free market and from the whims of consumer sovereignty.

State Encouragement
In seeking security and corporate growth, the technostructure is not entirely on its own. It is aided by a government, which establishes fiscal, monetary, and welfare policies to assure an adequate level of aggregate demand while subsidizing technological research and development.

The cooperation between the technostructure and the state depends, of course, on the consent of the people. They are taught to believe, through "systematic public bamboozlement," that sustained economic growth and steadily rising incomes are *the* national goals. But this process is self-defeating. As people become more educated, they begin to realize that the costs of their material gains are the sacrifices they must make of leisure, fellowship, cultural enrichment, and the like. In short, they must sacrifice those ingredients that determine the quality of life. The result can only be mounting dissatisfaction with the prevailing system.

Conclusion: More Government
What is the solution for improving the quality of life? The answer is that there must be a vast expansion of the public sector—both economically and politically—in order to lessen the interest in economic growth for its own sake and to permit greater emphasis on The Higher Things in Life. Otherwise, political forces must sooner or later arise that will seek to wrest the privilege of economic decision making away from the "corporate technostructure."

In short, what Galbraith advocates is closer ties between big corporations and the government. At one extreme, these ties may consist of outright government ownership of large businesses. A more moderate solution might be some form of private—public partnership to assure government involvement in business decisions. Either approach, according to Galbraith, would provide both a more realistic response by large corporations to the public's needs and desires and a painless transition to socialism.

Regulatory Reform

Business has more freedom in the United States than in almost any other country of the world. But even here, certain restrictions are placed on business practices. These limitations are not new. Some of them date back to the late nineteenth century, when the first wave of government regulation occurred.

Since then, two broad types of regulation—economic and social—have come into existence. Both types raise important questions about the appropriate role of government in a complex society and about the steps that can be taken to fulfill that role.

Today's regulatory structure consists of the "old" and "new."

Economic Regulation

The growth of government regulation has occurred in stages. The earlier form of regulation may conveniently be referred to as economic, or "old-style," regulation. It is conducted by government agencies that were created for the purpose of regulating specific industries, markets, and business practices. Commonly referred to as "alphabet agencies," the major ones were established many decades ago. They include:

The older, economic type of regulation focuses on specific industries, markets, and business practices.

- Interstate Commerce Commission (ICC)—1887

- Federal Trade Commission (FTC)—1914

- Federal Power Commission (FPC)—1920

- Food and Drug Administration (FDA)—1931

- Federal Deposit Insurance Corporation (FDIC)—1933

- Federal Communications Commission (FCC)—1934

- Securities and Exchange Commission (SEC)—1934

- National Labor Relations Board (NLRB)—1935

- Civil Aeronautics Board (CAB)—1938

From their inception, these agencies have been concerned primarily with economic issues. For example, the Interstate Commerce Commission, initially created to prevent abusive market practices on the part of the railroads, was subsequently authorized to regulate interstate rates and routes of all surface carriers. The Federal Trade Commission was established to prevent unfair competitive practices in the marketplace. The Federal Power Commission came into existence in order to oversee the newly burgeoning hydroelectric industry. The Food and Drug Administration was created for the purpose of testing drugs, cosmetics, and food products before they are offered to the public.

In general, these agencies have focused attention on prices, markets, and the obligation of industry to provide the public with adequate service.

Social Regulation

A more recent form of regulation that emerged in the 1960s may be called social, or "new-style," regulation. Although all regulation is fundamentally "social" in that it affects people's well-being, the newer type is concerned with social issues relating to production. These include

The newer, social type of regulation focuses on products, production, and public issues.

problems of pollution, product safety, and product reliability. A number of agencies have been created to administer social regulations. Among them:

- Equal Employment Opportunity Commission (EEOC)—1965

- Environmental Protection Agency (EPA)—1970

- National Highway Traffic Safety Administration (NHTSA)—1970

- Occupational Safety and Health Administration (OSHA)—1970

- Consumer Product Safety Commission (CPSC)—1972

- Drug Enforcement Agency (DEA)—1973

- Nuclear Regulatory Commission (NRC)—1975

- Federal Energy Regulatory Commission (FERC)—1977

- Food Safety and Quality Service (FSQS)—1977

Social regulation seeks to fulfill specific tasks aimed at protecting the public.

These new-style agencies tend to be *functionally* oriented, in that they are solely concerned with fulfilling specific tasks. For example, the Equal Employment Opportunity Commission investigates complaints of discrimination by workers. The Environmental Protection Agency monitors discharges and emissions from factories. The National Highway Traffic Safety Administration sets rules for fuel efficiency and safety standards for automobiles. The Occupational Safety and Health Administration enforces worker-protection requirements for employees.

Because of their functional orientation, the agencies have been criticized in some quarters as being overly zealous. That is, in carrying out their missions, they have not always given adequate consideration to the adverse impacts of their actions on such factors as business-sector productivity, growth, innovation, employment, cost to the consumer, and inflation.

Consequences of Regulation

These and related criticisms must be examined more closely. In particular, although many regulations have had desirable effects, some have not. You can get an idea of the types or problems that arise from regulatory policies by examining several of their adverse consequences in terms of the economy's fundamental goals.

Efficiency

Some regulations have socially desirable consequences, but others have contributed to impairing efficiency.

How do regulatory policies affect the factors that determine efficiency—such as competition, productivity, innovation, and risk taking? According to a number of studies done at universities and research organizations, the overall impact of regulations has not been favorable. Both economic regulation, which operates mainly through market restrictions, and social regulation, which relies primarily on direct legislation, have generally reduced rather than enhanced efficiency.

Market Restrictions Many of the older regulatory agencies have defined as their objective the maintenance of "orderly markets" for the industries they regulate. This objective has typically been attained by strictly limiting the entry of new competitors and by regulating rates, routes, and specific business practices. The airline and trucking industries provide two interesting examples.

The Civil Aeronautics Board was created in 1938 to regulate commercial airlines. From that year until 1978, when the industry was deregulated, the CAB "managed" the airlines market in three major ways:

Regulation of airline rates and routes provides a case study of how the government operated a cartel.

• It blocked entry by potential competitors. No new airline was granted a charter to enter the industry, despite the fact that nearly 200 applications were filed.

• It controlled routes and rates. Routes were allocated among the airlines on the basis of "public need," and rates were set according to what was considered "fair." Without prior approval, which often took years, neither the routes nor the rates could be adjusted to meet changing market conditions.

• It instituted cross-subsidization. Airlines were permitted to charge regulated higher fares on profitable trunk-line routes between major cities. In return, they were also required to service many smaller cities, even if this were possible only at a loss. In effect, therefore, some passengers simply cross-subsidized others.

The CAB thus operated a "cartel in the public interest." That is, it provided what it considered to be "adequate service at reasonable prices." However, it did this by preventing the free market from allocating scarce resources to their most highly valued uses.

The airline industry was deregulated by Congress in 1978, and the CAB was scheduled to go out of existence in 1985. Since 1978, therefore, price competition has prevailed in air transportation. As a result, new and more efficient firms have entered the industry while less efficient ones have been driven out. And many areas with low population densities that were previously serviced by large-capacity aircraft are now serviced more efficiently by small commuter planes.

But regulation dies hard. The Federal Aviation Administration (FAA), which regulates airline safety, has authority to grant landing rights at the nation's airports. Small airlines and potential competitors claim that the FAA has used this authority to protect the established carriers from competition.

Following in the path of the airlines, Congress authorized deregulation of the trucking industry in 1980. For many decades prior to that time, the Interstate Commerce Commission maintained an "orderly market" for truckers by limiting entry, establishing rates, and determining the conditions under which products could and could not be transported. However, the industry has been only partially deregulated. The ICC, claiming that it is responding to mandates of the courts, continues to limit entry and to maintain some rate stability.

Direct Legislation Most of the newer regulatory agencies consider their task to be that of protecting the public rather than serving it. Consequently, they have tended to rely on legislation rather than the marketplace as a means of achieving their objectives. Several examples illustrate the consequences of this approach.

The newer types of regulation are more concerned with protecting the public than with influencing market behavior.

1. Drug Regulations The Food and Drug Administration requires all drugs to undergo extensive testing before they can be prescribed by physicians. This is true even of drugs that have long been used in foreign countries. These regulations have delayed approval of some drugs by many years. Consequently, critics contend, efforts to minimize risk to consumers have been costly in two ways:

- According to some estimates, more lives have been lost than have been saved, not to mention the costs in terms of pain and suffering that many patients might have been relieved of.

- The United States no longer ranks as highly as it once did in pharmaceutical research.

More use should be made of taxes, subsidies, and other market mechanisms for curbing pollution.

2. Environmental Regulations In order to curb pollution, the Environmental Protection Agency (EPA) has imposed costs on firms without always achieving the desired results. This is partly because it has failed to make sufficient use of such market-oriented mechanisms as taxes, subsidies, and emission fees. Instead, it has relied on licenses, zoning laws, and other types of direct controls. These have limited the ability of firms to seek efficient ways of reducing their overall levels of pollution.

Some safety regulations have increased firms' production costs while providing no significant improvements in safety.

3. Safety Regulations The Occupational Safety and Health Administration (OSHA) has added considerably to the costs of production of many firms while often achieving little in the way of desirable results. For instance, in a study of OSHA's safety rules conducted by the Brookings Institution, a prominent research organization located in Washington, D.C., it was concluded that "study after study demonstrates little or no effect of worker safety regulation upon the accident rate." And studies done at other institutions have arrived at similar results.

On the basis of these and numerous other research findings, can it be said that regulations in general have reduced the economy's efficiency? The answer is not a simple *yes* or *no*.

Economists who have studied the effects of regulations generally concur on two points:

1. Those economic regulations that prohibit *all* restrictive agreements, *most* horizontal mergers, and various anticompetitive pricing practices have helped the market work more effectively. As a result, they have enhanced efficiency.

2. Most of the remaining economic regulations, and some social regulations, have imposed high costs on firms without providing corresponding improvements in benefits. These have impeded the market's ability to function effectively. Consequently, they have impaired efficiency.

Equity, Stability, and Growth

Regulations have had their greatest impact on efficiency. However, a few words may be said about their effects on society's other economic goals.

With respect to equity, it may seem that regulations provide the fairest way of dealing with a problem. Upon closer examination, however, it is often found that the benefits and costs of many regulations are not distributed equitably. Of course what is equitable is often a value judgement about which rational people disagree, and many regulations do at least redress situations in which the distribution of advantages and burdens was decidedly unequal.

With respect to stability, some regulations contribute to the inflation rate. For example, certain laws require firms to spend money in ways that increase production costs without providing equal increases in benefits. These types of regulations create upward pressures on prices.

Finally, with respect to growth, it is apparent that many regulations limit competition. This causes reductions in productivity, innovation, and risk taking. The result is to retard expansion of the nation's output and hence to retard the rate of improvement in society's standard of living.

In general:

Any regulations that impede rather than enhance the functioning of free markets cause adverse changes in existing relationships between economic entities—households, businesses, and government. The result must inevitably be a redistribution of benefits and costs, upward pressure on prices, and a slower rate of improvement in living standards.

Some regulations have provided unequal distributions of benefits and costs, contributed to inflation, and impeded economic growth.

Practical Guidelines for Regulatory Reform

In view of these criticisms, what can be done to reduce both the burden of government regulations and the plethora of agencies that administer them? The question is important because regulations create not only social benefits but social costs as well. Moreover, the latter sometimes exceed the former. Therefore, practical guidelines are needed for determining when existing regulations should be eliminated and when new ones should be introduced.

Because regulations can have adverse consequences, guidelines are needed for implementing and evaluating all types of legislative rules.

Economic Impact: Benefit–Cost Analysis

One way to improve the regulatory process is to require government agencies to file periodic economic-impact statements. These would disclose both the benefits and costs of a regulation, thus improving the effectiveness of government decisions.

For example, benefits are measured by all of the gains that accrue to society as a result of using resources to comply with a particular regulation. The benefits may include increased production of goods and services as well as improvements in health and safety. Costs are measured in terms of sacrificed benefits—those that society would have obtained by employing the resources in their best alternative use. The costs include the expenses of government administration and those of business compliance, as well as the opportunity cost of lost output.

It is obvious that many benefits and costs consist of "intangibles" that cannot be measured. Nevertheless, by thinking in terms of the additional or *incremental* benefits and costs of a regulatory policy, more intelligent decisions can be made concerning its economic impact. Three examples of actual cases show why.

Automobile Emission Standards A University of Chicago study found that, in order to achieve a certain emission standard, the incremental cost would be $4 billion and the incremental benefit (in terms of environmental improvement) would be $5 billion. But, in order to achieve the next higher level of emission control, the incremental cost would be $6 billion and the incremental benefit would be $1 billion. On the basis of these data, the first level of emission control is justifiable because the incremental benefit exceeds the incremental cost, resulting in a net gain of $1 billion to society. The second level, however, is not justifiable because the incremental cost exceeds the incremental benefit, resulting in a net *loss* to society of $5 billion.

Chemical Products A Harvard University study found that complying with OSHA's benzene regulations entailed an incremental cost of $300 million annually and an incremental benefit of one life saved. However, it was also estimated that four lives were likely to be lost for every $300 million worth of control equipment produced. Thus, the regulations risked four lives to save one life.

Transportation for the Handicapped Public transportation systems have been required to install special lifts on buses and trains at incremental costs involving hundreds of millions of dollars. Studies show that the lifts are used by a very small proportion of handicapped persons. As a result, some communities have found that providing free door-to-door taxi service (called "dial-a-cab") is a much less costly solution.

"Sunset" Laws

A second way of improving the regulatory process is for Congress to adopt "sunset" legislation. This consists of laws that are scheduled to expire on specified dates. If regulatory activities were subject to such legislation, Congress would have to review them periodically—say, every five years—to decide whether they should be renewed. If they were not renewed, the "sun" would be allowed to "set" on them.

Regulatory Budgets

A third step toward achieving greater efficiency in regulation is to require the preparation of regulatory budgets. These are annual statements disclosing the direct costs to government (including agency salaries and other expenses) of administering regulations and the direct costs to business of complying with them. The cost data used are those regularly recorded for accounting purposes. Hence they are relatively easy to compile because no estimates of opportunity costs are required. The resulting figures are astonishing. They have been estimated at hundreds of billions of dollars—much higher than many political leaders realize.

Free-Market Alternative

A fourth approach to regulatory reform is to develop an alternative to regulation. This means that greater reliance should be placed on looking for ways to enhance, rather than hinder, the functioning of a free market. Two related steps toward achieving this goal may be mentioned.

Ways should be sought to make the free market work better before turning to restrictive regulations as a means of correcting deficiencies.

Improve Consumer Knowledge It is usually more efficient to inform consumers fully about products or hazards than to require goods to meet certain standards. This allows individuals to decide for themselves how they want to balance benefits and costs. Nutritional labels on foods and warning labels on cigarettes provide examples of this approach.

Set Incentive Standards It is usually more efficient to establish production standards that encourage progress than to mandate specific requirements. This provides regulated firms with a stronger incentive to meet prescribed standards in new and different ways. Thus if Congress, rather than simply outlawing discharges, would use tax penalties and tax credits as devices to reduce pollution, it would stimulate innovation and reward technological advancement.

To conclude:

There is substantial agreement in Washington concerning these guidelines for reform. Indeed, they have been adopted by a number of agencies in their efforts to deregulate certain activities. Nevertheless, many regulations that yield questionable positive (if not negative) net benefits to society still exist. Their costs in terms of society's economic goals, therefore, are borne by everyone.

What You Have Learned in This Chapter

1. The antitrust laws are intended to curb monopoly and to maintain competition in the American economy. The chief antitrust laws are the Sherman Antitrust Act, the Clayton Antitrust Act, the Federal Trade Commission Act, the Robinson–Patman Act, the Wheeler–Lea Act, and the Celler Antimerger Act. Taken together and in a broad sense, they forbid restraint of trade, monopolization, price discrimination, and unfair competition. Major groups exempt from the antitrust laws are the regulated transport industries and labor unions.

2. The courts have consistently struck down restrictive agreements. This trend will continue because restrictive agreements are conspiracies against the public.

3. With respect to monopoly and combination, the "reasonableness" of a firm's market behavior continues to be a factor considered by the courts. As for mergers, vertical and conglomerate types are not scrutinized as closely as are horizontal mergers. A horizontal merger is likely to be attacked if it results, or is likely to result, in a significant reduction in competition.

4. Patent abuse and the power of patent monopoly have been significantly weakened in the past several decades. It appears that the courts will continue to move in the direction of preventing the abuses of the patent grant. Similarly, with respect to trademark abuse, the courts have acted increasingly to prevent the use of trademarks to promote price discrimination, market exclusion, and market sharing (that is, cartel arrangements) among competitors.

5. Concentration ratios are typically used to evaluate the extent of "monopoly power." According to the available evidence, economic concentration in manufacturing may not be significantly greater today than it was in previous decades. In general, however, concentration ratios do not really measure monopoly power. This is because the results can differ widely according to the way in which the calculations are made. The choice of base, unit, and measure of output can all influence the outcome.

6. Many critics contend that the antitrust laws have not succeeded in enhancing competition. Some of these critics argue in favor of placing greater reliance on the marketplace instead of the courts. Others contend that there should be greater government involvement in the management of large corporations.

7. Many government economic and social regulations have contributed to impairing both efficiency and equity. Therefore, some practical guidelines for improving regulatory practices include (a) making greater use of benefit–cost analysis; (b) adopting "sunset" legislation; (c) utilizing regulatory budgets; and (d) placing greater reliance on the market system.

For Discussion

1. *Terms and concepts to review:*
antitrust laws
Sherman Antitrust Act (1890)
unfair competition
Clayton Antitrust Act (1914)
price discrimination
interlocking directorate
Federal Trade Commission Act (1914)
Federal Trade Commission
Robinson–Patman Act (1936)
Wheeler–Lea Act (1938)
Celler Antimerger Act (1950)
injunction
consent decree
restrictive agreement
conscious parallel action
rule of reason
merger
vertical merger
horizontal merger
conglomerate merger
patent

tying contract
restrictive license
cartel
market share
concentration ratio
aggregate-concentration ratio

2. "The rationale underlying restrictive agreements among competitors is based on the potential danger arising from the existence of the power of sellers to manipulate prices. Where this power does not exist, the laws pertaining to restrictive agreements are practically meaningless. Thus, there is no point in holding unlawful an agreement among competitors to fix prices, allocate customers, or control production, when the competitors involved are so small that they lack significant power to affect market prices." Evaluate this statement.

3. Suppose that tomorrow morning all grocers in Chicago, without previous public notice, were to raise their prices for milk by 3 cents per liter. Would this action prove the existence of an agreement or constitute an offense on the part of the grocers? What would your answer be if the automobile manufacturers without notice announced a 5 percent price increase next year on all new model cars? Explain.

4. If all the companies in an oligopolistic industry quote identical prices without prior agreement by following the prices of the industry leader, is this evidence of a combination or conspiracy?

5. In an industry characterized by price leadership without prior arrangement, is there likely to be a charge of combination or conspiracy leveled against that industry if: (a) prevailing prices are announced by the industry's trade association rather than by a leading firm; (b) all firms in the industry report their prices to their industry trade association; (c) all firms in the industry quote prices on a basing point system (that is, the delivered price is the leader's price plus rail freight from the leader's plant); (d) all firms follow the leader not only in price, but in product and sales policies as well? (These four questions should be answered as a group rather than individually.)

6. In the Columbia Steel case (1948), the Supreme Court said: "We do not undertake to prescribe any set of percentage figures by which to measure the reasonableness of a corporation's enlargement of its activities by the purchase of the assets of a competitor. The relative effect of percentage command of a market varies with the setting in which that factor is placed." Does this conflict with Judge Hand's statement in the Alcoa case? Explain.

7. "Since there are 'good' monopolies and 'bad' monopolies, a company should be judged by its total contribution to society—not by its market behavior alone." Do you agree? Explain.

8. "Many trustbusters and economists forget that *concentration is a function of consumer sovereignty,* and that the same consumers who make big businesses big can make them small or even wipe them out by simply refraining from the purchase of their products. This is a not-so-obvious principle of our free enterprise system which needs to be better understood." Do you agree? Discuss.

9. "To say that the degree of competition depends on the number of sellers in the marketplace is like saying that football is more competitive than tennis." Discuss. (**Hint** Can you describe different forms of competition, in addition to price competition, that exist in American industry?)

10. It is generally stated that growth, stability, and flexibility are three primary objectives of mergers.
   (a) With respect to growth, it has been said that "a firm, like a tree, must either grow or die." Evaluate this statement.
   (b) Why may instability be a motive for merger? Instability of what?
   (c) What is meant by flexibility as a motive for merger? (**Hint** Compare *flexibility* with *vulnerability.*)

11. Section 7 of the Clayton Antitrust Act of 1914 and its amendment, the Celler Antimerger Act of 1950, states: "No corporation engaged in commerce shall acquire, directly or indirectly, the whole or any part of the stock or other share capital and no corporation subject to the jurisdiction of the Federal Trade Commission shall acquire the whole or any part of the assets of another corporation engaged also in commerce, where in any line of commerce in any section of the country, the effect of such acquisition may be substantially to lessen competition, or to tend to create a monopoly."

Assume that you are an economist for a large corporation and that you are asked to prepare a report on why this legislation should be repealed. What main points would you bring out in your argument?

Labor Economics and Labor Relations

Learning guide

Watch for answers to these important questions

How did American labor unions evolve? What sorts of obstacles did they face? What kinds of assistance did they receive in their long and turbulent history?

What is collective bargaining? How does it work? What are the major components of a typical collective bargaining agreement?

How do unions seek to raise wages in the labor market? Are unions "good" or "bad"?

STRIKE THREATENS TO DISRUPT PRODUCTION

UNEMPLOYMENT HIGHER IN THE GHETTOS

UNION WAGE DEMANDS ARE TOP PRIORITY

EXTRA PAY FOR HOLIDAYS A NEW TARGET

These are the kinds of headlines you frequently encounter in the news media. They describe labor problems that involve all of us, not only in our personal capacities as consumers, employees, or employers, but also as citizens concerned with significant economic issues.

You will find in this chapter that a study of labor problems involves, in a very fundamental way, a study of unions. This includes how they have evolved, how they bargain with management, and how they may affect the general welfare. Information of this sort is, at best, only partly known and, at worst, generally misunderstood.

You will also learn that *the primary and continuous objective of all unions is to improve the wages and working conditions of their members by bargaining with employers.* Through a process of negotiation, unions and management work out arrangements for higher wages and salaries, new and better pension plans, holidays and vacations with pay, health and welfare plans, shorter hours, and safer working conditions. This bargaining approach to the solution of labor problems is a characteristic feature of labor economics and industrial relations in the United States and in some other advanced countries.

This chapter explains the rise of unions and their current role in the economy.

History of American Unionism: The Labor Movement

A union is an organization of workers that seeks to gain monopolistic power in the market place.

The development of labor unions in the United States during the nineteenth and twentieth centuries is often referred to as the *labor movement*. It is a fascinating story that plays an integral role in the nation's political and economic history.

What is a *union*? It may be defined as an organization of workers that seeks to gain a degree of monopoly power in the sale of its services so that it may be able to secure higher wages, better working conditions, and other economic improvements for its members. The development of unionism spans roughly four periods:

1. The local movement: Revolution to the Civil War.

2. The national movement: post–Civil War to the Depression.

3. The era of rapid growth: Depression to World War II.

4. The age of maturity: post–World War II to the present.

The Local Movement: Revolution to the Civil War

In Commonwealth vs. Hunt (1842), the court recognized the right of workers to bargain collectively with employers.

Although labor organizations were started prior to the Revolutionary War, they were all very short-lived and of no significant consequence. Not until the last quarter of the eighteenth century did some of the unions have sufficient durability to survive for a number of years. These were localized *craft unions*, composed of workers in a particular trade, such as bakers, carpenters, longshoremen, printers, shoemakers, and teamsters. Throughout the history of unionism, the crafts have always been the first to organize. This is largely because their specialized skills or abilities put them in a relatively stronger position to gain monopolistic power in the marketplace.

In 1842, in the landmark Massachusetts case of *Commonwealth* v. *Hunt*, a court held a trade union to be lawful. It also declared that unions could bargain collectively with employers over wages, hours, and related issues.

This led to some small improvements in working conditions during the 1840s and 1850s. The most significant developments were the gradual decline in the length of the average working day from about 13 hours to 10 or 11 hours in most factories, and the passage of 10-hour laws by many states. Laws were also passed to regulate child labor, but these were seldom enforced.

The National Movement: Post–Civil War to the Great Depression

The union movement experienced its initial rapid rate of growth during the last third of the nineteenth century.

After the Civil War (1865), the growth of national craft unions quickened perceptibly with the spread of industrialism across the country and the expansion of the railroads into the West. Unions became increasingly "national" as they embraced formerly local unions, which became local branches of their national organization. The movement for an 8-hour working day was begun. Then the first signs of the long, bitter, and almost unbelievably hostile opposition to labor's struggle for union recognition and survival began to take shape.

Knights of Labor

In 1869, seven tailors met in Philadelphia and founded the Noble and Holy Order of the Knights of Labor—or simply the *Knights of Labor.* This was a national labor organization that attempted to unify all types of workers, regardless of their craft and without regard to race, sex, nationality, or creed. The organization was powerful and influential. It won several strikes against the railroads, and its membership rose rapidly to a peak of 730,000 in 1886.

> The Knights' program called for various improvements and reforms. They included: establishment of the 8-hour day; equal pay for equal work by women; abolition of child and convict labor; public ownership of utilities; the establishment of cooperatives; and, in general, the peaceful replacement of a competitive society with a socialistic system. Strikes were to be used as weapons only after all other means had failed.

The Knights of Labor was a curious group, with one foot in the past and the other in the future. It championed the cause of workers in general, but it rejected the traditional organizing of workers by crafts, preferring instead the mass unionization of both unskilled and skilled workers. This philosophy ultimately contributed to its decline. After 1886, membership in the group fell rapidly, for three major reasons:

1. Opposition by craft leaders, who saw no reason why the bargaining position of labor's elite—the skilled workers—should be wasted on efforts to secure benefits for the unskilled.

2. Dissension among leading members and groups over whether a more aggressive approach through strikes and collective bargaining should replace the slower evolutionary methods of political and social change.

3. Accusations (which were never proved) that the union was connected with anarchist activities, such as the violence and bombing that occurred in Chicago's Haymarket riot in 1886—a notorious incident in American labor history. (See Box 1.)

As a result of these problems, the Knights of Labor steadily lost ground in the labor movement and finally ceased to exist in 1917.

The Knights of Labor, established in 1869, was the first national union to engage in a mass effort aimed at organizing all types of workers.

Box 1
The Haymarket Riot: Haymarket Square, Chicago, May 4, 1886

By 1886 the movement for the 8-hour day had gained wide support by striking workers in many cities. In Chicago, about 80,000 workers were demonstrating when a group of alleged anarchists took advantage of the excitement by throwing a bomb into the crowd in front of the McCormick Harvester Works at Haymarket Square. A riot ensued. Nearly a dozen people (including seven policemen) were killed, and many others were injured. Although the anarchists bore the brunt of public indignation, organized labor in general, and the Knights of Labor in particular suffered heavily.

Culver Pictures

American Federation of Labor

During the late nineteenth century, the American Federation of Labor (AFL) began to replace the Knights of Labor as the dominant labor union.

In the early 1880s, representatives of several craft unions, dissatisfied with the philosophy and policies of the Knights of Labor, formed their own group, which became known in 1886 as the *American Federation of Labor.* Under the leadership of Samuel Gompers, who served as its president from 1886 until his death in 1924 (except for one year when he was succeeded by William Green), the AFL led and dominated the labor movement. Its philosophy was based on three fundamental principles:

1. **Business Unionism** This was a practical policy of seeking "bread-and-butter" improvements in wages and working conditions. These were to be achieved through evolution rather than revolution, without engaging in the class struggles of society.

2. **Federalism** This was an organizational policy of maintaining autonomous national and international craft unions, each controlling its own trade specialty.

3. **Voluntarism** This was a policy of opposition to government interference, either for or against labor. It concerned all matters pertaining to labor organization, labor negotiations with management, and related activities.

The concept of unionism adopted by the AFL was thus much different from that held by the Knights of Labor. As the Knights declined in importance, the AFL grew, with its membership exceeding 1 million shortly after the turn of the century. By World War I, after surviving decades of extraordinary and often violent public hostility toward unions, the AFL found that it was clearly voicing the views of a majority of organized workers. Union membership exceeded 5 million, and workers had earned substantial gains in wages and working conditions.

But then the growth of unionism started to take a turn for the worse. The government withdrew its limited protection of labor's right to organize, and employers refused to recognize labor unions. As a result, unions lost members. Lethargy and lack of aggressiveness engulfed American labor as technological changes, unfavorable court decisions, the growth of company unions (those limited to the employees of particular firms), and a period of national prosperity all contributed to the dampening of union activity. By the early 1930s, union membership had declined to less than 3 million. (See also Box 2.)

The Era of Rapid Growth: Depression to World War II

Many antilabor practices were declared illegal during the 1930s.

The fortunes of organized labor underwent a dramatic reversal during the Depression of the 1930s. The first piece of pro-labor legislation passed by Congress was the *Norris–LaGuardia Act* of 1932, which modified or eliminated the worst abuses against organized labor:

1. The hated *yellow-dog contract*—which required the employee to promise, as a condition of employment, not to join a labor union—was declared illegal.

2. The conditions under which court injunctions could be issued against unions were greatly restricted. (Prior to that time, judges were often inclined to issue court orders, backed up by police force, to terminate a strike.)

Box 2
Industrial Workers of the
World—The "Wobblies"

Historical Pictures Service, Chicago

The Hand That Will Rule the World—One Big Union

The early 1900s saw the formation of the *Industrial Workers of the World* (IWW), a labor union of immigrants who were mostly unskilled factory workers, miners, lumbermen, and dock workers. Popularly known as the "Wobblies," the organization's members had a militant style with the slogan: "Labor Produces All Wealth. All Wealth Must Go to Labor." Their goal was to unite all workers into "One Big Union," to tear down capitalism by force, and to replace it with socialism. The IWW reached a membership peak of about 100,000 by 1912, but it declined thereafter as a result of internal dissension and the imprisonment of nearly 100 of its leaders on charges of treason. The organization, however, did not become extinct.

Although still relatively small, the IWW in recent decades has concentrated mainly on organizing workers in small plants that major unions have ignored as too insignificant. According to its leaders, the Wobblies' bargaining demands today are "basically the normal types of demands for (better) working conditions and rates of pay, but flavored with a different perspective." Violence, they say, is avoided for the most practical of reasons: "The other side has more capacity."

The major publication of the IWW was a weekly magazine called *Solidarity*. The accompanying song, "Solidarity Forever," composed in 1915 by an IWW member, has long been the anthem of the entire American labor movement. It is by far the best-known union song in the United States.

Solidarity Forever!

(Tune: "Battle Hymn of the Republic")

When the Union's inspiration through the workers' blood shall run,
There can be no power greater anywhere beneath the sun,
Yet what force on earth is weaker than the feeble strength of one?
But the Union makes us strong.

Chorus:
Solidarity forever!
Solidarity forever!
Solidarity forever!
For the Union makes us strong.

Is there aught we hold in common with the greedy parasite
Who would lash us into serfdom and would crush us with his might?
Is there anything left for us but to organize and fight?
For the Union makes us strong.

It is we who plowed the prairies; built the cities where they trade;
Dug the mines and built the workshops; endless miles of railroad laid.
Now we stand, outcast and starving, 'mid the wonders we have made;
But the Union makes us strong.

All the world that's owned by idle drones, is ours and ours alone.
We have laid the wide foundations; built it skyward stone by stone.
It is *ours*, not to slave in, but to master and to own,
While the Union makes us strong.

They have taken untold millions that they never toiled to earn.
But without our brain and muscle not a single wheel can turn.
We can break their haughty power; gain our freedom when we learn
That the Union makes us strong.

In our hands is placed a power greater than their hoarded gold;
Greater than the might of armies, magnified a thousand-fold.
We can bring to birth the new world from the ashes of the old,
For the Union makes us strong.

Historical Pictures Service, Chicago

The prolabor legislation of the 1930s enabled the union movement to grow rapidly.

The stage was now set. Under President Franklin Delano Roosevelt's administration of the 1930s, other favorable labor legislation was passed. These laws set standards for minimum wages, maximum hours, and child labor, and created the U.S. Employment Service and the social security system. But none of these was more important for the union movement than the National Labor Relations Act of 1935, which was hailed as labor's Magna Carta.

The *National Labor Relations Act* (also known as the *Wagner Act*) of 1935 is the basic labor relations law of the United States. The act has three major provisions:

1. It guarantees the right of workers to organize and to bargain collectively through representatives of their own choosing.

2. It forbids the employer from engaging in "unfair labor practices." These include:

(a) Interfering or discriminating against workers who form unions or engage in union activity.

(b) Establishing a *company union* or organization of workers that is limited to a particular firm.

(c) Refusing to bargain in good faith with a duly recognized union.

3. It established the *National Labor Relations Board* (NLRB) to enforce the act and to supervise free elections among a company's employees to determine which union, if any, is to represent the workers.

With this firm legal umbrella provided by Congress—especially the right of labor to organize and to bargain collectively—the labor movement embarked on the fastest and longest upward journey in its history. Thousands of workers went back into their old unions and thousands of others joined new ones. As shown in Exhibit 1, union membership totaled 10 million by 1940.

Congress of Industrial Organizations

The Congress of Industrial Organizations (CIO), favoring "vertical" or industrial unions, was established in the mid-1930s because it opposed the "horizontal" or craft-union bias of the AFL.

In the mid-1930s, several union leaders in the AFL launched an attack against the craft bias of the Federation. They argued that craft unions were "horizontal" unions, which were not well adapted to the needs of workers in modern mass-production industries. Instead, *industrial unions* or "vertical" unions were needed to organize all workers in a particular industry—for example, automobile manufacturing and coal mining. Although the Federation never refused to recognize industrial unions—indeed, the insurgent leaders were all heads of industrial unions that were affiliated with the AFL—the parent organization had been relatively unsuccessful in organizing workers in mass-production industries.

A controversy thus arose within the AFL leadership that lasted for several years. Finally, in 1938, the insurgent unions were expelled from the Federation. As a result, they banded together to form an independent rival union called the *Congress of Industrial Organizations* (CIO).

The CIO was immediately successful in organizing millions of previously unorganized workers in the automobile, steel, and other mass-production industries. But the AFL also continued to make huge gains. Both the AFL and the CIO emerged from World War II stronger than ever before. However, with the termination of wartime economic controls, prices rose faster than wages, and strikes broke out in many major industries during 1945 and 1946. These strikes raised a great

Exhibit 1
Union Membership
Since 1900

THE GROWTH OF UNION MEMBERSHIP

The union movement experienced its most rapid growth during the 1930s and 1940s.

TOTAL UNION MEMBERSHIP AS A PERCENTAGE OF THE CIVILIAN LABOR FORCE

Since the 1950s, union membership has averaged less than 25 percent of the civilian labor force.

Source: U.S. Department of Labor.

wave of antiunion sentiment both in and out of Congress, resulting in the passage of new restrictive labor legislation. Thus came the end of an era in the history of the labor movement.

The Age of Maturity: Post—World War II to the Present

In June 1947, after numerous major strikes, a new labor–management relations act was passed. It provided the most detailed and extensive regulation of unions and industrial relations in the nation's history.

    The *Labor–Management Relations Act* (*Taft–Hartley Act*) of 1947 amended the 1935 National Labor Relations Act (Wagner Act). The Taft–Hartley Act retains for labor the rights that had been given it by the Wagner Act, but Taft–Hartley includes additional provisions:

1. It outlaws the following "unfair labor practices" of unions:
  (a) Coercion of workers to join a union.
  (b) Failure of a union to bargain with an employer in good faith.
  (c) *Jurisdictional strikes* (or disagreements between two or more unions as to which shall perform a particular job). *Secondary boycotts* (or attempts by a union through strikes, picketing, and the like to stop one employer from doing business with another employer).

The Taft–Hartley Act (1947) declared illegal many of the abusive practices of unions.

Featherbedding (or "make-work" rules, which are designed to increase the amount of labor or labor time on a particular job).

2. It outlaws the *closed shop*, whereby an employer is required to make current union membership a condition of employment. But it permits the *union shop*, which allows nonunion employees to be hired on the condition that they join the union after they are employed.

3. It requires unions to file financial reports with the NLRB, and it requires union officials to sign affidavits stating that they are not members of the Communist Party.

4. It prohibits strikes called before the end of a 60-day notice period prior to the expiration of a collective-bargaining agreement, in order to give conciliation agencies enough time to try to resolve disputes before a walkout occurs.

5. It enables the President to obtain an 80-day court injunction in order to provide a "cooling-off" period in cases involving strikes that endanger the national health or safety.

The Taft–Hartley Act also permits state legislatures to pass *right-to-work laws*. These are state laws that make it illegal to require membership in a union as a condition of employment. About 20 states, mostly in the South and Midwest, adopted such laws. Their main effect was to outlaw the union shop. In practice, however, these laws have been relatively weak in many states.

The Taft–Hartley Act was strongly denounced by unions for almost a decade after its passage. In retrospect, however, many economists and labor leaders now agree that the law does not appear to have put the unions at a disadvantage in bargaining, nor does it seem to have been a significant obstacle in the path of union growth.

Despite strong opposition by labor, the Taft–Hartley Act did not really "enslave" workers or hurt the union movement, as critics thought it would.

The AFL–CIO

Most, but not all, labor organizations joined either the AFL or the CIO. Those unions not affiliated with any federation of labor organizations are called *independent unions*. They may be national or international, and they are not limited to workers in any one firm.

For a number of years during and after World War II, labor leaders in both the AFL and the CIO dreamed of merging the two federations into a single and powerful union. Finally, in 1955, a single organization known as the *American Federation of Labor–Congress of Industrial Organizations (AFL–CIO)* was formed. The purposes of the organization, as paraphrased from its constitution, may be stated briefly. They are: (a) to improve wages, hours, and working conditions for workers; (b) to realize the benefits of free collective bargaining; and (c) to strengthen America's democratic traditions by protecting the labor movement from Communists, Fascists, and other totalitarians.

By the mid-1950s, with the merger of the AFL and the CIO, organized labor became a mature and powerful influence in the economy.

The union movement thus entered an age of maturity and power, and with it came mounting opposition by the foes of organized labor. Some union leaders were charged with mismanagement and embezzlement of union funds, and others were charged with extorting money from employers and employees under the threat of invoking "labor trouble." The AFL–CIO dealt with these problems by adopting Codes of Ethical Practices and by expelling several unions. In 1959, Congress passed a new law, the Labor–Management Reporting and Disclosure Act, which again indicated that the government would discipline labor as a whole in order to protect it from a few of its corrupt leaders.

The *Labor–Management Reporting and Disclosure Act* (*Landrum–Griffin Act*) of 1959 amended the National Labor Relations Act. The amendments included:

1. A requirement that all unions and union officers submit detailed financial reports.

2. Severely tightened restrictions on secondary boycotting and picketing.

3. A requirement of periodic secret-ballot elections of union officers.

4. Restriction of ex-convicts and Communists from positions as union officers.

The Future: Stabilization or Expansion?

What will be the future of the American labor movement? Many informed observers believe that union membership will stabilize at somewhat less than 25 percent of the labor force. There are several reasons for this belief:

Certain characteristics and attitudes of the public will limit the growth of unions, stabilizing their membership at about its present percentage of the labor force.

1. Changing Composition of the Labor Force The proportion of blue-collar workers, who are the chief source from which most unions draw their membership, has declined steadily from almost 50 percent of the civilian labor force after World War II to about half that today. Meanwhile, the proportion of white-collar workers has increased correspondingly. Most of the unorganized blue-collar workers are employed in small manufacturing plants and in the trade and service industries, all of which are more difficult to unionize.

2. Changing Attitudes Toward Unions The public as well as some political leaders in Congress have become less sympathetic toward unions. This is a result of what sometimes appear to be unreasonably prolonged strikes, the discovery of fraudulent practices among union officials, and the growing belief—whether true or not—that union pressures for wage increases are a chief cause of rising prices or cost-push inflation.

Other labor experts contend that union membership will continue to expand because there is still a large pool of unorganized labor in agriculture, trade, the professions, and the service industries. In any case:

> Unions have become big businesses, with millions of members and hundreds of millions of dollars in welfare funds (such as pension funds, unemployment funds, and the like). As a result, they have come increasingly to seek a new type of leadership in the form of professional *administrators*. These are people capable of dealing effectively with Congress, management, the public, and the rising proportion of more educated members—rather than leaders who are merely effective organizers.

Some of labor's bitter experiences in its struggle for recognition are depicted in Box 3.

Collective Bargaining

The chief objective of unions has been to improve the status of workers. That goal is now achieved for the most part through the method of *collective bargaining*. This is a process of negotiation between representatives of a company's management and a union for the purpose of arriving at mutually acceptable wages and working conditions for employees.

Box 3
**Bloody Battles During
Labor's Formative Years**

Violence and bloodshed often accompanied strikes, especially during the decades of struggle for union recognition. Since the 1940s, labor–management differences have almost always been settled by peaceful negotiation. In the photograph on the left, workers defy pickets at a Ford plant in Dearborn, Michigan, during a UAW–CIO strike in 1941. In the photograph on the right, pickets flee the clubs of policemen during a strike in Chicago in 1937.

Brown Brothers

Historical Pictures Service, Chicago

If a union represents a majority of workers in a firm, it may be "certified" by the government's National Labor Relations Board and recognized by management as the collective-bargaining agent for the employees. Representatives of the union and of management then meet together at the bargaining table to work out a *collective agreement*, or contract. The two sides are rarely in accord when they begin, but the bargaining process is one of give and take by both parties until a contract is agreed upon. The union representatives then take the contract back to their members for a vote of acceptance or rejection. If the members reject it, they may send their union representatives back to continue the bargaining process, or they may decide to reinforce their demands by going on strike.

When a collective agreement is ratified both by union and by management, it becomes a legally binding contract as well as a guiding principle of labor–management relations for the period of time specified in the agreement. More than 95 percent of all such agreements in existence today were successfully negotiated without any strikes or work stoppages.

Collective-bargaining contracts differ greatly in their scope and content. However, the major issues with which such agreements deal may be divided into four broad groups:

1. Wages and other benefits.

2. Industrial relations.

3. Multiunit bargaining.

4. Settlement of labor–management disputes.

Wages and Other Benefits

You may read in a newspaper that a labor–management negotiation has resulted in a $1-per-hour "package," consisting of 60 cents in wages and 40 cents in other benefits. Such packages are composed of two parts:

1. Basic Wages—payments received by workers for work performed, based on time or output.

2. Supplementary or Fringe Benefits—compensation to workers other than basic wages, such as bonuses, pension benefits, holiday pay, or vacation pay.

The term "wages" is thus a complex one in many collective-bargaining discussions and may give rise to various issues and problems.

Basic Wages: Time or Incentive Payments?

If you were a worker, would you want to be paid on the basis of "time," or would you prefer some sort of incentive system that compensated you according to how much you produced?

About 70 percent of American workers in manufacturing are paid on the basis of time—by the hour, day, week, or month—with extra compensation for work done during nights, weekends, and holidays. The remaining 30 percent of manufacturing workers receive their basic compensation through some type of incentive payment that is related to output or profit. Compensation may be in the form of wages, commissions, bonuses, and so on.

> Many employers have criticized the concept of time payment by arguing that it provides no incentive for workers to produce, since it relates earnings received to time worked rather than to output. Unions, however, have usually preferred time pay because it compensates workers on a uniform basis rather than penalizing the slower ones and rewarding the faster ones.

Time-payment systems tend to prevail in industries in which an individual's production cannot be precisely measured or in which rate of output is largely controlled by established technology. Examples include the automobile, chemical, and machine-tool industries. On the other hand, incentive systems have been effective in competitive industries in which labor costs are a high proportion of total costs and workers' outputs are measurable. Examples exist in some clothing and textile operations.

The great majority of unions have not strongly opposed incentive systems as such. However, they have been very much concerned with the rules of operation of such systems and with problems they pose.

For example:

1. How should a worker be compensated if a machine breaks down or if there is a stoppage of material flow due to causes beyond his or her control?

2. Since it may be possible to measure the outputs of only certain types of workers in a plant (such as maintenance personnel or assembly-line operators), can an equitable incentive and time system be established for all workers in the plant?

3. Will management provide an adequate staff of accountants, time-study engineers, and personnel experts to see that the incentive system continues to operate effectively and equitably?

A collective bargaining agreement typically consists of a "package" of wages and other benefits.

Most unions have always opposed incentive payments, preferring that wages be set at hourly rates.

Profit Sharing

Many companies have introduced a different type of incentive system known as profit sharing. These firms distribute to their workers a share of the profits after certain costs (such as wages, materials, and overhead) have been covered. Profit-sharing plans of various types (including bonuses) have existed since the early nineteenth century and are not uncommon in American industry. In general, profit sharing is most widespread in firms and industries with the following characteristics:

1. Consistent and relatively large profits, so that profit sharing becomes a worthwhile incentive.

2. Year-round stability of the work force (as opposed to high seasonal instability), thus permitting a permanent body of employees to build up an interest and equity in the company.

3. High turnover of key personnel, for whom profit sharing can have significant holding power.

4. Relatively weak or no unionization.

Unions have tended to oppose profit-sharing arrangements, preferring that workers be paid for what they do.

The first three characteristics are readily understandable, but why the fourth? The answer is that unions have ordinarily opposed profit sharing for two major reasons:

1. It establishes an employer–employee "partnership" in profits and thereby weakens the influence of unions.

2. It makes the employee's compensation dependent on profits. These in turn are determined in large part by managerial policies (such as pricing practices, product design, and technology) over which the worker has no direct control.

As a result:

> Unions have *usually* opposed profit sharing, arguing that workers should be paid for what they do. They should not be penalized when a company loses money or be rewarded with a share of the profits when it makes money.

Wage Structure and Job Classification

Employers have tended to prefer the use of multiple rates within each job classification. Unions, on the other hand, have usually preferred single-rate classifications.

Should all workers in a particular job classification, such as welders or assemblers, receive a single rate of pay? Or should there be a range of wages for each job based on years of experience, merit, length of service, and other factors? Such questions are obviously important for many collective-bargaining discussions.

In recent decades most manufacturing firms have adopted formal wage structures. This has been accomplished largely through the process of *job classification.* That is, the duties, responsibilities, and characteristics of jobs are described and the jobs are point-rated (perhaps by established formulas based on engineering studies of workers in such jobs). Then the jobs are grouped into graduated classifications with corresponding wage rates and wage ranges. Employers prefer job classification because it systematizes the wage structure and facilitates the handling of problems dealing with wage administration.

> Some of the chief problems of job-classification plans revolve around the issue of single rates versus rate ranges for each job grouping. Unions have tended to favor the single-rate approach because it reduces friction and dissension among workers in each rank. Employers, on the other hand, have usually preferred the use of rate ranges because it permits them to grant rewards on the basis of merit within each rank.

Supplementary or Fringe Benefits

Wage supplements or fringe benefits, such as pensions, insurance, and welfare plans, have grown remarkably in recent decades. This trend is likely to persist as long as union negotiators continue to emphasize the need for worker "security" in their bargaining with employers. Moreover, the various plans are becoming increasingly liberal. Health plans, for example, once included only hospitalization. Now they often cover outpatient care, free eyeglasses, psychiatric and dental care, and so on. Similarly, such additional benefits as sick leaves, time off with pay, and vacation allowances have all expanded substantially.

Supplementary wages or fringe benefits raise at least two fundamental questions:

1. Whereas wages used to be paid exclusively for time worked, there is a significant trend in the payment of some wages for time *not worked*. Therefore:

> If the trend toward more and more labor costs going into fringe benefits continues, will payment for time worked decrease in importance, and will our traditional mode of payment therefore become outdated?

2. To an employer, total fringe-benefit payments vary mostly with the number of employees rather than with the hours worked per employee. This is because workers receive the same vacations, holidays, group insurance, and so on, whether they put in 30, 40, or 50 hours per week. This means that it may be cheaper for an employer to pay existing workers at overtime rates than to hire new employees. Therefore:

> If the growth trend of fringe benefits continues, will it add so much to employers' costs that the propensity to employ will be reduced?

Will the growth of fringe-benefit payments raise production costs sufficiently to reduce employment?

Industrial Relations

A second major area of collective bargaining pertains to *industrial relations*—the rules and regulations governing the relationship between union and management. Because the subject of industrial relations is quite broad, attention may be focused on a few of the more important topics.

Union Security

"In unity there is strength." This is the fundamental principle upon which unionism is based. It follows that a primary objective of unions is "union security," or strength. A union's ability to attain security is determined by two major factors: the type of recognition that it is accorded and its financial arrangement for collecting dues. The more common forms of union recognition are the closed shop and the union shop, and the typical method of dues collection is the "checkoff." Let us see what these concepts entail.

Union security measures are concerned with strengthening the power and position of unions.

Closed Shop A plant or business establishment in which the employer agrees that all workers must belong to the union before they can be employed is known as a *closed shop*. This arrangement tends to be advantageous to the union and disadvantageous to the firm. A closed shop benefits the union by enabling it to control entry into the job or trade, thereby strengthening the union's bargaining position. However, it harms employers by depriving them of their right to hire whom they wish.

The Taft–Hartley Act of 1947 made the closed shop illegal for firms engaged in interstate commerce. The act only drove the closed shop underground, however. The closed shop does not exist in principle in union–management contracts, but it does exist in fact in certain skilled trades and industries, such as printing, construction, and transportation.

Union Shop A plant or business establishment in which the employer is free to hire whom he or she wants, but agrees to require that the employee join the union within a specified time after being hired (usually 30 days) as a condition for continuing in employment, is called a *union shop*.

The union shop, as distinguished from the closed shop, requires an employee to join the union after becoming employed.

The union shop is the most common form of union recognition found in industry today. There are two major reasons for this:

1. The Taft–Hartley Act of 1947 made the closed shop illegal.

2. There is a tendency for various industries to switch to the union shop from other less common types of union-recognition arrangements.

Both the closed shop and the union shop have certain obvious disadvantages to employers. The major disadvantage is that both types of shops give the union greater bargaining strength. Hence, management has often argued in favor of the *open shop*. This is a plant or business establishment in which the employer is free to hire union or nonunion members. Unions have always opposed the open shop on the grounds that it often results in a closed nonunion shop because of the antiunion hiring preferences of many employers.

Checkoff If a union is to continue to function, it must have an efficient means of collecting dues from its members. In the old days, unions often stationed strong-arm men at plant gates on paydays in order to enforce the payment of dues. Those workers who held back their union dues risked a bloody nose or even a fractured skull. But with the growth of unionism and union recognition, the *checkoff* system was introduced. The employer, with the written permission of the workers, withholds union dues and other assessments from paychecks and then transfers the funds to the union. This simplifies the dues-collection process and assures the prompt and regular payment of dues.

The checkoff system allows management to withhold union dues from workers' paychecks.

Restricting Membership and Output

Unions enhance their security through various forms of membership and output restriction.

Many unions seek to obtain higher incomes for their members by restricting membership. This creates a scarcity of their particular kind of labor. Membership may be controlled in several ways: (1) varying apprenticeship requirements; (2) sponsoring state licensing for those in the trade (examples are barbers, electricians, and plumbers); (3) varying initiation fees; and (4) establishing seniority agreements that provide for the order in which workers may be laid off and rehired.

Many unions also seek to restrict their members' output in order to increase the demand for labor and thereby to secure higher wages. Output restriction may be accomplished by shortening the working day, limiting the output per worker, and opposing the introduction of labor-saving technology.

Thus, whereas management may seek to increase profits by raising productive efficiency, unions are primarily interested in improving earnings and working conditions for their members. Because these objectives often conflict, the means that are chosen to achieve them must be ironed out around the bargaining table.

Multiunit Bargaining

Perhaps the most controversial issue in the practice of collective bargaining involves multiunit agreements.

> Multiunit bargaining (sometimes inaccurately called "industry-wide bargaining") is a collective-bargaining arrangement covering more than one plant. It may occur between one or more firms in an industry and one or more unions, and it may take place on a national, regional, or local level. Although it can be national in scope and very inclusive, it is rarely completely industry-wide.

A number of examples can be used to illustrate the scope and diversity of multiunit bargaining.

• In the automobile and steel industries, one employer such as General Motors or United States Steel owns a number of plants and bargains with a single union—the United Automobile Workers or the United Steel Workers.

• In the construction and retailing industries, two or more employers in an industry may bargain with one or more national unions. The bargaining will usually be subdivided geographically into national, regional, and local areas.

• In the bituminous-coal industry, all employers bargain with one industrial union on a national basis. In the railroad industry, on the other hand, employers bargain with several groups and must consider the demands of all groups in arriving at a settlement.

• In various Western cities, bargaining has developed on an area-wide basis between employer associations and unions that cut across industry lines.

• A practice called *coalition bargaining* has also gained wide use. The AFL–CIO tries to coordinate and establish common termination dates for contracts with firms that deal with a number of unions at plants throughout the United States and Canada. In this way, the AFL–CIO can strengthen its bargaining position by threatening to close down all plants simultaneously.

Multiunit bargaining in the United States is thus a widespread and complex process that varies by industry, geography, and the nature of the issues involved. This explains why the expression "industry-wide bargaining" is usually not completely accurate.

The chief advantages of multiunit bargaining are these:

1. It strengthens the union wage structure within markets and industries by making union–management contracts easier to negotiate and enforce.

2. It increases labor stability by making it more difficult for a rival union to enter an industry.

However, because of its large-scale and often national nature, multiunit bargaining poses several important problems:

1. It gives unions a strong degree of monopoly power, which, coupled with the employer's fear of a widespread strike, often enables unions to extract highly inflationary wage settlements.

2. It tends to focus on the national settlement of basic economic issues

Multinunit bargaining is a collective-bargaining approach involving one or more firms in an industry and one or more unions.

Multinunit bargaining strengthens the position of unions and tends to focus on the national settlement of basic issues.

involving wages and working conditions. Thus it leaves such important "noneconomic" issues as work standards and working rules for settlement at the local plant level. This often results in disproportionately higher costs to local employers because they lack the funds for counteroffers after national issues have been settled.

3. It frequently allows matters of local concern to become subjects of national negotiations. This might lead to strikes, even though the issues may eventually be referred back to, and settled at, the local level.

Settling Labor–Management Disputes

Strikes are one of several methods of settling labor–management disputes.

The collective-bargaining process can be likened to a game of strategy between opposing players, with each side threatening to employ its own unique weapons in order to defeat the other.

The employer's major weapons include injunctions and lockouts. An *injunction* is a court order forbidding an individual or group of individuals (such as a union) from taking a specified action. Employers' use of this device has been severely restricted since the Norris–LaGuardia Act of 1932. A *lockout* is the closing down of a plant by an employer in order to keep workers out of their jobs.

The union's major weapons include boycotts and strikes. A *boycott* (sometimes called a *primary boycott*) is a campaign by workers to discourage people from dealing with an employer or buying the company's products. A *strike* is a mutual agreement among workers to stop working, without resigning from their jobs, until their demands are met.

Experience indicates that it is rarely necessary for either side to use its maximum economic strength. In general:

> Although the power to strike is labor's ultimate weapon, it is a major and costly one that unions do not use lightly. An analysis of data since 1935 indicates that, on an annual basis, the amount of working time lost because of strikes has never been as high as 2 percent of total labor-days worked and has averaged less than 1 percent of that amount. This is far less than the proportion of time lost from work because of the common cold.

Arbitration and Mediation (Conciliation)

What happens if labor–management negotiations break down? In such a case, the unsuccessful bargainers may have to resolve their disagreements through processes known as arbitration and mediation.

By either of two methods, arbitration or mediation, disagreements between labor and management may be resolved through the efforts of an impartial third party.

Arbitration This is an effective method of settling differences between two parties. It involves the use of an impartial third party, called an arbitrator, who is acceptable to both sides and whose decision is binding and legally enforceable on the contesting parties. The arbitration procedure consists of the company and the union submitting their disagreement to the arbitrator. After hearing all the evidence, the arbitrator issues a decision. It is based not on what the arbitrator believes to be wise and fair but upon how he or she understands the language of the contract to apply to the case at hand. Thus, an arbitrator is like a judge: An arbitrator relates the case to the contract, just as a judge relates a case to the law.

Voluntary arbitration is provided for in the great majority of all collective-bargaining agreements in effect today. There is no doubt that the existence and extensive use of this type of arbitration has helped to reduce the number of strikes.

Another plan that has often been proposed as a key to industrial peace, especially in the case of prolonged strikes, is "compulsory arbitration." As the name implies, this *requires* labor and management to submit their differences to an arbitrator. Obviously, however, compulsory arbitration is not a substitute for free collective bargaining. Where it has been tried in some advanced democratic countries, it has caused more turmoil than peace and has not stopped strikes.

Mediation This process, sometimes also called *conciliation*, is a means by which a third party, the mediator, attempts to reconcile the differences between contesting parties. The mediator may attempt to maintain constructive discussions, to search for common areas of agreement, or to suggest compromises. However, the mediator's decisions are not binding, and they need not be accepted by the contesting parties. The federal government provides most mediation services through an independent agency called the Federal Mediation and Conciliation Service, while most states and some large municipalities provide similar services.

The Economics of Unions: Efficiency and Equity

Labor unions have important influences on the economy. The ways in which they affect economic efficiency (resource allocation) and equity (income distribution) are particularly relevant. Let us see how.

How Unions May Raise Wages

Chief among the unions' many objectives is the raising of wages. Many interesting models of wage determination can be developed to illustrate different kinds of competitive and monopolistic market situations. Three of the more common ones are illustrated in Exhibit 2. The supply and demand curves in each diagram relate the price of labor, expressed in wages, and the quantity of labor supplied and demanded.

Unions may seek to raise the wages of members through various types of restrictive practices.

Featherbedding Model

Figure (*a*) of Exhibit 2 illustrates what happens when the union seeks to increase the demand for labor—that is, to shift the demand curve to the right—through the use of *featherbedding* techniques. These are "make-work" rules or practices designed by unions to restrict output by artificially increasing the amount of labor or labor time employed on a particular job. There are a number of examples. The Painters Union has limited the width of brushes and the sizes of rollers. The Meat Cutters Union has required prewrapped meat to be rewrapped on the job. The Trainmen's Union has demanded that railroads eliminate the use of radio telephones by crew and revert back to hand signals and lanterns. And the Railroad Brotherhood was able for years to maintain a "fireman" on diesel locomotives, which have no boiler fire.

Most featherbedding practices are imposed under the guise of promoting health or safety. In reality, however, they are often self-protective devices that reflect the insecurity of workers in a declining industry. There is a fundamental need, therefore, for adequate retraining programs to permit the shifting of workers to new jobs. Otherwise, featherbedding practices—like other restrictive devices, whether they

Exhibit 2
How Unions May Raise Wages in Competitive Markets

(a) FEATHERBEDDING MODEL

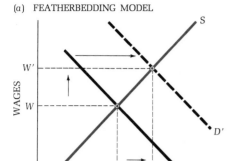

(b) CRAFT-UNION MODEL

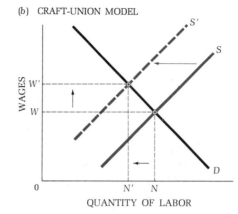

(c) INDUSTRIAL-UNION MODEL

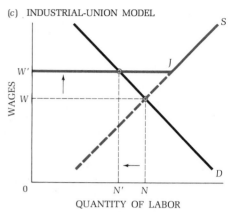

Figure (a): *Increase the demand for labor.* Through featherbedding or other restrictive and make-work practices, unions may succeed in shifting the demand for labor to the right from D to D'. This will increase the equilibrium quantity of labor from N to N' and the equilibrium wage from W to W'.

Figure (b): *Decrease the supply of labor.* If a craft union can restrict the supply of labor by shifting the supply curve from S to S', it will reduce the equilibrium quantity of labor from N to N' and raise the equilibrium wage from W to W'.

Figure (c): *Organize all workers in an industry.* An industrial union covering an entire industry would seek a wage level such as W', which is above the equilibrium wage at W. The supply curve of labor would thus change from its normal shape (which includes the dashed portion) to W'JS, and the equilibrium quantity would therefore decline from N to N'.

are employed by unions, by business firms, or by professional associations, must ultimately result in higher prices to consumers as well as a misallocation of society's resources.

Craft-Union Model

Figure (b) represents the situation in which a craft union composed of workers in a particular trade, such as carpenters or electricians, seeks to restrict the supply of labor in order to raise wages. The union may do this by imposing high obstacles to entry for those seeking membership. Examples of such obstacles are long apprenticeship requirements, high initiation fees, or closed membership periods. In the more general sense, unions have often sought to restrict the overall supply of labor in the economy by supporting legislation to (1) curb immigration, (2) shorten the workweek, (3) reduce child labor, and (4) assure compulsory retirement. The model in Figure (b), therefore, applies to all such policies, since their effect is to shift the supply curve of labor to the left.

Industrial-Union Model

The union represented in Figure (c) seeks to organize all workers in an industry and to impose a wage that is above the equilibrium wage. This changes the supply curve, as explained in the exhibit. Thus, at the union-imposed wage of W', employers can hire as many as $W'J$ units of labor, and they can hire no labor at less than this wage. The new supply curve $W'JS$ is thus perfectly elastic over the segment $W'J$, signifying that the industry can buy this much labor at the union wage. If the industry wants more than $W'J$ units of labor, it will have to pay a higher wage. As shown in the diagram, the industry will demand only N' units of labor at the wage rate imposed by the union.

Conclusion: Are Unions Too Big?

These models of how unions may seek to raise wages illustrate the following basic criticism often leveled against them:

> Unions are monopolies. As such, they engage in restrictive practices in order to achieve benefits (wages) above the free-market equilibrium levels that would exist in a competitive system. They thereby cause resource misallocation, unemployment, and inflation.

Keep in mind, however, that the same restrictive charges can equally well be leveled against any organization that has a substantial degree of monopoly power—whether it be a business firm, a professional association, or any other type of institution.

Exhibit 3 examines this criticism from both sides of the fence by comparing the charges often made against unions and their responses to these charges. These and other criticisms of unions have led to suggestions that their monopolistic power should be restricted or controlled. At least four common remedies, along with an equal number of responses by unions, have been proposed:

1. Subject Unions to the Antitrust Laws

Labor's Reply The antitrust laws were designed for profit-motivated corporations, not welfare-motivated unions. These laws involve complex issues that are not directly applicable to union practices and objectives, and it would be logically wrong as well as socially and economically unjust to subject unions to them.

The question of whether unions are too large and therefore have excessive market power is not easily answered. There are some persuasive arguments on both sides of the issue.

Exhibit 3 Are Unions Too Big?	The Charges Against Unions	How the Unions Reply
	1. Unions fix the price of labor through the exertion of their monopoly power and thereby extract excessively high wages.	1. Despite the alleged monopoly power of unions, the average worker's take-home pay is still inadequate.
	2. Unions monopolize job opportunities through the use of the union shop.	2. The union shop is simply an application of the democratic principle of majority rule.
	3. Unions have the power to shut down whole industries as a result of multiunit bargaining.	3. Multiunit bargaining is necessary in order to stabilize wage rates among competing employers.
	4. Unions have become financial giants because of their tax-exempt status and the use of the dues-checkoff system.	4. The assets of unions have made possible many significant advances in social welfare, and these assets are minute compared to the assets of giant corporations.
	5. Unions, because of their great monopolistic power, can determine the life or death of thousands of individual businesses.	5. Unions seek countervailing power against the firms with which they bargain. They try to benefit workers, not drive firms out of business.

Several proposals aimed at reducing the market power of unions have been made.

2. Prohibit Multiunit Bargaining

Labor's Reply Multiunit bargaining enables small businesses to present a united front against union demands. Otherwise, small businesses would be overpowered by unions.

3. Break Large Unions Up into Local Bodies

Labor's Reply Breaking up large unions into smaller ones would make them even more monopolistic in setting the price of labor. There would be several unions in each major industry, with each union monopolizing its own labor supply and seeking the highest possible wage from its employer. The union in General Motors, for example, would press for its own demands without concern for whether Ford, Chrysler, or American Motors could match those demands.

4. Outlaw the Union Shop

Labor's Reply Since workers elect the union that will represent them, the existence of union shops is democracy in action. Besides, eliminating the union shop would not necessarily reduce a union's ability to employ weapons such as boycotts and strikes.

To conclude:

> The problem of union monopoly is a complex one. Although there is no doubt that unions possess varying degrees of monopoly power, there is no simple solution to the question of what should be done about it. Most observers would probably agree, however, that an attack against specific abuses rather than a sweeping attack against unions in general provides the most realistic and desirable approach.

Issue
Voluntary Overtime: The Backward-Bending Labor Supply Curve

If your employer asks you to work overtime, should you have the right to refuse? This has sometimes been a major issue in labor–management negotiations.

At the present time, agreements between unions and managements often stipulate that workers must put in extra hours of weekend work—at premium rates—when it is requested. Management contends that this provision in the labor contract is necessary if a business is to be operated efficiently. When demand is high, companies often have to run their plants 6 or 7 days a week. "It would be impossible," says an executive of a large agricultural implements firm, "to manage a complex system of interrelated manufacturing and assembly lines unless there is assurance of a constant work force. The decision of a few key employees not to work overtime could force the closing of our entire plant."

How do the unions reply? Their answer is simple. "Our members want the right to say 'No thanks,'" says a prominent union president. Many other union leaders agree. Those representing a number of basic industries have declared their intention to make voluntary overtime a bargaining issue in future contract negotiations.

Varied Experiences

Many workers resist overtime because, with already large paychecks, they value their leisure more than the additional wages they would get for putting in extra hours—even at premium rates. Some observers believe, however, that this feeling is merely a by-product of prosperity. In recession, workers are faced with the difficulty of getting along on straight-time pay and are anxious to pick up any overtime they can get.

Various companies have settled the overtime question in different ways. In some firms, labor contracts require only a "reasonable amount of overtime." In others, only junior workers are required to accept it; senior employees can reject the extra hours if less experienced workers can be found to fill the need. In still other firms, outside help is brought in to complete necessary work. But this practice is held in disfavor by most companies because it is costly and inflexible.

Regardless of what happens in various collective-bargaining negotiations, the problem of voluntary overtime is bound to surface from time to time. It is much too important an issue, both for labor and management, to lie dormant for very long.

Questions

1. Should workers be required to accept available overtime? In answering this question, keep in mind that, if they refuse, they may deprive others of the right to work available overtime.

2. The refusal of an employee to work overtime means that his or her supply curve of labor is backward-bending—as shown by the S curve in Figure (a).
  (a) Interpret the curve. Why does it have this peculiar shape?
  (b) If the wage at J is the maximum hourly wage desired, what will be the worker's income at this wage?

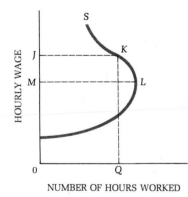

(a) INDIVIDUAL WORKER

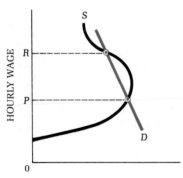

(b) ENTIRE INDUSTRY

3. In Figure (b), the demand and supply curves of labor for an entire industry are shown. If the equilibrium wage is at R, will this equilibrium be stable or unstable? What if the wage is at P? Explain. (Hint An equilibrium is stable when a small departure from it sets into motion forces that automatically restore the equilibrium.)

What You Have Learned in This Chapter

1. The chief overall objective of unions is to improve the wages and working conditions of their members by bargaining with employers. Much of the history of the union movement in America can be viewed as an attempt to achieve this goal.

2. The period from the Revolution to the Civil War witnessed the beginnings of the American labor movement. Some craft unions were started despite the opposition of employers and the generally unsympathetic attitudes of the courts.

3. From the end of the Civil War to the Depression was the formative period of unionism. The Knights of Labor, followed by the American Federation of Labor, dominated the labor movement.

4. From the depression years of the 1930s until the end of World War II, the labor movement expanded rapidly. Favorable legislation that guaranteed labor's right to organize and bargain collectively with employers was passed. The Congress of Industrial Organizations emerged in this period and was extremely successful in organizing industrial unions.

5. After World War II, unions entered an age of maturity. The following have been among the chief events since then:

(a) Congress sought to curb some of the power of labor unions by passing the National Labor Relations Act (Taft–Hartley Act) of 1947. This law prohibited the closed shop, outlawed "unfair labor practices" of unions, and imposed other regulations on union practices.

(b) The AFL and the CIO merged in 1955 to form one huge labor organization for the purpose of strengthening the bargaining position of workers.

(c) The Labor–Management Reporting and Disclosure Act (Landrum–Griffin Act) of 1959 constrained further the power of unions by requiring unions and union officers to submit periodic financial reports and by imposing other restrictions on various union practices.

6. Unions try to improve the status of workers by bargaining collectively with management. Although there is no "typical" collective-bargaining agreement, the major issues usually involve matters pertaining to wages, industrial relations, multiunit bargaining, and the settlement of labor–management disputes.

7. Supply-and-demand models may be constructed to illustrate how unions seek to raise the wages of their members. Thus, in a featherbedding model, the union tries to shift the demand curve for labor to the right. In a craft-union model, the union tries to shift the supply curve of labor to the left. In an industrial-union model, the union seeks to impose a wage floor above the market equilibrium level.

8. The basic criticism of unions is that they are monopolies that engage in restrictive practices in order to raise wages above free-market equilibrium levels. Hence, they cause economic inefficiency (resource misallocation), unemployment, and inflation. Unions reply that they exert countervailing power against the firms with which they bargain and that they thereby benefit not only workers but also society as a whole.

For Discussion

1. *Terms and concepts to review:*
union
craft union
Norris–LaGuardia Act (1932)
yellow-dog contract
National Labor Relations (Wagner) Act (1935)
company union
National Labor Relations Board
industrial union
Labor–Management Relations (Taft–Hartley) Act (1947)
jurisdictional strike
secondary boycott
featherbedding
closed shop
union shop
open shop
right-to-work laws
independent union
AFL–CIO
Labor–Management Reporting and Disclosure Act (1959)
collective bargaining
industrial relations
checkoff
multiunit bargaining
coalition bargaining
injunction
lockout
boycott
strike
arbitration
mediation
conciliation

2. Outline the highlights of the labor movement from the time of the Revolution to the present.

3. Some prolabor factions have argued that the Taft–Hartley Act was a major setback to the labor movement and unfair to organized labor. If you were a *defender* of the act, how would you criticize this viewpoint? Give some examples.

4. If you were a union leader bargaining for better wages and working conditions, what criteria would you use to support your arguments? What kinds of issues might you want to negotiate?

5. What would be the probable effects of a law that required all labor–management disputes to be settled by government arbitration?

6. Which has a greater degree of monopoly power—a union's monopoly of a labor market or a firm's monopoly of a product market? Why?

7. Do unions really raise wages? That is, do wages in unionized industries rise faster than they would if those industries were non-unionized? What are some of the basic considerations to take into account in answering this question?

30
CHAPTER

Social Problems: Insecurity, Poverty, and Discrimination

Learning guide
Watch for the answers to these important questions

What chief social measures exist today to provide protection against the insecurity of old age, unemployment, disability, ill health, and death?

How can we explain the fact that in a country as rich as ours, more than 10 percent of the people are poor?

What can be done about the problems of poverty and deprivation that confront many millions of Americans? In general, what are the economic effects of proposed programs for social reform?

What are the economic effects of discrimination? What can economics contribute to a better understanding of discrimination?

This chapter examines the ways in which economics can help solve the problems of insecurity, poverty, and discrimination.

Security or insecurity? Welfare or "illfare"? Equality or inequality?

These are the alternatives that are sometimes posed by critics in their discussions of America's social problems. Among the most important of these problems are insecurity, poverty, and discrimination. Some of the critics also contend that a concern for social reform makes people dependent upon their government and is therefore contrary to the American tradition. This tradition is based on the Puritan ethic of self-reliance, industry, and thrift.

Anyone who is familiar with the history of social reform in America knows that these contentions are nothing new. From the nineteenth century to the present, we have seen the abolition of slavery, the introduction of free public education, the passage of protective legislation for labor, the provision of public charity for the needy, and the enactment of social security legislation providing some protection against the losses that may result from old age, disability, ill health, and unemployment. And always there were those who cried that such measures of protection were alien to the American tradition. In view of our history, it seems evident that our tradition may not be as simple and puritanical as these stalwart defenders make it out to be.

Thus, we shall find in this chapter that today's social reform measures are no different in their underlying philosophy from those that were introduced a century or more ago. The differences that do exist are to be found in the scope of their objectives and in the details of the specific measures.

Insecurity and Social Security

Most families are insecure in the sense that they stand a chance of suffering economically from a loss of income. Such losses may occur as a result of unemployment, illness, injury, retirement, or death of the breadwinner. Because of the hardships consequent upon such losses, our present program of social security was instituted during the Great Depression of the 1930s.

The *Social Security Act* of 1935 (with its many subsequent amendments) is the basic comprehensive social security law of the United States. It provides for:

1. Social insurance programs for old age, survivors, disability, and health insurance (OASDHI) and unemployment payments to insured persons.

2. A public charity program in the form of welfare services, institutional care, food, housing, and other forms of assistance.

Some of the provisions of the act are administered and financed by the federal government, some by state and local governments, and some by all three levels of government. (See Exhibit 1.)

Against this background, some of the act's main features may be examined. This will provide you with a better understanding of the underlying logic and philosophy of our social security system.

Our social security system consists of a social insurance program and a public charity program.

Social Insurance Programs

The several insurance programs that are contained in the Social Security Act are diverse in their coverage, benefits, financing, and administration. They can be classified, however, into categories designed to provide financial protection against (1) old age, disability, ill health, and death, and (2) unemployment.

Social insurance programs are concerned with protecting people from the economic hardships of old age, disability, ill health, and unemployment.

Old Age, Survivors, Disability, and Health Insurance (OASDHI)

The OASDHI program embraces what most people commonly refer to as "social security." It is actually an annuity scheme—a special type of compulsory saving program—that provides cash benefits when earnings are cut off by old age, total disability, or death. The benefits vary according to the amount of social security taxes collected from the employer and the employee. These taxes and benefits have increased over the years, presumably to compensate for inflation. More than 90 percent of all employed persons are eligible for benefits, including retirement benefits at age 65. A similar proportion of mothers and children are eligible to receive survivors' payments if the head of the family dies. There is also medical and hospital insurance for those over 65 (known as Medicare) and a program that provides for the health needs of people with modest incomes (known as Medicaid).

Unemployment Insurance

The unemployment insurance program is administered by the individual states within a general framework established by the federal government. The program provides for *unemployment benefits*—weekly payments to covered workers who are involuntarily unemployed for a specified number of weeks. Today more than three-fourths of the civilian labor force is eligible for unemployment benefits.

Exhibit 1
Social Welfare Expenditures Under Public Programs

Social welfare programs have expanded to embrace much more than "social security"—protection against loss of earnings from retirement, disability, and death as conceived in the Social Security Act of 1935.

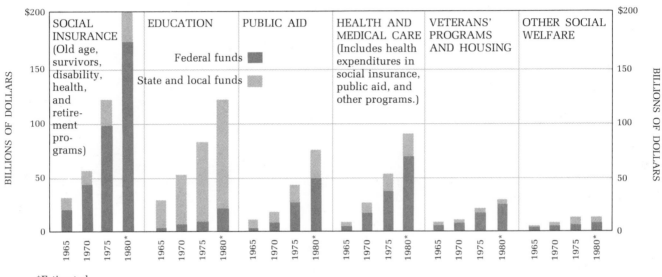

SOCIAL INSURANCE (Old age, survivors, disability, health, and retirement programs)

EDUCATION

Federal funds

State and local funds

PUBLIC AID

HEALTH AND MEDICAL CARE (Includes health expenditures in social insurance, public aid, and other programs.)

VETERANS' PROGRAMS AND HOUSING

OTHER SOCIAL WELFARE

BILLIONS OF DOLLARS

*Estimated

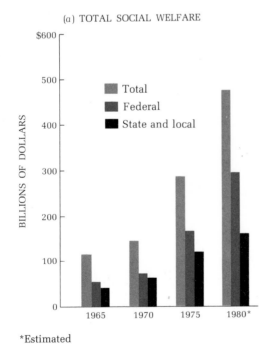

(a) TOTAL SOCIAL WELFARE

BILLIONS OF DOLLARS

Total
Federal
State and local

*Estimated

Source: U.S. Bureau of the Census.

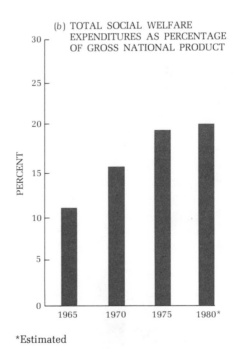

(b) TOTAL SOCIAL WELFARE EXPENDITURES AS PERCENTAGE OF GROSS NATIONAL PRODUCT

PERCENT

*Estimated

Charitable Programs—Welfare

The noninsurance part of the social security system consists of charitable or welfare programs administered by federal, state, and local governments, to which the federal government contributes substantially. These programs are often referred to as special assistance programs because they are intended to help special categories of needy persons. The more important programs include aid to the disabled, medical assistance to the needy, food distribution and relief programs, housing subsidies and assistance for low-income groups, and welfare services in the form of institutional care for the needy.

In addition to these, there are general assistance programs administered and financed exclusively by various state and local governments.

Charitable (or welfare) programs provide aid to special groups of needy persons.

Evaluating Social Security

The social security system—including both federal and state programs —provides a measure of protection against most major forms of insecurity. Nevertheless, it has been the subject of severe criticisms—particularly with respect to financing.

As the average age of the population and the number of retired people both increase, the burden of paying for social security will fall increasingly on fewer workers.

Despite its insurance provisions, social security is in no meaningful sense an insurance program. This is because our social security system differs from a system based on private insurance in several fundamental ways:

• Individual benefits are determined by many factors other than taxes ("premiums") paid.

• Participation and "contributions" are compulsory. Thus, individuals are unable to select and pay for the particular benefits they wish to receive.

• The tax used to finance the program is a payroll tax based on a fixed percentage of wages up to a specified minimum wage level. Therefore, the burden of the tax is regressive, bearing most heavily on low- and middle-income groups.

In addition, the payroll tax has a destabilizing effect on the national economy. Because it is a tax on wages, increases in the tax rate legislated during recessions delay recovery by reducing income available for spending.

Financing the Program

In view of these shortcomings, a fairer way of paying for social security is needed. Three alternative approaches to reform may be considered:

Three major approaches to financing social security are possible.

1. Restructure the Payroll Tax The payroll tax could be revised to permit exemptions and deductions similar to those used for the income tax. This would greatly reduce if not eliminate the tax on families in poverty. Any loss in revenue resulting from the restructuring of the tax could be made up by a small percentage increase in the income tax.

2. Substitute the Income Tax The payroll tax could be replaced by the income tax as a means of financing social security. This would require a substantial increase in income-tax rates in order to produce larger yields. However, since a major adjustment in the rate schedule of the income tax is not likely to be undertaken at any one time, it would probably be more feasible to restructure it in small steps. This would permit the full burden of the payroll tax to be transferred gradually and in an equitable way.

Exhibit 2

Social Security: Will It Be There When You Need It?

Public-opinion surveys show that confidence in the social security program is ebbing. The basic reason is that the average age of the population is increasing because of reduced birth and death rates. Therefore, the social security system will be calling upon fewer workers, ages 20 to 70, to support more retired people after the turn of the century.

Maximum annual social security taxes on employee and employer, along with maximum benefits, are expected to soar in the years ahead.

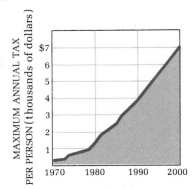

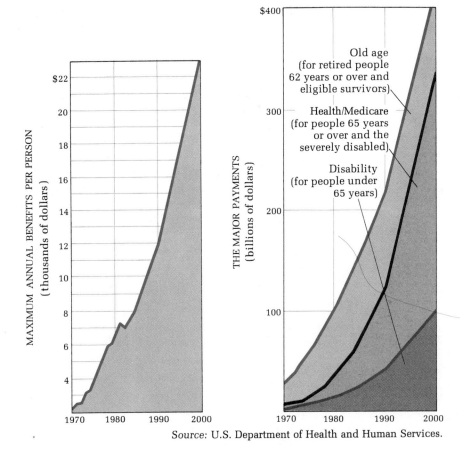

Source: U.S. Department of Health and Human Services.

3. Finance Benefits from General Revenues The costs of social security could be paid out of the general funds of the U.S. Treasury. Certain benefits are already financed in this way. By extending the procedure to cover all benefits out of general revenues, the financing of social security would be made more equitable, because the taxes supplying the general fund are largely progressive.

These reforms are not mutually exclusive. They could be combined in various ways to produce a fairer method of paying for social security. At the very least, if the payroll tax is retained, an equitable system of exemptions for low-income families should be provided, and a deliberate effort should be made to avoid worsening recessions by untimely tax increases.

Conclusion: Short-Run and Long-Run Measures

The need for tax reform to finance social security is only one step in the right direction. As shown in Exhibit 2, the costs and benefits of social security are rising sharply. They will continue to soar in the years ahead as fewer workers are called upon to support an increasing number of retirees.

Does this mean that taxes to finance social security benefits should be raised? That may be one solution. But others are currently under consideration in Congress:

1. Raise the Minimum Retirement Age This will encourage people to remain in their jobs for longer periods. However, some studies have concluded that the morale, and therefore the productivity, of workers would be adversely affected if they were required to extend their working years in order to qualify for social security benefits.

2. Reduce the Cost-of-Living Adjustments Automatic cost-of-living increases, enabling social security benefits to keep up with rising prices, were legislated by Congress in the early 1970s. As a result, social security recipients constitute perhaps the only group in society whose annual real income has not suffered from inflation. Because of this, a chief proposal being considered in Washington would link social security benefits to society's real income (measured by real gross national product). In that way, recipients as a group would share the losses from inflation more equally with the rest of the population.

These proposals are "short-term" solutions that will stave off a social security crisis for a few years. In order to achieve a more permanent solution, other steps must be taken.

In addition to alternative means of financing social security, measures to reduce its costs can also be undertaken.

> For the long run, policies are needed that will encourage greater investment in capital formation and in human resources *today*. This will assure that more and better factories and equipment, along with a more skilled labor force, will be available in the future. In that way, workers in later years will be more productive. Hence, with their higher real incomes, they will be better able to support the aged.

Affluence and Poverty: America's Underdeveloped Nation

America's aggregate wealth is unmatched by that of any nation in history. Its fields and factories generate a superabundance of foods, goods, and gadgets; most of its families possess automobiles and television sets; and the great majority of families own their homes.

The signs of affluence are everywhere—except among the 25 million Americans who live in poverty and deprivation. This group is larger than the population of many countries. It is composed of men, women, and children of all races who live near or below the bare subsistence level. Some interesting statistics about people living in poverty in the United States are shown in Exhibit 3.

What Is Poverty?

For many years, economists and statisticians have grappled with the problem of defining and measuring poverty. Central to the concept is the *poverty line*—a sliding income scale that varies between rural and urban locations according to family size. The poverty line for an urban family of four—which is regarded as fairly typical—was approximately $10,000 annually in the early 1980s.

Of course, many of the people who fall below the line, such as a married medical-school student or an elderly couple on social security who

Exhibit 3
Persons Below Low-Income (Poverty) Level, by Family Status, Race, Sex, and Residence

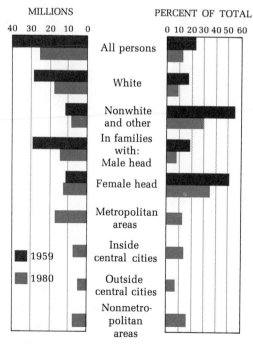

Source: U.S. Bureau of the Census.

own their home and car, are poor only by definition. Nor does the poverty line distinguish between costs of living in different areas of the country. A low income goes a lot farther in Meridian, Mississippi, than in San Francisco or New York City. Nevertheless, in view of the following facts, a simple income measure of poverty understates the real dimensions of the situation:

1. A poverty-line income for a family of four allows for practically no dental or medical care. It also permits no movies, newspapers, or books and only very small quantities of clothing, meat, fruits, and vegetables.

2. More than 10 percent of the total population is classified as poor. Contrary to a widespread belief, blacks do not constitute a majority in the group. Of 25 million poor Americans, approximately 18 million are white.

3. Most of the population lives in cities and towns. Therefore, it is not surprising that the majority of the poor are urban dwellers.

In general, there is no simple and unique definition of poverty—or even of "poorness." It is an economic and psychological state of being that varies for different people from time to time and from place to place. (See Box 1.)

Box 1
The Paradox of Poverty in the United States

What constitutes poverty? In some of the poorest counties of the nation, the great majority of homes lack baths and inside toilets, and a large minority have no running water. Their inhabitants, by present-day American standards, would be classified as poverty-stricken.

But let us examine the situation more closely.

In the early 1980s, among households with annual incomes under $10,000, the goods shown in the graph were owned.

The poor in America thus have many of the accoutrements of an affluent society. This is the *paradox of poverty*. The American poor are not the same as the starving

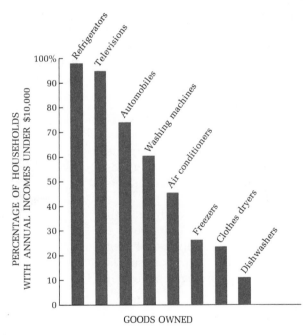

Source: U.S. Bureau of the Census.

poor of India or the Far East, but they are poor nevertheless.

In Calcutta, the "street people" live their entire lives on the city's sidewalks.

Bruce Davidson/Magnum

George Sturm/Black Star

What Are the Causes and Costs of Poverty?

We may distinguish among three different types of poverty, according to the economic, social, and personal factors that cause them.

Poverty arises from several different sources. Each must be dealt with in different ways.

1. Cyclical Poverty A fall in aggregate demand for goods and services may cause a depression or a deep recession. The result is mass unemployment and widespread poverty. However, with the growth of modern macroeconomic theory and policy, political leaders have learned how to reduce such severe setbacks in the economy, and this cause of poverty is no longer as serious a problem as it once was.

2. Community Poverty A region may lose its economic base or its major source of income and employment, thereby leaving an entire population in a state of economic deprivation. Some industrial areas, such as those in the north-central states, have suffered heavy unemployment because technology and machinery have replaced manual labor in their principal industries. This type of poverty can be remedied only through regional economic development programs or outward migration.

3. Personal Poverty Poverty has always existed among some individuals and families, in times of prosperity as well as in depression, in high-income regions and in low-income ones. It is due to personal and social factors, some of which are beyond individual control. For example, aside from that small proportion of the poor to whom sociologists refer as the "disreputable poor" (the tramps, beggars, derelicts, and so on), there are families that are poverty-stricken because of racial prejudice, inadequate training and job opportunities, physical or mental handicaps, desertion by the breadwinner, and various other causes.

Poverty levies serious social costs. Some sociological studies have concluded that poverty causes ill health and emotional disturbance and helps to spread disease. It *may* also contribute to delinquency, vice, and crime. All these impose heavy costs on the community, which must maintain more police and fire protection, more courts and jails, more public-health and sanitation facilities, and more welfare programs.

Poverty is an economic problem with many undesirable social consequences.

Further, there is evidence that poverty breeds poverty—that the children of the poor grow up and marry others who are similarly deprived. They tend to have more children than they can provide with an adequate start in life. These children are likewise raised in a poverty environment, and so the cycle perpetuates itself from one generation to the next.

Can We Eliminate Poverty?

Considering the high cost of poverty, what can be done about America's nation of the poor? In order to launch an attack on the problem, Congress passed the *Economic Opportunity Act* of 1964. This law declared that a national policy goal will be:

> to eliminate the paradox of poverty in the midst of plenty in this Nation by opening to everyone the opportunity for education and training, the opportunity to work, and the opportunity to live in decency and dignity.

The Economic Opportunity Act opened a door to waging a war on poverty. In addition, a number of specific proposals—beyond those involving improvements in the welfare system itself—have been advanced. These proposals fall loosely into three groups: (1) family allowances or guaranteed annual incomes, (2) negative income taxes, and (3) combinations of both.

Family Allowances or Guaranteed Annual Incomes

A family-allowance plan would give every family, regardless of income, an annual stipend based on the number and age of its children.

Many sociologists and social workers have suggested the adoption of a *family-allowance system*. Under this plan, every family in the country, rich or poor, would receive from the government a certain amount of money based exclusively on the number and age of its children. Those families that are above certain designated income levels would return all or part of the money with their income taxes; those below specified income levels would keep it. More than 60 nations, including Canada and all the European countries, give such family allowances.

A modified version of the family-allowance plan is the *guaranteed annual income*. This would award all families under the poverty line a straight allowance for each parent plus specified amounts for each child according to the size of the family. If the family's income were to rise, the payment would be reduced until a break-even level a little higher than the poverty line were reached.

Under both the family-allowance and guaranteed-annual-income plans, families would not be as well or better off by not working. Nevertheless, there is substantial opposition to these proposals in Congress. This is partly because of the fear that the programs would be too costly, and partly because many legislators believe that the plans place more emphasis on governmental "big brother" paternalism than on providing jobs.

Negative Income Taxes

A negative income tax would provide the poor with a kind of reverse income tax.

A scheme that has received widespread interest and support from liberal and conservative economists, business executives, and political leaders has been the *negative income tax*. This would guarantee the poor a certain minimum income through a type of reverse income tax. A poor family, depending on its size and private income level, would be paid by the government enough either to reduce or close the gap between what it earned and some explicit minimum level of income, which might be equal to, or modestly above, the government's designated poverty line. The size of the payments, of course, would depend on the specific formula adopted. A hypothetical illustration appears in Exhibit 4.

Several major advantages are claimed for this proposal.

1. Administrative Efficiency The present governmental administrative machinery—the Internal Revenue Service and the Treasury—would handle records and disburse payments, so that a new government agency would not be needed.

2. Income Criterion Income deficiency would be the sole criterion for establishing eligibility for subsidy, instead of the plethora of criteria that have existed in the past. Many more millions of poor families would thus be eligible. With the resulting expanded coverage, many poor families would have an income "floor" under them and could begin to break the cycle of poverty that has kept some of them on welfare for several generations.

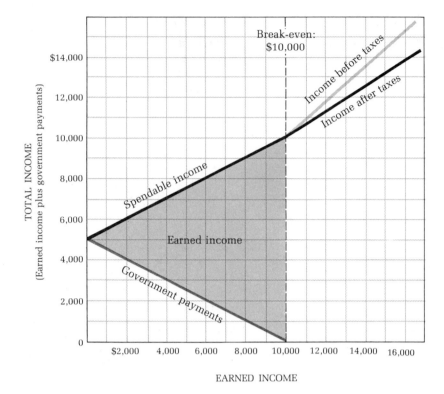

EARNED INCOME

Exhibit 4

How the Negative Income Tax Might Work

(annual data—hypothetical)

This is how the negative income tax might work for a family of four, consisting of two adults and two children:

1. As the family's income increases, the government payments decrease according to this formula:

$$\frac{\text{government}}{\text{payments}} = \$5,000 - \tfrac{1}{2}(\text{earned income})$$

Thus, you can verify with the formula or from the table that if earned income is zero, the family receives a government payment of $5,000 per year. If earned income rises to $2,000, the family receives a government payment of $4,000, giving it a spendable income of $6,000. Similarly, at an earned income of $4,000, the government payment is $3,000, thus making spendable income $7,000.

2. The break-even point occurs at an earned income of $10,000. At this point, government payments are zero, and at higher income levels the family begins to pay income taxes.

(1) Earned income	(2) Government payments $5,000 − ½(1)	(3) Spendable income (1) + (2)
$ 0	$5,000	$ 5,000
1,000	4,500	5,500
2,000	4,000	6,000
3,000	3,500	6,500
4,000	3,000	7,000
5,000	2,500	7,500
6,000	2,000	8,000
7,000	1,500	8,500
8,000	1,000	9,000
9,000	500	9,500
10,000	0	10,000

3. Note that the following equation is always true:

$$\frac{\text{spendable}}{\text{income}} = \text{earned income} + \frac{\text{governments}}{\text{payments}}$$

3. Incentive Maintenance If a family's income were to increase, payments from the government would decrease by some proportion, but not by as much as the increase. Thus, the incentive to work in order to gain more income would not be reduced.

Despite these advantages, however, there are various difficulties that must also be recognized.

1. High Cost The negative income tax could not be administered, as many of its proponents claim, with only a small addition to the staff of the Internal Revenue Service. Checks would have to be sent out monthly or weekly, and effective controls to prevent abuse would need to be established. This large task would require substantial changes in the administrative structure of the IRS.

2. Opposition by Middle-Income Groups Workers in the middle-income groups would receive no benefits from the negative income tax, as they would from a family-allowance plan. In addition, they would undoubtedly resent paying taxes to subsidize families whose annual incomes were in some cases only a few hundred dollars less than their own.

Combining the Family-Allowance and the Negative-Income-Tax Plans

Both family allowances and negative income taxes have their advantages and disadvantages. In view of this, can a plan be developed that combines the best features of both? One possibility, which may be called an

An income-allowance system that combines both the family allowance and negative income-tax plans can be devised.

"income-allowance plan," is illustrated for a family of four in Exhibit 5. The same model can be adapted to larger or smaller families.

Look at the table first. The essential feature of the plan is that it grants an annual monetary allowance to each member of a family—regardless of the family's income. (Of course, an upper limit can be set on the total amount granted to any family, and separate allowances can be provided for those covered by OASDHI insurance.) Assuming that the allowance is $500 for every man, woman, and child and that the tax rate is 30 percent on earned income (income other than the allowance), the way in which the plan would affect a family of four is shown in the table. Note that, at any level of earned income before tax, the family's earned income after the 30 percent tax, plus its fixed income allowance of $2,000, equals its disposable income.

These ideas are also conveyed in the figure. The 45-degree line serves as a benchmark. Along this line, the family's earned income would equal its disposable income if there were no taxes or allowances. However, since taxes and allowances exist, their influences on income are shown by the two remaining lines.

A unique feature of this plan is that it merges the concept of a negative income tax with the existing positive-income-tax schedule. This occurs in the chart where the disposable-income line reaches point A, which corresponds to an earned income before tax of $10,000 and a disposable income of $9,000. Beyond this point, income allowances are zero and the 30 percent tax no longer exists. In its place, the present positive tax schedule prevails. The rates in this schedule will determine the steepness of the line segment AB. A wide range of rates is possible, and no family need end up paying more taxes than it is now paying.

Conclusion: Income Plans Are Not the Whole Answer

A sound income-allowance plan must combine proper work-incentive and job-training programs.

Virtually all income plans have at least three variables in common:

1. An income "floor"—a minimum level of income to be received by everyone.

2. A positive "tax" rate, which decreases the government allowance as income increases.

3. A break-even level of income at which the government allowance is zero.

The problem in setting up an income plan, of course, involves the correct selection of these variables while maintaining effective work incentives. The minimum-income and break-even levels should not be set so high as to discourage people from seeking work or to subsidize those who do not need assistance.

In other words:

> All income plans have the same goal—to put money into the hands of the poor. At best, therefore, income plans can only relieve the symptoms of poverty—not its causes. To cure the disease itself, an income plan must be combined with proper work-incentive and job-training programs. But perhaps even more fundamental is the need to develop better methods for defining and measuring poverty. (See Box 2.)

Exhibit 5
Income-Allowance Plan for a Family of Four
(annual data—hypothetical)

Assumptions: (1) 30% tax on earned income; (2) income allowance = $2,000 (that is, $500 per person).

Both the table and chart show that, at lower income levels, the family pays less in taxes than it receives in allowances. At higher income levels, the reverse is true. For example, when earned income before tax is $3,000, the family pays $900 in taxes and re-ceives $2,000 in allowances, so it has a net gain of $1,100. When earned income before tax is $8,000, the family pays $2,400 in taxes and still receives $2,000 in allowances—a net loss of $400.

When the family's earned income before tax exceeds $10,000, the income allowance ceases and the present positive tax schedule goes into effect. The rate structure of the tax schedule determines the slope of the line segment AB in the figure. Note that the following equation is always true:

$$\frac{\text{disposable}}{\text{income}} = \frac{\text{earned income}}{\text{after tax}} + \frac{\text{income}}{\text{allowance}}$$

Earned income before tax	Income tax at 30%	Earned income after 30% tax		Income allowance		Disposable income
$ 0	$ 0	$ 0	+	$2,000	=	$2,000
1,000	300	700	+	2,000	=	2,700
2,000	600	1,400	+	2,000	=	3,400
3,000	900	2,100	+	2,000	=	4,100
4,000	1,200	2,800	+	2,000	=	4,800
5,000	1,500	3,500	+	2,000	=	5,500
6,000	1,800	4,200	+	2,000	=	6,200
7,000	2,100	4,900	+	2,000	=	6,900
8,000	2,400	5,600	+	2,000	=	7,600
9,000	2,700	6,300	+	2,000	=	8,300
10,000	3,000	7,000	+	2,000	=	9,000

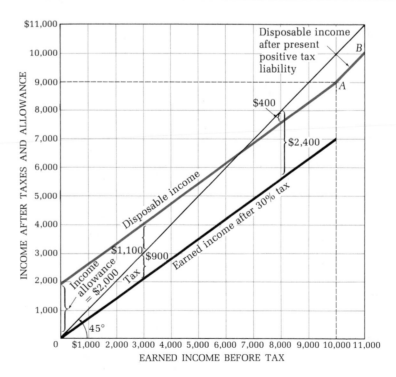

Attacking Poverty Through the Labor Market

Minimum-wage legislation and employment-training programs provide two approaches to dealing with poverty.

One of the problems encountered in trying to eliminate poverty is that a very large proportion of the poor constitute a mixed bag of underutilized human resources. They include not only involuntarily unemployed but also large numbers of discouraged jobless people who have given up looking for work; part-time workers who want, but are unable to find, full-time employment; and full-time workers who hold jobs at inadequate pay.

In view of this, what measures besides family allowances, negative income taxes, and income allowances can be undertaken to improve the lot of America's poor—and thereby wage the war against poverty on yet another front? There are two approaches that operate directly through the labor market, rather than through income redistribution. These are (1) minimum-wage adjustments and (2) employment-training programs.

Minimum Wages

Minimum-wage legislation has had a long history, both at home and abroad. The objectives of such legislation are:

1. To prevent firms from paying substandard wages when labor-market conditions enable them to do so.

2. To establish a wage floor representing some minimal level of living.

3. To increase purchasing power by raising the incomes of low-wage workers.

In the United States, the basic federal minimum-wage law is the *Fair Labor Standards Act* of 1938. Commonly called the Wages and Hours Law, the act has been amended from time to time for the purposes of raising the statutory wage minimum and providing coverage for broader categories of workers.

Analyzing the Effects of Minimum Wages

What are the economic consequences of minimum wages? The answers are not certain because minimum wages have *many* effects and implications in addition to those pertaining to poverty prevention. Before ex-

---

Box 2
Can Poverty Be Redefined?

The government's definition of poverty is based solely on cash income. The definition does not take into account such noncash benefits as food stamps, medical care, and subsidized housing.

What happens when the dollar value of these benefits is included in poor people's incomes? According to a Census Bureau study, the number of families living below the poverty line declines dramatically. The decrease amounts to about 42% if medical services are included and about 16% if they are not. (The reason for excluding medical services is to avoid the impression that those in the worst health are the best off.)

What does this imply with respect to government anti-poverty programs? "People will read into it what they want," said a Census Bureau official. "Conservatives will argue that the poverty problem has been grossly overstated; liberals will say that the figures prove the success of social programs."

However, no action on redefining poverty can be taken until the monetary value of government benefits received by lower- and middle-income families are compared. Among the benefits received by the latter are tax deductions for mortgage interest and tax exemptions on municipal-bond interest and company-paid benefits.

---

amining the issues, you can gain a better appreciation of the problem by analyzing the effects of minimum wages in terms of a supply-and-demand model.

In Exhibit 6, Figure (a), the curves labeled S and D represent the supply of workers and the demand for workers in a competitive labor market. The upward-sloping supply curve indicates that more units of labor will be supplied at a higher wage than at a lower one. The downward-sloping demand curve indicates that a larger quantity of labor will be demanded at a lower wage than at a higher one. If no minimum wage is imposed, the equilibrium price at which labor will be bought and sold —the equilibrium wage—will be at W, and the equilibrium quantity will be at N.

Arguments Against Minimum Wages If society feels that the equilibrium wage is too low, it will support legislation to establish a minimun wage at some higher level. Suppose that the legal minimum is set at W'. At that wage level, the quantity of labor demanded will be $W'J$ and the quantity supplied will be $W'K$. There will thus be a surplus of labor equal to the amount JK. This surplus denotes a pool of labor that is unemployed as a result of government's imposition of a minimum wage. The pool consists of two "types" of unemployed people:

Minimum-wage legislation causes unemployment among workers whose productivities are not high enough to warrant employment at the legal minimum.

1. Those who were previously employed at a wage of W and have become unemployed at a wage of W'.

2. Those who were not previously in the labor force at the wage of W but have decided to enter it at the wage of W'.

Note that the higher the minimum wage, the greater the pool of unemployed. For example, if the minimum wage is raised to the level represented by W'', the new labor surplus will be the amount LM, as compared to the previous smaller surplus JK.

> On the basis of supply-and-demand analysis, opponents of minimum wages conclude that legally set wage floors cause unemployment. The workers who become unemployed are those whose productivities are not high enough to allow them to earn the legal minimum. As a result, they either remain permanently unemployed or seek work in low-wage marginal industries not covered by the minimum-wage law. This depresses wages in those industries still further.

Arguments in Favor of Minimum Wages How do those who favor wider use of minimum wages as a means of alleviating poverty respond to these conclusions? They offer arguments such as the following:

1. The market for labor is not as competitive as the supply-and-demand model assumes. Instead, there is a high degree of employer *monopsony* —monopolistic power—in the hiring of resources. As a result, employers are able to exploit low-skilled workers by paying them less than their productivities warrant. Therefore, by raising minimum wages and by broadening coverage, government can reduce exploitation without causing unemployment.

2. Increases in minimum wages raise both consumer purchasing power and production costs. However, low-income workers spend practically all of their increased wages, creating further increases in income and consumption for others. The resulting expansions in total demand, therefore, more than offset the rise in production costs, thereby stimulating a higher level of employment rather than creating unemployment.

Exhibit 6
Effect of Minimum Wages in a Competitive Labor Market

In a competitive market the equilibrium wage at W and the quantity of labor at N are determined by the intersection of the supply and demand curves for labor. If a minimum wage is imposed, a surplus of labor (unemployment) results. Thus, at minimum wage 1, the surplus is JK; at minimum wage 2, the surplus is LM. In general, the higher the minimum wage, the greater the surplus.

The long-run trend of the minimum-wage rate has been steadily upward. The rate is somewhat less than one-half (usually 40–45 percent) of the average wage rate in manufacturing.

The people who are hurt by minimum-wage legislation are those who lack the skills and training to be hired at the legal wage. These are mostly young people, former homemakers entering the labor force, and members of some racial minority groups.

Russ Kinne/Photo Researchers

(a) SUPPLY-AND-DEMAND MODEL

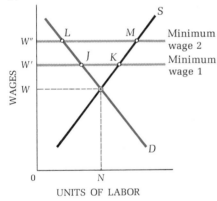

(b) STEADY RISE OF THE FEDERAL MINIMUM WAGE

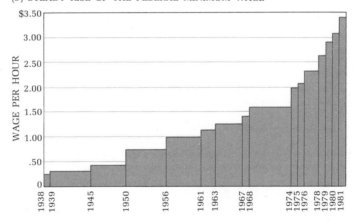

3. Enforced higher wages encourage employers to develop better ways of utilizing their resources. This leads to improvements in efficiency, resulting in benefits for everyone—business firms, workers, consumers, and society as a whole.

Conclusion: What Does the Evidence Show?

In view of the wide differences between opposing camps, what can be said of the link between minimum wages, unemployment, and poverty? This problem has been the subject of hundreds of research investigations, both by government and by academic economists. Out of numerous studies conducted at national, regional, and industry-wide levels, covering periods of cyclical upswings and downswings, the following conclusions emerge:

1. Statutory wage minimums do *not* unqualifiedly aid the poor—as is frequently claimed. Although minimum wages help some workers, they cause unemployment among those who are the least well off in terms of marketable skills or location. These are largely the competitively disadvantaged groups in society—most notably young people, racial minorities, and women.

2. Although minimum wages are a cause of unemployment, it is not known *how much* unemployment they cause. The amounts can vary widely by industry, geographic area, and stage of the business cycle.

The rising trend of minimum wages is shown in Figure (*b*) of Exhibit 6.

In general, minimum-wage legislation may be an effective device for eliminating substandard wages, and there is some evidence that it has been an effective means of reducing poverty. But because minimum wages attack the effect rather than the cause, other measures are needed if the problem of poverty is ever going to be solved.

Minimum wages cause more unemployment among minority groups. But the amount of unemployment caused by minimum wages is unknown.

Employment-Training Policies and the Dual-Labor-Market Theory

A second approach to attacking poverty via the labor market is through *employment-training policies.* These are deliberate efforts undertaken in the private and public sectors to develop and use the capacities of human beings as actual or potential members of the labor force. Many different groups are involved in formulating and implementing such policies. They include government agencies at the national and local levels, employers, unions, colleges, and voluntary organizations. Despite such diversity, however, there is widespread agreement that one of the nation's major employment-training problems is to find adequate jobs for its poor.

Most middle-class Americans believe—because they have been taught to believe—that anyone who really wants to work can find a "good job." The facts indicate that this is not so. Evidence suggests that there exists what may appropriately be called a *dual labor market* This market consists of two submarkets:

Employment-training policies provide another approach to dealing with poverty through the labor market.

1. A primary labor market, in which jobs are characterized by relatively high wages, favorable working conditions, and employment stability.

2. A secondary labor market, in which jobs, when they are available, pay relatively low wages, provide poor working conditions, and are highly unstable.

Blue-collar workers, many of whom are union members, and white-collar workers constitute most of the primary market. In contrast, the competitively disadvantaged poor—the unskilled, the undereducated, and the victims of racial prejudice—are largely confined to the secondary market.

In view of this:

Employment-training policies for the disadvantaged, at the very least, must provide employment opportunities for individuals who want to work but are unable to find a job. More specifically, such policies must seek to accomplish two goals: (1) to provide opportunities for those in the secondary market to qualify for primary employment, and (2) to improve the quality of secondary employment.

Conclusion: Coordinated Efforts Needed

Employment-training policies must be combined with some type of income-allowance plan in order to wage a successful war against poverty.

What can be done to reach these goals? A number of specific measures have existed for many years. Others have been suggested, some of which are in various stages of discussion within the government. Generally speaking, all such policies follow three main avenues of attack:

1. They seek to break down discriminatory employment practices through government legislation, subsidies, and employer education.

2. They try to upgrade workers from the secondary to the primary market through training and job-experience programs.

3. They attempt to qualify people for employment in the primary market by providing education, counseling, and related services.

> Despite these efforts, employment-training policies by themselves cannot solve the poverty problem. Such policies have to be coordinated with other measures—such as a negative-income-tax plan or an income-allowance plan—if significant advances are to be made. But even this may not go far enough in helping poor people to find adequate jobs unless our present methods of matching workers with jobs can be integrated effectively into a total employment-training system.

Economics and Discrimination: Racism and Sexism

One of the most important social problems of our time, and one that exists in all societies, is *discrimination*. This term is widely used today to refer to the differential treatment of persons.

The most pervasive types of discrimination are racism and sexism. From what you now know about economics, it is interesting to see some of the ways in which these common forms of discrimination can be analyzed in terms of supply and demand. Two practical situations that may be considered are (1) the effect of neighborhood integration on property values, and (2) discrimination in employment.

Neighborhood Integration and Property Values

Economic principles can be used to analyze discrimination in housing.

You will often hear it said that, when blacks move into a white neighborhood, property values decline. Although there is insufficient scientific evidence to confirm or refute this hypothesis, it is instructive to examine conditions under which it may or may not be true.

In Exhibit 7, the curves S and D represent the normal supply and demand for housing in an unintegrated (white) neighborhood. The equilibrium price of housing is at P and the equilibrium quantity at Q. Now suppose that a black family buys a house in the area. If neither the neighbors nor potential buyers harbor any racial prejudices, the supply and demand curves will be unaffected and the equilibrium price and quantity will remain at their present levels.

Suppose, however, that some of the neighbors have a prejudice against blacks. If those neighbors do not want to live in an integrated area, they might decide to sell their houses at a price below what they would have accepted earlier. The supply curve of housing will therefore shift to the right from S to S'. As a result, the equilibrium price will decline to the level at P_1 and the equilibrium quantity will increase to the level at Q_1.

Of course, sellers are not the only ones who can discriminate against blacks. Some potential buyers may, too. If buyers discriminate, they will be willing to buy less housing at any given price than they were willing to buy before. The effect of this action is to shift the demand curve to the left—from D to D' in the diagram. The intersection of the new demand curve D' with the new supply curve S' determines a still lower equilibrium price and a lower quantity—namely, P_2 and Q_2—than existed when sellers discriminated but buyers did not.

Conclusions: Whites Cause Decline

Several important conclusions emerge from this analysis:

First, property values will be unaffected by neighborhood integration if neither white sellers nor white buyers discriminate against blacks.

Second, property values will be driven down by neighborhood integration if white sellers or white buyers discriminate. The amount by which property values deteriorate will depend on the intensity of discrimination—the extent to which the supply curve is shifted to the right or the demand curve is shifted to the left—as a result of integration.

In general:

Property values do not decline because of integration per se. They decline because some *whites discriminate against blacks*, thereby bringing about the deterioration in property values that whites fear.

Discrimination in Employment

There is a great variety of occupations which women have begun to claim as fields for individual effort from which no intelligent, refined man who views things as they really are would seek to exclude them.

Scientific American,
September 1870

More than a century has elapsed since *Scientific American's* editorial. Yet there is much evidence that women are still a long way from job equality with men. Despite substantial progress, various studies show that women often earn up to one-third less simply because they are women. (See the table in Exhibit 8.)

Much the same is true of certain minority groups. Blacks, Asians, homosexuals, and members of many other groups have long been victims of discrimination in employment. Some of the effects of this discrimination, and some of the effects that would occur if discrimination were eliminated, are described in the following discussion. discussion.

Two-Market Model

An opportunity for discrimination exists when a market can be divided into homogeneous submarkets. Price and quantity can then be established in each submarket through the separate interactions of supply and demand. An illustration of this is shown in the two-market model of Exhibit 8. Figure (a) represents a primary labor market for males. Figure (b) depicts a secondary labor market for females. (The same model could be used to analyze discrimination between whites and blacks, skilled and unskilled, or other competing groups.)

In Figure (a), the demand curve D for labor in the primary market intersects the supply curve of males, S_M. This results in an equilibrium wage rate for males at W_M and an equilibrium quantity of male employment, Q_M.

Exhibit 7
Effects of Neighborhood Integration

If, as a result of integration, either the supply curve of housing shifts to the right or the demand curve for housing shifts to the left, the equilibrium price of housing will decline. But the decrease will be caused by those who discriminate, not by those who are discriminated against.

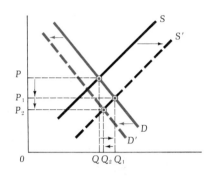

Discriminatory practices can often be analyzed by dividing a total market into its constituent submarkets.

Because women are excluded from the primary market, they must seek employment elsewhere—namely, in the secondary market represented by Figure (b). In this market, occupations are less productive than in the primary market. As a result, Figure (b) shows that the demand for women's services is less, and the supply of females looking for jobs is smaller, than the demand for and supply of men's services in Figure (a). The economic consequence of this is that the equilibrium wage rate for females, W_F, and the equilibrium quantity of female employment, Q_F, are less than W_M and Q_M.

How can this situation be corrected? The ideal solution would be to eliminate discrimination by permitting women to compete with men in the primary market. If this were done, the supply curve of females S_F in Figure (b) would be added to the S_M curve in Figure (a), yielding a new total market supply curve of males and females, S_{M+F}.

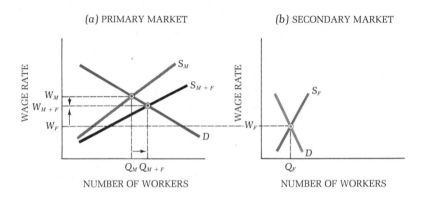

(a) PRIMARY MARKET   (b) SECONDARY MARKET

Exhibit 8
Sexism in the Labor Market

Discrimination based on sex results in women earning less than men for the same work. It also causes greater total unemployment and lower productivity.

Occupation	Weekly median pay		
	Women	Men	Women's pay as a percentage of men's
Clerical workers	$220	$328	67%
Computer specialists	355	488	73
Editors and reporters	324	382	85
Engineers	371	547	68
Lawyers	407	574	71
Nurses	326	344	95
Physicians	401	495	81
Sales workers	190	366	52
Teachers (elementary)	311	379	82
Waiters	144	200	72

Conclusion: Favorable Effects of Eliminating Discrimination

As you can see from Figure (a), the elimination of discrimination would have several major effects.

First, total employment would be raised from the level at Q_M to the level at Q_{M+F}. This would also lead to increased production because women would be employed in more productive jobs than before. Consequently, society would benefit by receiving a larger volume of output for the same labor input that went to the segregated markets.

Second, the equilibrium wage of females would increase, and the equilibrium wage of males would decrease, to the level at W_{M+F}. Further, the increase in wages received by women would more than offset the decrease in wages received by men. Society, therefore, would experience a *net monetary gain.*

Perhaps most important:

> The increased wages received by women would not come at the expense of reduced wages received by men. It would come from the *gain in productivity* and the additional output that would result from the elimination of discrimination.

Of course, these conclusions depend on the responsiveness (elasticities) of demand and supply, and on the relative productivities of males and females. Such considerations should be kept in mind if a more complete analysis of discrimination is undertaken.

What You Have Learned in This Chapter

1. The U.S. social security system is based primarily on the Social Security Act of 1935 and its many subsequent amendments. Through social insurance, the system provides a measure of protection against old age, unemployment, disability, ill health, and death. Through charity, the social security system provides welfare services for the needy. However, the payroll tax that contributes to financing the system is regressive, bearing down most heavily on low- and middle-income groups.

2. Poverty is one of today's most fundamental issues, affecting about 25 million Americans. The basic types of poverty are cyclical poverty, community poverty, and personal poverty. The great social costs of poverty have resulted in many proposals for reform.

3. Various income schemes and assistance plans have been proposed to revise and improve our welfare system. Among the most popular are family allowances, the guaranteed annual income, and the negative income tax. No matter which approach or combination of approaches is adopted, it must be combined with a work-incentive and job-training program if it is to remove people from a lifetime on the dole and make them productive, useful members of society.

4. The problem of poverty can be attacked through the labor market. Two approaches that have been considered are (a) minimum-wage adjustments, and (b) employment-training programs. The preponderance of evidence indicates that minimum wages create adverse employment effects—particularly among competitively "disadvantaged groups" —but the size of the effects are not known. On the other hand, employment-training programs, to be successful, must recognize the existence of a dual labor market and seek to provide opportunities for those in the secondary market to qualify for primary employment.

5. Economic analysis demonstrates that two common forms of discrimination, racism and sexism, create misallocations of society's resources. Further, these misallocations are caused by those who do the discriminating, not by those who are discriminated against.

For Discussion

1. *Terms and concepts to review:*
Social Security Act (1935)
unemployment benefits
poverty line
family-allowance plan
guaranteed annual income
negative income tax
Fair Labor Standards Act (1938)
monopsony
employment-training policies
dual labor market

2. What are the main features of our social security system? Is the system adequate? Explain.

3. Why not solve the problem of poverty by simply redistributing income equally to everyone?

4. It has been suggested that there is a remarkable inverse relationship between human fertility and "hot baths." The latter represents the reasonable creature comforts of life, such as a basic but adequate amount of food, clothing, housing, and sanitation facilities. If such a relationship exists, it might be better to break the poverty cycle by providing poor people with these goods. What do you think of this argument? (**Note** Do you think the same argument could apply to such underdeveloped, overpopulated regions as India and the Far East?)

5. In contrast to question 4, suppose that providing income allowances to poor families increased their birth rates. What might this imply about the elasticity relationship between the supply of children and family income? Explain the various implications of this.

6. Evaluate the income plans described in the chapter as proposals for attacking the problem of poverty.

7. Two measures have often been advocated by political leaders as means of encouraging employers to provide on-the-job training for the disadvantaged: (a) tax incentives and (b) contract or employment subsidies. Which measure is likely to be more effective? Discuss.

8. If blacks rather than whites tend to buy into a newly integrated neighborhood, would property values decline? Illustrate with supply and demand curves.

9. "If job discrimination against females were eliminated, the increase in wages received by women would more than offset the decrease in wages received by men. Therefore, society as a whole would be better off because its net satisfactions would be increased." Do you agree? (**Hint** What does "better off" mean?)

31
CHAPTER

Urban Problems: Can the Cities Be Saved?

Learning guide
Watch for the answers to these important questions

What are the major economic problems confronting the nation's cities? How do education, housing, transportation, and urban finance create interrelated issues of major concern to all state and local governments?

Why would a free market in education improve the educational system? What major proposals have been advanced for "freeing" education?

What types of housing problems exist in most large urban areas? Can specific measures be proposed for widening consumer choices and reducing prices in the urban housing market?

Why are most urban transportation systems said to be unbalanced? How can proper transport pricing and technology serve to reduce imbalances?

What is the nature of the fiscal dilemma facing most cities? Can measures be adopted to resolve the problems? How may Washington play a role in the changing relationship among federal, state, and local governments?

This chapter surveys the major economic problems facing the nation's cities.

The eminent philosopher Alfred North Whitehead once remarked: "The major advances in civilization are processes which all but wreck the societies in which they occur."

According to some observers, American society is already close to being wrecked. Since World War I, the everyday life of the average person in the West has undergone greater changes than it had since the dawn of the Christian era. One of the chief reasons is that a revolution in agricultural technology has shifted a high proportion of the population from the farms to the cities.

In 1918, 50 percent of the nation's population was rural, as shown in Exhibit 1. Today, about 70 percent of the population is urban and living on only 1 percent of the land. By the year 2000, more than 80 percent of the population will be living in urban areas, and much of the remaining 20 percent will be at least "semiurbanized."

This trend toward urbanization has created social and economic problems of enormous significance. Among them are problems of mass transit, suburban sprawl, medical care, education, crime control, housing, urban renewal, and urban unemployment, to mention only a few. As a result, the problems of American cities are among the most seriously debated issues of our time.

The social problems of urbanization are inseparable from the economic ones. To highlight and analyze some of the more important aspects of this extremely complex subject, we shall focus most of our attention on the economic issues.

An Overview of Urban Problems

The problems of American cities result from a unique set of pressures. Some of them are deeply rooted in the nation's history; others go back only a few decades. Taken together, these problems have raised issues and initiated controversies that will be with us for many years to come. Because it is impossible to analyze all the problem areas, we may begin by sketching a few that are of major concern.

Education

One of the most technologically *unprogressive* segments of the economy is education. It has had to expand its resources to meet the needs of a growing population and to transmit the results of a knowledge explosion. However, it has not expanded efficiently—especially in urban areas, where the demands upon it have been greatest. Society has borne the cost in the form of higher taxes and a decline in the quality of schooling, at least as measured by grades recorded on standardized examinations. New ways must be sought to improve the efficiency and quality of education. Perhaps the most promising possibility is to move the public schools out of the public sector, where they have been dominated by rigid bureaucratic controls, and into the private sector, where they can compete freely for consumers' dollars. Some city governments have already taken steps in this direction, and others are giving it serious consideration.

Housing

American cities have long had to face the task of assuring an adequate number of decent homes for everyone. Considerable government aid has been given to the middle-income groups, but not enough to the poor. As a result, the cities are still confronted with a mounting demand for low-cost dwellings. Added to this are the problems of discrimination, which blacks and other minority groups encounter in the housing market. These are among the more important difficulties that make "the housing problem" a multidimensional issue of great social, as well as economic, significance.

Transportation

The ability to move goods and people is basic to the life of a city. Automobiles and trucks have come to play a dominant role, but they cannot carry the burden alone. Hence, the cities must now create properly balanced transportation systems, including highways, buses, trains, subways, and parking spaces. Such systems seek to optimize the use of transportation facilities with minimum congestion and maximum efficiency. At the present time, many urban transportation ills are apparent. They include frequent overcrowding, poor service, inequitable sharing of financial burdens, and inadequate planning for future needs and costs. With the growth of population and industry, these problems will become progressively worse unless new transportation policies are formulated.

Exhibit 1
Urbanization in the United States

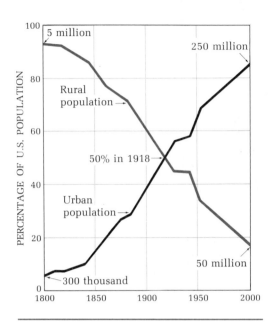

Urban Finance

The most fundamental economic challenge facing the cities is to find ways of raising the money needed to pay for urban improvements. The problems are manifold. Increases in low-income urban populations have brought greater demands for such community services as education, public health, and public safety. Middle- and upper-income groups, as well as businesses, have been moving out of urban areas and into the suburbs, thus eroding the tax base of the cities. Local governments have become fragmented and increasingly inefficient in their efforts to meet new and expanding area-wide needs. What steps can be taken to reduce these difficulties? There are several, but they require for their success that officials at all levels of government be committed to making them work.

The Market for Education

Several methods can be used to improve the efficiency and quality of public education.

One major problem of all large cities is the public educational system. Critics have accused the public schools of being rigid bureaucracies. Conservatives, liberals, and radicals, regardless of race, have complained that the political mechanisms that are supposed to make public schools accountable to their communities have either failed to work or have worked very clumsily. As a result, only the rich now have a choice —they can either move to other school districts or enroll their children in expensive private schools. Most middle- or low-income parents, on the other hand, have no alternative but to keep their children in the local public school. Parents who belong to one of several religious faiths may be able to send their children to a low-cost church school—but such schools are relatively few.

What can be done to correct the situation? One controversial suggestion is to weaken the monopoly powers of public schools by making them more competitive. The argument can be reduced to two basic propositions:

> **1.** If public schools are to provide variety and excellence, they must be subjected to the competitive pressures of a free market in which parents and children exercise consumer sovereignty by paying their money and taking their choice.

> **2.** If consumers are given this opportunity, they will usually choose the better schools and, in so doing, will force the quality of all schools to improve.

This argument has been advanced by many critics from the right and the left. Like all proposed panaceas, it suffers from oversimplification. Nevertheless, it has considerable merit when viewed as part of a larger, comprehensive effort at school reform. Although there are various means, political and fiscal, of encouraging a free market in education, four proposals in particular have received the greatest attention:

1. Decentralization of school systems.

2. Creation of publicly financed private schools.

3. Performance contracting.

4. The voucher system.

An analysis of each of these approaches will provide an understanding of the role that competition can play in a program for school reform.

Decentralization of School Systems

A proposal that is frequently suggested to encourage competition is that school systems be decentralized. This would make them more responsive to the particular needs of their own communities. Most of the people who favor this approach do not base their beliefs on the presumed benefits of competition per se. Instead, they act on the conviction that the interests of minority groups in large cities have been totally disregarded by the monopolistic system. Some community leaders in these cities are therefore demanding control over the schools on the grounds that children are receiving an education that is not only inferior but also dominated by the values of the white middle class.

Would total decentralization of large school systems create the beneficial effects of competition that the advocates of this approach seek? Probably not—for several reasons:

Decentralization of school systems is often advocated. However, there are better methods of achieving desired goals.

Fragmentation of School Systems

Each relatively homogeneous community—whether white or black, rich or poor—would be given monopolistic control over its schools. This would fragment the school systems, reduce their efficiency, and return them to the situation that existed in the 1890s. At that time school administrators cried for consolidation rather than decentralization in the hope of bringing about greater economies of scale.

Resistance to Pedagogical Reform

The biases and bigotries of each community would be given a disproportionate influence over the education of the community's children, most of whom are not likely to remain in the same district after their schooling is completed. Further, because teachers are professionals who seek to apply professional standards, they would resent working under local pressures and find it extremely difficult to introduce pedagogical reform.

Student Immobility

Parents who are dissatisfied with the decentralized school system in one district may in principle be able to move to another. Whether they can do so *in fact* is doubtful. In New York, Chicago, and other major cities, the better schools would be unable to absorb the large numbers who would want to enroll. And in the suburbs, students from lower- and middle-income minority groups would continue to be effectively restricted from the better schools located in middle-income white communities.

Because of these educational drawbacks, total decentralization is not likely to materialize—mainly for economic reasons. There is a growing awareness on the part of all concerned that excessive decentralization can be too costly a way to achieve the benefits of competition.

Large-scale decentralization may be too costly a method of improving educational quality.

Publicly Financed Private Schools

A second proposal for providing free consumer choice in education is the use of public money to create both public and private schools. The latter would be designed to meet the needs of particular minority groups. This means that a typical large city would have not only its own public schools but also private schools run by different religious, racial, and ethnic groups for their own constituents. The private schools might receive public financial support based on enrollment, community income levels, or other criteria—somewhat as certain private American universities receive partial financial aid from the federal government.

This proposal is actually another form of decentralization. The difference is that it bases decentralization on religion, race, and culture instead of geographic location. This would create competition among schools—but not necessarily in terms of educational quality. Even though such schools would theoretically be open to all, they would in effect be segregated by religious, racial, and cultural differences. Admittedly, segregation has long existed in many school districts. However, publicly financed private schools would tend to perpetuate and perhaps even encourage it, certainly not to reduce it.

Performance Contracting

Under performance contracting, school systems would allow firms to bid for the opportunity of supplying the community with its educational needs.

A third competitive scheme proposes that each school district specify the exact educational program it wants and then invite private firms to bid for the opportunity of supplying the desired "package." The firm with the lowest price would be awarded the contract. This scheme would stimulate competition and growth in the educational-systems industry, thereby encouraging the development of better teaching machines, learning materials, and other pedagogical aids. Parents, children, and taxpayers would all benefit because they would be getting the program they want at the lowest possible cost, and school districts would be making the most efficient use of the limited funds available to them.

This plan, known as *performance contracting*, has had considerable appeal. Its chief difficulty is that its results are not always easily measurable. Although certain parts of education are well defined and involve the acquisition of basic skills that can be measured, many other parts are ill defined and consist of learning how to relate, interpret, and appreciate. These latter parts are not ordinarily susceptible to the type of measurement that would be needed for evaluating the effectiveness of performance contracts. As a result, this proposal, which has been tried in some school systems and has been strongly resisted by teachers and administrators, has had only limited success.

The Voucher System

Under a voucher system, families would be able to choose the schools they want.

A fourth proposal for increasing competition is to give money, or more specifically "vouchers," to families with children and let them choose the school they want—public, parochial, or private. The vouchers would be equivalent in value to the community's expenditures per public-school pupil. For each pupil in a given family enrolled in a given school, the family would give the school one voucher. The city would then reimburse the school by the amount of the voucher. This scheme has long been advocated by leading educators and economists.

According to its supporters, the voucher system would promote competition in several ways.

1. Schools would be pressured into stating their objectives and programs clearly—and into living up to them, at the risk of being squeezed out of the market.

2. Assuming an "open-enrollment" policy, parents would be free to choose the type of school that seemed best to them—traditional or progressive, private or public.

3. If "bonus" vouchers for poor or disadvantaged youngsters were provided, as some supporters of the plan have suggested, schools that have significant numbers of such pupils could better afford to develop programs that meet the needs of those students.

4. Some of the better suburban schools, faced with mounting educational expenditures and deficits, might be encouraged to recruit poor students from the inner cities. This would help bring about a greater degree of socioeconomic and racial integration.

The voucher system, therefore, would provide lower-income families with a range of choices in education that is roughly comparable to that enjoyed by the middle class. This by itself may make it worthy of adoption. Nevertheless, those who support the plan are well aware of its controversial nature and shortcomings. Among them:

The voucher system would provide families with a wide range of choices.

1. It might encourage the creation of racially segregated schools—a trend that would run counter to the stated objectives of the government.

2. It would lead to public support of parochial schools, thereby violating the Constitutional principle of separation of church and state.

3. It would encourage the establishment of weak schools and "diploma mills" by sharp operators seeking to exploit the public's lack of knowledge of educational programs and curricula.

Several suggestions have been made to overcome these objections. For example, racial segregation could be prevented by requiring each school to fill at least half of its openings by lottery among its applicants. Administrative controls could be introduced to minimize public subsidization of religious instruction. And, last but not least, state-supervised educational and accreditation standards could be vigorously enforced to prevent the establishment of fly-by-night schools.

The voucher system has been adopted on a limited, experimental basis by only a few, relatively small, school districts. Unfortunately, it has never been tried on a wide enough scale to permit firm conclusions to be drawn.

Conclusion: Comprehensive Reform for Greater Efficiency

There is substantial agreement that increased competition is needed to improve the efficiency of education in this country. One of the first steps that should be taken is to weaken the monopolistic power of public education. If each school system were to turn itself into an educational marketplace in which children and their parents could afford to choose the type of school they want, it would become more sensitive to the real needs of children and their parents. However:

Competition in education would improve efficiency, but it would not be the whole answer.

> Competition in education is not a complete solution. Educational quality should not be decided exclusively in the marketplace, because most parents and children are not capable of evaluating the product they are buying. Nevertheless, they should have some significant influence over its quality. Therefore, what is needed is a comprehensive program of reform in which some competitive elements represented by the proposals outlined here can play a part.

Housing in the Inner Cities

Because of economic, political, and technological obstacles, private enterprise has not been able to meet the housing needs of most major cities.

The desperate shortage of adequate living space for the poor is one of the major failures of American cities. Large-scale and costly efforts by government to solve the problem have met with only limited success. Nor has entrepreneurial initiative succeeded where government has failed. The provision of low-income housing in the inner cities is one activity in which exclusive reliance on private enterprise has proved to be inadequate.

What are the reasons for this? There are many, including problems of taxation, financing, technology, racial discrimination, law, and politics. Because of these complexities, it is doubtful that private enterprise can ever solve the problems of low-income urban housing, or the closely related problems of urban renewal, without the help of a comprehensive housing policy by government. Such a policy has been developing for decades, but it has been painfully slow in its evolution and frequently muddled in its administration.

Government Housing Policies

Although government has failed to complete the development of an effective housing policy, it has not been unconcerned with resolving important issues. Over the years it has:

1. Regulated private housing through zoning laws, building codes, and rent controls.

2. Promoted private housing construction by making available needed supplies of credit.

3. Engaged in the ownership and operation of public housing.

4. Subsidized urban-renewal programs by private builders.

Regulation of Private Housing

The regulation of private housing has led to misallocations of dwelling space.

Government has been directly involved in the regulation of private housing in two major ways. One is by specifying the conditions under which dwellings can be built. The other is by limiting the rents that tenants must pay.

Most local governments have zoning laws that control the allocation of land for commercial and industrial buildings and for residential dwellings of the single- and multiple-family type. They also have building and housing codes that specify standards of ventilation, sanitation, and structural safety. Unfortunately, as illustrated later in this chapter, many of these laws are unduly restrictive, and their enforcement has been weakened by political influences. As a result, their economic effect has been to limit the quantity and types of housing that are most needed for large cities. Consequently, they have also contributed —along with rising population and income—to the upward pressure on rents in these areas.

To curb such pressures, particularly during wartime, government has sometimes imposed rent controls to keep rents from soaring. Rent ceilings may be necessary during emergencies. As a permanent policy, however, they can be more harmful than beneficial—for several reasons:

1. They cause a misallocation of dwelling space, because families who can afford higher-rent apartments are encouraged to remain in inexpensive rent-controlled apartments instead of moving to make room for lower-income newcomers.

2. They limit the returns to landlords as compared with returns on invested funds in other fields, thereby encouraging neglect and even abandonment of buildings.

3. They curb the supply of rental housing and usually cause it to decline.

Over the long run, all three of these factors tend to injure tenants rather than to help them. The experiences of various cities with rent controls, both in the United States and abroad, strongly confirm these conclusions. For example, largely because of political pressure, New York City has retained rent controls in one form or another since World War II. Consequently, it has suffered drastically from all of the effects enumerated above. Apartment buildings in the slum areas of the city are often without adequate heat or sanitation, and many have been literally abandoned by their owners in order to obtain income-tax losses. (See Box 1.)

Promotion of Private Housing

Since the 1930s, the federal government has encouraged the construction of private housing and promoted home ownership through various agencies, including the Federal Housing Administration and the Veterans Administration. It has sought to achieve these goals by expanding the supply of housing credit—through federally chartered savings and loan associations, provisions for mortgage insurance, creation of a secondary market for mortgages, and other devices. This program has succeeded in promoting home ownership by middle-income families, but it has done little to increase the supply of housing for the poor.

Various government-supported "easy financing" programs have promoted home ownership for middle-income, but not low-income, families.

Box 1
Abandoned Buildings in New York City

Rent control in New York and some other cities has contributed to a housing shortage for low-income groups. It has also encouraged many landlords to abandon their buildings in favor of tax losses.

Peter Karas/Freelance Photographers Guild

Exhibit 2

Urban Renewal Decreases the Supply of Housing

Given the demand curve *D* for housing, the destruction of blighted housing by urban renewal decreases the available supply of housing. The supply curve of housing thus shifts to the left from *S* to *S'*. As a result, the equilibrium price rises from *P* to *P'*, and the equilibrium quantity falls from *Q* to *Q'*. In other words, the poor pay more for less housing.

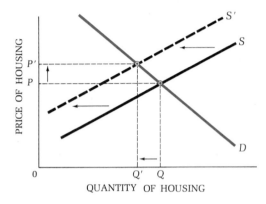

Methods must be found to close the gap between housing costs and what low-income families can pay.

Public Housing

Since the 1930s government has been involved in public housing—housing that is privately designed and built but owned and operated on a rental basis by public authorities. Under the Housing Act of 1937 and its subsequent amendments, the federal government is authorized to extend financial aid to state and local governments in order to help them provide low-rent housing to low-income families. Municipal governments, through the sale of bonds, contribute 10 percent of the total capital investment for each public-housing project, and the federal government pays the remaining 90 percent. The municipal public-housing authorities collect the rents and operate the projects with the objective of breaking even on operating costs. In effect, however, the federal government subsidizes virtually all of these projects because the interest received by municipal bondholders is exempt from federal income taxes, and the projects themselves are exempt from local property taxes. Although public-housing policies have largely succeeded in expanding the supply of low-rent housing, Congressional appropriations, as explained later in this chapter, have not solved many of the practical problems involved in the provision of adequate housing.

Urban Renewal

During the 1950s, there began a pronounced shift in emphasis from the construction of new housing for the poor to the rehabilitation of the cities. Sponsored jointly by federal and municipal governments, and financed primarily by the former, the objective of urban renewal has been to rebuild old or decayed neighborhoods in order to attract industry, stimulate commercial activity, encourage affluent people to return from the suburbs to the cities, and, in general, restore property values and tax yields.

Although urban-renewal programs in the downtown centers of many cities have been impressive, they have also failed in a number of respects. Reconstruction has usually been confined to limited areas without relation to an overall plan. Projects have usually been selected for their commerical value and "show appeal" rather than for their usefulness to the community as a whole. Tremendous hardships have been imposed on many of the people—most of them blacks—who have been evicted from renewal areas but have been given few if any alternative areas to which they can move. And the livelihood of many small-scale neighborhood businesspeople has been destroyed because they are unable to relocate at rents they can afford.

The overall effects of urban renewal, in terms of its shifting the supply curve of housing, are explained in Exhibit 2.

Problems of Housing

The enormous need for city housing poses staggering problems of a complex nature. The first and most fundamental problem is the gap between the housing costs and what low-income families can pay. With the shortage of land in large cities, the kind of housing that is most needed is apartment buildings, either new or rehabilitated. Even if such buildings could be made available in the quantity and density desired, government estimates show that the rental rates for one- or two-bedroom apartments would be beyond the means of most low-income families.

In fact, more than two-thirds of such families could not afford to pay even *half* the estimated rents.

A second problem is that government programs to provide housing for the poor have been inadequate. Congress has created one program after another over the past several decades, but many have been insufficiently funded and very poorly conceived. In fact, they have often overlapped and even conflicted with earlier programs. As a result, they create chaos together with fantastic amounts of red tape, while exerting relatively little impact on urban problems. Nor has urban renewal been of much help. This is because most localities have been concerned with broadening their tax bases and have used urban-renewal programs to construct new commercial development or housing for middle-income or affluent families rather than for low-income families.

Housing programs designed to help low-income families have generally been unsuccessful.

A third problem is that, although rehabilitation of slum housing is an alternative to the construction of new housing, it is not an overall solution. There are several reasons for this. Rehabilitation does not increase the total supply of housing units. It displaces people without successfully relocating them. It is not cheaper than new housing—especially when planning and the costs of rehabilitation are considered. And, it does not reduce the social and cultural barriers that separate the poor from the rest of society.

Approaches to a Solution

There is widespread agreement that ways must be found to broaden the choices available to consumers in the urban housing market. Three general approaches that would lower the price of dwellings are especially noteworthy. These are (1) the adoption of a uniform national building code, (2) government-funded rent supplements, and (3) government-funded interest subsidies.

Uniform National Building Code

Local building codes vary widely in the several thousand jurisdictions in the United States. Most such codes set standards far above what is needed for safety and durability. Many of them also unreasonably restrict the materials and production methods that must be used. The codes are often designed to protect special-interest groups, such as building-components manufacturers and trade unions, rather than to provide the largest possible supply of safe housing at the lowest possible prices.

A uniform national building code that specifies performance and safety standards rather than materials and methods would improve construction efficiency and reduce costs.

To correct this situation, builders' associations, construction engineers, and governmental advisory groups have long advocated a uniform national building code. Ideally, such a code should specify performance and safety standards rather than materials and methods. This would encourage components manufacturers as well as builders to develop new, cost-saving substitutes. Until such a uniform national code is established, there is little hope of improving production efficiency in the home-building industry—an industry that consists mainly of small firms catering to a highly fragmented housing market.

Rent Supplements

A direct approach to widening the housing market for the poor is for the government to supplement a portion of the rental payments of low-income families. This might be done by the government's making up the difference in rents for those families below a specified income level who cannot obtain decent housing at rental rates not exceeding one-fourth of their incomes. (The figure of one-fourth is typically used as a national average by budget-counseling services and welfare agencies, but higher or lower figures might be more appropriate in different regions.) Thus, the tenant pays one-fourth of his or her income toward rent, and the government pays the balance up to the "fair market value." As the tenant's income rises, the government's supplement falls until the tenant is paying the full rent and the government is paying nothing.

The chief disadvantage of this plan is in its administration. Tenants and landlords must be audited periodically to see that the government is not being overcharged. But the plan has several factors in its favor:

1. It gives tenants a wider choice in seeking apartments rather than confining them to public housing projects.

2. It avoids the stigma of "poorness" attached to public housing.

3. It does not reduce the tenant's incentive to work.

Rent supplements thus have some of the features of a negative income tax.

A system of rent supplements was established by the government in 1965. Despite its advantages—including the fact that it is less costly to administer than public housing—it has been politically unpopular and has been supported only on a limited scale with relatively small budgets.

Interest Subsidies

To encourage home ownership by low-income families, the government could subsidize interest payments on housing. That is, it could contribute a proportion of the monthly interest that a family must pay on its home mortgage. To help poorer families who would rather rent than buy, an equivalent arrangement could be made. With this system, the government would pay the landlord a proportion of the contractual interest and the landlord in turn would reduce the tenant's rent. In both instances, the government's interest subsidy varies inversely with the family's income. As the latter rises toward some specified level, the former declines toward zero.

This type of plan was adopted in the Housing and Urban Development Act of 1968. However, it was geared toward helping families whose incomes are just above the poverty line rather than those whose incomes are below it. On the whole, the act made a substantial start toward expanding the supply of new dwellings for low- and moderate-income families. But it was only a start. Extensions of the act are needed if decent housing is to be provided for the poorest segments of the population.

An analysis of rent supplements and interest subsidies, in terms of supply and demand, is presented in Exhibit 3.

Conclusion: A Unified Plan for Greater Equity

Any solution to city housing problems requires some sort of government subsidy. There is a gap between what low-income families can pay for housing and what private enterprise can supply at a reasonable profit. Subsidies are a realistic means of closing this gap.

Through the use of rent supplements and interest subsidies, government could improve both efficiency and equity in the housing market.

Exhibit 3
Rent Supplements and Interest Subsidies Increase the Demand for Housing

Figure (a): In the short run, the stock of housing in existence is fixed. Therefore, the supply curve S is a vertical line—that is, supply is perfectly inelastic or unresponsive to changes in price. Consequently, factors that tend to increase the demand for housing, such as rent supplements and interest subsidies, cause the demand curve to shift to the right—from D to D'. This brings about a rise in the equilibrium price from P to P', while the equilibrium quantity Q remains the same. As a result, the entire increase in housing expenditures is absorbed by landlords as increased rents.

Figure (b): In the long run, the supply of housing has been found to be relatively elastic. That is, it has been highly responsive to changes in price. Consequently, an increase in demand from D to D' leads to the higher equilibrium price P' and the larger equilibrium quantity Q'.

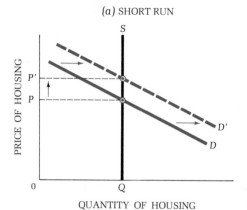

(a) SHORT RUN

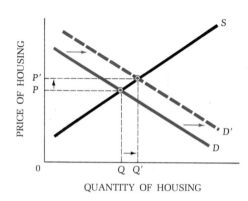

(b) LONG RUN

The most common types of subsidies, in the form of below-market interest rates, rent supplements, and long-term mortgages, can continue, but more extensive plans are also needed:

> An effective and far-reaching program would be one in which the federal government acquires the land it needs, provides for the construction of dwelling units by private enterprise, and pays no property taxes as long as the buildings are occupied by low-income families. However, because the cities cannot afford to lose the taxes on these properties, the federal government could relieve the cities of other financial obligations. Among the major ones that might be considered are health, education, and welfare costs.

The adoption of such a plan would improve social equity by permitting business and government to work together in meeting the housing needs of all low-income groups.

Transportation Systems

Any discussion of urban problems must include transportation. The central task is to reduce the excessive use of automobiles and to encourage other forms of transportation, such as trains and buses.

Why this imbalance? One reason is that rising real incomes have encouraged people to make greater use of automobiles than of public transportation. Another is the Federal Highway Act itself. This law allows 90 percent federal funding for freeways, thereby providing cities with virtually costless highways, which have been too tempting to resist. The result has been mounting traffic congestion, a tearing apart of the cities as well as the countryside, and the creation of distorted transportation systems that tend to increase the private and social costs of movement.

A city's transportation system consists of all the vehicles and "fixed plant" necessary to move people and goods from one place to another. It may thus include not only automobiles, taxis, buses, and trains, but also streets, freeways, stations, parking spaces, and similar facilities. There is no doubt that continued investment in all of these will occur in many large cities during the coming years. However, it is desirable that the growth of urban transportation systems be economically sensible. Therefore, two classes of policy proposals should be considered:

1. Transportation pricing.

2. Technological improvements and innovations in transportation systems.

Transportation Pricing

We know from the study of supply and demand that a price system rations the use of existing goods among buyers who are willing to pay the market price. Further, a price system guides the distribution of resources to their highest-valued uses. Can a price system be used to help correct urban transportation problems?

There is excessive traffic congestion in our cities because of an imbalance between automobiles and other forms of transportation. Most cities have created this imbalance themselves by subsidizing the use of automobiles and discouraging the use of mass transit. They have done this by constructing and maintaining streets and freeways without charging users sufficiently high fees to allow a proper allocation of this resource. Therefore, if the situation is to be corrected, a fundamental principle must be recognized:

> At any given time, the supply of streets, bridges, and other traffic facilities is fixed. If during some period there is congestion on the roads or a shortage of parking spaces, this means that the quantity demanded of the facility at that moment exceeds the quantity supplied. Therefore, a higher price is needed to bring the two quantities into balance—to "clear" the market.

At the present time, the use of most roads is allocated to users on the basis of time delays that motorists are willing to tolerate. Thus, everyone who uses a road at any given moment enjoys the same service. During rush hours, however, a person whose time is more valuable pays a higher price in terms of delays than the person whose time is less valuable. This means that the former, in effect, "subsidizes" the latter.

Variable Tolls

A *variable toll system* would greatly reduce if not eliminate the overall problems of "congestion" and "shortage." For example, if higher tolls were charged during morning and evening rush hours on major free-

A city's transportation system includes all of the resources needed to move people and goods from one place to another.

Congestion of a facility exists whenever the quantity demanded exceeds the quantity supplied at a given price.

ways connecting the suburbs with the cities, users whose time was relatively more valuable to society would still travel regularly at those hours. Others, however, either would shift their travel to alternative roads or to off-peak times or would seek different forms of transportation, such as rapid transit.

Of course, there may be some technical problems in implementing such a proposal, but the solution is well within the grasp of modern technology. In some cases it would be feasible to introduce existing toll systems of the types currently found on various turnpikes and highways. But these might gradually be replaced with such devices as magnetic car identifiers built into the roadways and automated computer systems. Such systems would permit motorists to be billed monthly for the benefits they derive from the use of the roads. A considerable amount of research on this has already been conducted in the United States and elsewhere. In fact, some of the world's largest cities have been experimenting with differential pricing systems in which fares or tolls are based on time, distance, and direction of travel.

Economic analysis thus suggests that, with the development of diverse transportation facilities in the cities, the adoption of a variable toll system would correct much of the imbalance that exists between private automobiles and public transportation. With this system, motorists would continue to have a free choice as to the alternative streets and the amount of street space they wish to utilize. Thus, scarce public streets would be allocated according to the *benefit principle*. This principle holds that people should be "taxed" for a service in proportion to the benefit they receive from it.

A variable toll system makes use of the price mechanism as a way of allocating scarce transportation resources. However, its effective implementation requires some relatively minor technological changes in existing transportation systems.

Public Transit Systems

Variable tolls, as opposed to flat fares, are equally desirable for public transit systems, including subways and buses. Such systems are used at full capacity during the morning and evening peak periods, but they are usually underutilized the rest of the time. Low or even free off-peak fares would relieve much of the rush-hour congestion. Further, such a pricing scheme could be adopted at little or no additional cost to the transit system (other than the expense of installing new turnstiles or fare boxes). This is because the cost of operating the vehicles is substantially the same whether they are full or empty.

A variable toll structure for public transit systems would allocate these resources more efficiently than single-rate tolls.

It is sometimes contended that differential transit fares would burden the poor, because they rely heavily on public transportation. This argument has three major weaknesses.

First, the poor tend to live closer to the inner cities and to travel shorter distances. Hence, a fare based on mileage would actually benefit them.

Second, many of the urban poor who travel to get to work, such as those who perform domestic service in the suburbs or work as cleaning personnel in office buildings, travel against the major flow of traffic or at off-peak times. Therefore, they too would benefit from a differential fare system.

Third, some studies have shown that the poor tend to rely as much or more on public transportation for nonwork trips, so a lower fare during off-peak hours would be to their advantage.

In general, therefore, although some lower-income families would undoubtedly be hurt by a differential fare structure, it appears that many more would benefit.

Technological Improvements and Innovations

In addition to establishing an appropriate pricing system for rationing the use of transportation facilities, various technological improvements and supplemental policies are possible. Three independent classes of proposals, none of which would require a massive investment in new facilities, may be considered.

Changes in existing laws and regulations can go a long way toward improving transportation efficiency in large cities.

1. Electronic Control Systems These would regulate access to urban freeways through strategically placed sensors and traffic signals. Such controls have been employed successfully in a number of cities in the United States and Europe. They are likely to be adopted on a large scale in the coming years.

2. Subsidies These can be used to reorient bus services in the inner cities. Various studies indicate that present bus systems often do not provide adequate connection and transfer points to meet the needs of the working poor—especially those who must commute by bus to work in the suburbs.

3. Taxicab and Jitney Services These can be expanded. Merely by relaxing somewhat the restrictions that nearly all cities impose on the supply of taxis, their number could be increased and the rates reduced. Also, by permitting the use of jitneys—that is, cars or station wagons that carry passengers at nominal rates over a regular route (a very common form of public transportation in many foreign and in some American cities)—much of the problem of automobile congestion in the cities would be eliminated.

Conclusion: An Efficient "Transport Mix"

The cities can do a great deal at relatively little cost to relieve the transportation pressures they now face. These pressures differ from city to city. Therefore:

The money that is saved by improving transportation efficiency can be used to meet other urban needs.

> Experimentation with new and flexible approaches is needed to find an efficient "transport mix"—one suited to the special requirements of each city. The money that can be saved from optimum use of a well-designed transportation system might better be spent on education, housing, pollution abatement, and other measures that will make the city a more desirable place in which to live.

A major problem in urban transportation is described in Box 2.

Financing Local Government: Our Urban Fiscal Dilemma

Any discussion of urban policies must eventually deal with the difficult problem of financing public services. Why does a problem exist? Wilkins Micawber, a character in Charles Dickens's novel *David Copperfield*, described a situation that epitomizes the financial squeeze that many of our cities are experiencing today:

> Annual income twenty pounds, annual expenditure nineteen six: result, happiness.
> Annual income twenty pounds, annual expenditure twenty pounds ought and six: result, misery.

Joe Munroe/Photo Researchers

Charles Harbutt/Magnum Photos

Ray Ellis/Photo Researchers

Box 2
Urban Transportation:
Economic Solutions to
Imbalances

The major transportation problem facing large cities is to get hundreds of thousands —and in some cases millions —of people to and from work in the central business districts with safety, minimum congestion, and reasonable comfort. The economic difficulties of accomplishing this include problems of costs, revenues, pricing, and financing.

Costs are a problem because mass-transit systems such as commuter trains and subways suffer from a limited ability to adjust variable costs to fluctuations in passenger volume. They also require large amounts of capital investment to provide for modernization and expansion.

Revenues are inadequate because political pressures have forced regulatory agencies to keep tolls and fares low—too low to meet operating costs, let alone replace obsolete equipment. Pricing policies create other difficulties; distorted fare structures have caused some facilities to be overused while others are relatively idle. Financing is hard to obtain because efforts to support mass-transit operations out of general funds have met with considerable resistance. Many people feel that mass transit benefits only commuters, rather than the public as a whole; and most cities and states are financially hard pressed.

Fast, efficient mass transit is vital to the economic health of our big cities. Two guidelines for policy may be suggested:

• Public funds should subsidize both capital investment and operating costs for mass transit. Attempts to cover constantly rising operating expenses by increasing fares have diverted commuters to highways.

• Tolls for the use of highways, bridges, and tunnels should more closely reflect the private and social costs of commuting by private car. The excess revenues should be allocated to mass transit. Such action would help to offset current highway-biased subsidy arrangements.

Can variable toll systems, which charge higher prices during peak periods and lower prices during off-peak periods, help reduce imbalances in the utilization of transportation facilities?

The costs of urban public services have risen faster than urban tax revenues. As a result, many cities find themselves facing fiscal problems.

This is indeed the essence of America's urban fiscal dilemma. The reasons for it can be summarized briefly:

1. As our population expands and our economy grows richer, we not only purchase more goods and services from the private sector but also increase our demands on the public sector.

2. To meet these demands, urban governments must increase their expenditures on virtually all types of public services. These include sanitation, police and fire protection, education, health, welfare, transportation, recreation, and cultural facilities.

3. While cities have been left to grapple with soaring municipal costs, the groups that pay the heaviest share of taxes—business firms and middle-income families—have for decades been moving to the suburbs. These groups have been replaced by an ever-expanding population of the poor, who are especially in need of (but unable to afford) the more expensive education, welfare services, and health services, in addition to other public benefits.

Because of these conditions, most cities face a growing fiscal problem. To raise the revenue needed to pay for public services, taxes must be increased. However, taxes in the cities are already burdensome, and further increases may only hasten the exodus of people and businesses to nearby suburbs, where taxes are lower and various other aspects of business and family life are more favorable.

Most cities have frequently had deficits amounting to many millions of dollars—deficits that they have covered by dipping into reserves, by borrowing against future budgets, and by selling long-term notes. Not since the depression of the 1930s, however, has the plight of many city treasuries been as bleak as it has been in recent years.

Several methods exist for coping with the fiscal problems of cities.

How should the various levels of government direct their limited resources to combat poverty, crime, pollution, eyesores, and slum unemployment while improving education, housing, mass transit, and the other amenities of a better urban life? The solution rests on finding more effective ways of raising revenues while improving the efficiency of local government. Several proposals for achieving these objectives may be considered:

1. Minimize fiscal disparities.

2. Utilize revenue sharing.

3. Impose user charges.

4. Restructure the property tax.

5. Establish metropolitan government.

A broad approach to financing urban government should draw on all these proposals.

Minimize Fiscal Disparities

Cities provide many goods and services whose benefits and costs are not appropriately apportioned. People benefit in varying degrees from the expenditures of local governments, and they pay in varying degrees for the values they receive. But the disparities between costs and benefits may be wide because the people who work in the city and the people who visit the city are not always the same people as the taxpayers who own property or live in the city. As a result of these misalignments, there tend to be wide differences not only in the taxable bases and expenditure requirements of the more than 80,000 local governmental units in the United States but also in the quantity and quality of services provided by these units.

"Spillover" Effects

The divergencies of costs and benefits have created extensive "spillover" effects among a wide array of urban government programs. These range from health, education, and welfare services to environmental protection. Two examples of the many "spillover" effects may be given.

Many public services provide spillover effects because of the differences between costs and benefits.

1. The mounting education and welfare budgets of most major cities have been caused in large part by our national agricultural policy. In recent decades, Washington has promoted the subsidization and mechanization of the South's cotton and tobacco fields, driving out millions of workers who have then streamed into the cities looking for jobs. Most of these people are poor and unskilled, and many of them are illiterate. Hence, either they have become public charges or, at best, they have been able to find menial employment at the minimum wage. Meanwhile, many of the "expatriates"—the former residents of the cities— continue to work in the cities and to hold the higher-paying jobs while turning over the bulk of their tax dollars to the suburban municipalities in which they reside.

2. In the area of environmental protection, it was once thought that air and water pollution were strictly local problems peculiar to a few cities. But now it is recognized that geographic boundaries in such matters are largely irrelevant and that the issues are of national or even international concern. Canadian residents, for example, have filed suits in U.S. courts against American firms for contaminating the air over Canada.

In these and many other situations, the disparities between costs and benefits should be minimized. The most effective way to accomplish this is for the federal government to absorb a much larger share of the financial burden. At the present time, state and local governments pay almost all the costs of public safety, transportation (except highways), elementary and secondary education, water supply and treatment, parks and recreation, and garbage collection. In addition, they pay a substantial part of the costs of health, welfare, and social security programs. If a larger portion of the costs of these local activities could be transferred to Washington, many of the spillover effects would be greatly reduced or eliminated and the city governments would be relieved of enormous tax responsibilities.

Spillovers would be greatly reduced if Washington were to absorb more of the financial burden of public services.

Utilize Revenue Sharing

One approach to relieving the mounting fiscal pressures facing states and cities is for the federal government to engage in *revenue sharing*. Such a plan requires that the federal government *automatically* turn over a portion of its tax revenues to state and local governments each year. The justification for this is based on certain fundamental facts and relationships involving both revenues and expenditures.

First, the federal government collects most of the taxes levied; state and local governments collect a relatively minor proportion. The federal government's chief source of revenue is the income tax. Because of its progressive rate structure, the tax yields approximately a 1.5 percent increase in revenues for every 1 percent increase in the nation's total output of final goods and services—its gross national product (GNP). The state and local governments, on the other hand, receive the great bulk of their revenues from property, sales, and other taxes. These tend to increase by about 1 percent for every 1 percent increase in GNP.

Second, state and local spending has been increasing at rates of about 7 percent to 10 percent per year—roughly twice as fast as the growth in GNP. At the same time, state and local governments have met growing public resistance to increases in taxes, the imposition of new taxes, and the sale of bonds—these being the only methods available to finance rising municipal expenditures.

States and cities have long advocated a policy of revenue sharing. This is because it enables them to receive a larger share of the taxes collected by Washington.

According to revenue-sharing advocates, *the salvation of states and cities lies in their receiving a greater share of federal tax revenues.* Of course, the federal government has long poured out money to states and localities, but this has been largely in the form of grants-in-aid for specific programs to which Washington has attached many bureaucratic strings and controls. What the governors and mayors want is a kind of philosophical Jeffersonianism. This is an arrangement whereby the federal government gives out blocks of grants for broad general purposes while allowing all or most of the spending decisions to be made at the state or local level. In this way, by sharing a percentage of its revenues on a fixed basis with hard-pressed states and cities, the federal government can encourage much greater local initiative.

Revenue sharing was approved by Washington in 1972. However, state and local government leaders often complain that the program is inadequate and has not been consistently implemented. Although these criticisms are as much political as economic, there is considerable agreement that revenue sharing when properly applied has been successful.

Impose User Charges

Urban governments should make greater use of fees—or user charges—for the services they provide.

Local governments obtain their revenues from various sources. These include taxation, license fees, interest earnings, special assessments, sales of property, charges for municipal services, and so on. The last item, often called "user charges," offers promising opportunities for additional revenues.

At present, many people receive the benefits of city hospitals, public housing, treated water, mass transit, refuse collection, and public schools. Many people also help support part of the costs of these locally provided services through special payments, rents, and fees, as well as through taxation. The issue is whether the cities should revise their systems of user charges for these services, and whether they should charge for services that are presently financed out of tax revenues.

The answer to both questions is *yes*—for several reasons:

First, a revision of user charges is based on the recognition that, if certain types of services are available too cheaply or at flat rates, their limited supply will be rationed by congestion whenever the quantity demanded exceeds the quantity supplied at the existing price. As mentioned earlier, any mass-transit facility during a rush hour serves as a striking illustration. In such cases, a *differential* pricing structure would provide not only a better rationing mechanism than a single price but a larger total revenue as well.

Second, by imposing charges on certain services that are currently financed entirely from tax revenues, and by varying the charges according to their use, a more efficient utilization of resources and a greater volume of total revenue can be realized. Public libraries, museums, and marinas provide typical examples. The services of these facilities are usually offered free or at little cost to residents of the suburbs as well as the cities. Because the poor make relatively less use of these amenities, the overall effect is for middle- and upper-income households to be subsidized in large measure from taxes paid by low-income groups.

User charges have a number of advantages. Among the more important are these:

User charges would permit greater efficiency in the provision of public services.

1. They enable the municipal government to know the value of its services to its users.

2. They reduce benefit spillovers resulting from geographic differences.

3. They permit greater efficiency of production, less oversupply of services, and larger total revenues than are permitted by tax financing.

But user charges also have at least two closely related limitations. First, they are inappropriate for financing "public goods"—goods whose benefits are available to everyone—such as clean streets, traffic lights, and public safety. Second, they are difficult to apply where specific benefits to users are hard to identify and measure.

Restructure the Property Tax

A fourth approach to improving the finances of local governments would be to revise the existing structure of the property tax. This tax, with its diverse rates and bases, is imposed only at the state and local levels, not at the federal level. Although local governments have other sources of revenue, such as sales and excise taxes, income taxes, utility revenue, and liquor-store revenue, the property tax is nevertheless their largest single source of funds. This tax helps pay the local share of school costs as well as a large part of the expenses incurred for public safety, sanitation, street lighting, and most other community services.

The property tax provides the largest single source of revenue to local governments. Unfortunately, it has several undesirable effects.

Despite its widespread use, the property tax suffers from a number of shortcomings. Three are particularly important.

1. It requires tax assessors to "guess" the market value of taxable property. This is because the true market value cannot be known unless the property is sold. As a result, wide differentials and inequities of assessment exist both within and between districts.

2. The tax is extremely regressive at the lower end of the income scale. It bears down much harder on poorer families than richer ones because housing is such a large part of consumer spending for lower-income groups.

3. It causes "fiscal zoning"—that is, the control of land use in order to maximize the tax base. For example, it encourages laws requiring large minimum lot sizes, thereby raising land costs and discouraging the construction of smaller homes for moderate-income families.

These and other factors make the property tax one of the most controversial in the entire tax structure. Nevertheless, it continues to exist, partly because it raises so much revenue and partly because it is the major tax that local governments are permitted by their states to levy.

The Land-Value Tax

A tax on land (exclusive of buildings) would have several advantages and would overcome the excessive reliance of urban governments on property taxes.

The many bad economic effects of the property tax have resulted in various proposals for its revision. The most desirable and feasible way to correct its deficiencies would be to restructure it in favor of a land-value tax. This is a tax on bare sites exclusive of any buildings or other structures that stand on them. This idea was first proposed by the American economist Henry George in his book *Progress and Poverty* (1879). George advocated such a tax on land as a "single tax" to replace all others. Here, however, it is suggested as a partial but substantial substitute for the property tax only.

The fundamental idea is to tax the annual unearned gains from land. This is the economic rent or surplus that accrues to the owners of land not because of improvements they have made upon it but because of community development and population growth that have caused the market value of land to rise. Three chief arguments are advanced in favor of such a tax.

1. It discourages land from being held out of productive use.

2. It encourages the building of structures on the land.

3. It returns to society the increases in the value of land resulting from economic growth.

The major criticism of the tax is that it is difficult to administer. This is because it cannot distinguish between increases in the value of land resulting from economic growth and increases resulting from improvements made on the land.

What is needed is a revision of the property tax so that it bears down more heavily on land than on buildings.

Even though this criticism is valid, its adverse effects can certainly be mitigated through appropriate tax laws. Experience in other countries that make use of land-value taxation, including such mixed economies as Canada, Australia, and New Zealand, indicates that such laws are feasible and workable.

> At present, the property tax in the United States is relatively light on land and heavy on buildings. Hence, the tax favors landowners, who tend to be in the higher-income groups, and speculators, who find it more profitable to hold land for future resale than to build upon it. By restructuring the property tax so that it bears down more heavily on land than on buildings, these undesirable effects would be greatly reduced without causing revenue losses to local governments. In fact, various studies have concluded that a land-value tax averaging about 5 percent nationally would yield the same total revenue that is now produced by property taxes on land and buildings.

Establish Metropolitan Government

A fifth means of coping with the challenges facing local governments is one that realizes the need for regional attacks on pressing urban problems. This approach is as much political as it is economic. It is based on the recognition that local government authority in most metropolitan areas is too fragmented to provide for overall balanced systems of land use, transportation, public health, and the like. For example, many large urban areas, such as those that include Chicago, New York, Philadelphia, and Pittsburgh, have considerably more than 500 local governmental units each. The effects of such proliferation are fiscal duplication, administrative inefficiency, and suburban separatism, which hurts minority groups.

To help correct these deficiencies, some form of consolidation is needed. One of the more feasible possibilities is to set up a "two-tier" system of metropolitan government in urban regions. Such a system could consist of an area government and local governments, with functions assigned to each. At the area level, the functions assigned could be those that have broad overlapping interests or that offer advantages of economies of scale. Examples are planning, zoning, water supply, sewage disposal, transportation, and public health. At the local levels, community governments could administer their own police departments, fire services, and school systems. Some functions, of course, could also be shared at both levels, if it were advantageous to do so.

There are three major advantages to such a plan.

1. Efficiency would be increased by consolidating some of the functions of smaller governmental units.

2. Governmental units at all levels would become more responsive to human needs and preferences as a result of decentralizing some of the functions of the larger cities.

3. The relationship of local governmental units to the states and federal government would be strengthened by a more rational allocation of functions among the various levels of government.

Metropolitan government has been adopted to varying degrees by some cities in the United States and Canada. But most local officials oppose the idea because they fear the loss of power. Consequently most states have been reluctant to pass the necessary enabling legislation. Ideally, if Washington would expand the program of grants that it already provides for some regional activities, it could offer additional incentives to the states and to local governments by rewarding them financially for initiating plans for the establishment of some form of metropolitan government.

Conclusion: Changing Federal–State Relations

In almost every presidential administration, efforts are undertaken by the federal government to develop "new" economic programs and relationships with state and local governments. Among the more recent examples are two arrangements that have received wide attention—the New Federalism and enterprise zones.

The New Federalism

Should social programs be administered by the federal government or by the states? Those who favor federal administration contend that Washington can avoid much duplication of efforts while assuring that benefits are distributed uniformly. Those who favor state administration argue that state governments are closer to the people and therefore have a better understanding of local needs.

As with virtually all political issues, the solution entails some sort of compromise. One possibility would be for the states to take over all programs in social welfare, community development, education, and local transportation. In return, Washington could provide the states with excise-tax revenues from alcohol, gasoline, tobacco, and telephone services while assuming the cost of health care (Medicaid) for the poor. The increased cost of this arrangement to the states would roughly equal the gain they would realize in higher savings and tax revenues.

Local governments could provide certain services more efficiently if they would consolidate some of their facilities and efforts.

A greater consolidation and sharing of service facilities would promote the concept of metropolitan government.

The "New Federalism" seeks to develop more efficient ways of financing and administering social programs.

Returning certain social programs to the states would not necessarily improve their efficiency.

A program of this kind, called the "New Federalism," was initially proposed by President Reagan. Its purpose was to help streamline the federal government and to return more authority to the states. The program, however, suffers from several shortcomings:

1. At present, the federal government's criteria for allocating tax revenues to the states are based on such factors as population, per-capita income, local tax rates, and unemployment rates. These factors differ widely among states. Therefore, unless a single formula can be developed that is acceptable to most states, any method of allocation will be regarded as inequitable.

2. Within each state, the funding of existing social programs must compete with other state spending priorities. Returning programs to the states, therefore, could result in their spending less for important social programs. Further, it is likely that many states would deliberately cut down on social-welfare spending in order to encourage the poor to move to other states with higher welfare benefits.

3. There is no reason to believe that most social programs can be administered more efficiently at state and local levels than at the federal level. Indeed, state and local bureaucracies are as inefficient and unresponsive as those of the federal government, and they are growing much faster. Therefore, some critics contend, improvements in efficiency can be attained more readily by reducing the number of social programs than by merely transferring them to other levels of government.

Enterprise Zones

Enterprise zones would provide free-trade enclaves in urban areas, thereby encouraging their economic development. To be successful, however, the zones must provide substantial advantages to businesses.

One way of changing existing relationships among federal, state, and local governments would be to aid distressed urban areas by creating "enterprise zones." These are free-trade enclaves with special tax exemptions, located in the blighted, high-unemployment sections of central cities. The purpose of the zones is to attract businesses, thereby stimulating employment and urban development.

Enterprise zones have existed in certain European countries for some time. On the basis of European experiences and making allowances for American conditions, it seems clear that several *incentive* considerations must be kept in mind if the concept is to be implemented successfully.

1. Businesspeople in the urban enterprise zones should be able to expect profits, or rates of return on their investments, to be high enough to compete with those of businesses in suburban areas—or even in more distant areas. This means that the appropriate *infrastructure*—the "social overhead capital" needed as a basis for modern production, such as adequate land, utilities, and municipal services—must be available.

2. Most skilled workers have left the core cities to seek better opportunities elsewhere. Therefore, job training is likely to be an expensive overhead cost, except for retailing and other service-oriented businesses that can utilize relatively unskilled workers.

3. Tax exemptions by themselves are not enough. There may also have to be exemptions from minimum-wage laws, labor legislation, and unnecessarily strict health and safety regulations. In those European countries in which tax concessions alone have been used, enterprise zones have at best been only moderately successful.

In conclusion:

State and local governments must deal with the complex problem of financing public services. Proposals for accomplishing this have ranged from making fundamental revisions in tax structures to establishing regional governments. Because of the difficulties of implementing such measures, it seems inevitable that Washington's involvement in urban problems will become more pronounced. Whatever specific policies are adopted, it is certain that changing federal–state relations, or establishing new forms of federalism, will have profound effects on the future of urban areas.

What You Have Learned in This Chapter

1. Critics have accused the public schools—especially those in large cities—of being rigidly controlled educational monopolies. This makes them insensitive to community desires and unresponsive to the need for change. By subjecting them to competition in a free market, it is argued, the quality of all schools will improve. Four proposals have been advanced for increasing competition: decentralization of school systems, creation of publicly financed private schools, performance contracting, and the voucher system.

2. The inner cities have long been faced with the problem of providing adequate housing for the poor. Government has tried to help, but sometimes has done more harm than good. The ultimate solution rests on developing an appropriate system of federal subsidies to help support low-income housing. The federal government should also absorb the health, education, and welfare costs of the cities so that the latter can afford to exempt all low-income housing from property taxes.

3. The transportation crisis of the cities is due primarily to an imbalance between private automobiles and public transportation. This results in congestion, time delays, and a general misallocation of transportation facilities. Two broad steps can be taken toward developing a balanced transportation system.
  (a) The introduction of an appropriate pricing system, in the form of variable tolls, to ration the use of scarce transportation facilities.
  (b) The introduction of technological improvements and economic innovations, such as electronic control systems, mass-transit subsidy schemes, and relaxed restrictions on the use of taxicab and jitney services.

4. The most fundamental problem of the cities is to finance needed urban improvements and social programs. This requires that they resolve their present fiscal difficulties. Recommended measures include minimizing fiscal disparities, utilizing revenue sharing, imposing user charges, restructuring the property tax, and establishing metropolitan government.

5. Because the cities will experience great difficulties in resolving their fiscal dilemmas, the federal government will become more involved in urban problems. This will lead to changing economic relationships among all levels of government.

For Discussion

1. *Terms and concepts to review:*
benefit principle
revenue sharing
infrastructure

2. Can you propose some guidelines for improving public education in the United States by suggesting the kinds of decisions that should be centralized and decentralized at different levels of state and local government?

3. "If the government would stop interfering in the housing market, the price of housing would adjust to the free interaction of supply and demand and there would be no problem." Do you agree? Explain.

4. Various public transit systems have considered raising their fares during morning and evening rush hours and lowering them at other times. Despite the advantages of such schemes, they have rarely been adopted. Why?

5. If the cities need more money to finance urban improvements, why do they not simply raise taxes or borrow?

6. It may be argued that, when a city makes available "free" museums, "free" golf courses, "free" tennis courts, "free" marinas, and so on, it is redistributing income *from the poor to the rich!* How might this happen? What can be done about it?

32
CHAPTER

Energy and Environmental Economics

Learning guide

Watch for the answers to these important questions

How can a supply-and-demand model be used to illustrate surpluses and shortages of energy? Why is a "high-price" policy a surplus policy? Why is a "low-price" policy a shortage policy?

Which types of energy policies has the United States followed in the past? What were the overall consequences of those policies?

How can demand-reduction and supply-expansion policies help to stabilize energy prices and to reduce dependence on foreign energy sources? Can provisions be made for reducing the burdens of high energy prices on low-income groups?

What types of analytical approaches are useful for dealing with environmental problems? What difficulties are encountered in implementing these approaches?

What policy options exist for reducing environmental damage? How much do they cost? Who should pay for them?

This chapter deals with the economics of natural resources, particularly energy and the environment.

Are there sufficient physical resources available to keep the economy growing at desired rates in the years ahead? Is our nation passing from an era of abundant supplies of natural resources into one of persistent shortages?

These questions are being asked with increasing frequency. From time to time, apparent deficiencies of energy and certain other raw materials, and pollution of air and water, have alerted nearly everyone to resource and environmental issues. For this reason, a course in economics today would be incomplete if it did not devote some time to analyzing these important problems.

This chapter focuses on economic controversies concerning two fundamental classes of resources—energy and the environment (that is, land, air, and water). As you will see, an understanding of the basic issues goes a long way toward formulating public policies aimed at improving efficiency and equity in the use of all types of resources.

Energy Policies

Since the early 1970s, the Arab-dominated Organization of Petroleum Exporting Countries (OPEC), through cooperation of its thirteen member nations, has managed to increase greatly the world price of oil. By severely limiting output, OPEC has succeeded in boosting sharply the average price of exported oil. The consequences of this action, combined with the ability of OPEC to exercise a strong influence over world oil prices, has led political leaders everywhere to consider alternative measures for coping with future energy needs and prices. Two distinct approaches will be explored here: (1) free-market policy and (2) demand-reduction and supply-expansion policies. Each is intended to reduce domestic dependence on foreign sources of energy—and ideally to stabilize, if not reduce, energy prices.

Before undertaking an analysis of the policy alternatives, it is useful to keep certain facts in mind.

First, the economics of energy resources concerns these resources as *commodities*. These include oil, gas, and coal, as well as hydroelectric and nuclear power, both of which are produced from natural resources.

Second, as a nation's output of goods and services grows, so does its need for energy and other natural-resource commodities required to fuel that growth. Consequently, consumption of raw materials has been rising rapidly in all advanced countries. This has led many observers to conclude that the world is moving from an age of relative resource abundance to an era of relative resource scarcity. But, as we shall see:

The basic energy "problem" is not that the needed resources are unavailable. There are great quantities of raw materials in the ground. The problem is economic: *What* energy resources will society choose to extract? *How* will they be extracted? *For whom* will they be extracted?

Free Markets

Economists may not know very much. But we do know one thing very well: how to produce shortages and surpluses. Do you want to produce a shortage of any product? Simply have government fix and enforce a legal *maximum* price on the product which is less than the price that would otherwise prevail. . . . Do you want to produce a surplus of any product? Simply have government fix and enforce a legal *minimum* price above the price that would otherwise prevail.

Milton Friedman and Robert V. Roosa

This quotation explains why some people argue in favor of a free market for energy, particularly for oil and natural gas. Past government intervention, these critics claim, has intensified rather than alleviated energy problems, resulting in gross inefficiencies and inequities. Because indictments such as these affect all of us, the fundamental economic issues are worthy of examination.

Surpluses and Shortages

In Exhibit 1, the S and D curves represent the normal supply and demand curves for a commodity such as energy. The diagram shows three types of market situations that may occur. Their occurrence depends on whether government legislators choose to pursue a free-market policy, a "high-price" policy resulting in a surplus, or a "low-price" policy resulting in a shortage.

1. Free-Market Policy Suppose that the supply and demand for energy are allowed to interact freely and that no governmental constraints are imposed on prices and quantities. It follows that the intersection of the S and D curves will determine an equilibrium price at P and an equilibrium quantity at Q. As a result, there will be no energy shortages or surpluses. The market will be cleared because sellers will be offering, and buyers will be purchasing, precisely the same quantity of energy *at the equilibrium price.*

Exhibit 1
Surpluses and Shortages of Energy

In a free market, the equilibrium price of energy will be at P and the equilibrium quantity will be at Q. But if government institutes measures to raise the price, say to P', the quantity supplied will exceed the quantity demanded by an amount equal to the distance KL. There will thus be a surplus of this amount. Conversely, government measures that cause a reduction in price, say to P", will result in quantity demanded exceeding quantity supplied. There will thus be a shortage of an amount equal to the distance MN.

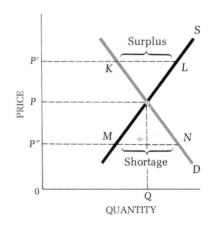

2. "High-Price" Policy What if government legislators wish to pursue a high-price policy? In that case, they will adopt measures that will cause the price of energy to be higher than the free-market equilibrium price. This means that the price will rise, say, from P to P '. At this higher price, the quantity supplied will exceed the quantity demanded by an amount equal to the distance KL. This amount, therefore, represents a surplus of energy *at the higher price.* A high-price policy may thus also be thought of as a *surplus policy.*

3. "Low-Price" Policy As a third possibility, government legislators may choose to follow a low-price policy. In that case, they will adopt measures that will cause the price of energy to be lower than the free-market equilibrium price. Thus, if the price is brought down from P to P″, the quantity demanded at this reduced price will exceed the quantity supplied by an amount equal to the distance MN. This amount, therefore, represents a shortage of energy *at the lower price.* A low-price policy may thus also be thought of as a *shortage policy.*

We are now in a position to define the correct meaning of surplus and shortage—two widely misused and misunderstood terms:

> A *surplus* is an excess. It is the amount by which the quantity supplied of a commodity exceeds the quantity demanded at a given price, as when the given price is above the free-market equilibrium price. A *shortage* is a deficiency. It is the amount by which the quantity demanded of a commodity exceeds the quantity supplied at a given price, as when the given price is below the free-market equilibrium price. Therefore, because a shortage or surplus can exist only *at a given price,* the terms "shortage" and "surplus" have no meaning unless the quantities demanded and supplied of a commodity are related to a particular price.

Oil and Natural-Gas Policies

What are the implications of these ideas for America's energy policies?

For several decades prior to the early 1980s, both the oil and natural-gas industries were subject to extensive regulations. These took the form of legislation designed to create either "high" prices (and therefore surpluses) or "low" prices (and therefore shortages). For example:

High-Price or Surplus Policy Prior to the early 1970s, legislation was enacted that permitted oil-producing states to set quotas (limits) on output and the federal government to set quotas on imports. By thus restricting our total supply, domestic crude-oil prices were kept well above world prices. The way in which this was done is explained in terms of a supply-and-demand model in Exhibit 2.

What were the results of this policy? To begin with, consumers were injured because they had to pay higher prices for petroleum products. In addition, efficient producers were injured because they could not reduce costs by making fuller utilization of their wells. For the most part, the only group to benefit from a surplus policy was the one given the most generous production quotas. This group consisted of the numerous politically influential, but mainly inefficient, small owners of property rights.

Low-Price or Shortage Policy In the early 1970s, the United States reversed its oil policy. As the world price of oil rose due to monopolistic export restrictions established by OPEC, Washington imposed ceiling prices on most domestically produced oil. This created shortages and

Exhibit 2
High-Price (Surplus) Policy for Oil

Government policy sought to establish a "high" price, such as P ', which is above the equilibrium price at P. This was achieved by setting quotas (limits) on domestic oil production and on imports, thereby reducing the quantity from Q to Q '. The supply curve of oil therefore changed from its normal shape (which includes the dashed portion) to P 'JS.

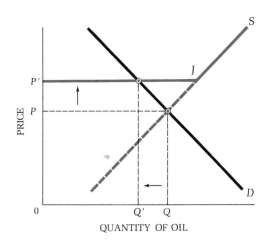

prevented the market from clearing at the higher equilibrium price. Most small, inefficient producers, however, were protected from these adverse consequences by special legislation. Laws were passed requiring large refiners to sell some of their oil to small refiners at lower prices. In effect this procedure taxed the larger, lower-cost firms in order to subsidize the smaller, higher-cost ones.

At the same time, serious shortages of natural gas, another major source of energy, were developing. They were due to ceiling prices imposed on interstate gas sales by the Federal Power Commission. Of course, the officially stated reason for establishing ceiling prices is always the same—"to provide just and reasonable rates to consumers and a fair return to producers." But as you learned in earlier chapters and as explained below, ceiling prices can also have adverse effects.

Free-Market Policy Oil and most natural gas were deregulated in the early 1980s, and their prices have been allowed to seek their free-market levels. But politicians know an unpopular policy when they see it. It is possible, therefore, that some form of energy regulation, resulting either in surpluses or in shortages, will again be established. Because of this, the following overall consequences of previous regulatory policies should be understood.

Government regulation of oil and natural gas resulted in inefficiencies and inequities. These are likely to recur under any new forms of regulation.

> Government regulation of oil and natural gas caused both resource misallocation and social inequities—in two ways:
>
> **1.** Federal and state controls over oil resulted in favoring some firms over others. The burden of this favoritism was borne by consumers and by low-cost producers.
>
> **2.** Federally imposed ceiling prices on natural gas sold in interstate commerce resulted in shortages and in reduced incentives to explore for new gas. This caused many households and businesses to purchase alternative forms of energy, such as higher-priced electricity and oil, for heating purposes.

Demand Reduction and Supply Expansion

A second approach to achieving greater energy independence is for the nation to seek ways of curbing energy consumption or ways of stimulating energy production, or both. What are the economic implications of such efforts? The answer can be best understood by realizing that the growing world demand for energy will assure rising long-run trends of crude-oil and natural-gas prices. However, these rising price trends will have different impacts on the demand for, and the supply of, energy.

Energy Demand: Present and Future Consumption

High prices for crude oil and natural gas will encourage conservation. Household and business consumers of energy will find it more economical to improve insulation in buildings, to purchase smaller and more efficient automobiles, and to pay greater attention to the energy requirements of appliances and machines. When the prices of oil and natural gas are high enough, consumers will also find it worthwhile to install solar-powered air-conditioning systems, where geographically feasible, and to seek ways of substituting other energy sources (such as coal and atomic power) for oil and natural gas. These effects will change the composition of energy inputs and establish a balance that reflects society's preferences for alternative energy goods.

Economic policies designed to discourage consumption are more desirable than outright regulation of production.

Thus, conservation does not mean that energy resources must be left in the ground on the assumption that society will value these resources more highly in the future than it does in the present. Balanced use of resources today is an essential part of making our economy grow. Materials that are incorporated into today's capital goods help to increase tomorrow's production. Therefore:

> True conservation requires that resources be managed in a manner that reflects society's preferences between present and future consumption. This means that an increase in the value of energy today, relative to its expected future value, should lead to a more rapid rate of recovery today. If government regulations and policies prevent this from happening, the nation's resources are misallocated in relation to consumers' preferences. Society thus suffers a net loss caused by inefficiencies and inequities.

Energy Supply: Providing Incentives to Produce

Methods that may be used to encourage production include price guarantees and a system of variable tariffs to provide some degree of import protection.

Rising energy prices will help stimulate exploration and development. But if the large capital investments needed to expand energy output are to be undertaken, producers must be given adequate incentives. Two measures would be particularly appropriate—selective price guarantees and a variable tariff.

Selective Price Guarantees To encourage the development of new products, such as shale oil or synthetic gas from coal, the government could guarantee producers the price of these commodities for a specified number of years. If the market price of the goods rises above the guaranteed price, no government action is necessary. But if the market price falls below the guaranteed price, the government could compensate producers with direct payments to make up the difference.

The chief advantage of this proposal is that it would allow the prices of new energy to be determined in a free market by supply and demand. Government would compensate producers for the difference between the market price they receive and a higher, target price.

The chief disadvantage of the proposal is that the government would have to decide which new energy sources to support. This might discourage production of nonsupported energy sources, thereby leading to increasing government support of the total market. However, the danger of this happening can be reduced if, in its legislation, Congress specifies the life of the plan.

It may be noted that a plan of this type, called a *direct-payments plan*, has long existed for certain farm commodities. On the basis of this experience, there is strong reason to believe that such a plan would encourage producers to seek ways of expanding the output of energy.

Variable Tariff To encourage domestic capital investment, producers must be protected from decisions of oil-exporting countries to disrupt the market for political or economic reasons. Government can provide this protection with a *tariff*—a tax—on the importation of oil and natural gas. Moreover, the tariff should be variable rather than fixed, so that upward or downward adjustments can be made quickly and easily in response to changing international conditions.

A tariff, like any other form of protection, causes resource misallocation and therefore entails economic costs. However, the consequences of a tariff are less adverse than those of the other major protective device —an *import quota*. This is a law that limits the number of units of a commodity that may be imported during a given period. Although relative prices are distorted by a tariff, it nevertheless allows the public to receive the benefits of any low-cost imports that may be obtained. This is because a tariff permits market forces to allocate society's resources. An import quota, on the other hand, stifles competition and creates vested interests among importers, who must apply to the government for import licenses and quota allocations. As a result, import quotas tend to become discriminatory, favoring some importers over others, at the public's expense.

Conclusion: Efficiency and Equity

What broad policy alternatives exist for reducing domestic dependence on foreign sources of energy?

One point of view favors a free market. If oil and natural gas are not regulated, it is argued, energy prices will adjust to the level at which optimum rates of development are encouraged and substitution of less costly alternatives is worthwhile.

A free market in energy, combined perhaps with subsidies and tax measures to help low-income groups, would be more efficient and equitable than regulation.

Another view holds that a free market leads to high prices. These, in the long run, may stimulate development, but at the expense of hardships borne by members of lower-income groups, who spend a larger percentage of their incomes on energy. Critics of a free market therefore advocate price controls and a search for alternative fuels through various government incentives and central planning.

As with many economic controversies, there are important truths in both points of view. An appropriate resolution, therefore, would be one that recognizes the following:

> Experience demonstrates that government cannot successfully program society's future energy supplies. Attempts to do so lead to prolonged surpluses or shortages—and hence to inefficiencies and inequities. Therefore, the adoption of a free market in energy, with provisions for reducing (through subsidies or tax measures) the burdens of adjustment among low-income groups, should be one of our major national goals.

Some interesting trends that may reveal the future of energy production and consumption are discussed in Box 1.

Environmental Policies

The Walrus and the Carpenter
Were walking close at hand;
They wept like anything to see
Such quantities of sand:
"If this were only cleared away,"
They said, "it *would* be grand!"

"If seven maids with seven mops
Swept it for half a year,
Do you suppose," the Walrus said,
"That they could get it clear?"
"I doubt it," said the Carpenter,
And shed a bitter tear.

Lewis Carroll, *Through the Looking Glass* (1872)

The penultimate Western man, stalled in the ultimate traffic jam and slowly succumbing to carbon monoxide, will not be cheered to hear from the last survivor that the gross national product went up by a record amount.

John Kenneth Galbraith

As the carpet of increased choice is being unrolled before us by the foot, it is simultaneously being rolled up behind us by the yard.

E. J. Mishan

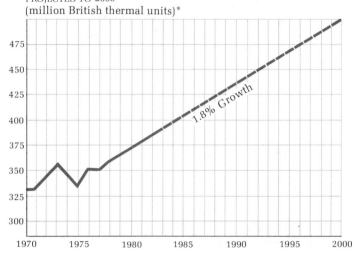

PER–CAPITA CONSUMPTION OF ENERGY IN THE U.S.,
PROJECTED TO 2000
(million British thermal units)*

1.8% Growth

Box 1
Energy: What Future?

The coming years will see substantial changes in America's energy policies. Washington realizes that incentives are needed to spur exploration and production. Otherwise, if the gap between U.S. energy consumption and production continues to grow, it will have to be filled by energy imports. This would increase the nation's reliance on foreign sources of supply, a consequence that political leaders want to avoid.

For natural gas, the future looks particularly bright. There are enough sources underground to provide ample quantities of natural gas through the next century. But at what price? This remains to be seen. If energy prices go high enough, it will become profitable to convert coal into gas and to unlock natural gas trapped in hard rock formations. Still more gas can come from future technologies that are known but are not yet cost-effective at present prices for energy.
Source: American Gas Association.

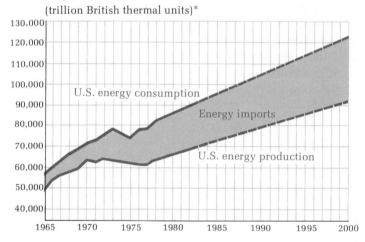

AMOUNT OF ENERGY IMPORTED TO THE U.S.,
PROJECTED TO 2000
(trillion British thermal units)*

U.S. energy consumption

Energy imports

U.S. energy production

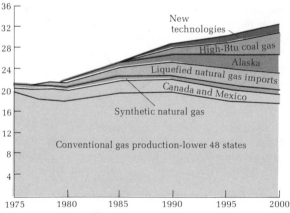

SOURCES OF GAS
(trillions of cubic feet)

New technologies
High-Btu coal gas
Alaska
Liquefied natural gas imports
Canada and Mexico
Synthetic natural gas
Conventional gas production-lower 48 states

*One Btu—British thermal unit—is the amount of energy needed to raise the temperature of 1 pound of water 1 degree Fahrenheit.

These quotations, particularly the last two by prominent economists, suggest that there is a direct relationship between economic growth and the level of pollution. The relationship is such that, as the nation's production increases, so does the inevitable by-product of production, pollution. Further, both of them grow at compound (although not necessarily equal) rates.

What policies exist for curbing pollution? Before answering this question, we should examine some basic economic principles that are useful for analyzing environmental problems.

Economic Analysis for Environmental Improvement

One major challenge of pollution stems from the widespread difference between private costs and social costs. According to classical economic theory, the operation of a free market assures that the price system will automatically allocate resources to their socially most efficient uses. It appears, however, that the price system is not always effective in dealing with environmental factors. As firms seek to maximize profits, adverse side effects are generated in the form of polluted environments, which become social costs—those that are borne by society. The problem, therefore, is to develop modified market mechanisms, as well as nonmarket mechanisms, for allocating resources when the internal or private costs of firms differ substantially from their social costs. Three analytical approaches are useful for this purpose. They are called (1) marginal or incremental analysis, (2) benefit–cost analysis, and (3) cost-effectiveness analysis.

A major cause of pollution arises from resource misallocation due to disparities between private and social costs.

As you will see, the ideas underlying these methods of analysis are applicable not only to pollution control but to a wide variety of other socioeconomic problems as well.

Marginal or Incremental Analysis

One of the most fundamental rules of economics that serves as a guide for making rational decisions is the "marginal" or "incremental" principle:

Marginal or incremental analysis provides a means of judging the optimal level of pollution.

> The net gain of any activity is maximized at the point at which the incremental (added, or "marginal") cost of that activity is equal to its incremental benefit. Thus, expenditures on pollution abatement will result in added costs as well as added benefits. But the degree of pollution will be at an optimum level from *society's* point of view when the incremental cost of reducing it further is equal to the incremental benefits derived therefrom.

For example, suppose that an upstream steel mill discharges its wastes into a river. If by spending a dollar on pollution abatement the mill can save downstream fisheries at least a dollar, it should do so—from the standpoint of society's well-being.

As was pointed out above, a problem arises because of the fundamental distinction between private costs and social costs. The upstream steel mill, for example, disposes of its wastes in a manner that affects others. It does not, however, pay for this disposal. Instead, the mill treats the stream as a free good, and hence the mill's costs of production are lower than they would otherwise be. The downstream fisheries, on the other hand, incur higher private costs because they must absorb the pollutants of the upstream mill.

Therefore, to the extent that prices reflect all production costs, the upstream mill's prices are understated and the downstream fisheries' prices are overstated. The result is a net loss to society because of a failure of all firms concerned to equate their private and social costs. The general consequences are therefore undesirable:

1. Society gets too much steel and not enough fish.

2. Consumers of fish, by paying higher prices, subsidize consumers of steel.

3. Therefore, economic resources are not allocated in the most efficient way.

Most private decisions produce side effects of one type or another. Some may be favorable and some unfavorable. Social scientists refer to such consequences as *externalities*. In the case of pollution, the undesirable externalities can be reduced by special taxes, charges, subsidies, or laws. A fundamental challenge, of course, is to develop methods of evaluating each type of action.

Benefit–Cost Analysis

One method that has been developed for such purposes is known as *benefit–cost analysis*. As shown below, it is a technique of evaluating alternative programs by comparing, for each program, the value today—called the *present value*—of all expected future benefits with the present value of all expected future costs. The calculation employed to arrive at an estimate utilizes a percentage figure representing the opportunity cost of capital. This is a rate equal to what the funds would have earned in their best alternative use of equal risk.

Example Suppose that the present value of expected benefits to be derived from a particular pollution-abatement program is estimated to be $1 million and the present value of expected costs is $0.9 million. Then the ratio of benefit to cost is 1.11 to 1. This suggests that the program may be worth undertaking, depending on how it ranks with alternative investment projects. This is because the benefit/cost ratio is greater than 1. That is, the incremental benefit exceeds the incremental cost, because each $1 of investment stands to return $1.11 in benefits. On the other hand, if the ratio turned out to be less than 1, the incremental cost would exceed the incremental benefit, and the program would not be warranted.

Benefit–cost analysis has been used since the 1930s, primarily in government investment projects for flood control and river-valley development. It has also been employed to evaluate pollution-abatement projects as well as other socioeconomic programs. Among them have been employment training, family planning, vocational rehabilitation, and disease control. Despite its extraordinary success in some of these areas, certain major limitations prevent its widespread application:

1. Benefits Are Difficult to Define and Measure In the case of a smog-abatement program, for instance, certain benefits are relatively easy to establish. Examples are the savings in painting and cleaning expenses that will result from purer air. But how do we define the effects on human life? If the program reduces the death rate from respiratory diseases, the benefit/cost ratio will rise. But if people live longer, the benefit/cost ratio will decline *if* older people become ill more often and require more medical care. Similarly, in a program to reduce the pollution of a lake or river, it may be possible to forecast the probable financial benefits to fisheries in terms of the higher earnings they are

Benefit–cost analysis provides a means of evaluating an antipollution program.

Unfortunately, there are some practical difficulties in implementing a benefit–cost analysis.

likely to receive. But how do we establish the nonmonetary benefits of the program to the community?

2. Priorities May Conflict with Benefits Even if all the monetary benefits of a program could be established, the resulting benefit/cost ratio would not always reflect the relative need for the program from society's overall standpoint. For example, a particular pollution-abatement project may yield an expected benefit/cost ratio of 1.2 to 1. A separate project for training the hard-core unemployed may produce an expected benefit/cost ratio of 1.1 to 1. Does this mean that society's limited supply of funds should be taken from the latter and put into the former? Not necessarily. An attack on hard-core unemployment may have nonmonetary, but socially desirable, consequences that simply do not lend themselves to benefit–cost analysis.

Cost-Effectiveness Analysis

The difficulty of defining and measuring benefits led to the introduction of another method of efficiency planning known as *cost-effectiveness analysis*. This is a technique of selecting from alternative programs the one that will attain a given objective at the lowest cost. It is most useful in situations whose benefits cannot be measured in terms of money. Thus, cost-effectiveness analysis is of no use in deciding whether it would be better to develop a program for abating pollution or for reducing the number of deaths from traffic accidents. However, given the decision to spend on one of these, cost-effectiveness analysis may be used to select the alternative that will cost least.

Cost-effectiveness analysis provides an alternative (and somewhat easier) means of evaluating an antipollution program.

As a hypothetical example, a cost-effectiveness analysis of deaths resulting from smog might reach the following conclusions.

On the average, a reduction of one death could be achieved for each of the following expenditures per person:

1. $90,000 on the development of clean-burning fuels.

2. $60,000 on the installation of furnace and engine filtering devices.

3. $45,000 on the provision of improved medical treatment.

4. $18,000 on the vigorous enforcement of existing smog-abatement laws.

5. $150 on the production of special "gas masks" or breathing devices for all citizens.

If the only factor to be considered were the cost, it follows that the last choice is the one to be adopted because it achieves the given objective at the lowest cost.

Unfortunately, there are many types of environmental problems—as well as urban and social-welfare problems—for which cost-effectiveness analysis has not yet demonstrated its usefulness. For example, should the limited funds available for general pollution abatement be spent for smog control, water purification, or waste disposal? This question is critical. Yet the question may not be specific enough for cost-effectiveness analysis to answer. This is because a common objective must first be defined and measured, and the costs of alternative actions for achieving that objective must be identified, as in the hypothetical example above. These, of course, are the fundamental difficulties. However, as more and better information becomes available, cost-effectiveness analysis will continue to gain in importance as a powerful tool for program evaluation.

Some antipollution programs cannot be readily evaluated by cost-effectiveness techniques.

Four Environmental Policies

Environmental policies may utilize either market or nonmarket methods.

How much does it cost to undertake antipollution programs? Who pays for them? These questions are at the heart of environmental policy.

Unfortunately, we do not always know the net gain—the benefits relative to the costs—of eliminating a particular pollutant from the environment. Hence, we may spend too much money reducing some types of pollution that are not very damaging and not enough reducing those types that are. Until our knowledge is more complete, the government must use guesswork in some cases, but it must discourage polluters. We will consider four proposals for curbing pollution:

1. Levy emission fees on polluters.
2. Sell pollution "rights."
3. Subsidize pollution-abatement efforts.
4. Impose direct regulations.

Meanwhile, some images relating to the problem appear in Box 2.

Levy Emission Fees on Polluters

Many economists and legislators have increasingly emphasized the idea that the costs of pollution should be built into the price-profit system as an incentive feature. In simplest terms, this approach involves the use of metering devices to measure the amount of pollution emitted by factories. Fees would then be imposed for every unit of pollutant discharged.

The levying of emission fees would promote greater efficiency on the part of polluting firms.

A pollution-control board—a state or federal agency—could determine safe limits of emission. Then the fees it charged could be varied not only by the amount of waste emitted but also by the hour of the day, by the day of the week, and by geographic location. By setting its own multiple-fee schedules on these bases, the board could exert a strong influence on *how much, when,* and *where* pollutants were discharged. And because the emission fees would become part of a firm's costs of operation, the board would be using the price mechanism as a carrot as well as a stick.

Several arguments are offered in favor of this approach:

1. It would permit the imposition of variable charges on the generation of pollutants. Historically, governmental systems for controlling pollutants have usually been on a yes-or-no basis. However, as indicated above, we do not yet know enough about the different kinds of pollutants simply to prohibit them or to permit them without qualification. By levying emission fees, it would be possible to impose degrees of control as the need arises.

2. It would enable government to distribute the damage caused by pollution more evenly throughout the country. By charging lower emission fees in sparsely populated areas and higher fees in the more densely populated regions, factories would be encouraged to locate away from the cities, where they could pollute with less social damage.

3. It would cause firms to calculate the costs of waste, as well as the costs and benefits of abatement, and to consider these alternatives in their production and pricing decisions. Businesses would thus be stimulated to seek methods of reducing waste—perhaps by "recycling" it back into production or by developing socially harmless methods of disposal.

Box 2
Environmental Pollution

Ray Ellis/Photo Researchers

DeSazo-Rapho/Photo Researchers

Give me your . . . huddled masses yearning to breathe free,
The wretched refuse of your teeming shore.

Emma Lazarus, The New Colossus (1903)

Rhoda Galyn/Photo Researchers

Dave Repp/Photo Researchers

. . . And Man created the plastic bag and the tin and alumi-
num can and the cellophane wrapper and the paper plate.
And this was good because Man could then take his automo-
bile and buy all his food in one place and He could save that
which was good to eat in the refrigerator and throw away that
which had no further use. And soon the earth was covered
with plastic bags and aluminum cans and paper plates and
disposable bottles and there was nowhere to sit down or
walk. And Man shook his head and cried: "Look at this God-
awful mess."

Art Buchwald

If you with litter will disgrace,
And spoil the beauty of this place,
May indigestion rack your chest
And ants invade your pants and vest.

Sign at the entrance of the
Pleasure Gardens of Ceylon

Exhibit 3
A Market for Pollution "Rights"

One way to attack the pollution problem is through the price system. For each specific type of pollution, the government would determine the maximum amount that is within safe limits—such as the number of tons of raw sewage per year that, if dumped into a lake, would disintegrate by normal bacterial processes. It could then sell *rights to pollution* in a free market. Each "right" would permit the owner to dump a specified quantity of sewage per year into the lake.

The supply curve S in this case would therefore be a vertical line. The demand curve D, however, would be downward-sloping. This indicates that some polluters would find it cheaper to buy the pollution rights than to invest in pollution-abatement equipment, while others would not. Hence, the equilibrium price would settle at P and the equilibrium quantity would settle at Q. Note that this quantity is less than the amount at Q', the amount that would prevail if the price of a pollution right were zero.

Over the years, the growth in income and population would cause the demand curve to rise—say to D'. This would bring about a higher equilibrium price, P'.

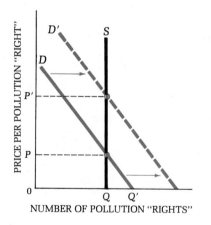

NUMBER OF POLLUTION "RIGHTS"

The rebuttals to these arguments can be readily anticipated. Essentially, the opponents of emission fees make the following points:

1. Only certain types of pollution can be measured with metering devices.

2. Many factors other than emission fees, such as the availability of a suitable labor supply and access to raw materials and markets, influence the geographic location of firms.

3. Benefits and costs are impossible to measure precisely.

For these reasons, those who object to the levying of emission fees argue that such a system would at best have only limited advantages.

Sell Pollution "Rights"

A second proposal for dealing with the problem of pollution is to establish a system of marketable licenses. Each license would give its owner the "right" to pollute—up to a specified amount in a given place during a particular period of time. These licenses or rights could be bought and sold in an organized market—not unlike the stock market or the commodities market. Their prices would fluctuate according to the forces of supply and demand, reflecting the general desire of polluters to dispose of wastes. The basic economic features of the proposal are explained in greater detail in Exhibit 3.

At a very low price, any firm that wanted to pollute could do so at relatively little cost. If the price were very high, some form of supplementary rights would have to be issued to financially weaker firms in order to enable them to pollute, while limiting (through special taxes or other means) the opportunities for financially stronger firms to do the same. A similar type of scheme might also be developed for households.

This approach to pollution control would not be adaptable to all forms of pollution. But for those to which it would be suited, its fundamental advantage would be its operation through the free market and the use of the price system as a mechanism for coping with pollution problems.

Subsidize Pollution-Abatement Efforts

A third approach to curbing pollution is through government subsidization schemes for firms. This system could take various direct and indirect forms. Among them: outright payments for the reduction of pollution levels, subsidies for particular control devices, and exemptions from local property taxes on pollution-abatement equipment. Also, special fast depreciation allowances and tax credits for the purchase of pollution-control equipment could be granted.

If subsidization of any type were to be employed in a pollution-control scheme, the following guidelines should be kept in mind:

1. Give Outright Payments It would be better to give business firms direct payments for the reduction of pollution levels than to offer tax credits for investing in pollution-abatement equipment. Direct or outright payments would leave businesses free to adopt the least costly means of reducing the discharge of pollutants. Tax credits on equipment, on the other hand, would discourage firms from investigating all alternative methods of pollution abatement, including the possibility of burning nonpolluting fuels.

2. Subsidize Profitable Equipment If firms are to be subsidized for investing in pollution controls, the subsidies should be given for equipment that is likely to enhance businesses' net profits either by adding to revenues or by reducing costs. A pollution-control device that was not expected to increase profits would leave firms with very little incentive to acquire it—even if the government offered to pay part of the cost.

3. Develop Pollution Standards Subsidy payments should be tied to the amounts by which pollutants were reduced *below* the levels that would have prevailed without the payments. Such standards are extremely difficult (if not impossible) to estimate, especially for new firms. Yet, failure to establish guidelines of this type would make any subsidization scheme largely ineffective.

4. Make Users Pay Subsidy payments would violate the "benefit principle" of equity if, as is most likely, the subsidies were financed out of general tax revenues. According to the benefit principle—which has strong support on moral and ethical grounds—pollution-control measures should be part of the costs of production. That is, consumers who buy products ought to pay the antipollution costs of production just as labor, capital, and other inputs are paid for. In other words, even though all of society benefits from subsidies to control pollution, it can be argued that consumers who buy the products that are responsible for pollution should pay the costs of reducing it.

5. Avoid Tax Credits Moral and ethical principles of fairness would be violated if indirect subsidies were given in the form of tax credits to firms that invest in pollution-abatement equipment. Such credits would mean that some taxpayers would have to pay higher taxes than otherwise. This would introduce further biases into the tax system, resulting in resource misallocation.

These guidelines and the difficulties of implementing them make it clear that subsidy schemes, although frequently proposed, are not necessarily the best approach for public policy.

Impose Direct Regulations

A fourth method of pollution control would be to invoke the legislative powers of government at all levels. This would involve the use of licenses, permits, zoning regulations, registration, and other controls. Violators would be subject to civil and criminal proceedings. Direct regulations such as these are wholly within the province of federal and state governments, which, under the "general welfare" and "police power" clauses of the Constitution, have the authority to pass laws protecting the health and promoting the safety of citizens.

Direct regulation is a nonmarket method of dealing with pollution.

The general objection to direct regulation of pollution is the same as the objection to direct regulation of anything else. Regulation leads to rigidities and, in many cases, unwieldy and inefficient forms of control. A law that sets a limit on pollution levels will cause a greater misallocation of resources than, say, a system of emission fees. This is because the latter can accomplish the same overall reductions in pollution while leaving firms free to adjust to the realities of their own particular production situations as they think best.

Does this mean that direct regulations should be avoided at all costs? Not necessarily. In a capitalistic economy, direct regulations may very well be needed. However, they should be adopted only after all other market-oriented mechanisms have been found unsuitable.

Conclusion: Which Policy Should Be Adopted?

No one environmental policy is suitable for all purposes. Different policies may be needed, but market methods should be explored before resorting to nonmarket (direct-regulation) methods.

It is impossible to say which of the four approaches to pollution control —emission fees, pollution "rights," subsidization, or direct regulations —would be best. There are different kinds and sources of pollution, many of which are not well understood. Hence, a method of control that might work effectively for curbing air or water contamination might not be suitable for reducing noise levels or land exploitation. Each class of pollution problems must therefore be analyzed separately, and a specific control system must designed for each.

If such a procedure were followed, it might very well be found that different combinations of policies are needed for different kinds of pollution. In the meantime, most present pollution controls are in the form of direct regulation. This leaves few or no bases for judging the effectiveness of alternative control schemes.

What about technology as a solution? To many critics, technology is the culprit that has been responsible for creating the mess. Cans and bottles accumulate because they cannot be burned. The automobile turns cities into parking lots and landscapes into paved highways. Environmentalists now fear that people will be tempted to turn again to technology—perhaps to the dream of building air-conditioned geodesic domes over the cities, or to visions of colonizing outer space—as an answer to our environmental problems. But these are only fantasies. More realistically:

> Technology will no doubt play a vital role in helping to rescue society from its propensity to create pollution. However, our most fundamental need, if we are to survive on this planet, is to *create a value system that will enable us to assess the various parts of the environment.* As philosopher Lewis Mumford once stated: "Any square mile of inhabited earth has more significance for man's future than all of the planets in the solar system."

Issue
Property Rights and Pollution: Who Owns What?

Curing pollution is simple. All we have to do is invoke the market system. We can do this by letting people own, buy, and sell *property* rights in what are now publicly owned resources.

If this were done, people would find it less profitable to pollute. As with any commodity, the value society places on environmental resources would reflect their best alternative uses. Only when resources are "too cheap" do they tend to be "overused" or polluted, as is the case with much of our air, land, and water.

Unfortunately, the implementation of these ideas may sometimes be difficult. The reasons, however, may be more political than economic, because private rather than public ownership may be required.

Everyone's Property Is No One's Property[1]

Pollution most frequently occurs in, or is conveyed through, such public goods as air, rivers, lakes, oceans, and commonly owned lands, such as public parks and streets. In most cases, *rights* to use these resources (public goods) are held by all of us in common or are simply unspeci-

---

[1] W. Lee Hopkins, "An Economic Solution to Pollution," *Business Review*, Federal Reserve Bank of Philadelphia, September 1970. Adapted.

fied by law. When rights to resources (goods) are vague or held in common, the rule is "first come, first served."

For example, people have less incentive to maintain the purity of a lake or stream when they do not have the right to capture the value of doing so. Water in a private lake tends to be put to its highest-valued uses (including those in the future) when the owner stands to gain. If the owner can capture that value by selling the lake, he or she has an incentive to protect the quality of the water. Unfortunately, no such incentive exists for our commonly owned air, water, and land. As a result, these resources are not being put to the uses most highly valued by society—they are "overconsumed" (polluted), while other goods are "overproduced." One means of coping with this problem is to specify salable property rights in our commonly owned resources (or public goods).

Privatizing Public Goods[2]

Public goods are goods that cannot be provided for some without being provided for others. The normal market mechanism for achieving consumer sovereignty is therefore inapplicable. Those who would benefit from the provision of such goods will not pay for the benefits because they can enjoy the goods without paying for them if the goods are provided for anybody else. Everybody will wait for somebody else to buy the goods in the hope of being able to enjoy a free ride.

This is not a new problem. Indeed, in the beginning, before the invention of property rights, all goods were public. It did not pay anyone to improve on traditional procedures because any resulting increase in output would be free to everyone in the tribe. It did not pay anyone to build a house if he could instead find someone who had built one and then move in with him (or kick him out). Only with the establishment of privatization, or private property, was the decentralization of deci-

Arthur Tress

Paul Conklin/Monkmeyer Press Photo Service

---

[2] Abba P. Lerner, "The Economics and Politics of Consumer Sovereignty," *The American Economic Review, Papers and Proceedings*, May 1972. Adapted.

sion making that is necessary for efficient production made possible. Our problem now is that the invention and application of the special devices needed to *privatize* public goods have been too slow. Privatizing is nothing more than establishing the institutional arrangements by which the individual or group who pays for the benefit gets it and the one who does not pay for it does not get it.

However, not all public goods can be privatized. There will still be services that, if provided for some, are inevitably made available for all. For such services, the market mechanism cannot work. Everybody will refrain from buying them in the hope that someone else will. And nobody will be willing to pay the total cost of a benefit to all.

Need for Agreement

Where this is the case, agreement is necessary for combined action. This is what government is for. A citizen will agree to be compelled to contribute to the cost of a project, provided that enough others also are compelled, so that the benefit exceeds the contribution (or tax). Of course, not all goods can be privatized. But it is our failure to privatize where privatization is possible that is responsible for most of the ills of pollution.

Ken Lambert/Free Lance Photographers Guild

Questions

1. Is it necessary for environmental resources to be privately owned in order to reduce their pollution? How else might the market system be invoked while retaining public ownership?

2. If privatization of environmental resources is so desirable, why has it not been undertaken on a large scale?

What You Have Learned in This Chapter

1. A surplus or shortage of a commodity can exist only at a given price. Therefore, it is meaningless to use such terms as "surplus" or "shortage" unless a specific price is understood.

2. If the United States wishes to improve the allocation of energy resources, two major options are available: (a) free markets, and (b) demand reduction and supply expansion. After decades of experience with government-mandated regulations and controls, there is widespread agreement that a free market in energy has the best chance of meeting the nation's goals.

3. In general, the difficulty of implementing and maintaining free markets in energy is more political than economic. Therefore, various regulations aimed at protecting special interests can easily arise. This prevents the realizations of efficiency and equity that free markets bring.

4. The natural environment includes three major types of resources—air, land, and water. These have been polluted and exploited by businesses and households because society has failed to evaluate the real costs of using various environmental resources. That is, society has not assigned appropriate prices to cover utilization costs and has instead made the resources available "free." As a result, two methods that are gaining increasing use for correcting these shortcomings and for improving decision making about environmental issues are benefit–cost analysis and cost-effectiveness analysis.

5. Several approaches to pollution control are possible. Among them: (a) levy emission fees on polluters, (b) sell pollution "rights," (c) subsidize pollution-abatement efforts, and (d) impose direct regulations. Because relatively little is known about the many causes and effects of pollution, it is virtually certain that no one of these policies would be suitable in all cases. Instead, various combinations would be desirable. At present, however, most policies are in the form of direct regulations.

For Discussion

1. *Terms and concepts to review:*
surplus
shortage
direct-payments plan
benefit–cost analysis
cost-effectiveness analysis

2. Using supply and demand curves, illustrate the concept of direct payments. Could a direct-payments plan lead to an eventual "surplus" of oil? Explain.

3. Using supply and demand curves, describe the effects on price and output of a subsidy to sellers. How do these effects compare with those of a direct-payments plan in question 2?

4. "If all land and inland waters were privately owned, this would be a first step in controlling pollution." Explain the justification for this statement.

5. Of the various environmental-policy alternatives suggested in this chapter, which one would probably be the most practical and least costly to administer, all other things being equal? Explain your answer.

Selected Topics:
International Economics and
the World's Economies

33
CHAPTER

International Economics: Foreign Trade and Protection

Learning guide
Watch for the answers to these important questions

Why do nations engage in trade? What principles underlie international trade and the benefits that nations receive from it?

Why do nations impose barriers to trade? What types of barriers are most common?

What arguments are commonly made in favor of import protection? Are any of them valid? How can they be evaluated?

What is the foreign-trade multiplier? How does it help us to understand fluctuations in economic activity in today's world of interdependent nations?

This chapter surveys the major principles and problems of international trade.

The study of international economics is becoming more important as the countries of the world become increasingly interdependent economically. Many of the issues that can either tie nations closer together or drive them apart have their roots in economics.

In general, the study of international economics is concerned with the same fundamental questions as domestic economics. Thus, the problems of *what* to produce, *how much* to produce, and *for whom* to produce it are still foremost. The difference is that these questions are studied for several economies or nations rather than for one.

On the microeconomic side, for example, international economics may show how the price systems of different countries interact to affect resource allocation and income distribution. On the macroeconomic side, there may be concern with the ways in which imports, exports, and investment expenditures among nations affect their levels of income, employment, and economic growth. Microeconomic and macroeconomic principles are often employed simultaneously in the study of international economics.

To begin with, we will concentrate on one broad segment of international economics—trade among nations. The remaining aspects of international economics, financial principles and policies, will be considered in a subsequent chapter.

Major Features of World Trade

It is appropriate to begin the study of international trade by asking two questions: (1) Of what relative significance is world trade to nations? (2) What are the distributional patterns of trade between the United States and the major regions of the world?

The Importance of World Trade

American students are not as familiar with the importance of international trade as are students in most other countries. This is because in many nations the volume of exports or imports may be as much as 40 percent of GNP. But only roughly 10 percent of the GNP of the United States is sold abroad, and approximately the same percentage is purchased abroad.

However, neither the dollar volume of U.S. trade with other nations nor the U.S. products involved in it are trivial—as you can see from Exhibit 1. In total dollar volume, the amounts are far larger than the international trade carried on by any other country. In terms of relative importance, agricultural goods represent less than 20 percent of our combined imports and exports, and nonagricultural goods represent more than 80 percent of these totals.

World trade is becoming increasingly important to the United States.

Patterns of U.S. Trade

Where do our imports come from? Where do our exports go? Exhibit 1 shows clearly that the least industrialized areas of the world are neither America's biggest suppliers nor its biggest customers. Europe (which includes most of the leading industrial countries of the world), Canada, Asia (notably Japan), and Mexico are America's largest markets for purchases and sales of goods.

Of course, changes in the world's economies since the early part of this century have brought changes in our patterns of trade. For example, trade with Asia has grown in relative importance, while trade with Europe, although still large in absolute terms, has declined substantially.

Our biggest competitors in world markets are also our best customers.

Why Do Countries Trade?

Imagine what would happen if you tried to be completely self-sufficient. You would have to grow your own food, make your own clothing, build your own means of transportation, construct your own shelter, make your own furniture, treat your own illnesses, and provide for all your needs and desires. Obviously, you would not be able to do many things because you would lack the necessary material resources, time, and skills. Hence, your level of living would be much lower than it is now.

How could you correct the situation? You could *specialize*—that is, you could concentrate on the things you do best. In that way, you could produce more than enough for yourself and sell or trade your surpluses for the other things you want. That is essentially what we all do. A carpenter, a salesperson, a doctor, a teacher, a bricklayer—each "specializes" in the activity that he or she does best and thereby earns enough to buy the goods and services produced by others.

Specialization also exists among nations:

Resources are distributed unevenly through the world. Some countries have more or better land, or labor, or capital than others, so it may pay for them to *specialize*. In this way, a larger quantity and a greater variety of goods are produced, which nations can exchange with one another. As with individuals, the quantity and variety of goods would be less if each nation tried to be self-sufficient.

Countries trade in order to acquire the goods and services they want at lower costs than if they were produced domestically.

Exhibit 1
Foreign Trade of the United States

International trade is playing an increasingly important role, both in the U.S. economy and in the world economy. But the patterns of trade are undergoing continuous change.

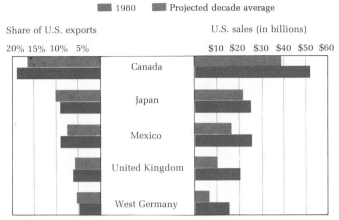

OUR BEST CUSTOMERS

Canada
Japan
Mexico
United Kingdom
West Germany

Share of U.S. exports — U.S. sales (in billions)

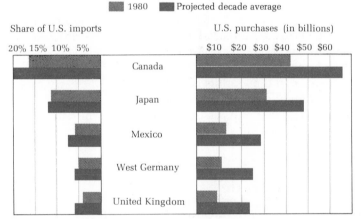

OUR MAIN SUPPLIERS

Canada
Japan
Mexico
West Germany
United Kingdom

Share of U.S. imports — U.S. purchases (in billions)

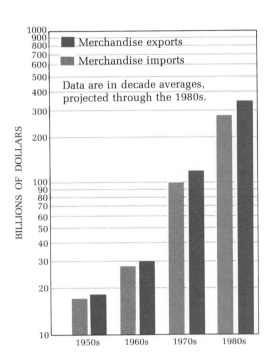

■ Merchandise exports
■ Merchandise imports

Data are in decade averages, projected through the 1980s.

BILLIONS OF DOLLARS

1950s   1960s   1970s   1980s

U.S. Merchandise Exports and Imports, 1980s (billions of dollars)

	Merchandise exports		Merchandise imports	
	1980	Decade average*	1980	Decade average*
Item				
Agricultural products	$ 41	$ 48	$ 17	$ 21
Nonagricultural products†	175	232	224	322
	$216	$280	$241	$343
Region				
Africa	$ 9.1		$32.3	
Asia	60.2		78.8	
Australia and Oceania	4.9		3.4	
Europe	71.4		47.8	
Canada	35.4		41.5	
Mexico and Central America	21.3		22.7	
South America	17.4		14.4	

* Based on projections from 1970 through 1990.
† Minerals, fuels, chemicals, manufactured goods, and machinery.
Source: U.S. Department of Commerce.

These ideas can be better understood by examining the principles and consequences that underlie the exchange of goods between nations and regions.

Law of Absolute Advantage

The simplest and most obvious reason for trade is provided by what is known as the *law of absolute advantage*. This principle states that a basis for trade between regions exists when each, because of natural or acquired endowments, can provide the other with a good or service for less than it would pay to produce the product at home.

Thus, the United States buys coffee from Brazil, and Brazil buys machinery from the United States. Libya buys lumber from Sweden, and Sweden buys oil from Libya. Florida buys cars made in Michigan, and Michigan buys oranges grown in Florida.

In general, this kind of trading helps both parties. Imagine how costly it would be, for example, if some Florida business managers tried to acquire the factories and skilled workers needed to make automobiles, or if some Michigan business executives tried to build the huge hot-houses that would be needed for growing orange trees in Michigan.

Note For convenience, we ordinarily speak of countries or regions as buyers and sellers of products. But the governments of those areas are not doing all the buying and selling. Most international trade is carried on by private firms. Only in command economies do governments engage significantly in trade.

A basis for trade may exist if one country has an absolute advantage over another in the production of a commodity.

The Concept of Comparative Advantage

The reasons for trade are not always as obvious as those in the examples given above. Trade between individual people or nations can be profitable even if one of the parties can produce *both* products more efficiently than the other. This involves a concept known as "comparative advantage."

For example, some doctors may be good typists. Yet a doctor generally hires a typist, even though the typist may not type as well as the doctor does. This is because the time spent at medical practice is more profitable than the time spent at the typewriter. Thus, suppose a doctor can do a necessary day's typing in 1 hour, whereas the typist who is hired takes 3 hours to do the same amount of typing. If the doctor earns $60 per hour by practicing medicine, and pays the typist $6 per hour, the doctor gains $42 per day by performing only medically related tasks. To put the example in a different but equivalent way, the doctor can earn enough money in 18 minutes by practicing medicine to pay for 3 hours of the typist's time.

A basis for trade may exist even if one country has an advantage over another in the production of both traded commodities but has a relative or comparative advantage in one of these.

An Application to Nations

Applying the same principle to nations, let us take the case of England and Portugal, both producing two products—cloth and wine. (This was the kind of example used in 1817 by the great English classical economist David Ricardo. He was the first to explain the mutual advantages of trade between nations in terms of what is now known as the law of comparative advantage.)

Exhibit 2
Illustration of Comparative Advantage

The curves *DE* and *D'E'* are production-possibilities curves for each country. Without trade between the two nations, England may choose to be self-sufficient in both cloth and wine by producing a combination represented by point *K*. Similarly, Portugal may choose to be self-sufficient by producing a combination represented by point *K'*.

Production from One Day's Labor at Full Employment

	Cloth output (yards per day)	Wine output (gallons per day)	Cost ratio (cloth:wine)
England	30	10	3:1
Portugal	30	30	1:1

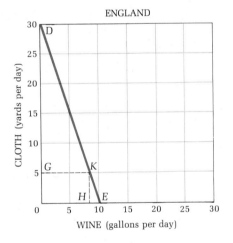

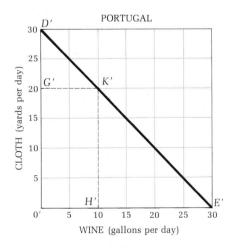

An illustration based on hypothetical data appears in Exhibit 2. It is clear from the table that Portugal is equally as efficient as England in the production of cloth but three times as efficient as England in the production of wine. Therefore, Portugal has a comparative (or relative) advantage in wine production.

In the graphs of Exhibit 2, the data are presented in the form of production-possibilities curves. You will recall that these are normally shown as curved lines that are bowed outward. Here, however, the "curves" are shown as straight lines. This is because we are assuming for simplicity that production takes place under conditions of *constant* rather than increasing costs.

Thus, in England, the intersection of the production-possibilities curve *DE* with the two axes of the chart tells us that one day's labor can produce either 30 yards of cloth or 10 gallons of wine—or any particular combination in between as determined by any given point along the line. Hence, the steepness (slope) of *DE* measures the relative cost of the two products in England and is constant at the ratio 3:1. Similarly, in Portugal, the intersection of *D'E'* with the two axes signifies that one day's labor can produce either 30 yards of cloth or 30 gallons of wine—or any specific combination in between as determined by any given point along the line. Therefore, the steepness of *D'E'* measures the relative cost of the two products in Portugal and is constant at the ratio 1:1.

How much will each country produce? It is impossible to answer this question without knowing the demands for each product in the two countries. However, if we assume that there is no trade between them, it may be inferred that each will try to be self-sufficient by producing some cloth and some wine, as denoted by any given point on each nation's production-possibilities curve. Thus, England might choose the point *K*, representing 0*G* yards of cloth and 0*H* gallons of wine. On the other hand, Portugal might choose the point *K'*, representing 0'*G'* yards of cloth and 0'*H'* gallons of wine.

Introducing Trade

What will happen if the two countries decide to engage in unrestricted trade? Let us assume for simplicity the following conditions:

1. There are no transportation costs between the two countries.

2. Competitive conditions prevail in both nations.

3. Because labor is the only scarce factor of production, the prices of the products are equal to their relative labor costs.

This means that the costs, and therefore the prices, in both countries are as follows:

price in England: 3 yards cloth = 1 gallon wine
price in Portugal: 1 yard cloth = 1 gallon wine

Obviously, *compared with wine, cloth is cheaper in England than in Portugal. Compared with cloth, wine is cheaper in Portugal than in England.* Therefore, England will import wine from Portugal and Portugal will import cloth from England. As exports of Portuguese wine enter England, the supply of wine in England will increase and its price will fall. Similarly, as exports of English cloth enter Portugal, the supply of cloth in Portugal will increase and its price will fall.

The Gains from Trade

The price ratios in England and Portugal will thus become equal to one another. Why? Because, as we have assumed, there is competition in both nations and there are no trade restrictions or transportation costs between them.

Therefore:

> The two countries will constitute in effect a *single market* with a *single price ratio*. At this new price ratio, it will pay for England to specialize in the production of cloth and for Portugal to specialize in the production of wine. Then both nations can trade a portion of these outputs with one another. In that way the two countries can end up with more wine and more cloth than if each country tried to produce both products by itself.

The point is illustrated graphically in Exhibit 3. Figure (*a*) is constructed by combining the two previous figures from Exhibit 2. Thus, the figure for England is in the same relative position as before, but the figure for Portugal is "flipped over" so that its origin is in the upper right-hand corner at 0'. The construction procedure is illustrated in Figure (*b*).

Figure (*a*) has several interesting features:

1. The dashed line *DL* defines the trading possibilities for both countries. Because it is a straight line, it has a constant price ratio (or slope) that is somewhere between the price ratios represented by the two production-possibilities curves, *DE* and *D'E'*.

2. An "exchange point" will tend to be established in the vicinity of *P*. This is because at a point such as this both England and Portugal can have more cloth and more wine by specializing and trading than by trying to be self-sufficient. For example, suppose that England specializes entirely in cloth and produces 30 (= 0*D*) yards of it per day. If it consumes 9 (= 0*M*) yards of cloth, it can export the remaining 21 (= *MD*) yards and acquire 14 (= *MP*) gallons of wine in return. It thus ends up at the point *P*, at which it has *more* cloth and *more* wine than when it was self-sufficient at the point *K*.

3. Similarly, if Portugal specializes completely in wine, it can produce 30 (= 0'*E'*) gallons per day. If it consumes 16 (= 0'*N'*) gallons of this, it has 14 (= *N'E'*) gallons left over, which it can export to England in return for 21 (= 0'*M'*) yards of cloth. In this way Portugal also ends up at the point *P*, at which it consumes both *more* cloth and *more* wine than when it was self-sufficient at the point *K'*.

4. Both countries thus benefit from international specialization and exchange. The amount by which a country benefits from trade is called the *gains from trade*. As you will see, this concept plays an important role in the trading policies of nations.

It is interesting to note from the figure that only in the vicinity of point *P* along the line *DL* will both countries gain by having both more wine and more cloth. At exchange points that are much higher or lower, one country may gain while the other loses, relative to the condition in which each was self-sufficient without trade. At point *S*, for example, England will gain by having more cloth and more wine than it had at point *K*. However, Portugal will lose by having more wine and less cloth than it had at point *K'*. At point *T*, on the other hand, England

Exhibit 3

Exhibit 3
The Terms of Trade and the Gains from Trade

Figure (*a*) combines the two separate figures from Exhibit 2, as shown here in Figure (*b*).

The lines *DE* and *D'E'* are the production-possibilities curves from the previous exhibit. Before trade begins, England is producing at point *K* and Portugal at point *K'*. As a result of trade, both countries may extend their production frontiers to *P*, at which point each country receives more of both goods than before. These increased benefits of trade are called the *gains from trade*.

The dashed line *DL* is the new price line representing the trading possibilities of both nations. Its steepness (slope) measures the *terms of trade*. This is the amount of goods that each nation must give up (or export) for one unit of goods that it receives (or imports). The line must fall somewhere between the two old price lines *DE* and *D'E'* in order for trade to occur. If it falls to the left of *DE* (or to the right of *D'E'*), it will be cheaper for England (or for Portugal) to produce both products and not trade.

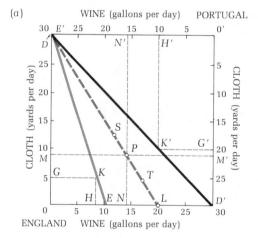

(*a*)

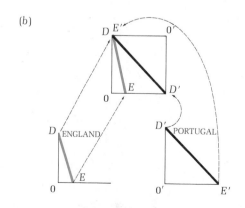

(*b*)

will have less cloth and more wine. However, Portugal will have more of both. Therefore:

> Only in the vicinity of point *P* can *both* countries experience the mutual benefits of having more of *both* products. Consequently, under conditions of competition and unrestricted trade, the exchange point will tend to settle at or near *P*.

The Terms of Trade

The terms of trade are the number of units of a good that must be given up by each party to a transaction for one unit of a good received.

Each country thus gains by specializing in what it can produce with the greatest comparative or relative advantage. The gains will then be divided between the two countries according to the new price ratio, which, as you have seen, is simply the slope of the trading-possibilities line *DL* in the figure.

Thus, the closer that the line *DL* is to *DE*, the higher will be the price of wine relative to cloth. Therefore, the greater will be Portugal's gain relative to England's. If *DL* should coincide with *DE*, which is unlikely, Portugal will receive all the gains from trade and England will receive none. These principles work in reverse, of course, if the line *DL* shifts in the opposite direction toward *D'E'*.

In general, the new price line *DL* must always be somewhere between the old price lines *DE* and *D'E'* in order for trade to occur. If *DL* is, say, to the left of (or steeper than) *DE*, the trading price of wine will be *greater* than the old price ratio in England. England will then find it cheaper to produce its own wine than to import it from Portugal. Similarly, if the line *DL* is to the right of *D'E'*, it will pay for Portugal to produce its own cloth instead of trading with England.

The terms of trade reflect the sacrifice, or opportunity cost, of exchange.

These ideas involve the concept of *terms of trade*. It may be defined as the number of units of goods that must be given up for one unit of goods received by each party to a transaction. (Graphically, the terms of trade are measured by the slope of the line *DL* in the chart.) In any transaction, the terms of trade are determined by the relative demands of the trading parties. In general:

> The terms of trade are said to move *in favor of* the party that gives up fewer units of goods for one unit of goods received. On the other hand, the terms of trade move *against* the party that gives up more units of goods for one unit of goods received.

You will see that the terms of trade play a vital and intensely practical role in evaluating exchange relations between nations.

Conclusion: An Important Law

The foregoing ideas make it possible to formulate a principle of fundamental significance in economics, especially in international economics. It is based on the concept of comparative advantage, which was developed earlier, but the concept may now be expressed more formally as a law.

Law of Comparative Advantage Suppose that one nation can produce each of two products more efficiently than another nation and can produce one of these commodities with comparatively greater efficiency than it can the other commodity. Then it should specialize in production of the product in which it is most efficient and leave production of the other product to the other country. By engaging in trade, the two nations will then have more of both goods. This principle is also applicable to individual people and to regions as well as to nations.

The law of comparative advantage thus leads to an important conclusion:

The law of comparative advantage provides a general explanation of the benefits of trade.

> Free and unrestricted trade among nations encourages international specialization according to comparative advantage. It thereby *tends* to bring about three favorable results:
>
> **1.** The most efficient allocation of world resources as well as a maximization of world production.
>
> **2.** A redistribution of relative product demands, resulting in greater equality of product prices among trading nations.
>
> **3.** A redistribution of relative resource demands to correspond with relative product demands, resulting in greater equality of resource prices among trading nations.

It is important to emphasize that these outcomes are *tendencies* rather than certainties. The reason is that they are based on such idealistic assumptions as the existence of competition and the absence of trade restrictions (including transportation costs). Because these assumptions are not entirely realized in practice, the consequences of free trade will deviate somewhat from these tendencies.

Instruments of Protection

Despite the fundamental advantages of completely free trade—namely, encouragement of the most efficient allocation of world resources and the maximization of world production—nations have not been quick to adopt it. They have often chosen instead to institute various methods of protecting their home industries by imposing barriers to free trade. The reasons usually advanced for such actions will be explained later. First, however, the chief forms of protection may be noted briefly.

Despite the advantages of international specialization and trade, nations erect trade barriers of various kinds.

Tariffs

Tariffs have played a very significant role in various political and sectional disputes in the United States. A *tariff* is a customs duty or tax imposed by a government on the importation (or exportation) of a good. Tariffs may be specific (based on a tax per unit of the commodity) or ad valorem (based on the value of the commodity). There are a number of reasons, some of them rather complex, why a government might impose a tariff. For present purposes, however, it will be simplest for us to think of a tariff as a tax on imports exclusively. Further, it will be assumed that tariffs are imposed either for the primary purpose of protecting domestic industry from foreign competition or for providing the government with more revenue.

Exhibit 4 presents a history of tariff levels in the United States. Because a tariff is a law that must be approved by Congress, it is often named after the legislator who sponsored it. As the figure shows, the trend since 1930 has been sharply downward, with average rates less than 10 percent since 1970.

Exhibit 4
Average Tariff Rates in the United States
(duties collected as a percentage of dutiable imports)

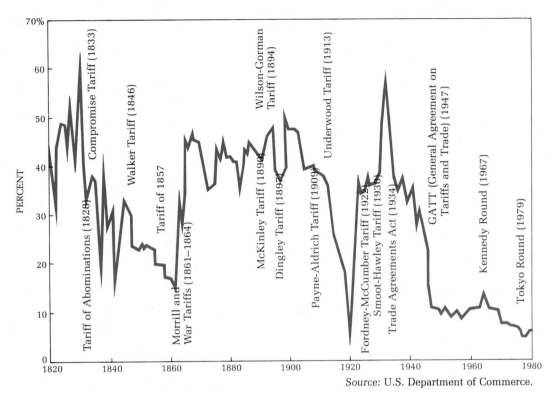

Source: U.S. Department of Commerce.

Tariffs have often been a political football in American history. Although tariff rates have fluctuated widely, the trend has been sharply downward since the early 1930s. Since the post–World War II years, America has been a leading low-tariff nation.

Quotas and Other Nontariff Barriers

Tariffs are not the only means that nations employ to protect their home industries. Another common instrument of protection is the *import quota*. This places a precise legal limit on the number of units of a commodity that may be imported during a given period. Countries may also impose other nontariff barriers to trade. Examples are customs procedures and laws involving import financing; foreign-exchange requirements; and various regulations involving labeling, health, safety, and shipping, some of which are expressly designed as protectionist devices. Quotas and other nontariff barriers have become relatively more significant than tariffs as protective instruments in many countries, including the United States.

What are the economic consequences of protection? In general:

All forms of protection tend to impede the full advantages of international specialization that are to be gained from free or unrestricted trade. When a nation adopts protective devices, such as tariffs or quotas, it causes a shift of resources from more efficient to less efficient uses and restricts consumers' freedom of choice.

An interesting example of nontariff barriers is described in Box 1.

Arguments for Protection

The law of comparative advantage and the economic benefits of free trade have never been successfully refuted, despite many heroic attempts to do so. Nevertheless, efforts by special-interest groups to obtain import protection are common. American history is replete with long and eloquent pleas by business managers, union representatives, and political leaders contending that theirs is a "different" situation requiring special consideration. Most of these arguments for protection can be grouped into one of the following categories:

1. Infant-industry argument.
2. National-security argument.
3. Diversified-economy argument.
4. Wage-protection argument.
5. Employment-protection argument.

You will see below that there are fallacies in all these arguments. But before you read on, you should understand the following fundamental point:

> We can sell abroad only if we buy abroad. When the United States imports from foreign countries, those countries earn thereby most of the dollars they need to purchase American exports. In general, *exports are the cost of trade and imports are the return from trade,* not the other way around. Over the long run, a nation must export (sacrifice goods) in order to import (acquire goods).

Box 1
Nontariff Barriers: When Is a Salami a Bologna?

In France, it is illegal to advertise whiskey and gin—allegedly because they are bad for the health. Without the pressures of advertising, the French tend to drink domestic wines and brandies instead of importing scotch and gin.

Similar restrictions on trade exist in other countries. The United States, for example, prohibits the importation of French candies—presumably because their colorants are unsafe. Japan prohibits the exportation of calculators containing integrated circuits made in other countries. And the Netherlands prohibits exports of pharmaceuticals not manufactured by members of a Dutch trade association.

But perhaps most interesting is the question: When is a sausage not a sausage? The not-so-simple answer is: When it is exported and bumps into another country's definition of a sausage. The definition may be expressed in terms of size, shape, casing, color, the mix of ingredients, and, in some instances, the number of links per string. Anything that does not conform to a particular country's definition of a sausage is ruled a nonsausage and may not be imported.

No less interesting are the difficulties involved in defining an importable cow. The classic nontariff barrier is the provision of a German tariff law of 1902, now obsolete, affecting the importation of cattle. This granddaddy of nontariff barriers was designed to exclude Dutch and Russian cattle competitive with German types but to allow entry of Swiss cattle. It did so with a definition that gave an extra-low duty rate to "large dappled mountain cattle or brown cattle reared at a spot 300 meters above sea level and which have at least one month's grazing at a spot at least 800 meters above sea level."

The old German law, while not mentioning any country, achieved its aim with what amounted to a description of Swiss cattle-raising practices. Modern nontariff barriers, however, are not so diplomatic. The catalog of such barriers seems infinite, and as more is found out about them, almost every country, including the United States, is seen to be a serious offender.

As you will see in the following paragraphs, this basic principle is essential for understanding the fallacies that underlie nearly all arguments for protection—*including those for tariffs and quotas.*

Infant-Industry Argument

When George Washington was inaugurated in 1789, he appointed Alexander Hamilton as the first Secretary of the Treasury. In 1791, Hamilton issued his famous *Report on Industry and Commerce.* In this volume, he articulated with remarkable depth and clarity the economic problems of the time and proposed the nation's first protective tariff system. A fundamental justification for this system was the new nation's need to protect its growing infant industries.

An *infant industry* is an underdeveloped industry that may not be able to survive competition from abroad. The infant-industry argument for protection says that such industries should be shielded temporarily with high tariffs or quotas until the industries develop technological efficiency and economies of scale that will enable them to compete with foreign industries.

This type of plea was the basis on which tariffs were established for a number of industries during the nineteenth and twentieth centuries. But economists have come to recognize three major shortcomings of this argument:

1. Tariffs or other protective devices become the vested interests of particular business and political groups. When that happens, protective measures become extremely difficult to eliminate.

2. Some protected industries never grow out of the "infant" stage. That is, they never become able to compete effectively with more mature industries in other countries.

3. An increase in tariffs or quotas results in higher prices to domestic consumers. Therefore, if an industry must be shielded from foreign competition, a subsidy would be more desirable because it tends to increase output as well as to reduce costs and prices. Above all, a subsidy is visible and must be voted periodically by Congress, which makes it easier to eliminate when it has outlived its intended function.

National-Security Argument

From time to time, representatives of various industries have made major efforts, through government and the news media, to gain protection from the onslaught of foreign competition. For example, some years ago the chairman of the board of the U.S. Steel Corporation asked a congressional committee: "Can we be assured of the strong industrial base in steel we need for modern defense if one-quarter or more of the steel we require were imported from countries lying uncomfortably close to the Soviet Union or China?"

This quotation provides a superb illustration of the "national-security argument." The argument is based on the assumption that a nation should be as self-sufficient as possible in the production of goods needed for war and defense.

On the face of it, this plea for protection seems persuasive. On closer examination, however, the following criticisms become apparent:

1. It is primarily a military argument rather than an economic one. Therefore, it should be decided by the proper military authorities in a calm and rational manner without the distorting influence of people who have a direct business interest in the outcome. Those with a knowledge of economics can help by pointing out the costs of protection in terms of resource misallocation and a reduced standard of living.

2. Many industries are important, in one way or another, to defense or national security and could qualify equally well for increased protection.

3. As pointed out in the discussion of the infant-industry argument, a subsidy is preferable to a tariff or quota if some form of shielding is necessary.

Diversified-Economy Argument

"Don't put all your eggs in one basket." This maxim is as applicable to nations as it is to individual people—at least according to the "diversified-economy" theorists. They contend that increased protection is desirable because it enables a nation to build up a variety of industries for greater economic stability. In that way, they say, a highly specialized economy—such as Bolivia's tin economy or Chile's copper economy—will suffer less from adverse swings in the world's demand for its chief exports.

The use of import-protection measures to encourage diversification of industries is a weak argument for large industrialized economies.

This argument contains some elements of truth. A single-crop or single-product economy is highly vulnerable to swings in demand—which may be permanent. For example, the introduction of man-made fibers has impoverished or severely damaged those economies that concentrated on the production of natural fibers.

But the diversified-economy argument also has some shortcomings:

1. It is of little significance to an economy that is already diversified and advanced, such as that of the United States.

2. It assumes that the government is more clairvoyant than private investors and thus better able to envision the future economic benefits flowing from new and diversified industries.

3. It overlooks not only the inefficiencies that may result from forced, "unnatural" diversification but also the consequent increase in cost, which may more than offset any economic gains.

Wage-Protection Argument

Because wages in the United States are higher than in most other industrialized nations, some people argue that tariffs or quotas are needed to protect American workers from the products of cheap labor abroad.

Protecting high-cost domestic labor from cheap foreign labor is not in itself a valid argument for import barriers.

In essence, advocates of this argument are contending that a high-wage nation cannot compete with a low-wage nation. In reality, however, the contention is false. The products of high-wage U.S. labor compete daily in world markets with the products of low-wage labor. The fact is that, for many products, high wages do not of themselves prevent or even hinder trade among nations.

Three criticisms and qualifications of the wage-protection argument are particularly important:

We must know why domestic labor is more costly than foreign labor, and we must know what can be done about it.

1. It assumes that labor is the only resource entering into production. In fact, labor is a resource that is combined in each nation with varying quantities of capital and land. As a result, the products of countries may often be characterized as *labor-intensive*, *capital-intensive*, or *land-intensive*, depending on the relative proportions of resources that are employed in production.

2. Low-wage countries will have an advantage over high-wage countries *only* in trading products that are labor-intensive. These are goods for which wages are a large proportion of total costs. High-wage countries may be better off not competing with low-wage countries in trading these products.

3. Even where labor-intensive products are concerned, however, high-wage countries may be able to compete effectively with low-wage countries if labor productivity in the former is high enough to compensate for lower wage levels in the latter.

A recent example of the wage-protection argument is the subject of Box 2.

Employment-Protection Argument

The use of import barriers to protect domestic employment is a costly measure that invites retaliation by other countries.

Supporters of trade protection often argue that tariffs or quotas are desirable because they reduce imports relative to exports and thus encourage a favorable balance of trade—that is, a surplus of exports over imports. This, in turn, stimulates the export industries and helps to bring about a higher level of domestic income, employment, and production.

Is this a valid plea for protection? Like the previous arguments, it may seem persuasive, but the following considerations should be kept in mind:

1. Any benefits in the form of higher income and employment, if they occur, are not likely to last long. The history of tariffs and quotas shows

Box 2
Labor Fights for Quota Protection

The American labor movement has been actively supporting protectionism since the late 1960s. According to many union leaders, liberal trade policy is an anachronism. Quotas are needed to protect high-paid American workers from the products of cheap labor abroad.

Wide World Photos

that, in the long run, nations tend to retaliate with their own protective measures, leaving all nations worse off than before.

2. Tariffs and quotas tend to result in higher prices, thus penalizing domestic consumers while benefiting inefficient domestic producers. In the long run, this encourages a movement of resources out of more efficient industries into less efficient (protected) ones, thereby raising costs and reducing comparative advantage.

3. In international trade, goods pay for goods. Hence, in the long run, a nation that exports must also import. Protective measures tend to impede the operation of this principle and, therefore, to limit rather than to encourage higher real income and employment in the long run.

Conclusion: Tariffs Preferred to Quotas

It is clear from these arguments that any kind of protective measure benefits some groups at the expense of the rest of society. Nevertheless, it is likely that nations will always employ certain forms of protection—for political as well as for economic reasons. If this is so, which type of protection is economically preferable—tariffs or quotas? The answer is best understood in terms of a society's four major goals—efficiency, equity, stability, and growth.

Tariffs and quotas both lead to resource misallocation and therefore higher prices.

Efficiency

A tariff causes less resource misallocation and permits greater efficiency in domestic markets than an import quota. This is because, although imports are taxed under a tariff, the foreign supply of the commodity available in the domestic market is nevertheless flexible. As a result, an increase in the domestic demand for the good can be met by an increase in the volume of imports, with little or no change in the domestic price or in production. Even if the domestic price should rise, it can never exceed the unprotected price by more than the amount of the import duty.

Tariffs permit market adjustments to occur both in prices and in import quantities.

Under an import quota, on the other hand, the foreign supply of the commodity available domestically is inflexible. Consequently, an increase in domestic demand simply raises the domestic price relative to the unprotected price without any limit as to the differential between them.

Quotas place a limit on imports, thus permitting market adjustments to occur only in prices.

In general, therefore:

> A tariff causes less resource misallocation than an import quota. This is because market adjustments under a tariff are mostly changes in import quantities, whereas market adjustments under an import quota are simply changes in domestic prices.

Equity

A tariff allows for less inequity than an import quota. With a tariff, dependency of domestic buyers on particular suppliers is reduced, and there is greater assurance that the benefits of any low-cost importation that may be done are fully realized by the public rather than by the recipients of quota allocations. With an import quota, on the other hand, importers must apply for government licenses. The allocation of licenses is usually determined by noneconomic factors and without taking consumer choice and producer cost into account. Thus:

Import quotas, unlike tariffs, tend to be discriminatory. The reason is that such quotas favor some importers over others, enabling the former to reap larger profits at the latter's (and at the public's) expense.

Stability and Growth

Tariffs and quotas cause higher domestic prices, but a tariff permits greater price stability than does a quota. This is because the foreign supply of a commodity available in the domestic market is flexible under a tariff but inflexible under a quota. Consequently, changing supply and demand conditions result in smaller fluctuations in price, but greater fluctuations in import quantities, under a tariff than under a quota.

Finally, with respect to growth, it is true that both tariffs and quotas encourage expansion of protected industries. However, in the long run, the final result of either is a net loss in the economy's overall growth. This is because resources are encouraged to shift out of industries in which the nation has a comparative advantage into protected industries which entail relatively high costs of production.

To conclude:

Tariffs and import quotas both entail economic costs. Although relative prices are distorted by tariffs, they nevertheless permit market forces to allocate society's resources. Alternatively, import quotas stifle competition, create vested interests in quota allocation, and are discriminatory in their effects. Therefore, if some degree of trade protection is desired for whatever reason, the country would be better off with tariffs than with import quotas.

A fitting conclusion to this discussion of trade protection is presented in Box 3.

The Foreign-Trade Multiplier

How does foreign trade affect a nation's income and employment? To answer this question, we must think of imports and exports in a special way. Imports should be regarded as *withdrawals* from a nation's circular flow of income because they represent money earned at home but not put back into the income stream through consumption expenditures. Thus, if Americans decide to buy more foreign-made cars and fewer American-made ones, the American automobile industry will sell less. As a result, it will reduce its investment expenditures and lay off workers. These unemployed workers will then buy fewer appliances, vacation trips, houses, and other goods. Their reduced demands for these products and services will in turn result in a further decline in investment and employment. The *initial* increase in imports, therefore, will eventually bring about a *multiplied* decrease in national income and output.

Exports should be regarded as *injections* into a nation's circular flow of income because they represent money received from foreigners who have bought American goods. For example, if West Germans decide to buy less of their own goods and more American products, some American firms will find the demand for their products increasing. These firms will then expand their investment in plant and equipment and hire more workers, who in turn will buy more of other products and thereby encourage the expansion of other industries. The *initial* increase in exports, therefore, eventually brings about a *multiplied* increase in national income and output.

On the whole, tariffs do not impair efficiency, equity, stability, and growth as much as import quotas do.

Because of the foreign-trade multiplier, an increase in net exports can result in a magnified increase in national income and employment.

These ideas suggest the existence of a "foreign-trade multiplier"—one of many multiplier concepts in economics. It may be described in the following way:

The *foreign-trade multiplier* is a principle that states that fluctuations in net exports (that is, exports minus imports) may generate magnified variations in national income. This principle is based on the idea that a change in exports relative to imports has the same multiplier effect on national income as a change in expenditure "injections" into the income stream. Similarly, a change in imports relative to exports has the same multiplier effect on national income as does a change in "withdrawals" or "leakages" from the income stream.

In general, an increase in exports tends to raise domestic income, but the increased income also induces some imports. These imports act as "leakages." They tend to reduce the full multiplier effect that would exist if imports remained constant. The foreign-trade multiplier thus helps explain the fluctuations in economic activity that occur in today's world of interdependent nations.

Box 3
Who Will Be the Sacrificial Lamb?

Despite all the economic arguments that can be presented in favor of free trade, many prominent people, including some business executives, labor leaders, and politicians, continue to plead for protection.

"There is no question that my industry's needs for price relief from the below-cost-of-production price levels now prevailing in the so-called "world" market will cost consumers more and will contribute to further inflation.

"However, if such relief is not provided, much, if not all, of the domestic sugar producing industry will disappear. The inflationary effect of what my industry seeks will pale into nothing compared to that induced by total or even greater reliance on foreign suppliers for this vital commodity."

A. E. Benning, Chairman
and Chief Executive Officer
The Amalgamated Sugar Co.
Ogden, Utah

"South African ferrochrome producers, using predatory prices, are destroying producers in a drive to control U.S. supply of this critical material. Without import relief, there would then be nothing to prevent a South African ferrochrome cartel from extracting monopoly prices or withholding supply from U.S. steel producers and thus substantially disrupting this essential industry."

A. D. Gate
Committee of Producers
of High Carbon Ferrochrome
Washington, D.C.

"A very large proportion of the imported footwear is produced in factories owned or controlled by American manufacturers. It is sold in the American market at the same price it would command if it had been made here. Thus the cost differential between the low-wage foreign operation and the modest wages of American shoe workers becomes a profit differential for manufacturers, wholesalers and retailers. The consumer gets no share in it.

"Are we now to tell the typical shoe worker, aged 50, that he must cheerfully surrender his job to a 12-year-old girl in Taiwan or a peasant working behind his cottage in Spain? Can we make him whole by offering him a course in bricklaying or bus driving? He will not buy it. And neither, we think, will the nation."

George O. Fecteau, President
United Shoe Workers
of America

"Thousands of our members have become sacrificial lambs on the altar of foreign trade.

"The flood of foreign-made tires is being felt by our members in that segment of the rubber industry. If nothing is done to check this trend, thousands of tire plant jobs will be eliminated. We cannot and will not stand still for this.

"Our people don't want to hear ideological phrases of the learned economists' theories on free trade. What all our members really want is a steady job."

Peter Bommarito, President
United Rubber Workers

"Comparative advantage [says] let each country produce what they make best and we have unlimited free trade and the end result is prices are cheaper and everybody's life is better.

"There is one catch. If the comparative advantage is that some countries work children, have no minimum wage, no 40-hour workweek, no other protections, no free unions, then obviously they have an advantage of exploitation and it should not be subsidized by the workers of this country. In fact, it ought to be opposed."

Edmund G. Brown, Jr.
Governor, State of California

Case
Import Protection Can Be Good

Everyone agrees that import protection leads to inefficiency and higher prices. Everyone, that is, except those in the protected industries, including labor leaders. Since the 1960s, after decades of exalting the virtues of free trade, American labor made an abrupt about-face. It went on record supporting import restraints, arguing that they are necessary to protect domestic jobs and wages. To buttress their arguments that restraints can actually improve efficiency and reduce prices, labor leaders are fond of quoting from a U.S. Department of Labor study, "Price Behavior of Products Under Import Relief," published in 1979. The chief conclusions of the study may be summarized briefly.

The imposition of import relief need not have inflationary consequences if the affected domestic industry is able to use the (temporary) relief period to improve its technology, productivity, and price competitiveness. Import relief gives a domestic industry that has been seriously injured by imports a "breathing spell," during which it can take steps to increase efficiency and improve its competitive position. Conventional analysis of import relief typically ignores this possibility.

The Bureau of International Labor Affairs conducted an examination of price and efficiency in industries granted import relief. The study found that the manufacturing industries that were provided relief from injurious imports—speciality steel, nonrubber footwear, and color television receivers—had smaller price increases during the relief period than other comparable commodities. Meanwhile, the productivity increases were greater than the increases in the economy as a whole and greater than the increases in comparable industrial categories. The evidence thus suggests that the presumed inflationary impact of import relief can be greatly overstated, if potential gains in efficiency in the temporarily protected industries are not considered.

Reasons for Improved Efficiency

Analysis of each of the three affected industries revealed that, after the provision of import relief, capacity utilization rates rose. The industries increased their investment rates and introduced new technology with the effect of improving efficiency and lowering costs of production. These measures contributed to better price performance during the period in which import relief was instituted.

These results suggest that an effort should be undertaken to reexamine the methodology used in estimating the inflationary impact of import relief. It is imperative that policy makers have better information in order to judge whether to grant import relief.

Conclusion

Accurate estimates of the inflationary costs of protection need to be balanced against the costs of dislocation that may occur if protection is not granted. As it now stands, forecasts of the inflationary impact of protection are inadequate because they overlook potential positive responses by the protected industries. Without more accurate information, legislators must make decisions on the basis of inadequate estimates of social costs and, therefore, inaccurate assessments of net social benefits.

What familiar argument for protection is supported by this study?

What You Have Learned in This Chapter

1. Trade is important in the world economy. In quantitative terms, merchandise imports or exports may be as much as 40 percent of GNP for many major countries. In qualitative terms, many goods that countries import are virtually impossible to produce domestically.

2. Nations can raise their material standards of living by specializing and trading instead of trying to be self-sufficient. Two basic principles of specialization are the law of absolute advantage and the law of comparative advantage. The latter is more general because it demonstrates that nations can mutually benefit from specialization and trade even if each has only a relative rather than a complete advantage over the other in the production of commodities. The *gains* from trade are the benefits that nations receive; the *terms* of trade are the sacrifices they must make of the goods they give up in return for the goods they receive.

3. Despite the mutual benefits of free trade, nations have instituted various forms of protection. These common instruments of protection consist of tariffs, import quotas, and other protective devices. The last includes unusual customs procedures and laws pertaining to import financing, foreign-exchange requirements, and regulations involving labeling, health, safety, and shipping.

4. Many arguments may be advanced in favor of protection. Each needs qualification, and most involve logical fallacies. In general, if some form of protection is to be imposed, a tariff is less objectionable on economic grounds than an import quota.

5. The foreign-trade multiplier is one of many multiplier concepts in economics. It is a principle that states that fluctuations in a nation's net exports may cause magnified changes in its national income.

For Discussion

1. *Terms and concepts to review:*
law of absolute advantage
gains from trade
terms of trade
law of comparative advantage
tariff
import quota
infant industry
foreign-trade multiplier

2. Examine the following production-possibilities table based on hypothetical data:

Country	Labor input (days)	Output of:	
		Shoes (pairs)	Beef (pounds)
Italy	3	100	75
Argentina	3	50	60

(a) Which country, if any, has an absolute advantage in production? A comparative advantage? Explain.

(b) What is the *range* of possible barter terms—that is, the range within which the two countries may exchange goods? (**Hint** What are the *domestic terms of trade* in each country?)

(c) What will determine the actual terms of exchange? Explain carefully.

3. The Constitution of the United States (Article 1, Sec. 10) states: "No State shall, without the consent of the Congress, lay any imposts or duties on imports or exports, except what may be absolutely necessary for executing its inspection laws." Do you think the Founding Fathers were wise to pass this law? What would happen to the American standard of living if each state were allowed to impose protective barriers to trade?

4. "If you believe in the free movement of goods between nations, you should logically believe in the free movement of people, too. This means that cheap foreign labor should be admitted to the United States, even if it results in the displacement of American labor." Do you agree? Explain your answer.

5. An editorial in the *Washington Inquirer* stated that: "The United States should develop a large shipbuilding industry. Such an industry would provide more jobs and higher incomes for workers. Moreover, the ships could be used for passenger and cargo service in peacetime, and could be quickly converted for military purposes in case of war. In view of these advantages, it would be wise for the U.S. government to protect the domestic shipbuilding industry from foreign competition until it can grow to a stronger competitive position." Do you agree with this editorial? Explain.

6. Abraham Lincoln is reputed to have remarked: "I don't know much about the tariff. But I do know that when I buy a coat from England, I have the coat and England has the money. But when I buy a coat in America, I have the coat and America has the money." Can you show that Lincoln was correct only in the first sentence of his remark?

International Economics: Foreign Exchange and Payments

Learning guide
Watch for the answers to these important questions

Why does money flow between countries? What function is performed by foreign-exchange markets?

What is a balance-of-payments statement? What are its major components? What do these components disclose?

What is meant by balance-of-payments disequilibrium? How does it arise?

How may a nation adjust to balance-of-payments equilibrium? What are the major consequences of the various policies that may be followed? What policies do nations follow today?

This chapter surveys the major principles and problems of international finance.

At one time, the study of international economics dealt primarily with the problems of trade between nations. But this has long since ceased to be true. The economic relations among countries depend as much on financial considerations as on trade. Hence, an understanding of international finance is essential in dealing with world economic problems.

What do we mean by international finance? In the most general sense, it deals with the monetary side of international trade. The study of international finance is therefore concerned with the nature of international transactions. These include their forms of payment, the ways in which they are recorded for purposes of analysis and interpretation, their economic effects on the nations involved, and the methods by which their undesirable consequences can be minimized. Once you have some familiarity with these complex issues, you will better understand many of the most critical problems faced by nations today.

International Payments and Foreign Exchange

Each nation has its own unit of currency. This means that, when transactions are conducted across national borders, one currency must be converted into another.

For example, if a French importer buys machinery from the United States, the American exporter eventually receives payment in dollars, not in French francs. Similarly, if an American tourist visits England, he or she pays for hotel rooms, restaurant meals, and other goods and services in British pounds, not in dollars. The instruments used to make international payments are called collectively *foreign exchange*. These instruments consist not only of currency but also of checks, drafts, and bills of exchange, which are simply orders to pay currency.

Function of the Foreign-Exchange Markets

International transactions go on all the time. As a result, some people have dollars that they want to exchange for pounds and others have pounds that they want to exchange for dollars. How do these people acquire the foreign exchange they desire?

The answer is that foreign exchange is bought and sold in organized markets through dealers, just as stocks, bonds, wheat, copper, and numerous other commodities are bought and sold. In the United States, the foreign-exchange dealers are the large commercial banks located in New York, San Francisco, and various other major cities. Overseas, the major foreign-exchange centers include London, Zurich, Paris, Brussels, Tokyo, and Hong Kong. Therefore, if you want to acquire or dispose of foreign exchange, you can easily do so by communicating directly with a dealer or by going through the local commercial bank, which will arrange the transaction through one of the large banks dealing in foreign exchange.

The foreign-exchange markets permit the conversion of one currency into another.

The most fundamental function performed by organized foreign-exchange markets is that they provide a ready means for transferring purchasing power from one country to another and from one currency to another. Without foreign-exchange markets, international trade would be virtually limited to barter.

Effects of International Transactions

Suppose that an American exporter sells a machine to a British importer. The importer might pay for it by purchasing a draft from the bank—that is, an order to pay a specified number of British pounds to the American exporter. The exporter then converts the draft into American dollars by selling the draft to a foreign-exchange dealer. The number of dollars the dealer pays for the draft depends on the rate of exchange between dollars and pounds. (The dealer, like any broker, will also impose a commission charge.)

International transactions result in flows of money between countries and enable countries to purchase each other's goods.

The American exporter now has the dollars, and the foreign-exchange dealer has a draft payable in British pounds. What will each of them do? Because they are in business, they are likely to deposit the funds in their own bank accounts so that they can continue to write the checks they need to carry on their activities. Thus, the American exporter will deposit the dollars in an American bank, and the American foreign-exchange dealer will send the draft to England for deposit in a British bank. The dealer, by having such an account, can write a draft or check against it and sell it to an American importer who needs pounds to pay for goods purchased from a British exporter.

What are the results of these activities? In general, international transactions have two economic effects:

1. An export transaction increases the supply of money in the exporting country and reduces it in the importing country. For an import transaction, the reverse is true. (Can you explain why?)

2. By exporting, a nation obtains the foreign monies it needs to acquire imports. In other words, a nation that sells abroad can also buy abroad. (Japan, for example, sells motorcycles, television sets, and other goods to the United States and is thereby able to obtain the dollars it needs to buy American machines, agricultural goods, and other products.)

The Balance of Payments

So far, we have assumed that economic relations among nations are based solely on international trade. In reality, this is not the whole story. Foreign exchange is demanded and supplied as a result of various other important types of transactions besides importing and exporting. It is necessary, therefore, that we examine the nature of these transactions.

Corporations prepare periodic reports, such as balance sheets and income (or profit-and-loss) statements, summarizing in money terms the results of their business activities. These reports are used by bankers, business executives, stockholders, creditors, or any other interested parties—even by the government—to evaluate a company's financial position.

Each nation also prepares a somewhat similar periodic report called a "balance of payments." The report summarizes in money terms the results of a nation's international economic activities by showing how some transactions cause an outflow of funds and others an inflow. It should be apparent, therefore, that a nation's balance of payments is of concern not only to economists but also to business managers, bankers, government leaders, and anyone interested in world affairs.

An Illustrative Model of the Balance of Payments

What does a balance-of-payments statement actually look like? How is it interpreted? We can best answer these questions by first analyzing the structure of an idealized balance-of-payments form such as the one shown in Exhibit 1.

As you have just learned, a nation's balance of payments is a financial summary of its international transactions. The first thing to notice is that these money flows are represented in the last two columns of the statement by "debits" and "credits"—two terms that are widely used in discussions of the balance of payments:

> A *debit* is any transaction that results in a money outflow or payment to a foreign country; it may be represented on a balance-of-payments statement by a negative sign. A *credit* is any transaction that results in a money inflow or receipt from a foreign country; it may be represented on a balance-of-payments statement by a positive sign. (**Note** These definitions are applicable only in international economics. If you take a course in accounting, you will find that the terms "debit" and "credit" are defined differently.)

The balance-of-payments model shown in Exhibit 1 is self-explanatory. All you have to do is go down the list to see that each item would logically result in either an outflow or an inflow of money and hence would be recorded as either a debit or a credit.

The balance of payments is divided into two major categories: (1) current account and (2) capital account. In the first category, the subclassification at the top denoting merchandise trade usually involves the largest debits and credits in balance-of-payments statements. Thus, a merchandise import is a debit item because it results in a money outflow or payment. A merchandise export is a credit item because it results in a money inflow or receipt.

The remaining items can be interpreted in a similar way. Those requiring further clarification will be explained shortly.

Exhibit 1
General Model of the Balance of Payments

	Debit (money outflows or payments) (−)	Credit (money inflows or receipts) (+)		Debit (money outflows or payments) (−)	Credit (money inflows or receipts) (+)
I. CURRENT ACCOUNT			II. CAPITAL ACCOUNT		
A. Merchandise trade			**A. Official reserve assets**		
1. Merchandise imports	x		1. Increase in government-held international reserve assets	x	
2. Merchandise exports		x	2. Decrease in government-held international reserve assets		x
B. Service transactions			**B. Other government assets abroad**		
1. Transportation			1. Increase in government loans and other claims	x	
a. Rendered by foreign carriers	x		2. Decrease in government loans and other claims		x
b. Rendered by domestic carriers		x			
2. Travel expenditures			**C. Long-term**		
a. In foreign countries	x		1. Purchased securities from foreigners	x	
b. By foreigners here		x	2. Sold securities to foreigners		x
3. Interest and dividends			**D. Short-term***		
a. Paid to foreigners	x		1. Increase of bank balances abroad	x	
b. Received from abroad		x	2. Decrease of foreign-held bank balances here	x	
4. Banking and insurance services			3. Increase of foreign-held bank balances here		x
a. Rendered by foreign institutions	x		4. Decrease of bank balances abroad		x
b. Rendered to foreigners by domestic institutions		x			
5. Government expenditures			Errors and omissions		
a. By home government abroad	x				
b. By foreign governments here		x			
C. Unilateral transfers					
1. Private					
a. Remittances sent abroad	x				
b. Remittances received from abroad		x			
2. Governmental					
a. Grants to other countries	x				
b. Grants from other countries		x			

*Also includes private currency holdings and claims not listed.

Source: Adapted with substantial changes from Delbert Snider, *Introduction to International Economics,* 5th ed., Homewood, Ill.: Irwin, 1971.

The Balance of Payments Always Balances (in Accounting)

If you take a basic course in accounting, you will learn to apply a principle known as *double-entry bookkeeping.* This principle holds that every transaction is of a twofold nature and must be expressed, for accounting purposes, in the form of *both* debits and credits. In other words, for any given debit there must be one or more credits whose total will precisely equal the debit. Similarly, for any given credit there must be one or more debits whose total will precisely equal the credit.

This idea can be illustrated with reference to the balance-of-payments model in Exhibit 1. Suppose, for example, that an American firm exports equipment worth $1 million to a foreign country. This part of the transaction is a merchandise export and appears as a credit item on the U.S. balance of payments. The importing country may pay for the goods in any one or a combination of several ways. These are recorded as debit items on the U.S. balance of payments. For instance:

1. The importing country may pay in dollars by decreasing its foreign-held bank balances in the United States. This is shown in the capital account, subclass D, item 2.

2. The importing country may pay in its own currency, which has the effect of increasing U.S. bank balances held abroad. This is shown in the same subclass as before, but in item 1.

3. The importing country may receive the equipment as a gift under the U.S. foreign-aid program, in which case it is a unilateral transfer similar to a grant. This is shown in the current account, subclass C, item 2a.

Double-entry bookkeeping assures, in principle, that *total debits equal total credits*—or, in other words, that the *balance of payments always balances* in an accounting sense. In practice, however, because a country's balance of payments summarizes millions of individual international transactions, it is rarely accurate down to the last dollar. Hence, total debits will be either less than or greater than total credits. To correct this, a balance-of-payments statement will often show an item called "errors and omissions" or "statistical discrepancy." This item, which equals the difference between actual total debits and actual total credits, is added to the smaller of these two totals to bring them into balance.

However, the fundamental reason why a balance-of-payments statement always balances may be summarized as follows:

> A country, like a household, cannot spend more than its current income unless it draws on its cash reserves, sells some of its assets, borrows, or receives gifts. All of these are credit items on its balance-of-payments statement. Similarly, a country cannot spend less than its current income unless it accumulates cash reserves, acquires some assets, lends, or gives gifts. All of these are debit items. Therefore, total debits must always equal total credits.

From an accounting viewpoint, the balance of payments always balances. However, we must look deeper in order to understand the economic implications of "balance" in the balance of payments.

The Two Major Accounts

The balance-of-payments model, as we have seen, contains two major accounts. Let us survey briefly the contents of each.

Current Account

This includes all imports and exports of goods and services, and is the most basic account in the balance of payments. It is the stuff of which international economic relations are composed. The other (capital) account fulfills what are largely auxiliary functions by facilitating the flow of goods and services.

The subclass called "unilateral transfers" is somewhat like the capital account (see below). That is, unilateral transfers are capital movements and gifts for which there are no return commitments or claims. Thus, a personal remittance to a resident of a foreign country involves no commitment for repayment and is classified as a unilateral transfer.

A nation's balance of payments consists of a current account and a capital account.

Capital Account

This is composed entirely of governmental and private paper claims and obligations. Thus:

The subclass called "official reserve assets" consists of changes in international reserve assets. These are used for settling accounts between government central banks. Such intergovernmental settlements usually arise because of deficits or surpluses in the current account or in the other components of the capital account. International reserve assets serve to finance those deficits and surpluses. Examples of international reserve assets are convertible currencies (those that are in wide demand and are therefore readily exchangeable, such as U.S. dollars, Japanese yen, British pounds, and West German marks) and gold.

The next subclass, "other government assets abroad," is self-explanatory. It includes changes in government loans and other claims against foreigners.

In the remainder of the capital account, the long-term component consists of loans and investments maturing in more than one year. The short-term component consists of claims maturing in less than one year and of foreign-exchange and bank balances. These short-term capital movements may flow into or out of a country to make up for differences in payments and receipts resulting from a gap between imports and exports or from other transactions.

Against this background, let us summarize what is meant by "balance of payments":

> The *balance of payments* is a statement of the money value of all transactions that take place between a nation and the rest of the world during a given period. These transactions may consist both of imports and exports of goods and services and of movements of short-term and long-term investments, gifts, currency, and gold. The transactions may be classified for convenience into two categories: current account and capital account.

The Balance of Payments of the United States

An abbreviated version of the U.S. balance of payments is shown in Exhibit 2. Note that the balance of trade is not the same thing as the balance of payments, although many people confuse the two. The *balance*

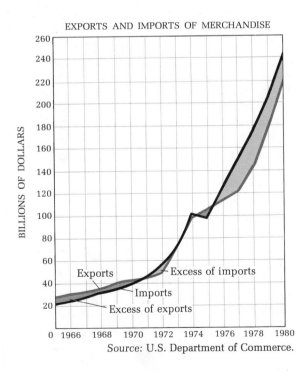

EXPORTS AND IMPORTS OF MERCHANDISE

BILLIONS OF DOLLARS

Exports

Imports

Excess of imports

Excess of exports

0 1966 1968 1970 1972 1974 1976 1978 1980

Source: U.S. Department of Commerce.

Exhibit 2
United States Balance of Payments, 1980

The balance on current account reflects current patterns of trade and the net flow of gifts and grants to foreign countries. The balance on capital account reflects the net value of long-term financial claims between the United States and the rest of the world.

	Credit (+), debits (−) (millions of dollars)
CURRENT ACCOUNT	
Exports of goods and services	$344.7
Imports of goods and services	−333.9
Unilateral transfers, net	−7.7
Balance on current account	**3.1***
CAPITAL ACCOUNT	
U.S. assets abroad, net	−84.8
Foreign assets in the U.S., net	50.3
Balance on capital account	**−34.5**
Balance on current and capital accounts	**−31.4**
Statistical discrepancy	31.4
Overall balance	**$ 0.0**

*The figures above do not quite add up to this total, due to rounding.

of trade is that part of a nation's balance of payments that deals with merchandise imports and exports. A "favorable" balance of trade exists when the value of a nation's exports exceeds the value of its imports. An "unfavorable" balance of trade exists when the value of a nation's imports exceeds the value of its exports.

What about the "balance" in the balance of payments? Here the concept is somewhat more complicated. In simplest terms, a nation's overall balance of payments always balances by virtue of the principle of double-entry bookkeeping. However, it is important to understand the economic circumstances under which specific balances are achieved. Therefore, the remainder of this chapter is devoted to a discussion of essential ideas involving balance-of-payments adjustments.

Economic Balance and Imbalance

Although a nation's balance of payments always balances in the accounting sense—in the sense that total debits always equal total credits—it need not balance in an economic sense. Before explaining the reasons why, two important sets of concepts associated with balance-of-payments analysis must be clarified. These are (1) autonomous and compensatory transactions and (2) equilibrium and disequilibrium.

Autonomous and Compensatory Transactions

It is useful to think of a nation's balance of payments as a record that reports two very different types of transactions—autonomous and compensatory.

Autonomous Transactions

Autonomous transactions are undertaken for reasons that are independent of the balance of payments. If you refer back to the general model in Exhibit 1, you will see that the main classes of autonomous transactions are merchandise trade and services, unilateral transfers, and long-term capital movements. The reasons for calling these autonomous are not hard to see. Merchandise trade and services are a response to relative differences in prices at home and abroad. Unilateral transfers are a response to private and governmental decisions based on personal, military, or political considerations. Long-term capital movements are a response to relative differences in expected rates of return on financial investments at home and abroad. These autonomous transactions are thus unrelated to the balance of payments as such, and they may result in total money receipts being greater or less than total money payments.

Autonomous transactions (such as trade, unilateral transfers, and long-term capital movements) occur for economic and political reasons; they are independent of the balance of payments.

Compensatory Transactions

In contrast, *compensatory transactions* are undertaken as a direct response to balance-of-payments considerations. Compensatory transactions may be thought of as balancing items that arise in order to accommodate differences in money inflows and outflows resulting from autonomous transactions.

If you look back at the general model in Exhibit 1, you will see that there are two main classes of compensatory transactions. These are shifts in the official reserve transactions account (consisting of international reserve assets, such as major currencies and gold holdings) and short-term capital movements. Because these primarily involve

Compensatory transactions (such as movements in currency, gold, and short-term capital) occur in order to adjust imbalances caused by autonomous transactions.

changes in international reserve assets at home and abroad and in bank balances, it seems clear that they serve largely as adjustment items to correct for imbalances in autonomous transactions. Thus, in a sense, if you borrow to pay a debt, you are financing a deficit in your personal "balance of payments" by means of a compensatory transaction—the money borrowed.

Equilibrium and Disequilibrium

How do autonomous and compensatory transactions affect the economic position of a nation in relation to other nations? The answer to this question involves the notion of equilibrium and disequilibrium. As you already know, a market price or quantity is in equilibrium when it is in a state of balance among opposing forces, and it is in disequilibrium when there is no such balance. The same ideas of equilibrium and disequilibrium can be applied to a nation's international economic position as reflected in its balance of payments:

> *Balance-of-payments disequilibrium* exists when, over a given period (usually several years), the sum of autonomous credits does not equal the sum of autonomous debits. A *deficit disequilibrium* occurs when total autonomous debits exceed total autonomous credits. On the other hand, a *surplus disequilibrium* occurs when total autonomous credits exceed total autonomous debits.

A disequilibrium in the balance of payments occurs when total autonomous debits and credits are persistently unequal for a prolonged period.

The existence of compensatory transactions is evidence of a nation's balance-of-payments disequilibrium. In practice, of course, you cannot always expect the sum of autonomous receipts and payments to match each other exactly—any more than you can expect total supply and demand in a competitive market to be precisely equal at all times. This is because numerous decision-making entities (mostly households and firms) are involved. But you do expect periodic deficits and surpluses to balance out approximately over a period of a few years. When this does not occur, it is necessary to find the reason why.

The most common reason for a country's failure to attain a balance between deficits and surpluses is that it has suffered a persistent deficit disequilibrium for a number of years. This means that the nation has spent more than it has earned and hence must have been either drawing on its cash reserves, selling its assets, borrowing, or receiving gifts from other countries.

Adjusting to Equilibrium

How can a nation correct a disequilibrium in its balance of payments? The answer is straightforward. Because disequilibrium is the result of a gap between a country's total autonomous payments and receipts, the factors that determine these autonomous transactions must undergo a change so that the nation's total money outflows and inflows can be brought into balance. The problem can best be approached by analyzing the adjustment process that would take place under four sets of circumstances:

Adjustment to balance-of-payments equilibrium may be analyzed under four sets of circumstances.

1. Freely fluctuating exchange rates.
2. Price and income changes.
3. The gold standard.
4. Government controls.

Exhibit 3
**Supply of, and Demand for,
British Pounds**

An increase in the demand for British pounds
will raise the equilibrium price from P to P'
and the equilibrium quantity from N to N'.

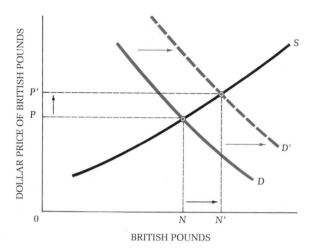

It is instructive to see how adjustments in the balance of payments are
brought about under each of these conditions.

Adjustment Through Freely Fluctuating Exchange Rates

Nations' currencies are traded in the foreign-exchange market.

The *foreign-exchange rate* is the price of one currency in terms of another. If in the wheat market the price of wheat were $1 per bushel, this
would mean that anyone could take $1 to the market and exchange it for
a bushel of wheat. Further, anyone could take a bushel of wheat to the
market and exchange it for $1. Similarly, if in the foreign-exchange mar-
ket the dollar price of British pounds were $2 = £1, it would mean that
anyone could take $1 to the market and exchange it for £0.50 or anyone
could take £1 to the market and exchange it for $2.

The foreign-exchange market is a competitive market that behaves
according to the laws of supply and demand. This means that fluctuations in the price of foreign exchange are the result of changes in the
demand and supply curves of buyers and sellers. The basic idea is illustrated in Exhibit 3. In this simple model, the "commodity" being
bought and sold is British pounds and the price is expressed in terms of
dollars. (A similar situation could be depicted in which the commodity
is dollars and the price is expressed in terms of British pounds.) For
simplicity, we are assuming that there are only two countries, the United
States and Britain. The interaction of the demand curve for pounds
with the supply curve of pounds thus determines the equilibrium price
at P and the equilibrium quantity at N.

In the foreign-exchange market, Americans (such as importers and tourists) are always wanting to buy pounds; and Britons are always wanting to buy dollars. Hence, at any given time there are "dollars looking for pounds" and there are "pounds looking for dollars." This makes an active market in foreign exchange.

The Adjustment Process

In order to understand how international adjustments take place under freely fluctuating exchange rates, let us begin by assuming a state of equilibrium in which the exchange rate in Exhibit 3 is at P and there is neither a deficit nor a surplus in the American balance of payments. If American imports of British goods were then to rise, and if this increase were not offset by long-term capital movements or unilateral transfers from Britain to the United States, the American demand for pounds would also increase. That is, the demand curve would shift to the right from D to D'. As the price rose toward the new equilibrium level at P', British pounds would become more expensive for Americans to buy, thereby causing the United States to reduce its purchases of British goods. At the same time, American dollars would become cheaper for Britons, thereby causing Britain to expand its purchases of American goods. This slowing down of American imports from Britain and expansion of American exports to Britain would continue until a new equilibrium in the U.S. balance of payments was reached in accord with the equilibrium price in the foreign-exchange market. Thus:

Balance-of-payments equilibrium is achieved automatically under a system of freely fluctuating exchange rates.

Freely fluctuating exchange rates perform at least three important functions:

1. They automatically correct a disequilibrium in the balance of payments through the free play of international market forces.

2. They may make imports cheaper and exports dearer, or vice versa, by altering the price of foreign exchange without *necessarily* affecting domestic or foreign price levels.

3. To the extent that they operate independently of domestic price and income levels, they bear the burden of balance-of-payments adjustments without imposing constraints on the domestic economy (as will be explained shortly).

Despite these desirable features, freely fluctuating exchange rates have some disadvantages:

Freely fluctuating exchange rates can have undesirable effects on a country's trade.

1. They make it difficult and risky for traders to commit themselves for weeks or months in advance to international transactions. The reason is that the exchange rate may change between the time goods are ordered and the time they are received. This uncertainty may reduce trade between nations.

2. Freely fluctuating exchange rates turn the terms of trade against a nation whose currency is depreciated in the foreign-exchange market. For example, an increase in the demand for British pounds results in a price increase or *appreciation* in the dollar price of pounds and a price decrease or *depreciation* in the pound price of dollars. This means that the United States must export more goods to Britain to earn the same total revenue that it earned before.

3. Freely fluctuating exchange rates *may* stimulate or depress a nation's export industries by making its currency either cheaper or dearer in international markets. This could tend to encourage fluctuations in income and employment.

Adjustment Through Price and Income Changes

You have learned that exchange-rate adjustments can bring about an equilibrium in the balance of payments while domestic price and income levels remain stable. A moment's reflection will make it evident that it is also true that changes in domestic price and income levels can restore equilibrium in a nation's balance of payments while exchange rates remain stable. Let us see why.

Price Changes

If a nation maintains fixed exchange rates, it may be able to achieve balance-of-payments equilibrium through adjustments in its price level.

In terms of the previous example, if there is a deficit in the U.S. balance of payments due to an excess of imports over exports, a deflation of American prices can have the same effect as a depreciation of the dollar in the foreign-exchange market. This is because, if prices in the United States are reduced, it becomes cheaper for Britons to buy American goods. American exports to Britain will therefore increase, and this will tend to eliminate the U.S. balance-of-payments deficit. (Equivalently, an inflation in Britain can have the same effect as an appreciation of the pound in the foreign-exchange market. Can you explain why?)

How might a deflation be brought about? There are three possibilities:

1. Some deflationary pressures will be induced automatically through market forces because the excess of American imports over exports will cause a reduction in the United States money supply.

2. Contractionary economic (monetary and fiscal) policies may have to be invoked in order to exert a downward push on prices.

3. U.S. manufacturers may try to reduce or stabilize prices in order to compete with foreigners.

It is possible that a trade-off exists between price changes and the level of employment. To the extent that this is true, reductions in prices will tend to increase unemployment and thereby bring about a recession. The question, therefore, is whether such a high cost should be incurred in order to achieve balance-of-payments equilibrium. Many political leaders believe that it should not and that some other solution should be sought.

Income Changes

If a nation maintains fixed exchange rates, it may be able to achieve balance-of-payments equilibrium through adjustments in its income level.

A country's balance of payments is also related to its national income. Thus, if the domestic level of income increases while exchange rates and domestic prices remain stable, people will tend to import more goods from abroad and to take more trips abroad. (For balance-of-payments purposes, an American tourist visiting a foreign country is equivalent to the United States importing "scenery" from that country.) A deficit in the U.S. balance of payments, therefore, can be corrected through a decrease in the domestic level of income. (Equivalently, it can also be corrected through an increase in other nations' levels of income, because American exports will increase if foreign income rises.)

The disadvantages of adjustment through domestic income reduction, however, are essentially the same as those of price deflation. Contractionary economic (monetary and fiscal) policies would have to be invoked in order to cause a downward pressure on national income. This in turn would probably induce a recession and unemployment—a trade-off that most people would not willingly accept for the sake of achieving balance-of-payments equilibrium.

Before proceeding with this important problem, it will be helpful to conclude the discussion thus far with an important principle:

> The influence of adjustments in exchange rates, price levels, and income levels on a balance-of-payments disequilibrium will depend on the relative responsiveness of demand to changes in prices and incomes.

Two examples will help to illustrate this idea:

1. Foreign demand for our nation's exports depends in part on our level of prices. Other things remaining the same, a 10 percent reduction in domestic prices will have the same effect as a 10 percent depreciation in the price of our currency on the foreign-exchange market, as far as correcting a deficit in our balance of payments is concerned.

2. Our demand for other countries' exports depends in part on our level of income. Other things remaining the same, there is *some* percentage reduction in domestic income that will correct our balance-of-payments deficit, but that percentage can only be estimated.

Factors such as these are of considerable practical significance. Indeed, they have played extremely important roles in the international financial policies of nations, as will be seen later. Therefore, you will find it helpful to look up the meaning of *income elasticity of demand* in the Dictionary at the back of the book.

Adjustment Under the Gold Standard: The Classical Model

A very interesting process of adjustment takes place when the trading nations' monetary systems are on a gold standard. This situation existed for several dozen countries during the half century before World War I and for some years thereafter (until the onset of the depression in the early 1930s). Because of this, international adjustments under a gold standard can be considered part of classical (that is, pre-1930s) economic theory. As you will see, however, the theory has important implications for today's world economy.

The Gold Standard

If a nation were on a gold standard, it would be obliged to buy and sell gold to the public in exchange for paper money at a *fixed legal rate* and to permit gold to be imported and exported without restrictions. Under such circumstances, the exchange rate would tend to be stable and would never fluctuate beyond very narrow limits.

In 1930, for example, when the United States and England were both on a gold standard, the U.S. Treasury was required by law to buy and sell gold to the public at a price of $20.67 per ounce. Similarly, the Bank of England was required by law to buy and sell gold at a price of £4.25 per ounce. Therefore, because an ounce (which is equal to 480 grains) of gold could be exchanged for $20.67 in the United States or for £4.25 in England:

$$\$20.67 = £4.25 \ (= 1 \text{ ounce, or 480 grains, of gold})$$

In practice, nations have been reluctant to undergo the pain of price and income adjustments for the sake of achieving balance-of-payments equilibrium.

Under a gold standard, gold flows freely into and out of a country.

Hence, the par rate of exchange between the two countries was determined by the ratio $20.67 ÷ £4.25, or

$$\$4.86 = £1 \ (= 0.24 \text{ ounce, or } 113 \text{ grains, of gold})$$

In 1930, the cost (including insurance and freight) of shipping 0.24 ounce of gold between New York and London was about $0.02. As a result, the exchange rate or dollar price of pounds remained within the range of $4.84 to $4.88, for the following reasons:

1. Suppose the price of pounds in the foreign-exchange market were to rise, say, to $4.89. It would then be cheaper for an American importer to acquire 113 grains of gold for $4.86 and ship the gold to London at a cost of 2 cents in order to pay the British exporter. The importer would *in effect* be paying $4.88 for a pound instead of $4.89.

2. Suppose the price in the foreign-exchange market were to fall, say, to $4.83. A British importer would then be better off to acquire gold for £1 (=$4.86) and ship the gold to New York at a cost of 2 cents in order to pay the American exporter. The importer would *in effect* be getting $4.84 for a pound instead of $4.83.

The gold points provide upper and lower limits within which exchange rates can fluctuate.

The upper and lower limits of foreign exchange were thus $4.88 and $4.84, respectively. These were known as the *gold points*. Gold points delimit the range within which the foreign-exchange rates of gold-standard currencies will fluctuate. Thus, the gold points are equal to the par rate of exchange plus and minus the cost (including insurance) of shipping gold. The upper and lower gold points for a nation are called its *gold-export point* and its *gold-import point*, respectively. This is because gold will be exported when the foreign-exchange rate rises above the upper level and imported when the rate falls below the lower level. One nation's gold-export point is thus another nation's gold-import point, and vice versa.

To conclude, therefore:

> A gold standard provides free convertibility between paper money and gold, as well as the unrestricted shipment of gold into and out of the country. Consequently, the exchange rate under such circumstances tends to remain stable within the limits set by the gold points.

The Adjustment Process

Under the classical gold standard, balance-of-payments adjustments occurred automatically through gold inflows and outflows.

How does the existence of a gold standard affect the restoration of equilibrium due to a trade deficit in a nation's balance of payments? This in effect was a key question that the nineteenth-century classical economists asked. Their answer was that the adjustment is brought about *automatically* through changes in the price level. Why? Because they assumed that the price level is directly related to the quantity of money in circulation, which in turn is tied to the volume of gold being held by nations.

Thus, if a country experiences a disequilibrium in its balance of payments as a result of a trade deficit, its demand for foreign exchange will rise so that the exchange rate increases at least to the gold-export point. As gold leaves the country, the quantity of money will decrease, which in turn will reduce prices. With lower prices, the country's exports will rise and its imports fall, thereby correcting the disequilibrium.

What happens if a country experiences a disequilibrium in its balance of payments due to a trade surplus? The process is exactly the opposite. The country's demand for foreign exchange will fall, the exchange rate will drop, gold will be imported, prices will increase, and exports will fall while imports rise until equilibrium is again restored.

Classical Theory of Income and Employment Determination

This explanation of the adjustment process, it should be emphasized, was the classical economists' solution. Logically, it was an integral part of the classical theory of income and employment determination because it was based on two assumptions:

1. Full Employment of Resources This condition assures that an increase in the quantity of money would bring about an increase in the general price level.

2. Flexible Prices and Wages This condition assures that prices and wages would respond readily to changes in total spending.

Are these assumptions valid? With the development and extension of economic ideas since the 1930s, the first assumption (of full employment) has been viewed by many economists as a special rather than a general condition. Further, the second assumption (of flexible prices and wages—especially on the downward side) is obviously incorrect in our modern economy, where both big businesses and big unions exert monopolistic influences in the marketplace.

This leads to the following conclusion:

The gold standard has both desirable and undesirable features. On the one hand, it provides for stable exchange rates, which tend to reduce risks and encourage international trade while automatically correcting international disequilibrium. On the other hand, it requires that each nation submit to painful processes of deflation (or inflation) by subordinating its domestic economy to the dictates of external economic relations in order to achieve international equilibrium.

The adjustment process under a gold standard was part of classical thinking because it rested on the assumptions of classical theory.

Adjustment Through Government Controls

The methods of adjustment described thus far rely in different ways on market forces to correct a disequilibrium in the balance of payments. Now we shall turn to a final and radically different method of adjustment. This is the suppression of market forces through the imposition of direct government controls on international transactions. The list of specific controls is almost endless, but for analysis they can be grouped into two categories: exchange controls and trade controls.

Exchange Controls

One way in which a nation might seek to correct a deficit in its balance of payments is to limit the freedom of its residents to import goods and services and to export funds. To accomplish this objective, the government would impose direct controls over those types of international transactions that are to be curbed, while leaving others relatively uncontrolled or even "free."

Under such a system, all foreign-exchange earnings must be sold to the government and all foreign exchange needed to pay for international

Governments can try to maintain balance-of-payments equilibrium by controlling exchange rates.

transactions must be bought from the government. The rates at which the government buys and sells foreign exchange are officially established and need not be equal. This is typically accomplished through the adoption of a "multiple exchange system." Thus, the government may set a relatively high price or rate of exchange on the foreign exchange needed to import unessential luxury goods and a relatively low rate on the importation of vitally needed raw materials and capital goods. It may also designate some types of transactions as unrestricted and sell portions of its foreign exchange to the highest bidders.

In general:

> Exchange controls require that the government, rather than the free market, decide the order of priority for the importation of goods and services. This decision may then be implemented by allocating the limited supply of foreign exchange among competing uses.

Exchange controls have been used mainly by command economies, but also by mixed economies during wars or other emergencies.

Nations have instituted exchange controls for various reasons. The more important ones have been to provide better centralized control over the economy, to reduce wide economic fluctuations, to eliminate persistent deficits in the balance of payments, and to assure essential imports for hastening economic growth and development. The chief advantage of controls is that *some* method of adjustment must be employed to correct a significant disequilibrium caused by a balance-of-payments deficit. Among governments that use them, exchange controls may *look* like the least undesirable and least painful of the various choices that have been discussed. This is especially true in command economies. They use controls extensively, and their citizens have never known other alternatives.

In general, exchange controls are bound to lead to resource misallocation.

On the other hand, exchange controls also have several disadvantages:

1. By preventing or even limiting the importation of certain goods, controls may shift the demand for these goods to domestic producers. But, because these goods are available in very limited quantities, the effect may be to stimulate inflation at home as well as an exodus of resources out of export industries. This will encourage a drop in exports and aggravate rather than cure the deficit disequilibrium.

2. Because exchange controls prevent the free expression of market forces, they encourage the creation of an illegal black market in foreign exchange.

3. By curbing imports, controls help to bring on deflation in those countries whose export industries are adversely affected. This may encourage retaliatory measures by the injured nations, thereby reducing trade.

Trade Controls

Governments may also use trade controls to adjust their balances of payments.

A government may use another general class of measures, called *trade controls*, to adjust a disequilibrium caused by a balance-of-payments deficit. These may take such forms as tariffs and quotas to curb imports, special taxes on outflows of capital and on tourists going abroad, and subsidies to encourage the export industries. Measures such as these, as we have already learned, prevent the operation of the law of comparative advantage, misallocate world resources, and discourage the flow of trade. As with exchange controls, trade controls may also invite economic retaliation by other nations.

Conclusion: Today's Policies

Which of the four methods of achieving balance-of-payments equilibrium do countries actually employ? No nation today is on a gold standard, so the adjustment process under this classical model can be eliminated. This leaves exchange rates, price and income changes, and government controls as relevant alternatives.

Exchange Rates

If a nation permits the price of its own currency to fluctuate freely in the foreign-exchange market, any disequilibrium in its balance of payments will be corrected quickly and automatically. But, as pointed out earlier, this and other advantages of freely fluctuating exchange rates can entail certain sacrifices that the country's political leaders are not always willing to accept. Therefore, they may be inclined to seek a compromise between completely free and completely fixed exchange rates. Such a compromise consists of what is known as "managed" or "dirty floating." Under this type of policy, the nation's central bank interferes in the foreign-exchange market by buying and selling the country's currency in order to keep its price within narrow limits. In this way, by stabilizing the price of its currency within a range, say, of one or two percentage points, the nation is able to achieve some of the advantages of fluctuating exchange rates while avoiding some of the costs.

"Managed floating" is a compromise between completely fixed and completely flexible exchange rates.

Price and Income Changes

A nation that adopts a policy of managed floating will also have to maintain relatively stable prices and incomes. Otherwise the country will find itself under increasing pressure to realign its exchange rate as economic conditions change and the nation's currency becomes either more or less valuable in relation to other currencies. But, as you learned earlier, political leaders are not inclined to permit the desire for balance-of-payments equilibrium to determine domestic economic policies. Therefore, although such policies can contribute to balance-of-payments disequilibrium, they are not generally designed to avoid it.

Government Controls

Exchange and trade controls substitute government regulations for free-market decisions. All countries have employed controls during periods of war or other emergencies for the purpose of allocating scarce foreign exchange between high-priority and low-priority uses. However, only command economies use controls during peace. The purpose of controls is to assure the exportation and importation of those goods needed to fulfill a nation's plans for development.

Most mixed economies today engage in managed floating. Command economies make extensive use of exchange and trade controls.

To conclude:

Most mixed economies today adhere to a policy of managed exchange rates. Relatively minor use is made of general economic (price and income) policies for the express purpose of achieving balance-of-payments equilibrium. Command economies, on the other hand, make extensive use of exchange and trade controls. These are designed to help the planners in command economies manage their countries' economic growth.

It is interesting to note by how much (or by how little?) the policies of nations today differ from those of several centuries ago. See "Leaders in Economics," page 750.

The Bettmann Archive

Leaders in Economics

Thomas Mun
1571–1641
Mercantilist

At the end of the fifteenth century, a new philosophy of *statism* emerged in Western Europe. Absolute monarchy had replaced the decentralized structure of feudalism; the oceans had been conquered and were no longer considered barriers to trade; and the expansion of world commerce had occurred simultaneously with the development of banking and credit institutions. These factors encouraged dramatic struggles for power by kings and princes, resulting in ultranationalistic policies that tended to make all states enemies, as each sought to achieve world military and economic leadership.

Mercantilism
These developments gave rise to what is known as *mercantilism*—a set of doctrines and practices aimed at promoting national prosperity and the power of the state. This was to be achieved in three ways:

1. Accumulating precious metals (mainly gold and silver) through the maintenance of favorable trade balances, or excesses of exports over imports.

2. Achieving economic self-sufficiency through imperialism (empire building).

3. Exploiting colonies for the benefit of the mother country by monopolizing the raw materials and precious metals of the colonies while reserving them as exclusive markets for exports.

Mercantilism reached its peak in the seventeenth century, serving as a political and economic ideology in England, France, Spain, and Germany.

Favorable Balance of Trade
The majority of those who wrote on mercantilist theory were businesspeople. The most notable was Thomas Mun, a leading English merchant and for many years a director of the famous British East India Company. His book, *England's Treasure by Forraign Trade,* was published posthumously by his son in 1664.

This treatise is regarded as the outstanding exposition of mercantilist doctrine. It stressed the importance to England of maintaining a favorable balance of trade—a doctrine of fundamental significance in mercantilism because it was a key means of accumulating gold and silver. The book was also the first work to show that it was not the specific balance of trade with any particular nation that was the important consideration but the total balance with all nations. The former could be unfavorable, according to Mun, as long as the latter was favorable.

In Germany, the chief goal of mercantilism was to increase the revenue of the state. Hence, it became known as *cameralism* (after *Kammer,* the name of the royal treasury), and its principles were extensively implemented as government policy during the eighteenth century.

Case
Trading in Foreign Exchange: The Fastest Game in Town

Do fluctuating currency values affect businesses engaged in international trade? Would a company dealing abroad be incurring undue risks if it failed to protect itself against changes in the value of the dollar? The answer to both questions is *yes*. However, management can achieve the financial protection required by trading in the most universal of all commodities—money. Such trading is conducted in what is called the "foreign-exchange market." It is a money center in which the world's leading currencies—dollars, marks, pounds, yen, francs, and so forth—are bought and sold. Some are traded by investors seeking protection against future currency fluctuations, the rest by speculators hoping to make a profit. As a result of these divergent goals, international trade is able to flourish in a world of fluctuating exchange rates.

Fast Action

Who are the currency traders? As with the stock and commodity markets, the foreign-exchange market has its own mixed bag of participants. Among them: banks, corporations, oil-rich sheiks from the Middle East, millionaires from almost every country, businesspeople, and ordinary citizens. The leading professionals in the field, however, are mainly individual specialists and representatives of major banks. But these experts, popularly referred to as the "gnomes of Zurich," have had their share of setbacks, as events since the 1970s attest:

• New York's Franklin National Bank, once the twentieth-largest bank in America, and West Germany's Herstatt Bank, one of Europe's biggest, suffered financial failure (bankruptcy) as a result of foreign-exchange losses.

• Union Bank of Switzerland and the Swiss branch of Lloyd's Bank—both highly reputable institutions—lost $150 million and $75 million, respectively, from dealings in foreign exchange.

• The Vatican, acting on the advice of an eminently successful Italian financier, lost $60 million on foreign-exchange transactions.

If these experts are unable to beat the fast-moving foreign-exchange market, how can a company dealing abroad hope to do so? The answer is, it cannot; therefore, it should not try. Instead, it should write *forward contracts,* thereby shifting the consequences of exchange-rate fluctuations to speculators who are willing to bear the risks.

How Forward Contracts Work

The essential idea behind a forward contract is simple. The seller of the contract agrees to deliver a stipulated amount of foreign exchange for a specified price at a certain future date. The buyer promises to accept. Basically, the entire process consists of five steps:

Step 1: A U.S. manufacturer agrees to export goods to an English buyer six months from now in exchange for £1,000. The manufacturer, however, does not know what £1,000 will be worth in U.S. dollars in six months. Therefore, the firm wants to protect itself from risk.

Step 2: The manufacturer writes (sells) a contract to a U.S. bank, agreeing to deliver £1,000 to the bank in six months in exchange for $1,900 at that time. The bank is thus guessing that the exchange rate in six months will be $1.90 = £1.

Step 3: The U.S. bank telephones its correspondent bank in London and borrows £1,000 *today.* Assuming that the exchange rate today is $2.00 = £1, the U.S. bank sells the pounds for $2,000 and lends out the money to its U.S. customers for six months.

Step 4: Six months later, the U.S. manufacturer delivers goods to the English buyer and is paid £1,000. The manufacturer then takes pounds to the U.S. bank and receives $1,900 as agreed (step 2). The U.S. bank also gets back its $2,000 in repaid loans (step 3).

Step 5: The U.S. bank pays back the £1,000 it borrowed six months earlier from the London bank. The remaining dollars cover the U.S. bank's service charges, interest expenses on pounds borrowed, and profits.

This is one of the more common ways in which forward contracts operate. As a result of selling a contract, the manufacturer has "hedged" his risk by protecting himself against an unforeseen fall in the price of pounds.

Conclusion: Speculation Promotes Trade

Two groups, each with different goals, participate in the foreign-exchange market. One group, the *hedgers,* is concerned with *reducing risks* of currency fluctuations. Another group, the *speculators,* seeks to *earn profits* by assuming risks that hedgers wish to avoid. Speculators, therefore, engage both in buying and selling forward contracts in the hope of profiting from fluctuations in currency prices. Of course, speculators who guess future currency prices incorrectly can incur huge losses—as often happens. Nevertheless, speculators are a necessary part of the foreign-exchange market—a market that facilitates international trade by enabling business firms to hedge their risks of currency losses.

Foreign-exchange trading, whether in the international monetary market or in the trading rooms of the world's major banks, is a hectic experience for buyers and sellers alike.

Régis Bossu/Sygma

Questions

1. In the example of forward contracts given above, who is the hedger? Who is the speculator? Explain. What would have been the effect on each party if the price of pounds six months later (step 4) had fallen to $1.80? Risen to $2.20?

2. "Speculators are no different from gamblers. Like gamblers, speculators create no product and hence perform no useful social function." Evaluate.

What You Have Learned in This Chapter

1. Because nations carry on their business in different currencies, foreign-exchange markets exist in which currencies and related instruments can be bought and sold. The existence of such markets enables nations to engage in international transactions.

2. The international transactions of a nation are summarized periodically in a financial statement known as the balance of payments. This records money inflows and outflows, classified in categories of accounts.

3. In accounting terms, a nation's balance of payments always balances. This is because the sum of money inflows must equal the sum of money outflows—by virtue of the principle of double-entry bookkeeping. But, in an economic sense, the balance of payments may not balance when exchange rates are fixed because certain transactions may not be sustainable.

4. Balance-of-payments disequilibrium may be corrected by (a) movements in exchange rates; (b) adjustments in price and income levels; (c) gold flows, with consequent price and income adjustments if nations are on a gold standard; and (d) government controls over foreign exchange and foreign trade. The first three rely on market forces to bring about the needed adjustment; the fourth suppresses market forces by substituting the hand of government.

For Discussion

1. *Terms and concepts to review:*
foreign exchange
debit
credit
balance of payments
balance of trade
autonomous transactions
compensatory transactions
balance-of-payments disequilibrium
foreign-exchange rate
gold points
mercantilism
cameralism

2. In a free market, if the dollar rate of exchange for French francs rises, what happens to the French rate of exchange for dollars? Explain.

3. How does each of the following transactions affect the supply of money in the United States?
   (a) The United States sells Chevrolets to England.
   (b) France sells perfume to the United States.
   (c) An American tourist visits Japan.
   (d) A Japanese tourist visits the United States.

4. Which of the following transactions results in a debit, and which in a credit, in the U.S. balance of payments?
   (a) An American student buys a new Honda motorcycle.
   (b) An American tourist flies Air France to Paris.
   (c) General Motors pays a dividend to a British stockholder.
   (d) The U.S. Army builds a new military base overseas.
   (e) An American resident buys shares of stock in a British corporation.
   (f) An American resident sends money to his relatives in another country.

5. Can there be a net positive or net negative balance in the balance of payments?

6. Why are autonomous debits and credits not likely to be equal?

7. Compare the processes of adjustment to disequilibrium under (a) freely fluctuating exchange rates; (b) price and income changes; (c) the gold standard; (d) government controls. (**Suggestion** Think in terms of what these systems have in common, and develop your answer accordingly.)

35
CHAPTER

International Economics: Past and Present Policies

Learning guide

Watch for the answers to these important questions

What factors brought about the weakening of the world economy between World War I and World War II? What important lessons were learned from the economic experiences of the 1930s?

How did the United States help to rebuild the economies of Western Europe and Japan after World War II? What important developments occurred in postwar international trade and finance that altered the course of the world economy?

What difficulties of balance-of-payments adjustments arose under the system of fixed exchange rates? Why were political leaders reluctant to adopt the necessary measures for adjustment?

How do floating exchange rates differ from adjustable and crawling rates? What are the advantages and disadvantages of each?

This chapter surveys the history of international commercial and financial policies.

Lord Rothschild, a world-famous British financier of the nineteenth century, was once asked by a friend to explain the international financial system. He replied, "My dear chap, there are only two men in the world who understand the international financial system—a young economist in the Treasury and a rather junior man in the Bank of England. Unfortunately, they disagree."

There is no doubt that most people are unfamiliar with the international monetary system. This is true despite the fact that the dollar has at times been under attack by foreigners; our gold policy (or lack of it) is regarded by some groups as a national scandal; and American tourists visiting abroad are occasionally astounded to discover that the value of their dollars, in terms of foreign currencies, can sometimes rise or decline considerably between breakfast and dinner.

These are only a few of the myriad aspects of the complex world of international finance. Furthermore, the world of international trade is equally complex. This chapter reviews the background and consequences of these complexities and discusses recommendations for improving the community of sovereign nations held together by economic interdependence.

The Interwar Period: Weakening and Disintegration of the World Economy

In the decades before World War I, most major countries were closely integrated through a well-developed network of trade and finance. The essential features of this complex system may be characterized briefly:

1. Nations and regions tended to specialize on the basis of their factor endowments. This made multilateral trade necessary.

2. Tariffs for the most part affected only moderately the international flow of goods according to the principle of comparative advantage.

3. London was the center of finance and trade. Its supporting facilities of banks, brokerage houses, insurance companies, shipping firms, and communication lines extended throughout the world.

4. Nearly all major nations and many minor ones—several dozen in all—were on the gold standard. This permitted the easy convertibility of currencies, which was necessary for carrying on international transactions smoothly and efficiently.

Prior to World War I, most major nations were on a gold standard and the world economy functioned with reasonable efficiency.

This was also an era of rapid advances in technology and large migrations of labor and capital. These fundamental changes were assimilated by the system, though not, to be sure, without some major political and economic upheavals. The balances of payments of most trading nations tended to adjust fairly smoothly to gold movements, while exchange rates remained stable.

This, briefly, was the nature of the relatively harmonious international economic setting that prevailed until the eve of World War I. In the next three decades, however, the world economy experienced a series of deep disturbances. These included: (1) structural weakening during the 1920s, (2) disintegration during the 1930s, and (3) disruption during World War II.

Structural Weakening During the 1920s

World War I destroyed the economic relations between nations that had been developing through nearly five decades of peace in Europe. International commercial and financial links were broken, markets were disorganized, and the marketing system was shattered. All belligerent nations except the United States abandoned the gold standard; the American government officially discouraged gold withdrawals from banks; and gold exports were subjected to strict legal controls. These steps were necessary to prevent the hoarding of gold and its flight to safer havens in neutral nations—common occurrences in periods of crisis.

During the 1920s, signs that the world economy was weakening became increasingly apparent.

After the war, there were violent inflations in continental Europe, and the restoration of the gold standard became a major objective of international policy. Between 1925 and 1929, more than 40 countries returned to gold. Only a few continued to operate on the basis of inconvertible paper money. But the new gold standard established during this period was based on economic conditions and philosophies different from those that existed before 1914. Some of the more important changes that took place may be noted briefly.

Changes in National Objectives

Governments began to place less emphasis on the automatic operation of an international monetary system provided by the gold standard and more emphasis on *domestic* economic stability. The war and postwar years brought severe monetary disturbances, inflation, and then depression. With the establishment of the Federal Reserve System in the United States just before World War I and the creation of similar institutions in many other countries during the 1920s, government officials became increasingly involved in efforts to stabilize prices and economic activity through central-bank monetary policy.

Increased Government Intervention

In many countries, the decade after the war was marked by the beginnings of a retreat from laissez-faire as farmers, labor unions, consumers, and other special-interest groups pressed for greater government protection and reforms. This gave rise to growing nationalism. As a result, the United States and other nations, including Australia, Great Britain, India, and Japan, enacted new protective trade legislation during the 1920s.

Conclusion: Increased Importance of the U.S. Economy

By the end of the 1920s, the world's major trading nations had gone through a realignment. The United States emerged as a dominant economic power.

The changing national objectives and government policies weakened the international monetary mechanism by making it more rigid. At the same time, the United States gained increasing dominance in the international economy. By 1929, it had become the world's largest exporter, the second largest importer (after Great Britain), and the world's chief creditor. This meant that, with other nations heavily dependent on it, the United States would have to maintain a stable, high level of income and employment and a steady flow of lending to other nations if the well-being of the world economy was to be preserved. Any sudden changes in American economic stability, tariff rates, or credit flows could affect access to markets and produce severe international repercussions. This, as you will see, is precisely what happened.

Disintegration During the 1930s

During the 1930s, the world economy was subjected to a series of devastating blows.

In the United States, prosperity began its rise in 1922 and reached a peak in the first half of 1929. During this period American investment, income, and employment climbed to unprecedented heights. But then the overall decline in economic activity set in. First came a drop in industrial production in July 1929. This was followed by a collapse of the stock market three months later, and finally by a precipitous decline in American spending and investment abroad.

How did the major trading nations respond to these depressing effects on world commerce? There were several types of reaction, which will be examined next. As you will see later, these reactions significantly affected the international economic policies of nations after World War II.

Higher Tariffs

In the United States and other major countries, there was a marked tendency to subordinate international trade to national interests. The United States made access to its domestic market difficult by passing the Smoot–Hawley Tariff of 1930. This new law broadened the range of protected commodities to over 25,000, and provided for increases in some 800 rates covering a wide variety of both agricultural and industrial goods. Great Britain, which had been the citadel of free trade for 80 years, abandoned its policy and adopted a protective tariff in 1932. Similarly, other countries attempted to control their foreign trade by establishing tariffs, quotas, special exchange allocations, bilateral trade agreements for the trading of specific products, and monopolistic state-controlled trading systems. In general, the actions undertaken during this period more than offset years of effort by the League of Nations (the predecessor of the United Nations) to establish freer international trade.

Financial Crisis and the Abandonment of Gold

A second major development of international significance occurred in the spring of 1931. Two major European banks failed due to technical insolvency—their liabilities exceeded their assets. The fear of further bank failures spread, causing financial panics accompanied by heavy "runs" on various nations' gold and foreign-exchange reserves. In Britain, which was especially hard hit because British banks were overextended on loans to foreigners, the gold drain reached crisis proportions. Consequently, on September 21, 1931, Parliament announced that the Bank of England would no longer be required by law to sell gold. This meant that Britain had officially gone off the gold standard.

In the months that followed, the international depression deepened, and financial panics were repeated in various nations. As a result, by the end of 1932, twenty-four countries had followed England in abandoning the gold standard.

Devaluation of the Dollar

The United States was not, of course, immune to the effects of the Depression. The period 1929–1932 was one of severe deflation. Moreover, some 5,000 banks—about one-third of the nation's total—became insolvent. As a result, early in 1933, a wave of currency and gold hoarding ensued. This forced President Franklin Delano Roosevelt to declare a bank "holiday," to place an embargo on the export of gold, and to prevent banks and the Treasury from paying out the precious metal. These steps placed the United States on a *gold bullion standard*. This meant that gold was nationalized by the Treasury, taken out of domestic circulation as money, and made available in the form of gold bullion only for industrial uses and international transactions in return for other money.

In addition, the government made a further attempt at currency stabilization when it devalued the dollar in 1934.

> *Devaluation* is an official act that makes a domestic currency cheaper in terms of gold or foreign currencies. Historically, it was typically undertaken to increase a nation's exports and to reduce its imports.

Thus on January 31, 1934, the United States devalued the dollar relative to gold by approximately 41 percent. This was accomplished by raising the Treasury's buying and selling price of gold from $20.67 per ounce to $35 per ounce. This act made it cheaper for foreigners to buy dollars and more expensive for Americans to buy foreign currencies.

Consequences of Devaluation

Other countries responded to the devaluation by imposing higher tariffs and other trade restrictions. But the devalued dollar, which was now stabilized in relation to other depreciated currencies, exerted mounting balance-of-payments pressures for devaluation on the remaining gold-standard countries with their overvalued currencies. During the mid-1930s, this (in combination with the growing fear of war in Europe) resulted in a heavy net inflow of capital and gold to the United States for

An increase in tariffs, the abandonment of the gold standard, and the devaluation of the dollar were measures that had widespread international economic effects. In addition, the growing fear of war in Europe compounded the uncertainty that prevailed at home and abroad.

safekeeping. Between 1934 and 1938, the remaining gold-standard nations—Belgium, Switzerland, France, and the Netherlands—unable to sustain any further drain, abandoned gold and devalued their currencies. Thus came the end of an era. (See Box 1.)

Conclusion: International Agreements

By the eve of World War II, the leading trading countries of the Western world had learned at least two important lessons:

1. *Fiscal—monetary management.* By releasing their currencies from gold, nations could be free to manage their economies by fiscal and monetary means without the fear of losing reserves and without the need to be regulated by international gold movements.

2. *Foreign retaliation.* Devaluation, however, is not ordinarily a one-way street; it usually causes opposing reactions by other nations in the form of trade restrictions or retaliatory devaluation.

The remaining highlights of the immediate pre—World War II years may be summarized briefly.

1. The United States and most Western European countries entered an agreement that, for international purposes, represented a compromise between the rigidities of the gold standard and domestic currency management. Thus:

(a) Each country established its own government stabilization fund to buy and sell foreign exchange in the open market in quantities necessary to maintain reasonable stability of its own currency in relation to foreign currencies.

(b) Competitive devaluation for the purpose of expanding exports was renounced.

By the end of the 1930s, governments had learned to manipulate their economies.

Box 1
Dollar Devaluation and the Gold Standard

In the winter of 1934, a notorious crime occupied the attention of most Americans. Dollar devaluation was only a secondary concern. Hence, when President Roosevelt devalued the dollar on January 31, 1934, few people anticipated the worldwide implications of this act. Within the next four years the gold standard faded into extinction, never again to be restored by any nation.

(c) The central banks of the participating countries were authorized to buy gold without limit, but gold served largely as an equilibrating device for balance-of-payments purposes.

On the whole, exchange-rate equilibrium was restored among the democratic trading nations, whereas such totalitarian countries as Germany and the USSR maintained tightly controlled systems for allocating foreign exchange.

2. In the area of international trade, the United States established a *Reciprocal Trade Agreements program.* This is a plan for expanding American exports through legislation that authorized the President to negotiate U.S. tariff reductions with other nations in return for parallel concessions. The program consists of the Trade Agreements Act of 1934, with subsequent amendments, and related legislation. An interesting feature of the Reciprocal Trade Agreements program has been the widespread use of what is known as a *most-favored-nation clause.* Its inclusion in a trade treaty means that each of the signatories agrees to extend to the other the same preferential tariff and trade concessions that each may in the future extend to nonsignatories. That is, the signatories extend to one another the same treatment that each gives to its "most favored nation." The great majority of trading countries have adhered to this principle since 1948.

Toward the eve of World War II, the United States entered an exchange stabilization agreement with other countries and established a reciprocal trade program.

Disruption During World War II: Lend-Lease

World War II (1939–1945) disrupted world trade. The belligerents as well as the leading neutral nations were largely prevented from engaging in exchange transactions with the United States and the Allies. In order to help the allied nations to buy the goods they needed but could not pay for, the United States instituted a system known as *lend-lease* in accordance with the Lend-Lease Act of 1941. It provided advances in goods and supplies in return for reciprocal help from the recipient countries in the form of care and housing for American troops. In money terms, the value of the grants given by the United States far exceeded the value of the services that it received in return. But as Prime Minister Winston Churchill remarked to Parliament, lend-lease was not intended to provide for an equal exchange; indeed, it was "the most unsordid act in the history of any nation."

Post–World War II International Commerce

In the summer of 1944, few people were concerned about the problems of international trade and finance. Allied troops were engaged in the great battle for the Normandy beachhead; a group of German army officers had tried unsuccessfully to assassinate Adolf Hitler; and a politically obscure man named Harry S. Truman was emerging as the potential running mate of President Roosevelt in his bid for a fourth term.

At the same time, an event of less colorful but highly durable significance was taking place in the lovely rural setting of Bretton Woods, New Hampshire. There, in the Mount Washington Hotel, at the foot of New England's highest mountain, the United Nations Monetary and Financial Conference was holding an international meeting destined to affect the world's economic structure for decades to come. Present at the meeting were representatives from 16 governments, including Lord Keynes in his capacity as advisor to the British treasury.

At the end of World War II, the groundwork was laid for a new set of international commercial policies.

The primary result of this historic gathering was the formation of a plan for a new and remarkable international financial system. The original agreement was developed largely by the British and American delegations. It was signed by 35 nations, but the membership subsequently increased to more than three times that number. We shall examine the nature of this system and related aspects of world trade a bit later.

European Economic Recovery

The first international commercial policies adopted after World War II consisted of aid programs designed to rebuild the industries of war-torn countries.

When the war ended, the European economy had been devastated. For five years after the war, Europe's balance of payments on current account suffered from a substantial trade deficit. Among the factors that were responsible for this deficit were the pressure of inflation, the reduction of productive capacity caused by the war, and the loss of overseas export markets.

The immediate task, of course, was to rebuild the European economy while financing its deficit. Most of the responsibility fell to the United States, which extended approximately $17 billion in foreign aid between 1945 and 1948. About half of this was in the form of outright gifts and half in the form of loans. But it was recognized that these were merely stopgap measures and that more consistent and far-reaching policies were necessary. The result was the formulation of two important types of American aid programs that had a substantial influence on the economic development of other nations.

European Recovery Program (Marshall Plan)

On June 5, 1947, Secretary of State George C. Marshall delivered a commencement address at Harvard University. In his speech, he proposed what came to be known as the *European Recovery Program* (ERP), or *Marshall Plan*. Financed by the United States, the plan was a comprehensive blueprint for the economic recovery of European countries. The plan's purposes were (1) to increase the productive capacity of these countries, (2) to stabilize their financial systems, (3) to promote their mutual economic cooperation, and (4) to reduce their dependence on U.S. assistance. Out of this came the Organization for European Economic Cooperation, an association initially comprising 17 European countries working in concert to assure their own economic recovery.

The Marshall Plan ended in 1951, after providing more than $10 billion in aid. About 90 percent of this was in outright grants and the rest was in loans. There is widespread agreement that the program was a success. It contributed substantially to raising the average level of industrial production among participating nations by more than half their 1947 level and to suppressing a decade of rapid inflation.

Mutual Security Administration

By late 1951, the emphasis of American foreign policy had shifted from direct economic aid to European nations to the containment of communism. The immediate cause of this change in attitude was the outbreak of the Korean War in June 1950. For military reasons, the ERP was absorbed by the Mutual Security Administration, which provided both military and economic assistance to various nations throughout the world.

Since the early 1950s, a substantial part of American economic aid has been directed at the underdeveloped countries of Africa, Asia, and Latin America. A great deal of aid has gone to assist those governments that are regarded as bulwarks against communism, regardless of whether they are otherwise democratic or autocratic. As a result, America has been criticized for propping up repressive regimes and is often regarded by the peoples of such countries as a supporter of dictatorship and even of political terrorism.

Trade Liberalization and Regional Integration

Even during World War II, it was evident to many political leaders that a new multilateral trading system would be needed after the war—one that provided for liberalization and economic integration of world trade. A significant step in this direction, as we have seen, was the Reciprocal Trade Agreements program adopted by the United States. This program empowered the President to agree on mutual tariff reductions with other countries and to incorporate most-favored-nation clauses in such agreements. After the war, various trading nations endorsed and adopted additional measures designed to strengthen world commerce. The more important ones are examined briefly.

In addition to American aid programs, policies were adopted by various other countries that were aimed at promoting multilateral trade.

General Agreement on Tariffs and Trade (GATT)

The first major postwar step toward liberalization of world trade was the *General Agreement on Tariffs and Trade* (GATT). This is an international agreement signed in 1947 by 23 countries, including the United States. GATT is dedicated to four basic principles: (1) nondiscrimination in trade through adherence to unconditional most-favored-nation treatment; (2) reduction of tariffs by negotiation; (3) elimination of import quotas (with some exceptions permitted); and (4) resolution of differences through consultation. The number of nations participating in GATT has since increased by several dozen, and it has been an important and successful force for the liberalization of world trade.

Regional Integration

Despite the fact that nations have erected trade barriers to shield themselves from one another, the underlying desire for free trade has nevertheless been persistent. Although worldwide free trade may never become a reality, regional free-trade agreements among two or more nations are commonplace. Such agreements have typically taken three forms: free-trade areas, customs unions, and common markets.

1. **Free-Trade Area** This is an association of trading nations that agree to impose no restrictive devices, such as tariffs or quotas, on one another. However, each country is free to impose whatever restrictions it wishes on nonparticipants. The best-known example is the European Free Trade Association (EFTA), established in 1960. Its members have included Austria, Great Britain, Sweden, Norway, Denmark, Switzerland, and Portugal. Similar organizations have been established or proposed among Latin American, Asian, and African countries.

2. **Customs Union** This is an agreement among two or more trading nations to abolish trade barriers (such as tariffs and quotas) among themselves and to adopt a common external policy of trade (such as a com-

mon external tariff) with all nonmember nations. The most familiar example is Benelux (which consists of Belgium, the Netherlands, and Luxembourg). Similar plans have been adopted or proposed in other geographic areas.

3. Common Market This is an association of trading nations that agree (a) to impose no trade restrictions (such as tariffs or quotas) among participants; (b) to establish common external barriers (such as a common external tariff) to nonparticipants; and (c) to impose no national restrictions on the movement of labor and capital among participants. The most significant example has been the European Economic Community (EEC), or European Common Market, established in 1958. Among its members have been Belgium, Denmark, France, Great Britain, West Germany, Ireland, Italy, Luxembourg, and the Netherlands.

A free-trade area, a customs union, and a common market (in that order) represent increasing degrees of economic integration. Of these, the common market is the most significant. What can be said about its economic effects?

On the favorable side:

A common market yields two major benefits:

1. It encourages a more efficient allocation of member nations' resources in accordance with the laws of comparative advantage.

2. It expands the size of the market for member nations, thereby enabling their industries to gain the economies (lower unit costs) of large-scale production.

On the unfavorable side:

A common market places a trade barrier—typically a tariff wall—between the member countries as a whole and all nonmember nations. The result may be a diversion of trade between the two groups, thereby causing an economic loss for all parties concerned.

Reduction of Trade Barriers

The United States has long sought to foster greater economic unification with other nations. Toward this end, it has passed various "trade acts" as part of its Reciprocal Trade Agreements program. These laws, designed to encourage U.S. trade expansion, have widened the powers of the Presidency by enabling the President to reduce trade barriers. Specifically, the President can:

1. Negotiate reductions in tariff and certain nontariff barriers for broad categories of goods instead of on specific commodities.

2. Lower tariffs by substantial percentages on the basis of reciprocal trade agreements, provided that such agreements include most-favored-nation clauses so that the benefits of reduced tariffs are extended to other countries.

3. Grant vocational, technical, and financial assistance to American employees and businesses that are adversely affected by tariff reduction.

As a result of these trade-expansion acts, numerous nations have become involved in duty reductions. However, some countries whose industries were injured by tariff reductions have found themselves faced with increased pressures for protection. This has led them either to adopt or to consider adopting various forms of nontariff barriers to trade. Among these are quotas, license requirements, and border taxes.

Many countries have adopted regional free-trade agreements, of which the common market is the most familiar.

The United States has followed policies designed to reduce trade barriers and to promote world trade.

Post–World War II International Finance

The postwar developments in international trade were paralleled by equally momentous changes in international finance. When the representatives of the allied nations met in Bretton Woods, New Hampshire, in 1944 to construct an orderly system of international monetary cooperation that would be conducive to global trade, the experiences of the 1930s were still fresh in everyone's mind. It was clear that neither a system of freely fluctuating exchange rates nor one of fixed rates that would permit easy devaluations was the way to strengthen the financial relations of nations in the postwar world.

At the end of World War II, the groundwork was laid for a new set of international financial policies.

International Monetary Fund

One of the most important products of the Bretton Woods conference was the formation of the *International Monetary Fund* (IMF). This is an organization that was established by the United Nations in 1945 for the purposes of eliminating exchange restrictions, encouraging exchange-rate stability, and providing for worldwide convertibility of currencies to promote multilateral trade based on international specialization. Today, well over 100 nations are members of the Fund.

The IMF has helped many countries to overcome temporary balance-of-payments deficits. It has also served as a powerful force in helping to maintain relatively stable exchange rates. These and related matters are taken up in further detail later in the chapter.

From Dollar Shortage to Dollar Surplus

The United States emerged from the war as a large creditor to the allied countries. After the war, American lending continued to mount into the billions of dollars as the United States shifted its emphasis from the provision of military goods to the provision of civilian goods for the war-torn nations. The latter, of course, had little if anything to export in return. Nor did they have the gold or dollar reserves with which to pay for the American goods they received. Hence, a "dollar shortage" became one of the most talked-about problems of the postwar decade as the United States continued to show a rather persistent deficit in its balance of payments after 1950.

During the 1950s, the international economy experienced a "dollar shortage" because the United States was the world's major creditor nation.

Further, because gold and dollars were the major source of international monetary reserves, the dollar (and to a lesser extent the British pound) became known as a *key currency*—in effect, a substitute for gold in meeting international obligations. This meant that, during the 1950s, while the United States was accumulating a huge deficit in its balance of payments, other countries—mainly the European nations—were adding to their reserves. These were primarily in the form of dollar deposits in U.S. banks or short-term government securities.

By the mid-1950s, the European and Japanese economies were not only rehabilitated but thriving. The United States, however, was still spending heavily by maintaining large troop commitments overseas, providing economic aid to underdeveloped countries, and experiencing a mounting outflow of American tourists going abroad. All this added up to continued deficits and a huge accumulation of dollars in Europe and Japan. Thus, by the late 1950s it was recognized throughout the world that the dollar shortage had been *transformed* into a serious and dangerous dollar surplus in foreign countries.

"Defending the Dollar"

By 1960, the world was in the midst of a "dollar surplus" as the United States continued to spend heavily abroad.

How might the deficit be corrected? There were three plausible choices: (1) domestic deflation; (2) devaluation of the dollar; and (3) reductions in foreign outlays. The first two choices would increase international earnings by expanding U.S. exports relative to imports. The third would simply decrease U.S. expenses.

The first choice was ruled out because deflation would lead to an increase in the unemployment rate in the United States, which was already averaging more than 5 percent in the early 1960s. The second choice was also ruled out because devaluation by a major trading country such as the United States would have brought on a chain of competitive devaluations by most other countries. This left the third choice—reduction of foreign outlays—as a means of "defending the dollar."

The measures adopted in the early 1960s took several major forms. Families of servicemen stationed overseas were sent back to the United States. The limits on duty-free goods that could be brought back by returning American tourists were cut. European countries were exhorted to carry a larger share of the mutual defense burden and of foreign aid. Special taxes and "voluntary restraints" were imposed on the outflow of American capital. Nations in debt to the United States were asked to speed up their payments. Trading nations were urged to end their remaining restrictions against American imports.

What were the consequences? These measures did not succeed in eliminating the deficit. At best, they may have helped to keep it from becoming still larger. But in any case they were more than straws in the wind, for they portended a series of international monetary crises that shook the financial world.

International Monetary Crises

The gold-exchange standard had succeeded in stabilizing exchange rates and promoting international trade.

In terms of what it set out to do, the 1944 conference at Bretton Woods was a smashing success. It stabilized exchange rates and created an international monetary system that was highly productive of world trade and investment. This was accomplished by establishing a modified type of gold standard called a *gold-exchange standard*. It had two distinctive features:

1. The dollar was tied to gold. That is, the U.S. Treasury agreed to make gold and dollars mutually convertible, to foreign central banks *only*, at the rate of $35 per ounce of gold.

2. Each nation tied its currency to the dollar. That is, each nation fixed an exchange rate or par value for its currency in relation to the dollar and agreed to maintain that rate within a 1 percent range by buying and selling its currency against the dollar.

This meant that businesspeople anywhere in the world could trade with Britain, for example, and be certain that the value of the pound would not vary by more than a few cents above or below its established rate. As before, however, nations still needed monetary reserves to settle their international monetary deficits. Under the pure gold standard, such reserves consisted of gold. However, under the postwar gold-exchange standard, reserves consisted primarily of gold and dollars and to a lesser extent of British pounds. The dollars, as we have seen, were derived largely from U.S. deficits and held mainly in the form of bank deposits and short-term government securities. Because of this, the United States became known as the "world's banker," with the dollar serving as the key or reserve currency.

As American and British deficits continued to mount, and as inflationary forces pushed up prices not only in the United States but also in England and various other important trading nations, the accumulation of pressures erupted in large speculative flows of major currencies. These endangered the international payments system. Recurring doubts arose as to whether the United States would be willing and able to maintain convertibility of the dollar into gold at the fixed price of $35 for an ounce of gold. As a result, increasing proportions of dollars were converted into gold during the 1960s. Most of the conversions were done by foreign speculators and others who thought it would be safer or more profitable to hold the yellow metal instead of the green paper.

During the 1960s, nations became increasingly alarmed at the growing "dollar surplus." There was growing doubt about America's ability to maintain convertibility of the dollar into gold.

Finally, in the late 1960s, three sets of events capped a decade of international monetary crisis.

Special Drawing Rights ("Paper Gold")

After 1958, the European countries began to press the United States to reduce its balance-of-payments deficit. The United States, in return, urged throughout the 1960s that a plan be developed for increasing international liquidity in the absence of dollar outflows. In 1969, after nearly five years of discussion and four years of negotiation, *Special Drawing Rights* (SDRs)—popularly known as "paper gold"—were approved by the International Monetary Fund.

Special Drawing Rights were adopted by the IMF as one way of helping nations to finance balance-of-payments deficits.

SDRs are supplementary reserves in the form of account entries or "claims" on the books of the IMF. The claims are allocated among participating countries in accordance with their relative economic strength as determined by their national income, population, and volume of world trade. SDRs can be drawn upon by governments to help finance balance-of-payments deficits. The purpose of the "paper gold" is to provide an orderly growth of reserves to meet the expanding needs of world trade.

Devaluation

On November 19, 1967, the twenty-sixth Sunday after Trinity, some churchgoers in England heard a somber but very relevant text from Anglican pulpits. The lesson was from James, chapter 5, verses 1 to 3:

International economic pressures forced Britain to devalue the pound in order to reduce its deficit by stimulating exports.

Go to now, ye rich men, weep and howl for your miseries that shall come upon you.

Your riches are corrupted, and your garments are moth-eaten.

Your gold and silver is cankered; and the rust of them shall be a witness against you, and shall eat your flesh as it were fire. Ye have heaped treasure together for the last days.

Why this curious reading from scripture? The answer is that, while the creation of SDRs was being discussed among governments, Britain was indulging herself in an easy-money policy that was contributing to inflation, trade deficits, and financial strains. On November 18, 1967, she succumbed to international economic pressures and devalued the pound from $2.80 to $2.40, a decrease of 14.3 percent. This was the third devaluation for Britain in 36 years. It was intended to give the country a sharper competitive edge in world markets as well as the breathing time needed to repair its foundering economy and deficit-ridden balance of payments.

Whether or not a devaluation succeeds in eliminating a deficit depends on many factors—among them the various policy measures taken at home to curb inflation. Such measures, which Britain adopted in the late 1960s, included heavy new taxes, broad wage controls, and a tight national budget. As you have already learned, if an austerity policy is sufficiently harsh and if it is combined with an appropriately restrictive monetary policy, it can succeed in curbing inflation and thereby make a devaluation yield lasting economic benefits.

A Two-Tier System for Gold

A group of nations agreed to stabilize the price of gold on the world market. They established a two-price system for gold.

Following the devaluation of the pound in 1967, confidence in the dollar was further weakened by inflation in the United States and the expectation that the dollar would have to be devalued. Consequently, a rush to buy gold developed late in the year. Most of the buyers were speculators who planned to make a quick profit by reselling the gold at the higher price that would obtain after the expected devaluation.

In the meantime, seven countries known as the Gold Pool nations—the United States, Great Britain, West Germany, Belgium, Italy, the Netherlands, and Switzerland—had been stabilizing the price of gold. Since 1961, they had been holding the free-market price of gold in world markets at the American price of $35 per ounce. They did this by pooling their gold and standing ready to buy or sell as the need arose. But with the onset of the new "gold rush," there was a danger that the gold holdings of these nations would be depleted, thus endangering the entire international monetary system.

The speculative fever reached a dramatic climax in March 1968 with the announcement of a two-tier (or two-price) system for gold by the Gold Pool nations. Henceforth, they said, their central banks would exchange existing gold stocks among themselves at the historic official price of $35 per ounce but would no longer buy or sell gold in private markets. This would leave the private-market price of gold to rise or fall like that of any other commodity.

This action further demonetized gold—that is, reduced its influence in the monetary system and thereby removed its threat to the dollar. Thus, by the end of the 1960s, the dollar seemed victorious over gold for several reasons. The West German mark had been revalued upward, and the French franc had been devalued, both to more realistic levels. Britain's trade balance had improved. Further, South Africa, the world's largest producer of gold, was mining the metal faster than the free market could absorb it, thus creating a huge "overhang" of potential supply. These factors contributed to bringing the free price of gold down to the near-$35 level that had prevailed for most of the three previous decades.

End of an Era

For a brief time it seemed as if the period of recurring international monetary crises was over. But these hopes were short-lived. To the dismay and disapproval of foreign governments, the United States continued to spend more overseas than it earned and refused to take measures that would enable it to curb its outflow of funds.

By 1970 the chronic deficit had ballooned to the point of crisis. U.S. imports were rising far faster than exports. Banks and corporations were putting billions of dollars annually into investments abroad. And defense spending, swollen by the Vietnam war, was a hemorrhage through which other billions of dollars leaked out.

Moreover, foreigners were holding billions of dollars they did not want. In the summer of 1971 certain countries, headed by France and Switzerland, rushed to convert their dollar holdings into gold. By July only $10 billion in gold was left in Fort Knox. The crunch came on August 15, 1971, when President Nixon announced to the world that the U.S. "gold window" was closed. Henceforth, the government would no longer exchange dollars for gold with foreign central banks. Thus, the system of fixed exchange rates based on the Bretton Woods agreement, with which the free world had lived for 27 years, came to an end.

In August, 1971, after a substantial drain of gold, President Nixon closed the U.S. "gold window." Thenceforth, the United States would no longer exchange gold for dollars.

Recent Developments: Managed or "Dirty" Floating

Events since the termination of the Bretton Woods agreement have been accompanied by further changes in international economic relations. The more important developments may be summarized briefly:

• In December 1971, and again in February 1973, the United States devalued the dollar—first against gold and then against SDRs. In addition, the German mark and Japanese yen were revalued upward, resulting in a substantial net, or effective, dollar devaluation.

• In November 1973, the two-tier system for gold was abandoned by the Gold Pool nations. This left them free to pursue whatever actions they wished with respect to gold.

• In 1972 and 1973, after several further monetary crises, the Japanese yen, the British pound, and some other important currencies were set "afloat." This meant that their values were to be determined by the free play of supply and demand. Subsequently, various other nations' currencies were officially swept afloat by the tidal waves of selling that continued to strike the U.S. dollar.

Does this mean that currencies today are left alone to respond to international market forces? Not exactly. Experience shows that floating rates tend to be managed or "dirty" rather than clean. That is, central banks frequently intervene in the market to keep their weak currencies from falling too sharply. Despite these efforts, however, some currencies nevertheless decline while others rise, reflecting international confidence—or lack of it—in a country's economy.

Since the early 1970s, most countries have engaged in the practice of "managed" or "dirty" floating.

As a result of these developments, representatives of the United States and other major trading nations have met on a number of occasions since 1973 to work out an improved world monetary system. The key question that must be answered is whether it is possible to devise new rules of the game that will permit greater exchange-rate stability in international economic relations. Some interesting comparisons of exchange rates are shown in Exhibit 1.

Problems of International Adjustment Under Fixed Exchange Rates

Looking back over these historical developments, it is appropriate to ask why international monetary crises have occurred. The reasons can be easily understood by considering a summary of the conditions that oc-

Under a system of fixed exchange rates, the stability of the international monetary system was threatened whenever major trading nations ran prolonged deficits or surpluses.

Exhibit 1

Can Exchange Rates Be Stabilized?

Whenever exchange rates seem to be settling down, something happens to create a new round of instability. In most cases a nation's currency loses value in relation to other currencies because of that nation's higher rate of inflation.

These developments emphasize the difficulty—or impossibility—of maintaining stable exchange-rate agreements once the market decides that a particular currency is overvalued.

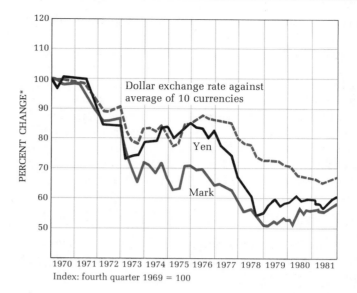

Dollar exchange rate against average of 10 currencies

Index: fourth quarter 1969 = 100

curred under a system of fixed exchange rates such as prevailed in the Bretton Woods agreements:

1. In the world market, the quantity supplied of a nation's currency tended to exceed the quantity demanded when that country ran a *deficit* in its balance of payments. This occurred when the nation payed out more money than it took in, by spending, investing, or giving it away. To buy its currency back, the monetary authority had to spend its reserves of convertible currencies or gold (by selling the gold to foreign central banks) or borrow from the International Monetary Fund.

2. Similarly, in the world market the quantity demanded of a nation's currency tended to exceed the quantity supplied when the country ran a *surplus* in its balance of payments. In that case the nation was taking in more money than it was paying out. Therefore, the central bank had to sell its currency in return for foreign exchange in order to meet foreign demand. This resulted in an accumulation of reserves, mostly dollars, which the central bank in the surplus country did not always wish to hold.

3. The international monetary system was threatened whenever major nations continued to run large deficits or surpluses for prolonged periods of time. The problem, therefore, was for each of the leading trading countries to maintain a tendency toward balance between its money inflows and outflows.

What difficulties did nations encounter in achieving international monetary balance? It is to this problem that we now turn our attention.

The Reluctance to Adjust

The heart of any international monetary system is its adjustment mechanism—the process by which nations achieve payments balance.

Under the old gold standard, the adjustment was automatic. That is, a nation with a deficit in its balance of payments tended to lose gold, and the loss of gold brought about a domestic deflation, which resulted in increased exports and decreased imports. This meant, however, that the domestic economic goal of full employment through appropriate fiscal and monetary policies had to take second place to international economic adjustment—a situation that all nations found untenable.

Under the Bretton Woods system, exchange rates remained fixed. Consequently, the process of adjustment was left to nations themselves. This meant that countries had to be willing to adopt either deflationary policies to correct persistent balance-of-payments deficits or "reflationary" policies to reduce balance-of-payments surpluses. Of course, the pressure on deficit nations to change their domestic policies depended on how long their reserves held out or how long they could continue to borrow. Surplus nations, on the other hand, tended to gain reserves, and hence they were able to avoid adjustment almost indefinitely.

In general, nations that are committed to the maintenance of full employment do not find it easy to adopt a policy of domestic deflation. Under fixed exchange rates, the United States and Britain were prime examples. Both went through long periods of deficits, but both were able to delay adjustments because the dollar and the pound served as reserve currencies. Eventually, when the United States was forced to adjust in the 1960s because it was losing gold, it took the easier and less effective route. It employed indirect forms of exchange controls such as special taxes on foreign earnings and the imposition of limits on capital exports, corporate overseas investing, and bank lending abroad.

When countries are committed to fixed exchange rates, they are not usually willing to undergo the price and income adjustments necessary to correct balance-of-payments disequilibria.

What have we learned from historical experience? Under a system of fixed exchange rates, such as the one that existed in the Bretton Woods era, the most positive approach a government could take to correct an imbalance was to change the par value of its currency. But this was considered to be the most drastic of measures—for two reasons:

1. If a country had been suffering from deficits, a *depreciation* of its currency in order to restore balance involved a sacrifice of international prestige. Depreciation meant that the country's political leaders were admitting to the world that they had been unable to manage domestic economic affairs properly.

2. If a country had been experiencing surpluses in its balance of payments, an *appreciation* or upward revaluation of its currency may have caused some domestic unemployment, especially in its export industries. Obviously, this was a step that elected political leaders were not easily persuaded to take.

The Inevitability of Adjustment

Ultimately, of course, nations found it necessary to adjust. This was because the forces that created international imbalances—inflation and deflation—also caused domestic economic difficulties that required correction. But the adjustment was often a long time in coming, and, in the meantime, nations bumped along from one crisis to another.

Eventually, countries do adjust, but the process is often painful.

Was this the world that those at Bretton Woods envisaged in 1944? The answer is *no*. They never thought that the dollar would remain the world's key currency for several decades after the war, nor that it would be a currency whose supply might someday exceed the quantity that central banks wished to hold. Likewise, they never foresaw the possibility that there would someday be a huge market for *Eurodollars*. These are dollar deposits in banks outside the United States, mostly in

Europe. Eurodollars, which are held by American or foreign banks, corporations, and individuals, represent dollar obligations that are constantly crossing national frontiers in search of the highest return. Hence, under fixed exchange rates, Eurodollars could affect balances of payments and even turn pressure on a currency into an international monetary crisis. Some interesting aspects of this are described in Box 2.

Floating, Adjustable, or Crawling Rates?

In view of this historical background, what can be done to improve the world's monetary system? Central bankers and economists are interested in three types of proposals: floating exchange rates, adjustable pegs, and crawling pegs.

Box 2
Eurocurrency: Questions and Answers That Worry Some Experts

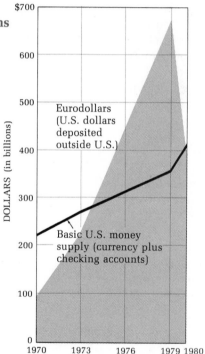

When interest rates soar at home, domestic companies often seek cheaper loans in the "Euromarket." Although it originated in Europe, the Euromarket has become a world market in which leading banks, large corporations, governments, and wealthy individuals negotiate short- and long-term financing in major currencies.

What Is Eurocurrency?
It is money on deposit in financial institutions outside the country of its origin. Examples are U.S. dollars on deposit at banks outside the United States, Swiss francs outside Switzerland, West German marks outside West Germany, and so on. The quantities involved, which determine the size of the Eurocurrency market, are equivalent to *trillions* of dollars.

Are Eurodollars the Same as Eurocurrency?
No. Eurodollars are the portion of Eurocurrency denominated in dollars. Until the late 1960s, Eurodollars constituted almost the entire Eurocurrency market. Since then, marks, francs, pounds, and yen have gained in importance. However, the supply of Eurodollars amounts to hundreds of billions of dollars—considerably more than America's basic money supply consisting of currency and checking-account deposits.

What Is So Special About the Euromarket?
It is largely unregulated, and there are no reserve requirements. Therefore, banks can make cheaper loans and pay higher interest to depositors because there are no laws requiring a certain percentage of deposits to be kept idle as reserves.

Why Are Government Officials Worried About It?
For two reasons:

1. If the Eurocurrency market continues to expand relative to domestic markets, central banks will find it increasingly difficult to control the volume of money and credit.
2. Some central bankers believe that the Euromarket increases the severity of foreign-exchange fluctuations.

For both reasons, therefore, it is felt that the Euromarket is becoming an important contributor to world economic instability. Some experts, however, disagree. They contend that the Euromarket has caused increased competition among large banks, resulting in more foreign loans than in the past.

Floating Exchange Rates

Floating exchange rates leave currencies uncontrolled and free to fluctuate according to supply and demand. Thus, a decrease in the price of a nation's currency in the foreign-exchange market encourages that country's exports and discourages its imports. On the other hand, an increase in the price of a nation's currency has the opposite effect. There are thus two chief advantages of freely floating exchange rates:

1. They provide for automatic adjustment in the balance of payments without the intervention of a central authority.

2. They eliminate the need for stabilization funds and international reserves.

But there are also two chief disadvantages of freely floating rates:

1. They may restrict the expansion of world trade by leaving importers, exporters, creditors, and others in a state of great uncertainty about future exchange rates.

2. They may encourage speculation in foreign exchange, which could accentuate price swings and cause a destabilization of world trade.

Many experts believe that these undesirable consequences might eventually lead to more rather than fewer trade controls. This is one reason why central banks often intervene to prevent exchange rates from fluctuating too freely.

It may be noted that one of the disadvantages of freely floating rates —namely, uncertainty about future exchange rates—can be reduced significantly through the use of what is known as the "forward exchange market." This market provides importers and exporters with some insurance against losses or gains resulting from future fluctuations in foreign exchange. See Exhibit 2.

Exhibit 2

Currency Protection in the Forward Exchange Market (90-day forward spread—hypothetical data)

Forward exchange is foreign exchange that is bought (or sold) at a given time and at a stipulated current or "spot" price but is payable at a future date. Thus, by buying or selling forward exchange, importers and exporters can protect themselves against the risks of future fluctuations in the current exchange market.

The spread between spot and future prices can vary considerably, as the figure shows. Currencies that are in strong demand tend to sell at a premium, while those that are in a weaker position sell at a discount. In the latest months shown, for example, French importers of West German goods paid heavily by buying forward marks at a premium, thus restricting their purchases of Volkswagens. But West German importers found forward francs so cheap they could afford to buy a lot more French wine.

Exhibit 3
How the Crawling Peg Works

Under the crawling peg system, a deficit nation finds that its exchange rate stays at the lower level of the allowable band of fluctuation. So its exchange rate is allowed to move downward in predictable fashion until the effects of lowering the rate bring the balance of payments back into equilibrium. On the other side, the exchange rate of a surplus nation is increased in a manner that gradually reduces its surplus. The merit of the crawling peg is that its movements are predictable and it facilitates the adjustment process, both for deficit nations and for surplus nations.

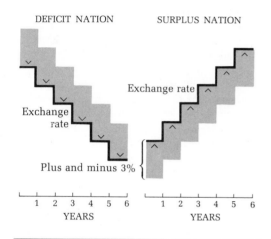

"Managed" exchange rates are likely to continue because they enable countries to maintain better control over their international financial environment.

Adjustable Pegs

An *adjustable peg* system permits controlled changes in the par rate of exchange after a long-run disequilibrium in the balance of payments. It also allows for short-run variations in the exchange rate within a few percentage points around the par value. (This was essentially the Bretton Woods system.) The most desirable feature of such a system is that it operates efficiently only if the par rate is consistent with the nation's long-run equilibrium in its balance of payments. In that case, the adjustment problem is entirely of a short-term nature. The most undesirable feature is that the threat of speculation and disruption of foreign-exchange markets exists when a change in the basic par rate becomes necessary.

Crawling Pegs

Under a *crawling peg* system, the par value of a nation's exchange rate is allowed to change automatically by small increments, downward or upward. These changes are permitted when, in actual daily trading on the foreign-exchange markets, the price of a nation's currency persists on the "floor" or "ceiling" of the governmentally established range for a specified period of time. The changes in the par value are kept small and gradual (probably about 3 percent annually) in order to discourage speculation, but they are sufficient to correct for fundamental imbalances in the balance of payments.

The crawling peg system thus represents a compromise between floating exchange rates and the adjustable peg. Although the crawling peg does not eliminate the need for international reserves, it permits smaller reserves than fixed rates do. And, because everyone knows how far and in what direction exchange rates are moving, speculation tends to be minimal while world trade and investment continue to expand.

A graphic illustration of how the crawling peg system works is given in Exhibit 3.

Conclusion: Permanent Agreement Doubtful

The choice between a system of adjustable exchange rates and one that permits either floating or crawling rates has been discussed for years by bankers, economists, and political leaders. Governments tend to believe that an adjustable exchange-rate system is best. Many economists, on the other hand, especially those in the academic world, have come increasingly to favor the more flexible systems, such as the floating rate or crawling peg. Despite international meetings held to discuss the matter, it is doubtful that any enduring arrangements will ever emerge. In the words of one European central banker:

> The system of fixed exchange rates [under Bretton Woods] *succeeded because it was needed.* It accomplished its objectives—to encourage world trade and to stimulate Europe's economic development. Those achievements were realized by the early 1960s. Since then, the lesson of history has been that it is unrealistic to assume that any government would go along with a permanent policy of exchange rates based on some agreed-upon mechanism that could easily be discarded in a period of adversity.

Case
Multinational Corporations: The "New" Foreign Investment

The great English classical economist David Ricardo demonstrated in the early nineteenth century that unrestricted operation of the law of comparative advantage makes everybody better off. Each nation, he said, should be free to specialize in producing the goods it can produce most efficiently and to leave the production of *other* goods to the countries that can produce *them* most efficiently. The nations of the world can then have more goods by engaging in trade.

Today the neon signs of American, European, and Japanese multinational corporations light the skylines of most of the major cities throughout the world. These companies have spawned subsidiaries and branches in order to exploit their own comparative advantages. They have discovered that economies of scale can be enhanced by locating in foreign markets, and that the advantages of such economies outweigh the regulations and financial risks that global operations may entail.

The international economic implications of multinationals are discussed frequently in the news media. The more important issues are worth examining.

What Are Multinationals?

Boeing, Lockheed, McDonnell-Douglas, and other U.S. aircraft manufacturers do business around the globe, but are they multinationals? Not really, because virtually all of their manufacturing is done in the United States. Accordingly, they are *inter*national rather than *multi*national.

Are all multinationals American? Most lay observers think they are. But, in fact, the first companies with manufacturing, mining, or oil-producing facilities in several countries were British and Dutch. Some of these companies survive, among them the mighty Royal Dutch/Shell group of companies, one of the world's largest oil concerns, and the Anglo-Dutch Unilever group. In recent years other large European and Japanese companies have entered the multinational ranks. But even if it is hard to define a multinational precisely, recognition is somewhat simpler:

> A multinational is a large company that produces in at least four countries, does business still farther afield, and employs people of many nationalities.

Under Attack

Multinationals have been severely criticized for being too big, too powerful, and too rich. Some critics, for example, point out that General Motors' annual income from sales is larger than the gross national products of some of the countries in which it does business, suggesting that GM is more powerful than those nations. But a top executive at IBM rebuts that charge as nonsense. "Wherever a multinational operates," he says, "it must observe local laws. And if a country wishes to, it can expropriate the local subsidiary. Can a multinational expropriate a country?" Not now, perhaps; but it was not so long ago that the United Fruit Company controlled some 4 million acres of land in Latin America and that Liberia was known as the "Firestone Republic."

Today, the financial resources of the major multinationals are so huge that they can challenge or even wreck some nations' economic

Beryl Goldberg

The 50 Largest U.S. Multinationals, 1981

Rank	Company	Total revenue (millions)	Foreign revenues as % of total
1	Exxon	$108,108	70.1%
2	Mobil	65,458	62.9
3	Texaco	57,628	67.0
4	Standard Oil of California	44,224	53.9
5	Ford Motor	38,247	48.4
6	General Motors	62,699	25.0
7	IBM	29,070	48.1
8	Phibro-Salomon	25,109	53.3
9	Citicorp	18,275	62.0
10	Intl Tel & Tel	23,197	47.3
11	Gulf Oil	28,252	36.7
12	BankAmerica	15,085	52.7
13	Chase Manhattan	10,651	65.0
14	E I Du Pont de Nemours	22,790	29.5
15	General Electric	27,854	20.9
16	Dow Chemical	11,873	47.9
17	Standard Oil of Indiana	30,372	16.4
18	Occidental Petroleum	15,335	31.7
19	J P Morgan	6,778	63.3
20	Safeway Stores	16,580	24.7
21	Sun Co	15,967	25.6
22	Manufacturers Hanover	7,476	53.3
23	Eastman Kodak	10,337	38.0
24	Xerox	8,691	44.5
25	Goodyear	9,153	41.0
26	Procter & Gamble	11,416	32.8
27	Phillips Petroleum	15,966	21.3
28	F W Woolworth	8,310	40.9
29	Union Carbide	10,168	31.4
30	Colgate-Palmolive	5,261	58.7
31	United Technologies	13,668	22.1
32	Dart & Kraft	10,211	28.5
33	Tenneco	15,462	18.8
34	CPC International	4,343	64.4
35	Chemical Bank New York	5,658	47.2
36	Pan Am World Airways	3,797	70.0
37	R J Reynolds Industries	9,766	27.2
38	Coca-Cola	5,889	45.0
39	Bankers Trust New York	4,656	55.0
40	Minnesota Mining & Mfg	6,508	39.3
41	Continental Illinois	6,287	37.8
42	Johnson & Johnson	5,399	44.0
43	Atlantic Richfield	27,798	8.4
44	Getty Oil	12,887	17.8
45	Chrysler	10,822	20.2
46	International Harvester	7,041	30.3
47	Sperry	5,427	39.3
48	Halliburton	8,508	24.7
49	First Chicago	4,326	48.3
50	Beatrice Foods	9,024	23.1

Source: Forbes.

and monetary policies. Rightly or wrongly, the multinationals as a group have often been blamed for causing, or at least intensifying, the international monetary problems that have damaged the world economy in recent decades.

Financial Management

The reason, quite simply, is that if the multinationals' corporate treasurers decide a nation's currency is overvalued, they will shift into a safer one. This may raise the demand for it, while reducing demand for the one they have quit. Similarly, the multinationals may withhold investment in those countries that they think are politically unstable or subject to chronic inflation and put their money in other nations they think offer better prospects. Good business, yes; but the corporations' individual and collective decisions can have a profound influence on the wealth of nations.

In contrast, the purely national corporation, because it is usually smaller than the typical multinational and is committed to one country, enjoys less freedom to shift money and resources around the world as the prospects of profit dictate. Nor can the national company as easily shift manufacturing operations from a high-cost country to one characterized by low wages. Multinationals can, however, and frequently do. Understandably, labor unions accuse them of exporting jobs. However, the multinational frequently has little choice, because to compete effectively against products already being produced in low-cost countries it must move to them.

Furthermore, many manufacturing operations in developing nations produce components that are exported for assembly in the multinationals' major markets, which are the rich industrial countries. In that sense, the strategy may even create jobs at home.

A favorite governmental charge against the multinationals is that they avoid taxes by "transfer-pricing" techniques. That is, multinationals allegedly manipulate the prices that subsidiaries pay to each other in order to take profits where taxes are lowest, thereby depriving higher-tax governments of their revenues. There is plenty of evidence that some multinationals do indeed use this technique. But the companies' executives point out that tax avoidance is no crime and ask rhetorically whether their strategy should be to take their profits where taxes are highest.

Conclusion: International Regulation?

Quite clearly, the multinationals will continue to be under attack for a long time, not only for the practices outlined above, but also for their sheer size and their basic nature. To many observers, including some leading business executives, the spectacle of a giant corporation run by a few people making decisions that affect the lives of millions of people and perhaps dozens of countries is extremely distasteful. The attack on multinationals is thus as much political as economic.

The probability is that out of all the scrutiny and discussion will emerge an international consensus on the regulation of these giant corporations, with the majority of countries adopting identical or very similar laws. The process is likely to be slow, however. Although most nations agree that the multinationals need regulation, agreement about regulation virtually ends there. Each country has its own distinct ideas about what the rules ought to be.

The 10 Largest Foreign Multinationals and Their Investment in the U.S., 1981

Foreign investor	Country	U.S. company	Percent owned	Industry	Revenue (millions)
1. Anglo American Corp of So Africa Ltd *Minerals & Resources*	So Africa Bermuda	Phibro-Salomon	27%	metal trading, brokerage	$25,098
		Engelhard Corp	28	metals	2,192
		Inspiration Consol Copper	50	copper	165
Hudson Bay M&S	Canada	Terra Chemicals	100	fertilizer	350
					27,805
2. Royal Dutch/ Shell Group	Netherlands, UK	Shell Oil	69	oil	21,629
		Scallop Corp	100	oil	
		Massey Coal	50	coal	
		Billiton Metals & Ores	100	metals	4,700
		Ocean Minerals	48	metals	
		Billiton Exploration	100	metals	
					26,329
3. Seagram Co Ltd	Canada	Joseph E. Seagram & Sons	100	spirits & wines	1,466
		EI Du Pont	20	chemicals, energy	22,790
					24,256
4. British Petroleum Plc	UK	Standard Oil Ohio	53	energy	13,457
5. Fried Flick Group	Germany	WR Grace	28	chemicals, multicompany	6,521
6. Tengelmann Group	Germany	Great A&P Tea	50	supermarkets	6,227
7. B.A.T. Industries Plc	UK	BATUS	100	paper, retailing, tobacco	4,600
		Germaine Monteil	100	cosmetics	1,194
		Marshall Field	80	retailing	
					5,794
8. Générale Occidentale SA	France	Grand Union	100	supermarkets	4,137
		Diamond Intl	41	packaging, lumber	1,289
					5,426
9. Beneficiaries of US Philips Trust	Netherlands	North Am Philips	62	electronics	3,030
		Signetics	100	semiconductors	344
					3,374
10. Bayer AG	Germany	Mobay Chemical	100	chemicals	1,270
		Miles Laboratories	100	health care	770
		Cutter Laboratories	100	health care	353
		Helena Chemical	100	chemicals	
		Haarmann & Reimer	100	chemicals	637
		Agfa-Gevaert	100	photographics	
					3,030

Source: Forbes.

Questions

1. A multinational company may have operations in—among other countries—the United States and South Africa. In the United States the company supports the ideal of equal opportunity regardless of race and religion. In South Africa, it goes along with discrimination against blacks. Is the company merely being prudent, or is it morally flawed? How *should* it behave?

2. A U.S. company has the choice of serving export markets by building a plant either in North Carolina or in Taiwan. In North Carolina, it can expect a net profit after taxes equaling 5 percent of sales. In Taiwan, it can expect 15 percent. Where should it locate?

3. In some Middle Eastern countries, bribes to government officials are more than merely customary—they are also the price of doing business. Should a multinational pay the bribes and take the business or follow strict ethical principles and let the business go?

What You Have Learned in This Chapter

1. For several decades before World War I, most national economies were closely integrated through a well-developed network of trade and finance. Despite rapid advances in technology and heavy migrations of labor and capital, the international economic setting remained relatively harmonious until the outbreak of the war.

2. World War I disrupted national trading and financial relationships. Although efforts were made at postwar reconstruction, there was a structural weakening of the international economy during the decade of the 1920s as nations shifted their economic goals toward greater internal stability and control at the expense of automatic external adjustment.

3. The world economy, particularly the interdependence of nations, underwent major deterioration during the Depression of the 1930s. Governments sought to protect themselves from economic crises by imposing higher tariffs, by going off the gold standard, and by devaluing their currencies. Although some significant steps toward international economic reform were made during the late 1930s, the outbreak of World War II prevented further progress.

4. After World War II, most of the war-torn nations of the world became beneficiaries of American economic aid. Major steps were taken toward trade liberalization through GATT and toward economic integration through the development of common markets. In the area of international finance, the Bretton Woods conference of 1944 established the IMF and a world monetary arrangement that was enormously successful in encouraging international trade.

5. By the 1960s, however, it was apparent that economic conditions had changed so much that the world's monetary system was out of date. The volume of world trade increased faster than reserves, causing international monetary crises that resulted in exchange controls and devaluations. Among the measures taken to alleviate the pressures were the introduction of SDRs and a two-tier (or two-price) system for gold. Finally, in the face of continued adversity, the Bretton Woods system of fixed exchange rates was abandoned in late 1971. Since then, countries have allowed their currencies to float in foreign-exchange markets.

6. Three proposals have been suggested to improve the world's monetary system: (1) floating exchange rates, (2) an adjustable peg system, and (3) a crawling peg system. Political considerations being what they are, however, it is unlikely that any system of exchange-rate stability will be adhered to by all nations under all circumstances.

For Discussion

1. *Terms and concepts to review:*
gold bullion standard
devaluation
Reciprocal Trade Agreements program
most-favored-nation clause
European Recovery Program (ERP)
General Agreement on Tariffs and Trade (GATT)
free-trade area
customs union
common market
International Monetary Fund (IMF)
gold-exchange standard
Special Drawing Rights (SDRs or "paper gold")
Eurodollars
floating exchange rates
forward exchange
adjustable peg
crawling peg

2. What major features would you stress if you were to write a research paper on the history of international commercial and financial policies?

3. If a country's balance of payments is in equilibrium and the nation experiences a decline in exports, does its balance of payments go into disequilibrium? What happens if floating exchange rates prevail?

4. Devaluation (or exchange depreciation) stimulates a nation's exports while curbing its imports; upward revaluation (or exchange appreciation) has the opposite effect. In view of this, would you recommend the use of devaluation and revaluation as useful countercyclical policies to combat recessions and inflations, similar to the way we currently use fiscal–monetary policies for such purposes? Explain.

5. From the experiences of the 1960s, would you say that the dollar was overvalued or undervalued in world markets? What could have been done to correct the situation?

6. Why do you suppose that many "anti-Keynesians" often propose that the United States go back to a gold standard?

7. The various economic regions of the United States (such as the Northeast or the Southwest) are somewhat like countries, each with its own particular type of economy. However, unlike countries, they all use the same currency, dollars, which puts them in effect on a fixed exchange rate with respect to one another. What happens when some of these regions experience deficits and the others experience surpluses? How do they adjust? How does the regional adjustment process compare with that of nations?

8. Deficits in the U.S. balance of payments were welcomed in the early 1950s but viewed with great concern a decade later. Why?

9. It is often said that the Bretton Woods arrangement resulted in a compromise between fixed and floating exchange rates. Is this true? Explain. What would have been a better compromise?

36

CHAPTER

The Less Developed Countries: Special Growth Problems of Nations in Poverty

Learning guide

Watch for the answers to these important questions

What is meant by "economic development"? Why is the concept difficult to apply?

What are the "stages" of economic development? What main features characterize the various stages? What are the chief advantages and disadvantages of subdividing the process of economic development into stages?

Are there any fundamental principles of economic development? What must be known about agriculture, population, and capital in order to understand their roles as broad determinants of development?

How do international considerations affect economic development? What roles are played by foreign investment and foreign aid? What special issues do these activities raise?

This chapter explains the major growth problems faced by the world's less developed countries.

While millions of inhabitants of advanced industrial nations worry about eating too much, several billion people in dozens of poverty-stricken countries worry about starving. The poverty-stricken countries constitute much of Latin America, Africa, and Asia. It is here that most of the 3 billion citizens of the underdeveloped world live, the majority of them ill fed, poorly housed, and illiterate.

What is the economic destiny of nations in poverty? Because the poor nations contain three-fourths of the world's population, it is the affluent nations that are in the minority. Hence, it is important to understand both the problems faced by poor countries and the measures that can be taken to help solve these problems.

As you will see, nations in poverty are part of the larger picture of economic growth and development, and there are international implications as well. Although there is no explicit or unified theory of economic development, some of today's most significant insights stem from Adam Smith's *The Wealth of Nations* (1776). This was written before the main thrust of the industrial revolutions but after many important agricultural revolutions.

The Meaning of Economic Development

The poor nations are usually referred to as *less developed countries* (LDCs), underdeveloped countries, or developing countries. They are usually characterized by the following conditions:

- Poverty levels of income and hence little or no saving.

- High rates of population growth.

- Substantial majorities of the labor force employed in agriculture.

- Low rates of adult literacy.

- Extensive *disguised unemployment*. This is a condition in which employed resources (usually labor resources) are not being used in their most efficient ways. The concept is also known as *underemployment*.

- Heavy reliance on one or a few items (mainly agricultural) for export.

- Government control by a wealthy elite, which often opposes any changes that would harm its economic interests.

The LDCs tend to have several common characteristics.

Among underdeveloped nations, these characteristics are tendencies rather than certainties. Exceptions can be found to all of them.

How many countries of the world are considered to be "less developed"? Which ones are they? From time to time, the United Nations has designated dozens of countries as LDCs. Among them are Indonesia, Burma, India, Pakistan, Egypt, Nigeria, Syria, Morocco, Paraguay, Ecuador, Honduras, Turkey, and Colombia. Exhibit 1 provides a birds-eye view of the less developed world.

What Is Economic Development?

The fundamental challenge facing each poor country is to transform the status of its economy from underdeveloped to developed. Economic development is the process by which a nation attains an upward transformation of its entire socioeconomic system. This means that there are improvements in the quality of resources as well as positive changes in attitudes, institutions, and values of the society.

Exhibit 1
The Less Developed Countries

Most of the less developed countries are in the tropics—that is, between the Tropic of Cancer and the Tropic of Capricorn. Of course, these countries show various degrees of underdevelopment, ranging from severe to relatively moderate.

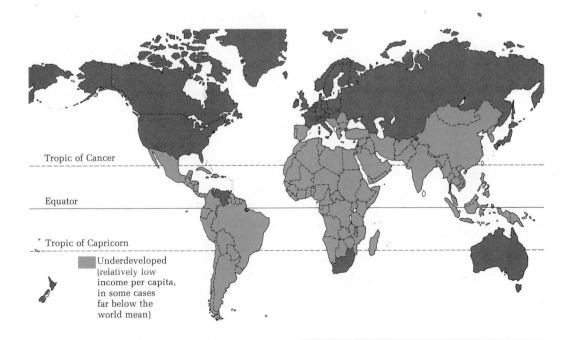

Tropic of Cancer

Equator

Tropic of Capricorn

Underdeveloped (relatively low income per capita, in some cases far below the world mean)

This characterization of economic development is more of a description than a definition. For economic purposes, a more precise statement is needed:

Economic development is the process whereby a nation's real per-capita output or income (its gross national product, or GNP) increases over a long period of time. A nation's rate of economic development is thus measured by its per-capita rate of economic growth.

In order for you to appreciate the implications of this definition, you will need to examine the meanings of some of the terms it uses.

1. The statement that economic development is a "process" refers to the idea that it is a continuous action or series of changes taking place in a definite manner. This suggests that certain causal forces are at work. These must be identified so that their influences on a nation's economic development can be understood.

2. The statement that economic development is measured on a "per-capita" basis indicates that data must be corrected for population change. A nation that experiences an increase in total real output is not necessarily better off materially. In order for there to be material improvement, the gain in output must more than offset any increase in population so that there are more goods for everyone.

3. The statement that economic development takes place "over a long period of time" makes a distinction between the short run and the long run. A short-run spurt in economic growth may be the result of fortuitous circumstances, whereas a long-run expansion in production is generally the result of fundamental change. Thus, it is one thing for a society to experience an increase in real per-capita output over a period of several years. It is quite another for that society to sustain the increase for perhaps a decade or more.

In addition to increases in real income per capita, there are other objectives of economic development. Among these are greater equality in the distribution of income, a rising minimum level of income, and reduction of disguised unemployment. However, these are generally regarded as secondary goals—mainly because they are strongly influenced in each country by existing social structures and institutions. Therefore, in a developing country, there is some likelihood that these secondary goals will be at least partially attained if the primary goal of a sustained increase in real income per capita—and more broadly a general improvement in the entire social system—is realized.

A Study in Contrasts

It is useful to compare the gap, at different points in time, between per-capita incomes in the less developed countries and those in the advanced countries. This enables us to see whether the gulf has widened, narrowed, or remained the same. Economists frequently make such comparisons, and the results are astonishing:

Over the long run, the income gap between the richest countries and the poorest ones has been widening. Indeed, in some periods the income of the richest countries has been as much as 15 or 20 times that of the poorest. As a result, an increasing proportion of all goods and services—now more than 80 percent—is produced in countries in which less than 25 percent of the world's people live.

This trend portends serious consequences for the world community. However, it is not enough simply to measure differences in the economic progress of nations. We must see clearly why these differences occur. This requires that we understand the factors determining a nation's economic development. These factors include the quantity and quality of human and natural resources, the rate of capital accumulation, the degree of specialization and scale of production, and the rate of technological progress. They also include environmental factors—namely, the political, social, cultural, and economic framework within which growth and development take place. Once we comprehend the significance of these factors, it becomes easy to appreciate why the rich nations are getting richer while the poor ones are getting relatively poorer.

This fact can be illustrated by comparing the United States with most underdeveloped countries. The United States has a large labor force with a relatively high proportion of skilled workers. It has numerous business leaders who are experienced and disciplined. It has a substantial and diversified endowment of natural resources, an extensive system of transportation and power, an efficient and productive technology financed by an adequate supply of savings, and a stable and comparatively uncorrupt government. And, not to be overlooked, it has a culture in which the drive for profit and material gain is generally accepted. These factors in combination have stimulated America's economic development.

In the less developed countries, on the other hand, most of these conditions are absent. The people in the labor force are largely unskilled and inefficient, and many of them are chronically ill or undernourished. Saving is small or even negative, resulting in low rates of investment and capital accumulation. The cultural environment favors the clergy, the military, or government administration, while frowning upon commerce, finance, and entrepreneurship. Furthermore, government is often either unstable or, if not, dictatorial, corrupt, and inefficient. Paradoxically, many poor countries are rich in natural resources. However, because most of these countries lack the other ingredients, they cannot sustain economic development.

Many LDCs do not possess the combination of cultural and physical conditions needed for sustained growth.

Stages of Development

The primary challenge of economic development is to get the less developed countries started on a path toward rising real income per capita. For most LDCs, this task usually requires a major transformation of the economic and social structures of the country. You can gain some appreciation of what such a transformation entails by observing the stages of growth through which an LDC might pass as it progresses from underdevelopment to the status of a fully developed country.

W. W. Rostow, a distinguished economic historian who also served as special assistant to several Presidents, has constructed descriptive "models" of economic development. They consist of five phases (shown in Exhibit 2) that characterize the growth of nations.

The process of economic growth can be viewed in terms of "stages" of development.

Stage 1: The Traditional Society

The traditional stage is the earliest stage of a society's development. In this period, the economy is largely primitive. It is characterized by three major conditions:

Exhibit 2
The Stages of Development

The process of economic development, as explained by Rostow, can be divided into five stages. The model provides useful insights into the changes that occur as a nation is transformed from a traditional to a technically progressive society. (**Note** The lengths of the stages, of course, should not be thought of as uniform. In reality, some may be much longer than others, depending on the characteristics of the particular country—its culture, its institutions, and many other factors.)

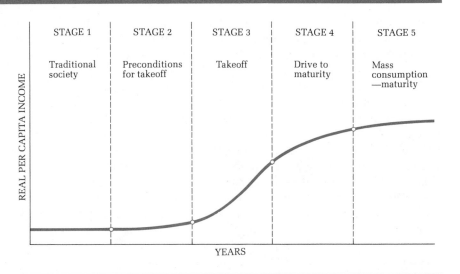

1. There is an absence of modern science and technology.

2. Resources are overallocated in agriculture and underallocated in manufacturing.

3. A rigid social structure exists that impedes economic change.

As a result of these conditions, productivity is low and real income or output per capita is barely at a subsistence level.

Historically, almost all countries and regions were in the traditional stage of development during the early Middle Ages (fifth century to tenth century), and many remained in the traditional stage during the later Middle Ages (tenth century to fifteenth century). Even today, there are economies in Asia, Latin America, and the Middle East that are almost entirely (if not completely) traditional.

Stage 2: The Preconditions for Takeoff

The second stage is transitional. It is a period in which the conditions needed for upward movement are being formed. The chief characteristics of this period are these:

1. New scientific techniques are being applied to agriculture and manufacturing.

2. Financial institutions, such as banks, are emerging to mobilize capital and provide funds for new investment.

3. Improvements in transportation and communication are occurring, permitting a widening of commerce.

At the same time, a fundamental political change—the building of a centralized national state—is taking place. Although low-productivity methods are still widespread, there may be some cases in which traditional activities exist side by side with modern ones. Obstacles to development are gradually being overcome, but real income or output per capita is rising slowly.

Historically, these conditions occurred widely in western Europe between the end of the Middle Ages (about the fifteenth century) and the Age of Enlightenment (the eighteenth century). Today the majority of poor nations are in this stage of development.

Stage 3: The Takeoff

The third stage of development—the takeoff—is the great watershed of economic growth. It occurs when the old obstacles and resistances to steady expansion are finally overcome. Some important conditions that characterize this stage are these:

The takeoff stage is the "springboard" for those nations that reach it. Many LDCs have not yet arrived at this stage.

1. Modern technology and organizational methods in agriculture and industry are being adopted.

2. Net investment is rising, usually toward levels of roughly 10 percent of national income.

3. There is a birth of major new industries, which in turn stimulates the development of many subsidiary industries.

While this is happening, the agricultural sector is likely to be undergoing a revolutionary improvement in productivity. Labor is being released to work in the cities, while farms are providing raw materials to meet the expanding demands of the industrial sector. As a result of all these conditions, real income or output per capita begins to rise significantly.

Historically, for those countries that have experienced takeoff, this stage has usually lasted about two or three decades. In Britain, for example, it covered most of the last quarter of the eighteenth century. In the United States and France, it occurred during the three decades preceding 1860. In Germany, it took place during the third quarter of the nineteenth century. In Japan, it covered the fourth quarter of the nineteenth century. And in Canada and the Soviet Union, it occurred during the quarter-century preceding the outbreak of World War I. In recent decades, several other countries, including Brazil, Egypt, Israel, Lebanon, Mexico, South Korea, and Taiwan, have either reached or entered the takeoff stage. For some of these countries, however, rapid growth has been severely interrupted by wars.

In general:

> The takeoff stage is a period in which savings are rising, there is an expanding entrepreneurial class capable of directing savings into new investment, and the economy is exploiting hitherto unused natural resources and methods of production.

Stage 4: The Drive to Maturity

After takeoff there follows a new stage—the drive to maturity. This is a period of sustained, if fluctuating, progress as modern technology is extended over a wide range of economic activity. Several important features of this period may be noted:

1. Investment in new plant and equipment is maintained at a relatively high rate, usually between 10 and 20 percent of national income.

2. The rapid rate of investment permits the growth of output to exceed the increase in population.

3. The economy assumes a significant role in world trade as new import requirements arise and new export commodities are developed.

On the whole, this is a period in which the economy undergoes significant structural changes as production techniques improve, the growth of new industries accelerates, and the growth of older industries levels off. As a consequence, society experiences sustained increases in real income or output per capita.

Historically, it has taken most advanced countries about 40 years to complete the drive to maturity. Britain, France, and the United States accomplished it during the last four decades of the nineteenth century. Japan achieved it in the first half of the present century. Of course, none of the developing countries has yet reached this stage.

In general terms:

> The drive to maturity is a period of resource diversification. The economy moves beyond the industries that initiated the takeoff and develops the capacity and technology to produce efficiently a broad range of commodities.

Stage 5: Mass Consumption—Maturity

The mass-consumption stage is the final (mature) stage for advanced countries. The United States, Japan, and most countries of Western Europe have attained it.

The final stage of development is reached with the coming of a high level of mass consumption. As a society achieves this level of maturity, several things happen:

1. An increasing proportion of resources is directed to the production of consumers' durables and services.

2. The percentage of skilled workers in the labor force rises, as does the percentage of the total population living in cities.

3. A progressively larger share of resources is allocated to society's welfare and security.

The stage of mass consumption is thus an age of affluence. For the United States, it began around the end of World War I (1918). But it was in the years after the end of World War II (1945) that the signs became most evident. A large-scale migration from rural to urban areas, from farms to factories, occurred as people became increasingly aware of, and eager to share, the consumption fruits of a mature economy. Automobiles, major appliances, and social welfare services became widely diffused, as real income or output per person rose to the point at which society could afford to have more than just the basic necessities.

In the 1950s, western Europe and Japan entered this stage. The USSR became technically ready for it during that period. However, political and social problems of adjustment faced by Soviet leaders have retarded the launching of this phase.

Conclusion: Two Shortcomings of the Model

The Rostow model has some shortcomings and should not be viewed as an accurate representation of all historical processes.

Does Rostow's model of the stages of development provide useful insights into the development process? There is no doubt that it does. However, the model suffers from at least two important shortcomings. These may impede its use as a guide for formulating public policy.

1. Economic development cannot be divided into precise stages. Growth is a continuous process, not a discrete one. Therefore, any attempt to separate it into distinct periods must be highly arbitrary. No two people viewing the past growth of a society would necessarily agree on the exact points at which one stage ended and another began. Nor would any two people necessarily agree on whether the society had even experienced a particular stage.

2. It is not necessary for investment to rise rapidly before sustained growth can take place, as in Rostow's takeoff stage. Some countries have experienced steady development resulting from gradually rising levels of investment over a long period. Nor is it necessary for an agricultural revolution—a modernization of farming techniques—to precede an industrial revolution in order for resources to be transferred from the rural to the industrial sector. As you will see, the experiences of LDCs since about 1950 indicate that agriculture and industry may expand simultaneously while sustained development is taking place.

In conclusion, therefore:

Rostow's model of the stages of development provides many useful insights into the changes that occur as a country is transformed from a traditional to a technically progressive society. Therefore, the model should be viewed as a useful tool, not as a precise explanation of a historical process.

Some Principles and Problems of Development

Although there is no single or unified theory of development, various principles and policies would undoubtedly serve as ingredients if such a theory should ever evolve. Moreover, a modern theory would have to embrace several social sciences rather than economics alone. This will become evident as we discuss the following important concepts and issues of development theory:

Development theory rests on some fundamental concepts. These will play a role in any systematic model that may be developed.

1. The need for agricultural development.

2. Escaping from the "population trap."

3. Investing in physical capital.

4. Investing in human capital.

5. Labor-intensive versus capital-intensive projects.

6. Small versus large projects.

7. Private versus social profitability.

The Need for Agricultural Development

In underdeveloped countries, the great bulk of human resources is devoted to agriculture. These resources tend to be inefficiently employed. As a result, there is a great deal of disguised unemployment or "underemployment."

Agriculture, for the most part, produces the nation's food and raw materials. Therefore, in order for economic development to take place out of domestic resources, agricultural efficiency must improve. This is necessary in order to produce a surplus of output over and above what the agricultural sector itself consumes. As this happens, human and material resources are spared from farming to work in manufacturing. This helps to expand the industrial sector while consuming the surplus of the agricultural sector.

It may be necessary for an agricultural revolution to precede or accompany an industrial revolution in order for development to take place.

These facts suggest a proposition of fundamental importance in economic development:

> In most LDCs there is a close relationship between the agricultural sector and the industrial sector. The relationship is such that the growth of the industrial sector is strongly influenced by prior or simultaneous technical progress in the agricultural sector.

The operation of this important principle has been amply demonstrated in economic history. For example, the development of towns during the Middle Ages was accompanied by, and to a significant extent preceded by, improved methods of agricultural production. Notable was the adoption of the three-field system. Also, the industrial revolution of the eighteenth and nineteenth centuries in Europe and the United States was strongly influenced by an agricultural revolution. This was marked by a number of major innovations, including the introduction of root crops, horse-hoeing husbandry, four-course rotation, and scientific animal breeding. These developments were of such great importance that they actually overshadowed in certain respects the accompanying industrial revolutions. (See Box 1.)

Land Reform

Despite widespread popular belief, land reform can actually retard rather than enhance economic development.

Agricultural development rarely occurs without land reform. In many underdeveloped countries, agricultural land is owned by a few rich families but is farmed by large numbers of poor families. Proponents of land reform have almost always advocated the division of land ownership among the families working it. Presumably, the broadening of ownership would yield important psychological and political values as well as economic incentives.

The evidence, however, does not always bear this out. Various studies of land reform have found that the fragmenting of land ownership by itself may actually reduce farm productivity rather than raise it. This is true unless land reform is accompanied by other measures. These include:

1. The implementation of new farming techniques, such as improvements in plant strains, irrigation systems, and fertilization programs.

2. The increased availability of credit—through the creation of local banks or cooperative credit societies—for investment-minded farmers.

The need for these agricultural reforms is readily seen:

> Legislation that breaks up large landholdings will also eliminate landlords and, therefore, the services they provide. These are mainly tools and credit. Hence, not only must land reform be accompanied by the provision of sufficient technical and financial resources to replace what is lost, it must also provide for the enhancement of agricultural productivity.

Escaping from the "Population Trap"

To solve their economic problems, the less developed countries must either avoid or extricate themselves from the "population trap." That is, their real GNP must continue to increase faster than their population.

Although not all underdeveloped countries are "overpopulated," most of them are. In poor regions in Asia, parts of Latin America, and Africa, population presses heavily on physical resources. Accumula-

Box 1
Agricultural Development and Economic Growth: A Novel Interpretation

It is an instructive exercise in the interpretation of economic history to consider how far the introduction to agriculture of root crops (such as the turnip) is responsible for the economic development of the past three centuries.

Root crops did two main things: They eliminated the fallow (plowed but unseeded) field and they made scientific animal breeding possible. The fallow field had been necessary to eliminate weeds, but the practice of planting roots in rows between which horses could pull the implements necessary to cultivate the ground made the fallow field unnecessary. Also, the roots enabled the farmer to feed his stock through the winter and thereby eliminate the need for the traditional mass slaughter of farm animals at Christmas. This made selective breeding possible, with astounding results.

1. The increased production of food probably was the principal cause of the amazing fall in mortality, especially infant mortality, in the middle years of the eighteenth century. Most of the rise in population of the Western world was due to this.

2. The extra food enabled more babies to live and thus provided the inhabitants for the industrial cities.

3. The new techniques enabled agriculture to produce a large surplus and thus made it possible to feed the hungry people of the new towns.

Thus, even if there had been no startling changes in industrial techniques, it is probable that the agricultural revolution itself would have produced many of the phenomena we usually associate with the industrial revolution. And it is possible that the vast developments in agricultural techniques that have taken place in recent decades may foreshadow a new revolution in economic life as great as that of the last century.

Source: Adapted, with substantial changes, from Kenneth E. Boulding, *Economic Analysis,* 3rd ed., New York, Harper & Row, 1955, p. 719n.

W. E. Ferguson/FPG

Terry Qing/FPG

U.S. farming methods, geared to big farms, heavy mechanization, and few farmers, are not easily adaptable to conditions in many of the developing countries. These countries typically have many small farms that are intensively cultivated by large numbers of farmers. More than half the farms in most developing countries are less than 12 acres in size. The type of agricultural revolution that is needed in these countries in order to raise their productivity is to provide farmers with the right incentives and the necessary agricultural inputs.

Exhibit 3
Can Population Be Controlled Through the Price System?

Can the price system be used to help plan the size of a nation's population?

Population control might be exercised through the sale of "birth rights." The government, for example, might decide that each married couple should be entitled to two "free births." Beyond that, a couple would have to pay a price if they wanted to have more children. How much would they have to pay? The answer would depend on the current market price of birth-right certificates, each certificate permitting a woman to have one completed pregnancy.

The government would issue a fixed amount of these certificates for a period of time. Hence, the supply curve S would be a vertical line. However, the demand curve D would be normal or downward-sloping. Through the free interaction of supply and demand, the equilibrium price would settle at P; the equilibrium quantity would, of course, be at Q.

Over a period of time, income (and perhaps population) would grow. Therefore, the demand curve would shift rightward to D'. The government might then decide to issue additional certificates, as shown by the new supply curve S'. This would result in a different equilibrium price at P' and an equilibrium quantity at Q'. The additional certificates the government decided to issue would depend on the degree of control it wished to exercise over the market price and the size of the population.

Question There are obvious social and economic difficulties in implementing such a system. Can you name them? Can you also suggest ways of overcoming some of the difficulties?

tion, or saving, is therefore difficult. Why? Because the level of production is low and resources are committed primarily to agriculture in order to produce the bare necessities of consumption. As long as the pressure on food supplies continues, large numbers of people must subsist at the barest survival level. This makes it extremely difficult if not impossible for the nation to extricate itself from the population trap.

What can be done to alleviate the problem? One approach, of course, would be for large numbers of people to emigrate from overpopulated to underpopulated regions. But numerous legal, social, and economic obstacles make this solution unfeasible.

SUPPLY OF, AND DEMAND FOR, "BIRTH RIGHTS"

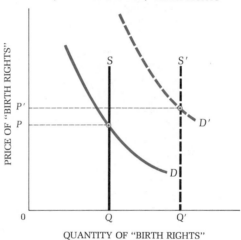

QUANTITY OF "BIRTH RIGHTS"

The most practical alternative is to meet the population problem head-on. Various studies have demonstrated quite conclusively that it is cheaper to increase real incomes per capita by slowing population growth than by investing in new factories, irrigation, and so on. Studies have also shown that it is not so much the absolute *size* of the population as the population *growth rate* that lessens improvements in real income per capita. Because of this, a number of developing countries, including China, Indonesia, Taiwan, India, and Pakistan, have instituted family-planning programs. These have ranged from simple counseling services to large-scale voluntary sterilization schemes (usually vasectomies). A chief difficulty is that any population-control scheme may interfere with local religious traditions, which often impede if not prevent the development of effective programs.

An interesting *economic* approach to the problem is proposed in Exhibit 3. Although it is not likely that such a plan would ever be adopted, it provides a thought-provoking topic for discussion.

Investing in Physical Capital

Many economists and government officials used to believe that massive infusions of capital were alone sufficient to induce economic development. Increases in real output, it was contended, were attributable almost entirely to expansions in the stock of capital rather than to increases in labor employment or improvements in technology.

Where did this assumption come from? It was based on the economic concept of *marginal productivity*. This is defined as the increase in output resulting from a unit change in a variable input while all other inputs are held fixed. The concept is associated with the famous *law of diminishing returns* (the formal meaning of which you can look up in the Dictionary at the back of the book). In simplest terms, the law tells you that the more you have of a particular type of resource, the less productive or useful is any one unit of it.

Now, because most underdeveloped countries have an excess of labor, the marginal productivity of labor in such countries is low or close to zero (or perhaps even negative). And because most underdeveloped countries have an insufficient amount of capital, the marginal productivity of capital is high. Consequently, the infusion of large doses of capital appeared to be the most effective means of raising real GNP per capita.

Recent Findings

This conclusion, although largely correct, has been greatly modified over the years. Research studies and experiences in less developed countries during the past several decades have revealed some interesting findings:

1. There are limits to the amount of new capital that LDCs can "absorb" or utilize effectively in any given period. These limits are set by such factors as the availability of related skilled labor and the level of effective demand for the output of the new capital. It does little good, obviously, to build a railroad if there is not enough skilled labor to operate and maintain it or not enough demand for goods transported by the railroad to support it.

2. The marginal productivity of farm labor may be low because it is employed in densely populated areas where arable land is relatively scarce. Yet in many LDCs large sections of fairly fertile lands are underpopulated for cultural or political reasons, or simply because the lands are located in undesirable or inaccessible areas. Of course, some injections of capital may help. But increases in output would be greater if the infusions of capital were accompanied by shifts of farm labor from overpopulated to underpopulated areas.

As a general rule, therefore:

Both extra capital and extra labor of an appropriate type are needed to obtain extra output. The notion that in the LDCs the marginal productivity of capital is high while that of labor is low is undoubtedly correct. However, it is true only in an overall sense. When used in proper combinations, the marginal productivities of *related* kinds of skilled labor and capital are likely to be quite high.

Investing in Human Capital

Investments in physical capital must be accompanied by investments in human capital if increased productivity is to accelerate economic development. The "quality" of a population, as measured by its skills, education, and health, is more important than its size in influencing a nation's cultural and economic progress. It is no accident that the populations of advanced countries have higher average levels of education and longer life spans than those of underdeveloped countries.

Infusion of capital alone to stimulate development is usually not enough. Indeed it may even be wasteful. Instead capital must be combined with related kinds of labor in order to encourage economic growth.

Four main areas call for particular attention:

Most LDCs should devote more effort to training technicians rather than scientists.

1. Emphasis on Basic Technical Training Underdeveloped countries usually suffer from a glut of unskilled workers and a shortage of skilled workers. These nations should place more emphasis on vocational instruction and less on academic training. For example, primary-school and secondary-school curricula should be oriented toward technical education and on-the-job training in such fields as agriculture, commerce, industry, and construction. This would be more useful than concentrating on preparing students for passing entrance examinations at universities in Britain, France, and the United States.

2. Development of Middle-Level Skills Most LDCs suffer from a shortage of people with middle-level skills. For example, there is usually a much greater need for technicians than for scientists and engineers. If universities and educational institutes were to focus on the development of these middle-level skills, it would enhance productivity.

3. Utilization of Foreign Experts The LDCs have long suffered from a serious "brain drain." This results when their talented younger people going to universities in advanced nations remain there instead of returning to their home countries, where they are desperately needed. Underdeveloped nations may not always be able to eliminate this form of emigration. However, they can minimize it by making greater use of foreign experts in domestic education and training programs.

4. Investment in Public Health Large-scale health programs are needed to reduce disease and mortality rates in LDCs. Of course, reductions in mortality rates result in greater population growth. This adds to the burden of people pressing against limited resources. The solution, however, is not to reduce public health but to supplement it with voluntary birth-control programs. Only when men and women gain some degree of control over their lives does investment in human capital become a force for cultural as well as economic change.

Labor-Intensive Versus Capital-Intensive Projects

The distinction between labor-intensive and capital-intensive projects is more relevant at the interindustry level than at the intraindustry level.

Should an underdeveloped country that is trying to industrialize concentrate on labor-using or capital-using investment projects? This question can be addressed in terms of what may conveniently be called a "labor-intensity" versus a "capital-intensity" criterion.

1. Labor-Intensity Criterion This standard applies when labor is excessive relative to capital. Emphasis should then be placed on projects that make maximum use of the abundant factor of production, labor, and minimum use of the scarce factor, capital. Such an approach would tend to reduce the degree of disguised unemployment while increasing industrial output.

2. Capital-Intensity Criterion According to this standard, capital-using projects should be favored even if labor is excessive. The reason is that the potential gains in productivity that are achieved by maximizing the amount of capital per worker will more than offset the loss of output resulting from unemployment. This is particularly true, it is argued, when the developing country must face competition for its manufactured products from more advanced industrial economies.

To a considerable extent, the controversy over labor-intensive versus capital-intensive investments is academic and irrelevant to modern manufacturing processes. In most industries there is little room for substitution between capital and labor. This is because production processes within plants are predetermined by technology. Combinations of labor and capital are established by engineering rather than according to economic requirements. A given plant is designed with a predetermined capacity to be operated by a certain number of workers. Although some variations in output may be made within a single-shift operation, multiple shifts are the only way in which large changes in output can be realized.

These facts suggest the following conclusions:

The labor-intensity versus capital-intensity criterion is usually of little practical value in implementing investment decisions within a particular industry. On the other hand, the criterion assumes greater realism when it is used to compare *interindustry* investments for the purpose of noting which projects will tend to be more labor-using (or capital-saving) and which more capital-using (or labor-saving). Such comparisons can help in deciding the types of industries that should be promoted by a developing country.

Unfortunately, these economic conclusions are often overshadowed by political considerations, as shown in Exhibit 4.

Small Versus Large Projects

Should LDCs try to develop large and complex production operations, or should they concentrate first on small-scale industries? Practical considerations favor the latter approach. In most underdeveloped countries, it is highly probable that one or more of the necessary ingredients of industrialization is lacking. These include adequate capital, transportation facilities, suitable marketing channels, modern technical knowledge, and effective managerial skills.

Small projects demand fewer of the scarce ingredients. At the same time, they develop needed entrepreneurship, can be instituted more rapidly, and can begin to impart their beneficial economic effects to the community more quickly. Large industrial projects, on the other hand, have less chance of succeeding under these conditions, and their payoffs in terms of economic benefits to the nation are likely to lie far in the future.

Jerry Frank/DPI
Automobile assembly plant in Latin America.

Information Service of India
Durgapur steelworks in West Bengal.

Ethiopian Airlines
A Boeing 707 of Ethiopian Airlines.

The limitations of this conclusion must be recognized, however. The distinction between "small" and "large" projects is not always clear-cut. Moreover, large and small projects are often complementary rather than competitive. A large manufacturing plant, for instance, will frequently stimulate the development of many small plants to provide parts and services. Hence, it cannot be stated as a firm rule that one size or scale of manufacturing is always preferable to another.

As a practical matter, the alternatives must be identified and measured in each case. For certain types of manufacturing, a large, integrated production process may be necessary in order to gain economies that will permit internationally competitive pricing. For other types of manufacturing, differences in scale may hinge on factors other than productive efficiency. Some considerations are size of market and availability of the right type of labor supply. Thus in many LDCs, modern manufacturing plants and paved roads have been provided by foreign aid, while ox-drawn wagons are used to transport the goods. Clearly, therefore, cost is not the only factor to be considered when deciding on the size of the plant to be constructed.

Private Versus Social Profitability

The private rate of return on a project may or may not equal its social rate of return. The latter reflects the project's value to society.

Every real investment yields two kinds of returns. One may be called the "private" rate of return; the other can be referred to as the "social" rate of return. Under certain theoretical conditions they may be identical. In reality, however, they usually differ, sometimes by a wide margin. Let us see why.

The *private rate of return* on an investment is the financial rate. This is the rate that business managers try to anticipate prior to investing their funds. It is therefore the same as the *marginal efficiency of investment* studied in macroeconomic theory. In simplest terms, the private rate of return is the expected net profit after taxes in relation to costs. The rate may be expressed as a percentage annual return upon either the total cost of the project or upon the net worth of the stockholder-owners. From the viewpoint of investors, this rate is the most important criterion, because it measures the profitability of the investment.

The *social rate of return* is the net value of the project to the economy. The social rate is estimated on the basis of the net increase in output that a project, such as a new industry, may be expected to bring, directly or indirectly, to the area being developed. The industry's contribution is measured by subtracting the cost to society of the resources used from the value of what the industry produces. Therefore, the concept of a social rate of return is that of a net return.

As a general rule:

A difference usually exists between the private and social rates of return. There are two reasons:

1. The costs of various inputs to the private owner may be different from the cost to the economy.

2. The value of the sales receipts to the private owner may be different from the value to the economy of having the goods produced.

An Illustrative Example

As a practical illustration, you might think in terms of a factory in a certain area. This investment may yield a high private rate of return to its owners. If the factory employs a significant segment of the area's labor force, it may also seem to be yielding a high social rate of return. However, before we can be sure of this, we would have to analyze such offsetting factors as the resources used by the factory and the adverse externalities or spillovers.

After these considerations are taken into account, the difference between the private and social rates may be quite substantial. Indeed, a project may have a high private rate of return and a low—possibly even negative—social rate. This might be true, for example, if the factory pollutes its environment. Alternatively, a high social rate and a low private rate may also be encountered. This usually happens with certain types of public-works projects.

These two examples are extremes. Between them is a range of projects that are suitable for a particular community in accordance with its stock of human and material resources. This is the range that must be sought out, identified, and developed by the government agencies and organizations that are encouraging industrialization.

Some International Aspects of Development

The fundamental task of LDCs is to increase their productivity by improving their methods of production. This requires investment in physical and human capital. Examples are power facilities, factories, machines, education, public health, and the like.

LDCs face the difficult task of devising policies aimed at attracting foreign investment.

Because the LDCs for the most part are poor, they do not generate enough savings to finance their own capital formation. Therefore, they must acquire the needed investment from abroad by obtaining private foreign investment, foreign aid, or a combination of the two.

Attracting Private Foreign Investment

What economic measures might underdeveloped countries consider in order to attract investment from private foreign sources?

1. Infrastructure Facilities The governments of LDCs might undertake to provide the necessary *infrastructure*. This is the economic and social overhead capital needed as a basis for modern production. Examples of infrastructure are roads, telephone lines, power facilities, schools, and public-health services. Many advanced countries as well as international agencies have had a long history of providing LDCs with generous loans on relatively easy terms for the purpose of building infrastructure facilities.

2. Insurance Protection When considering investment in certain politically volatile LDCs, foreign corporations are concerned with security of life and property. Insurance provisions could help reduce such risks. The governments of LDCs might consider establishing insurance companies, or contracting with foreign insurance companies, for this purpose. The plan could be financed partly by the recipient governments and partly by the governments of the lending countries. An international financing agency of the United Nations, such as the World Bank (discussed later in this chapter), could provide the necessary administrative assistance. Some progress in this direction has, in fact, been made, but observers contend that much work remains to be done.

3. Nonnationalization Guarantees Potential investors must be given reasonable assurance that their assets will not be nationalized (that is, expropriated) by the governments of recipient nations. At the very least, investors should be guaranteed "fair compensation" in the event of nationalization. They should also be assured that disputed claims will be settled by the International Court of Justice at The Hague.

4. Profit and Capital Transfers Businesspeople are not likely to invest in LDCs without the knowledge that a certain share of profits can be transferred out of the country each year. In addition, specific provisions are needed to permit capital mobility. For example, laws could be formulated that place minimum restrictions on the transfer of ownership between foreigners, in the event that investors wish to sell their assets.

5. Tax Concessions LDCs can offer a variety of tax inducements to attract foreign capital. As examples, income taxes and property taxes on preferred types of investments can be reduced or postponed for a specific number of years. Several underdeveloped nations have had success with such policies. However, to use tax concessions effectively, care must be taken not to drive out existing firms by giving competitive advantages to new foreign companies.

The foregoing ideas suggest this conclusion:

> In order to attract foreign capital, LDCs must create a *favorable climate for investment*. This requires the adoption of economic policies designed to protect property rights, permit capital mobility, and enhance profits.

Foreign Aid

Even under the best of circumstances, some LDCs may not be able to attract sufficient private foreign investment to meet total capital requirements for takeoff into sustained growth. In that case, help in the form of foreign aid from other nations is needed. *Foreign aid* consists of loans, grants, or assistance by one government to another for the purpose of accelerating economic development in the recipient country. Box 2 shows the results of some foreign aid.

**Box 2
Hydroelectric Project
in Ghana**

This gigantic construction project, financed by foreign aid, is one of the largest ever undertaken in Africa or Asia. The huge conduits carry water from the dam to the turbine house. Numerous other construction and agricultural projects have been provided to LDCs by foreign aid.

Ian Berry/Magnum

Major Sources of Foreign Aid

Since the end of World War II (1945), several national and international organizations have been established to provide foreign aid of various types. Some of the more important agencies will be noted briefly.

World Bank The *International Bank for Reconstruction and Development*, popularly known as the World Bank, was established by a United Nations charter in 1944. The Bank's functions were to provide loans and credit for postwar reconstruction and to promote development of poorer countries. The Bank's chief function today is to finance basic development projects, such as dams, communication and transportation facilities, and health programs. It does this by insuring or otherwise guaranteeing private loans or, when private capital is not available, by providing loans itself. The Bank has also established affiliated agencies to finance higher-risk investment projects for both private and public enterprises in underdeveloped countries.

IDCA The most important American organization concerned with foreign assistance is the *International Development Cooperation Agency* (IDCA). Created in 1979, it represents a major restructuring and consolidation of previous development programs operated by different U.S. agencies and various multilateral organizations. IDCA has two major functions. The first is to advise government on development policies. The second is to administer funds voted annually by the U.S. Congress for the purpose of providing economic, technical, and defense assistance to nations that are identified with the free world. IDCA includes within its organization the Agency for International Development (AID), the federal government's chief foreign-aid unit, which was previously part of the U.S. State Department.

Other Nations The United States is not the only source of assistance to underdeveloped countries. The Soviet Union, China, and other nations have come to play increasingly important roles. This is not surprising, because, for any country that provides it, foreign aid may be motivated as much by political as by economic considerations.

Issues in Foreign Aid

What are some of the economic issues that arise in the provision of foreign aid? The basic questions involve the classes, amounts, conditions, and forms of aid that should be given.

1. Projects or Programs? Should the United States confine its aid to specific capital projects, or should it provide aid for general programs? The World Bank, the U.S. Congress, and AID have tended to follow the project approach. This is because specific projects appear more concrete and less wasteful. Economists, however (including those at AID), tend to prefer the program approach. The reason is that it permits greater flexibility, a more general use of the underdeveloped country's resources, and a recognition of the fact that capital projects that are really needed will probably be undertaken sooner or later anyhow. This latter view seems to make more sense. In the long run, a nation's economic development is not dependent on single projects. Rather, it depends on a total program whose effectiveness is determined by the way in which it manages its own general resources.

Foreign aid is provided by a major international organization as well as by many individual nations.

Foreign aid has become a controversial issue, replete with political as well as economic considerations.

Various criteria have been proposed for granting foreign aid. Virtually no one objects to providing aid in the form of food and medicine for nations hit by disasters, but the granting of aid for development purposes is controversial.

2. How Much Aid Should the United States Give? Various criteria for granting aid have been proposed. For example:

• Aid should be provided until income per capita in the recipient country has been raised by a certain percentage.

• Sufficient aid should be given to make up a deficit in the recipient country's balance of payments. In simplest terms, this means that, when a nation's outflow of money exceeds the inflow, foreign aid should make up the difference.

• Aid should be provided in proportion to a recipient country's needs as measured by its income per capita.

No matter how rational these and other criteria may seem, they ignore the fact that foreign aid is more a tool of foreign policy than an application of economic logic. Demonstrations outside an American embassy, the destruction of a U.S. government facility, or the thwarting of a communist coup can influence congressional appropriations for assistance more than the rational dictates of economic experts.

3. Should Conditions Be Imposed on Foreign Aid? Many political leaders feel that assistance should be provided to any poor country that is trying to improve its economic position. But problems and dilemmas of a political and quasi-political nature tend to cloud this simple criterion. For instance:

• Should aid be given to some communist countries, such as Poland or Yugoslavia, but not to others, such as China or Cuba?

• Should we confine aid only to the noncommunist countries?

• Should we see to it that the benefits of aid to a given country are spread throughout the society rather than being concentrated in a single socio-economic class?

• Should aid be given only to countries that accomplish reforms (such as tax, budget, and land reforms), or should it be given without restrictions?

These are typical of the problems that face the United States in its foreign-assistance programs. Some people have proposed that aid be given with no strings attached. However, this would ordinarily be a foolish course for the United States to follow. With few exceptions, the U.S. should at least approve of the goals for which the aid is to be used and impose conditions that will assure reasonable efficiency in the attainment of these goals.

4. Should Foreign Assistance Take the Form of Loans or Grants? The answer to this question involves not only economic considerations but moral, ethical, and social ones as well. In many Muslim countries, for instance, charging interest on loans carries an unfavorable connotation because it implies that the lender is taking unfair advantage of the distress of the borrower.

Nevertheless, some guide for policy decisions is needed. Perhaps the most feasible guide is an "international welfare criterion." This might be a standard that provides grants to countries whose per-capita incomes are below a specified level and loans to countries above that level. In the past, our foreign-aid policies have often been inconsistent in the use of this or any other standard.

In conclusion:

Experience shows that average growth rates of many underdeveloped countries have sometimes been extremely impressive for as much as a decade or more. But averages can be deceptive. Actually, there is still a wide disparity in performance among the underdeveloped nations and regions of the world. A study of the development process indicates that foreign assistance *in conjunction with* private investment is necessary if the LDCs are to make the most effective use of their human and material resources.

Issue
Foreign Aid: A Bottomless Pit?

America's foreign-aid programs were launched with the best of intentions after World War II. But after several decades and hundreds of billions of dollars given away, the programs started showing signs of falling apart. An increasing number of citizens—from ordinary taxpayers to political leaders and scholars—have criticized not only specific aid projects but also the underlying philosophy of the entire aid program. The criticisms have been political as well as economic. Among them:

• Some of the largest recipients of American aid have opposed the United States in critical international situations. India, for instance, has been helped numerous times by American food shipments, but it has repeatedly denounced U.S. diplomatic and military actions. Further, critics say, why should India be given assistance if it could afford to undertake the enormous cost of developing an atomic bomb?

• The United States has used aid as a tool for promoting foreign policy. The State Department, for example, has sometimes even supported dictatorships that rule by terror and suppression when these dictatorships served as bulwarks against communism.

• Soft loans (at low interest rates) and grants to LDCs have been wasted on such inefficient monuments as steel mills, automobile assembly plants, and state airlines. If the underdeveloped countries had to rely more heavily on commercial loans, their governments would be concerned with allocating resources to agricultural and regional development programs more closely attuned to national needs.

Foreign Aid: Averages by Donor Countries (latest comparative data)

IN MILLIONS OF U.S. DOLLARS		PERCENT OF GNP
$401.7	SWEDEN	.72%
$428.8	NETHERLANDS	.62%
$1,638.4	FRANCE	.60%
$131.4	NORWAY	.57%
$713.4	CANADA	.50%
$721.8	BRITAIN	.38%
$1,434.6	W. GERMANY	.36%
$3,439.0	U.S.	.25%
$1,126.2	JAPAN	.25%

Source: **United Nations.**

As a percentage of GNP, the average amount of foreign aid by the United States ranks near the bottom.

• The widely believed "cycle-of-poverty" thesis, which holds that poor countries are trapped in a quagmire of poverty and stagnation, is an unsupported hypothesis. All developed countries were at one time poor, with low per-capita incomes and little or no accumulated capital. Yet these nations advanced, usually without significant outside capital or external grants. For example, Hong Kong, an overcrowded colony with few natural resources and a limited domestic market, has made remarkable progress since the 1960s. Groups that have advanced outside their native countries and with no significant financial or technical assistance from others include the Chinese in Southeast Asia, the Indians in East Africa, and the Lebanese in West Africa.

In light of these views, can foreign aid do for the poor countries what it did for the war-torn economies of western Europe during the 1940s and 1950s? Clearly not, according to the critics. They point out that, in the western European nations, the motivations and institutions favorable to development were already present. In most LDCs, on the other hand, the extension of grants and loans under the euphemism of foreign aid amounts to pouring billions of dollars into a bottomless pit.

Dissent on Development: Western Guilt Complex

Among the growing number of political leaders and scholars who take this position is an economist at the London School of Economics, P. T. Bauer. In various controversial books and articles, Bauer challenges the conventional wisdom that foreign aid is essential for narrowing the income gap between rich and poor countries. Income statistics, he says, often hide more than they reveal. There is no significant difference between the per-capita income levels of the richest underdeveloped countries and the poorest developed ones. Further, he points out, some underdeveloped countries, such as the oil-rich Arab states, have per-capita incomes that are among the highest in the world.

One of Bauer's objectives is to shatter the guilt complex of Western countries. There is an unfounded belief, he says, that advanced countries are somehow responsible for the poverty of the underdeveloped world. In a review of Bauer's writings, Edwin McDowell, a member of the editorial staff of the *Wall Street Journal,* paraphrased Bauer this way:

> Actually, Western prosperity was generated by its own population, not achieved at anyone's expense. Those countries were already materially much more advanced than the underdeveloped countries when they established contact with the latter in the 18th and 19th centuries. Even now many developed countries, including some of the richest, have few economic contacts with the underdeveloped world.

> Moreover, some of the richest Western countries were colonies in their earlier history, notably the U.S., Canada, Australia, and New Zealand. And some were already prosperous while they were still colonies. This certainly does not prove that colonialism is a necessary or admirable precondition of material progress. However, along with the contemporary experience of Hong Kong, it tends to refute the assumption (enunciated as a general principle by the U.N.) that colonial status and economic progress are incompatible.

> Nevertheless, belief that Western economic gains were achieved at the expense of the underdeveloped world has led donors to favor economic development assistance as a form of partial restitution and has led recipients to view it as an admission of Western guilt. In part that accounts for what the author describes as the "economics of resentment." It consists of the

anomaly of donor countries beseeching poor nations not to refuse their aid, combined with recipient governments showing their thanks by pursuing policies hostile to donors.

Conclusion: Bad Economics and Bad Sociology

In a more general sense, Bauer is critical of the social implications of foreign aid. He questions the underlying premise of development—whether it is moral to try to transform human society. "The attitudes and motivations which promote material success are not necessarily or even usually those which confer happiness, dignity, sensitivity, a capacity to love, a sense of harmony, or a reflective mind." Therefore, the attempt to change fundamental attitudes and beliefs for the sake of material progress is not only bad economics, but also bad sociology.

Many people, of course, disagree with these views. Those who support foreign aid argue that the United States should not abandon its tradition of helping needy people. As the critics point out, however, providing food and medicine to nations hit by disasters is one thing, while continuing massive military and economic transfusions for every country that wants them is quite another.

Whatever the outcome of the debate, two things are certain: The days of a generous U.S. aid policy are over, and it is no longer possible to discuss problems of development intelligently without coming to grips with the practical issues raised by foreign aid.

Questions

1. Much foreign aid to LDCs is in the form of military aid. Does this tend to stimulate their economies? If so, why do some critics object to such aid? If not, why is such aid given? Discuss.

2. Can you suggest some objective economic guidelines for providing aid to LDCs?

3. "It is morally wrong for rich countries not to help poor ones." Is this an economic argument? Explain.

What You Have Learned in This Chapter

1. The per-capita income gap between the richest nations and the poorest nations appears to be widening over the long run. This is due to differences in the factors that account for economic development. Among them: the quantity and quality of human and natural resources, the rate of capital accumulation, the degree of specialization and scale of production, the rate of technological progress, and the environmental (political, social, cultural, and economic) framework.

2. A nation may be considered to pass through various "stages" of development as it is transformed from a traditional to a technically progressive society. These stages help explain the social and economic changes that take place during growth.

3. The economic process of development can be analyzed within a framework of certain fundamental ideas. Some of the more important are these:

(a) The need for an agricultural revolution to release underemployed resources for industrialization.
(b) The need to reduce birth rates so as to relieve the pressure of population against resources.
(c) The recognition that investment in physical capital is necessary, but that physical capital alone will not stimulate development.
(d) The realization that investment in human capital, as well as in physical capital, is important.
(e) The distinction between labor-intensive and capital-intensive projects.
(f) The possible superiority of small-scale over large-scale projects.
(g) The distinction between private and social profitability, which is a useful guide for judging the desirability of an investment project.

4. One of the ways in which LDCs can acquire capital is by attracting private foreign investment. This requires that LDCs adopt measures that will create a favorable climate for investment. Examples of such measures are provisions for the following:

(a) Infrastructure facilities.
(b) Insurance protection for life and property.
(c) Nonnationalization guarantees.
(d) Profit and capital transfers.
(e) Tax concessions.

5. Another way in which LDCs can acquire capital as well as technical assistance is by foreign aid. The International Bank for Reconstruction and Development (World Bank), with its affiliates, helps to finance loans for investment projects in underdeveloped countries. The United States, through its technical cooperation and assistance programs, has also been a source of foreign aid. So have many other countries, including the Soviet Union and China.

6. A number of problems and dilemmas of foreign aid are of continuous concern to government officials. They involve such issues as these:

(a) The purposes for which aid should be given.
(b) The amount of aid to be provided.
(c) The conditions under which aid may be extended.
(d) The forms that aid may take.

Because political and foreign-policy considerations play a significant role in foreign aid, it is probably impossible to establish a firm set of guidelines that will be applicable in all situations.

For Discussion

1. *Terms and concepts to review:*
less developed countries
disguised unemployment
economic development
private rate of return
social rate of return
infrastructure
foreign aid
International Bank for Reconstruction and Development
International Development Cooperation Agency

2. It is sometimes suggested that underdeveloped nations that are seeking to industrialize should simply follow the historical paths taken by the more advanced nations. After all, why not benefit from the experiences of others? Evaluate this argument.

3. In the early years of America's post–World War II aid program (1945–1955), it was argued by many critics that the provision of health and sanitation facilities to LDCs would worsen their situation rather than improve it. The reason is that health and sanitation programs would *reduce* the LDCs' death rates. This argument is still heard today. Can you explain the logic of it?

4. Among the early investments commonly undertaken by LDCs are (a) an international airline and (b) a steel mill. Does this make sense? Explain.

5. Rapid economic development requires that a nation save and invest a substantial proportion of its income. What would you advise for the many LDCs whose savings rates are low or virtually zero because the great majority of their population is close to starvation?

6. "Rapid population growth is by far the single most serious obstacle to overcome as far as most LDCs are concerned." Can you suggest some *economic* approaches to the solution of this problem?

7. A Gloomy Dissent on South Asia. To Gunnar Myrdal, a leading Swedish economist and Nobel laureate, prospects for real growth in at least one part of the underdeveloped world—South Asia—are gloomy indeed. That is the clear implication of *Asian Drama*, a three-volume, 2,221-page inquiry into development in eight countries. Reporting on many years of study and observation, Myrdal concluded that growth in much of South Asia is hamstrung by hostile social, cultural, and political institutions. Thus, development plans that seek to manipulate strictly economic factors are doomed to failure. Instead, says Myrdal, countries must massively reform their institutions before any real growth will take place. Among his proposals:

(a) Governments must be strengthened— for better policy making and greater immunity from ethnic, social, and geographic divisions.
(b) Patterns of land ownership must be changed—to give the people who work the land an incentive to improve it.
(c) Population growth must be slowed— because, says Myrdal, it "holds the threat of economic stagnation or deterioration."
(d) Education must be modernized—to make it an instrument of development policy.

Evaluate Myrdal's proposals.

Radical Viewpoints, Old and New

Learning guide

Watch for the answers to these important questions

What major types of radical philosophy have grown up as reactions to capitalism?

Who was Karl Marx? What radical theories did he propose that have become the ideology of more than one-third of the inhabited globe?

What are the strengths and weaknesses of Marx's theories? What can we gain from understanding them?

How do concepts of socialism and radicalism today differ from those developed by Marx in the third quarter of the nineteenth century?

The history of radicalism is a history of social protest. Protest against what? All the economic, social, political, and cultural ailments of capitalism.

Social protest is by no means new, of course. It can be found in writings dating back at least as far as the Old Testament. But two characteristics distinguish radicalism from most earlier rebellions against established orders.

First, it is decidedly economic in nature. Second, it is international in scope and appeal. Radicalism, as we know it today, has roots less than two centuries old. But in that time—brief, as history goes—the movement has split into two factions. The first, socialism, seeks to right wrongs primarily through democratic procedures. The second, communism, regards parliamentary democracy as a tool of capitalism.

Each of these broad factions has, in turn, split into further groups. But despite the many different types of radical theory that flourish in various parts of the world, all groups have this much in common: *They seek to change the structure of capitalistic institutions and to establish new institutions for the purpose of building a better world.*

Reactions to Capitalism: Four Radical Philosophies

Modern socialism, like capitalism, grew out of the industrial revolution. You have already learned that such early British classical economists as Adam Smith, Thomas Malthus, and David Ricardo sought to explain and justify the economic transformation that took place in England during the late eighteenth and early nineteenth centuries. Thus they advocated policies of economic liberalism, namely laissez-faire and free or unrestricted international trade. At the same time, however, other scholars, both in Britain and on the Continent, were challenging the classicists with ideas of their own, based on events that were taking place in Europe's major industrial nations.

This chapter surveys the nature of radicalism and the foundations on which it rests.

Radicalism represents a reaction to perceived failures of capitalism.

Four main radical philosophies have emerged since the last century.

In England, for example, the factory system had already taken hold. Critics of the new order were appalled by frightful working conditions (including cases of cruelty toward young children in the factories and mines), crowded and filthy cities, and mobs of angry workers displaced by the introduction of new machines. In France, years of wars and waste had brought crushing taxes for the support of a corrupt government, resulting in the Revolution of 1789, one of the greatest social upheavals in world history. And in Germany, manufacturers were seeking to build up industrial establishments that could compete with those in Britain.

Against this setting arose several major reactions to capitalism. These reactions took the form of four great radical philosophies, listed here in chronological order.

1. Utopian socialism.

2. Marxian socialism and communism.

3. Syndicalism.

4. Christian socialism.

It is useful to sketch briefly the historical backgrounds of these movements before proceeding to a closer examination of the second and most important one, Marxian socialism and communism.

Utopian Socialism

There have always been activists who have striven for a better world. In that sense, it is correct to refer to such individuals as "socialists"—that is, as social reformers.

The first and perhaps the best book on social reform was written by Sir Thomas More (1478–1535), a famous English statesman under Henry VIII, as well as saint and martyr in the Roman Catholic Church. More's great satirical classic, *Utopia* (which is often required reading in English literature courses), was an attack on the evils of poverty, waste, idleness, and the institution of private property. The last, of course, is fundamental to capitalism.

Utopian socialism advocated the development of model communities in which the means of production were socially owned.

More was critical of social conditions in England and certain other European states during the early sixteenth century. As a solution, he proposed creation of a "utopia"—an ideal city-state (somewhat similar to the one described in Plato's *Republic*). In this society everyone would be happily employed, there would be ample opportunity for cultural enrichment, and democracy would prevail, with all citizens working for the good of society. (The word *utopia*, incidentally, which was invented by More, is Greek for "no place.")

In the centuries that followed, More's book stimulated a flood of publications advocating social reform—a flood that has lasted until the present day. First among the major reformist writers were the *utopian socialists.* These were English and French theorists of the early nineteenth century who proposed the creation of model communities, largely self-contained, in which the instruments of production would be collectively owned and government would be primarily on a voluntary and wholly democratic basis. The chief propagators of such plans were, in England, Robert Owen (1771–1858) and, in France, Charles Fourier (1772–1837).

Robert Owen was by far the best known of the utopian socialists. In the gloomy squalor of factory life in Britain, this young Horatio Alger rose from apprentice to co-proprietor and manager, in his twenties, of a huge cotton mill at New Lanark in Scotland.

Here, in the first quarter of the nineteenth century, he built a model community of neat houses and free schools for his workers and their families. The community attracted many thousands of visitors, including political dignitaries, social reformers, writers, and businesspeople from around the world. Owen shortened the workday, improved working conditions, and rewarded each employee in proportion to his actual hours of labor. Later he constructed similar model communities—one of them in the United States, in New Harmony, Indiana. All of them, however, turned out to be administrative and financial failures.

Owen's place as a social reformer is significant. He played a key role during the early nineteenth century in giving England its first effective factory laws for the protection of workers. In retrospect, of course, it is now evident that Owen was a prophet of improvements he never lived to see, for his ideas profoundly influenced the betterment of industrial life in Britain and the United States.

In 1884, a movement known as *Fabian socialism* was founded in England. An outgrowth of utopian socialism, it advocated gradual or evolutionary reform within a democratic framework. The movement attracted many prominent people over the years. Some of its most active supporters were economists Beatrice and Sydney Webb, who helped to build the British Labour Party; the distinguished Anglo-Irish dramatist George Bernard Shaw; and the noted economist and historian G. D. H. Cole.

Fabian socialism, a late-nineteenth-century outgrowth of utopian socialism, stood for evolutionary (rather than revolutionary) reform.

Marxian Socialism and Communism

Toward the middle of the nineteenth century, there occurred in Europe a series of events that strongly influenced the future course of the world.

In December 1847, on one of London's typically damp and cold winter days, a small but clamorous group of labor leaders met at a convention of the newly formed Communist League. There were strong currents of anxiety and trepidation in the air, for although England was relatively calm at the time, the Continent was on the verge of an upheaval. Through an almost continuous belt stretching from France to Russia, there was seething discontent over the long-prevailing miseries of poverty, injustice, and political and social intolerance. No one doubted that a series of revolutions would sweep Europe in the coming months.

Among those who attended this historic meeting were two relatively young and unknown radical intellectuals. One was Karl Marx, aged twenty-nine; the other was his close friend and associate, Friedrich Engels, aged twenty-seven. They had been commissioned by the League to prepare a statement of principles and a program for action that would help incite the masses and foment revolt against the existing order of society. Their tract opened with the following inflammatory, dramatic, and ominous words:

Marxian socialism had its beginnings in the middle of the nineteenth century.

> A spectre is haunting Europe—the spectre of Communism. All the powers of old Europe have entered into a Holy Alliance to exorcise this spectre; Pope and Czar, Metternich and Guizot, French radicals and German police-spies.

After pages of historical analyses and predictions, their treatise ended with the following exhortation:

> The Communists disdain to conceal their views and aims. They openly declare that their ends can be attained only by the forcible overthrow of all existing social conditions. Let the ruling classes tremble at a Communist revolution. The proletarians have nothing to lose but their chains. They have a world to win.

WORKING MEN OF ALL COUNTRIES, UNITE!

In the following month, January 1848, this statement of principles and objectives was published as a pamphlet under the title *Communist Manifesto*. It is significant not for its economic content, for it had practically none. Its importance lies in the manner in which it presented Marx as a brilliant and forceful revolutionary.

But there is another side to Marx—that of a painstaking scholar and deep philosophical economist—which is of much greater significance. In most of the three decades that followed publication of the *Communist Manifesto*, Marx devoted almost all his working time to developing an extensive and extraordinary "scientific" theory, which was eventually published as a mammoth treatise entitled *Das Kapital* (translated *Capital*) (vol. I, 1867). This was the "Doomsday Book of Capitalism"—a powerfully written work in which Marx predicted the revolutionary overthrow of the capitalistic system and its ultimate replacement by a *classless* society. This society would be composed only of workers, or proletarians, who would own and operate the means of production for the benefit of all.

Marx called this ultimate state "communism" in order to distinguish it from various "unscientific" forms of socialism, such as utopian socialism, which existed during his time. Much of the spirit of his ideas was incorporated in the Russian, Chinese, and Cuban revolutionary systems of communism that were established in the twentieth century. In some Western nations, in contrast, various evolutionary or moderate Marxian systems were also founded, represented largely by social-democratic types of political parties. These groups have preferred to retain the title of "socialism" in order to help bridge the gap between certain features of Marxian theory and the rest of the socialist movement. In general, Marxism is by far the most significant of the radical philosophies to have emerged as a reaction to capitalism.

Marxism is by far the most significant of the radical philosophies that have emerged in reaction to capitalism.

Syndicalism

The third great radical philosophy spawned by the industrial revolution was syndicalism. This movement, which was both a strategy of revolution and a plan for social reorganization, was influenced by the wave of anarchism (the belief that all government is evil and should be eliminated) that spread through parts of Europe during the late nineteenth and early twentieth centuries.

The advocates of *syndicalism* demanded the abolition of both capitalism and the state, which they viewed as instruments of oppression, and the reorganization of society into industry-wide associations or syndicates of workers. Thus, there would be a syndicate of all the steel mills, which would be owned and operated by the workers in the steel industry; a syndicate of all the coal mines made up of workers in the coal industry; and so on. In this way, the syndicates, which were fundamen-

Syndicalism sought to organize workers into industry-wide groups. These would then overthrow capitalism by initiating a general strike and seizing the nation's factories.

tally trade unions, would replace the state, each syndicate governing its own members in their activities as producers but leaving them free from interference in all other matters. The chief exponent of syndicalism was the French social philosopher Georges Sorel (1847–1922). Ironically, his views later influenced the growth of fascism during the 1930s.

In the United States, the syndicalists organized a revolutionary industrial union in 1905 called the Industrial Workers of the World (IWW). Popularly known as the Wobblies, the union was founded in Chicago by Eugene V. Debs, William D. Haywood, and Daniel De Leon— all of them well-known names in the history of radicalism. The group's avowed aim was to overthrow capitalism and to establish socialism by calling a general strike throughout industry, locking out employers, and seizing the nation's factories. Despite the organization's success in gathering a peak membership of 100,000 before World War I and in leading over 150 strikes, it suffered from growing internal dissension and nearly fell apart after the war. However, it continued to survive. Today, with its distinctly moderate, nonrevolutionary philosophy, it is a small but vigorous union.

Syndicalists in the United States organized the IWW, popularly known as the Wobblies.

Christian Socialism

The late nineteenth century also saw the rise of the Christian socialists, whose ideas were the most moderate of the four great radical philosophies. The movement was started in France by a Catholic priest. It then spread to England, where it caught on among a number of Protestant intellectuals and clerics, and subsequently reached the United States. Variations of it still exist in these and other countries.

Christian socialism viewed the worker not merely as a commodity but as a "commodity with a soul."

In general *Christian socialism* is a movement of various church groups to preach the "social gospel"—a type of social legislation and reform that is grounded in theology. It seeks to improve the well-being of industrial workers by advocating the formation of labor unions, the passage of legislation, and above all by appealing to employers to respect the dignity of workers as people and as Christians, rather than as so much muscle or physical power. It also repudiates the Marxian doctrine of the class war or revolution. Among the leading forces of this movement have been Pope Leo XIII, the "working-man's Pope," whose famous encyclical *Rerum Novarum* (1891) enunciated these principles; Pope Pius XI, whose encyclical *Quadragesimo Anno* (1931) reaffirmed them; and the Protestant theologians Reinhold Niebuhr and Paul Tillich.

The Economic Theories of Karl Marx

None among the various radical philosophies that emerged as reactions to capitalism during the nineteenth century has had deeper or more widespread effects than that of Karl Marx. Indeed, his views, in one form or another, are the basic beliefs of more than one-third of the inhabited globe.

Marx, a "philosophical economist," was deeply influenced by the writings of the eminent early-nineteenth-century German philosopher Georg Hegel, and in particular by the Hegelian *dialectic*. This technical term denotes a method of logic or reasoning in Hegelian philosophy. It holds that any concept, which may be called a *thesis*, can have meaning only when it is related to its opposite or contradictory concept, called an *antithesis*. The interaction of the two then forms a new concept or understanding called a *synthesis*. Thus, the concept of "high" (thesis) evokes the opposite concept of "low" (antithesis), and the two then interact to form the new concept of "height" (synthesis). Similarly, contradictory concepts like "light" and "dark," "truth" and "falsity," "being" and "not being" interact to form new concepts, each of which brings us a step closer to understanding the ever-changing nature of the real world.

In Hegelian philosophy, the dialectic process, through its *reconciliation of opposites*, becomes a method of interpreting history. Thus, in the evolution of cultures, we observe a process in which the higher form of culture clashes with, and triumphs over, the lower form. In the development of art, one "period" interacts with, and is succeeded by, another. In the history of religion, primitive and simplistic types of worship struggle against, but eventually give way to, more sophisticated forms and concepts. In general, history is a record of progress from lower to higher manifestations of the dialectic principle.

How did these Hegelian ideas influence Marx's thinking? We can seek to answer this question by sketching briefly the fundamental doctrines that appear in his enormous work *Das Kapital:*

1. Economic interpretation of history.
2. Theory of value and wages.
3. Theory of surplus value and capital accumulation.
4. The class struggle.
5. Theory of socialistic and communistic evolution.

These doctrines constitute the framework of Marxian theory. Although they are attributed to Marx, they were formulated during his many years of association with his close friend and intellectual collaborator, Friedrich Engels. Each man had a profound influence on the other.

Economic Interpretation of History

Marx sought to discover the basic principles of history. His method was to construct what he regarded as a completely logical system in which he presented in scientific fashion the laws of historical development, the sources of economic and social power, and a prediction of the inevitable future.

In order to predict the future course of events, Marx had to understand the causal forces that were at work. This, he believed, could only be done by studying the past. Hence, he looked for the fundamental causes of historical events, and he found them in the economic environments in which societies develop.

According to Marx, all great political, social, intellectual, and ethical movements of history are determined by the ways in which societies organize their social institutions to carry on the basic economic activities of production, exchange, distribution, and consumption of goods. Although economic motives may not always be the sole cause of human behavior, every fundamental historical development is basically the result of changes in the way in which one or more of these economic activities is carried out. This, in essence, is the *economic interpretation of history*.

Dialectic, in Hegelian philosophy, is a method of reasoning that holds that every action evokes an opposite reaction. This becomes a way of interpreting historical progress.

In Marx's view, all great historical movements can be attributed to economic forces.

Thus, in the Marxian system, economic forces are the prime cause of change—the alpha and omega of history—and they operate with the inevitability of natural laws to determine the development of a society. Even the Protestant Reformation of the sixteenth century, which for all intents and purposes was a major religious movement in world history, was cloaked in ideological veils, according to Marx. These veils concealed its true causes, which were basically economic.

Dialectical Materialism

This philosophy became known as *dialectical materialism*. As the method of historical analysis used by Marx, it employed Hegel's notion that historical change is the result of conflicting forces and that these forces are basically economic or materialistic. In the Marxian view of history, every economic system, based on a set of established production, exchange, distribution, and consumption relationships, grows to a state of maximum efficiency and then develops internal contradictions or weaknesses that cause it to decay. By this time, the roots of an opposing system have already begun to take hold. Eventually this new system displaces the old one while absorbing its most useful features. This dynamic process continues, with society being propelled from one historical stage to another as each new system triumphs over the old.

Historical change, said Marx, results from the interactions of conflicting economic forces.

Theory of Value and Wages

The second major doctrine in Marxian economics is the theory of value and wages. This, of course, was also a fundamental area of concern to the classical economists who preceded Marx—including Smith, Ricardo, and others. But Marx, unlike the classical economists, used these concepts to a different end in explaining the historical development and future course of capitalism.

To Marx, the term "value" had the same meaning as it had to other orthodox economists both before and after. *Value* is the power of a commodity to command other commodities in exchange for itself. This power is measured by the proportional quantities in which a commodity exchanges with all other commodities. Likewise, to Marx and other economists, the *price* of a commodity is its power to command money in exchange for itself. Price is simply the "money name" of the value of a commodity.

Marx contended that the value of a commodity is determined by the socially necessary labor time embodied in its production.

But what determines the value of a commodity? The answer, according to Marx, is labor. In his words:

> That which determines the magnitude of the value of any article is the amount of . . . labor-time socially necessary for its production. . . . Commodities, therefore, in which equal quantities of labor are embodied, or which can be produced in the same time, have the same value. The value of one commodity is to the value of another, as the labor-time necessary for the production of one is to that necessary for the production of the other. As values, all commodities are only definite masses of congealed labor-time.

In general terms, therefore, if it takes twice as much labor-time to produce coats as hats, the price of coats will be twice the price of hats. Note from the last sentence of the quotation that Marx did not restrict his concept of labor-time to direct or current labor spent on the production of commodities. He included indirect or "congealed" labor as well, such as the labor-time necessary to construct the factories and machines that are then used to produce other goods.   Therefore:

> *Because capital and other commodities are congealed labor,* they are all reducible to the common denominator of labor-time.   Therefore, they will exchange for one another at prices that are proportional to the amount of labor-time they contain.

Marx argued that competition among capitalists forces them to pay workers a subsistence level of wages.

From this theory of value, it was a short step for Marx to develop his theory of wages.   In his view, a mature capitalistic society consists of only two classes.   One of these is a capitalist class, which owns and controls the means of production.   The other is a working class, which owns and controls nothing and is subservient to the capitalist class.   (The land-owning class, at this relatively advanced stage of capitalism's development, had been absorbed by the capitalist class and had declined to a position of minor importance.)   This leads to the following theory of wages:

> The capitalist class finds, in its competitive struggle to earn profits, that it must pay the lowest possible level of wages to the working class.   The wages it will pay, therefore, will be at a subsistence level.   This is a wage level that is just high enough for the working population to maintain itself, based primarily on its physical or biological needs and to a lesser extent on its social and customary needs.

This theory of wages, it may be noted, did not originate with Marx.   It was the familiar *subsistence theory of wages,* which Marx adopted from the classical economists who preceded him.

Theory of Surplus Value and Capital Accumulation

When Marx combined his theories of value and wages, the logical outcome was the third feature of his theoretical system: the doctrine of surplus value.   From this, there emerged the natural process of capital accumulation.

Surplus Value

Surplus value, said Marx, is the difference between the value of what the worker produces and the value of what the worker receives.

In Marx's model, surplus value arises in the following way.   When workers are employed in the production of a commodity, it is the capitalist who sets the length of the working day.   Thus, on the one hand, the value of what the workers produce is determined by the labor-time embodied in the commodity.   On the other hand, the wage that the workers receive is determined by the "subsistence level" of living.   The workers do not stop producing when the value of what they create is equal to their subsistence wage.   Instead they continue to produce, and the value that they create over and above their subsistence wage represents "surplus value," which goes to the capitalist.   In numerical terms, the capitalist may set the working day at 12 hours, but the workers may each produce a value equal to their subsistence wage in 7 hours.   The remaining 5 hours of their labor-time is, therefore, surplus value, which is literally appropriated or stolen by the capitalist.

To Marx, surplus value is the driving force of the capitalistic system —the key incentive that prompts capitalists to carry on production.   Efforts on the part of capitalists to increase surplus value may take various forms.   Among them:

1. Increasing the length of the working day.

2. Intensifying or speeding up the workers' production (by offering "piece rates" or other incentives).

3. Introducing labor-saving machinery, thereby permitting some workers to be released while those who remain are made to work longer hours or more intensively.

Capital Accumulation

What do capitalists do with the surplus value that, according to Marx, has been literally stolen from the labor of workers? Marx's answer is that capitalists use part of the surplus for their personal consumption and part to acquire more labor and machines. They acquire these, of course, because they expect to get back more money than they lay out. The inflow of surpluses, over and above the capitalists' money outlays, continues in an unending series from one production operation to the next, thereby generating a sequence of capital accumulations. Thus, whereas the mainstream classical economists of the nineteenth century contended that capitalists were engaging in "saving" when they acquired funds to hire more labor for production, Marx argued that the funds which capitalists "saved" were stolen from workers in the form of surplus value.

These ideas, which lie at the heart of the Marxian model of capitalism, may be summarized briefly:

> *Surplus value* is the difference between the value that workers create (as determined by the labor-time embodied in a commodity that they produce) and the value that they receive (as determined by the subsistence level of wages). Surplus value is not created by capitalists; it is appropriated by them through their exploitation of the worker. Hence, capitalists are robbers who steal the fruits of the laborers' toil. The accumulation of capital comes from surplus value and is the key to, as well as the incentive for, the development of a capitalistic system.

It is interesting to note that Marx harbored no particular animosity toward capitalists as such, even though he characterized them as greedy robber barons. In Marx's view, it was the competitive capitalistic system itself that was evil. Capitalists were merely participants in the great race. They had to exploit and accumulate or else they would be exploited and their assets would be accumulated.

The Class Struggle

What are the consequences of capitalistic production? In order to answer this question, Marx turned to an examination of the past and again used the method of dialectical analysis—thesis and antithesis—to interpret the historical process.

All history, he said, is composed of struggles between classes. In ancient Rome, it was a struggle between patricians and plebeians and between masters and slaves. In the Middle Ages, it was conflict between guildmasters and journeymen and between lords and serfs. And in the modern society that has sprouted from the ruins of feudal society, class antagonisms have narrowed down to a struggle between two opposing groups—the oppressing capitalist class or bourgeoisie and the oppressed working class or proletariat. The former derive their income from *owning* the means of production and from exploiting the labor of workers. The latter own nothing but their labor power and, because they are dependent for a living upon the receipt of a wage, must sell their labor power in order to exist.

What is the role of the state in this two-class society? Marx's answer was precise: "The state," he said, "is nothing but the organized collective power of the possessing classes." It is an agency controlled by the bourgeoisie to advance its own interests, and its power "grows stronger in proportion as the class antagonisms with the state grow sharper." The state, in short, is an agency of oppression.

The Consequences of Capitalist Production

Marx contended that the class struggle and other contradictions within capitalism would lead to worsening economic conditions.

The class struggle might go on indefinitely, according to Marx, were it not for certain "contradictions" that automatically and inevitably develop within the capitalistic system. Among the more important ones are these:

1. Increasing Unemployment The capitalists' drive to increase their surplus value and to accumulate capital results in the displacement of labor. (This, in modern terminology, is technological unemployment.) It leads to ever-increasing misery as a "reserve army of the unemployed" builds up.

2. Declining Rate of Profits As capital accumulates, a growing proportion of it goes into physical capital, such as labor-saving machinery, which yields no surplus value. A declining proportion of it goes into human capital or labor, which is the sole producer of surplus value. Hence, the capitalists' rate of profit—or the surplus value that they appropriate from labor—tends to be a declining percentage of the total capital that is accumulated.

3. Business Cycles With increasing unemployment, a declining rate of profit, and the tendency for wages to remain at the subsistence level, uncertainty and instability are inevitable. Depressions recur "each time more threateningly" as capitalists find themselves under continual competitive pressure to acquire more capital and to displace workers.

4. Concentration and Monopolization of Capital Competition among capitalists thus becomes increasingly intense. A dog-eat-dog situation develops as small capitalists are either fatally weakened or absorbed by a few larger ones. In this way, capital becomes concentrated in large-scale industrial units or monopolies. As Marx put it, "hand in hand with this centralization" of capital goes the "expropriation of many capitalists by the few."

5. Finance Capitalism and Imperialism Marx implied that a fifth "contradiction" would emerge from the monopoly stage of capitalistic development. The nature of this contradiction was amplified in the early twentieth century by V. I. Lenin, the founder of the USSR. Lenin argued that the growing tendency toward concentration and monopolization of capital would produce an economy dominated by "finance capital." In such a situation, huge business trusts or monopolies, in conjunction with a handful of large banks, control and manipulate the masses. Those who manage finance capital will then reach out beyond their own national boundaries, forming cartels and international combines to dominate and control the markets and resources of other nations. When this happens, the economy has reached the stage of "capitalistic imperialism"—the highest stage of capitalism.

Summary

Marx concluded that these conditions, especially the first, imposed miseries and hardships on workers that they would not tolerate indefinitely. The working class, he said, would eventually revolt against the capitalist class and bring about a system in which economic justice prevails. Before we examine the nature of this change, let us summarize the foregoing Marxian ideas briefly.

> The *class struggle* represents an irreconcilable clash of interests between the bourgeoisie or capitalist class and the proletariat or working class. The source of this clash is the surplus value that capitalists steal from workers. This results, over the long run, in increasing unemployment, a declining rate of profit, business cycles, concentration of capital, and finance capitalism and imperialism.

According to Marx, the class struggle will eventually be resolved when the proletariat overthrows the bourgeoisie and establishes a new and equitable economic order.

Eventually, said Marx, the working class would overthrow capitalism and establish a new and equitable economic system.

Theory of Socialist and Communist Evolution

Marx held that capitalism must someday receive its death blow at the hands of the workers. When this happens, capitalism will be succeeded by socialism, which Marx regarded as a *transitory stage* on the road to communism. This stage will have two major characteristics:

Marx predicted that capitalism would be succeeded first by socialism and subsequently by full communism.

1. "Dictatorship of the proletariat." This is a state of affairs in Marxian socialism in which the bourgeoisie has been toppled from power and is subject to the control of the working class. In other words, the "expropriators have been expropriated," and capitalists' properties are under the management of the proletariat, who are also in control of the state.

2. Payment according to work performed. This means that laborers will earn wages, each receiving "for an equal quantity of labor an equal quantity of products," and "he who does not work shall not eat."

Socialism, in Marxian ideology, may thus be defined as a transitory stage between capitalism and full communism. That is, *Marxian socialism is a stage in which the means of production are owned by the state, the state in turn is controlled by workers ("dictatorship of the proletariat"), and the economy's social output is distributed by the formula, "From each according to his ability, to each according to his labor."*

> *Communism*, in Marxian ideology, is the final, perfect goal of historical development. It means:
>
> **1.** A classless society in which all people live by earning and no person lives by owning.
>
> **2.** The state is nonexistent, having been relegated to the museum of antiquities "along with the bronze ax and the spinning wheel."
>
> **3.** The wage system is abolished and all citizens live and work according to the formula, *"From each according to his ability, to each according to his needs."*

This last quotation, it may be noted, represents the essence of pure communism and is one of the most famous phrases in all of literature. Indeed, since it was first written, it has appeared in more than a thousand works of fiction and nonfiction, excluding textbooks. (See "Leaders in Economics," page 812.)

Leaders in Economics

Karl Heinrich Marx
1818–1883
Founder of "Scientific Socialism"

If it is true that people are ultimately judged by the influence of their ideas, then Karl Marx surely ranks as one of the most important persons who ever lived. His thoughts have shaped the policies of nations and affected the lives of millions of people.

Marx was born in Trier (Treves), Germany, the son of a successful lawyer with liberal philosophical leanings. Educated at the University of Bonn and the University of Berlin, he received his doctorate in philosophy from the University of Jena in 1841 at the age of twenty-three.

Early Views
In Marx's undergraduate years, his radical ideas began to flourish when he fell in with an extremist student group called the Young Hegelians—disciples of the German philosopher Georg Hegel. During the 1840s, while Marx was still in his twenties, he spent short periods in Germany, France, and Britain. In all three countries, he was always one step ahead of the police, who continually sought to expel him because of his incendiary articles extolling communism and revolution in newspapers and other periodicals, as well as his attacks against religion and utopian socialism. "Religion," he once wrote (in a quotation that has since become famous), ". . . is the sigh of the oppressed creature . . . the opium of the people." As for utopian so-

Historical Pictures Service, Chicago

Friedrich Engels (*left*) with Karl Marx and his family.

cialism, it was "unscientific" because it lacked an understanding of the role of history and of the certainty of the class struggle.

Wife and Friend
It was also during the 1840s that Marx became involved with the two most important people of his life. One of them was Jenny von Westphalen, daughter of an aristocrat who was a public administrator of Trier. The other was a gallant named Friedrich Engels, the son of a wealthy industrialist.

Marx married Jenny, whom he had known since childhood; she was literally "the girl next door." The match itself was a study of opposites. She was slender, beautiful, and genteel; he was short, stocky, and caustic. But they loved each other deeply, and she gave up her refined and prestigious life in Trier in return for his unstinting devotion to her and to their children. Their life together was one of great hardship and extreme poverty as they moved from one slum to another while Marx struggled

to earn a living—a task that, as a writer, he never mastered.

Marx met Engels during a brief stay in Paris in 1843. The two men struck up an immediate intellectual rapport. This fact was especially surprising because Engels's father was a rich businessman who owned factories in Germany and England, and the young Engels never exhibited any aversion to the social and monetary advantages that this background afforded him. Engels became Marx's lifelong friend, collaborator, and alter ego, as well as his benefactor. Indeed, there is no evidence that Marx ever had any other close friends.

In 1849, after being hounded by police and expelled from three countries, Marx moved to London, where he lived, except for brief intervals, until the time of his death. Here he existed in the depths of poverty, depending for bare survival on small and irregular remunerations of $5 to $10 that he received for articles submitted to the New York *Tribune*, and

on the benevolence of Engels, who, for some unexplained reason, led a double life. He was fully in accord with Marx's anticapitalistic views, yet he also managed his father's factory in Manchester and even held a seat on the Manchester Stock Exchange.

Major Works
Marx sacrificed everything for his research, an activity that engaged his full time and effort from morning until night in the great library of the British Museum. The result, after many years of painstaking work, was the publication, in 1867, of Volume I of his enormous treatise, *Das Kapital*. But his health was never good. In 1881, after the death of two of his five children, his devoted and tired wife Jenny also died, and Marx followed her two years later. His eulogy was delivered by Engels and the funeral was attended by eight persons.

Engels labored on Marx's notes for the next several years, thereby making possible the publication of volumes II and III of *Das Kapital* (1885, 1894). Four additional volumes, entitled *Theorien über den Mehrwert* (*Theories of Surplus Value*) were published from still other notes in the period 1905–1910. On the basis of these and other writings, Marx has come to be regarded as an economist of major significance.

Keep in mind, though, that it was Lenin who fashioned the content of communism. Marx predicted its eventual occurrence, but it remained for Lenin to design the structure. This he did in his writings and speeches during the first two decades of the present century, and in his founding of the USSR after the Revolution of 1917.

Evaluation of Marxian Theory

Now that we have sketched the main features of Marxian theory, it is appropriate to discuss its achievements and failures. It is evident that Marx sought to reach three major objectives:

1. To develop a *theory of history* that would explain the fundamental causes of capitalistic development.

2. To formulate *theories of value, wages, and surplus value* that would describe the basic processes at work in the capitalistic economy.

3. To establish a foundation for *revolutionary socialism and communism.*

We may evaluate Marx's theories in terms of these objectives.

Theory of History

As you recall, Marx's interpretation of history was based on *economic* thesis and antithesis. Although he recognized that political, social, and other factors influenced historical development, he regarded them as distinctly subordinate. To him, the basic or causal forces were fundamentally economic, those central to the activities and institutions of production, exchange, distribution, and consumption of goods.

Critics have pointed out that this is a one-sided, oversimplified interpretation because it leaves out, or fails to give sufficient weight to, the many noneconomic forces and institutions in history. Despite this criticism, many distinguished historians have long believed that Marx's interpretation of history provided the first deep awareness of the importance of economic forces in the historical process.

In the past several decades, modern historians have increasingly incorporated economic causation in their historical studies. Although it cannot be said that Marx was solely responsible for this trend, there is general agreement that his approach to the study of history played a significant role.

In his theory of history, Marx sought to explain the fundamental causes of the development of capitalism.

Theories of Value, Wages, and Surplus Value

Marx's theory of value, we have seen, was a *labor* theory of value. In essence, his argument can be stated in the form of a syllogism. This is a type of reasoning in formal logic consisting of two premises or assumptions and a logical conclusion that follows directly from them. Thus, according to Marx:

> Labor creates all value.
>
> Labor does not receive all the value it has created.
>
> Therefore, labor is being cheated.

It should be remembered that, according to Marx, the first premise is true because capital and all other commodities are nothing more than congealed labor. The second premise is true because labor receives only a subsistence wage, which is less than the value it creates. And the conclusion is true because capitalists appropriate the surplus value of labor for themselves.

Was Marx correct? We can answer this question by offering the following criticisms of his ideas, based on economic principles and concepts presented in previous chapters.

In his theory of surplus value, Marx sought to explain how capitalists exploit workers by stealing what is rightfully theirs.

Neglect of Entrepreneurial Functions

Marx overlooked the role of the entrepreneur as an organizer and risk taker.

By attributing all value to labor alone, Marx neglected the functions performed by the entrepreneur as a risk taker and organizer of the factors of production. Without the entrepreneur, labor would be an amorphous mass. It is the entrepreneur who gives "shape and form" to labor by bringing workers together, providing them with capital, and giving them a purpose for working. In a socialistic or communistic society, these functions might be performed by the government or by a committee of workers, but they are functions that must be performed by somebody.

Failure to Recognize Demand

Marx overlooked the role of demand as one of the determinants of value.

Marx's theory of value, based as it was on the labor-time embodied in a commodity, failed to recognize that the normal value of a good is as much a result of demand as of supply. In a competitive capitalistic system, as you already know, the concept of long-run normal value is that of an equilibrium value or price that reflects diverse consumer demands bidding for the services and products of scarce factors of production. This means that consumers must be willing and able to buy and to express their preferences through the price system if prices are to serve the function of inducing both human and nonhuman resources into production. Marx did not fully understand this role of the price system. Hence his theory of value provided an inaccurate and unrealistic measure of the real values at which commodities are exchanged.

Inadequate Analytical Support of Surplus Value

Marx's explanation of surplus value lacks analytical support and is unsubstantiated by evidence.

Surplus value, according to Marx, arises because workers are paid a subsistence wage that is less than the value of the commodities that they create. The question we must now ask is whether this theory of surplus value is plausible. The answer appears to be *no*, for the following reasons:

1. Definition of Subsistence Is Vague Marx did not use the concept of subsistence in a consistent manner, nor did he define it as a determinate quantity. At certain times, he employed the term in a biological sense to refer to the goods needed for physical well-being. At other times, he used it to mean the "conventional" goods to which people become "socially accustomed."

2. Competition Will Eliminate the Surplus Marx placed strong emphasis on the competitive forces that exist in a capitalistic society—and in particular on the highly competitive relationships among capitalists themselves. If wages are sufficiently flexible to adjust to the "socially accustomed" level of living, there is every reason to believe that the surplus itself will be eliminated as capitalist employers bid higher and higher wages for the services of employees. This is because, if a worker yields a surplus to *his* or *her* capitalist employer, it will pay for *some other* capitalist employer to hire the worker away at a higher wage. Competition among capitalists will thus bid wages up to a level at which the surplus no longer exists.

These are among the chief reasons to conclude that Marx's theory of surplus value lacks analytical support. Further, there is no concrete evidence to indicate that there exists in the capitalistic system a fund of value of the type that Marx conceived in his concept of surplus value.

This does not necessarily mean, however, that a surplus does not exist. Modern radical economists believe that it does, as you will see later in this chapter.

Revolutionary Socialism and Communism

Marx predicted that the increasing misery of workers would prompt the proletariat to overthrow capitalism and to replace it first by socialism and then by communism. This, he said, would be the inevitable result of the "internal contradictions" that were inherent in capitalism and that would eventually destroy it.

Most of Marx's predictions have not materialized.

Was Marx's prediction correct? For the most part, no—at least not in the sense that he meant. But despite the mistakes that exist in the Marxian model, the views of its author have long been accepted by hundreds of millions of people in many nations. In some totalitarian countries, his theory was adopted intact; in many nontotalitarian nations, a brand of "modified" or "revised" Marxism developed. We may refer to the latter as *post-Marxism*. This type of socialism is not necessarily antagonistic to capitalism. However, it seeks to achieve socialistic goals through a much greater degree of government regulation and control than exists in market-oriented capitalistic systems. More will be said about this later.

Conclusions: Three Questions

We may conclude this evaluation of Marxian theory by answering briefly three fundamental questions that are often asked.

Despite the shortcomings of Marx's conclusion, he nevertheless identified some critical problems.

Have Marx's Deductions Been Borne Out?

Some of Marx's deductions of the "economic consequences of capitalist production" have evidently not been realized. There are several reasons for this.

First, the proletariat, far from experiencing increasing misery, has in fact experienced a long-run growth of real wages and a rising standard of living.

Second, the rate of profits has not declined, nor have business cycles been entirely an overproduction phenomenon, as Marx claimed.

Third, the workers and the capitalists, at least in the United States, have not aligned themselves into two distinct and opposing classes. Indeed, they often overlap to the extent that the great majority of corporation stockholders are also workers. In the United States, most corporate stock is owned by households, not only directly, but also indirectly through pension funds.

There is thus no question that some of Marx's most important theoretical deductions have turned out to be wrong.

Are There Elements of Truth in Marx's Predictions?

Despite his incorrect predictions of economic events, we cannot conclude that Marx was totally wrong. Some of his prophecies contained important truths. For example:

1. It is undeniable that technological, cyclical, and structural unemployment have continued to plague the capitalistic system.

2. There has certainly been a growth in the concentration of capital and monopoly power since the time of Marx's writing during the third quarter of the nineteenth century. However, there is considerable disagreement among economists as to the direction of monopoly trends during most of the present century.

3. Although capitalism has not ended in final collapse, it was certainly dealt a serious blow in 1930 with the emergence of a prolonged and desperate depression that eventually ushered in many new measures of social reform.

On this score, therefore, some of Marx's prophecies were disturbingly accurate.

What Is the Value of Marxian Theory?

We are thus led to conclude that Marx put his finger on some of the most important economic problems of our society. Among these problems are unemployment, business cycles, and industrial concentration and monopoly. Most of our efforts in previous chapters were devoted to the development of methods for curing these ills within a framework of capitalism. It is appropriate, therefore, that we now turn our attention to examining the ways in which modern socialism—a system rooted in Marxian ideology—seeks to solve these and other economic problems.

Development and Meaning of Socialism

During the present century, socialism has evolved into two main factions—one evolutionary, the other revolutionary.

When the nineteenth century drew to a close, Marxism had already become an international movement of considerable significance. But it was a movement whose members had divergent viewpoints. As a result, the followers of Marx began to divide into two factions. One of these consisted of a large and heterogeneous majority called "revisionists"; the other was composed of a smaller but more homogeneous minority known as "strict Marxists."

The basic philosophies of these two groups are implied by their names:

> The revisionists believe that the theories of Marx must be *revised* in order to accord with conditions of the times. Revisionists argue that socialism should be achieved by peaceful and gradual means through a process of evolution rather than revolution.

> The strict Marxists, on the other hand, adhere to a literal interpretation of their master's teachings. They contend that the workers of the world form one great brotherhood that must revolt in order to overthrow the capitalistic system and establish a dictatorship of the proletariat.

Since the early part of this century, the revisionists have been in control of most of the socialist parties of Western nations. Further, since the 1930s, socialistic governments have been in power at one time or another in a number of democratic countries. These include Great Britain, France, Sweden, Norway, Denmark, Australia, and New Zealand. In most of these and various other nations, socialist leaders were placed in office—and subsequently voted out of office—through free elections. This suggests that, when we talk about socialism, we are referring to *democratic* socialism of the liberal reformist type. This is distinguished from *authoritarian* socialism, such as exists in the USSR, eastern Europe, Cuba, and China.

Socialism Between World Wars I and II

In order to appreciate the meaning of modern democratic socialism, it may be helpful to have a brief sketch of the historical development of socialist thought and practice in the period between the two world wars.

During the 1920s and 1930s, peaceful Marxian socialists, both in Europe and in America, launched a renewed and vigorous attack against the shortcomings of capitalism. Expressions like "economic inequality," "chronic unemployment," "private wealth and public poverty," and "degeneration of social and cultural values" became familiar shibboleths. In Europe, social democratic parties were strongly committed to revisionist Marxism, the solidarity of the working class, and the ultimate establishment of socialism by democratic means as a way of correcting the deficiencies of the capitalistic system. This was an era of great ferment in socialist activity.

The Theoretical Model

At the same time, some economists at European and American universities began to grapple with a question that eventually evolved into one of the most interesting controversies in the history of economics. The essence of the problem may be summarized by recalling that, in the theoretical or pure model of capitalism, there are at least three important features:

A famous theoretical model of democratic socialism that was developed during the 1930s was based on trial-and-error pricing conducted by a central planning board.

1. The means of production are privately owned.

2. Product and resource prices are freely determined by supply and demand in competitive markets.

3. Resources are allocated efficiently in accordance with consumer choice.

Now, if we adopt the classical definition of socialism as an economy in which the means of production are owned by society, the question we ask is this:

> Can a socialistic economic system, seeking to be democratic rather than authoritarian and lacking the prices that are freely established in competitive markets, achieve the same degree of efficiency in resource allocation as the pure model of capitalism? Further, can it do so without destroying the basic economic freedoms of consumer and occupational choice?

These questions, it may be noted, are the fundamental theoretical problems of democratic socialism.

Notice that the issue is complicated by the fact that the system must remain democratic. It might be easier to achieve greater efficiencies in resource use by *telling* consumers what they can have and by *ordering* workers to their jobs, but such actions would be completely contrary to the basic philosophy of democratic socialism.

This problem became the subject of widespread discussion in the 1930s and was finally resolved in 1938 with the publication of a remarkable theoretical model of a socialist economy. The chief architect of the model was a well-known Polish economist, Oskar Lange.

According to this theoretical model, a democratic socialist economy could be administered by a Central Planning Board, which would set prices *as if* the competitive market had set them. The Board would, for example, manipulate prices in the product and resource markets with the objective of equating quantities supplied with quantities demanded, thereby assuring that equilibrium was maintained without surpluses or shortages. In this way the Board, through *trial and error,* would guide the factors of production into their most efficient uses in accordance with the wishes expressed by households. *All this would be done through the operation of a price system that would permit freedom of consumer and occupational choice.*

This type of economy, the socialist theorists contended, would yield a double benefit.

First, it would achieve efficient resource utilization, as in the theoretical competitive model of capitalism.

Second, and simultaneously, it would overcome the major disadvantages of real-world capitalism. It would do so by bringing about (1) a more equitable distribution of income resulting from the elimination of private ownership, (2) an adjustment of production according to consumer demands, and (3) a continuous high level of employment assured by government's stable investment policies.

Postwar Developments: The Meaning of Modern Socialism

The outbreak of World War II prevented these ideas from being pursued further. Nor were they taken up again after the war—for three major reasons:

After World War II, contemporary socialist thinkers changed their objectives from total *social control of industry to* partial *control accompanied by central planning.*

1. Mixed capitalistic countries of Western Europe underwent exceptionally high rates of economic growth during the postwar years. These experiences contributed greatly to discrediting the socialistic belief that capitalism was an outmoded economic system.

2. Several conservative governments in Western Europe adopted many far-reaching social-welfare measures, which socialist leaders had long advocated.

3. Various nationalization policies (that is, government takeovers of major industries) in some West European nations turned out unsuccessfully. Indeed, they created problems of excessive bureaucratization and inefficiency that were even greater than the problems that nationalization had been designed to solve.

These developments led to a substantial change in orthodox socialist thinking. Many social democratic parties abandoned their traditional opposition to private property and their goal of *total* social ownership. They turned their attention instead to "improving the mix" in already mixed economies. The following definition of socialism reflects the modified views of contemporary socialist thinkers:

> *Socialism* is a movement that seeks to improve economic efficiency and equity by establishing (1) public ownership of all important means of production and distribution and (2) some degree of centralized planning to determine what goods to produce, how to produce them, and to whom they should be distributed.

As you can see, therefore, the core of socialism is *economic.* Socialism's goal is to transform capitalism by altering its most fundamental feature—the institution of private property.

Today's Radical Socialism

In recent decades, a new wave of radical socialism has swept across the major Western democracies. The members of this movement are mostly political and social activists who take an aggressive stand on many fundamental issues. For example, they press for greater social and economic equality, more "worker control" over economic enterprises, nationalization of large firms, and an end to war-making and imperialism by advanced nations. Unlike many other socialists, the newer radicals regard centralized authority with disdain. Hence, they are not admirers of the USSR or of any system that suppresses freedom of expression.

Since the 1960s, a new form of radical socialism has grown in importance.

The radical socialists have not developed a complete philosophy. However, they have many interesting things to say about economic matters. We can gain an appreciation of some of their main ideas by focusing attention on two fundamental areas: the problem of resource allocation and the nature of surplus value.

Resource Allocation: Free Markets Versus Cooperative Planning

As you have seen in a number of earlier chapters, the free market plays a central role in capitalistic societies. Through the unhampered interaction of supply and demand, the market mechanism accomplishes several major objectives:

1. It provides producers with information about consumer preferences.

2. It allocates society's resources in accordance with these preferences.

3. It encourages the most economical choice of production techniques.

4. It synthesizes the individual buying and selling decisions of millions of households and firms.

For these reasons, it is easy to understand why the free market has often been extolled by distinguished political and economic leaders. (See Box 1.)

Despite these apparent virtues, modern radical socialists are not persuaded that the free market is the most desirable device for allocating resources. On the contrary, they believe strongly that the market mechanism is both socially and economically objectionable—even evil—for the following reasons:

Today's radicals see much to criticize in modern mixed economies.

1. Inefficiency and Instability The free market causes unemployment and inflation. Government policies may at times succeed in reducing inefficiency and instability. But history shows clearly that government policies are often ill conceived and improperly administered because they are designed to preserve the market mechanism rather than replace it.

2. Inequity The market system perpetuates economic and social inequalities—unjustified disparities in the distribution of income, wealth, and power. Two fundamental institutions of capitalism, private property and inheritance, are among the root causes of economic inequality. In addition, a third institution—the market system—permits inequalities to continue.

Wide World Photos

Library of Congress

"I am convinced that if it were the result of deliberate human design, and if the people guided by the price changes understood that their decisions have significance far beyond their immediate aim, this mechanism would have been acclaimed as one of the greatest triumphs of the human mind. Its misfortune is the double one that it is not the product of human design and that the people guided by it usually do not know why they are made to do what they do."

Friedrich A. Hayek

"The free market is not only a more efficient decision maker than even the wisest central planning body, but even more important, the free market keeps economic power widely dispersed. It is thus a vital underpinning of our democratic system."

John F. Kennedy

Today's Marxists do not subscribe to these views of President Kennedy or Nobel prize winner Hayek. To the radical socialists, the market mechanism fosters inequality and oppression rather than equity and freedom.

---

3. Social Imbalance The free market causes an inefficient distribution of resources between private and social goods—a lack of *social balance.* This happens because the market system, through advertising and promotion, favors the production of private goods (such as automobiles, television sets, and stereos) for which consumers can voluntarily express their preferences by prices offered. At the same time, the free market suppresses the production of social goods (such as schools, libraries, and public hospitals), which come into existence only through compulsory taxes. In other words, as a result of the market system, too much private expenditure goes to satisfy superficial wants artificially created, while many fundamental public needs are neglected because they cannot compete successfully for the same resources.

Today's radical socialists thus conclude:

The market system is inefficient, inequitable, and immoral. It perpetuates a class structure that associates wealth with privilege and poverty with oppression. These problems cannot be solved within the framework of existing capitalistic institutions. Therefore, the institutions themselves must be changed before any significant improvements in human welfare can be realized.

In other words, radical socialists believe that the market system should be replaced by some alternative decision-making process that promotes society's well-being—economic as well as moral and cultural.

Cooperative Planning

If free markets are strongly opposed by modern Marxists, what mechanism do they advocate for providing information and allocating resources? The most obvious answer would appear to be central planning—a method long used in varying degrees by socialistic countries. Under central planning, the government decides *what* goods will be produced, *how* they will be produced, and *to whom* the output will be distributed. At the very least, therefore, central planning requires government to exercise substantial control over most, if not all, important phases of economic activity.

Modern radicals oppose centralized or "top-down" planning because it is authoritarian and inefficient.

This solution poses a basic problem for today's radical socialists. Most of them are as strongly opposed to traditional forms of central planning as to free markets—for two reasons:

1. Bureaucratic Inefficiency Experiences in socialistic countries show that central planning leads to bureaucracy—excessive multiplication and concentration of power in administrative bureaus—with resulting inefficiency and waste. The benefits of central planning are thus lost to society through resource misallocation and reduction of output.

2. Authoritarian Management The growth of bureaucracy, as the evidence also shows, results in autocratic or "top-down" decision making. Management imposes sacrifices upon workers without their prior advice or consent.

Modern radical socialists are thus led to the conclusion that a third method of resource allocation—one that avoids what they regard as the undesirable consequences of both the free market and central planning—is needed. The method they advocate may be called "participative decision making" or "cooperative planning."

Today's radicals advocate extensive "social involvement" in the planning process.

> According to today's radical socialists, cooperative planning is the ideal method of resource allocation. Cooperative planning entails (1) educating people to their "true needs," (2) eliminating "economic waste" caused by unproductive labor, and (3) preserving democratic traditions through worker participation in decision making at both the company and national levels. Adoption of cooperative planning would lead to "production for use" (rather than for profit) within a social framework oriented toward collaboration (rather than competition) for mutual benefit.

These ideas—particularly the expressions in quotation marks—require some further comment. As you will see, they are directly related to the notion of *surplus value*, a concept of fundamental importance both in Marxian and modern radical thinking.

The Nature of Surplus Value

Marx defined a society's "surplus" as the difference between the value of goods created by workers and the subsistence wage they actually receive. In other words, Marx viewed a capitalistic economy's surplus as consisting of profits, rent, and interest—the sum of which rightfully belongs to workers but is expropriated (literally stolen) by capitalists.

Today's new radicals believe that Marx's definition of surplus was adequate for his time, but that the concept must be broadened to reflect the greater complexity of today's advanced capitalistic economies. Accordingly, modern adherents of Marxism define economic surplus in a capitalistic society as the *difference between the market value of all final goods and services produced during a period and the socially necessary costs of producing them.* Thus, if the total market value of all final goods and services produced in the economy during a given year—called gross national product or GNP—is $1 billion, and the socially necessary costs of producing that output are $400 million, then the society's economic surplus for that year is $600 million.

Modern radicals have redefined surplus value by distinguishing between costs that are socially necessary and those that are not.

The question that must be asked, of course, is what is the meaning of "socially necessary costs"? Today's Marxists define this concept for measurement purposes as the sum of three types of expenditures:

1. Replacement Investment This is the value of plant and equipment used up or depreciated each year in producing the nation's final output—its GNP. This amount of investment expenditure is thus necessary to replace that part of GNP that is worn out.

2. Payments for Productive Labor This class of expenditures consists of wages paid to workers producing "socially useful output"—an expression widely employed but not clearly defined by modern radical socialists. They hold that, in a capitalistic economy, a substantial share of the surplus is used to support largely "unproductive" activities—among them excessive advertising and administration (both in business and government). In a socialistic economy, most of these expenditures would be socially unnecessary, leaving a larger proportion of society's resources to be employed in more constructive activities.

3. Minimal Costs of Government This class of expenditures consists of those costs of government needed to provide essential services. These include education, public health, judicial administration, police and fire protection, planning, and perhaps some minimal level of national defense. (The "minimal level," however, is not clearly defined by radicals.) All other expenditures on government in capitalistic societies—such as expenditures for war and imperialism—are wasteful. They serve only to absorb a large part of the surplus that could better be used for producing needed social goods.

In the modern radical view, surplus value includes not only what Marx said it did, but also socially unnecessary costs.

In summary, therefore:

Modern radical socialists define economic surplus as consisting not only of profits, rent, and interest, as Marx did, but also of socially unnecessary costs in both the private and the public sectors. This concept of economic surplus is, therefore, much broader than the view held by Marx.

These ideas can be expressed by two simple equations.

According to Marx:
$$\text{economic surplus} = \text{profits} + \text{rent} + \text{interest}$$

According to the modern radical socialists:
$$\text{economic surplus} = \text{profits} + \text{rents} + \text{interest} + \text{socially unnecessary costs}$$

What Happens to the Surplus?

Radical socialists believe that, over the long run, the economy's surplus tends to rise—both in absolute terms and as a percentage of GNP. According to some estimates, the surplus today in the United States is more than 60 percent of GNP, having risen from somewhat less than 50 percent since the 1930s.

This growing surplus, the radicals say, exists because of insufficient consumption and investment opportunities available in a mature capitalistic economy. As a result, resources are increasingly utilized in "unproductive" outlets and activities. These include:

1. **Nonprice Competition** This consists of methods of competition that do not involve changes in selling price, such as advertising, product differentiation, superficial model changeovers, and so on.

2. **Bureaucracy** This is the overabundance of administrative bureaus and agencies, especially in government.

3. **War and Imperialism** "War" includes other military activities. Imperialism refers to the exploitation of weaker nations both by government and by large corporations, which may function together in a vast "military–industrial complex."

Today's radicals believe, as did Marx, that capitalism is doomed.

> Radical socialists thus conclude that these inherent contradictions within capitalism must eventually lead to its collapse—either through revolution or war or through a fundamental transformation of its basic institutions. In fact, according to many radical socialists, the end of capitalism may already be in sight. This is evidenced by the social and economic disruption experienced by today's advanced capitalistic countries, the warlike policies that they pursue, and the growing importance to them of government.

Conclusion: Identifying Fundamental Issues

You can see from the foregoing analysis that radical economists have had much to criticize about capitalism's institutions and processes. What solutions to society's ills do these critics offer? The answer is not clear. Although they advocate public ownership of capital, administration by "workers' councils," and cooperative planning, these are only means toward an end. There is much that the radicals do not explain. For example:

Modern radical socialism leaves many questions unanswered. Perhaps its chief contribution consists in raising important issues.

• How can resources be allocated without markets?

• How can planning be achieved without bureaucracy?

• How can greater social and economic equality be realized without competition?

• How can collective ownership exist without destroying individual initiative?

• And, in general, how can national governments of large, complex societies make important social and economic decisions without seriously impairing efficiency and democratic processes?

In view of this, what conclusion can we draw about the merits of radical socialism?

> Perhaps the chief contribution of modern radicalism has been its identification of important issues. By pointing out the shortcomings of our economic system, radical socialists have made us more aware of capitalism's failure to achieve desired goals of efficiency and equity. And, by focusing attention on such problems as private versus public ownership, the unequal distribution of wealth and power, and externalities and market failures, today's radicals have put their finger on some of the most fundamental issues of our time.

Issue
Is Capitalism Dying?

The United States has experienced several recessions during the latter half of this century. In recent years, unemployment and inflation rates exceeding 10 percent have not been uncommon. These strains on the economic system have stirred debates among scholars as to whether American capitalism has entered its final era—a crisis stage leading to decline and fall, perhaps before the end of this century.

Notable among the supporters of this belief are many of today's radical socialists. Their ideas of impending disaster stem largely from the writings of Karl Marx. According to these radicals, what the United States has experienced since the mid-1970s has not just been severe business cycles, as most conventional economists contend, but rather wrenching changes in the system's fundamental structure. To support this view, radicals offer the following analysis.

Marxian Dynamics

In Marxian theory, as well as in modern radical thinking, an advanced capitalistic economy develops certain "contradictions" which lead eventually to the system's collapse. Many of today's radicals believe that these contradictions are already apparent—as evidenced by certain developments in recent history:

Business Cycles. The depression of the early 1980s registered the highest unemployment rate since the depression of the 1930s. In accordance with Marxian logic, the sharp downturn was the result of the growing influence of two long-term trends:

1. The drive for capital accumulation, particularly labor-saving equipment, resulting in the displacement of labor and in an ever-increasing level of unemployment.

2. A declining rate of profit, arising from the inability of physical capital (as distinguished from human capital—that is, labor) to produce surplus value.

Market Concentration. With the worsening of economic conditions—manifested especially by a declining rate of profit—capitalists have sought ways to protect their self-interest by absorbing weaker firms. This has led to the concentration of capital in large-scale industrial units or monopolies.

Imperialistic Multinationalism. The effects of monopolization are ultimately realized on an international scale with the emergence of a new form of business enterprise—the multinational corporation. Operating across national boundaries, the huge multinational organizations dominate markets and control the resources of other countries. This is what Lenin called the stage of "capitalistic imperialism"—the highest and final stage of mature capitalism.

The radicals conclude that the United States entered this last stage in the 1960s, followed shortly thereafter by Japan and West Germany. Therefore, it is only a matter of time, probably not more than a few decades, before these bastions of capitalism either collapse or are drastically transformed by the internal dynamics of their own system.

What Future?

Today's Marxists recognize that policy makers in government and in business seek ways to escape from crisis and to sustain steady growth. Among the tools and techniques used for these purposes are fiscal and monetary policies, the laying off of workers, the cutting of services, and intermittent experiments in wage—price controls and economic planning. But these are only temporary palliatives, for there is no escape from the growing dilemma of inflation versus unemployment. As the squeeze on workers continues, they will respond increasingly with strikes and demonstrations, thereby sowing the seeds for what will be a revolution at worst or an extreme leftward shift in political ideology at best. In any case, a sure sign of these impending developments, the radicals contend, is the growing oppression that the working class is experiencing as a result of government's failure to resolve the contradictions inherent in today's advanced capitalistic societies.

Questions

1. Radicals base much of their belief in the eventual collapse of capitalism on a declining rate of profit. Do the data in the accompanying table support the radicals' contention? (*Hint:* What are the long-term trends of percentage rate of return on stockholders' equity and on sales?)

2. What do you think is the strongest argument the radicals have to support their view? Do you believe the argument will be resolved? If not, is capitalism doomed, as many radicals contend? Explain.

Sales, Profits, and Stockholders' Equity, in All Manufacturing Corporations
(billions of dollars)

Year	Sales	Profit after federal income taxes	Stockholders' equity
1950	$ 181.9	$12.9	$ 83.3
1955	278.4	15.1	120.1
1960	345.7	15.2	165.4
1965	492.6	27.5	211.7
1970	708.8	28.6	306.8
1975	1,065.2	49.1	423.4
1976	1,203.2	64.5	462.7
1977	1,328.1	70.4	496.7
1978	1,496.4	81.1	540.5
1979	1,741.8	98.7	600.5
1980	1,896.8	92.4	664.9

Source: Federal Trade Commission.

What You Have Learned in This Chapter

1. The major reactions to capitalism have been utopian socialism, Marxian socialism and communism, syndicalism, and Christian socialism. Of these, the Marxian reaction has had the most significant impact on the political and economic relationships of nations.

2. Karl Marx was strongly influenced by the early-nineteenth-century German philosopher Georg Hegel, and particularly by the latter's use of the dialectic. This is a form of discourse in which history is interpreted as the reconciliation of opposites. The approach provided much of the basis for Marx's (and Engels's) theories. There are five major features of Marx's model: (a) economic interpretation of history, (b) theory of value and wages, (c) theory of surplus value and capital accumulation, (d) class struggle, and (e) theory of socialist and communist evolution.

3. Critics of Marx have pointed out major shortcomings: (a) Marx's economic interpretation of history is oversimplified and one-sided—although, thanks at least in part to Marx, there has been a growing emphasis on economic causation in modern historical studies. (b) Marx's theories of value, wages, and surplus value neglected the entrepreneurial functions, failed to recognized the role of demand in the determination of value, and rested on inadequate analytical foundations.

Despite these criticisms, there are elements of truth in Marx's predictions, and much is to be gained from a knowledge of Marxian theory as an aid in understanding some of the pronouncements and policies of communist nations today.

4. Socialism in most of the Western world is conceived as a democratic process—in the sense that socialist leaders may be voted into or out of office in free elections. The goal of the majority of today's democratic socialists is the establishment of the "welfare state" through evolutionary rather than revolutionary methods.

5. An important force in modern socialism is today's radical socialists. They (as distinguished from conventional democratic socialists) oppose free markets, bureaucratic central planning, and, in general, the social and economic inequities inherent both in market and in command economies. Although many fundamental problems have been identified by modern radical socialists, it is not clear that their proposed methods of solution (public ownership, cooperative planning, and so forth) are superior to those available in present-day mixed economies.

For Discussion

1. *Terms and concepts to review:*
utopian socialism
Fabian socialism
syndicalism
Christian socialism
economic interpretation of history
dialectical materialism
value
price
subsistence theory of wages
surplus value
class struggle
Marxian socialism
communism
"dictatorship of the proletariat"
socialism

2. Why should a student of today be familiar with the nature and origins of radical ideas, some of which are well over a century old?

3. What is meant by an "interpretation of history"? Can you suggest several different types of interpretations? In your previous history courses in high school or college, which interpretations were stressed?

4. Marx was aware that direct labor is only one of several inputs used in production and that raw materials, machines, and other resources were also necessary. How, then, could he argue that labor alone was the basis of value?

5. According to Marx, would there be such a thing as surplus value if capitalists paid workers "what they were worth"? Explain.

6. Do you believe that there is such a thing as a "class struggle" in the Marxian sense? Why or why not? (**Hint** Can we divide a complex social structure into dichotomous or opposed subclasses? By what criteria?)

7. If we prove that Marx's theory of surplus value is logically incorrect, does this mean that workers *in fact* are not exploited in our capitalistic system? Explain by defining what you mean by "exploitation." (**Hint** If you were a profit-maximizing employer, would you hire someone to work for you if the added value he or she created were less than the wages you paid?)

8. What major shortcoming do you find in the Marxian model of capitalism?

9. Marxism, it has been said, is like religion: "For those who believe, no explanation is necessary; for those who do not believe, no explanation is possible. Logical arguments, therefore, are not the grounds for acceptance or rejection. It is emotion, not logic, that is the influencing factor. This is why Marxism remains as the basic ideology of several nations and many millions of people throughout the world." Do you agree? Can you add anything to the proposition?

10. Radical socialists have referred to democratic socialists as "coddlers of capitalism." Can you suggest why?

11. Is it possible to have political and social freedom in a command economy? Is it possible to have a market economy without political and social freedom? Explain.

Economic Planning: The Visible Hand in Mixed and in Command Economies

38

CHAPTER

Learning guide

Watch for the answers to these important questions

What is economic planning? Why do some countries engage in it?

What are econometric models? What is input–output analysis? How do some countries use these tools to facilitate economic planning?

How does the USSR engage in economic planning? What means are used to stimulate production? Are economic freedoms in the USSR the same as, or different from, those in mixed economies?

To what extent has the USSR been more, or less, successful than the United States in achieving each of the four goals of economics? Why is it difficult, and perhaps even meaningless, to make comparisons of efficiency between the USSR and the United States?

What three broad socioeconomic goals did China try to achieve between 1949 and 1979? How have these goals been modified since then under China's changed leadership? What specific problems, achievements, and failures has China realized in pursuing the goals of efficiency, equity, stability, and growth?

As you know, the market system is the basis of capitalism, and it is a fundamental mechanism for allocating resources in mixed economies. Through the unhampered interaction of supply and demand, producers are provided with information about consumer preferences. As a result, competition assures that society's resources are allocated in accordance with these preferences, the most economical choice of production techniques is encouraged, and the individual buying and selling decisions of millions of households and firms are synthesized. This method of resource allocation, including its achievements and failures, has occupied our attention in most of the earlier chapters.

An alternative way in which a society can allocate its scarce resources is by economic planning. An *economic plan* is a detailed scheme, formulated beforehand, for achieving specific objectives by governing the activities and interrelationships of those entities—firms, households, and governments—that have an influence on the desired outcome. This method of resource allocation plays a key role in command economies. However, certain types of economic plans are also employed in many mixed economies.

Why should we study economic planning? There are two reasons. First, *planned economies*—economic systems in which the government

This chapter explains the theories and techniques of planning in selected countries.

directs resources for the purpose of deciding *what* to produce, *how* to produce it, and possibly *for whom* to produce it—are playing an increasingly important role in the world today. Second, the problems that economic planning tries to solve are fundamental to every type of economic system. Therefore, an understanding of planning principles and experiences can provide us with guides for evaluating and improving public policies.

Why Plan? Four Fundamental Goals

All countries seek the same economic goals of efficiency, equity, stability, and growth.

Why do some countries undertake economic planning? The reason is obvious. Countries plan in order to achieve specific economic goals that, it is believed, would not be realized, or would be attained too slowly, if markets were allowed to operate freely. What are these economic goals? As you will recall, four that are fundamental to all economies—mixed as well as command—are efficiency, equity, stability, and growth. A review of these concepts will help to refresh your understanding of certain fundamental ideas.

Efficiency

In general, *efficiency* is the ability to make the best use of available resources to attain a desired result. Two important types of efficiency are "technical" and "economic."

Note These terms were discussed many times in earlier chapters. If you do not recall their specific meanings and implications, you should look them up *now* (under "efficiency") in the Dictionary at the back of the book.

Technical efficiency, which exists when a society is producing at some point on its production-possibilities curve, is a primary goal of *all* economies because every society wants to make maximum use of available resources. Economic efficiency, which includes technical efficiency while also reflecting consumer preferences, is a primary goal of market-oriented economies but not necessarily of command economies. This is because the planners in command economies are not always interested in fully satisfying the wants of consumers. As a result of these differences in goals, you can appreciate why we are not always able to compare the performance of a command economy with that of a market-oriented one.

Equity

Every economic system seeks answers to three fundamental questions: *What* goods should society produce? *How* should those goods be produced? *For Whom* should they be produced? The first two questions deal with resource-utilization problems. Therefore, they are concerned with matters of efficiency. The third question deals with income distribution—the division of society's output among its people. Hence, it is concerned with matters of equity or justice.

As you learned in previous chapters, equity is a philosophical *concept* and it is also an economic *goal*. There is no scientific basis for concluding that a particular standard of income distribution is either just or unjust. Although many standards of distribution are possible, three have received the widest attention:

1. **Contributive Standard** "To each according to the market value of his or her contribution to society's output."

2. **Needs Standard** "To each according to his or her needs."

3. **Equality Standard** "To each equally."

Do you recall from earlier chapters the economic implications of these distributive standards? You can review them now by looking up the terms in the Dictionary at the back of the book.

Stability and Growth

Stability and growth are the two remaining fundamental goals of every economic system. These terms have close economic interrelations. By maintaining stability, an economy avoids substantial inflationary and deflationary price movements and is better able to promote continuous full employment of all resources. This in turn leads to a robust volume of economic activity and to the encouragement of steady *economic growth*—a rising level of real output per capita. As a result, all income groups in society benefit, even if each receives a constant proportion of an expanding economic pie.

Conclusion: Free Market Versus Centralized Control

Every society seeks four fundamental economic goals: efficiency, equity, stability, and growth. Some societies, however, try to attain these goals by constructing plans—schemes of action or procedure designed to accomplish certain objectives. When an economic entity (such as a household, firm, or government) undertakes planning, it seeks to do a systematic job of setting goals, determining resources needed to meet the goals, and matching the two according to a time schedule. Although centralized planning is a key feature of command economies, most democratic countries also engage in some degree of planning. A chief problem these countries face, of course, is to achieve what they regard as a proper compromise or middle ground between free markets and centralized control. (See Box 1.)

Some countries seek to achieve their economic goals primarily through the free market. Others try to achieve their goals through planning.

Tools of Economic Planning

If economic planning is to be effective, government efforts must be directed toward influencing behavior both at the macroeconomic and at the microeconomic level. What analytical procedures are available for such purposes? There are several, but those that have gained increasing use as tools of economic planning are econometric models and input–output analysis.

Econometric Models

If you were in a high government position responsible for overall economic planning, one of your chief functions would be to identify and analyze relations between important variables that have an influence on the economy's performance. Some examples of such variables are consumption expenditures, investment expenditures, interest rates, prices, production, money supply, employment, and productivity. How would you go about combining these and other factors into a set of meaningful relations that can be used as a guide for forecasting and planning?

One way of attacking the problem is by the use of *econometrics*. This approach integrates economic theory, mathematics, and statistics. That is, it expresses economic relations in the form of mathematical equations and verifies the resulting models by statistical methods. By constructing theoretical models that can be quantified and tested with actual data, econometrics seeks to explain economic behavior.

Econometric models were first introduced on a substantial scale during the 1930s. Among the pioneers in the field were Professors Ragnar Frisch of Norway and Jan Tinbergen of the Netherlands. In recognition of their monumental contributions, both men were honored in 1969 by being made the first recipients of the Alfred Nobel Memorial Prize in Economic Science. Today, as a result of the trailblazing efforts of Frisch and Tinbergen, large-scale econometric models have gained wide use. Consisting of hundreds of equations, they are employed as forecasting and planning devices by some corporations as well as by a number of national governments.

Box 1
Mixed Economies: The Many Shades of Capitalism

Capitalism is a system characterized by private ownership of the means of production. This implies that there is a relatively free market in which entrepreneurs can enter businesses of their choice. In addition, it implies that production is motivated by the drive for profit.

Capitalism is also usually associated with personal freedom. In reality, however, the two may be independent. For example, Nazi Germany (1933–1945) was capitalist because most of its industries were privately owned. But the government was a dictatorship that deprived people of certain political and social freedoms. Yugoslavia, on the other hand, is also a dictatorship, but most of its industries are state-owned and are managed by workers within a relatively free-market framework.

Further "models" can be identified among the world's leading capitalist countries:

United States and West Germany
These countries come closest to the traditional concept of capitalism. Most businesses are privately owned and operated for profit. Government provides certain basic services (for example, education, national defense, postal service) and exercises varying degrees of regulation over certain others. Government also tries to direct the economy toward its economic goals by employing tax, spending, and money-supply policies.

Britain, France, and Italy
Most industries in these countries are privately owned, except for those deemed "basic." Among the latter are coal, railroads, and steel in Britain; oil, steel, cement, and an auto company in France; and public transportation systems and some financial institutions in Italy. France has also adopted so-

called "indicative planning." That is, government and industry representatives jointly establish broad production targets for key industries. These industries then receive government tax and credit incentives to achieve desired goals. (**Note** In the early 1980s, under a new administration, France initiated an extensive program aimed at nationalization of many major firms. It remains to be seen how far this program will be carried.)

Scandinavia: Denmark, Norway, and Sweden
Scandinavian capitalism, which is often mistaken for socialism, is more accurately called "welfare statism." The Swedish version is the most thoroughly developed. Although about 90 percent of Sweden's enterprises are privately rather than governmentally owned, income taxes on profits are as high as 80 percent. These revenues are used to promote investment and to finance an extensive system of social benefits providing cradle-to-grave care

for everyone. As a result, the Swedish standard of living is one of the highest in the world. But these benefits have been accompanied by considerable inflationary pressures—due largely to budget deficits and monetary expansions incurred to finance social programs.

Japan
Most Japanese enterprises are privately owned. But industry and government work closely together. The largest firms, especially those engaged heavily in exporting, receive substantial government preferences. These include tax privileges, easy credit from state-connected banks, and similar benefits. Japan's economic system is thus a type of industry–government cartel. Both sectors cooperate to achieve maximum production and employment. This is accomplished in part by limiting imports and, some critics claim, by dumping in overseas markets, thereby "exporting" unemployment to Japan's major trading partners.

Planning in the Netherlands

The nation that has made the greatest use of econometrics for government planning is the Netherlands. Denmark, Norway, and Sweden have also placed heavy reliance on this planning technique. The approach used by the Dutch, however, may be regarded as typical of the way in which econometric planning procedures can be employed by a government that wishes to use them.

In the Netherlands, a Central Planning Bureau founded by Jan Tinbergen serves as the planning agency for the Dutch economy. The Bureau constructs econometric models that are designed to do two things —*forecast* and *simulate*. Both activities provide the basis for planning.

When used for forecasting, the models are employed to predict the short-term and long-term course of such economic variables as consumption expenditures, investment expenditures, prices, interest rates, and gross national product. These predictions serve the government as a guide for judging future trends in the economy.

When used for simulation, the models are employed to replicate operations within the economy and the outcomes of different policies. The government may want to know, for example, what the effects will be on total output, income, interest rates, and employment if personal income taxes are increased by 10 percent or decreased by 5 percent. The alternative tax rates are fed into the model, and the resulting outcomes are computed. Similarly, alternative raw-materials quantities, factory-utilization rates, and so on, are "plugged" into the model to determine how much production will be available to fulfill expected demands at specified prices.

In these ways, the Central Planning Bureau arrives at numerical estimates of the various inputs needed to reach alternative targets. The Bureau then provides the information to representatives of labor, management, and government, all of whom work together to construct a final plan.

An illustration of an econometric model is presented in Exhibit 1. You can see from the explanation in the exhibit why such models are gaining increasing use in many countries as tools for forecasting and planning.

The Netherlands makes extensive use of econometric models as planning tools.

Input–Output Analysis

If the demand for automobiles were to increase by 20 percent, how much of an increase could be expected in the sales of rubber, steel, automobiles, and glass to the automobile industry? One way of answering this question would be through the use of input–output analysis.

Input–output analysis is a method of studying the interrelations between industries (or sectors) of an economy. A model in the form of a table is constructed in which each of the economy's industries is listed twice: once down the left side as a seller of outputs and once across the top as a buyer of inputs. Within the body of the table are squares called "cells," which show in numerical terms the sales–purchase relation among the industries portrayed in the model.

A highly simplified illustration of an input–output model for an economy comprising four industries is shown in Exhibit 2. A more realistic model would contain dozens or even hundreds of industries. The model is "read" in the following way:

Input–output analysis uses a special type of table for studying the interrelations among industries and sectors.

Exhibit 1

Mathematizing the Economy—An Econometric Model

Although an econometric model is usually an elaborate system of mathematical equations, some of the flavor of econometrics can be experienced from a simple model. This is illustrated by the following five-equation system, which describes a national economy:

$$\text{consumption expenditures} = a + b(\text{national income}) \tag{1}$$

$$\text{investment expenditures} = c + d(\text{profits in previous period}) \tag{2}$$

$$\text{taxes} = e(\text{gross national product}) \tag{3}$$

$$\begin{array}{c}\text{gross national}\\\text{product}\end{array} = \left(\begin{array}{c}\text{consumption}\\\text{expenditures}\end{array}\right) + \left(\begin{array}{c}\text{investment}\\\text{expenditures}\end{array}\right) + \left(\begin{array}{c}\text{government}\\\text{expenditures}\end{array}\right) \tag{4}$$

$$\text{national income} = (\text{gross national product}) - (\text{taxes}) \tag{5}$$

In the equations above, each of the letters a, b, c, d, and e are mathematical constants, called parameters. Each represents some particular number derived by statistical procedures. Once the parameters are determined, the model can be "solved" by making various substitutions and calculating the results.

The first three equations in the model are "behavioral." They tell how the dependent variable on the left side behaves in relation to the independent variable on the right. Thus, the first equation states that consumption expenditures depend on—are a function of—national income. The second says that investment expenditures are a function of the previous period's profits. The third states that taxes are a function of—or some proportion of—gross national product.

The last two equations are "definitional." They express identities or truisms about the economy. Equation (4), for example, shows

that gross national product is the sum of three classes of expenditures—consumption, investment, and government. Equation (5) says that national income is the difference between gross national product and taxes.

Of course, since the model is intended to be a simplification of reality, the equations necessarily omit certain variables that might be included in a more detailed model. Nevertheless, even this basic model could be used reasonably well for forecasting the dependent variables—those on the left sides of the equal signs. First, however, good estimates must be obtained of the five parameters, a through e, and of the two variables, "profits in the previous period," shown in equation (2), and "government expenditures," shown in equation (4). Once the forecasts are made, planning can be facilitated by organizing resources to meet desired goals.

Interpreting the Rows

Each row (reading across from left to right) shows the value of output sold by each industry at the left to the industries listed across the top of the table. For example, in the period covered, the rubber industry sold $300 million worth of goods to itself for further production, $100 million to the steel industry, $500 million to the automobile industry, and nothing of significance to the glass industry. The interindustry sales total was therefore $900 million. In addition, direct consumption of rubber by other sources amounted to $200 million. The rubber industry's total output was therefore $1,100 million.

The remaining rows for each industry are interpreted similarly. Thus, the dollar figure in each cell tells you how an industry's total output (shown at the right end of the table) was distributed among the various buyers listed across the top.

Exhibit 2

Input–Output Table for an Economy with Four Industries
(millions of dollars; hypothetical data for a given period)

An input–output table shows certain interdependencies between industries in an economy. Reading from left to right, the dollar figure in each cell tells you the *sales* (outputs) that each industry listed at the left made to the industries shown across the top. Similarly, reading down from the top to bottom, the dollar figure in each cell tells you the *purchases* (inputs) that each industry shown across the top acquired from the industries listed at the left. The numbers in parentheses are called *input coefficients.* They indicate the proportions of total inputs (shown at the bottom) that the industries at the top of each column received from the industries at the left. Of course, for each industry at the top of the table, the sum of its input coefficients must equal 1 (or 100 percent).

Output (sellers) \ Input (buyers)	Rubber industry	Steel industry	Automobile industry	Glass industry	Interindustry sales total	Direct consumption*	Total output
Rubber industry	$300 (.27)	$100 (.06)	$500 (.25)		$900	$200	$1,100
Steel industry	$200 (.18)	$400 (.25)	$600 (.30)	$100 (.17)	$1,300	$300	$1,600
Automobile industry	$100 (.09)	$200 (.13)	$400 (.20)	$200 (.33)	$900	$1,100	$2,000
Glass industry			$400 (.20)	$100 (.17)	$500	$100	$600
Other resources	$500 (.45)	$900 (.56)	$100 (.05)	$200 (.33)	$1,700		$1,700
Total input	$1,100	$1,600	$2,000	$600	$5,300	$1,700	$7,000

* Consists of all other sales, including direct sales to households, government, foreign sources, and sales for capital formation (that is, investment goods).

Interpreting the Columns

Each column (reading down from top to bottom) shows the value of input purchased by each industry at the top from the industries listed along the left side of the table. For example, in the period covered, the steel industry bought $100 million worth of goods from the rubber industry, $400 million worth of steel for its own use, $200 million worth of goods from the automobile industry, and nothing of significance from the glass industry. In addition, it purchased $900 million worth of "other resources." Therefore, the value of total input purchased by the steel industry was $1,600 million.

The remaining columns for each industry are interpreted in the same way. The dollar figure in each cell shows how an industry's total input (shown at the bottom of the table) was distributed among the various sellers listed at the left.

Calculating the Input Coefficients

With this information given, the table enables us to calculate the value of each input needed to produce an additional dollar's worth of output. The resulting numbers, called *input coefficients,* are shown in parentheses in each cell. Each input coefficient is obtained from the formula

$$\text{input coefficient} = \frac{\text{industry's specific input}}{\text{industry's total input}}$$

For example, reading down from the top of the table, the steel industry's specific input from the rubber industry was \$100 million, while the steel industry's total input was \$1,600 million. Therefore, the steel industry's input coefficient, *IC*, for rubber is

$$\text{STEEL}\,IC_{rubber} = \frac{\$100}{\$1,600} = .06$$

Similarly, reading down again from the top of the table, the glass industry's specific input from the automobile industry was \$200 million, while the glass industry's total input was \$600 million. Hence, the glass industry's input coefficient for autos is

$$\text{GLASS}\,IC_{autos} = \frac{\$200}{\$600} = .33$$

The remaining input coefficients are calculated similarly. Notice that the sum of the input coefficients in each column must equal 1.

Application to Forecasting and Planning

The input–output table can now be used to answer the question posed at the beginning of this section:

If the demand for automobiles were to increase by 20 percent, how much of an increase could be expected in the sales of rubber, steel, automobiles, and glass to the automobile industry?

A 20 percent increase in the demand for automobiles would increase their direct consumption from \$1,100 million to \$1,320 million. This additional output of \$220 million worth of automobiles would be matched by the following input increases in the automobile industry:

rubber:	0.25 × \$220 million =	\$ 55 million
steel:	0.30 × \$220 million =	66 million
automobiles:	0.20 × \$220 million =	44 million
glass:	0.20 × \$220 million =	44 million
other resources:	0.05 × \$220 million =	11 million
	Total value of additional inputs =	\$220 million

The total value of additional inputs to the automobile industry thus equals the value of its additional output, \$220 million.

Note There are also numerous secondary, tertiary, and even more remote effects on the automobile and other industries because of the circular repercussions of production decisions among the industries. For example, more automobiles require more steel, rubber, and other inputs, which also require more automobiles, and so on.

An input coefficient shows the values of the inputs that are needed to produce an additional output of a given value.

When an input–output table is completed, it shows how much of each additional input is needed to provide a given increase in output.

You can now appreciate the usefulness of input–output analysis:

An input–output model serves two important planning functions:

1. It indicates the impacts of changes in demand on industry supplies.

2. It suggests where potential bottlenecks may arise in the flow of goods between industries.

For these reasons, input–output analysis permits changes to be anticipated before they occur. This enables plans to be formulated in order to minimize disruptions in resource use.

Uses and Difficulties

The pioneering work on input–output analysis was done by Wassily Leontief at Harvard University. Leontief devoted most of his professional career—some forty years, from the 1930s to the 1970s—to deriving the data needed for compiling massive input–output tables encompassing hundreds of industries. In 1973, in recognition of his scholarship, the Swedish government awarded Leontief the Nobel Prize in Economic Science. As a result of his efforts, many corporations and some governments (including the government of the USSR) today make substantial use of input–output analysis for forecasting and planning their economic activities.

Despite the advances made in input–output analysis, it still suffers from certain problems. Among them:

An input–output model is based on past economic relationships and on a particular classification of industries. Both of these may be subject to criticism.

• The data in input–output tables are based on past relations in the economy. To be more useful for forecasting and planning, the dollar flows and coefficients should ideally reflect current, if not future, relations. This will be impossible, however, until more and better information, and improved methods of analyzing it, become available.

• The division of an economy into specific industries raises many problems of definition and classification. Should television production be treated as a separate industry, or should it be grouped with television equipment, electronic equipment, or communications equipment? One classification may be too narrow or refined; another, too broad or aggregated.

These and other difficulties have only retarded, rather than prevented, the implementation of input–output techniques. Much progress has already been made in overcoming these obstacles.

Conclusion: More Scientific Planning

During the past several decades, a growing number of corporations and governments have placed increasing reliance on scientific planning techniques—including econometrics and input–output analysis. The reasons can be attributed to two major factors:

Econometrics and input–output analysis are planning tools used by many corporations and governments.

1. Continuing integration of economic theory and mathematics. This makes possible the formulation of complex economic concepts in precise mathematical terms.

2. Rapid advances in computer science. This enables huge quantities of data to be processed and analyzed.

As a result, models of economic systems can now be constructed on much larger scales than was previously possible. This suggests the following conclusion:

> In the final analysis, the usefulness of any model depends on the accuracy and completeness of its information. As research and data-collection methods improve, econometrics and input–output analysis will gain wider adoption as scientific planning tools in industry and government.

It is significant to note that econometrics, input–output analysis, and related techniques are more than just analytical tools. As a result of their development and implementation, the nature of economics has undergone dramatic changes in recent decades. (See "Leaders in Economics" on page 837.)

Planning in the USSR

The Soviet Union provides an example of a command economy that engages extensively in planning.

Any study of economic planning would be incomplete without a discussion of the USSR. This nation has been actively engaged in planning longer than any other country.

The USSR came into existence as a direct reaction to capitalism. In November 1917, the revolutionary Bolshevik (later known as Communist) party of Russia, under the leadership of V. I. Lenin, overthrew the government and, five years later, established the Union of Soviet Socialist Republics. The ultimate objective of the party, which identified itself with the "dictatorship of the proletariat," was to establish Marxian socialism and eventually full communism in the Soviet Union and throughout the world. This, it was said, would end the "want, misery, and injustice of capitalist society."

Has this goal been achieved? We can best answer the question by examining the present structure of the Soviet economy within a framework of four distinguishing features:

1. Soviet economic institutions and organization.

2. Soviet economic planning.

3. Reorganization and changes in the Soviet economy.

4. The challenge of economic growth.

Soviet Economic Institutions and Organization

Every society is characterized by certain institutions—established ways of doing things based on customs, practices, or laws. Acting in combination, these institutions affect the society's organizational structure. We examine here the more important institutions in the Soviet economy.

Social Ownership of Industry

The Soviet Union defines its economic system as socialist, not communist. Socialism, according to Marxian doctrine, is a preparatory stage in the attainment of full communism. Unlike the United States, therefore, all means of industrial production in the USSR that require the use of hired labor are owned by "society," represented by the government. Although some people, such as professionals and artisans, can work for themselves, they must do so without the help of hired labor. Except for a few special cases (for example, domestic servants), no person may employ another for a wage or for private gain.

Wide World Photos
Ragnar Frisch

United Press International
Jan Tinbergen

United Press International
Wassily Leontief

Leaders in Economics

Ragnar Frisch
1895–1973

Jan Tinbergen
1903–

Wassily Leontief
1906–
*Econometrics and
Input–Output Analysis*

Adam Smith and Karl Marx founded systems of economic thought. Yet it is doubtful whether these intellectual giants, if they were students today, could pass a graduate course in economic theory. This is because of the two men's lack of mathematical sophistication in explaining economic ideas. Smith's *The Wealth of Nations* (1776) confines its examples to the use of arithmetic, while Marx's *Das Kapital* (vol. I, 1867) never goes beyond simple algebra. Today the highest status—not only in economics but in all the social and man-

agement sciences—is accorded those whose competence in their particular field is buttressed by the ability to use higher mathematics in formulating essential ideas.

Worldwide Recognition
The evidence of this on an international scale became apparent in 1969 when the Swedish Royal Academy of Science bestowed jointly on Norway's Ragnar Frisch and Holland's Jan Tinbergen the first Alfred Nobel Memorial Prize in Economic Science. Both men, the Academy noted, had distinguished themselves since the 1930s by developing pioneering applications of higher mathematics to economic theory and measurement—the integration of which is known as "econometrics."

In 1973 an American economist—Wassily Leontief—who had immigrated from the USSR several decades earlier and had spent most of his professional career at Harvard University, became another

recipient of the Nobel Prize in Economic Science. Leontief was honored for his outstanding work in developing input–output analysis. This is a highly sophisticated approach to studying complex relationships among industries, regions, and sectors of an economy.

Modern Tools
Today econometrics and input–output analysis are standard tools for forecasting and planning in various countries. As societies become more complex, these tools and other procedures employing advanced mathematical techniques will gain increasing use by governments and corporations. Hence, there is no doubt that, if Adam Smith and Karl Marx were students and aspiring social scientists today, they would be devoting a good deal of their efforts to mastering differential and difference equations, matrix algebra, statistics, and other subjects in higher mathematics.

In the USSR, both industry and agriculture are socially owned.

In general, the publicly owned enterprises in the USSR are not significantly different in form from similar types of American publicly owned firms such as the Tennessee Valley Authority, the U.S. Postal Service, and municipally owned public utilities. Furthermore:

> Public ownership in the Soviet Union does not apply to consumer goods. Virtually all consumer goods are privately owned. And, as in the United States, people may own automobiles, houses, furniture, clothing, government bonds, savings deposits, and so on.

Social Ownership of Agriculture

Agriculture in the USSR is organized along somewhat more complex lines. Two types of farms are in operation, both types socially owned:

1. **State Farms** These are agricultural lands owned and operated as state enterprises under government-appointed managing directors. Workers and administrators are hired to run the farms and are usually paid set wages and, if their work exceeds basic norms of output, bonuses as well.

2. **Collective Farms** These are agricultural cooperatives. They consist of communities of farmers who pool their resources, lease land from the government on a long-term basis, and divide the profits among the members according to the amount and kind of work done by each. Collective farms, which are subject to detailed government regulation, are the dominant form of agriculture in the Soviet Union.

Collective farms were introduced in the late 1920s as a compromise between socialistic principles and political expediency. They were meant to reduce the hostile resistance of the agrarian class (at that time about 80 percent of the Soviet population) to total centralization and control of agriculture. Under the collectivization laws, the farms must sell the bulk of their output to the government at low, pre-set prices. However, they can dispose of the rest of their output as they wish— usually through farmers' markets or bazaars. These are free markets where prices and quality are generally higher than in government stores.

Economic Incentives

The Soviet Union often uses monetary incentives to achieve certain economic objectives.

A fundamental feature of the Soviet economy is its widespread use of monetary rewards. They are used to induce people to exert the efforts needed to accomplish specific tasks. Two major forms of economic incentive exist:

1. **Differential Rewards** These are paid to people in occupations requiring different skills. For example, within the high-income groups are academic research scientists, ballet and opera stars, and university professors of science. In the middle-income groups are engineers, physicians, teachers, and skilled workers. In the lower-income groups are technicians, semi-skilled workers, and unskilled workers.

2. **Productivity Incentives** These are provided for workers and managers alike. For workers in industry and on state farms, basic pay rates are usually calculated not in relation to the number of hours of work but in relation to the number of units produced. In addition, special graduated rates are paid to those who exceed the norm. (It is interesting to note that, in the United States and other noncommunist countries, piecework payments of this type have long been bitterly criticized by labor unions as exploitative.) Management incentives, on the other hand, consist of

bonuses and various types of fringe benefits, including housing and free meals at the plant.

Are economic incentives of this type contrary to Marxian thinking? The Soviets think not:

> In a *socialistic* society, the Soviet planners say, people have not yet been prepared for full communism. Therefore, incentives may be needed to persuade individuals to produce at their full potential.

Freedom of Consumer and Occupational Choice

In the competitive model of capitalism, there is *both consumer sovereignty and freedom of consumer choice*. That is, consumers register their demands for goods through the price system, and producers compete with one another to fulfill those demands. In such a system the consumer is theoretically king. This means that consumers not only decide *what* goods are produced but also are free to choose *how much* they want from the supplies that are available.

In the Soviet economy, the state decides which consumer goods, and how much of each, will be produced (except for the free-market portion of goods produced by collective farms). It then places these goods in government stores—normally without rationing—at equilibrium prices that it believes will clear the market in a given period. Consumers are free to purchase the products or not, as they see fit, at the established prices. Hence, it is correct to say that, generally speaking, *there is freedom of consumer choice in the Soviet Union, but there is not consumer sovereignty.*

Under normal conditions, there is also *freedom of occupational choice.* As was suggested above, the state sets differential wage and salary structures according to types of occupation, skill, geographic location, and other conditions. Workers are largely free to choose the kinds of jobs for which they can qualify.

Broadly speaking, therefore:

> Soviet households have much the same freedoms of consumer and occupational choice as do households in the United States and most other countries. Although there are exceptions, the Soviet leaders have found through hard experience that the preservation of such freedoms provides for more orderly markets and much greater administrative efficiency.

Money and Taxes

The monetary unit in the USSR is the ruble. But in effect two kinds of money circulate:

1. Currency This is used for transactions within the household sector and between households and the state.

2. Bank Money This is used in the government sector among state enterprises.

These currencies are convertible into one another for business purposes (for example, to pay wages), but such conversion is under strict government control. The dual monetary system is designed to prevent the excessive issue of currency in the household sector and to facilitate budgetary control over state enterprises.

Taxes in the Soviet Union, as a percentage of national income, are much higher than in the United States, and probably higher than in most other countries. This is because of the Soviet government's greater pro-

The USSR permits both occupational freedom and freedom of consumer choice, but not consumer sovereignty.

The USSR uses a dual monetary system— one for households and one for government– business transactions. The government's major sources of revenue are profits taxes and sales taxes.

portion of total expenditures. These include: military outlays; welfare spending on socialized medicine, free education, and numerous other benefits; complete operation of state enterprises; and the financing of most new investment in industry, trade, communication, and transport. What are the chief sources of the revenue that pays for these expenditures? In the United States, it would be primarily a graduated personal income tax and to a lesser extent a corporation income tax. The latter averages roughly 50 percent of corporate profits. In contrast:

> The bulk of the Soviet government's revenue comes from a profits tax on state enterprises and a sales tax—called a "turnover" tax—on goods sold to the public. Although the rates vary, the profits tax has tended to bring in about 40 percent of the state's annual revenue and the sales tax about 30 percent.

Soviet Economic Planning

The USSR has been a planned economy since the 1920s, but its economic plans have varied from time to time. Economic plans have taken the form of enormous comprehensive blueprints for coordinating the parts of most or all of the economy. Beginning in 1928, the state embarked on a series of Five-Year Plans (with occasional shorter or longer plans at various times), each with the purpose of achieving certain objectives. There is no need for us to explore the details of each of these plans. However, it will be useful to examine their general features.

The Problems of Balance and Flexibility: Input–Output Analysis

Economic planning in the Soviet Union is done on a nationwide basis, for geographic regions as well as for industries.

Some of the difficulties that arise very early in the planning process involve the problems of achieving appropriate balance and flexibility among the interrelated parts of the economy.

In formulating a five-year plan, for example, production targets are established not only for enterprises and industries but also for geographic regions of the economy. If the plan is to be ideal, it must utilize fully all resources in the most efficient way. This is the task of input–output analysis—a basic tool of planning in the Soviet Union. Thus, the quantities of inputs to be produced, such as iron, steel, and glass, must be balanced by the quantities of outputs that use those inputs, such as houses, automobiles, and agricultural machinery. Otherwise, there will be excess production of some of these commodities relative to others, with the result that certain resources will be used inefficiently.

These difficulties are further complicated by the fact that the planned balances must be dynamic rather than static. That is, they must allow for growth in the quantities of outputs and inputs to be produced over a period of time. This requires that the plan be sufficiently flexible to permit readjustment of any of its parts at any point during the life of the plan in the event that the desired targets are not being met as originally intended.

The Formulation of Objectives

The various five-year plans that have guided the USSR since 1928 have emphasized different objectives based on economic, social, political, and military considerations. For the most part, the biggest problem has been deciding on the proportion of the nation's limited resources to be devoted to the production of consumer goods, capital goods, and military goods. In general, the plans have had four major objectives:

1. To attain the highest standard of living in the world by overtaking the advanced capitalistic countries in output per capita as rapidly as possible.

2. To build a major military complex with the most modern nuclear capabilities.

3. To provide for universal health and education so as to further the nation's growth and scientific progress.

4. To achieve a substantial degree of economic independence from the outside world.

On the whole, the effort to attain these goals has made it necessary for the Soviet planners to follow a threefold strategy.

* First, place a major reliance on agriculture to supply the food and raw materials needed for rapid industrialization.

* Second, give high priority to the use of the country's limited resources for the development of heavy industry, such as steel, machinery, fuel, and power.

* Third, give low priority to the production of consumer goods.

Agriculture and heavy industry have been given the highest priorities in Soviet planning; the production of consumer goods has been given the lowest priority.

The consequences of these policies on the Soviet Union have been painful. Standards of living have remained low compared to the United States, and agriculture has experienced repeated failures and setbacks. These have been the cause of serious concern to government leaders.

The Details of Planning

A comprehensive economic plan of the type prepared in the USSR is extraordinarily detailed. It includes a number of "subplans," such as an output plan, a capital budget or expenditures plan, a financial plan, a labor-utilization plan, and various regional plans. A few words may be said about the problems of preparing the first two of these plans: the output plan and the capital budget.

Output Plan In the preparation of the output plan, the government leaders must be concerned both with consumer preferences and sacrifices in production.

An output plan must consider the alternative inputs and the costs of utilizing them for particular production purposes.

The Soviets recognize that, on the one hand, it would be irrational to produce goods that consumers desire if the production of such goods interfered with the overall objectives of the plan. On the other hand, it would be equally irrational to produce goods that consumers do not desire—that is, would not purchase in sufficient quantities at specified prices. This helps explain why advertising exists in the Soviet Union, although on a much smaller scale than in the United States. Advertising not only seeks to influence the marketing of new products but also helps to clear the market of unsold goods.

Soviet planners must take alternative production costs into account when they set output targets. Labor costs are relatively easy to measure because they are reflected by wage rates. These serve as an indication of the "real costs" of labor—the sacrifices in production that must be made in order to attract labor out of alternative employments. But the means by which the Soviet leaders measure nonlabor costs of production are not always so clear. For example, some experts in the field believe that the Soviet authorities do not attempt to include in their estimates of money costs all the real sacrifices in production resulting from the use of natural resources, capital funds, and land. Nor do they include the costs of distributing goods (such as warehousing and transportation) in their calculation of national income, because they regard distribution activities as unproductive. Thus:

> Soviet attitudes toward alternative costs and distribution are due partly to the difficulties of measurement, partly to the influence of Marxian ideology, and partly to the belief that certain types of price and cost calculations are "capitalistic economics." As a result, there is no doubt that the Soviet planners often sacrifice economic efficiency in order to attain desired objectives.

Capital Budget How do the Soviet authorities determine the output of specific types of producers' goods? For example, how do they decide between a bulldozer and a power shovel, or between a truck and a railroad flatcar?

Such decisions are governed by the capital budget. This is a list of specific investment projects arranged in decreasing order of priority according to each project's *coefficient of relative effectiveness* (CRE). This technical term, used in the USSR, means the expected payoff or percentage rate of return on a capital investment. It is akin to the concept of "marginal efficiency of investment" used in Western economics. A particular investment project is thus either accepted or rejected by the planning authorities according to whether its CRE is above or below the prescribed minimum. In general:

> The CRE is a device for rationing the scarce supply of capital among alternative uses. The method of calculating the CRE is quite similar to procedures used by business economists and financial managers in the United States. The factors that enter into the calculation include economic costs, interest rates, and the returns and expenses expected on the project over its estimated life.

The capital budget allocates scarce funds for specific projects. The funds are rationed according to the expected profitability of the projects.

Adoption and Supervision of the Plan

When the Soviet planners complete their plan, it is reviewed by the government, by the representatives of labor and management, and by the Communist party. The advice and suggestions of these groups may then be incorporated by the planners before they submit it to the Politburo—the highest organ of the Communist party—for the resolution of disputes and final approval. Supervision of the plan is then entrusted to various agencies whose responsibility is to see it through to fulfillment. In the process of supervision, however, the plan is revised periodically to correct for unforeseen developments and errors. In effect, therefore, the "plan" is actually a series of plans rather than a rigid once-and-for-all arrangement.

The planning process involves participation by various groups.

Reorganization and Changes

Of course, an effective plan should be responsive to changing needs. In recognition of this, Soviet planners have at times instituted various reforms. For example:

Decision Making This is done at the enterprise level and has been partially decentralized. Company managers are given greater freedom in hiring workers, setting wages, varying product mixes, contracting with suppliers, and making small investments in new equipment.

Incentive Systems These have been introduced in order to encourage greater output. Workers and managers can strive for bonuses and other benefits based on the efficiency of their enterprise. Efficiency is measured by the ratio of a firm's profit to total assets (that is, by a firm's return on assets). This relates the productivity of assets to goods *sold* rather than merely to goods produced.

Marketing Programs These have been instituted in order to stimulate consumer demand. Advertising is employed to help move goods from dealers' shelves, and prices are reduced when sales become sluggish.

What have been the results of these reorganizations and changes? In general:

Soviet reforms have been introduced to encourage greater overall efficiency. However, the reforms in large part have met with limited success—for political as well as economic reasons:

1. Central planners have not been willing to surrender the real power needed to make decentralization work.

2. The economy has not undergone the organizational and administrative changes required to permit the introduction of new production and distribution methods.

3. Soviet workers have not been sufficiently interested in monetary incentives because of the limited quantity and variety of consumer goods available on which increased incomes can be spent.

As a consequence, greater pressures are frequently put on the Soviet government to provide a larger quantity and better quality of consumer goods.

Accomplishments and Failures

The major economic goal of the USSR has been the attainment of rapid growth. Other objectives—stability, equity, and efficiency—have not been neglected. However, they have been of secondary importance. How successful have the Soviets been in realizing their desired ends?

Growth

Unfortunately, various problems of definition and measurement are encountered in dealing with Soviet data. These difficulties make comparisons with mixed economies much harder. Nevertheless, the available figures suggest the following growth patterns:

1. Since 1950, the growth of real gross national product (GNP) in the Soviet Union has averaged approximately 6 percent per year. This compares with about 4 percent for the United States and somewhat higher rates for West Germany and Japan.

2. Real GNP in the Soviet Union has increased relative to the United States, but the rate of increase has slowed down. In 1950, for example, the USSR's real GNP was one-third that of the United States; in 1960 it was 44 percent, and since 1970 it has averaged close to one-half. (See Exhibit 3.)

How can we explain this substantial growth record? What is the Soviets' magic formula for success? Actually, their growth record is due simply to a consistent economic policy that has stressed several factors:

1. The maintenance of a high proportion (between one-fourth and one-third) of gross investment to GNP.

Soviet planning has suffered setbacks and deficiencies for several reasons.

Exhibit 3

Economic Growth—USSR and the United States

Since 1950, the USSR has grown somewhat faster than the United States—but it still lags far behind the United States in total output. At present, the Soviet economy is roughly half as big as the American economy.

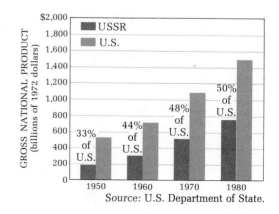

Source: U.S. Department of State.

2. The granting of major priority to the development of such heavy industries as steel, machinery, and power, all of which have magnified or multiplier effects on income and output.

3. The construction and importation of vast quantities of modern equipment.

4. The training of hundreds of thousands of technicians to operate and maintain the physical plant.

These factors have been combined with a rapid increase in the nonagricultural labor force, which has helped to provide the supply of labor needed in the industrial sector.

Stability

Fluctuations in investment expenditures are a chief cause of business cycles. In a command system, in which government makes the strategic decisions, it is easier to manage such expenditures than in a capitalistic system, in which decisions are left up to each firm. As a result, the Soviet economy has maintained high employment and stable prices for much longer periods than have mixed economies.

Equity

The USSR has made substantial progress in attaining stability and equity.

The distribution of income in the USSR is quite uneven. The highest rewards go to political and military leaders, who constitute an elite group in Soviet society. In addition, enterprise managers not only earn much higher salaries than ordinary workers but also receive substantial fringe benefits in the form of superior housing, longer vacations, and in some cases a free car. Similarly, physicists, opera singers, and others in certain preferred occupations (determined by government) are paid considerably more than semiskilled and unskilled workers. Therefore, contrary to Marxian doctrine, *incomes are not generally distributed according to "needs."*

However, there are not the extremes of high and low incomes in the USSR that exist in many mixed economies, and all Soviet citizens receive state-subsidized education, health care, housing, and other benefits at relatively little or no direct costs. On the whole, therefore, despite some considerable disparities, the distribution of income—both money income and real income—is substantially more equal in the USSR than in most advanced mixed economies.

Efficiency

The USSR has been least successful in attaining efficiency.

The Soviet Union has been considerably less successful with respect to efficiency than with its other goals. The factors responsible have been both technical and economic. The agricultural sector has lagged far behind the industrial sector in productivity. The reasons are due mainly to short growing seasons, inadequate incentives to stimulate productivity, and heavy investment of resources in industry and defense at the expense of agriculture. Productivity has also suffered in the industrial sector. This is evidenced, as mentioned earlier, by the fact that various reforms designed to increase output—including efforts at management decentralization and the provision of incentives for workers—have not been particularly successful. On the whole, therefore, it may be said that Soviet planners have failed to achieve technical efficiency—the maximum ratio of physical outputs to available physical inputs.

Nor have the Soviets come anywhere close to attaining economic efficiency—maximum production in accordance with consumers' preferences. This is because a central planning board, rather than a free market, is the mechanism for determining what goods will be produced. Because the central planners have historically given top priority to the production of capital goods relative to consumer goods, the quantities and qualities of the latter have generally fallen far below the levels prevailing in advanced mixed economies.

Conclusion: Better Planning

As a consequence of these experiences, Soviet planners have given up on broad reform. They have undertaken instead to improve central planning and management systems in order to reduce inefficiencies and improve productivity. In general:

The overall objective of the USSR is to improve the quality of planning by making better use of planning methods.

> Since about 1970, Soviet emphasis has shifted from more planning to better planning—through the application of modern economic and scientific management principles. Imports from the West, ranging from agricultural goods to advanced equipment and systems, are rising as a result of these efforts. The ultimate goal is to meet the needs of restive consumers, whose living standards are far below those in other industrial nations.

Planning in China

In 1949, the Communist People's Liberation Army swept victoriously into Peking, the ancient capital of China. Under the leadership of Mao Zedong, it took control of a largely underdeveloped, war-devastated economy containing one-fourth of the world's population in an area one-third larger than the continental United States.

China's economic goals are closely integrated with its social ones. It has sought to develop a classless, collective, and cooperative society.

During the next thirty years, China pursued policies aimed at achieving three broad socioeconomic goals:

1. A *classless* society, in which all people are equal.

2. A *collective* society, in which all resources are publicly owned and employed for the nation's benefit.

3. A *cooperative* society, in which everyone lives, works, and sacrifices for the common good.

The ideological goals of China under Chairman Mao can thus be summed up in three words: *classless, collective,* and *cooperative.* Although the country did not achieve all three objectives, Chinese society came closer than any other communist nation in realizing its goals.

In the late 1970s, after the death of Mao, China underwent a change in political leadership. As a result, the nation's ideology has been somewhat modified. However, the economy continues to be characterized in varying degrees by certain special features, as explained in the following paragraphs.

Organization: Industry and Agriculture

One of the distinguishing characteristics of the Chinese economy is the way in which its industrial and agricultural sectors are organized. Both were gradually transformed from private to public ownership during the first decade of communist rule. Consequently, since 1960, almost all economic activities of any significance have been controlled by the state.

China's industrial and agricultural sectors are organized to facilitate central planning.

The organization of the industrial sector was patterned after the Soviet system. Ministries of production were created to serve as administrative agencies within individual industries or groups of industries. There is a Ministry of Electric Power, a Ministry of Steel, a Ministry of Textiles, and so on. In most cases, the various ministries are part of a complex network designed to direct government investment, production, and marketing plans—both nationally and locally. Although some degree of decentralization exists, its advantages are outweighed by bureaucratic structures that have been built up between the various ministries and enterprises. These have contributed significantly to the inefficiency and waste that are common in the administration of many industries and to the resulting losses in productivity that are reflected at all levels.

The agricultural sector, which provides China with most of its food and raw materials, is the foundation of the economy. A substantial part of agricultural activity is organized into communes. These are groups of villages that own their own land and assign production teams to farm it. The communes consume a portion of the output produced and sell the rest. State farms also exist, but these are government-owned enterprises operated as agricultural experiment stations for the purpose of developing new and improved farming methods.

To conclude:

China's industrial and agricultural sectors are organized in such a way as to facilitate centralized economic planning. A certain amount of decentralization exists: Enterprise managers are given limited discretion in determining prices, resource utilization, and output volumes, provided their decisions do not conflict with political ideology and national goals.

Planning Strategies and Experiences

Economic planning has occupied the attention of Chinese political leaders for decades. What have been the results of their efforts? This question can best be answered by sketching some of the highlights of China's recent planning experiences.

Efficiency

Because of limited consumer sovereignty and high underemployment, China has done poorly in achieving efficient resource allocation.

As you know, an economy is said to be economically or allocatively efficient when it has achieved maximum output with its available resources and is producing goods that consumers are willing and able to purchase. Does China's command economy meet this test of efficiency? The answer is *no*—for two major reasons:

1. In China, the production of most goods is determined by the state—not by consumers through their spending decisions. This is still true, even though the government has permitted somewhat freer markets since the late 1970s. Consequently, there is freedom of consumer choice, in that consumers can select from the goods available. But there is relatively little consumer sovereignty, because markets do not play a dominant role in relating consumer preferences to production decisions.

2. China suffers from considerable disguised unemployment, best termed *underemployment*. There are many reasons for this. For example, most of the labor force is unskilled and uneducated, making it difficult for workers to adapt to modern technology, even when it is available. Transportation facilities are largely primitive, slowing down the movement of goods and people. And restrictions are imposed on specialization and resource mobility, limiting the migration of workers between industries and between farms and cities.

Equity

In a capitalistic economy, the four classes of income payments are wages, rent, interest, and profit. In China, most rent and interest payments are confined to special state-determined uses for the purpose of influencing resource allocation. Profits, on the other hand, are encouraged. But they are either remitted to the state or used by enterprises for reinvestment and expansion and for incentive bonuses to workers and managers. Wages, therefore, remain the major form of income payment.

The government's policy has been to narrow inequalities in income over the years. This has been accomplished in various ways:

Despite reductions in class distinctions and the elimination of wide differences in income and wealth, there are still significant economic inequities among the people of China.

1. Properties of the rich were either confiscated or taxed away during the 1950s. Consequently, there is no wealthy class. Nor is there any destitute or impoverished class, because no one is permitted to fall below a minimum standard of living.

2. Various social benefits have been instituted. Among them are free education, health care, old-age homes, and retirement facilities. In addition, there are state-provided vocational, cultural, recreational, and child-care programs.

3. Price and wage policies designed to reduce class differences have been implemented. As a result, a discriminatory pricing system provides lower prices for "essential" goods and higher prices for nonessentials. In addition, the long-run goal of the wage policy is to reduce the gap between the lowest and highest wage rates by gradually increasing the lowest relative to the highest.

Although these accomplishments are noteworthy, they might paint an exaggerated picture of China's gains in equity. Many wide differences in income per capita still exist. Certain professionals and factory managers, for example, earn many times more than the average worker. And the average level of income in the urban sector is approximately four times higher than it is in the rural sector. Despite these disparities, however, China has made considerable progress toward eliminating the extremes of low and high incomes. Box 2 provides examples of this progress.

Stability

The achievement of relatively stable wages and prices has been one of the notable accomplishments of China's central planners. Stability has been attained through the coordination of several major policies:

China has achieved considerable price stability through the use of specific policies and controls.

1. Incentive Systems By the use of incentives, employees are continually encouraged to put forth their greatest productive effort. In addition, many enterprises have cooperative committees, which permit workers to participate with managers in decision-making activities. Taken together, all these measures are designed to stimulate productivity while maintaining stability (as explained in the following paragraphs) within the framework of China's ideological goals.

Box 2
China: Striving for
Efficiency and
Equity—with Tears

United Press International

Jill Hartley/Photo Researchers

China's struggle for greater efficiency has been impeded by many factors, cultural as well as economic. As a result, China must make do with a good deal of primitive capital and obsolete technology in the long struggle toward industrialization. Thus, bicycles, carts, horses, and manpower are the chief means of moving people and goods in the country's industrial areas. In addition, China lacks modern capital equipment to undertake most large-scale construction activity. Consequently, large numbers of workers are employed continuously to build dikes, canals, roads, and bridges.

In the struggle for equity, the nation's policies have had a profound influence on Chi-

nese society and culture. Never before in the country's long history have so many changes been made in such a short time. In the past few decades, legal equality was established between the sexes. Medical and sanitation facilities were greatly expanded in the cities and villages. Education was revised and extended by establishing full-time day schools, part-time evening and correspondence schools, and combined work-study programs. And language reform was undertaken to promote simplification and unification of China's many dialects, with the eventual goal of replacing the pictographic characters with more easily learned phonetic symbols. While China is still poor, compared with

Eric Kroll/Taurus Photos

United Press International

Eastfoto

Western nations, there is no doubt that most of its people have acquired more material necessities in the latter half of this century than they ever had in previous centuries.

However, these achievements have not been painless. China is still a monolithic, oppressive totalitarian state. Terror and brutalities exist (although they are often hidden), and life is controlled. Consequently, China, with its billion people, is a difficult country for Western democracies to understand. But it is a country that, in today's world, the developed nations are learning not to ignore.

Eastfoto

2. Wage–Price Policy Of course, gains in productivity result in declining unit labor costs and, therefore, in rising profit margins. How do China's planners distribute the benefits of higher profits? In two ways. One is by decreasing prices while keeping wages constant, thereby increasing workers' real incomes. The other is by investing a percentage of profits in new capital, thereby enlarging the base for achieving future gains in productivity and real income. China's wage–price policy thus consists of converting a portion of productivity improvements into higher real income. This is done partly by reducing prices and partly by raising wages.

3. Fiscal–Monetary Controls China's fiscal and monetary policies have helped considerably to maintain price stability. Fiscal control is exercised through the national budget, and most government expenditures are financed by taxes. Monetary control is exercised by the nation's central bank—the People's Bank of China. This institution holds accounts of all enterprises and determines the allocation of financial resources. Because the government limits deficit financing, minimizes borrowing from abroad, and maintains a stable money supply, much of the upward pressure on prices that prevails in mixed economies has been considerably less pronounced in China.

As pointed out earlier, none of these policies is pursued independently. All three are coordinated by China's planners to assure a high degree of wage–price stability.

Growth

China has managed to maintain favorable growth rates through heavy capital investment.

The Chinese regard capital investment as an important requirement for growth. Accordingly, China's planners have adhered to a low-wage policy—for two major reasons. One is to provide more funds for capital formation. The other is to minimize inflationary pressures by keeping the aggregate demand for consumer goods in line with the limited supply of such goods. The result of this policy has been a continuous high rate of capital investment. It is estimated to average between 30 and 40 percent of gross national product—and in some periods as high as 40 to 50 percent—compared with a range of only 10 to 20 percent for most mixed economies.

The consequence of China's investment planning has been a steady expansion of economic growth at an average rate of about 4 percent per year. This is approximately in line with long-run growth rates experienced by the United States and some other mixed economies. By Western standards, however, China is still a very poor country with a low average level of living. Whether Chinese leaders can turn their country into an economic superpower by the year 2000 depends on the nation's ability to adhere to an optimum policy capable of sustaining a high rate of growth.

The Four Modernizations and the Eight-Character Policy

In 1978, China's new leaders announced a monumentally ambitious plan designed to launch the nation into the twenty-first century. Called the Four Modernizations, the plan is a twenty-year blueprint for improving agriculture, industry, science, and the military. The details of the plan, including projected growth rates of production and real income, undergo frequent revisions. Nevertheless, the Four Modernizations, which China's news media have called "The New Long March," consists of three phases:

Phase 1 Nationwide mechanization of agriculture accompanied by a reorganization of industry.

Phase 2 Large and sustained annual increases in factory and in agricultural production.

Phase 3 Diversification of production, with greater emphasis on sophisticated consumer goods and such high-technology items as electronic products and computers. As for the military, it appears that this will be given the lowest priority in the overall plan for mechanization.

The first two phases were initially intended to be completed during the 1980s. The third phase was then to be initiated and completed by the end of this century. However, these plans have been revised many times since they were first introduced. Today the Four Modernizations is more of a philosophy than a formal plan. As the Chinese themselves (who are fond of slogans) put it, they prefer to adhere to the following Eight-Character Policy, which permits planning flexibility when needed:

China's overall planning objective has been to modernize and expand its agriculture and industry. But the means of achieving this goal have undergone frequent change.

READJUSTING
imbalances between
agriculture and industry

RESTRUCTURING
industrial management
and financial administration

CONSOLIDATING
factories to gain greater
economies of scale

IMPROVING
techniques of management,
technology, and production

These expressions, of course, are vague enough to fit any type of plan.

Conclusion: Limited Market Socialism

China, in 1978, thus made a complete turnaround from the previous thirty years of communist rule and isolation. In an effort to modernize itself and become an economic superpower by the year 2000, it has opened its doors to the advanced nations. Whether the turnaround will continue remains to be seen, for China is still a totalitarian nation with a somewhat divided leadership. Nevertheless, it is a nation whose economic system is now substantially different from the preceding one.

Today, China is making more use of the free market as a means of achieving planning goals.

China's current economic system may be described as limited market socialism. That is, most of the means of production are still owned by government. However:

• Cooperation and trade with foreign nations are recognized as important conditions for growth.

• Wages more closely match each worker's output, and profit-sharing bonuses are used as incentives for workers and managers.

• Managers make greater use of anticipated profits as a guide for determining what goods to produce and how to produce them.

• Government makes greater use of realized profits as a guide for allocating credit to particular industries.

Exhibit 4

Can China Catch Up?

(latest comparable data, 1980)

China's leaders announced their new plans for economic growth in 1978. But their chances of catching up to the USSR (not to mention the United States) by the year 2000 are practically zero.

For example, China's 1980 GNP must grow at an average annual rate of 5 percent in order to match the Soviet Union's 1980 GNP by the end of the century. The comparable growth rate needed to equal America's 1980 GNP is 8 percent. Therefore, for China to realize even *half* of its stated goal by the year 2000 would require some sort of economic miracle.

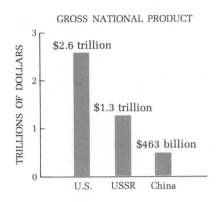

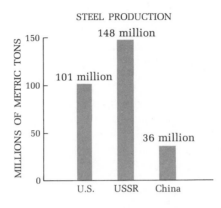

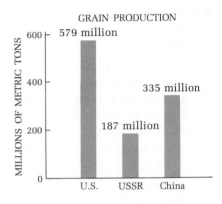

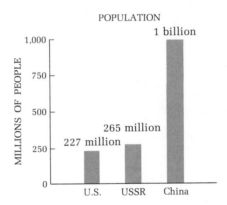

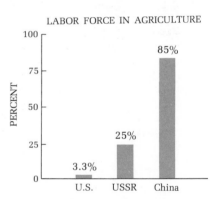

Sources: Central Intelligence Agency; U.S. Department of Commerce; Joint Economic Committee of Congress.

China's political leaders, it is said, are always looking for a quick solution to complex economic problems. At present, they are focusing on rapid modernization. But the difficulties of achieving their desired goals are likely to be much greater than they and their economic planners imagine.

For example, the nation's GNP must grow considerably faster than the average annual rate of 4 percent experienced thus far. In addition, the country must maintain political stability, curb population growth, and greatly improve productive efficiency in agriculture and manufacturing. Otherwise, China will be unable to expand exports in those commodities in which it has relative advantages over competing nations. Hence, it will not be able to earn the funds necessary to import modern plant and equipment from other countries.

These facts, as well as those presented in Exhibit 4, are a few of the hard realities that China must face as it attempts to race toward modernization.

The Convergence Hypothesis:
A Meeting of East and West?

> The only choice is either bourgeois or socialist ideology. There is no middle course.
>
> V. I. Lenin

Is this view of Lenin's really true? Some scholars in both the East and West think not. They believe in a *convergence hypothesis*. This hypothesis proposes that capitalism and communism, driven by the process of industrialization, will eventually merge to form a new kind of society. In it, the personal freedoms and profit motive of Western capitalistic democracies will blend with the government controls that exist in a communistic (especially in the Soviet) economy.

Some scholars predict that a rapprochement between East and West will inevitably occur.

Perhaps the most dramatic statement of this rapprochement between East and West was made some years ago by the distinguished Soviet physicist Andrei Sakharov. In a 10,000-word essay that was smuggled to the West, he wrote:

> The continuing economic progress being achieved under capitalism should be a fact of great theoretical significance for any dogmatic Marxist. It is precisely this fact that lies at the basis of peaceful coexistence and it suggests, in principle, that if capitalism ever runs into an economic blind alley it will not necessarily have to leap into a desperate military adventure. Both capitalism and socialism are capable of long-term development, borrowing positive elements from each other and actually coming closer to each other in a number of essential aspects.

The only hope for world peace, Sakharov concluded, was a coalescence of socialistic and capitalistic systems. Otherwise, we stand on the brink of disaster.

Three Basic Assumptions

The convergence hypothesis, of course, is an adaptation of the familiar Marxian doctrine that economic forces determine a nation's political and social development. But it departs from orthodox Marxism by challenging the conviction that communism is the only route to attaining the highest form of social evolution. Thus, in the simplest sense, the key factor is the ongoing process of industrialization. As former Harvard economist John Kenneth Galbraith put it years ago, advancing technology has different implications for the United States and for the Soviet Union. In the United States, it must lead to increased intellectual curiosity and freedom; in the USSR, it must lead to much greater government planning and control.

The institutional and cultural differences between East and West are probably too great to allow convergence to occur.

The convergence hypothesis rests on three basic assumptions:

1. Industrialization leads to urbanization and to many common challenges of effective resource organization and management. The skills, training, and desires of a steel worker in Pittsburgh are not significantly different from those of one in Magnitogorsk. Hence the two workers tend to evolve toward a similar way of life.

2. Industrialization inevitably produces a more complex society with problems of specialization and exchange that are common to all advanced economies.

3. Industrialization raises living standards and improves economic well-being. This, in turn, leads to intellectual independence and probably to ideological nonconformity.

Conclusion: Many Gaps Remain

On the basis of these assumptions, there appear to be more surface similarities today between the United States and the USSR than there were several decades ago. Thus, in order to make its economy work better, the United States has accepted a degree of "socialism" and welfare statism that in the more distant past would have been unthinkable. The Soviet Union, on the other hand, has followed a policy of greater freedom and decentralization since the mid-1960s.

Are we to conclude from this that the convergence hypothesis is becoming a reality? The answer is *no*:

> Even if communism is capable of achieving its economic goals, the evidence does not show that the political and social objectives of the United States are anywhere present in communist countries. Therefore, even if the Soviet Union and the United States actually do come closer in the economic sphere, there are still major if not unbridgeable gaps between the traditions, value systems, and goals of the two societies.

Case
China: "The New Long March"

> The Chinese people's march toward the great goal of the Four Modernizations echos from the foothills of the Yenshan Mountains to the shores of the Yellow Sea to all corners of the world. It has aroused worldwide attention. We are setting out to conquer on our New Long March the mountains, seas, plains, oilfields and mines of our motherland. We want to scale the heights of science and technology. We want to develop normal trade relations with other countries of the world.
>
> The Beijing *People's Daily*

To achieve their goals, China's leaders have embarked on a dramatic and ambitious journey. The new doctrine does not represent an abandonment of, but rather a retreat from, the repressive communist ideology that prevailed from 1949 to 1978.

Thus, the once sacred goals of national self-reliance and independence from outside resources are now gone. In their place, China's leaders have instituted new forms of "market socialism." For example:

• Greater initiative and autonomy are encouraged at the level of individual enterprise.

• Realistic pricing practices designed to allocate goods and resources are being implemented in certain industries.

• Steady wage increases, bonuses, paid vacations, and other material incentives are being employed to spur greater production and productivity.

• Thousands of students and plant managers are being sent to Japan and the advanced Western democracies to study "capitalistic" technology and management methods. In addition, huge contracts are being signed with major firms in these countries to set up new plants in China.

• Tourists are encouraged to visit China and to exchange cultural experiences. China now hosts hundreds of thousands of tourists annually, compared to a relative handful prior to 1978.

Chinese newspaper headline translates: "The New Long March."

"Take advantage of every moment to race to the year 2000."

Paolo Koch/Photo Researchers

What do China's leaders promise the people in return for their efforts? A higher material standard of living—a greater quantity and variety of consumer goods—than the nation has ever had. Ideally, this will also be accompanied by more political and social freedoms than the Chinese have hitherto experienced.

The ultimate goal of China's modernization plans is to achieve a higher material standard of living. Large quantities and wide varieties of consumer goods are thus being introduced to a much greater extent than ever before.

Eastfoto

James Andanson/Sygma

China has invited an economic invasion by Western democracies. Pierre Cardin has been hired to design high-fashion clothing. Coca-Cola is being sold throughout much of the country. U.S. Steel is helping to build giant iron-ore refining facilities. Pan American Airways is developing a luxury hotel chain. The Japanese and Germans are building steel mills and chemical plants. The British are supplying industrial equipment. The Dutch are providing port facilities. The Swedes are constructing railroads. And the French are developing telecommunications satellites and nuclear power plants. Meanwhile, the Chinese are learning English and other foreign languages in an effort to establish closer contact with the formerly "barbaric" foreigners.

Wide World Photos

Eric Kroll/Taurus Photos

Agricultural development has one of the highest priorities in China's plans. Most farms are organized into communes. These are groups of villages that own their own land and assign production teams to farm it. The communes consume a proportion of the output and sell the rest. Because the organization of most communes is relatively primitive, the greatest difficulties will be encountered in trying to mechanize them. The Chinese, however, expect to achieve this goal by the mid-1990s.

An Optimum Economic Policy

What steps should China take to assure a steady and self-sustaining expansion of GNP?

China's long-run policy should seek to accomplish three major goals:

1. *Reduce Population Growth:* This requires organized educational birth-control programs on a national scale.

2. *Improve Agricultural Efficiency:* This requires the adoption of new technology and practices, such as the use of improved seeds, fertilizers, pesticides, and farm equipment.

3. *Expand Foreign Trade:* This requires specializing in the production of labor-intensive commodities embracing a wide array of agricultural and handicraft products, along the lines dictated by the law of comparative advantage.

China's economic planners, in varying degrees, have been pursuing these objectives for many years. Whether the country's leadership, however, is capable of sustaining a large-scale organized effort in this direction for the next several decades remains to be seen.

What You Have Learned in This Chapter

1. Countries engage in economic planning to achieve specific economic goals. The chief ones are efficiency, equity, stability, and growth.

2. Among the basic tools of scientific economic planning are econometrics and input–output analysis. These techniques are gaining increasing use by corporations as well as by governments. Some mixed as well as some command economies use these methods for planning purposes.

3. Since the late 1920s, the Soviet system has been a command economy. Its primary objective has been to raise itself to the status of a major industrial and military power. Through state ownership of industry and extensive planning, it has succeeded in achieving these goals. But its citizens have paid a heavy cost in terms of deprivation of consumer goods and lack of political and economic freedoms.

4. Chinese leaders, in their formal planning efforts, are emphasizing a high rate of investment in heavy industry, accompanied by a reorganization of agriculture to achieve greater efficiency in food and raw-materials production. Despite some serious setbacks, the long-run growth of China's GNP has been reasonably satisfactory—averaging about 4 percent annually. China's ability to sustain or increase this rate of expansion will depend on whether it can maintain political stability, curb population growth, improve agricultural productivity, and expand exports in those commodities in which it has comparative advantages—such as agricultural and handicraft products.

5. Some observers contend that the process of industrialization must lead eventually to a convergence of communism and capitalism—a meeting of East and West. Even if this hypothesis were valid on economic grounds, which is doubtful, it overlooks the traditions and goals that make the USSR and the United States vastly different in their institutions and value systems.

For Discussion

1. *Terms and concepts to review:*
economic plan
planned economy
efficiency
economic growth
econometrics
input–output analysis
state farms
collective farms
coefficient of relative effectiveness (CRE)
underemployment
convergence hypothesis

2. In terms of goals, political leaders often place a higher priority on equity than on efficiency, stability, or growth. Can you suggest why?

3. Fill in the required data, including the input coefficients, for the accompanying input–output table.

(a) Suppose that there is a 10 percent increase in foreign demand for manufactured goods. Would any of the numbers in the table be affected? Explain.

Input–Output Table for an Economy (millions of dollars; hypothetical data)

Output (sellers) \ Input (buyers)	Agricultural sector	Manufacturing sector	Service sector	Intersector sales total	All other sales	Total output
Agricultural sector	$100 ( )	$200 ( )	$50 ( )		$150	
Manufacturing sector	$300 ( )	$400 ( )	$200 ( )		$100	
Service sector	$50 ( )	$150 ( )	$100 ( )		$100	
Other resources	$50 ( )	$250 ( )	$50 ( )			
Total input					$350	

(b) Would other sectors of the economy be affected by an increase in foreign demand for manufactured goods? Does it make any difference if the manufacturing sector is operating at full capacity or at less than full capacity? Discuss.

(c) In terms of your answer to part (b), can you explain why an input–output table may serve as a model to depict an economy in general equilibrium?

4. Since the USSR is a centrally directed and collectivist economy, there is no competition as in American capitalism. True or false? Explain.

5. Why would a socialist economy, such as that of the USSR, want to employ the capitalistic device of providing economic incentives? What types of incentives do they use?

6. Is there freedom of consumer choice in the USSR? Is there consumer sovereignty? Explain.

7. Which would you suggest as a better guide for judging the efficiency of firms in the United States and in the USSR—profits or sales? What are some of the assumptions underlying your answer?

8. What criteria would you use in judging whether one nation's economy is better than another's? Are there noneconomic criteria, too?

9. Why do the Soviet authorities want to engage in the complex and difficult task of planning? Why do they not simply let a free-market system allocate the resources and distribute the income for them?

10. What are some of the "capitalistic" practices that the USSR has adopted over the years? Do the Soviets view these as a step toward capitalism? Explain.

11. What is the economic function of profits, and of the anticipation of profits, in a market economy? In the Chinese economy?

12. There is considerable evidence that, in advanced Western societies and even in the USSR, the use of material incentives serves to spur worker productivity and thereby to encourage greater output. In view of this, why did Chinese leaders under communism (prior to 1978) usually oppose the use of material incentives?

Acknowledgements

Part I p. xxviii
  © Joel Gordon, 1975

Introduction p. 2
  Thomas Banchoff and David Salesin

Chapter 1 p. 11
  Andrew Popper/Picture Group

Chapter 2 p. 34
  Ken Love/Black Star

Chapter 3 p. 53
  © Beryl Goldberg, 1982

Chapter 4 p. 71
  Dennis Brack/Black Star

Part 2 p. 94
  Doug Wilson/Black Star

Chapter 5 p. 96
  Frank Fisher/Liaison Photo Agency

Chapter 6 p. 115
  Andrew Sacks/Black Star

Chapter 7 p. 135
  Bob East III/Picture Group

Chapter 8 p. 157
  Jan Lukas/Photo Researchers

Chapter 9 p. 172
  Dennis Brack/Black Star

Part 3 p. 198
  Fred Ward/Black Star

Chapter 10 p. 200
  Edward Klamm/Black Star

Chapter 11 p. 219
  Paolo Koch/Photo Researchers

Chapter 12 p. 240
  Courtesy Federal Reserve Bank of
  New York

Chapter 13 p. 256
  Sybil Shelton/Peter Arnold

Part 4 p. 276
  John Neubauer/Alpha, FPG

Chapter 14 p. 278
  Tom Nebbia/DPI

Chapter 15 p. 298
  Gregory Heisler/Liaison Photo
  Agency

Chapter 16 p. 323
  Teri Leigh Stratford/Photo
  Researchers

Chapter 17 p. 348
  Charles Marden Fitch/FPG

Part 5 p. 372
  Leif Skoogfors/Woodfin Camp

Chapter 18 p. 374
  Bryce Flynn/Picture Group

Supplement p. 400
  Arnold Zann/Black Star

Chapter 19 p. 412
  © Beryl Goldberg, 1982

Supplement p. 423
  Jan Lukas/Photo Researchers

Chapter 20 p. 432
  George Hunter/Alpha, FPG

Part 6 p. 452
  Eli Heller/Picture Group

Chapter 21 p. 454
  Joe Munroe

Supplement p. 474
  David Strick/Black Star

Chapter 22 p. 487
  Jack Spratt/Picture Group

Chapter 23 p. 505
  Alvis Upitis/Black Star

Chapter 24 p. 526
  Charles Schneider/FPG

Chapter 25 p. 538
  Dave Repp/Photo Researchers

Chapter 26 p. 557
  Robert M. Mottar/Photo Researchers

Part 7 p. 575
  Paolo Koch/Photo Researchers

Chapter 27 p. 576
  George Gerster/Photo Researchers

Chapter 28 p. 598
  Frank Fisher/Liaison Photo Agency

Chapter 29 p. 629
  United Press International

Chapter 30 p. 652
  Sepp Seitz/Woodfin Camp

Chapter 31 p. 672
  Sepp Seitz/Woodfin Camp

Chapter 32 p. 696
  David Moore/Black Star

Part 8 p. 714
  M. E. Warren/Photo Researchers

Chapter 33 p. 716
  Hedrich-Blessing/FPG

Chapter 34 p. 734
  Hiroyuki Matsumoto/Black Star

Chapter 35 p. 754
  Steve Allen/Peter Arnold

Chapter 36 p. 778
  Joseph Nettis/FPG

Chapter 37 p. 801
  Dan Porges/Peter Arnold

Chapter 38 p. 827
  Lee Lockwood/Black Star

Index

Budget
  deficits and surpluses, 79, 181–184, 190–192
  line (indifference curves), 424
  management, 181–184, 190–192
  policies, 184, 190–192
Budgeting, 78–80
Bureaucracy, 586
  economics of, 587–589
Business-cycle forecasting, methods of, 119–121
Business cycles, 115–122
Business monopoly, 599
Businesses
  organization of, 65–67
  size of, 67–68
Business unionism, 632

C

Cameralism, 750
Capital account in balance of payments, 731–732
Capital
  accumulation of, and growth, 306
  as a factor of production, 12
Capital consumption allowance, 107
Capital deepening, 319
Capitalism, 23, 25–28
  "death" of, Issue, 824–825
Capital-intensity criterion, 790
Capital market, 207–209
Capital-output ratio, 310–311
Carol, Robin, 597
Carroll, Lewis, 701
Celler Antimerger Act, 604
Certificates of deposit (CDs), negotiable, 206
Chamberlin, Edward Hastings, Leader in Economics, 520
Change in amount consumed, 147
Changes in consumption, 147
Checkable deposits, 201–202, 205
Checkoff, 642
China
  economic planning in, 845–852, 854–856
  limited market socialism in, 851–852
Christian socialism, 805
CIO, 634
Circular flow of economic activity, 28
  limitations of model of, 29–30
Circular merger, 604
Clark, John Bates, Leaders in Economics, 536
Classical economics
  definition of, 139
  essentials of, 137–139
  Keynesian response to, 139–140
Classical economists, Portfolio, 154
Classical theory in international economics, 745–747
Class struggle, 809–810
Clayton Antitrust Act, 600
Closed shop, 636, 641

Coalition bargaining, 643
Coincident indicators, 121
Collective agreement, 638, 639–641
Collective bargaining, 637–645
Collective decision making, 78–80
Collective goods. See Public goods
Command economy, 20
Commercial bank, 209–210
Commercial paper, 206
Commodity-futures market, 400–411
  basis in, 403, 409
  economics of, 407
  hedging in, 404–409
  margin buying in, 403
  speculation in, 408–409
  trading examples in, 401–402, 404–407
  trading floor of, 410
Common market, 762
Communism, Marxian, 811
Communist Manifesto, 803–804
Comparative advantage, 351–352, 719–722
  free trade and, 357–358
  law of, 351–352, 722
Comparative statics, 559
Compensation of employees, 55
Compensatory transactions in balance of payments, 740
Competition, as an institution of capitalism, 26
Competitive industries in business cycles, 118
Competitive wage model, 540
Complementary goods, 43
  cross elasticity of, 391
Composition, fallacy of, 6
Comptroller of the Currency, 216
Concentration ratio, 515, 616
  aggregrate, 618
  critique of, 616–618
Conciliation, 645
Congestion charges, 590
Conglomerate merger, 604, 608–611
Congress of Industrial Organizations, 634
Conscious parallel action, 606
Consent decree, 605
Conspiracies, 606
Constant dollars, GNP in, 97–98
Consumer equilibrium and utility equations, 415–417
Consumer price index, 128–129
Consumer sovereignty, 47
Consumer's surplus, 418–419
Consumption, 142
  change in, 147
  change in amount of, 147
Consumption function, 143
Contestable market, 516
Contributive standard, 62
  in general equilibrium, 568
Convergence hypothesis, 853–854
Cooperative planning, 82
Corporate profits, 55
Corporation, definition of, 66
Corporation income tax, 85–86

Correspondence principle, 563
Cost-effectiveness analysis and environmental policies, 705
Cost-push inflation, 127–129
Costs
  economic, 434
  explicit, 434
  implicit, 434
  long-run, 435–436, 438–442
  and normal profit, 434
  opportunity, 433
  outlay, 433
  short-run, 435–436, 438–442
Cotton gin, 309
Countervailing power, 516
Craft union, 630, 646
Crawling pegs, 772
Credit, 736
  in balance-of-payments, 358–360
Credit instrument, 205
Creeping inflation, 128
Cross elasticity of demand, 390–393
Cross-licensing, 614
Crowding out, 182, 186, 195, 293–294
Currency, 201, 205
Current account in balance of payments, 731
Current dollars, GNP in, 97–98
Customer loan demands, 234
Customs union, 761–762
Cyclically balanced budget, 190
Cyclical unemployment, 123

D

Davenport, Henry J., 561
Death taxes, 86
Debit, 736
  in balance of payments, 358–360
Debt-management guidelines, 196
Debt, public, economics of, 192–195
Decentralized school systems, 675
Declining value of the dollar, 131
Decreasing-cost industry, 592
"Defending the dollar," 764
Deficit, budget, 79
Deflating GNP, 97–98
Demand, 34–38
  and buyers' incomes, 42
  and change in quantity demanded, 41
  change in, 42, 46–47
  curve, 35–36
  definition of, 35
  expectations, 43
  law of, 36
  market, 38
  nonmonetary factors and, 44
  price and, 36
  schedule, 35
Demand and supply, review of, 375
Demand curve and indifference curves, 429–430
Demand deposit, 201, 205
Demand price, 76, 418

Demand-pull inflation, 127
Dennison, Edward, 312
Deposit banking, 219–239
Deposit contraction, 229–230
Deposit expansion, 222–230
    by the banking system, 224–227
    by a single bank, 222–224
Deposit-expansion multiplier, 227–228
Depository Institutions Deregulation and
    Monetary Control Act, 222
Depreciation
    of foreign exchange, 769
    in national income accounting, 105, 107
Deregulation in supply-side economics,
    334–335
Devaluation, 368, 757–759, 765–766
Dialectical materialism, 807
Differentiated products, 506
Diminishing marginal utility, 414–415
Diminishing returns, law of, 436–438
Direct-payments plan and energy policy,
    700
Direct tax, 90
"Dirty floating," 367, 749, 767–768
Discount, 603
Discount rate, 242–243
Discouraged workers, 123
Discretionary fiscal policy, 181–188
    evaluation of, 185–188
Discrimination
    price, 602
    by race and sex, 668–670
Diseconomies of scale, 445–447
Disequilibrium, 41
"Dismal science," 315–321
Disposable income, 109
Dissolution, 605
Diversified-economy argument, 727
Dividend, 66
Division, fallacy of, 6
Division of labor, 14–15
Dollar shortage, 763
Dollar surplus, 763
Domestic-exchange equations, 349–350
Double counting, 98
Drug regulations, 623
Dual banking system, 215–216
Dual labor market, 667
Duopoly, 512–514
DuPont Cellophane case, 396
Durable-goods industries in business cy-
    cles, 118
Dynamic model, 394, 560

E

Econometrics, 120, 829–832
Economic cost, 434
Economic development, 779–797
    definition of, 779–780
    fashions in, 791
    international aspects of, 793–797
    principles of, 785–793
    stages of, 781–785

Economic efficiency. *See* Efficiency
Economic goals, 15–18
    conflicts and trade-offs between, 18–19
Economic good, 19
Economic growth. *See* Growth
Economic indicators, 120
Economic interpretation of history, 806–
    807
Economic man, 25
Economic plan, 827
Economic planning, 827–856
    in China, 845–852, 854–856
    goals of, 828–829
    stagflation policy and, 344–345
    tools for, 829–836
    in USSR, 836–845
Economic regulation, 621
Economic rent, 543
    models of, 544–545
    Ricardo on, *Reading,* 556
Economic system, 3
Economics, 3
Economies of scale, 445–447
Education, 312
    financing of, 675–676
    market for, 674–677
    reform of, 677
Efficiency
    economic, 16–17
    as an economic goal, 15–17
    general equilibrium and, 568
    technical, 15–16
Eight-Character Policy, 850–852
Elasticity
    cross, 390–393
    income, 388–390
    price, 374–383
Emission fees, 706
Employment discrimination, 669–670
Employment-protection argument, 728
Employment ratio, 124
Employment-training policies, 339–340,
    667–668
Energy policies, 696–701
Engels, Friedrich, 812
Enterprise zones, 694
Entrepreneurship, as a factor of produc-
    tion, 13
Environmental policies, 701–712
    benefit-cost analysis and, 704
    cost-effectiveness analysis and, 705
    marginal analysis and, 703
    property rights and, 710–712
Equality standard, 64
Equation of exchange, 257–258
Equilibrium, 557–572
    price and quantity, 41
    stability of, 558–561
    See also General equilibrium, Partial
    equilibrium
Equity
    as an economic goal, 17
    in income distribution, 17
    in taxation, 87–90

Eurocurrency, 769–770
Eurodollars, 203, 205
European Common Market, 762
European Recovery Program, 760–761
Evans, Oliver, 309
Excess reserves, 222
Exchange controls, 369, 747–749
Excise taxes, 86
Exclusion principle, 73
    in public-goods theory, 577–582
Exclusive (tying) contracts, 602
Expectations and market demand, 43
Expectations theory, 327–329
Expenditure multiplier, 176
Explicit cost, 433, 434
Exports and imports, 349
External economies of scale, 446–447
Externalities, 74

F

Fabian socialism, 803
Factors of production, 12–14
    functional classification of, 13–14
    returns to owners of, 13–14
Fallacies in reasoning, 5, 6
False-cause fallacy, 5
Family-allowance plan, 660
Fawcett, Millicent Garrett, 156
FDIC, 216
Feasible region, 238
Featherbedding, 636, 646
Federal Advisory Council, 215
Federal agency notes, 206
Federal Deposit Insurance Corporation,
    216
Federal funds, 207
Federal-funds rate and monetarist policy,
    294
Federalism, 632
Federal Open-Market Committee, 215
Federal Reserve Bank, 214
Federal Reserve System, 211–215
    organization and functions of, 213–215
Federal Trade Commission Act, 600–603
Feigen, Bernard, 595
Feldstein, Martin, 334
Financial intermediaries, 209–211
Financial markets, 204–209
Financing local government, 686–695
Firm, 65
Fiscal dividends, 180
Fiscal drag, 180
Fiscalism, 279–280, 291, 293
    unresolved issues in, 289–291
Fiscal-monetary issues, 279–296
Fiscal policy, 172–196
    evaluation of, 187–189
    formulas for, 176–177
    multiplier effects and, 185–186
    public choice and, 187
    timing and, 185
Fisher, Irving, *Leaders in Economics,* 261
Fitch, John, 309

Dictionary of Economic Terms and Concepts

This Dictionary includes the definitions of every technical word, phrase, and concept given in the text, as well as definitions of many other terms of significance in economics. It also presents cross references and brief examples that explain the significance of important terms. Hence the Dictionary will be a convenient and permanent source of reference—not only for this course, but for future courses you may take in economics, other social sciences, and business.

A

ability-to-pay principle: Theory of taxation that holds that the fairest tax is based on the financial means of the taxpayer—regardless of any benefit he or she may receive from the tax. Financial means may be determined by either wealth or income. The U.S. personal income tax is founded on this idea.

absolute advantage, law of: Principle that states that a basis for trade exists between nations or regions when each of them, as a result of natural or acquired superiorities, can provide a good or service that the other wants at a lower cost than if each were to provide it for itself. This law accounts for much of the world's trade.

absolute-income hypothesis: Proposition that states that a family's propensity to consume (that is, the amount it spends on consumption) depends on its *level* of income—the absolute amount available for spending. This concept of the propensity to consume was the one used by Keynes. (*Contrast with* **relative-income hypothesis; permanent-income hypothesis.**)

acceleration curves: Short-run inflation–unemployment relationships showing how the inflation rate speeds up with expansionary fiscal–monetary policies and slows down with contractionary ones. (*See* **Phillips curve.**)

accelerator principle: Proposition that net investment in capital goods depends upon *changes* in the level of output (that is, GNP). This is because capital goods are durable. Therefore, if existing production capacity is adequate, it is possible to produce a constant level of output with existing equipment, replacing it as it wears out. No net investment needs to be undertaken. But if aggregate demand increases, the economy, operating at full capacity, will have to undertake additional investment in order to produce an increase in output. Therefore, net investment is a function of *changes* in the level of output. Thus:

$$\text{net investment} = \text{accelerator} \times \text{change in GNP}$$

and hence

$$\text{accelerator} = \frac{\text{net investment}}{\text{change in GNP}}$$

The accelerator itself is a mathematical constant—a number such as 1.0, 1.5, 2.0, and so on—that is estimated by statistical procedures.

accounts payable: A company's debts to suppliers of goods or services.

accounts receivable: Amounts due to a firm from customers.

accrued expenses payable: Obligations, such as wages and salaries, interest on borrowed funds, and pensions.

adjustable peg: System that permits governmentally controlled changes in the par rate of foreign exchange after a nation has had long-run disequilibrium in its balance of payments. It allows also for short-run variations within a narrow range of a few percent around the par value.

ad valorem subsidy: Fixed percentage subsidy based on the price or value of a commodity.

ad valorem tax: Fixed percentage tax on the price or value of a commodity. *Examples:* sales taxes, property taxes, and most import duties.

aggregate concentration ratio: A measure of the relative size of firms within a large segment of the economy. The ratio measures the percentage share of sales, assets, value added, profits, employment (or any other indicator of size) accounted for by the largest firms across entire sectors or subsectors of the economy. The "largest firms" may range from a few dozen to several hundred, depending on the size of the sector being measured. (*Contrast with* **concentration ratio.**)

aggregate demand: Total value of output that all sectors of the economy are willing to purchase at any given time or level of income.

aggregate supply: Total value of output produced or available for purchase by the economy at any given time or level of income.

Agricultural Adjustment Act (1938): Basic farm law (with subsequent amendments) of the United States. It has, at various times, provided for (1) price supports of selected farm products at specified levels; (2) production control through acreage allotments of certain crops; (3) marketing agreements and quotas between the Department of Agriculture and producers in order to control the distribution of selected commodities; (4) payments to farmers and others who follow approved soil conservation practices; and (5) parity payments to farmers for selected agricultural staples.

allocative efficiency: *See* **efficiency.**

Aluminum Company of America (Alcoa) case (1945): Major antitrust case against Alcoa. The company was the dominant firm in aluminum production, accounting for 90 percent of the nation's output. Even though Alcoa did not aggressively seek to attain a monopoly, but rather found that monopoly had been "thrust upon" the company, it was a "passive beneficiary" of monopoly, according to Judge Learned Hand, who therefore found the company in violation of the Sherman Antitrust Act. This stringent interpretation was thus contrary to the traditional *rule of reason* that had prevailed since the Standard Oil case of 1911. As it happened, Judge Hand's rigid interpretation was greatly tempered in subsequent antitrust cases, and has not been strictly applied since 1945.

American Federation of Labor–Congress of Industrial Organizations (AFL–CIO): League of labor unions formed in 1955 by a merger of the AFL and CIO. Its purposes are to improve the wages, hours, and conditions of workers and to realize the benefits of free collective bargaining. It exercises no authority or control over member unions other than requiring them to abide by its constitution and code of ethical practices.

American Tobacco case (1911): Major antitrust case in which the Supreme Court found the "tobacco trust" to be in violation of the Sherman Act. The trust consisted of five major tobacco manufacturers controlling 95 percent of domestic cigarette production. However, the Court did not condemn the trust for that fact. It was the trust's "unreasonable" market behavior,

driving competitors out of business, that caused the Court's condemnation.

annually balanced budget: Philosophy that holds that total revenues and expenditures in the government's budget should be balanced or brought into equality every year.

antitrust laws: Acts passed by Congress since 1890 to prevent monopoly and to maintain competition. The chief ones are (1) the Sherman Antitrust Act (1890); (2) the Clayton Antitrust Act (1914); (3) the Federal Trade Commission Act (1914); (4) the Robinson–Patman Act (1936); (5) the Wheeler–Lea Act (1938); and (6) the Celler Antimerger Act (1950).

Aquinas, St. Thomas (1225–1274): Medieval philosopher who wrote on economic problems during the early stages of modern capitalism. He attempted to harmonize reason with faith by applying principles of Aristotelian philosophy to biblical teaching and canonical dogma. Thus he held that the individual's right to private property accords with natural law; commerce is to be condoned to the extent that it maintains the household and benefits the country; fairness and truthfulness in commercial dealings are essential virtues; and so on. In general, these and other ideas of Aquinas make him one of the important leaders in early economic thought.

arbitrage: Act of buying a commodity in one market and simultaneously selling it in a dearer market at a higher price. Arbitrage tends to equalize prices of a commodity in different markets, except for differences in the costs of transportation, risk, and so on.

arbitration: Settlement of differences between parties (such as a union and management) by the use of an impartial third party called an arbitrator who is acceptable to both sides and whose decision is binding and legally enforceable on the contesting parties. The arbitrator issues a decision based not on what he thinks is wise and fair but on how he thinks the language of the contract applies to the case. (*Contrast with* **mediation.**)

Arrow, Kenneth Joseph (1921–): Leading American economist and Nobel laureate (1972). He is noted for his work in welfare economics, mathematical programming, and growth theory. Arrow served on the President's Council of Economic Advisors in 1962 and has been on the faculties of the University of Chicago, Harvard University, and Stanford University.

Arrow's impossibility theorem: Proposition that proves that no voting system is perfect because group decisions cannot be both rational and fair. The reason is that five conditions are needed to meet all requirements of rationality and fairness: (1) the voter must be able to rank alternatives in a consistent manner; (2) the voter must be free to choose any possible ranking of alternatives; (3) the voting outcome must please as many people as possible while displeasing as few as possible; (4) no individual may dictate a decision to the voting group; and (5) the voting system must preserve the ranking of a given set of alternatives if there is added to it another set of alternatives. Arrow's theorem demonstrates that, because of logical inconsistencies, these conditions cannot be applied simultaneously. Therefore, it is impossible to construct a "perfect" voting system—one that is completely rational and fair.

assets: Resources or things of value owned by an economic entity, such as an individual, household, or firm. *Examples:* cash, property, and the rights to property.

automatic fiscal stabilizers: Nondiscretionary or "built-in" features that automatically cushion recession by helping to create a budget deficit and curb inflation by helping to create a budget surplus. *Examples:* (1) income tax receipts; (2) unemployment taxes and benefits; (3) agricultural price supports; and (4) corporate dividend policies.

automatic transfer services (ATS): A combined interest-bearing savings and zero-balance checking account offered by many banks. When a check written against the account is presented for payment, the bank switches the necessary funds from savings to checking. A more apt description, therefore, would be automatic transfer *of savings* (rather than *services*). ATS accounts are one of several forms of savings-type checkable deposits.

autonomous consumption: Consumption independent of income. It is the part of total consumption that is unrelated to income. (*Compare* **induced consumption.**)

autonomous investment: Investment independent of income, output, and general economic activity. (*Compare* **induced investment.**)

autonomous transactions: Settlements among nations that arise from factors unrelated to the balance of payments as such. The main classes are merchandise trade and services, long-term capital movements, and unilateral transfers.

average-cost price: See **full-cost price.**

average fixed cost: Ratio of a firm's total fixed cost to the quantity it produces. Also, the difference between average total cost and average variable cost. Thus,

$$\text{average fixed cost} = \frac{\text{total fixed cost}}{\text{quantity of output}}$$

Also,

average fixed cost = average total cost
$$- \text{ average variable cost}$$

average–marginal relationship: Mathematical relationship between all corresponding average and marginal curves. The relationship is such that: when an average curve is rising, its corresponding marginal curve is above it; when an average curve is falling, its corresponding marginal curve is below it; and when an average curve is either at a maximum or at a minimum, its corresponding marginal curve intersects (is equal to) it.

average product: Ratio of total output or product to the amount of variable input needed to produce that volume of output. Thus,

$$\text{average product} = \frac{\text{total product}}{\text{variable input}}$$

average propensity to consume: Ratio of consumption to income:

$$\text{average propensity to consume} = \frac{\text{consumption}}{\text{income}}$$

It thus reveals the proportion of income that is spent on consumption.

average propensity to save: Ratio of saving to income:

$$\text{average propensity to save} = \frac{\text{saving}}{\text{income}}$$

It thus reveals the proportion of income that is saved (that is, not spent on consumption).

average revenue: Ratio of a firm's total revenue to its quantity of output sold—or, equivalently, its price per unit of quantity sold. Thus,

average revenue
$$= \frac{\text{total revenue}}{\text{quantity}} = \frac{(\text{price})(\cancel{\text{quantity}})}{\cancel{\text{quantity}}} = \text{price}$$

average revenue product: Ratio of total revenue to the quantity of an input employed. Thus,

$$\text{average revenue product} = \frac{\text{total revenue}}{\text{quantity of input employed}}$$

average tax rate: Ratio or percentage of a total tax to the base on which it is imposed. *Example:*

average personal income tax rate
$$= \frac{\text{total personal income tax}}{\text{total taxable income}}$$

average total cost: Ratio of a firm's total cost to the quantity it produces. Also, the sum of average fixed cost and average variable cost. Thus,

$$\text{average total cost} = \frac{\text{total cost}}{\text{quantity of output}}$$

Also,

average total cost
$$= \text{average fixed cost} + \text{average variable cost}$$

average variable cost: Ratio of a firm's total variable cost to the quantity it produces. Also, the difference between a firm's average total cost and average fixed cost. Thus,

$$\text{average variable cost} = \frac{\text{total variable cost}}{\text{quantity of output}}$$

Also,

average variable cost
$$= \text{average total cost} - \text{average fixed cost}$$

B

Bain index: Measure of a firm's monopoly power, based on the divergence between price, P, and average total cost, ATC. A modified version of the index in which the divergence is expressed as a proportion of price is

$$\text{Bain index} = \frac{P - ATC}{P}$$

The index will be zero (no monopoly power) when the firm is earning only normal profit (that is, $P = ATC$). On the other hand, the index will be greater than zero when the firm is earning an economic or excess profit (that is, $P > ATC$). Basic shortcomings of the index are that (1) large profits do not necessarily indicate the existence of strong monopoly power, since large profits may be the result of greater efficiency or of different accounting methods used for depreciation and asset valuation; (2) it is a static rather than dynamic measure and therefore cannot be applied to firms that experience rapid changes in technology, demand, and so on.

balanced budget: Budget with total revenues and total expenditures that are equal.

balanced-budget multiplier: Hypothesis that asserts that, if government spending and taxes are increased or decreased simultaneously by equal amounts, *NNP* will be increased or decreased by the same amount. *Example:* An equal increase in government spending and taxes of $20 billion will raise *NNP* by $1 \times \$20$ billion = $20 billion. (Similarly, an equal decrease of $20 billion will lower *NNP* by $1 \times \$20$ billion = $20 billion.) The reason for this is that the effects of equal increases in government spending and taxes are opposite. Therefore, the two multiplier processes cancel each other out—except on the first round, when the full amount of government spending is added to *NNP*.

balance of payments: Statement of the money value of all transactions between a nation and the rest of the world during a given period, such as a year. These transactions may consist of imports and exports of goods and services, and movements of short-term and long-term investments, gifts, currency, and gold. The transactions may be classified into several categories, of which the two broadest are the current account and the capital account.

balance-of-payments disequilibrium: Circumstance that exists when, over an unspecified period lasting several years, a nation's autonomous credits do not equal its autonomous debits. A deficit disequilibrium exists when total autonomous debits exceed total autonomous credits. A surplus disequilibrium occurs when total autonomous credits exceed total autonomous debits.

balance of trade: That part of a nation's balance of payments dealing with merchandise imports and exports. A "favorable" balance of trade exists when the value of exports exceeds the value of imports. An "unfavorable" balance exists when the value of imports exceeds the value of exports.

balance sheet: Statement of a firm's financial position on a given date. It shows what the firm owns (its assets), what it owes (its liabilities), and the residual or equity of the owners (the net worth).

Bank of the United States: Chartered for the period 1791 to 1811, the Bank's function was to assist the Treasury in its fiscal activities and to provide an adequate supply of currency to meet the needs of business. The Bank's performance was generally satisfactory, but its charter was not renewed. Primary opposition came from farmers, who felt that the Bank favored urban commercial interests over rural agricultural ones and that the Bank's financial power was too great.

banker's acceptance: Promise by a bank to pay specific bills for one of its customers when the bills become due. It may be thought of as a bank-guaranteed "post-dated" check written by one of its customers and accepted by the bank for payment. The bank thus assumes the customer's debt and guarantees payment on the post-dated day. In the interim, if the bank should need short-term funds, it can sell the check at a discount from face value in the money market. (*See also* **bill of exchange; draft.**)

barter: Simple exchange of one good for another without the use of money.

basic wages: Payments received by workers for work performed, based on time or output.

basis: In the futures market, the difference between the cash and futures price of a commodity:

Basis = futures price − cash price

The difference is approximately equal to the carrying costs (including freight, insurance, storage, and so forth) of moving the product from local rural markets to major terminal markets, such as Chicago, Omaha, and Kansas City.

"bathtub theorem": A model in the form of a physical analogy—a bathtub. The level of water in the tub represents the economy's output or income. Thus, water flowing into the tub represents "injections." These may consist of investment, government spending, or exports. The effects of these expenditures are to increase aggregate demand and thus to raise the water level in the tub (that is, to increase income and employment). Water flowing out of the tub represents "withdrawals." These are "leakages" from total income, which may consist of saving, taxes, and imports. The effects of such leakages are to decrease aggregate demand and thus to lower the water level in the tub (that is, to decrease income and employment).

benefit−cost analysis: Method of evaluating alternative investment projects by comparing for each the (discounted) present value of all expected benefits or net receipts with the (discounted) present value of all expected costs or sacrifices. Once such comparisons are made, a rational basis exists for choosing one investment project over the other.

benefit−cost (B/C) ratio: Ratio of the present value of benefits (net receipts) of an investment to the present value of costs:

$$B/C = \frac{\text{present value of benefits}}{\text{present value of costs}}$$

The *B/C* ratio thus gives the present value of net receipts per dollar of investment cost. The ratio must equal at least 1 in order for the investment to be recovered (that is, repaid by its net receipts).

benefit principle: Theory of taxation that holds that a fair tax is one that is levied on people according to the services or benefits they receive from government. The chief difficulties are that: (1) for many goods, benefits cannot be readily determined (for example, national defense, public education, police and fire protection); and (2) those who receive the benefits are not always able to pay for them (for example, recipients of welfare or unemployment compensation).

bilateral monopoly: Market structure in which a monopsonist buyer faces a monopolist seller. The equilibrium quantity may be determinate. However, the price level for that quantity is logically indeterminate. That is, the price will end up somewhere between the minimum price preferred by the monopsonist and the maximum price preferred by the monopolist.

bill of exchange: Draft (or type of "check") used between countries. (*See also* **draft.**)

bimetallic standard: Monetary standard under which the national unit of currency (such as the dollar) is defined in terms of a fixed weight of two metals, usually gold and silver. The United States was on this standard during the nineteenth century, but it usually worked unsatisfactorily because of the operation of Gresham's Law. (*See also* **Gresham's Law; mint ratio.**)

black market: Illegal market in which a good is sold for more than its legal ceiling price. The good may or may not be rationed. If it is, experience indicates that the criteria used for rationing are virtually certain to create skullduggery and inequities. (*Compare* **white market.**)

Board of Governors: Group of seven people that supervises the Federal Reserve System. Members are appointed by the President and confirmed by the Senate for terms of 14 years each, one term expiring every 2 years.

bond: Agreement to pay a specified sum (called the "principal") either at a future date or periodically over the course of a loan, during which time a fixed rate of interest may be paid on certain dates. Bonds are issued by corporations and by the federal, state, and local governments. They are typically used for long-term financing.

boycott: Campaign to discourage people from dealing with a particular firm. (Sometimes called a "primary boycott.")

break-even point: Level of output at which a firm's total revenue equals its total cost (or its average revenue equals its average total cost) so that its net revenue is zero. At a break-even point as defined in economics, a firm is normally profitable, since total cost in economics includes normal profit.

Brown Shoe case (1962): Major antitrust case in which the Supreme Court struck down a merger between Brown Shoe and Kinney Shoe as a violation of the Clayton Antitrust Act. Although both companies were shoe manufacturers and retailers with relatively small market shares, the merger, it was held, would nevertheless "foreclose competition from a substantial share of the market for shoes without producing countervailing economic or social advantages." The Court also held that the merger might increase market concentration in a few cities where both companies had retail stores.

budget: Itemized estimate of expected revenues and expenditures for a given period in the future.

budget deficit: Budget in which total expenditures exceed total revenues.

budget surplus: Budget in which total revenues exceed total expenditures.

Burns, Arthur Frank (1904–): American economist and expert on business cycles, fiscal policy, and monetary policy. He served as President of the National Bureau of Economic Research, as a professor of economics at Columbia University, and in various high-level government positions, including head of the President's Council of Economic Advisors and Chairman of the Board of Governors of the Federal Reserve System.

business cycles: Recurrent but nonperiodic fluctuations in general business and economic activity that take place over a period of years. They occur in aggregate variables, such as income, output, employment, and prices, most of which may move at approximately the same time in the same direction, but *at different rates.* Business cycles are thus accelerations and retardations in the rates of growth of important economic variables.

C

cameralism: Form of mercantilism extensively implemented by German governments during the eighteenth century. Its chief objective was to increase the revenue of the state. [The word comes from *Kammer* ("chamber"), the named applied to the royal treasury.]

capital: 1. As a factor of production, capital is a produced means of further production (such as capital goods or investment goods in the form of raw materials, machines, or equipment) for the ultimate purpose of manufacturing consumer goods. Hence human resources are also part of an economy's capital. **2.** As money, capital represents the funds that businesspeople use to purchase capital goods. **3.** In accounting, capital may sometimes represent net worth or the stockholders' equity in a business.

capital consumption allowance: Expression used in national-income accounting to represent the difference between "gross" and "net" private domestic investment. It consists almost entirely of depreciation and is often used as if it were synonymous with it.

capital deepening: Increases in an economy's stock of capital at a faster rate than the growth of its labor force, thus expanding the volume of capital per worker and raising average output per worker.

capitalism: Economic system characterized by private ownership of the factors of production and their operation for profit under predominantly competitive conditions.

capital market: Center where long-term credit and equity instruments, such as bonds, stocks, and mortgages, are bought and sold.

capital–output (or capital/output) ratio: Concept sometimes used in a "total" sense, and sometimes in a "marginal" sense. Thus: **1.** The "total" capital–output ratio is the ratio of an economy's total stock of real capital to the level of its income or output. **2.** The "marginal" capital–output ratio is the change in an economy's income or output resulting from a unit change in its stock of real capital. Thus a ratio of 3/1 means that three units of additional capital produce one unit of additional output.

capital stock: Unit of ownership in a corporation. It represents the stockholder's proprietary interest. Two major classes are common stock and preferred stock.

capital widening: Increases in an economy's stock of capital at the same rate as the growth of its labor force, thus maintaining the same volume of capital per worker and hence the same average output per worker.

cartel: Association of producers in the same industry, established to increase the profits of its members by adopting common policies affecting production, market allocation, or prices. A cartel may be domestic or international in scope. In the United States, organizations of independent business enterprises established for mutually beneficial purposes are called *trade associations,* not cartels. The latter term has been reserved exclusively for foreign or international associations. However, when a trade association or similar group fixes prices, restricts output, or allocates markets for its members, it behaves in *effect* like a cartel.

Celler Antimerger Act (1950): Major antitrust law. An extension of Section 7 of the Clayton Antitrust Act, it prohibits a corporation from acquiring the stock *or assets* of another corporation if the effect would be a substantial lessening of competition or a tendency toward monopoly. *Note:* Prior to this law, only the acquisition of *stock* by competing corporations was illegal under the Clayton Antitrust Act.

certificate of deposit (CD): *See* **negotiable certificate of deposit.**

Chamberlin, Edward Hastings (1899–1967): American economist who was one of the pioneers in developing the theory of monopolistic competition. His doctoral dissertation, *The Theory of Monopolistic Competition* (Harvard, 1933), became a standard work in the field. In this and in subsequent editions and articles, Chamberlin emphasized the role of product differentiation, advertising, and differences in consumer preferences as factors contributing to the existence of "partial" or "competing monopolists." Chamberlin thus identified a new form of market structure, monopolistic competition, the theory of which has become an essential part of microeconomics.

change in amount consumed: Increase or decrease in the amount of consumption expenditure due to a change in income. It may be represented by a movement along a consumption-function curve.

change in consumption: Increase or decrease in consumption, represented by a shift of the consumption-function curve to a new position. The shift results from a change in any of the factors that were assumed to remain constant when the curve was drawn. These may include (1) the volume of liquid assets owned by households, (2) expectations of future prices and incomes, (3) anticipations of product shortages, and (4) credit conditions.

change in demand: Increase or decrease in demand, represented by a shift of the demand curve to a new position. The shift results from a change in any of the factors that were assumed to remain constant when the curve was drawn. These may include (1) buyers' money incomes, (2) the prices of related goods, (3) buyers' tastes or preferences, (4) the number of buyers in the market, and (5) buyers' expectations about future prices and incomes.

change in quantity demanded: Increase or decrease in the quantity demanded of a good due to a change in its price. It may be represented by a movement along a demand curve.

change in quantity supplied: Increase or decrease in the quantity supplied of a good due to a change in its price. It may be represented by a movement along a supply curve.

change in supply: Increase or decrease in supply represented by a shift of the supply curve to a new position. The shift results from a change in any of the factors that were assumed to remain constant when the curve was drawn. These may include (1) the state of technology, (2) resource prices or the costs of the factors of production, (3) the prices of other goods, (4) the number of sellers in the market, and (5) sellers' expectations regarding future prices.

checkoff: Procedure by which an employer, with the written permission of the worker, withholds union dues and other assessments from paychecks and then transfers the funds to the union. This provides an efficient means by which the union can collect dues from its members.

Christian socialism: Movement, since the late nineteenth century, by various church groups to preach the "social gospel"— a type of social legislation and reform that seeks to improve the well-being of the working classes by appealing to Christian ethical and humanitarian principles.

circular flow of economic activity: Model demonstrating the movement of goods, resources, payments, and expenditures among sectors of the economy. A simple model may include the household and business sectors and the product and resource markets—but other models may be constructed that are more complex.

Clark, John Bates (1847–1938): Leading American economist whose major treatise, *The Distribution of Wealth* (1899), was the first American work in pure economic theory. The book developed what is essentially the modern version of the marginal-productivity theory. This theory demonstrates that a (perfectly competitive) capitalistic society distributes incomes to resource owners in proportion to the market values of their contribution to production. The theory was thus used by others to justify capitalism as a fair (equitable) system. Clark, it should be noted, had much in common with his British contemporary, Alfred Marshall. Both used similar methodologies in analyzing economic problems. Clark, however, tended to be more theoretical and abstract.

classical economics: Body of economic thought dominant in the Western world from the late eighteenth century until the 1930s. Among its chief proponents were Adam Smith (1723–1790), Jean Baptiste Say (1767–1832), Jeremy Bentham (1748–1832), Thomas Robert Malthus (1766–1834), David Ricardo (1772–1823), Nassau William Senior (1790–1864), and John Stuart Mill (1806–1873). It emphasized human self-interest and the operation of universal economic laws that tend automatically to guide the economy toward full-employment equilibrium if the government adheres to a policy of laissez-faire or noninterventionism.

class struggle: In the theories of Karl Marx, an irreconcilable clash between the bourgeoisie (or capitalist class) and the proletariat (or working class) arising out of the surplus value that capitalists appropriate from workers. The class struggle will eventually be resolved when the proletariat overthrows the bourgeoisie and establishes a new and equitable economic order.

Clayton Antitrust Act (1914): A major antitrust law aimed at preventing unfair, deceptive, dishonest, or injurious methods of competition. It made the following practices and arrangements illegal, where their effect is a substantial lessening of competition or a tendency toward monopoly: (1) price discrimination, except where there are differences in grade, quality, or quantity sold, or where the lower prices make due allowances for cost differences in selling or transportation, or where the lower prices are offered in good faith to meet competition; (2) tying contracts between sellers and purchasers; and (3) intercorporate stockholdings among competing corporations. It also makes illegal, regardless of the effect on competition, (4) interlocking directorates, if the corporations involved are competitive and if any one of them has capital, surplus, and undivided profits in excess of $1 million.

closed shop: A firm that agrees that an employee must be a union member before being employed and must remain a union member after becoming employed. It is illegal under the Labor–Management Relations (Taft–Hartley) Act of 1947.

coalition bargaining: Method of bargaining by which a federation of unions (such as the AFL–CIO) tries to coordinate and establish common termination dates for contracts with firms that deal with a number of unions at their plants throughout the economy. Its purpose is to enable the federation to strengthen union bargaining positions by threatening to close down all plants simultaneously.

Coase theorem: Proposition that demonstrates that, if (1) property rights are clearly defined and (2) the number of affected parties is small, individuals seeking to maximize their well-being will negotiate the internalization of their own externalities. The resulting allocation of resources will be efficient and will have been arrived at by private agreement—without a solution imposed by an outside authority (that is, government). Basically, the parties involved will find that, if transactions costs (the costs including time and effort of negotiating contracts) are low because few people are involved, mutual gains will be realized from voluntary agreements. Thus, for example, a farmer whose crops are damaged by the wandering cattle of a neighboring rancher can pay the rancher to reduce his output of cattle. When all costs and benefits are taken into account, an efficient output of crops as well as of cattle is attained without an externally (governmentally) imposed decision.

cobweb theorem: Generic name for a theory of cyclical fluctuations in the prices and quantities of various agricultural commodities—fluctuations that arise because, for certain agricultural products, (1) the quantity demanded of the commodity at any given time depends on its price at that time, whereas (2) the quantity supplied at any given time depends on its price at a previous time when production plans were initially formulated. Hogs and beef cattle have been notable examples.

coefficient of relative effectiveness (CRE): Term used in the Soviet Union to mean the expected payoff or percentage rate of return on a capital investment; akin to the concept of marginal efficiency of investment in Western economics.

coincident indicators: Time series that tend to move approximately "in phase" with the aggregate economy and hence are measures of current economic activity.

collective agreement: A collective-bargaining contract worked out between union and management, describing wages, working conditions, and related matters.

collective bargaining: Negotiation between a company's management and a union for the purpose of agreeing on mutually acceptable wages and working conditions for employees.

collective farms: Agricultural cooperatives in the USSR consisting of communities of farmers who pool their resources, lease land from the government, and divide the profits among the members according to the amount and kind of work done by each. This type of farming, which is subject to detailed government regulation, dominates agriculture in the USSR.

collective good: *See* **public good.**

command economy: Economic system in which an authoritarian government exercises primary control over decisions concerning what and how much to produce; it may also, but does not necessarily, decide for whom to produce. (*Compare* **planned economy.**)

commercial bank: Financial institution, chartered by federal or state governments, primarily engaged in making short-term industrial and commercial loans by creating demand or checking deposits and retiring loans by canceling demand deposits. It may also perform other financial functions, such as holding time or savings deposits and making long-term mortgage loans.

commercial paper: Unsecured promissory notes, usually in minimum denominations of $10,000, sold by several hundred major corporations. The most familiar example is GMAC paper, sold by General Motors Acceptance Corporation, to finance the purchase of General Motors cars.

common market: Association of trading nations that agrees: (1) to impose no trade restrictions, such as tariffs or quotas, among participants; (2) to establish common external barriers (such as a common external tariff) to nonparticipants; and (3) to impose no national restrictions on the movement of labor and capital among participants. *Example:* European Economic Community (EEC).

common stock: Shares that have no fixed rate of dividends and hence may receive higher dividends than the fixed rate on preferred stock, if the corporation's earnings are sufficiently high.

Commonwealth (Mass.) v. Hunt (1842): The first case in which a (Massachusetts) court held a trade union to be a lawful organization. It declared that workers could form a union to bargain collectively with employers.

communism: 1. In the theories of Karl Marx, the final and perfect goal of historical development. It is characterized by: (a) a classless society in which all people live by earning and no person lives by owning; (b) the disappearance of the state; and (c) the abolition of the wage system so that all citizens live and work according to the motto: "*From each according to his ability, to each according to his needs.*" **2.** In most communist countries today, an economic system based on (a) social ownership of property, including most of the means of production and distribution; (b) government planning and control of the economy; and (c) a scheme of rewards and penalties to achieve maximum productive effort. *Note:* Communist leaders claim that the system that exists in communist countries today is socialism of the type that Marxian ideology holds as being preparatory to the attainment of full communism.

company union: A labor union limited to a particular firm. It is usually unaffiliated with any other union.

comparative advantage, law of: Principle that states that, if one nation can produce each of two products more efficiently than another nation and can produce one of these commodities more efficiently than the other, it should specialize in the product in whose production it is most efficient and leave production of the alternative product to the other country. Then, by engaging in trade, the two nations will have more of both goods. This principle is applicable to individuals and regions as well as to nations.

comparative statics: Method of analysis in which the effects of a change in one or more of the determining conditions in a static model are evaluated by comparing the results after the change with those before the change. *Example:* Comparing the effects on equilibrium prices and quantities (in a supply-and-demand model) resulting from a shift in supply or demand curves. It is like comparing two "snapshots" of a phenomenon —one taken before the change and one after.

compensatory (accommodating) transactions: Settlements among nations that are a direct response to balance-of-payments considerations. They may be thought of as balancing items that arise to accommodate differences in money inflows and outflows resulting from so-called autonomous transactions. The two main classes are short-term capital movements and shifts in gold holdings.

competition: Rivalry among buyers and sellers of goods or resources. Competition tends to be directly related to the degree of diffusion (as opposed to the concentration) of market power and the freedom with which buyers and sellers can enter or leave particular markets. It is sometimes used to mean perfect (pure) competition, depending on whether it is employed in that context.

complementary goods: Commodities that are related such that at a given level of buyers' incomes, an increase in the price of one good leads to a decrease in the demand for the other, and a decrease in the price of one good leads to an increase in the demand for the other. *Examples:* ham and eggs; hamburgers and buns. (*Compare* **substitute goods.**)

compounding: Process by which a given amount, expressed in dollars, is adjusted at interest to yield a future value. That is, interest when due is added to a principal amount and thereafter earns interest. *Example:* At 6 percent, a principal of $1, plus interest, amounts to a sum of $1.06 after one year, and to an additional 6 percent, for a sum of $1.124, after two years, and so on. Compounding is thus the opposite of **discounting.**

compound interest: Interest computed on a principal sum and also on all the interest earned by that principal sum as of a given date.

Comptroller of the Currency: Federal agency that charters all national banks. It also oversees the operations of national banks and of those state banks that are members of the Federal Reserve System.

concentration ratio: Percentage of an industry's output accounted for by its largest firms—typically, by its four largest. The percentage (or ratio) is usually based either on sales, value added, or value of shipments. Sometimes, however, other measures of size, such as assets or employment, are used.

conglomerate merger: Amalgamation under one ownership of unlike plants producing unrelated products. It reflects a desire by the acquiring company to spread risks, to find outlets for idle capital funds, to add products that can be sold with the firm's merchandising knowledge and skills, or simply to gain economic power on a broader front.

conscious parallel action: Identical price behavior among competing firms. It may or may not be the result of collusion or prior agreement, but it has, nevertheless, been held illegal by the courts in various antitrust cases.

consent decree: A means of settling cases in equity among the parties involved (such as a defendant firm and the Department of Justice). The defendant does not admit guilt, but agrees nevertheless to cease and desist from certain practices and to abide by the rules of behavior set down in the decree. This is the chief instrument employed by the Justice Department and by the Federal Trade Commission in the enforcement of the Sherman and Clayton Acts. The majority of antitrust violations are settled in this manner.

conspicuous consumption: Expression originated by Thorstein Veblen (1857–1929) to mean that those above the subsistence level (that is, the so-called "leisure class") are mainly concerned with impressing others through their standard of living, taste, and dress—in Veblen's words, through "pecuniary emulation." ("Keeping up with the Joneses" is a popular expression of this concept.)

constant-cost industry: Industry that experiences no increases in resource prices or in costs of production as it expands, despite new firms entering it. This will happen only when the industry's demand for the resources it employs is an insignificant proportion of the total demand for those resources.

constant dollars: Expression reflecting the actual prices of a previous year or the average of actual prices of a previous period of years. Hence economic data are often quoted in constant dollars. (*Compare* **current dollars.**)

Consumer Price Index (CPI): Average of prices of goods and services commonly purchased by families in urban areas. Generally referred to as a "cost-of-living index," the CPI is published by the Bureau of Labor Statistics of the U.S. Department of Labor.

consumer sovereignty: Concept of the consumer as "king"—in the sense that the consumer registers his or her preferences for goods by "dollar votes" in the marketplace. In a highly competitive economy, competition among producers will cause them to adjust their production to the changing patterns of consumer demands. In less competitive circumstances, where monopolistic forces and other imperfections exist, resources will not be allocated in accordance with consumer wishes.

consumer's surplus: Difference between what a consumer pays and the maximum amount he or she would be willing to pay for a given quantity of a commodity.

consumption: Expenditures on consumer goods and services.

consumption function: Relationship between consumption expenditures and income such that, as income increases, consumption increases, but not as fast as income. The expression **propensity to consume** is often used synonymously. (*Note:* Since the word "function" is employed here in its mathematical sense to mean a variable whose value depends on the value of another variable, the expression "consumption function" can also be used to designate *any* type of relationship between consumption and income—not necessarily the type defined above. However, the above type is the most common one.)

contestable market: One that is characterized by ease of exit—the ability to leave the market at little cost. Companies already in such a market are under pressure to maintain a low-price policy. This discourages outsiders from entering, capturing some of the industry's profits, and getting out quickly. Airlines and trucking provide good examples of contestable markets because the principal assets—planes and trucks—though expensive, are both mobile and readily resalable.

contributive standard: Criterion of income distribution popularly expressed by the phrase, "To each according to his or her contribution." It means that, if the market value of one person's production is twice that of another's, then the first person should be paid twice as much as the second. This is the predominant criterion of income distribution in market-oriented economies. You will consider the contributive standard a just or equitable one only if you believe that each person is entitled to the fruits of his or her labor. (*Compare* **equality standard; needs standard.**)

convergence hypothesis: Conjecture that capitalism and communism, driven by the process of industrialization, will eventually merge to form a new kind of society in which the personal freedoms and profit motive of Western capitalistic democracies blend with the government controls that exist in a communistic (especially Soviet) economy.

corporation: Association of stockholders created under law but regarded by the courts as an artificial person existing only in the contemplation of the law. The chief characteristics of a corporation are (1) limited liability of its stockholders; (2) stability and permanence; and (3) ability to accumulate large sums of capital for expansion through the sale of stocks and bonds.

correspondence principle: Proposition that demonstrates that, in order for comparative statics (the comparison of equilibrium positions in static states) to be meaningful, it is first necessary to develop a dynamic analysis of stability.

cost: Sacrifice that must be made to do or to acquire something. What is sacrificed may be money, goods, leisure time, security, prestige, power, or pleasure.

cost–benefit analysis: *See* **benefit–cost analysis.**

cost-effectiveness analysis: Technique of selecting from alternative programs the one that attains a given objective at the lowest cost. It is a type of analysis most useful when benefits cannot be measured in money.

cost-push inflation: Condition of generally rising prices caused by factor payments to one or more groups of resource owners increasing faster than productivity or efficiency. It is usually attributed to monopolistic market power possessed by some resource owners, unions, or business firms. "Wage-push" and "profit-push" are the most common forms of cost-push inflation.

countervailing power: Proposition that the growth of market power by one group in the United States may tend to stimulate the growth of a counterreaction and somewhat offsetting influence by another group. *Examples:* Big labor unions face big corporations at the bargaining table; chain stores deal with large processing and manufacturing firms; and big government faces big business and big unions.

craft union: Labor union composed of workers in a particular trade, such as bakers, carpenters, or teamsters. It is thus a "horizontally" organized union.

crawling peg: System of foreign-exchange rates that permits the par values of a nation's currency to change automatically by small increments, downward or upward, if in actual daily trading on the foreign exchange markets the price in terms of other currencies persists on the "floor" or "ceiling" of the governmentally established range for a specified period.

credit: 1. A promise by one party to pay another for money borrowed or for goods and services received. Credit may therefore be regarded as an extension of money. **2.** In international economics, any transaction that results in a money inflow or receipt from a foreign country. It may be represented on a balance-of-payments statement by a plus sign.

credit instrument: Written or printed financial document serving as either a promise or an order to transfer funds from one person to another.

creeping inflation: Slow but persistent upward movement in the general level of prices over a long period of years, typically at an average annual rate of up to 3 percent.

cross elasticity of demand: Percentage change in the quantity purchased of a good resulting from a 1 percent change in the price of another good. Thus:

$$\text{cross elasticity of demand}$$
$$= \frac{\text{percentage change in the quantity purchased of } X}{\text{percentage change in the price of } Y}$$
$$= \frac{(Q_{X2} - Q_{X1})/(Q_{X2} + Q_{X1})}{(P_{Y2} - P_{Y1})/(P_{Y2} - P_{Y1})}$$

in which Q_{X1} and Q_{X2} represent quantities purchased of X before and after the change in the price of Y, and P_{Y1} and P_{Y2} represent the corresponding prices of Y before and after the change. The cross elasticity of demand thus measures the responsiveness of changes in the quantities purchased of a good to changes in the price of another good. In general, the higher the coefficient of elasticity, the greater the degree of substitutability. (For example, competing brands of goods in the same industry, such as competing brands of television sets, have high positive cross elasticities.) A coefficient of zero indicates goods that are nonsubstitutes or are unrelated. (Examples are lettuce and beer, hats and books.) A negative coefficient indicates goods that are complementary. (Examples are watches and watchbands, cameras and film, shirts and ties.)

crowding out: Proposition that states that large increases in government spending, whether financed by taxing, borrowing, or printing new money, are likely to reduce business investment spending. There are two reasons: (1) Resources that might otherwise be used by the private sector are diverted to public use. (2) Interest rates tend to be pushed up when government spending is financed by borrowing or printing money. This increases the costs of business borrowing and forces many firms out of the financial markets. For both reasons, therefore, private incentives to work, save, and invest may be diminished, thus reducing productive capital investment.

currency: Paper money. (Coins are not part of currency.)

current assets: Cash and other assets that can be turned quickly into cash.

current dollars: An expression reflecting actual prices of each year. Hence economic data are often quoted in current dollars. (*Compare* **constant dollars.**)

current liabilities: Debts that fall due within a year.

customs union: Agreement among two or more trading nations to abolish trade barriers, such as tariffs and quotas, among themselves and to adopt a common external policy of trade (such as a common external tariff with all nonmember nations). *Example:* Benelux (Belgium, the Netherlands, and Luxembourg).

cyclically balanced budget: Philosophy that holds that total revenues and expenditures in the government's budget should be balanced or brought into equality over the course of a business cycle.

cyclical unemployment: Unemployment that results from business recessions or depressions because aggregate demand falls too far below the full-employment level of aggregate output and income.

D

death taxes: Taxes imposed on the transfer of property after death. They consist of estate and inheritance taxes and are imposed by federal and state governments at progressive rates.

debit: In international economics, any transaction that results in a money outflow or payment to a foreign country. It may be represented on a balance-of-payments statement by a minus sign.

decreasing-cost industry: Industry that experiences decreases in resource prices or in its costs of production as it expands because of new firms entering it. This situation might arise for a while as a result of substantial external economies of scale.

deduction: In logical thinking, a process of reasoning from premises to conclusions. The premises are more general than the conclusions, so deduction is often defined as reasoning from the general to the particular. (Opposite of **induction.**)

deflation: 1. Statistical adjustment of data by which an economic time series expressed in current dollars is converted into a series expressed in constant dollars of a previous period. The purpose of the adjustment is to compensate for the distorting effects of inflation (that is, the long-run upward trend of prices) through a reverse process of "deflation." **2.** Decline in the general price level of all goods and services—or, equivalently, a rise in the purchasing power of a unit of money. (*Compare* **inflation.**)

demand: Relation expressing the various amounts of a commodity that buyers would be willing and able to purchase at possible alternative prices during a given period of time, all other things remaining the same. This relation may be expressed in a table (called a **demand schedule**), in a graph (called a **demand curve**), or in a mathematical equation.

demand curve: Graph of a demand schedule, showing the number of units of a commodity that buyers would be able and willing to purchase at various possible prices during a given period of time, all other things remaining the same.

demand deposit: Promise by a bank to pay immediately an amount of money specified by the customer who owns the deposit. It is thus "checkbook money" because it permits transactions to be paid for by check rather than with currency. However, unlike other types of checkable deposits, a demand deposit does not pay interest to its owner.

demand, law of: Principle that states that the quantity demanded of a commodity varies inversely with its price, assuming that all other things that may affect demand remain the same. These "all other" things include (1) buyers' money incomes; (2) the prices of related goods in consumption; and (3) tastes and other nonmonetary determinants, such as consumer preferences, number of buyers in the market, or characteristics of buyers.

demand price: Highest price a buyer is willing to pay for a given quantity of a commodity.

demand-pull inflation: Condition of generally rising prices caused by increases in aggregate demand at a time when available supplies of goods are becoming more limited. Goods may go into short supply because resources are fully utilized or because production cannot be increased rapidly enough to meet growing demand.

demand schedule: Table showing the number of units of a commodity that buyers would be able and willing to purchase at various possible prices during a given period of time, all other things remaining the same.

demand-side economics: Measures aimed at achieving efficiency through policies designed to regulate purchasing power. Keynesian economics, because it tends to focus on fiscal and monetary policies to control aggregate demand, has been characterized as demand-side economics. (*Contrast with* **supply-side economics.**)

deposit-expansion multiplier: Proposition that states that an increase in *excess* reserves of the banking system can cause a magnified increase in total deposits; similarly, a decrease in the banking system's *legal* reserves may cause a magnified decrease in total deposits. The total cumulative expansion (or contraction) will at most be some multiple of the required reserve ratio. The deposit-expansion multiplier can be expressed by the formula

$$\text{deposit-expansion multiplier} = \frac{1}{\text{required reserve ratio}} = \frac{1}{R}$$

Therefore, if we let D represent the change in demand deposits for the banking system as a whole, and E the amount of excess reserves, then

$$D = E \times \text{deposit-expansion multiplier}$$

or

$$D = E \times \frac{1}{R}$$

(*Example:* If $E = \$1,000$ and $R = 10$ percent, then $D = \$1,000 \times 1/0.10 = \$10,000$. Thus excess reserves of $1,000 can result in as much as a $10,000 increase in demand deposits.) There are "leakages," however, that prevent this multiplier from exerting its full impact. They include (1) the leakage of cash into circulation, since some deposits will be withdrawn in cash and some checks will be "cashed" instead of deposited; (2) a margin of excess reserves that banks for one reason or another may not lend out; and (3) the failure of businesspeople to borrow all that the banks want to lend.

Depository Institutions Deregulation and Monetary Control Act (1980): *See* **Monetary Control Act of 1980.**

depreciation: Decline in the value of a fixed asset, such as plant or equipment, due to wear and tear, destruction, or obsolescence resulting from the development of new and better techniques.

depression: Lower phase of a business cycle in which the economy is operating with substantial unemployment of its resources and a sluggish rate of capital investment and consumption resulting from little business and consumer optimism.

derived demand: Demand for a product or resource based on its contribution to the product for which it is used. *Examples:* The separate demands for bricks, lumber, and so on, are derived partly from the demand for construction; the demand for steel is derived partly from the demand for automobiles.

devaluation: Official act that makes a domestic currency cheaper in terms of foreign currencies (or in terms of gold under a gold standard). It is typically designed to reduce a nation's balance-of-payments deficits by increasing exports while reducing imports. (*Contrast with* **revaluation**.)

dialectical materialism: Logical method of historical analysis. In particular, it was used by Karl Marx, who employed the philosopher Hegel's idea that historical change is the result of inherently conflicting or opposing forces in society and that the forces are basically economic or materialistic.

"dictatorship of the proletariat": Expression used by Karl Marx to describe a stage of Marxian socialism in which the bourgeoisie (or capitalist class) has been toppled from power and, along with its properties, is under the management of the proletariat (or working class), which is also in control of the state.

diminishing marginal utility, law of: In a given period of time, the consumption of a product while tastes remain constant may at first result in increasing marginal (that is, incremental) satisfactions or utilities per unit of the product consumed, but a point will be reached beyond which further units of consumption of the product will result in decreasing marginal utilities per unit of the product consumed. This is the point of diminishing marginal utility. *Note:* Even though marginal utility may rise at first, *it must eventually fall.* It is the diminishing phase of marginal utility that is relevant and serves as the basis for the law.

diminishing returns (variable proportions), law of: In a given state of technology, the addition of a changing or variable factor of production to other fixed factors of production may at first yield increasing marginal (that is, incremental) returns per unit of the variable factor added, but a point will be reached beyond which further additions of the variable factor will yield diminishing marginal returns per unit of the variable factor added. This is the point of diminishing marginal returns. *Note:* Even though marginal returns may rise at first, *they must eventually fall.* It is the diminishing phase of marginal returns that is relevant and serves as the basis for the law.

direct payments: Method of subsidizing sellers while permitting the price of a commodity to be determined in a free market by supply and demand. If the price turns out to be "too low," sellers are compensated by a subsidy from the government for the difference between the market price received and some higher, predetermined target price. If the market price turns out to be equal to or greater than the target price, no subsidized compensation is provided. Under this system, therefore, consumers pay and sellers receive the market price of the commodity, but sellers *may in addition* receive a subsidy. (*Note:* A plan of this type has long existed for certain farm commodities.)

direct tax: Tax that is not shifted—that is, its burden is borne by the persons or firms originally taxed. *Examples:* personal income taxes, social security taxes paid by employees, and death taxes.

discounting: Process by which a given amount, expressed in dollars, is adjusted at interest to yield a present value. *Example:* At 6 percent, $1.06 one year hence has a present value of $1; $1.124 two years hence has a present value one year hence of $1.06, and a present value today of $1. Discounting is thus the opposite of **compounding**.

discount rate: Interest rate charged to depository institutions on their loans from the Federal Reserve Banks. It is called a "discount rate" because the interest on a loan is discounted when the loan is made, rather than collected when the loan is repaid.

disequilibrium: State of imbalance or nonequilibrium. *Example:* a situation in which the quantities supplied and demanded of a commodity at a given price are unequal, so there is a tendency for market prices and/or quantities to change. Any economic entity or system, such as a household, a firm, a market, or an economy, that is not in equilibrium is said to be in disequilibrium.

disguised unemployment (underemployment): Situation in which employed resources are not being used in their most efficient ways.

disinvestment: Reduction in the total stock of capital goods caused by failure to replace it as it wears out. *Example:* the consumption or using up of factories, machines, and so forth at a faster rate than they are being replaced so that the productive base is diminishing.

disposable personal income: Income remaining after payment of personal taxes.

dissaving: Expenditure on consumption in excess of income. This may be accomplished by drawing on past savings, borrowing, or receiving help from others.

dividend: Earnings that a corporation pays to its stockholders. Payments are usually in cash, but they may also be in property, securities, or other forms.

division of labor: Specialization in productive activities among workers, resulting in increased production because it (1) permits development and refinement of skills; (2) avoids the time that is wasted in going from one job to another; and (3) simplifies human tasks, thus permitting the introduction of labor-saving machines.

double coincidence of wants: Situation that is necessary in a barter exchange: each party must have what the other wants and must be willing to trade at the exact quantities and terms suitable to both.

double taxation: Taxation of the same base in two different forms. A typical example is the corporate income tax: the corporation pays an income tax on its profits, and the stockholder pays an income tax on the dividends he receives from those profits.

draft: Unconditional written order by one party (the creditor or drawer) on a second party (the debtor or drawee) directing the second party to pay a third party (the bearer or payee) a specified sum of money. An ordinary check, therefore, is an example of a draft.

dual banking system: Expression referring to the fact that all commercial banks in the United States are chartered either as national banks or as state banks. This organizational structure, not found in any other country, is a unique outgrowth of American political history.

dual labor market: Labor market consisting of two submarkets: (1) a primary labor market, in which jobs are characterized by relatively high wages, favorable working conditions, and employment stability; and (2) a secondary labor market, in which jobs, when they are available, pay relatively low wages, provide poor working conditions, and are highly unstable. Blue-collar workers, many of whom are union members, account for most of the participants in the primary market, whereas the competitively "disadvantaged poor"—the unskilled, the undereducated, and the victims of racial prejudice—are confined to the secondary market.

dumping: Sale of the same product in different markets at different prices. *Example:* A monopolist might restrict his output in the domestic market and charge a higher price because demand is relatively inelastic, and "dump" the rest of his output in a foreign market at a lower price because demand there is relatively elastic. He thereby gains the benefit of lower average total costs on his entire output (domestic plus foreign) and earns a larger net profit than if he sold the entire output in the domestic market—which he could do only by charging a lower price per unit on all units sold.

duopoly: Oligopoly consisting of two sellers. Hence it may be either a perfect duopoly or an imperfect one, depending on whether the product is standardized or differentiated.

dynamic model: One in which economic phenomena are studied by relating them to preceding or succeeding events. The influence of time is therefore taken explicitly into account. A dynamic model is thus like a "motion picture" as distinguished from a "snapshot." (*Compare* **static model.**)

E

econometrics: Integration of economic theory, mathematics, and statistics. It consists of expressing economic relationships in the form of mathematical equations and verifying the resulting models by statistical methods.

economic costs: Payments made to the owners of the factors of production to persuade them to supply their resources in a particular activity.

economic development: Process whereby a nation's real per-capita output or income (its GNP) increases over a long period of time. A nation's rate of economic development is thus measured by its per-capita rate of economic growth.

economic efficiency: *See* **efficiency**

economic good: Scarce commodity—that is, any commodity for which the market price is greater than zero at a particular time and place. (*Compare* **free good.**)

economic growth: Rate of increase in an economy's full-employment real output or income over time—that is, the rise in its full-employment output in constant prices. Economic growth may be expressed in either of two ways: (1) as the increase in total full-employment real GNP or *NNP* over time, or (2) as the increase in per-capita full-employment real GNP or *NNP* over time. The "total" measure is employed to describe the expansion of a nation's economic output or potential, whereas the "per-capita" measure is used to express its material standard of living and to compare it with other countries.

economic indicators: Time series of economic data, classified as leading, lagging, or coincident indicators. They are used in business-cycle analysis and forecasting.

economic interpretation of history: Proposition advanced by Karl Marx (and others) that the great political, social, intellec-

tual, and ethical movements of history are determined by the ways in which societies organize their social institutions to carry on the basic economic activities of production, exchange, distribution, and consumption of goods. Thus economic forces are the prime cause of fundamental historical change.

economic man: The notion that each individual in a capitalistic society, whether he or she be a worker, businessperson, consumer, or investor, is motivated by economic forces and hence will always act to obtain the greatest satisfaction for the least sacrifice or cost. Satisfaction may take the form of profits to a businessperson, wages or leisure hours to a worker, pleasure to a consumer from the goods that he or she purchases, and so on.

economic plan: Detailed method, formulated beforehand, for achieving specific economic objectives by governing the activities and interrelationships of those economic entities, namely firms, households, and governments, that have an influence on the desired outcome.

economic (pure) profit: Payment to a firm in excess of its economic costs, including normal profit. It is the same as **net revenue.**

economic rent: Payment to an owner of a unit of a factor of production, in an industry in equilibrium, in excess of the factor's supply price or opportunity cost. The payment is thus in excess of the minimum amount necessary to keep the factor in its present occupation. Economic rent is therefore a surplus to the recipient.

economics: Social science concerned chiefly with the way society chooses to employ its limited resources, which have alternative uses, to produce goods and services for present and future consumption.

economic system: Relationships between the components of an economy (such as its households, firms, and government) and the institutional framework of laws and customs within which these organisms operate to determine *what, how,* and *for whom* goods are produced.

economies (diseconomies) of scale: The decreases (increases) in a firm's long-run average costs as the size of its plant is increased. Those factors that give rise to economies of scale are (1) greater specialization of resources; (2) more efficient utilization of equipment; (3) reduced unit costs of inputs; (4) opportunities for economical utilization of by-products; and (5) growth of auxiliary facilities. Diseconomies of scale may eventually set in, however, due to (1) limitations of (or "diminishing returns" to) management in its decision-making function and (2) competition among firms in bidding up prices of limited resources.

efficiency: Ability to make the best use of what is available to attain a desired result. Two specific types of efficiency are "technical" and "economic." **1. Technical efficiency:** Condition that exists when a production system—a firm, an industry, an economy—is achieving maximum output by making the fullest utilization of available inputs. The system is then producing on its production-possibilities curve. This means that no change in the combination of resources can be made that will increase the output of one product without decreasing the output of another. **2. Economic (allocative) efficiency:** Condition that exists when a production system has achieved technical efficiency *and* is fulfilling consumer preferences by producing the combination of goods that people want—are willing and able to buy—with their present incomes. This means that no change in the combination of resources or of output can be implemented that will make someone better off without making someone else worse off—each in his or her own estimation. (*Note:* Economic efficiency is synonymous with **Pareto optimality.**)

elasticity: Percentage change in quantity demanded or supplied resulting from a 1 percent change in price. Mathematically, it is the ratio of the percentage change in quantity (demanded or supplied) to the percentage change in price:

$$\text{elasticity, } E = \frac{\text{percentage change in quantity}}{\text{percentage change in price}}$$

$$= \frac{(Q_2 - Q_1)/(Q_2 + Q_1)}{(P_2 - P_1)/(P_2 + P_1)}$$

in which Q_1 and Q_2, and P_1 and P_2, denote the corresponding quantities and prices before and after the change. This coefficient of elasticity (which is usually stated numerically without regard to algebraic sign) may range from zero to infinity. It may take any of five forms:

perfectly elastic	$(E = \infty)$
relatively elastic	$(E > 1)$
unit elastic	$(E = 1)$
relatively inelastic	$(E < 1)$
perfectly inelastic	$(E = 0)$

The preceding definition refers to what is known as *price elasticity* of demand or supply. It is one of several types of elasticities that exist in economics and is the one that is commonly understood unless otherwise specified. In general, elasticity may be thought of as the responsiveness of changes in one variable to changes in another, where responsiveness is measured in terms of percentage changes.

Employment Act of 1946: Act of Congress that requires the government to maintain high levels of employment, production, and purchasing power. To assist the President in this task, the act authorizes him to appoint a panel of experts known as the Council of Economic Advisors.

employment ratio: Percentage of the working-age population (16 years of age and older) that is employed.

employment-training policies: Deliberate efforts undertaken in the private and public sectors to develop and use the capacities of human beings as actual or potential members of the labor force.

Engel's Laws: Set of relationships between consumer expenditures and income derived by a nineteenth-century German statistician, Ernst Engel, and based on research into workingmen's purchases in Western Europe during the 1850s. The relationships state that, as a family's income increases: (1) the percentage it spends on food decreases; (2) the percentage it spends on housing and household operations remains about constant (except for the part spent on fuel, light, and refrigeration, which decreases); and (3) the percentage it spends on all other categories and the amount it saves increase (except for medical care and personal care items, which remain fairly constant). In general, the *total* amount spent increases as a family's income increases. *Note:* Strictly speaking, only the first relationship above is attributed to Engel; the other two are mod-

ernized versions of his early findings, based on more recent research.

entrepreneurship: Factor of production that is defined as the function performed by those who assemble the other factors of production, raise the necessary money, organize the management, make the basic business policy decisions, and reap the gains of success or the losses of failure. The entrepreneur is the innovator and the catalyst in a capitalistic system. He need not be exclusively an owner or a manager; the entrepreneurial function may be performed by either or both, depending on the size and complexity of the firm.

equal advantage, law of: In a market economy, owners of resources will always transfer them from less desirable to more desirable uses. As this happens, the occupations *out of* which resources are transferred often tend to become more desirable, while the occupations *into* which resources are transferred tend to become less desirable. This transfer process continues until all occupations are equally desirable. At this point, there is no gain to be made by further transfer of resources. Hence the economy is in equilibrium. *Note:* The term "desirable" includes both monetary and nonmonetary considerations. The latter helps explain why permanent differences in monetary rewards may exist between various occupations.

equality standard: Criterion of income distribution popularly expressed by the phrase, "To each equally." You will regard the equality standard as a just or equitable one only if you assume that all people are alike in the *added* satisfaction or utility they get from an extra dollar of income. If this assumption is false—if an additional dollar of income actually provides a greater gain in utility to some people than to others—then justice is more properly served by distributing most of any increase in society's income to those who will enjoy it more. In reality, there is no conclusive evidence to suggest that people are either alike or unlike in their capacities to enjoy additional income. Therefore, no scientific basis exists for assuming that an equal distribution of income is more equitable than an unequal one. (*Compare* **contributive standard; needs standard.**)

equation of exchange: Expression of the relation between the quantity of money (M), its velocity of circulation (V), the average price (P) of final goods and services, and the physical quantity (Q) of those goods and services:

$$MV = PQ$$

The equation states that the total amount of money spent on goods and services (MV) is equal to the total amount of money received for goods and services (PQ). (*See also* **quantity theory of money.**)

equilibrium: State of balance between opposing forces. An object in equilibrium is in a state of rest and has no tendency to change.

equilibrium conditions: Set of relationships that defines the equilibrium properties of an economic entity such as a household, a firm, or an entire economy.

equilibrium price: 1. Price of a commodity determined in the market by the intersection of a supply curve and a demand curve. (Also called **normal price.**) **2.** Price (and corresponding equilibrium quantity) that maximizes a firm's profit.

equilibrium quantity: 1. Quantity of a commodity determined in the market by the intersection of a supply curve and a demand curve. **2.** Quantity (and corresponding equilibrium price) that maximizes a firm's profit.

equity: Justice or fairness. In economics, equity refers to justice with respect to the distribution of income or of wealth within a society. Because justice is subjective rather than objective, equity may be thought of as a philosophical concept but an economic goal. However, there is no scientific way of concluding that one standard or mechanism for distributing income is just and therefore "good" while another is unjust and therefore "bad." Each society or type of economic system establishes its own standards of distribution. Nevertheless, economics can help to evaluate the material consequences of any standard that a society adopts. (*See also* **contributive standard; equality standard; needs standard.**)

escalator clause: Provision in a contract whereby payments such as wages, insurance or pension benefits, or loan repayments over a stated period are tied to a comprehensive measure of living costs or price-level changes. The consumer price index and the implicit price index (GNP deflator) are the measures most commonly used for this purpose.

estate tax: Progressive (graduated) tax imposed by the federal government and by most state governments on the transfer of all property owned by a decedent at the time of death. Exemptions, deductions, and rates vary widely among the states.

Eurodollars: Dollar deposits in banks outside the United States, mostly in Europe. They are held by American and foreign banks, corporations, and individuals and represent dollar obligations that are constantly being shifted from one country to another in search of the highest return.

European Recovery Program (ERP): Commonly known as the "Marshall Plan" (after Secretary of State George C. Marshall, who proposed it in 1947), this was a comprehensive recovery blueprint for European countries, financed by the United States, for the purposes of (1) increasing their productive capacity, (2) stabilizing their financial systems, (3) promoting their mutual economic cooperation, and (4) reducing their dependence on U.S. assistance. The ERP was terminated in 1951 after considerable success, and its functions were absorbed by other government agencies and programs.

excess reserves: Quantity of a bank's legal reserves over and above its required reserves. Thus:

excess reserves = legal reserves − required reserves

Excess reserves are the key to a bank's lending power.

excise tax: Tax imposed on the manufacture, sale, or consumption of various commodities, such as liquor, tobacco, and gasoline.

exclusion principle: Basis for distinguishing between nonpublic and public goods. A good is nonpublic if anyone who does not pay for it can be excluded from its use; otherwise, it is a public good.

expenditure multiplier: Principle that states that changes in total spending, consisting of consumption and investment, can bring about magnified changes in income. The expenditure multiplier (M_E) is thus the same as the investment multiplier, except that the independent variable is broadened to include spending rather than investment only. *See* **multiplier.**

explicit costs: Money outlays of a firm recorded in its books of account. (*Compare* **implicit costs.**)

external economies and diseconomies of scale: Conditions that bring about decreases or increases in a firm's long-run average costs as a result of factors that are entirely outside of the firm as a producing unit. They depend on adjustments of the industry and are related to the firm only to the extent that the firm is a part of the industry. *Example:* External economies may result from improvements in public transportation and marketing facilities as an industry develops in a particular geographic area; however, diseconomies may eventually set in as firms bid up the prices of limited resources in the area.

externalities: External benefits or costs for which no compensation is made. (Externalities are also called **spillovers.**)

F

Fabian socialism: Form of socialism founded in England in 1884. It emerged as an outgrowth of utopian socialism by advocating gradual and evolutionary reform within a democratic framework.

factors of production: Human and nonhuman productive resources of an economy, usually classified into four groups: land, labor, capital, and entrepreneurship.

Fair Labor Standards Act (Wages and Hours Law) of 1938: An act, with subsequent amendments, that specifies minimum hourly wages, overtime rates, and prohibitions against child labor for workers producing goods in interstate commerce.

family-allowance plan: Plan that provides every family, rich or poor, with a certain amount of money based exclusively on the number and age of its children. Families above certain designated income levels return all or a portion of the money with their income taxes, but those below specified income levels keep it. More than 60 countries have family allowance plans.

Fawcett, Millicent Garrett (1847–1919): English economic educator whose book, *Political Economy for Beginners* (1870), was largely a simplification and abridgement of classical economics as expressed by Mill in 1848. (*See* **Mill, John Stuart.**) Her book was highly successful, went through ten editions over a period of forty years, and established her as an outstanding popularizer of classical economic ideas.

featherbedding: Labor union "make-work" rules designed to increase the labor or labor-time on a particular job. Outlawed by the Labor–Management Relations (Taft–Hartley) Act of 1947.

Federal Advisory Council: Committee within the Federal Reserve System that advises the Board of Governors on important current developments.

federal agency discount notes: Short-term credit instruments sold (issued) by certain government agencies. Among these are the Federal Home Loan Bank, the Federal National Mortgage Association, and the Federal Farm Credit Bank System. The money raised by these agencies is used to provide mortgages and other types of loans.

Federal Deposit Insurance Corporation (FDIC): Government agency that insures deposits (demand and time) at commercial and savings banks. Each insured bank pays an annual premium equal to a fraction of its total deposits, in return for which the FDIC insures each account up to $100,000 against loss due to bank failure. In addition to its insurance function, the FDIC supervises insured banks and presides over the liquidation of banks that do fail. Two parallel agencies that perform similar functions are the Federal Savings and Loan Insurance Corporation, which insures deposits in savings and loan associations, and the National Credit Union Administration, which provides deposit insurance for federally chartered credit unions. National banks (chartered by the federal government) are required to be insured by the FDIC, and state-chartered banks may apply if they wish. Since the late 1930s, practically all banks have been covered by insurance, thereby eliminating bank runs and permitting greater bank stability.

federal funds: Unsecured loans that banks and certain other depository institutions make to one another, usually overnight, out of their excess reserves. The purchase and sale of federal funds is limited to banks, savings institutions, and certain government agencies.

federal-funds rate: Interest rate at which banks borrow excess reserves from other banks' accounts at the Fed, usually overnight, to keep required reserves from falling below the legal level. In general, the lower the volume of excess reserves, the higher will be the federal-funds rate. Therefore, the federal-funds rate is an important indicator that the Fed watches to decide whether it should add to banks' reserves or take them away. For short periods of time, the Fed can largely control the federal-funds rate. For example, the rate can be raised by selling Treasury bills to the banking system, thereby pulling out reserves. Conversely, the rate can be lowered by buying bills from the system, thereby putting in reserves. As part of its policy-making function, the Fed tries to maintain a federal-funds rate that is consistent with other monetary goals.

Federal Open Market Committee: The most important policy-making body of the Federal Reserve System. Its chief function is to establish policy for the System's purchase and sale of government and other securities in the open market.

Federal Reserve Bank: One of the 12 banks (plus branches) that make up the Federal Reserve System. Each serves as a "banker's bank" for the member banks in its district by acting as a source of credit and a depository of resources, and by performing other useful functions.

Federal Reserve System: Central banking system created by Congress in 1913. It consists of (1) 12 Federal Reserve Banks— one located in each of 12 districts in the country; (2) a Board of Governors; (3) a Federal Open Market Committee and various other committees; and (4) several thousand member banks, which hold the great majority of all commercial bank deposits in the nation.

Federal Trade Commission: Government agency created in 1914. It is charged with preventing unfair business practices by enforcing the Federal Trade Commission Act and by exercising concurrently with the Justice Department the enforcement of prohibitive provisions of the Clayton Antitrust Act as amended by the Robinson–Patman Act.

Federal Trade Commission Act (1914): A major antitrust law of the U.S. Its chief purpose is to prevent unfair (that is, deceptive, dishonest, or injurious) methods of competition and, as amended by the Wheeler–Lea Act (1938), to safeguard the pub-lic by preventing the dissemination of false and misleading advertising of food, drugs, cosmetics, and therapeutic devices.

financial intermediaries: Business firms that serve as middlemen between lenders and borrowers by creating and issuing financial obligations or claims against themselves in order to acquire profitable financial claims against others. Examples of such firms are commercial banks, mutual savings banks, savings and loan associations, credit unions, insurance companies, and all other financial institutions. In general, they are wholesalers and retailers of funds.

financial markets: The money and capital markets. In the former, short-term credit instruments are bought and sold; in the latter, long-term credit and equity instruments are bought and sold.

firm: Business organization that brings together and coordinates factors of production—capital, land, labor, and entrepreneurship—for the purpose of producing a good or service.

First Bank of the United States: *See* **Bank of the United States.**

fiscal drag: Tendency of a high-employment economy to be held back from its full growth potential because it is incurring budgetary surpluses. Such surpluses may arise because, other things being equal, a progressive tax system tends to generate increases in revenues relative to expenditures during periods of high employment.

fiscalism: Macroeconomic theory and policies that follow in the tradition of John Maynard Keynes. Fiscalism places major reliance on manipulation of the federal budget to stabilize the economy. In addition, fiscalist theory concludes that an increase in the money supply leads to a reduction in the interest rate. This causes an increase in the amount of business investment and therefore in aggregate demand. Unemployed resources are drawn into production, and the economy moves toward full employment while prices adjust accordingly. The fiscalist model is thus characterized by (1) a predominantly monetary theory of the interest rate, (2) a predominantly non-monetary theory of the price level, and (3) no distinction between market and real rates of interest. (*Contrast with* **monetarism.**)

fiscal policy: Deliberate exercise of the government's power to tax and spend in order to achieve price stability, help dampen the swings of business cycles, and bring the nation's output and employment to desired levels.

Fisher equation: *See* **equation of exchange.**

Fisher, Irving (1867–1940): One of America's foremost economists during the first half of the twentieth century. A professor at Yale University, he authored many books and articles on diverse topics, including statistics and monetary theory. Among his many contributions was the "Fisher equation," which he used to explain the cause-and-effect relationship between the money supply and the price level. (*See* **equation of exchange** and **quantity theory of money.**)

fixed assets: Durable assets of an enterprise used to carry on its business, such as land, buildings, machinery, equipment, office furniture, automobiles, and trucks.

fixed costs: Costs that do not vary with a firm's output. *Examples:* rental payments, interest on debt, property taxes.

floating exchange rates: Foreign-exchange rates determined in a free market by supply and demand.

"forced" saving: Situation in which consumers are prevented from spending part of their income on consumption. Some examples include: (1) prices rising faster than money wages, causing a decrease in real consumption and hence an increase in real (forced) saving; (2) a corporation that plows back some of its profit instead of distributing it as dividend income to stockholders; and (3) a government that taxes its citizens and uses the funds for investment, thereby preventing the public from utilizing a portion of its income for the purchase of consumer goods.

foreign aid: Loans, grants, or assistance from one government to another for the purpose of accelerating economic development in the recipient country.

foreign exchange: Instruments used for international payments. Such instruments consist not only of currency, but also of checks, drafts, and bills of exchange (which are orders to pay currency).

foreign exchange rate: Price of one currency in terms of another.

foreign-trade multiplier: Principle that states that fluctuations in net exports (that is, imports minus exports) may generate magnified variations in national income. It is based on the idea that a change in exports relative to imports has the same multiplier effect on national income as a change in expenditure "injections" into the income stream. Similarly, a change in imports relative to exports has the same multiplier effect on national income as a change in "withdrawals" from the income stream. In general, an increase in exports tends to raise domestic income, but the increased income also encourages some imports, which act as "leakages." These tend to reduce the full multiplier effect that would exist if imports remained constant.

forward exchange: Foreign exchange bought (or sold) at a given time and at a stipulated current or "spot" price, but payable at a future date. By buying or selling forward exchange, importers and exporters can protect themselves against the risks of fluctuations in the current exchange market.

forward prices: Proposed plan for reducing price uncertainty and encouraging greater stability in agriculture through the use of the price system as an adjustment mechanism. Under the plan, a government-appointed board would predict in advance of breeding or seeding time the equilibrium prices of commodities, based on expected supply and demand. The government would then guarantee those predicted or forward prices in two ways: by storage programs and direct payments to farmers, if actual prices should fall below forward prices, and by a direct tax on farmers, if actual prices should rise above forward prices.

four-firm concentration ratio: See **concentration ratio.**

free good: Good for which the market price is zero at a particular time and place.

free-rider problem: Tendency of people to avoid paying for a good's benefits when they can be obtained free. Public goods (such as national defense, air-traffic control, and so on) provide examples because the benefits of such goods are indivisible and therefore cannot be denied to individuals, whether they pay or not. Those who do not pay are thus "free riders." If many

people become free riders, there might be no way of knowing how much of a public good should be provided. In that case, some form of collective action, usually through government, is taken.

free-trade area: Association of trading nations whose participants agree to impose no restrictive devices, such as tariffs or quotas, on one another but are free to impose whatever restrictive devices they wish on nonparticipants. *Example:* The European Free Trade Association (EFTA).

frictional unemployment: Unemployment due to maladjustments in the economic system resulting from imperfect labor mobility, imperfect knowledge of job opportunities, and a general inability of the economy to match people with jobs instantly and smoothly. A common form of frictional unemployment consists of people who are temporarily out of work because they are between jobs.

Friedman, Milton (1912–): A leading American economist and Nobel laureate (1976) who did pioneering work in the study of consumption theory, monetary economics, and other fields. Most of his career was spent as a professor at the University of Chicago, where he was the foremost exponent of the "Chicago School" of economic thought. This approach to economics extolls free markets, a minimal role for government, and other libertarian views. Friedman thus follows in the tradition of Adam Smith and most other classical economists.

full-cost (average-cost) price: Price for a given volume of output that is at least high enough to cover all of a firm's costs of production—that is, its average total cost for that volume of output. If demand is great enough to enable the firm to sell its entire output at that price, the firm will earn a normal profit. If it can sell its output at a still higher price, it will earn an economic (or pure) profit.

full employment: Condition in which all the economy's resources available for employment are being utilized with maximum efficiency. In terms of society's human resources (which serve as an imperfect but practical representation of "all" resources), full employment means that the entire civilian labor force is working, except for those who are temporarily out of work or who are changing jobs.

Full Employment and Balanced Growth (Humphrey–Hawkins) Act (1976): Federal law with three major provisions: (1) Requires the President to set long-term and short-term production and employment goals, including an annual unemployment-rate target of 4 percent, and to identify means for attaining the goals through public-employment programs, employment-training policies, and so on. (2) Requires the Federal Reserve to declare semiannually its monetary policies and their relation to the President's goals. (3) Requires the government to undertake actions that will achieve the goal of full employment while striving for a zero-percent inflation rate.

full-employment budget: Estimate of annual government expenditures and revenues that would occur if the economy were operating at full employment. Any resulting surplus (or deficit) is called a full-employment surplus (or deficit).

"functional finance": Philosophy that holds that the government should pursue whatever fiscal measures are needed to achieve noninflationary full employment and economic growth—without regard to budget balancing per se. The federal budget is thus viewed functionally as a flexible fiscal tool for achieving economic objectives rather than as an accounting statement to be balanced periodically.

functional income distribution: Payments in the form of wages, rents, interest, and profits made to the owners of the factors of production in return for supplying their labor, land, capital, and entrepreneurial ability.

G

gains from trade: Net benefits or increases in goods that a country receives as a result of trading with others. This concept also applies to trading between small economic entities, such as regions and individuals.

Galbraith, John Kenneth (1908–): American economist whose writing, in the tradition of the "institutionalist school," is perhaps closest to that of Thorstein Veblen. Like Veblen, Galbraith criticized America's capitalistic institutions and processes. Among his chief propositions are these: (1) The market system, dominated by big business, does not perform the way the "conventional wisdom" of traditional economics says that it does. (2) Modern industry is run by a "technostructure" of elite specialists who bamboozle consumers through advertising, thereby insulating big business from the free market. (3) A larger public sector is needed, both economically and politically, to reduce the power of large corporations and to "educate" the people to appreciate "the higher things in life."

General Agreements on Tariffs and Trade (GATT): International commercial agreement signed in 1947 by the United States and many other countries for the purpose of achieving four basic long-run objectives: (1) nondiscrimination in trade through adherence to unconditional most-favored-nation treatment, (2) reduction of tariffs by negotiation, (3) elimination of import quotas (with some exceptions), and (4) resolution of differences through consultation.

general equilibrium theory: Explanation or model of the interrelations between prices and outputs of goods and resources in different markets and the possibility of simultaneous equilibrium among all of them. It is primarily of theoretical interest, but it focuses attention on the fact that, in the real world, markets are often interdependent.

general price level: Expression representing the "average" level of prices in the economy. It is often represented by the **Implicit Price Index**, although no index can accurately reflect all prices.

George, Henry (1839–1897): Prominent American economist whose book, *Progress and Poverty* (1879), ranks as one of the most widely read economic treatises of all time. In the book he advocated a *single tax* on land as the source of all government revenue. In support of his proposal, he argued that, unlike other factors of production, land is provided by nature. Therefore, rent to landlords is an unearned surplus that increases as population grows, depriving the landless of their birthright to a share of the surplus. The solution is government taxation of all land rent. If this were done, no other taxes would be needed. (*See* **single tax**.)

gift tax: Progressive (graduated) tax imposed by the federal government and by some state governments. It is paid by the donor or person who makes the gift, not the donee or recipient of it. Exemptions, deductions, and rates vary widely among the states.

Gini coefficient of inequality: A measure of the degree of inequality in a distribution. On a Lorenz diagram, it equals the numerical value of the area between the Lorenz curve and the diagonal line divided by the entire area beneath the diagonal line. The ratio may vary between 0 (no inequality) and 1 (complete inequality).

GNP deflator: *See* **Implicit Price Index.**

gold-bullion standard: Monetary standard under which (1) the national unit of currency (such as the dollar, pound, or mark) is defined in terms of a fixed weight of gold; (2) gold is held by the government in the form of bars rather than coin; (3) there is no circulation of gold in any form within the economy; and (4) gold is available solely to meet the needs of industry (as in jewelry and dentistry) and to settle international transactions among central banks or treasuries. This is the standard that the United States and most advanced nations adopted when they went off the gold-coin standard in the early 1930s.

gold (coin) standard: Monetary standard under which (1) the national unit of currency (such as the dollar, pound, or franc) is defined by law in terms of a fixed weight of gold; (2) there is a free and unrestricted flow of the metal in any form into and out of the country; (3) gold coins are full legal tender for all debts; (4) there is free convertibility between the national currency and gold coins at a defined rate; and (5) there are no restrictions on the coinage of gold. Nearly 50 countries of the world were on this standard in the late nineteenth and early twentieth centuries.

gold-exchange standard: Monetary standard under which a nation's unit of currency is defined in terms of another nation's unit of currency, which in turn is defined in terms of, and is convertible into, gold. This standard prevailed in the noncommunist world from 1944 to 1971 and is primarily of international economic significance. Thus, in this period, the U.S. dollar was defined as equal to $1/35$ of an ounce of gold and was convertible to foreign central banks at this rate. Each foreign central bank, in turn, defined the par value of its own currency in terms of the U.S. dollar and maintained it at that level. The entire system operated by international agreement (under the **International Monetary Fund**).

gold points: Range within which the foreign exchange rates of gold-standard countries will fluctuate. Thus the gold points are equal to the par rate of exchange plus and minus the cost (including insurance) of shipping gold. The upper and lower gold points for a nation are called its "gold-export point" and its "gold-import point," respectively, because gold will be exported when the foreign exchange rate rises above the upper level and will be imported when the rate falls below the lower level. One nation's gold-export point is thus another nation's gold-import point, and vice versa.

goldsmiths' principle: Banks can maintain a fractional—rather than 100 percent—reserve against deposits, because customers will not ordinarily withdraw their funds at the same time. Hence the banks can earn interest by lending out unused or excess reserves. This principle was discovered centuries ago by the English goldsmiths, who held gold in safekeeping for customers.

government monopoly: Monopoly both owned and operated by either a federal or a local government. *Examples:* The U.S. Postal Service, many water and sewer systems, and the central banks of most countries.

grants-in-aid: Financial aid at the intergovernmental level that consists of (1) revenues received by local governments from their states and from the federal government; and (2) revenues received by state governments from the federal government. These revenues are used mainly to help pay for public welfare assistance, highways, and education.

Great Leap Forward: Ambitious economic plan undertaken by China during 1958–1960 to accelerate enormously its rate of economic growth. The plan was unrealistic and forced the country into a major economic crisis.

greenbacks: Paper money (officially called United States Notes) issued by the Treasury to help finance the Civil War, 1861–1865. The currency was not redeemable in specie (gold or silver coins) and was the first official legal-tender money issued by the federal government. (*Note:* The U.S. dollar today is sometimes called a "greenback," but this is a colloquial rather than a literal term.)

Gresham's Law: Principle which asserts that cheap money tends to drive dear money out of circulation. Thus, if two kinds of metals, such as gold and silver, circulate with equal legal-tender powers (as happened in the United States under the bimetallic standard during the nineteenth century), the cheaper metal will become the chief circulating medium while the dearer metal will be hoarded, melted down, or exported, thereby disappering from circulation. The law is named after Sir Thomas Gresham, Master of the Mint under Queen Elizabeth I during the sixteenth century. (*See also* **mint ratio; bimetallic standard.**)

gross national disproduct: Sum of all social costs or reductions in benefits to society that result from producing the gross national product. *Example:* Pollution of the environment is part of gross national disproduct, to the extent that it is caused by production of the gross national product.

gross national income (GNI): The equivalent of gross national product from the "income" viewpoint. It consists of national income at factor cost (that is, the sum of wages, rent, interest, and profit) plus two nonincome or business-expense items: indirect business taxes and capital consumption allowance.

gross national product (GNP): Total market value of all final goods and services produced by an economy during a year.

growth: *See* **economic growth**

guaranteed annual income: Plan that awards all families under a certain "poverty line" level a straight allowance for each parent plus specified amounts for each child according to the size of the family. No family receives less than a designated amount; and, as a family's income rises, the payment from the government is reduced until a break-even level (which is a little higher than the poverty line) is reached.

H

hard-core unemployed: People who are unemployed because they lack the education and skills for today's complex economy. (Discrimination may also be a contributing factor.) They consist mainly of certain minority groups, such as blacks, Chicanos, the "too-old," the "too-young," high-school dropouts, and the permanently displaced (who are victims of technological change).

hedging: Purchase and sale of a commodity in two different markets at the same time and a corresponding offsetting sale and purchase of the same commodity in the two markets at a later time. The markets involved are the cash or spot market, in which a physical commodity is bought and sold, and the futures or forward market, in which contracts for subsequent delivery of the physical commodity are bought and sold. Hedging helps firms to reduce inventory costs, adjust to changing market conditions, and plan future supplies of goods needed for production. Hence it also leads to lower prices.

Hicks, John R. (1904–): Leading British economist and Nobel laureate. He contributed significantly to the reconstruction of demand theory through the development of indifference-curve analysis. His work thus follows in the tradition of general equilibrium theory as formulated by Leon Walras and Vilfredo Pareto in the late nineteenth century. Among Hick's other leading contributions have been a refinement of the marginal-productivity theory of wages and an integrated analysis of Keynesian with classical theory.

"high-powered money": *See* **monetary base.**

hog–corn price ratio: Number of bushels of corn required to buy 100 pounds of live pork:

$$\text{hog–corn price ratio} = \frac{\text{price of live hogs per 100 pounds}}{\text{price of corn per bushel}}$$

When the ratio is relatively low, hog production decreases because farmers find it more profitable to sell their corn in the market than to use it for feeding hogs. Conversely, when the ratio is relatively high, hog production increases because farmers use the corn to feed more hogs and to market them at heavier weights.

horizontal equity: Doctrine that states that "equals should be treated equally." *Example:* Persons with the same income, wealth, or other taxpaying ability should, in order to bear equal tax burdens (or make equal subjective sacrifices), pay the same amount of tax. (*Compare* **vertical equity.**)

horizontal merger: Amalgamation under one ownership of plants engaged in producing similar products. The products might be close substitutes, such as competing brands of cement, or moderate substitutes, such as tin cans and jars. The objective is to round out a product line that is sold through the same distribution channels, thereby offering joint economies in selling and distribution efforts.

Hotelling's paradox: Proposition that states that monopolistically competitive firms must, in order to attract each other's customers, make their products as similar to existing products as possible without destroying the differences. Therefore, as a type of market structure, monopolistic competition leads to maximum differentiation of products with minimum differences between them. (This proposition was formulated analytically in 1929 by a distinguished economist and statistician, Harold Hotelling. Because the theory of monopolistic competition had not yet been formulated, Hotelling's model was based on what he called "industries composed of many firms and similar goods.")

household: All persons living in the same home. A household may thus consist of one or more families.

human resources: Productive physical and mental talents of the people who constitute an economy.

Humphrey–Hawkins bill: *See* **Full Employment and Balanced Growth Act (1978).**

hyperinflation: Situation in which prices are rising with little or no increase in output; hence it is also sometimes called "runaway" or "galloping" inflation.

hypothesis: A working guess about the behavior of things, or an expression about the relationship between variables in the real world. In economics, the "things" may include consumers, workers, business firms, investors, and so on, and the variables may include prices, wages, consumption, production, or other economic quantities.

I

imperfect competition: A classification of market structures that falls between the two extremes of perfect competition and monopoly. It consists of monopolistic competition and oligopoly.

implicit costs: Costs of self-owned or self-employed resources that are not recorded in a company's book of account. *Example:* the alternative interest return, rental receipts, and wages that a self-employed proprietor forgoes by owning and operating his own business.

Implicit Price Index (GNP deflator): Weighted average of the price indexes used to deflate the components of GNP. Thus, for any given year,

$$\text{GNP in constant prices} = \frac{\text{GNP in current prices}}{\text{Implicit Price Index (= IPI)}}$$

Therefore,

$$\text{IPI} = \frac{\text{GNP in current prices}}{\text{GNP in constant prices}}$$

Because of its comprehensiveness, the IPI is the best single measure of broad price movements in the economy.

import quota: Law that limits the number of units of a commodity that may be imported during a given period.

impossibility theorem: *See* **Arrow's impossibility theorem.**

incidence: Range of occurrence or influence of an economic act. It is a term used primarily in the study of taxation and refers to the economic entity (such as a household or a firm) that bears the ultimate burden of a tax.

income: Gain derived from the use of human or material resources. A flow of dollars per unit of time. (*Compare* **wealth.**)

income-consumption curve: In indifference-curve analysis, a line showing the amounts of two commodities that a consumer will purchase when his income changes while the prices of the commodities remain the same. Geometrically, it is a line connecting the tangency points of price lines and indifference curves as income changes while prices remain constant.

income distribution: Division of society's output (that is, income society earns) among people. Income distribution thus concerns the matter of who gets how much, or what proportion, of the economy's total production. (*See* **functional income distribution; personal income distribution.**)

income effect: Change in quantity of a good demanded by a buyer due to a change in his real income resulting from a change in the price of a commodity. It assumes that the buyer's money income, tastes, and the prices of all other goods remain the same. (*Compare* **substitution effect.**)

income elasticity of demand: Percentage change in the quantity purchased of a good resulting from a one-percent change in income. Thus,

income elasticity of demand
$$= \frac{\text{percentage change in quantity purchased}}{\text{percentage change in income}}$$
$$= \frac{(Q_2 - Q_1)/(Q_2 + Q_1)}{(Y_2 - Y_1)/(Y_2 + Y_1)}$$

in which Q_1 and Q_2 represent the quantities purchased before and after the change in income and Y_1 and Y_2 represent the corresponding levels of income before and after the change. Thus the income elasticity of demand denotes the responsiveness of changes in quantity purchased to changes in income, where responsiveness is measured in terms of percentge changes.

income statement: Financial statement of a firm showing its revenues, costs, and profit during a period. Also known as a profit-and-loss statement.

income tax: Tax on the net income, or the residual that remains after certain items are subtracted from gross income. The two types of income taxes are the personal income tax and the corporation income tax.

income velocity of money: Average number of times per year that a dollar is spent on purchasing a part of the economy's annual flow of final goods and services—its GNP. It equals the ratio of GNP to the quantity of money. (*See also* **equation of exchange.**)

incomes policy: Laws aimed at curbing inflation by establishing conditions under which businesses' production costs (especially wages), prices, and profits may be allowed to increase. *Examples:* Wage and price controls.

inconvertible paper standard: Monetary standard under which the nation's unit of currency may or may not be defined in terms of any metal or other precious substance; however, there is no free convertibility into these other forms. Historically, this standard has existed on a domestic basis in all countries since the worldwide abandonment of gold in the 1930s.

increasing-cost industry: Industry that experiences increases in resource prices or in its costs of production as it expands because of new firms entering it. This will happen when the industry's demand for the resources it employs is a significant proportion of the total demand for those resources.

increasing costs, law of: Principle that states that, on an economy's production-possibilities curve relating two kinds of goods, the real cost of acquiring either good is not the money that must be spent for it but the increasing amount of the alternative good that the society must sacrifice or "give up" because it cannot have all it wants of both goods.

Independent Treasury Act (1846): Law that created the Independent Treasury System (1846–1863). During its life, the law enabled the Treasury to act as its own bank, receiving and disbursing its own funds, thus making it independent of the banking system. The Independent Treasury System also engaged in the purchase and sale of government bonds, thus affecting the quantity of money. This procedure, which decades later was called *open-market operations*, became an integral part of the Federal Reserve System after its establishment in 1913.

independent union: Labor union not affiliated with any federation of labor organizations. It may be national or international, and it is not limited to workers in any one firm.

indexation: Assignment of inflation-adjusting escalator clauses to long-term contracts. Thus wages, rents, interest payments, and even the tax system can be readjusted in proportion to price changes so that people's gains due to inflation are not taxed away, thereby reducing real income. *Example:* If your income goes up by 10 percent when prices go up by 10 percent, you have no more purchasing power than before. Yet your income tax will rise because you will be pushed into a higher tax bracket. This situation can be avoided by indexing the income tax, thereby "correcting" it for inflation. (*See* **escalator clause**.)

index numbers: Figures that disclose the relative changes in a series of numbers, such as prices or production, from a base period. The base period is usually defined as being equal to an index number of 100, and all other numbers in the series both before or after that period are expressed as percentages of that period. Index numbers are widely used in reporting business and economic data.

indifference curve: Graph of an indifference schedule. Every point along the curve represents a different combination of two commodities, and each combination is equally satisfactory to a recipient because each one yields the same total utility.

indifference schedule: Table showing the various combinations of two commodities that would be equally satisfactory or yield the same total utility to a recipient at a given time.

indirect tax: Tax that can be shifted either partially or entirely to someone other than the individual or firm originally taxed. *Examples:* sales taxes, excise taxes, taxes on business and rental properties.

induced consumption: That part of total consumption that is related to income.

induced investment: Tendency of rising income, output, and economic activity to stimulate higher levels of investment. That part of total investment that is related to aggregate income or output. It may also be directly related to induced consumption, which in turn is related to income. (*Compare* **autonomous investment**.)

induction: Process of reasoning from particular observations or cases to general laws or principles. Most human knowledge is inductive or empirical since it is based on the experiences of our senses. (Opposite of **deduction**.)

industrial relations: Rules and regulations governing the relationship between union and management. It often deals with such matters as union security (for example, the type of recognition that the union is accorded, or its financial arrangement for collecting dues) and methods of controlling the quantity and kind of union membership through apprenticeship requirements, licensing provisions, initiation fees, and seniority rules.

industrial union: Labor union consisting solely of workers from a particular industry, such as a union of coal miners or a union of steel workers. It is thus a "vertically" organized union.

industry: Group of firms producing similar or identical products.

infant industry: Underdeveloped industry that, in the face of competition from abroad, may not be able to survive the early years of struggle before reaching maturity.

inferior good: A good whose consumption varies inversely with money income (prices remaining constant) over a certain range of income. *Examples:* potatoes, used clothing, and other "cheap" commodities bought by poor families. The consumption of these commodities declines in favor of fancier foods, new clothing, and the like as the incomes of low-income families rise.

inflation: Rise in the general price level (or average level of prices) of all goods and services. Equivalently, it is a decline in the purchasing power of a unit of money (such as the dollar). The general price level thus varies inversely with the purchasing power of a unit of money. For example, if prices double, purchasing power decreases by one-half; if prices halve, purchasing power doubles.

inflationary gap: Amount by which aggregate demand exceeds aggregate supply at full employment, thereby causing inflationary pressures.

infrastructure: A nation's economic and social overhead capital needed as a basis for modern production. *Examples:* roads, telephone lines, power facilities, schools, and public health.

inheritance tax: Tax imposed by most state governments on property received from persons who have died. It is primarily progressive (graduated) in rate structure, but exemptions, deductions, and rates vary widely among the states.

injunction: Court order requiring that a defendant refrain from certain practices or that he take a particular action.

innovation: Adoption of a new or different product or of a new or different method of production, marketing, financing, and so on. It thus establishes a new relation between the output and the various kinds of imputs (capital, land, labor, and so forth) in a production process. In a more formal sense, it is the setting up of a new production function.

innovation theory: Explanation originated by Joseph Schumpeter (1883–1950) that attributes business cycles and economic development to innovations that forward-looking businesspeople adopt in order to reduce costs and increase profits. Once an innovation proves successful, other businesspeople follow with the same or with similar techniques, and these innovations cause fluctuations in investment that result in business cycles. The innovation theory has also been used as a partial explanation of how profits arise in a competitive capitalistic system.

institutions: Those traditions, beliefs, and practices which are well established and widely held as a fundamental part of a culture. *Example:* Institutions of capitalism include private property, economic individualism, laissez-faire, and free markets. (*Note:* In sociology, social systems are often characterized by their institutions. Examples of sociological institutions are marriage, the family, and so on. Institutions are thus the pillars or foundations on which a social system rests.)

interest: 1. Return to those who supply the factor of production known as "capital" (that is, the payment for supplying the funds with which businesspeople buy capital goods). **2.** Price paid for the use of credit or loanable funds over a period of time. It is stated as a rate—that is, as a percentage of the amount borrowed. Thus an interest rate of 10% annually means that the borrower pays 10 cents per $1 borrowed per year, or $10 per $100 borrowed per year, and so on. (*Note:* This definition of interest assumes that borrowers and lenders expect prices to be stable. If they are not, there will be a difference between the actual (or market) rate of interest and the real rate. See **real rate of interest.**)

interlocking directorate: Situation in which an individual serves on two or more boards of directors of competing corporations.

internal economies and diseconomies of scale: Conditions that bring about decreases or increases in a firm's long-run average costs or scale of operations as a result of size adjustments within the firm as a producing unit. They occur irrespective of adjustments within the industry and are due mainly to physical economies or diseconomies. *Example:* Internal economies may result from greater specialization and more efficient utilization of the firm's resources as its scale of operations increases, but internal diseconomies may eventually set in because of the limited decision-making abilities of the top management group.

International Bank for Reconstruction and Development (World Bank): Established by the United Nations in 1945 to provide loans for postwar reconstruction and to promote development of less developed countries. The Bank's chief function is to aid the financing of basic development projects, such as dams, communication and transportation facilities, and health programs, by insuring or otherwise guaranteeing private loans or, when private capital is not available, by providing loans from its own resources and credit. Affiliated agencies also exist to help finance higher-risk investment projects in underdeveloped countries.

International Development Cooperation Agency (IDCA): The most important American organization concerned with foreign aid. Created in 1979, it represents a major restructuring and consolidation of previous development programs operated by different U.S. agencies and various multilateral organizations. IDCA has two major functions. The first is to advise government on development policies. The second is to administer funds voted annually by Congress for the purpose of providing economic, technical, and defense assistance to nations that are identified with the free world. (IDCA includes within its organization the Agency for International Development, the government's chief foreign-aid unit, which was previously part of the U.S. State Department.)

International Monetary Fund (IMF): Established by the United Nations in 1944 for the purpose of eliminating exchange restrictions, encouraging exchange-rate stability, and providing for worldwide convertibility of currencies in order to promote multilateral trade based on international specialization. More than 100 nations are members of the Fund.

inventory: Stocks of goods that business firms have on hand, including raw materials, supplies, and finished goods.

investment: Spending by business firms on new job-creating and income-producing goods. It consists of replacements of, or additions to, the nation's stock of capital, including its plant, equipment, and inventories (that is, its nonhuman productive assets).

"invisible hand": Expression coined by Adam Smith in *The Wealth of Nations* to convey the idea that each individual, if left to pursue his self-interest without interference by government, would be led, as if by an invisible hand, to achieve the best good for society.

involuntary unemployment: Situation in which people who want work are unable to find jobs at the wage rates prevailing for the skills and experience they have to offer.

isoquant: Curve along which each point represents a different combination of two inputs or factors of production (such as capital and labor) and each combination yields the same level of total output.

J

Jevons, William Stanley (1835–1882): English neoclassical and mathematical economist who made major contributions to value and distribution theory, capital theory, and to statistical research in economics. He is best known as a leading contributor to marginal utility analysis. "Value," he pointed out, "depends entirely upon utility." In equilibrium, marginal utilities are proportionate to prices. "From this, the ordinary laws of supply and demand are a necessary consequence." Jevon's major work in economics was his book, *Theory of Political Economy* (1871).

job classification: Process of describing the duties, responsibilities, and characteristics of jobs, point-rating them (perhaps by established formulas based on engineering time studies of workers in such jobs), and then grouping the jobs into graduated classifications with corresponding wage rates and wage ranges.

jurisdictional strike: Strike caused by a dispute between two or more craft unions over which shall perform a particular job. Outlawed by the Taft–Hartley Act, 1947.

K

Keynes, John Maynard (1883–1946): British economist and founder of the New Economics. His most widely known work was his book *The General Theory of Employment, Interest and Money* (1936), in which he reorganized thinking about macroeconomic problems. The following chief features characterize the so-called Keynesian "system": (1) the dependency of consumption on income, called the **consumption function;** (2) the **multiplier** relationship between investment expenditures and income; (3) the **marginal efficiency of investment** as a measure of businesses demand for investment; and (4) the use of **fiscal policy** and **monetary policy** to maintain full employment. In contrast to the classical theory, Keynes showed that our economic system could remain in equilibrium at any level of employment, not necessarily full employment. Therefore, he concluded, active fiscal and monetary policies by government are needed to maintain high levels of resource utilization and economic stability. (*See also* **Keynesian economics.**)

Keynesian economics: Body of economic thought that originated with the British economist John Maynard Keynes (1882–1946) in the 1930s. It has since been extended and modified to the point where many of its basic analytical tools and ideas are now an integral part of general economic theory. In contrast to classical economics, which emphasized the automatic tendency of the economy to achieve full-employment equilibrium under a government policy of laissez-faire, Keynesian economics seeks to demonstrate that an economy may be in equilibrium at any level of employment. The theory, therefore, concludes that appropriate government fiscal and monetary policies are needed to maintain full employment and steady economic growth with a minimum rate of inflation.

kinked demand curve: A "bent" demand curve, and a corresponding discontinuous marginal revenue curve, facing an oligopolistic seller. The kinked curve signifies that, if the seller raises the price above the kink, sales will fall off rapidly because other sellers are not likely to follow the price upward. If the seller reduces the price below the kink, sales will expand relatively little because other sellers are likely to follow the price downward. The market price, therefore, tends to stabilize at the kink.

Knights of Labor: National labor organization founded in 1869. It rejected the traditional organizing of workers by crafts, preferring instead the mass unionization of both unskilled and skilled workers. The Knights championed the cause of workers and achieved many liberal improvements and reforms, but began to decline in the late 1880s due to several factors: (1) opposition by craft leaders who preferred organization along craft lines; (2) internal dissension among leading members and groups; and (3) suspicion—unproved—that it was involved in Chicago's Haymarket riot and bombing of 1886. By 1917, it had ceased to exist.

Kuznets, Simon Smith (1901–): Russian-born American economist who made major contributions to the study of national income accounting, economic growth, productivity, and related areas. He is the "father" of national income accounting because much of his efforts toward improving the theory and measurement of national income during the 1930s became a foundation for subsequent methods by the U.S. Department of Commerce. In 1971, at the age of 70, Kuznets was awarded the Nobel Prize in Economic Science.

L

labor: 1. Factor of production that represents those hired workers whose human efforts or activities are directed toward production. **2.** All personal services, including the activities of wageworkers, professional people, and independent businesspeople. "Laborers" may thus receive compensation not only in the form of wages but also as salaries, bonuses, commissions, and the like.

labor force: The employable population, defined for measurement purposes as all people 16 years of age or older who are employed plus all those who are unemployed but actively seeking work.

Labor–Management Relations (Taft–Hartley) Act (1947): An amendment to the National Labor Relations (Wagner) Act of 1935. It retains the rights given to labor by the 1935 Act but also: (1) outlaws "unfair labor practices" of unions, such as coercion of workers to join unions, failure to bargain in good faith, jurisdictional strikes, secondary boycotts, and featherbedding; (2) outlaws the closed shop but permits the union shop; (3) requires unions to file financial reports with the NLRB and union officials to sign affidavits to the effect that they are not Communists; (4) prohibits strikes called before the end of a 60-day notice period prior to the expiration of a collective-bargaining agreement; and (5) enables the President to obtain an 80-day court injunction against strikes that endanger national health or safety.

Labor–Management Reporting and Disclosure (Landrum–Griffin) Act (1959): Act that amended the National Labor Relations Act of 1935 by (1) requiring detailed financial reports of all unions and union officers; (2) severely tightening restrictions on secondary boycotting and picketing; (3) requiring periodic secret-ballot elections of union officers; and (4) restricting ex-convicts and Communists from holding positions as union officers.

Laffer curve: A hypothetical relationship between tax revenues and the tax rate. The relationship is such that, as the tax rate increases from zero to 100 percent, tax revenues rise correspondingly from zero to some maximum level and then decline to zero. The optimum rate is thus the one that produces the maximum revenue. Rates that are lower than optimum are deemed "normal" because tax revenues can be increased by raising the rate. Rates that are higher than optimum are regarded as prohibitive because they impair personal and business incentives and are thus counterproductive. Therefore, when the tax rate is in the prohibitive range, tax reductions should bring increased economic activity and higher, not lower, tax revenues. (*Note:* There is no concrete evidence to support this assumed relationship between tax revenues and the tax rate.)

lagging indicators: Time series that tend to follow or trail aggregate economic activity.

laissez-faire: "Leave us alone"—an expression, coined in France during the late seventeenth century, that today is interpreted to mean freedom from government intervention in all economic affairs.

land: Factor of production that includes land itself (in the form of real estate) as well as mineral deposits, timber, water, and other nonhuman or "natural" resources.

law: Expression of a relationship between variables, based on a high degree of unvarying uniformity under the same conditons. (Often used synonymously with **principle**.)

leading indicators: Time series that tend to move ahead of aggregate economic activity, thus reaching peaks and troughs before the economy as a whole.

legal monopoly: Privately owned firm that is granted an exclusive right by government to operate in a particular market. In return, government may impose standards and requirements pertaining to the quantity and quality of output, geographic areas of operation, and the prices or rates that are charged. The justification of legal monopoly is that unrestricted competition in the industry is socially undesirable. Public utilities are typical examples of legal monopolies.

legal reserves: Assets that a bank or other depository institution (such as a savings and loan association or credit union) may lawfully use as reserves against its deposit liabilities. For a member bank of the Federal Reserve System, legal reserves consist of deposits held with the district Federal Reserve Bank plus currency held in the vaults of the bank—called "vault cash." Any other highly liquid financial claims, such as government securities, are classified as *nonlegal reserves*. For a nonmember bank or other depository institution, legal reserves include vault cash and deposits held with the district Federal Reserve Bank or with an approved institution. The latter includes any depository institution (such as a member bank) that holds a reserve balance with the Federal Reserve.

Lerner index: Measure of a firm's monopoly power, based on the divergence between price, P, and marginal cost, MC, expressed as a proportion of price. Thus

$$\text{Lerner index} = \frac{P - MC}{P}$$

When a firm is in equilibrium, the index will range between 0 and 1. It will be zero (no monopoly power) for a firm in perfect competition, since $P = MC$. At the other extreme, the index will be 1 (complete monopoly power) in the rare case of a firm whose marginal costs are zero. Basic shortcomings of the formula are that (1) marginal-cost data for a firm are not generally known and cannot be readily derived; and (2) it is a static rather than dynamic measure.

less developed (underdeveloped) country: A nation that, in comparison with the more developed countries, tends to exhibit such characteristics as (1) poverty level of income and hence little or no saving, (2) high rate of population growth, (3) substantial majority of its labor force employed in agriculture, (4) low proportion of adult literacy, (5) extensive disguised unemployment, and (6) heavy reliance on a few items for export.

liabilities: Monetary debts or things of value owned by an economic entity (such as an individual, household, or business firm) to creditors.

limited liability: Restriction of the liability of an investor, such as a stockholder in a corporation, to the amount of his investment.

liquidity: Ease with which an asset can be converted into cash quickly without loss of value in terms of money. Liquidity is thus a matter of degree. Money is perfectly liquid, wheres any other asset possesses a lower degree of liquidity—depending on the condition above.

liquidity preference (theory of interest): Theory formulated by J. M. Keynes (1883–1946). The theory contends that households and businesses would rather hold their assets in the most liquid form—cash or checking accounts. The reason is to satisfy three motives: (1) the "transactions motive," to carry out everyday purchasing needs; (2) the "precautionary motive," to meet possible unforeseen conditions; and (3) the "speculative motive," to take advantage of a change in interest rates. These motives determine the demand for money, whereas the monetary authority determines its supply. The demand for, and supply of, money together determine the equilibrium rate of interest.

liquidity trap: Condition in which an increase in the supply of money will not further reduce the rate of interest, because the total demand for money at that relatively low interest rate (expressed in terms of a liquidity-preference curve) is infinite. This means that, at the low rate of interest, everyone would rather hold money in idle balances than risk the loss of holding long-term securities offering poor yields. (In geometric terms, the liquidity trap exists at that rate of interest where the liquidity-preference curve becomes perfectly horizontal.)

loanable-funds theory of interest: Theory that holds that the interest rate is determined by the demand for, and the supply of, loanable funds only, as distinguished from *all* money. The sources of demand for loanable funds are businesses that want

to invest, households that want to finance consumer purchases, and government agencies that want to finance deficits. The sources of supply of loanable funds are the central banking system, which influences the supply of money (and hence the supply of loanable funds) in the economy, and households and businesses that make loanable funds available out of their past or present savings.

lockout: Closing down of a plant by an employer in order to keep workers out of their jobs.

logarithmic scale: Special type of scale used in graphing. The scale is spaced in logarithms. As a result, equal *percentage* changes between numbers are represented by equal distances along the scale. For example, a 100 percent change is always the same distance on the scale whether the change is from 1 to 2, 2 to 4, 3 to 6, 5 to 10, 10 to 20, or 50 to 100. In contrast, a conventional scale is spaced arithmetically. Therefore, equal *amounts* of change between numbers are represented by equal distances along the scale. Thus the changes from 1 to 2, 2 to 3, 6 to 7, 15 to 16, and so on, are all the same distances on an arithmetic scale. A logarithmic scale is useful for comparing *ratios* of change between data. In contrast, an arithmetic scale is used to compare *amounts* of change between data.

long run: Period that is long enough for a firm to enter or leave an industry and to vary its output by varying all its factors of production, including its plant scale.

long-run average cost curve (planning curve): Curve that is tangent to, or envelops, the various short-run average total cost curves of a firm over a range of output representing different scales or sizes of plant. Thus it shows what the level of average costs would be for alternative outputs of different-sized plants.

long-run industry supply curve: Locus or "path" of a competitive industry's long-run equilibrium points. That is, the long-run industry supply curve connects the stable equilibrium points of the industry's supply and demand curves over a period of time, both before and after these curves have adjusted completely to changed market conditions. The long-run industry supply curve may be either upward-sloping, horizontal, or downward-sloping, depending on whether the industry is an increasing-, constant-, or decreasing-cost industry.

Lorenz diagram: Graphic device for comparing the actual distribution of a variable with an equal distribution of that variable. It is most often employed to compare a society's actual distribution of income among families with an equal distribution. For example, each axis of the chart is scaled from 0 to 100 percent. Then the cumulative percentage relationships between two variables, such as "percent of income" and "percent of families," are plotted against each other. The resulting (Lorenz) curve of actual income distribution is then compared to a 45° diagonal line representing equal income distribution. The degree of difference between the two curves indicates the extent of income inequality. Similar curves may be constructed to show other types of distributions (such as distribution of wealth or distribution of wages in a factory).

M

macroeconomics: The part of economics that deals with the economy as a whole, or with large subdivisions of it. It analyzes the economic "forest" rather than the "trees."

Malthusian theory of population: First published by Thomas Malthus in 1798 and then revised in 1803, this theory states that population tends to increase as a geometric progression (1, 2, 4, 8, 16, 32, and so forth) while the means of subsistence increase at most only as an arithmetic progression (1, 2, 3, 4, 5, 6, and so forth). This is because a growing population applied to a fixed amount of land results in eventually diminishing returns to workers. Human beings are therefore destined to misery and poverty unless the rate of population growth is retarded. This may be accomplished either by (1) preventive checks, such as moral restraint, late marriages, and celibacy or, if these fail, by (2) positive checks, such as wars, famines, and disease.

Malthus, Thomas Robert (1776–1834): English classical economist. Best known for his theory that held that population would tend to outrun the food supply. The result would be a bare subsistence level of survival for the laboring class. (*See* **Malthusian theory of population.**) Malthus, in his book *Principles of Political Economy* (1820), also developed the concept of "effective demand," which he defined as the level of aggregate demand necessary to maintain full employment. If effective demand declined, he said, overpopulation would result. He thus anticipated a fundamental concept in modern macroeconomics.

manpower policies: See **employment-training policies.**

Marcet, Jane Haldimand (1769–1858): English economic educator whose book, *Conversations on Political Economy* (1816), conveyed in dialogue form the teachings of her classical-economic predecessors and contemporaries—Smith, Say, Malthus, and Ricardo. She thus contributed significantly to the teaching of economics.

marginal cost: Change in total cost resulting from a unit change in quantity. Marginal cost is thus the additional cost of one more unit of output. It is calculated by a formula:

$$\text{marginal cost} = \frac{\text{change in total cost}}{\text{change in quantity}}$$

Marginal cost is also the change in total variable cost resulting from a unit change in quantity. The reason is that total cost changes because total variable cost changes, whereas total fixed cost remains constant.

marginal-cost price: Price (or production) of output as determined by the point at which a firm's marginal cost equals its average revenue (demand). This is an optimum price for society, because the value of the last unit to the marginal user (measured by the price he pays for the last unit, which is equal to the price he pays for any other unit) is equivalent to the value of the resources used to produce that unit. However, this marginal-cost price will leave the firm suffering a loss if it results in a price below the firm's average total cost.

marginal efficiency of investment: Expected rate of return on an addition to investment. More precisely, it is the expected rate of return over the cost of an additional unit of a capital good. It is determined by such factors as (1) the demand for the product that the investment will produce; (2) the level of production costs in the economy; (3) technology and innovation; and (4) the stock of capital available to meet existing and future market demands.

marginal product: Change in total product resulting from a unit change in the quantity of a variable input employed. It is calculated by a formula:

$$\text{marginal product} = \frac{\text{change in total product}}{\text{change in a variable input}}$$

Marginal product thus measures the gain (or loss) in total product from adding an additional unit of a variable factor of production.

marginal-productivity theory of income distribution: Principle that states that, when there is perfect competition for inputs, a firm will purchase factors of production up to the point at which the price or marginal cost of the factor is equal to its marginal revenue productivity. Therefore, in real terms, each factor of production will be paid a value equal to what it contributes to total output—that is, it will be paid what it is "worth."

marginal propensity to consume: Change in consumption resulting from a unit change in income. it is calculated by a formula:

$$\text{marginal propensity to consume} = \frac{\text{change in consumption}}{\text{change in income}}$$

It thus reveals the fraction of each extra dollar of income that is spent on consumption.

marginal propensity to invest: Change in investment resulting from a unit change in aggregate output. It is calculated by a formula:

$$\text{marginal propensity to invest} = \frac{\text{change in investment}}{\text{change in aggregate output}}$$

marginal propensity to save: Change in saving resulting from a unit change in income. It is calculated by a formula:

$$\text{marginal propensity to save} = \frac{\text{change in saving}}{\text{change in income}}$$

It thus reveals the fraction of each extra dollar of income that is saved.

marginal propensity to spend: Change in total spending on consumption and investment resulting from a unit change in aggregate output or income. The marginal propensity to spend, *MPE*, consists of the marginal propensity to consume, *MPC*, and the marginal propensity to invest, *MPI*. Thus, out of any change in aggregate output or income,

$$MPE = MPC + MPI$$

marginal rate of substitution: 1. In demand theory, the rate at which a consumer is willing to substitute one commodity for another along an indifference curve. It is the amount of change in the holdings of one commodity that will just offset a unit change in the holdings of another commodity, so that the consumer's total utility remains the same. Thus, along an indifference curve,

$$\text{marginal rate of substitution} = \frac{\text{change in commodity } Y}{\text{change in commodity } X}$$

The marginal rate of substitution is always negative because one commodity must be decreased when the other is increased in order to keep total utility the same (that is, to remain on a given indifference curve). **2.** In production theory, the marginal rate of substitution is the change in one type of productive input that will just offset a unit change in another type of productive input, so that the total level of production (along an **isoquant**) remains the same. Some examples of productive inputs are capital and labor, fertilizer and land.

marginal revenue: Change in total revenue resulting from a unit change in quantity. It is calculated by a formula:

$$\text{marginal revenue} = \frac{\text{change in total revenue}}{\text{change in quantity}}$$

Marginal revenue thus measures the gain (or loss) in total revenue that results from producing and selling an additional unit.

marginal revenue product: Change in total revenue resulting from a unit change in the quantity of a variable input employed. It is calculated by a formula:

$$\text{marginal revenue product} = \frac{\text{change in total revenue}}{\text{change in a variable input}}$$

Marginal revenue product thus measures the gain (or loss) in total revenue from adding an additional unit of a variable factor of production.

marginal tax rate: Ratio, expressed as a percentage, of the change in a total tax resulting from a unit change in the base on which it is imposed. *Example:*

$$\text{marginal personal income tax rate} = \frac{\text{change in total personal income tax}}{\text{change in total taxable income}}$$

marginal utility: Change in total utility resulting from a unit change in the quantity of a commodity consumed. It is calculated by a formula:

$$\text{marginal utility} = \frac{\text{change in total utility}}{\text{change in quantity consumed}}$$

Marginal utility thus measures the gain (or loss) in satisfaction from an additional unit of a good.

margin requirements: 1. Percentage down payment required of a borrower to finance the purchase of stock. This rate is set by the Federal Reserve System's Board of Governors. An increase in margin requirements is designed to dampen security purchases; a decrease, to encourage them. **2.** Percentage down payment required of a borrower to finance the purchase of futures contracts in the futures market. The rate is set by the exchange's regulatory commission.

market economy: Economic system in which the questions of what to produce, how much to produce, and for whom to produce are decided in an open market through the free operation of supply and demand. There are no "pure" market economies, but several specialized markets (such as the organized commodity exchanges) closely approximate some of the properties of a pure market system. (*Compare* **command economy.**)

market price: Actual price that prevails in a market at any particular moment.

market rate of interest: Actual or money rate of interest that prevails in the market at any given time. (*Contrast with* **real rate of interest.**)

market share: Percentage of an industry's output accounted for by an individual firm. Measures of output usually employed are sales, value added, or value of shipments.

Marshall, Alfred (1842–1924): English economist who synthesized neoclassical thinking around the turn of the century and made many pioneering contributions as well. Among these were making a formal distinction between the short run and the long run and describing the equilibrium of price and output resulting from the interaction of supply and demand. He also formulated the concept of elasticity, made the distinction between money cost and real cost, and framed many other economic concepts. Much of modern microeconomics stems from Marshall's work. His best-known book, *Principles of Economics*, went through eight editions and was a standard reference and text in economics from 1890 until the 1930s.

Martineau, Harriet (1802–1876): English economic educator whose book, *Illustrations of Political Economy* (1834), emphasized the teaching of economics through applications and real-life experiences. She was thus a pioneer in the use of the "case method" of teaching—along the lines used today in many business and in some economics courses.

Marx, Karl Heinrich (1818–1883): Prussian-born and German-educated founder, with Friedrich Engels (1820–1895), of so-called "scientific socialism." This consists of a body of ideas that were best expressed in Marx's most important economic work, *Das Kapital* (translated "Capital"), the first volume of which was published in 1867. The main concepts rest on five fundamental doctrines: (1) **economic interpretation of history:** Economic forces are the prime cause of fundamental historical change. (2) **theory of value and wages:** The value of any commodity is determined by the amount of labor-time embodied in its production. The wages that capitalists pay to labor are held at a subsistence level that is just high enough to allow the working population to sustain itself and to rear children. (3) **theory of surplus value and capital accumulation:** The value of goods that workers produce is greater than the value, in the form of subsistence wages, that workers receive. The difference, called "surplus value," rightfully belongs to workers, but it is literally stolen from them by capitalists. Part of this surplus is used by capitalists for their personal consumption and part to acquire more labor and machines in order to perpetuate and expand the capitalistic system. (4) **class struggle:** The capitalists' drive to increase their surplus value and to accumulate capital results in the displacement of labor and in mounting unemployment. This leads to an irreconcilable clash of interests between the working class and the capitalist class. (5) **theory of socialist and communist evolution:** The working class (called the "proletariat"), experiencing increasing misery, will eventually rise and overthrow the capitalistic system by force. The proletariat will then dictate the establishment of a new system characterized in its early stage by socialism and in its mature stage by full communism. The motto of socialism will be: "From each according to his ability, to each according to his labor." The motto of communism will be: *"From each according to his ability, to each according to his needs."* This last quotation describes the ultimate goal of Marxism and the essence of pure communism.

median: Special type of average that divides a distribution of numbers into two equal parts—one-half of all cases being equal to or greater than the median value, and one-half being equal to or less.

mediation: Method of settling differences between two parties (such as a union and management) by the use of an impartial third party, called a mediator, who is acceptable to both sides but makes no binding decisions. The mediator tries to maintain constructive discussions, search for common areas of agreement, and suggest compromises. Federal, state, and most large local governments provide mediation services for labor–management disputes. Mediation is also sometimes called "conciliation." (*Contrast with* **arbitration.**)

member bank: Bank that belongs to the Federal Reserve System. All national banks (chartered by the federal government) must be members. State banks may join if they meet certain requirements.

mercantilism: Set of doctrines and practices aimed at promoting national prosperity and the power of the state by (1) accumulating precious metals (mainly gold and silver) through the maintenance of favorable trade balances, (2) achieving economic self-sufficiency through imperialism, and (3) exploiting colonies by monopolizing their raw materials and precious metals while reserving them as exclusive markets for exports. Mercantilism reached its peak in the seventeenth century, serving as a political and economic ideology in England, France, Spain, and Germany.

merger: Amalgamation of two or more firms under one ownership. The three common forms are: (1) *horizontal*, uniting similar plants and products; (2) *vertical*, uniting dissimilar plants in various stages of production; and (3) *conglomerate*, uniting dissimilar plants and products.

merit good: Product provided by government because society deems some minimum amount of the commodity worth (or meritorious) of production. Merit goods share, in different degrees, some of the properties of both public and private goods. Among numerous examples of merit goods are municipal golf courses, public libraries, national parks, public education, and public hospitals. These and other merit goods are subject to the *exclusion principle*, even though it may not always be invoked. (*See* **exclusion principle: public good.**)

microeconomics: The part of economics that is concerned with the study of specific economic units or parts of an economic system, such as its firms, industries, and households, and the relationships between these parts. It analyzes the "trees" of the economy as distinct from the "forest."

Mill, John Stuart (1806–1873): Last of the major English classical economists. His two-volume treatise, *Principles of Political Economy* (1848), was a masterful synthesis of classical ideas. Mill advocated laissez-faire, but he was also a strong supporter of social reforms. Among them: worker education, democratic producer cooperatives, redistribution of wealth, shorter working days, taxation of unearned gains from land, and social control of monopoly. Mill supported these measures because he mistrusted government and wanted to guarantee to individual workers the benefits of their contributions to production. Therefore, although Mill was often called a socialist, he was in fact a "moderate conservative" by today's standards. He believed too strongly in individual freedom to advocate major government involvement in the economy.

minimum differences, principle of: *See* **Hotelling's paradox.**

mint ratio: Under a bimetallic standard, the ratio of the weight of one metal to the other, and their equivalent in terms of the national unit of currency (such as the dollar), as defined by the government. For example, during the nineteenth century, when the United States was on a bimetallic standard, the government defined the mint ratio for many years as

15 grains of silver = 1 grain of gold = $1

The mint ratio was therefore 15:1. Since it remained fixed by law, it resulted in either gold or silver being driven out of circulation, depending on the relative market values of the two metals. (*See also* **bimetallic standard; Gresham's Law.**)

Mitchell, Wesley Clair (1874–1948): Leading American economist during the first half of the twentieth century. Mitchell was a professor of economics at Columbia University and a founder of the National Bureau of Economic Research, one of the world's major centers for quantitative research in aggregative economic activity. Mitchell's lifework was the study of business cycles, their history, nature, and causes. Much of what is known today about economic fluctuations has grown out of the pioneering research done by Mitchell.

mixed economy: Economic system in which the questions of what to produce, how much to produce, and for whom to produce are decided for some goods by the free market and for other goods by a central government authority. There are varying forms and degrees of mixed economies.

model: Representation of the essential features of a theory or of a real-world situation, expressed in the form of words, diagrams, graphs, mathematical equations, or combinations of these.

monetarism: Macroeconomic theory and policies that follow in the tradition of Irving Fisher. Monetarists contend that an increase in the money supply leads to an increase in prices. This causes the actual or market rate of interest to rise relative to the "real" rate—the rate that would prevail if prices were stable. The difference between the market rate and real rate represents an "inflation premium." This is an amount that lenders require and borrowers are willing to pay because both expect prices to continue rising. Monetarists conclude from their analysis that the effects on aggregate demand of temporary budgetary changes are uncertain. Therefore, steady monetary growth is preferable to discretionary fiscal actions. Thus, stated in concise terms, the monetarist model is characterized by (1) a predominantly monetary theory of the price level, (2) a predominantly nonmonetary theory of the interest rate, and (3) a distinction between market and real rates of interest. (*Contrast with* **fiscalism.**)

monetary asset: Claim against a fixed quantity of money, the amount of which is unaffected by inflation or deflation. *Examples:* bonds, accounts receivable, savings deposits, promissory notes, and cash. For every monetary asset, there is an equal monetary liability. (*See also* **monetary liability.**)

monetary base: *Net* monetary liabilities of government—the Fed and the Treasury—held by the public. It equals the sum of currency held by the public plus legal reserves. The monetary base may be called "high-powered" money because it supports the money supply (currency plus checkable deposits), which, because of our fractional-reserve banking system, is a *multiple* of the monetary base. The size of the monetary base thus affects the total monetary assets of the public.

Monetary Control Act of 1980: Major revision of bank legislation. It authorized the Federal Reserve System (1) to impose uniform reserve requirements on similar classes of deposits at *all* depository institutions and (2) to charge fees for its services and make them available to all depository institutions on an equal basis. In addition, the Act removed a wide range of restrictions on depository institutions, enabling them to become more directly competitive.

monetary liability: Promise to pay a claim against a fixed quantity of money, the amount of which is unaffected by inflation or deflation. For every monetary liability, there is an equal monetary asset. (*See also* **monetary asset.**)

monetary policy: Deliberate exercise of the monetary authority's (that is, the Federal Reserve's) power to induce expansions or contractions in the money supply in order to achieve price stability, to help dampen the swings of business cycles, and to bring the nation's output and employment to desired levels.

monetary standard: Laws and practices that determine the quantity and quality of a nation's money and establish the conditions, if any, under which its currency is ultimately redeemable.

monetary theory (of business cycle): Explanation of economic fluctuations in terms of financial factors, such as changes in the quantity of money and credit and changes in interest rates. Upswings occur when credit and borrowing conditions become favorable enough for businesspeople to borrow; downswings occur when the banking system begins to restrict its expansion of money and credit.

money: anything that is widely used and freely accepted in payment for goods and services. In modern society, money has at least these four functions: (1) as a medium of exchange for conducting transactions; (2) as a measure of value for expressing the prices of things; (3) as a standard of deferred payments, which permits borrowing or lending for future repayment; and (4) as a store of value, which permits saving for future spending.

money illusion: Situation in which a rise in all prices and incomes by the same proportion leads to an increase in consumption, even though real incomes remain unchanged.

money income: Amount of money received for work done. (*Compare* **real income.**)

money market: Center where short-term credit instruments such as U.S. Treasury bills, corporations' commercial paper or promissory notes, and bankers' acceptances are bought and sold.

money-supply rule: Guide for economic expansion advanced by some economists, especially by Milton Friedman. The "rule" states that the Federal Reserve should expand the nation's money supply at a steady rate in accordance with the economy's long-term growth trend and capacity to produce, such as 3 to 4 percent per year for the United States. More than this would lead to strong inflationary pressures; less would tend to be stagnating if not deflationary.

money wages: Wages received in cash. (*Compare* **real wages.**)

monopolistic competition: Industry or market structure characterized by a large number of firms of different sizes producing heterogeneous (similar but not identical) products, with relatively easy entry into the industry.

monopoly: Industry or market structure characterized by a single firm producing a product for which there are no close substitutes. The firm thus constitutes the entire industry and is a "pure" monopoly.

monopoly price: The profit-maximizing price for an imperfect competitor. It is the price (and the corresponding output) at which $MC = MR$ and $MC < P$. At this price, the value of the last unit to the marginal user (measured by the price he or she pays for the last unit, which is equal to the price paid for any other unit) is greater than the value of the resources used to produce that unit.

monopsony: Market structure characterized by only a single buyer of a good or service. It may be thought of as a "buyer's monopoly."

moral suasion: Oral or written appeals by the Federal Reserve board to member banks, urging them to expand or restrict credit but without requiring them to comply.

most-favored-nation clause: Provision in a trade treaty by which each signatory country agrees to extend to the others the same preferential tariff and trade concessions that it may in the future extend to nonsignatories (that is, the same treatment that each gives to its "most favored nation"). Most trading countries have adhered to this principle since 1948.

multiple expansion of bank deposits: Process by which a loan made by one bank is used to finance business transactions and ends up as a deposit in another bank. Part of this may be used by the second bank as a required reserve, the rest being lent out for business use so that it is eventually deposited in a third bank; and so on. The total amount of credit granted by the banking system as a whole will thus be a multiple of the initial deposit. (*See also* **deposit-expansion multiplier.**)

multiplier: Principle that states that changes in investment can bring about magnified changes in income, as expressed by the equation: multiplier × change in investment = change in income. The multiplier coefficient is given by the formula

$$\text{multiplier} = \frac{\text{change in income}}{\text{change in investment}}$$

$$= \frac{1}{MPS} = \frac{1}{1 - MPC}$$

in which *MPS* stands for the marginal propensity to save and *MPC* the marginal propensity to consume. (*Note:* This multiplier is sometimes called the "simple multiplier," the "investment multiplier," or the "expenditure multiplier." The last expression emphasizes the idea that *any* change in spending, whether by households, businesses, or government, and whether for consumption or for investment, can have a multiplier effect on income. However, the term *investment* is used in this definition because that is the variable that is usually assumed to change.)

multiunit bargaining: Collective-bargaining arrangement covering more than one plant. It may occur between one or more firms in an industry and one or more unions, and it may take place on a national, regional, or local level. It is sometimes called "industry-wide bargaining"—usually inaccurately, because it rarely affects an entire industry.

municipals: Marketable financial obligations—mostly bonds—issued by state and local governmental authorities (the latter including cities, towns, school districts, and so on). Interest income paid to their owners is exempt from federal income taxes and usually also from state income taxes of the state in which they are issued.

N

national bank: Commerical bank chartered by the federal government. Such banks are required to belong to the Federal Reserve System. A minority of banks today are national banks, but they hold considerably more than half the deposits of the banking system and are larger than most state-chartered banks.

National Banking Act (1863): Legislation aimed at standardizing banking practices and reaffirming the existence of our dual banking system. The law contained the following main provisions. (1) Opportunities for banks to be federally chartered, thus making them national banks. (2) Issuance of Treasury currency backed largely by government bonds. (3) Federal taxation of state bank notes, thus forcing them out of existence. (4) Holding of cash reserves against notes and deposits.

national income (at factor cost): 1. Total of all net incomes earned by, or ascribed to, the factors of production—that is, the sum of wages, rent, interest, and profit that accrues to the suppliers of labor, land, capital, and entrepreneurship. [*Note*: It should not be confused with the total income received by people from all sources (that is, personal income). The difference between the two is based on various accounting considerations.] **2.** In general terms and in theoretical discussions, the expression "national income" is often used in a simple generic sense to represent the income or output of an economy.

National Labor Relations (Wagner) Act (1935): Basic labor relations law of the United States. It (1) guarantees the right of workers to organize and bargain collectively through representatives of their own choosing, (2) forbids employers to engage in unfair labor practices, such as discrimination or interference, and (3) authorizes the National Labor Relations Board to enforce the act and supervise free elections among a company's employees.

National Labor Relations Board: Government agency established under the National Labor Relations Act of 1935 to enforce that act, to investigate violations of it, and to supervise free elections among a company's employees in order to determine which union, if any, is to represent them in collective bargaining.

Natural Gas Act (1938): Legislation granting the Federal Power Commission (FPC) authority over the interstate transportation of natural gas and empowering the Commission to regulate rates and services.

natural monopoly: Firm that experiences increasing economies of scale (that is, long-run decreasing average costs of production) over a sufficiently wide range of output, enabling it to supply an entire market at a lower unit cost than two or more firms. Electric companies, gas companies, and railroads are classic examples.

natural unemployment rate: Employment level at which only frictional and structural unemployment exist, not cyclical unemployment arising from a deficiency in aggregate demand. The natural unemployment rate can be lowered by improving labor markets—through job training, combating discrimina-tion in hiring, and so on—but not by overexpansionary fiscal and monetary policies.

near-monies: Assets that are almost, but not quite, money. They can easily be converted into money because their monetary values are known. *Examples*: time or savings deposits, U.S. government bonds, and cash values of insurance policies.

needs standard: Criterion of income distribution popularly expressed by the phrase, "To each according to his or her needs." This is the distributive principle of pure communism and an approximate criterion for apportioning income in most families. If you regard the needs standard as a just or equitable one, you are assuming that a central authority is capable of determining what constitutes your (and everyone else's) needs. (*Compare* **equality standard; contributive standard.**)

negative income tax: Plan for guaranteeing the poor a minimum income through a type of reverse income tax. A poor family, depending on its size and income, would be paid by the government enough either to reduce or to close the gap between what it earns and an explicit minimum level of income. That level might be equal to or above the government's designated "poverty line." As the family's income increases, the government's payment declines to zero.

negotiable certificate of deposit (CD): Large-denomination notes (minimum: $100,000) issued by major banks. They sell these securities to corporations and large individual investors, who buy them for their interest payments. (*Note*: Most banks also issue deposits or savings certificates for smaller investors. However, these are merely special types of time deposits. They are smaller in size and not marketable, unlike negotiable CDs.

negotiable order of withdrawal (NOW): A check written against an interest-bearing account. NOW accounts are offered by most banks and other depository institutions. Such accounts are one of several forms of savings-type checkable deposits.

neoclassical economics: Approach to economics that flourished in Europe and the United States between 1870 and World War I. Among its leaders were William Stanley Jevons in England, Carl Menger in Austria, Leon Walras in Switzerland, Vilfredo Pareto in Switzerland, Alfred Marshall in England, and John Bates Clark and Irving Fisher in the United States. The neoclassicists were primarily concerned with refining the principles of price and allocation theory, "marginalism," the theory of capital, and related aspects of economics. They made early and extensive use of mathematics, especially differential and integral calculus, in the development of their analyses and models. Much of the structure of modern economic science is built on their pioneering work.

net national product: Total sales value of goods and services available for society's consumption and for adding to its stock of capital equipment. It represents society's net output for the year and may be obtained by deducting a capital-consumption allowance from gross national product.

net-profit ratio: Ratio of a firm's net profit after taxes to its net sales. It is one of several general measures of a company's performance.

net revenue: A firm's "pure" or net profit, which is equal to its total revenue minus its total cost.

net worth: Difference between the total assets or things of value owned by a firm or individual and the liabilities or debts that are owed.

nonprice competition: Methods of competition that do not involve changes in selling price. *Examples:* advertising, product differentiation, and customer service.

nontariff barriers: Laws or regulations, other than tariffs, used by nations to restrict imports. For instance, in order to "protect" the health and safety of their citizens, many countries establish much higher standards of quality for various kinds of imported goods than for similar goods produced domestically. Food products and automobiles provide some typical examples. Actually, nontariff barriers (other than import quotas) are direct but subtle protective devices that are never publicly identified as such. Hence, they have become major forms of trade protection used by many countries.

normal good: A good whose consumption varies directly with money income, prices remaining constant. Most consumer goods are normal goods. (Same as **superior good.**)

normal price: The dynamic equilibrium price toward which the market price is always tending but may never reach.

normal profit: Least payment that the owner of an enterprise will accept as compensation for his entrepreneurial function, including risk taking and management. Normal profit is part of a firm's total economic costs, since it is a payment that the owner must receive in order to keep him from withdrawing his capital and managerial effort and putting them into an alternative enterprise.

normative economics: Approach to economics that deals with what "ought to be" rather than with what "is." Because it involves statements that are value judgments, much of it cannot be empirically verified. (*Compare* **positive economics.**)

Norris–La Guardia Act (1932): Act of Congress that outlawed the yellow-dog contract and greatly restricted the conditions under which court injunctions against labor unions could be issued.

notes payable: Promises to pay the holder, such as a bank, a sum of money within the year at a stated rate of interest.

O

Okun's Law: Relationship between changes in unemployment and the rate of economic growth (measured by changes in real GNP). The law, based on long-run trends, states that unemployment (1) decreases less than 1 percent for each percentage point that the annual growth of real GNP exceeds its long-term average and (2) increases less than 1 percent for each percentage point that the annual growth of real GNP falls short of its long-term average. The economy, therefore, must continue to grow considerably faster than its long-term average rate in order to achieve a substantial reduction in the unemployment rate. (The law is attributed to Arthur Okun, chairman of the Council of Economic Advisors under President Lyndon Johnson.)

oligopoly: Industry or market structure characterized by only a few firms selling either (1) a homogeneous or undifferentiated product—the industry is then called a "perfect" or "pure" oligopoly—or (2) heterogeneous or differentiated products—the

industry is then called an "imperfect" oligopoly. Some examples of perfect oligopolies are the copper, steel, and cement industries. Some examples of imperfect oligopolies are the automobile, soap, detergent, and household-appliance industries.

oligopsony: Industry or market structure characterized by only a few buyers of a commodity. *Example:* Natural-gas pipeline companies are oligopsonists in that there are only a few of them that purchase gas for transportation from any given field.

open-market operations: Purchases and sales of government securities by the Federal Reserve System. Purchases of securities are expansionary because they add to commercial banks' reserves; sales of securities are contractionary because they reduce commercial banks' reserves.

open shop: Business firm in which the employer is free to hire either union members or nonmembers.

operating profit ratio: Ratio of a firm's operating profit to its net sales.

opportunity cost: Value of the benefit that is forgone by choosing one alternative rather than another. It is also called "alternative cost," because it represents the implicit cost of the forgone alternative to the individual, household, firm, or other decision-making entity. The opportunity cost of any decision is thus the value of the sacrificed alternative. Because it may often be subjective, opportunity cost is not entered in a firm's public accounting records. (*Compare* **outlay costs.**)

outlay costs: Money expended to carry on a particular activity. They are the explicit costs that are entered in a firm's public accounting records, such as its income statement, to arrive at a measure of profit. *Examples:* wages and salaries, rent, and other money expenditures of a firm.

overinvestment theory (of business cycles): Explanation that holds that economic fluctuations are caused by too much investment in the economy as businesspeople try to anticipate rising demands during an upswing, and by sharp cutbacks in investment during a downswing when businesspeople realize they expanded too much in the previous prosperity.

P

paradox of thrift: Proposition that demonstrates that, if people as a group try to increase their saving, they may end up by saving less. The conclusion of the paradox is that an increase in saving may be desirable for an individual or family, but, for an entire economy, it will lead to a reduction in income, employment, and output if it is not offset by an increase in investment. The concept was first introduced by Bernard Mandeville in *The Fable of the Bees* (1714) and was later recognized in the writings of several classical economists. It subsequently became an integral part of the Keynesian model.

Pareto optimality: Condition that exists in a social organization when no change can be implemented that will make someone better off without making someone else worse off—each in his or her own estimation. Because an economic system is a type of social organization, Pareto optimality is synonymous with *economic efficiency.* (*See also* **efficiency.**)

Pareto, Vilfredo (1848–1923): Italian economist and sociologist who developed many elegant mathematical formulations of economic concepts, especially those pertaining to general equilibrium theory. His work provided a foundation for indifference-curve analysis. He showed that a theory of demand could be developed without dependence on utility, by observing consumer purchases of combinations of goods that are equally acceptable. Heavily influenced by Leon Walras, Pareto succeeded him as Professor of Political Economy at the University of Lausanne, Switzerland. (See **Pareto optimality**.)

parity price: Price that yields an equivalence to some defined standard. *Examples:* (1) In agriculture, a price for an agricultural commodity that gives the commodity a purchasing power (in terms of the goods that farmers buy) equivalent to the purchasing power that it had in a previous base period. (2) In international economics, the price or exchange rate between the currencies of two countries that makes the purchasing power of one currency substantially equivalent to the purchasing power of the other.

parity ratio: In agriculture, an index of the prices farmers receive divided by an index of the prices they pay. It is used to measure the economic well-being of agriculture as a whole.

partial-equilibrium theory: Explanation or model of a particular market, assuming that other markets are in balance. It thus ignores the interrelations of prices and quantities that may exist between markets. *Example:* Ordinary supply-and-demand analysis is normally of a partial-equilibrium nature, since it usually focuses on a single market while neglecting others.

participation rate (labor force): Number of people in the civilian labor force as a percentage of the civilian population. Only persons 16 years of age or older are included in the calculation.

partnership: Association of two or more individuals to carry on, as co-owners, a business for profit. The partners are solely responsible for the activities and liabilities of the business.

patent: Exclusive right conferred by government on an inventor, for a limited time. It authorizes the inventor to make, use, transfer, or withhold an invention (which might be done even without a patent), but it also gives the inventor the right to exclude others or to admit them on his or her own terms (which can be done only with a patent). Patents are thus a method of promoting invention by granting temporary monopolies to inventors.

patent monopoly: Firm that exercises a monopoly because the government has conferred upon it the exclusive right—through issuance of a patent—to make, use, or vend its own invention or discovery.

peak-load pricing: A practice that utilizes the fact that demand elasticities for some products differ at certain times. Therefore, instead of charging the same price at all times, the seller charges a higher price during peak-demand periods, when demand is more inelastic, and a lower price at other times. In this way, the selling firm reallocates its limited facilities during periods of high demand, thus reducing consumption and obtaining a more even use of its facilities at all times. *Example:* Telephone companies charge higher long-distance rates during the daytime (a peak period) and lower rates during the night (an off-peak period). Some electric utilities have also practiced peak-load pricing based on different time periods.

perfect competition: Name given to an industry or market structure characterized by a large number of buyers and sellers all engaged in the purchase and sale of a homogeneous commodity, with perfect knowledge of market prices and quantities, no discrimination in buying or selling, and perfect

mobility of resources. (*Note:* The term is usually employed synonymously with *pure competition*, although there is a technical distinction. Pure competition does not require perfect knowledge or perfect resource mobility, and hence it does not produce as smooth or rapid an adjustment to equilibrium as does perfect competition. However, both types of competition lead to essentially the same results in economic theory.)

permanent-income hypothesis: Proposition that states that a family's propensity to consume (that is, the amount it spends on consumption) depends on its anticipated long-run or permanent income—the average income expected to be received over a number of years. In addition, the theory holds that a family's consumption is approximately proportional to its permanent income. This hypothesis is thus an alternative theory of the consumption function. (*Contrast with* **absolute-income hypothesis; relative-income hypothesis**.)

personal income: In national-income accounting, the total income received by persons from all sources.

personal income distributions: Shares of total income received by people. The shares are often expressed in terms of percentages of aggregate income received by each fifth of all families, or in terms of the percentage of families falling within specific income classes.

Phillips curve: Curve that represents a trade-off between unemployment and inflation. Every point along the curve denotes a different combination of unemployment and inflation, and a movement along the curve reflects the reduction in one of these at the expense of a gain in the other.

Phillips Petroleum case (1954): Major regulation case in which the Supreme Court authorized the Federal Power Commission to regulate natural-gas prices that producers charge interstate pipeline companies. This was the first time in the nation's history that the Supreme Court ordered a regulatory commission to expand the scope of its authority.

planned economy: Economic system in which the government, according to a preconceived plan, plays a primary role in directing economic resources for the purpose of deciding what to produce, how much, and possibly for whom. A planned economy may or may not be a command economy, depending on whether the government operates within a substantially authoritarian or democratic framework. (See also **command economy**.)

planning-program-budgeting system (PPBS): Method of revenue and expenditure management based on (1) determination of goals, (2) assessment of their relative importance to society, and (3) allocation of resources needed to attain the goals at least cost. In more general terms, PPBS is a budgeting method that relates expenditures to specific goals or programs so that the costs of achieving a particular program can be identified, measured, planned, and controlled.

plant: Establishment that produces or distributes goods and services. In economics, a "plant" is usually thought of as a firm, but it may also be one of several plants owned by a firm.

Point Four Program: Part of the Foreign Economic Assistance Act of 1950. The Program seeks to raise living standards in less developed countries by making available to them U.S. technical and financial assistance, largely in the areas of agriculture, public health, and education. Much of this work is now carried out by agencies of the United Nations and by several U.S. agencies.

positive economics: An approach to economics that deals with what "is" rather than with what "ought to be." Much of positive economics involves the use of statements that can be verified by empirical research (that is, by an appeal to the facts). (*Compare* **normative economics.**)

potential GNP: The level of aggregate output that would exist if the economy were at full employment.

poverty line: Measure of poverty among families, defined in terms of a sliding income scale that varies between rural and urban locations according to family size.

precautionary motive: Desire on the part of households and businesses to hold part of their assets in liquid form so that they can be prepared for unexpected contingencies. This motive is influenced primarily by income levels rather than by changes in the interest rate, and it is one of the chief sources of demand for loanable funds in the modern theory of interest.

preferred stock: Shares of stock that receive priority (that is, preference) over common stock at a fixed rate in the distribution of dividends—or in the distribution of assets, if the company is liquidated.

prepayments: Business expenditures made in advance for items that will yield portions of their benefits in the present and in future years. *Examples:* advance premiums on a fire-insurance policy; expenses incurred in marketing a new product.

present value: Discounted value of future sums of money. The discount is taken at a specified interest rate for a specified period of time. Present value is thus a sum of money adjusted for interest over time.

price: The exchange value of a commodity—that is, the power of a commodity to command some other commodity, usually money, in exchange for itself.

price–consumption curve: In indifference-curve analysis, a line that connects the tangency points of price lines and indifference curves by showing the amounts of two commodities that a consumer will purchase when his or her income and the price of one commodity remain constant while the price of the other commodity varies.

price discrimination: Practice by a seller of charging different prices to the same or to different buyers for the same good, without corresponding differences in costs. (It may also consist of charging buyers the same price despite corresponding differences in costs.)

price leadership: Adherence by firms in an oligopolistic industry, often tacitly and without formal agreement, to the pricing policies of one of its members. Frequently, but not always, the price leader will be the largest firm in the industry and other firms will simply go along with the leader by charging the same price.

price line (budget line): In indifference-curve analysis, a line representing all the possible combinations of two commodities that a consumer can purchase at a particular time, given the market prices of the commodities and the consumer's money budget or income.

price system: Mechanism that allocates scarce goods or resources by rationing them among those buyers and sellers in the marketplace who are willing and able to deal at the going prices. The term is often used to express the way prices are established through the free play of supply and demand in competitive markets composed of many buyers and sellers. In reality, of course, there may be "noncompetitive" price systems in markets where buyers or sellers are relatively few in number.

primary reserves: A bank's legal reserves (consisting of vault cash and demand deposits with the Federal Reserve Bank) and demand deposits with other banks.

prime rate: Interest rate charged by banks on loans to their most credit-worthy customers.

principle: Fundamental law or general truth. It is often stated as an expression of a relationship between two or more variables. (*See also* **law.**)

private benefit: Utility that accrues to an individual, household, or firm as a result of a particular act. (*Compare* **social benefit.**)

private cost: Disutility (including economic cost) that accrues to an individual, household, or firm as a result of a particular act. (*Compare* **social cost.**)

private property: Basic institution of capitalism that gives each individual the right to acquire economic goods and resources by legitimate means and to use or dispose of them as he or she wishes. This right may be modified by society to the extent that it affects public health, safety, or welfare.

private rate of return: The business or financial rate of return on an investment—that is, the rate that businesspeople try to anticipate before investing their funds. In financial terms, it is the expected net profit after taxes and all costs, including depreciation, and may typically be expressed as a percentage annual return upon either the total cost of a project or the net worth of the stockholder owners.

private sector: That segment of the total economy consisting of households and businesses, but excluding government.

"process of creative destruction": An expression coined by the economist Joseph Schumpeter (1883–1950) to describe the growth of a capitalistic economy as a process of replacing the old with the new—that is, old methods of production, old sources of supply, and old skills and resources with new ones.

Producer Price Index (PPI): Average of selected items priced in wholesale markets, including raw materials, semifinished products, and finished goods. The PPI is published monthly by the Bureau of Labor Statistics of the U.S. Department of Labor.

production function: Relationship between the number of units of inputs that a firm employs and the corresponding units of output that result.

production-possibilities curve: Curve that depicts all possible combinations of total output for an economy. The curve assumes: (1) a choice between producing either one or both of two kinds or classes of goods; (2) full and efficient employment of all resources (that is, no underemployment); and (3) a fixed supply of resources and a given state of technological knowledge.

productivity: Relationship between the output of goods or services and one or more of the inputs used to produce the output. Productivity is calculated from a ratio:

$$productivity = \frac{output}{input}$$

A distinction is made between two measures of productivity—partial and total-factor. *Partial productivity* uses only one input in the denominator, as in output per worker or yield per acre. *Total-factor productivity* uses a "weighted" sum of all measurable inputs (land, labor, capital) employed in production. Because of the difficulty of measuring *all* inputs in a production process, partial rather than total-factor productivity is the most widely used type of measure.

product markets: Markets in which businesses sell the outputs that they produce (in contrast with resource markets in which they buy the inputs they need in order to produce).

profit: 1. Return to those who perform the entrepreneurial function. The residual (if any) after the payment of wages, rent, and interest to the owners of labor, land, and capital. **2.** Difference between total revenue and total cost. It is the same as net revenue, a residual or surplus over and above normal profit that accrues to the entrepreneur-owner after all economic costs, including explicit (outlay) costs and implicit (opportunity) costs, have been deducted from total revenue.

progressive tax: Tax whose percentage rate increases as the tax base increases. The U.S. personal income tax is an example. The tax is graduated so that, other things being equal and assuming no loopholes, a person with a higher income pays a greater percentage of his income and a larger amount of tax than a person with a lower income.

promissory note: Commitment by one person to pay another a specified sum of money by a given date, usually within a year. It is thus an "I.O.U." Such notes are used by individuals, corporations, and government agencies.

propensity to consume: Relationship between consumption expenditures and income such that, as income increases, consumption increases, but not as fast as income. The expression **consumption function** is often used synonymously.

propensity to save: Relationship between saving and income such that, as income increases, saving increases, but faster than income.

property resources: Nonhuman productive resources of an economy, including its natural resources, raw materials, machinery and equipment, and transportation and communication facilities.

property tax: Tax on any kind of property, whether real property (land and buildings) or personal property (such as stocks, bonds, and home furnishings).

proportional tax: Tax whose percentage rate remains constant as the tax base increases; hence, the amount of the tax paid is proportional to the tax base. The property tax is an example. Thus, if the tax rate remains constant at 10 percent, a taxpayer who owns $10,000 worth of property pays $1,000 in taxes, and a taxpayer who owns $100,000 worth of property pays $10,000 in taxes.

proprietorship: Simplest form of business organization, in which the owner or proprietor is solely responsible for the activities and liabilities of the business.

prosperity: Upper phase of a business cycle, in which the economy is operating at or near full employment and a high degree of business and consumer optimism is reflected by a vigorous rate of capital investment and consumption.

psychological theory (of business cycles): Explanation of economic fluctuations in terms of people's responses to political, social, and economic events. These responses, the theory holds, set off cumulative waves of optimism and pessimism, causing cycles in economic activity.

public choice: Branch of economics concerned with the study of nonmarket collective decision making, or the application of economics to political science. The goal of public choice is to develop ways of improving efficiency in the public sector, particularly in the provision of social goods.

public good: One that is not subject to the exclusion principle. That is, the good's benefits are indivisible and hence no one can be excluded from its consumption for not paying. Therefore, most public goods, but not all, are produced by the public sector because the private sector is usually unable or unwilling to provide them. Other characteristics of a public good are (1) very low (or even zero) incremental or marginal costs and (2) spillover costs to some groups and spillover benefits to others. *Examples:* national defense, fire protection, air-traffic control, radio broadcasting, and most television transmission.

public sector: That segment of the total economy consisting of all levels of government. It is thus exclusive of the household and business segments, which constitute the private sector.

public works: Government-sponsored construction, defense, or development projects that usually (but not always) entail public investment expenditures that would not ordinarily be undertaken by the private sector of the economy.

pure competition: *See* **perfect competition** for similarities and differences.

pure interest rate: Theoretical interest rate on a long-term, riskless loan, where the interest payments are made solely for the use of someone else's money. In practice, this rate is often approximated by the interest rate on long-term negotiable government bonds.

pure market economy: Competitive economic system characterized by many buyers and sellers, so that prices are determined by the free interaction of supply and demand.

Q

quantity theory of money: Classical theory of the relationship between the price level and the money supply. It holds that the level of prices in the economy is directly proportional to the quantity of money in circulation, such that a given percentage change in the stock of money will cause an equal percentage change in the price level in the same direction. The theory assumes that the income velocity of circulation of money remains fairly stable and that the quantity of goods and services is constant because the economy always tends toward full employment. (*See also* **equation of exchange.**)

R

rate of return: The interest rate that equates the present value of cash returns on an investment with the present value of the cash expenditures relating to the investment. That is, the rate of return on an investment is the interest rate at which the investment is repaid by its net receipts (that is, the difference between total receipts and total costs).

ratio (logarithmic) scale: Scale on a graph on which equal distances represent equal percentage changes. (It is equivalent to plotting the *logarithms* of the same data on an ordinary arithmetic scale.)

rational-expectations theory: Belief that people form expectations about recurring or *systematic* government fiscal–monetary policies and then refer to those expectations in their economic decision-making. Consequently, by the time the government's policies become known, the public has already acted on them, thereby offsetting their effects. This means that, to assure economic stability, government should choose the right policy and stick to it. That is, government should adhere to a policy of balanced budgets and steady growth of the money supply. Failure to do so will lead to public policies that are self-defeating and inflationary. In other words, the theory holds that the only policy moves that cause changes in people's behavior are the ones that are not expected—the surprise moves. Once the public learns to expect a policy, it no longer alters people's behavior.

rationing: Any method of restricting the purchases or use of a good. Government may, for various reasons, institute a system of rationing when, over an extended period of time, the quantity demanded of a good exceeds the quantity supplied at a given price.

real asset: Claim against a fixed amount of a commodity or the right to a commodity, the money value of which is affected by inflation or deflation. *Examples:* house, car, and most other goods and services. (*See also* **real liability.**)

real income: Purchasing power of money income or the quantity of goods and services that can be bought with money income. (*Compare* **money income.**)

realized investment: Actual investment out of any realized level of income. Equal to the sum of planned and unplanned (inventory) investment.

real liability: Promise to pay a fixed amount of a commodity, or right to a commodity, the money value of which is affected by inflation or deflation. (*See also* **real asset.**)

real output: Value of physical output unaffected by price changes.

real rate of interest: In classical theory, the interest rate measured in terms of goods. It is the rate that would prevail in the market if the general price level remained stable. Factors determining it are "real demand" for funds by businesses and "real supply" of funds by households. The former, in turn, is determined by the productivity of borrowed capital, and the latter by the willingness of consumers to abstain from present consumption.

real wages: Quantity of goods that can be bought with money wages. Real wages thus depend on the prices of the goods bought with money wages.

recession: Downward phase of a business cycle, in which the economy's income, output, and employment are decreasing and a falling off of business and consumer optimism is reflected by a declining rate of capital investment and consumption.

recessionary gap: Amount by which aggregate demand falls short of full-employment aggregate supply, thereby pulling down the real value of the nation's output.

Reciprocal Trade Agreements program: Plan for expanding American exports through legislation that authorizes the President to negotiate U.S. tariff reductions with other nations in return for parallel concessions. The program consists of the Trade Agreements Act of 1934, with subsequent amendments, and related legislation.

recovery: Upward phase of a business cycle, in which the economy's income, output, and employment are rising and a growing degree of business and consumer optimism is reflected by an expanding rate of capital investment and consumption.

refunding: Replacement or repayment of outstanding bonds by the issuance of new bonds. It is thus a method of prolonging a debt by paying off old obligations with new obligations.

regressive tax: Tax whose percentage rate decreases as the tax base increases. In this strict sense, there is no regressive tax in the United States. However, if we compare the rate structure of the tax with the taxpayer's net income rather than with its actual base, the term "regressive" applies to any tax that takes a larger share of income from low-income taxpayers than from high-income taxpayers. Most proportional taxes are thus seen to have regressive effects. A sales tax, for instance, is the same for rich people as for poor people. But the latter spend a larger percentage of their incomes on consumer goods. Therefore, the sales taxes they pay—assuming that there are few if any exemptions—are a greater proportion of their incomes.

rent: Return to those who supply the factor of production known as "land."

relative-income hypothesis: Proposition that states that a family's propensity to consume (that is, the amount it spends on consumption) depends on its previous peak level of income or on the relative position that the family occupies along the income scale. A family's spending behavior is thus influenced by the highest past income levels to which it has become accustomed and by the incomes of other families in the same socioeconomic environment. This hypothesis, therefore, is an alternative theory of the propensity to consume. (*Contrast with* **absolute-income hypothesis; permanent-income hypothesis.**)

repurchase agreement (RP or "repo"): A type of collateralized loan. The borrower sells the lender a credit instrument, usually a government security, and simultaneously agrees to buy it back on a later date at the same price, plus interest at a specified rate. The lender (investor) thus holds a security as collateral for a loan of fixed maturity at a fixed interest rate. Banks, often in need of short-term funds, are major users of RPs. They are sold to corporations and to large individual customers who have surplus cash balances to lend.

required reserves: Minimum amount of legal reserves that a bank is required by law to keep behind its deposit liabilities. Thus, if the reserve requirement is 10 percent, a bank with demand deposits of $1 million must hold at least $100,000 of required legal reserves.

resale price maintenance: Practice whereby a manufacturer or distributor of a branded product sets the minimum retail price at which that product can be sold, thereby eliminating price competition at the retail level.

resource markets: Markets in which businesses buy the inputs or factors of production they need to carry on their operations.

restrictive agreement: Conspiracy of firms that restrains trade among separate companies. It may involve a direct or indirect form of price fixing, output control, market sharing, coercion, exclusion of competitors, and so on. It is illegal under the antitrust laws.

restrictive license: Agreement whereby a patentee permits a licensee to sell a patented product under restricted conditions. The restrictions may include the patentee's limiting the geographic area in which the licensee may operate, level of output, or limiting the price the licensee may charge in selling the patented good.

return on net worth: Ratio of a firm's net profit after taxes to its net worth. It provides a measure of the rate of return on stockholders' investment.

return on total assets: Ratio of a firm's net profit after taxes to its total assets. It measures the rate of return on, or the productivity of, total assets.

revaluation: Official act that makes a domestic currency dearer in terms of foreign currencies (or in terms of gold under a gold standard). (*Contrast with* **devaluation**.)

revenue sharing: Plan by which the federal government turns over a portion of its tax revenues to state and local governments each year.

Ricardo, David (1772–1823): English classical economist, generally regarded as the "greatest of the classical economists." Richardo was responsible for refining and systematizing much of classical economic thinking. He formulated theories of value, rent, wages, and international trade, some of which have since been modified but many of which have endured to the present. In general, Ricardo held a scientific view of the economy; therefore, the task of economists, he believed, was to discover the laws that determine economic behavior. Among Ricardo's chief contributions that are of major relevance today are the **law of diminishing returns**—one of the most fundamental laws of economics; the theory of economic rent (studied in microeconomics); and the **law of comparative advantage** (studied in international economics).

right-to-work laws: State laws that make it illegal to require membership in a union as a condition of employment. These laws exist mostly in southern and midwestern states; their main effect is to outlaw the union shop, but in practice they have been relatively ineffective.

risk: Quantitative measurement of the mathematical probability (or "odds") that a given undesirable outcome (such as a loss) will occur. Because risk is predictable, losses that arise from risk can be estimated in advance and can be "insured" against —either by the firm itself or by an insurance company. *Examples:* The losses resulting from rejects on an assembly line can be "self-insured" by being built into the firm's cost structure; the possibility of fire damage can be externally insured by an insurance company.

Robinson, Joan (1903–): English economist who is best known for her distinguished treatise *The Economics of Imperfect Competition*, published in 1933. In this book, she identified and developed the new concept of monopolistic competition (which she called "imperfect competition"). This type of market structure, she emphasized, was characterized by "partial monopolies" producing similar products in order to fulfill diversified consumer preferences. Imperfect competition, she said, was thus a realistic market structure, the theory of which must be understood in order to evaluate the market behavior of a major segment of the private sector.

Robinson–Patman Act (1936): A major antitrust law of the United States, and an amendment to Section 2 of the Clayton Antitrust Act dealing with price discrimination. Commonly referred to as the "Chain Store Act," it was passed to protect independent retailers and wholesales from "unfair discriminations" by larger sellers who enjoy "tremendous purchasing power." The act declared the following illegal: (1) payment of brokerage fees when no independent broker is employed; (2) granting of discounts and other concessions to sellers (such as manufacturers) to buyers (such as wholesalers and retailers), unless such concessions are made to all buyers on proportionately equal terms; (3) price discrimination, except where the price differences make "due allowances" for differences in cost or are offered "in good faith to meet an equally low price of a competitor"; and (4) charging lower prices in one locality than in another, or selling at "unreasonably low prices," when either of these practices is aimed at "destroying competition or eliminating a competitor."

rule of reason: Interpretation of the courts (first announced in the Standard Oil case of 1911) that the mere size of a corporation, no matter how impressive, is no offense therefore not contrary to antitrust law. Instead, it requires "unreasonable" behavior in the form of actual exertion of monopoly power, as shown by unfair practices, for a firm to be held in violation of the antitrust laws. This interpretation, also known as the "good-trust-versus-bad-trust" criterion, was largely reversed in the Aluminum Company of America case in 1945. Nevertheless, the "reasonableness" of market behavior is still a factor that is often considered by the courts in antitrust cases.

rule of 72: Approximate formula for expressing the relationship between the number of years, Y, required for a quantity to double if it grows at an annual rate of compound interest, R. Thus, $YR = 72$. Therefore,

$$Y = \frac{72}{R} \quad \text{and} \quad R = \frac{72}{Y}$$

Example: At 6 percent interest compounded annually, a quantity will double in $Y = {}^{72}/_6 = 12$ years. Similarly, if a quantity doubles in 12 years, the compounded annual rate of growth is $R = {}^{72}/_{12} = 6$ percent.

S

sales tax: A flat percentage levy imposed on retail prices of selected items. The rates and the items taxed vary from state to state.

Samuelson, Paul Anthony (1915–): Leading American economist and the first American to receive the Nobel Prize in Economic Science. Samuelson's publications are extensive. His first treatise, *Foundations of Economic Analysis* (1947), based on his doctoral dissertation, explored the notion of equilibrium in many new and provocative ways. It also developed a concept of economic dynamics that was highly original and sophisticated. His hundreds of articles range through numerous areas of economics. Many of these articles, dealing with both macroeconomic and microeconomic topics, have become classics. In addition, Samuelson authored an introductory text that served as the standard work in the field for several decades.

"satisfice": A concept to convey the idea that, in reality, firms seek not to maximize profit but to achieve certain levels of satiation. *Example:* Firms try to attain a particular target level or rate of profit, and they try to achieve a specific share of the market or a certain level of sales.

saving: That part of income not spent on the consumption of goods and services.

Say, Jean Baptiste (1767–1832): French classical economist. He is best known for his popularization of Adam Smith's *Wealth of Nations* (1776) and for formulating the "Law of Markets"—the classical doctrine that supply creates its own demand. Say's Law thus asserted the impossibility of general overproduction. This idea was central to classical economic thought, because it led to the conclusion that markets were "self-correcting" if left free of government intervention.

Say's Law: An assertion that "supply creates its own demand." That is, the total supply of goods produced must always equal the total demand for them, since goods fundamentally exchange for goods while money serves only as a convenient medium of exchange. Therefore, any general overproduction is impossible. This assertion, named after the French economist Jean Baptiste Say (1767–1832), was fundamental in classical economic thought, for it led to the conclusion that the economy would automatically tend toward full-employment equilibrium if the government followed a policy of laissez-faire.

scarcity, law of: Principle that states that, at any given time and place, economic goods, including resources and finished goods, are scarce in the sense that there are not enough to provide all that people want. Therefore, these scarce goods can be increased, if at all, only through sacrifice of other resources or goods.

Schumpeter, Joseph Alois (1883–1950): Leading Austrian-American economist. His theories can be expressed in the form of several fundamental propositions. (1) The entrepreneur (that is, the businessperson) is the central actor—the prime mover of capitalism. (2) In striving for profit, the entrepreneur innovates by introducing new production techniques and new organizational methods. (3) Innovations cause economic growth, but they are also responsible for business cycles, which ultimately lead to the erosion of capitalism. (4) This erosion is already occurring because the capitalistic institutions that encouraged and nurtured entrepreneurship in the nineteenth and early twentieth centuries have either disappeared or undergone substantial change.

scientific method: A disciplined mode of inquiry represented by the processes of induction, deduction, and verification. The essential steps of the scientific method consist of (1) recognition and definition of a problem, (2) observation and collection of relevant data, (3) organization and classification of data, (4) formulation of hypotheses, (5) deductions from the hypotheses, and (6) testing and verification of the hypotheses. All scientific laws may be modified or challenged by alternative theoretical formulations, and hence the entire cycle consisting of these six steps is a self-correcting process.

seasonal fluctuations: Short-term swings in business and economic activity within the year that are due to weather and custom. *Examples:* upswings in retail sales during holiday periods, such as Christmas and Easter; changes between winter and summer buying patterns.

secondary boycott: Attempts by a union, through strikes, picketing, or other methods, to stop one employer from doing business with another employer. Outlawed by the Labor–Management Relations (Taft–Hartley) Act of 1947.

secondary reserves: A bank's earning assets that are near-liquid (that is, readily convertible into cash on short notice without substantial loss). *Examples:* short-term financial obligations, such as U.S. Treasury bills, high-grade commercial paper, bankers' acceptances, and call loans.

Second Bank of the United States: Chartered for the period 1816 to 1836, the Bank's functions were to serve as fiscal agent for the Treasury, issue its own notes, and finance both rural and commercial business interests. However, the Bank's generally conservative policies caused periods of financial strain throughout the economy. When Andrew Jackson, a "hard-money" advocate who opposed the issuance of paper money by banks, became the nation's President in 1828, he undertook measures to weaken the Bank's effectiveness. As a result, when the Bank's federal charter expired in 1836, it was not renewed.

selling costs: Marketing expenditures aimed at adapting the buyer to the product. *Examples:* advertising, sales promotion, and merchandising.

separation of ownership and control: The notion that, in a modern large corporation, there is a distinction between those who own the business (the stockholders) and those who control it (the hired managers). If stock ownership is widely dispersed, the managers may be able to keep themselves in power for their own benefit rather than for the primary benefit of the corporation and its stockholders.

shadow prices: Estimates of a commodity's prices that would prevail in a highly competitive market composed of many buyers and sellers. Shadow prices are established for accounting purposes as a means of valuing goods and resources that are not valued in the desired way by the price mechanism.

share draft: A check written against an interest-bearing account provided by a credit union. Share draft accounts are one of several forms of savings-type checkable deposits.

Sherman Antitrust Act (1890): A major antitrust law of the United States. It prohibits contracts, combinations, and conspiracies in restraint of trade, as well as monopolization or attempts to monopolize in interstate trade or foreign commerce. Violations are punishable by fines, imprisonment, or both.

shortage: The amount by which the quantity demanded of a commodity exceeds the quantity supplied at a given price, as when the given price is below the free-market equilibrium price. (*Compare* **surplus.**)

short run: Period in which a firm can vary its output through a more or less intensive use of its resources but cannot vary production capacity because it has a fixed plant scale.

simple multiplier: *See* **multiplier.**

single tax: Proposal advanced by the American economist Henry George (1839–1897) that the only tax a society should impose is a tax on land, because all rent on land is unearned surplus that increases as a result of natural progress and economic growth. Three major shortcomings leveled against this thesis are that the single tax (1) would not yield enough revenues to meet government's spending needs; (2) would be unjust, because surpluses would accrue to resource owners other than landlords if the owners were to gain some monopolistic control over the sale of their resources in the marketplace; and (3) would be difficult to administer because it would not distinguish between land and capital—that is, between the proportion of rent that represents a surplus and the proportion that results from improvements made on the land.

slope: Rate of change or steepness of a line as measured by the change (increase or decrease) in its vertical distance per unit of change in its horizontal distance. It may be calculated from a ratio:

$$\text{slope} = \frac{\text{change in vertical distance}}{\text{change in horizontal distance}}$$

Hence, a horizontal line has a zero slope, and a vertical line has an "infinite" slope. All straight lines that are upward or positively inclined have a slope greater than zero. (Analogously, all straight lines that are downward or negatively inclined have a slope less than zero.) Parallel lines have equal slopes. The slope of a straight line is the same at every point, but the slope of a curved line differs at every point. Geometrically, the slope of a curve at a particular point can be found by drawing a straight line tangent to the curve at that point. The slope of the line will then be equal to the slope of the curve at the point of tangency. In economics, all "marginals" are slopes or rate of change of their corresponding "totals." *Examples:* The marginal propensity to consume represents the rate of change or slope of its corresponding total propensity to consume; a marginal-cost curve is the slope of its corresponding total-cost curve; a marginal-revenue curve is the slope of its corresponding total-revenue curve; and so on. The concept of slope or rate of change (that is, "marginality") is unquestionably the most powerful and important analytical tool of economics.

Smith, Adam (1723–1790): Scottish philosopher and author of *The Wealth of Nations* (1776). This was the first comprehensive, systematic study of economics. The treatise earned Smith the appellation "Founder of Economics." In the book, he analyzed such concepts as specialization, division of labor, value and price determination, the distribution of income, the accumulation of capital, and taxation. He argued that, if individuals were left alone to pursue their self-interests, their behavior would, as if guided by an "invisible hand," lead to maximum benefits for society. He thus concluded that laissez-faire (that is, nonintervention of government) was essential to a society's economic efficiency. (*Note:* Smith's ideas became the foundation upon which the whole subsequent tradition of classical economics was constructed.)

social balance: Existence of an optimum distribution of society's resources between the private and public sectors—the former represented by the production of private goods, such as cars, clothing, and television sets, and the latter by the production of certain types of social goods, such as libraries, public health, and education.

social benefit: Utility that accrues to society as a result of a particular act, such as production or consumption of a commodity. (*Compare* **private benefit.**)

social cost: Disutility that accrues to society as a result of a particular act, such as production or consumption of a commodity. It includes real costs, the costs of sacrificed alternatives, and reductions in incomes or benefits caused by the act. It thus includes noneconomic as well as economic costs. (*Compare* **private cost.**).

social goods: Products provided by government, usually because society believes that such goods are not adequately provided by the private sector through the free market. Social goods include (1) *public goods,* such as national defense, public safety, and street lighting, and (2) *merit goods,* such as public education, libraries, and museums. (See **public good; merit good.**)

socialism: 1. In the theories of Karl Marx, a transitory stage between capitalism and full communism, in which the means of production are owned by the state, the state in turn is controlled by the workers ("dictatorship of the proletariat"), and the economy's social output is distributed by this formula: From each according to his ability, to each according to his labor. **2.** In its contemporary form, a movement that seeks primarily to improve economic efficiency and equity by establishing (a) public ownership of all important means of production and distribution and (b) some degree of centralized planning to determine what goods to produce, how they should be produced, and to whom they should be distributed.

social rate of return: Net value of a project to an economy (that is, of a town, city, state, or country). It is estimated on the basis of the net increase in output that a project such as a new industry may be expected to bring, directly or indirectly, to the area being developed. The industry's contribution is determined by subtracting from the value of what it produces the cost to society of the resources used. Hence the measure is intended to reflect all economic and social benefits as well as costs. (*Compare* **private rate of return.**)

Social Security Act (1935): The basic comprehensive social security law of the United States. It provides for two types of social security: (1) social insurance programs for old-age, survivors, disability, and health insurance (OASDHI), and for unemployment, both of which yield payments to insured persons; and (2) a public charity program in the form of welare services, institutional care, food, housing, and other forms of assistance. Some of the provisions of the act (with its many subsequent amendments) are administered and financed by the federal government, some by state and local governments, and some by all three levels of government.

social security tax: Payroll tax that finances the U.S. compulsory social-insurance program covering old-age and unemployment benefits. The taxes are paid both by employees and by employers, based on the incomes of the former.

Special Drawing Rights (SDRs or "paper gold"): Supplementary reserves (established in 1969) in the form of account entries on the books of the International Monetary Fund. SDRs, which are allocated among participating countries in accordance with their quotas, can be drawn upon by governments to help finance balance-of-payments deficits. They are meant to promote an orderly growth of reserves that will help the long-run expanding needs of world trade.

specialization: Division of productive activities among individuals and regions so that no one person or area is self-sufficient. Total production is increased by specialization, thus permitting all participants to share in a greater volume of output through the process of exchange or trade.

specie: Money in the form of gold or silver coins. The nominal or stated value of the coin should equal the market value of the metal contained in the coin, but this does not usually happen. The reason is that the market value of the gold or silver in the coin fluctuates according to supply and demand. Therefore, the metallic value of the coin may be greater or less than the nominal value stated on the coin. (*See* **mint ratio.**)

specific subsidy: Per-unit subsidy on a commodity. (*See also* **subsidy.**)

specific tax: Per-unit tax on a commodity. (*See also* **tax.**)

speculation: 1. In the popular sense, any business transaction involving considerable risk for the chance of receiving large gains. **2.** In the futures market, the purchase or sale of a futures contract without having an offsetting interest in the actual commodity. An increase in the price of the futures contract creates a profit for buyers of the contract (who are called "longs") and a corresponding loss for sellers of the contract (who are called "shorts").

speculative motive: Desire on the part of households and businesses to hold part of their assets in liquid form so that they can take advantage of changes in the interest rate. This motive is thus tied specifically to the interest rate and is one of the chief sources of demand for loanable funds in the modern theory of interest.

spillovers: External benefits or costs for which no compensation is made. (Spillovers are also called **externalities.**)

stable equilibrium: Condition in which an object or system (such as a price, firm, industry, or market) in equilibrium, when subjected to a shock sufficient to disturb its position, returns toward its initial equilibrium as a result of self-restoring forces. (In contrast, an equilibrium that is not stable may be either unstable or neutral.)

stagflation: Combination of "stagnation" and "inflation." It is a condition characterized by slow economic growth, high unemployment, and rising prices. Stagflation thus combines some of the features of recession and inflation.

Standard Oil case (1911): Major antitrust case in which Standard Oil of New Jersey was ordered broken up by the Supreme Court. The Court held Standard Oil to be in violation of the Sherman Antitrust Act because the company had engaged in "unreasonable market practices, including the attempt to drive others from the field and to exclude them from their right to trade." In this case, the Court introduced an important new criterion for judging monopoly behavior. (*See* **rule of reason.**)

state bank: Commercial bank chartered by a state government. Such banks may or may not be members of the Federal Reserve System.

state farms: Lands in the Soviet Union that are owned and operated as state enterprises under elected or governmentally appointed managing directors. Workers and technicians are hired to run the farms and are usually paid set wages. They may also be paid bonuses if their work exceeds basic norms of output.

static model: One in which economic phenomena are studied without reference to time—that is without relating them to preceding or succeeding events. Time, in other words, is not permitted to enter the analysis in any matter that will affect the results. A static model is thus like a "snapshot" as distinguished from a "motion picture." (*Compare* **dynamic model.**)

static multiplier: The multiplier without regard to the time required to realize its full effect. (*Compare* **truncated multiplier.**)

stock: Units of ownership interest in a corporation. The kinds of stock include common stock, preferred stock, and capital stock.

strategic-resource monopoly: Firm that has a monopoly because it controls an essential input to a production process. *Example:* DeBeers of South Africa owns most of the world's diamond mines.

strike: Agreement among workers to stop working, without resigning from their jobs, until their demands are met.

structural inflation: Condition of generally rising prices caused by uneven upward demand or cost pressures in some key industries, such as automobiles, construction, or steel, even if aggregate demand is in balance with aggregate supply for the economy as a whole.

structural unemployment: Type of unemployment, usually prolonged, resulting from fundamental alterations or "structural" variations in the economy, such as changes in technology, markets, or national priorities. Most types of workers—unskilled, skilled, or professional—are subject to structural unemployment as a result of any of these factors.

subsidy: Payment (usually by government) to businesses or households that enables them to produce or consume a product in larger quantities or at lower prices than they would otherwise.

subsistence theory of wages: Theory developed by some classical economists of the late eighteenth and early nineteenth centuries. It held that wages per worker tend to equal what the worker needs to "subsist"—that is, to maintain himself and to rear children. If wages per worker rose above the subsistence level, people would tend to have more children and the population would increase, thereby lowering real incomes per capita. Similarly, if wages per worker fell below the subsistence level, people would tend to have fewer children and the population would decline, thereby increasing real incomes per capita. Wages per worker would thus tend to remain at the subsistence level over the long run. This theory is also known as the "brazen (or iron) law of wages."

substitute goods: Commodities that are related such that, at a given level of buyers' incomes, an increase in the price of one good leads to an increase in the demand for the other and a decrease in the price of one good leads to a decrease in the demand for the other. *Examples:* gin and vodka; beef and pork. (*Compare* **complementary goods.**)

substitution effect: Change in quantity of a good demanded by a buyer resulting from a change in the good's price while the buyer's real income, tastes, and the prices of other goods remain the same. (*Compare* **income effect.**)

sunspot theory: Theory of business cycles proposed in England during the late nineteenth century. It held that sunspot cycles (disturbances on the surface of the sun) exhibited an extremely high correlation with agricultural cycles for a number of years; therefore, sunspots must affect the weather, the weather influences agricultural crops, and the crops affect business conditions. This theory received worldwide popularity when it was first introduced, but then fell into disrepute because the high correlation between sunspots and agricultural cycles did not endure; it was the result of accidental rather than causal factors.

superior good: A good whose consumption varies directly with money income, prices remaining constant. Most consumer goods are superior goods. (A superior good is also called a **normal good** because it represents the "normal" situation.)

supermultiplier: An enlargement of the simple multiplier, reflecting the inclusion of the marginal propensity to invest, *MPI*. It may be expressed by the formula

$$\text{supermultiplier} = \frac{1}{1 - (MPC + MPI)} = \frac{1}{1 - MPE}$$

in which *MPE* denotes the marginal propensity to spend.

supplementary (fringe) benefits: Forms of compensation to workers other than basic wages, such as bonuses, pension benefits, and holiday and vacation pay.

supply: A relation expressing the various amounts of a commodity that sellers would be willing and able to make available for sale at possible alternative prices during a given period of time, all other things remaining the same. This relation may be expressed as a table (called a supply schedule), as a graph (called a supply curve), or as a mathematical equation.

supply curve: Graph of a supply schedule, showing the number of units of a commodity that sellers would be able and willing to sell at various possible prices during a given period of time, all other things remaining the same.

supply, law of: Principle that states that the quantity supplied of a commodity usually varies directly with its price, assuming that all other things that may affect supply remain the same. These "all other" things include (1) resource prices, (2) prices of related goods in production, and (3) the state of technology and other nonmonetary determinants, such as the number of sellers in the market.

supply price: Least price necessary to bring forth a given output. Hence it is the lowest price a seller is willing to accept to persuade him to supply a given quantity of a commodity.

supply schedule: Table showing the number of units of a commodity that sellers would be able and willing to sell at various possible prices during a given period of time, all other things remaining the same.

supply-side economics: Measures aimed at achieving efficiency through policies designed to stimulate production. While there are many policies that may encourage increased production, the most fundamental supply-side policies are those that make direct use of *incentives*. For example, reductions in marginal tax rates—the taxes paid on the last few dollars of wages, interest, and dividends—provide direct incentives to work, save, and invest. (*Contrast with* **demand-side economics.**)

surplus: The amount by which the quantity supplied of a commodity exceeds the quantity demanded at a given price, as when the given price is above the free-market equilibrium price. (*Compare* **shortage.**)

surplus value: In the theories of Karl Marx, the difference between the value that a worker creates (as determined by the labor-time embodied in the commodity that the worker pro-

duces) and the value that he or she receives as determined by the subsistence level of wages. This surplus, according to Marx, is appropriated by the capitalist and is the incentive for the development of a capitalist system.

surtax: Tax imposed on a tax base in addition to a so-called normal tax. *Example:* a surtax on income in addition to the normal income tax. Note that a surtax is imposed on an existing tax base; it is not a "tax on a tax" as is popularly believed.

syndicalism: Economic system that demands the abolition of both capitalism and the state as instruments of oppression and, in their place, the reorganization of society into industry-wide associations or syndicates of workers. The syndicates, fundamentally trade unions, would replace the state. Each syndicte would then govern its own members in their activities as producers but leave them free from interference in all other matters. The chief exponent of syndicalism was the French social philosopher Georges Sorel (1847–1922), some of whose views later influenced the growth of fascism.

T

tariff: Customs duty or tax imposed by a government on the importation (or exportation) of a good. Tariffs may be (1) specific, in the form of a tax per unit of the commodity, or (2) ad valorem, based on the value of the commodity.

tax: A compulsory payment to government. Its purposes may be (1) to influence efficiency through resource allocation (so as to produce more of some commodities and less of others); (2) to influence equity through income and wealth distribution; (3) to influence economic stabilization; and (4) to influence economic growth.

tax avoidance: Legal methods or "loopholes" used by taxpayers to reduce their taxes. (*Compare* **tax evasion.**)

tax base: An object that is being taxed, such as income (in the case of an income tax), the value of property (in the case of a property tax), or the value of goods sold (in the case of a sales tax.)

tax-based incomes policy (TIP): A proposal for curbing inflation. The program provides tax benefits for those workers and firms that keep wage and price increases within established guidelines and tax penalties for those that do not. The guidelines, based on the economy's productivity and the current rate of inflation—perhaps an average of both—would be announced annually by government. In general, TIP is at best a short-run anti-inflation measure because it deals with the symptoms of inflation, not the cause.

tax evasion: Illegal methods of escaping taxes, such as lying about income or expenses. (*Compare* **tax avoidance.**)

tax incidence: Burden of a tax—that is, the economic entities, such as households, consumers, or sellers, that ultimately bear the tax.

tax multiplier: Relation between a change in personal income taxes and the resulting change in output, measured by *NNP*. For example, an increase in taxes reduces people's disposable income by that amount. Because consumption depends on income, the level of consumption will decrease by *MPC* multiplied by the change in income (or taxes). This in turn will cause a magnified drop in *NNP*, depending on the size of the expenditure multiplier, M_E. Thus the tax multiplier, M_T, may be expressed by the formula:

$$M_T = MPC \times M_E$$
$$= MPC \times \frac{1}{MPS}$$

tax rate: Amount of tax applied per unit of tax base, expressed as a percentage. *Example:* A tax of $10 on a base of $100 represents a tax rate of 10 percent.

tax shifting: Changing of the burden or incidence of a tax from the economic entity upon which it is initially imposed to some other economic entity. *Example:* Sales and excise taxes are imposed on the products of sellers, but these taxes are shifted in whole or in part through higher prices to buyers of the goods.

technical efficiency: *See* **efficiency.**

terms of trade: Number of units of goods that must be given up for one unit of goods received by each party (such as a nation) to a transaction. The terms are thus equal to the ratio at which goods are exchanged. In general, the terms of trade are said to move in favor of the party that gives up fewer units of goods for one unit of goods received and against the party that gives up more units of goods for one unit of goods received. In international economics, the concept of terms of trade plays an important role in evaluating exchange relationships between nations.

theory: Set of definitions, assumptions, and hypotheses put together in a manner that expresses apparent relationships or underlying principles of certain observed phenomena in a meaningful way.

time deposit: Money held in a depository-institution account of an individual or firm. Certain types of time deposits have specified maturity dates. For other types, the depository institution may require advance notice of withdrawal.

time preference: Human desire for a good in the present as opposed to the future. The desire is reflected by the price people are willing to pay for immediate possession of the good as opposed to the price they are willing to pay for future possession.

time series: A set of data ordered chronologically. Most of the published data of business and economics are expressed in the form of time series.

time value of money: The notion that dollars at different points in time cannot be made directly comparable unless they are first adjusted by a common factor—the interest rate. For example, if your money can earn 6 percent annually, then $1 today is worth $1.06 to you one year from today. Similarly, $1.06 next year is worth an additional 6 percent, or $1.124, two years from today. Conversely, $1.06 one year from today is worth $1 to you today; $1.124 two years from today is worth $1.06 a year from today, and is worth $1 today. (*See also* **compounding; discounting.**)

TIP: *See* **tax-based incomes policy.**

token money: Any object (usually coins) whose value as money is greater than the market value of the materials of which it is composed. *Example:* pennies, nickels, and so on.

total cost: Sum of a firm's total fixed costs and total variable costs.

total fixed costs: Costs that do not vary with a firm's output. *Examples:* rental payments, interest on debt, property taxes.

total–marginal relationship: Relationship between all corresponding total and marginal curves such that, when a total curve is increasing at an increasing rate, its corresponding marginal curve is rising; when a total curve is increasing at a decreasing rate, its corresponding marginal curve is falling; and when a total curve is increasing at a zero rate, as occurs when it is at a maximum, its corresponding marginal curve is zero. (*Note:* The case of decreasing total curves gives rise to negative marginal curves, but these situations need not be included in the definition because they are not ordinarily relevant or realistic in an economic sense.)

total revenue: A firm's total receipts; equal to price per unit times the number of units sold.

total variable costs: Costs that vary directly with a firm's output, rising as output increases over the full range of production. *Examples:* costs of raw materials, fuel, labor, and so on.

trade association: Organization of independent business enterprises (usually but not always in the same industry) established for mutually beneficial purposes. (*Note:* A trade association that behaves illegally by fixing prices, restricting output, or allocating markets for its members is similar to a cartel.) (*See also* **cartel.**)

Trade Expansion Act (1962): Part of the U.S. Reciprocal Trade Agreements program. This act broadened the powers of the President to (1) negotiate further tariff reductions on broad categories of goods; (2) lower or eliminate tariffs on those goods for which the European Common Market and the United States together account for at least 80 percent of total world exports; (3) lower tariffs by as much as 50 percent on the basis of reciprocal trade agreements, provided that such agreements include most-favored-nation clauses so that the benefits of reduced tariffs are extended to other countries; and (4) grant vocational, technical, and financial assistance to American employees and businesspeople whose industries are adversely affected by tariff reduction.

trade-possibilities curve: Curve that depicts the amounts of goods that countries may exchange with each other. The *slope* of the curve measures the **terms of trade.**

transmission mechanism: Process by which changes in the money supply bring about changes in people's spending behavior, thereby affecting prices, interest rates, and other economic variables. In the Keynesian model, the transmission mechanism or chain of causation is: money → interest rates → prices. In the monetarist model, the causal chain is: money → prices → interest rates.

transactions motive: Desire on the part of households and businesses to hold some of their assets in liquid form so that they can engage in day-to-day spending activities. This motive is influenced primarily by the level of income rather than by changes in the interest rate, and it is one of the chief sources of demand for loanable funds in the modern theory of interest.

transfer payments: Expenditures within or between sectors of the economy for which there are no corresponding contributions to current production. *Examples:* social security payments, unemployment compensation, relief payments, veterans' bonuses, net interest paid on government bonds and on consumer loans, and business transfers (such as charitable contributions and losses resulting from theft and debt defaults).

Treasury bills: Marketable financial obligations of the U.S. Treasury. They have minimum denominations of $10,000, and they usually mature in 3 months, 6 months, or 1 year.

Treasury bonds: Marketable financial obligations of the U.S. Treasury, maturing in more than 7 years from the date of issue. (These are *not* U.S. Savings Bonds, with which most people are familiar.)

Treasury notes: Marketable financial obligations of the U.S. Treasury, maturing in 1 to 7 years from date of issue.

trend: Long-run growth or decline of an economic time series over a period of years.

truncated multiplier: The multiplier applicable to a finite number of time periods. Its size approaches that of the static multiplier as the number of periods increases. However, it always realizes more than half the effect of the static multiplier within the first few periods. Thus the truncated multiplier for, say, four periods is measured by the formula

$$\text{truncated multiplier} \atop \text{for four periods} = 1 + MPC + (MPC)^2 = (MPC)^3$$

two-part tariff: Pricing method whereby the buyer pays two different sums: a fixed charge representing an access fee and another charge varying with use. This pricing method is suitable for a product with separable complementary demands. (*Examples:* public utilities charge a minimum fee and then levy an additional charge based on services rendered. An amusement park may charge an entrance fee and then impose separate charges for individual attractions.) In most cases, the fixed fee is intended to recover installation and maintenance costs, while the variable charges are designed to pay for the operation of specific services actually consumed.

tying contract (tie-in sale): Practice whereby a seller requires the buyer to purchase one or more additional or "tied" products as a condition for purchasing the desired or "tying" product. *Examples:* block bookings of motion pictures in which movie theaters are required to take "B" films as a condition for obtaining "A" films; the United Shoe Machinery Co., which once required shoemakers to purchase other materials as a condition for purchasing their shoe machinery.

U

uncertainty: State of knowledge in which the probabilities of outcomes resulting from specific actions are not known and cannot be predicted because they are subjective rather than objective phenomena. Uncertainties, therefore, are not insurable and cannot be integrated into the firm's cost structure.

underconsumption theory (of business cycles): Explanation of economic fluctuations that holds that recessions result from consumer expenditures lagging behind output because too large a proportion of society's income is not spent on consumption. According to the theory, society distributes income too inequitably to enable people to purchase all the goods produced.

underemployment (disguised unemployment): Condition in which employed resources are not being used in their most efficient ways.

unemployment: Situation that exists whenever resources are out of work or are not being used efficiently. There are various types of unemployment, such as technological, frictional, structural, disguised, involuntary, and cyclical. (Each of these is defined separately in this Dictionary.) The type most commonly meant, unless otherwise specified, is **involuntary unemployment.**

unemployment benefits: Weekly payments, administered by state governments, to "covered" workers who are involuntarily unemployed.

unfair competition: Deceptive, dishonest, or injurious methods of competitive behavior. Such practices are illegal under the antitrust laws.

union: Organization of workers that seeks to gain a degree of monopoly power in the sale of its services so that it may be able to secure higher wages, better working conditions, and other economic improvements for its members.

union shop: Business firm that permits a union nonmember to be hired on condition that he or she join the union after being employed.

U.S. Steel case (1920): Major antitrust case against U.S. Steel Corporation. The company, formed from a consolidation of many independent firms in 1901, accounted for nearly half the national output of iron and steel. Nevertheless, the Court found no evidence of wrongdoing and refused to order the breakup of the company. "The law does not make mere size an offense, or the existence of unexerted power an offense," said the Court. This was thus an application of the *rule of reason* by the Court, one of many such applications that have been made.

utility: Ability of a good to satisfy a want. Utility is determined by the satisfaction that one receives from consuming something.

utopian socialism: Philosophy advanced by a group of English and French writers in the early nineteenth century that advocated the creation of model communities, largely self-contained, in which the instruments of production were collectively owned and government was primarily on a voluntary and wholly democratic basis. The leading proponents were Robert Owen (1771–1858) in England and Charles Fourier (1772–1837) in France.

V

value: Power of a commodity to command other commodities in exchange for itself, as measured by the proportional quantities in which a commodity exchanges with all other commodities.

value added: Increment in value at each stage in the production of a good. The sum of the increments for all stages of production gives the total income—the aggregate of wages, rent, interest, and profit—derived from the production of the good.

value-added tax: Type of national sales tax paid by manufacturers and merchants on the value contributed to a product at each stage of its production and distribution.

variable costs: Costs that vary directly with a firm's output, rising as output increases over the full range of production. *Examples:* costs of raw materials, fuel, labor, and so on.

variable proportions, law of: See **diminishing returns, law of.**

Veblen, Thorstein Bunde (1857–1929): American institutional economist and critic of neoclassical economics. He emphasized the role of social institutions (that is, customs and practices) as major determinants of economic behavior. Among his many books, his first and best-known one was *The Theory of the Leisure Class* (1899). In this book he coined the famous phrase "conspicuous consumption" as a characteristic of the "leisure class." (*See* **conspicuous consumption.**)

verification: Testing of alternative hypotheses or conclusions by means of actual observation or experimentation—that is, by reference to the facts.

vertical equity: Doctrine that states that "unequals should be treated unequally." *Example:* Persons of different income, wealth, or other taxpaying ability should, in order to bear equal tax burdens (or make equal subjective sacrifices), pay different amounts of tax. (*Compare* **horizontal equity.**)

vertical merger: Amalgamation under one ownership of plants engaged in different stages of production of the same or similar goods, from raw materials to finished products. It may take the form of forward integration into buyer markets or backward integration into supplier markets. The chief objective is to achieve greater economies by combining different production stages and by regularizing supplies, thereby increasing profit margins. *Example:* A shoe manufacturer may merge with a chain of retail shoe stores, and with a leather-processing firm.

W

wages: **1.** Payment to those owners of resources who supply the factor of production known as "labor." This payment includes wages, salaries, commissions, and the like. **2.** The price paid for the use of labor. It is usually expressed as time rates, such as so much per hour, day, or week, or less frequently as rates of so much per unit of work performed.

wages-fund theory: Classical theory of wages best articulated by John Stuart Mill in 1848. It held that producers set aside a portion of their capital funds for the purpose of hiring workers needed for production. The amount of the fund depends on the stock of capital relative to the number of workers. In the long run, however, the accumulation of capital is itself limited or determined by the tendency toward a minimum "subsistence rate" of profits; hence the only effective way to raise real wages is to reduce the number of workers or size of the population. (*Note:* This theory was a reformulation of the **subsistence theory of wages.**)

Walras, Leon (1834–1910): French economist whose major work, *Elements of Pure Economics* (1874), was done at the University of Lausanne, Switzerland. He is regarded as one of the greatest economic theorists of all time. This is due to his mathematical formulations of the theory of general equilibrium "under a system of perfectly free competition." The model links the various markets of the economy through systems of equations, and shows the conditions needed to determine equilibrium prices and quantities. The Walrasian system thus represents the perfection of classical and neoclassical economics.

"wastes" of monopolistic competition: Expression used to denote overcrowded "sick" industries of monopolistic competition; the wastes are characterized by chronic excess capacity and inefficient operations. *Examples:* retail trades; textile manufacturing.

wealth: Anything that has value because it is capable of producing income. A "stock" of value as compared to a "flow" of income. (*Compare* **income.**)

welfare economics: Branch of economic theory concerned with the development of principles for maximizing social welfare.

Wheeler–Lea Act (1938): Amendment to the Federal Trade Commission Act. It was passed primarily to protect consumers, rather than just business competitors, from unfair (deceptive, dishonest, or injurious) methods of competition. Thus, injured consumers are given equal protection before the law with injured merchants. The act also prohibits false or misleading advertisements for food, drugs, cosmetics, and therapeutic devices.

white market: Legal market in which ration coupons for a commodity are transferable, permitting people who do not want all their coupons to sell them to those who do. A white market thus reduces, but does not eliminate, the inequities and skullduggery generally associated with rationing and a black market. (*Compare* **black market.**)

Y

yellow-dog contract: Contract that requires an employee to promise as a condition of employment that he will not belong to a labor union. Declared illegal in the Norris–La Guardia Act of 1932.

yield: Effective or going market rate of interest on a security. In a broader sense, it is the effective rate of return on any type of investment.

yield curve: Graph that shows, at a given time, the relationship between yields and maturities for debt instruments of equal risk (for example, treasury bonds). The yield curve thus expresses the *term structure of interest rates* for a particular class of debt instruments, which are alike in all respects except their maturity dates.

yield to maturity: Percentage figure reflecting the effective yield on a bond, based on the difference between its purchase price and its redemption price, taking into account any returns received by the bondholder in the interim.